BATMAN AND ROBIN

VOLUME 3 **DEATH OF THE FAMILY**

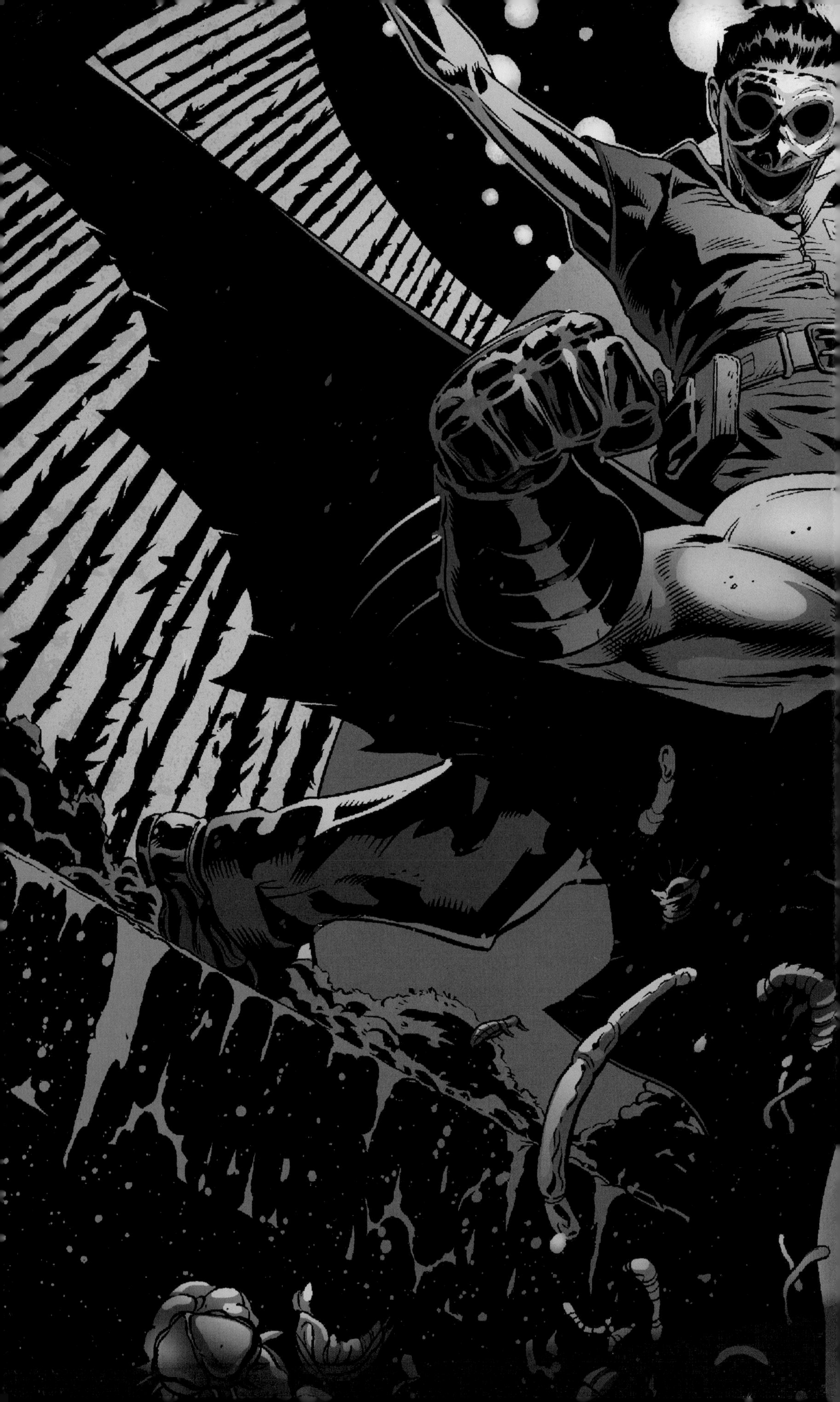

BATMAN AND ROBIN

VOLUME 3
DEATH OF THE FAMILY

PETER J. **TOMASI** SCOTT **SNYDER**
writers

PATRICK **GLEASON** ARDIAN **SYAF**
GREG **CAPULLO** pencillers

MICK **GRAY** VICENTE **CIFUENTES**
KEITH **CHAMPAGNE** JONATHAN **GLAPION** inkers

JOHN **KALISZ** FCO **PLASCENCIA** colorists

CARLOS M. **MANGUAL** RICHARD **STARKINGS**
COMICRAFT'S JIMMY **BETANCOURT** letterers

PATRICK **GLEASON**, MICK **GRAY** & JOHN **KALISZ**
collection cover artists

BATMAN created by BOB **KANE**

RACHEL GLUCKSTERN MIKE MARTS Editors – Original Series KATIE KUBERT Associate Editor – Original Series
RICKEY PURDIN Assistant Editor – Original Series RACHEL PINNELAS Editor
ROBBIN BROSTERMAN Design Director – Books ROBBIE BIEDERMAN Publication Design

BOB HARRAS Senior VP – Editor-in-Chief, DC Comics

DIANE NELSON President DAN DIDIO and JIM LEE Co-Publishers
GEOFF JOHNS Chief Creative Officer
JOHN ROOD Executive VP – Sales, Marketing and Business Development
AMY GENKINS Senior VP – Business and Legal Affairs NAIRI GARDINER Senior VP – Finance
JEFF BOISON VP – Publishing Planning MARK CHIARELLO VP – Art Direction and Design
JOHN CUNNINGHAM VP – Marketing TERRI CUNNINGHAM VP – Editorial Administration
ALISON GILL Senior VP – Manufacturing and Operations
HANK KANALZ Senior VP – Vertigo & Integrated Publishing JAY KOGAN VP – Business and Legal Affairs, Publishing
JACK MAHAN VP – Business Affairs, Talent NICK NAPOLITANO VP – Manufacturing Administration
SUE POHJA VP – Book Sales COURTNEY SIMMONS Senior VP – Publicity
BOB WAYNE Senior VP – Sales

BATMAN AND ROBIN VOLUME 3: DEATH OF THE FAMILY

DC Comics, 1700 Broadway, New York, NY 10019
A Warner Bros. Entertainment Company.
Printed by RR Donnelley, Salem, VA, USA. 10/25/13. First Printing.

HC ISBN: 978-1-4012-4268-8
SC ISBN: 978-1-4012-4617-4

SUSTAINABLE FORESTRY INITIATIVE

Certified Chain of Custody
At Least 20% Certified Forest Content
www.sfiprogram.org
SFI-01042
APPLIES TO TEXT STOCK ONLY

Library of Congress Cataloging-in-Publication Data

Tomasi, Peter, author.
Batman and Robin. Volume 3, Death of the Family / Peter Tomasi, Patrick Gleason, Mick Gray.
pages cm. — (The New 52!)
Collects BATMAN AND ROBIN #15-17, BATMAN AND ROBIN ANNUAL #1 and BATMAN #17"— Provided by publisher.
ISBN 978-1-4012-4268-8 (hardback)
1. Graphic novels. I. Gleason, Patrick, illustrator. II. Gray, Mick, illustrator. III. Title. IV. Title: Death of the Family.
PN6728.B36T645 2013

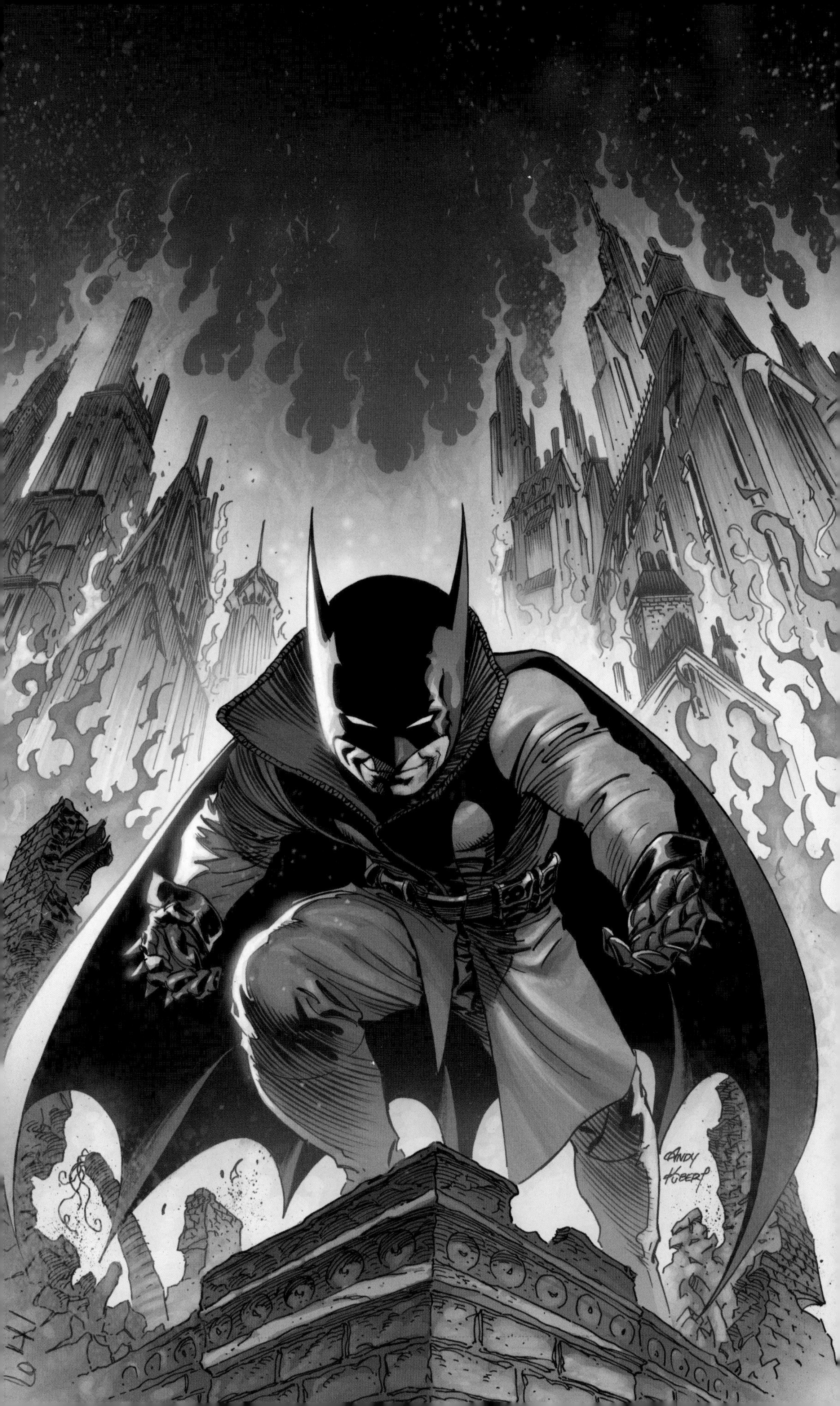
ANDY
KUBERT

BATMAN IMPOSSIBLE

PETER J. TOMASI writer **ARDIAN SYAF** penciller **VICENTE CIFUENTES** inker cover art by **ANDY KUBERT** with **BRAD ANDERSON**

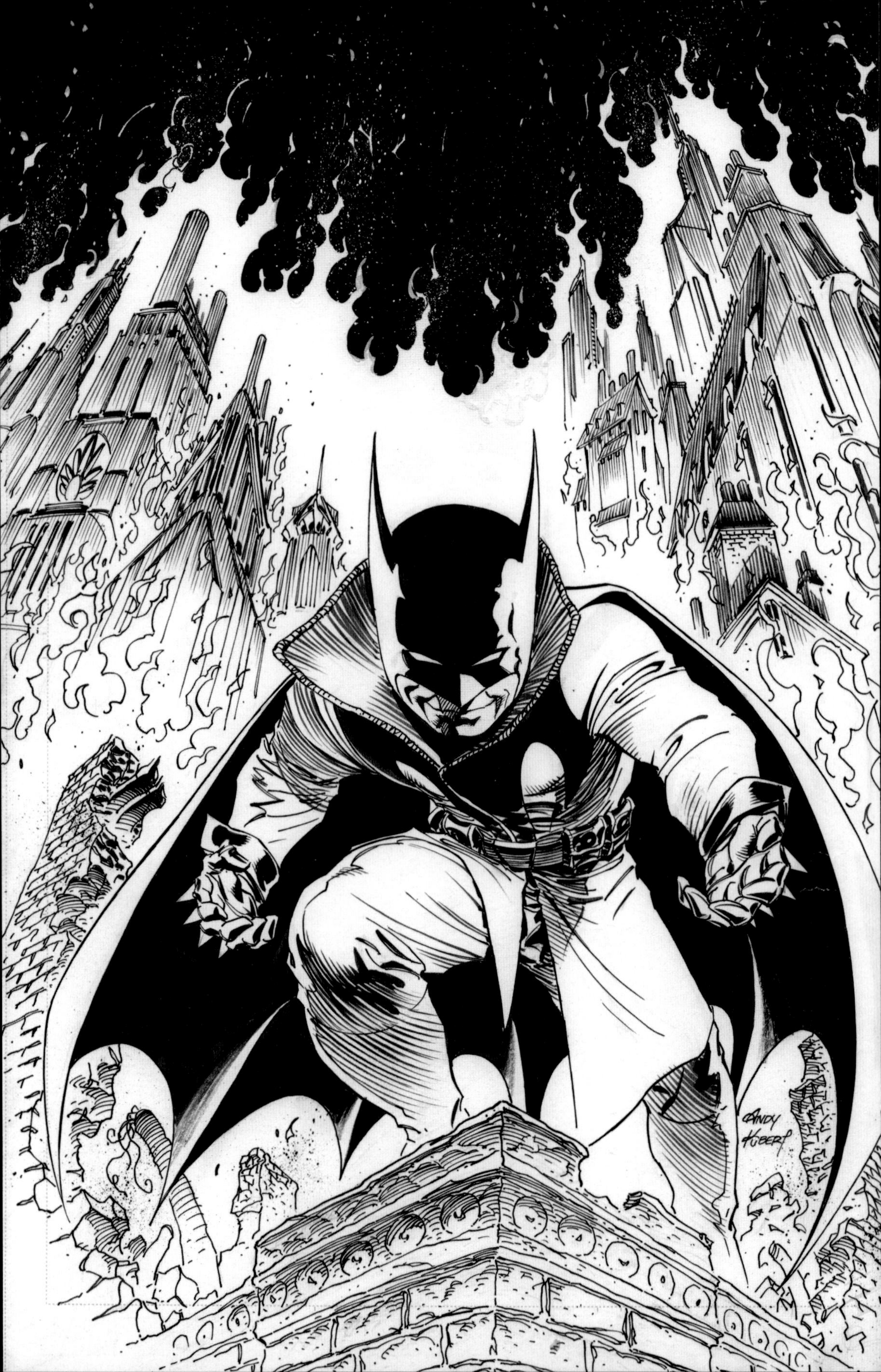
ANDY
KUBERT

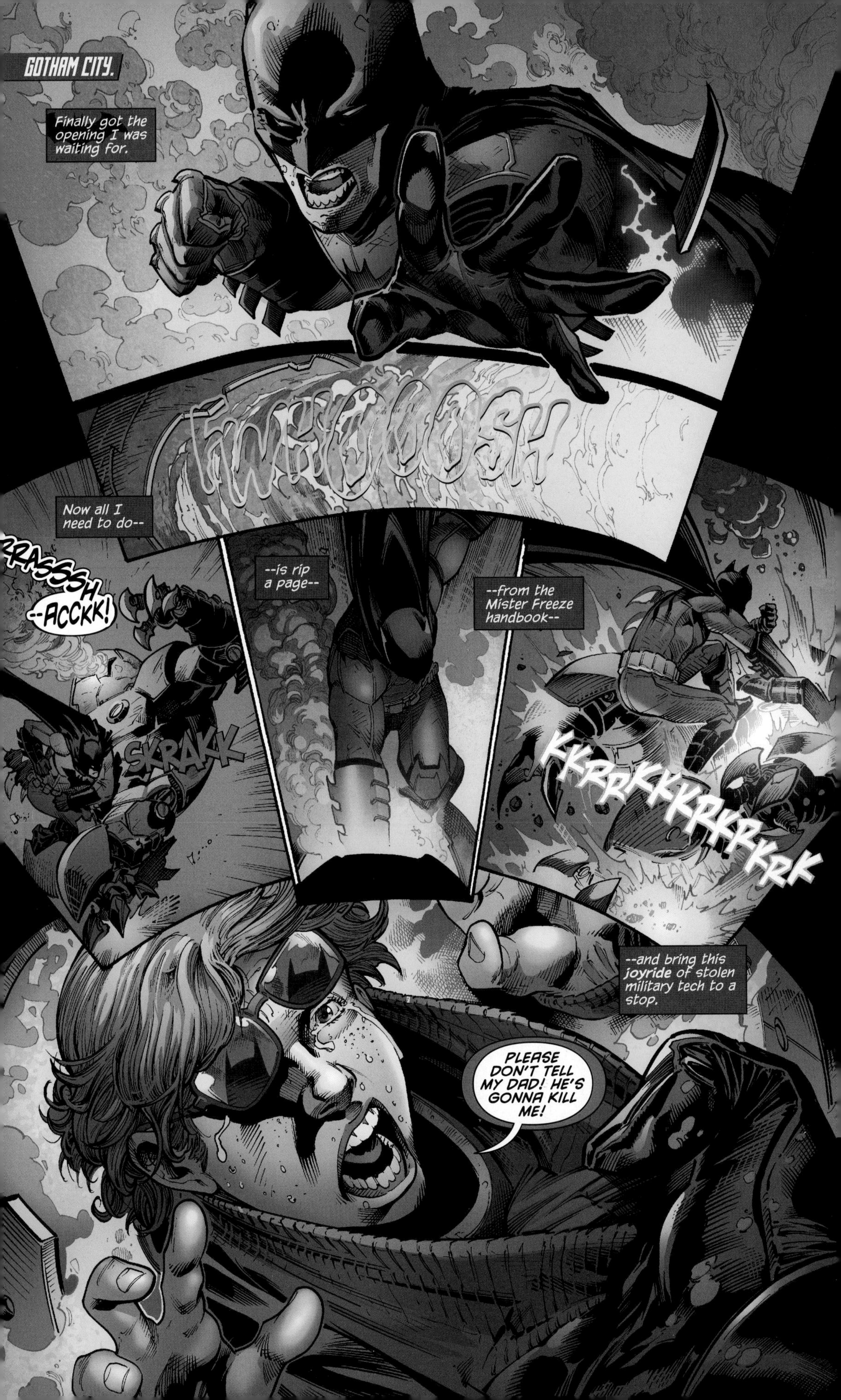
GOTHAM CITY.
Finally got the opening I was waiting for.
FWHOOOSH
Now all I need to do--
KRASSSH
--ACCKK!
SKRAKK
--is rip a page--
--from the Mister Freeze handbook--
KKRRKKKRKRKRKRK
--and bring this **joyride** of stolen military tech to a stop.
PLEASE DON'T TELL MY DAD! HE'S GONNA KILL ME!

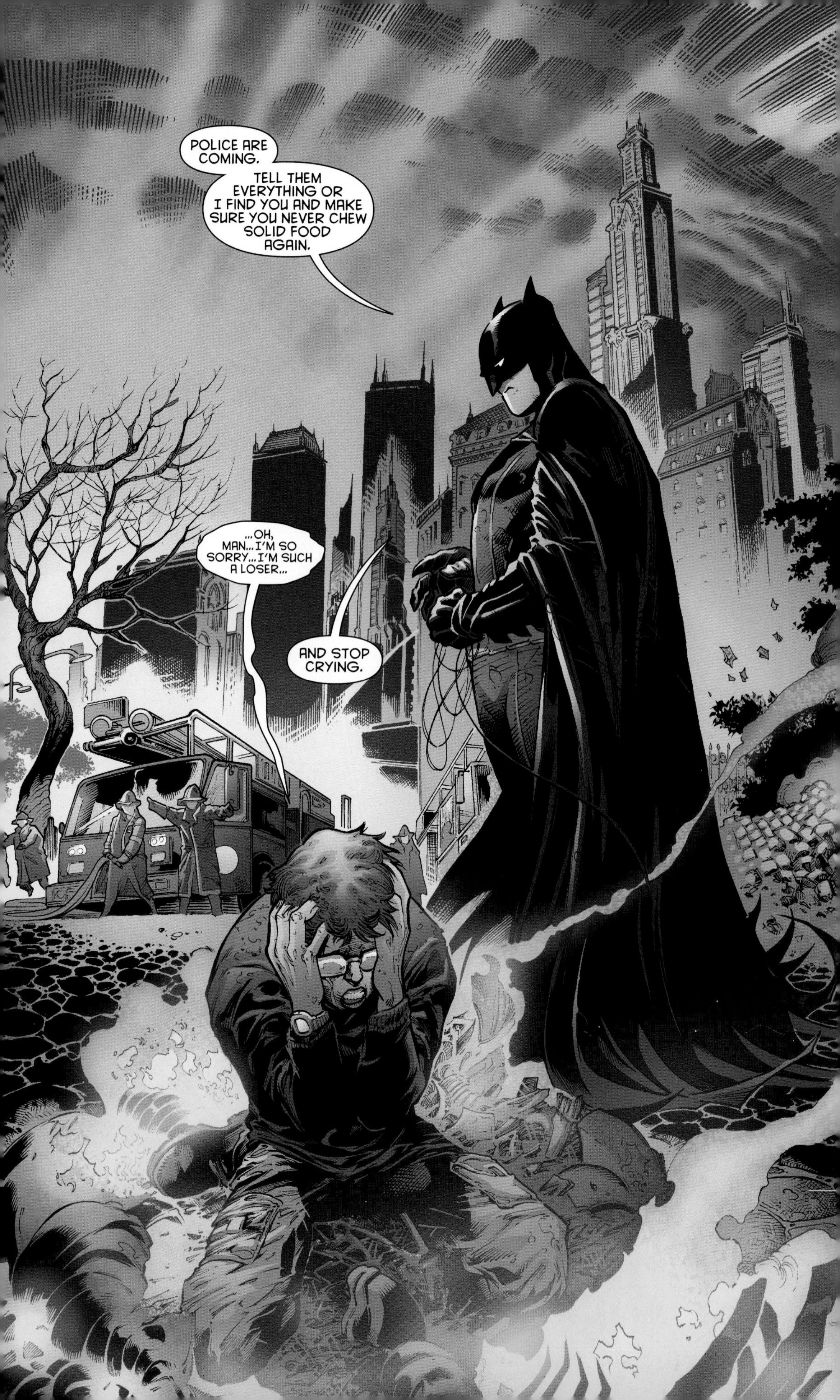
POLICE ARE COMING.
TELL THEM EVERYTHING OR I FIND YOU AND MAKE SURE YOU NEVER CHEW SOLID FOOD AGAIN.
...OH, MAN...I'M SO SORRY...I'M SUCH A LOSER...
AND STOP CRYING.

WAYNE MANOR.

HNN... ALFRED...

...NNN...

...COME ON...JUST A FEW MORE MINUTES...

STOP YOUR SOBBING, MASTER BRUCE.

...GNNN...

KRRKK

IT'S LUNCHTIME.

YOUR BREAKFAST IS READY.

DID DAMIAN CHECK IN?

IN A MANNER OF SPEAKING, YES.

EAT AND PUT ON THE NEW TED BAKER SUIT YOU BOUGHT. IT'S PERFECT FOR TRAVELING.

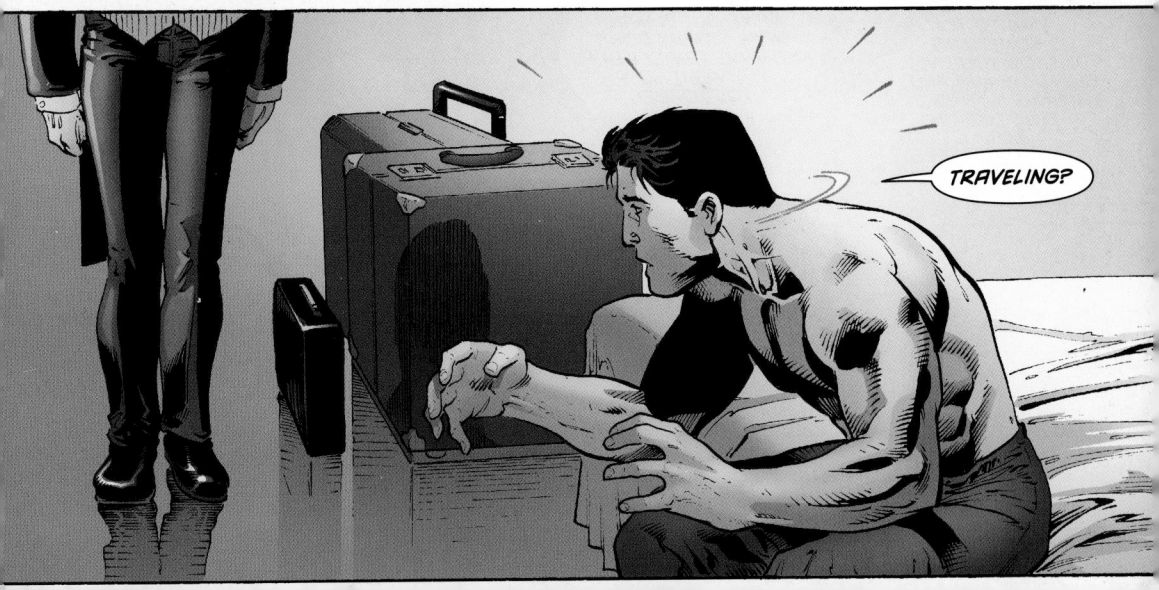

TRAVELING?

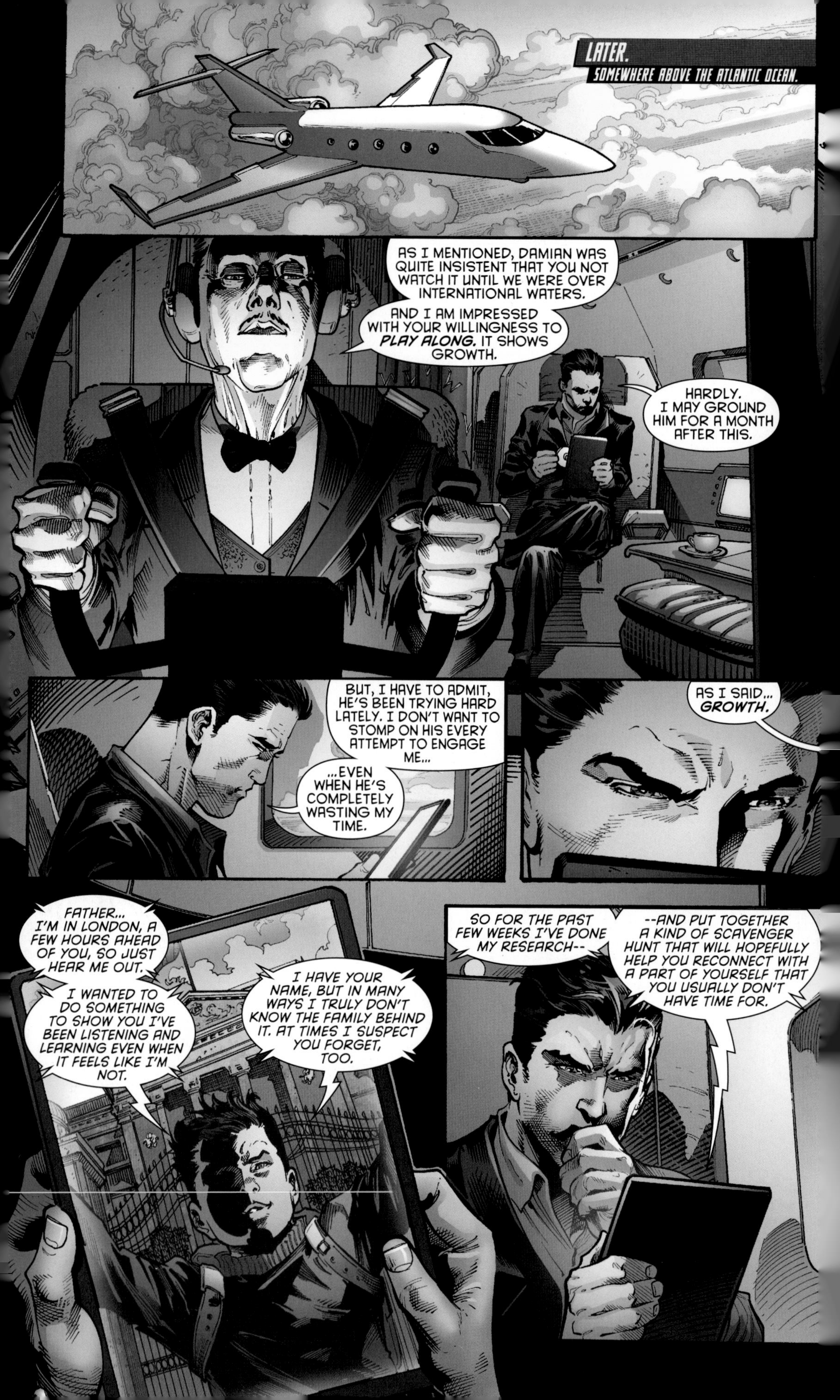
LATER.
SOMEWHERE ABOVE THE ATLANTIC OCEAN.
AS I MENTIONED, DAMIAN WAS QUITE INSISTENT THAT YOU NOT WATCH IT UNTIL WE WERE OVER INTERNATIONAL WATERS.
AND I AM IMPRESSED WITH YOUR WILLINGNESS TO PLAY ALONG. IT SHOWS GROWTH.
HARDLY. I MAY GROUND HIM FOR A MONTH AFTER THIS.
BUT, I HAVE TO ADMIT, HE'S BEEN TRYING HARD LATELY. I DON'T WANT TO STOMP ON HIS EVERY ATTEMPT TO ENGAGE ME...
...EVEN WHEN HE'S COMPLETELY WASTING MY TIME.
AS I SAID... GROWTH.
FATHER... I'M IN LONDON, A FEW HOURS AHEAD OF YOU, SO JUST HEAR ME OUT.
I WANTED TO DO SOMETHING TO SHOW YOU I'VE BEEN LISTENING AND LEARNING EVEN WHEN IT FEELS LIKE I'M NOT.
I HAVE YOUR NAME, BUT IN MANY WAYS I TRULY DON'T KNOW THE FAMILY BEHIND IT. AT TIMES I SUSPECT YOU FORGET, TOO.
SO FOR THE PAST FEW WEEKS I'VE DONE MY RESEARCH--
--AND PUT TOGETHER A KIND OF SCAVENGER HUNT THAT WILL HOPEFULLY HELP YOU RECONNECT WITH A PART OF YOURSELF THAT YOU USUALLY DON'T HAVE TIME FOR.

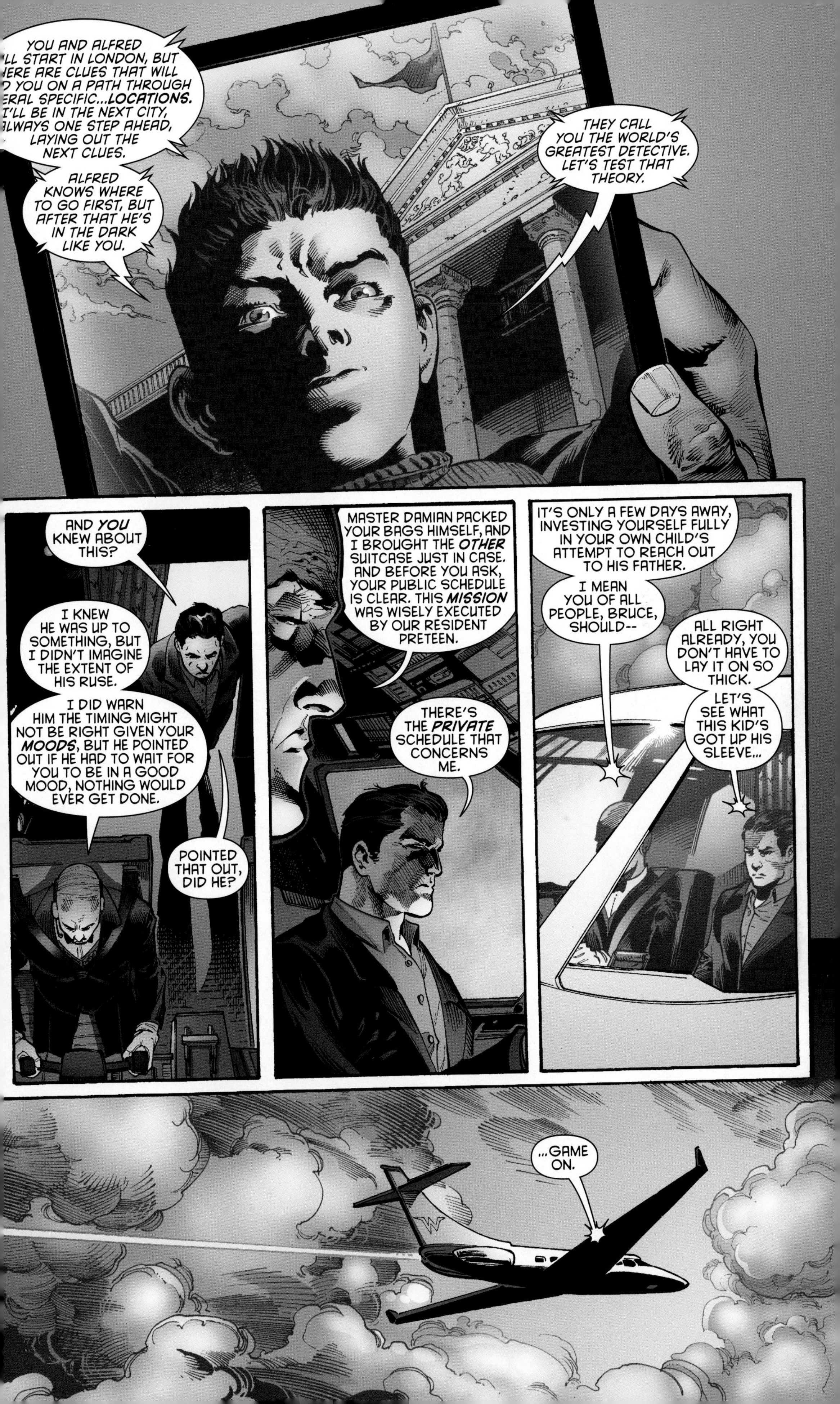
YOU AND ALFRED
'LL START IN LONDON, BUT
HERE ARE CLUES THAT WILL
D YOU ON A PATH THROUGH
ERAL SPECIFIC...LOCATIONS.
I'LL BE IN THE NEXT CITY,
ALWAYS ONE STEP AHEAD,
LAYING OUT THE
NEXT CLUES.
ALFRED KNOWS WHERE TO GO FIRST, BUT AFTER THAT HE'S IN THE DARK LIKE YOU.
THEY CALL YOU THE WORLD'S GREATEST DETECTIVE. LET'S TEST THAT THEORY.
AND YOU KNEW ABOUT THIS?
I KNEW HE WAS UP TO SOMETHING, BUT I DIDN'T IMAGINE THE EXTENT OF HIS RUSE.
I DID WARN HIM THE TIMING MIGHT NOT BE RIGHT GIVEN YOUR MOODS, BUT HE POINTED OUT IF HE HAD TO WAIT FOR YOU TO BE IN A GOOD MOOD, NOTHING WOULD EVER GET DONE.
POINTED THAT OUT, DID HE?
MASTER DAMIAN PACKED YOUR BAGS HIMSELF, AND I BROUGHT THE OTHER SUITCASE JUST IN CASE. AND BEFORE YOU ASK, YOUR PUBLIC SCHEDULE IS CLEAR. THIS MISSION WAS WISELY EXECUTED BY OUR RESIDENT PRETEEN.
THERE'S THE PRIVATE SCHEDULE THAT CONCERNS ME.
IT'S ONLY A FEW DAYS AWAY, INVESTING YOURSELF FULLY IN YOUR OWN CHILD'S ATTEMPT TO REACH OUT TO HIS FATHER.
I MEAN YOU OF ALL PEOPLE, BRUCE, SHOULD--
ALL RIGHT ALREADY, YOU DON'T HAVE TO LAY IT ON SO THICK.
LET'S SEE WHAT THIS KID'S GOT UP HIS SLEEVE...
...GAME ON.

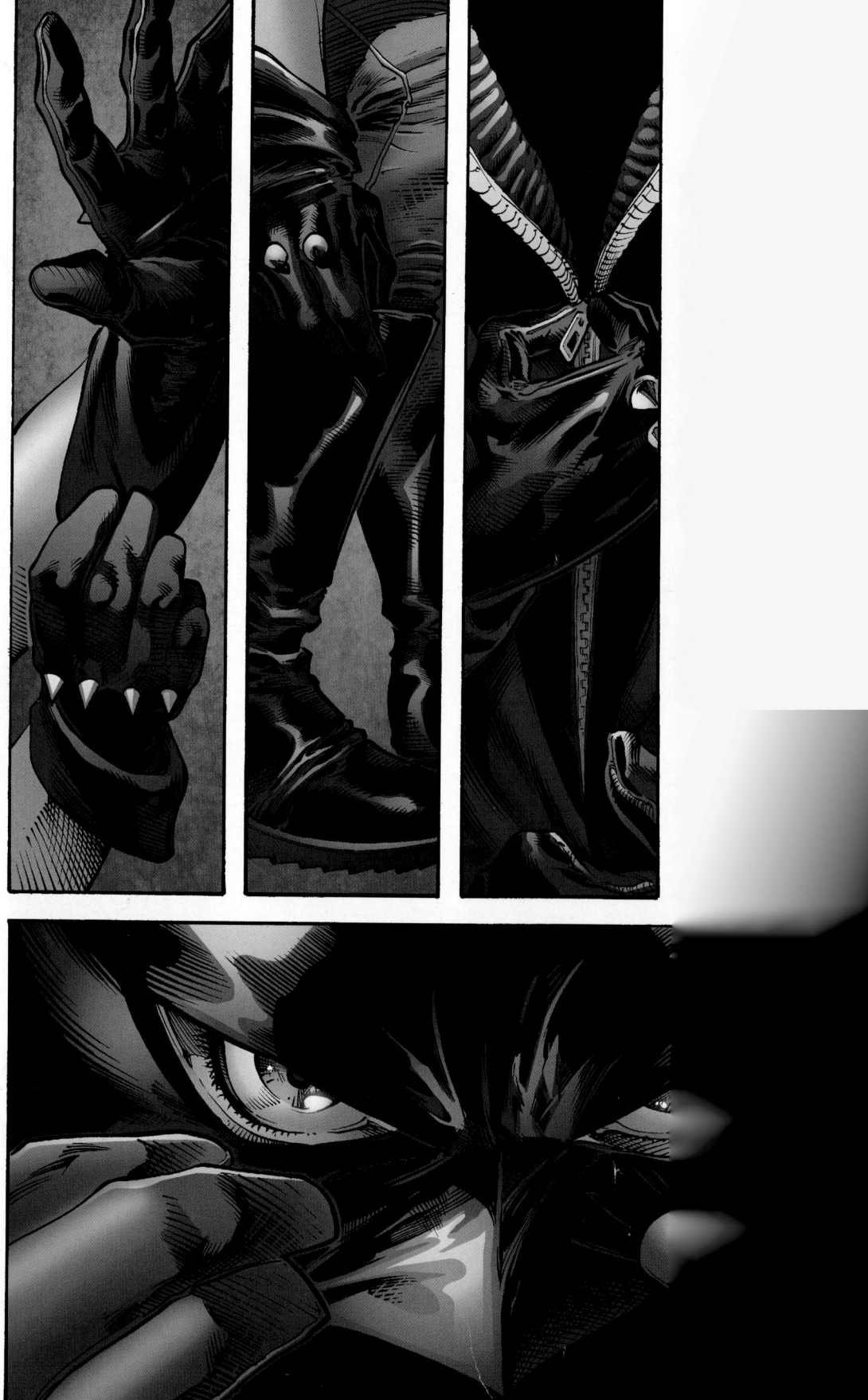

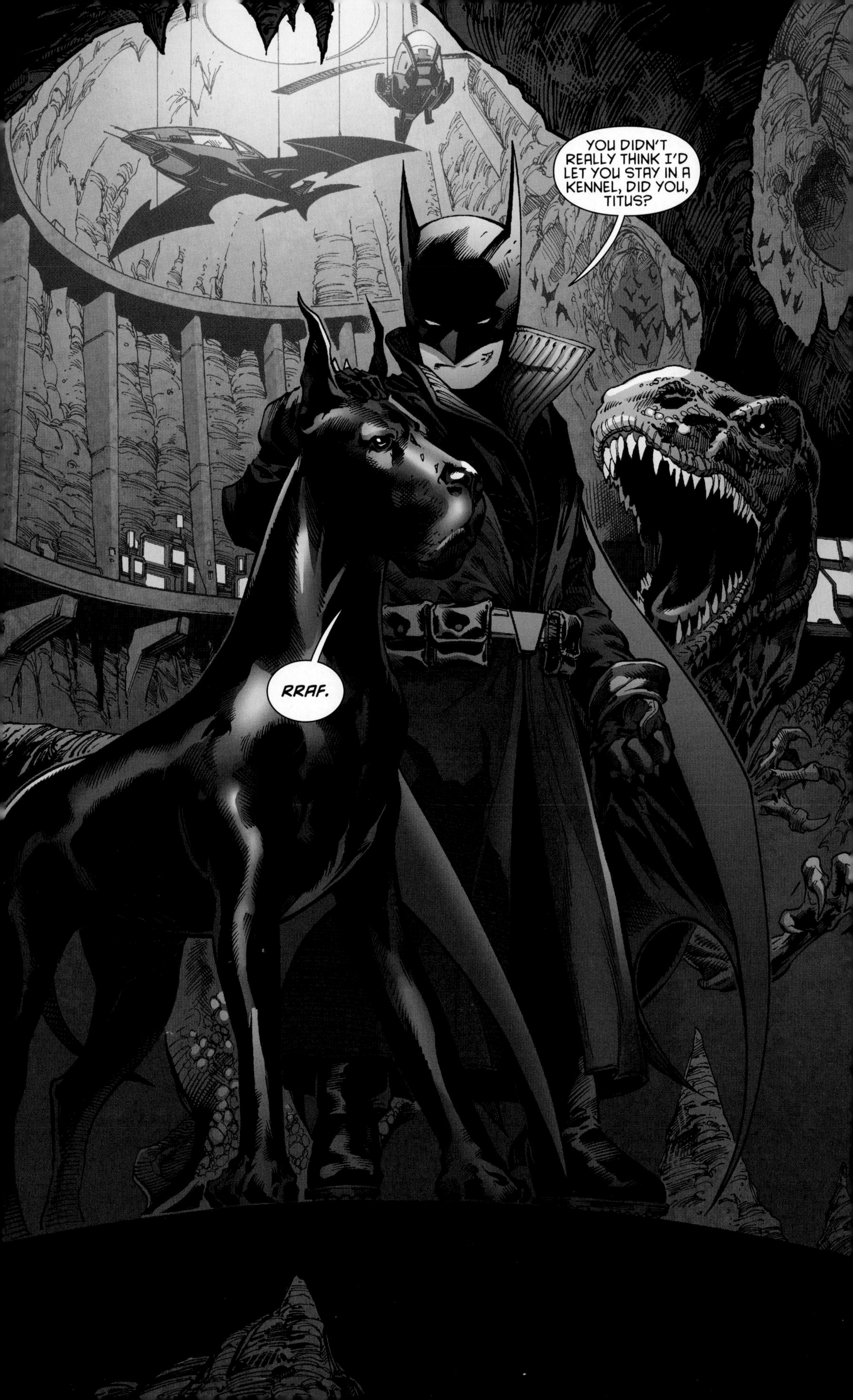
YOU DIDN'T REALLY THINK I'D LET YOU STAY IN A KENNEL, DID YOU, TITUS?
RRAF.

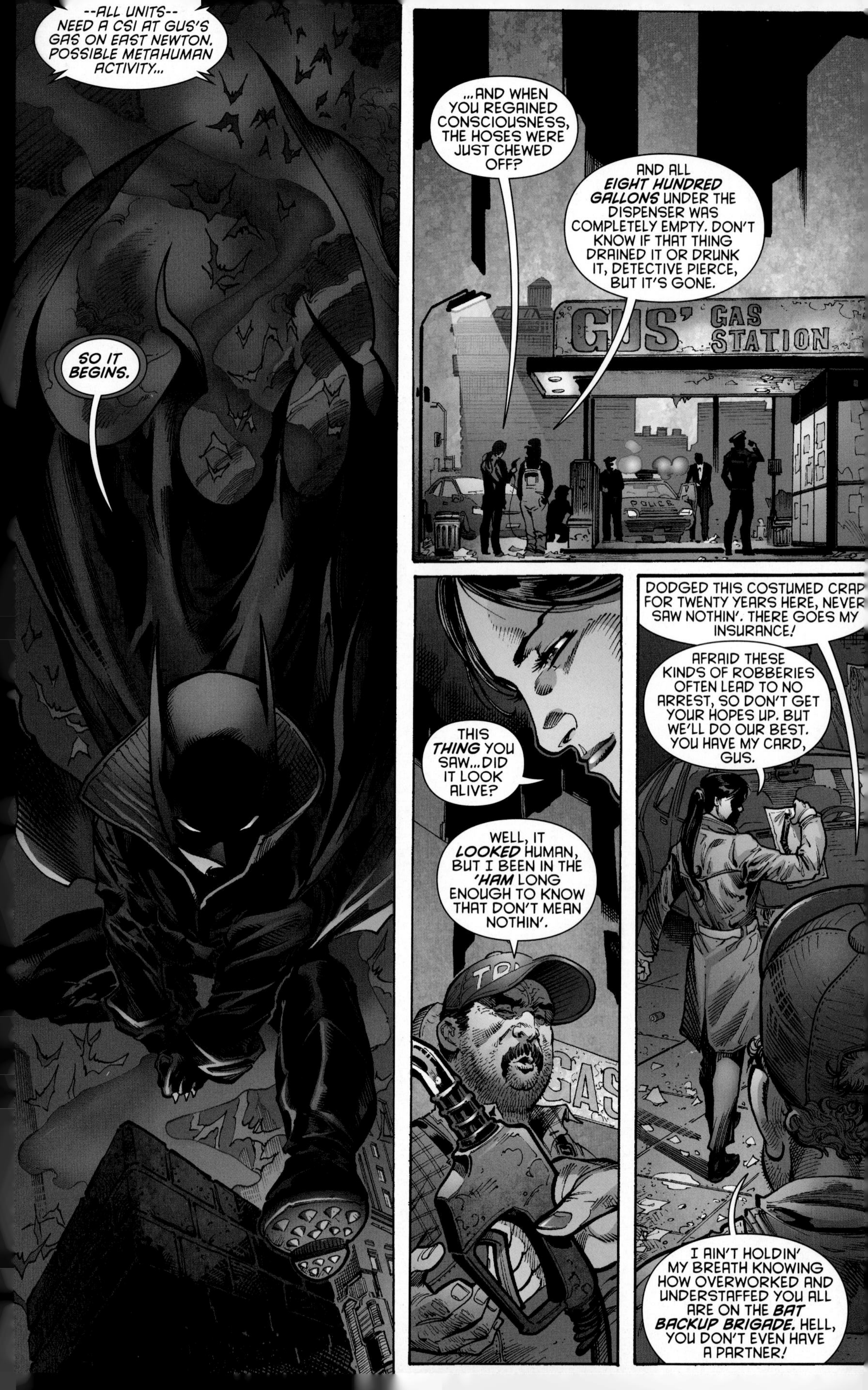
--ALL UNITS-- NEED A CSI AT GUS'S GAS ON EAST NEWTON. POSSIBLE METAHUMAN ACTIVITY...
SO IT BEGINS.
...AND WHEN YOU REGAINED CONSCIOUSNESS, THE HOSES WERE JUST CHEWED OFF?
AND ALL EIGHT HUNDRED GALLONS UNDER THE DISPENSER WAS COMPLETELY EMPTY. DON'T KNOW IF THAT THING DRAINED IT OR DRUNK IT, DETECTIVE PIERCE, BUT IT'S GONE.
GUS' GAS STATION
POLICE
THIS THING YOU SAW...DID IT LOOK ALIVE?
WELL, IT LOOKED HUMAN, BUT I BEEN IN THE 'HAM LONG ENOUGH TO KNOW THAT DON'T MEAN NOTHIN'.
DODGED THIS COSTUMED CRAP FOR TWENTY YEARS HERE, NEVER SAW NOTHIN'. THERE GOES MY INSURANCE!
AFRAID THESE KINDS OF ROBBERIES OFTEN LEAD TO NO ARREST, SO DON'T GET YOUR HOPES UP. BUT WE'LL DO OUR BEST. YOU HAVE MY CARD, GUS.
I AIN'T HOLDIN' MY BREATH KNOWING HOW OVERWORKED AND UNDERSTAFFED YOU ALL ARE ON THE BAT BACKUP BRIGADE. HELL, YOU DON'T EVEN HAVE A PARTNER!

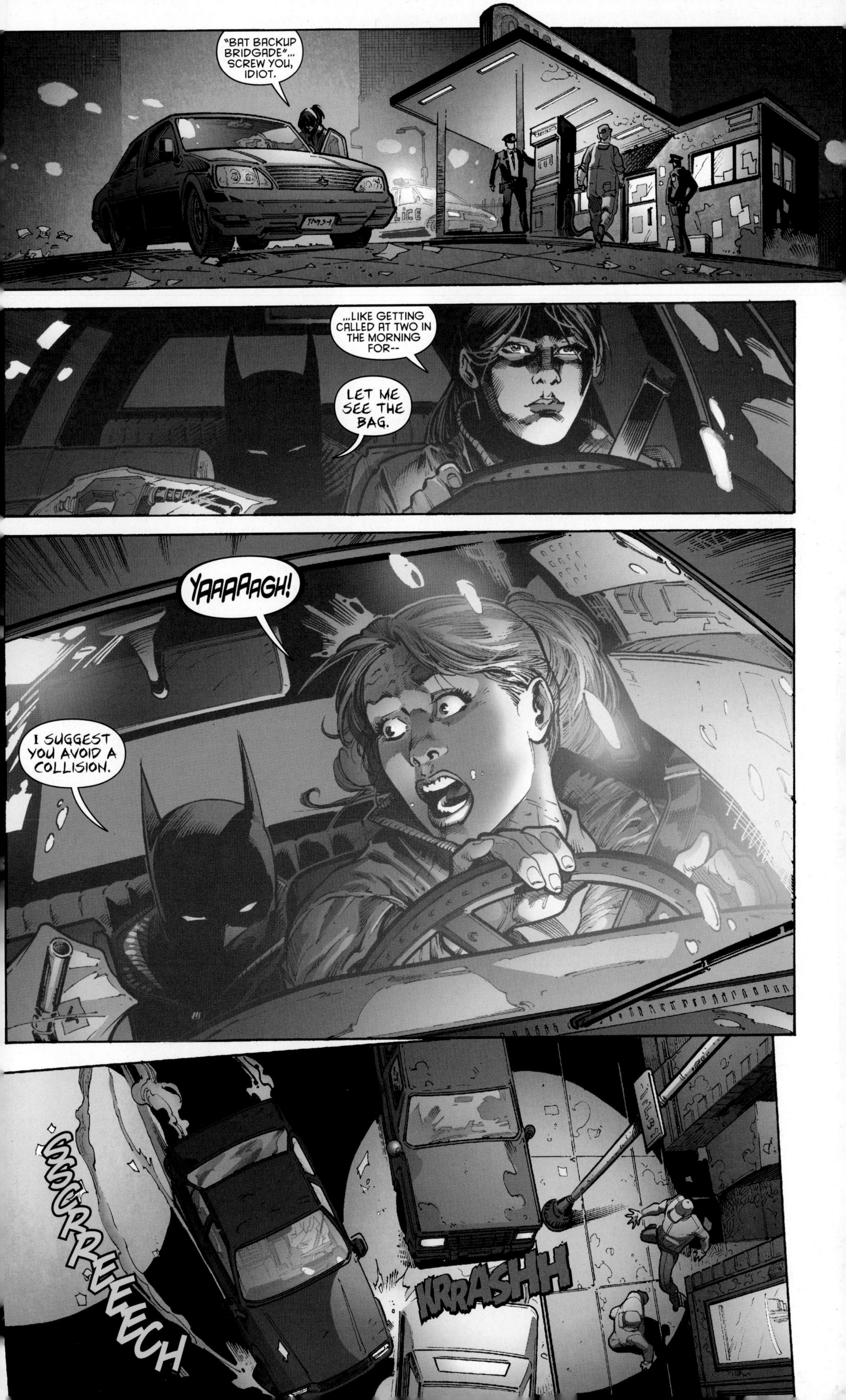
"BAT BACKUP BRIDGADE"... SCREW YOU, IDIOT.
...LIKE GETTING CALLED AT TWO IN THE MORNING FOR--
LET ME SEE THE BAG.
YAAAAAGH!
I SUGGEST YOU AVOID A COLLISION.
SSCREEEECH
KRRASHH

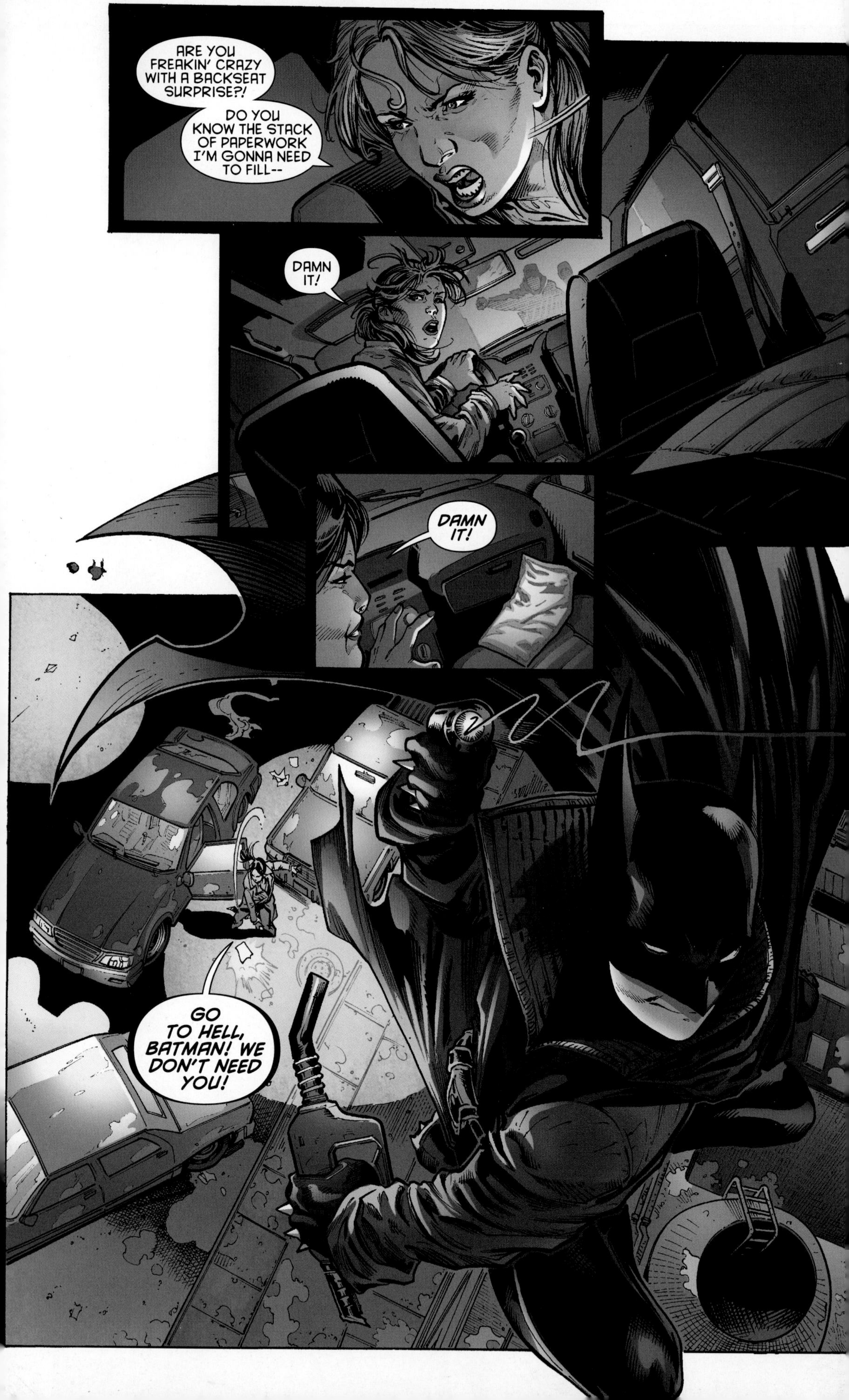
ARE YOU FREAKIN' CRAZY WITH A BACKSEAT SURPRISE?!
DO YOU KNOW THE STACK OF PAPERWORK I'M GONNA NEED TO FILL--
DAMN IT!
DAMN IT!
GO TO HELL, BATMAN! WE DON'T NEED YOU!

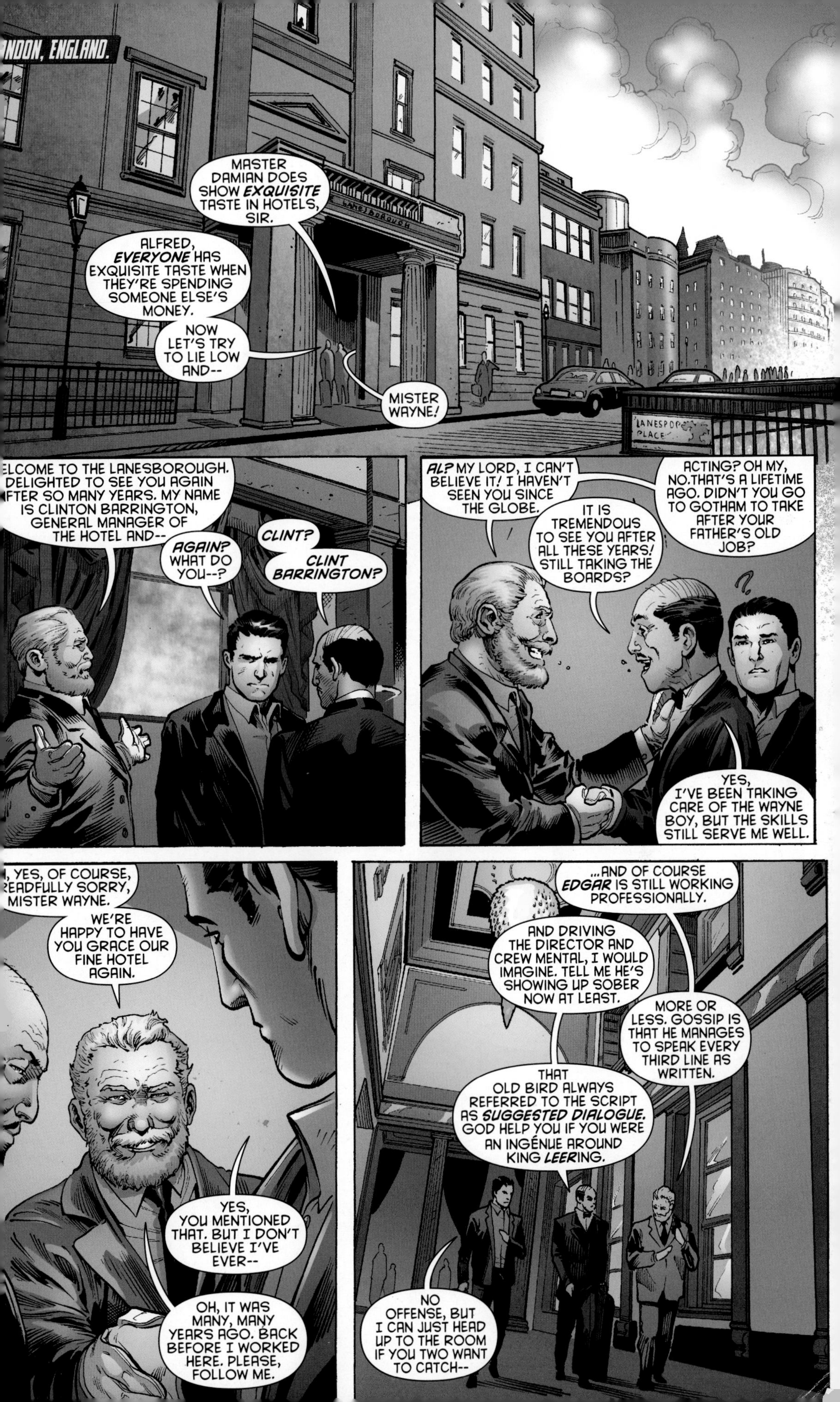
NDON, ENGLAND.
MASTER DAMIAN DOES SHOW EXQUISITE TASTE IN HOTELS, SIR.
ALFRED, EVERYONE HAS EXQUISITE TASTE WHEN THEY'RE SPENDING SOMEONE ELSE'S MONEY.
NOW LET'S TRY TO LIE LOW AND--
MISTER WAYNE!
LANESBOROUGH PLACE
ELCOME TO THE LANESBOROUGH. DELIGHTED TO SEE YOU AGAIN AFTER SO MANY YEARS. MY NAME IS CLINTON BARRINGTON, GENERAL MANAGER OF THE HOTEL AND--
AGAIN? WHAT DO YOU--?
CLINT?
CLINT BARRINGTON?
AL? MY LORD, I CAN'T BELIEVE IT! I HAVEN'T SEEN YOU SINCE THE GLOBE.
IT IS TREMENDOUS TO SEE YOU AFTER ALL THESE YEARS! STILL TAKING THE BOARDS?
ACTING? OH MY, NO. THAT'S A LIFETIME AGO. DIDN'T YOU GO TO GOTHAM TO TAKE AFTER YOUR FATHER'S OLD JOB?
?
YES, I'VE BEEN TAKING CARE OF THE WAYNE BOY, BUT THE SKILLS STILL SERVE ME WELL.
, YES, OF COURSE, READFULLY SORRY, MISTER WAYNE.
WE'RE HAPPY TO HAVE YOU GRACE OUR FINE HOTEL AGAIN.
YES, YOU MENTIONED THAT. BUT I DON'T BELIEVE I'VE EVER--
OH, IT WAS MANY, MANY YEARS AGO. BACK BEFORE I WORKED HERE. PLEASE, FOLLOW ME.
...AND OF COURSE EDGAR IS STILL WORKING PROFESSIONALLY.
AND DRIVING THE DIRECTOR AND CREW MENTAL, I WOULD IMAGINE. TELL ME HE'S SHOWING UP SOBER NOW AT LEAST.
MORE OR LESS. GOSSIP IS THAT HE MANAGES TO SPEAK EVERY THIRD LINE AS WRITTEN.
THAT OLD BIRD ALWAYS REFERRED TO THE SCRIPT AS SUGGESTED DIALOGUE. GOD HELP YOU IF YOU WERE AN INGÉNUE AROUND KING LEERING.
NO OFFENSE, BUT I CAN JUST HEAD UP TO THE ROOM IF YOU TWO WANT TO CATCH--

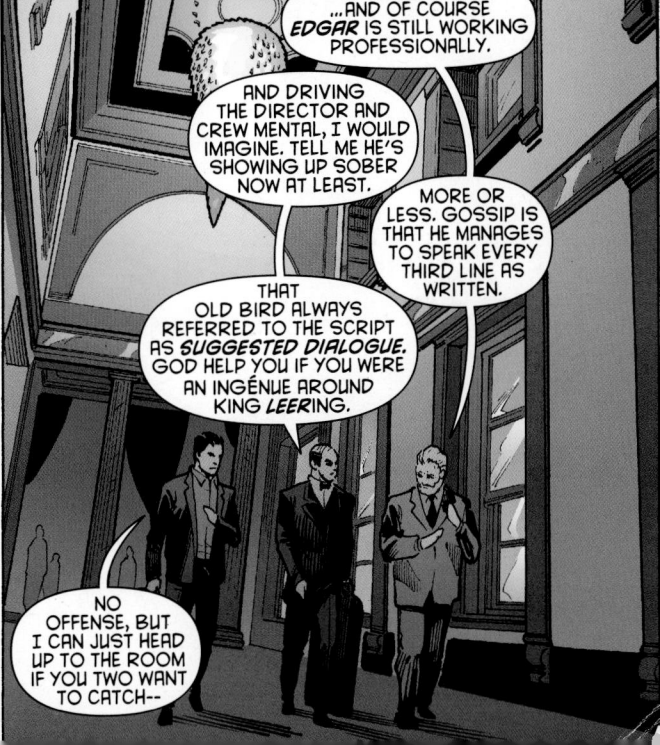

AH, HERE WE ARE...
...WE CALL IT: "UNFINISHED FRUIT."
CLINTON, I DON'T KNOW WHAT YOU'VE BEEN TOLD, BUT THAT PAINTING HAS NOTHING TO DO WITH ME.
IT MOST CERTAINLY DOES, MISTER WAYNE.
READ THE SIGNATURE.
MY... MOTHER...
SO IS THAT SMALL HAND-PRINT...?
YES IT IS.

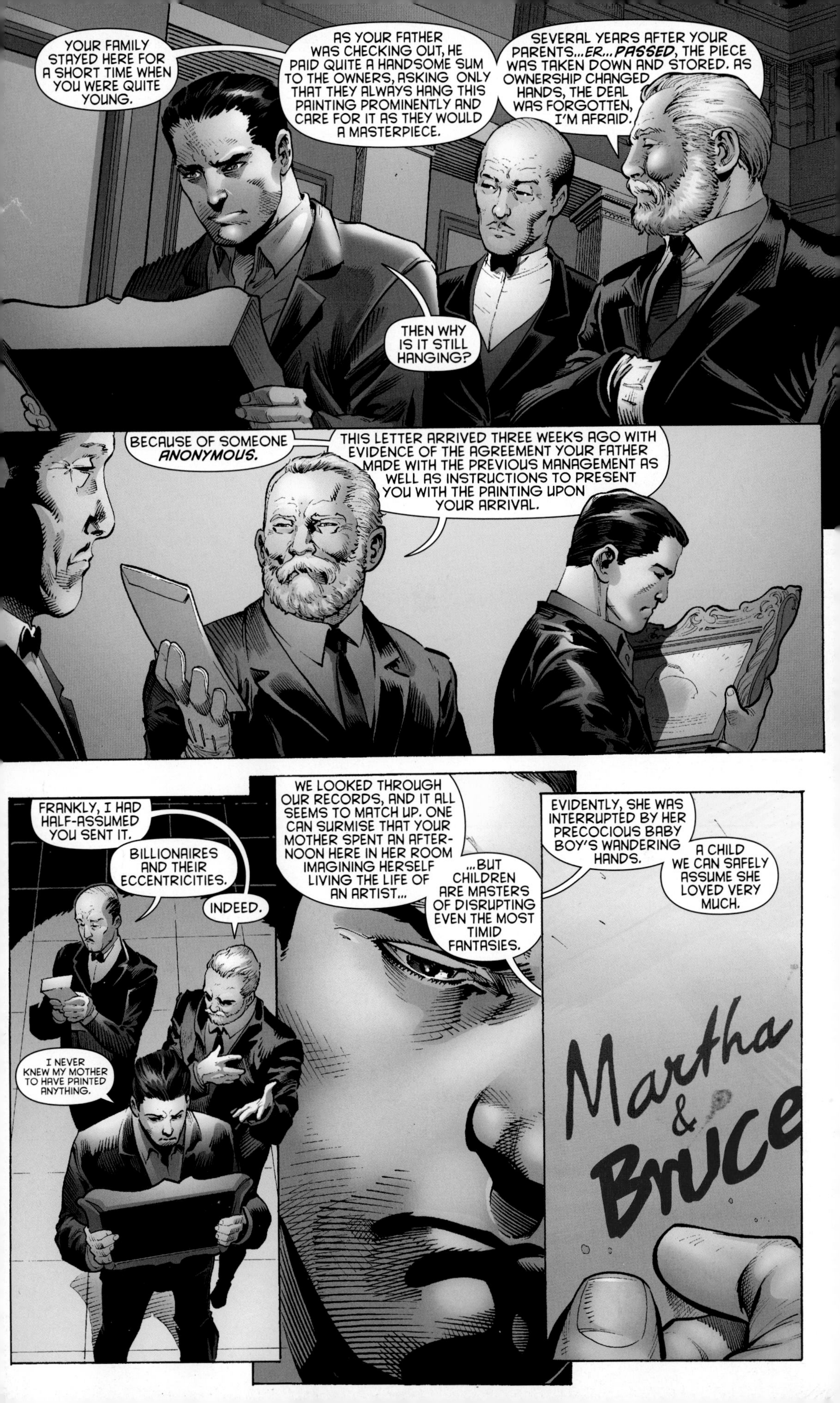
YOUR FAMILY STAYED HERE FOR A SHORT TIME WHEN YOU WERE QUITE YOUNG.
AS YOUR FATHER WAS CHECKING OUT, HE PAID QUITE A HANDSOME SUM TO THE OWNERS, ASKING ONLY THAT THEY ALWAYS HANG THIS PAINTING PROMINENTLY AND CARE FOR IT AS THEY WOULD A MASTERPIECE.
SEVERAL YEARS AFTER YOUR PARENTS...ER...PASSED, THE PIECE WAS TAKEN DOWN AND STORED. AS OWNERSHIP CHANGED HANDS, THE DEAL WAS FORGOTTEN, I'M AFRAID.
THEN WHY IS IT STILL HANGING?
BECAUSE OF SOMEONE ANONYMOUS.
THIS LETTER ARRIVED THREE WEEKS AGO WITH EVIDENCE OF THE AGREEMENT YOUR FATHER MADE WITH THE PREVIOUS MANAGEMENT AS WELL AS INSTRUCTIONS TO PRESENT YOU WITH THE PAINTING UPON YOUR ARRIVAL.
FRANKLY, I HAD HALF-ASSUMED YOU SENT IT.
BILLIONAIRES AND THEIR ECCENTRICITIES.
INDEED.
I NEVER KNEW MY MOTHER TO HAVE PAINTED ANYTHING.
WE LOOKED THROUGH OUR RECORDS, AND IT ALL SEEMS TO MATCH UP. ONE CAN SURMISE THAT YOUR MOTHER SPENT AN AFTER-NOON HERE IN HER ROOM IMAGINING HERSELF LIVING THE LIFE OF AN ARTIST...
...BUT CHILDREN ARE MASTERS OF DISRUPTING EVEN THE MOST TIMID FANTASIES.
EVIDENTLY, SHE WAS INTERRUPTED BY HER PRECOCIOUS BABY BOY'S WANDERING HANDS.
A CHILD WE CAN SAFELY ASSUME SHE LOVED VERY MUCH.
Martha & Bruce

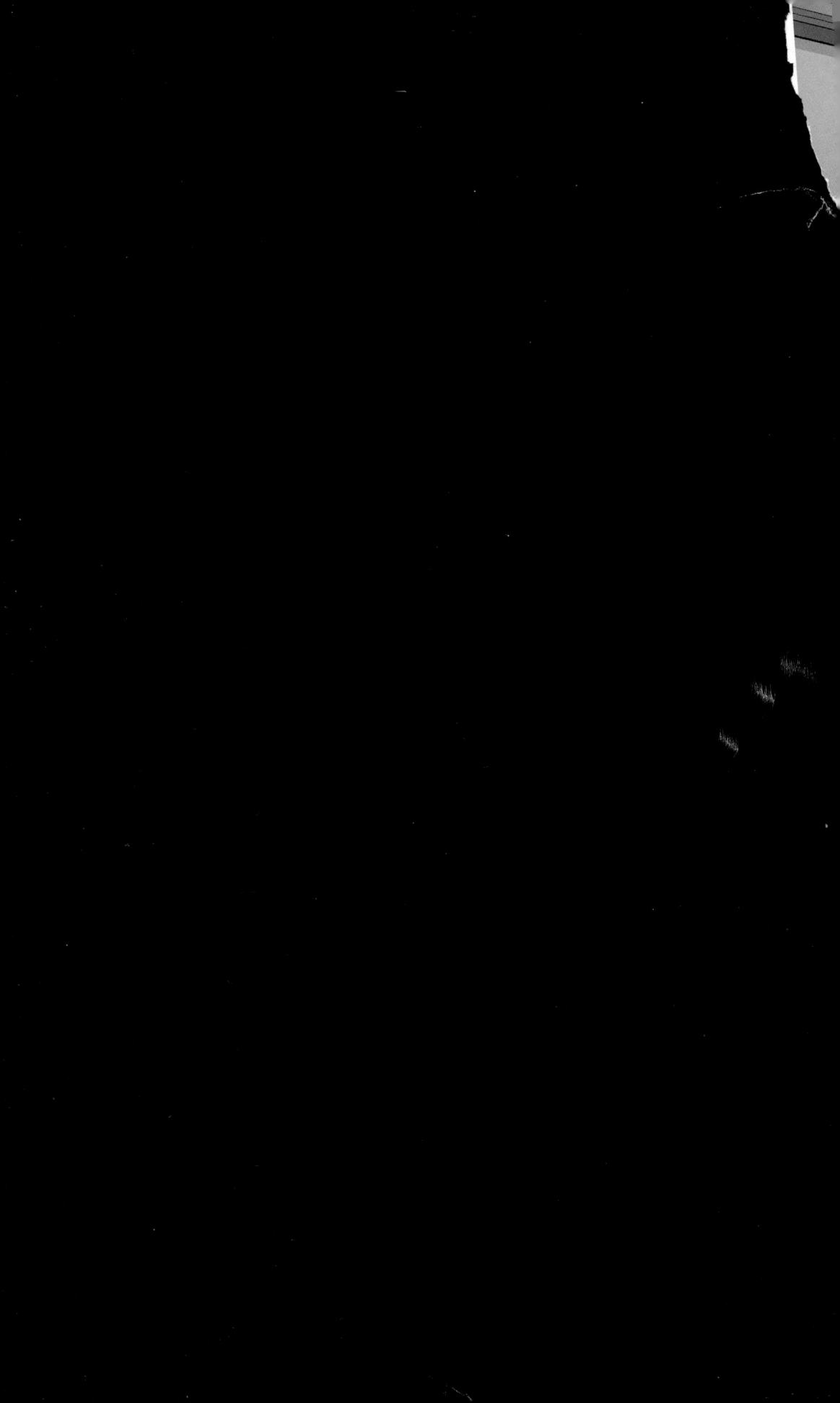

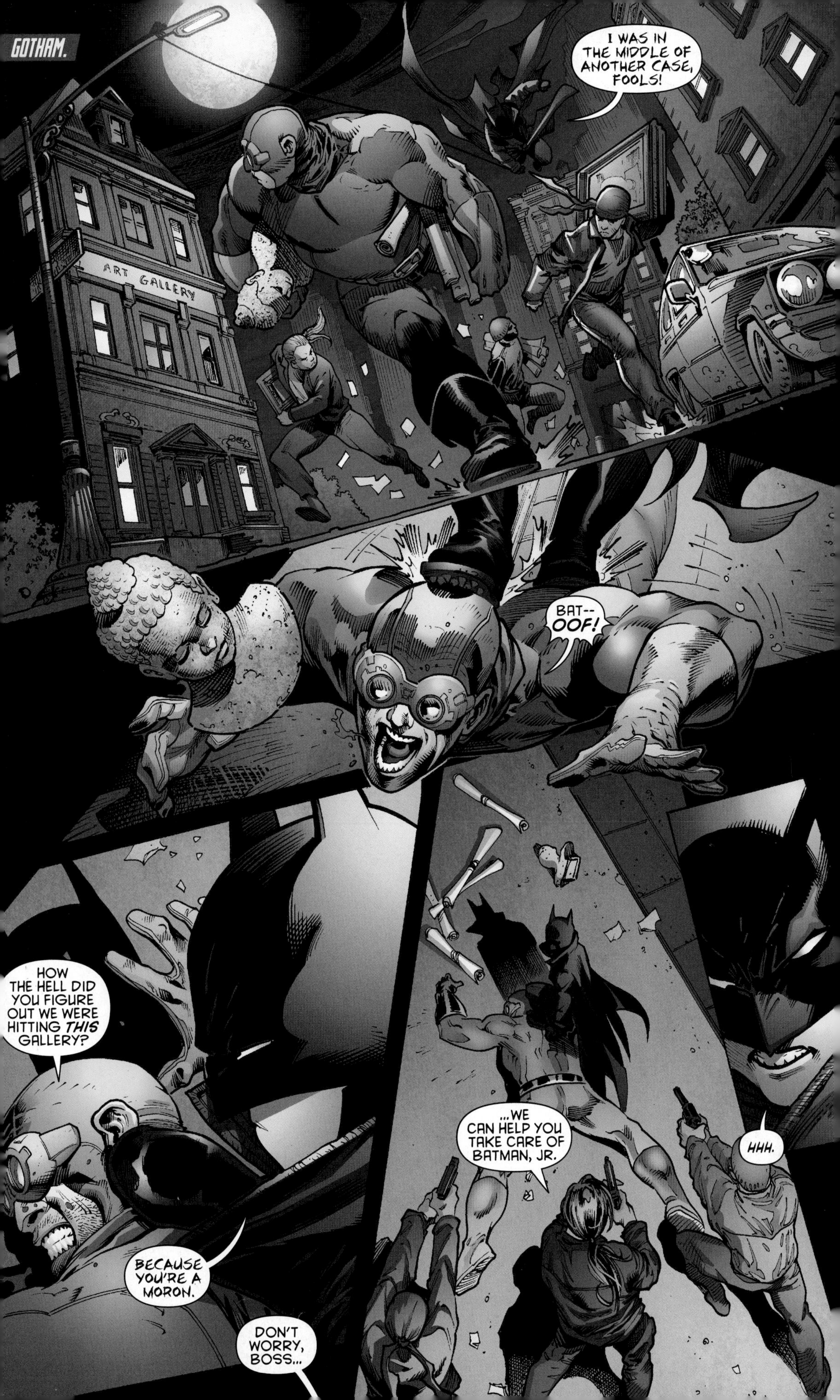
GOTHAM.
I WAS IN THE MIDDLE OF ANOTHER CASE, FOOLS!
ART GALLERY
BAT-- OOF!
HOW THE HELL DID YOU FIGURE OUT WE WERE HITTING THIS GALLERY?
BECAUSE YOU'RE A MORON.
DON'T WORRY, BOSS...
...WE CAN HELP YOU TAKE CARE OF BATMAN, JR.
HHH.

SEVENTEEN SECONDS LATER.

POOM

"THAT WAS VERY CONSIDERATE, DAMIAN."

IT WAS MY PLEASURE, FATHER. BUT YOUR QUEST ISN'T OVER.

I'M SURE YOU CAN EASILY FIGURE OUT YOUR NEXT STOP BASED ON THE CLUES YOU HAVE.

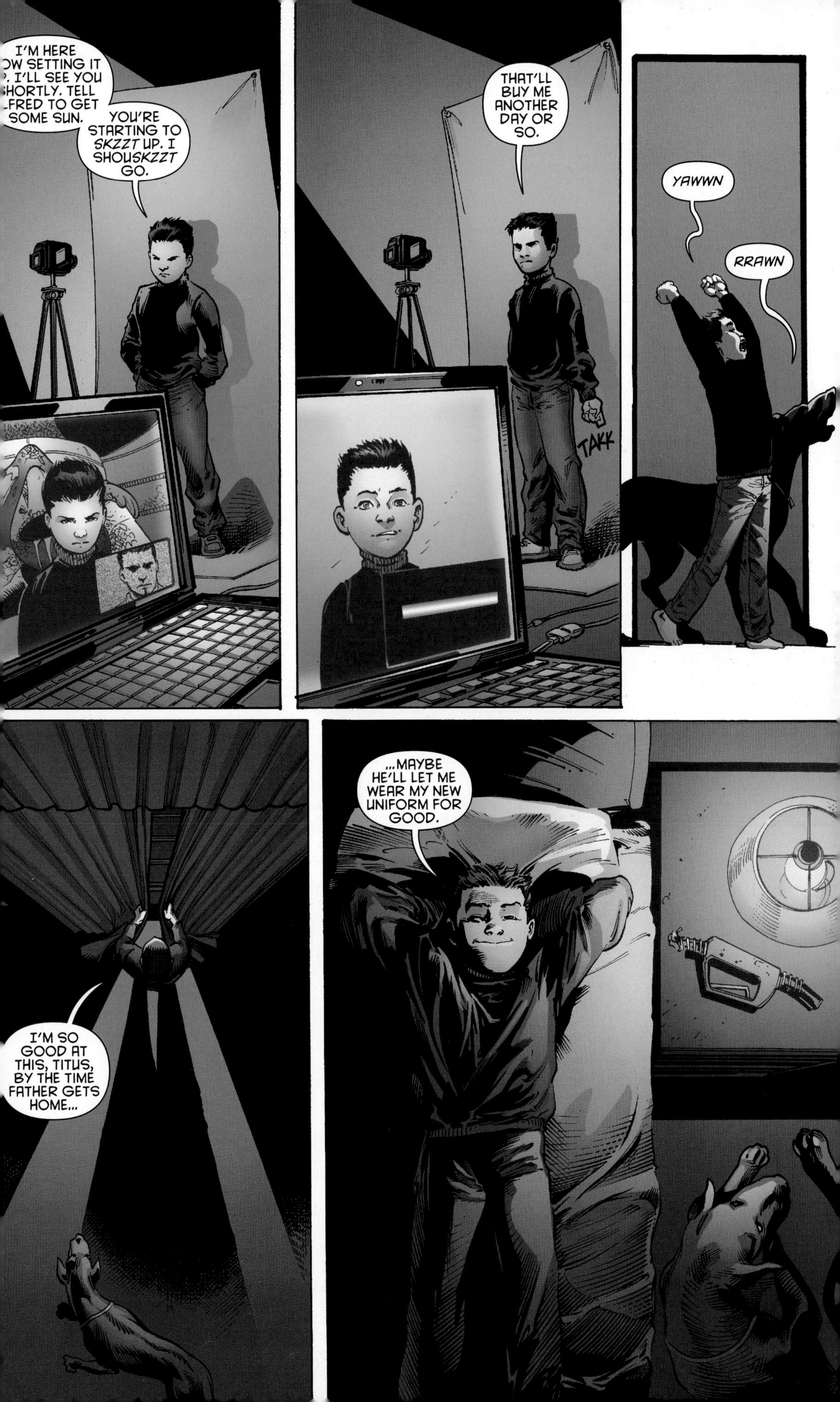
I'M HERE OW SETTING IT P. I'LL SEE YOU HORTLY. TELL FRED TO GET SOME SUN.
YOU'RE STARTING TO SKZZT UP. I SHOUSKZZT GO.
THAT'LL BUY ME ANOTHER DAY OR SO.
TAKK
YAWWN
RRAWN
I'M SO GOOD AT THIS, TITUS, BY THE TIME FATHER GETS HOME...
...MAYBE HE'LL LET ME WEAR MY NEW UNIFORM FOR GOOD.

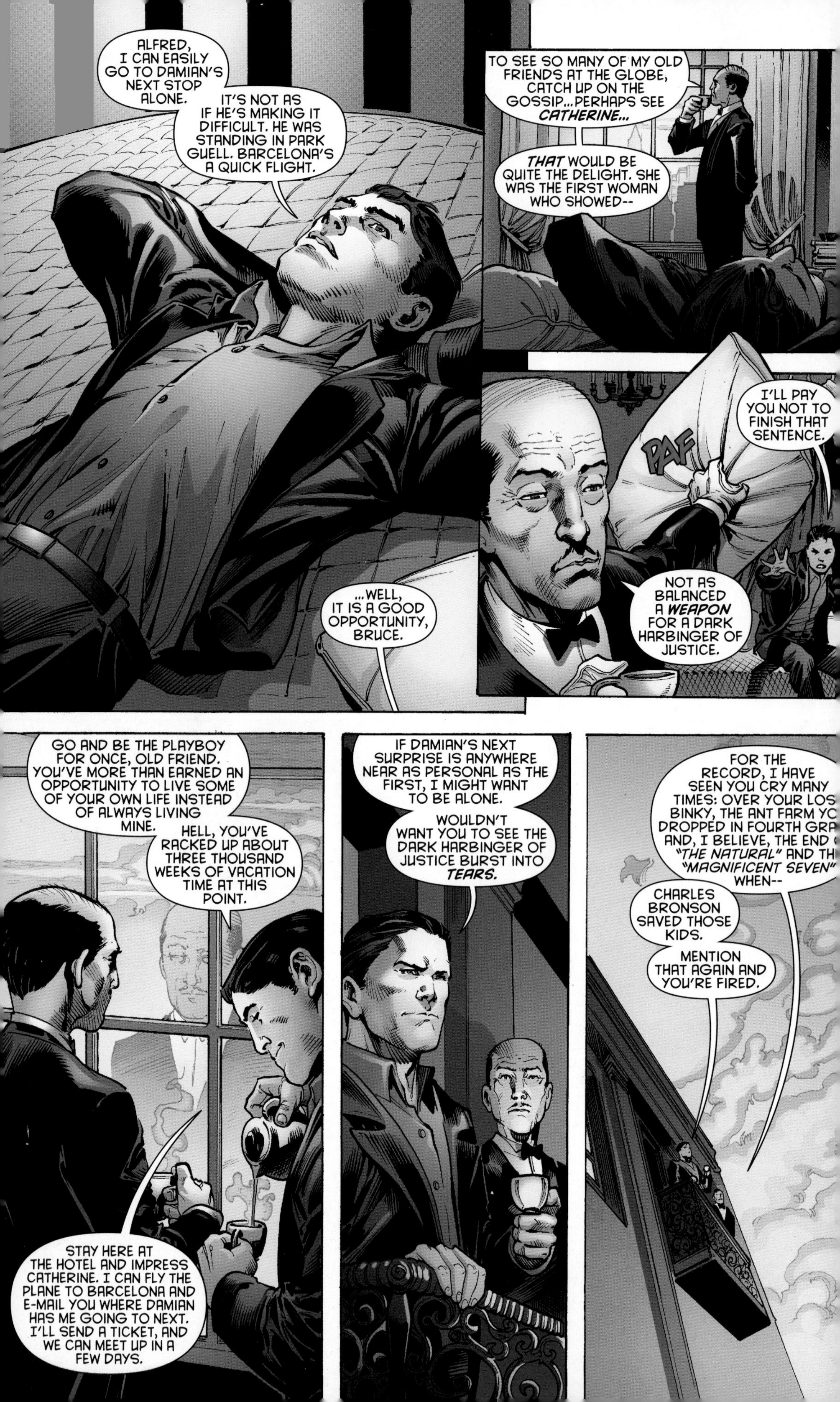
ALFRED, I CAN EASILY GO TO DAMIAN'S NEXT STOP ALONE.
IT'S NOT AS IF HE'S MAKING IT DIFFICULT. HE WAS STANDING IN PARK GUELL. BARCELONA'S A QUICK FLIGHT.
...WELL, IT IS A GOOD OPPORTUNITY, BRUCE.
TO SEE SO MANY OF MY OLD FRIENDS AT THE GLOBE, CATCH UP ON THE GOSSIP...PERHAPS SEE *CATHERINE...*
THAT WOULD BE QUITE THE DELIGHT. SHE WAS THE FIRST WOMAN WHO SHOWED--
PAF
I'LL PAY YOU NOT TO FINISH THAT SENTENCE.
NOT AS BALANCED A *WEAPON* FOR A DARK HARBINGER OF JUSTICE.
GO AND BE THE PLAYBOY FOR ONCE, OLD FRIEND. YOU'VE MORE THAN EARNED AN OPPORTUNITY TO LIVE SOME OF YOUR OWN LIFE INSTEAD OF ALWAYS LIVING MINE.
HELL, YOU'VE RACKED UP ABOUT THREE THOUSAND WEEKS OF VACATION TIME AT THIS POINT.
STAY HERE AT THE HOTEL AND IMPRESS CATHERINE. I CAN FLY THE PLANE TO BARCELONA AND E-MAIL YOU WHERE DAMIAN HAS ME GOING TO NEXT. I'LL SEND A TICKET, AND WE CAN MEET UP IN A FEW DAYS.
IF DAMIAN'S NEXT SURPRISE IS ANYWHERE NEAR AS PERSONAL AS THE FIRST, I MIGHT WANT TO BE ALONE.
WOULDN'T WANT YOU TO SEE THE DARK HARBINGER OF JUSTICE BURST INTO *TEARS.*
FOR THE RECORD, I HAVE SEEN YOU CRY MANY TIMES: OVER YOUR LOS BINKY, THE ANT FARM YO DROPPED IN FOURTH GRA AND, I BELIEVE, THE END *"THE NATURAL"* AND TH *"MAGNIFICENT SEVEN"* WHEN--
CHARLES BRONSON SAVED THOSE KIDS.
MENTION THAT AGAIN AND YOU'RE FIRED.

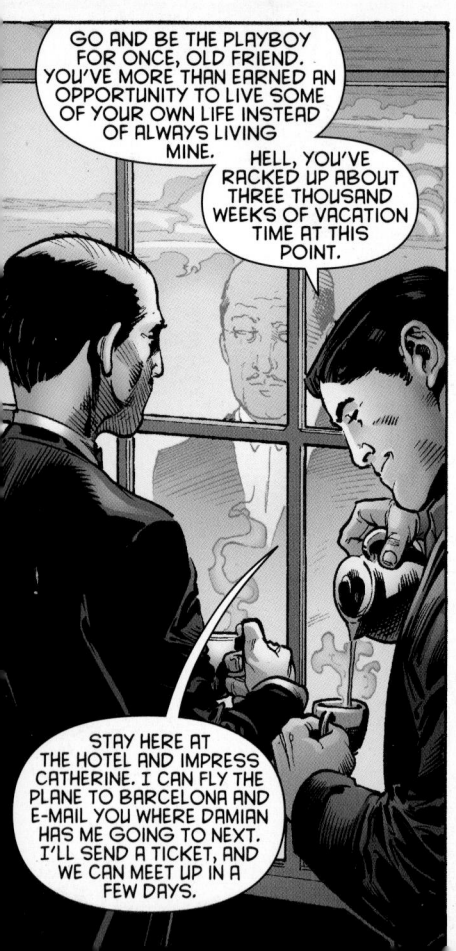

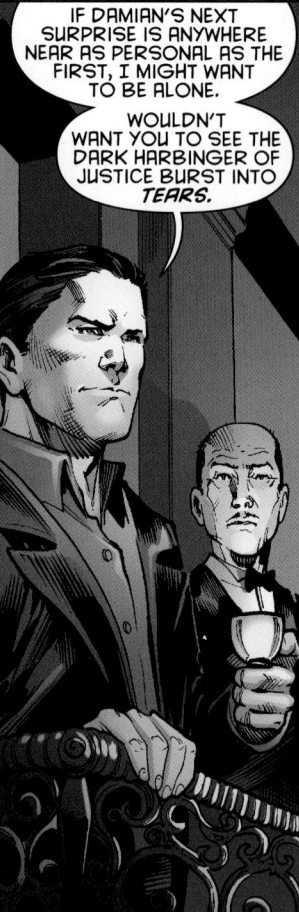

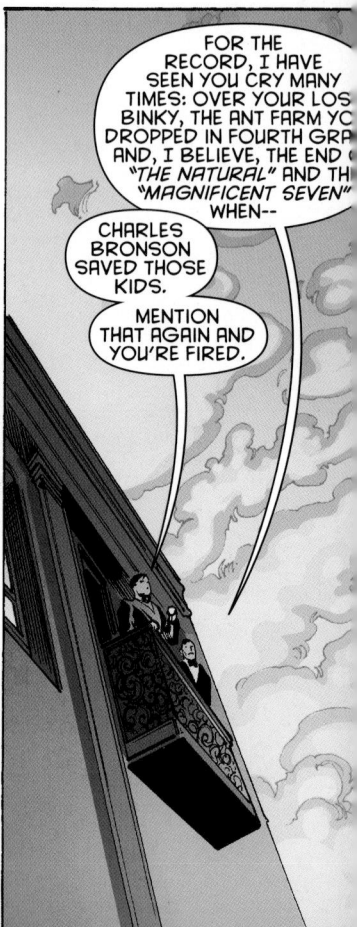

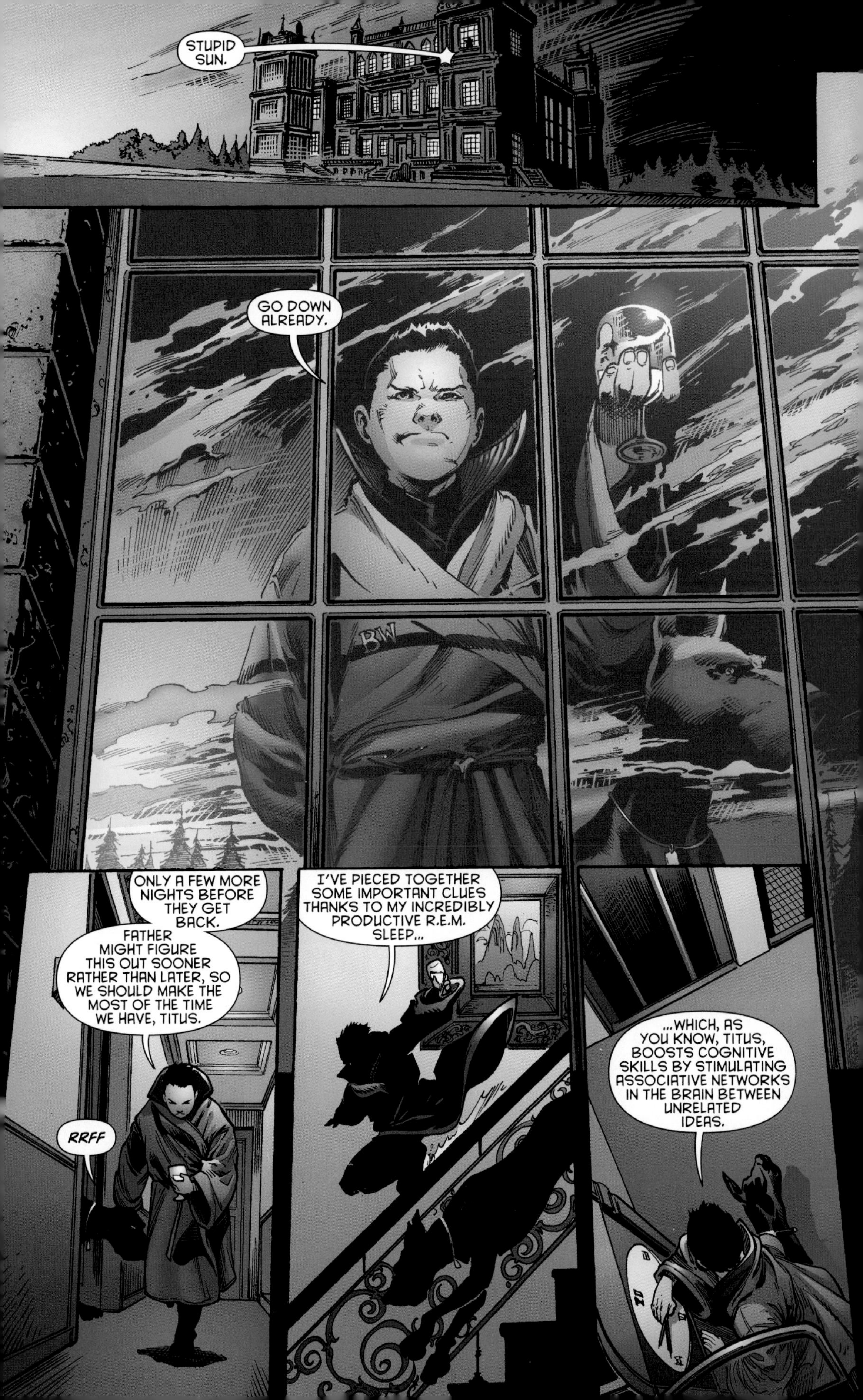
STUPID SUN.
GO DOWN ALREADY.
ONLY A FEW MORE NIGHTS BEFORE THEY GET BACK.
FATHER MIGHT FIGURE THIS OUT SOONER RATHER THAN LATER, SO WE SHOULD MAKE THE MOST OF THE TIME WE HAVE, TITUS.
RRFF
I'VE PIECED TOGETHER SOME IMPORTANT CLUES THANKS TO MY INCREDIBLY PRODUCTIVE R.E.M. SLEEP...
...WHICH, AS YOU KNOW, TITUS, BOOSTS COGNITIVE SKILLS BY STIMULATING ASSOCIATIVE NETWORKS IN THE BRAIN BETWEEN UNRELATED IDEAS.

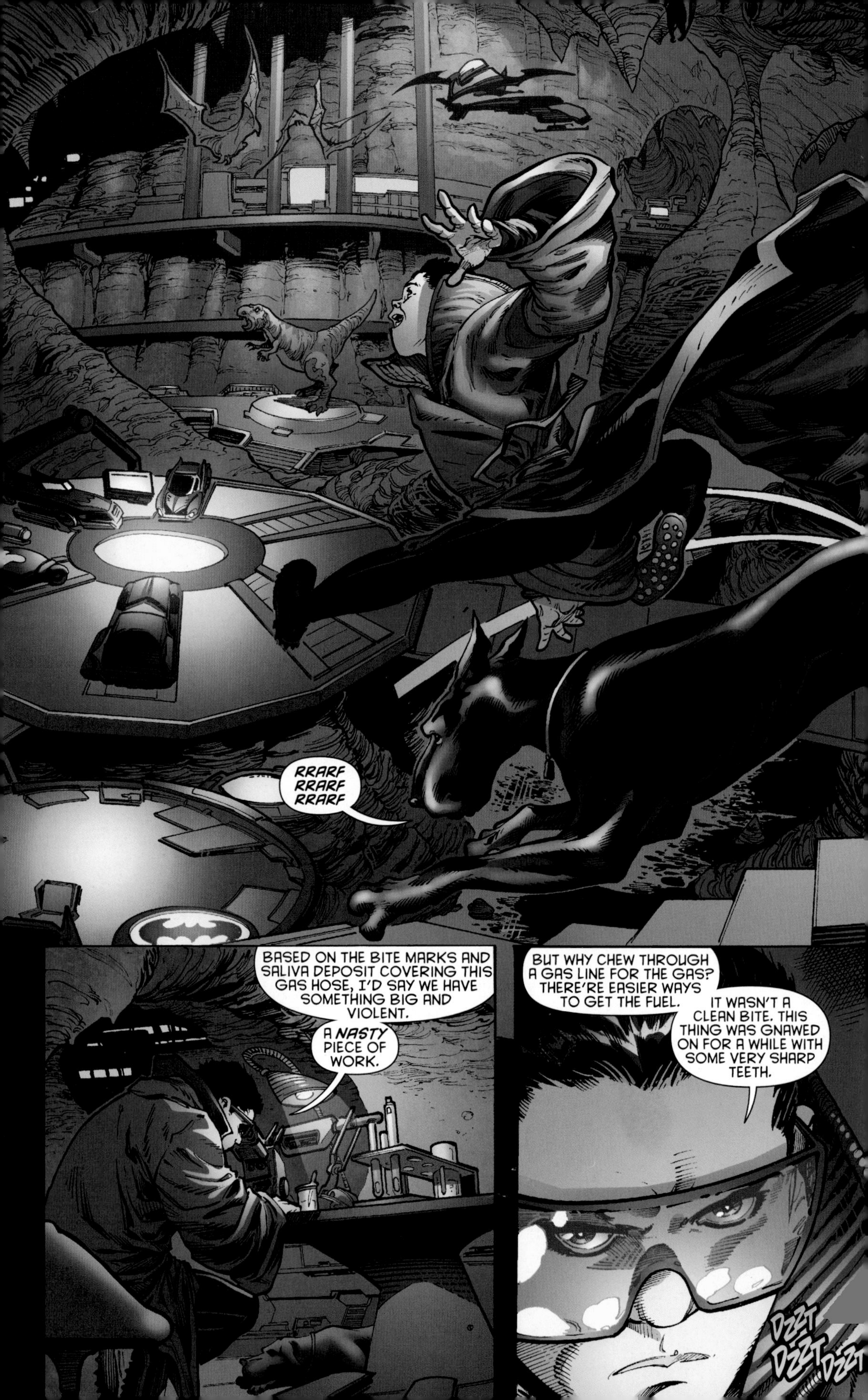
RRARF RRARF RRARF
BASED ON THE BITE MARKS AND SALIVA DEPOSIT COVERING THIS GAS HOSE, I'D SAY WE HAVE SOMETHING BIG AND VIOLENT.
A *NASTY* PIECE OF WORK.
BUT WHY CHEW THROUGH A GAS LINE FOR THE GAS? THERE'RE EASIER WAYS TO GET THE FUEL.
IT WASN'T A CLEAN BITE. THIS THING WAS GNAWED ON FOR A WHILE WITH SOME VERY SHARP TEETH.
DZZT DZZT DZZT

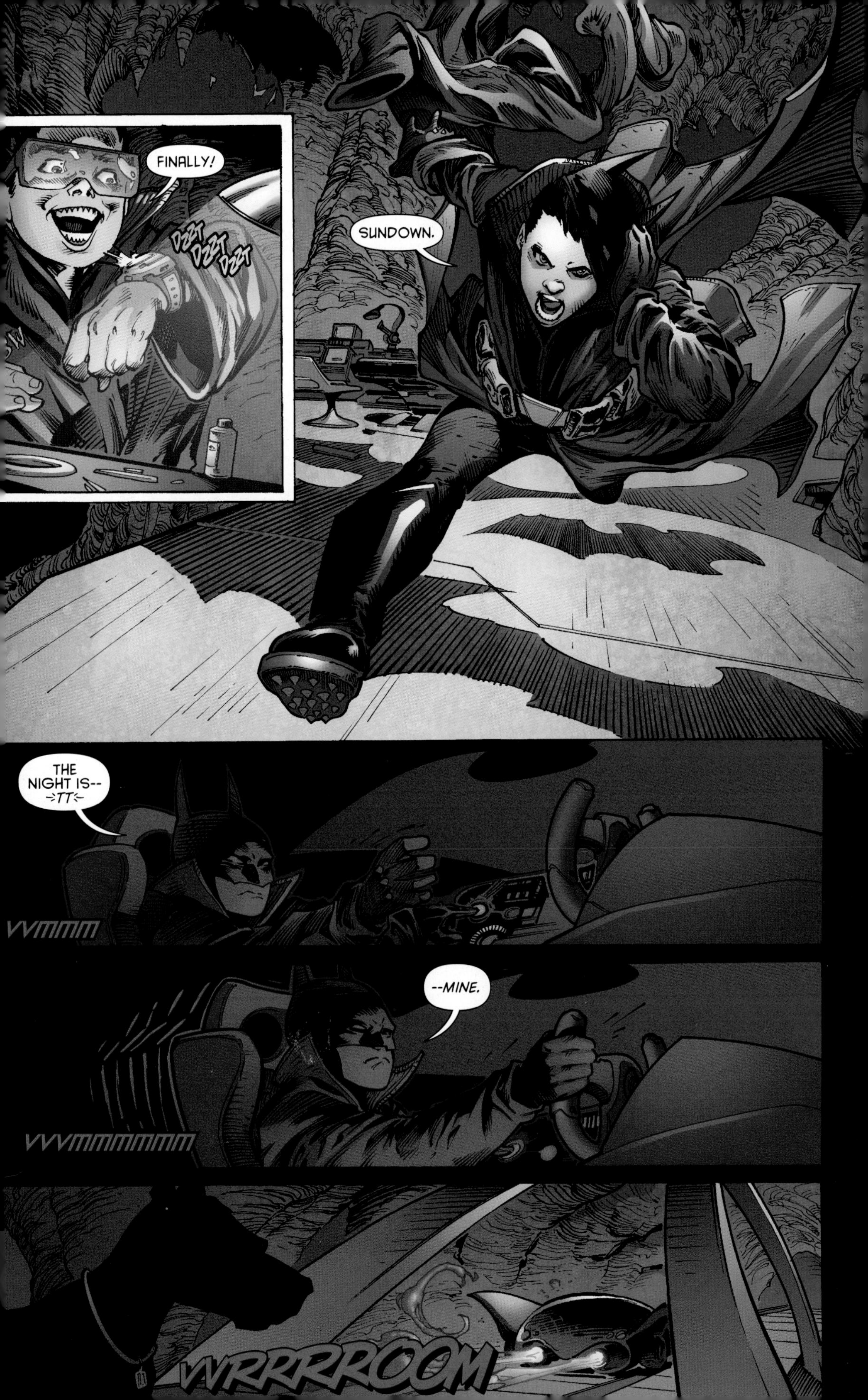
FINALLY!
DZZT DZZT DZZT
SUNDOWN.
THE NIGHT IS-- ->TT<-
VVMMM
--MINE.
VVVMMMMMMM
VVRRRROOM

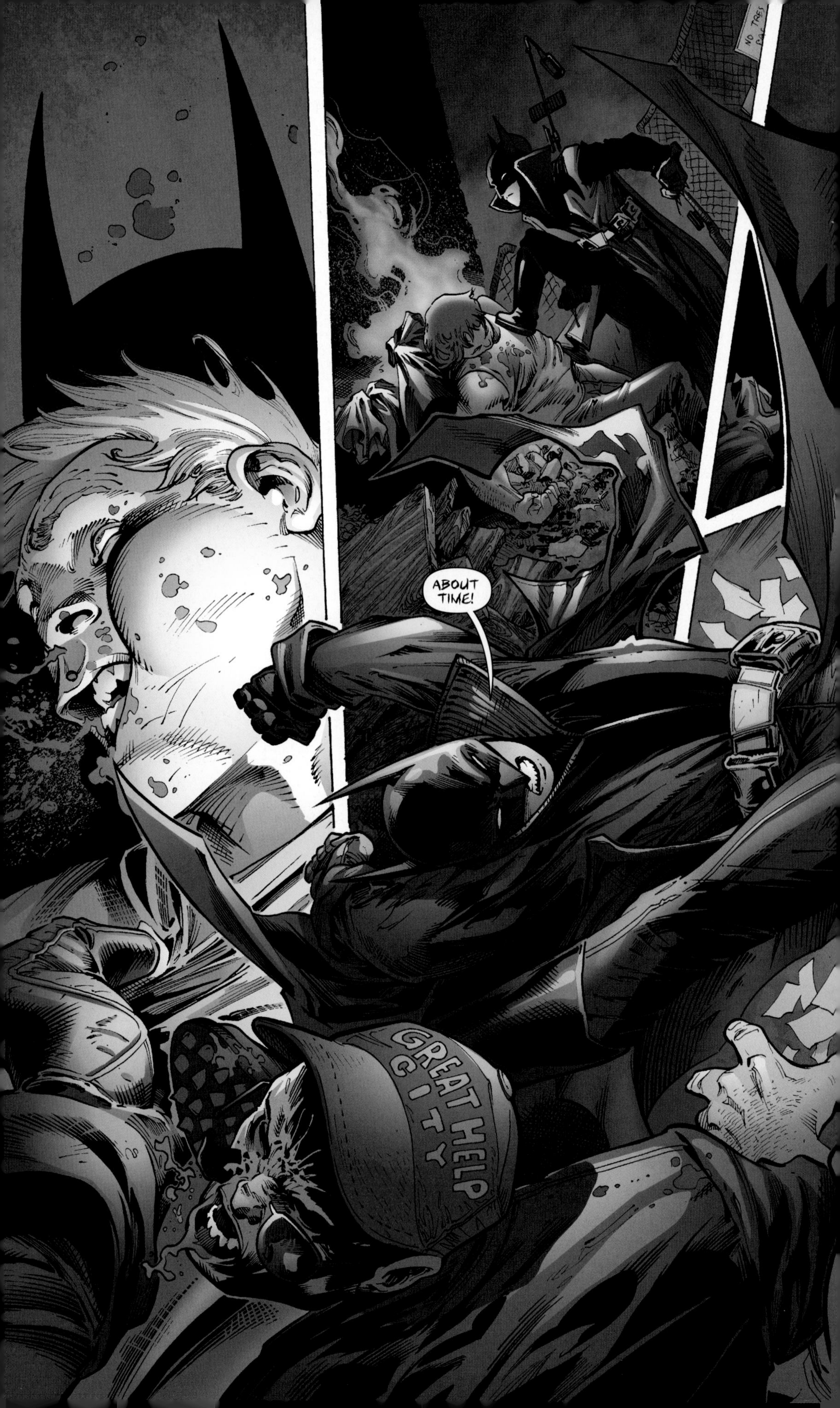
ABOUT TIME!
GREAT HELP CITY

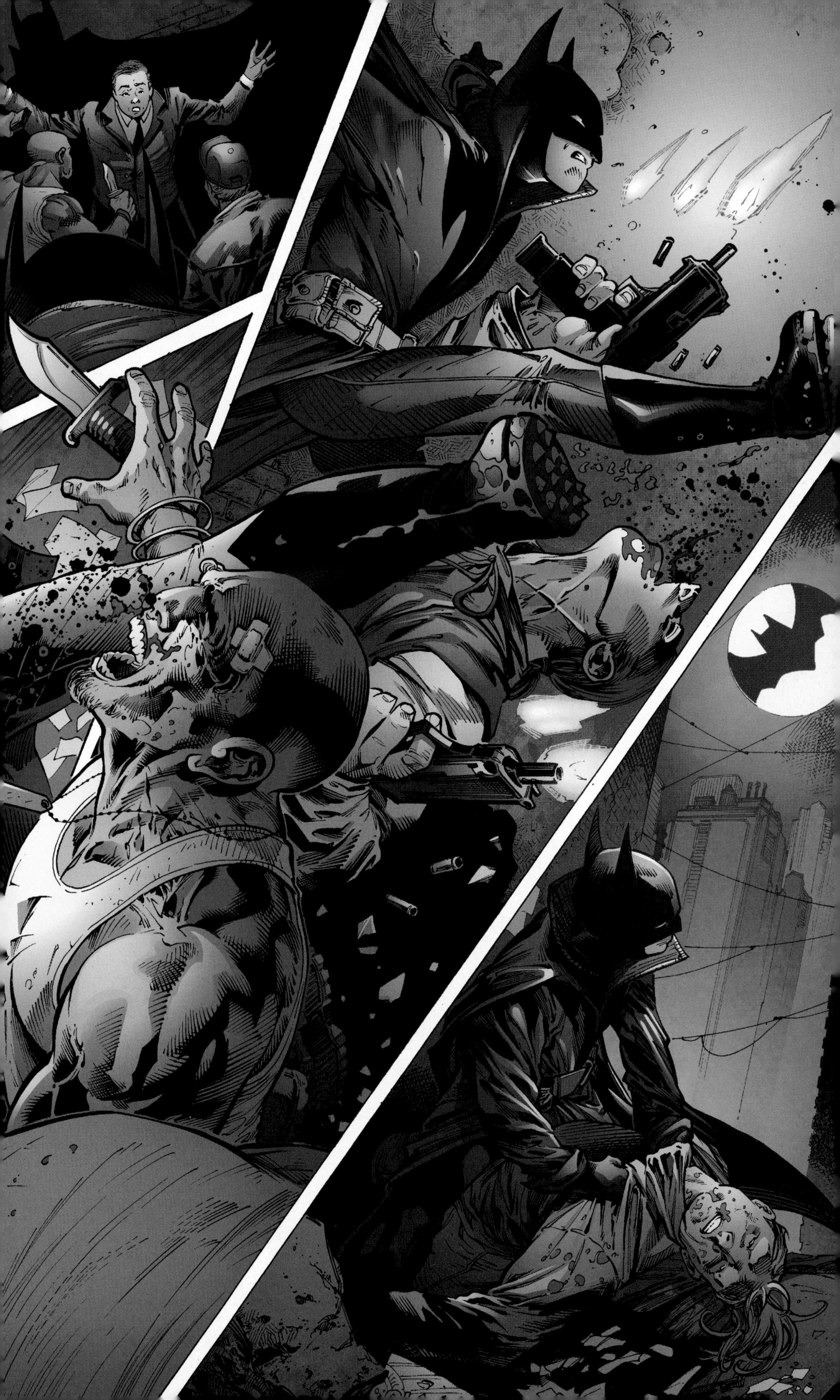

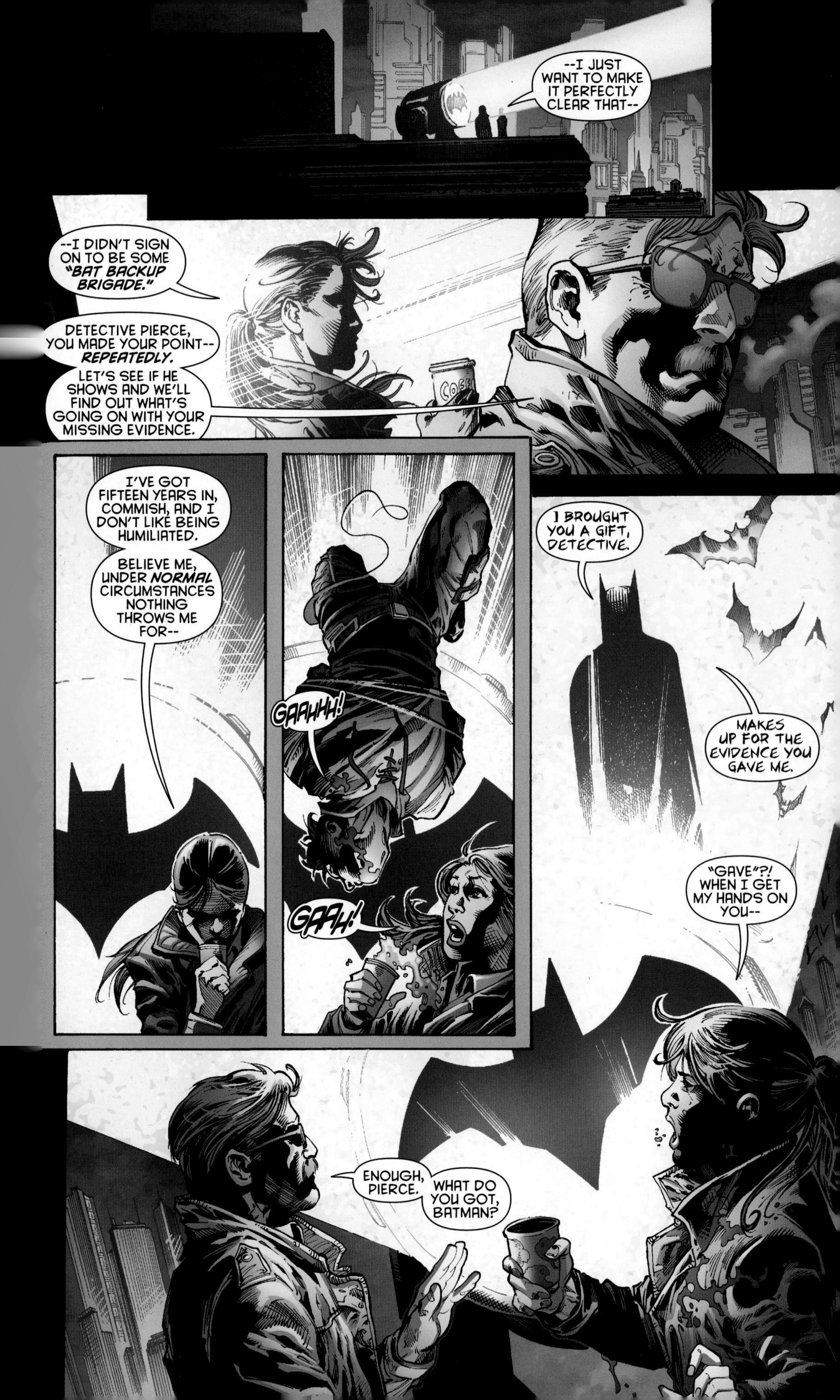
--I JUST WANT TO MAKE IT PERFECTLY CLEAR THAT--
--I DIDN'T SIGN ON TO BE SOME "BAT BACKUP BRIGADE."
DETECTIVE PIERCE, YOU MADE YOUR POINT-- REPEATEDLY.
LET'S SEE IF HE SHOWS AND WE'LL FIND OUT WHAT'S GOING ON WITH YOUR MISSING EVIDENCE.
COFF
I'VE GOT FIFTEEN YEARS IN, COMMISH, AND I DON'T LIKE BEING HUMILIATED.
BELIEVE ME, UNDER NORMAL CIRCUMSTANCES NOTHING THROWS ME FOR--
GAAHHH!
GAAH!
I BROUGHT YOU A GIFT, DETECTIVE.
MAKES UP FOR THE EVIDENCE YOU GAVE ME.
"GAVE"?! WHEN I GET MY HANDS ON YOU--
ENOUGH, PIERCE.
WHAT DO YOU GOT, BATMAN?

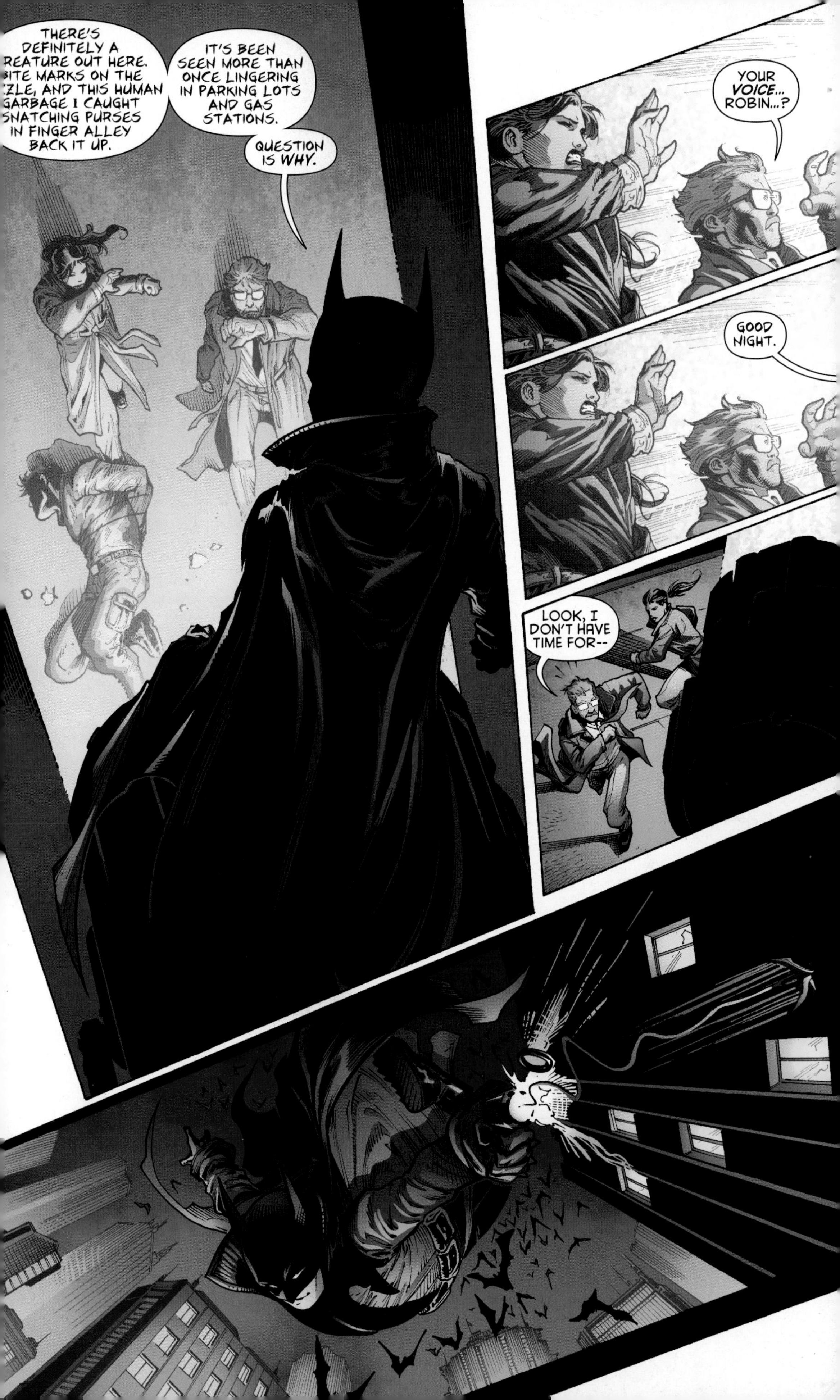

THERE'S DEFINITELY A REATURE OUT HERE. BITE MARKS ON THE ZLE, AND THIS HUMAN GARBAGE I CAUGHT SNATCHING PURSES IN FINGER ALLEY BACK IT UP.
IT'S BEEN SEEN MORE THAN ONCE LINGERING IN PARKING LOTS AND GAS STATIONS.
QUESTION IS WHY.
YOUR VOICE... ROBIN...?
GOOD NIGHT.
LOOK, I DON'T HAVE TIME FOR--

<HEY! KICK IT BACK!>*

*TRANSLATED FROM SPANISH.

<I'M LOOKING FOR A STATUE OF A LIZARD. YOU KNOW IT?>

<VERY NICE WORK, DETECTIVE.>

<NOW THEN... THE LIZARD?>

<I GUESS I AM A GOOD DETECTIVE.>

<...BECAUSE I KNOW IT'S A DRAGON AND I KNOW IT'S STRAIGHT AHEAD BY THE STAIRS.>

<BYE, MISTER WAYNE. YOUR SON IS CUTE!>

<I KNOW YOU HAVE AN AMERICAN ACCENT, SO YOU AREN'T FROM SPAIN. PLUS, JUDGING FROM YOUR SHOES, YOU'RE VERY RICH.>

Father.
Open this exactly 10'2" in front of the Lizard.

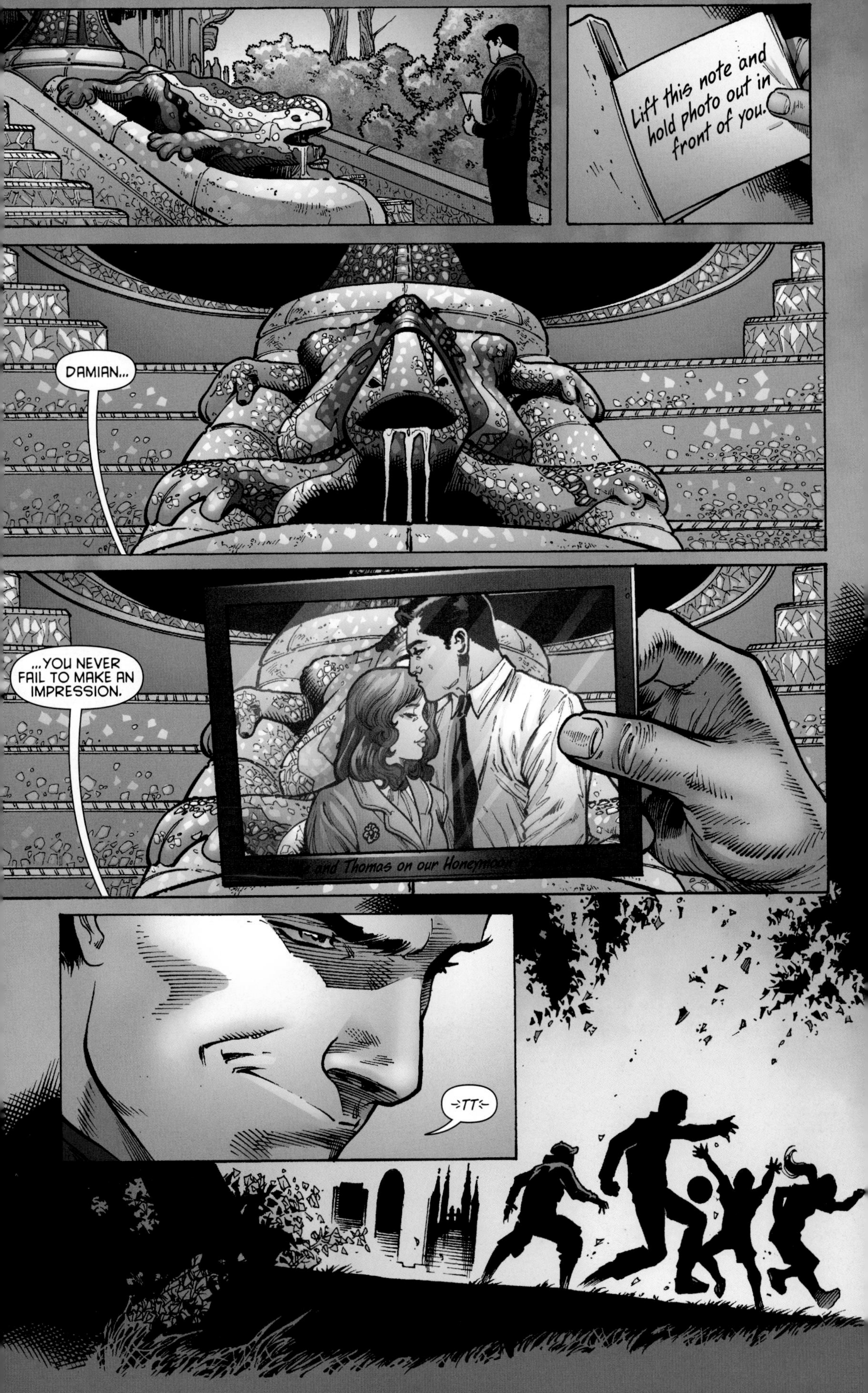
Lift this note and hold photo out in front of you.
DAMIAN...
...YOU NEVER FAIL TO MAKE AN IMPRESSION.
and Thomas on our Honeymoon
TT

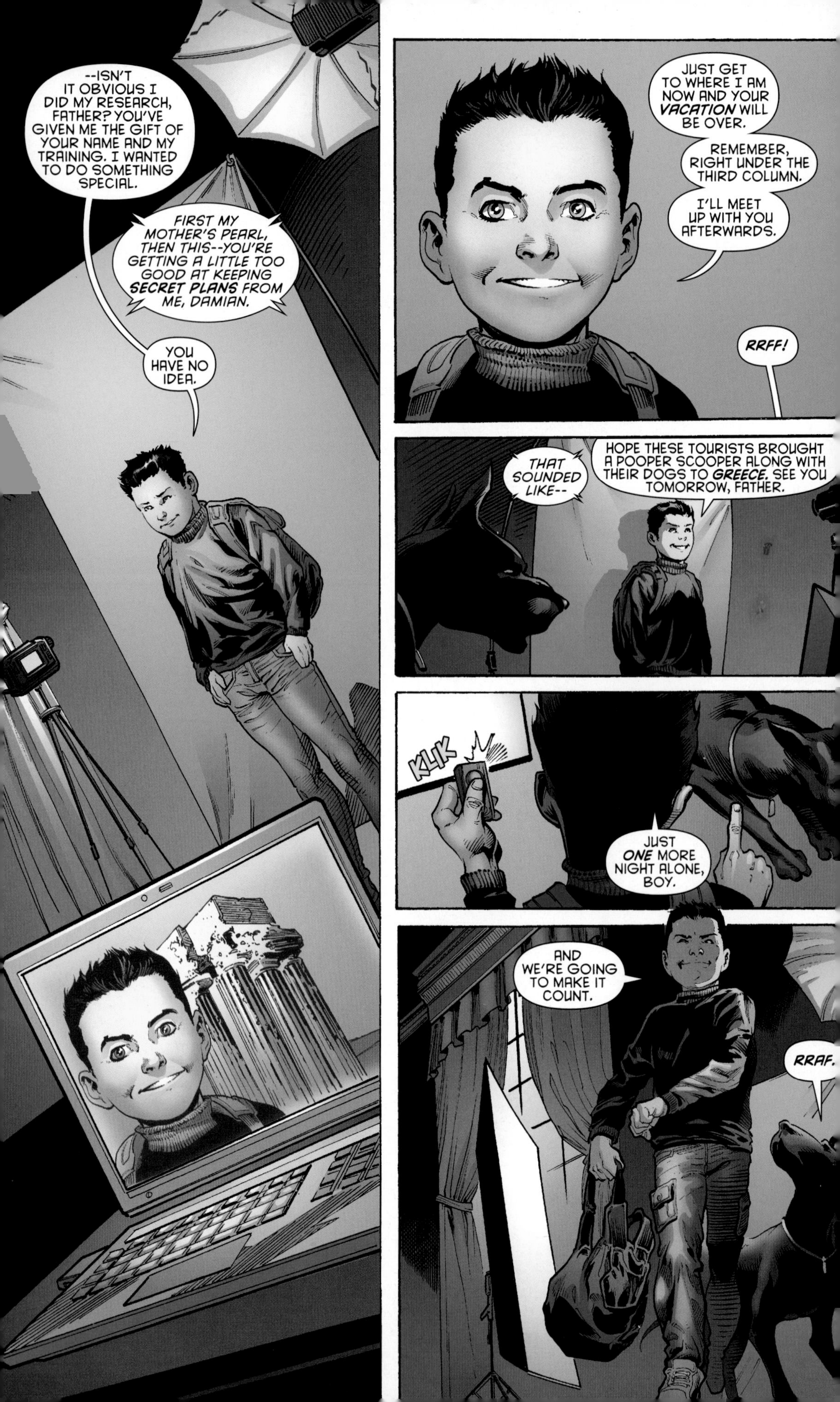
--ISN'T IT OBVIOUS I DID MY RESEARCH, FATHER? YOU'VE GIVEN ME THE GIFT OF YOUR NAME AND MY TRAINING. I WANTED TO DO SOMETHING SPECIAL.
FIRST MY MOTHER'S PEARL, THEN THIS--YOU'RE GETTING A LITTLE TOO GOOD AT KEEPING SECRET PLANS FROM ME, DAMIAN.
YOU HAVE NO IDEA.
JUST GET TO WHERE I AM NOW AND YOUR VACATION WILL BE OVER.
REMEMBER, RIGHT UNDER THE THIRD COLUMN.
I'LL MEET UP WITH YOU AFTERWARDS.
RRFF!
THAT SOUNDED LIKE--
HOPE THESE TOURISTS BROUGHT A POOPER SCOOPER ALONG WITH THEIR DOGS TO GREECE. SEE YOU TOMORROW, FATHER.
KLIK
JUST ONE MORE NIGHT ALONE, BOY.
AND WE'RE GOING TO MAKE IT COUNT.
RRAF.

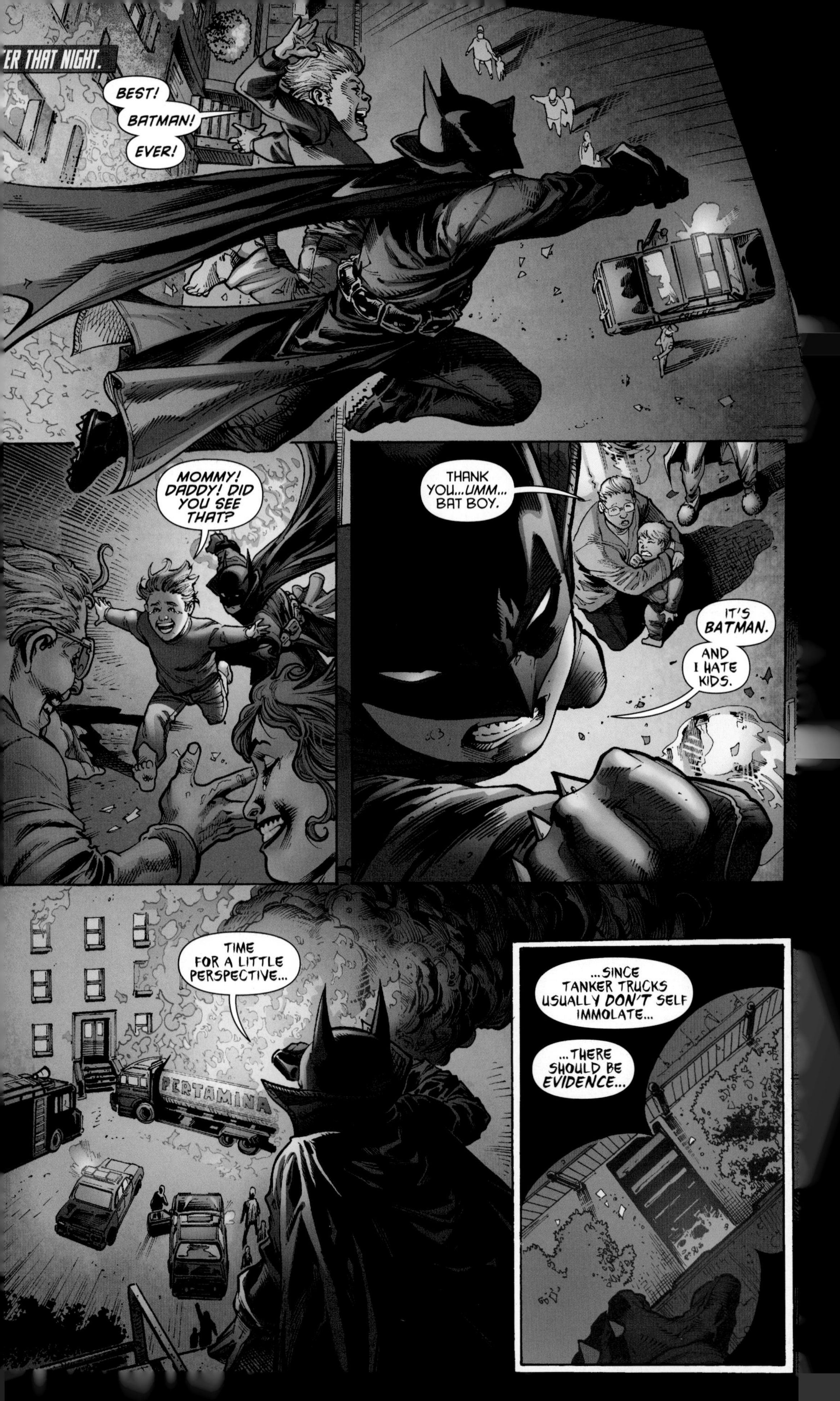

ER THAT NIGHT.
BEST!
BATMAN!
EVER!
MOMMY! DADDY! DID YOU SEE THAT?
THANK YOU...UMM... BAT BOY.
IT'S BATMAN.
AND I HATE KIDS.
TIME FOR A LITTLE PERSPECTIVE...
PERTAMINA
...SINCE TANKER TRUCKS USUALLY DON'T SELF IMMOLATE...
...THERE SHOULD BE EVIDENCE...

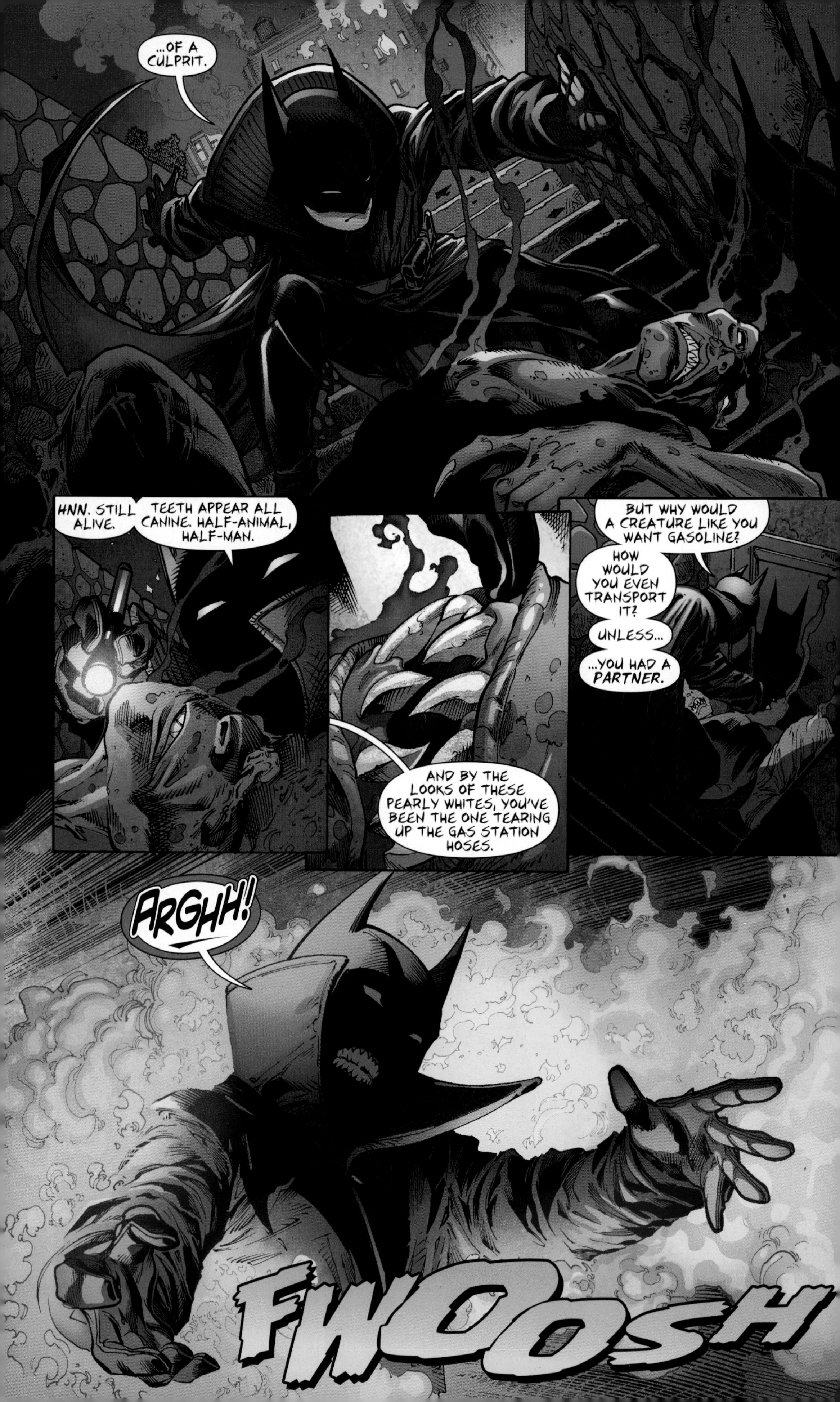
...OF A CULPRIT.
HNN. STILL ALIVE.
TEETH APPEAR ALL CANINE. HALF-ANIMAL, HALF-MAN.
AND BY THE LOOKS OF THESE PEARLY WHITES, YOU'VE BEEN THE ONE TEARING UP THE GAS STATION HOSES.
BUT WHY WOULD A CREATURE LIKE YOU WANT GASOLINE?
HOW WOULD YOU EVEN TRANSPORT IT?
UNLESS...
...YOU HAD A PARTNER.
ARGHH!
FWOOSH

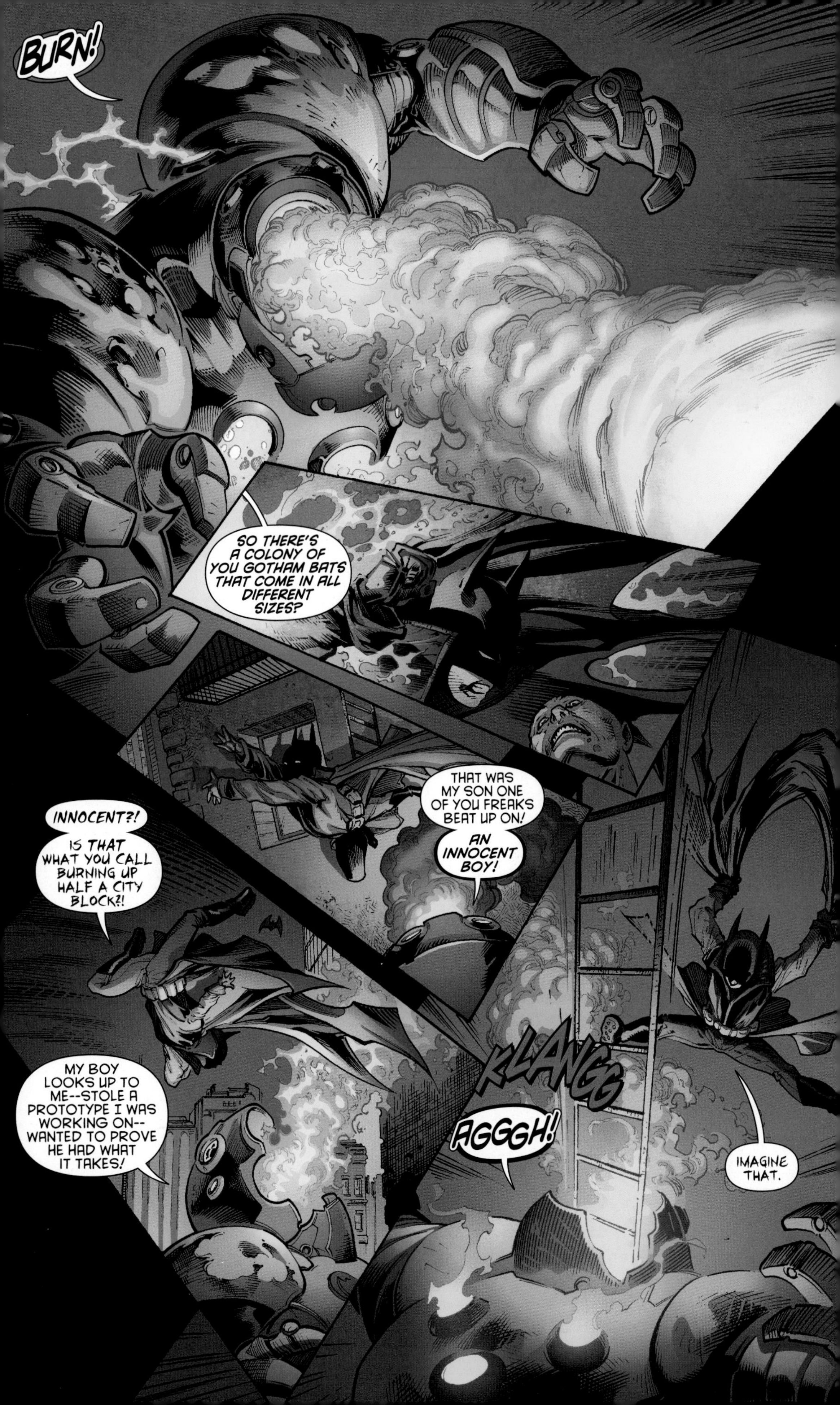
BURN!
SO THERE'S A COLONY OF YOU GOTHAM BATS THAT COME IN ALL DIFFERENT SIZES?
THAT WAS MY SON ONE OF YOU FREAKS BEAT UP ON!
AN INNOCENT BOY!
INNOCENT?!
IS THAT WHAT YOU CALL BURNING UP HALF A CITY BLOCK?!
MY BOY LOOKS UP TO ME--STOLE A PROTOTYPE I WAS WORKING ON--WANTED TO PROVE HE HAD WHAT IT TAKES!
KLANGG
AGGGH!
IMAGINE THAT.

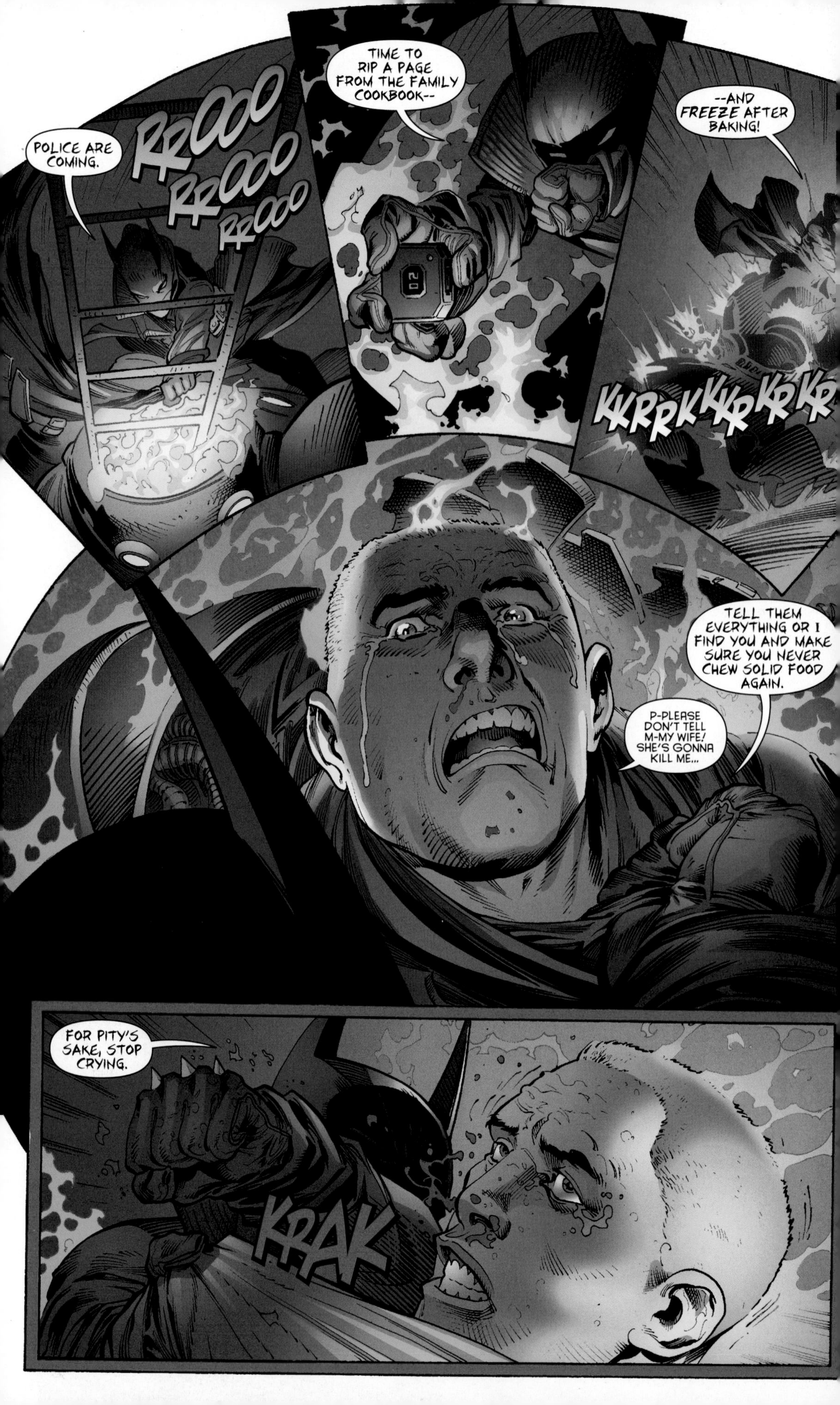
POLICE ARE COMING.
RRROOO RRROOO RRROOO
TIME TO RIP A PAGE FROM THE FAMILY COOKBOOK--
--AND FREEZE AFTER BAKING!
KKRRRKKKRKRKR
TELL THEM EVERYTHING OR I FIND YOU AND MAKE SURE YOU NEVER CHEW SOLID FOOD AGAIN.
P-PLEASE DON'T TELL M-MY WIFE! SHE'S GONNA KILL ME...
FOR PITY'S SAKE, STOP CRYING.
KRAK

KEEP YOUR HANDS UP AND DON'T MOVE!

D-DON'T SHOOT--I'LL MAKE A FULL CONFESSION--

I HIRED THAT LITTLE *WEASEL* CREATURE TO STEAL GAS FOR THE ARMOR'S WEAPON SYSTEM--

DID YOU NOW?

YES-- METAL ON METAL-- COULDN'T CHANCE A SPARK--NEEDED A GO-BETWEEN--

--THE WEASEL COULD KEEP THE CONNECTION ORGANIC AND ACT AS MUSCLE...

WHERE'D ALL THIS ARMOR COME FROM?

I BUILT IT...I WAS GOING TO HIRE MYSELF OUT TO GUYS LIKE FREEZE OR THE JOKER--MAKE MILLIONS...

NEED A PARAMEDIC OVER HERE--STILL GOT VITALS ON A PERP.

AND THE STUPIDITY NEVER ENDS.

I KNEW YOU WERE HIDING IN THE SHADOWS!

YOU'RE WELCOME.

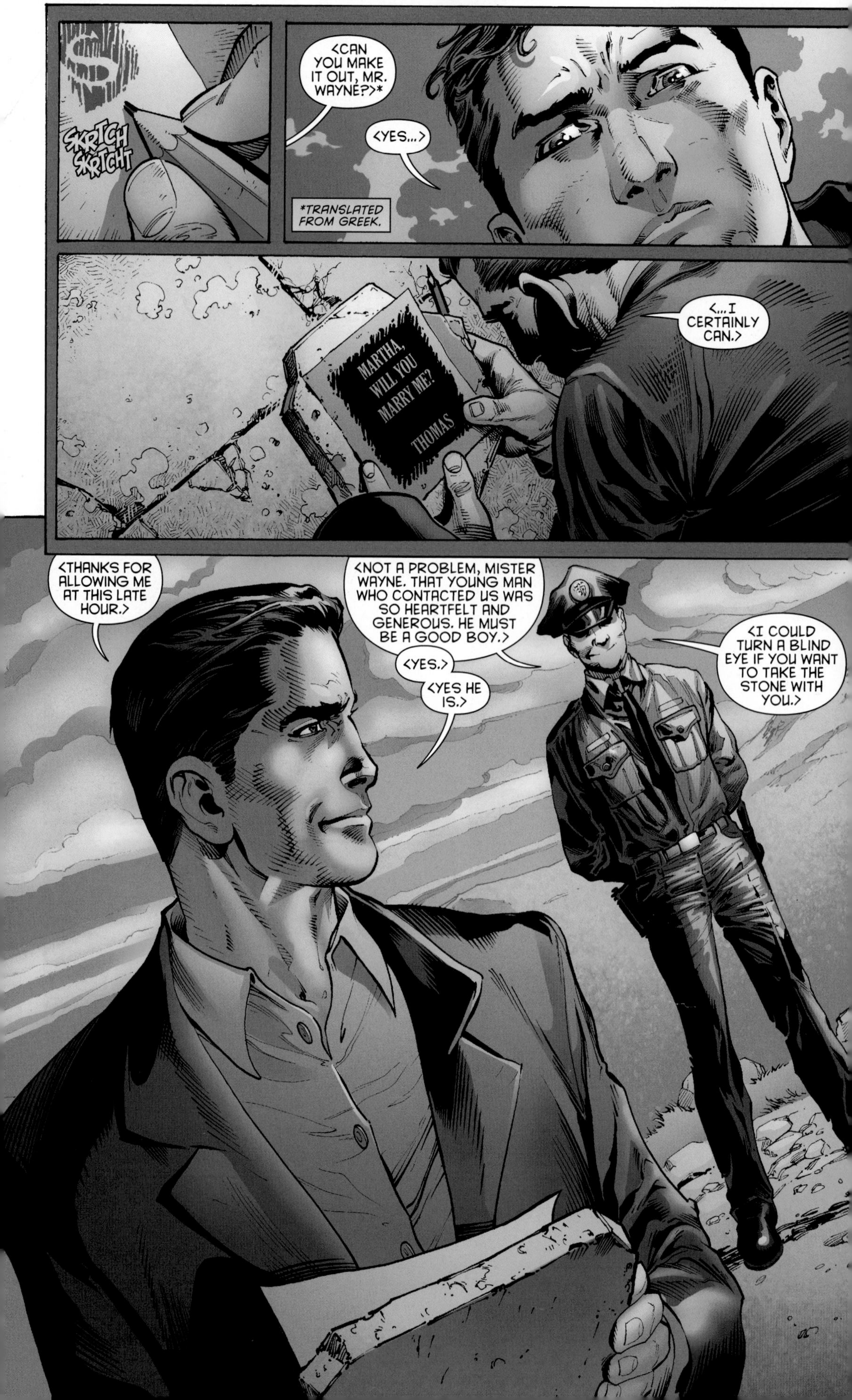

SKRTCH SKRTCHT
<CAN YOU MAKE IT OUT, MR. WAYNE?>*
<YES...>
*TRANSLATED FROM GREEK.
MARTHA, WILL YOU MARRY ME?
THOMAS
<...I CERTAINLY CAN.>
<THANKS FOR ALLOWING ME AT THIS LATE HOUR.>
<NOT A PROBLEM, MISTER WAYNE. THAT YOUNG MAN WHO CONTACTED US WAS SO HEARTFELT AND GENEROUS. HE MUST BE A GOOD BOY.>
<YES.>
<YES HE IS.>
<I COULD TURN A BLIND EYE IF YOU WANT TO TAKE THE STONE WITH YOU.>

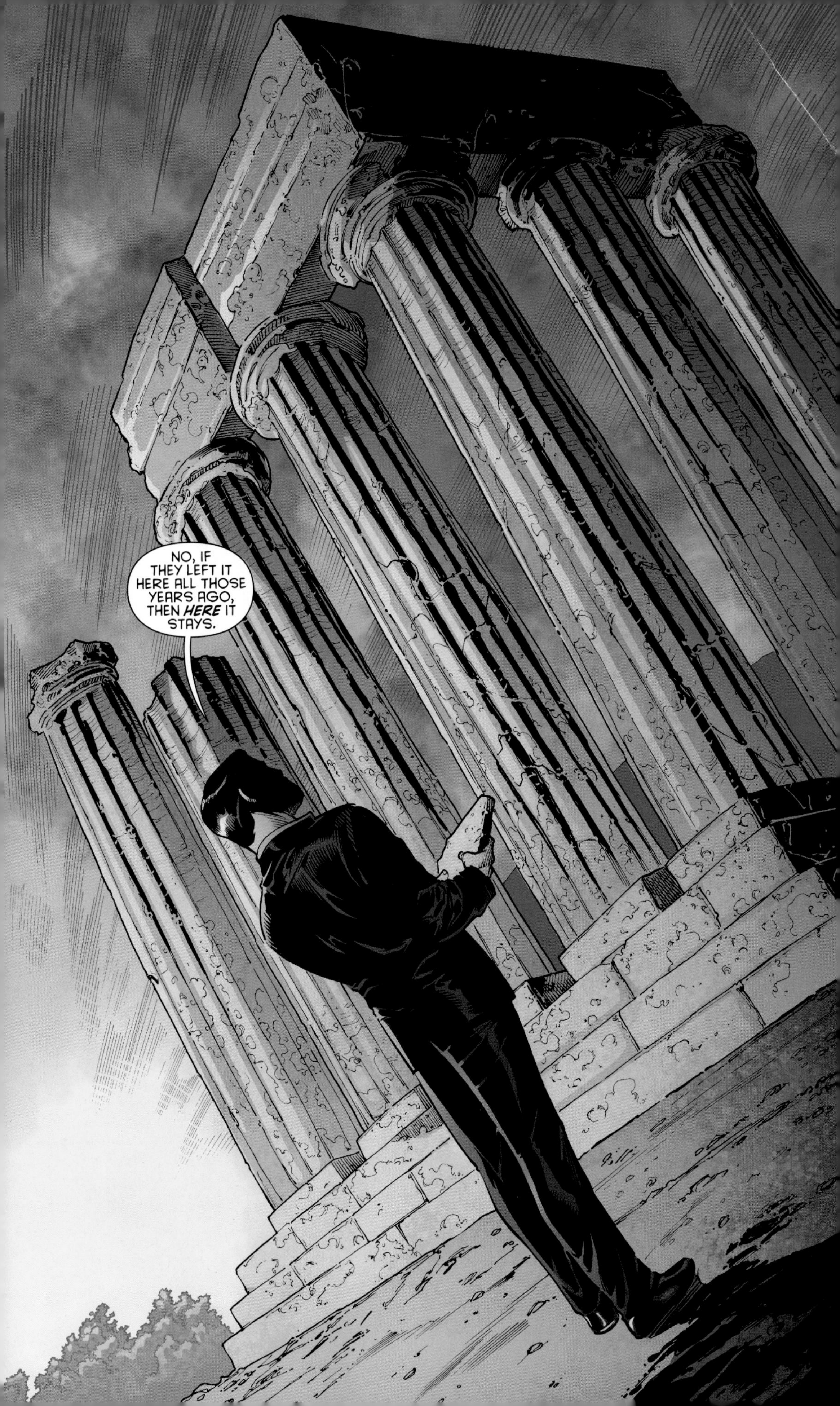
NO, IF THEY LEFT IT HERE ALL THOSE YEARS AGO, THEN *HERE* IT STAYS.

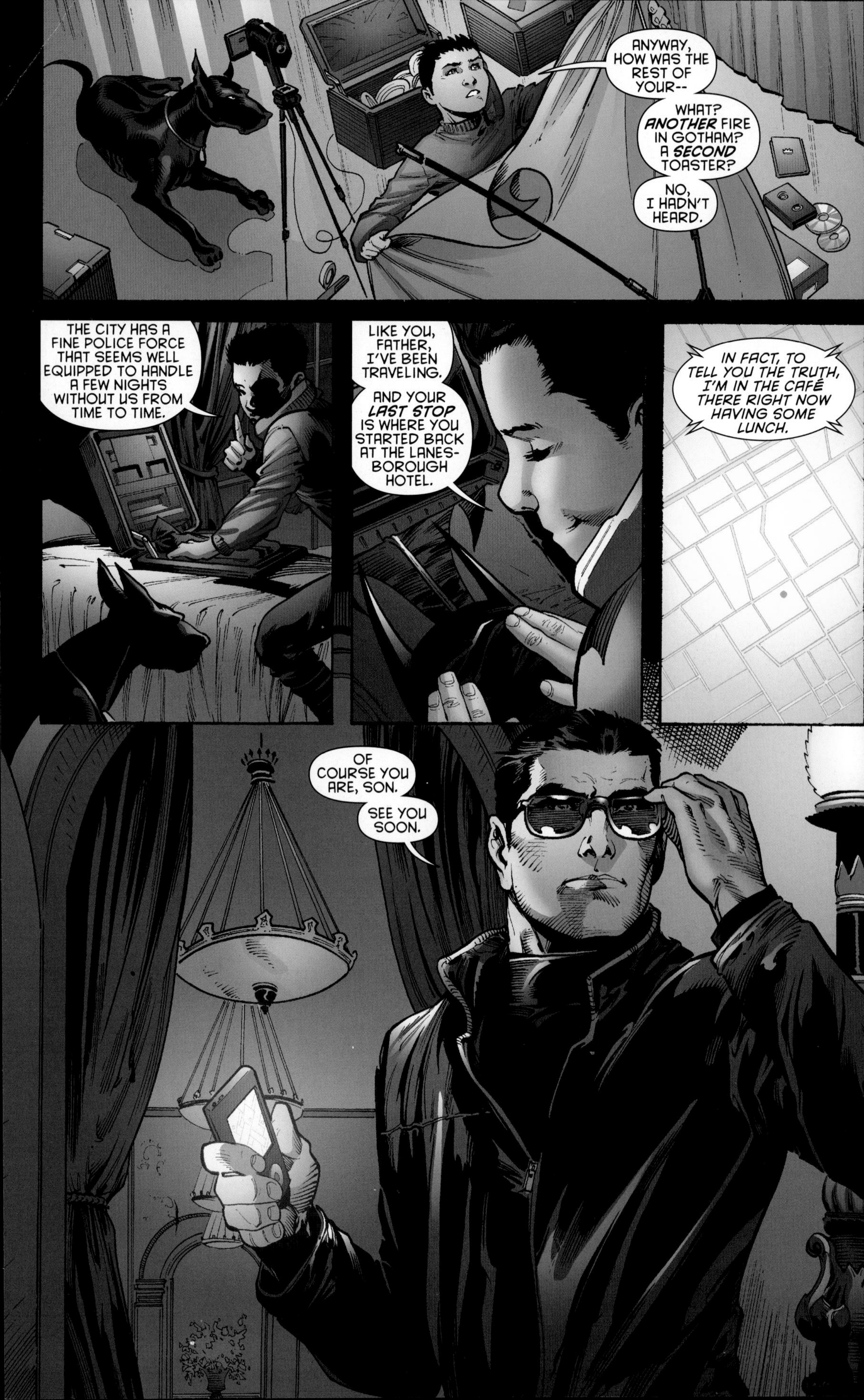
ANYWAY, HOW WAS THE REST OF YOUR--
WHAT? ANOTHER FIRE IN GOTHAM? A SECOND TOASTER?
NO, I HADN'T HEARD.
THE CITY HAS A FINE POLICE FORCE THAT SEEMS WELL EQUIPPED TO HANDLE A FEW NIGHTS WITHOUT US FROM TIME TO TIME.
LIKE YOU, FATHER, I'VE BEEN TRAVELING.
AND YOUR LAST STOP IS WHERE YOU STARTED BACK AT THE LANES-BOROUGH HOTEL.
IN FACT, TO TELL YOU THE TRUTH, I'M IN THE CAFÉ THERE RIGHT NOW HAVING SOME LUNCH.
OF COURSE YOU ARE, SON.
SEE YOU SOON.

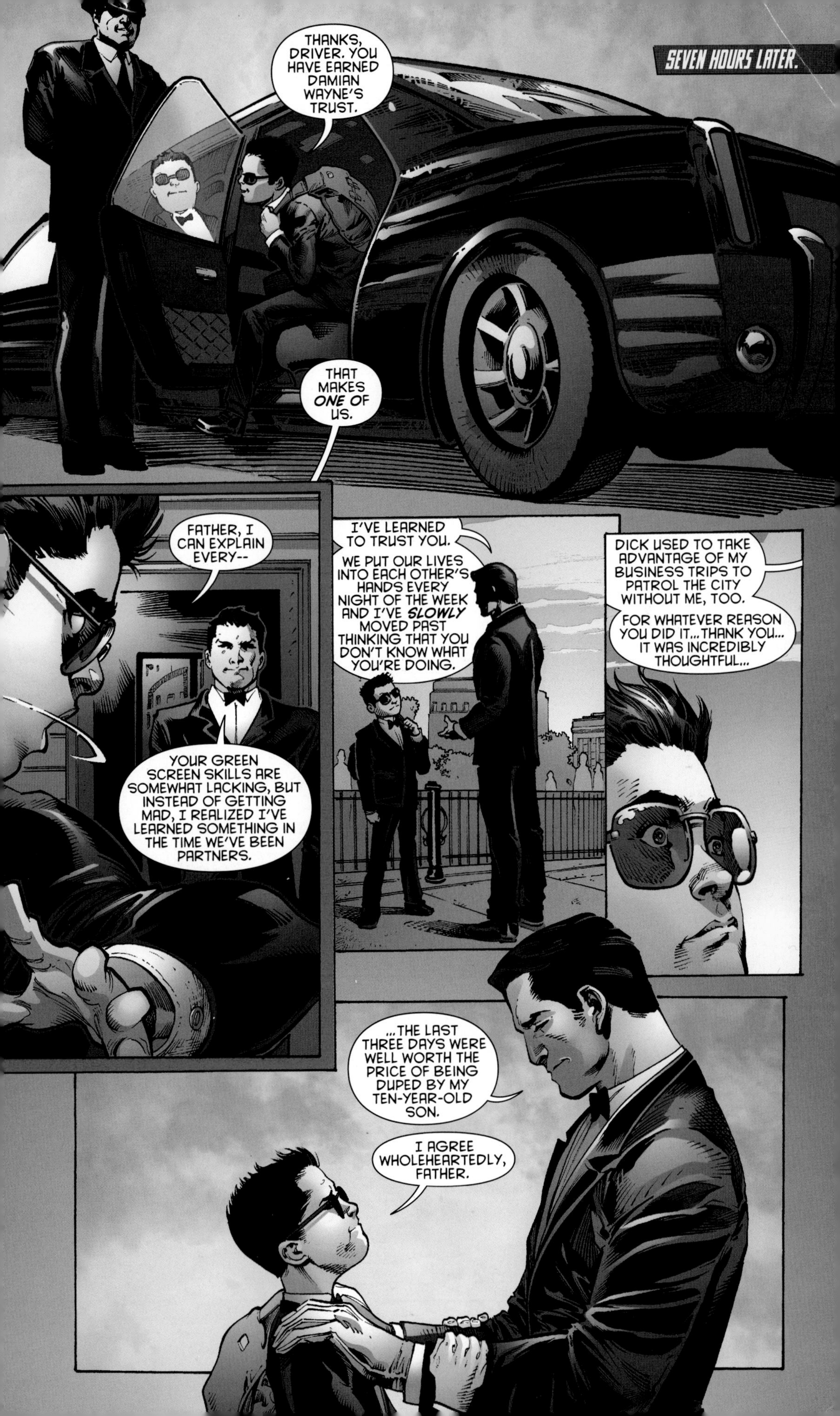
SEVEN HOURS LATER.
THANKS, DRIVER. YOU HAVE EARNED DAMIAN WAYNE'S TRUST.
THAT MAKES *ONE* OF US.
FATHER, I CAN EXPLAIN EVERY--
YOUR GREEN SCREEN SKILLS ARE SOMEWHAT LACKING, BUT INSTEAD OF GETTING MAD, I REALIZED I'VE LEARNED SOMETHING IN THE TIME WE'VE BEEN PARTNERS.
I'VE LEARNED TO TRUST YOU.
WE PUT OUR LIVES INTO EACH OTHER'S HANDS EVERY NIGHT OF THE WEEK AND I'VE *SLOWLY* MOVED PAST THINKING THAT YOU DON'T KNOW WHAT YOU'RE DOING.
DICK USED TO TAKE ADVANTAGE OF MY BUSINESS TRIPS TO PATROL THE CITY WITHOUT ME, TOO.
FOR WHATEVER REASON YOU DID IT... THANK YOU... IT WAS INCREDIBLY THOUGHTFUL...
...THE LAST THREE DAYS WERE WELL WORTH THE PRICE OF BEING DUPED BY MY TEN-YEAR-OLD SON.
I AGREE WHOLEHEARTEDLY, FATHER.

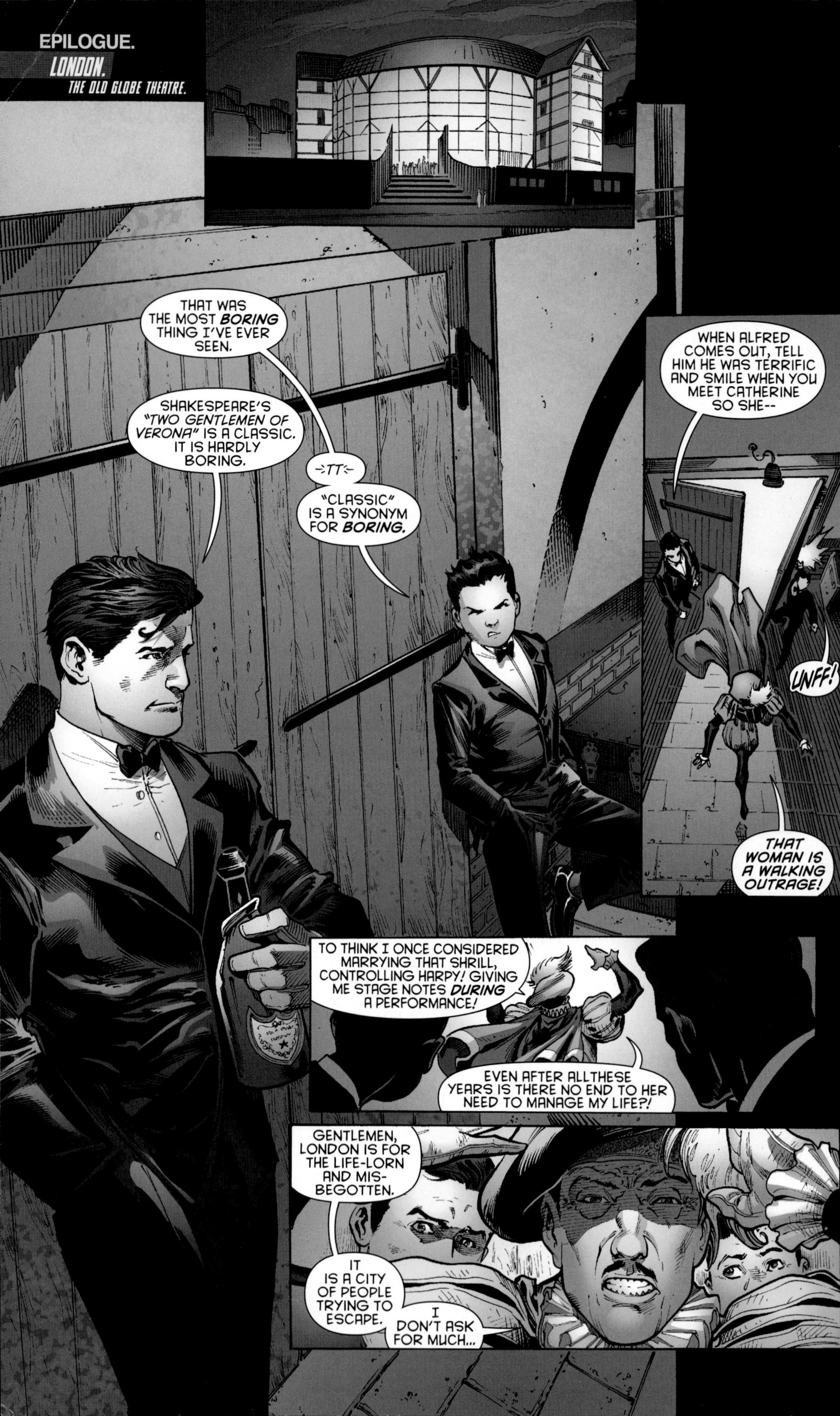
EPILOGUE.
LONDON.
THE OLD GLOBE THEATRE.
THAT WAS THE MOST BORING THING I'VE EVER SEEN.
SHAKESPEARE'S "TWO GENTLEMEN OF VERONA" IS A CLASSIC. IT IS HARDLY BORING.
TT
"CLASSIC" IS A SYNONYM FOR BORING.
WHEN ALFRED COMES OUT, TELL HIM HE WAS TERRIFIC AND SMILE WHEN YOU MEET CATHERINE SO SHE--
UNFF!
THAT WOMAN IS A WALKING OUTRAGE!
TO THINK I ONCE CONSIDERED MARRYING THAT SHRILL, CONTROLLING HARPY! GIVING ME STAGE NOTES DURING A PERFORMANCE!
EVEN AFTER ALLTHESE YEARS IS THERE NO END TO HER NEED TO MANAGE MY LIFE?!
GENTLEMEN, LONDON IS FOR THE LIFE-LORN AND MIS-BEGOTTEN.
IT IS A CITY OF PEOPLE TRYING TO ESCAPE.
I DON'T ASK FOR MUCH...

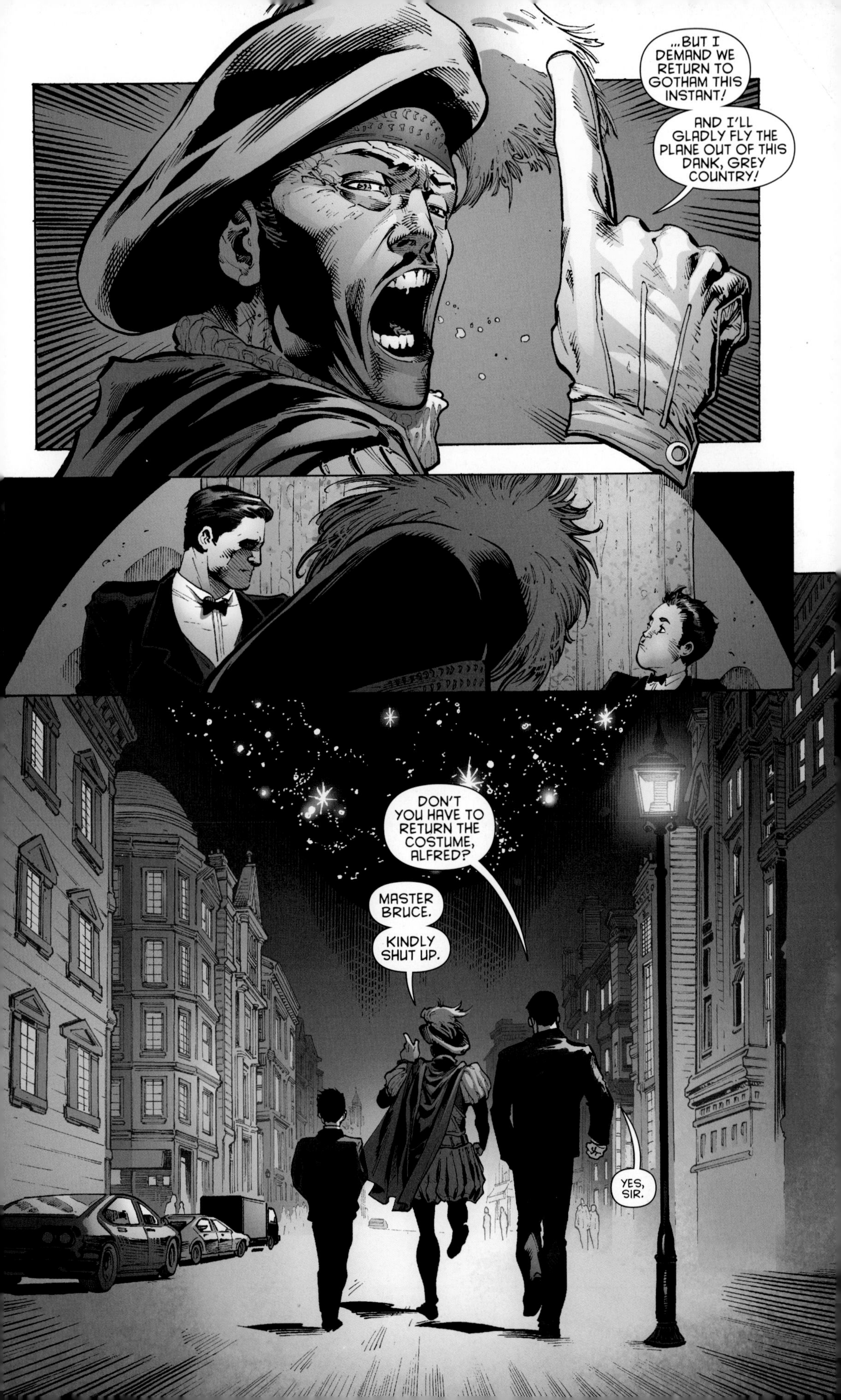
...BUT I DEMAND WE RETURN TO GOTHAM THIS INSTANT!
AND I'LL GLADLY FLY THE PLANE OUT OF THIS DANK, GREY COUNTRY!
DON'T YOU HAVE TO RETURN THE COSTUME, ALFRED?
MASTER BRUCE.
KINDLY SHUT UP.
YES, SIR.

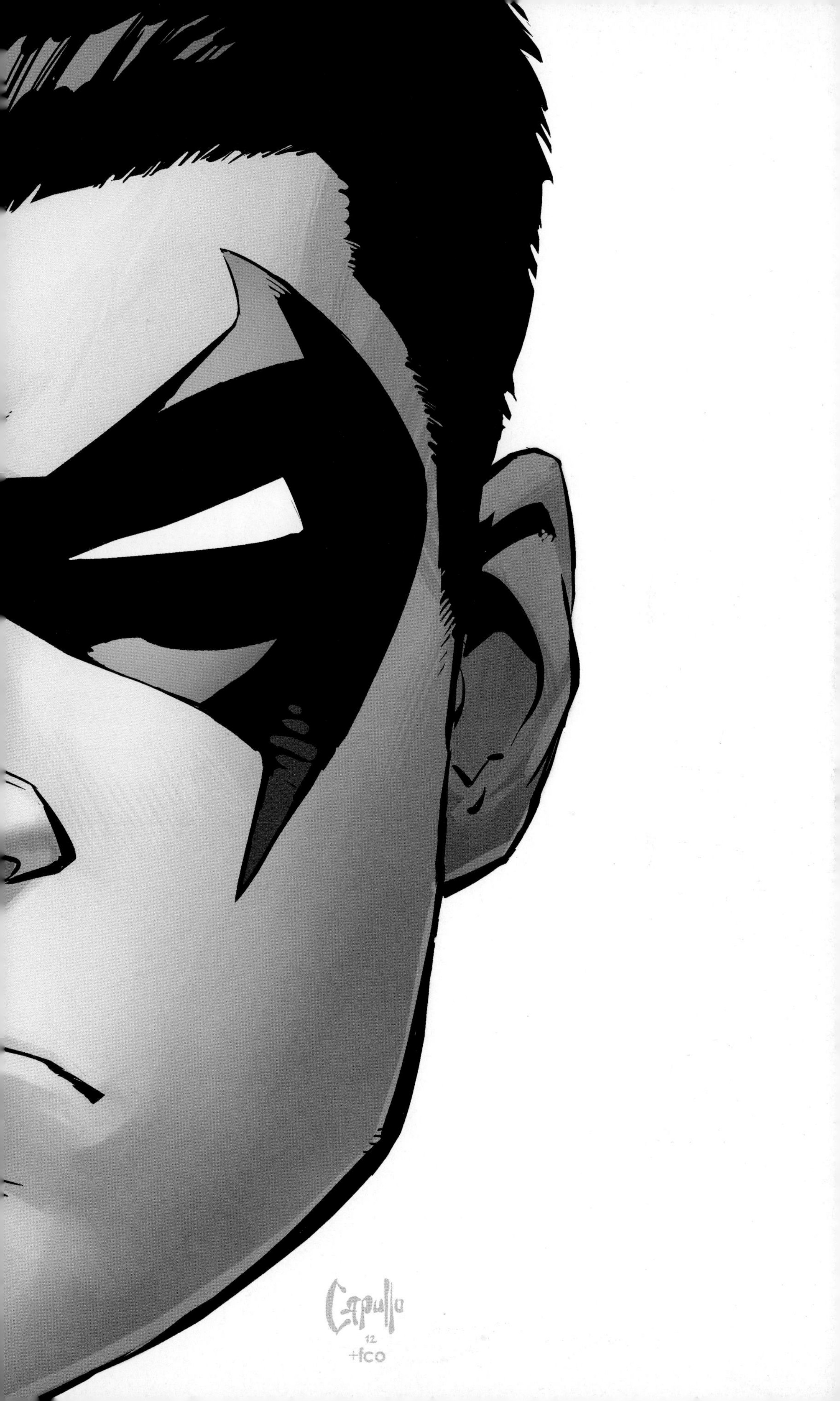
Capullo
12
+fco

DEATH OF THE FAMILY: LITTLE BIG MAN

PETER J. TOMASI writer PATRICK GLEASON penciller MICK GRAY inker cover art by GREG CAPULLO & FCO PLASCENCIA

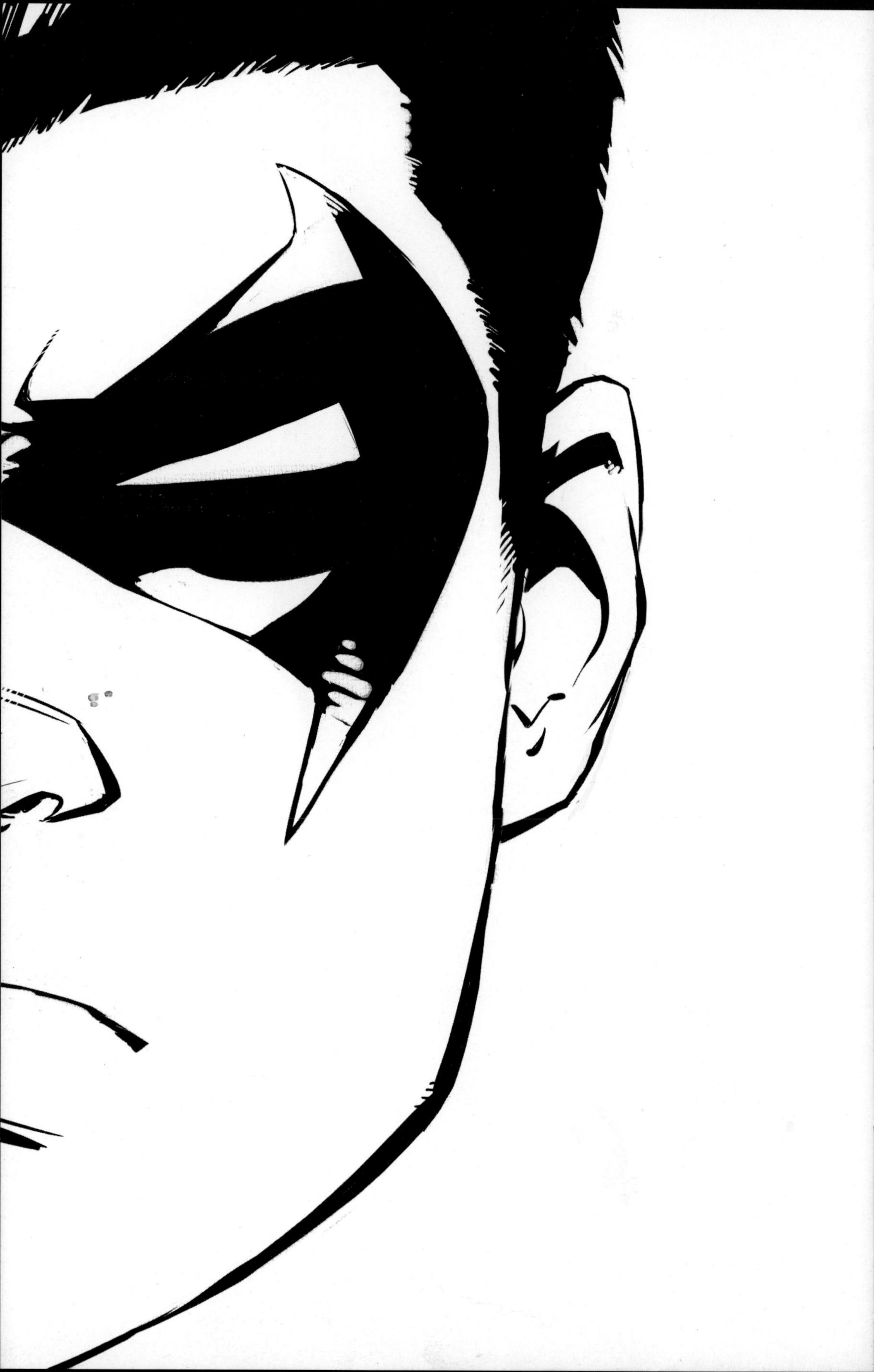

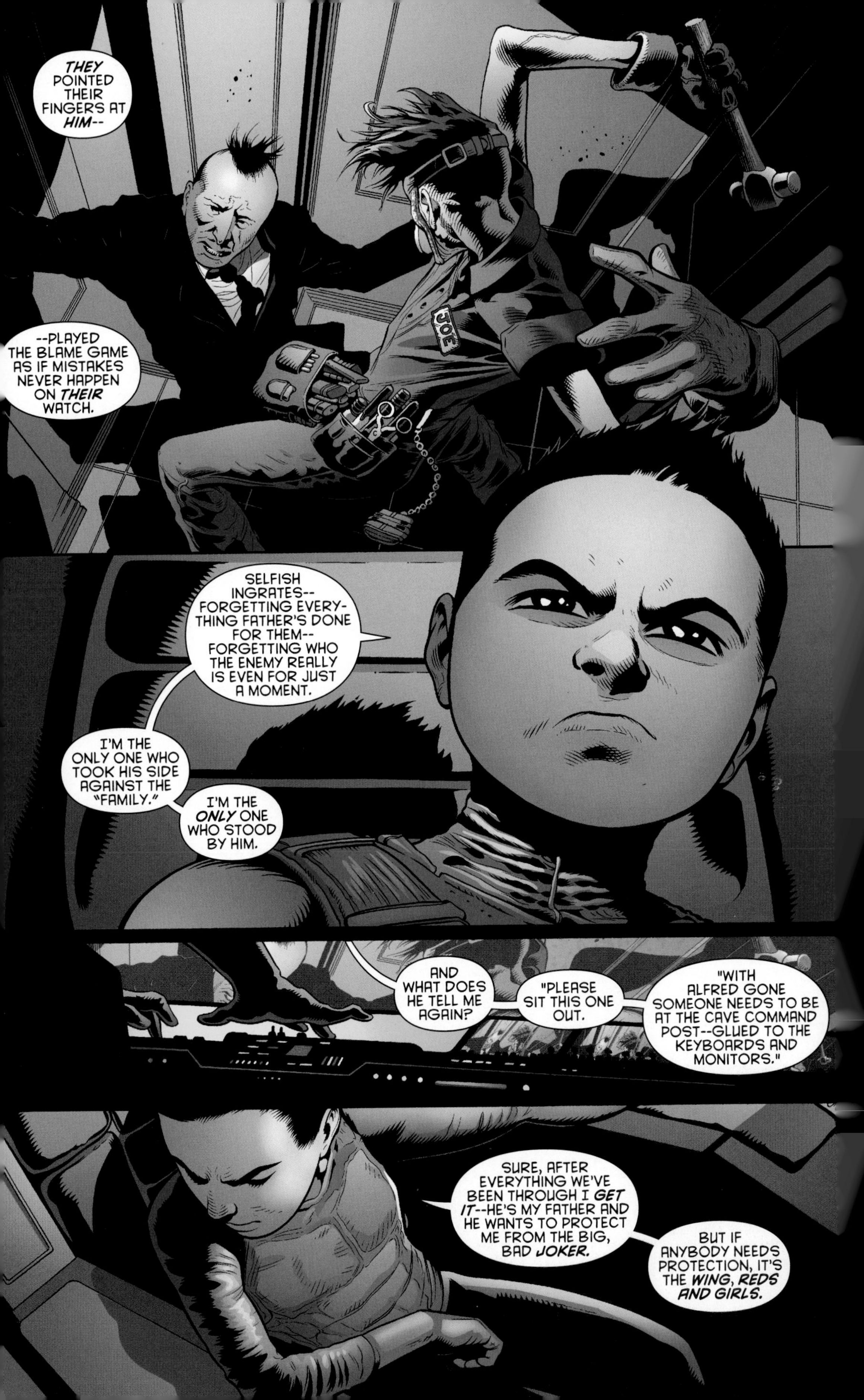
THEY POINTED THEIR FINGERS AT HIM--
--PLAYED THE BLAME GAME AS IF MISTAKES NEVER HAPPEN ON THEIR WATCH.
JOE
SELFISH INGRATES--FORGETTING EVERYTHING FATHER'S DONE FOR THEM--FORGETTING WHO THE ENEMY REALLY IS EVEN FOR JUST A MOMENT.
I'M THE ONLY ONE WHO TOOK HIS SIDE AGAINST THE "FAMILY."
I'M THE ONLY ONE WHO STOOD BY HIM.
AND WHAT DOES HE TELL ME AGAIN?
"PLEASE SIT THIS ONE OUT.
"WITH ALFRED GONE SOMEONE NEEDS TO BE AT THE CAVE COMMAND POST--GLUED TO THE KEYBOARDS AND MONITORS."
SURE, AFTER EVERYTHING WE'VE BEEN THROUGH I GET IT--HE'S MY FATHER AND HE WANTS TO PROTECT ME FROM THE BIG, BAD JOKER.
BUT IF ANYBODY NEEDS PROTECTION, IT'S THE WING, REDS AND GIRLS.

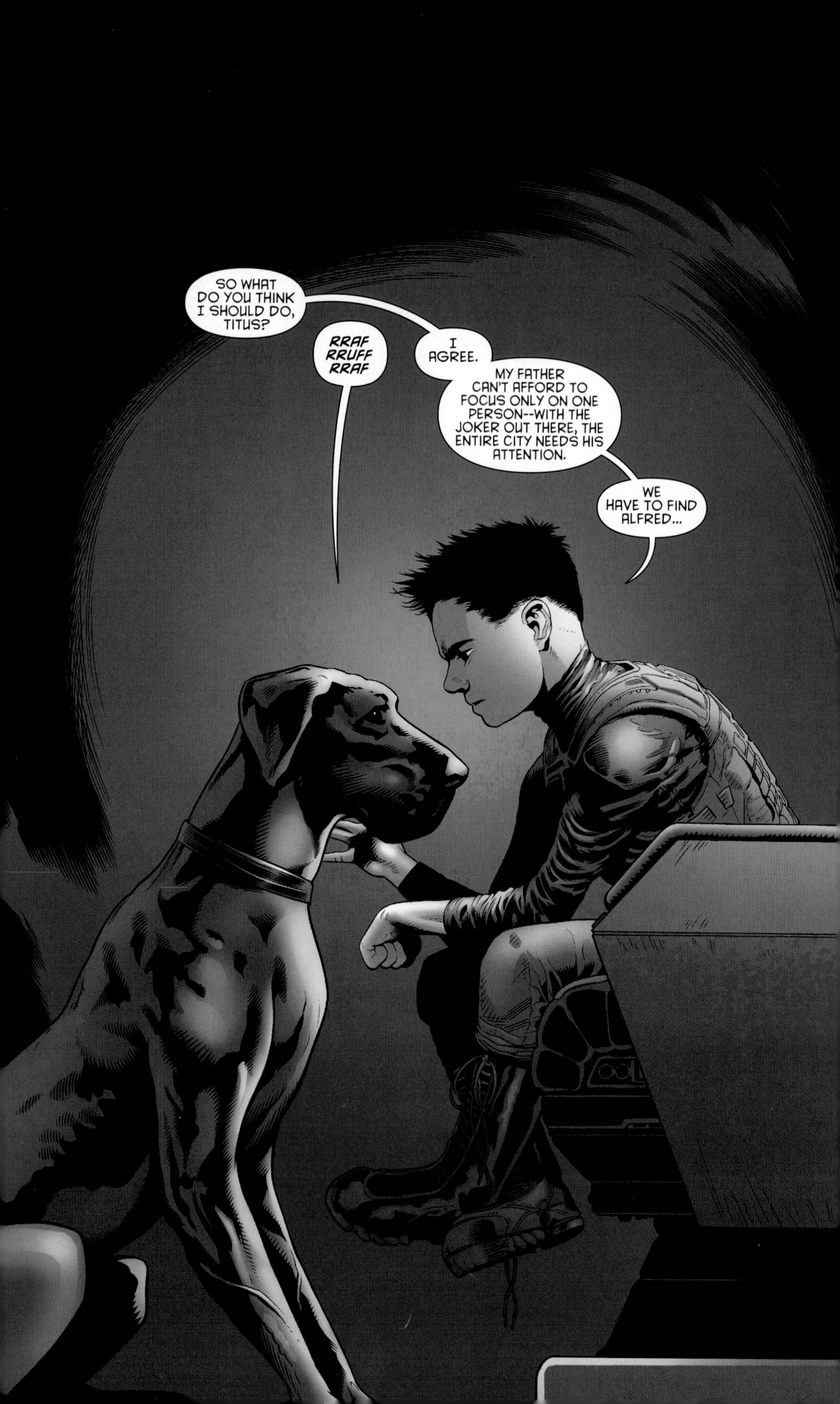
SO WHAT DO YOU THINK I SHOULD DO, TITUS?
RRAF RRUFF RRAF
I AGREE.
MY FATHER CAN'T AFFORD TO FOCUS ONLY ON ONE PERSON--WITH THE JOKER OUT THERE, THE ENTIRE CITY NEEDS HIS ATTENTION.
WE HAVE TO FIND ALFRED...

"...AND THE FIRST PLACE TO START IS THE SCENE OF ALFRED'S ABDUCTION."

WAYNE MANOR.

WE'VE COME UP EMPTY ON TIRE TREADS AND ANY PHYSICAL EVIDENCE, TITUS.

RRFF RRFF

NO FINGERPRINTS, HAIRS, OR EVEN SHOES WITH DISCERNIBLE SOLES...

...THE JOKER'S A TWISTED FREAK, NOT A GHOST...

SNURFF SNURFF

...URINE SAMPLE IS A MATCH FROM THE HYAENIDAE FAMILY OF SUBORDER FELIFORMS OF THE CARNIVORA.

AND THERE'S ONLY ONE PLACE THEY KEEP THOSE...

...HE HAD TO LEAVE SOMETHING BEHIND.

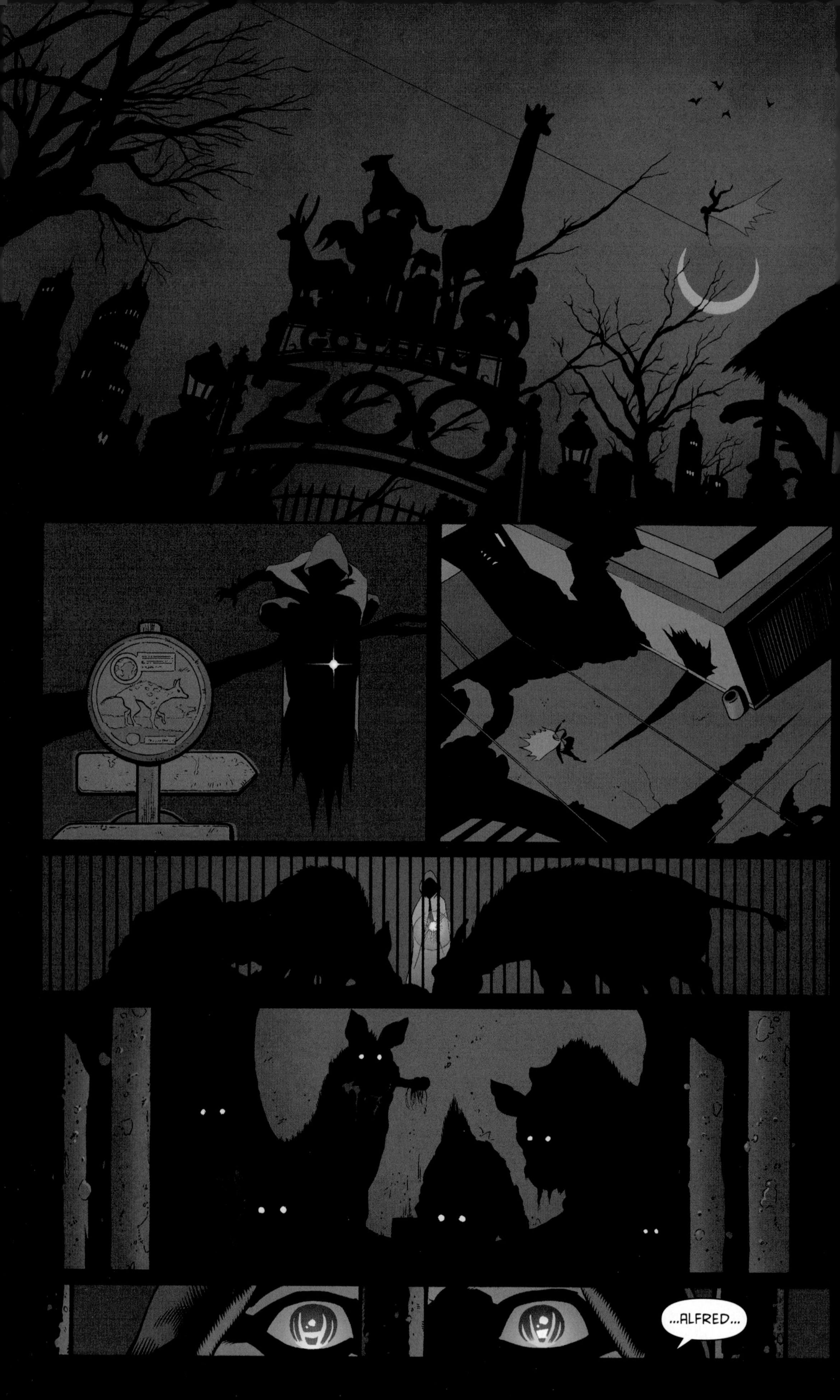
...ALFRED...

...NO...THE GUARD...

RRARRR   FRAKK

KZZZT

KLANK

RRNN

RRARR

KRAK

RRARRR

KRAK

WHAK

KRAKSNAPP

RRARRR

RRARRR

KRAKK

POOM

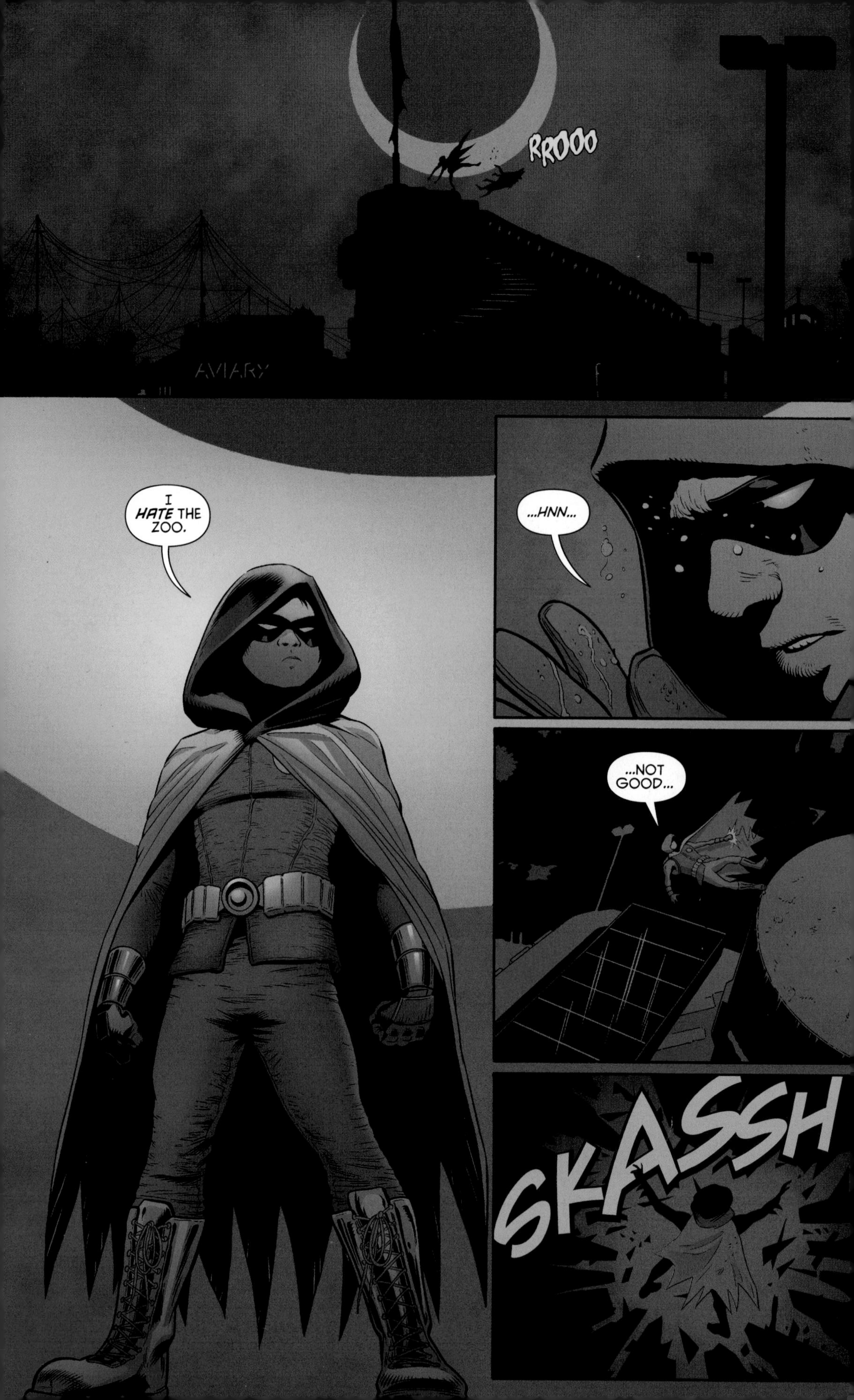
RROOO
AVIARY
I HATE THE ZOO.
...HNN...
...NOT GOOD...
SKASSH

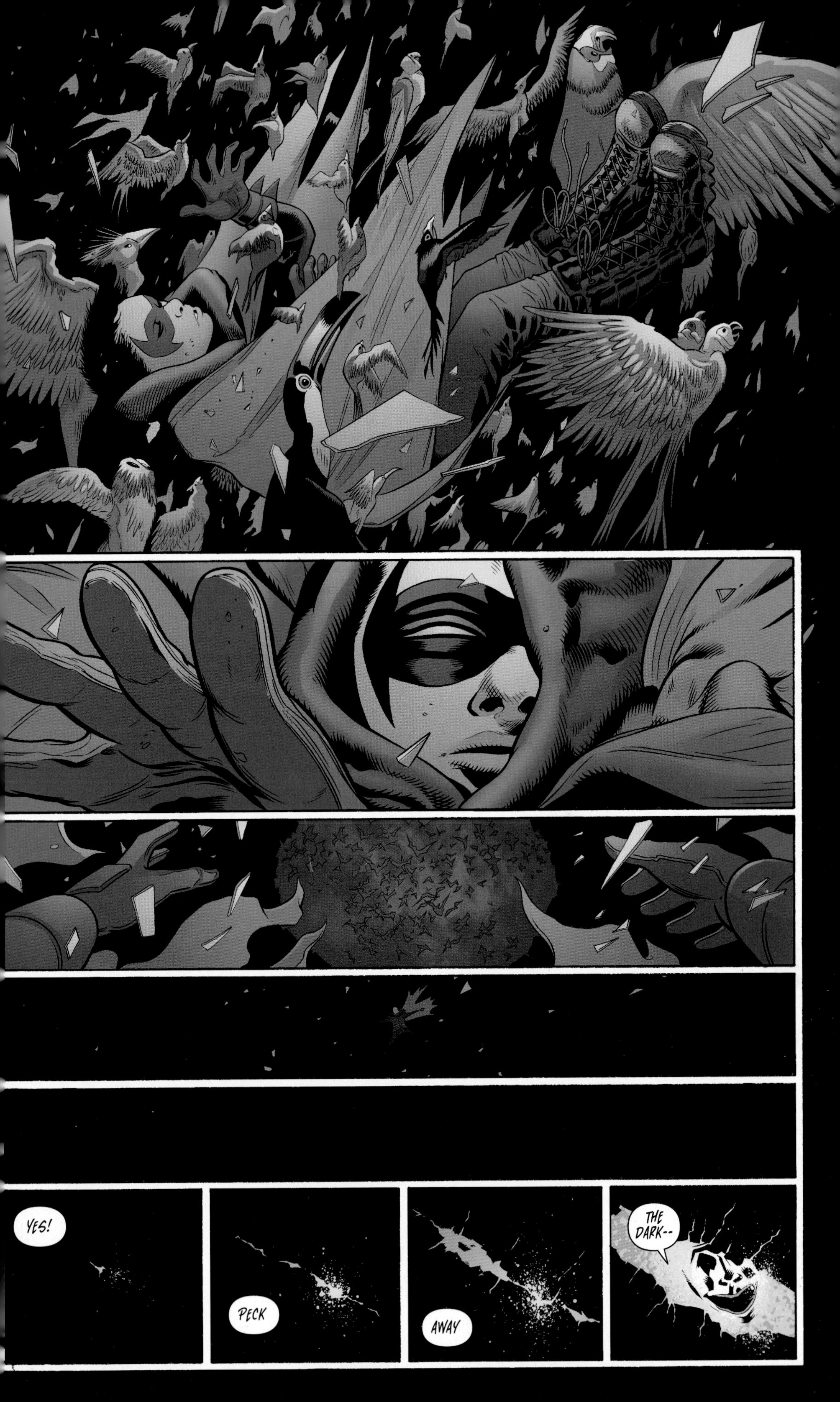
YES!
PECK
AWAY
THE DARK--

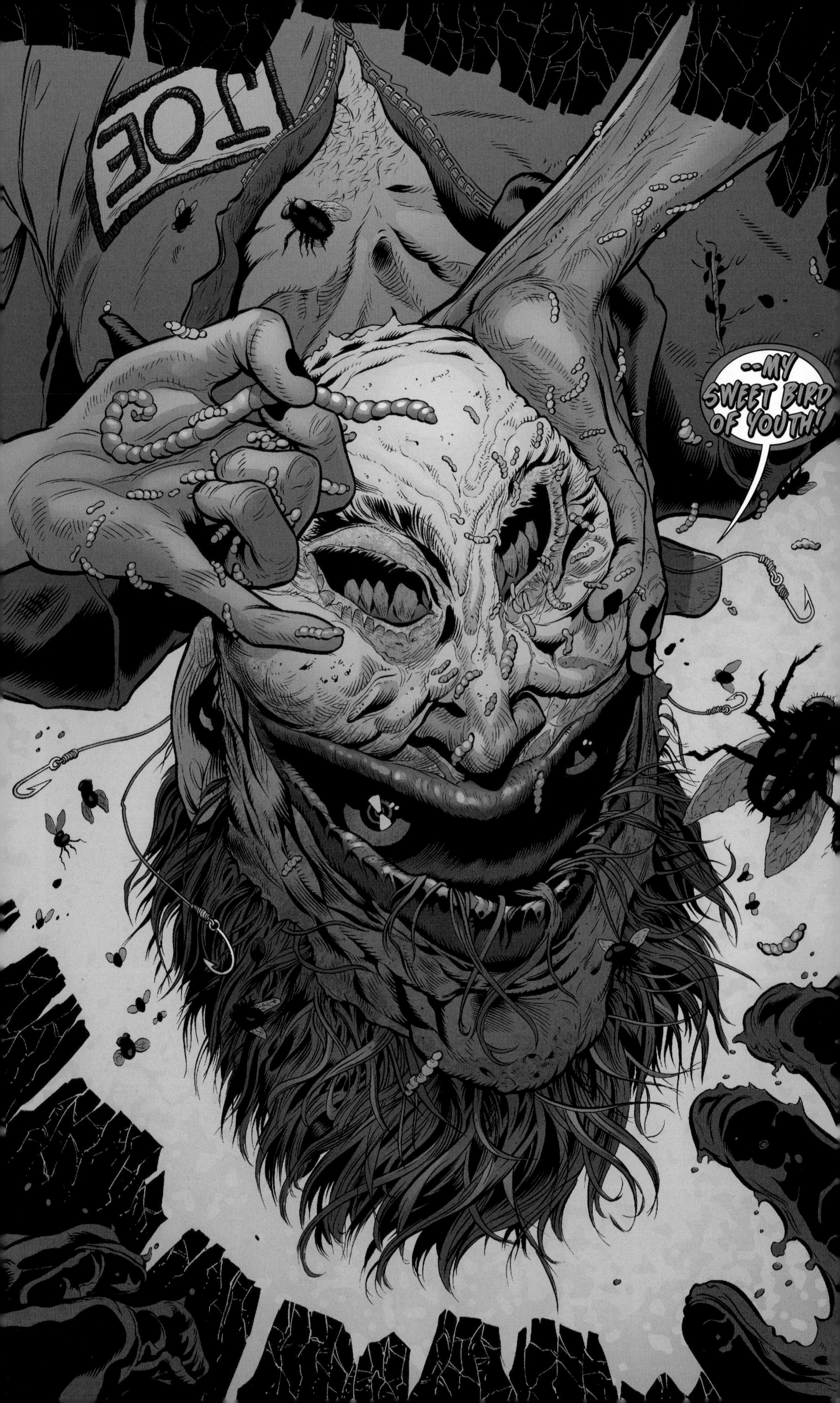
--MY SWEET BIRD OF YOUTH!

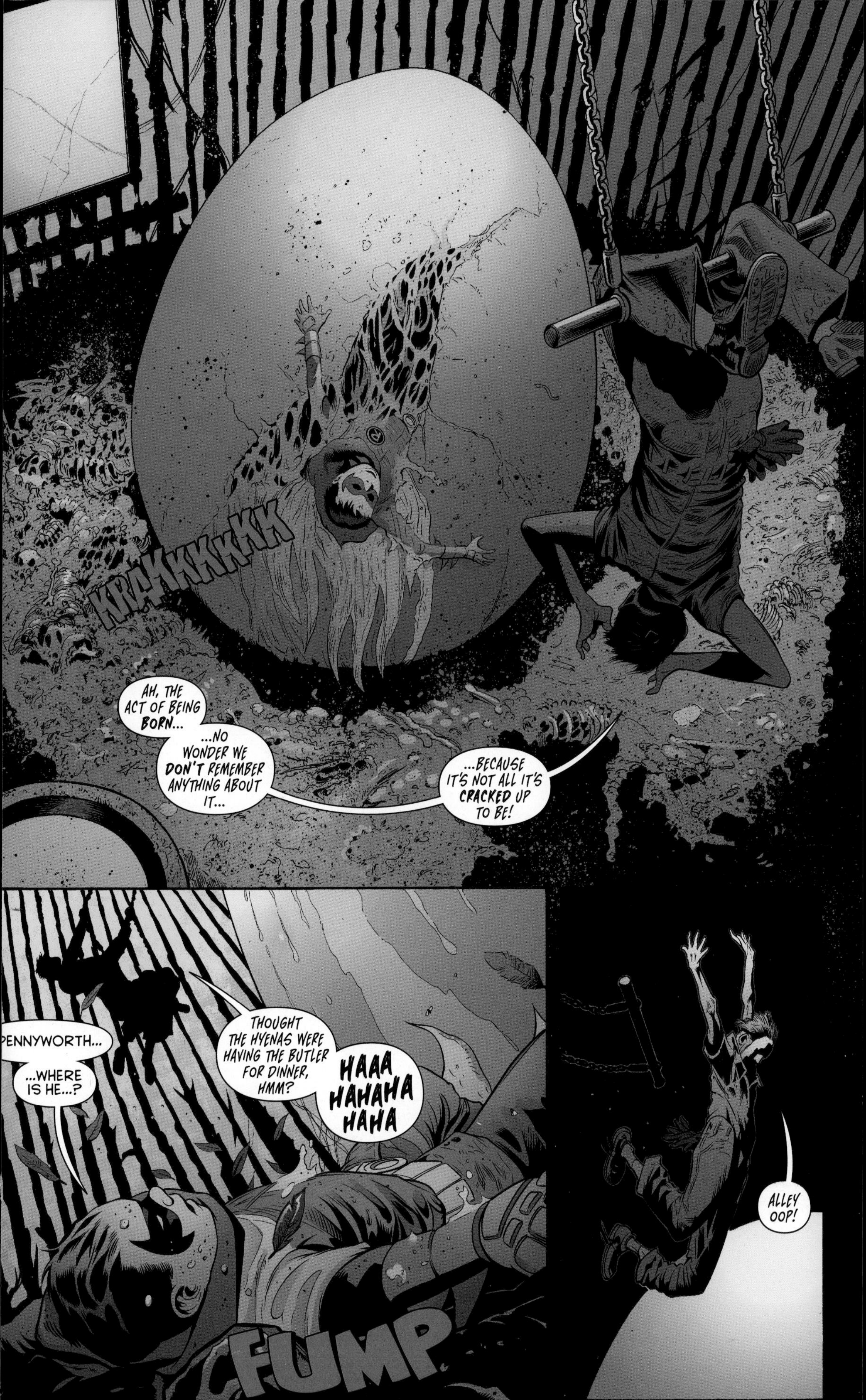
KRAKKKKKKK
AH, THE ACT OF BEING BORN...
...NO WONDER WE DON'T REMEMBER ANYTHING ABOUT IT...
...BECAUSE IT'S NOT ALL IT'S CRACKED UP TO BE!
PENNYWORTH...
...WHERE IS HE...?
THOUGHT THE HYENAS WERE HAVING THE BUTLER FOR DINNER, HMM?
HAAA HAHAHA HAHA
FUMP
ALLEY OOP!

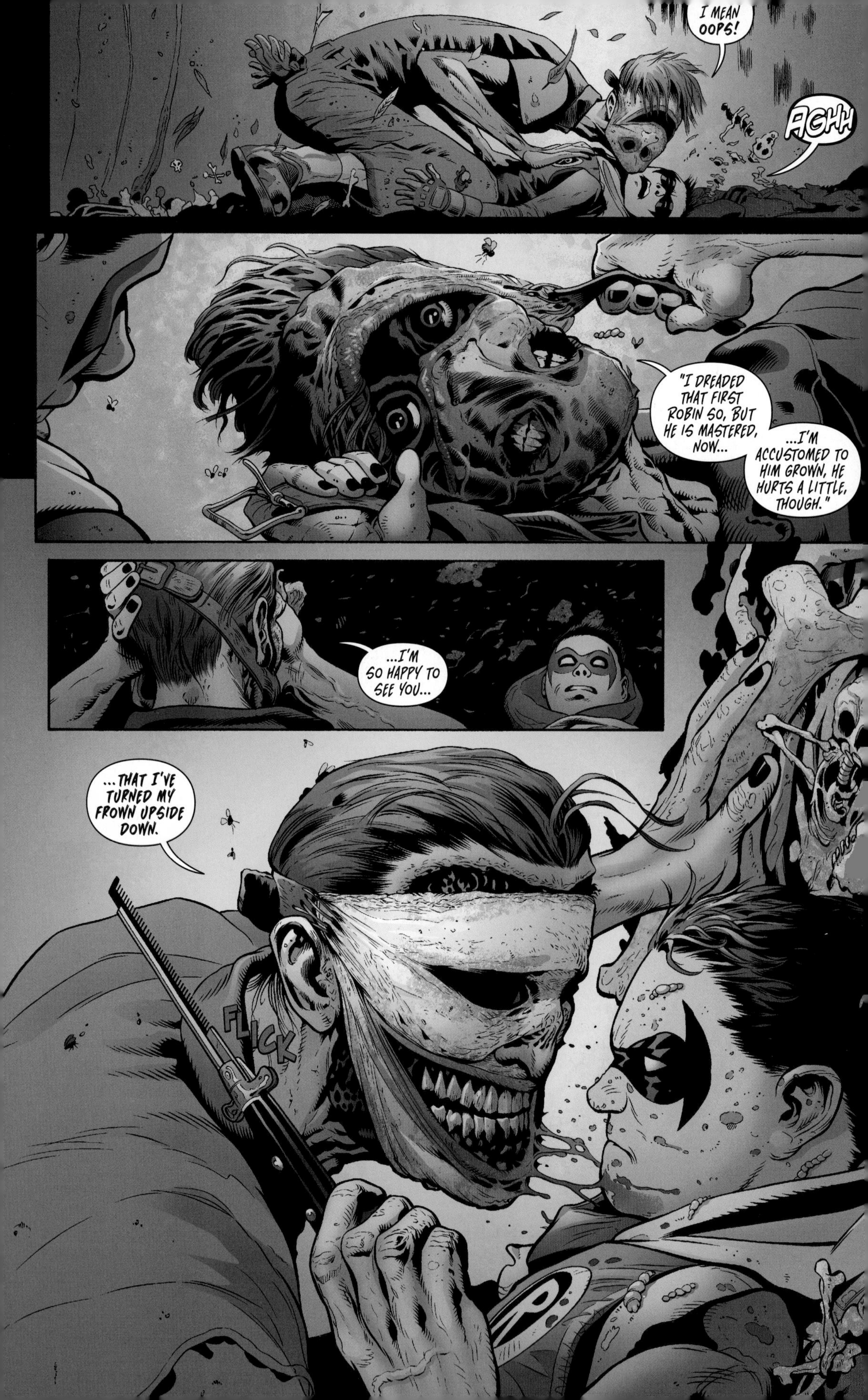
I MEAN OOPS!
AGHH
"I DREADED THAT FIRST ROBIN SO, BUT HE IS MASTERED, NOW...
...I'M ACCUSTOMED TO HIM GROWN, HE HURTS A LITTLE, THOUGH."
...I'M SO HAPPY TO SEE YOU...
...THAT I'VE TURNED MY FROWN UPSIDE DOWN.
FLICK

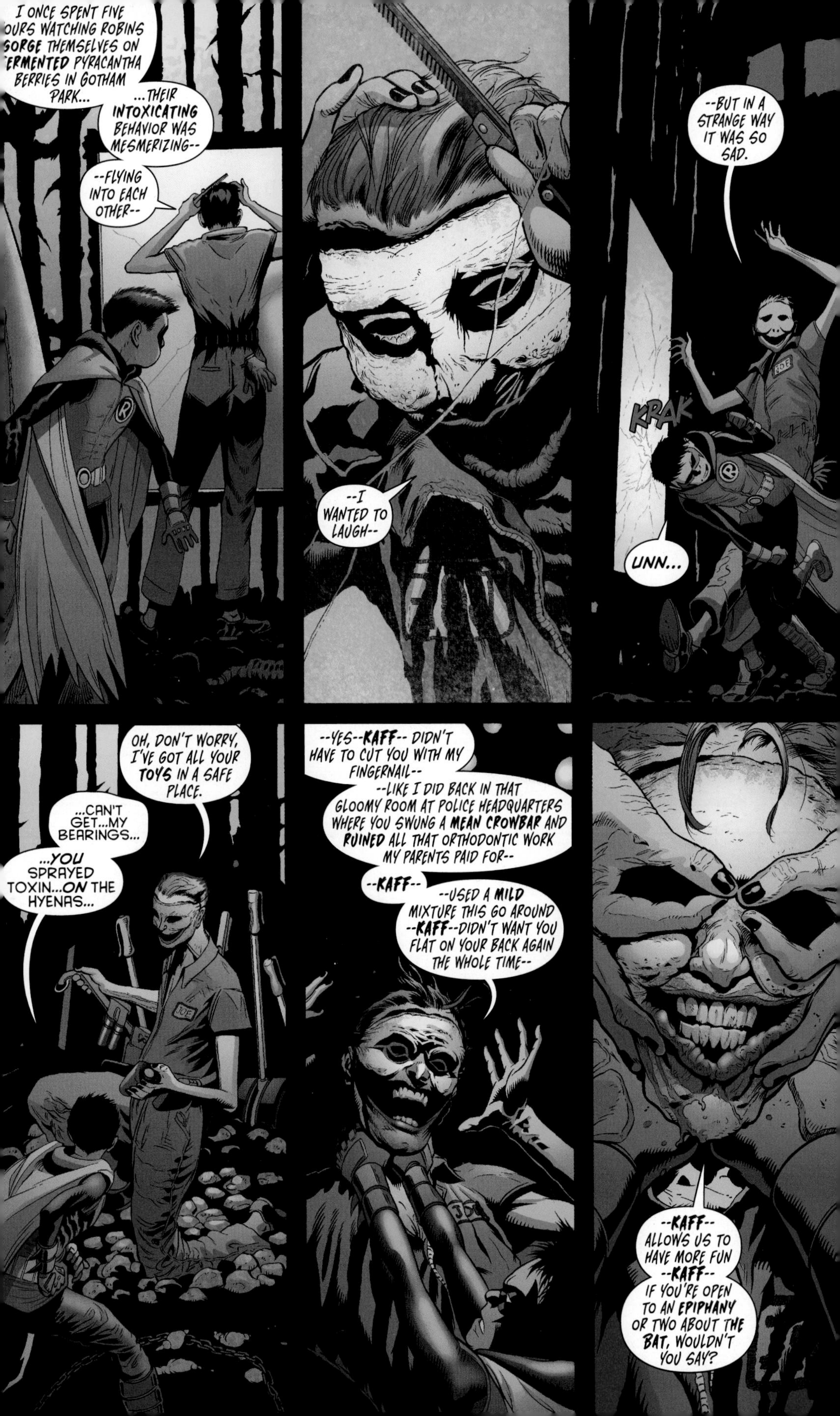
I ONCE SPENT FIVE HOURS WATCHING ROBINS GORGE THEMSELVES ON FERMENTED PYRACANTHA BERRIES IN GOTHAM PARK...
...THEIR INTOXICATING BEHAVIOR WAS MESMERIZING--
--FLYING INTO EACH OTHER--
--I WANTED TO LAUGH--
--BUT IN A STRANGE WAY IT WAS SO SAD.
KRAK
UNN...
OH, DON'T WORRY, I'VE GOT ALL YOUR TOYS IN A SAFE PLACE.
...CAN'T GET...MY BEARINGS...
...YOU SPRAYED TOXIN...ON THE HYENAS...
--YES--KAFF-- DIDN'T HAVE TO CUT YOU WITH MY FINGERNAIL--
--LIKE I DID BACK IN THAT GLOOMY ROOM AT POLICE HEADQUARTERS WHERE YOU SWUNG A MEAN CROWBAR AND RUINED ALL THAT ORTHODONTIC WORK MY PARENTS PAID FOR--
--KAFF--
--USED A MILD MIXTURE THIS GO AROUND --KAFF--DIDN'T WANT YOU FLAT ON YOUR BACK AGAIN THE WHOLE TIME--
--KAFF-- ALLOWS US TO HAVE MORE FUN --KAFF-- IF YOU'RE OPEN TO AN EPIPHANY OR TWO ABOUT THE BAT, WOULDN'T YOU SAY?

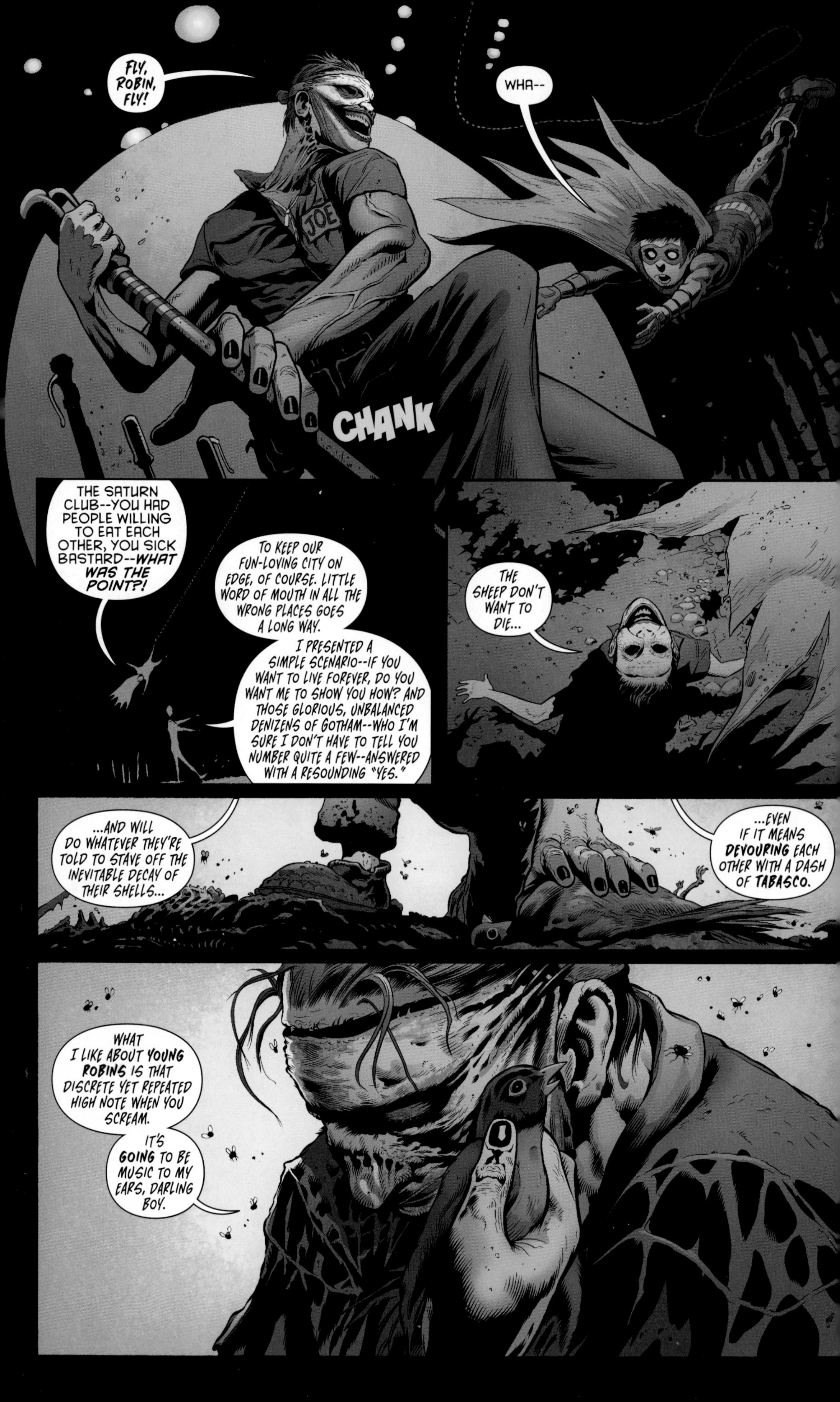
FLY, ROBIN, FLY!
WHA--
CHANK
THE SATURN CLUB--YOU HAD PEOPLE WILLING TO EAT EACH OTHER, YOU SICK BASTARD--WHAT WAS THE POINT?!
TO KEEP OUR FUN-LOVING CITY ON EDGE, OF COURSE. LITTLE WORD OF MOUTH IN ALL THE WRONG PLACES GOES A LONG WAY.
I PRESENTED A SIMPLE SCENARIO--IF YOU WANT TO LIVE FOREVER, DO YOU WANT ME TO SHOW YOU HOW? AND THOSE GLORIOUS, UNBALANCED DENIZENS OF GOTHAM--WHO I'M SURE I DON'T HAVE TO TELL YOU NUMBER QUITE A FEW--ANSWERED WITH A RESOUNDING "YES."
THE SHEEP DON'T WANT TO DIE...
...AND WILL DO WHATEVER THEY'RE TOLD TO STAVE OFF THE INEVITABLE DECAY OF THEIR SHELLS...
...EVEN IF IT MEANS DEVOURING EACH OTHER WITH A DASH OF TABASCO.
WHAT I LIKE ABOUT YOUNG ROBINS IS THAT DISCRETE YET REPEATED HIGH NOTE WHEN YOU SCREAM.
IT'S GOING TO BE MUSIC TO MY EARS, DARLING BOY.
JOE

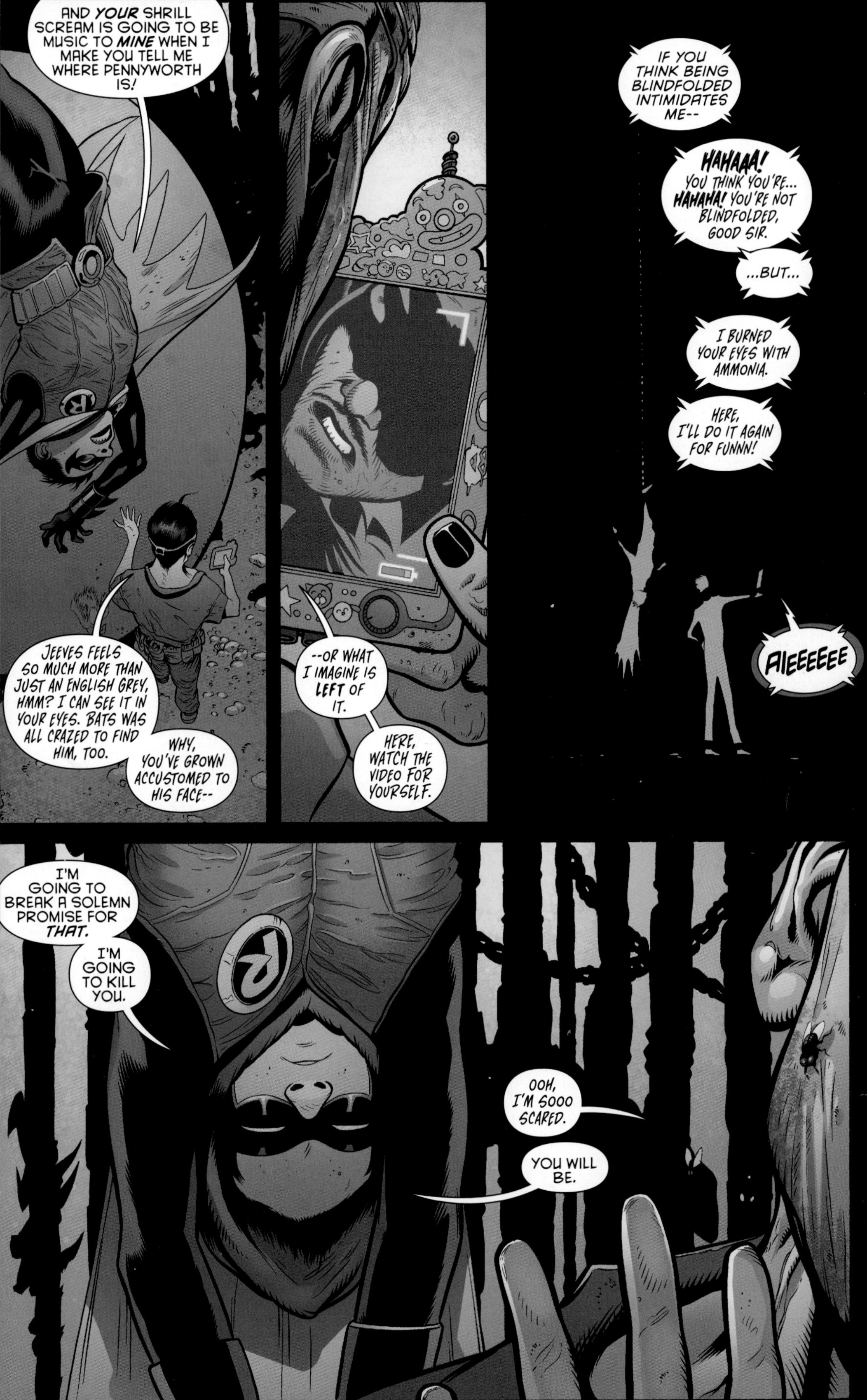
AND YOUR SHRILL SCREAM IS GOING TO BE MUSIC TO MINE WHEN I MAKE YOU TELL ME WHERE PENNYWORTH IS!
JEEVES FEELS SO MUCH MORE THAN JUST AN ENGLISH GREY, HMM? I CAN SEE IT IN YOUR EYES. BATS WAS ALL CRAZED TO FIND HIM, TOO.
WHY, YOU'VE GROWN ACCUSTOMED TO HIS FACE--
--OR WHAT I IMAGINE IS LEFT OF IT.
HERE, WATCH THE VIDEO FOR YOURSELF.
IF YOU THINK BEING BLINDFOLDED INTIMIDATES ME--
HAHAAA! YOU THINK YOU'RE... HAHAHA! YOU'RE NOT BLINDFOLDED, GOOD SIR.
...BUT...
I BURNED YOUR EYES WITH AMMONIA.
HERE, I'LL DO IT AGAIN FOR FUNNN!
AIEEEEEE
I'M GOING TO BREAK A SOLEMN PROMISE FOR THAT.
I'M GOING TO KILL YOU.
OOH, I'M SOOO SCARED.
YOU WILL BE.

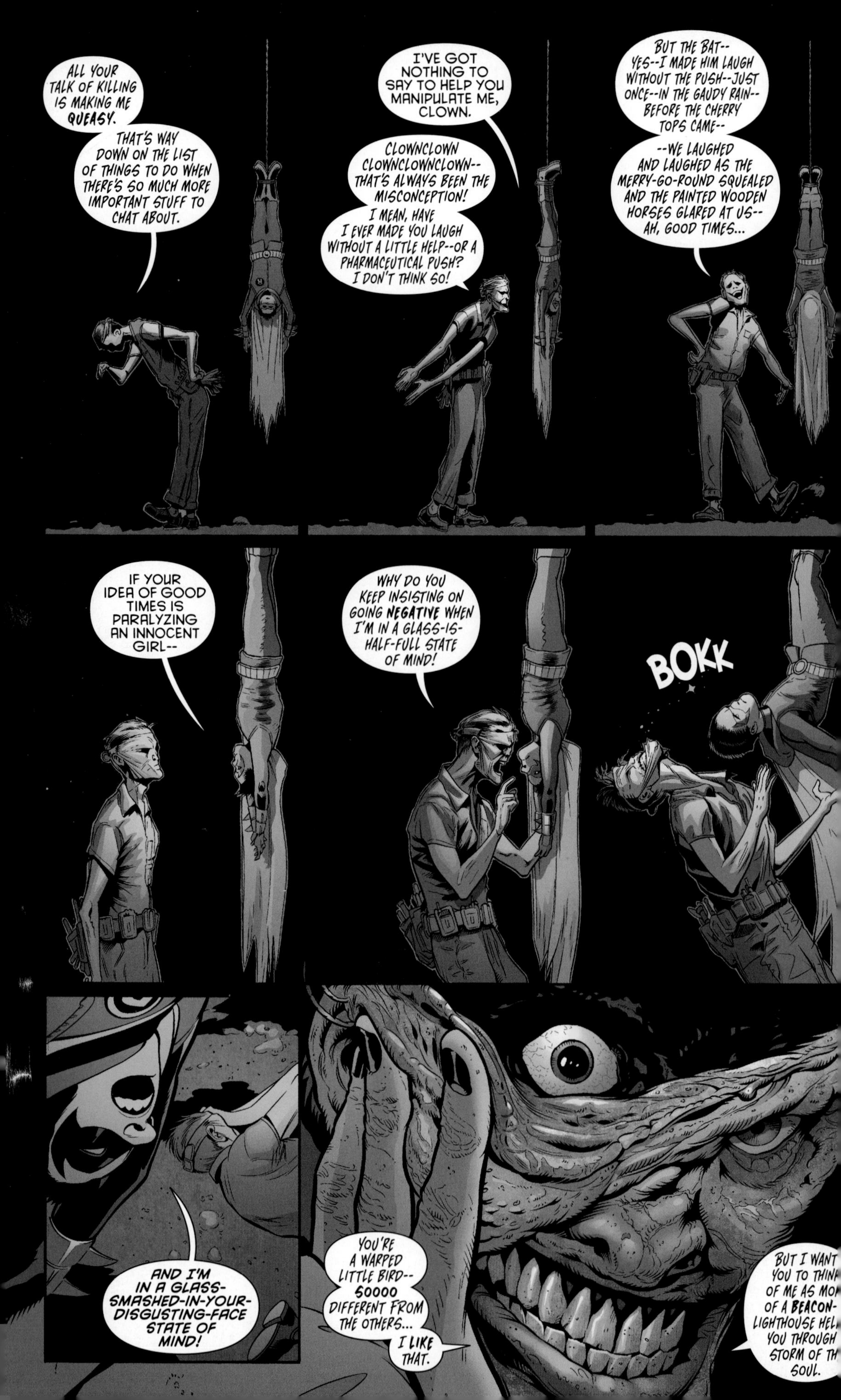

ALL YOUR TALK OF KILLING IS MAKING ME QUEASY.
THAT'S WAY DOWN ON THE LIST OF THINGS TO DO WHEN THERE'S SO MUCH MORE IMPORTANT STUFF TO CHAT ABOUT.
I'VE GOT NOTHING TO SAY TO HELP YOU MANIPULATE ME, CLOWN.
CLOWNCLOWN CLOWNCLOWNCLOWN-- THAT'S ALWAYS BEEN THE MISCONCEPTION!
I MEAN, HAVE I EVER MADE YOU LAUGH WITHOUT A LITTLE HELP--OR A PHARMACEUTICAL PUSH? I DON'T THINK SO!
BUT THE BAT-- YES--I MADE HIM LAUGH WITHOUT THE PUSH--JUST ONCE--IN THE GAUDY RAIN-- BEFORE THE CHERRY TOPS CAME--
--WE LAUGHED AND LAUGHED AS THE MERRY-GO-ROUND SQUEALED AND THE PAINTED WOODEN HORSES GLARED AT US-- AH, GOOD TIMES...
IF YOUR IDEA OF GOOD TIMES IS PARALYZING AN INNOCENT GIRL--
WHY DO YOU KEEP INSISTING ON GOING NEGATIVE WHEN I'M IN A GLASS-IS-HALF-FULL STATE OF MIND!
BOKK
AND I'M IN A GLASS-SMASHED-IN-YOUR-DISGUSTING-FACE STATE OF MIND!
YOU'RE A WARPED LITTLE BIRD-- SOOOO DIFFERENT FROM THE OTHERS...
I LIKE THAT.
BUT I WANT YOU TO THIN OF ME AS MO OF A BEACON- LIGHTHOUSE HEL YOU THROUGH STORM OF TH SOUL.

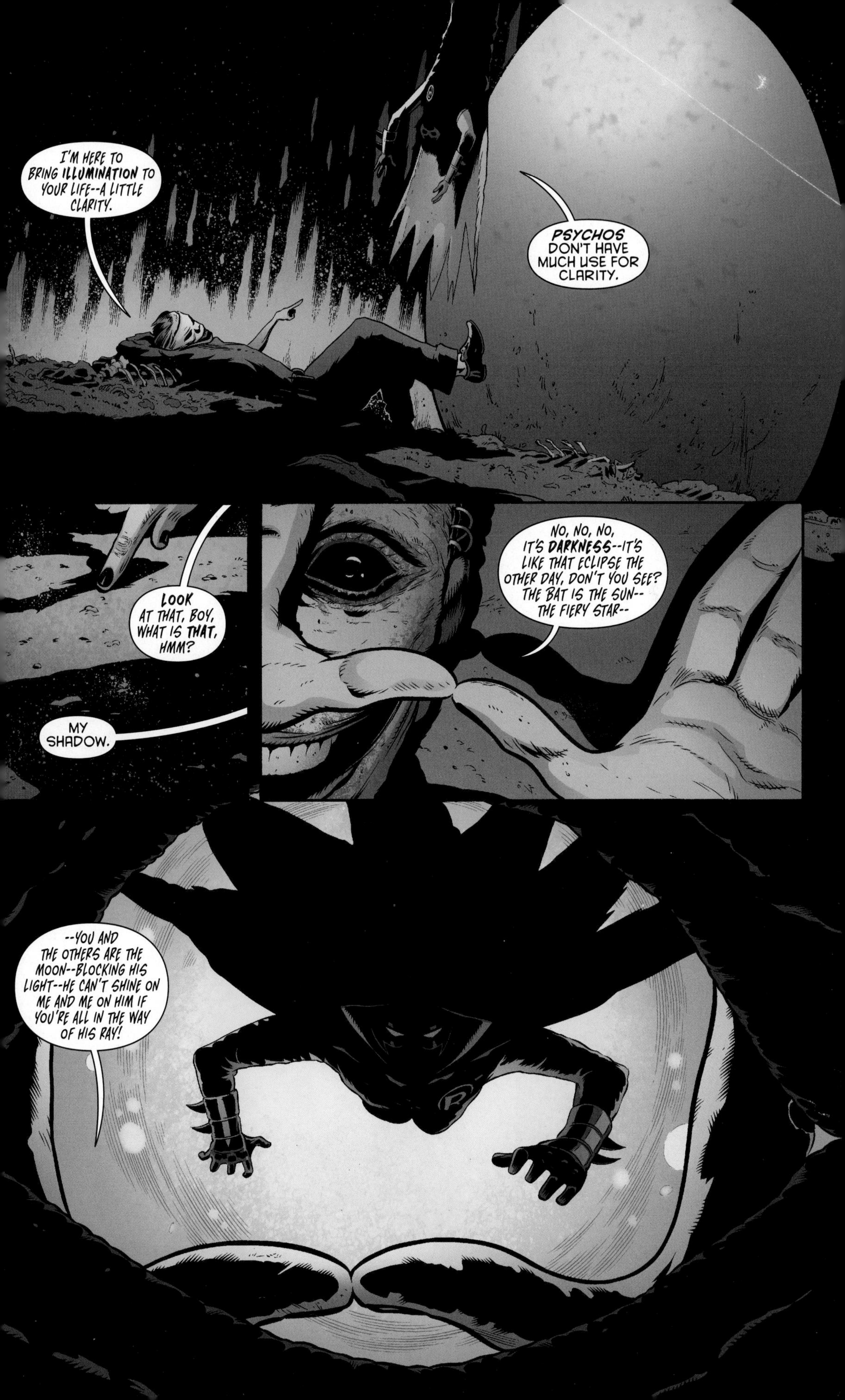
I'M HERE TO BRING ILLUMINATION TO YOUR LIFE--A LITTLE CLARITY.
PSYCHOS DON'T HAVE MUCH USE FOR CLARITY.
LOOK AT THAT, BOY, WHAT IS THAT, HMM?
MY SHADOW.
NO, NO, NO, IT'S DARKNESS--IT'S LIKE THAT ECLIPSE THE OTHER DAY, DON'T YOU SEE? THE BAT IS THE SUN--THE FIERY STAR--
--YOU AND THE OTHERS ARE THE MOON--BLOCKING HIS LIGHT--HE CAN'T SHINE ON ME AND ME ON HIM IF YOU'RE ALL IN THE WAY OF HIS RAY!

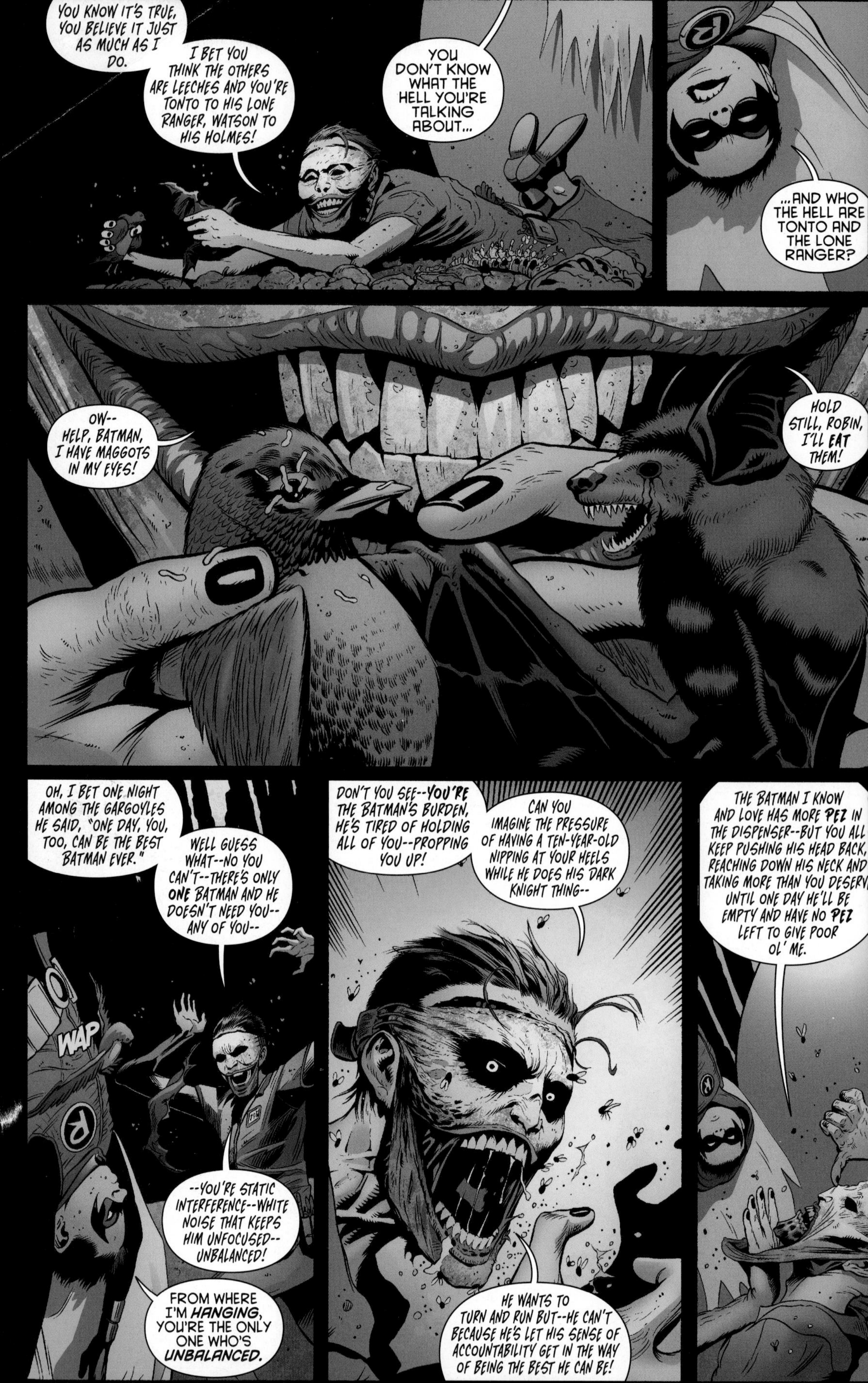

YOU KNOW IT'S TRUE, YOU BELIEVE IT JUST AS MUCH AS I DO.
I BET YOU THINK THE OTHERS ARE LEECHES AND YOU'RE TONTO TO HIS LONE RANGER, WATSON TO HIS HOLMES!
YOU DON'T KNOW WHAT THE HELL YOU'RE TALKING ABOUT...
...AND WHO THE HELL ARE TONTO AND THE LONE RANGER?
OW-- HELP, BATMAN, I HAVE MAGGOTS IN MY EYES!
HOLD STILL, ROBIN, I'LL EAT THEM!
OH, I BET ONE NIGHT AMONG THE GARGOYLES HE SAID, "ONE DAY, YOU, TOO, CAN BE THE BEST BATMAN EVER."
WELL GUESS WHAT--NO YOU CAN'T--THERE'S ONLY ONE BATMAN AND HE DOESN'T NEED YOU-- ANY OF YOU--
WAP
--YOU'RE STATIC INTERFERENCE--WHITE NOISE THAT KEEPS HIM UNFOCUSED-- UNBALANCED!
FROM WHERE I'M HANGING, YOU'RE THE ONLY ONE WHO'S UNBALANCED.
DON'T YOU SEE--YOU'RE THE BATMAN'S BURDEN, HE'S TIRED OF HOLDING ALL OF YOU--PROPPING YOU UP!
CAN YOU IMAGINE THE PRESSURE OF HAVING A TEN-YEAR-OLD NIPPING AT YOUR HEELS WHILE HE DOES HIS DARK KNIGHT THING--
HE WANTS TO TURN AND RUN BUT--HE CAN'T BECAUSE HE'S LET HIS SENSE OF ACCOUNTABILITY GET IN THE WAY OF BEING THE BEST HE CAN BE!
THE BATMAN I KNOW AND LOVE HAS MORE PEZ IN THE DISPENSER--BUT YOU ALL KEEP PUSHING HIS HEAD BACK, REACHING DOWN HIS NECK AND TAKING MORE THAN YOU DESERV UNTIL ONE DAY HE'LL BE EMPTY AND HAVE NO PEZ LEFT TO GIVE POOR OL' ME.

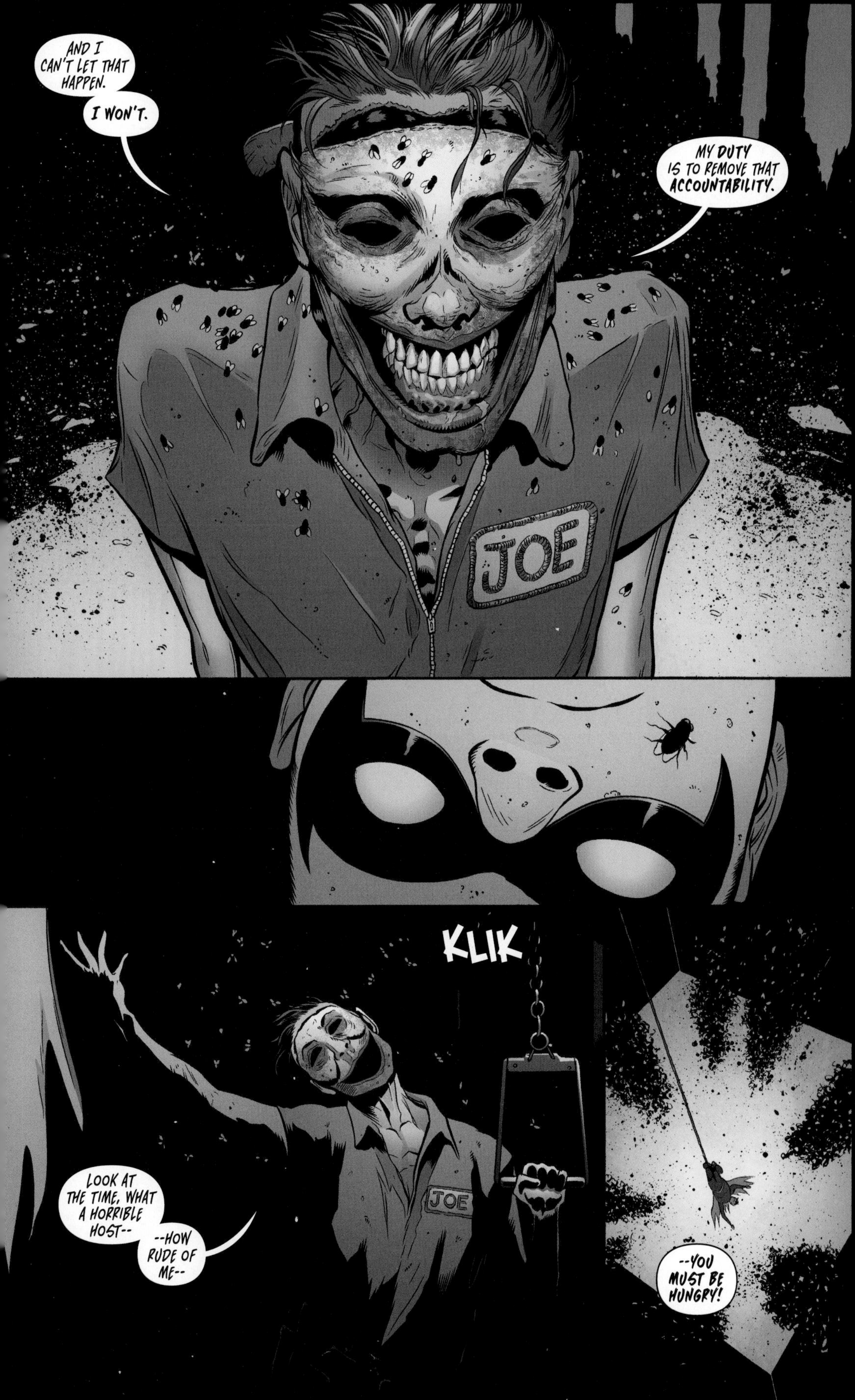
AND I CAN'T LET THAT HAPPEN.
I WON'T.
MY DUTY IS TO REMOVE THAT ACCOUNTABILITY.
JOE
KLIK
LOOK AT THE TIME, WHAT A HORRIBLE HOST--
--HOW RUDE OF ME--
JOE
--YOU MUST BE HUNGRY!

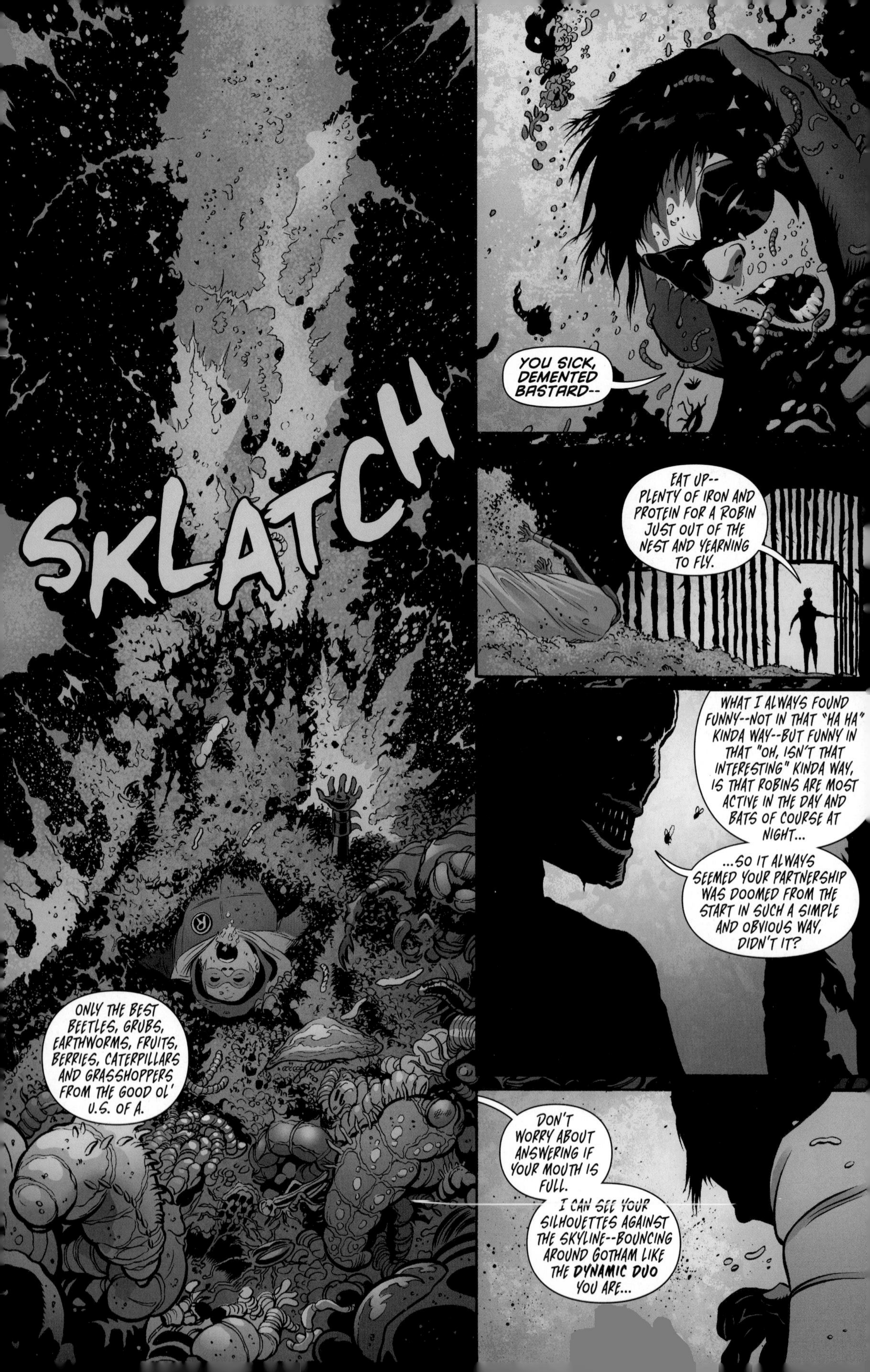
SKLATCH
ONLY THE BEST BEETLES, GRUBS, EARTHWORMS, FRUITS, BERRIES, CATERPILLARS AND GRASSHOPPERS FROM THE GOOD OL' U.S. OF A.
YOU SICK, DEMENTED BASTARD--
EAT UP-- PLENTY OF IRON AND PROTEIN FOR A ROBIN JUST OUT OF THE NEST AND YEARNING TO FLY.
WHAT I ALWAYS FOUND FUNNY--NOT IN THAT "HA HA" KINDA WAY--BUT FUNNY IN THAT "OH, ISN'T THAT INTERESTING" KINDA WAY, IS THAT ROBINS ARE MOST ACTIVE IN THE DAY AND BATS OF COURSE AT NIGHT...
...SO IT ALWAYS SEEMED YOUR PARTNERSHIP WAS DOOMED FROM THE START IN SUCH A SIMPLE AND OBVIOUS WAY, DIDN'T IT?
DON'T WORRY ABOUT ANSWERING IF YOUR MOUTH IS FULL.
I CAN SEE YOUR SILHOUETTES AGAINST THE SKYLINE--BOUNCING AROUND GOTHAM LIKE THE **DYNAMIC DUO** YOU ARE...

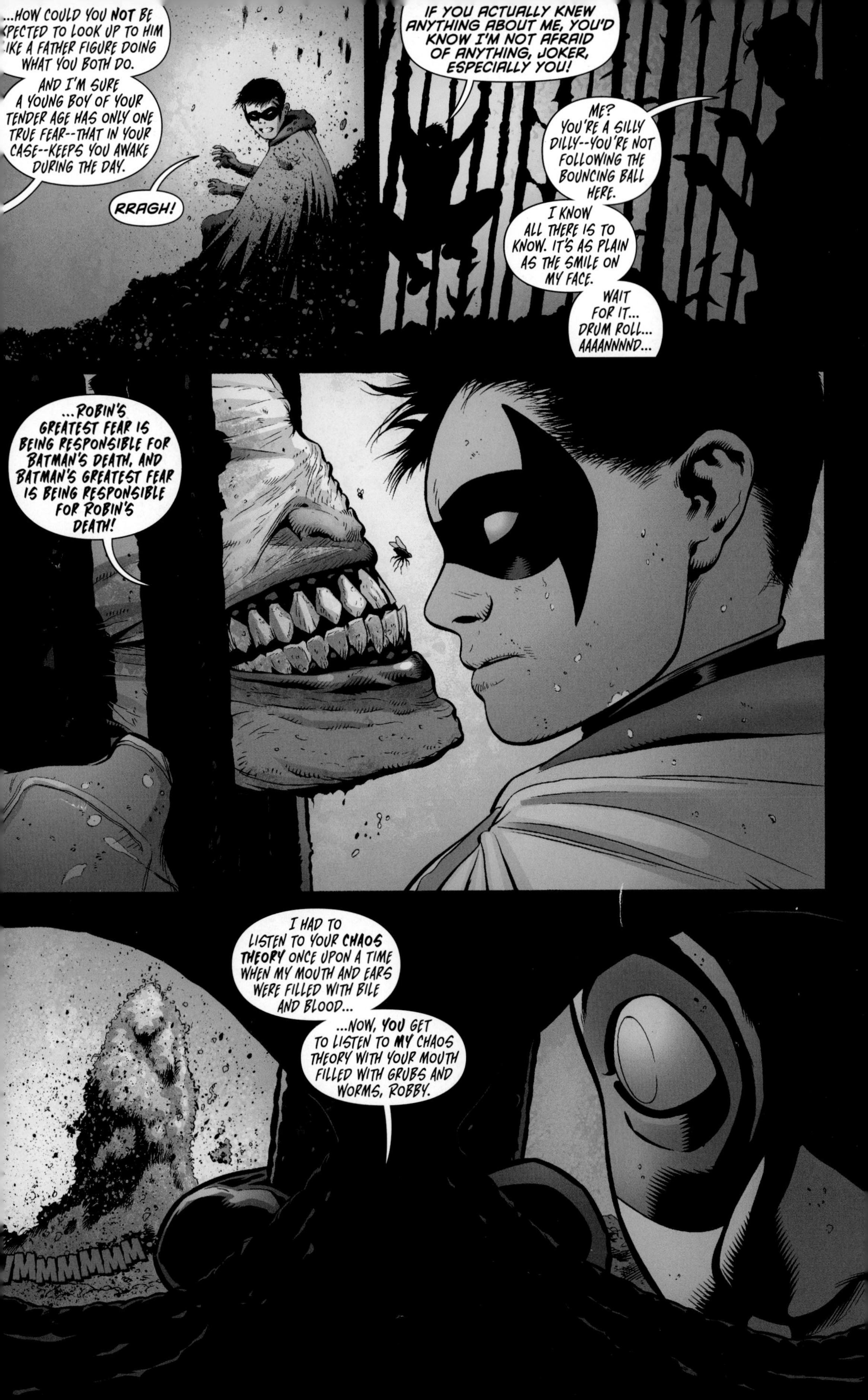
...HOW COULD YOU NOT BE EXPECTED TO LOOK UP TO HIM LIKE A FATHER FIGURE DOING WHAT YOU BOTH DO.
AND I'M SURE A YOUNG BOY OF YOUR TENDER AGE HAS ONLY ONE TRUE FEAR--THAT IN YOUR CASE--KEEPS YOU AWAKE DURING THE DAY.
RRAGH!
IF YOU ACTUALLY KNEW ANYTHING ABOUT ME, YOU'D KNOW I'M NOT AFRAID OF ANYTHING, JOKER, ESPECIALLY YOU!
ME? YOU'RE A SILLY DILLY--YOU'RE NOT FOLLOWING THE BOUNCING BALL HERE.
I KNOW ALL THERE IS TO KNOW. IT'S AS PLAIN AS THE SMILE ON MY FACE.
WAIT FOR IT... DRUM ROLL... AAAANNNND...
...ROBIN'S GREATEST FEAR IS BEING RESPONSIBLE FOR BATMAN'S DEATH, AND BATMAN'S GREATEST FEAR IS BEING RESPONSIBLE FOR ROBIN'S DEATH!
I HAD TO LISTEN TO YOUR CHAOS THEORY ONCE UPON A TIME WHEN MY MOUTH AND EARS WERE FILLED WITH BILE AND BLOOD...
...NOW, YOU GET TO LISTEN TO MY CHAOS THEORY WITH YOUR MOUTH FILLED WITH GRUBS AND WORMS, ROBBY.
MMMMMMM

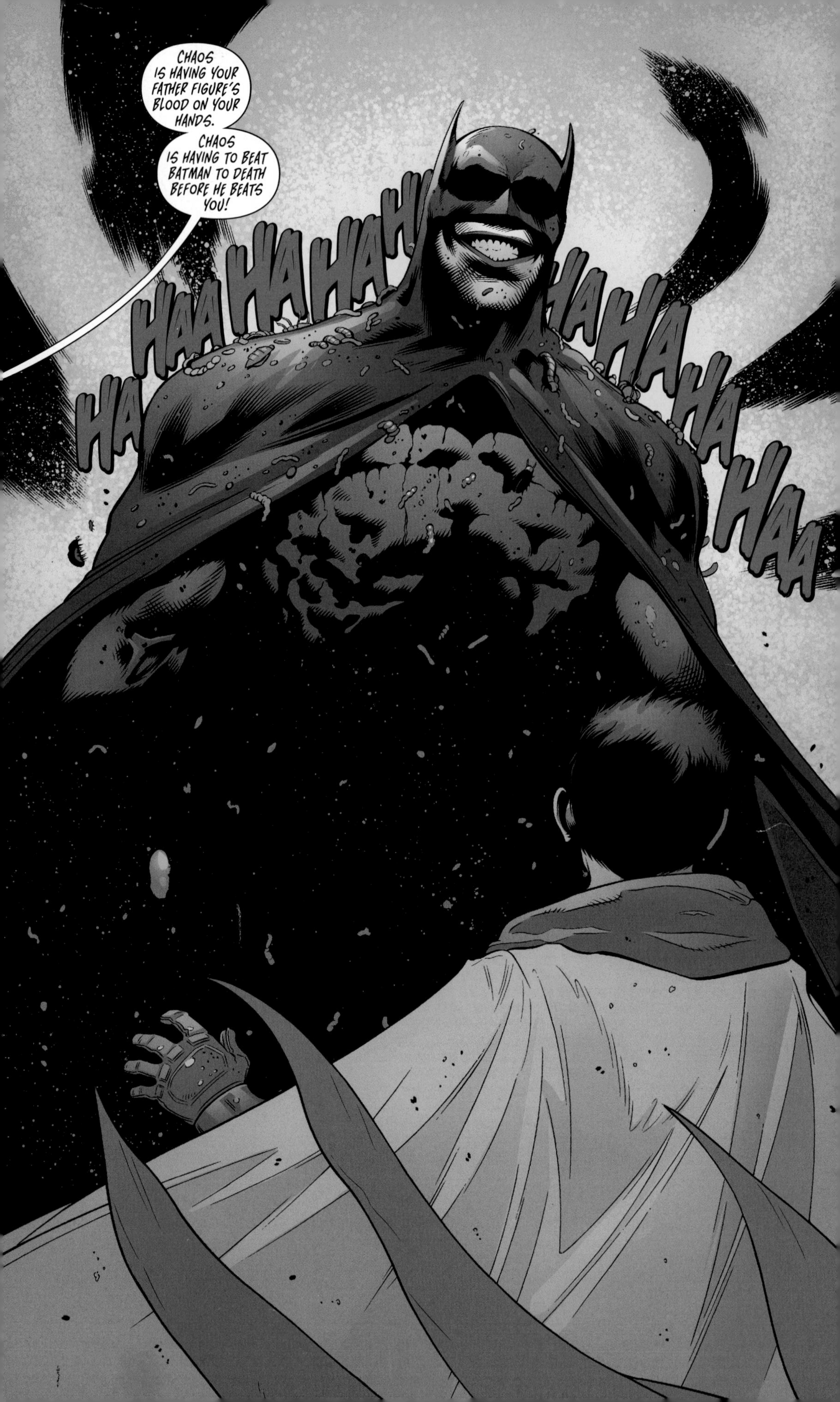
CHAOS IS HAVING YOUR FATHER FIGURE'S BLOOD ON YOUR HANDS.
CHAOS IS HAVING TO BEAT BATMAN TO DEATH BEFORE HE BEATS YOU!
HAHAAHAHAHAHAH
HAHAHAHAHAHAHAA

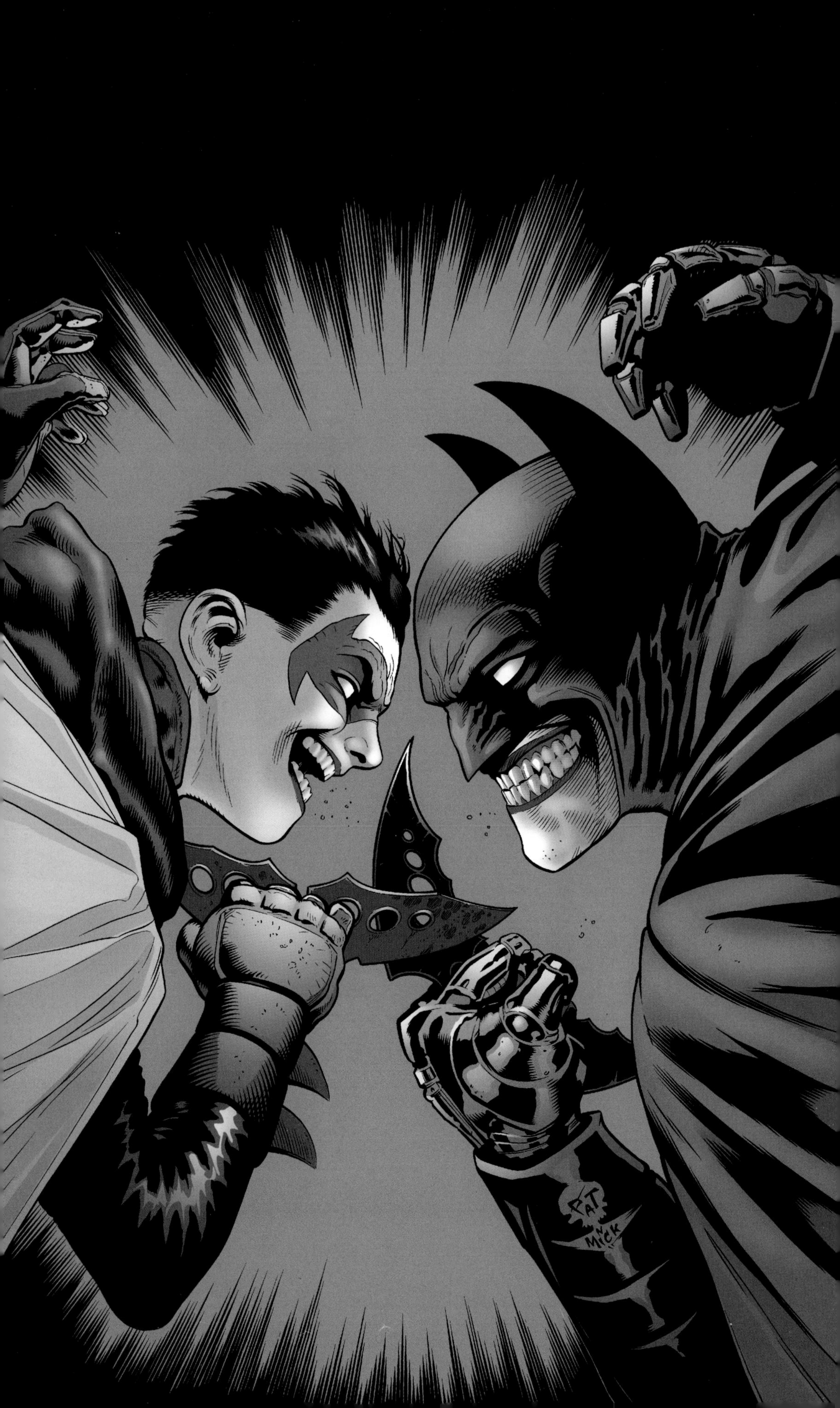

DEATH OF THE FAMILY: CAST A GIANT SHADOW

PETER J. TOMASI writer PATRICK GLEASON penciller MICK GRAY & KEITH CHAMPAGNE inkers cover art by PATRICK GLEASON, MICK GRAY & JOHN KALIS

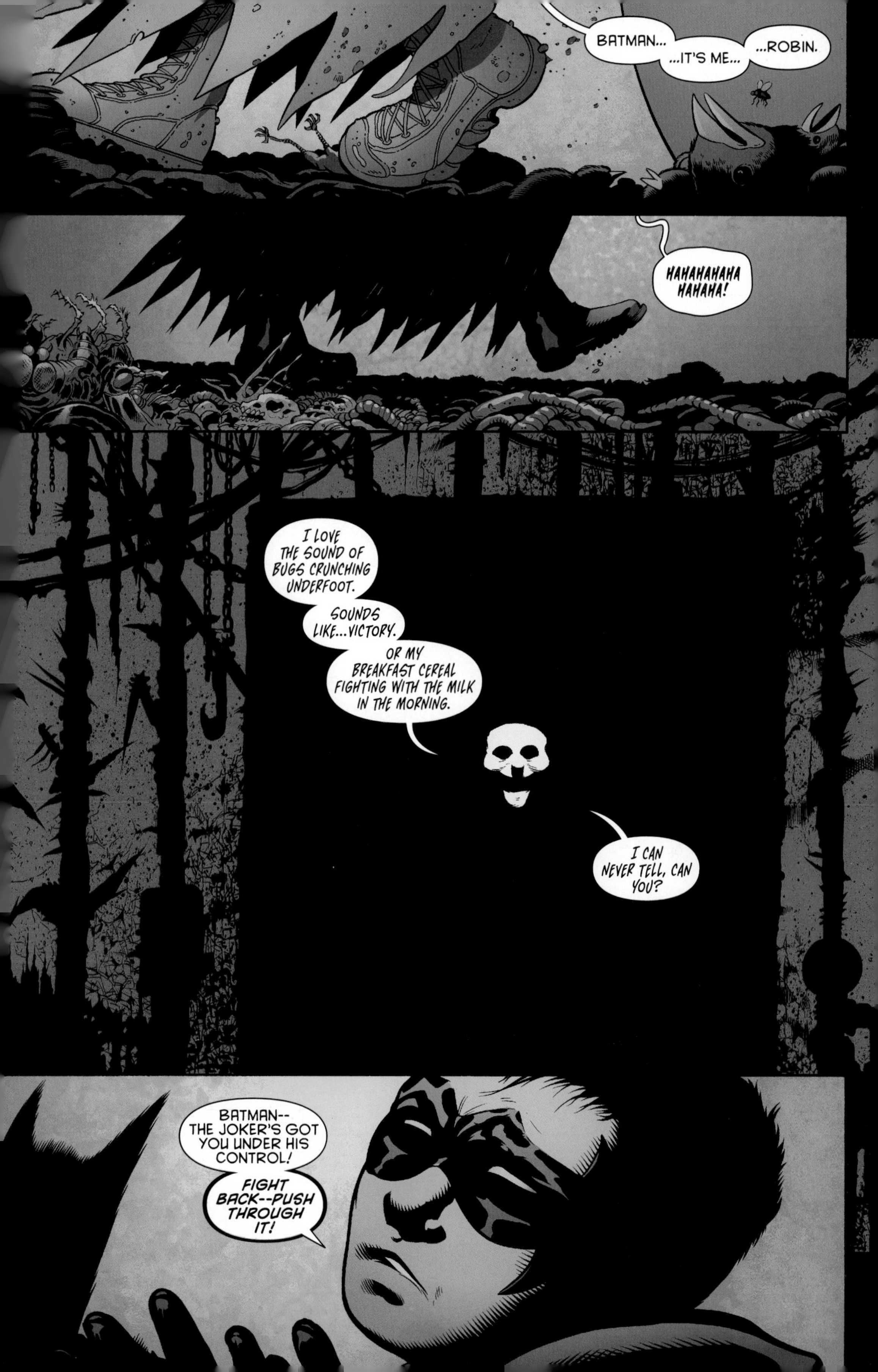
BATMAN...
...IT'S ME...
...ROBIN.
HAHAHAHAHA HAHAHA!
I LOVE THE SOUND OF BUGS CRUNCHING UNDERFOOT.
SOUNDS LIKE...VICTORY.
OR MY BREAKFAST CEREAL FIGHTING WITH THE MILK IN THE MORNING.
I CAN NEVER TELL, CAN YOU?
BATMAN-- THE JOKER'S GOT YOU UNDER HIS CONTROL!
FIGHT BACK--PUSH THROUGH IT!

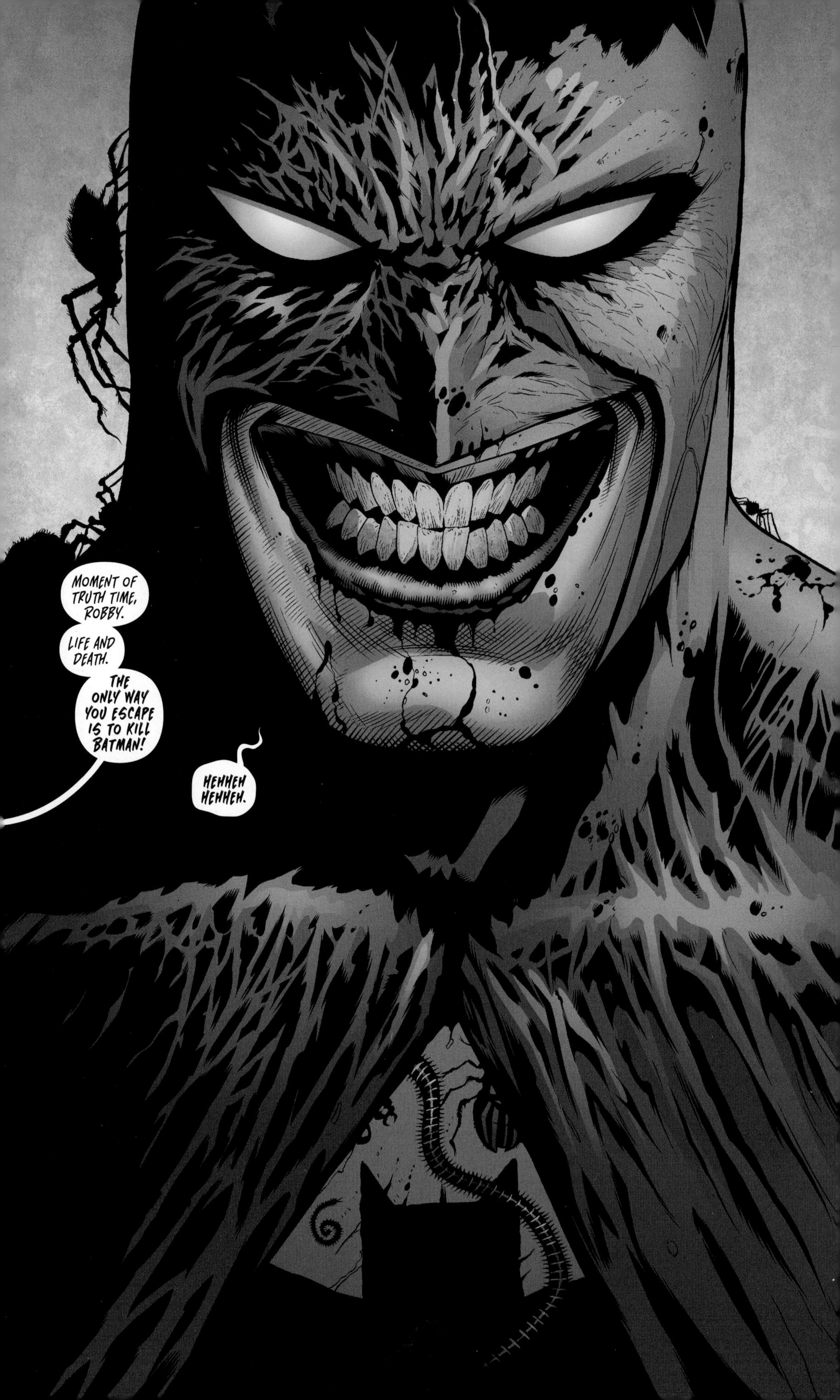
MOMENT OF TRUTH TIME, ROBBY.
LIFE AND DEATH.
THE ONLY WAY YOU ESCAPE IS TO KILL BATMAN!
HEHHEH HEHHEH.

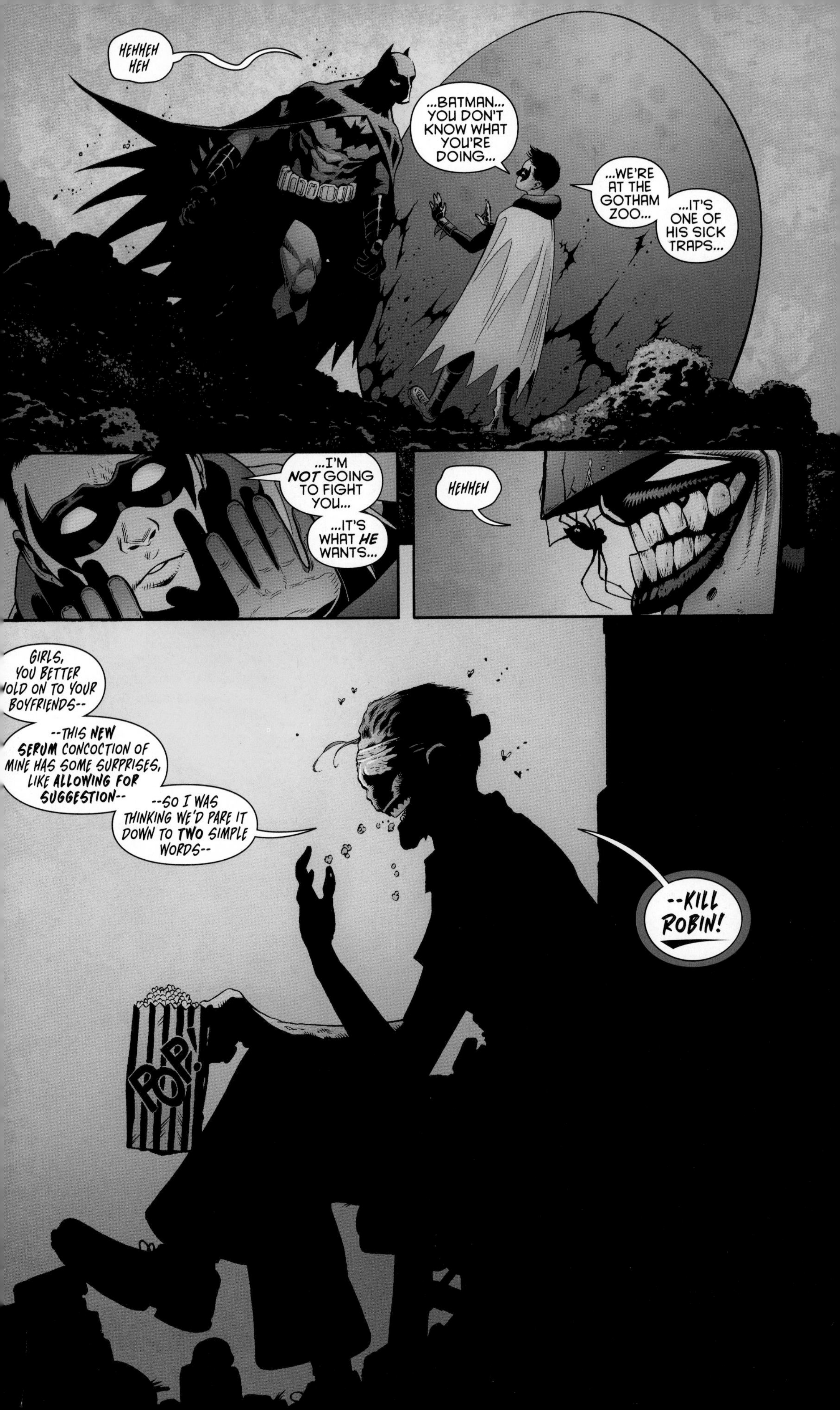
HEHHEH HEH
...BATMAN... YOU DON'T KNOW WHAT YOU'RE DOING...
...WE'RE AT THE GOTHAM ZOO...
...IT'S ONE OF HIS SICK TRAPS...
...I'M NOT GOING TO FIGHT YOU...
...IT'S WHAT HE WANTS...
HEHHEH
GIRLS, YOU BETTER OLD ON TO YOUR BOYFRIENDS--
--THIS NEW SERUM CONCOCTION OF MINE HAS SOME SURPRISES, LIKE ALLOWING FOR SUGGESTION--
--SO I WAS THINKING WE'D PARE IT DOWN TO TWO SIMPLE WORDS--
--KILL ROBIN!
POP!

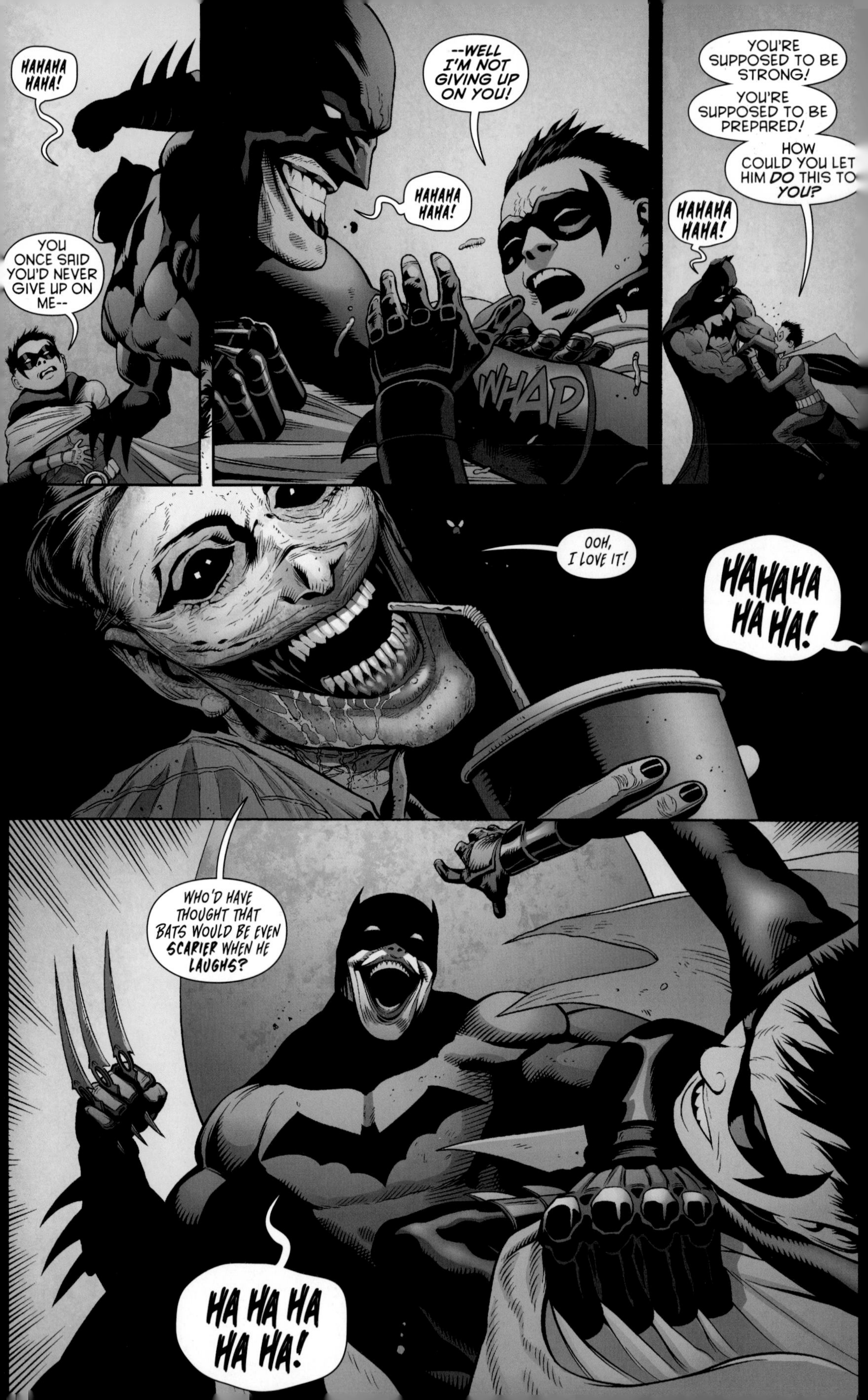
HAHAHA HAHA!
YOU ONCE SAID YOU'D NEVER GIVE UP ON ME--
--WELL I'M NOT GIVING UP ON YOU!
HAHAHA HAHA!
WHAP
YOU'RE SUPPOSED TO BE STRONG!
YOU'RE SUPPOSED TO BE PREPARED!
HOW COULD YOU LET HIM DO THIS TO YOU?
HAHAHA HAHA!
OOH, I LOVE IT!
HAHAHA HA HA!
WHO'D HAVE THOUGHT THAT BATS WOULD BE EVEN SCARIER WHEN HE LAUGHS?
HA HA HA HA HA!

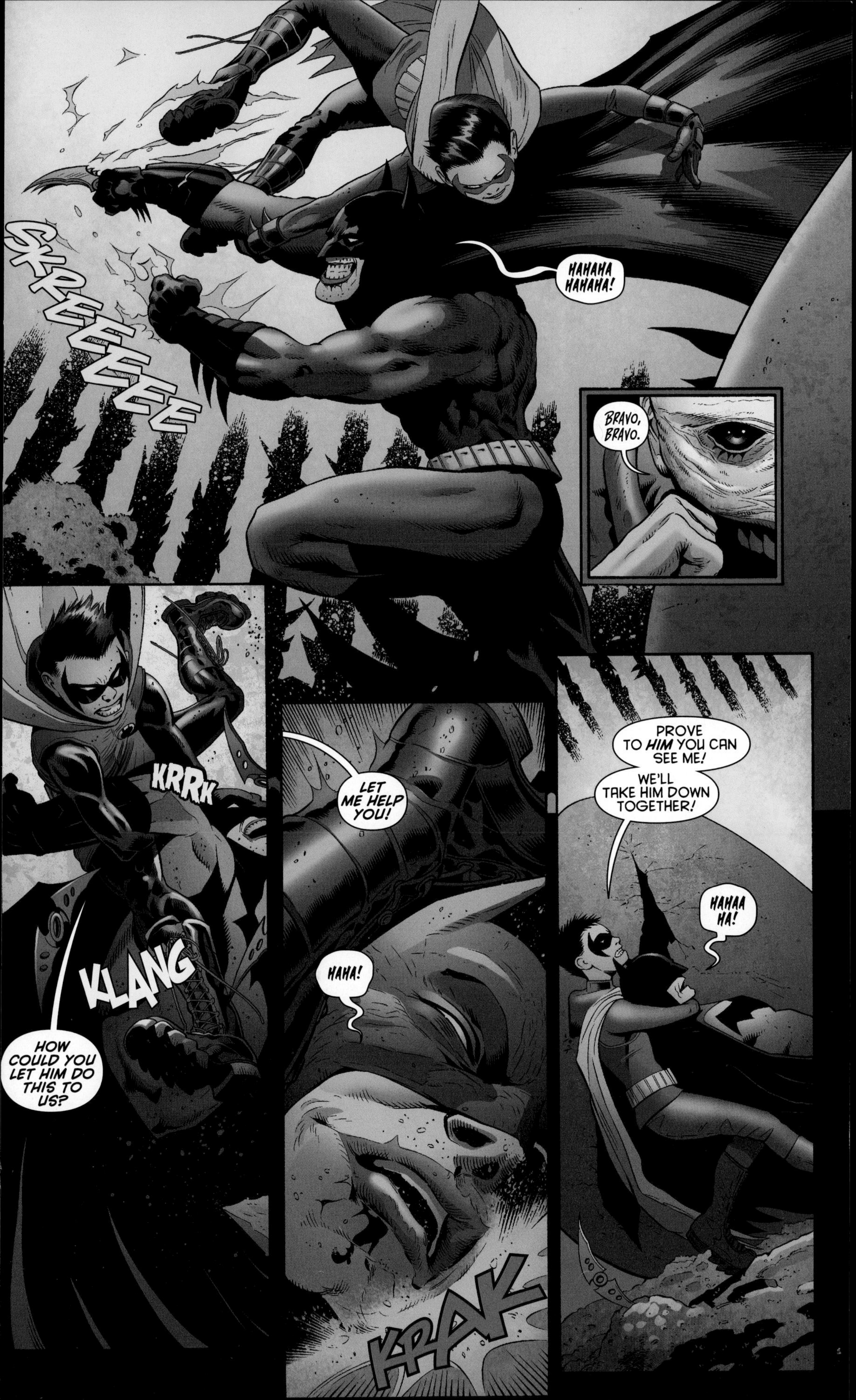
SKREEEEEE
HAHAHA HAHAHA!
BRAVO, BRAVO.
KRRK
KLANG
HOW COULD YOU LET HIM DO THIS TO US?
LET ME HELP YOU!
HAHA!
KRAK
PROVE TO HIM YOU CAN SEE ME!
WE'LL TAKE HIM DOWN TOGETHER!
HAHAA HA!

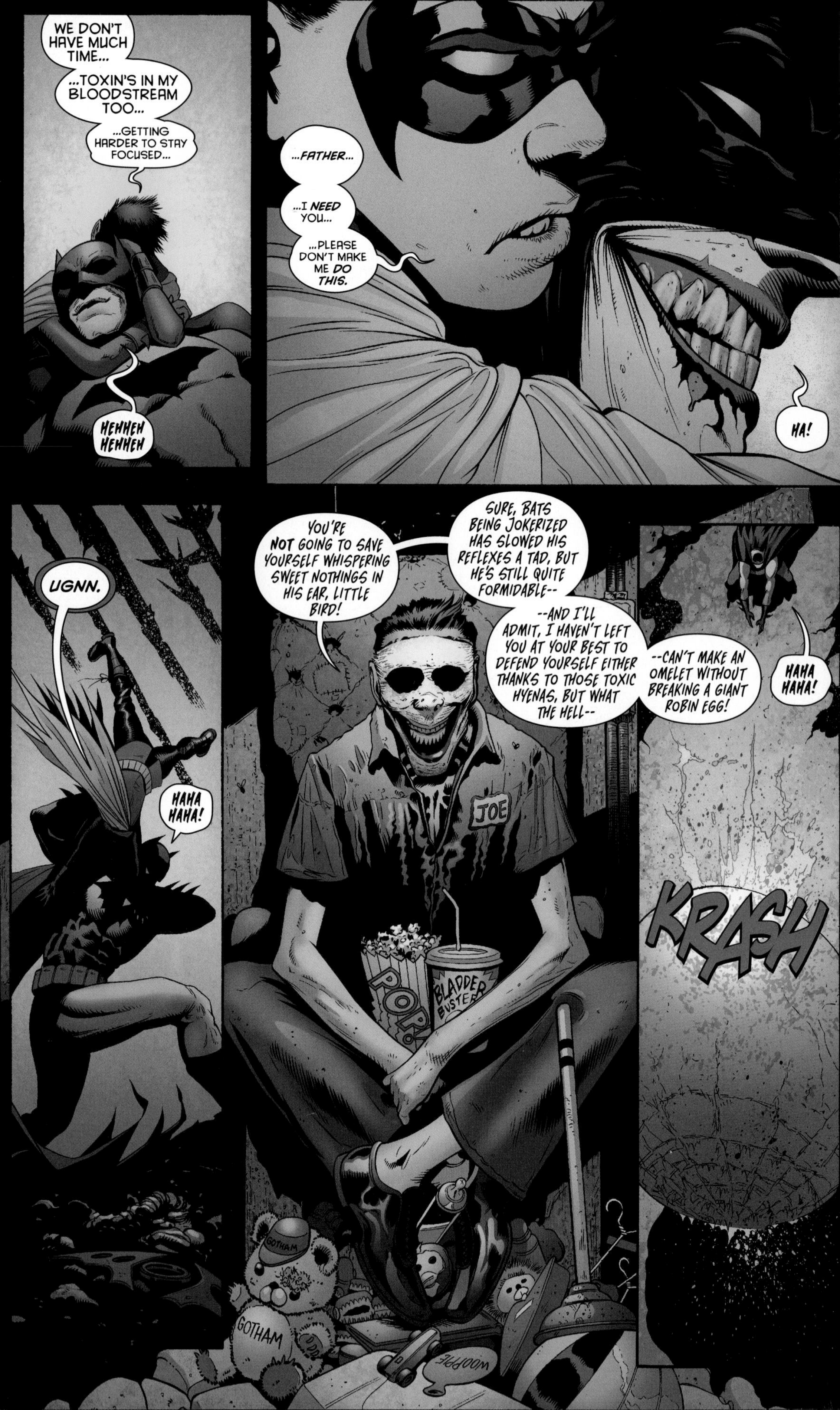
WE DON'T HAVE MUCH TIME...
...TOXIN'S IN MY BLOODSTREAM TOO...
...GETTING HARDER TO STAY FOCUSED...
HEHHEH HEHHEH
...FATHER...
...I NEED YOU...
...PLEASE DON'T MAKE ME DO THIS.
HA!
UGNN.
HAHA HAHA!
YOU'RE NOT GOING TO SAVE YOURSELF WHISPERING SWEET NOTHINGS IN HIS EAR, LITTLE BIRD!
SURE, BATS BEING JOKERIZED HAS SLOWED HIS REFLEXES A TAD, BUT HE'S STILL QUITE FORMIDABLE--
--AND I'LL ADMIT, I HAVEN'T LEFT YOU AT YOUR BEST TO DEFEND YOURSELF EITHER THANKS TO THOSE TOXIC HYENAS, BUT WHAT THE HELL--
--CAN'T MAKE AN OMELET WITHOUT BREAKING A GIANT ROBIN EGG!
HAHA HAHA!
KRASH
JOE
POP
BLADDER BUSTER
GOTHAM
GOTHAM
WOOPPEE

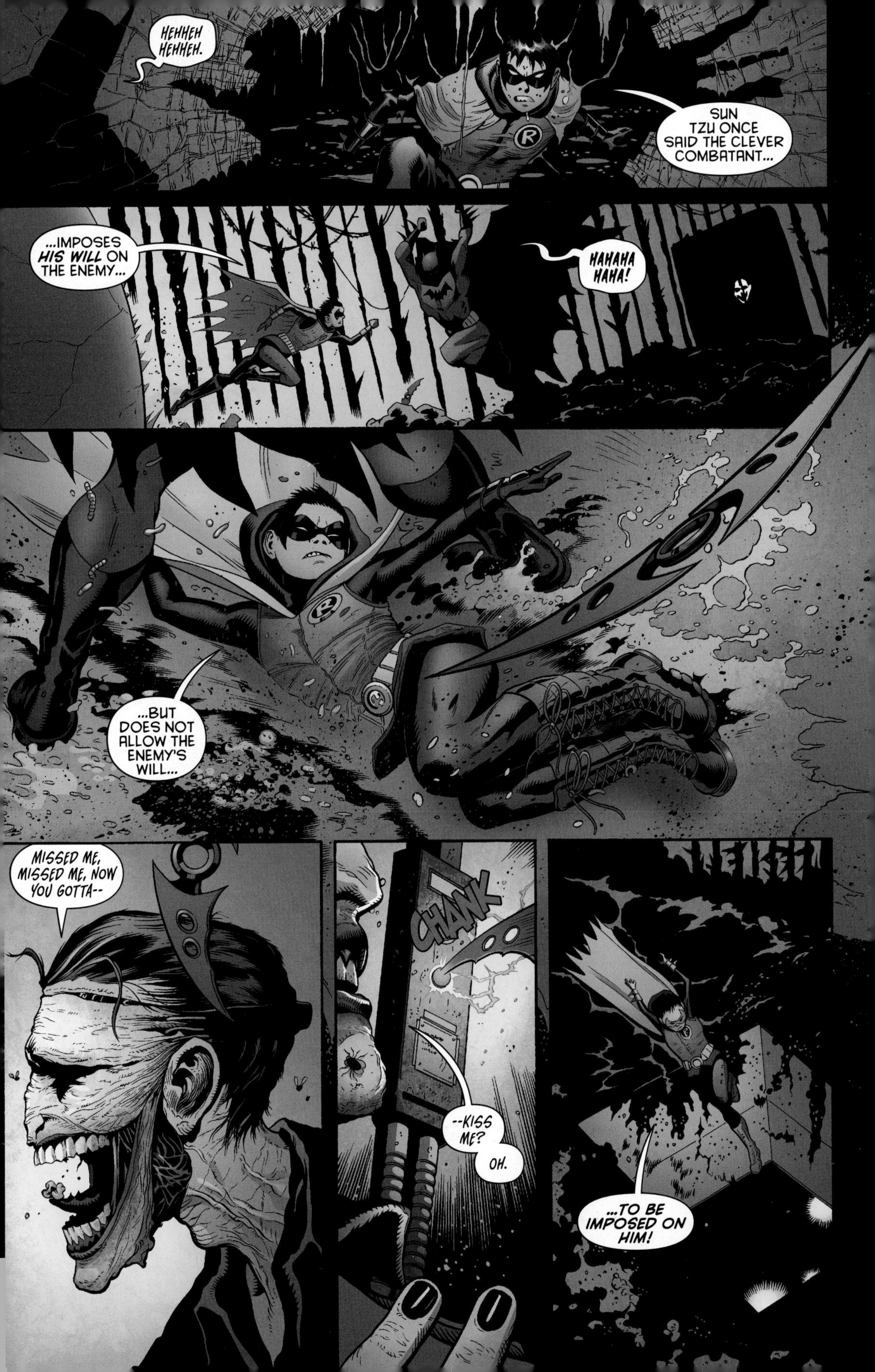
HEHHEH HEHHEH.
SUN TZU ONCE SAID THE CLEVER COMBATANT...
...IMPOSES HIS WILL ON THE ENEMY...
HAHAHA HAHA!
...BUT DOES NOT ALLOW THE ENEMY'S WILL...
MISSED ME, MISSED ME, NOW YOU GOTTA--
CHANK
--KISS ME?
OH.
...TO BE IMPOSED ON HIM!

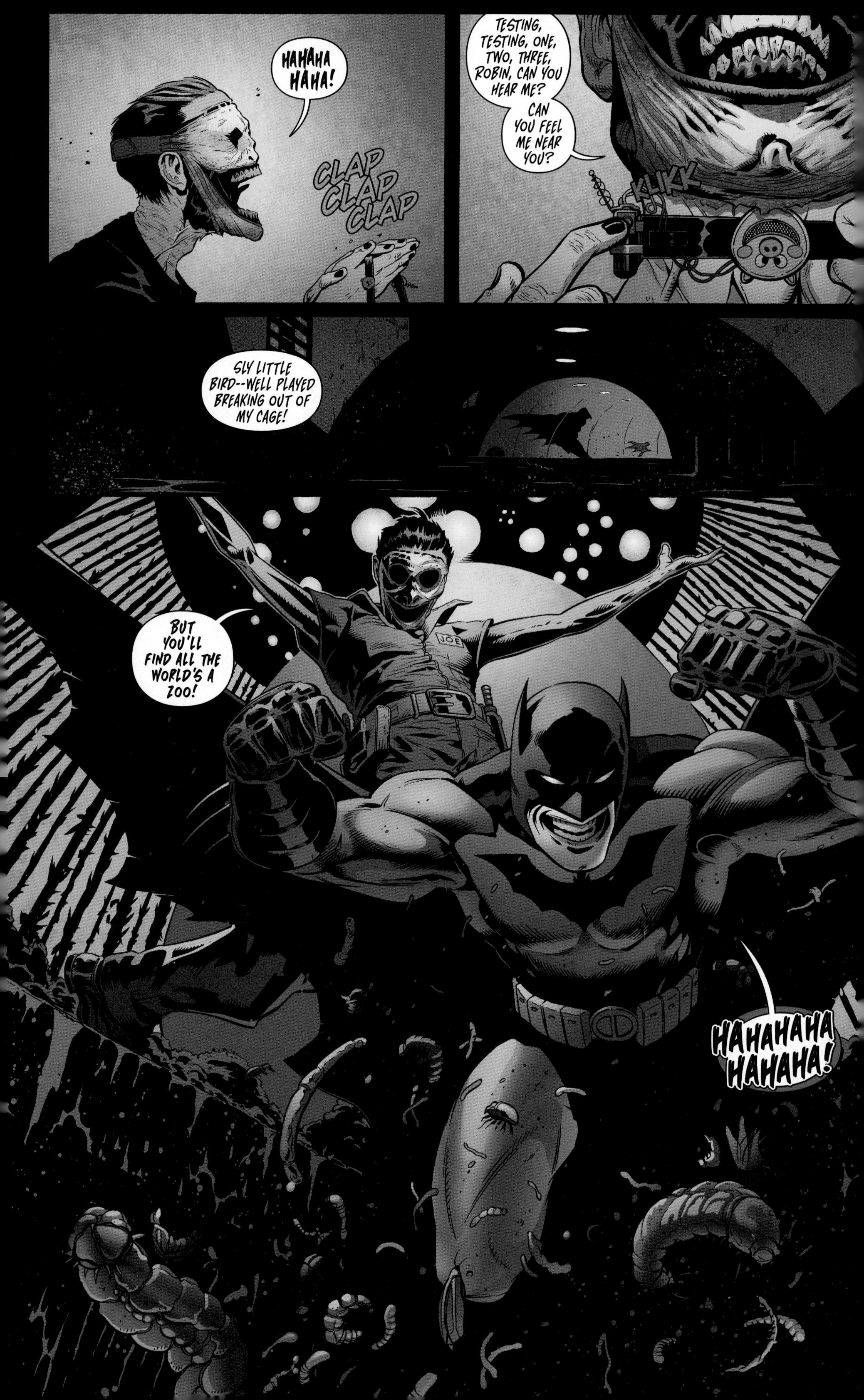
HAHAHA HAHA!
CLAP CLAP CLAP
TESTING, TESTING, ONE, TWO, THREE, ROBIN, CAN YOU HEAR ME?
CAN YOU FEEL ME NEAR YOU?
KLIKK
SLY LITTLE BIRD--WELL PLAYED BREAKING OUT OF MY CAGE!
JOE
BUT YOU'LL FIND ALL THE WORLD'S A ZOO!
HAHAHAHA HAHAHA!

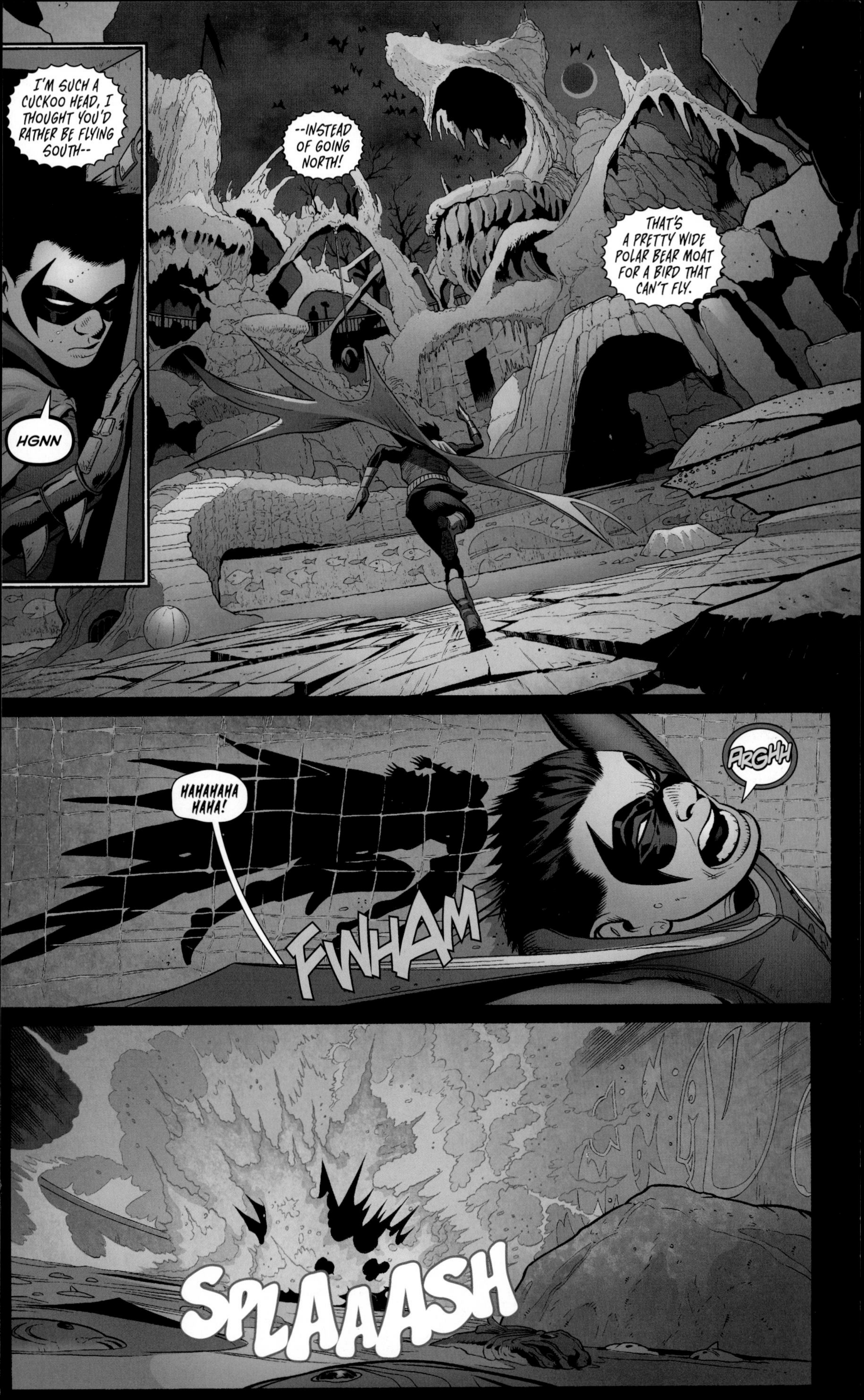

I'M SUCH A CUCKOO HEAD, I THOUGHT YOU'D RATHER BE FLYING SOUTH--
--INSTEAD OF GOING NORTH!
HGNN
THAT'S A PRETTY WIDE POLAR BEAR MOAT FOR A BIRD THAT CAN'T FLY.
HAHAHAHA HAHA!
ARGHH
FWHAM
SPLAAASH

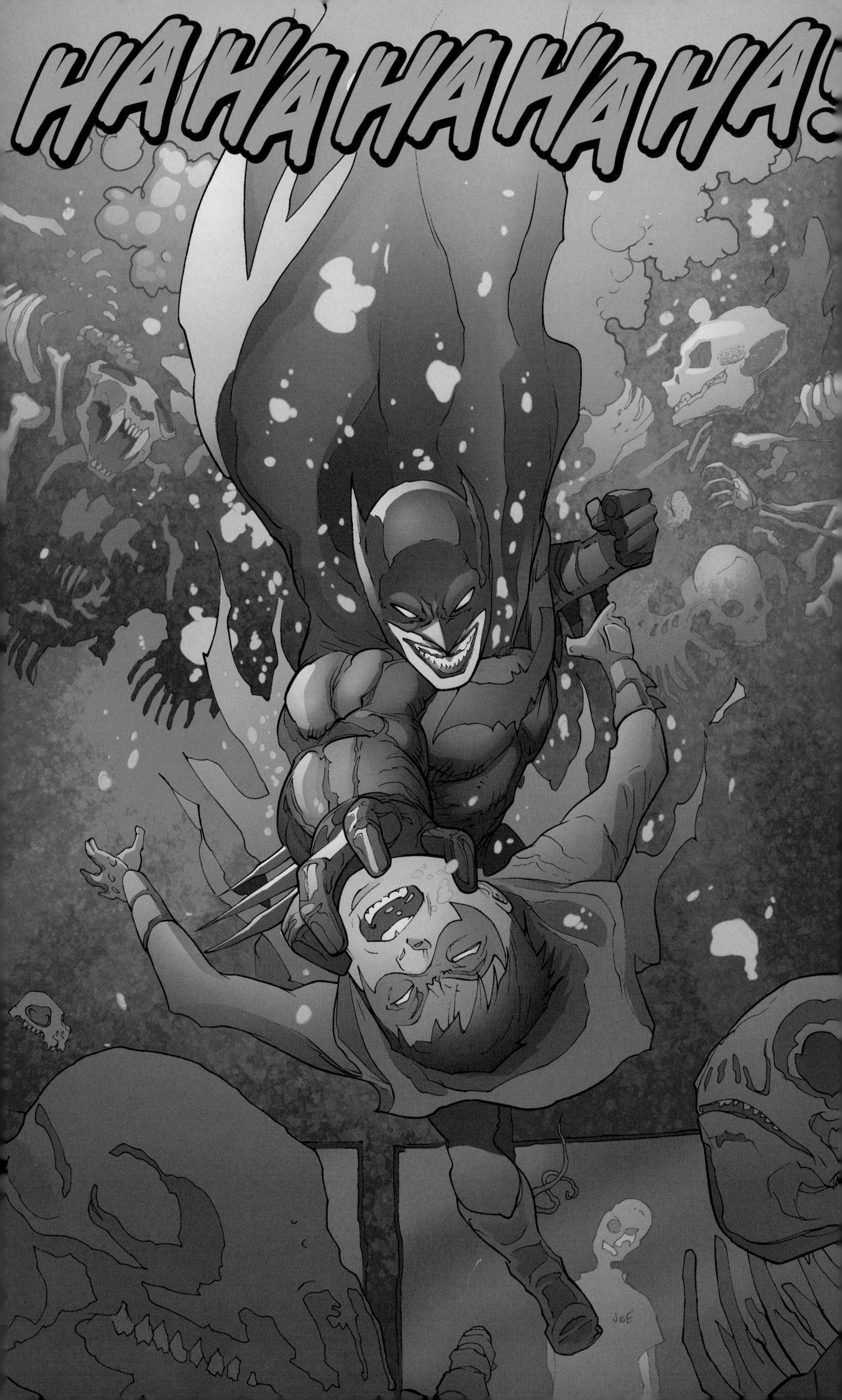
HAHAHAHAHAHA
JOE

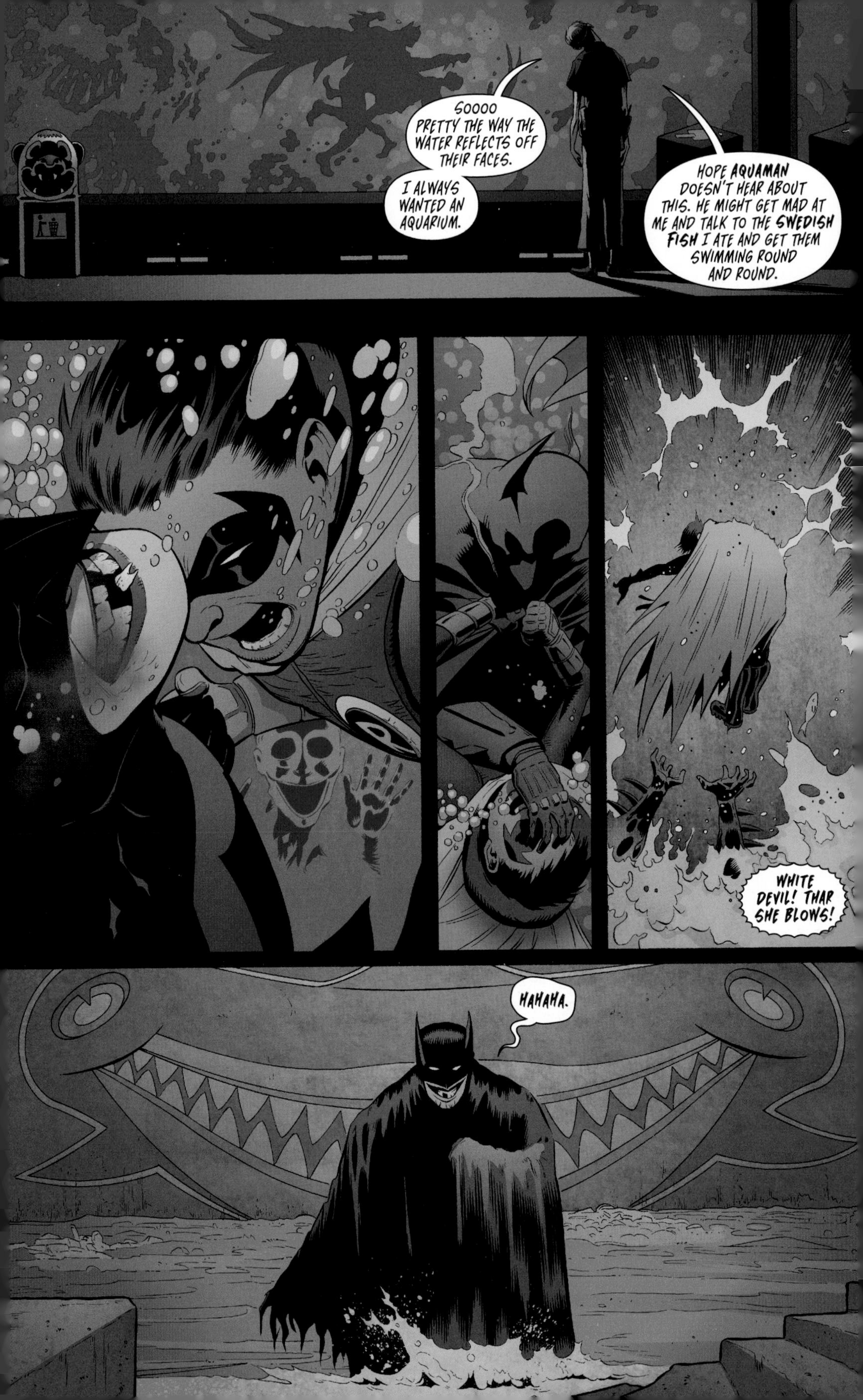
SOOOO PRETTY THE WAY THE WATER REFLECTS OFF THEIR FACES.
I ALWAYS WANTED AN AQUARIUM.
HOPE AQUAMAN DOESN'T HEAR ABOUT THIS. HE MIGHT GET MAD AT ME AND TALK TO THE SWEDISH FISH I ATE AND GET THEM SWIMMING ROUND AND ROUND.
WHITE DEVIL! THAR SHE BLOWS!
HAHAHA.

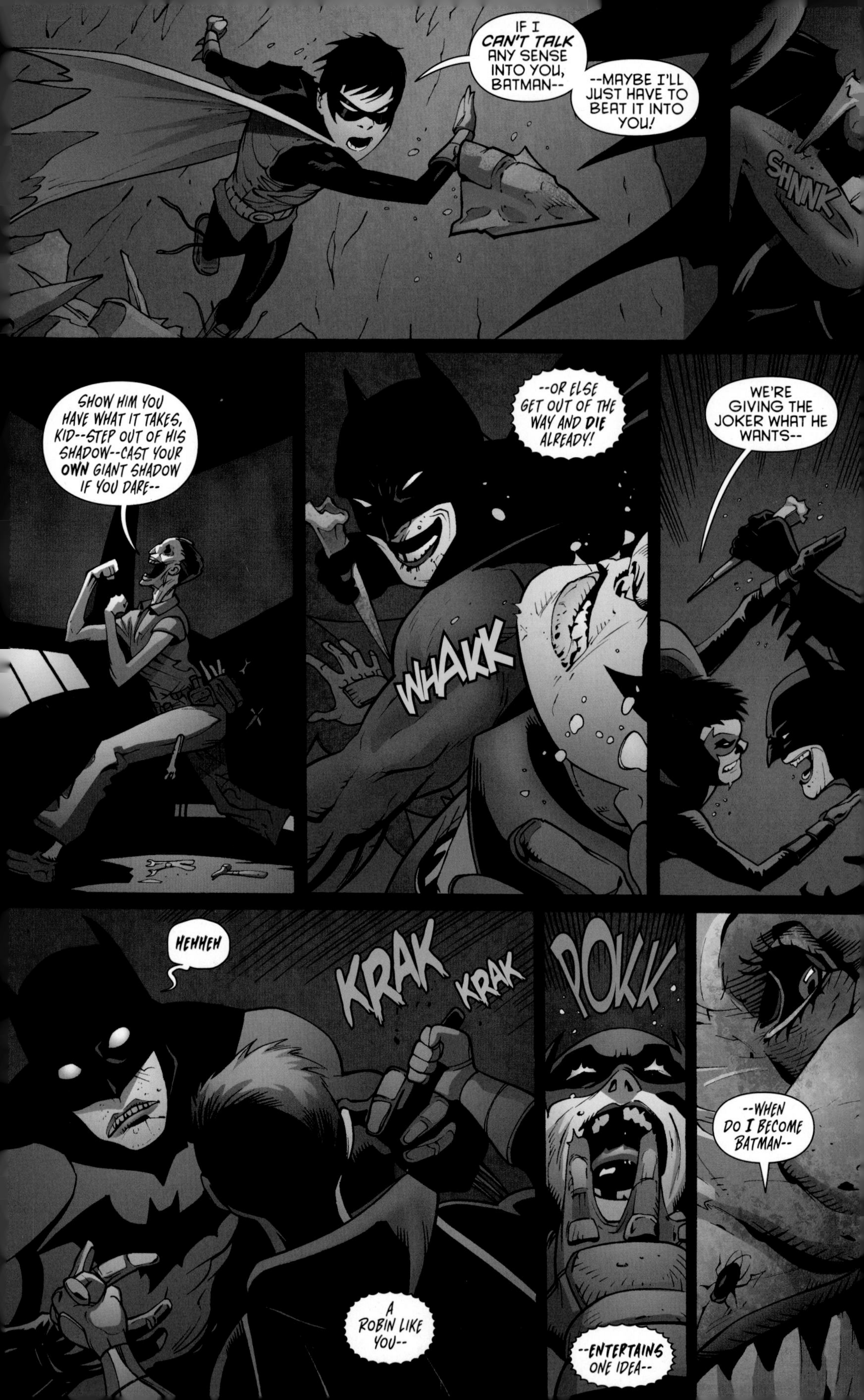
IF I CAN'T TALK ANY SENSE INTO YOU, BATMAN--
--MAYBE I'LL JUST HAVE TO BEAT IT INTO YOU!
SHNNK
SHOW HIM YOU HAVE WHAT IT TAKES, KID--STEP OUT OF HIS SHADOW--CAST YOUR OWN GIANT SHADOW IF YOU DARE--
--OR ELSE GET OUT OF THE WAY AND DIE ALREADY!
WHAKK
WE'RE GIVING THE JOKER WHAT HE WANTS--
HEHHEH
KRAK
KRAK
A ROBIN LIKE YOU--
POKK
--ENTERTAINS ONE IDEA--
--WHEN DO I BECOME BATMAN--

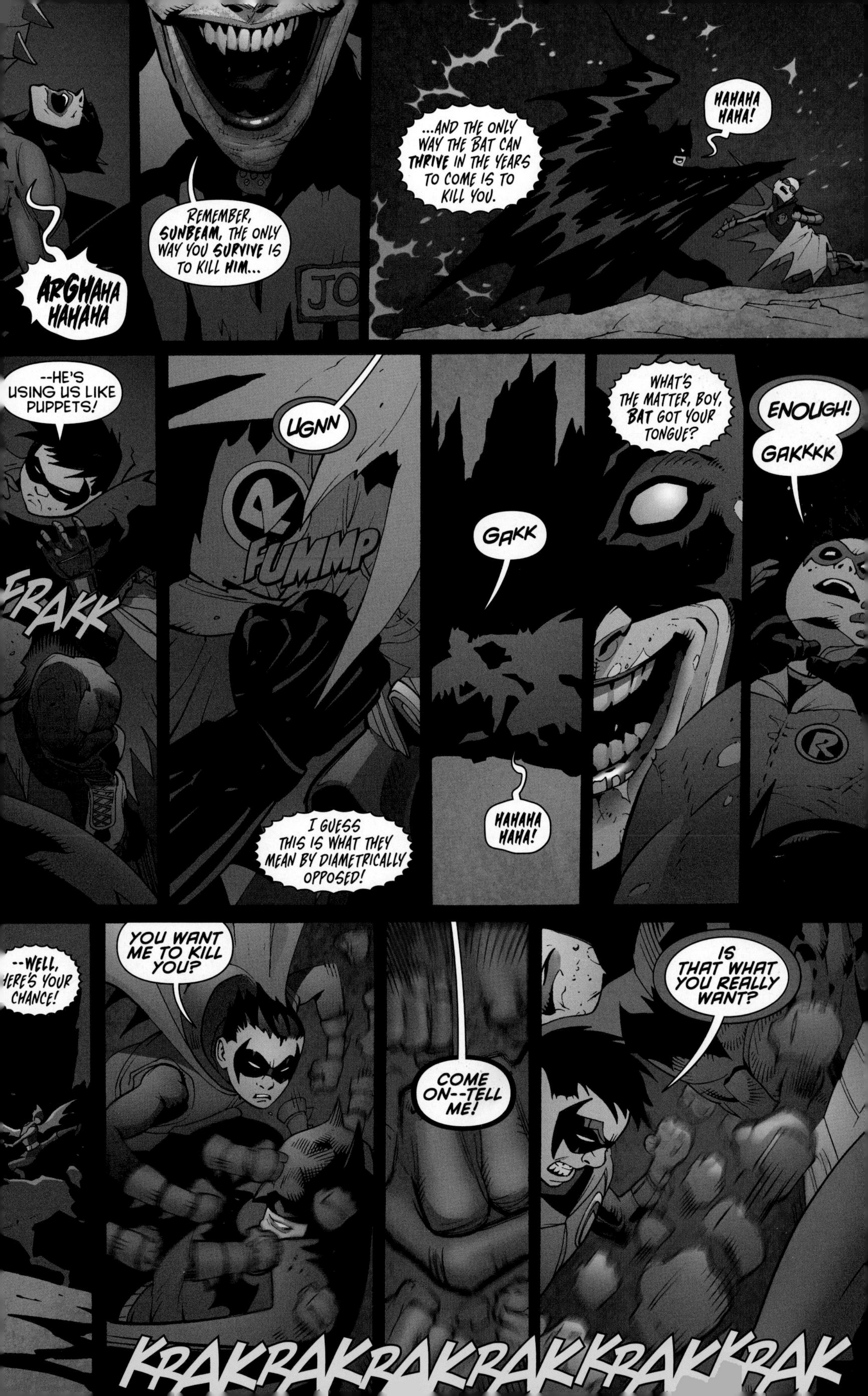
ARGHAHA HAHAHA
REMEMBER, SUNBEAM, THE ONLY WAY YOU SURVIVE IS TO KILL HIM...
...AND THE ONLY WAY THE BAT CAN THRIVE IN THE YEARS TO COME IS TO KILL YOU.
HAHAHA HAHA!
--HE'S USING US LIKE PUPPETS!
FRAKK
UGNN
FUMMP
I GUESS THIS IS WHAT THEY MEAN BY DIAMETRICALLY OPPOSED!
GAKK
HAHAHA HAHA!
WHAT'S THE MATTER, BOY, BAT GOT YOUR TONGUE?
ENOUGH!
GAKKKK
--WELL, HERE'S YOUR CHANCE!
YOU WANT ME TO KILL YOU?
COME ON--TELL ME!
IS THAT WHAT YOU REALLY WANT?
KRAKRAKRAKRAKKRAKKRAK

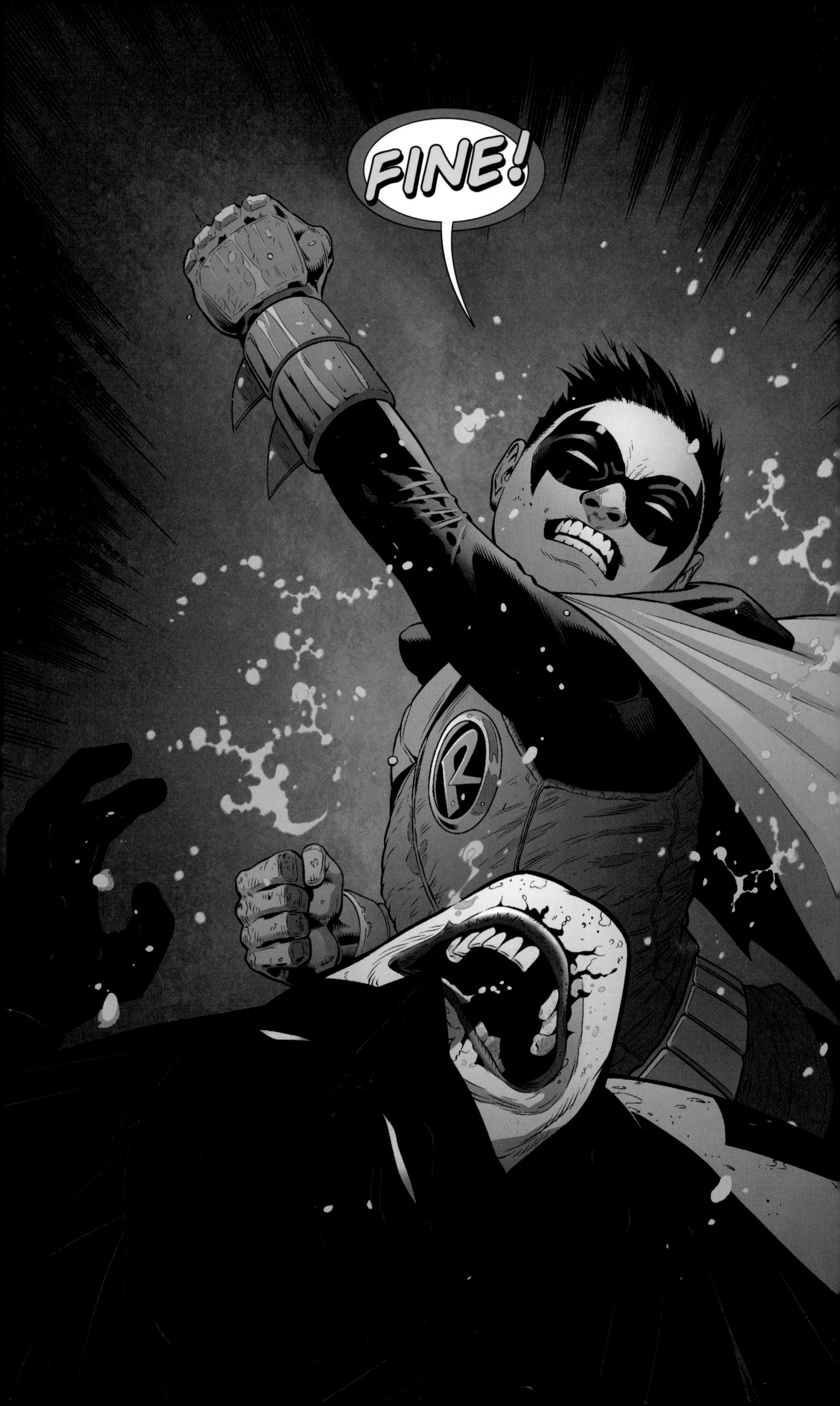
FINE!

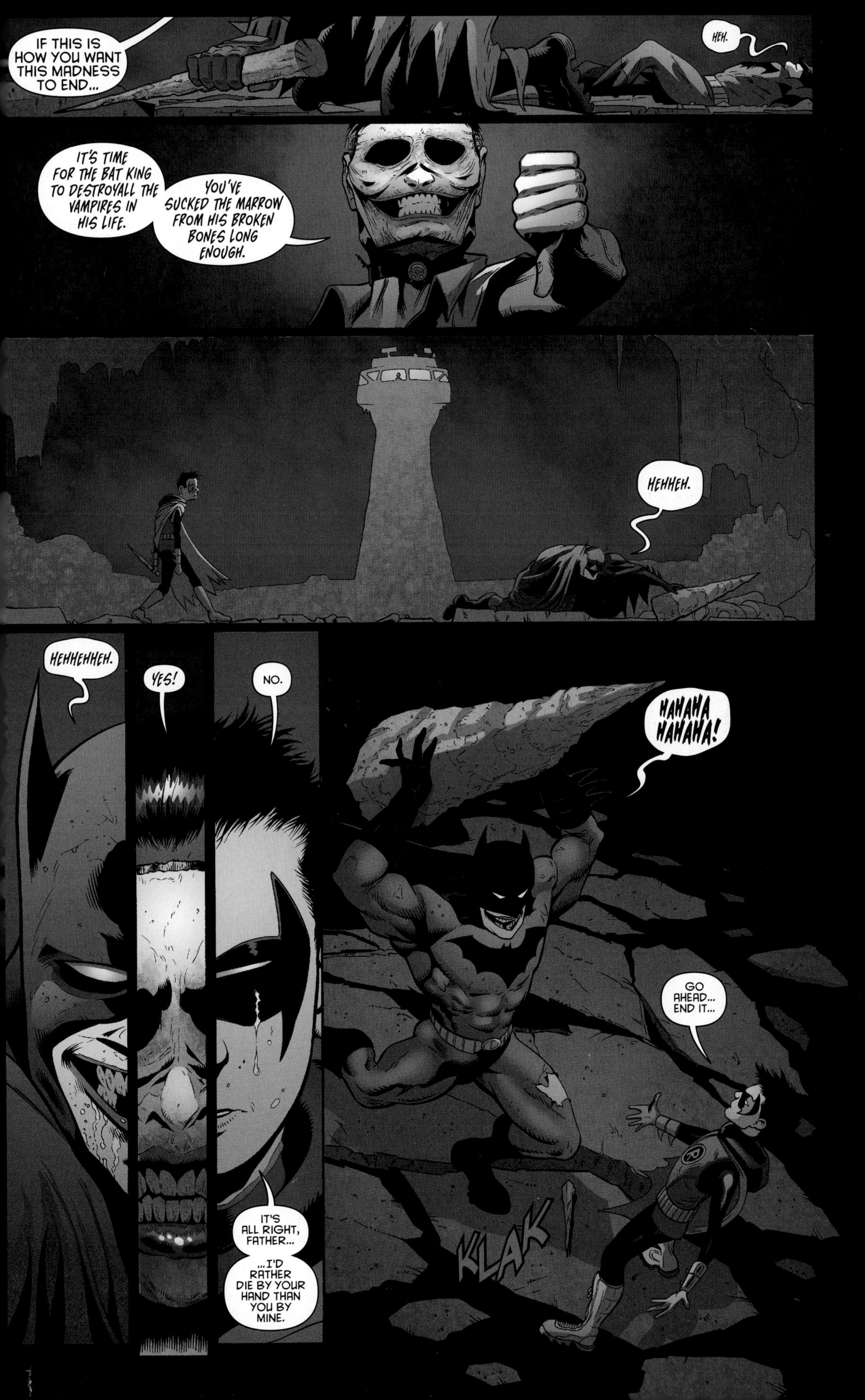
IF THIS IS HOW YOU WANT THIS MADNESS TO END...
HEH.
IT'S TIME FOR THE BAT KING TO DESTROYALL THE VAMPIRES IN HIS LIFE.
YOU'VE SUCKED THE MARROW FROM HIS BROKEN BONES LONG ENOUGH.
HEHHEH.
HEHHEHHEH.
YES!
NO.
HAHAHA HAHAHA!
GO AHEAD... END IT...
IT'S ALL RIGHT, FATHER...
...I'D RATHER DIE BY YOUR HAND THAN YOU BY MINE.
KLAK

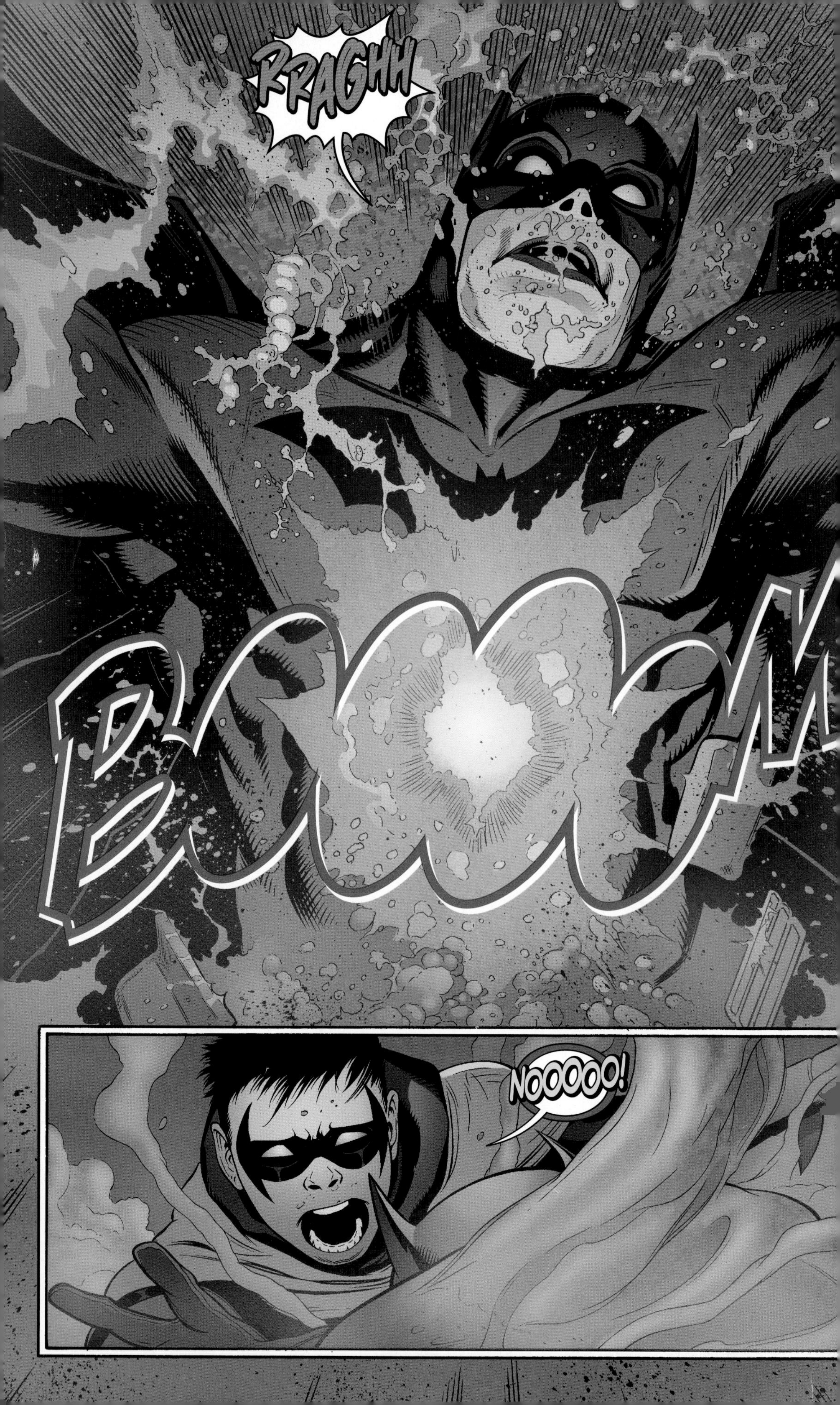
RRAGHH
BOOOOM
NOOOOO!

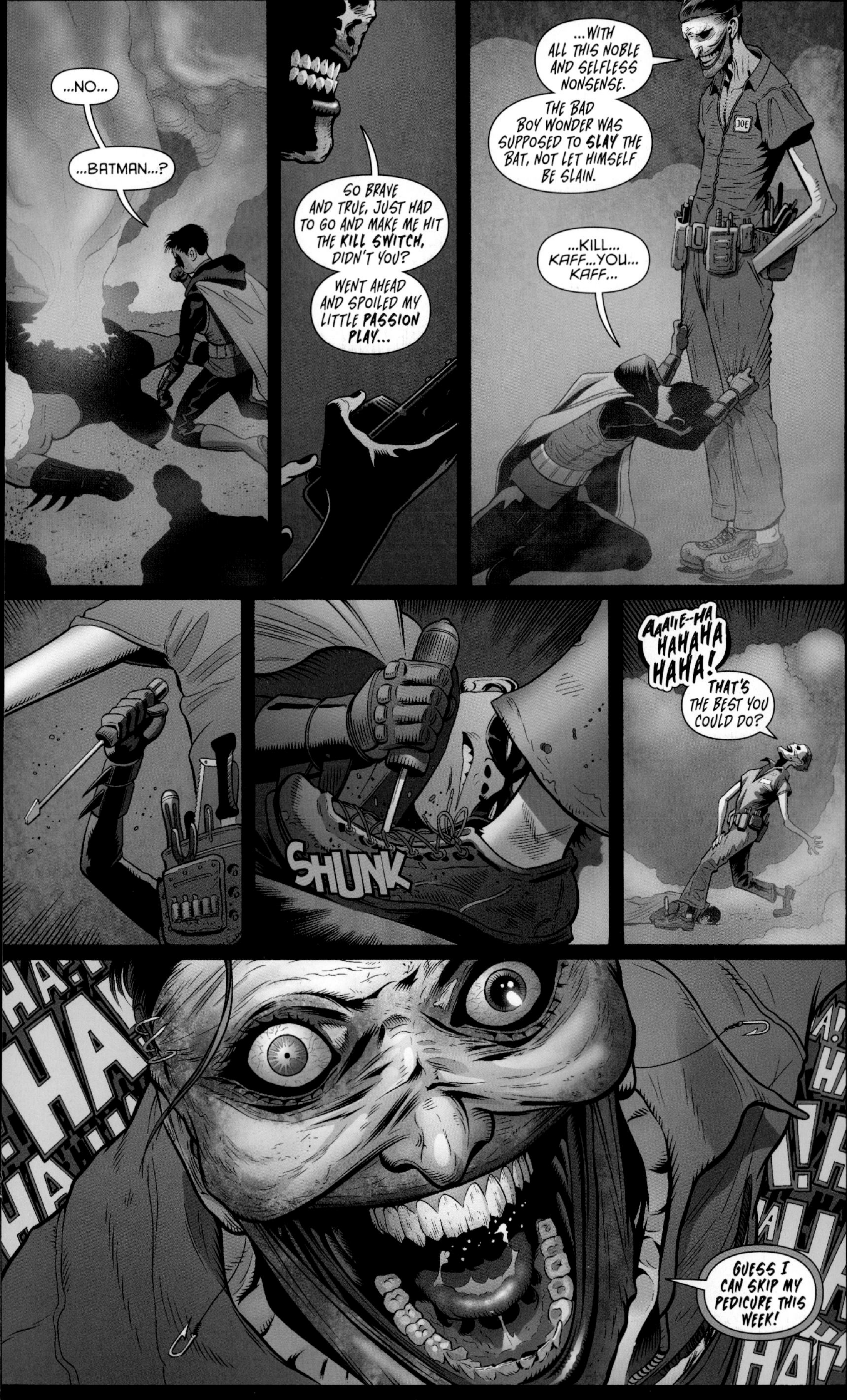
...NO...
...BATMAN...?
SO BRAVE AND TRUE, JUST HAD TO GO AND MAKE ME HIT THE KILL SWITCH, DIDN'T YOU?
WENT AHEAD AND SPOILED MY LITTLE PASSION PLAY...
...WITH ALL THIS NOBLE AND SELFLESS NONSENSE.
THE BAD BOY WONDER WAS SUPPOSED TO SLAY THE BAT, NOT LET HIMSELF BE SLAIN.
...KILL... KAFF...YOU... KAFF...
JOE
SHUNK
AAAIIE-HA HAHAHA HAHA!
THAT'S THE BEST YOU COULD DO?
GUESS I CAN SKIP MY PEDICURE THIS WEEK!

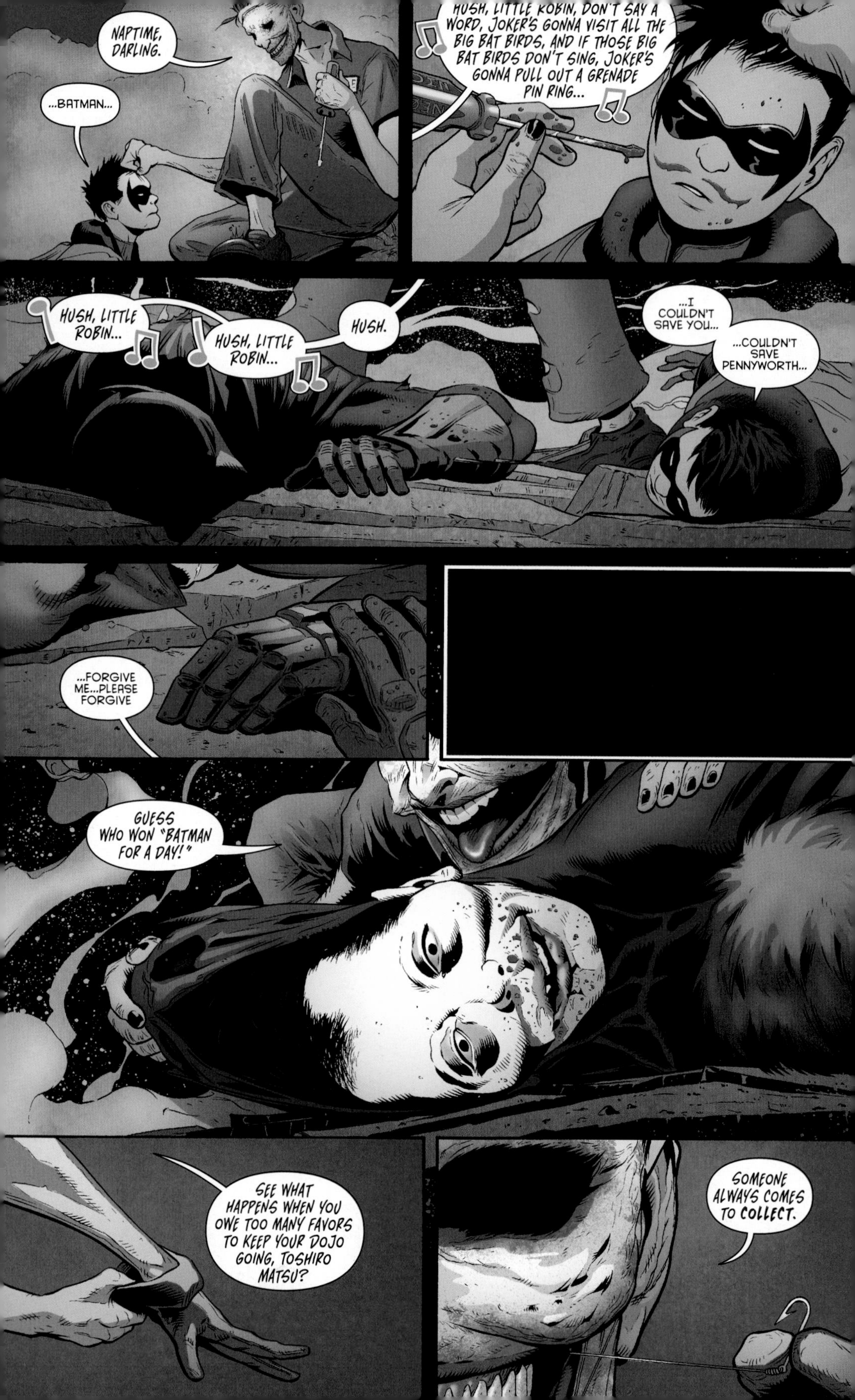
NAPTIME, DARLING.
...BATMAN...
HUSH, LITTLE ROBIN, DON'T SAY A WORD, JOKER'S GONNA VISIT ALL THE BIG BAT BIRDS, AND IF THOSE BIG BAT BIRDS DON'T SING, JOKER'S GONNA PULL OUT A GRENADE PIN RING...
HUSH, LITTLE ROBIN...
HUSH, LITTLE ROBIN...
HUSH.
...I COULDN'T SAVE YOU...
...COULDN'T SAVE PENNYWORTH...
...FORGIVE ME...PLEASE FORGIVE
GUESS WHO WON "BATMAN FOR A DAY!"
SEE WHAT HAPPENS WHEN YOU OWE TOO MANY FAVORS TO KEEP YOUR DOJO GOING, TOSHIRO MATSU?
SOMEONE ALWAYS COMES TO COLLECT.

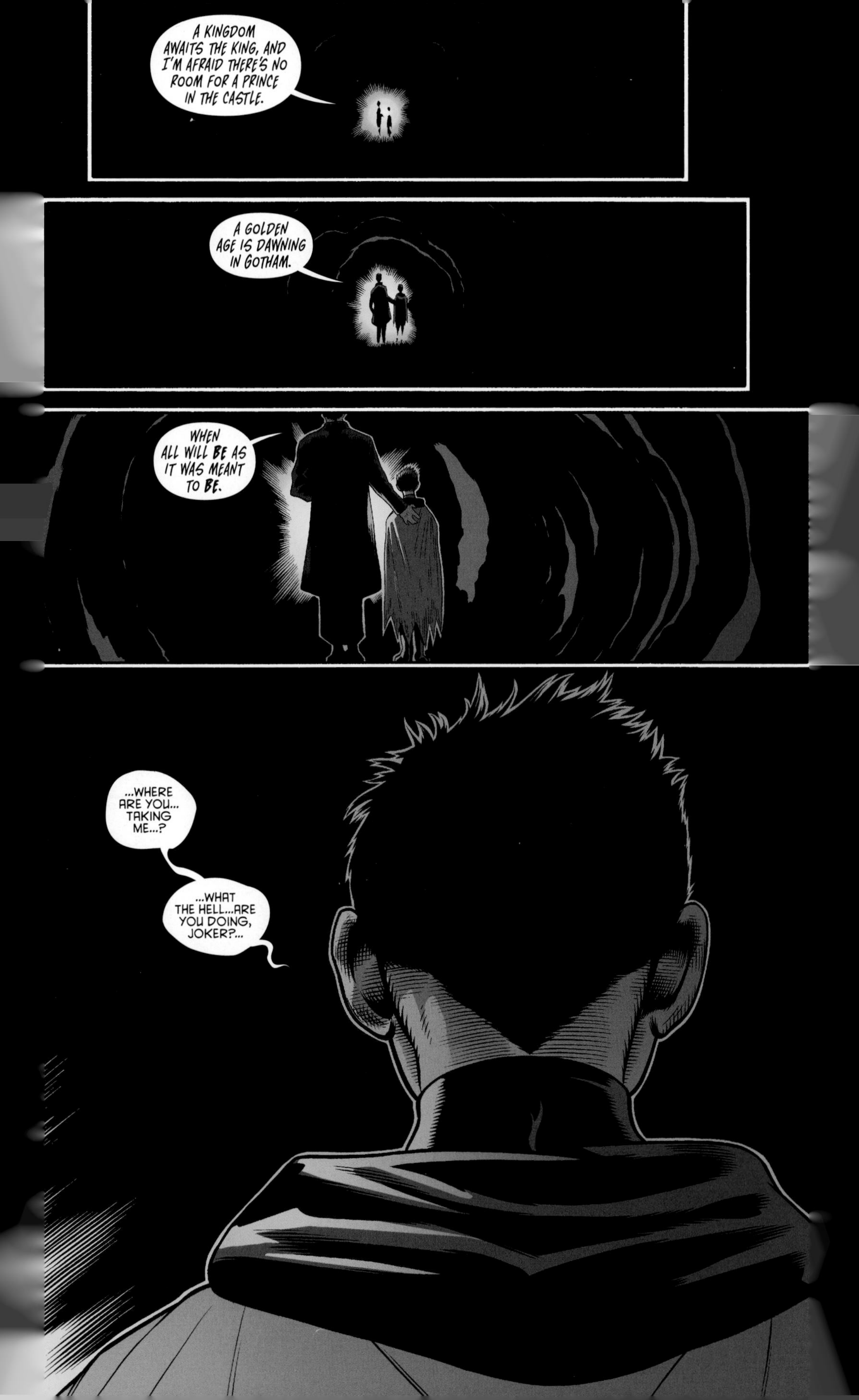
A KINGDOM AWAITS THE KING, AND I'M AFRAID THERE'S NO ROOM FOR A PRINCE IN THE CASTLE.
A GOLDEN AGE IS DAWNING IN GOTHAM.
WHEN ALL WILL BE AS IT WAS MEANT TO BE.
...WHERE ARE YOU... TAKING ME...?
...WHAT THE HELL...ARE YOU DOING, JOKER?...

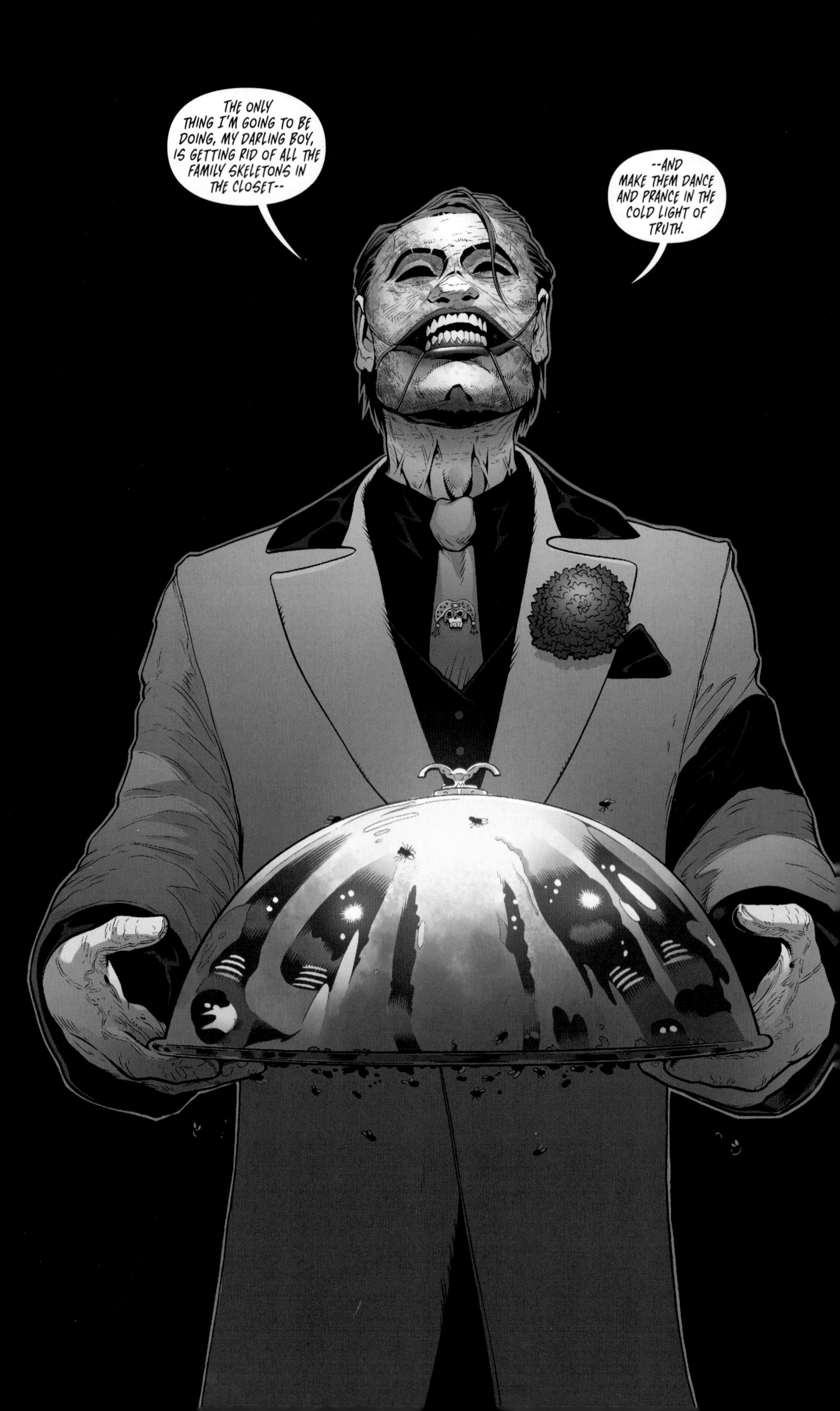
THE ONLY THING I'M GOING TO BE DOING, MY DARLING BOY, IS GETTING RID OF ALL THE FAMILY SKELETONS IN THE CLOSET--
--AND MAKE THEM DANCE AND PRANCE IN THE COLD LIGHT OF TRUTH.

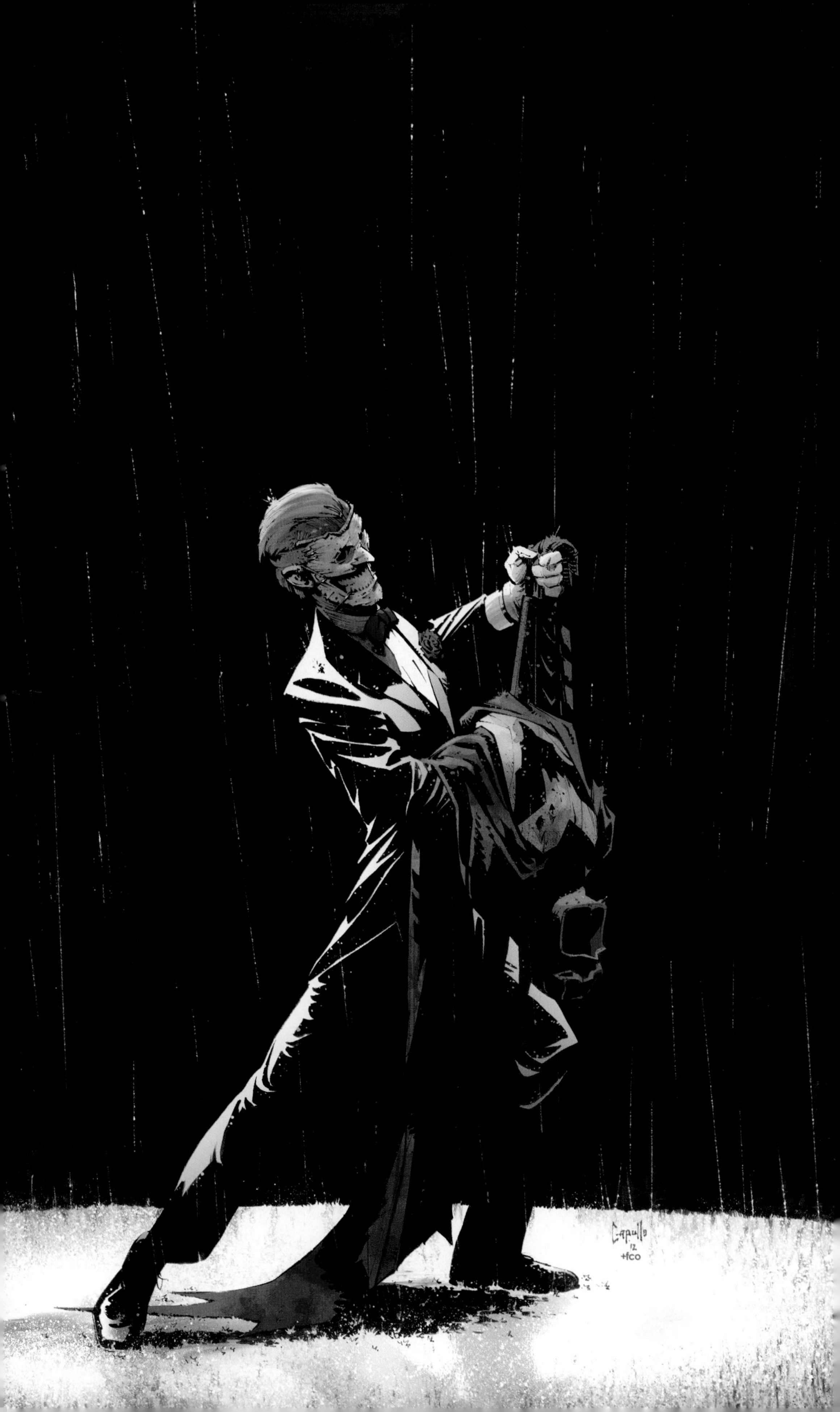

SCOTT SNYDER writer GREG CAPULLO penciller JONATHAN GLAPION inker cover art by GREG CAPULLO & FCO PLASCENCIA

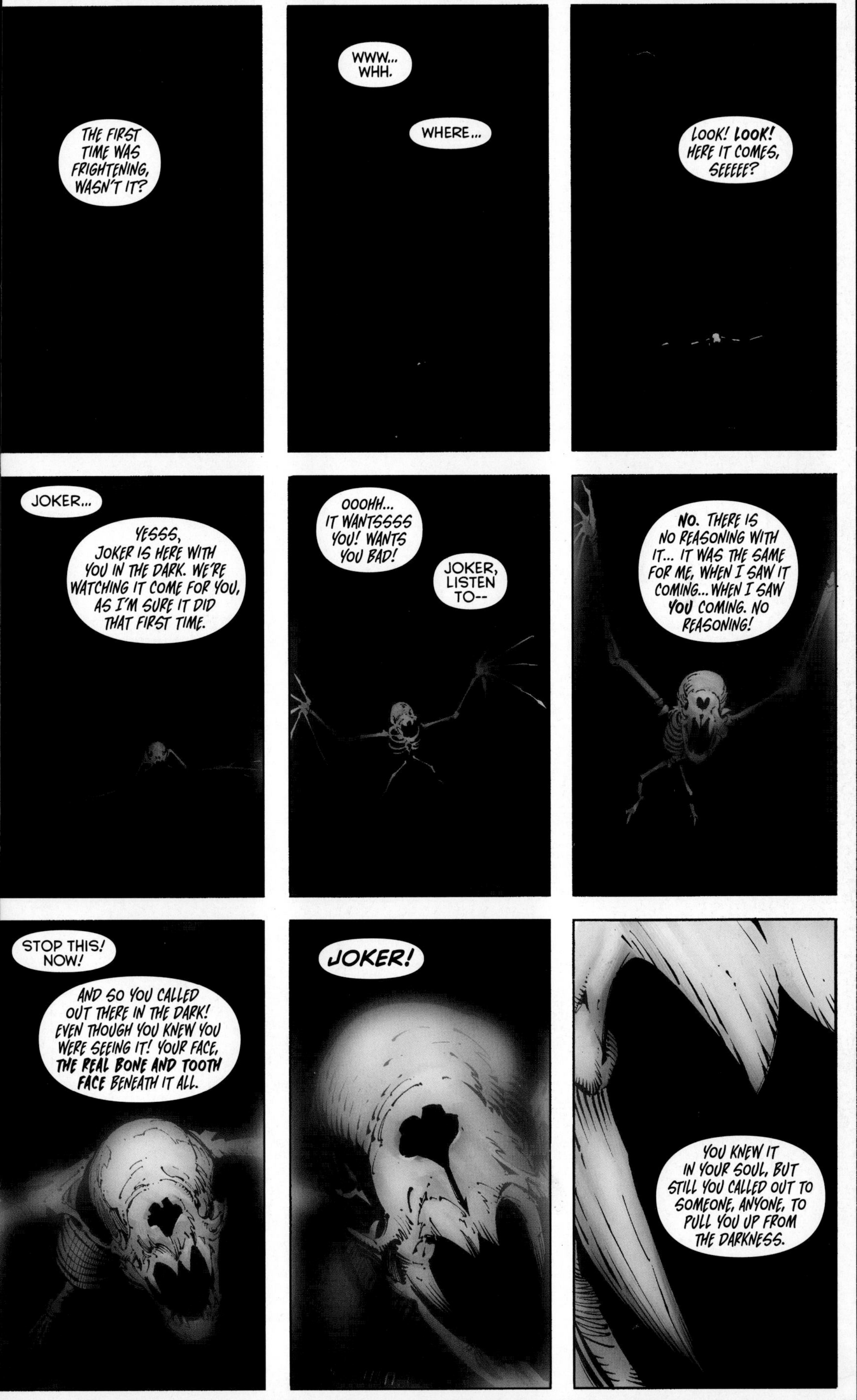
THE FIRST TIME WAS FRIGHTENING, WASN'T IT?
WWW... WHH.
WHERE...
LOOK! LOOK! HERE IT COMES, SEEEEE?
JOKER...
YESSS, JOKER IS HERE WITH YOU IN THE DARK. WE'RE WATCHING IT COME FOR YOU, AS I'M SURE IT DID THAT FIRST TIME.
OOOHH... IT WANTSSSS YOU! WANTS YOU BAD!
JOKER, LISTEN TO--
NO. THERE IS NO REASONING WITH IT... IT WAS THE SAME FOR ME, WHEN I SAW IT COMING... WHEN I SAW YOU COMING. NO REASONING!
STOP THIS! NOW!
AND SO YOU CALLED OUT THERE IN THE DARK! EVEN THOUGH YOU KNEW YOU WERE SEEING IT! YOUR FACE, THE REAL BONE AND TOOTH FACE BENEATH IT ALL.
JOKER!
YOU KNEW IT IN YOUR SOUL, BUT STILL YOU CALLED OUT TO SOMEONE, ANYONE, TO PULL YOU UP FROM THE DARKNESS.

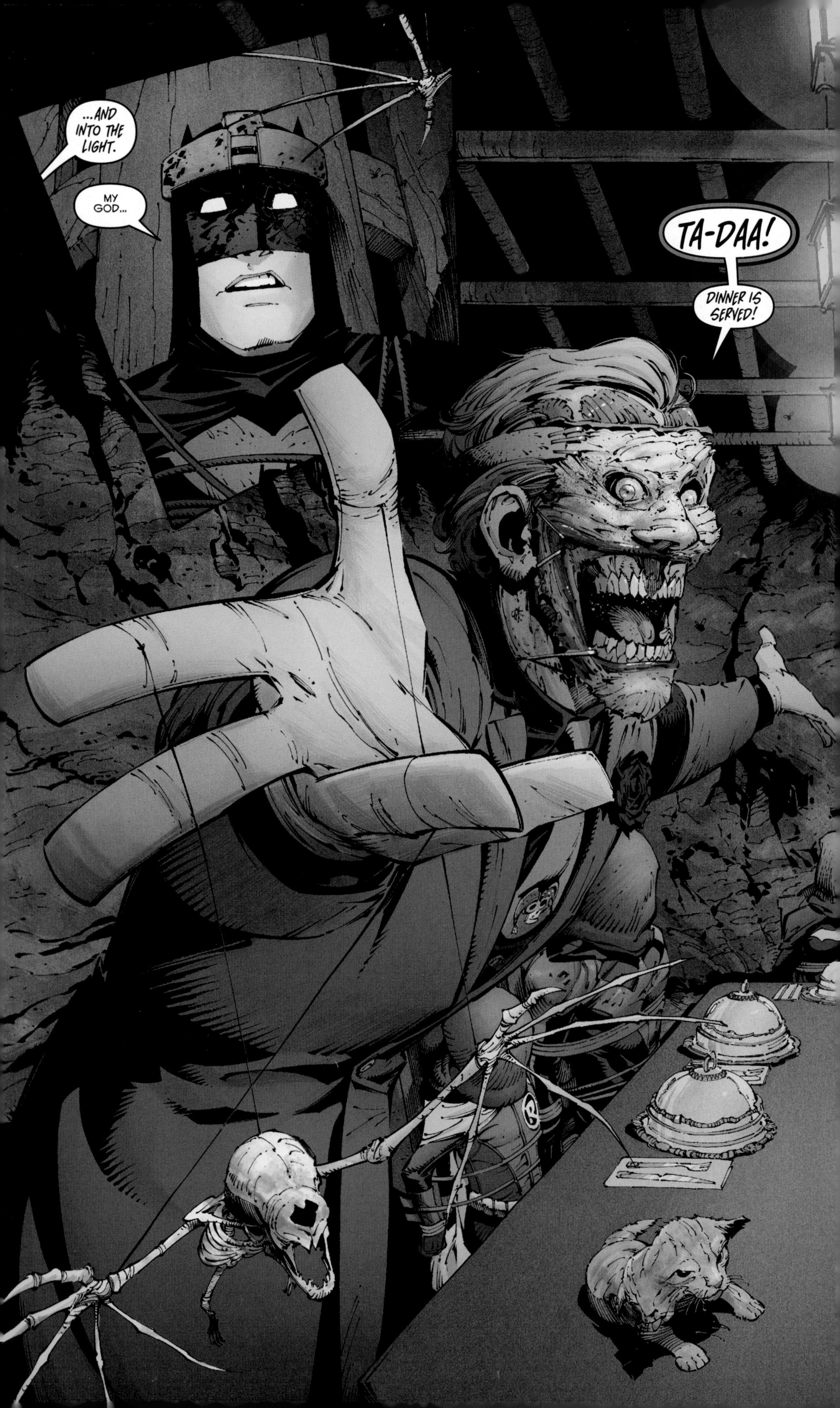
...AND INTO THE LIGHT.
MY GOD...
TA-DAA!
DINNER IS SERVED!

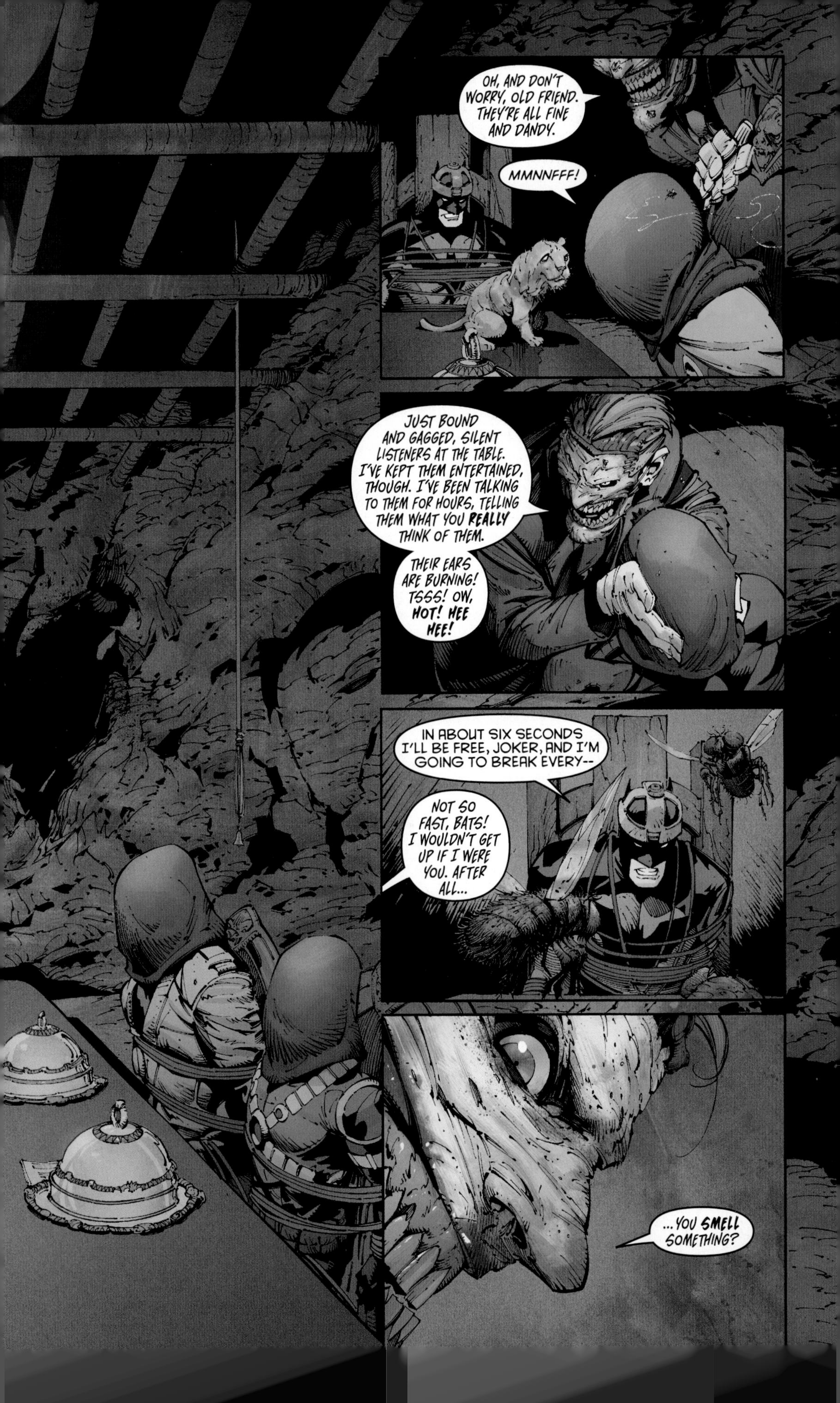
OH, AND DON'T WORRY, OLD FRIEND. THEY'RE ALL FINE AND DANDY.
MMNNFFF!
JUST BOUND AND GAGGED, SILENT LISTENERS AT THE TABLE. I'VE KEPT THEM ENTERTAINED, THOUGH. I'VE BEEN TALKING TO THEM FOR HOURS, TELLING THEM WHAT YOU REALLY THINK OF THEM.
THEIR EARS ARE BURNING! TSSS! OW, HOT! HEE HEE!
IN ABOUT SIX SECONDS I'LL BE FREE, JOKER, AND I'M GOING TO BREAK EVERY--
NOT SO FAST, BATS! I WOULDN'T GET UP IF I WERE YOU. AFTER ALL...
...YOU SMELL SOMETHING?

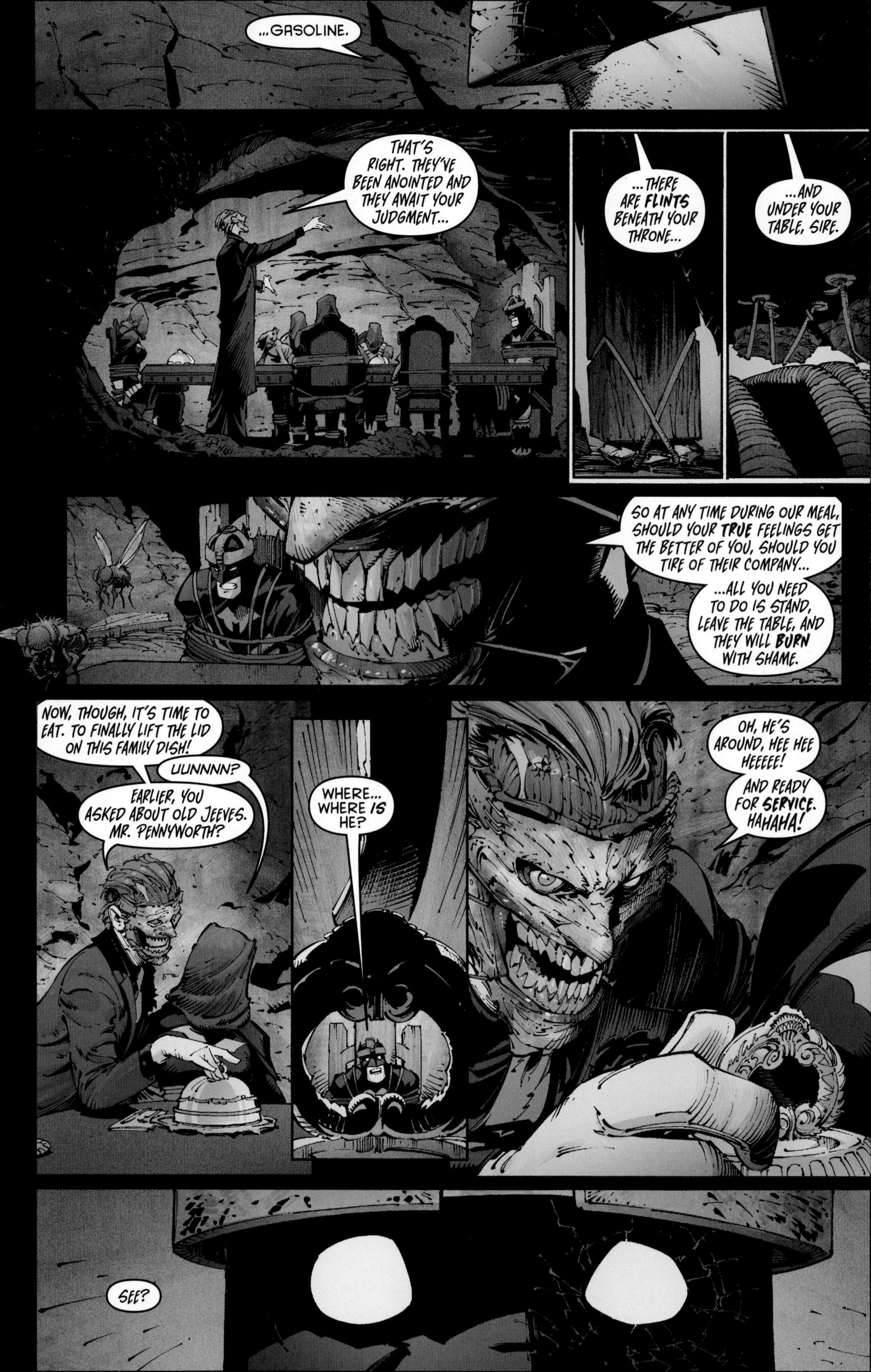
...GASOLINE.
THAT'S RIGHT. THEY'VE BEEN ANOINTED AND THEY AWAIT YOUR JUDGMENT...
...THERE ARE FLINTS BENEATH YOUR THRONE...
...AND UNDER YOUR TABLE, SIRE.
SO AT ANY TIME DURING OUR MEAL, SHOULD YOUR TRUE FEELINGS GET THE BETTER OF YOU, SHOULD YOU TIRE OF THEIR COMPANY...
...ALL YOU NEED TO DO IS STAND, LEAVE THE TABLE, AND THEY WILL BURN WITH SHAME.
NOW, THOUGH, IT'S TIME TO EAT. TO FINALLY LIFT THE LID ON THIS FAMILY DISH!
UUNNNN?
EARLIER, YOU ASKED ABOUT OLD JEEVES. MR. PENNYWORTH?
WHERE... WHERE IS HE?
OH, HE'S AROUND, HEE HEE HEEEEE!
AND READY FOR SERVICE. HAHAHA!
SEE?

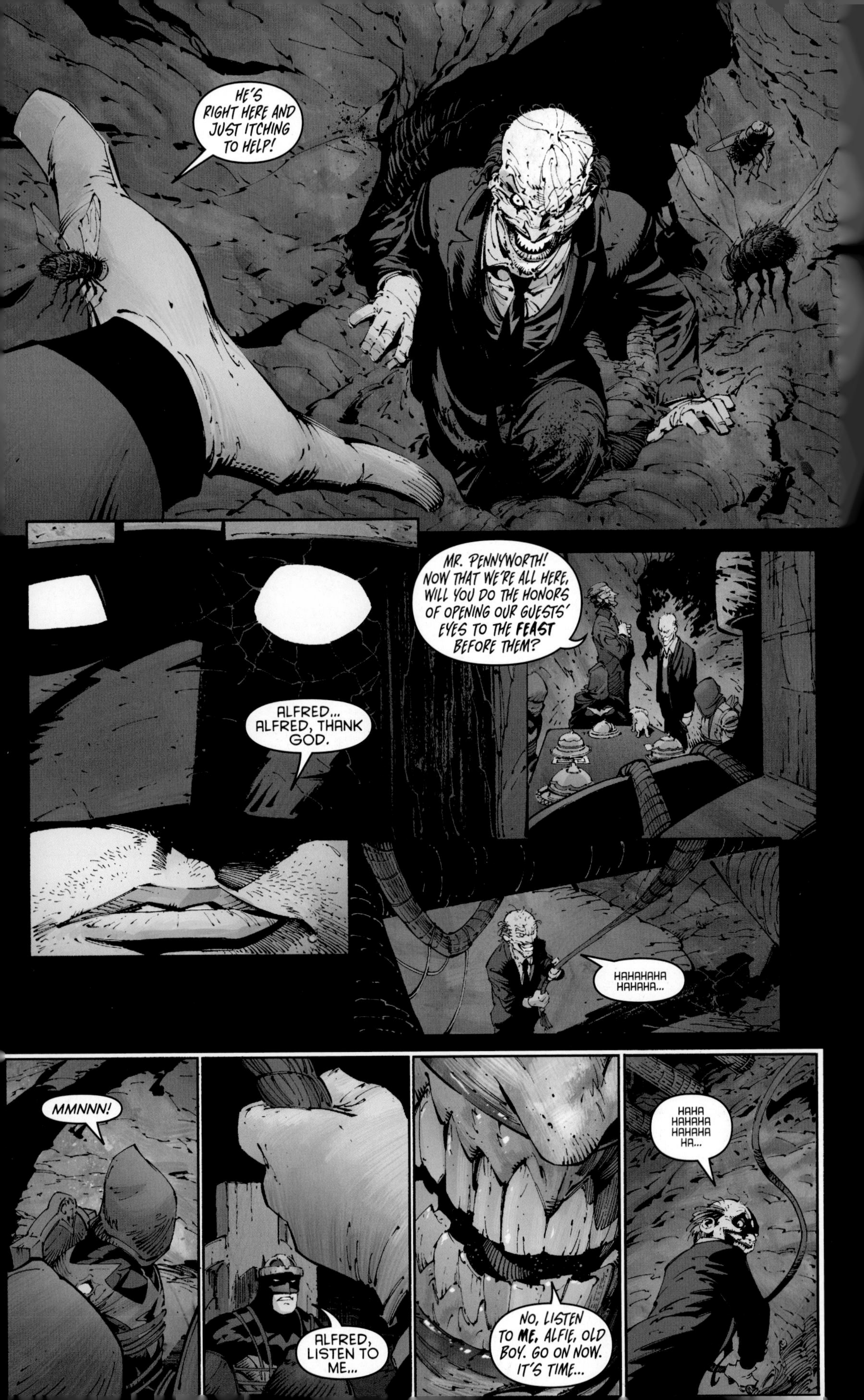
HE'S RIGHT HERE AND JUST ITCHING TO HELP!
MR. PENNYWORTH! NOW THAT WE'RE ALL HERE, WILL YOU DO THE HONORS OF OPENING OUR GUESTS' EYES TO THE FEAST BEFORE THEM?
ALFRED... ALFRED, THANK GOD.
HAHAHAHA HAHAHA...
MMNNN!
ALFRED, LISTEN TO ME...
NO, LISTEN TO ME, ALFIE, OLD BOY. GO ON NOW. IT'S TIME...
HAHA HAHAHA HAHAHA HA...

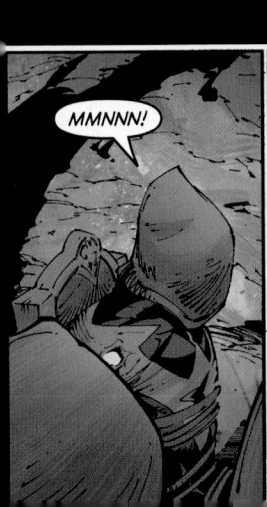

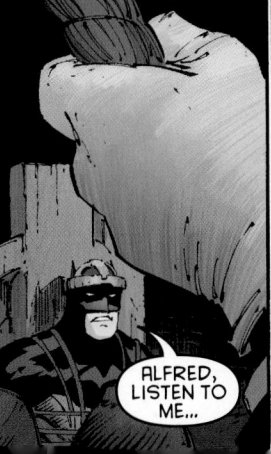

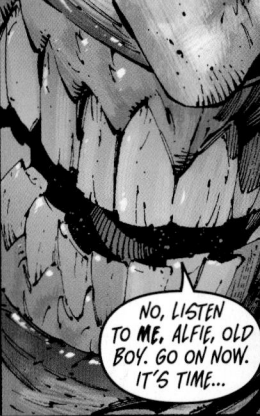

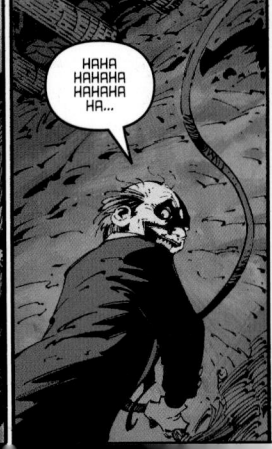

...TIME FOR THE FIRST COURSE!

NNNNGG!

PPLLLLLFFFF!

JOKER... WHAT HAVE YO DONE?!

WHAT HAVE I DONE? I'VE SIMPLY DRESSED THEM FOR THE PARTY!

OR RATHER, UNDRESSED THEM. TAKEN OFF THE CLOTHES THAT HAVE BEEN INVISIBLE TO EVERYONE BUT YOU, MY KING.

EXPOOOOOSED THEM.

AND SPEAKING OF EXPOSING, MR. PENNYWORTH, WOULD YOU SERVE US, PLEASSSSSSSE?

I SO HOPE YOU LIKE IT, EVERYONE...

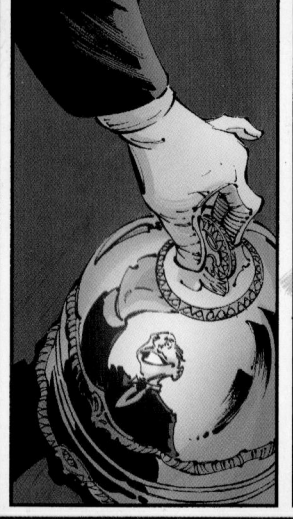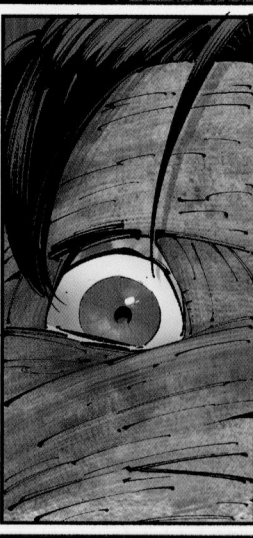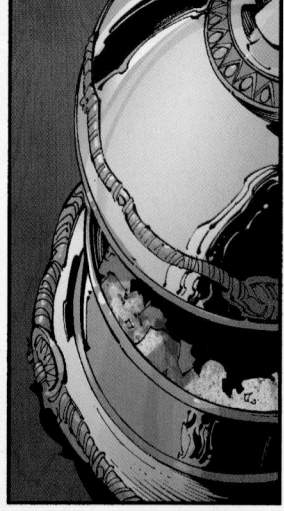

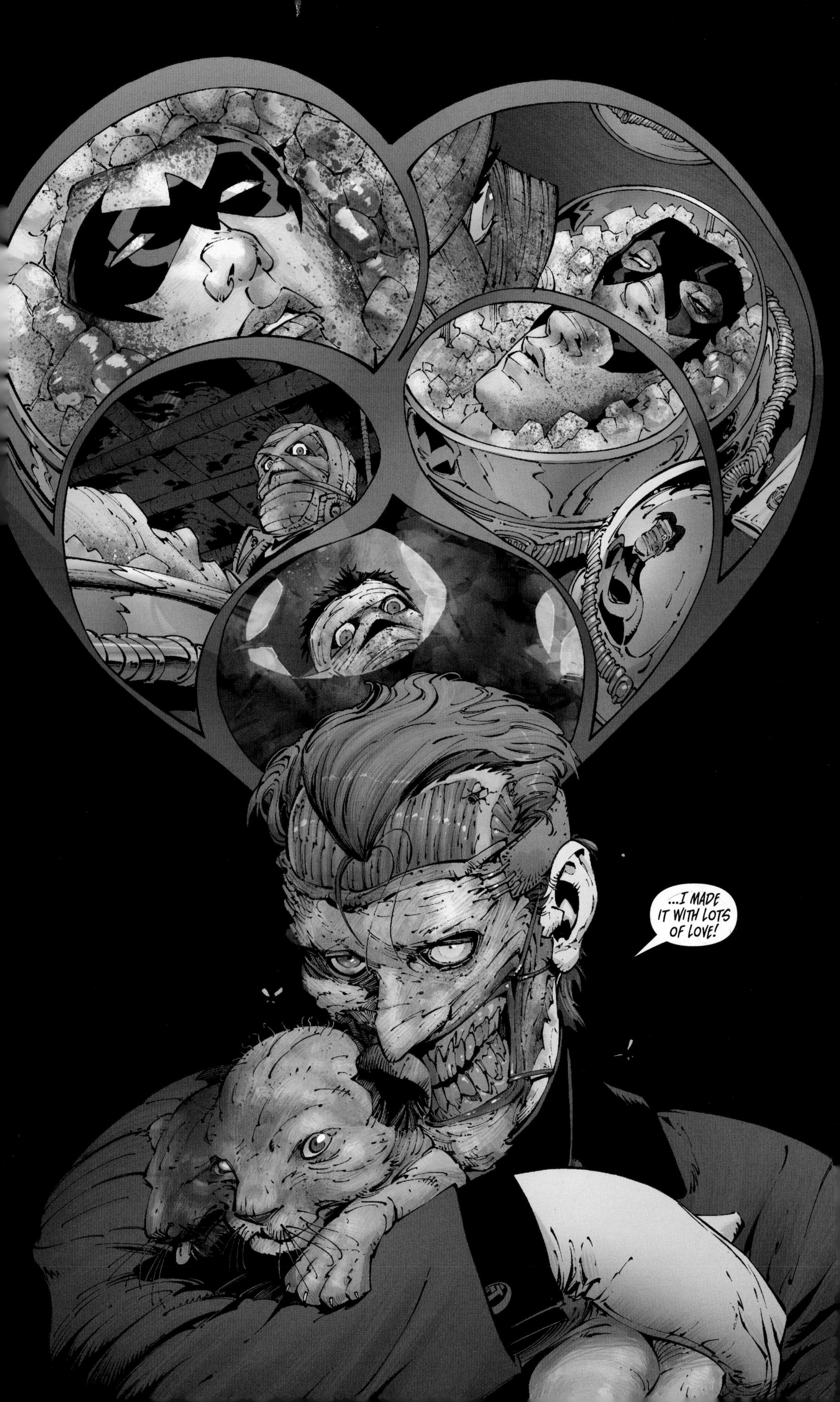
...I MADE IT WITH LOTS OF LOVE!

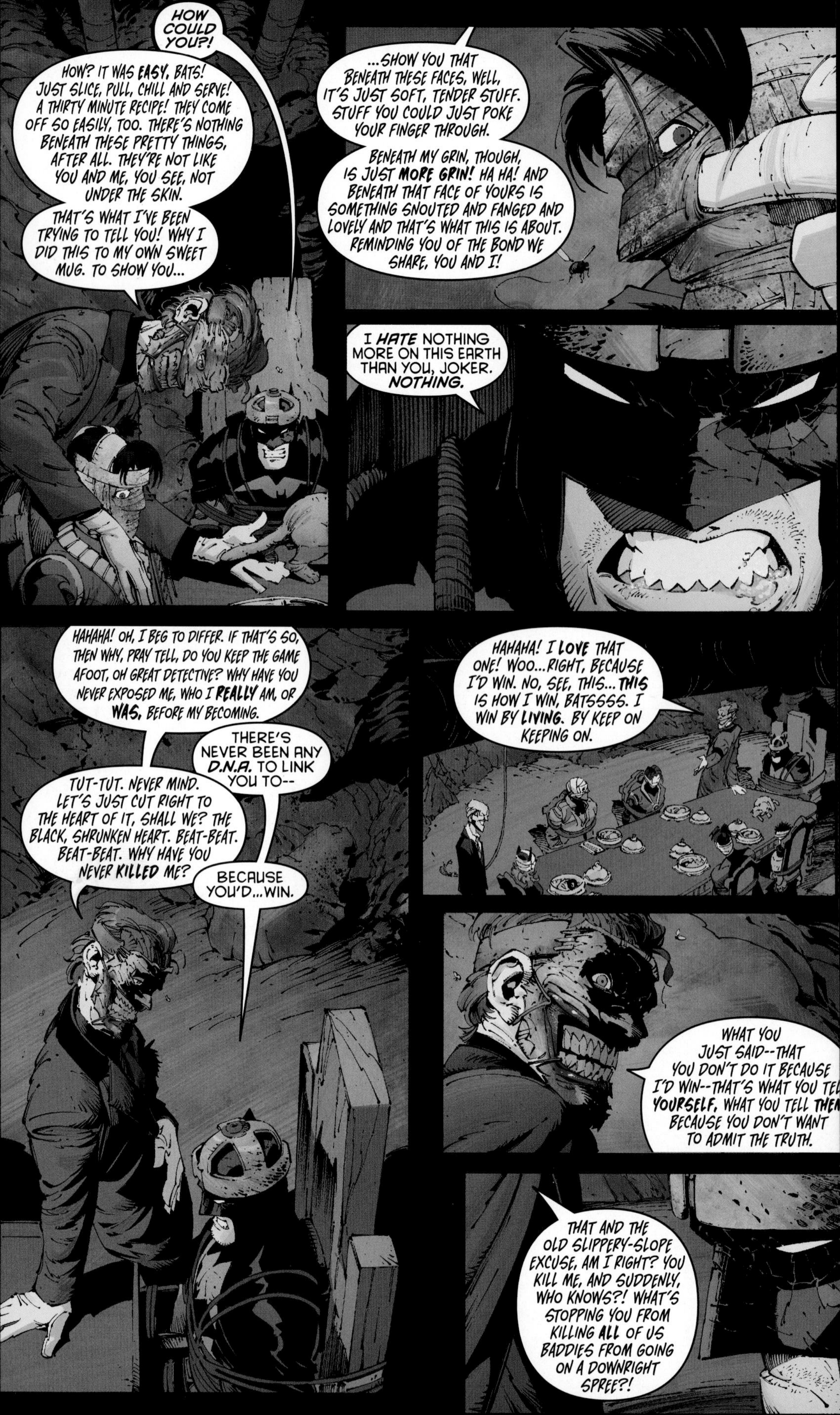
HOW COULD YOU?!
HOW? IT WAS EASY, BATS! JUST SLICE, PULL, CHILL AND SERVE! A THIRTY MINUTE RECIPE! THEY COME OFF SO EASILY, TOO. THERE'S NOTHING BENEATH THESE PRETTY THINGS, AFTER ALL. THEY'RE NOT LIKE YOU AND ME, YOU SEE, NOT UNDER THE SKIN.
THAT'S WHAT I'VE BEEN TRYING TO TELL YOU! WHY I DID THIS TO MY OWN SWEET MUG. TO SHOW YOU...
...SHOW YOU THAT BENEATH THESE FACES, WELL, IT'S JUST SOFT, TENDER STUFF. STUFF YOU COULD JUST POKE YOUR FINGER THROUGH.
BENEATH MY GRIN, THOUGH, IS JUST MORE GRIN! HA HA! AND BENEATH THAT FACE OF YOURS IS SOMETHING SNOUTED AND FANGED AND LOVELY AND THAT'S WHAT THIS IS ABOUT. REMINDING YOU OF THE BOND WE SHARE, YOU AND I!
I HATE NOTHING MORE ON THIS EARTH THAN YOU, JOKER. NOTHING.
HAHAHA! OH, I BEG TO DIFFER. IF THAT'S SO, THEN WHY, PRAY TELL, DO YOU KEEP THE GAME AFOOT, OH GREAT DETECTIVE? WHY HAVE YOU NEVER EXPOSED ME, WHO I REALLY AM, OR WAS, BEFORE MY BECOMING.
THERE'S NEVER BEEN ANY D.N.A. TO LINK YOU TO--
TUT-TUT. NEVER MIND. LET'S JUST CUT RIGHT TO THE HEART OF IT, SHALL WE? THE BLACK, SHRUNKEN HEART. BEAT-BEAT. BEAT-BEAT. WHY HAVE YOU NEVER KILLED ME?
BECAUSE YOU'D...WIN.
HAHAHA! I LOVE THAT ONE! WOO...RIGHT, BECAUSE I'D WIN. NO, SEE, THIS... THIS IS HOW I WIN, BATSSSS. I WIN BY LIVING. BY KEEP ON KEEPING ON.
WHAT YOU JUST SAID--THAT YOU DON'T DO IT BECAUSE I'D WIN--THAT'S WHAT YOU TELL YOURSELF, WHAT YOU TELL THEM BECAUSE YOU DON'T WANT TO ADMIT THE TRUTH.
THAT AND THE OLD SLIPPERY-SLOPE EXCUSE, AM I RIGHT? YOU KILL ME, AND SUDDENLY, WHO KNOWS?! WHAT'S STOPPING YOU FROM KILLING ALL OF US BADDIES FROM GOING ON A DOWNRIGHT SPREE?!

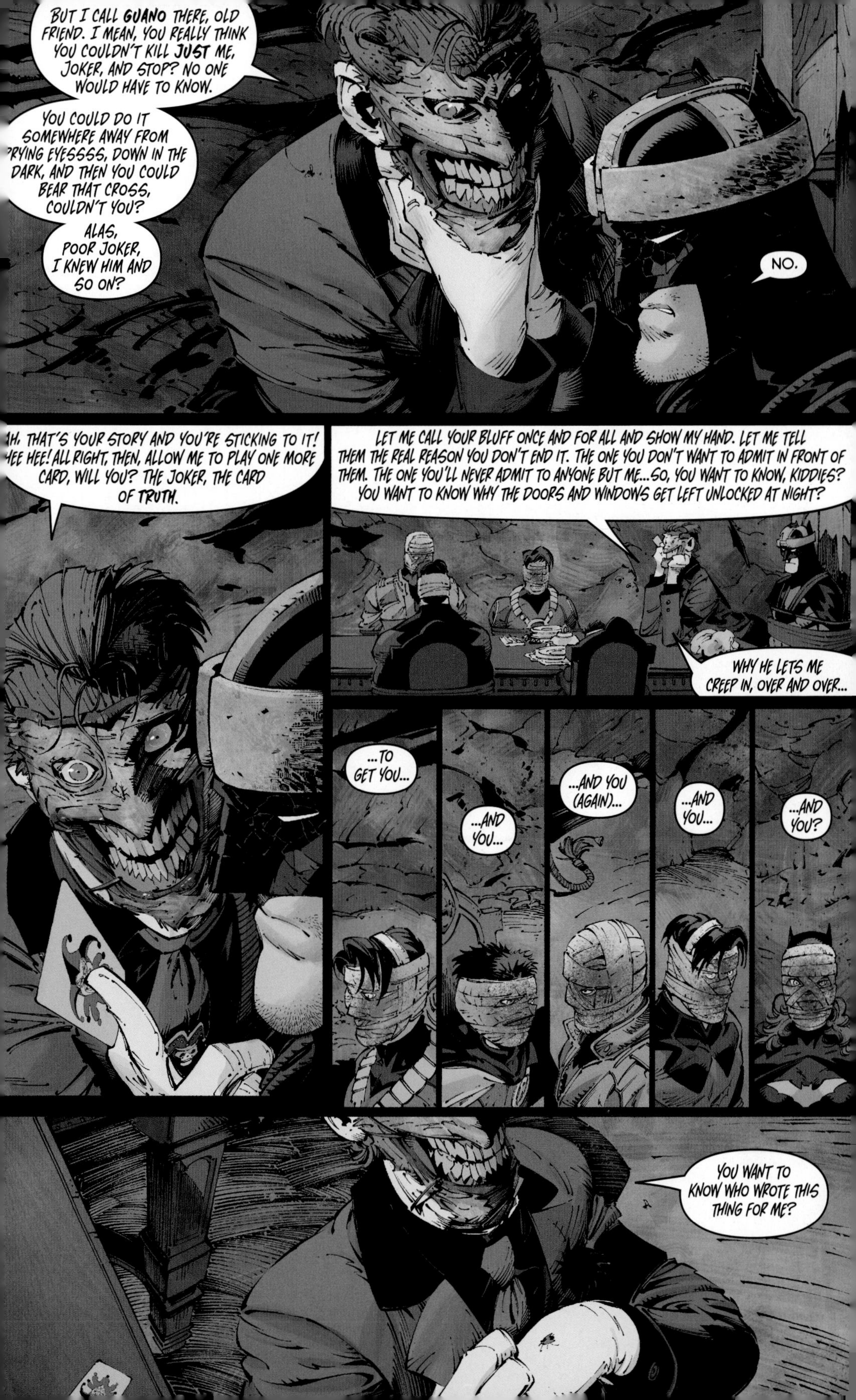
BUT I CALL GUANO THERE, OLD FRIEND. I MEAN, YOU REALLY THINK YOU COULDN'T KILL JUST ME, JOKER, AND STOP? NO ONE WOULD HAVE TO KNOW.
YOU COULD DO IT SOMEWHERE AWAY FROM PRYING EYESSSS, DOWN IN THE DARK, AND THEN YOU COULD BEAR THAT CROSS, COULDN'T YOU?
ALAS, POOR JOKER, I KNEW HIM AND SO ON?
NO.
AH, THAT'S YOUR STORY AND YOU'RE STICKING TO IT! HEE HEE! ALL RIGHT, THEN, ALLOW ME TO PLAY ONE MORE CARD, WILL YOU? THE JOKER, THE CARD OF TRUTH.
LET ME CALL YOUR BLUFF ONCE AND FOR ALL AND SHOW MY HAND. LET ME TELL THEM THE REAL REASON YOU DON'T END IT. THE ONE YOU DON'T WANT TO ADMIT IN FRONT OF THEM. THE ONE YOU'LL NEVER ADMIT TO ANYONE BUT ME...SO, YOU WANT TO KNOW, KIDDIES? YOU WANT TO KNOW WHY THE DOORS AND WINDOWS GET LEFT UNLOCKED AT NIGHT?
WHY HE LETS ME CREEP IN, OVER AND OVER...
...TO GET YOU...
...AND YOU...
...AND YOU (AGAIN)...
...AND YOU...
...AND YOU?
YOU WANT TO KNOW WHO WROTE THIS THING FOR ME?

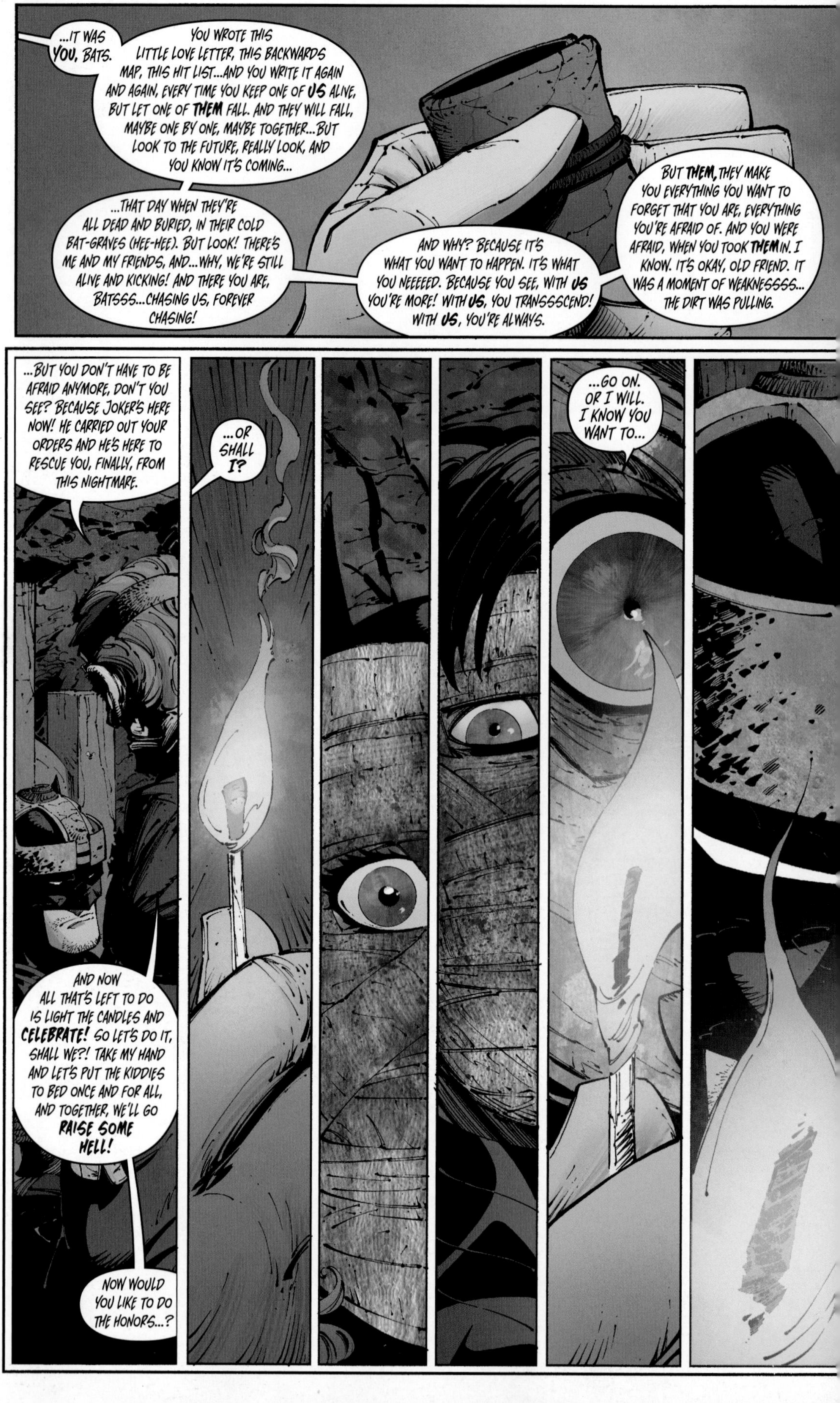
...IT WAS YOU, BATS.
YOU WROTE THIS LITTLE LOVE LETTER, THIS BACKWARDS MAP, THIS HIT LIST...AND YOU WRITE IT AGAIN AND AGAIN, EVERY TIME YOU KEEP ONE OF US ALIVE, BUT LET ONE OF THEM FALL. AND THEY WILL FALL, MAYBE ONE BY ONE, MAYBE TOGETHER...BUT LOOK TO THE FUTURE, REALLY LOOK, AND YOU KNOW IT'S COMING...
...THAT DAY WHEN THEY'RE ALL DEAD AND BURIED, IN THEIR COLD BAT-GRAVES (HEE-HEE). BUT LOOK! THERE'S ME AND MY FRIENDS, AND...WHY, WE'RE STILL ALIVE AND KICKING! AND THERE YOU ARE, BATSSS...CHASING US, FOREVER CHASING!
AND WHY? BECAUSE IT'S WHAT YOU WANT TO HAPPEN. IT'S WHAT YOU NEEEEED. BECAUSE YOU SEE, WITH US YOU'RE MORE! WITH US, YOU TRANSSSCEND! WITH US, YOU'RE ALWAYS.
BUT THEM, THEY MAKE YOU EVERYTHING YOU WANT TO FORGET THAT YOU ARE, EVERYTHING YOU'RE AFRAID OF. AND YOU WERE AFRAID, WHEN YOU TOOK THEM IN. I KNOW. IT'S OKAY, OLD FRIEND. IT WAS A MOMENT OF WEAKNESSSS... THE DIRT WAS PULLING.
...BUT YOU DON'T HAVE TO BE AFRAID ANYMORE, DON'T YOU SEE? BECAUSE JOKER'S HERE NOW! HE CARRIED OUT YOUR ORDERS AND HE'S HERE TO RESCUE YOU, FINALLY, FROM THIS NIGHTMARE.
AND NOW ALL THAT'S LEFT TO DO IS LIGHT THE CANDLES AND CELEBRATE! SO LET'S DO IT, SHALL WE?! TAKE MY HAND AND LET'S PUT THE KIDDIES TO BED ONCE AND FOR ALL, AND TOGETHER, WE'LL GO RAISE SOME HELL!
NOW WOULD YOU LIKE TO DO THE HONORS...?
...OR SHALL I?
...GO ON. OR I WILL. I KNOW YOU WANT TO...

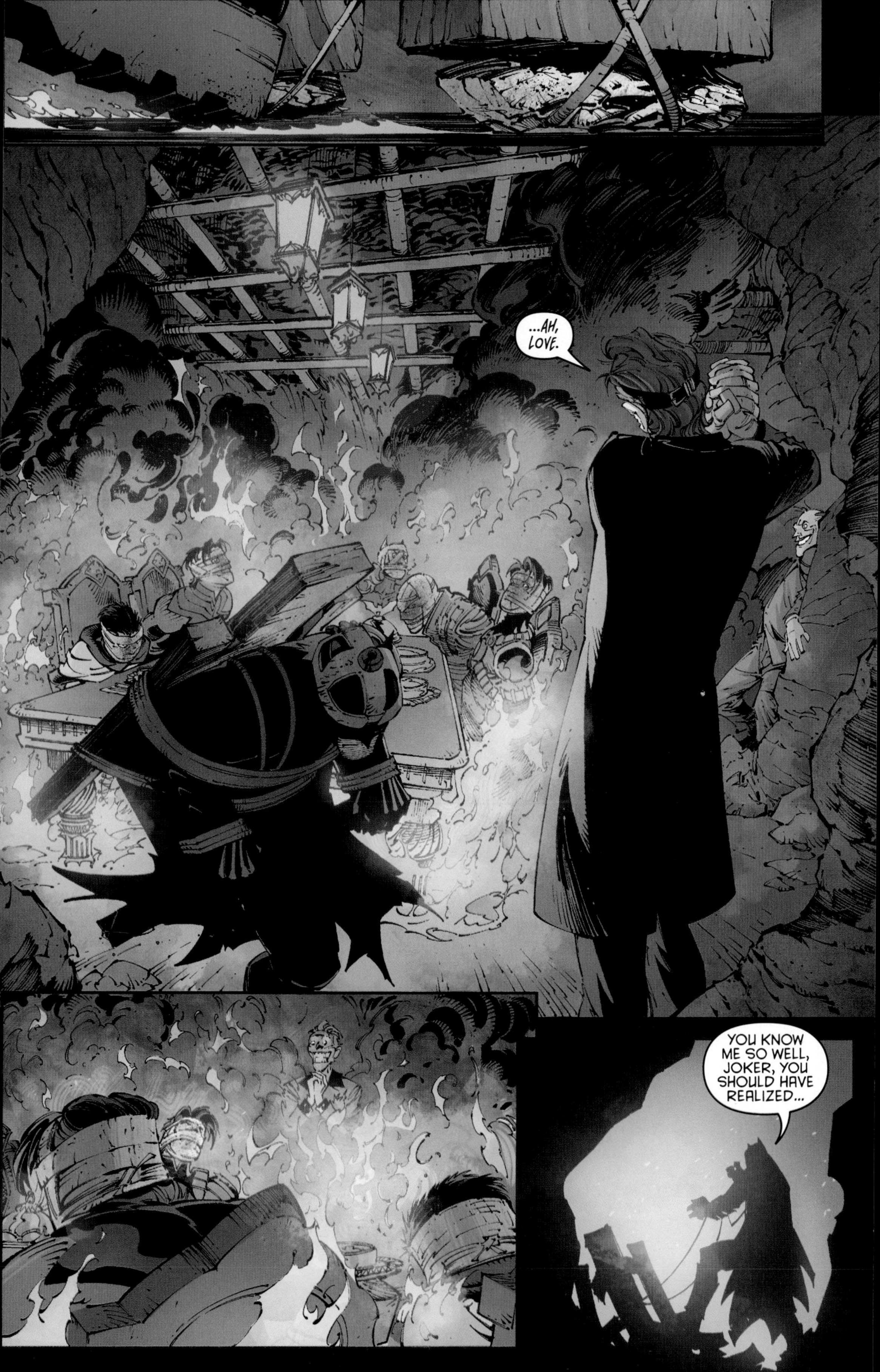
...AH, LOVE.
YOU KNOW ME SO WELL, JOKER, YOU SHOULD HAVE REALIZED...

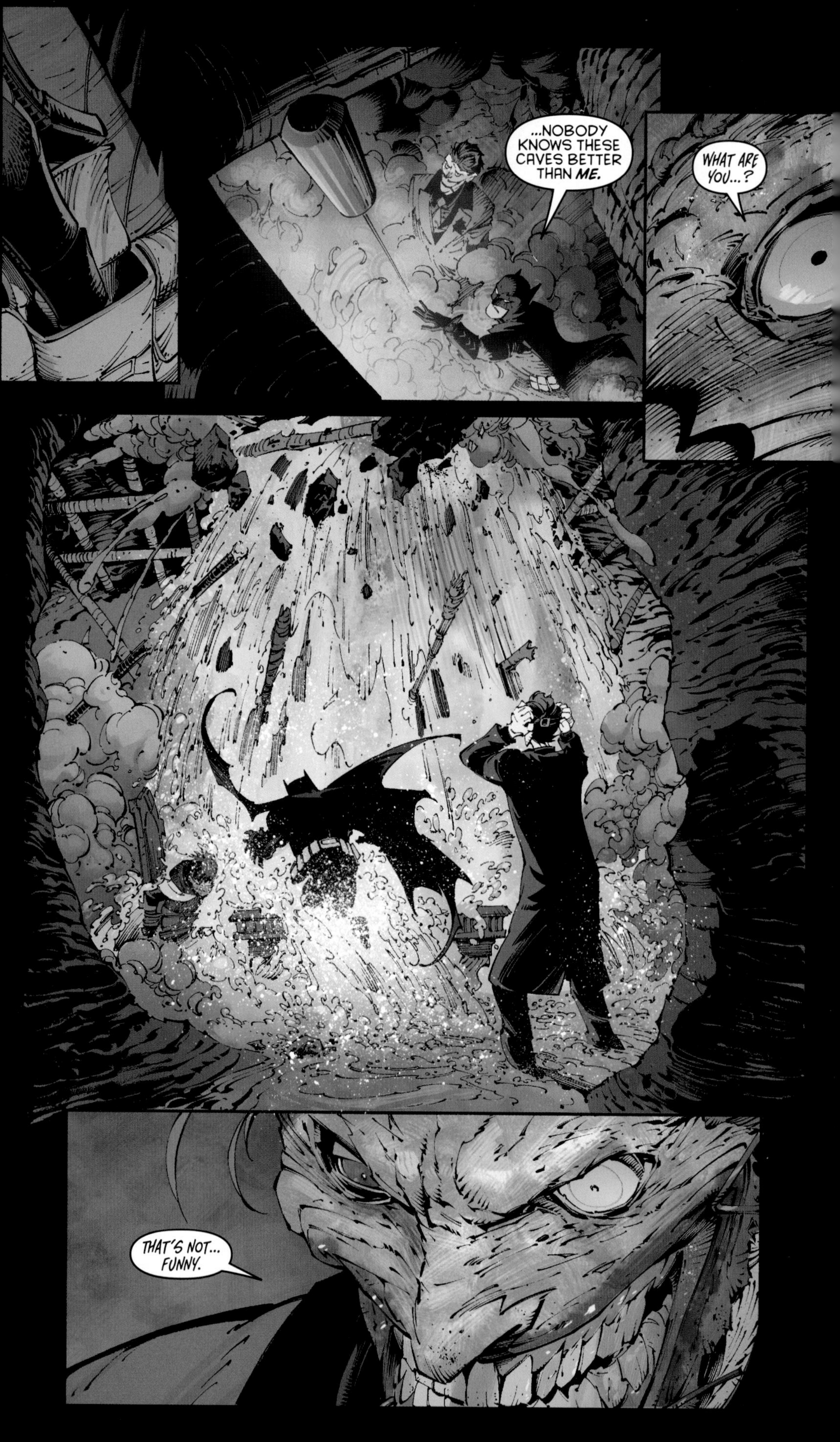
...NOBODY KNOWS THESE CAVES BETTER THAN *ME.*
WHAT ARE YOU...?
THAT'S NOT... FUNNY.

DAMIAN! DAMIAN, I HAVE YOU. YOU'RE...

...ALL RIGHT?

IS IT...BAD? TELL ME, I CAN TAKE IT. MY FACE IS NUMB.

SO IT WAS ALL A TWISTED *JOKE?*

KEEP ALFRED RESTRAINED. WE'LL GET HIM BACK TO THE CAVE AND--

GO.

GO AFTER HIM, BRUCE.

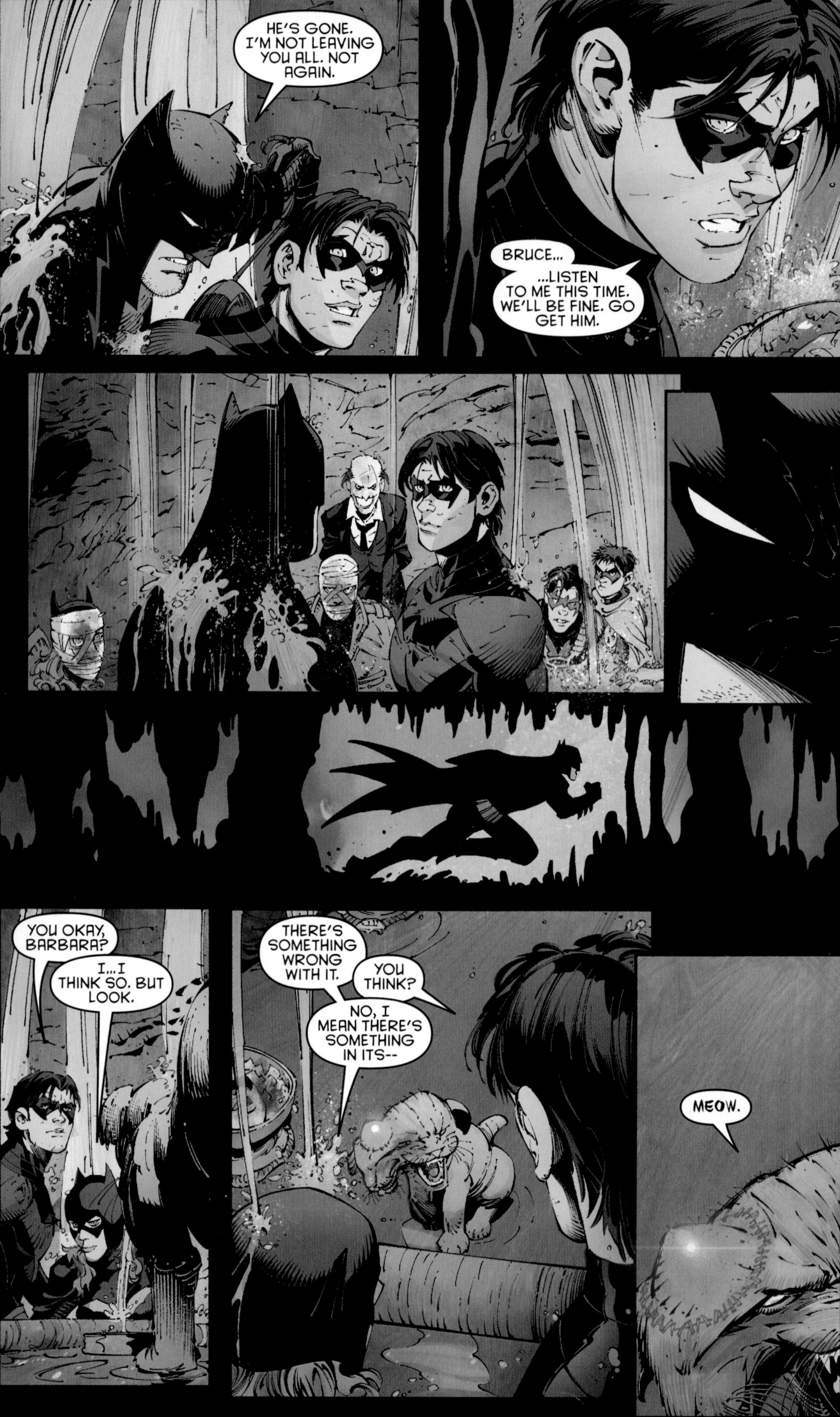
HE'S GONE. I'M NOT LEAVING YOU ALL. NOT AGAIN.
BRUCE...
...LISTEN TO ME THIS TIME. WE'LL BE FINE. GO GET HIM.
YOU OKAY, BARBARA?
I...I THINK SO. BUT LOOK.
THERE'S SOMETHING WRONG WITH IT.
YOU THINK?
NO, I MEAN THERE'S SOMETHING IN ITS--
MEOW.

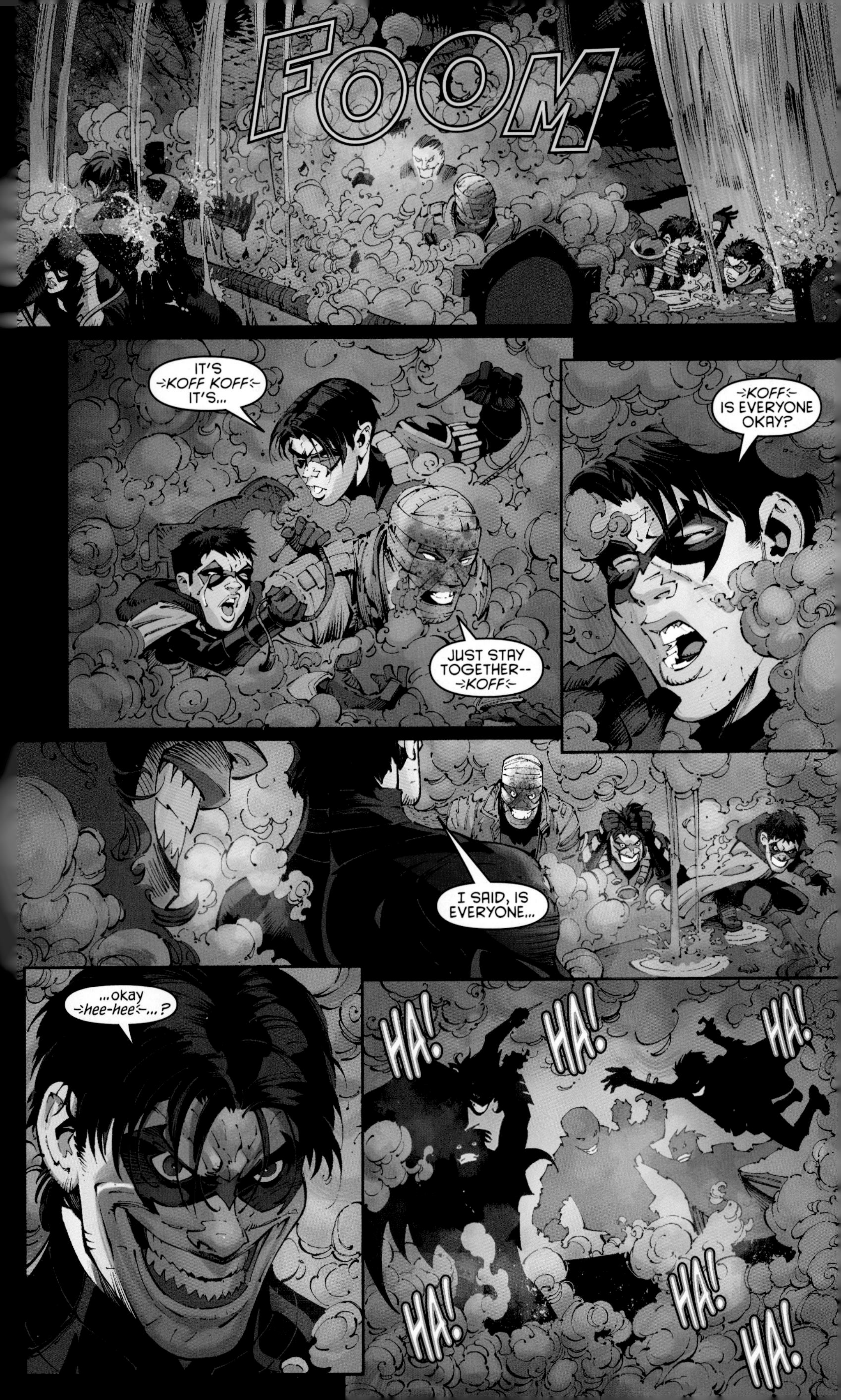
FOOM
IT'S -KOFF KOFF- IT'S...
JUST STAY TOGETHER-- -KOFF-
-KOFF- IS EVERYONE OKAY?
I SAID, IS EVERYONE...
...okay -hee-hee-...?
HA! HA! HA!
HA! HA! HA!

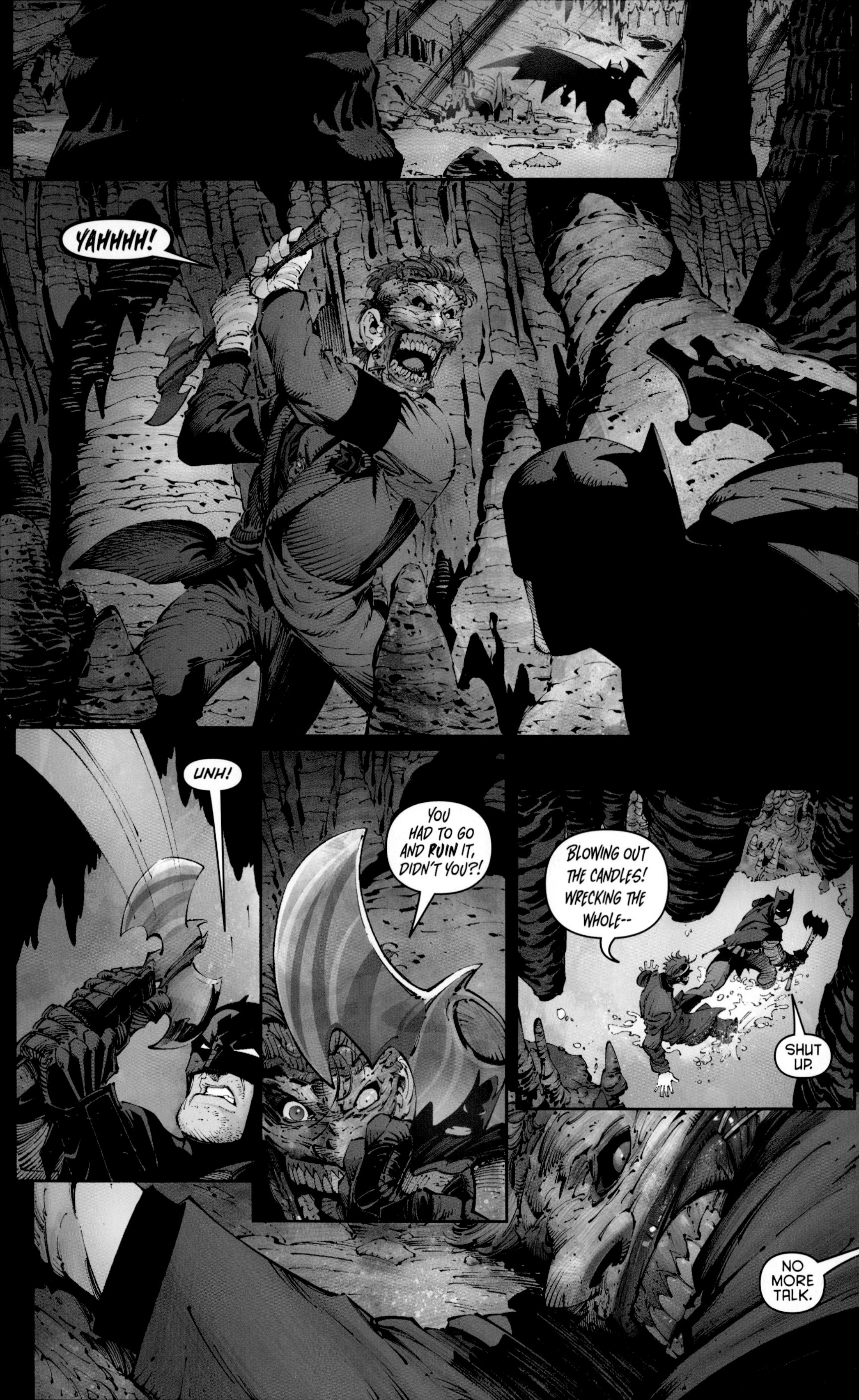
YAHHHH!
UNH!
YOU HAD TO GO AND RUIN IT, DIDN'T YOU?!
BLOWING OUT THE CANDLES! WRECKING THE WHOLE--
SHUT UP.
NO MORE TALK.

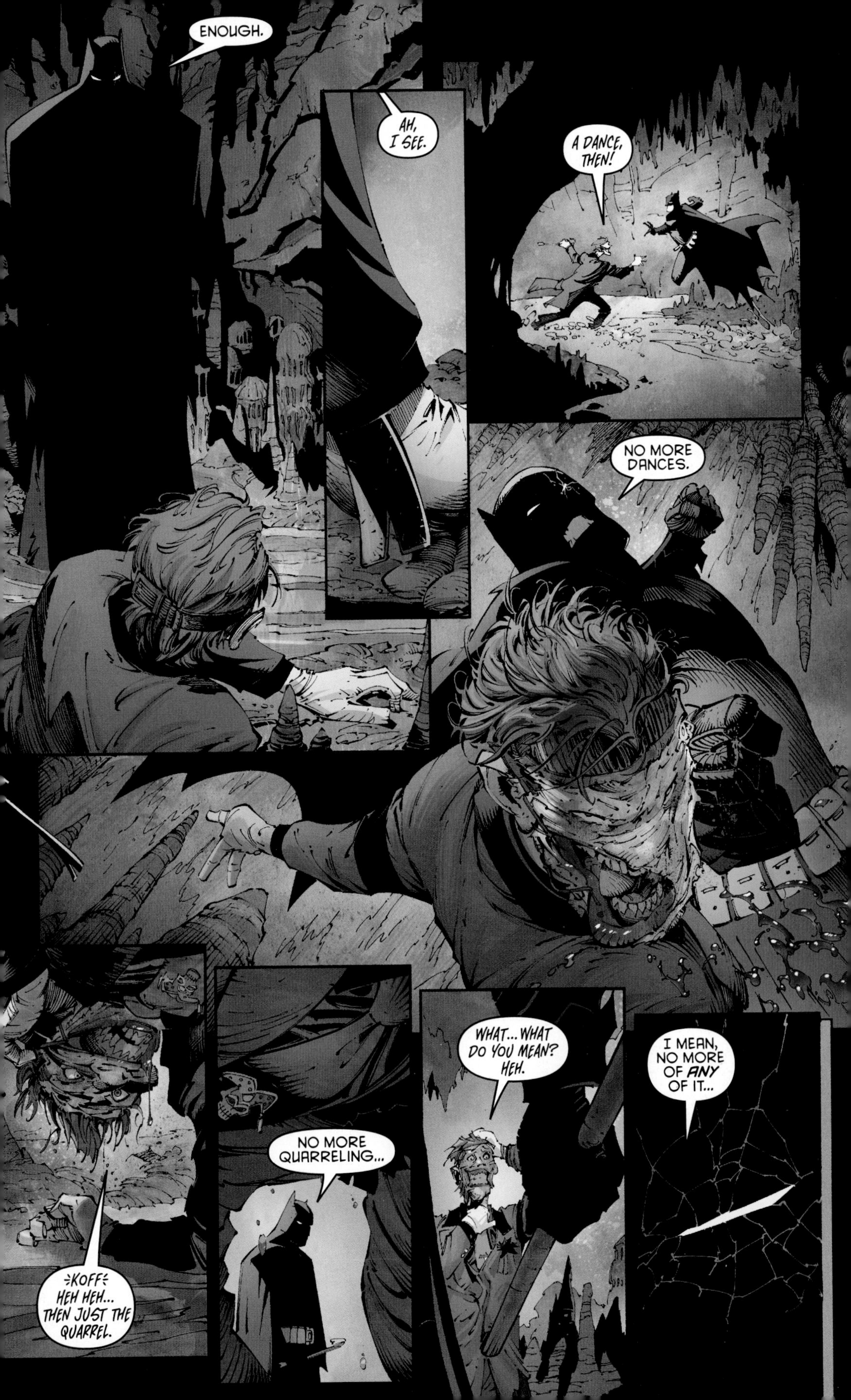
ENOUGH.
AH, I SEE.
A DANCE, THEN!
NO MORE DANCES.
≑KOFF≑ HEH HEH... THEN JUST THE QUARREL.
NO MORE QUARRELING...
WHAT... WHAT DO YOU MEAN? HEH.
I MEAN, NO MORE OF *ANY* OF IT...

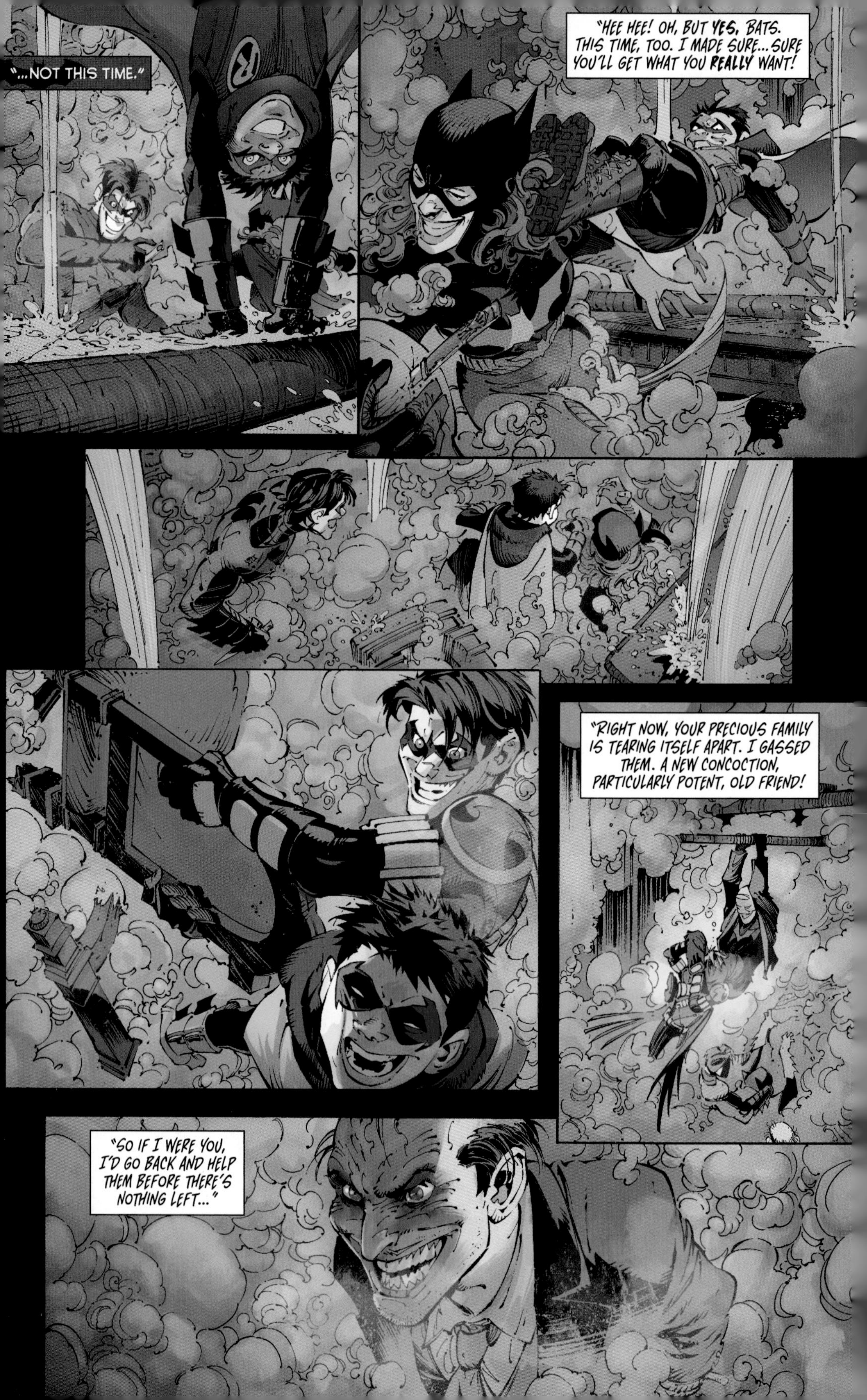
"...NOT THIS TIME."
"HEE HEE! OH, BUT YES, BATS. THIS TIME, TOO. I MADE SURE... SURE YOU'LL GET WHAT YOU REALLY WANT!
"RIGHT NOW, YOUR PRECIOUS FAMILY IS TEARING ITSELF APART. I GASSED THEM. A NEW CONCOCTION, PARTICULARLY POTENT, OLD FRIEND!
"SO IF I WERE YOU, I'D GO BACK AND HELP THEM BEFORE THERE'S NOTHING LEFT..."

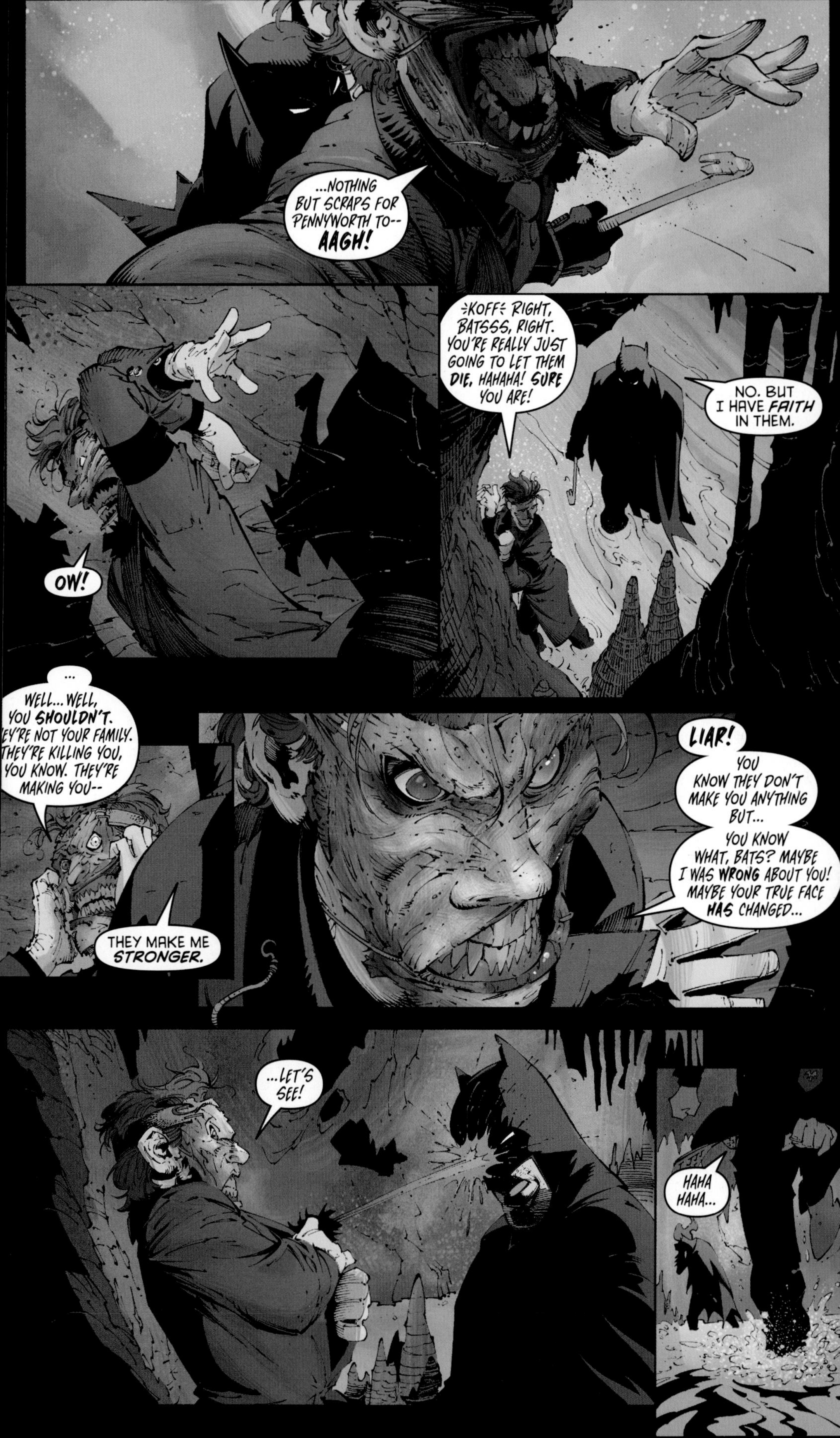
...NOTHING BUT SCRAPS FOR PENNYWORTH TO-- AAGH!
OW!
≠KOFF≠ RIGHT, BATSSS, RIGHT. YOU'RE REALLY JUST GOING TO LET THEM DIE, HAHAHA! SURE YOU ARE!
NO. BUT I HAVE FAITH IN THEM.
...
WELL... WELL, YOU SHOULDN'T. EY'RE NOT YOUR FAMILY. THEY'RE KILLING YOU, YOU KNOW. THEY'RE MAKING YOU--
THEY MAKE ME STRONGER.
LIAR!
YOU KNOW THEY DON'T MAKE YOU ANYTHING BUT...
YOU KNOW WHAT, BATS? MAYBE I WAS WRONG ABOUT YOU! MAYBE YOUR TRUE FACE HAS CHANGED...
...LET'S SEE!
HAHA HAHA...

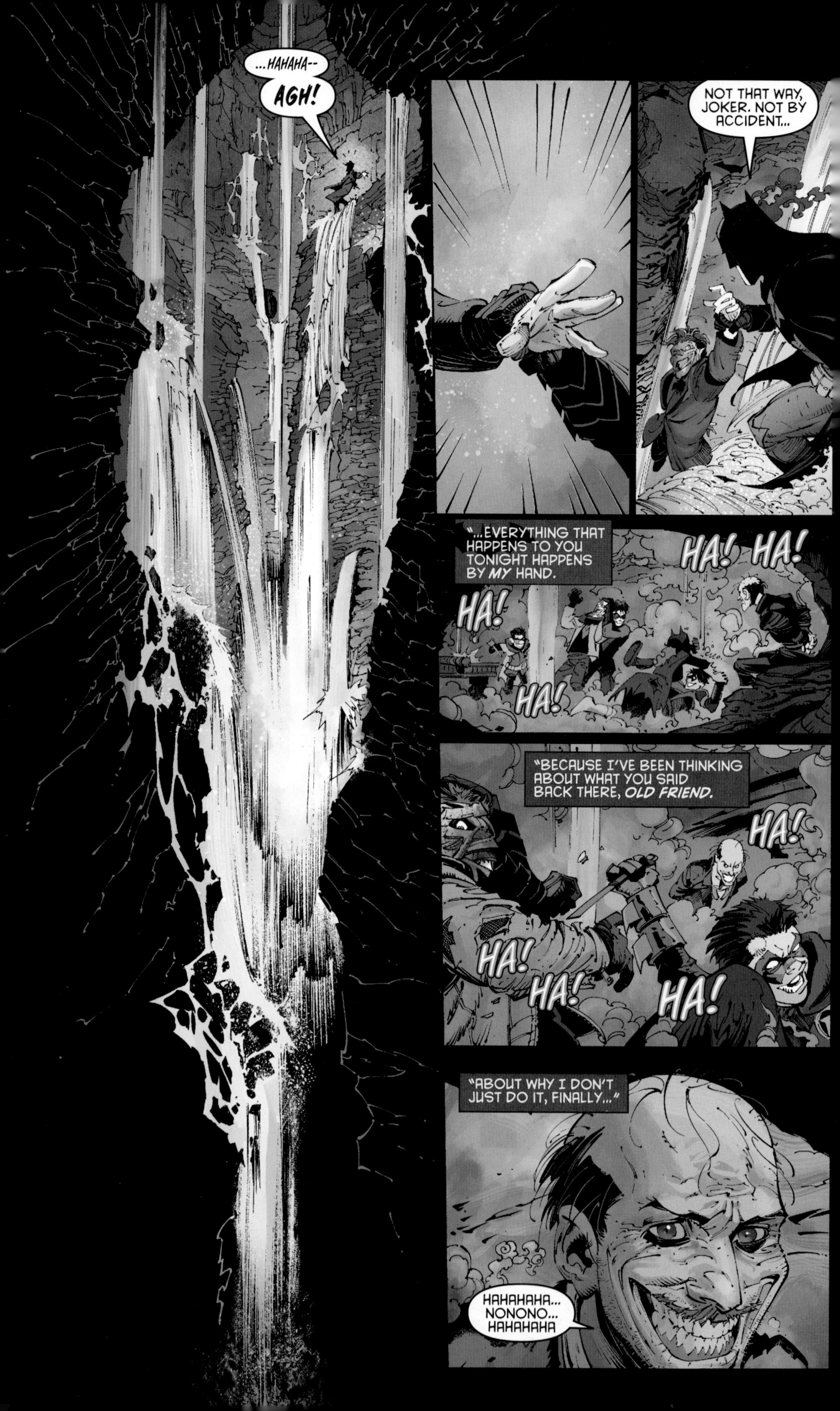
...HAHAHA--
AGH!
NOT THAT WAY, JOKER. NOT BY ACCIDENT...
"...EVERYTHING THAT HAPPENS TO YOU TONIGHT HAPPENS BY MY HAND.
HA! HA!
HA!
HA!
"BECAUSE I'VE BEEN THINKING ABOUT WHAT YOU SAID BACK THERE, OLD FRIEND.
HA!
HA!
HA!
HA!
"ABOUT WHY I DON'T JUST DO IT, FINALLY..."
HAHAHAHA... NONONO... HAHAHAHA

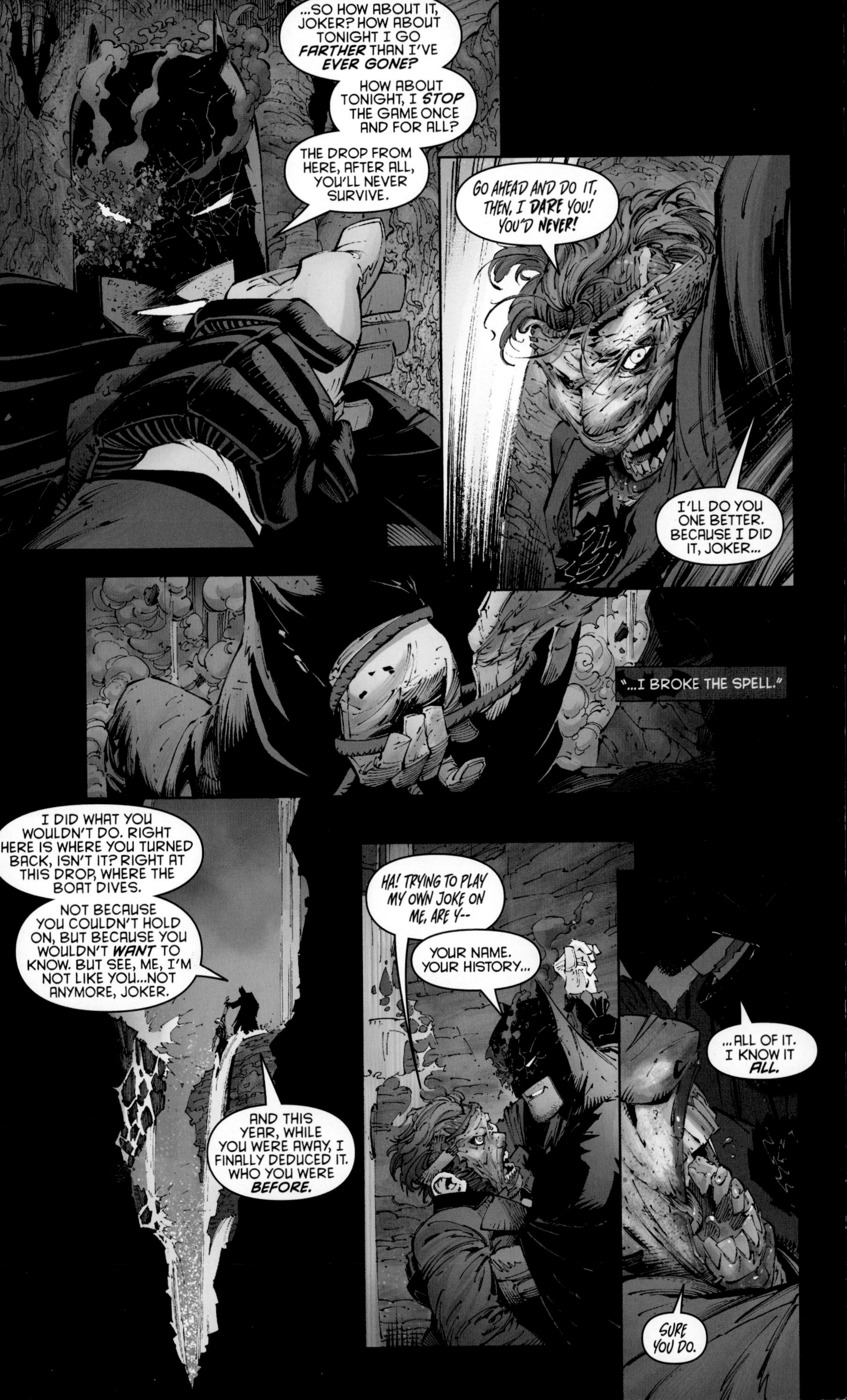
...SO HOW ABOUT IT, JOKER? HOW ABOUT TONIGHT I GO FARTHER THAN I'VE EVER GONE?
HOW ABOUT TONIGHT, I STOP THE GAME ONCE AND FOR ALL?
THE DROP FROM HERE, AFTER ALL, YOU'LL NEVER SURVIVE.
GO AHEAD AND DO IT, THEN, I DARE YOU! YOU'D NEVER!
I'LL DO YOU ONE BETTER. BECAUSE I DID IT, JOKER...
"...I BROKE THE SPELL."
I DID WHAT YOU WOULDN'T DO. RIGHT HERE IS WHERE YOU TURNED BACK, ISN'T IT? RIGHT AT THIS DROP, WHERE THE BOAT DIVES.
NOT BECAUSE YOU COULDN'T HOLD ON, BUT BECAUSE YOU WOULDN'T WANT TO KNOW. BUT SEE, ME, I'M NOT LIKE YOU...NOT ANYMORE, JOKER.
AND THIS YEAR, WHILE YOU WERE AWAY, I FINALLY DEDUCED IT. WHO YOU WERE BEFORE.
HA! TRYING TO PLAY MY OWN JOKE ON ME, ARE Y--
YOUR NAME. YOUR HISTORY...
...ALL OF IT. I KNOW IT ALL.
SURE YOU DO.

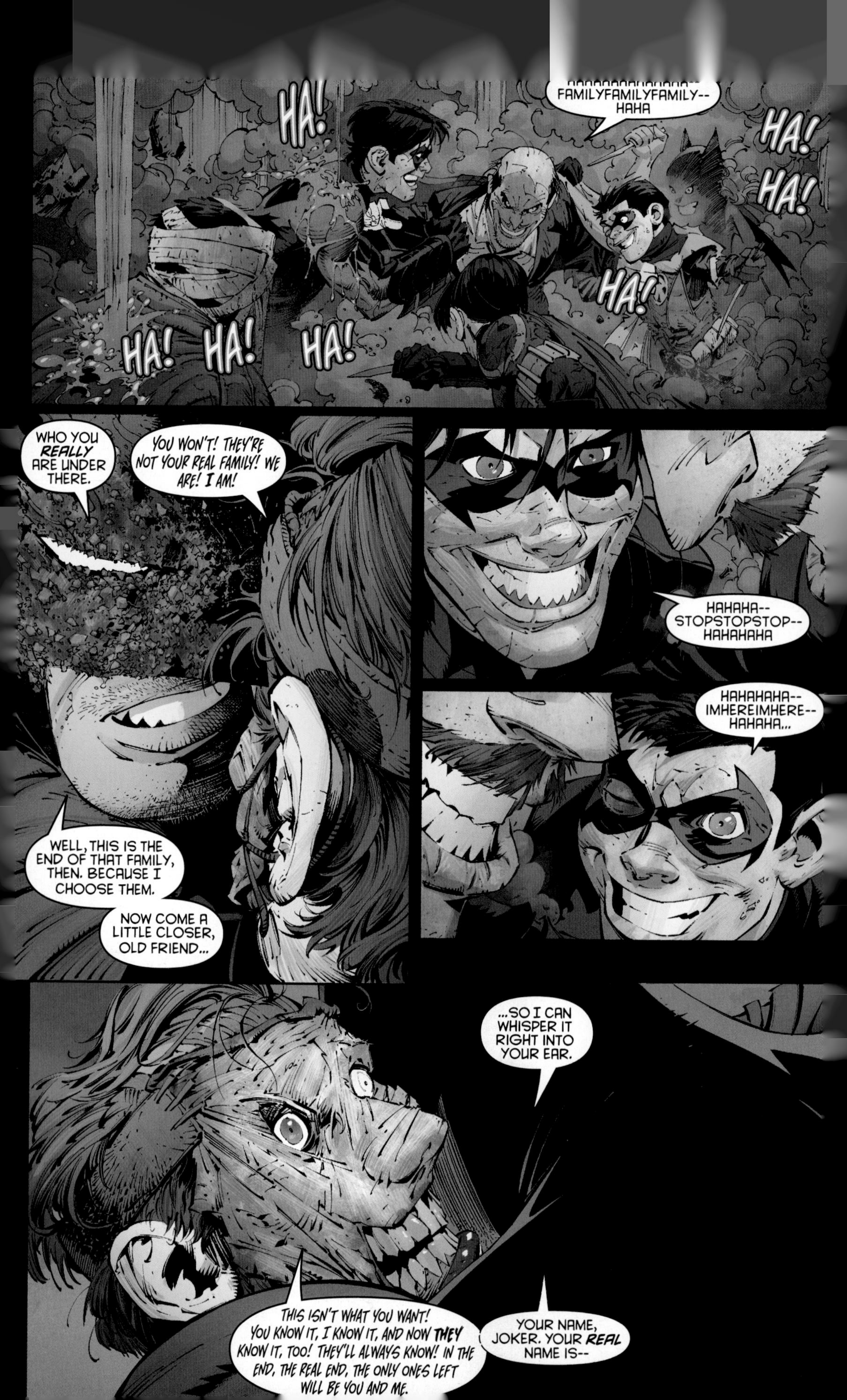

FAMILYFAMILYFAMILY--
HAHA
HA!
HA!
HA!
HA!
HA!
HA!
HA!
WHO YOU **REALLY** ARE UNDER THERE.
YOU WON'T! THEY'RE NOT YOUR REAL FAMILY! WE ARE! **I AM!**
HAHAHA-- STOPSTOPSTOP-- HAHAHAHA
HAHAHAHA-- IMHEREIMHERE-- HAHAHA...
WELL, THIS IS THE END OF THAT FAMILY, THEN. BECAUSE I CHOOSE THEM.
NOW COME A LITTLE CLOSER, OLD FRIEND...
...SO I CAN WHISPER IT RIGHT INTO YOUR EAR.
THIS ISN'T WHAT YOU WANT! YOU KNOW IT, I KNOW IT, AND NOW **THEY** KNOW IT, TOO! THEY'LL ALWAYS KNOW! IN THE END, THE REAL END, THE ONLY ONES LEFT WILL BE YOU AND ME.
YOUR NAME, JOKER. YOUR **REAL** NAME IS--

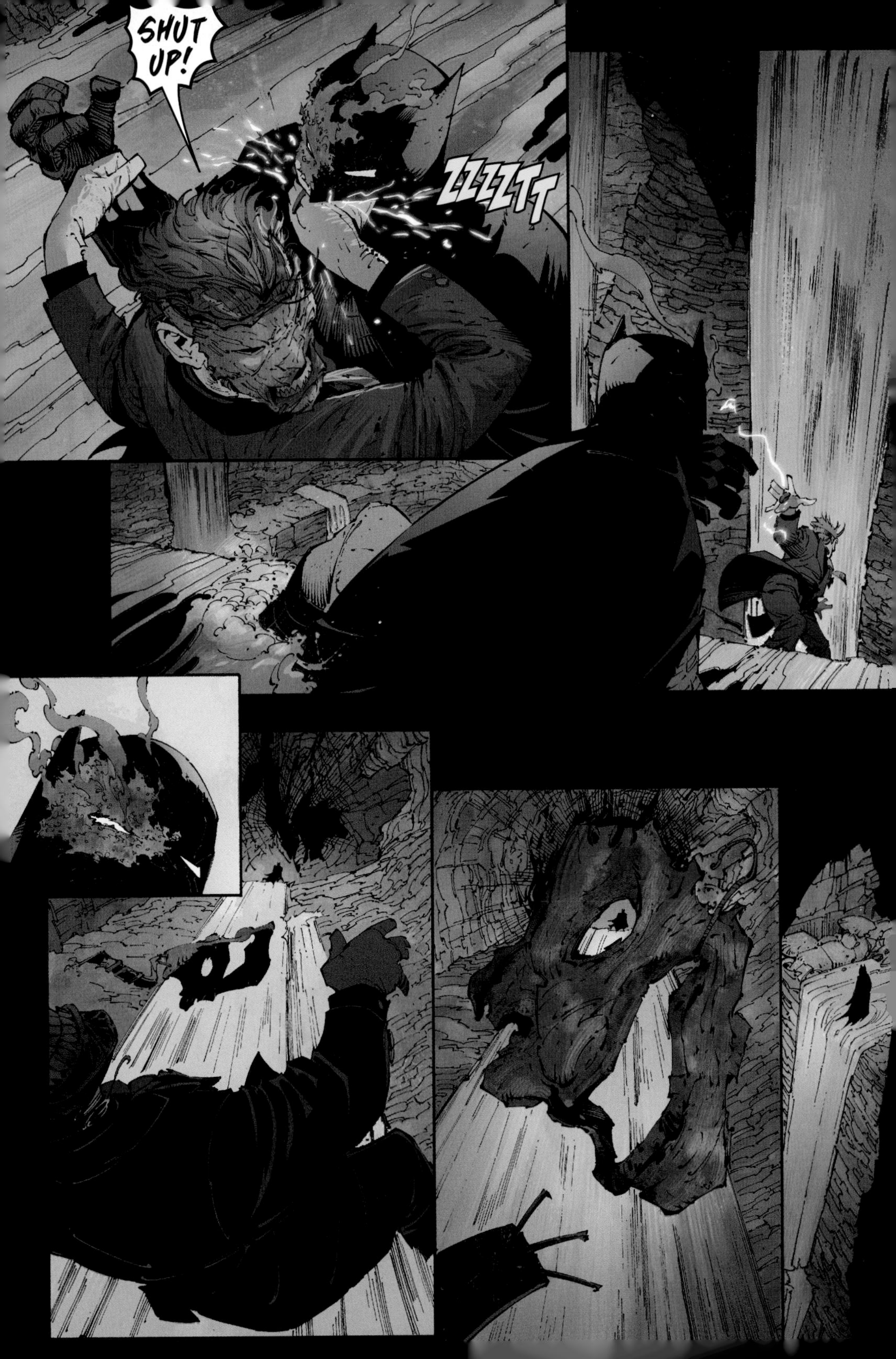
SHUT UP!
ZZZZTT

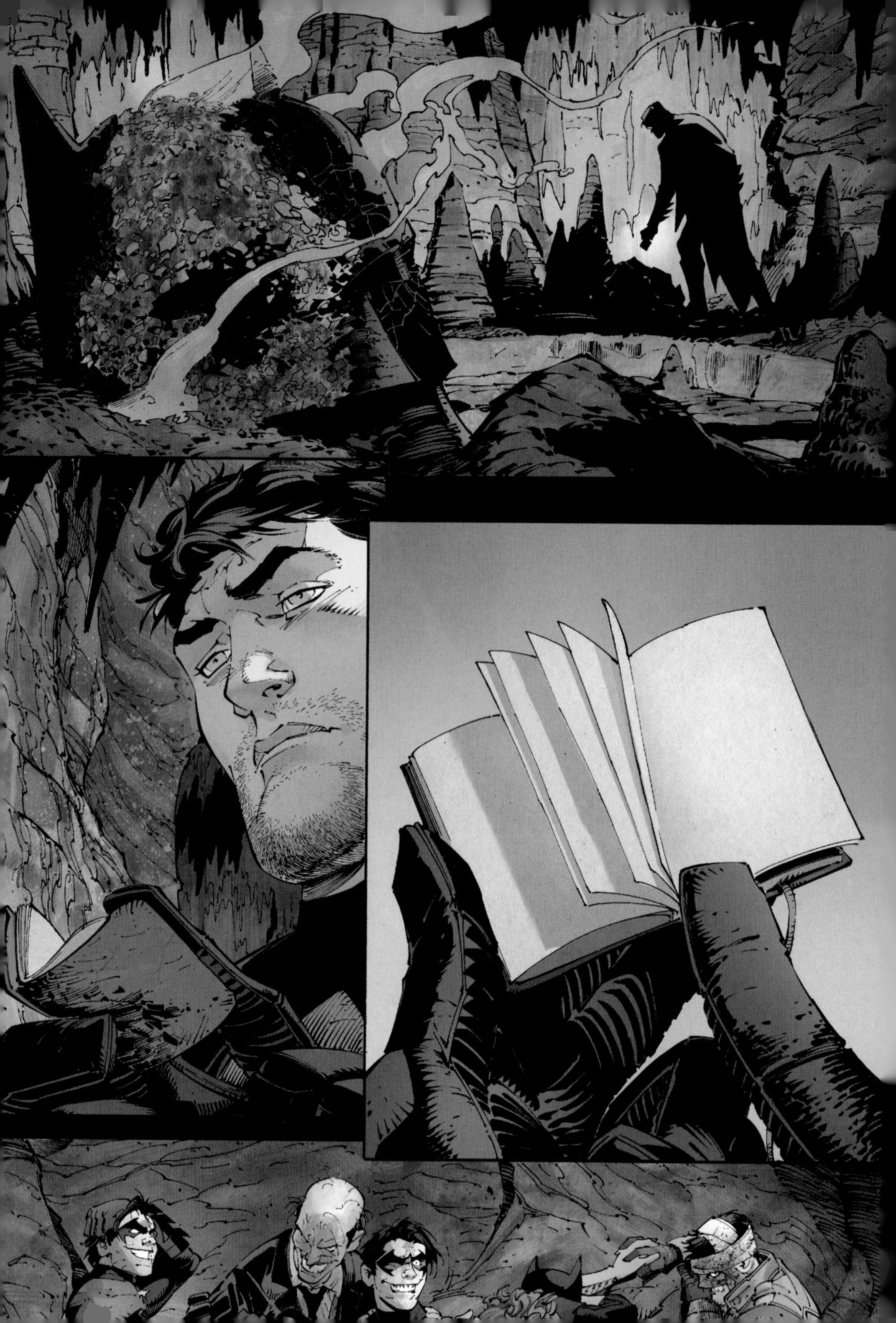

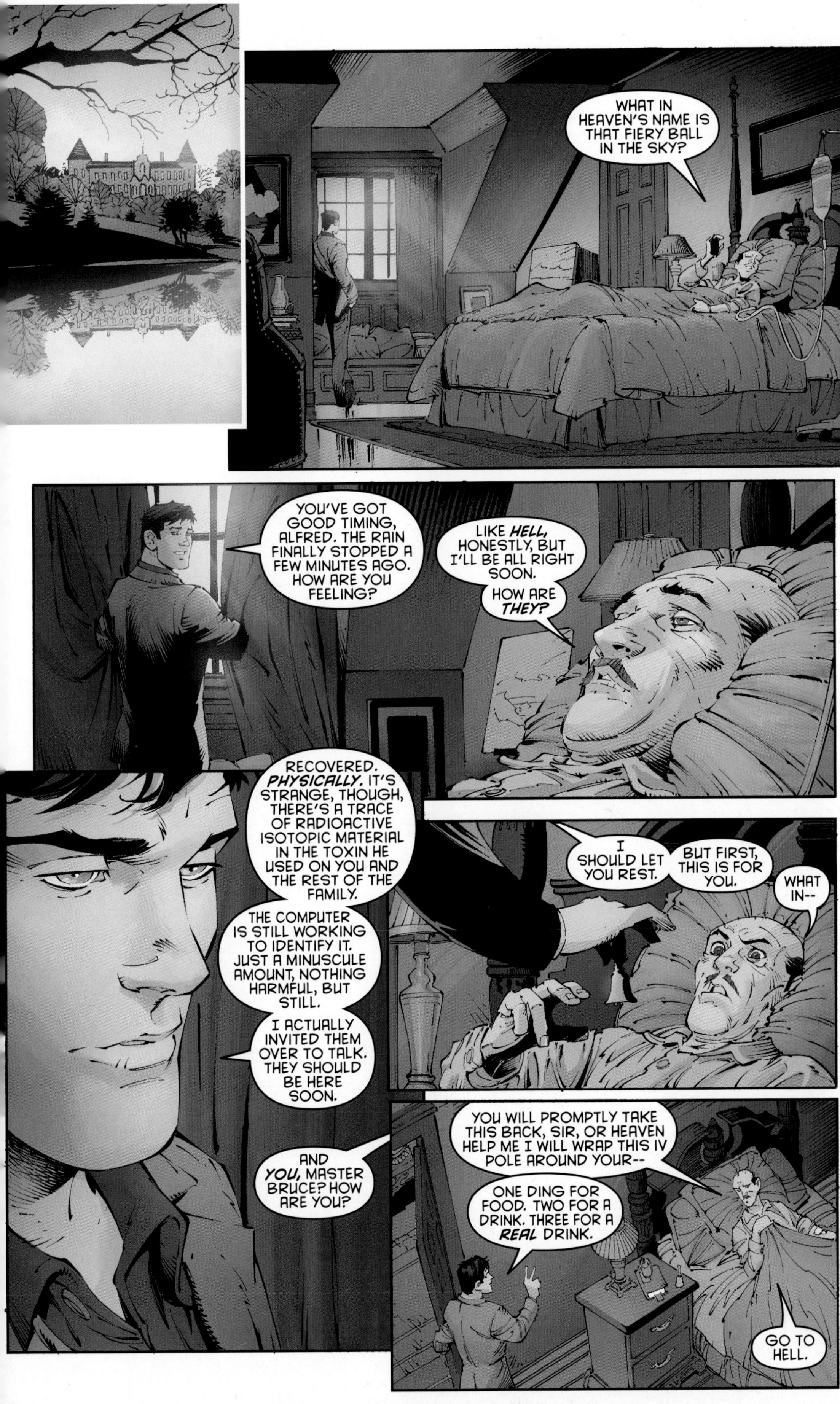
WHAT IN HEAVEN'S NAME IS THAT FIERY BALL IN THE SKY?
YOU'VE GOT GOOD TIMING, ALFRED. THE RAIN FINALLY STOPPED A FEW MINUTES AGO. HOW ARE YOU FEELING?
LIKE *HELL,* HONESTLY, BUT I'LL BE ALL RIGHT SOON.
HOW ARE *THEY?*
RECOVERED. *PHYSICALLY.* IT'S STRANGE, THOUGH, THERE'S A TRACE OF RADIOACTIVE ISOTOPIC MATERIAL IN THE TOXIN HE USED ON YOU AND THE REST OF THE FAMILY.
THE COMPUTER IS STILL WORKING TO IDENTIFY IT. JUST A MINUSCULE AMOUNT, NOTHING HARMFUL, BUT STILL.
I ACTUALLY INVITED THEM OVER TO TALK. THEY SHOULD BE HERE SOON.
AND *YOU,* MASTER BRUCE? HOW ARE YOU?
I SHOULD LET YOU REST.
BUT FIRST, THIS IS FOR YOU.
WHAT IN--
YOU WILL PROMPTLY TAKE THIS BACK, SIR, OR HEAVEN HELP ME I WILL WRAP THIS IV POLE AROUND YOUR--
ONE DING FOR FOOD. TWO FOR A DRINK. THREE FOR A *REAL* DRINK.
GO TO HELL.

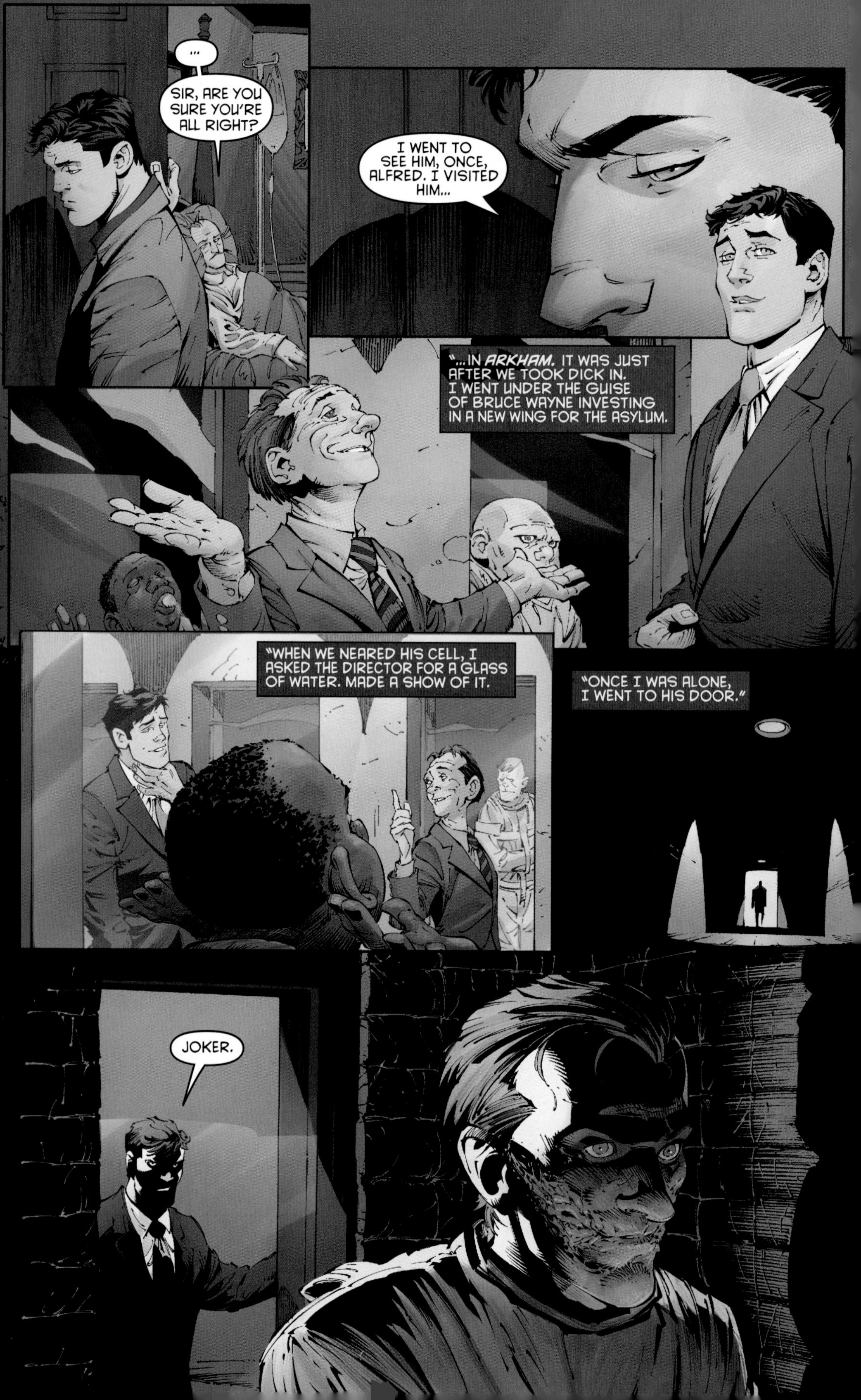
...
SIR, ARE YOU SURE YOU'RE ALL RIGHT?
I WENT TO SEE HIM, ONCE, ALFRED. I VISITED HIM...
"...IN ARKHAM. IT WAS JUST AFTER WE TOOK DICK IN. I WENT UNDER THE GUISE OF BRUCE WAYNE INVESTING IN A NEW WING FOR THE ASYLUM.
"WHEN WE NEARED HIS CELL, I ASKED THE DIRECTOR FOR A GLASS OF WATER. MADE A SHOW OF IT.
"ONCE I WAS ALONE, I WENT TO HIS DOOR."
JOKER.

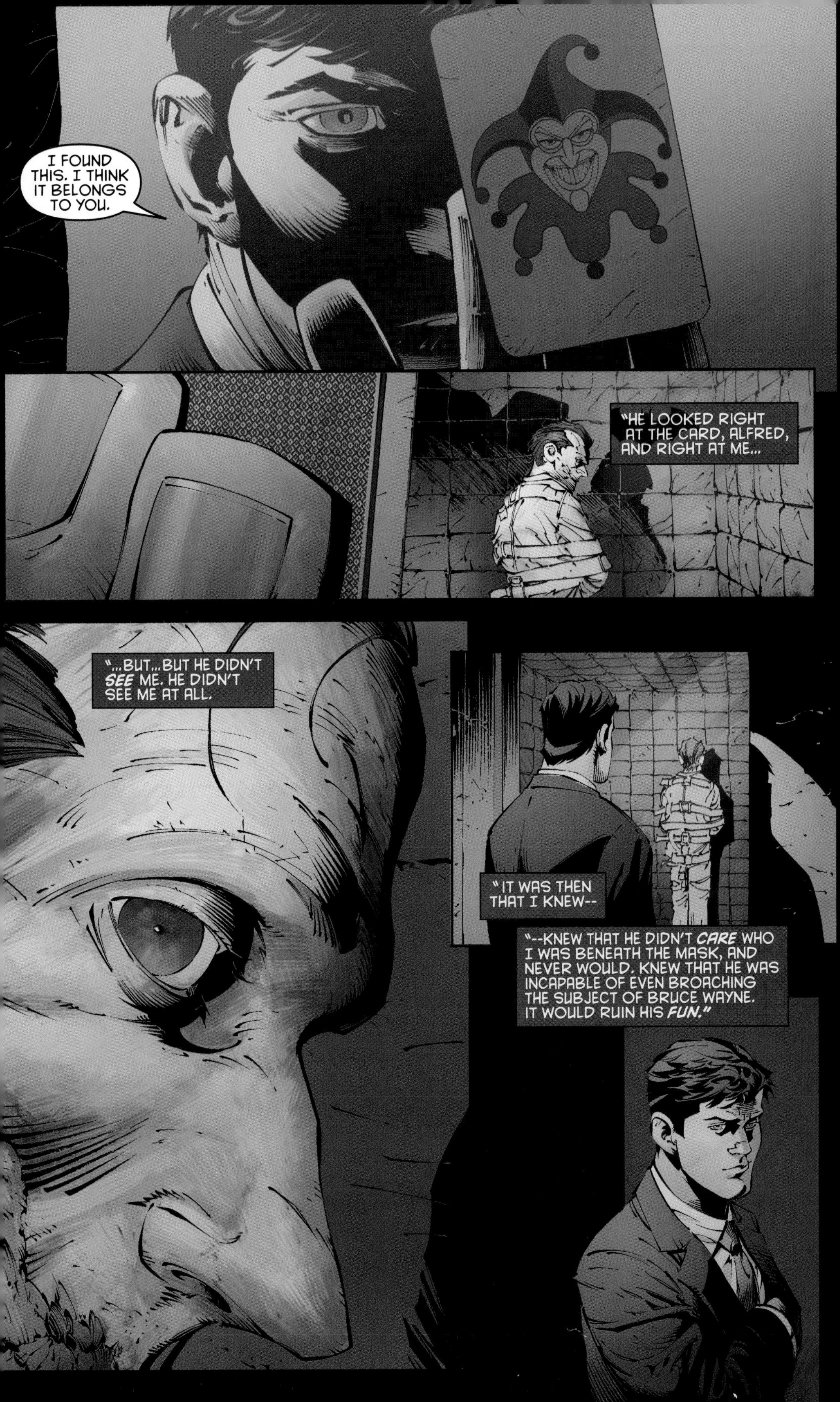
I FOUND THIS. I THINK IT BELONGS TO YOU.
"HE LOOKED RIGHT AT THE CARD, ALFRED, AND RIGHT AT ME...
"...BUT...BUT HE DIDN'T SEE ME. HE DIDN'T SEE ME AT ALL.
"IT WAS THEN THAT I KNEW--
"--KNEW THAT HE DIDN'T CARE WHO I WAS BENEATH THE MASK, AND NEVER WOULD. KNEW THAT HE WAS INCAPABLE OF EVEN BROACHING THE SUBJECT OF BRUCE WAYNE. IT WOULD RUIN HIS FUN."

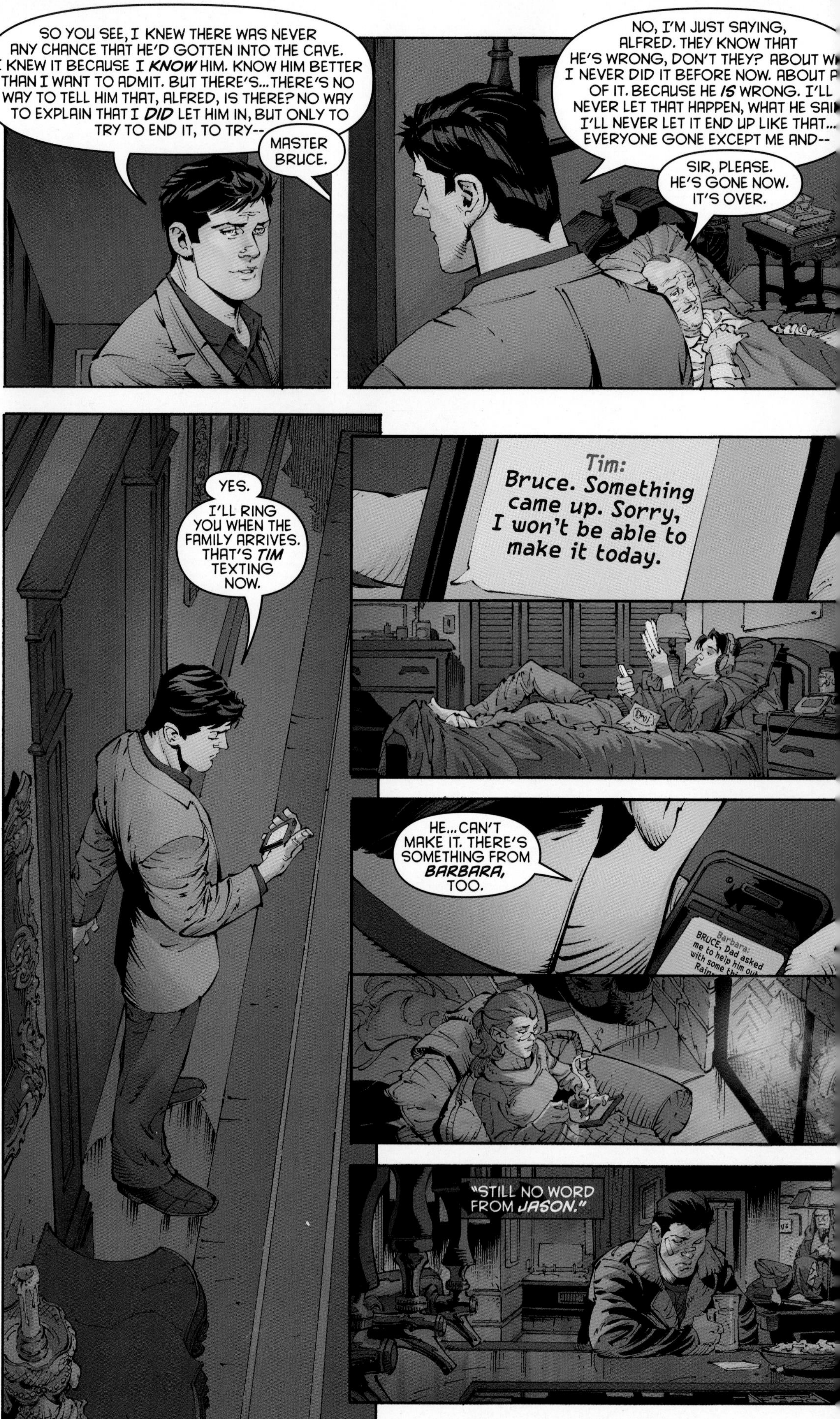
SO YOU SEE, I KNEW THERE WAS NEVER ANY CHANCE THAT HE'D GOTTEN INTO THE CAVE. I KNEW IT BECAUSE I KNOW HIM. KNOW HIM BETTER THAN I WANT TO ADMIT. BUT THERE'S... THERE'S NO WAY TO TELL HIM THAT, ALFRED, IS THERE? NO WAY TO EXPLAIN THAT I DID LET HIM IN, BUT ONLY TO TRY TO END IT, TO TRY--
MASTER BRUCE.
NO, I'M JUST SAYING, ALFRED. THEY KNOW THAT HE'S WRONG, DON'T THEY? ABOUT
I NEVER DID IT BEFORE NOW. ABOUT
OF IT. BECAUSE HE IS WRONG. I'LL NEVER LET THAT HAPPEN, WHAT HE SA
I'LL NEVER LET IT END UP LIKE THAT... EVERYONE GONE EXCEPT ME AND--
SIR, PLEASE. HE'S GONE NOW. IT'S OVER.
YES.
I'LL RING YOU WHEN THE FAMILY ARRIVES. THAT'S TIM TEXTING NOW.
Tim:
Bruce. Something came up. Sorry, I won't be able to make it today.
HE... CAN'T MAKE IT. THERE'S SOMETHING FROM BARBARA, TOO.
Barbara:
BRUCE, Dad asked
me to help him
"STILL NO WORD FROM JASON."

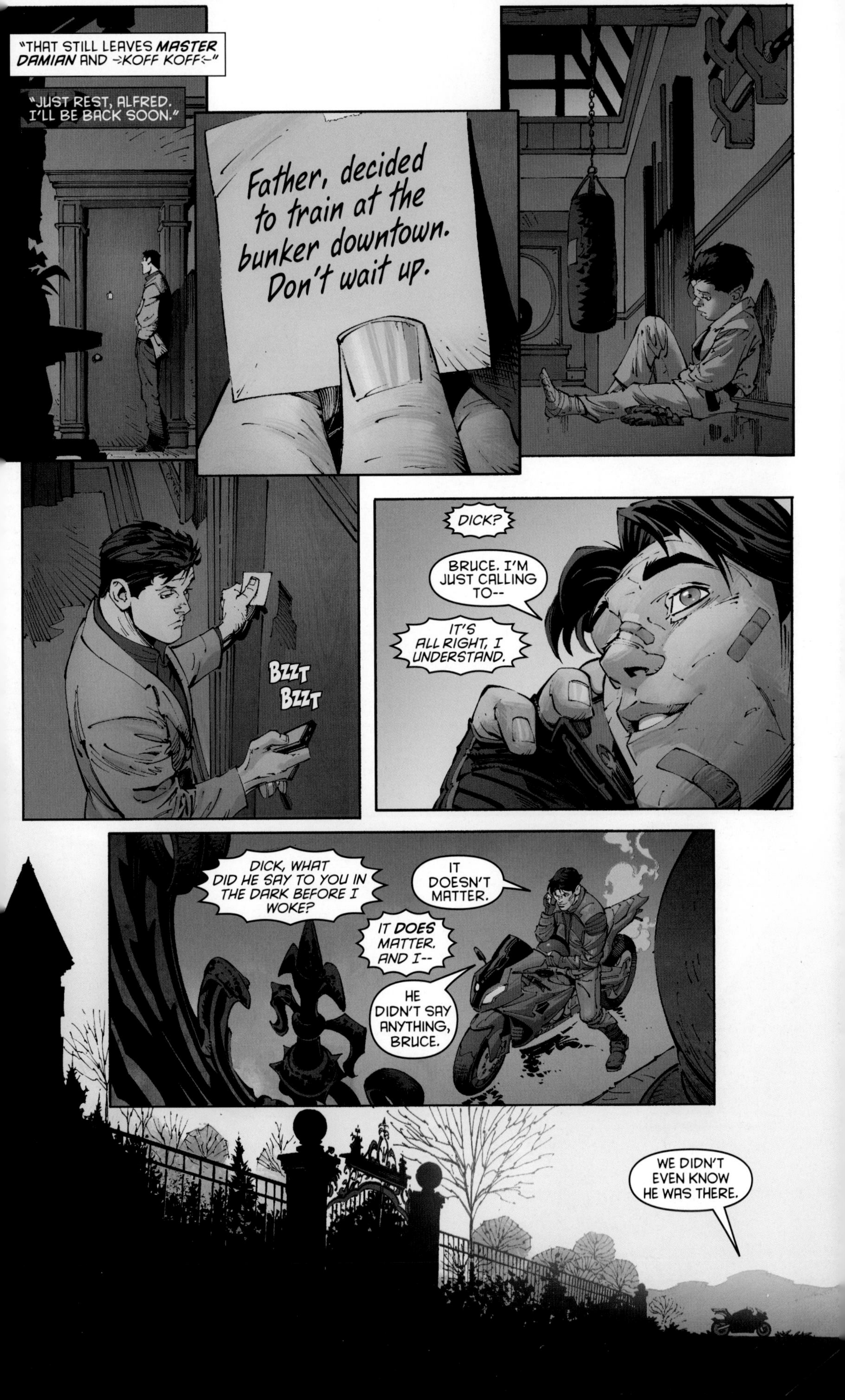
"THAT STILL LEAVES MASTER DAMIAN AND ⇢KOFF KOFF⇠"
"JUST REST, ALFRED. I'LL BE BACK SOON."
Father, decided to train at the bunker downtown. Don't wait up.
BZZT BZZT
DICK?
BRUCE. I'M JUST CALLING TO--
IT'S ALL RIGHT, I UNDERSTAND.
DICK, WHAT DID HE SAY TO YOU IN THE DARK BEFORE I WOKE?
IT DOESN'T MATTER.
IT DOES MATTER. AND I--
HE DIDN'T SAY ANYTHING, BRUCE.
WE DIDN'T EVEN KNOW HE WAS THERE.

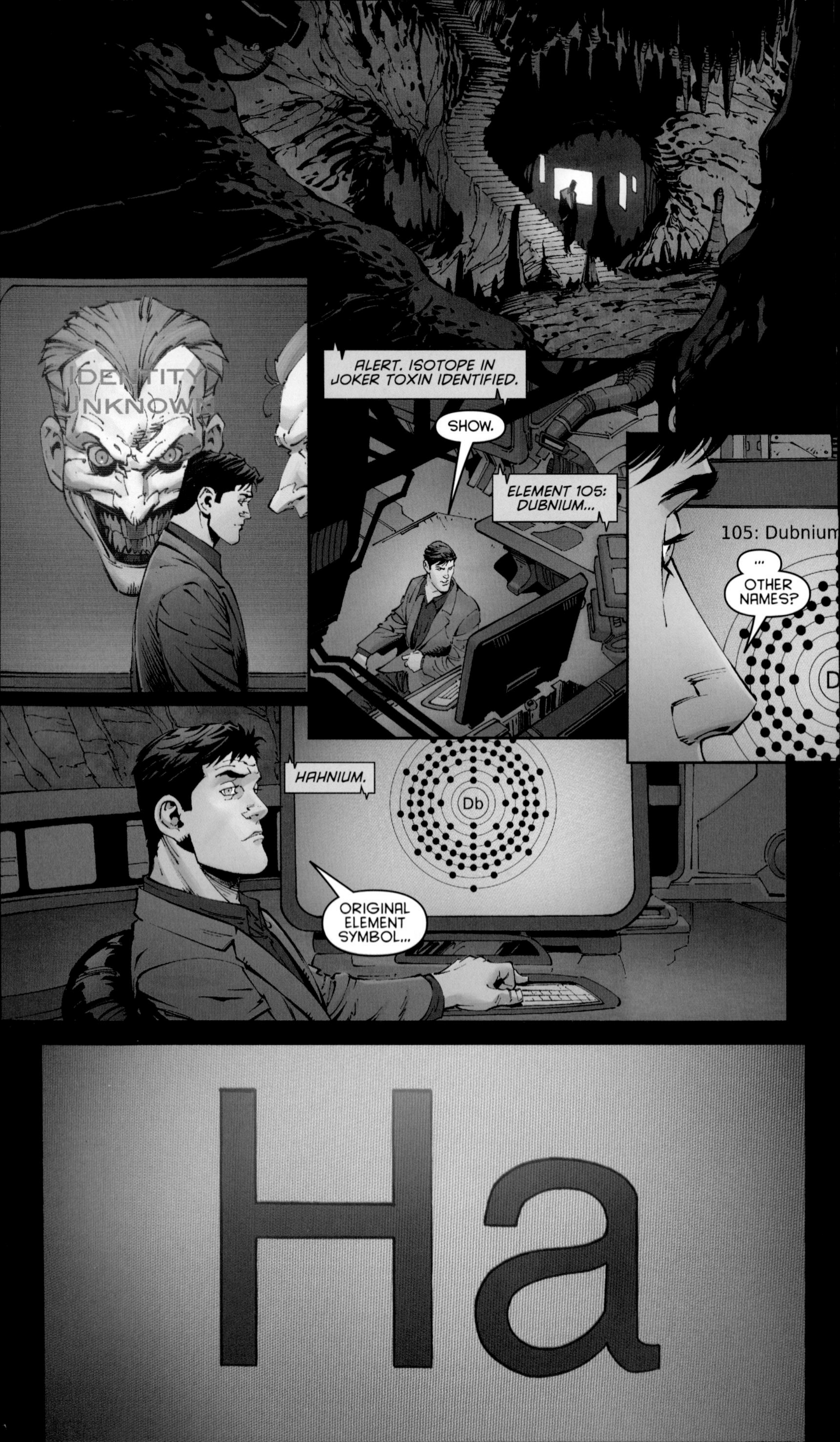
IDENTITY
ALERT. ISOTOPE IN JOKER TOXIN IDENTIFIED.
SHOW.
ELEMENT 105: DUBNIUM...
105: Dubnium
... OTHER NAMES?
HAHNIUM.
Db
ORIGINAL ELEMENT SYMBOL...
Ha

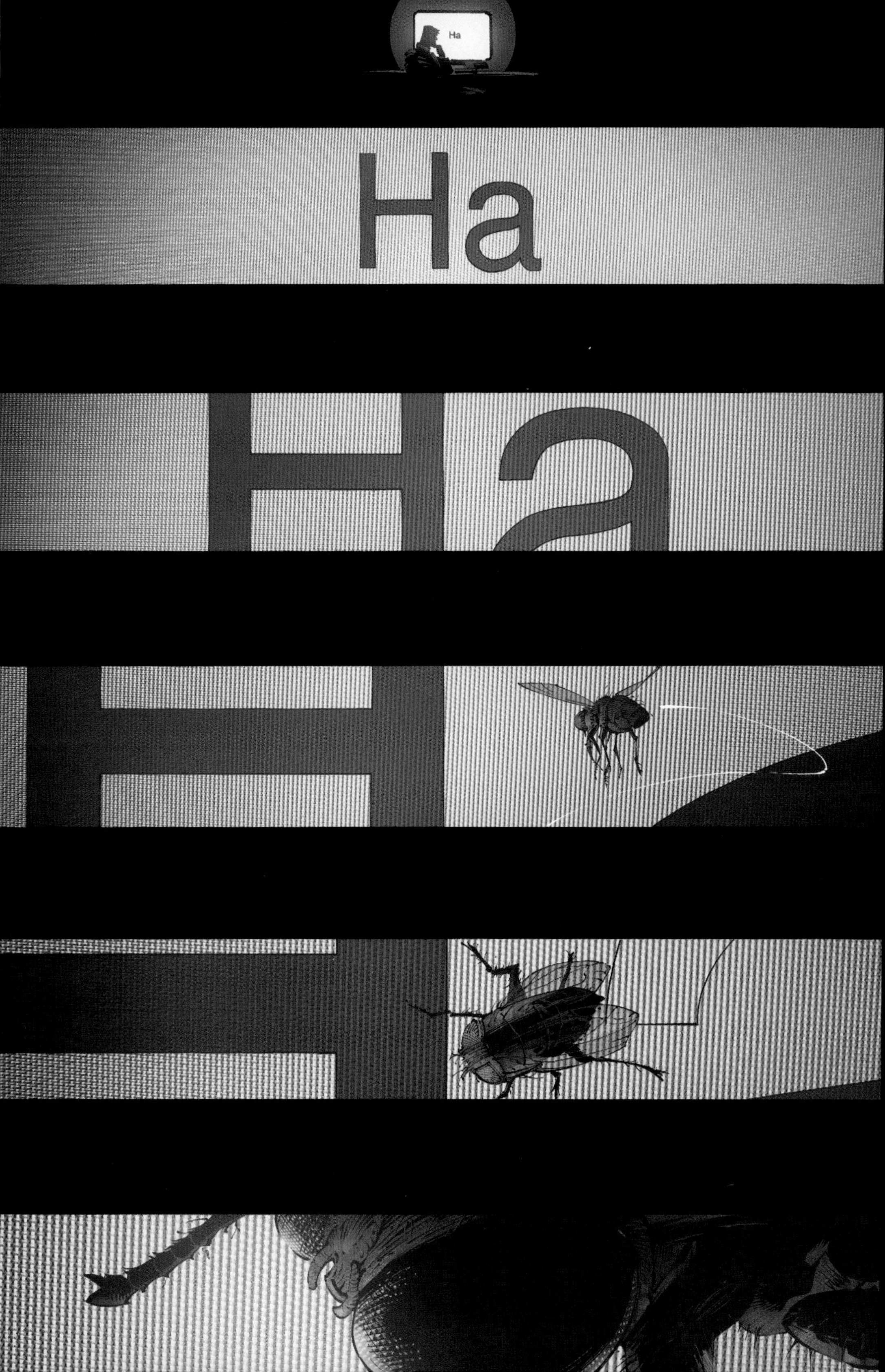
Ha
Ha

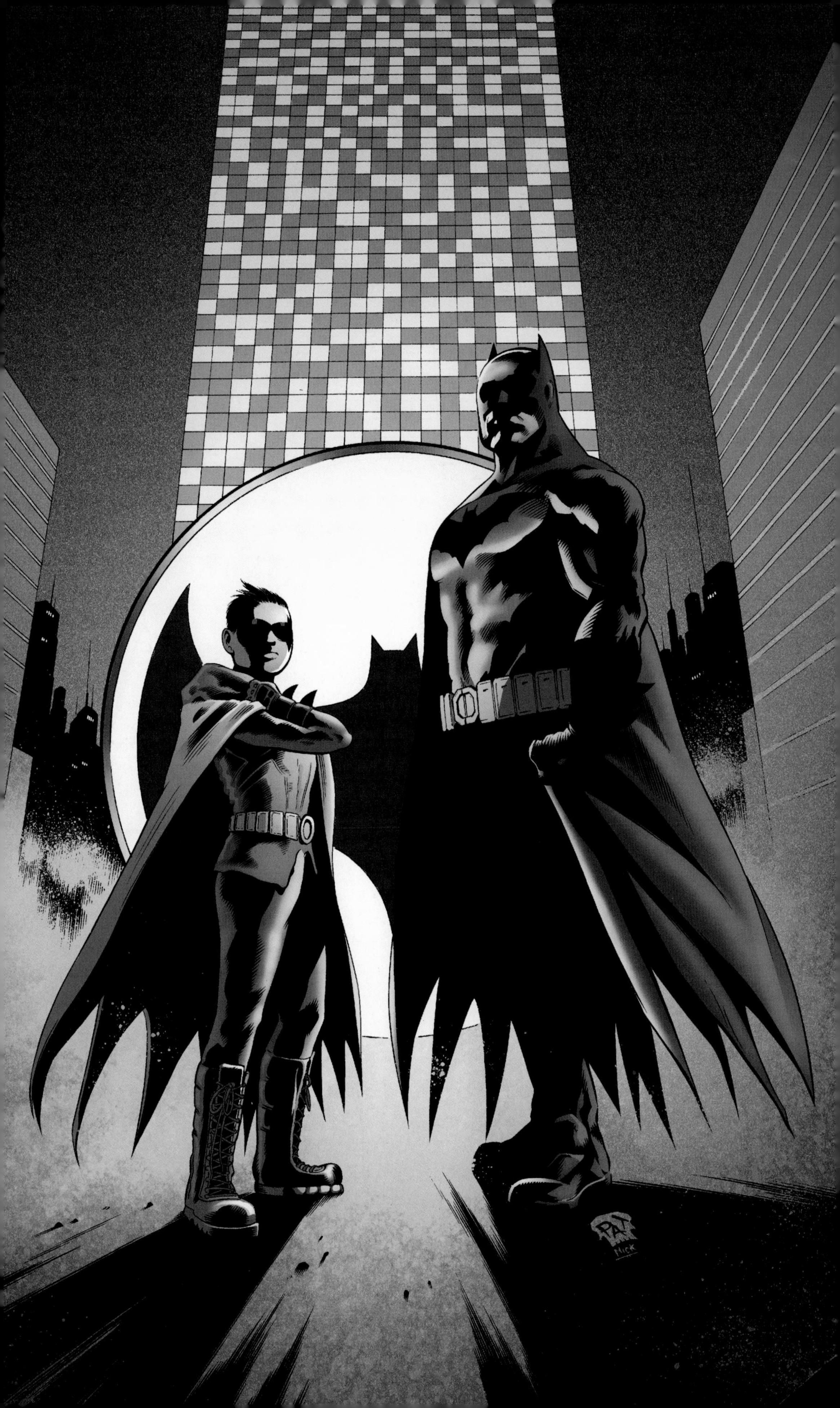

LIFE IS BUT A DREAM

PETER J. TOMASI writer **PATRICK GLEASON** penciller **MICK GRAY** inker cover art by **PATRICK GLEASON, MICK GRAY & JOHN KALISZ**

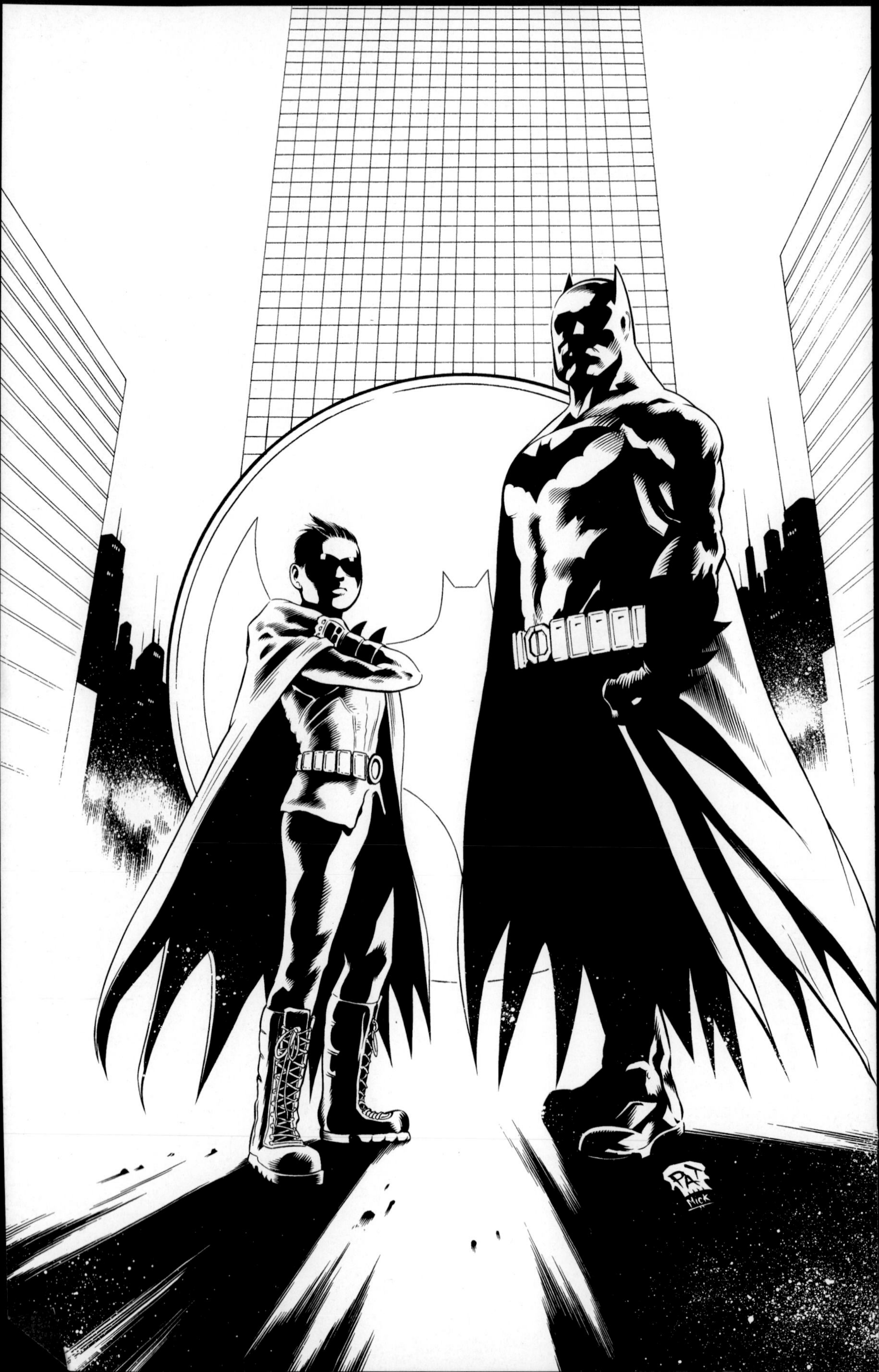

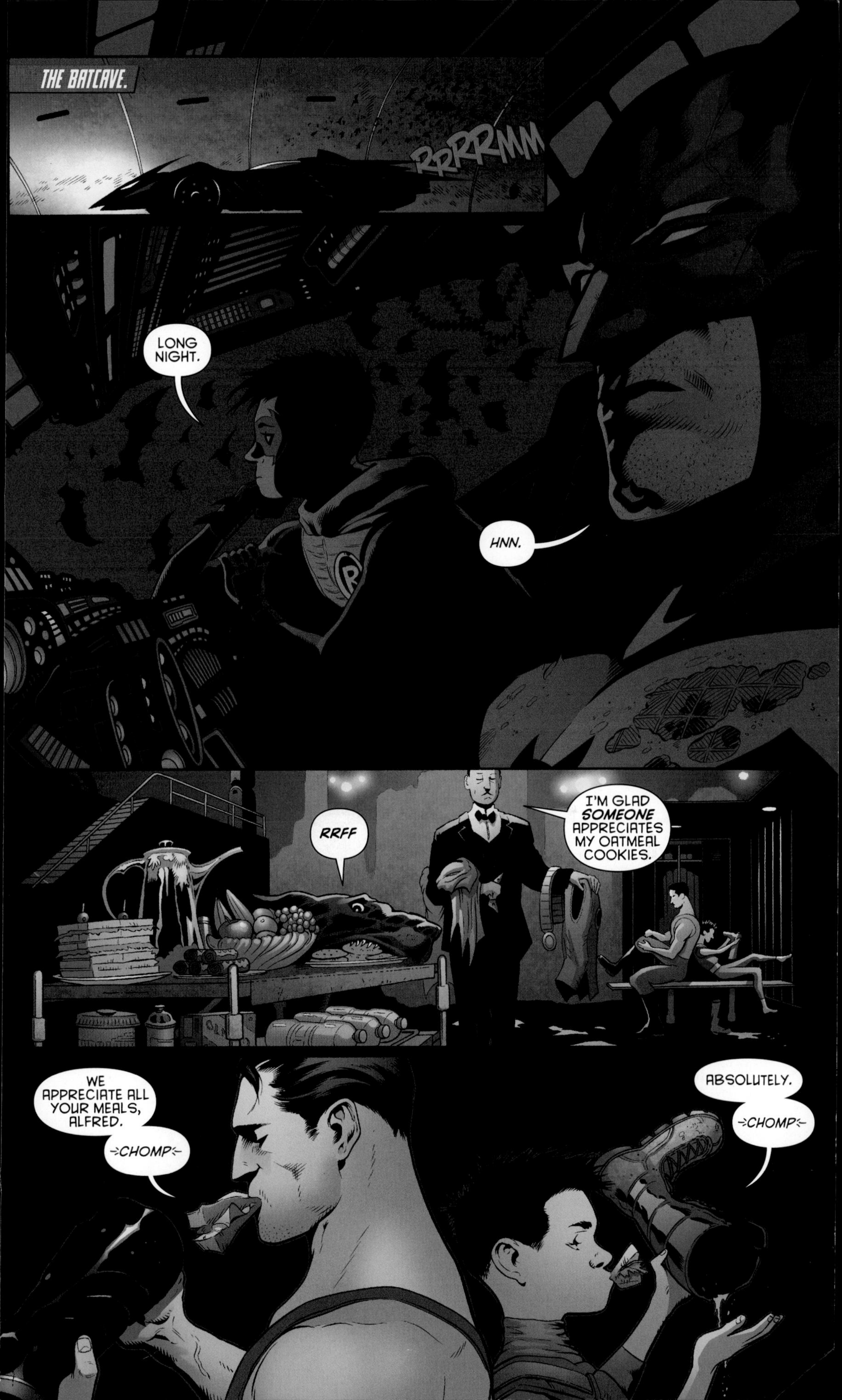
THE BATCAVE.
RRRRMM
LONG NIGHT.
HNN.
RRFF
I'M GLAD SOMEONE APPRECIATES MY OATMEAL COOKIES.
WE APPRECIATE ALL YOUR MEALS, ALFRED.
CHOMP
ABSOLUTELY.
CHOMP

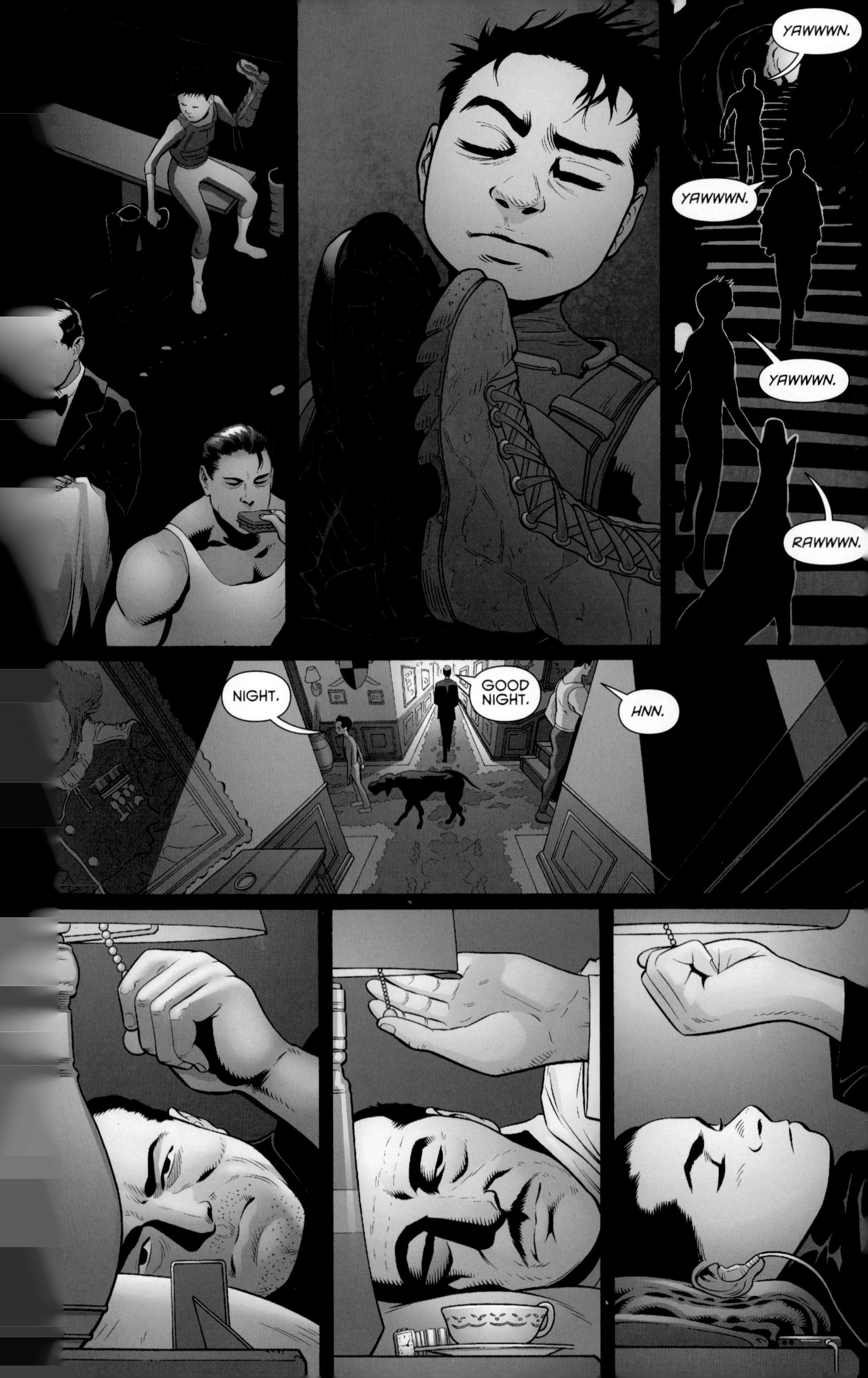
YAWWWN.
YAWWWN.
YAWWWN.
RAWWWN.
NIGHT.
GOOD NIGHT.
HNN.

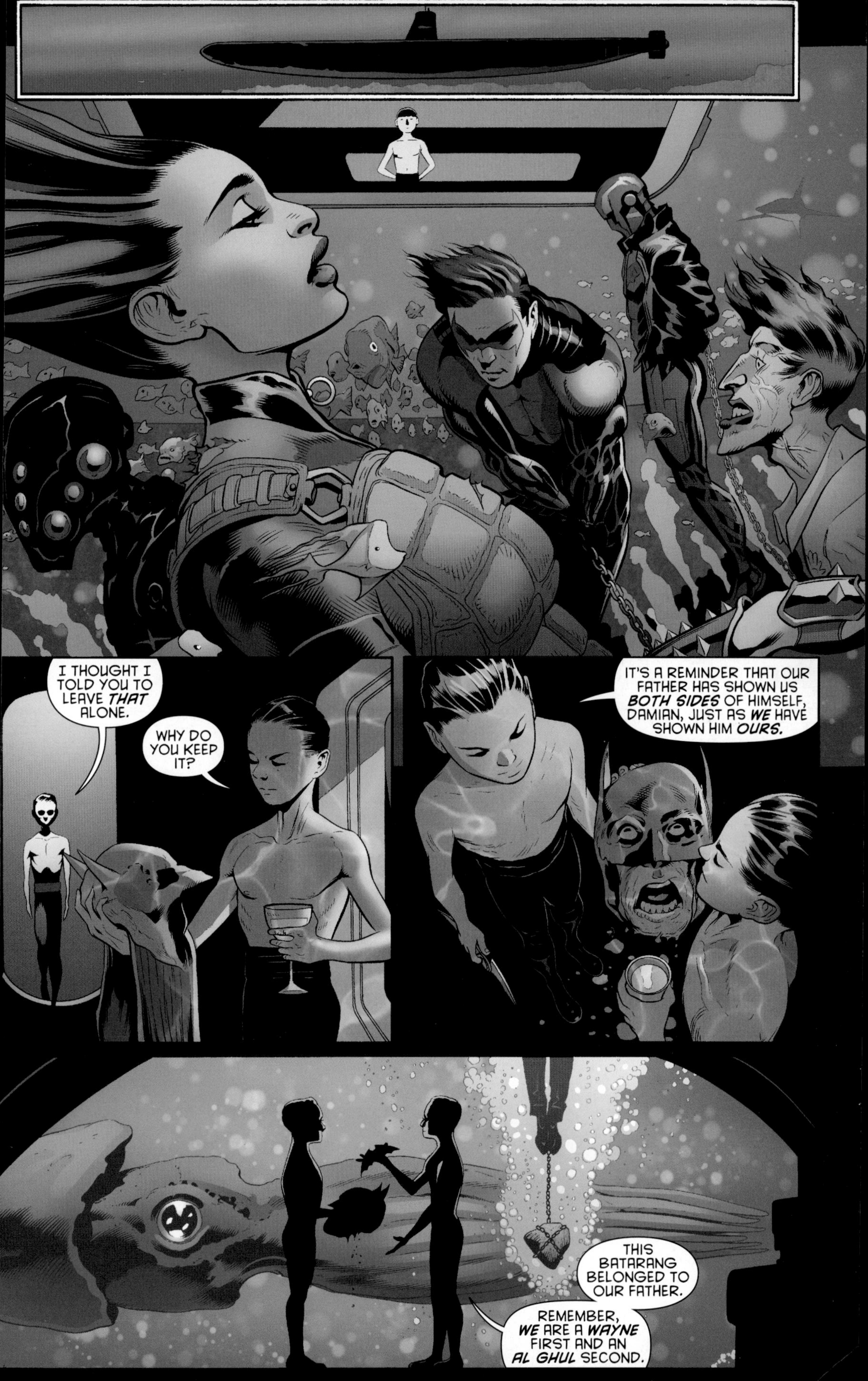
I THOUGHT I TOLD YOU TO LEAVE THAT ALONE.
WHY DO YOU KEEP IT?
IT'S A REMINDER THAT OUR FATHER HAS SHOWN US BOTH SIDES OF HIMSELF, DAMIAN, JUST AS WE HAVE SHOWN HIM OURS.
THIS BATARANG BELONGED TO OUR FATHER.
REMEMBER, WE ARE A WAYNE FIRST AND AN AL GHUL SECOND.

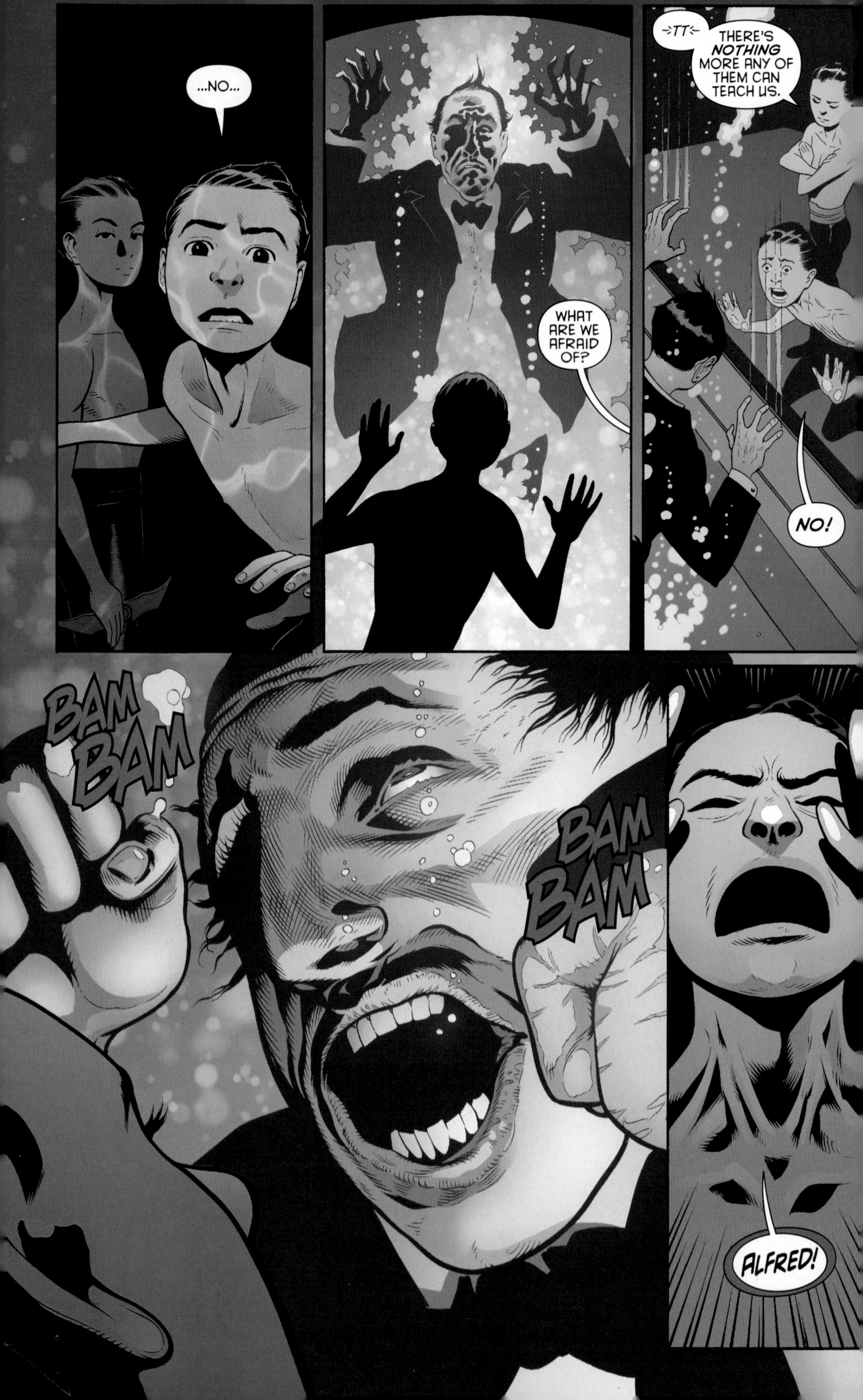
...NO...
WHAT ARE WE AFRAID OF?
-TT-
THERE'S NOTHING MORE ANY OF THEM CAN TEACH US.
NO!
BAM BAM
BAM BAM
ALFRED!

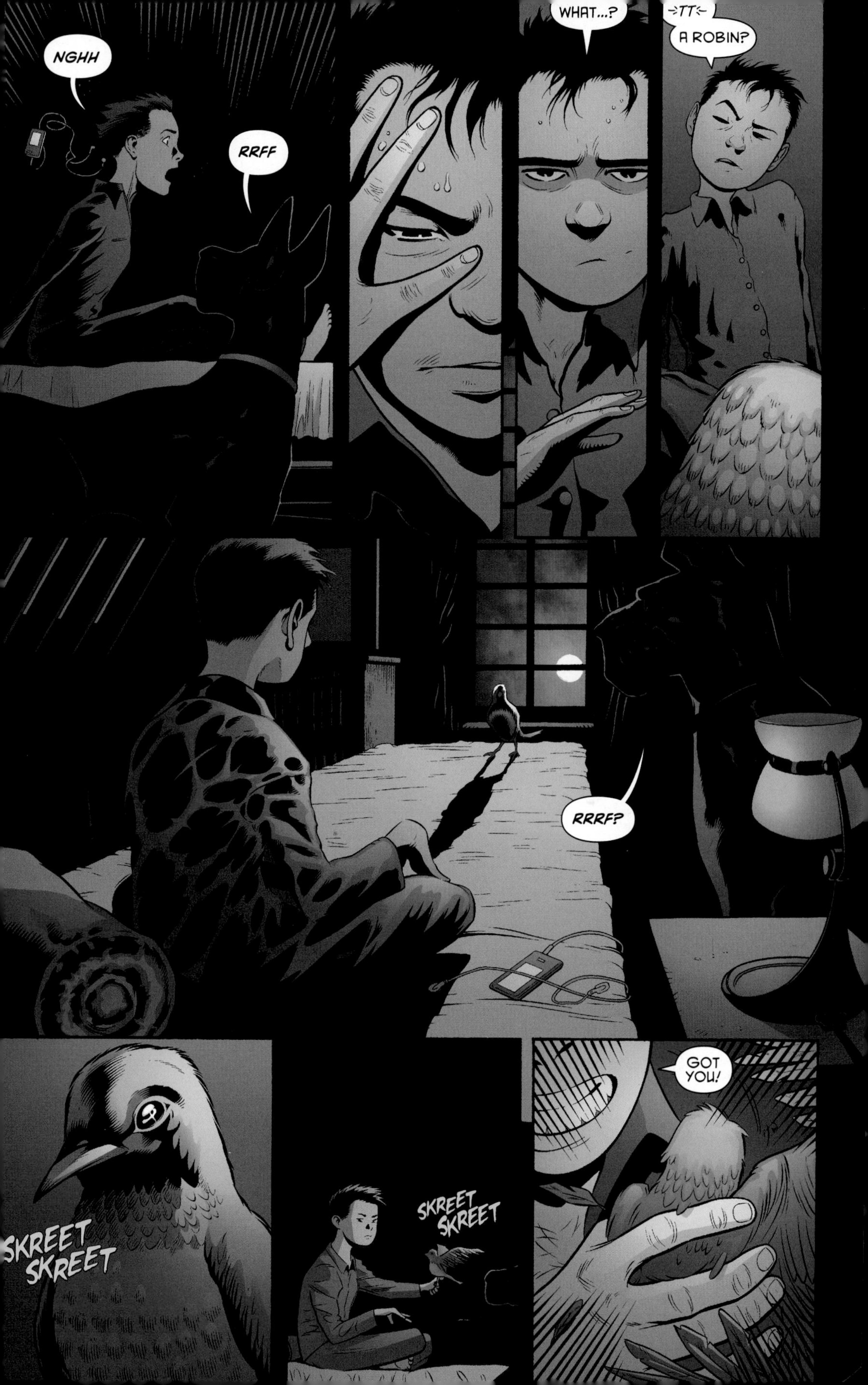
NGHH
RRFF
WHAT...?
TT
A ROBIN?
RRRF?
SKREET SKREET
SKREET SKREET
GOT YOU!

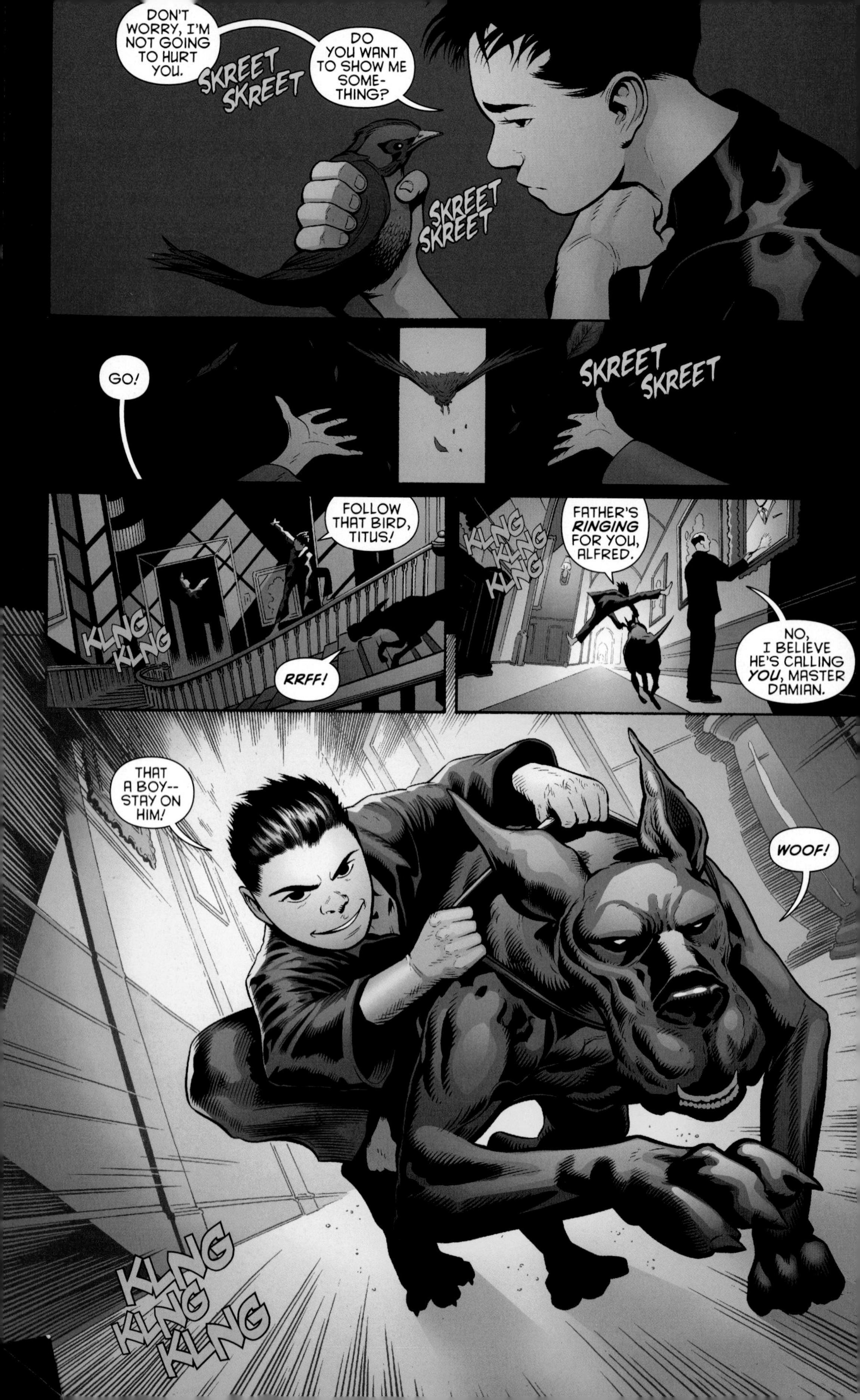
DON'T WORRY, I'M NOT GOING TO HURT YOU.
SKREET SKREET
DO YOU WANT TO SHOW ME SOME-THING?
SKREET SKREET
GO!
SKREET SKREET
FOLLOW THAT BIRD, TITUS!
KLNG KLNG
RRFF!
FATHER'S RINGING FOR YOU, ALFRED.
KLNG KLNG KLNG
NO, I BELIEVE HE'S CALLING YOU, MASTER DAMIAN.
THAT A BOY-- STAY ON HIM!
WOOF!
KLNG KLNG KLNG

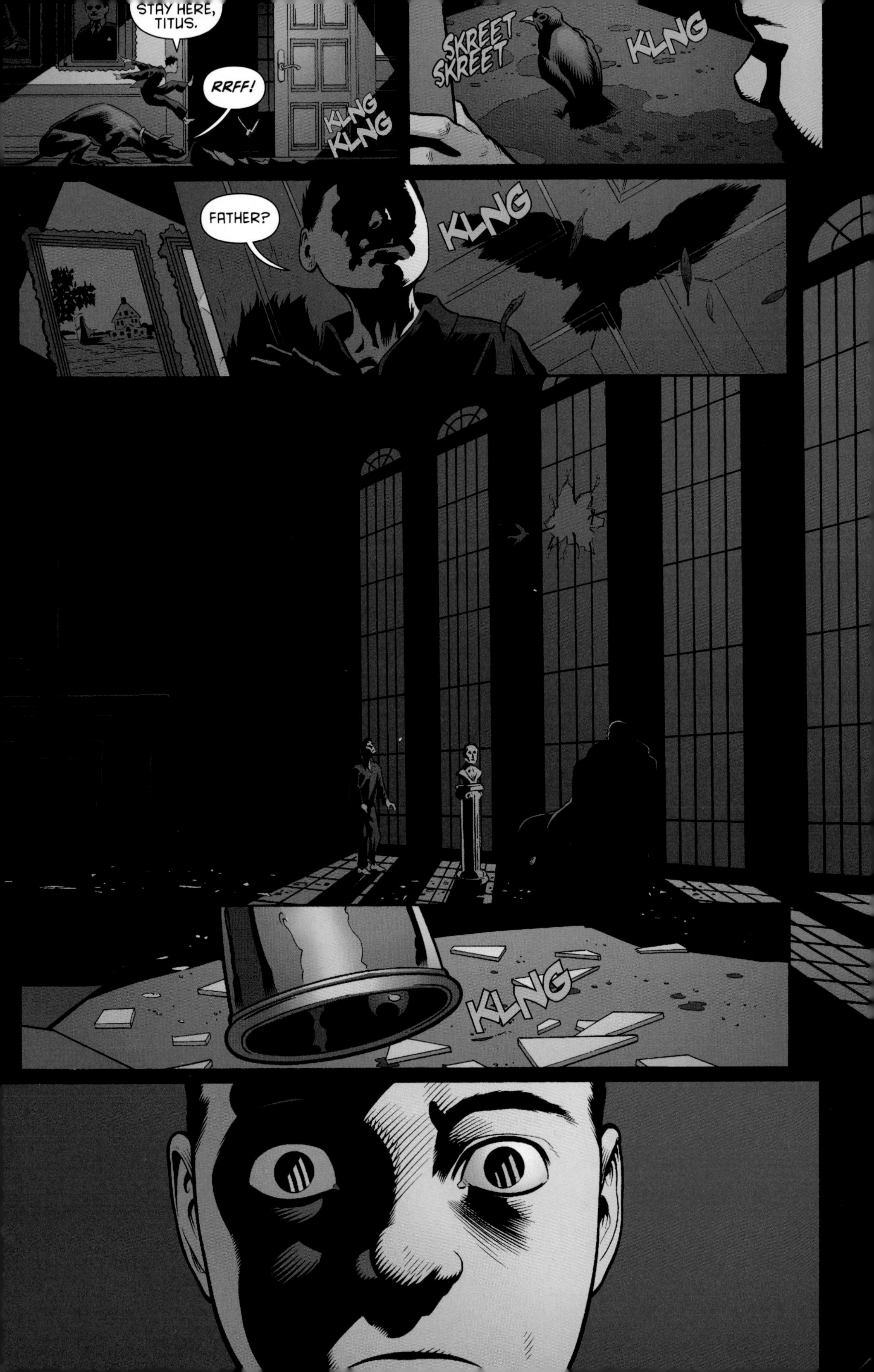
STAY HERE, TITUS.
RRFF!
KLNG KLNG
SKREET SKREET
KLNG
FATHER?
KLNG
KLNG

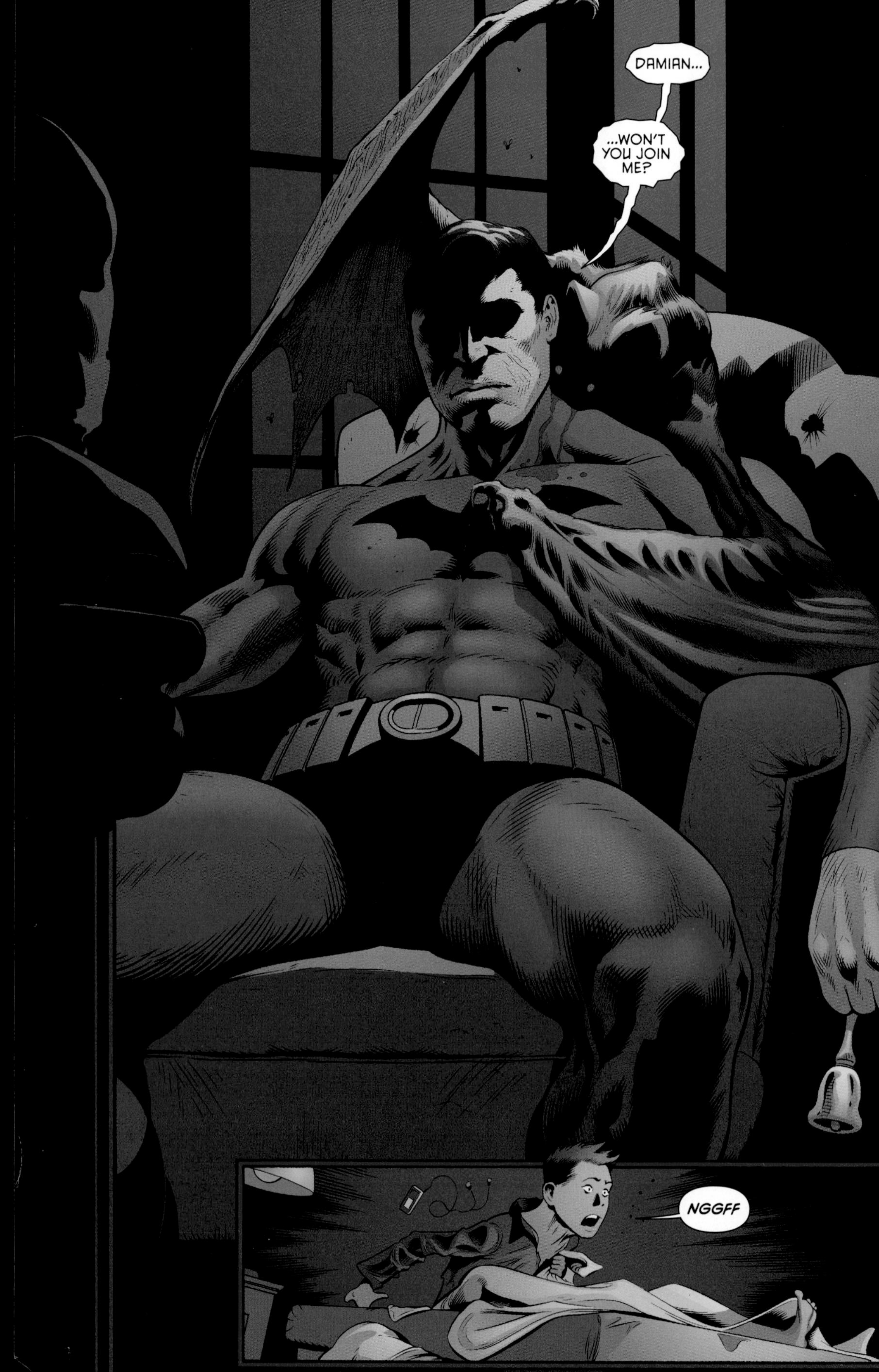
DAMIAN...
...WON'T YOU JOIN ME?
NGGFF

WHAT DO YOU THINK, ALFRED?

QUITE BEAUTIFUL, MASTER THOMAS. WOULD YOU LIKE ME TO WRAP IT?

ARE YOU QUESTIONING MY WRAPPING SKILLS?

ACTUALLY, THERE'S NO QUESTION THAT FOR SUCH A TALENTED SURGEON, YOU HAVE NO GIFT-WRAPPING ABILITY WHATSOEVER.

THEN SAVE ME FROM MYSELF, MISTER PENNYWORTH.

SAVE YOU, I SHALL, SIR.

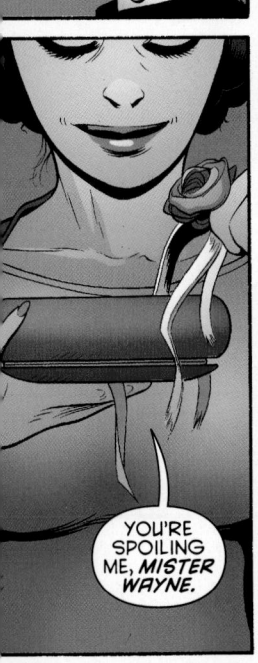

YOU'RE SPOILING ME, MISTER WAYNE.

I BELIEVE THAT'S MY SACRED DUTY FOR THE NEXT FIFTY YEARS OR SO, MRS. WAYNE.

WE LEAVING YET, DAD?

AND I THINK WE NEED A LITTLE HELPER TO PUT THESE ON.

...TOUGH TO FIT INTO THE LOOP...

GOOD JOB, BRUCE. YOUR HANDS ARE STEADIER THAN MINE.

NOTHING LIKE A NIGHT ON THE TOWN WITH MY HANDSOME BOYS.

MMM?

KRAK KRAK

KRAK KRAK

KRAK

MASTER BRUCE... DAMIAN, DO YOU NEED SOME ASSISTANCE?

KRAK KRAK KRAK

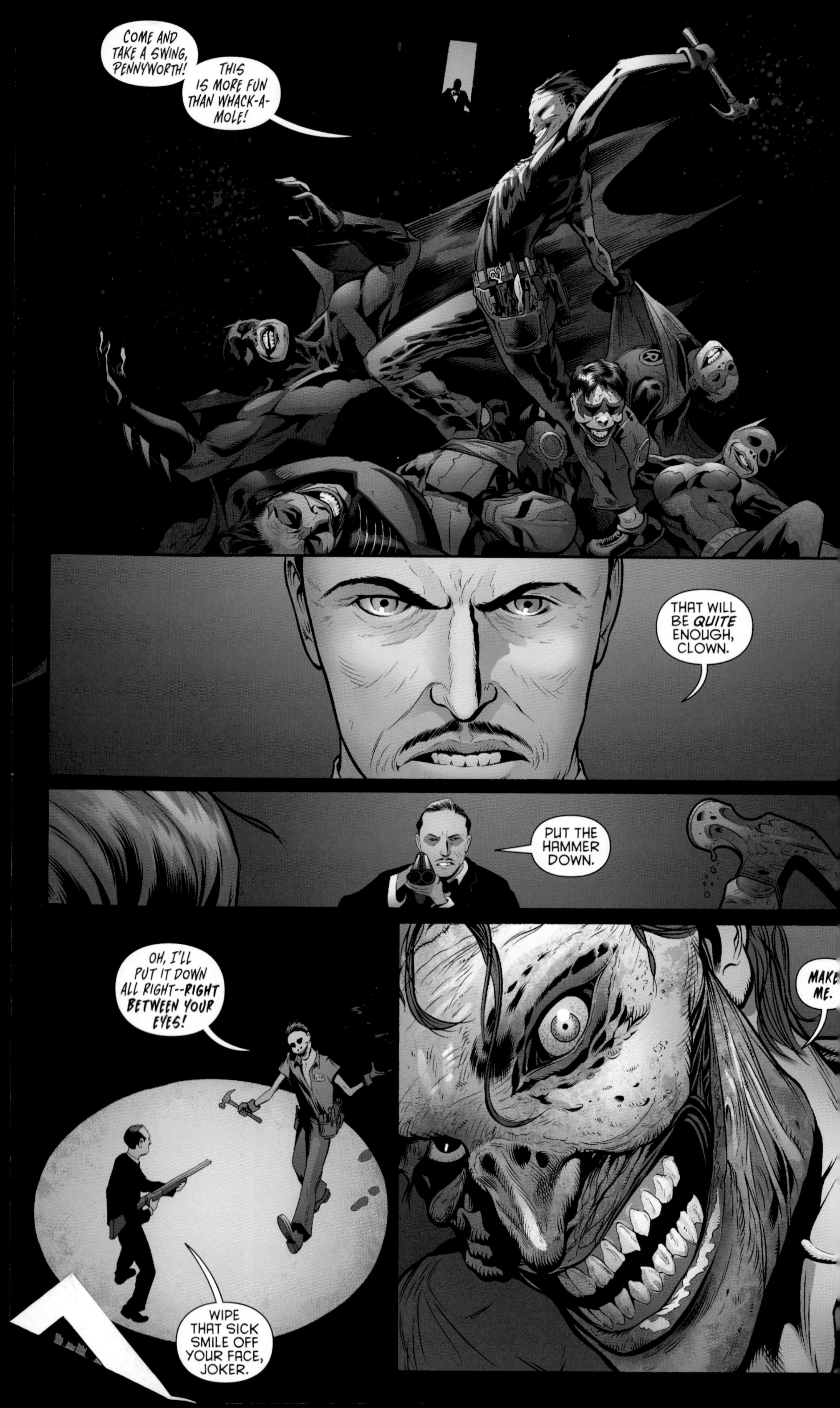
COME AND TAKE A SWING, PENNYWORTH!
THIS IS MORE FUN THAN WHACK-A-MOLE!
THAT WILL BE QUITE ENOUGH, CLOWN.
PUT THE HAMMER DOWN.
OH, I'LL PUT IT DOWN ALL RIGHT--RIGHT BETWEEN YOUR EYES!
WIPE THAT SICK SMILE OFF YOUR FACE, JOKER.
MAKE ME.

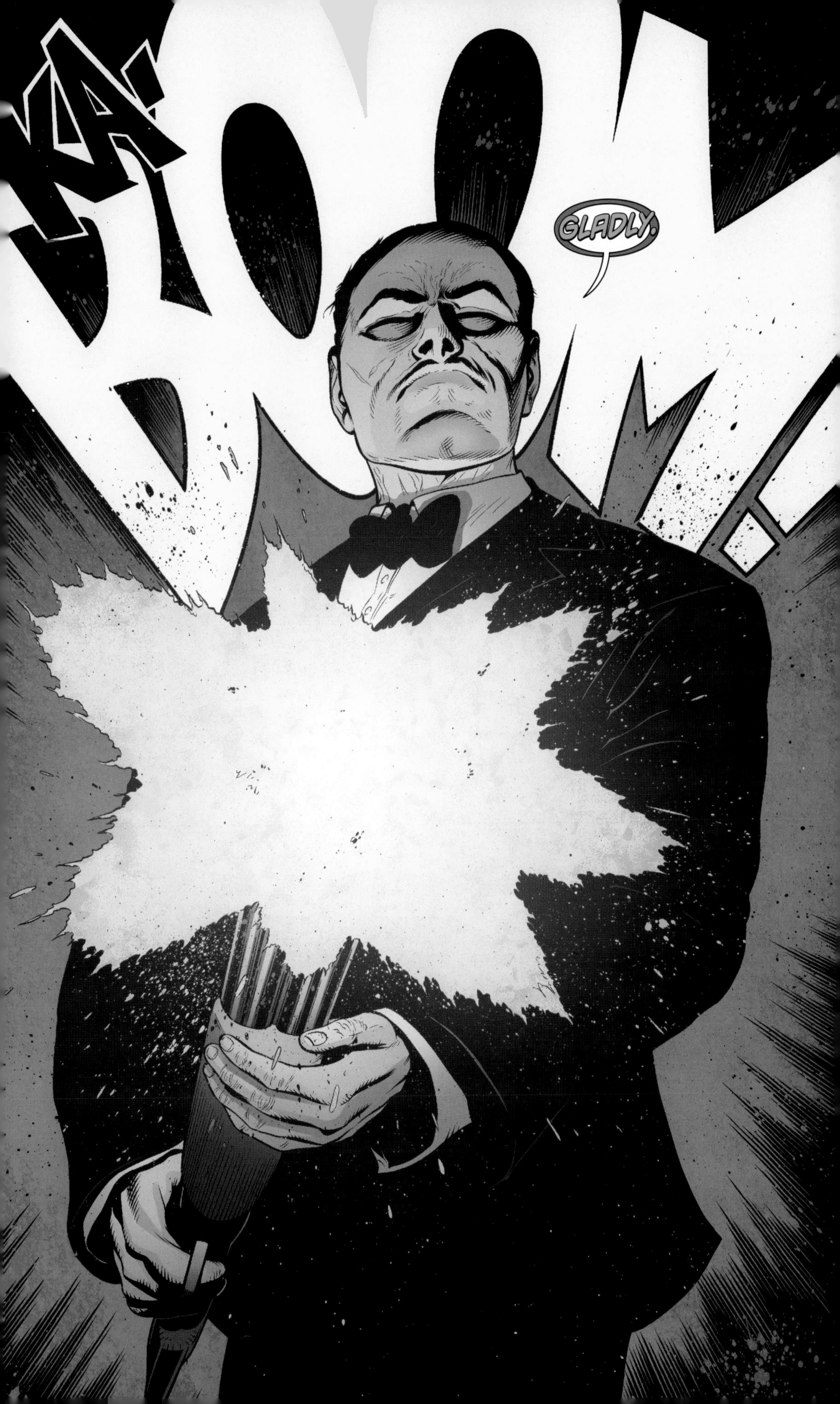
KA-BOOM!
GLADLY.

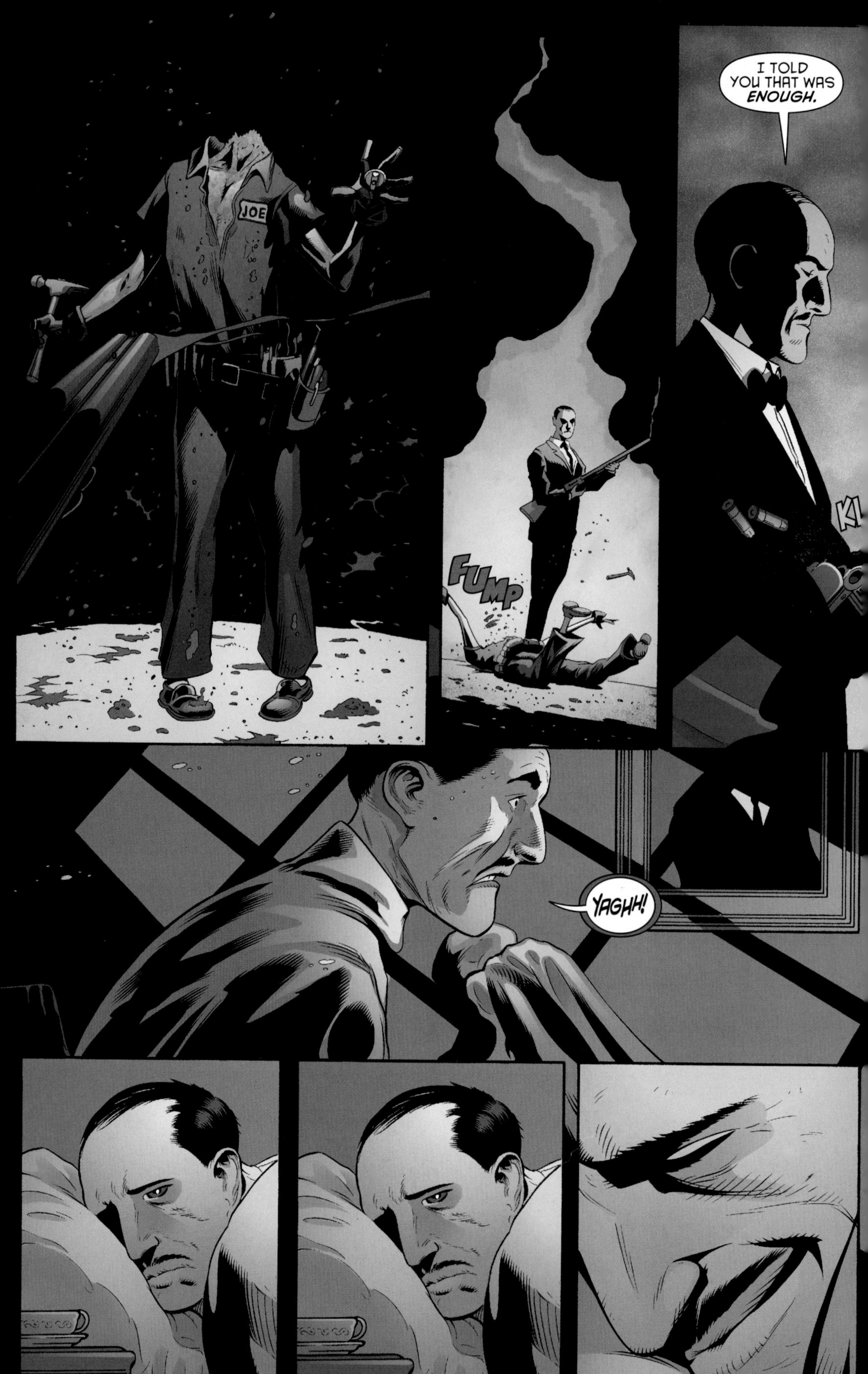
JOE
FUMP
I TOLD YOU THAT WAS *ENOUGH.*
KI
YAGHH!

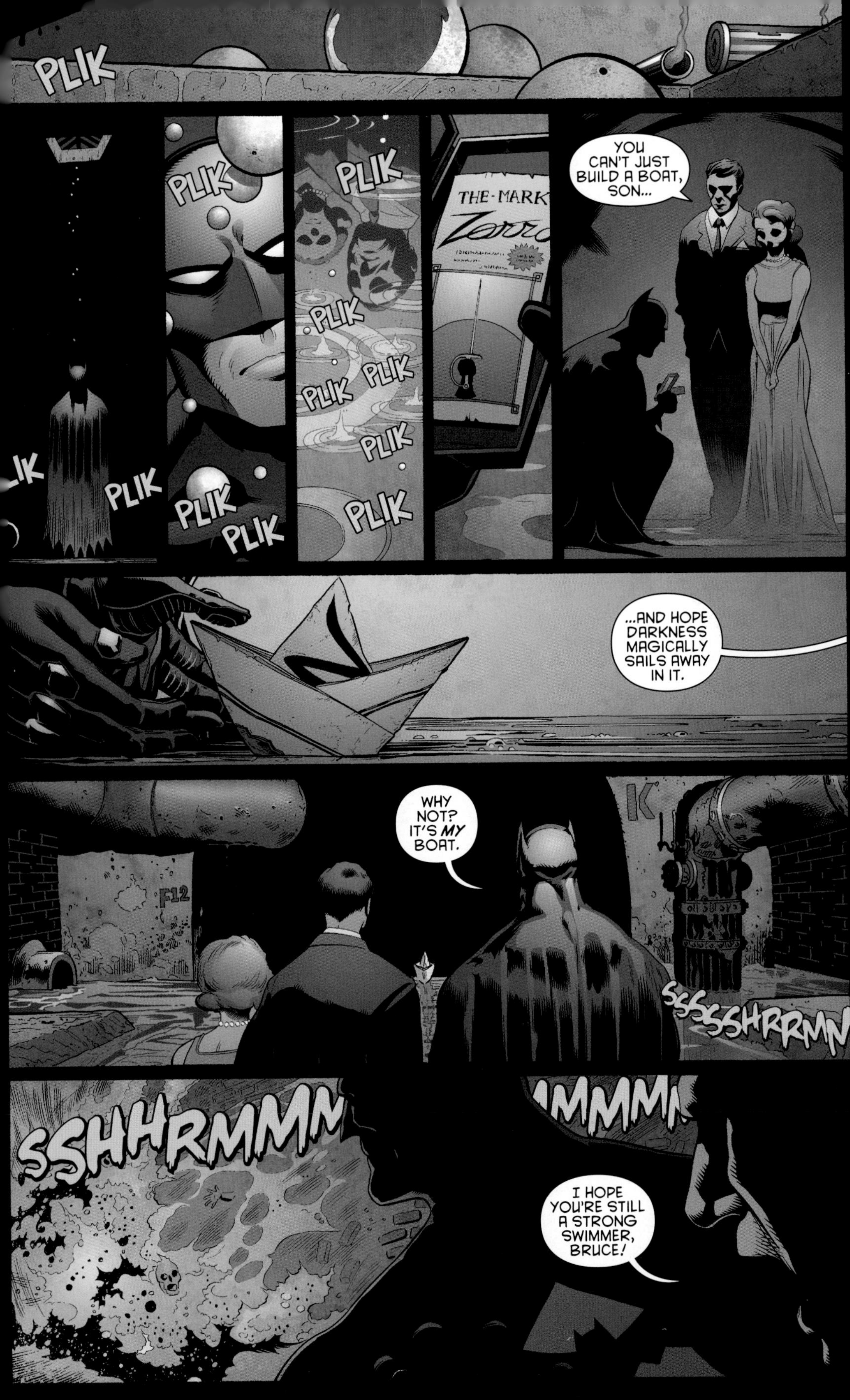
PLIK
PLIK
PLIK
PLIK
PLIK
PLIK
PLIK
PLIK
PLIK
PLIK
PLIK
THE-MARK
Zorro
YOU CAN'T JUST BUILD A BOAT, SON...
...AND HOPE DARKNESS MAGICALLY SAILS AWAY IN IT.
WHY NOT? IT'S *MY* BOAT.
F12
SSSSSHRRMN
SSHHRMMM
MMMM
I HOPE YOU'RE STILL A STRONG SWIMMER, BRUCE!

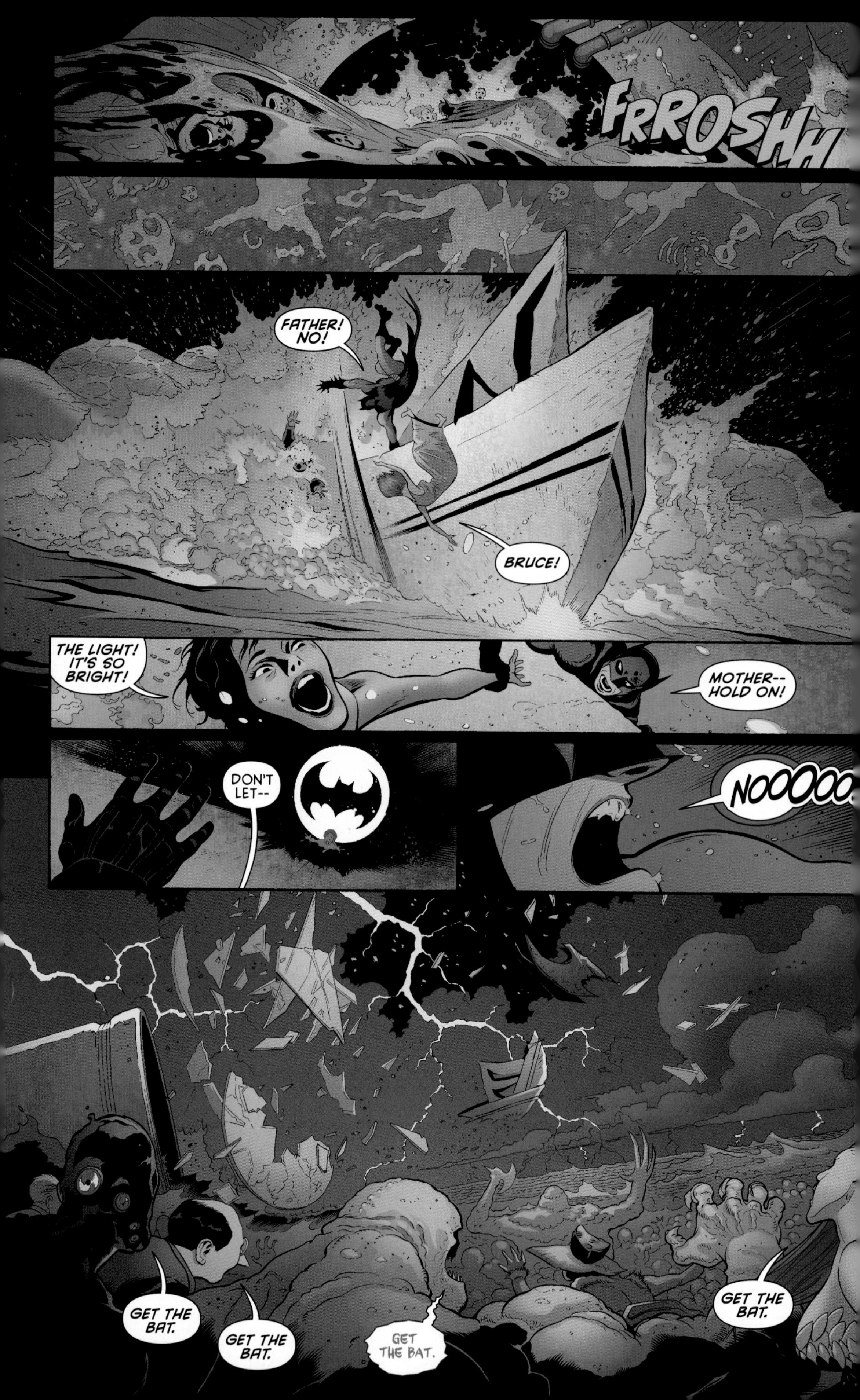
FRROSHH
FATHER! NO!
BRUCE!
THE LIGHT! IT'S SO BRIGHT!
MOTHER-- HOLD ON!
DON'T LET--
NOOOOO
GET THE BAT.
GET THE BAT.
GET THE BAT.
GET THE BAT.

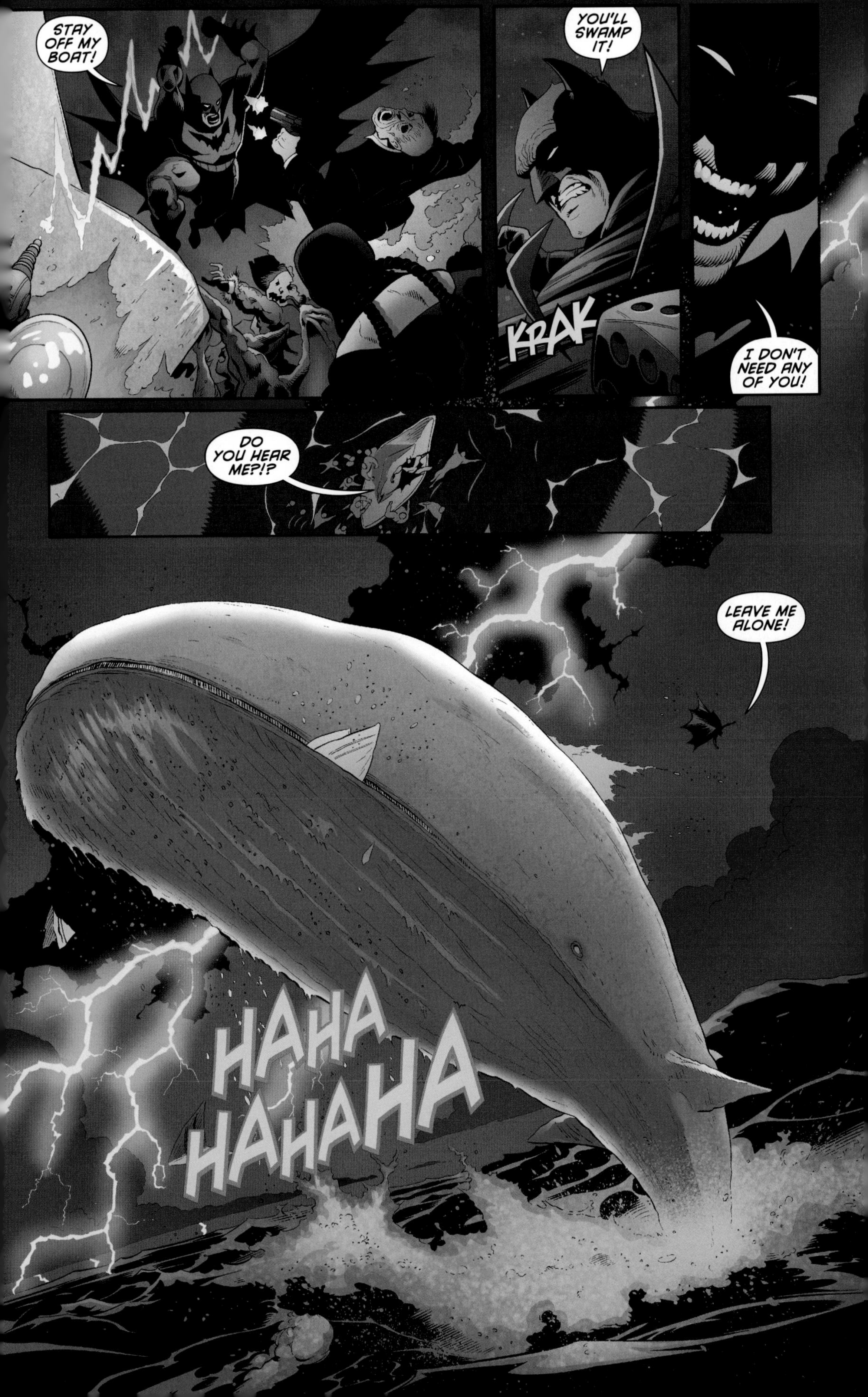
STAY OFF MY BOAT!
YOU'LL SWAMP IT!
KRAK
I DON'T NEED ANY OF YOU!
DO YOU HEAR ME?!?
LEAVE ME ALONE!
HAHA HAHAHA

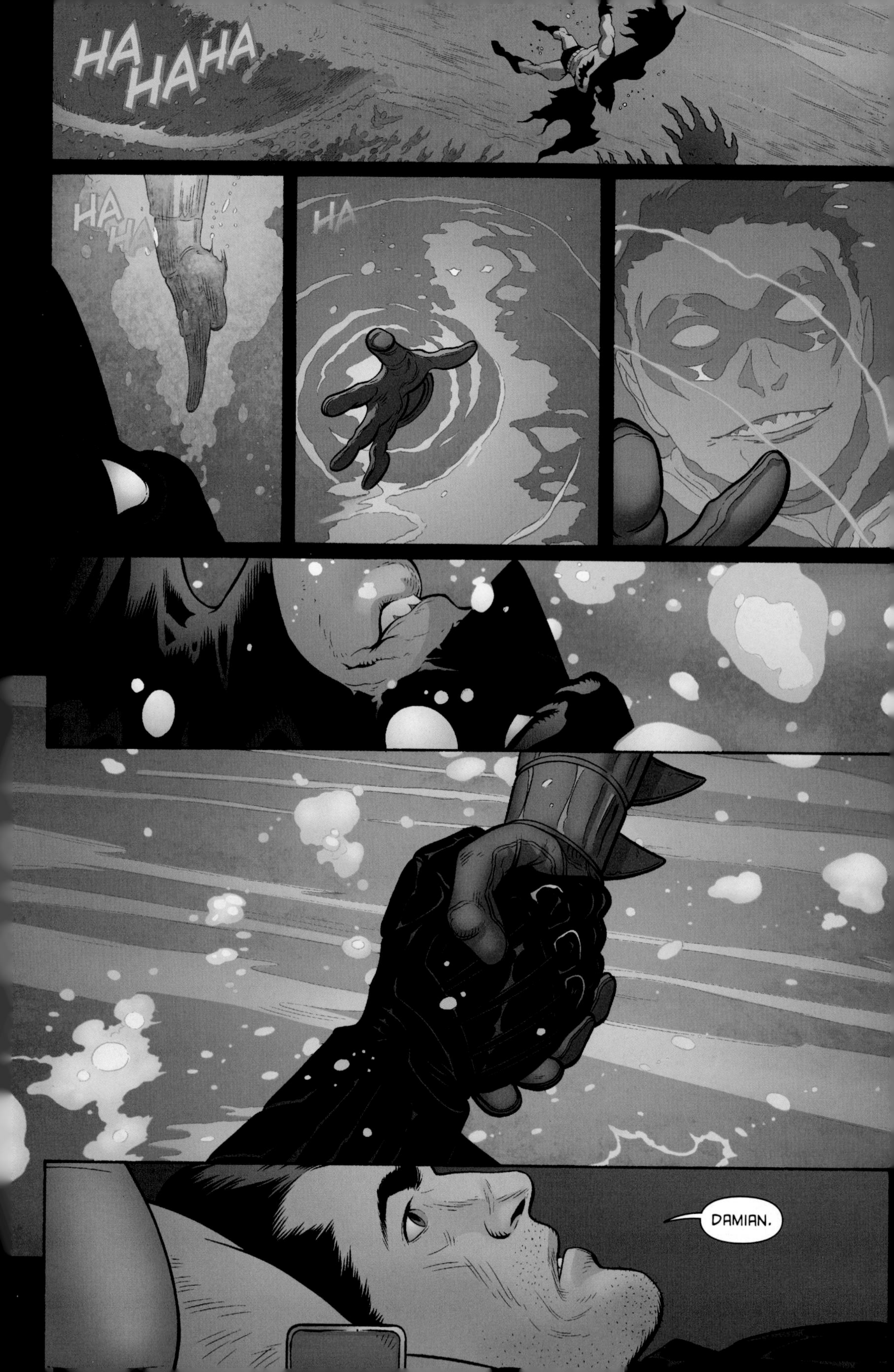
HA HAHA
HA HA
HA
DAMIAN.

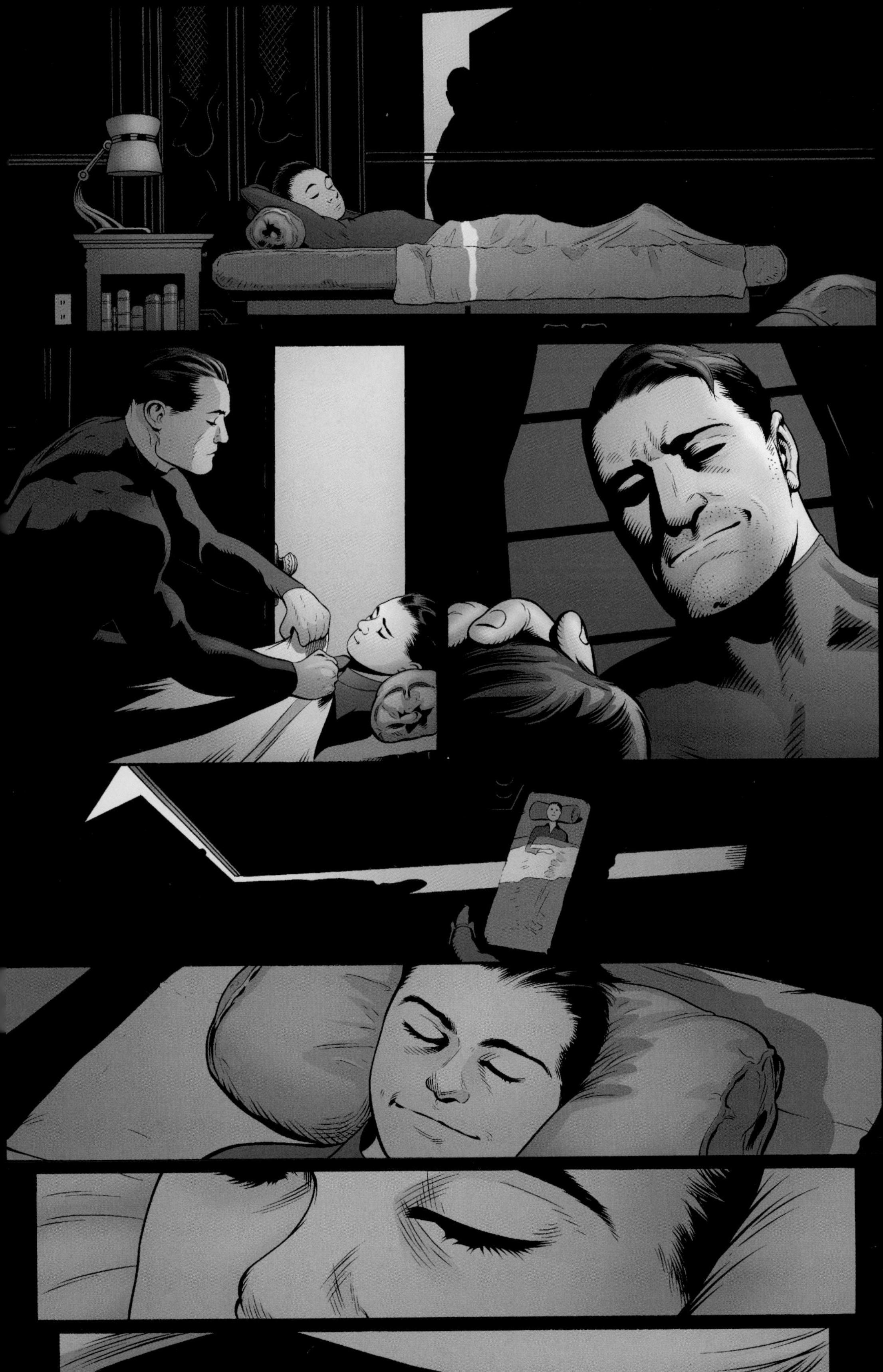

ANOTHER HARD DAY'S NIGHT OVER AND DONE.

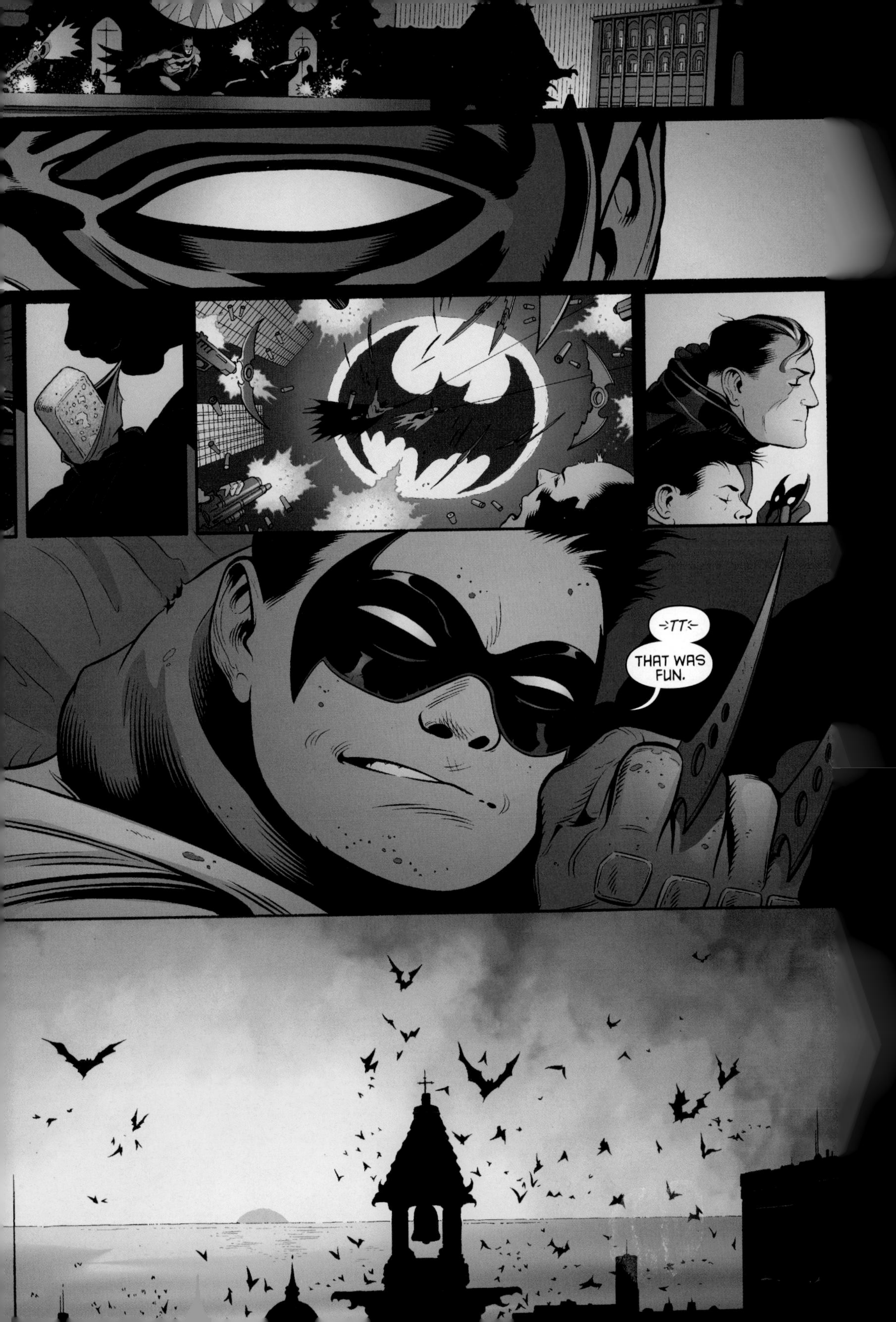
TT
THAT WAS FUN.

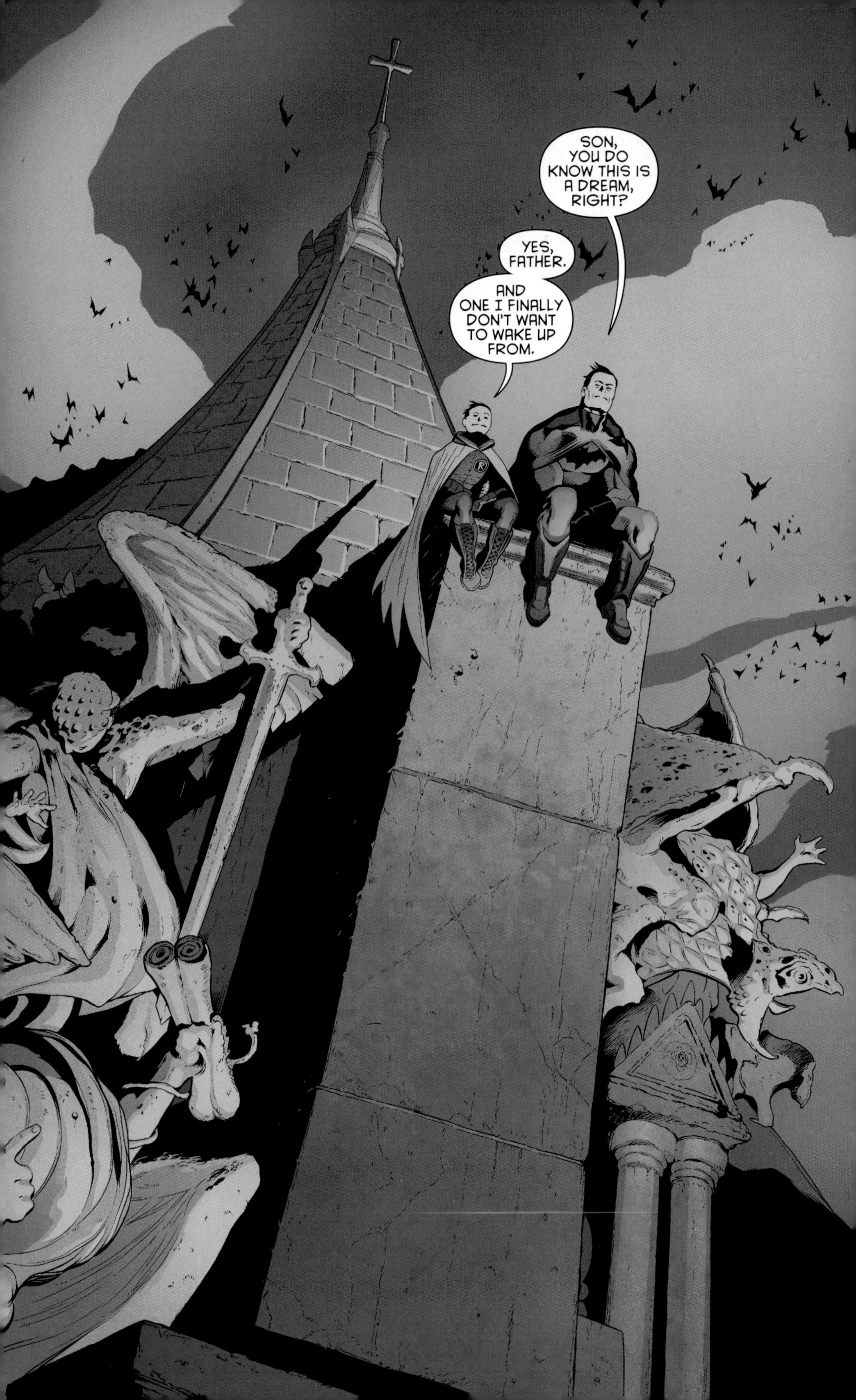
SON, YOU DO KNOW THIS IS A DREAM, RIGHT?
YES, FATHER.
AND ONE I FINALLY DON'T WANT TO WAKE UP FROM.

Unused Cover to BATMAN AND ROBIN #15 by Patrick Gleason

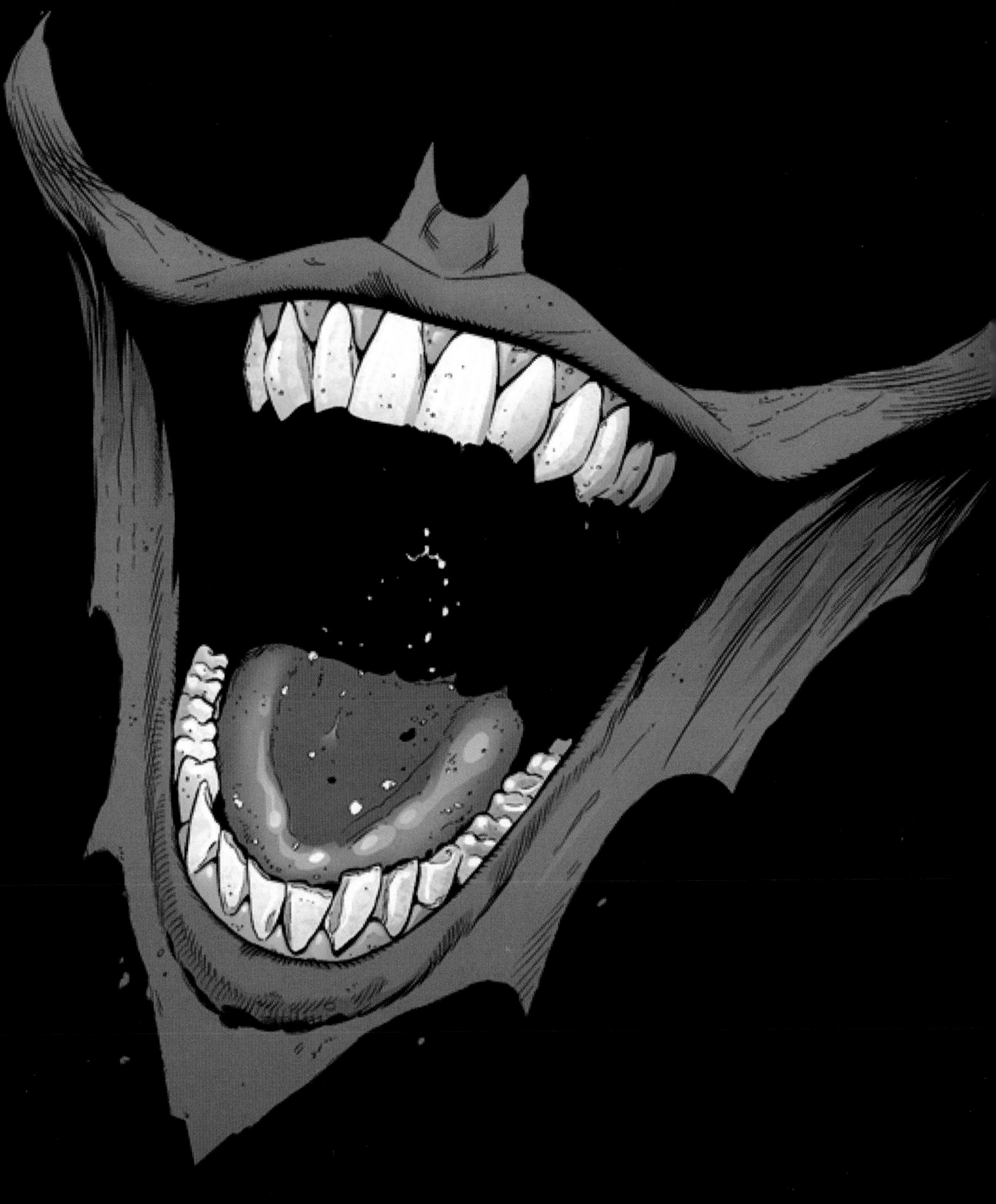

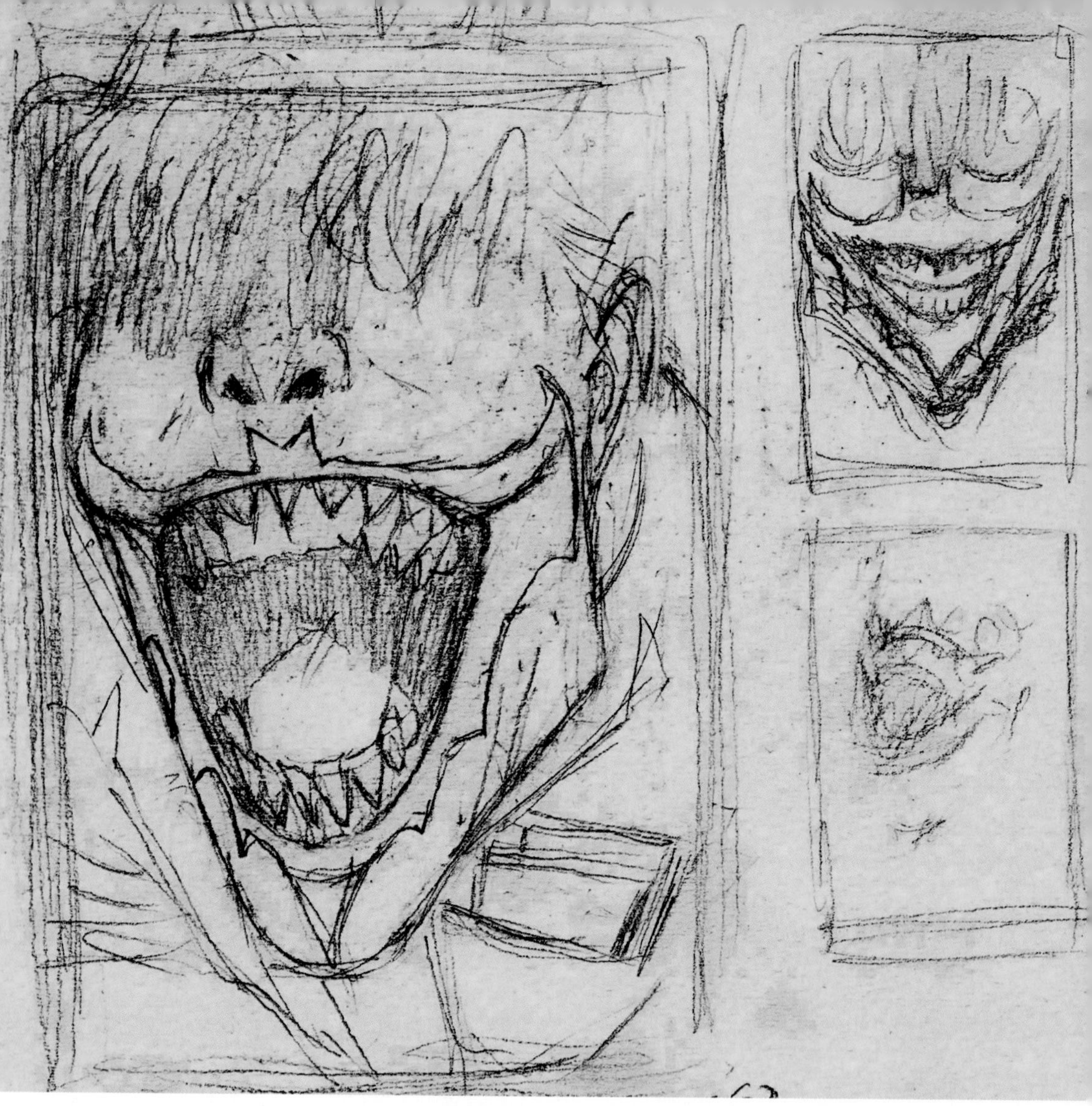
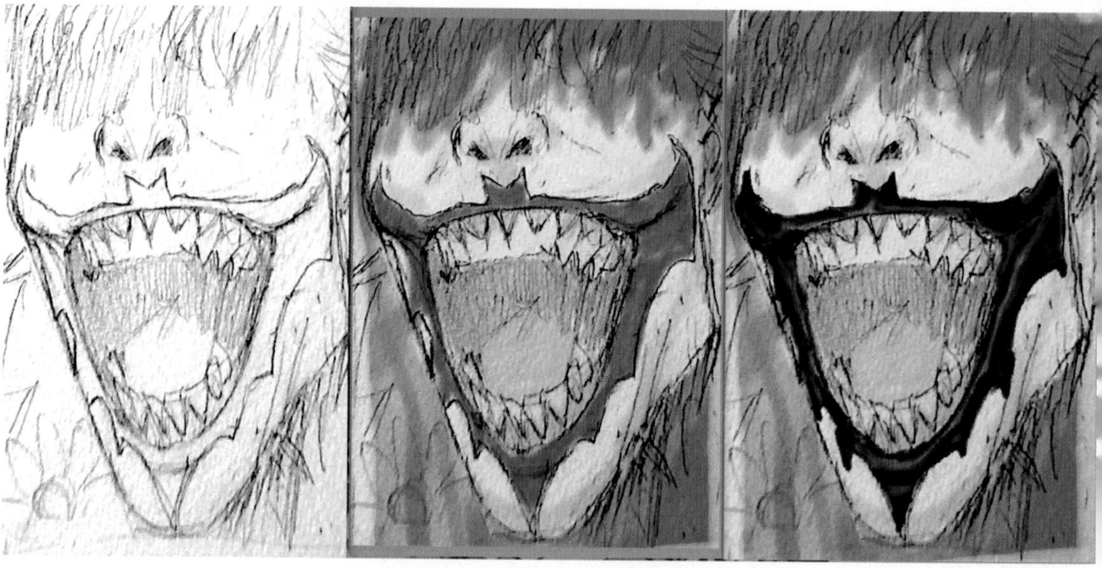

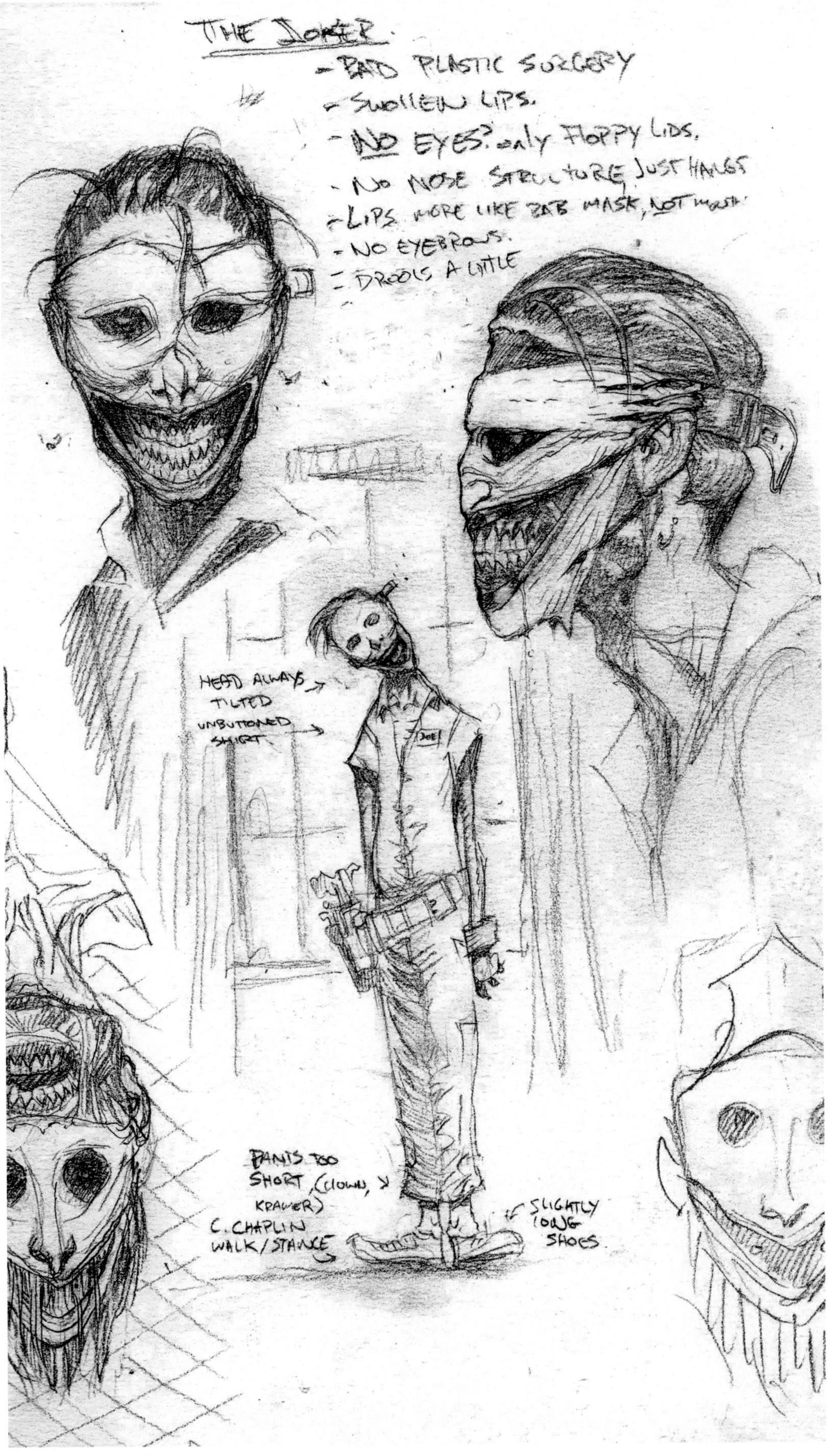
THE JOKER
- BAD PLASTIC SURGERY
- SWOLLEN LIPS.
- NO EYES? only FLOPPY LIDS.
- NO NOSE STRUCTURE JUST HANGS
- LIPS MORE LIKE BAD MASK, NOT MOUTH
- NO EYEBROWS.
- DROOLS A LITTLE
HEAD ALWAYS TILTED
UNBUTTONED SHIRT
JOE
PANTS TOO SHORT (CLOWN, & KRAMER)
C. CHAPLIN WALK/STANCE
SLIGHTLY LONG SHOES

PENCILS BY PATRICK GLEASON INKS BY MICK GRAY

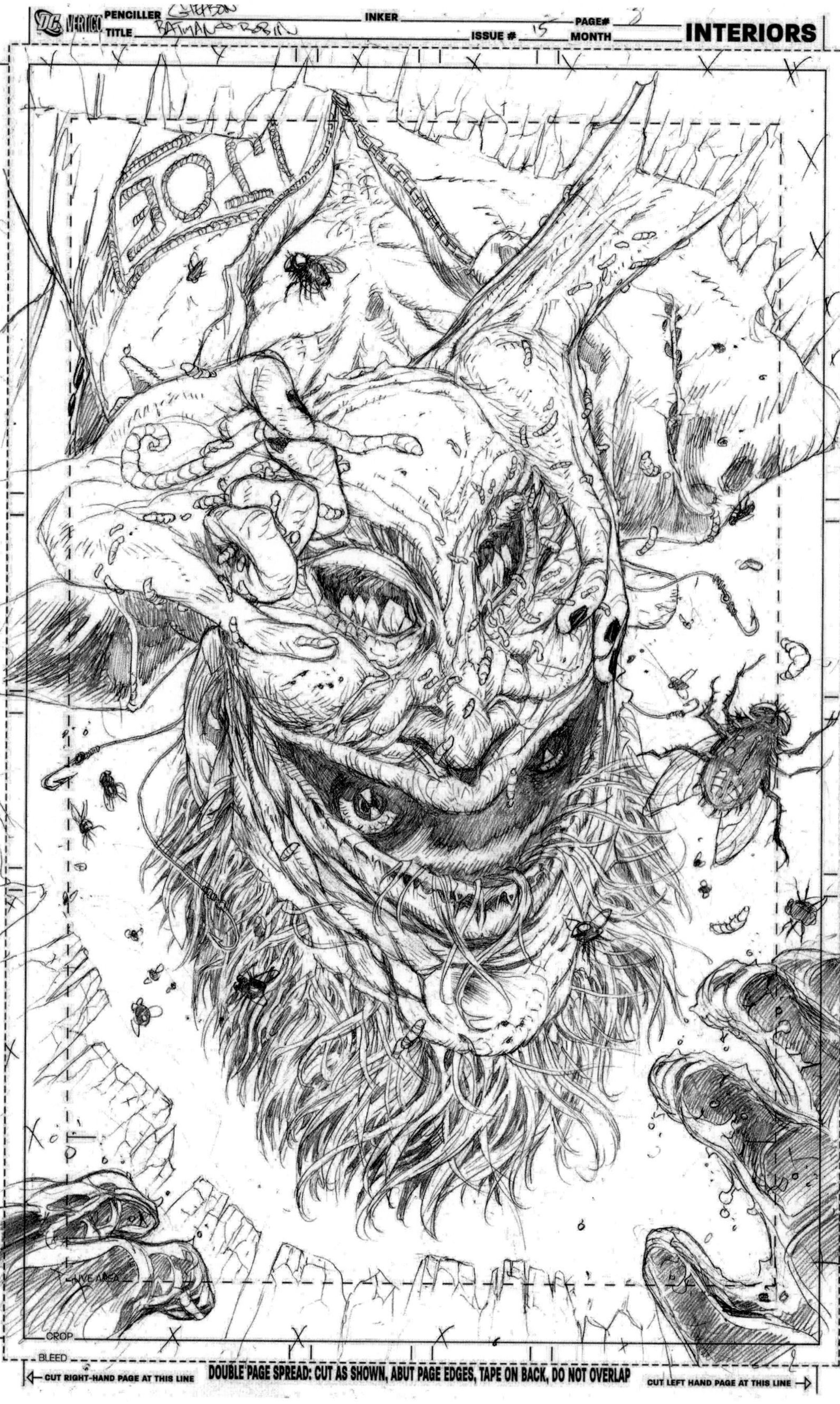

PENCILLER
INKER
PAGE#
TITLE
ISSUE # 15
MONTH
INTERIORS
MINIMUM BLEED 1/4" ALL AROUND
LIVE AREA
CROP
BLEED
CUT RIGHT-HAND PAGE AT THIS LINE
DOUBLE PAGE SPREAD: CUT AS SHOWN, ABUT PAGE EDGES, TAPE ON BACK, DO NOT OVERLAP
CUT LEFT HAND PAGE AT THIS LINE

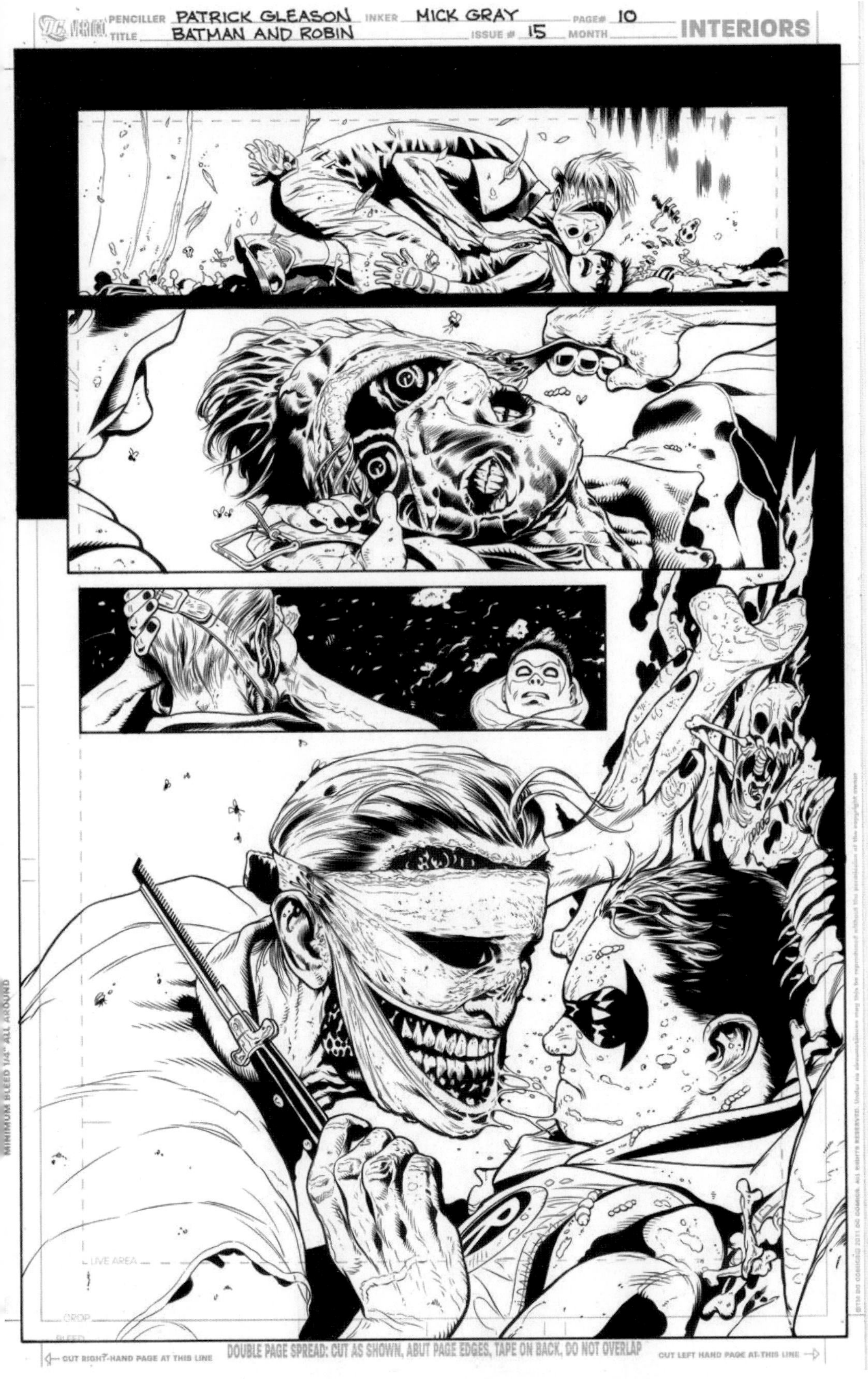
PENCILLER PATRICK GLEASON
INKER MICK GRAY
PAGE# 10
TITLE BATMAN AND ROBIN
ISSUE # 15
MONTH
INTERIORS
LIVE AREA
CROP
BLEED
CUT RIGHT-HAND PAGE AT THIS LINE
DOUBLE PAGE SPREAD: CUT AS SHOWN, ABUT PAGE EDGES, TAPE ON BACK, DO NOT OVERLAP
CUT LEFT HAND PAGE AT THIS LINE
MINIMUM BLEED 1/4" ALL AROUND

PENCILLER **PATRICK GLEASON** INKER **MICK GRAY** PAGE# **14**

TITLE **BATMAN AND ROBIN** ISSUE # **15** MONTH _____ **INTERIORS**

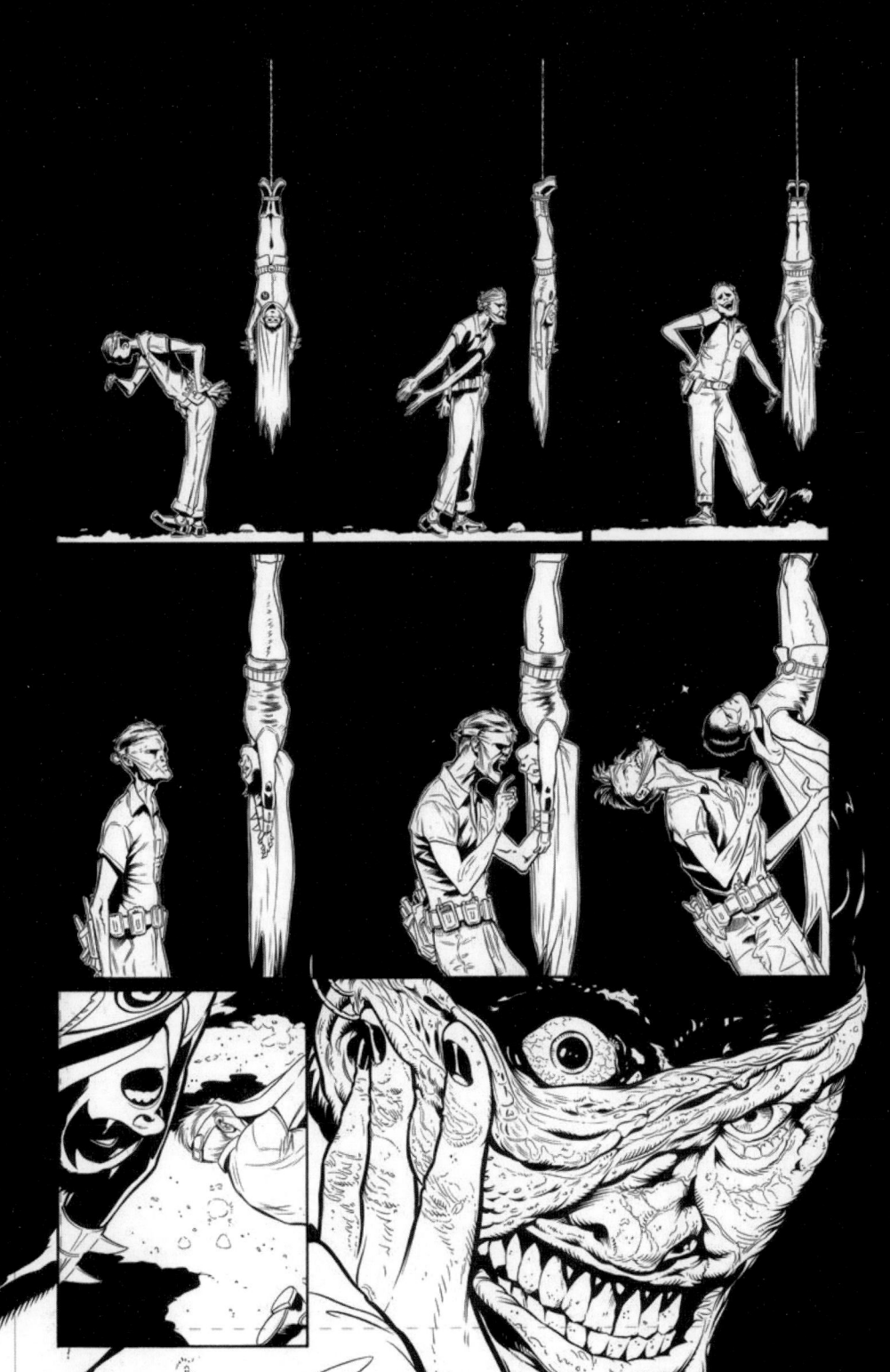

PAGE 2
panel 1
Angle on Bruce walking away, grabbing another sandwich, yawning, as Alfred continues to collect the banged up uniforms, tossing them into a cart. Damian, still sitting at the bench, is pulling off his remaining boot. Establish Bruce's boots on the floor if you can. By the by, they both should be wearing black Under Armor-type body suits for the rest of the scene, sleeves rolled up.

SILENT

panel 2
Angle on Damian as he presses the sole of Bruce's large boot to his smaller boot, simply staring at the size contrast as Titus looks on, a sandwich in his mouth. We're going for that feel of a boy putting his foot into a pair of his father's shoes.

SILENT

panel 3
Angle looking down from a few cave stairs ahead of them as Bruce, Damian, Alfred and Titus walk towards us. Alfred is carrying the tray of food. Damian is yawning, stretching his arms. Titus yawns too. Remember, they look exhausted.

BRUCE: Yawwwn.

ALFRED: Yawwwn.

DAMIAN: Yawwwn.

TITUS: Rawwwn

panel 4
We're upstairs now, angle on them all from behind walking into their respective bedroom doors. Titus is following Damian of course.

DAMIAN: Night.

ALFRED: Good night.

BRUCE: Hnn.

panels 5, 6, and 7
These should be across the bottom, right next to each other, each panel showing them lying in bed, reaching to shut off their respective lights.

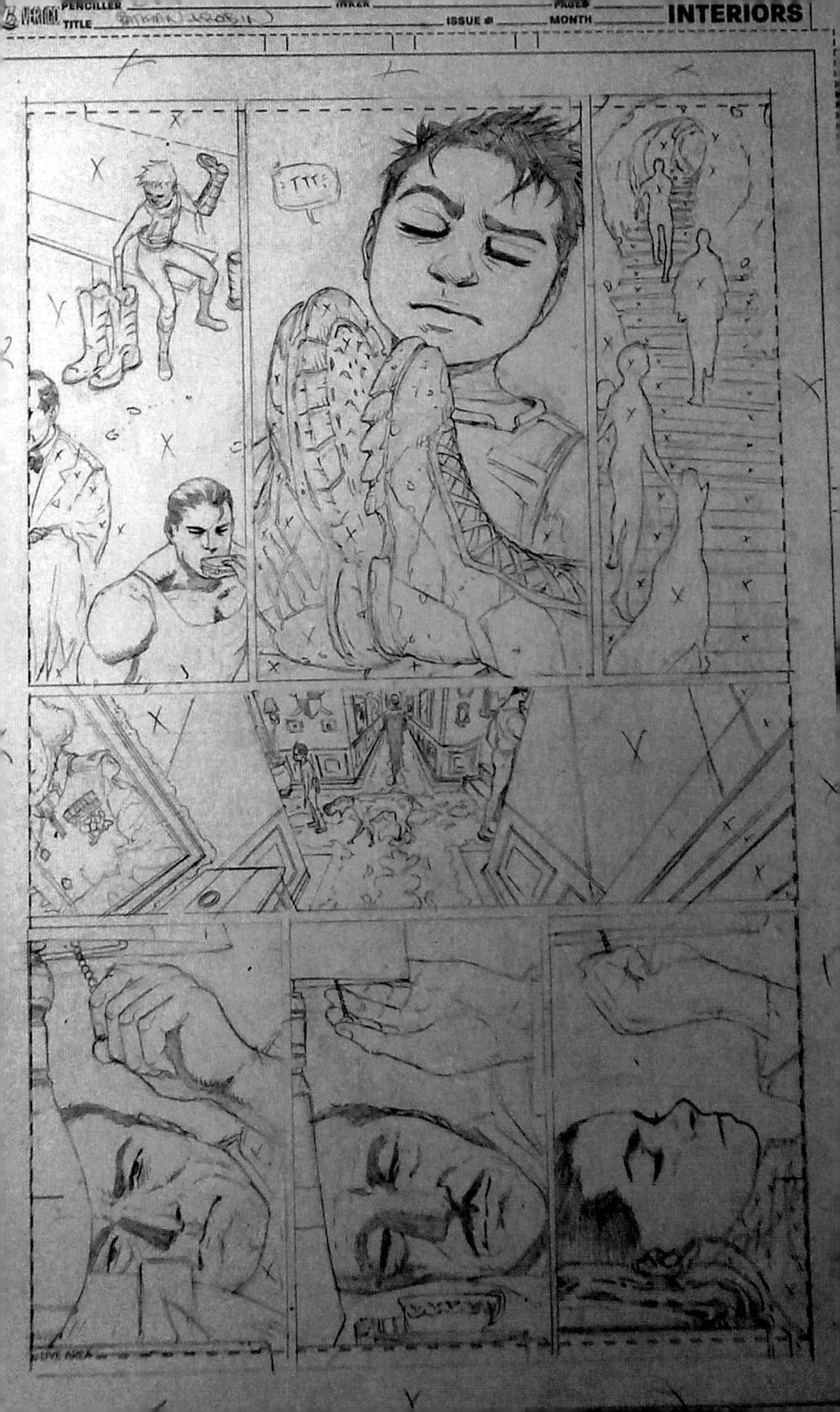

PAGE 3
panel 1
Pat, we're riffing off the sub scene in B&R #0, except angle it all different. Smallest on page.
Thin horizontal of the submarine moving under the sea.

SILENT

panel 2
In the sub, angle on DAMIAN 1, shirt off, glass of milk in hand, as he stares out at the
bodies under the water in front of his bay window. Fish pecking away, hands chained,
weighted down, various degrees of composition. The bodies in the foreground are of TALIA,
NIGHTWING, RED ROBIN, NOBODY and the JOKER (all responsible for little bits of
self-realization — teachers, if you will). The other bodies, if we even see them, should be
those of his OTHER TEACHERS from B&R #0.

SILENT

panel 3
Angle on Damian 1 as he's holding the BAT COWL by one of the ears as he drinks from his
glass. We can't see the front of the cowl or the bottom. Framed by the light in the hatchway
is the shadowed figure of DAMIAN 2. In other words he's talking to himself.

DAMIAN 2:　　　I thought I told you to leave *that* alone.

DAMIAN 1:　　　Why do you keep it?

panel 4
We see that Damian 1 is actually holding BATMAN'S SEVERED HEAD by the cowl ear, Bruce's
lifeless eyes stare at us through the cowls-slits, drops of blood drip from the neck as Damian 2
stands beside him.

DAMIAN 2:　　　It's a reminder that *our* father has shown us *both sides* of himself, just as *we*
have shown him *ours*.

panel 5
Angle on the 2 Damians facing each other, the bay window behind them like issue #0. Instead
of the shark let's see the bodies from panel 2 — only now a NEW BODY, chained at the feet,
hands free, is dropping into the water. There's a lot of bubbles from the weight surrounding
the body, so it obscures the identity of the person at this moment. Damian 1 is handing
Damian 2 a batarang. Damian 2, by the way, is still holding Batman's head.

DAMIAN 2:　　　This batarang belonged to our father.

DAMIAN 2:　　　Remember, *we* are a *Wayne* first and an Al Ghul second.

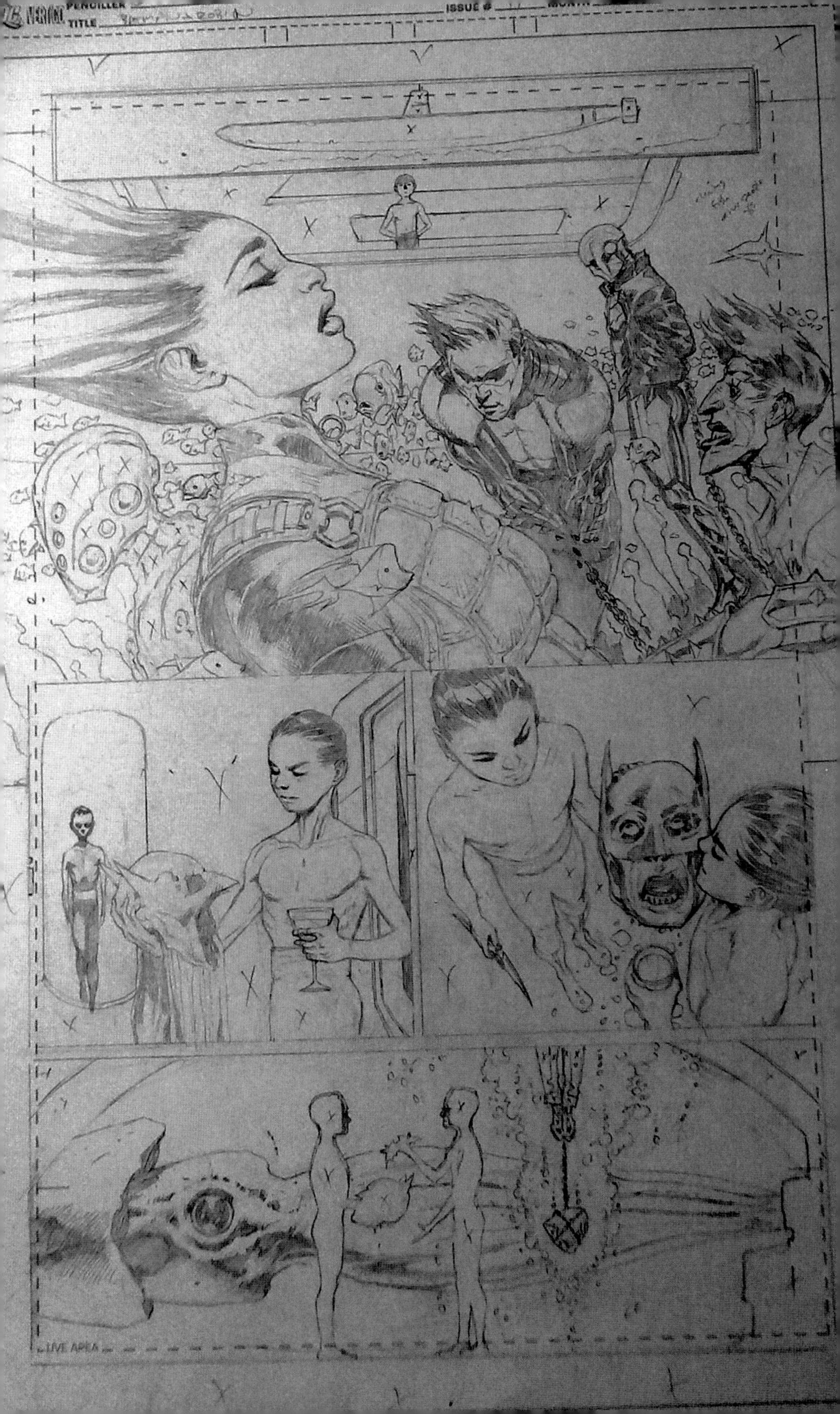
PENCILLER
ISSUE #
TITLE
LIVE AREA

DC COMICS™

START AT THE BEGINNING

BATMAN VOLUME 1
THE COURT OF OWLS

**BATMAN & ROBIN
VOLUME 1:
BORN TO KILL**

PETER J. TOMASI PATRICK GLEASON MICK GRAY

**BATMAN: DETECTIVE
COMICS VOLUME 1:
FACES OF DEATH**

TONY S. DANIEL

**BATMAN: THE DARK
KNIGHT VOLUME 1:
KNIGHT TERRORS**

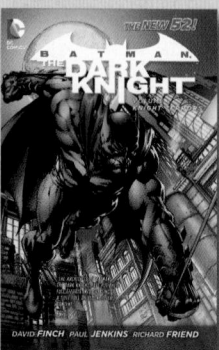

DAVID FINCH PAUL JENKINS RICHARD FRIEND

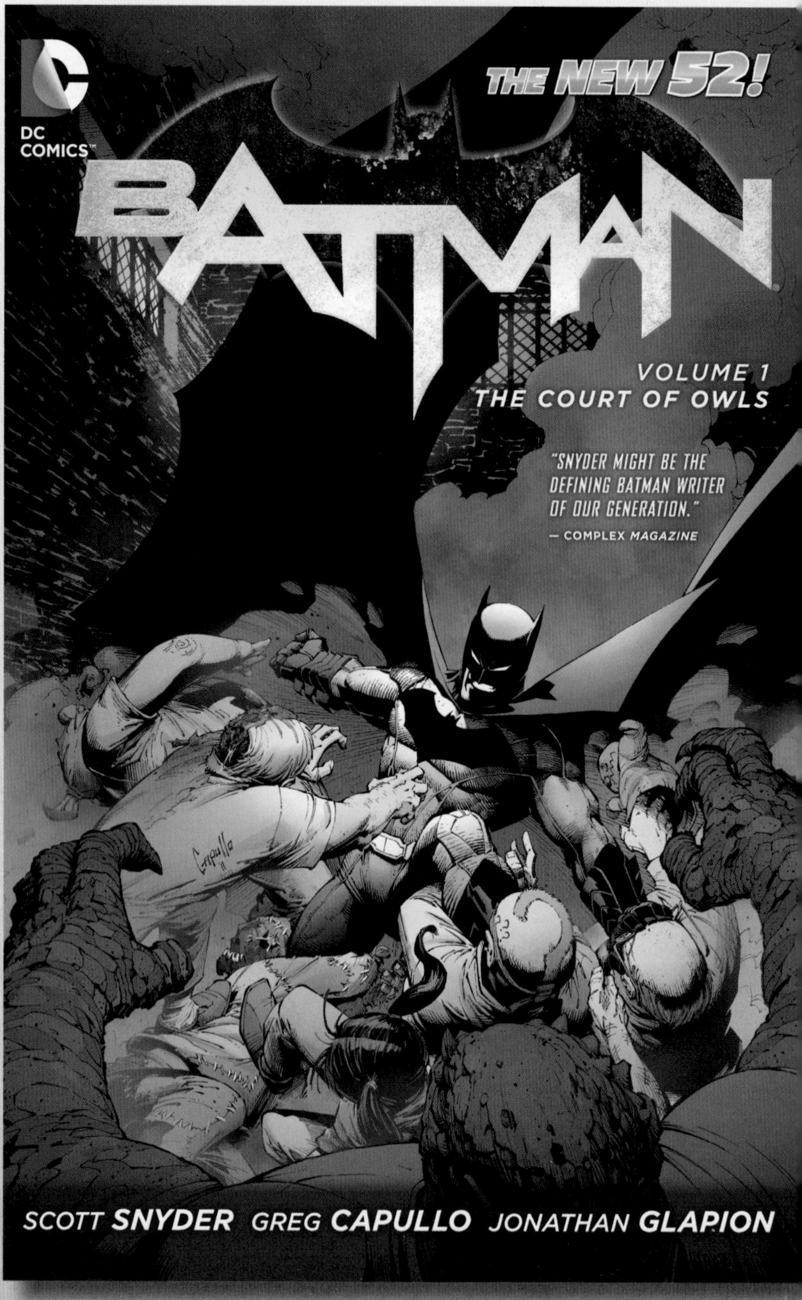

THE NEW 52!

DC COMICS™

BATMAN

VOLUME 1
THE COURT OF OWLS

"SNYDER MIGHT BE THE
DEFINING BATMAN WRITER
OF OUR GENERATION."
— COMPLEX MAGAZINE

SCOTT **SNYDER** GREG **CAPULLO** JONATHAN **GLAPION**

Your online portal to everything you need

connectED.mcgraw-hill.com

Look for these icons to access
exciting digital resources

Video

Audio

Review

? Inquiry

WebQuest

✓ Assessment

Concepts in Motion

Mc Graw Hill Education

LIFE iSCIENCE

Glencoe

Snow Leopard, *Uncia uncia*

The snow leopard lives in central Asia at altitudes of 3,000 m–5,500 m. Its thick fur and broad, furry feet are two of its adaptations that make it well suited to a snowy environment. Snow leopards cannot roar but can hiss, growl, and make other sounds.

The McGraw·Hill Companies

 Education

Send all inquiries to:
McGraw-Hill Education
8787 Orion Place
Columbus, OH 43240-4027

ISBN: 978-0-07-888002-5
MHID: 0-07-888002-5

Printed in the United States of America.

8 9 10 11 12 13 DOW 16 15 14

Contents in Brief

Authors and Contributors

Authors

American Museum of Natural History
New York, NY

Michelle Anderson, MS
Lecturer
The Ohio State University
Columbus, OH

Juli Berwald, PhD
Science Writer
Austin, TX

John F. Bolzan, PhD
Science Writer
Columbus, OH

Rachel Clark, MS
Science Writer
Moscow, ID

Patricia Craig, MS
Science Writer
Bozeman, MT

Randall Frost, PhD
Science Writer
Pleasanton, CA

Lisa S. Gardiner, PhD
Science Writer
Denver, CO

Jennifer Gonya, PhD
The Ohio State University
Columbus, OH

Mary Ann Grobbel, MD
Science Writer
Grand Rapids, MI

Whitney Crispen Hagins, MA, MAT
Biology Teacher
Lexington High School
Lexington, MA

Carole Holmberg, BS
Planetarium Director
Calusa Nature Center and
Planetarium, Inc.
Fort Myers, FL

Tina C. Hopper
Science Writer
Rockwall, TX

Jonathan D. W. Kahl, PhD
Professor of Atmospheric Science
University of Wisconsin-
Milwaukee
Milwaukee, WI

Nanette Kalis
Science Writer
Athens, OH

S. Page Keeley, MEd
Maine Mathematics and Science
Alliance
Augusta, ME

Cindy Klevickis, PhD
Professor of Integrated Science
and Technology
James Madison University
Harrisonburg, VA

Kimberly Fekany Lee, PhD
Science Writer
La Grange, IL

Michael Manga, PhD
Professor
University of California, Berkeley
Berkeley, CA

Devi Ried Mathieu
Science Writer
Sebastopol, CA

Elizabeth A. Nagy-Shadman, PhD
Geology Professor
Pasadena City College
Pasadena, CA

William D. Rogers, DA
Professor of Biology
Ball State University
Muncie, IN

Donna L. Ross, PhD
Associate Professor
San Diego State University
San Diego, CA

Marion B. Sewer, PhD
Assistant Professor
School of Biology
Georgia Institute of Technology
Atlanta, GA

Julia Meyer Sheets, PhD
Lecturer
School of Earth Sciences
The Ohio State University
Columbus, OH

Michael J. Singer, PhD
Professor of Soil Science
Department of Land, Air and
Water Resources
University of California
Davis, CA

Karen S. Sottosanti, MA
Science Writer
Pickerington, Ohio

Paul K. Strode, PhD
I.B. Biology Teacher
Fairview High School
Boulder, CO

Jan M. Vermilye, PhD
Research Geologist
Seismo-Tectonic Reservoir
Monitoring (STRM)
Boulder, CO

Judith A. Yero, MA
Director
Teacher's Mind Resources
Hamilton, MT

Dinah Zike, MEd
Author, Consultant, Inventor
of Foldables
Dinah Zike Academy; Dinah-
Might Adventures, LP
San Antonio, TX

Margaret Zorn, MS
Science Writer
Yorktown, VA

Consulting Authors

Alton L. Biggs
Biggs Educational Consulting
Commerce, TX

Ralph M. Feather, Jr., PhD
Assistant Professor
Department of Educational Studies and Secondary Education
Bloomsburg University
Bloomsburg, PA

Douglas Fisher, PhD
Professor of Teacher Education
San Diego State University
San Diego, CA

Edward P. Ortleb
Science/Safety Consultant
St. Louis, MO

Series Consultants

Science

Solomon Bililign, PhD
Professor
Department of Physics
North Carolina Agricultural and Technical State University
Greensboro, NC

John Choinski
Professor
Department of Biology
University of Central Arkansas
Conway, AR

Anastasia Chopelas, PhD
Research Professor
Department of Earth and Space Sciences
UCLA
Los Angeles, CA

David T. Crowther, PhD
Professor of Science Education
University of Nevada, Reno
Reno, NV

A. John Gatz
Professor of Zoology
Ohio Wesleyan University
Delaware, OH

Sarah Gille, PhD
Professor
University of California San Diego
La Jolla, CA

David G. Haase, PhD
Professor of Physics
North Carolina State University
Raleigh, NC

Janet S. Herman, PhD
Professor
Department of Environmental Sciences
University of Virginia
Charlottesville, VA

David T. Ho, PhD
Associate Professor
Department of Oceanography
University of Hawaii
Honolulu, HI

Ruth Howes, PhD
Professor of Physics
Marquette University
Milwaukee, WI

Jose Miguel Hurtado, Jr., PhD
Associate Professor
Department of Geological Sciences
University of Texas at El Paso
El Paso, TX

Monika Kress, PhD
Assistant Professor
San Jose State University
San Jose, CA

Mark E. Lee, PhD
Associate Chair & Assistant Professor
Department of Biology
Spelman College
Atlanta, GA

Linda Lundgren
Science writer
Lakewood, CO

Keith O. Mann, PhD
Ohio Wesleyan University
Delaware, OH

Charles W. McLaughlin, PhD
Adjunct Professor of Chemistry
Montana State University
Bozeman, MT

Katharina Pahnke, PhD
Research Professor
Department of Geology and Geophysics
University of Hawaii
Honolulu, HI

Jesús Pando, PhD
Associate Professor
DePaul University
Chicago, IL

Hay-Oak Park, PhD
Associate Professor
Department of Molecular Genetics
Ohio State University
Columbus, OH

David A. Rubin, PhD
Associate Professor of Physiology
School of Biological Sciences
Illinois State University
Normal, IL

Toni D. Sauncy
Assistant Professor of Physics
Department of Physics
Angelo State University
San Angelo, TX

Series Consultants, continued

Malathi Srivatsan, PhD
Associate Professor of Neurobiology
College of Sciences and Mathematics
Arkansas State University
Jonesboro, AR

Cheryl Wistrom, PhD
Associate Professor of Chemistry
Saint Joseph's College
Rensselaer, IN

Reading

ReLeah Cossett Lent
Author/Educational Consultant
Blue Ridge, GA

Math

Vik Hovsepian
Professor of Mathematics
Rio Hondo College
Whittier, CA

Series Reviewers

Thad Boggs
Mandarin High School
Jacksonville, FL

Catherine Butcher
Webster Junior High School
Minden, LA

Erin Darichuk
West Frederick Middle School
Frederick, MD

Joanne Hedrick Davis
Murphy High School
Murphy, NC

Anthony J. DiSipio, Jr.
Octorara Middle School
Atglen, PA

Adrienne Elder
Tulsa Public Schools
Tulsa, OK

Carolyn Elliott
Iredell-Statesville Schools
Statesville, NC

Christine M. Jacobs
Ranger Middle School
Murphy, NC

Jason O. L. Johnson
Thurmont Middle School
Thurmont, MD

Felecia Joiner
Stony Point Ninth Grade Center
Round Rock, TX

Joseph L. Kowalski, MS
Lamar Academy
McAllen, TX

Brian McClain
Amos P. Godby High School
Tallahassee, FL

Von W. Mosser
Thurmont Middle School
Thurmont, MD

Ashlea Peterson
Heritage Intermediate Grade Center
Coweta, OK

Nicole Lenihan Rhoades
Walkersville Middle School
Walkersvillle, MD

Maria A. Rozenberg
Indian Ridge Middle School
Davie, FL

Barb Seymour
Westridge Middle School
Overland Park, KS

Ginger Shirley
Our Lady of Providence Junior-Senior High School
Clarksville, IN

Curtis Smith
Elmwood Middle School
Rogers, AR

Sheila Smith
Jackson Public School
Jackson, MS

Sabra Soileau
Moss Bluff Middle School
Lake Charles, LA

Tony Spoores
Switzerland County Middle School
Vevay, IN

Nancy A. Stearns
Switzerland County Middle School
Vevay, IN

Kari Vogel
Princeton Middle School
Princeton, MN

Alison Welch
Wm. D. Slider Middle School
El Paso, TX

Linda Workman
Parkway Northeast Middle School
Creve Coeur, MO

Teacher Advisory Board

The Teacher Advisory Board gave the authors, editorial staff, and design team feedback on the content and design of the Student Edition. They provided valuable input in the development of *Glencoe Life iScience.*

Frances J. Baldridge
Department Chair
Ferguson Middle School
Beavercreek, OH

Jane E. M. Buckingham
Teacher
Crispus Attucks Medical Magnet High School
Indianapolis, IN

Elizabeth Falls
Teacher
Blalack Middle School
Carrollton, TX

Nelson Farrier
Teacher
Hamlin Middle School
Springfield, OR

Michelle R. Foster
Department Chair
Wayland Union Middle School
Wayland, MI

Rebecca Goodell
Teacher
Reedy Creek Middle School
Cary, NC

Mary Gromko
Science Supervisor K–12
Colorado Springs District 11
Colorado Springs, CO

Randy Mousley
Department Chair
Dean Ray Stucky Middle School
Wichita, KS

David Rodriguez
Teacher
Swift Creek Middle School
Tallahassee, FL

Derek Shook
Teacher
Floyd Middle Magnet School
Montgomery, AL

Karen Stratton
Science Coordinator
Lexington School District One
Lexington, SC

Stephanie Wood
Science Curriculum Specialist, K–12
Granite School District
Salt Lake City, UT

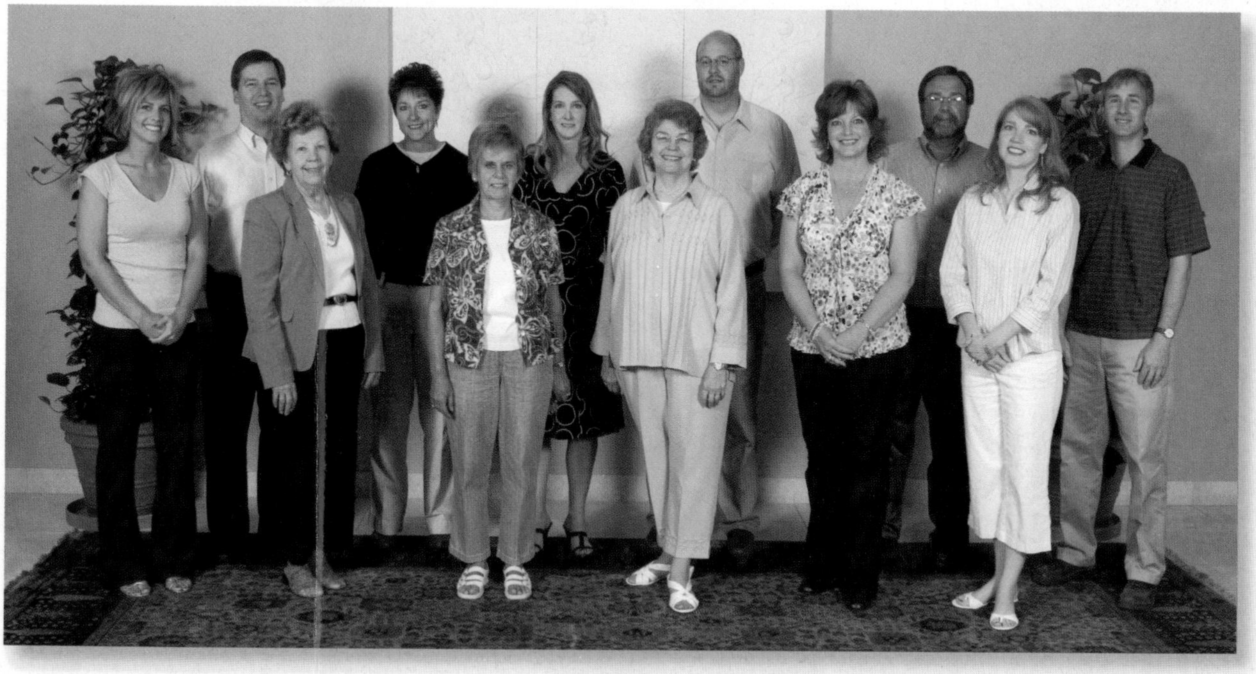

Online Guide

Get ConnectED

connectED.mcgraw-hill.com

Table of Contents
Glossary
Search
Chapter Resources
Lesson 1 Resources
Lesson 2 Resources
Lesson 3 Resources
Lesson 4 Resources
Chapter Lab
Chapter Review
Resources
Get Ready to Read
What do you think?
Before you read, decide if you agree or disagree with each of these statements. As you read this chapter, see if you change your mind about any of the statements.
1 The air you breathe is mostly oxygen.
2 Living things are made mostly of water.
3 Carbon, nitrogen, and other types of matter are used by living things over and over again.
4 Clouds are made of water vapor.
5 The Sun is the source for all energy used by living things on Earth.
6 All living things get their energy from eating other living things.
ConnectED Your one-stop online resource
connectED.mcgraw-hill.com
Video
Review
Inquiry
WebQuest
Assessment
Concepts in Motion
Multilingual eGlossary
Macmillan/McGraw-Hill
Glencoe
The McGraw-Hill Companies
Video
greenhouse gases
carbon dioxide
GLOBAL WARMING
Video

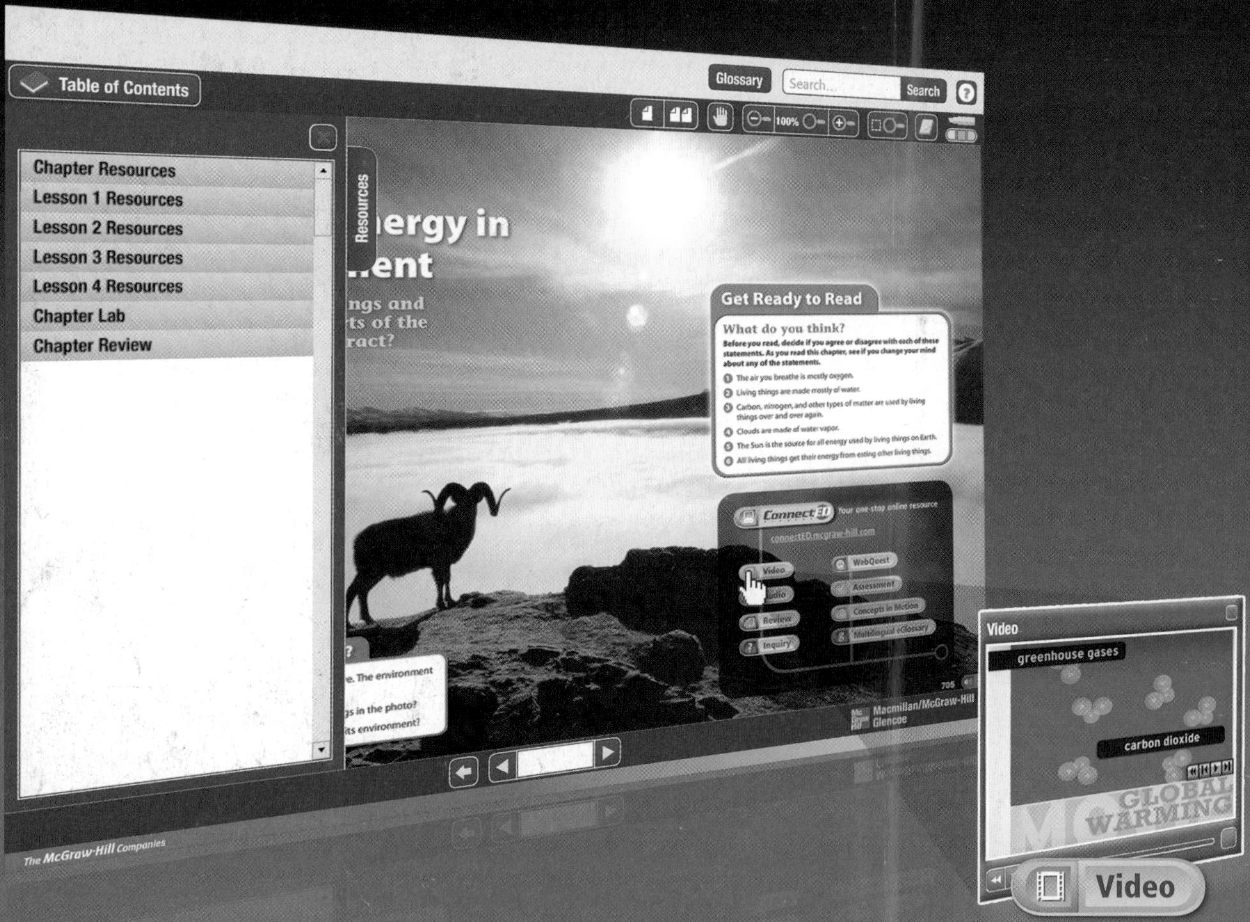

ConnectED

Your Digital Science Portal

Video

See the science in real life through these exciting videos.

Audio

Click the link and you can listen to the text while you follow along.

Review

Try these interactive tools to help you review the lesson concepts.

Inquiry

Explore concepts through hands–on and virtual labs.

WebQuest

These web-based challenges relate the concepts you're learning about to the latest news and research.

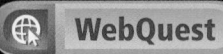

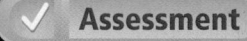

The icons in your online student edition link you to interactive learning opportunities. Browse your online student book to find more.

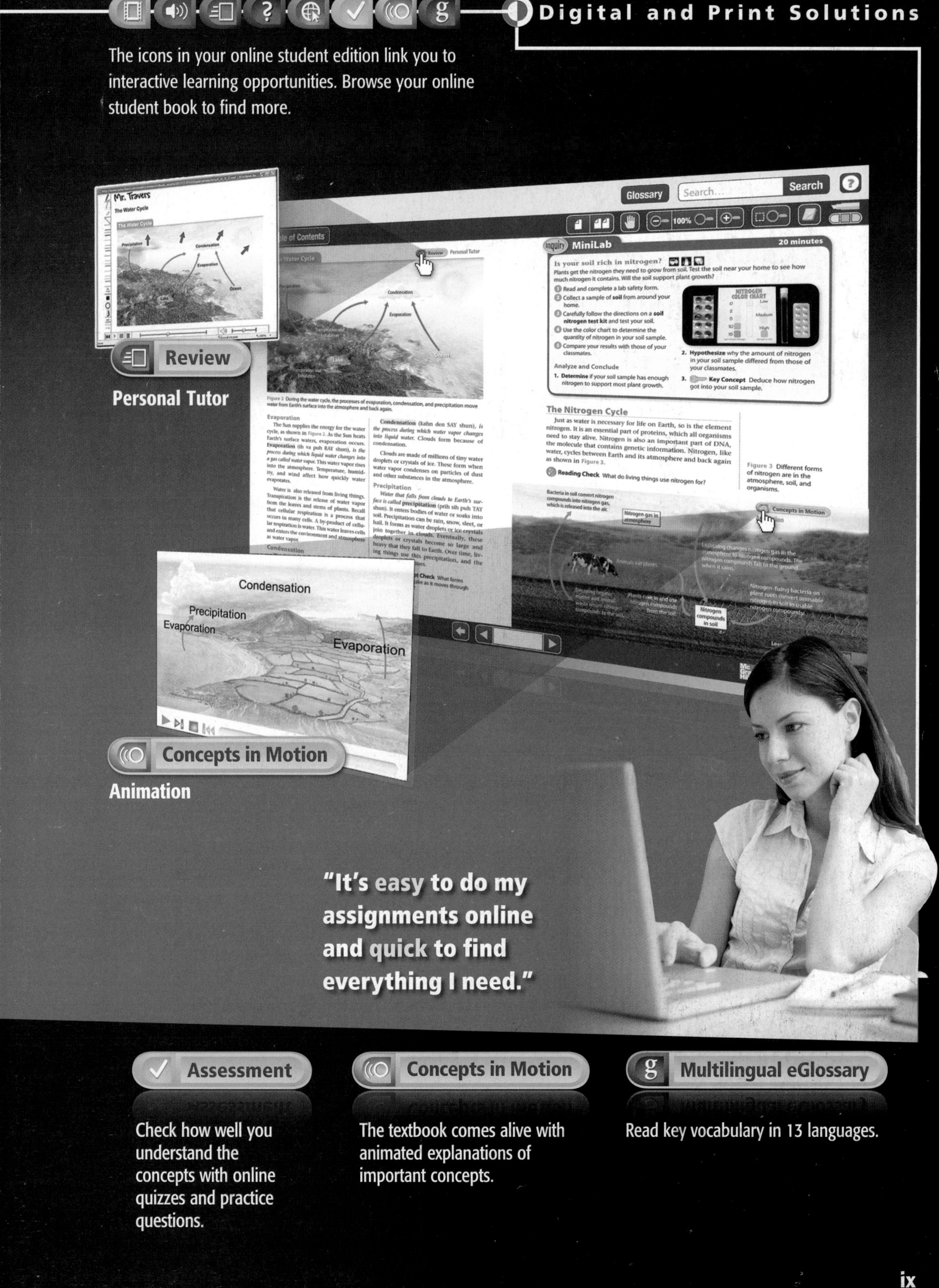
Glossary
Search...
Search
MiniLab
20 minutes
Is your soil rich in nitrogen?
The Nitrogen Cycle
Condensation
Precipitation
Evaporation
Evaporation

Review

Personal Tutor

Concepts in Motion

Animation

"It's easy to do my assignments online and quick to find everything I need."

Assessment

Check how well you understand the concepts with online quizzes and practice questions.

Concepts in Motion

The textbook comes alive with animated explanations of important concepts.

Multilingual eGlossary

Read key vocabulary in 13 languages.

Treasure Hunt

Your science book has many features that will aid you in your learning. Some of these features are listed below. You can use the activity at the right to help you find these and other special features in the book.

- **THE BIG IDEA** can be found at the start of each chapter.

- The Reading Guide at the start of each lesson lists 🔑 **Key Concepts,** vocabulary terms, and online supplements to the content.

- **Connect ED** icons direct you to online resources such as animations, personal tutors, math practices, and quizzes.

- **Inquiry** Labs and Skill Practices are in each chapter.

- Your **FOLDABLES®** help organize your notes.

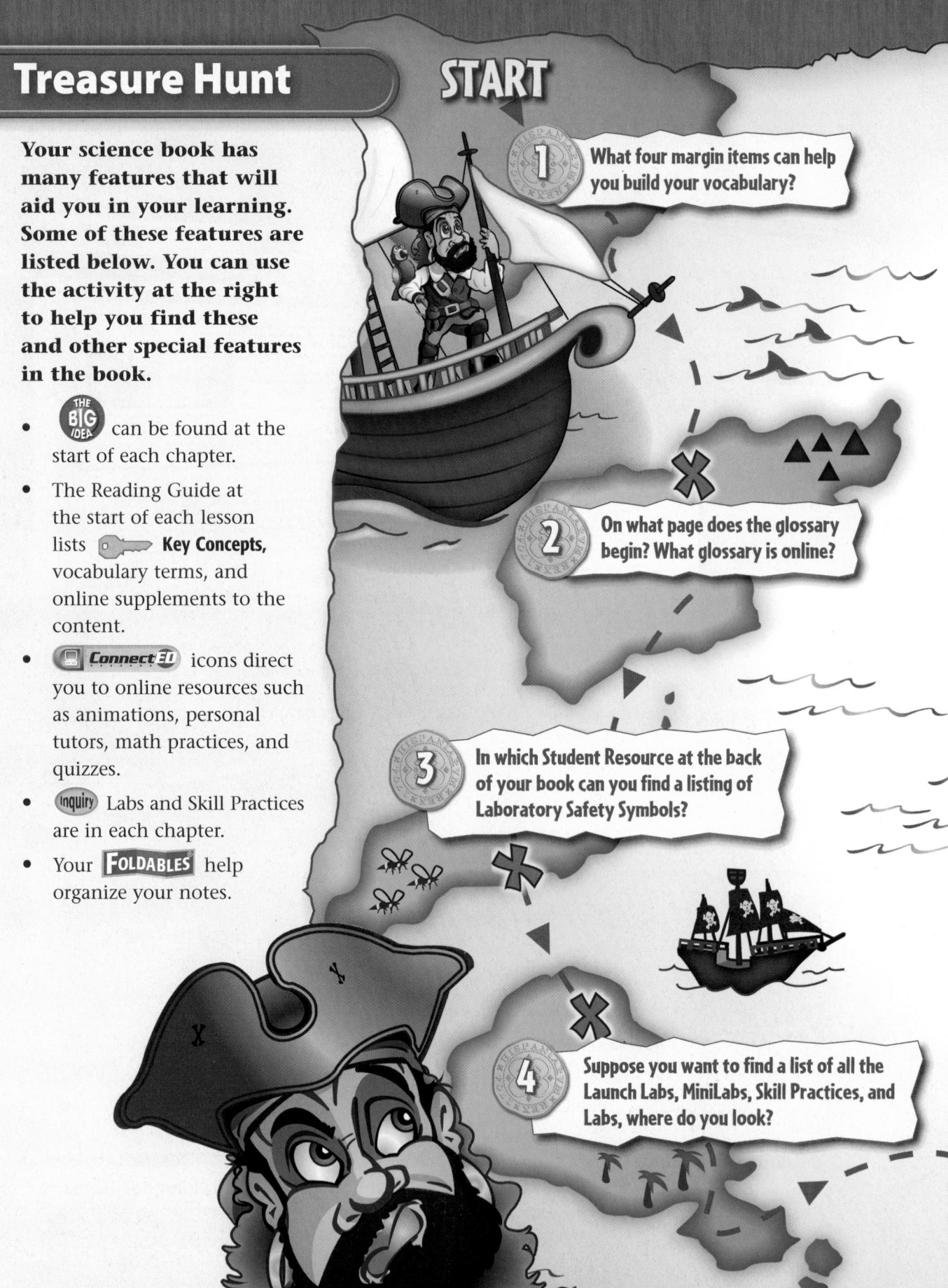

1 What four margin items can help you build your vocabulary?

2 On what page does the glossary begin? What glossary is online?

3 In which Student Resource at the back of your book can you find a listing of Laboratory Safety Symbols?

4 Suppose you want to find a list of all the Launch Labs, MiniLabs, Skill Practices, and Labs, where do you look?

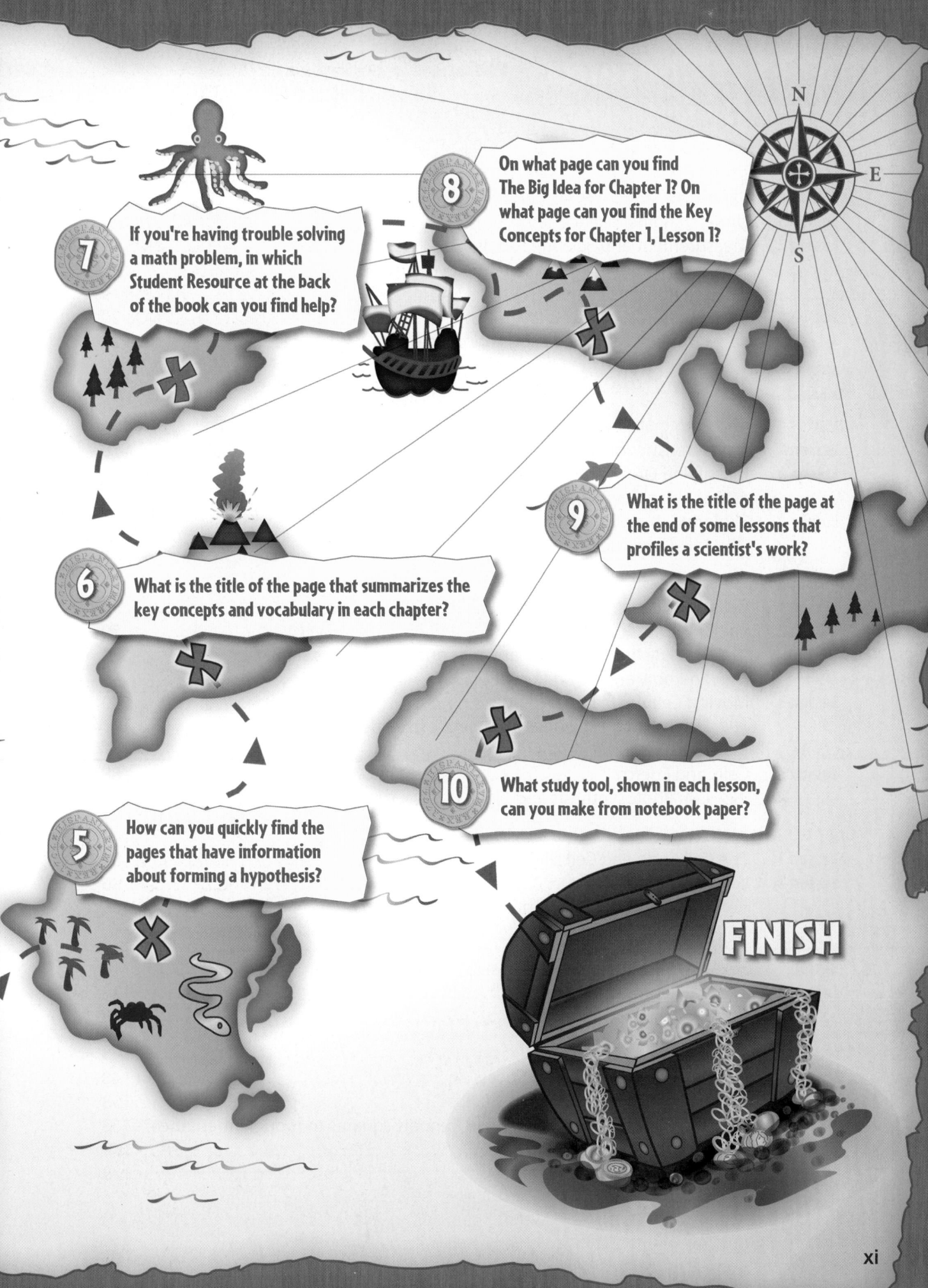

8 On what page can you find The Big Idea for Chapter 1? On what page can you find the Key Concepts for Chapter 1, Lesson 1?

7 If you're having trouble solving a math problem, in which Student Resource at the back of the book can you find help?

9 What is the title of the page at the end of some lessons that profiles a scientist's work?

6 What is the title of the page that summarizes the key concepts and vocabulary in each chapter?

10 What study tool, shown in each lesson, can you make from notebook paper?

5 How can you quickly find the pages that have information about forming a hypothesis?

FINISH

Table of Contents

Table of Contents

Table of Contents

Student Resources

TABLE OF CONTENTS

Inquiry

Inquiry Launch Labs

TABLE OF CONTENTS

Inquiry

Inquiry MiniLabs

TABLE OF CONTENTS

(Inquiry) Skill Practice

Inquiry

 **Labs**

Features

How Nature Works

Green Science

Science & Society

Careers in Science

Scientific Explanations

THE BIG IDEA

How can science provide answers to your questions about the world around you?

Inquiry **Vacuuming Corals?**

No, these two divers are collecting data about corals in waters near Sulawesi, Indonesia. They are marine biologists, scientists who study living things in oceans and other saltwater environments.

- What information about corals are these scientists collecting?

- What questions do they hope to answer?

- How can science provide answers to their questions and your questions?

Methods of SCIENCE

This chapter begins your study of the nature of science, but there is even more information about the nature of science in this book. Each unit begins by exploring an important topic that is fundamental to scientific study. As you read these topics, you will learn even more about the nature of science.

Models   Unit 1

Systems   Unit 2

Patterns   Unit 3

Graphs   Unit 4

Technology Unit 5

Reading Guide
Key Concepts 🔑
ESSENTIAL QUESTIONS

- What is scientific inquiry?
- What are the results of scientific investigations?
- How can a scientist minimize bias in a scientific investigation?

Vocabulary

science p. NOS 4

observation p. NOS 6

inference p. NOS 6

hypothesis p. NOS 6

prediction p. NOS 7

technology p. NOS 8

scientific theory p. NOS 9

scientific law p. NOS 9

critical thinking p. NOS 10

 Multilingual eGlossary

 Video BrainPOP®

Understanding Science

What is science?

The last time that you watched squirrels play in a park or in your yard, did you realize that you were practicing science? Every time you observe the natural world, you are practicing science. **Science** *is the investigation and exploration of natural events and of the new information that results from those investigations.*

When you observe the natural world, you might form questions about what you see. While you are exploring those questions, you probably use reasoning, creativity, and skepticism to help you find answers to your questions. People use these behaviors in their daily lives to solve problems, such as how to keep a squirrel from eating bird seed, as shown in **Figure 1.** Similarly, scientists use these behaviors in their work.

Scientists use a reliable set of skills and methods in different ways to find answers to questions. After reading this chapter, you will have a better understanding of how science works, the limitations of science, and scientific ways of thinking. In addition, you will recognize that when you practice science at home or in the classroom, you use scientific methods to answer questions just as scientists do.

Figure 1 Someone used reasoning and creativity to design each of these squirrel-proof bird feeders. However, some solutions don't work. Scientists use similar methods to try to solve problems.

Branches of Science

No one person can study all the natural world. Therefore, people tend to focus their efforts on one of the three fields or branches of science—life science, Earth science, or physical science, as described below. Then people or scientists can seek answers to specific problems within one field of science.

WORD ORIGIN

biology
from Greek *bios*, means "life"; and *logia*, means "study of"

Life Science

Biology, or life science, is the study of all living things. This forest ecologist, a life scientist who studies interactions in forest ecosystems, is studying lichens growing on Douglas firs. Biologists ask questions such as

- How do plants produce their own food?
- Why do some animals give birth to live young and others lay eggs?
- How are reptiles and birds related?

Earth Science

The study of Earth, including its landforms, rocks, soil, and forces that shape Earth's surface, is Earth science. These Earth scientists are collecting soil samples in Africa. Earth scientists ask questions such as

- How do rocks form?
- What causes earthquakes?
- What substances are in soil?

Physical Science

The study of chemistry and physics is physical science. Physical scientists study the interactions of matter and energy. This chemist is preparing antibiotic solutions. Physical scientists ask questions such as

- How do substances react and form new substances?
- Why does a liquid change to a solid?
- How are force and motion related?

Scientific Inquiry

As scientists study the natural world, they ask questions about what they observe. To find the answers to these questions, they usually use certain skills, or methods. The chart in **Figure 2** shows a sequence of the skills that a scientist might use in an investigation. However, it is important to know that, sometimes, not all of these skills are performed in an investigation, or performed in this order. Scientists practice scientific inquiry—a process that uses a variety of skills and tools to answer questions or to test ideas about the natural world.

Ask Questions

Like a scientist, you use scientific inquiry in your life, too. Suppose you decide to plant a vegetable garden. As you plant the vegetable seeds, you water some seeds more than others. Then, you weed part of the garden and mix fertilizer into some of the soil. After a few weeks, you observe that some vegetable plants are growing better than others. An **observation** *is using one or more of your senses to gather information and take note of what occurs.*

Observations often are the beginning of the process of inquiry and can lead to questions such as "Why are some plants growing better than others?" As you are making observations and asking questions, you recall from science class that plants need plenty of water and sunlight to grow. Therefore you infer that perhaps some vegetables are receiving more water or sunlight than others and, therefore, are growing better. An **inference** *is a logical explanation of an observation that is drawn from prior knowledge or experience.*

Hypothesize

After making observations and inferences, you are ready to develop a hypothesis and investigate why some vegetables are growing better than others. *A possible explanation about an observation that can be tested by scientific investigations is a* **hypothesis.** Your hypothesis might be: Some plants are growing taller and more quickly than others because they are receiving more water and sunlight. Or, your hypothesis might be: The plants that are growing quickly have received fertilizer because fertilizer helps plants grow.

Figure 2 This flow chart shows steps you or a scientist might use during a scientific investigation.

Visual Check What happens if a hypothesis is not supported?

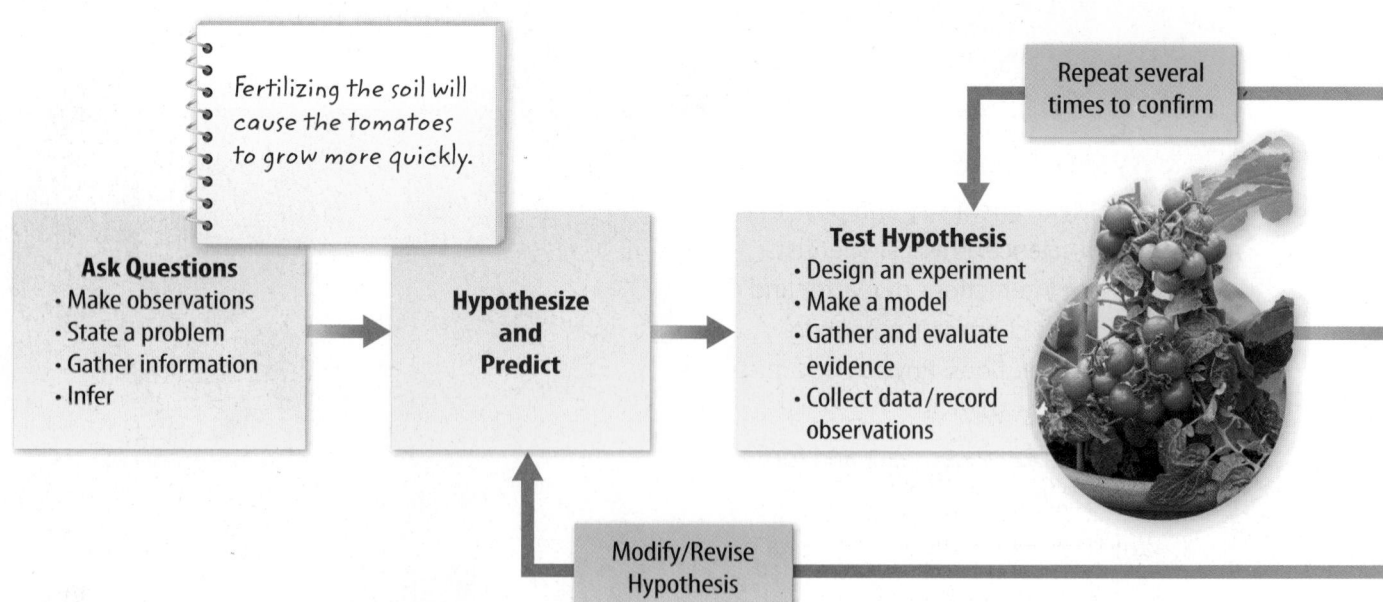

Fertilizing the soil will cause the tomatoes to grow more quickly.

Ask Questions
- Make observations
- State a problem
- Gather information
- Infer

Hypothesize and Predict

Test Hypothesis
- Design an experiment
- Make a model
- Gather and evaluate evidence
- Collect data/record observations

Repeat several times to confirm

Modify/Revise Hypothesis

Predict

After you state a hypothesis, you might make a prediction to help you test your hypothesis. *A* **prediction** *is a statement of what will happen next in a sequence of events.* For instance, based on your hypotheses, you might predict that if some plants receive more water, sunlight, or fertilizer, then they will grow taller and more quickly.

Test your Hypothesis

When you test a hypothesis, you often are testing your predictions. For example, you might design an experiment to test your hypothesis on the fertilizer. You set up an experiment in which you plant seeds and add fertilizer to only some of them. Your prediction is that the plants that get the fertilizer will grow more quickly. If your prediction is confirmed, it supports your hypothesis. If your prediction is not confirmed, your hypothesis might need revision.

Analyze Results

As you are testing your hypothesis, you are probably collecting data about the plants' rates of growth and how much fertilizer each plant receives. Initially, it might be difficult to recognize patterns and relationships in data. Your next step might be to organize and analyze your data.

You can create graphs, classify information, or make models and calculations. Once data are organized, you more easily can study the data and draw conclusions. Other methods of testing a hypothesis and analyzing results are shown in **Figure 2.**

Draw Conclusions

Now you must decide whether your data do or do not support your hypothesis and then draw conclusions. A conclusion is a summary of the information gained from testing a hypothesis. You might make more inferences when drawing conclusions. If your hypothesis is supported, you can repeat your experiment several times to confirm your results. If your hypothesis is not supported, you can modify it and repeat the scientific inquiry process.

Communicate Results

An important step in scientific inquiry is communicating results to others. Professional scientists write scientific articles, speak at conferences, or exchange information on the Internet. This part of scientific inquiry is important because scientists use new information in their research or perform other scientists' investigations to verify results.

 Key Concept Check What is scientific inquiry?

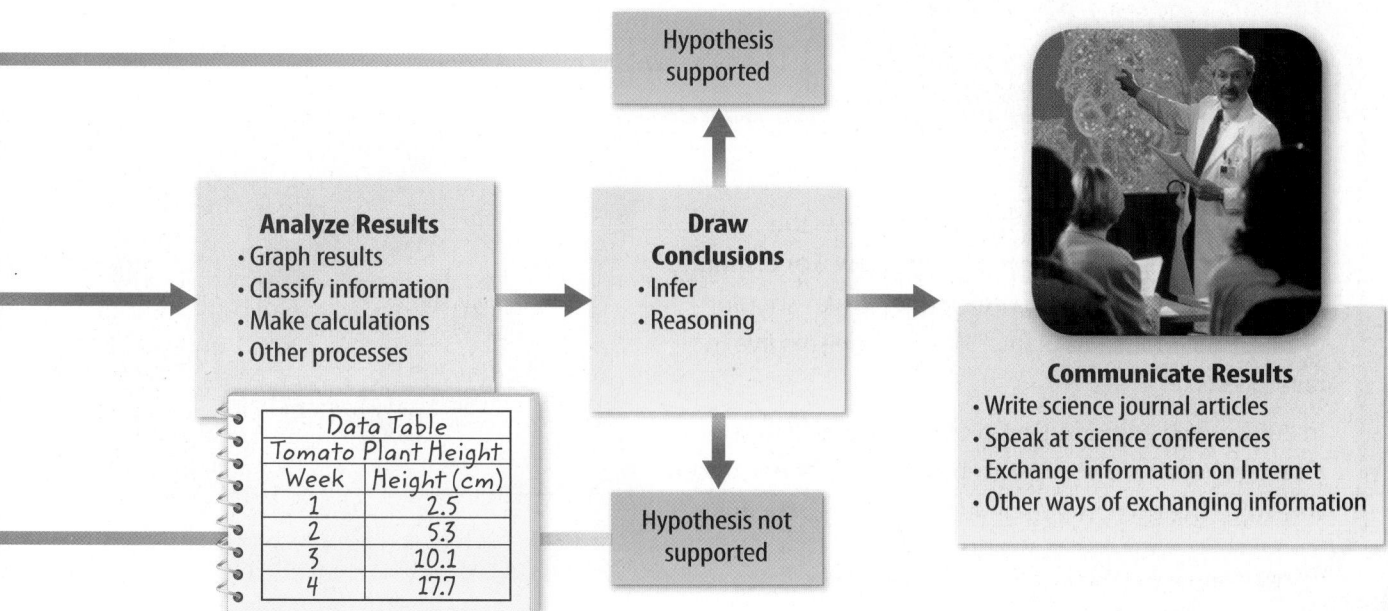

Analyze Results
- Graph results
- Classify information
- Make calculations
- Other processes

Data Table	
Tomato Plant Height	
Week	Height (cm)
1	2.5
2	5.3
3	10.1
4	17.7

Draw Conclusions
- Infer
- Reasoning

Hypothesis supported

Hypothesis not supported

Communicate Results
- Write science journal articles
- Speak at science conferences
- Exchange information on Internet
- Other ways of exchanging information

Results of Scientific Inquiry

Both you and scientists perform scientific inquiry to find answers to questions. There are many outcomes of scientific inquiry, such as technology, materials, and explanations, as shown below.

 Key Concept Check What are the results of scientific investigations?

Technology

The practical use of scientific knowledge, especially for industrial or commercial use is technology. Televisions, MP3 players, and computers are examples of technology. The C-Leg, shown to the right, is one of the latest designs of computer-aided limbs. The prosthetic leg has sensors that anticipate the user's next move, which prevents him or her from stumbling or tripping. In addition, this new technology has several modes that can enable the user to walk, stand for long periods of time, and even ride a bike.

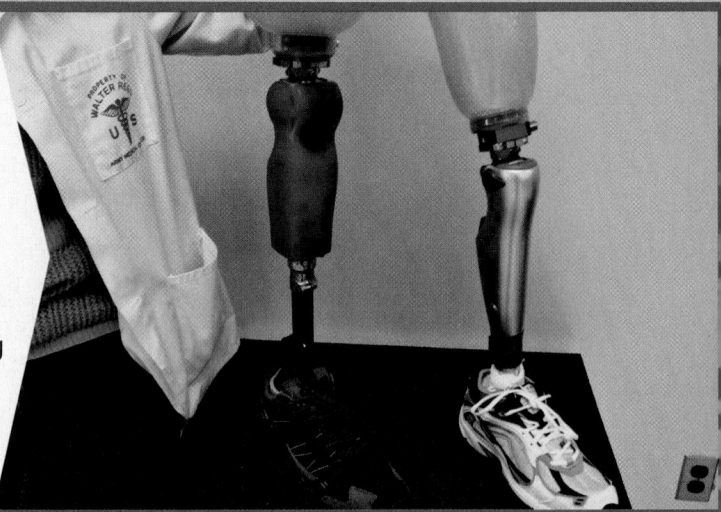

New Materials

Another possible outcome of an investigation is a new material. For example, scientists have developed a bone bioceramic. A bioceramic is a natural calcium-phosphate mineral complex that is part of bones and teeth. This synthetic bone mimics natural bone's structure. Its porous structure allows a type of cell to grow and develop into new bone tissue. The bioceramic can be shaped into implants that are treated with certain cells from the patient's bone marrow. It then can be implanted into the patient's body to replace missing bone.

Possible Explanations

Many times, scientific investigations answer the questions: *who, what, when, where,* or *how.* For example, who left fingerprints at a crime scene? When should fertilizer be applied to plants? What organisms live in rain forests?

In 2007, while exploring in Colombia's tropical rain forests, scientists discovered a new species of poisonous tree frog. The golden frog of Supatá is only 2 cm long.

Scientific Theory and Scientific Laws

Scientists often repeat scientific investigations to verify that the results for a hypothesis or a group of hypotheses are correct. This can lead to a scientific theory.

Scientific Theory The everyday meaning of the word *theory* is an untested idea or an opinion. However, a **scientific theory** *is an explanation of observations or events based on knowledge gained from many observations and investigations.* For example, about 300 years ago, scientists began looking at samples of trees, water, and blood through the first microscopes. They noticed that all of these organisms were made of tinier units, or cells, as shown in **Figure 3.** As more scientists observed cells in other organisms, their observations became known as the cell theory. This theory explains that all living things are made of cells. A scientific theory is assumed to be the best explanation of observations unless it is disproved. The cell theory will continue to explain the makeup of all organisms until an organism is discovered that is not made of cells.

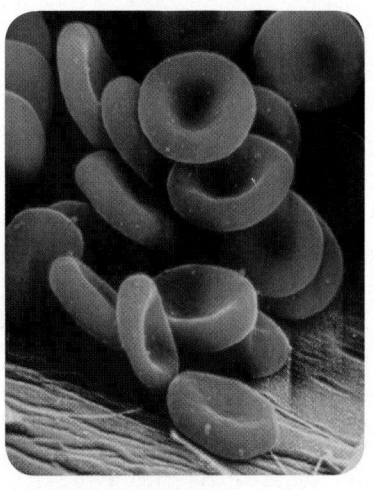

Figure 3 When you view blood using a microscope, you will see that it contains red blood cells.

Scientific Laws Scientific laws are different from societal laws, which are agreements on a set of behaviors. A **scientific law** *describes a pattern or an event in nature that is always true.* A scientific theory might explain how and why an event occurs. But a scientific law states only that an event in nature will occur under specific conditions. For example, the law of conservation of mass states that the mass of materials will be the same before and after a chemical reaction. This scientific law does not explain why this occurs—only that it will occur. **Table 1** compares a scientific theory and a scientific law.

FOLDABLES

Make a vertical two-column chart book. Label it as shown. Use it to organize your notes on scientific investigations.

Results of Scientific Investigations | Examples

Table 1 Comparing Scientific Theory and Scientific Law	
Scientific Theory	**Scientific Law**
A scientific theory is based on repeated observations and scientific investigations.	Scientific laws are observations of similar events that have been observed repeatedly.
If new information does not support a scientific theory, the theory will be modified or rejected.	If many new observations do not follow the law, the law is rejected.
A scientific theory attempts to explain why something happens.	A scientific law states that something will happen.
A scientific theory usually is more complex than a scientific law and might contain many well-supported hypotheses.	A scientific law usually is based on one well-supported hypothesis that states that something will happen.

Skepticism in Media

When you see scientific issues in the media, such as newspapers, radio, television, and magazines, it is important to be skeptical. When you are skeptical, you question information that you read or hear, or events you observe. Is the information truthful? Is it accurate? It also is important that you question statements made by people outside their area of expertise, and claims that are based on vague statements.

Evaluating Scientific Evidence

An important skill in scientific inquiry is critical thinking. **Critical thinking** *is comparing what you already know with the information you are given in order to decide whether you agree with it.* Identifying and minimizing bias also is important when conducting scientific inquiry. To minimize bias in an investigation, sampling, repetition, and blind studies can be helpful, as shown below.

 Key Concept Check How can a scientist minimize bias in a scientific investigation?

1 Sampling

A method of data collection that involves studying small amounts of something in order to learn about the larger whole is sampling. A sample should be a random representation of the whole.

2 Bias

It is important to reduce bias during scientific investigations. Bias is intentional or unintentional prejudice toward a specific outcome. Sources of bias in an investigation can include equipment choices, hypothesis formation, and prior knowledge.

Suppose you were a part of a taste test for a new cereal. If you knew the price of each cereal, you might think that the most expensive one tastes the best. This is a bias.

3 Blind Study

A procedure that can reduce bias is a blind study. The investigator, subject, or both do not know which item they are testing. Personal bias cannot affect an investigation if participants do not know what they are testing.

4 Repetition

If you get different results when you repeat an investigation, then the original investigation probably was flawed. Repetition of experiments helps reduce bias.

A   B   C

Most Popular Brand $2.00   Mediocre Brand $1.50   Least Popular Brand $0.50

Science cannot answer all questions.

You might think that any question can be answered through a scientific investigation. But there are some questions that science cannot answer, such as the one posed in **Figure 4.** Questions about personal opinions, values, beliefs, and feelings cannot be answered scientifically. However, some people use scientific evidence to try to strengthen their claims about these topics.

Safety in Science

Scientists follow safety procedures when they conduct investigations. You too should follow safety procedures when you do any experiments. You should wear appropriate safety equipment and listen to your teacher's instructions. Also, you should learn to recognize potential hazards and to know the meaning of safety symbols. Read more about science laboratory safety in the Science Skill Handbook at the back of this book.

Ethics are especially important when using living things during investigations. Animals should be treated properly. Scientists also should tell research participants about the potential risks and benefits of the research. Anyone can refuse to participate in scientific research.

Figure 4 Science cannot answer questions based on opinions or feelings, such as which paint color is the prettiest.

ACADEMIC VOCABULARY
ethics
(noun) rules of conduct or moral principles

Lesson 1 Review

✓ **Assessment** Online Quiz

? **Inquiry** Virtual Lab

Use Vocabulary

1 **Explain** the relationship between observations and hypotheses.

2 **Use the terms** *technology, scientific law,* and *scientific theory* in complete sentences.

3 **Contrast** inference and prediction.

4 **Compare and contrast** critical thinking and inference.

Understand Key Concepts 🗝

5 Which should NOT be part of scientific inquiry?
   A. bias   **C.** hypothesis
   B. analysis   **D.** testing

6 **Describe** four real-life examples of the results of scientific investigations.

7 **Discuss** four ways a scientist can reduce bias in scientific investigations.

Interpret Graphics

8 **Draw** a graphic organizer like the one below. In each oval, list an example of how to test a hypothesis using scientific inquiry.

Test Hypothesis

Critical Thinking

9 **Suggest** Why do you think people believe some theories even if they are not supported by credible evidence?

10 **Evaluate** In a magazine, you read that two scientific investigations attempted to answer the same question. However, the two teams of scientists came to opposite conclusions. How do you decide which investigation was valid?

Reading Guide

Key Concepts 🔑
ESSENTIAL QUESTIONS

- What is the difference between accuracy and precision?

- Why should you use significant digits?

- What are some tools used by life scientists?

Vocabulary

description p. NOS 12

explanation p. NOS 12

International System of Units (SI) p. NOS 12

accuracy p. NOS 14

precision p. NOS 14

significant digits p. NOS 15

g Multilingual eGlossary

Measurement and Scientific Tools

Description and Explanation

How would you describe the squirrel's activity in **Figure 5**? A **description** *is a spoken or written summary of observations.* Your description might include information such as: the squirrel buried five acorns near a large tree. A qualitative description uses your senses (sight, sound, smell, touch, taste) to describe an observation. *A large tree* is a qualitative description. However, a quantitative description uses numbers to describe the observation. *Five acorns* is a quantitative description. You can use measuring tools, such as a ruler, a balance, or a thermometer, to make quantitative descriptions.

How would you explain the squirrel's activity? An **explanation** *is an interpretation of observations.* You might explain that the squirrel is storing acorns for food at a later time. When you describe something, you report what you observe. But when you explain something, you try to interpret your observations. This can lead to a hypothesis.

Figure 5 A description and an explanation of a squirrel's activity contain different information.

The International System of Units

Suppose you observed a squirrel searching for buried food and recorded that it traveled about 200 ft from its nest. Someone who measures distances in meters might not understand how far the squirrel traveled. The scientific community solved this problem in 1960. It adopted *an internationally accepted system for measurement called the* **International System of Units (SI).**

SI Base Units and Prefixes

Like scientists and many others around the world, you probably use the SI system in your classroom. All SI units are derived from seven base units, as listed in **Table 2**. For example, the base unit for length, or the unit most commonly used to measure length, is the meter. However, you have probably made measurements in kilometers or millimeters before. Where do these units come from?

A prefix can be added to a base unit's name to indicate either a fraction or a multiple of that base unit. The prefixes are based on powers of ten, such as 0.01 and 100, as shown in **Table 3**. For example, one centimeter (1 cm) is one one-hundredth of a meter and a kilometer (1 km) is 1,000 meters.

Concepts in Motion   Interactive Table

Table 2 SI Base Units

Quantity Measured	Unit (symbol)
Length	meter (m)
Mass	kilogram (kg)
Time	second (s)
Electric current	ampere (A)
Temperature	Kelvin (K)
Substance amount	mole (mol)
Light intensity	candela (cd)

Table 3 Prefixes

Prefix	Meaning
Mega– (M)	1,000,000 (10^6)
Kilo– (k)	1,000 (10^3)
Hecto– (h)	100 (10^2)
Deka– (da)	10 (10^1)
Deci– (d)	0.1 (10^{-1})
Centi– (c)	0.01 (10^{-2})
Milli– (m)	0.001 (10^{-3})
Micro– (μ)	0.000 001 (10^{-6})

Conversion

It is easy to convert from one SI unit to another. You either multiply or divide by a power of ten. You also can use proportion calculations to make conversions. For example, a biologist measures an Emperor goose in the field. Her triple-beam balance shows the goose has a mass of 2.8 kg. She could perform the calculation below to find its mass in grams, X.

$$\frac{X}{2.8\,kg} = \frac{1,000\,g}{1\,kg}$$

$$(1\,kg)X = (1,000\,g)(2.8\,kg)$$

$$X = \frac{(1,000\,g)(2.8\,\cancel{kg})}{1\,\cancel{kg}}$$

$$X = 2,800\,g$$

Notice that the answer has the correct units.

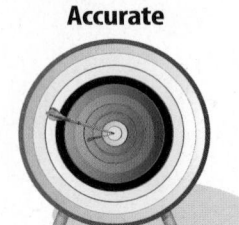
Accurate

An arrow in the center indicates high accuracy.

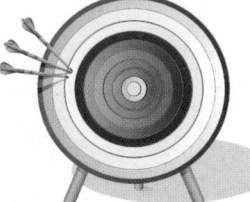
Precise but not accurate

Arrows far from the center indicate low accuracy. Arrows close together indicate high precision.

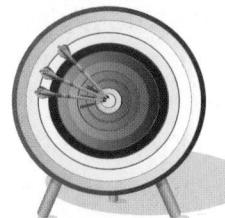
Accurate and precise

Arrows in the center indicate high accuracy. Arrows close together indicate high precision.

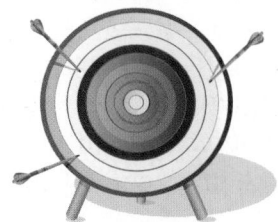
Not accurate or precise

Arrows far from the center indicate low accuracy. Arrows far apart indicate low precision.

Figure 6 The archery target illustrates accuracy and precision. An accurate shot is in the bull's-eye.

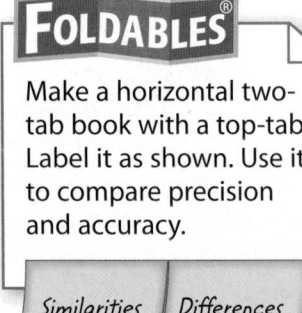

Make a horizontal two-tab book with a top-tab. Label it as shown. Use it to compare precision and accuracy.

| Similarities | Differences |

Precision and Accuracy

Precision and Accuracy

Suppose your friend Simon tells you that he will call you in one minute, but he calls you a minute and a half later. Sarah tells you that she will call you in one minute, and she calls exactly 60 seconds later. What is the difference? Sarah is accurate and Simon is not. **Accuracy** *is a description of how close a measurement is to an accepted or true value.* However, if Simon always calls about 30 seconds later than he says he will, then Simon is precise. **Precision** *is a description of how similar or close measurements are to each other,* as shown in **Figure 6.**

Table 4 illustrates the difference between precise and accurate measurements. Students were asked to find the melting point of sucrose, or table sugar. Each student took three temperature readings and calculated the mean, or average, of his or her data. As the recorded data in the table shows, student A had more accurate data. The melting point mean, 184.7°C, is closer to the scientifically accepted melting point, 185°C. Although not accurate, Student C's measurements are the most precise because they are similar in value.

 Key Concept Check How do accuracy and precision differ?

Table 4 The data taken by student A are more accurate because each value is close to the accepted value. The data taken by student C are more precise because the data are similar.

Table 4 Student Melting Point Data	Student A	Student B	Student C
Trial 1	183.5°C	190.0°C	181.2°C
Trial 2	185.9°C	183.3°C	182.0°C
Trial 3	184.6°C	187.1°C	181.7°C
Mean	184.7°C	186.8°C	181.6°C
Sucrose Melting Point (accepted value) 185°C			

Measurement and Accuracy

The tools used to take measurements can limit the accuracy of the measurements. Suppose you are measuring the temperature at which sugar melts, and the thermometer's measurements are divided into whole numbers. If your sugar sample melts between 183°C and 184°C, you can estimate the temperature between these two numbers. But, if the thermometer's measurements are divided into tenths, and your sample melts between 183.2°C and 183.3°C, your estimate between these numbers would be more accurate.

Significant Digits

In the second example above, you know that the temperature is between 183.2°C and 183.3°C. You could estimate that the temperature is 183.25°C. When you take any measurement, some digits you know for certain and some digits you estimate. **Significant digits** *are the number of digits in a measurement that are known with a certain degree of reliability.* The significant digits in a measurement include all digits you know for certain plus one estimated digit. Therefore, your measurement of 183.25°C would contain five significant digits, as explained in **Table 5.** Using significant digits lets others know how certain your measurements are. **Figure 7** shows an example of rounding to 3 significant digits?

 Key Concept Check Why should you use significant digits?

Figure 7 Since the ruler is divided into tenths, you know the rod is between 5.2 cm and 5.3 cm. You can estimate that the rod is 5.25 cm.

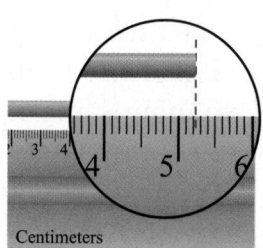

Math Skills

Significant Digits
The number 5,281 has 4 significant digits. Rule 1 in **Table 5** below states that all nonzero numbers are significant.

Practice
Use the rules in **Table 5** to determine the number of significant digits in each of the following numbers: 2.02; 0.0057; 1,500; and 0.500.

⊞ **Review**

• **Math Practice**
• **Personal Tutor**

SCIENCE USE v. COMMON USE·················

digital
Science Use of, pertaining to, or using numbers (numerical digits)

Common Use of or pertaining to a finger

Table 5 Significant Digits

Rules
1. All nonzero numbers are significant.
2. Zeros between nonzero digits are significant.
3. Final zeros used after the decimal point are significant.
4. Zeros used solely for spacing the decimal point are not significant. The zeros indicate only the position of the decimal point.

* The blue numbers in the examples are the significant digits.

Example	Significant Digits	Applied Rules
1.234	4	1
1.2	2	1
0.023	2	1, 4
0.200	3	1, 3
1,002	4	1, 2
3.07	3	1, 2
0.001	1	1, 4
0.012	2	1, 4
50,600	3	1, 2, 4

Scientific Tools

Scientific inquiry often requires the use of tools. Scientists, including life scientists, might use the tools listed on this page and the next page. You might use one or more of them during a scientific inquiry, too. For more information about the proper use of these tools, see the Science Skill Handbook at the back of this book.

Science Journal ▶

In a science journal, you can record descriptions, explanations, plans, and steps used in a scientific inquiry. A science journal can be a spiral-bound notebook or a loose-leaf binder. It is important to keep your science journal organized so that you can find information when you need it. Make sure you keep thorough and accurate records.

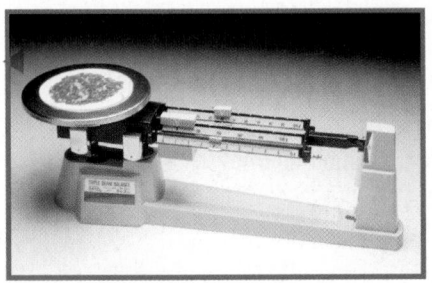

◀ Balances

You can use a triple-beam balance or an electric balance to measure mass. Mass usually is measured in kilograms (kg) or grams (g). When using a balance, do not let objects drop heavily onto the balance. Gently remove an object after you record its mass.

Thermometer ▶

A thermometer measures the temperature of substances. Although the Kelvin (K) is the SI unit for temperature, in the science classroom, you measure temperature in degrees Celsius (°C). Use care when you place a thermometer into a hot substance so that you do not burn yourself. Handle glass thermometers gently so that they do not break. If a thermometer does break, tell your teacher immediately. Do not touch the broken glass or the thermometer's liquid. Never use a thermometer to stir anything.

◀ Glassware

Laboratory glassware is used to hold, pour, heat, and measure liquids. Most labs have many types of glassware. For example, flasks, beakers, petri dishes, test tubes, and specimen jars are used as containers. To measure the volume of a liquid, you use a graduated cylinder. The unit of measure for liquid volume is the liter (L) or milliliter (mL).

◄ Compound Microscope

Microscopes enable you to observe small objects that you cannot observe with just your eyes. Usually, two types of microscopes are in science classrooms—dissecting microscopes and compound light microscopes, such as the one shown to the left. The girl is looking into two eyepieces to observe a magnified image of a small object or organism. However, some microscopes have only one eyepiece.

Microscopes can be damaged easily. It is important to follow your teacher's instructions when carrying and using a microscope. For more information about how to use a microscope, see the Science Skill Handbook at the back of this book.

((○) **Concepts in Motion**   Animation

Computers—Hardware and Software ►

Computers process information. In science, you can use computers to compile, retrieve, and analyze data for reports. You also can use them to create reports and other documents, to send information to others, and to research information.

The physical components of computers, such as monitors and keyboards, are called hardware. The programs that you run on computers are called software. These programs include word processing, spreadsheets, and presentation programs. When scientists write reports, they use word processing programs. They use spreadsheet programs for organizing and analyzing data. Presentation programs can be used to explain information to others.

Tools Used by Life Scientists

Magnifying Lens

A magnifying lens is a hand-held lens that magnifies, or enlarges, an image of an object. It is not as powerful as a microscope and is useful when great magnification is not needed. Magnifying lenses also can be used outside the lab where microscopes might not be available.

Slide

To observe items using a compound light microscope, you must place it on a thin, rectangular piece of glass called a slide. You must handle slides gently to avoid breaking them.

Dissecting Tools

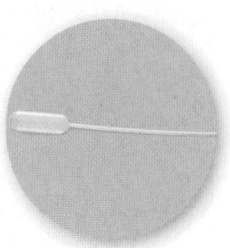

Scientists use dissecting tools, such scalpels and scissors, to examine tissues, organs, or prepared organisms. Dissecting tools are sharp, so always use extreme caution when handling them.

Pipette

A pipette is similar to an eyedropper. It is a small glass or plastic tube used to draw up and transfer liquids.

 Key Concept Check What are some tools used by life scientists?

Lesson 2 Review

✓ **Assessment**   Online Quiz

Use Vocabulary

1 **Define** *description* and *explanation* in your own words.

2 **Use the term** *International System of Units (SI)* in a sentence.

Understand Key Concepts

3 Which tool would a scientist use to view a tiny organism?
- **A.** computer
- **B.** compound microscope
- **C.** test tube
- **D.** triple-beam balance

4 **Describe** the difference between accuracy and precision.

5 **Explain** why scientists use significant digits.

Interpret Graphics

6 **Draw** a graphic organizer like the one below. Write the name of an SI base unit in each circle. Add additional circles to the graphic organizer as needed.

SI Base Unit

Critical Thinking

7 **Recommend** ways that computers can assist life scientists in their work.

 **Math Skills** ✕ ÷ + ─   Review ─ Math Practice ─

8 **Suppose** you measure the mass of a book and it is 420.0890 g. How many significant digits are in this measurement?

How can you build your own scientific instrument?

Materials

500-mL Erlenmeyer flask

rubber tubing, 15 cm

2-hole stopper

500-mL beaker

Also needed: short piece of plastic tubing, water, 100-mL graduated cylinder, plastic wrap (10 cm × 30 cm), bendable straws, food coloring (optional)

Safety

All organisms take in and release gases. Your cells take in oxygen and release carbon dioxide just like the cells of other animals, plants, fungi, protists, and some bacteria. However, many plant cells, some protists, and some bacteria also can take in carbon dioxide and release oxygen. In this lab, you will follow a procedure and build your own scientific instrument that measures the change in the volume of a gas.

Learn It

Scientists often **follow procedures** developed by other scientists to collect data. A procedure is a step-by-step explanation of how to accomplish a task. The steps in a procedure tell you what materials to use, how to them, and in what order to perform specific tasks. Some procedures are simple, while others are more complicated and require a lot of practice and skill.

Try It

1 Read and complete a lab safety form.

2 Into each, an Erlenmeyer flask and a beaker, pour 350 mL of water. Pour 100 mL of water into a graduated cylinder.

3 Seal the graduated cylinder with plastic wrap. Place your hand over the plastic wrap and turn the cylinder upside down. Carefully place the sealed end of the graduated cylinder into the beaker of water. Pull off the plastic wrap without losing any water from the graduated cylinder. Have a team member hold the it so that it doesn't tip over.

4 Place one end of a straw in one hole of a 2-hole stopper. Insert the plastic tubing into the other hole. Place one end of the rubber tubing over the plastic tubing.

5 Without lifting the cylinder above the water's surface, insert the free end of the rubber tubing inside the cylinder. Have a team continue to hold the cylinder.

6 Put the stopper in the flask. Record the initial reading of the water in the graduated cylinder in your Science Journal.

7 Gently blow into the straw and watch the change in volume of the water. Continue blowing into the straw until the graduated cylinder contains 50 mL of gas (air).

Apply It

8 **Draw a diagram** of your set up, also known as a eudiometer. Label all the parts, and describe their functions.

9 🔑 **Key Concept** Describe a scenario in which a life scientist would use this instrument to measure gases.

Reading Guide

Key Concepts
ESSENTIAL QUESTIONS

- How do independent and dependent variables differ?

- How is scientific inquiry used in a real-life scientific investigation?

Vocabulary

variable p. NOS 20

dependent variable p. NOS 20

independent variable p. NOS 20

constants p. NOS 20

g Multilingual eGlossary

Figure 8 Microalgae are plantlike organisms that can make oils.

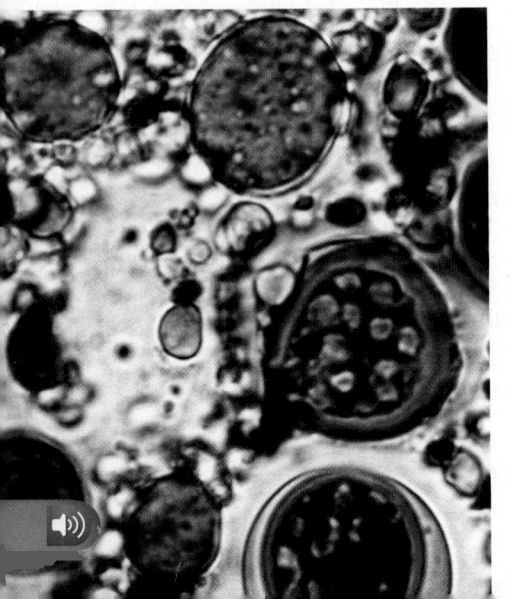

Case Study

Biodiesel from Microalgae

For the last few centuries, fossil fuels have been the main sources of energy for industry and transportation. But, scientists have shown that burning fossil fuels negatively affects the environment. Also, some people are concerned about eventually using up the world's reserves of fossil fuels.

During the past few decades, scientists have explored using protists to produce biodiesel. Biodiesel is a fuel made primarily from living organisms. Protists, shown in **Figure 8,** are a group of microscopic organisms that usually live in water or moist environments. Some of these protists are plantlike because they make their own food using a process called photosynthesis. Microalgae are plantlike protists.

Designing a Controlled Experiment

The scientists in this case study used scientific inquiry to investigate the use of protists to make biodiesel. They designed controlled experiments to test their hypotheses. In the margins of this lesson are examples of how scientists in the study practiced inquiry and the skills you read about in Lesson 1. The notebook pages contain information that a scientist might have written in a science journal.

A controlled experiment is a scientific investigation that tests how one variable affects another. A **variable** *is any factor in an experiment that can have more than one value.* In controlled experiments, there are two types of variables. The **dependent variable** *is the factor measured or observed during an experiment.* The **independent variable** *is the factor that you want to test. It is changed by the investigator to observe how it affects a dependent variable.* **Constants** *are the factors in an experiment that remain the same.*

Key Concept Check How do independent and dependent variables differ?

A controlled experiment has two groups—an experimental group and a control group. The experimental group is used to study how a change in the independent variable changes the dependent variable. The control group contains the same factors as the experimental group, but the independent variable is not changed. Without a control, it is difficult to know whether your experimental observations result from the variable you are testing or from another factor.

Biodiesel

The idea of engines running on fuel made from plant or plantlike sources is not entirely new. Rudolph Diesel, shown in **Figure 9,** invented the diesel engine. He used peanut oil to demonstrate how his engine worked. However, when petroleum was introduced as a diesel fuel source, it was preferred over peanut oil because it was cheaper.

 Reading Check What did Rudolph Diesel use as fuel?

Oil-rich food crops, such as soybeans, can be used as a source of biodiesel. However, some people are concerned that crops grown for fuel sources will replace crops grown for food. If farmers grow more crops for fuel, then the amount of food available worldwide will be reduced. Because of food shortages in many parts of the world, replacing food crops with fuel crops is not a good solution.

Aquatic Species Program

In the late 1970s, the U.S. Department of Energy began funding its Aquatic Species Program (ASP) to investigate ways to remove air pollutants. Coal-fueled power plants produce carbon dioxide (CO_2), a pollutant, as a by-product. In the beginning, the study examined all aquatic organisms that use CO_2 during photosynthesis—their food-making process. These included large plants, commonly know as seaweeds, plants that grow partially underwater, and microalgae. It was hoped these organisms might remove excess CO_2 from the atmosphere. During the studies, however, the project leaders noticed that some microalgae produced large amounts of oil. The program's focus soon shifted to using microalgae to produce oils that could be processed into biodiesel.

Figure 9 Rudolph Diesel invented the first diesel engine in the early 1900s.

Scientific investigations often begin when someone observes an event in nature and wonders why or how it occurs.

A hypothesis is a tentative explanation that can be tested by scientific investigations. A prediction is a statement of what someone expects to happen next in a sequence of events.

Observation A:
While testing microalgae to discover if they would absorb carbon pollutants, ASP project leaders noticed that some species of microalgae had high oil content.
Hypothesis A:
Some microalgae species can be used as a source of biodiesel fuel because the microalgae produce a large amount of oil
Prediction A:
If the correct species is found and the growing conditions are isolated, then large oil amounts will be collected.

Design an Experiment and Collect Data:
The ASP scientists developed a rapid screening test to discover which micro-algae species produced the most oil.
Independent Variable: amount of nitrogen available
Dependent Variable: amount of oil produced
Constants: the growing conditions of algae (temperature, water quality, exposure to the Sun, etc.)

Observation B:
Based on previous microalgae studies, starving microalgae of nutrients could result in more oil production.
Hypothesis B:
Microalgae grown with inadequate amounts of nitrogen alter their growth processes and produce more oil.
Prediction B:
If microalgae receive inadequate amounts of nitrogen then they will produce more oil.

Figure 10 Green microalgae and diatoms showed the most promise during testing for biodiesel production.

Which Microalgae?

Microalgae are microscopic organisms that live in marine (salty) or freshwater environments. Like many plants and other plantlike organisms, they use photosynthesis and make sugar. The process requires light energy. Microalgae make more sugar than they can use as food. They convert excess sugar to oil. Scientists focused on these microalgae because their oil then could be processed into biodiesel.

The scientists began their research by collecting and identifying promising microalgae species. The search focused on microalgae in shallow, inland, saltwater ponds. Scientists predicted that these microalgae were more resistant to changes in temperature and salt content in the water.

By 1985, a test was in place for identifying microalgae with high oil content. Two years later, 3,000 microalgae species had been collected. Scientists checked these samples for tolerance to acidity, salt levels, and temperature and selected 300 species. Of these 300 species, green microalgae and diatoms, as shown in **Figure 10**, showed the most promise. However, it was obvious that no one species was going to be perfect for all climates and water types.

Oil Production in Microalgae

Scientists also began researching how microalgae produce oil. Some studies suggested that starving microalgae of nutrients, such as nitrogen, could increase the amount of oil they produced. However, starving microalgae also caused them to be smaller, resulting in no overall increase in oil production.

Outdoor Testing v. Bioreactors

By the 1980s, the ASP scientists were growing micro-algae in outdoor ponds in New Mexico. However, outdoor conditions were very different from those in the laboratory. Cooler temperatures in the outdoor ponds resulted in smaller microalgae. Native algae species also invaded the ponds, forcing out the high-oil-producing laboratory microalgae species.

The scientists continued to focus on growing microalgae in open ponds, such as the one shown in **Figure 11.** Many scientists still believe that these open ponds are better for producing large quantities of biodiesel from microalgae. But, some researchers are now growing microalgae in closed glass containers called bioreactors, also shown in **Figure 11.** Inside these bioreactors, organisms live and grow under controlled conditions. This method avoids many of the problems associated with open ponds. However, bioreactors are more expensive than open ponds.

A biofuel company in the western United States has been experimenting with a low-cost bioreactor. A scientist at the company explained that they examined the ASP program and hypothesized that they could use long plastic bags, shown in **Figure 11,** instead of closed glass containers.

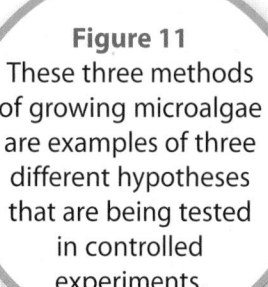

Open ponds are less expensive than bioreactors for growing microalgae.

Figure 11
These three methods of growing microalgae are examples of three different hypotheses that are being tested in controlled experiments.

Microalgae grown in plastic bags are very expensive to harvest.

Microalgae grow under controlled conditions in glass bioreactors.

Why So Many Hypotheses?

According to Dr. Richard Sayre, a biofuel researcher, all the ASP research was based on forming hypotheses. Dr. Sayre says, "It was hypothesis-driven. You just don't go in and say 'Well, I have a feeling this is the right way to do it.' You propose a hypothesis. Then you test it."

Dr. Sayre added, "Biologists have been trained over and over again to develop research strategies based on hypotheses. It's sort of ingrained into our culture. You don't get research support by saying, 'I'm going to put together a system, and it's going to be wonderful.' You have to come up with a question. You propose some strategies for answering the question. What are your objectives? What outcomes do you expect for each objective?"

 Reading Check Why is it important for a scientific researcher to develop a good hypothesis?

Increasing Oil Yield

Scientists from a biofuel company in Washington State thought of another way to increase oil production. Researchers knew microalgae use light energy, water, and carbon dioxide and make sugar. The microalgae eventually convert sugar into oil. The scientists wondered if they could increase microalgae oil production by distributing light to all microalgae. The experimental lab setup to test this idea is shown in **Figure 12.**

Observation C:
Microalgae use light energy, water, and carbon dioxide to make sugar, which is converted to oil.
Hypothesis C:
Microalgae will produce more oil if light is distributed evenly throughout because they need light energy to grow and produce more oil.
Prediction C:
If light is distributed more evenly then more microalgae will grow, and more oil will be produced.

Figure 12 Acrylic rods distribute light to microalgae below the water's surface. If microalgae receive light, they can photosynthesize and eventually produce oils. Without light, microalgae are not productive.

Bringing Light to Microalgae

Normally microalgae grow near the surface of a pond. Any microalgae about 5 cm below the pond's surface will grow less. Why is this? First, water blocks light from reaching deep into a pond. Second, microalgae at the top of a pond block light from reaching microalgae below them. Only the top part of a pond is productive.

Experimental Group

Researchers decided to assemble a team of engineers to design a light-distribution system. Light rods distribute artificial light to microalgae in a bioreactor. The bioreactor controls the environmental conditions that affect how the microalgae grow. These conditions include temperature, nutrient levels, carbon dioxide level, airflow, and light.

 Reading Check In the experimental group, what variables are controlled in the bioreactor?

Data from their experiments showed scientists how microalgae in well-lit environments grow compared to how microalgae grow in dimmer environments. Using solar data for various parts of the country, the scientists concluded that the light rod would significantly increase microalgae growth and oil production in outdoor ponds. These scientists next plan to use the light-rod growing method in outdoor ponds.

Field Testing

Scientists plan to take light to microalgae instead of moving microalgae to light. Dr. Jay Burns is chief microalgae scientist at a biofuel company. He said, "What we are proposing to do is to take the light from the surface of a pond and distribute it throughout the depth of the pond. Instead of only the top 5 cm being productive, the whole pond becomes productive."

 Reading Check What is the benefit of the light-distribution system?

> Scientists tested their hypothesis, collected data, analyzed the data, and drew conclusions.

Analyze Results:
The experimental results showed that microalgae would produce more oil using a light-rod system than by using just sunlight.
Draw a Conclusion:
The researchers concluded that the light-rod system greatly increased microalgae oil production.

Research scientists and scientists in the field rely on scientific methods and scientific inquiry to solve real-life problems. When a scientific investigation lasts for several years and involves many scientists, such as this study, many hypotheses can be tested. Some hypotheses are supported, and other hypotheses are not. However, information is gathered and lessons are learned. Hypotheses are refined and tested many times. This process of scientific inquiry results in a better understanding of the problem and possible solutions.

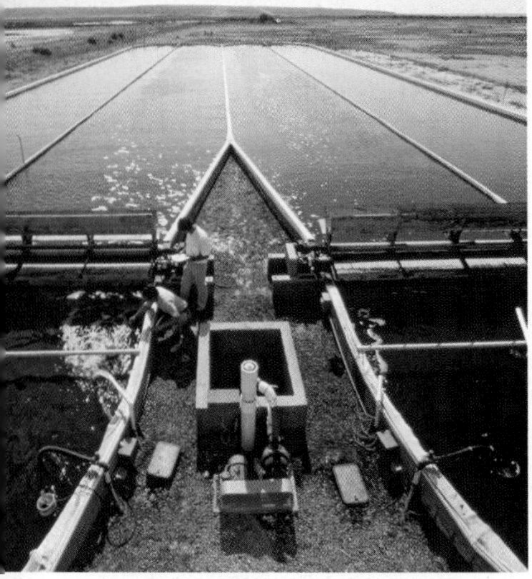

Figure 13 During cultivation, paddlewheels bring microalgae to the surface and expose them to light.

Another Way to Bring Light to Microalgae

Light rods are not the only way to bring light to microalgae. Paddlewheels, as shown in **Figure 13,** can be used to keep the microalgae's locations changing. Paddlewheels continuously rotate microalgae to the surface. This exposes the organisms to more light.

Key Concept Check Describe three ways in which scientific inquiry was used in this case study.

Why Grow Microalgae?

While the focus of this case study is microalgae growth for biodiesel production, there are other benefits of growing microalgae, as shown in **Figure 14.** Power plants that burn fossil fuels release carbon dioxide into the atmosphere. Evidence indicates that this contributes to global warming. During photosynthesis, microalgae use carbon dioxide and water, release oxygen, and produce sugar, which they convert to oil. Not only do microalgae produce a valuable fuel, they also remove pollutants from and add oxygen to the atmosphere.

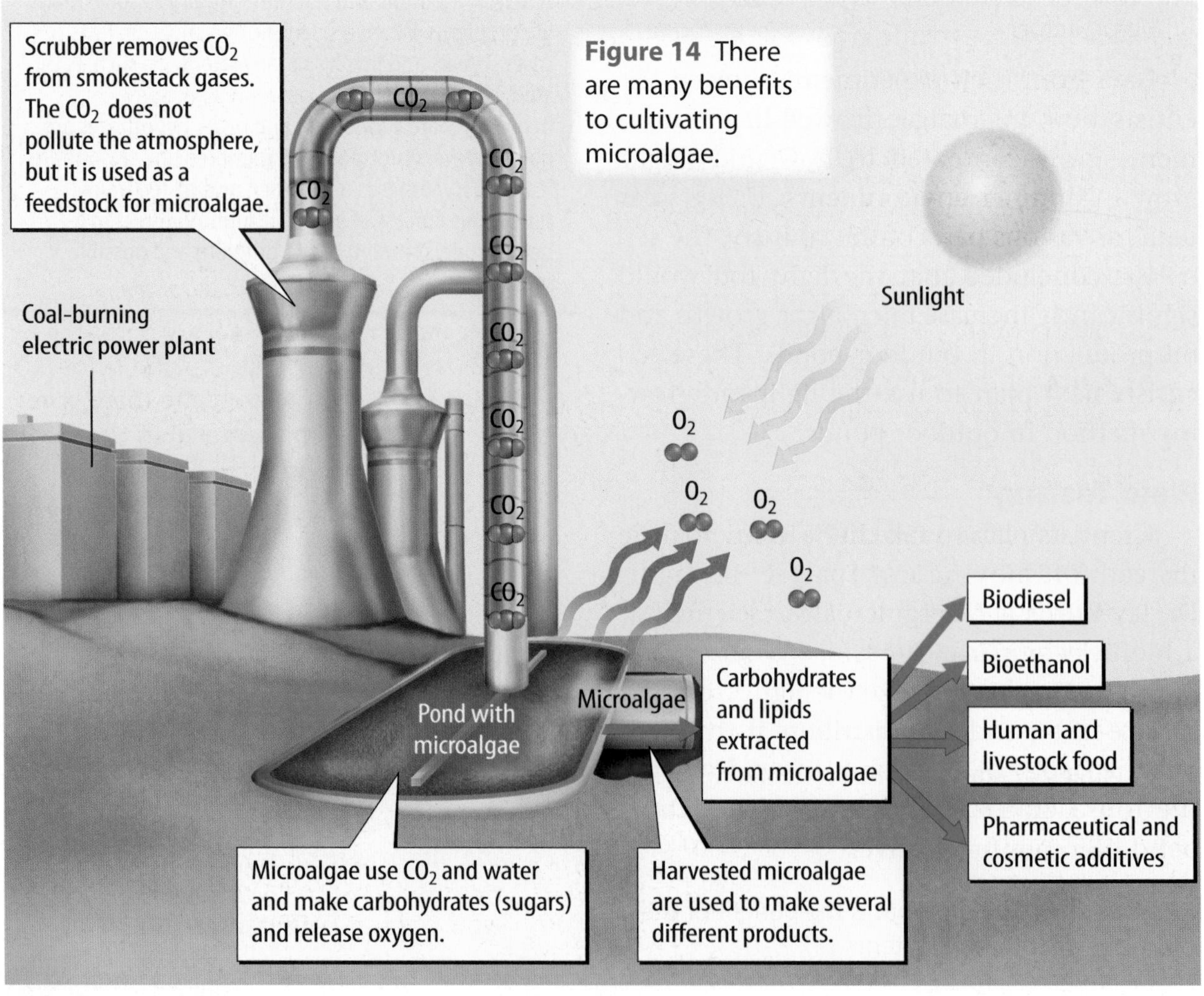
Scrubber removes CO_2 from smokestack gases. The CO_2 does not pollute the atmosphere, but it is used as a feedstock for microalgae.
CO_2
Coal-burning electric power plant
Sunlight
O_2
Pond with microalgae
Microalgae
Carbohydrates and lipids extracted from microalgae
Biodiesel
Bioethanol
Human and livestock food
Pharmaceutical and cosmetic additives
Microalgae use CO_2 and water and make carbohydrates (sugars) and release oxygen.
Harvested microalgae are used to make several different products.

Figure 14 There are many benefits to cultivating microalgae.

Are microalgae the future?

Scientists face many challenges in their quest to produce biodiesel from microalgae. For now, the costs of growing microalgae and extracting their oils are too high to compete with petroleum-based diesel. However, the combined efforts of government-funded programs and commercial biofuel companies might one day make microalgae-based biodiesel an affordable reality in the United States. In fact, a company in Israel has a successful test plant in operation, as shown in **Figure 15.** Plans are underway to build a large-scale industrial facility to convert carbon dioxide gases released from an Israeli coal-powered electrical plants into useful microalgae products. If this technology performs as expected, microalgae cultivation might occur near coal-fueled power plants in other parts of the world, too.

Currently, scientists have no final conclusions about using microalgae as a fuel source. As long as petroleum remains relatively inexpensive and available, it probably will remain the preferred source of diesel fuel. However, if petroleum prices increase or availability decreases, new sources of fuel will be needed. Biodiesel made from microalgae oils might be one of the alternative fuel sources used.

Figure 15 This microalgae test facility in Israel is reducing the amount of carbon dioxide pollution in the atmosphere.

Lesson 3 Review

✓ **Assessment** Online Quiz

Use Vocabulary

1 **Define** *variable* in your own words.

2 **Contrast** the terms *dependent variable, independent variable,* and *constants.*

Understand Key Concepts

3 Which factor does the investigator change during an investigation?
   A. constant
   B. dependent variable
   C. independent variable
   D. variable

4 **Give an example** of a scientific inquiry used in a real-life scientific investigation that is not mentioned in this chapter.

Interpret Graphics

5 **Organize Information** Copy and fill in a graphic organizer like the one below with information about the three types of oil production discussed in the study.

Critical Thinking

6 **Hypothesize** other methods to either increase the oil content of microalgae or to grow greater amounts of microalgae for biodiesel production.

7 **Evaluate** scientists' efforts to increase the oil content of microalgae and to grow microalgae more quickly. What would you do differently?

Materials

500-mL
Erlenmeyer
flask

one-hole
stopper with a
short pieces of
plastic tubing
in the hole

500-mL beaker

Also needed:
rubber tubing
(15 cm), water,
100-mL
graduated
cylinder,
plastic wrap
(10 cm × 30
cm), scissors,
bendable
straw, yeast,
sugar, triple-
beam balance,
stopwatch, ice,
thermometer

Safety

How can you design a bioreactor?

You are part of scientific team studying how yeast grows in a bioreactor. In a bioreactor, yeast uses sugar as an energy source and releases carbon dioxide gas as a waste product. One way you can tell how fast yeast grows is to measure the volume of gas the yeast produces.

Ask a Question

How do water temperature and sugar concentration affect yeast growth?

Make Observations

1. Read and complete a lab safety form.
2. Copy the data table shown on the next page into your Science Journal.
3. Place weighing paper or waxed paper on the triple-beam balance, and then zero the balance. Do not place solids directly on the balance. Measure 3 g of yeast. Use the paper to transport the yeast back to your lab station.

4. Repeat step 3 to measure 4 g of sugar.
5. Measure and pour 350 mL of water into both the Erlenmeyer flask and the beaker. Measure 100 mL of water in the graduated cylinder.
6. Seal the graduated cylinder with plastic wrap. Place you hand over the plastic wrap, and turn the graduated cylinder upside down. Carefully place the sealed end of the graduated cylinder into a beaker of water. Pull off the plastic wrap without losing any water from the cylinder. Have a team member hold the graduated cylinder so that it doesn't tip over.
7. Place one end of a 15-cm piece of rubber tubing over the short plastic or glass tubing in the stopper. Without lifting the cylinder above the water's surface, insert the free end of the long piece of tubing inside the graduated cylinder. Have a team continue to hold it. Record the initial reading of the water level in the graduated cylinder in your Science Journal.
8. Add the sugar and then the yeast to the Erlenmeyer flask. Place the stopper in the flask and swirl it to mix the contents. This flask is your bioreactor.
9. Record the volume of gas produced every 10 min for half an hour. To calculate the volume of gas produced for each 10 min time interval, subtract the initial volume from the final volume.

Form a Hypothesis

⑩ As a class, form a hypothesis that explains how a change in the amount of sugar in your bioreactor affects carbon dioxide production. Form a second hypothesis that explains how a change in temperature of the water affects carbon dioxide production.

Test Your Hypotheses

⑪ As a class, develop procedures to test your hypotheses. Use a range of temperatures and different amounts of sugar in your tests.

⑫ With your teammates, set up several bioreactors with the conditions you outlined in your procedures. Record the results from each bioreactor in a separate data table.

⑬ Using the class data, create two line graphs—one graph for each hypothesis.

Analyze and Conclude

⑭ **Analyze** What conditions resulted in the fastest growth of yeast?

⑮ **Compare** Which of the two variables had a greater influence on the growth of yeast? How did you draw that conclusion?

⑯ 🔵 **The Big Idea** Which scientific processes did you use in your investigation of bioreactors?

Communicate Your Results

Present your team's results to your class. Include visual aids and at least one graph.

Inquiry Extension

As part of your presentation, propose future research that your team will conduct on bioreactors. Describe other variables or other organisms your team will investigate. Explain the goal of your future research. Will you develop a product that can be marketed? Will you provide an explanation to solve a scientific problem? Will you develop a new technology?

Gas Produced	
Temperature of water _____	
Amount of sugar _____	

Time (min)	Eudiometer Reading (mL)
0	
10	
20	
30	

Lab Tips

☑ Make sure the graduated cylinder is not tilted when you take readings.

☑ If you use a recycled water bottle as your bioreactor, do not squeeze the bottle once you place the stopper in it or you can force air into the eudiometer.

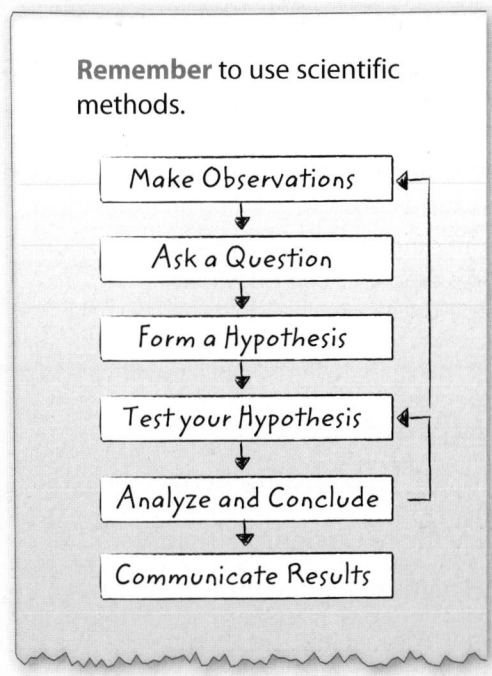

Remember to use scientific methods.

Make Observations → Ask a Question → Form a Hypothesis → Test your Hypothesis → Analyze and Conclude → Communicate Results

Study Guide and Review

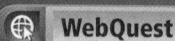

 **THE BIG IDEA** The process of scientific inquiry and performing scientific investigations can provide answers to questions about your world.

Key Concepts Summary 🔑

	Vocabulary
Lesson 1: Understanding Science • Scientific inquiry, also known as scientific methods, is a collection of skills that scientists use in different combinations to perform scientific investigations. • Scientific investigations often result in new **technology**, new materials, newly discovered objects or events, or answers to questions. • A scientist can help minimize bias in a scientific investigation by taking random samples, doing blind studies, repeating an experiment several times, and keeping accurate and honest records.	**science** p. NOS 4 **observation** p. NOS 6 **inference** p. NOS 6 **hypothesis** p. NOS 6 **prediction** p. NOS 7 **technology** p. NOS 8 **scientific theory** p. NOS 9 **scientific law** p. NOS 9 **critical thinking** p. NOS 10
Lesson 2: Measurement and Scientific Tools • **Precision** is a description of how similar or close measurements are to each other. **Accuracy** is a description of how close a measurement is to an accepted value. • **Significant digits** communicate the precision of the tool used to make measurements. • Life scientists use many tools, such as science journals, microscopes, computers, magnifying lenses, slides, and dissecting tools.	**description** p. NOS 12 **explanation** p. NOS 12 **International System of Units (SI)** p. NOS 12 **precision** p. NOS 14 **accuracy** p. NOS 14 **significant digits** p. NOS 15
Lesson 3: Case Study: Biodiesel from Microalgae • The **independent variable** is a factor in an experiment that is manipulated or changed by the investigator to observe how it affects a dependent variable. The **dependent variable** is the factor measured or observed during an experiment. • Scientific inquiry is used to gain information and find solutions to real-life problems and questions.	**variable** p. NOS 20 **dependent variable** p. NOS 20 **independent variable** p. NOS 20 **constants** p. NOS 20

Use Vocabulary

Explain the relationship between each set of terms.

1 scientific law, scientific theory

2 observation, explanation

3 hypothesis, scientific theory

4 description, explanation

5 International System of Units (SI), significant digits

6 variable, constant

Understand Key Concepts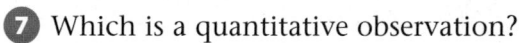

7 Which is a quantitative observation?

A. 15 m long

B. red color

C. rough texture

D. strong odor

8 Which is one way scientists indicate how precise and accurate their experimental measurements are?

A. They keep accurate, honest records.

B. They make sure their experiments can be repeated.

C. They use significant figures in their measurements.

D. They record small samples of data.

9 Which is NOT a source of bias?

A. accurate records

B. equipment choice

C. funding source

D. hypothesis formation

Critical Thinking

10 **Explain** What would be the next step in the scientific inquiry process below?

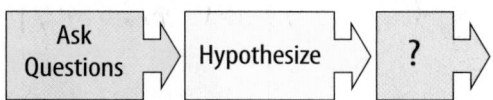

11 **Select** a science career that uses technology. Explain how that career would be different if the technology had not been invented.

12 **Identify** the experimental group, the control group, and controls in the following example. Explain your decision.

A scientist tests a new cough medicine by giving it to a group who have colds. The scientist gives another group with colds a liquid and tells them it is cough medicine. The people in both groups are women between the ages of 20 and 30 who normally are in good health.

Writing in Science

13 **Write** a five-sentence paragraph that includes examples of how bias can be intentional or unintentional and how scientists can reduce bias. Be sure to include topic and concluding sentences in your paragraph.

REVIEW THE B**I**G IDEA

14 What process do scientists use to perform scientific investigations? List a possible sequence of steps in a scientific inquiry and explain your reasoning.

15 What next step of scientific methods might these marine biologists perform?

Math Skills

Review

Math Practice

Significant Digits

16 How many significant figures are in 0.00840, 15.7, and 13.040?

LIFE: Structure & Function

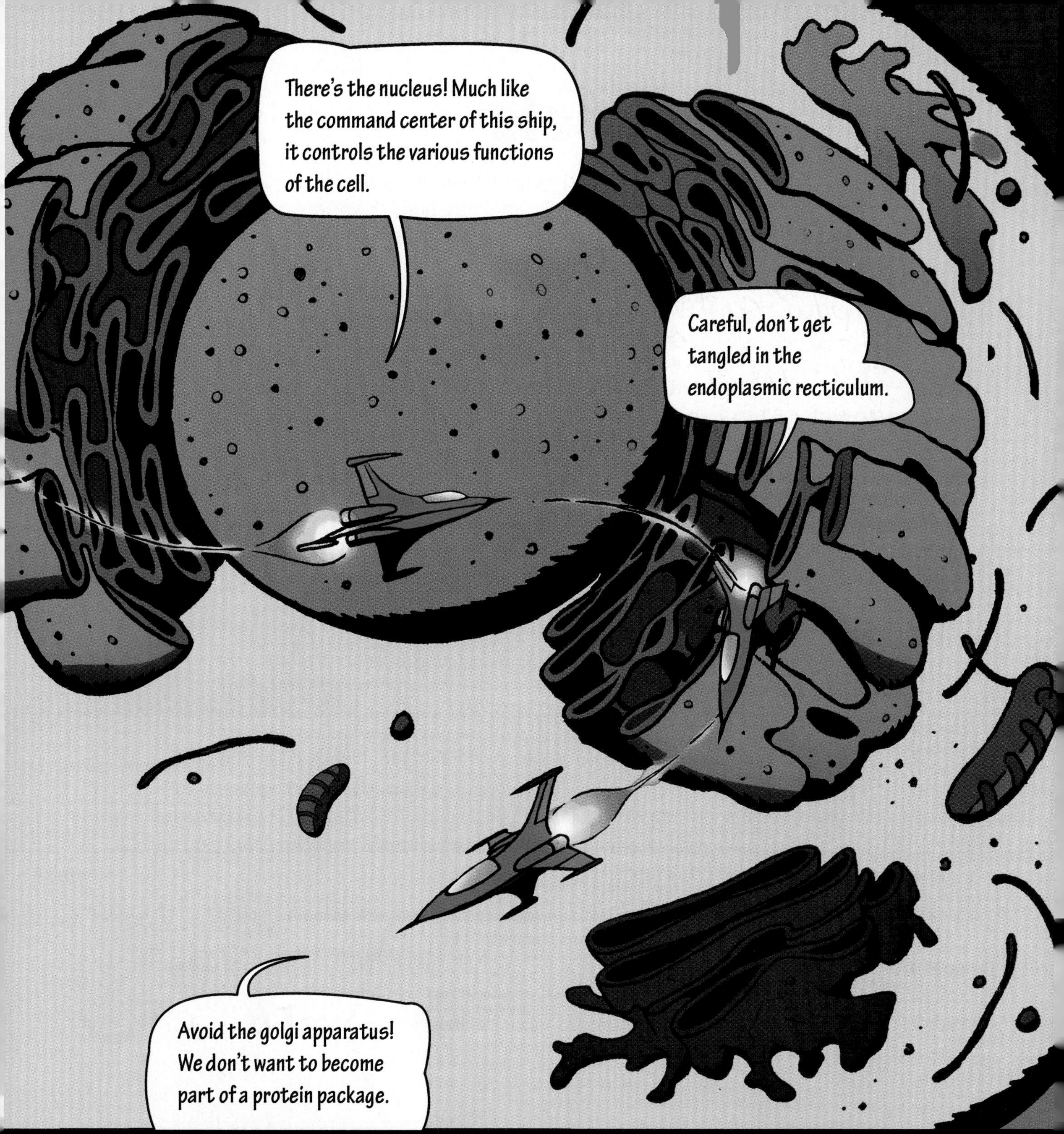
There's the nucleus! Much like the command center of this ship, it controls the various functions of the cell.
Careful, don't get tangled in the endoplasmic recticulum.
Avoid the golgi apparatus! We don't want to become part of a protein package.

1850 | 1900 | 1950

1858
Rudolf Virchow concludes that all cells come from preexisting cells.

1875
Walther Flemming introduces the term *mitosis* and notes that chromosomes split longitudinally during this process.

1953
James Watson and Francis Crick develop the double-helix model of DNA.

Inquiry
Visit ConnectED for this unit's **STEM** activity.

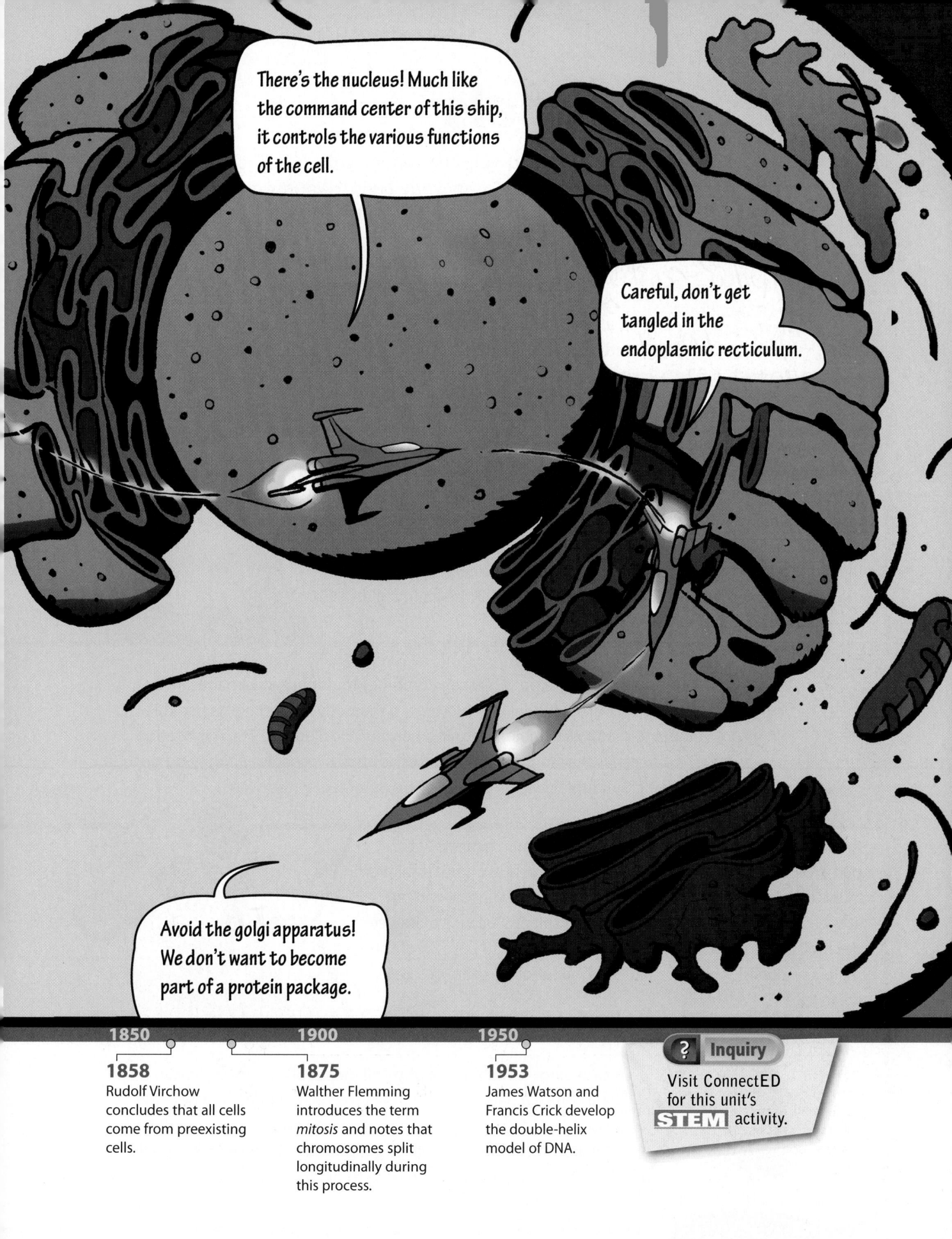

Models

What would you do without your heart—one of the most important muscles in your body? Worldwide, people are on donor lists, patiently waiting for heart transplants because their hearts are not working properly. Today, doctors can diagnose and treat heart problems with the help of models.

A **model** is a representation of an object, a process, an event, or a system that is similar to the physical object or idea being studied. Models can be used to study things that are too big or too small, happen too quickly or too slowly, or are too dangerous or too expensive to study directly. However, some models can replace organs or bones in the body that are not functioning properly.

A magnetic resonance image (MRI) is a type of model created by using a strong magnetic field and radio waves. MRI machines produce high-resolution images of the body from a series of images of different layers of the heart. For example, an MRI model of the heart allows cardiologists to diagnose heart disease or damage. To obtain a clear MRI, the patient must be still. Even the beating of the heart can limit the ability of an MRI to capture clear images.

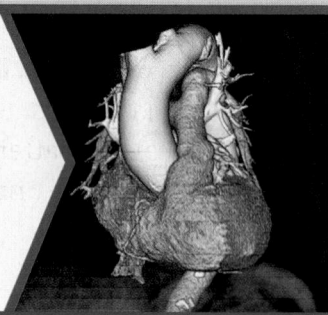

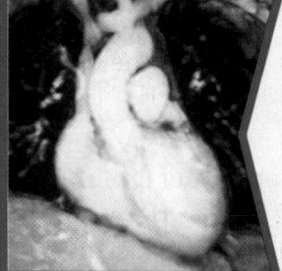

A computer tomography (CT) scan combines multiple X-ray images into a detailed 3-D visual model of structures in the body. Cardiologists use this model to diagnose a malfunctioning heart or blocked arteries. A limitation of a CT scan is that some coronary artery diseases, especially if they do not involve a buildup of calcium, may not be detected by the scan.

An artificial heart is a physical model of a human heart that can pump blood throughout the body. For a patient with heart failure, a doctor might suggest temporarily replacing the heart with an artificial model while they wait for a transplant. Because of its size, the replacement heart is suitable for about only 50 percent of the male population. And, it is stable only for about 2 years before it wears out.

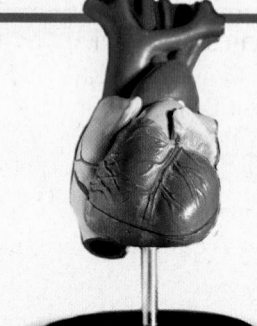

A cardiologist might use a physical model of a heart to explain a diagnosis to a patient. The parts of the heart can be touched and manipulated to explain how a heart works and the location of any complications. However, this physical model does not function like a real heart, and it cannot be used to diagnose disease.

Maps as Models

One way to think of a computer model, such as an MRI or a CT scan, is as a map. A map is a model that shows how locations are arranged in space. A map can be a model of a small area, such as your street. Or, maps can be models of very large areas, such as a state, a country, or the world.

Biologists study maps to understand where different animal species live, how they interact, and how they migrate. Most animals travel in search of food, water, specific weather, or a place to mate. By placing small electronic tracking devices on migrating animals biologists can create maps of their movements, such as the map of elephant movement in **Figure 1.** These maps are models that help determine how animals survive, repeat the patterns of their life cycle, and respond to environmental changes.

Limitations of Models

It is impossible to include all the details about an object or an idea in one model. A map of elephant migration does not tell you whether the elephant is eating, sleeping, or playing with other elephants. Scientists must consider the limitations of the models they use when drawing conclusions about animal behavior.

All models have limitations. When making decisions about a patient's diagnosis and treatment, a cardiologist must be aware of the information each type of model does and does not provide. CT scans and MRIs each provide different diagnostic information. A doctor needs to know what information is needed before choosing which model to use. Scientists and doctors consider the purpose and limitations of the models they use to ensure that they draw the most accurate conclusions possible.

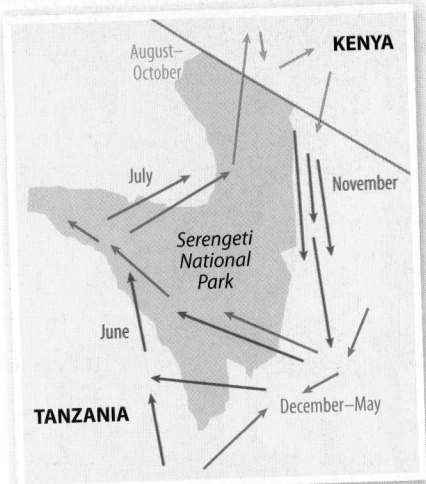

Figure 1 This map is a model of elephants' movements. The colored lines show the paths of three elephants that were equipped with tracking devices for a year.

Inquiry MiniLab   **40 minutes**

How can you model an elephant enclosure?

You are part of a zoo design firm hired to design a model of a new elephant enclosure that mimics a natural habitat.

1. Read and complete a lab safety form.
2. Research elephants and study the map above to understand the needs of elephants.
3. Create a detailed map of your enclosure using **colored pencils** and a **ruler.** Be sure to include the scale, labels, and a legend.
4. Trade maps with a classmate.
5. Using **salt dough** and **craft supplies,** build a physical 3-D model of the elephant enclosure.

Analyze and Conclude

1. **Describe** How did you decide on the scale for your map?
2. **Compare** What are some similarities between your map and your physical model?
3. **Contrast** What are the benefits and the limitations of your physical model?

Classifying and Exploring Life

THE BIG IDEA

What are living things, and how can they be classified?

Inquiry **Dropped Dinner Rolls?**

At first glance, you might think someone dropped dinner rolls on a pile of rocks. These objects might look like dinner rolls, but they're not.

- What do you think the objects are? Do you think they are alive?
- Why do you think they look like this?
- What are living things, and how can they be classified?

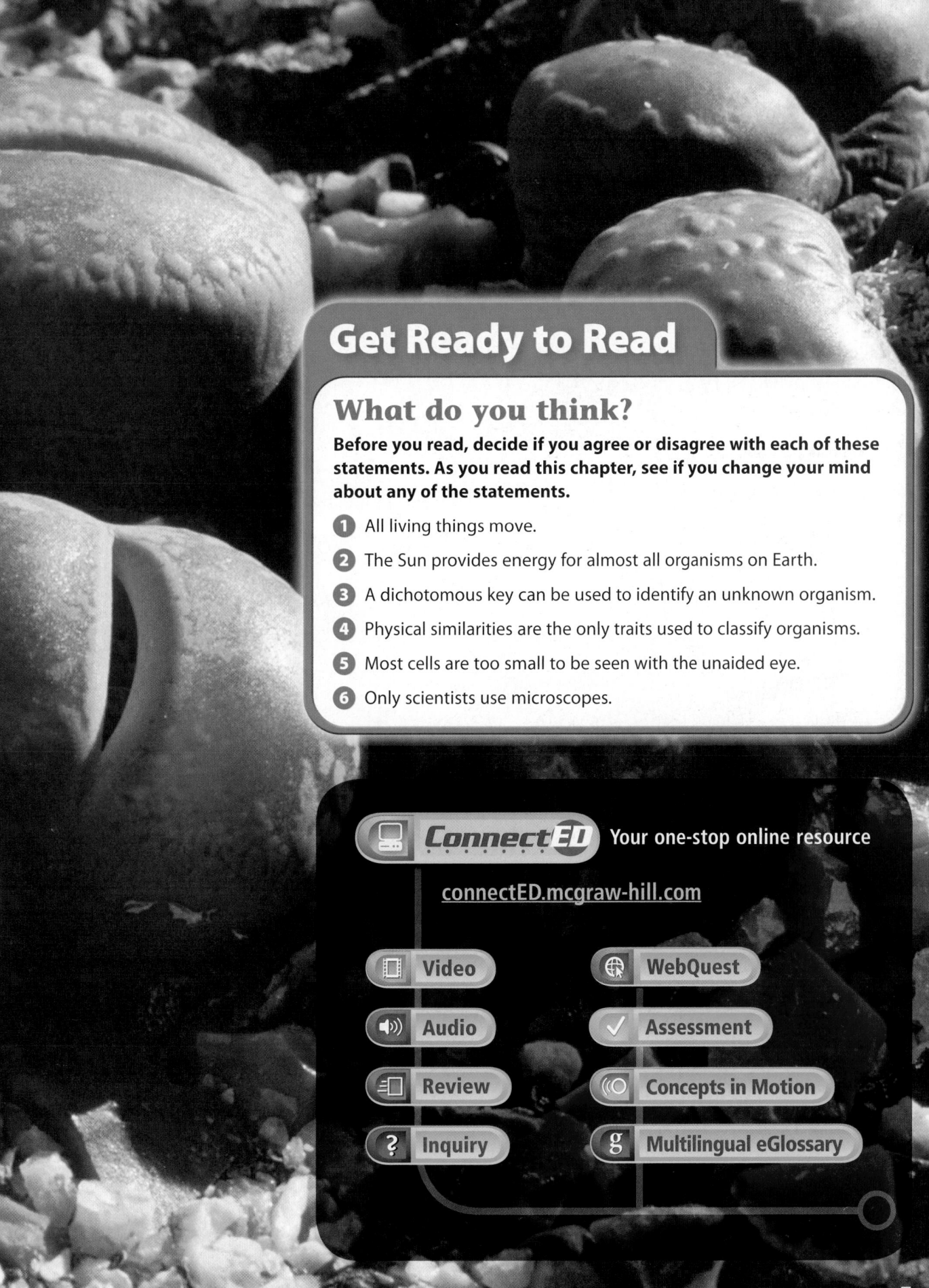

Get Ready to Read

What do you think?

Before you read, decide if you agree or disagree with each of these statements. As you read this chapter, see if you change your mind about any of the statements.

1 All living things move.

2 The Sun provides energy for almost all organisms on Earth.

3 A dichotomous key can be used to identify an unknown organism.

4 Physical similarities are the only traits used to classify organisms.

5 Most cells are too small to be seen with the unaided eye.

6 Only scientists use microscopes.

ConnectED Your one-stop online resource

connectED.mcgraw-hill.com

Video

WebQuest

Audio

Assessment

Review

Concepts in Motion

Inquiry

Multilingual eGlossary

Reading Guide

Key Concepts
ESSENTIAL QUESTIONS

- What characteristics do all living things share?

Vocabulary

organism p. 9

cell p. 10

unicellular p. 10

multicellular p. 10

homeostasis p. 13

g Multilingual eGlossary

Characteristics of Life

Inquiry What's missing?

This toy looks like a dog and can move, but it is a robot. What characteristics are missing to make it alive? Let's find out.

Launch Lab

Is it alive?

Living organisms have specific characteristics. Is a rock a living organism? Is a dog? What characteristics describe something that is living?

1. Read and complete a lab safety form.
2. Place three pieces of **pasta** in the bottom of a **clear plastic cup.**
3. Add **carbonated water** to the cup until it is 2/3 full.
4. Observe the contents of the cup for 5 minutes. Record your observations in your Science Journal.

Think About This

1. Think about living things. How do you know they are alive?

2. Which characteristics of life do you think you are observing in the cup?

3. **Key Concept** Is the pasta alive? How do you know?

Characteristics of Life

Look around your classroom and then at **Figure 1.** You might see many nonliving things, such as lights and books. Look again, and you might see many living things, such as your teacher, your classmates, and plants. What makes people and plants different from lights and books?

People and plants, like all living things, have all the characteristics of life. All living things are organized, grow and develop, reproduce, respond, maintain certain internal conditions, and use energy. Nonliving things might have some of these characteristics, but they do not have all of them. Books might be organized into chapters, and lights use energy. However, only those things that have all the characteristics of life are living. *Things that have all the characteristics of life are called* **organisms.**

Reading Check How do living things differ from nonliving things?

Figure 1 A classroom might contain living and nonliving things.

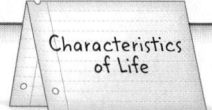
Organization

Your home is probably organized in some way. For example, the kitchen is for cooking, and the bedrooms are for sleeping. Living things are also organized. Whether an organism is made of one **cell**—*the smallest unit of life*—or many cells, all living things have structures that have specific functions.

Living things that are made of only one cell are called **unicellular** *organisms.* Within a unicellular organism are structures with specialized functions just like a house has rooms for different activities. Some structures take in nutrients or control cell activities. Other structures enable the organism to move.

Living things that are made of two or more cells are called **multicellular** *organisms.* Some multicellular organisms only have a few cells, but others have trillions of cells. The different cells of a multicellular organism usually do not perform the same function. Instead, the cells are organized into groups that have specialized functions, such as digestion or movement.

Growth and Development

The tadpole in **Figure 2** is not a frog, but it will soon lose its tail, grow legs, and become an adult frog. This happens because the tadpole, like all organisms, will grow and develop. When organisms grow, they increase in size. A unicellular organism grows as the cell increases in size. Multicellular organisms grow as the number of their cells increases.

Figure 2 A tadpole grows in size while developing into an adult frog.

Growth and Development

 **Concepts in Motion** Animation

✓ **Visual Check** What characteristics of life can you identify in this figure?

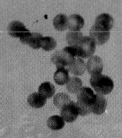

1 A frog egg develops into a tadpole.

2 As the tadpole grows, it develops legs.

Changes that occur in an organism during its lifetime are called development. In multicellular organisms, development happens as cells become specialized into different cell types, such as skin cells or muscle cells. Some organisms undergo dramatic developmental changes over their lifetime, such as a tadpole developing into a frog.

 Reading Check What happens in development?

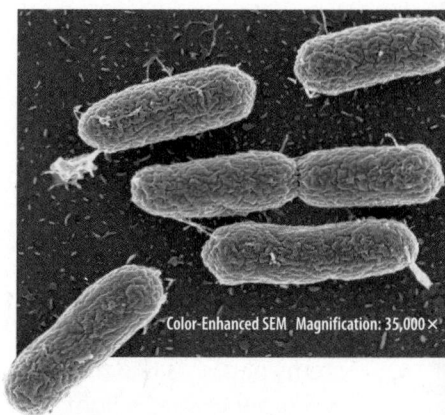

Color-Enhanced SEM   Magnification: 35,000×

Figure 3 Some unicellular organisms, like the bacteria shown here, reproduce by dividing. The two new organisms are identical to the original organism.

Reproduction

As organisms grow and develop, they usually are able to reproduce. Reproduction is the process by which one organism makes one or more new organisms. In order for living things to continue to exist, organisms must reproduce. Some organisms within a population might not reproduce, but others must reproduce if the species is to survive.

Organisms do not all reproduce in the same way. Some organisms, like the ones in **Figure 3,** can reproduce by dividing and become two new organisms. Other organisms have specialized cells for reproduction. Some organisms must have a mate to reproduce, but others can reproduce without a mate. The number of offspring produced varies. Humans usually produce only one or two offspring at a time. Other organisms, such as the frog in **Figure 2,** can produce hundreds of offspring at one time.

3 **The tadpole continues to grow as it develops into an adult frog.**

4 **An adult female frog can produce hundreds of eggs.**

Responses to Stimuli

If someone throws a ball toward you, you might react by trying to catch it. This is because you, like all living things, respond to changes in the environment. These changes can be internal or external and are called stimuli (STIHM yuh li).

Internal Stimuli

You respond to internal stimuli (singular, stimulus) every day. If you feel hungry and then look for food, you are responding to an internal stimulus—the feeling of hunger. The feeling of thirst that causes you to find and drink water is another example of an internal stimulus.

External Stimuli

Changes in an organism's environment that affect the organism are external stimuli. Some examples of external stimuli are light and temperature.

Many plants, like the one in **Figure 4,** will grow toward light. You respond to light, too. Your skin's response to sunlight might be to darken, turn red, or freckle.

Some animals respond to changes in temperature. The response can be more or less blood flowing to the skin. For example, if the temperature increases, the diameter of an animal's blood vessels increases. This allows more blood to flow to the skin, cooling an animal.

Figure 4 The leaves and stems of plants like this one will grow toward a light source.

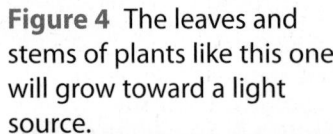 **MiniLab**

20 minutes

Did you blink?

Like all living organisms, you respond to changes, or stimuli, in your environment. When you react to a stimulus without thinking, the response is known as a reflex. Let's see what a reflex is like.

1. Read and complete a lab safety form.
2. Sit on a chair with your hands in your lap.
3. Have your partner gently toss a **soft, foam ball** at your face five times. Your partner will warn you when he or she is going to toss the ball. Record your responses in your Science Journal.
4. Have your partner gently toss the ball at your face five times without warning you. Record your responses.
5. Switch places with your partner, and repeat steps 3 and 4.

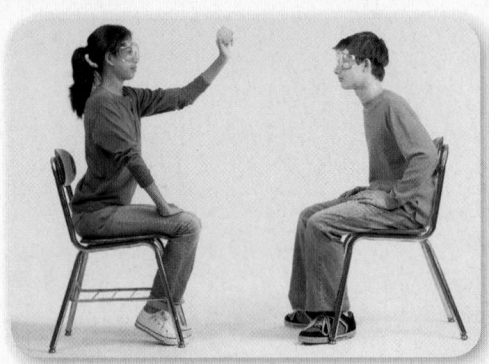

Analyze and Conclude

1. **Compare** your responses when you were warned and when you were not warned.

2. **Decide** if any of your reactions were reflex responses, and explain your answer.

3. **Key Concept** Infer why organisms have reflex responses to some stimuli.

Homeostasis

Have you ever noticed that if you drink more water than usual, you have to go to the bathroom more often? That is because your body is working to keep your internal environment under normal conditions. *An organism's ability to maintain steady internal conditions when outside conditions change is called* **homeostasis** (hoh mee oh STAY sus).

The Importance of Homeostasis

Are there certain conditions you need to do your homework? Maybe you need a quiet room with a lot of light. Cells also need certain conditions to function properly. Maintaining certain conditions—homeostasis—ensures that cells can function. If cells cannot function normally, then an organism might become sick or even die.

Methods of Regulation

A person might not survive if his or her body temperature changes more than a few degrees from 37°C. When your outside environment becomes too hot or too cold, your body responds. It sweats, shivers, or changes the flow of blood to maintain a body temperature of 37°C.

Unicellular organisms, such as the paramecium in **Figure 5**, also have ways of regulating homeostasis. A structure called a contractile vacuole (kun TRAK tul • VA kyuh wohl) collects and pumps excess water out of the cell.

WORD ORIGIN · · · · · · · · · · ·

homeostasis
from Greek *homoios*, means "like, similar"; and *stasis*, means "standing still"

Figure 5 This paramecium lives in freshwater. Water continuously enters its cell and collects in contractile vacuoles. The vacuoles contract and expel excess water from the cell. This maintains normal water levels in the cell.

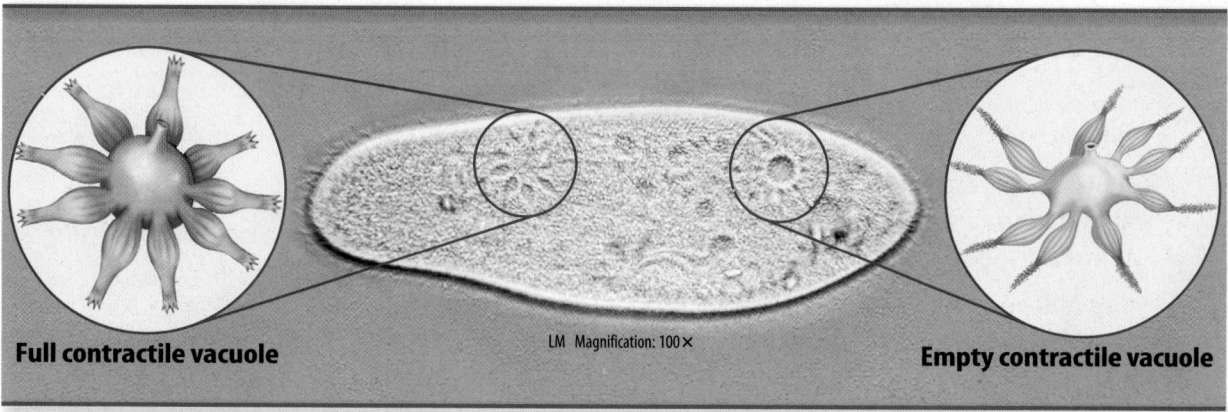

Full contractile vacuole　　　LM Magnification: 100×　　　**Empty contractile vacuole**

There is a limit to the amount of change that can occur within an organism. For example, you are able to survive only a few hours in water that is below 10°C. No matter what your body does, it cannot maintain steady internal conditions, or homeostasis, under these circumstances. As a result, your cells lose their ability to function.

Reading Check Why is maintaining homeostasis important to organisms?

Energy

Everything you do requires energy. Digesting your food, sleeping, thinking, reading and all of the characteristics of life shown in **Table 1** on the next page require energy. Cells continuously use energy to transport substances, make new cells, and perform chemical reactions. Where does this energy come from?

For most organisms, this energy originally came to Earth from the Sun, as shown in **Figure 6.** For example, energy in the cactus came from the Sun. The squirrel gets energy by eating the cactus, and the coyote gets energy by eating the squirrel.

Key Concept Check What characteristics do all living things share?

Energy Use

Review Personal Tutor

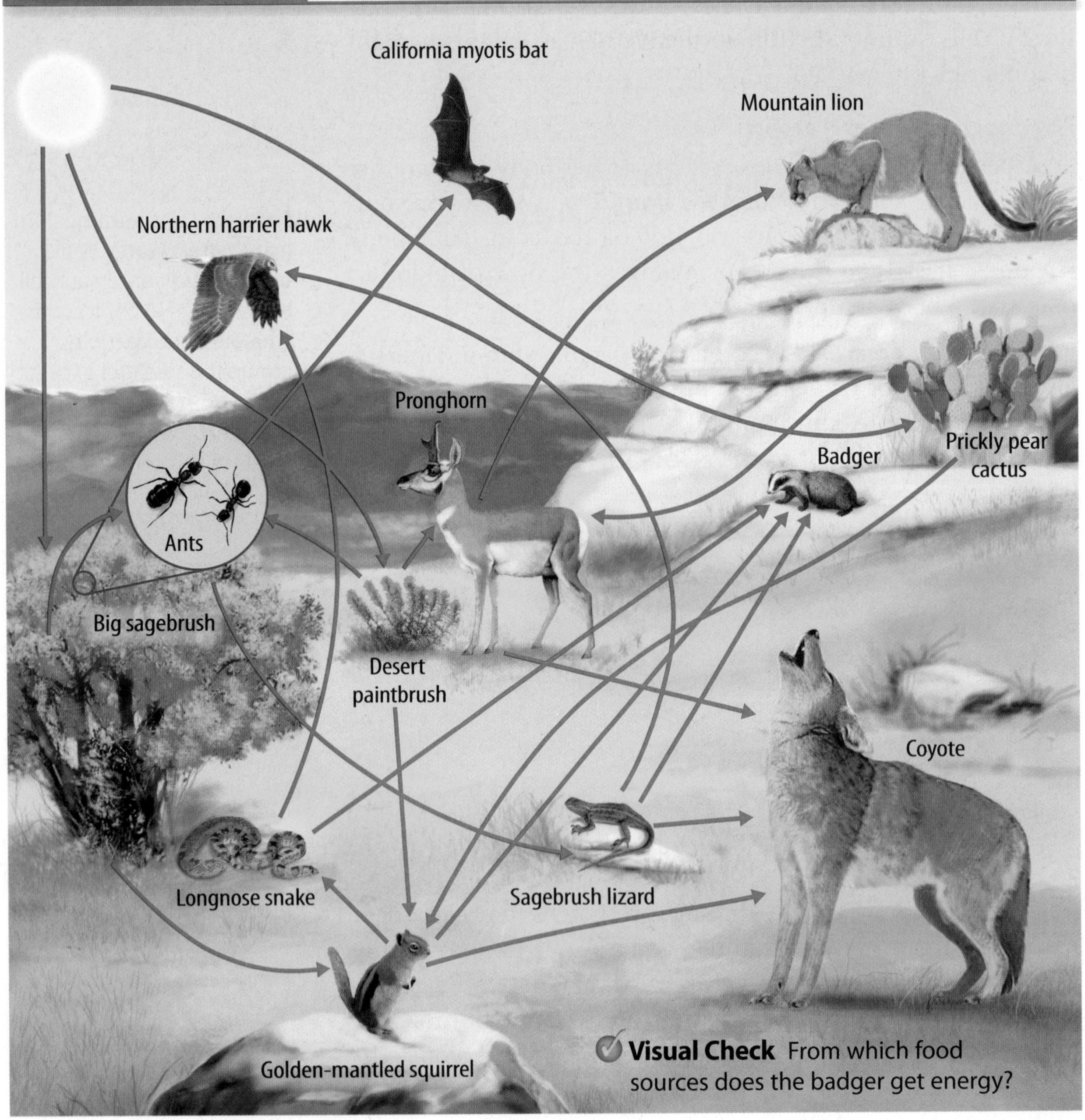

California myotis bat
Mountain lion
Northern harrier hawk
Pronghorn
Badger
Prickly pear cactus
Ants
Big sagebrush
Desert paintbrush
Coyote
Longnose snake
Sagebrush lizard
Golden-mantled squirrel
Visual Check From which food sources does the badger get energy?

Figure 6 All organisms require energy to survive. In this food web, energy passes from one organism to another and to the environment.

Table 1 Characteristics of Life | Concepts in Motion | Interactive Table

Characteristic	Definition	Example
Organization	Living things have specialized structures with specialized functions. Living things with more than one cell have a greater level of organization because groups of cells function together.	
Growth and development	Living things grow by increasing cell size and/or increasing cell number. Multicellular organisms develop as cells develop specialized functions.	
Reproduction	Living things make more living things through the process of reproduction.	
Response to stimuli	Living things adjust and respond to changes in their internal and external environments.	
Homeostasis	Living things maintain stable internal conditions.	
Use of energy	Living things use energy for all the processes they perform. Living things get energy by making their own food, eating food, or absorbing food.	

Lesson 1 Review

Visual Summary

An organism has all the characteristics of life.

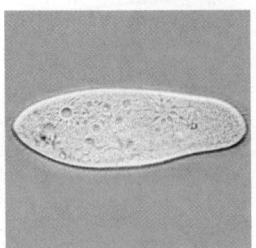

Unicellular organisms have specialized structures, much like a house has rooms for different activities.

Homeostasis enables living things to maintain a steady internal environment.

FOLDABLES

Use your lesson Foldable to review the lesson. Save your Foldable for the project at the end of the chapter.

What do you think NOW?

You first read the statements below at the beginning of the chapter.

1. All living things move.

2. The Sun provides energy for almost all organisms on Earth.

Did you change your mind about whether you agree or disagree with the statements? Rewrite any false statements to make them true.

Use Vocabulary

1. A(n) _____ is the smallest unit of life.

2. **Distinguish** between unicellular and multicellular.

3. **Define** the term *homeostasis* in your own words.

Understand Key Concepts

4. Which is NOT a characteristic of all living things?
   - **A.** breathing
   - **B.** growing
   - **C.** reproducing
   - **D.** using energy

5. **Compare** the processes of reproduction and growth.

6. **Choose** the characteristic of living things that you think is most important. Explain why you chose that characteristic.

7. **Critique** the following statement: A candle flame is a living thing.

Interpret Graphics

8. **Summarize** Copy and fill in the graphic organizer below to summarize the characteristics of living things.

9. **Describe** all the characteristics of life that are represented in the figure below.

Critical Thinking

10. **Suggest** how organisms would be different if they were not organized.

11. **Hypothesize** what would happen if living things could not reproduce.

The Amazing Adaptation of an Air-Breathing Catfish

Discover how some species of armored catfish breathe air.

Have you ever thought about why animals need oxygen? All animals, including you, get their energy from food. When you breathe, the oxygen you take in is used in your cells. Chemical reactions in your cells use oxygen and change the energy in food molecules into energy that your cells can use. Mammals and many other animals get oxygen from air. Most fish get oxygen from water. Either way, after an animal takes in oxygen, red blood cells carry oxygen to cells throughout its body.

Adriana Aquino is an ichthyologist (IHK thee AH luh jihst) at the American Museum of Natural History in New York City. She discovers and classifies species of fish, such as the armored catfish in the family Loricariidae from South America. It lives in freshwater rivers and pools in the Amazon. Its name comes from the bony plates covering its body. Some armored catfish can take in oxygen from water and from air!

Some armored catfish live in fast-flowing rivers. The constant movement of the water evenly distributes oxygen throughout it. The catfish can easily remove oxygen from this oxygen-rich water.

But other armored catfish live in pools of still water, where most oxygen is only at the water's surface. This makes the pools low in oxygen. To maintain a steady level of oxygen in their cells, these fish have adaptations that enable them to take in oxygen directly from air. These catfish can switch from removing oxygen from water through their gills to removing oxygen from air through the walls of their stomachs. They can only do this when they do not have much food in their stomachs. Some species can survive up to 30 hours out of water!

Meet an Ichthyologist

Aquino examines hundreds of catfish specimens. Some she collects in the field, and others come from museum collections. She compares the color, the size, and the shape of the various species. She also examines their internal and external features, such as muscles, gills, and bony plates.

Some armored catfish remove oxygen from air.

It's Your Turn

BRAINSTORM Work with a group. Choose an animal and list five physical characteristics. Brainstorm how these adaptations help the animal be successful in its habitat. Present your findings to the class.

Lesson 2

Reading Guide

Key Concepts
ESSENTIAL QUESTIONS

- What methods are used to classify living things into groups?
- Why does every species have a scientific name?

Vocabulary

binomial nomenclature p. 21
species p. 21
genus p. 21
dichotomous key p. 22
cladogram p. 23

g Multilingual eGlossary

Video BrainPOP®

Classifying Organisms

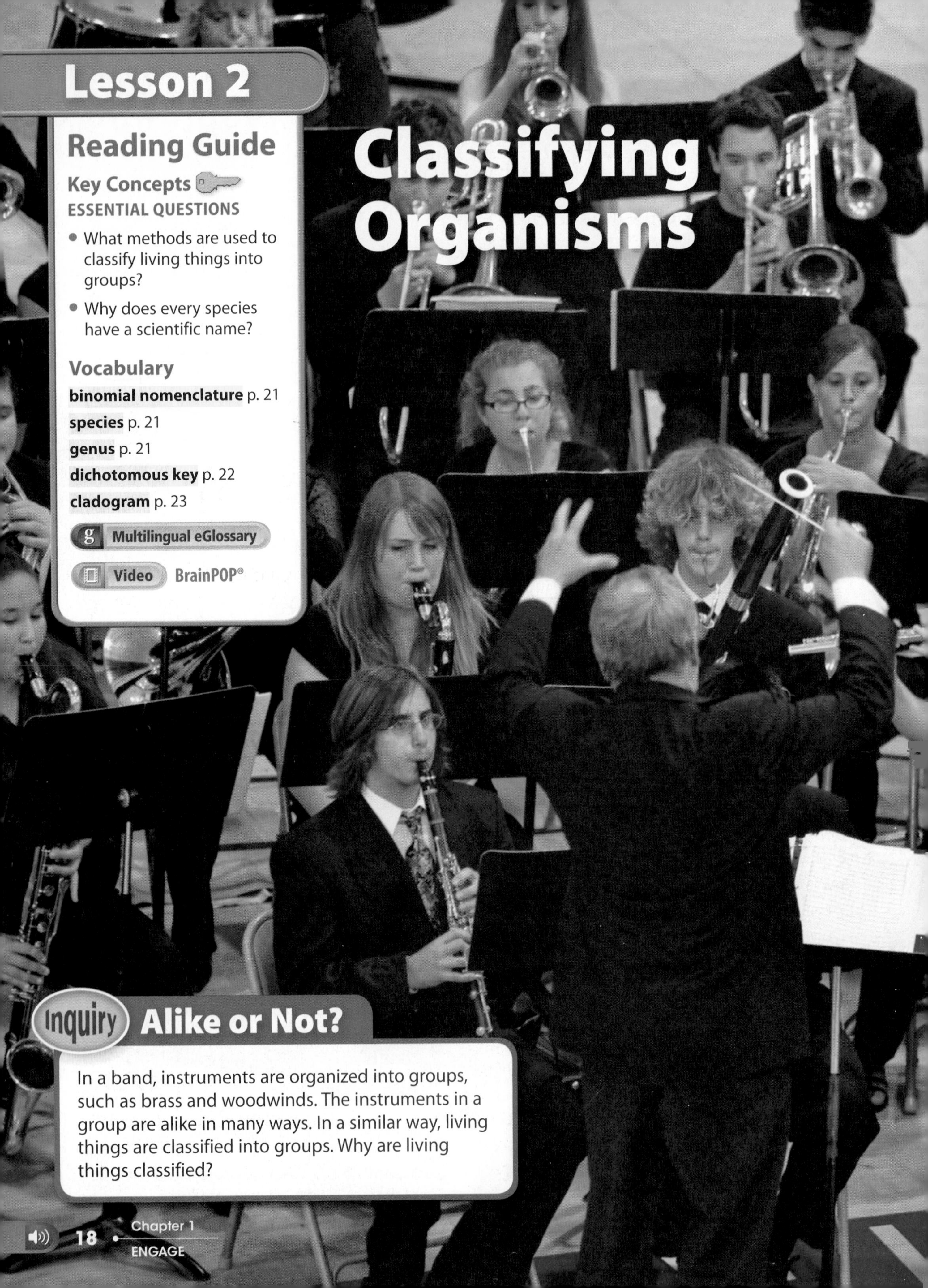

Inquiry Alike or Not?

In a band, instruments are organized into groups, such as brass and woodwinds. The instruments in a group are alike in many ways. In a similar way, living things are classified into groups. Why are living things classified?

How do you identify similar items?

Do you separate your candies by color before you eat them? When your family does laundry, do you sort the clothes by color first? Identifying characteristics of items can enable you to place them into groups.

1. Read and complete a lab safety form.

2. Examine twelve **leaves.** Choose a characteristic that you could use to separate the leaves into two groups. Record the characteristic in your Science Journal.

3. Place the leaves into two groups, *A* and *B,* using the characteristic you chose in step 2.

4. Choose another characteristic that you could use to further divide group A. Record the characteristic, and divide the leaves.

5. Repeat step 4 with group B.

Think About This

1. What types of characteristics did other groups in class choose to separate the leaves?

2. 🔑 **Key Concept** Why would scientists need rules for separating and identifying items?

Classifying Living Things

How would you find your favorite fresh fruit or vegetable in the grocery store? You might look in the produce section, such as the one shown in **Figure 7.** Different kinds of peppers are displayed in one area. Citrus fruits such as oranges, lemons, and grapefruits are stocked in another area. There are many different ways to organize produce in a grocery store. In a similar way, there have been many different ideas about how to organize, or classify, living things.

A Greek philosopher named Aristotle (384 B.C.–322 B.C.) was one of the first people to classify organisms. Aristotle placed all organisms into two large groups, plants and animals. He classified animals based on the presence of "red blood," the animal's environment, and the shape and size of the animal. He classified plants according to the structure and size of the plant and whether the plant was a tree, a shrub, or an herb.

Figure 7 The produce in this store is classified into groups.

✅ **Visual Check** What other ways can you think of to classify and organize produce?

Determining Kingdoms

SCIENCE USE v. COMMON USE

kingdom
Science Use a classification category that ranks above phylum and below domain

Common Use a territory ruled by a king or a queen

In the 1700s, Carolus Linnaeus, a Swedish physician and botanist, classified organisms based on similar structures. Linnaeus placed all organisms into two main groups, called **kingdoms.** Over the next 200 years, people learned more about organisms and discovered new organisms. In 1969 American biologist Robert H. Whittaker proposed a five-kingdom system for classifying organisms. His system included kingdoms Monera, Protista, Plantae, Fungi, and Animalia.

Determining Domains

The classification system of living things is still changing. The current classification method is called systematics. Systematics uses all the evidence that is known about organisms to classify them. This evidence includes an organism's cell type, its habitat, the way an organism obtains food and energy, structure and function of its features, and the common ancestry of organisms. Systematics also includes molecular analysis—the study of molecules such as DNA within organisms.

Using systematics, scientists identified two distinct groups in Kingdom Monera—Bacteria and Archaea (ar KEE uh). This led to the development of another level of classification called domains. All organisms are now classified into one of three domains—Bacteria, Archaea, or Eukarya (yew KER ee uh) —and then into one of six kingdoms, as shown in **Table 2.**

 Key Concept Check What evidence is used to classify living things into groups?

Table 2 Domains and Kingdoms

Domain	Bacteria	Archaea	Eukarya			
Kingdom	Bacteria	Archaea	Protista	Fungi	Plantae	Animalia
Example						
Characteristics	Bacteria are simple unicellular organisms.	Archaea are simple unicellular organisms that often live in extreme environments.	Protists are unicellular and are more complex than bacteria or archaea.	Fungi are unicellular or multicellular and absorb food.	Plants are multicellular and make their own food.	Animals are multicellular and take in their food.

Scientific Names

Suppose you did not have a name. What would people call you? All organisms, just like people, have names. When Linnaeus grouped organisms into kingdoms, he also developed a system for naming organisms. This naming system, called binomial nomenclature (bi NOH mee ul · NOH mun klay chur), is the system we still use today.

Binomial Nomenclature

Linneaus's naming system, **binomial nomenclature**, *gives each organism a two-word scientific name,* such as *Ursus arctos* for a brown bear. This two-word scientific name is the name of an organism's species (SPEE sheez). *A* **species** *is a group of organisms that have similar traits and are able to produce fertile offspring.* In binomial nomenclature, the first word is the organism's genus (JEE nus) name, such as *Ursus.* A **genus** *is a group of similar species.* The second word might describe the organism's appearance or its behavior.

How do species and genus relate to kingdoms and domains? Similar species are grouped into one genus (plural, genera). Similar genera are grouped into families, then orders, classes, phyla, kingdoms, and finally domains, as shown for the grizzly bear in **Table 3.**

Table 3 The classification of the brown bear or grizzly bear shows that it belongs to the order Carnivora.

Taxonomic Group	Number of Species	Examples
Domain Eukarya	About 4–10 million	
Kingdom Animalia	About 2 million	
Phylum Chordata	About 50,000	
Class Mammalia	About 5,000	
Order Carnivora	About 270	
Family Ursidae	8	
Genus *Ursus*	4	
Species *Ursus arctos*	1	

Table 3 Classification of the Brown Bear

Visual Check What domain does the brown bear belong to?

▲ **Figure 8** These trees are two different species. *Pinus alba* has long needles, and *Tsuga canadensis* has short needles.

FOLDABLES

Make a horizontal two-tab book to compare two of the tools scientists use to identify organisms—dichotomous keys and cladograms.

Uses of Scientific Names

When you talk about organisms, you might use names such as bird, tree, or mushroom. However, these are common names for a number of different species. Sometimes there are several common names for one organism. The animal in **Table 3** on the previous page might be called a brown bear or a grizzly bear, but it has only one scientific name, *Ursus arctos*.

Other times, a common name might refer to several different types of organisms. For example, you might call both of the trees in **Figure 8** pine trees. But these trees are two different species. How can you tell? Scientific names are important for many reasons. Each species has its own scientific name. Scientific names are the same worldwide. This makes communication about organisms more effective because everyone uses the same name for the same species.

 Key Concept Check Why does every species have a scientific name?

Classification Tools

Suppose you go fishing and catch a fish you don't recognize. How could you figure out what type of fish you have caught? There are several tools you can use to identify organisms.

Dichotomous Keys

A **dichotomous key** *is a series of descriptions arranged in pairs that leads the user to the identification of an unknown organism.* The chosen description leads to either another pair of statements or the identification of the organism. Choices continue until the organism is identified. The dichotomous key shown in **Figure 9** identifies several species of fish.

Dichotomous Key 🔑

1. a. This fish has a mouth that extends past its eye. It is an arrow goby.	**1a** 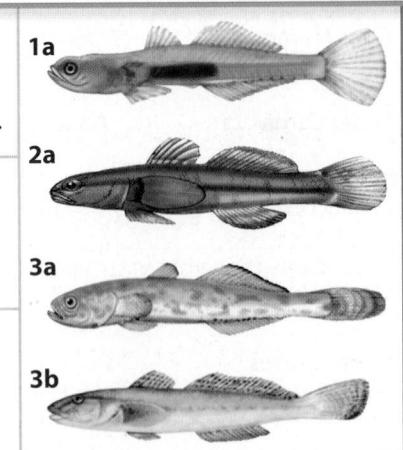
b. This fish does not have a mouth that extends past its eye. Go to step 2.	**2a**
2. a. This fish has a dark body with stripes. It is a chameleon goby.	
b. This fish has a light body with no stripes. Go to step 3.	**3a**
3. a. This fish has a black-tipped dorsal fin. It is a bay goby.	**3b**
b. This fish has a speckled dorsal fin. It is a yellowfin goby.	

▲ **Figure 9** Dichotomous keys include a series of questions to identify organisms.

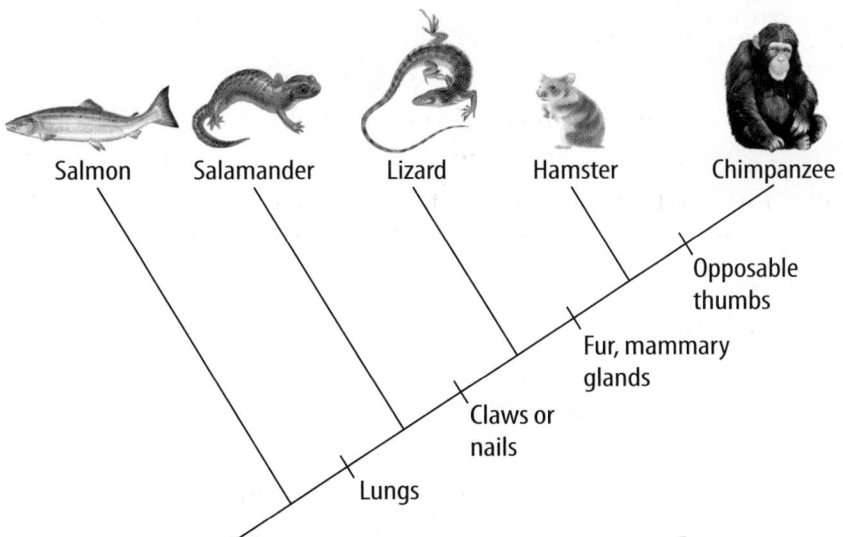

Salmon   Salamander   Lizard   Hamster   Chimpanzee

Opposable
thumbs

Fur, mammary
glands

Claws or
nails

Lungs

Figure 10 A cladogram shows relationships among species. In this cladogram, salamanders are more closely related to lizards than they are to hamsters.

(◎ Concepts in Motion)

Animation

Cladograms

A family tree shows the relationships among family members, including common ancestors. Biologists use a similar diagram, called a cladogram. *A* **cladogram** *is a branched diagram that shows the relationships among organisms, including common ancestors.* A cladogram, as shown in **Figure 10,** has a series of branches. Notice that each branch follows a new characteristic. Each characteristic is observed in all the species to its right. For example, the salamander, lizard, hamster, and chimpanzee have lungs, but the salmon does not. Therefore, they are more closely related to each other than they are to the salmon.

Inquiry MiniLab

20 minutes

How would you name an unknown organism?

Assign scientific names to four unknown alien organisms from a newly discovered planet.

1 Use the table to assign scientific names to identify each alien.

2 Compare your names with those of your classmates.

Analyze and Conclude

1. **Explain** why you chose the two-word names for each organism.

2. **Compare** your names to those of a classmate. Explain any differences.

3. 🔑 **Key Concept** Discuss how two-word scientific names help scientists identify and organize living things.

Prefix	Meaning	Suffix	Meaning
mon—	one	—antennius	antenna
di—	two	—ocularus	eye
rectanguli—	square	—formus	shape
trianguli—	triangle	—uris	tail

Lesson 2 Review

Visual Summary

All organisms are classified into one of three domains: Bacteria, Archaea, or Eukarya.

Every organism has a unique species name.

A dichotomous key helps to identify an unknown organism through a series of paired descriptions.

FOLDABLES®

Use your lesson Foldable to review the lesson. Save your Foldable for the project at the end of the chapter.

What do you think NOW?

You first read the statements below at the beginning of the chapter.

3. A dichotomous key can be used to identify an unknown organism.

4. Physical similarities are the only traits used to classify organisms.

Did you change your mind about whether you agree or disagree with the statements? Rewrite any false statements to make them true.

Use Vocabulary

1 A naming system that gives every organism a two-word name is _____ _____.

2 **Use the term** *dichotomous key* in a sentence.

3 **Organisms** of the same _____ are able to produce fertile offspring.

Understand Key Concepts 🔑

4 **Describe** how you write a scientific name.

5 **Compare** the data available today on how to classify things with the data available during Aristotle's time.

6 Which is NOT used to classify organisms?
   A. ancestry
   B. habitat
   C. age of the organism
   D. molecular evidence

Interpret Graphics

7 **Organize Information** Copy and fill in the graphic organizer below to show how organisms are classified.

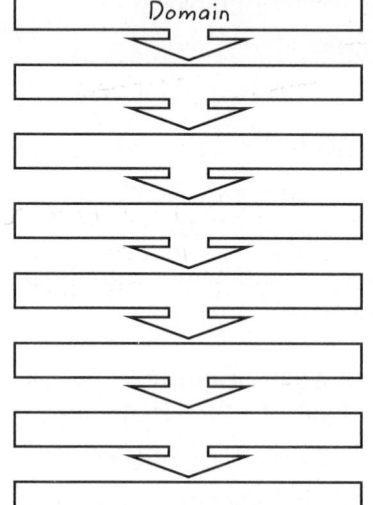

Critical Thinking

8 **Suggest** a reason scientists might consider changing the current classification system.

9 **Evaluate** the importance of scientific names.

How can you identify a beetle?

A dichotomous key is one of the tools scientists use to identify an unknown organism and **classify** it into a group. To use a dichotomous key, a scientist examines specific characteristics of the unknown organism and compares them to characteristics of known organisms.

Learn It

Sorting objects or events into groups based on common features is called classifying. When classifying, select one feature that is shared by some members of the group, but not by all. Place those members that share the feature in a subgroup. You can **classify** objects or events into smaller and smaller subgroups based on characteristics.

Try It

1 Use the dichotomous key to identify beetle A. Choose between the first pair of descriptions. Follow the instructions for the next choice. Notice that each description either ends in the name of the beetle or instructs you to go on to another set of choices.

2 In your Science Journal, record the identity of the beetle using both its common name and scientific name.

3 Repeat steps 1 and 2 for beetles B, C, and D.

Apply It

4 Think about the choices in each step of the dichotomous key. What conclusion can be made if you arrive at a step and neither choice seems correct?

5 Predict whether a dichotomous key will work if you start at a location other than the first description. Support your reasoning.

6 🗝 **Key Concept** How did the dichotomous key help you classify the unknown beetles?

Dichotomous Key

1A.	The beetle has long, thin antennae. Go to 5.
1B.	The beetle does not have long, thin antennae. Go to 2.
2A.	The beetle has short antennae that branch. Go to 3.
2B.	The beetle does not have short antennae that branch. It is a stag beetle, *Lucanus cervus*.
3A.	The beetle has a triangular structure between wing covers and upper body. It is a Japanese beetle, *Popillia japonica*.
3B.	The beetle does not have a triangular structure. Go to 4.
4A.	The beetle has a wide, rounded body. It is a June bug, *Cotinis nitida*.
4B.	The beetle does not have a wide, rounded body. It is a death watch beetle, *Xestobium rufovillosum*.
5A.	The beetle has a distinct separation between body parts. Go to 6.
5B.	The beetle has no distinct separation between body parts. It is a firefly, *Photinus pyralis*.
6A.	The beetle has a black, gray, and white body with two black eyespots. It is an eyed click beetle, *Alaus oculatis*.
6B.	The beetle has a dull brown body with light stripes. It is a click beetle, *Chalcolepidius limbatus*.

Lesson 3

Reading Guide

Key Concepts 🔑
ESSENTIAL QUESTIONS

- How did microscopes change our ideas about living things?

- What are the types of microscopes, and how do they compare?

Vocabulary

light microscope p. 28

compound microscope p. 28

electron microscope p. 29

 Multilingual eGlossary

Exploring Life

Inquiry Giant Insect?

Although this might look like a giant insect, it is a photo of a small tick taken with a high-powered microscope. This type of microscope can enlarge an image of an object up to 200,000 times. How can seeing an enlarged image of a living thing help you understand life?

Can a water drop make objects appear bigger or smaller?

For centuries, people have been looking for ways to see objects in greater detail. How can something as simple as a drop of water make this possible?

1 Read and complete a lab safety form.

2 Lay a sheet of **newspaper** on your desk. Examine a line of text, noting the size and shape of each letter. Record your observations in your Science Journal.

3 Add a large drop of **water** to the center of a piece of **clear plastic.** Hold the plastic about 2 cm above the same line of text.

4 Look through the water at the line of text you viewed in step 2. Record your observations.

Think About This

1. Describe how the newsprint appeared through the drop of water.

2. **Key Concept** How might microscopes change your ideas about living things?

The Development of Microscopes

Have you ever used a magnifying lens to see details of an object? If so, then you have used a tool similar to the first microscope. The invention of microscopes enabled people to see details of living things that they could not see with the unaided eye. The microscope also enabled people to make many discoveries about living things.

In the mid 1600s English scientist Robert Hooke made one of the most significant discoveries using a microscope. He observed and named cells. Before microscopes, people did not know that living things are made of cells. In the late 1600s the Dutch merchant Anton van Leeuwenhoek (LAY vun hook) made improvements to the first microscopes. His microscope, similar to the one shown in **Figure 11,** had one lens and could magnify an image about 270 times its original size. This made it easier to view organisms.

Key Concept Check How did microscopes change our ideas about living things?

Figure 11 Anton van Leeuwenhoek observed pond water and insects using a microscope like the one shown above.

 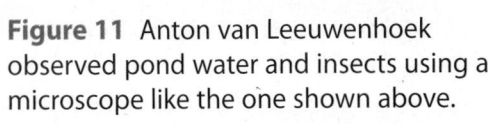

Use Multiplication

The magnifying power of a lens is expressed by a number and a multiplication symbol ($\times$). For example, a lens that makes an object look ten times larger has a power of 10$\times$. To determine a microscope's magnification, multiply the power of the ocular lens by the power of the objective lens. A microscope with a 10$\times$ ocular lens and a 10$\times$ objective lens magnifies an object 10 $\times$ 10, or 100 times.

Practice

What is the magnification of a compound microscope with a 10$\times$ ocular lens and a 4$\times$ objective lens?

🖥 **Review**

- **Math Practice**
- **Personal Tutor**

Types of Microscopes

One characteristic of all microscopes is that they magnify objects. Magnification makes an object appear larger than it really is. Another characteristic of microscopes is resolution—how clearly the magnified object can be seen. The two main types of microscopes—light microscopes and electron microscopes—differ in magnification and resolution.

Light Microscopes

If you have used a microscope in school, then you have probably used a light microscope. **Light microscopes** *use light and lenses to enlarge an image of an object.* A simple light microscope has only one lens. *A light microscope that uses more than one lens to magnify an object is called a* **compound microscope.** A compound microscope magnifies an image first by one lens, called the objective lens. The image is then further magnified by another lens, called the ocular lens. The total magnification of the image is equal to the magnifications of the ocular lens and the objective lens multiplied together.

Light microscopes can enlarge images up to 1,500 times their original size. The resolution of a light microscope is about 0.2 micrometers (μm), or two-millionths of a meter. A resolution of 0.2 μm means you can clearly see points on an object that are at least 0.2 μm apart.

Light microscopes can be used to view living or nonliving objects. In some light microscopes, an object is placed directly under the microscope. For other light microscopes, an object must be mounted on a slide. In some cases, the object, such as the white blood cells in **Figure 12,** must be stained with a dye in order to see any details.

✔ **Reading Check** What are some ways an object can be examined under a light microscope?

Compound Light Microscope 🔑

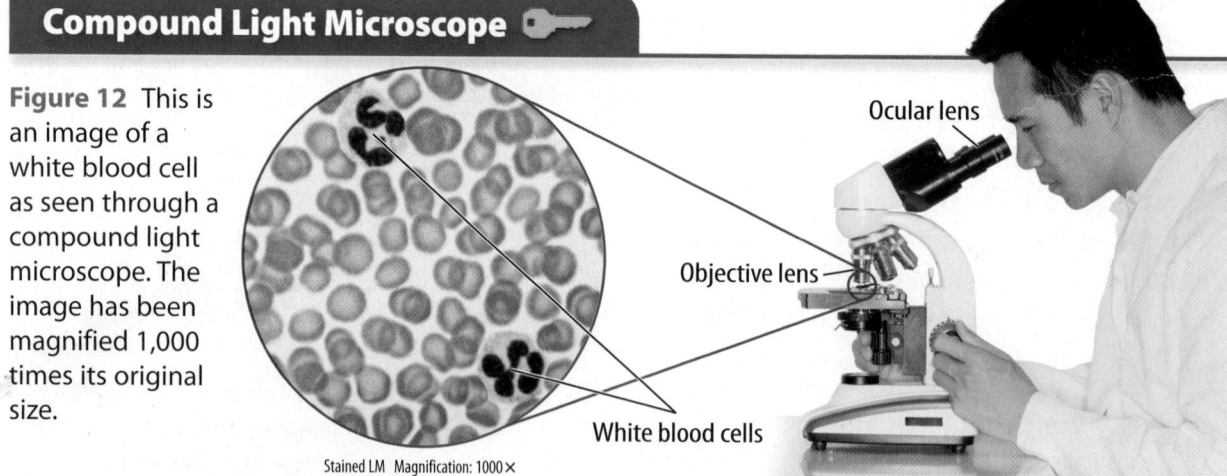

Figure 12 This is an image of a white blood cell as seen through a compound light microscope. The image has been magnified 1,000 times its original size.

Ocular lens

Objective lens

White blood cells

Stained LM Magnification: 1000$\times$

Electron Microscopes

You might know that electrons are tiny particles inside atoms. **Electron microscopes** *use a magnetic field to focus a beam of electrons through an object or onto an object's surface.* An electron microscope can magnify an image up to 100,000 times or more. The resolution of an electron microscope can be as small as 0.2 nanometers (nm), or two-billionths of a meter. This resolution is up to 1,000 times greater than a light microscope. The two main types of electron microscopes are transmission electron microscopes (TEMs) and scanning electron microscopes (SEMs).

TEMs are usually used to study extremely small things such as cell structures. Because objects must be mounted in plastic and then very thinly sliced, only dead organisms can be viewed with a TEM. In a TEM, electrons pass through the object and a computer produces an image of the object. A TEM image of a white blood cell is shown in **Figure 13.**

SEMs are usually used to study an object's surface. In an SEM, electrons bounce off the object and a computer produces a three-dimensional image of the object. An image of a white blood cell from an SEM is shown in **Figure 13.** Note the difference in detail in this image compared to the image in **Figure 12** of a white blood cell from a light microscope.

 Key Concept Check What are the types of microscopes, and how do they compare?

REVIEW VOCABULARY · · · ·

atom
the building block of matter that is composed of protons, neutrons, and electrons

FOLDABLES

Make a two-column folded chart. Label the front *Types of Microscopes*, and label the inside as shown. Use it to organize your notes about microscopes.

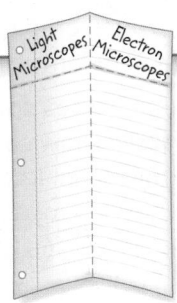

Figure 13 A TEM greatly magnifies thin slices of an object. An SEM is used to view a three-dimensional image of an object.

Electron Microscopes

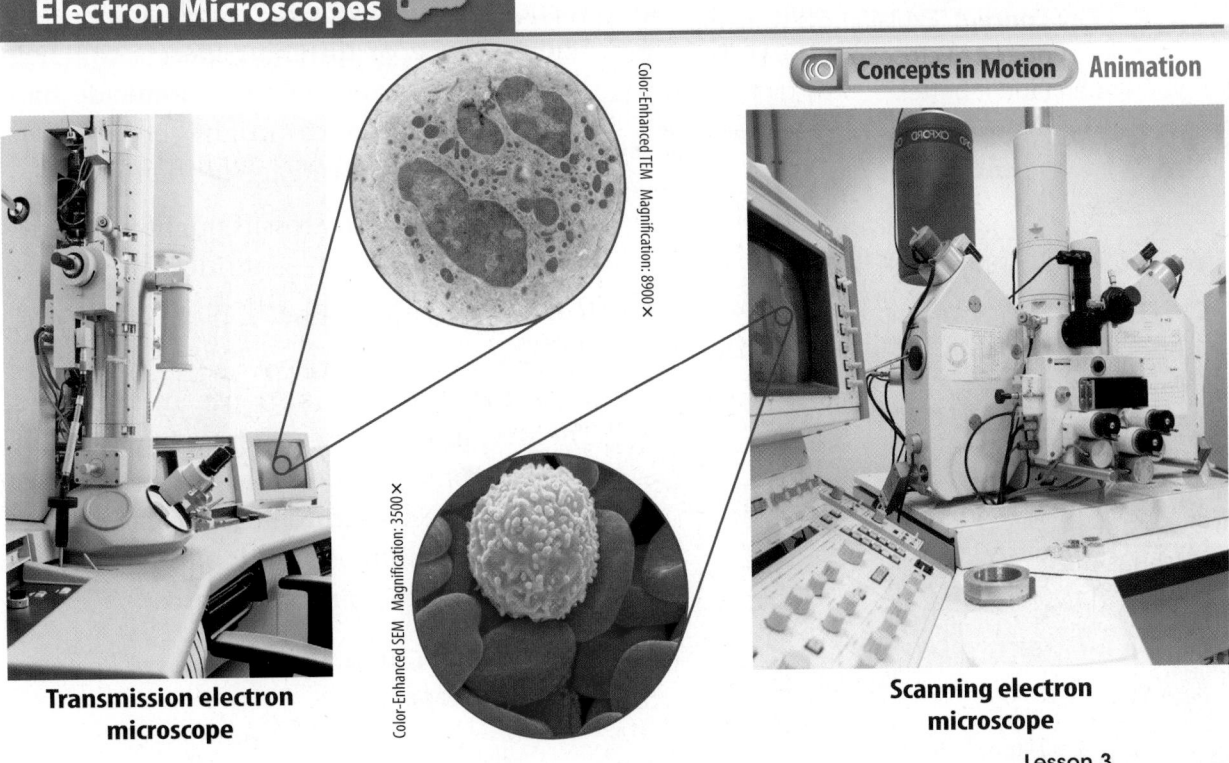

Concepts in Motion   Animation

Color-Enhanced TEM   Magnification: 8900×

Color-Enhanced SEM   Magnification: 3500×

Transmission electron microscope

Scanning electron microscope

inquiry MiniLab
20 minutes

How do microscopes help us compare living things?

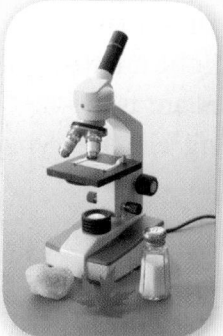

A microscope enables scientists to study objects in greater detail than is possible with the unaided eye. Compare what objects look like with the unaided eye to those same objects observed using a microscope.

1. Read and complete a lab safety form.

2. Examine a **sea sponge,** a **leaf,** and **salt crystals.** Draw each object in your Science Journal.

3. Observe **microscope slides of each object** using a **microscope** on low power.

4. Draw each object as it appears under low power.

Analyze and Conclude

1. **Compare** your sketches of the objects observed with your unaided eye and observed with a microscope.

2. 🔑 **Key Concept** Explain how studying an object under a microscope might help you understand it better.

WORD ORIGIN · · · · · · · · · · · · · · · · · ·

microscope
from Latin *microscopium,* means "an instrument for viewing what is small"

ACADEMIC VOCABULARY · · · · · · · · · · · · · ·

identify
(verb) to determine the characteristics of a person or a thing

Using Microscopes

The **microscopes** used today are more advanced than the microscopes used by Leeuwenhoek and Hooke. The quality of today's light microscopes and the invention of electron microscopes have made the microscope a useful tool in many fields.

Health Care

People in health-care fields, such as doctors and laboratory technicians, often use microscopes. Microscopes are used in surgeries, such as cataract surgery and brain surgery. They enable doctors to view the surgical area in greater detail. The area being viewed under the microscope can also be displayed on a TV monitor so that other people can watch the procedure. Laboratory technicians use microscopes to analyze body fluids, such as blood and urine. They also use microscopes to determine whether tissue samples are healthy or diseased.

Other Uses

Health care is not the only field that uses microscopes. Have you ever wondered how police determine how and where a crime happened? Forensic scientists use microscopes to study evidence from crime scenes. The presence of different insects can help identify when and where a homicide happened. Microscopes might be used to **identify** the type and age of the insects.

People who study fossils might use microscopes. They might examine a fossil and other materials from where the fossil was found.

Some industries also use microscopes. The steel industry uses microscopes to examine steel for impurities. Microscopes are used to study jewels and identify stones. Stones have some markings and impurities that can be seen only by using a microscope.

 Reading Check List some uses of microscopes.

Lesson 3 Review

Visual Summary

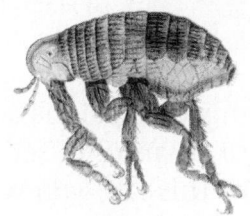

Living organisms can be viewed with light microscopes.

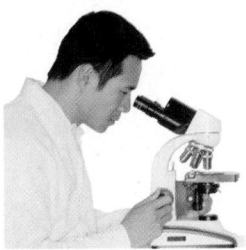

A compound microscope is a type of light microscope that has more than one lens.

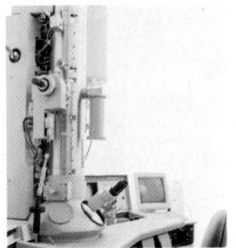

Living organisms cannot be viewed with a transmission electron microscope.

FOLDABLES

Use your lesson Foldable to review the lesson. Save your Foldable for the project at the end of the chapter.

What do you think NOW?

You first read the statements below at the beginning of the chapter.

5. Most cells are too small to be seen with the unaided eye.

6. Only scientists use microscopes.

Did you change your mind about whether you agree or disagree with the statements? Rewrite any false statements to make them true.

Use Vocabulary

1 **Define** the term *light microscope* in your own words.

2 A(n) _____ focuses a beam of electrons through an object or onto an object's surface.

Understand Key Concepts

3 **Explain** how the discovery of microscopes has changed what we know about living things.

4 Which microscope would you use if you wanted to study the surface of an object?
   A. compound microscope
   B. light microscope
   C. scanning electron microscope
   D. transmission electron microscope

Interpret Graphics

5 **Identify** Copy and fill in the graphic organizer below to identify four uses of microscopes.

6 **Compare** the images of the white blood cells below. How do they differ?

 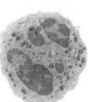 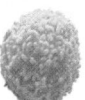

Critical Thinking

7 **Develop** a list of guidelines for choosing a microscope to use.

Math Skills

Review — Math Practice

8 A student observes a blood sample with a compound microscope that has a 10× ocular lens and a 40× objective lens. How much larger do the blood cells appear under the microscope?

Materials

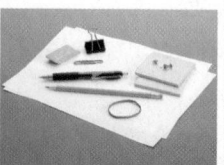

a collection of objects

Constructing a Dichotomous Key

A dichotomous key is a series of descriptions arranged in pairs. Each description leads you to the name of the object or to another set of choices until you have identified the organism. In this lab, you will create a dichotomous key to classify objects.

Question

How can you create a dichotomous key to identify objects?

Procedure

1 Read and complete a lab safety form.

2 Obtain a container of objects from your teacher.

3 Examine the objects, and then brainstorm a list of possible characteristics. You might look at each object's size, shape, color, odor, texture, or function.

4 Choose a characteristic that would separate the objects into two groups. Separate the objects based on whether or not they have this characteristic. This characteristic will be used to begin a dichotomous key, like the example below.

Dichotomous Key to Identify Office Supplies

The object is made of wood. Go to 1.
The object is not made of wood. Go to 2.
1. The object is longer than 20 cm. Go to 5.
3. The object is not longer than 20 cm. Go to 9.
2. The object is made of metal. Go to 6.
4. The object is not made of metal. Go to 10.

5 Write a sentence to describe the characteristic in step 4, and then write "Go to 1." Write another sentence that has the word "not" in front of the characteristic. Then write "Go to 2."

6 Repeat steps 4 and 5 for the two new groups. Give sentences for new groups formed from the first group consecutive odd numbers. Give sentences for groups formed from the second group consecutive even numbers. Remember to add the appropriate "Go to" directions.

7 Repeat steps 4–6 until there is one object in each group. Give each object an appropriate two-word name.

8 Give your collection of objects and your dichotomous key to another group. Have them identify each object using your dichotomous key. Have them record their answers.

Analyze and Conclude

9 **Evaluate** Was the other team able to correctly identify the collection of objects using your dichotomous key? Why or why not?

10 **The Big Idea** Summarize how dichotomous keys are useful in identifying unknown objects.

Communicate Your Results

Create a poster using drawings or photos of each object you identified. Include your two-word names for the objects.

 **Extension**

Teach a peer how to use a dichotomous key. Let the peer use your collection to have a first-hand experience with how a key works.

5

Lab Tips

☑ Base the questions in your key on observable, measurable, or countable characteristics. Avoid questions that refer to how something is used or how you think or feel about an item.

☑ Remember to start with general questions and then get more and more specific.

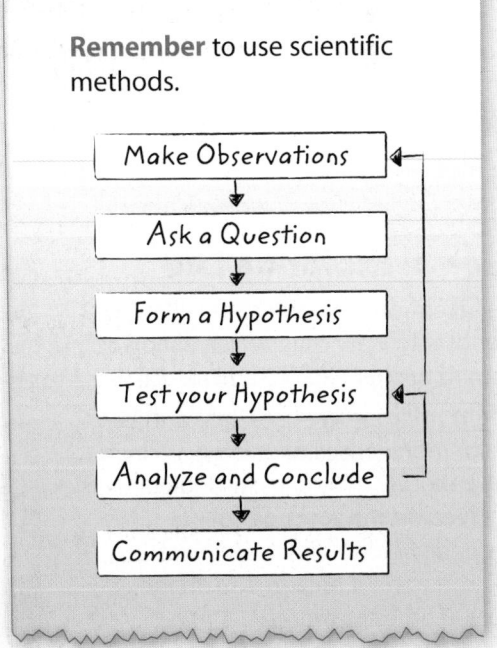

Remember to use scientific methods.

Make Observations → Ask a Question → Form a Hypothesis → Test your Hypothesis → Analyze and Conclude → Communicate Results

Chapter 1 Study Guide

 **All living things have certain characteristics in common and can be classified using several methods. The invention of the microscope has enabled us to explore life further, which has led to changes in classification.**

Key Concepts Summary

| Vocabulary |

Lesson 1: Characteristics of Life

- An **organism** is classified as a living thing because it has all the characteristics of life.
- All living things are organized, grow and develop, reproduce, respond to stimuli, maintain **homeostasis,** and use energy.

organism p. 9
cell p. 10
unicellular p. 10
multicellular p. 10
homeostasis p. 13

Lesson 2: Classifying Organisms

- Living things are classified into different groups based on physical or molecular similarities.
- Some **species** are known by many different common names. To avoid confusion, every species has a scientific name based on a system called **binomial nomenclature.**

binomial nomenclature
  p. 21
species p. 21
genus p. 21
dichotomous key p. 22
cladogram p. 23

Lesson 3: Exploring Life

- The invention of microscopes allowed scientists to view cells, which enabled them to further explore and classify life.
- A **light microscope** uses light and has one or more lenses to enlarge an image up to about 1,500 times its original size. An **electron microscope** uses a magnetic field to direct beams of electrons, and it enlarges an image 100,000 times or more.

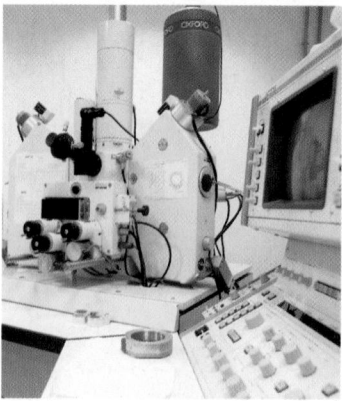

light microscope p. 28
compound microscope
  p. 28
electron microscope p. 29

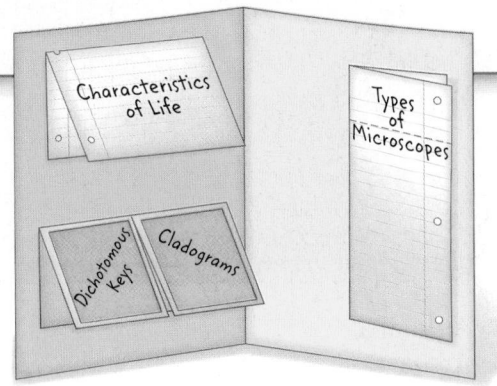
FOLDABLES® **Chapter Project**

Assemble your lesson Foldables as shown to make a Chapter Project. Use the project to review what you have learned in this chapter.

Characteristics of Life

Types of Microscopes

Dichotomous Keys

Cladograms

Use Vocabulary

1 A(n) _____ organism is made of only one cell.

2 Something with all the characteristics of life is a(n) _____.

3 A(n) _____ shows the relationships among species.

4 A group of similar species is a(n) _____.

5 A(n) _____ has a resolution up to 1,000 times greater than a light microscope.

6 A(n) _____ is a light microscope that uses more than one lens to magnify an image.

Concepts in Motion Interactive Concept Map

Link Vocabulary and Key Concepts

Copy this concept map, and then use vocabulary terms from the previous page to complete the concept map.

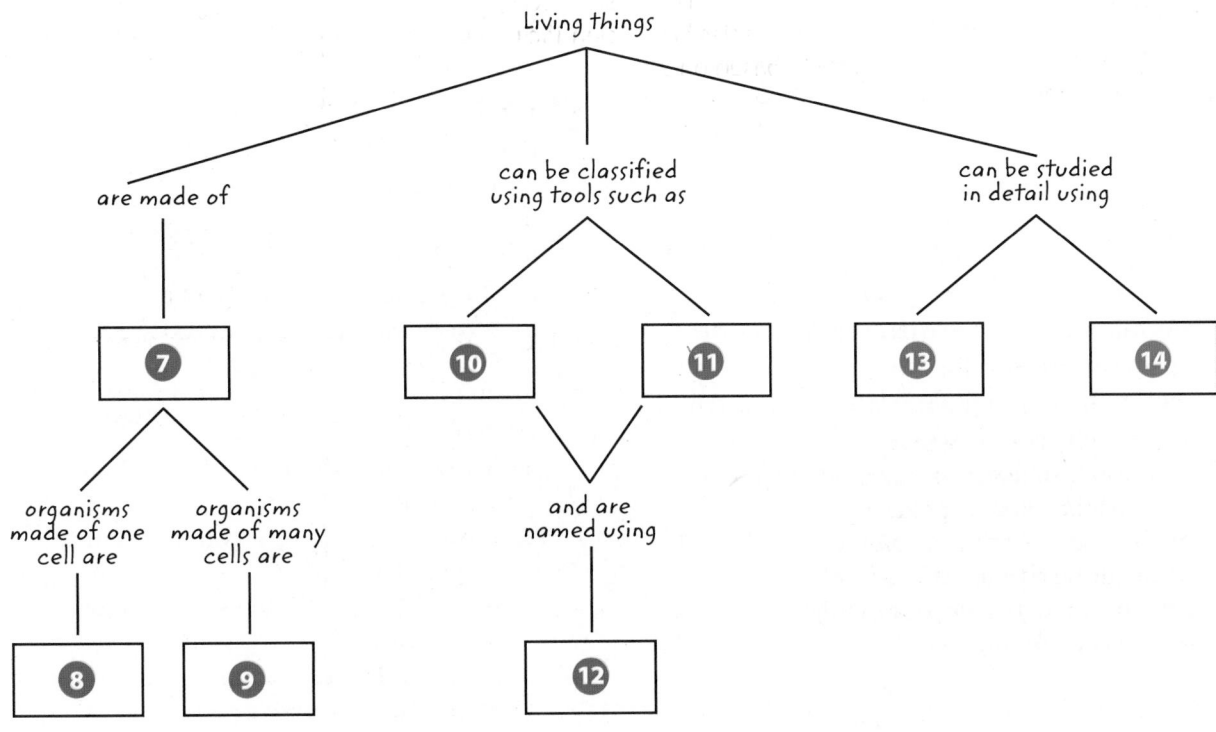

Chapter 1 Review

Understand Key Concepts

1 Which is an internal stimulus?

   A. an increase in moisture
   B. feelings of hunger
   C. number of hours of daylight
   D. the temperature at night

2 Which is an example of growth and development?

   A. a caterpillar becoming a butterfly
   B. a chicken laying eggs
   C. a dog panting
   D. a rabbit eating carrots

3 Based on the food web below, what is an energy source for the mouse?

   A. fox
   B. grass
   C. owl
   D. snake

4 Which shows the correct order for the classification of species?

   A. domain, kingdom, class, order, phylum, family, genus, species
   B. domain, kingdom, phylum, class, order, family, genus, species
   C. domain, kingdom, phylum, class, order, family, species, genus
   D. domain, kingdom, phylum, order, class, family, genus, species

5 The organism shown below belongs in which kingdom?

   A. Animalia
   B. Archaea
   C. Bacteria
   D. Plantae

6 Which was discovered using a microscope?

   A. blood
   B. bones
   C. cells
   D. hair

7 What type of microscope would most likely be used to obtain an image of a live roundworm?

   A. compound light microscope
   B. scanning electron microscope
   C. simple light microscope
   D. transmission electron microscope

8 Which best describes a compound microscope?

   A. uses electrons to magnify the image of an object
   B. uses multiple lenses to magnify the image of an object
   C. uses one lens to magnify the image of an object
   D. uses sound waves to magnify the image of an object

Critical Thinking

9 **Distinguish** between a unicellular organism and a multicellular organism.

10 **Critique** the following statement: An organism that is made of only one cell does not need organization.

11 **Infer** In the figure below, which plant is responding to a lack of water in its environment? Explain your answer.

12 **Explain** how using a dichotomous key can help you identify an organism.

13 **Describe** how the branches on a cladogram show the relationships among organisms.

14 **Assess** the effect of molecular evidence on the classification of organisms.

15 **Compare** light microscopes and electron microscopes.

16 **State** how microscopes have changed the way living things are classified.

17 **Compare** magnification and resolution.

18 **Evaluate** the impact microscopes have on our daily lives.

Writing in Science

19 **Write** a five-sentence paragraph explaining the importance of scientific names. Be sure to include a topic sentence and a concluding sentence in your paragraph.

REVIEW THE **BIG IDEA**

20 Define the characteristics that all living things share.

21 The photo below shows living and nonliving things. How would you classify the living things by domain and kingdom?

Math Skills ×÷+

Review

— Math Practice —

Use Multiplication

22 A microscope has an ocular lens with a power of 5× and an objective lens with a power of 50×. What is the total magnification of the microscope?

23 A student observes a unicellular organism with a microscope that has a 10× ocular lens and a 100× objective lens. How much larger does the organism look through this microscope?

24 The ocular lens on a microscope has a power of 10×. The microscope makes objects appear 500 times larger. What is the power of the objective lens?

Standardized Test Practice

Record your answers on the answer sheet provided by your teacher or on a sheet of paper.

Multiple Choice

1 What feature of living things do the terms *unicellular* and *multicellular* describe?

   A how they are organized

   B how they reproduce

   C how they maintain temperature

   D how they produce macromolecules

Use the diagram below to answer question 2.

2 Which characteristic of life does the diagram show?

   A homeostasis

   B organization

   C growth and development

   D response to stimuli

3 A newly discovered organism is 1 m tall, multicellular, green, and it grows on land and performs photosynthesis. To which kingdom does it most likely belong?

   A Animalia

   B Fungi

   C Plantae

   D Protista

4 Unicellular organisms are members of which kingdoms?

   A Animalia, Archaea, Plantae

   B Archaea, Bacteria, Protista

   C Bacteria, Fungi, Plantae

   D Fungi, Plantae, Protista

5 Which microscope would best magnify the outer surface of a cell?

   A compound light

   B scanning electron

   C simple dissecting

   D transmission electron

Use the diagram below to answer question 6.

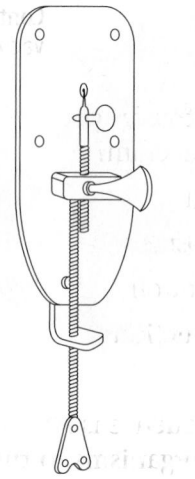

6 Which discovery was NOT made with the instrument above?

   A Bacterial cells have thick walls.

   B Blood is a mixture of components.

   C Insects have small body parts.

   D Tiny organisms live in pond water.

7 Which statement is false?

   A Binomial names are given to all known organisms.

   B Binomial names are less precise than common names.

   C Binomial names differ from common names.

   D Binomial names enable scientists to communicate accurately.

Use the diagram below to answer question 8.

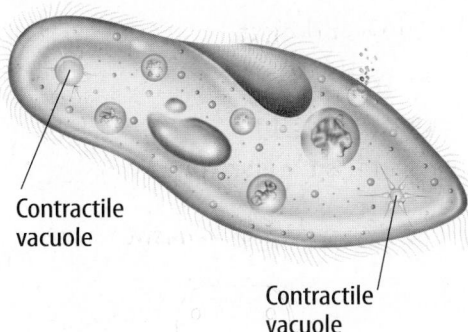

Contractile vacuole

Contractile vacuole

8 Which is the function of the structures in this paramecium?

   A growth

   B homeostasis

   C locomotion

   D reproduction

9 Which sequence is from the smallest group of organisms to the largest group of organisms?

   A genus → family → species

   B genus → species → family

   C species → family → genus

   D species → genus → family

10 Which information about organisms is excluded in the study of systematics?

   A calendar age

   B molecular analysis

   C energy source

   D normal habitat

Constructed Response

11 Copy and complete the table below about the six characteristics of life.

Characteristic	Explanation

12 Choose one characteristic of living things and explain how it affects everyday human life. From your own knowledge, give a specific example.

Use the diagram below to answer question 13.

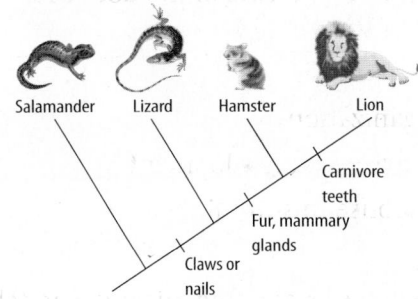

Salamander   Lizard   Hamster   Lion

Carnivore teeth

Fur, mammary glands

Claws or nails

13 Explain why the lion is more closely related to the hamster than the hamster is related to the salamander.

NEED EXTRA HELP?													
If You Missed Question...	1	2	3	4	5	6	7	8	9	10	11	12	13
Go to Lesson...	1	1	2	2	3	3	2	1	2	2	1	1	2

Chapter 2

Cell Structure and Function

THE BIG IDEA How do the structures and processes of a cell enable it to survive?

Inquiry Alien Life?

You might think this unicellular organism looks like something out of a science-fiction movie. Although it looks scary, the hairlike structures in its mouth enable the organism to survive.

- What do you think the hairlike structures do?

- How might the shape of the hairlike structures relate to their function?

- How do you think the structures and processes of a cell enable it to survive?

Get Ready to Read

What do you think?

Before you read, decide if you agree or disagree with each of these statements. As you read this chapter, see if you change your mind about any of the statements.

1 Nonliving things have cells.

2 Cells are made mostly of water.

3 Different organisms have cells with different structures.

4 All cells store genetic information in their nuclei.

5 Diffusion and osmosis are the same process.

6 Cells with large surface areas can transport more than cells with smaller surface areas.

7 ATP is the only form of energy found in cells.

8 Cellular respiration occurs only in lung cells.

ConnectED Your one-stop online resource

connectED.mcgraw-hill.com

Video

WebQuest

Audio

Assessment

Review

Concepts in Motion

Inquiry

Multilingual eGlossary

Cells and Life

Reading Guide

Key Concepts 🔑
ESSENTIAL QUESTIONS

- How did scientists' understanding of cells develop?
- What basic substances make up a cell?

Vocabulary

cell theory p. 44

macromolecule p. 45

nucleic acid p. 46

protein p. 47

lipid p. 47

carbohydrate p. 47

g Multilingual eGlossary

Inquiry Two of a Kind?

At first glance, the plant and animal in the photo might seem like they have nothing in common. The plant is rooted in the ground, and the iguana can move quickly. Are they more alike than they appear? How can you find out?

What's in a cell?

Most plants grow from seeds. A seed began as one cell, but a mature plant can be made up of millions of cells. How does a seed change and grow into a mature plant?

1 Read and complete a lab safety form.

2 Use a **toothpick** to gently remove the thin outer covering of a **bean seed** that has soaked overnight.

3 Open the seed with a **plastic knife,** and observe its inside with a **magnifying lens.** Draw the inside of the seed in your Science Journal.

4 Gently remove the small, plantlike embryo, and weigh it on a **balance.** Record its mass in your Science Journal.

5 Gently pull a **bean seedling** from the soil. Rinse the soil from the roots. Weigh the seedling, and record the mass.

Think About This

1. How did the mass of the embryo and the bean seedling differ?

2. **Key Concept** If a plant begins as one cell, where do all the cells come from?

Understanding Cells

Have you ever looked up at the night sky and tried to find other planets in our solar system? It is hard to see them without using a telescope. This is because the other planets are millions of kilometers away. Just like we can use telescopes to see other planets, we can use microscopes to see the basic units of all living things—cells. But people didn't always know about cells. Because cells are so small, early scientists had no tools to study them. It took hundreds of years for scientists to learn about cells.

More than 300 years ago, an English scientist named Robert Hooke built a microscope. He used the microscope to look at cork, which is part of a cork oak tree's bark. What he saw looked like the openings in a honeycomb, as shown in **Figure 1.** The openings reminded him of the small rooms, called cells, where monks lived. He called the structures cells, from the Latin word *cellula* (SEL yuh luh), which means "small rooms."

Figure 1 To Robert Hooke, the cells of cork looked like the openings in a honeycomb.

The Cell Theory

After Hooke's discovery, other scientists began making better microscopes and looking for cells in many other places, such as pond water and blood. The newer microscopes enabled scientists to see different structures inside cells. Matthias Schleiden (SHLI dun), a German scientist, used one of the new microscopes to look at plant cells. Around the same time, another German scientist, Theodor Schwann, used a microscope to study animal cells. Schleiden and Schwann realized that plant and animal cells have similar features. You'll read about many of these features in Lesson 2.

Almost two decades later, Rudolf Virchow (VUR koh), a German doctor, proposed that all cells come from preexisting cells, or cells that already exist. The observations made by Schleiden, Schwann, and Virchow were combined into one **theory.** As illustrated in **Table 1,** *the* **cell theory** *states that all living things are made of one or more cells, the cell is the smallest unit of life, and all new cells come from preexisting cells.* After the development of the cell theory, scientists raised more questions about cells. If all living things are made of cells, what are cells made of?

Key Concept Check How did scientists' understanding of cells develop?

REVIEW VOCABULARY

theory
explanation of things or events based on scientific knowledge resulting from many observations and experiments

Table 1 Scientists developed the cell theory after studying cells with microscopes.

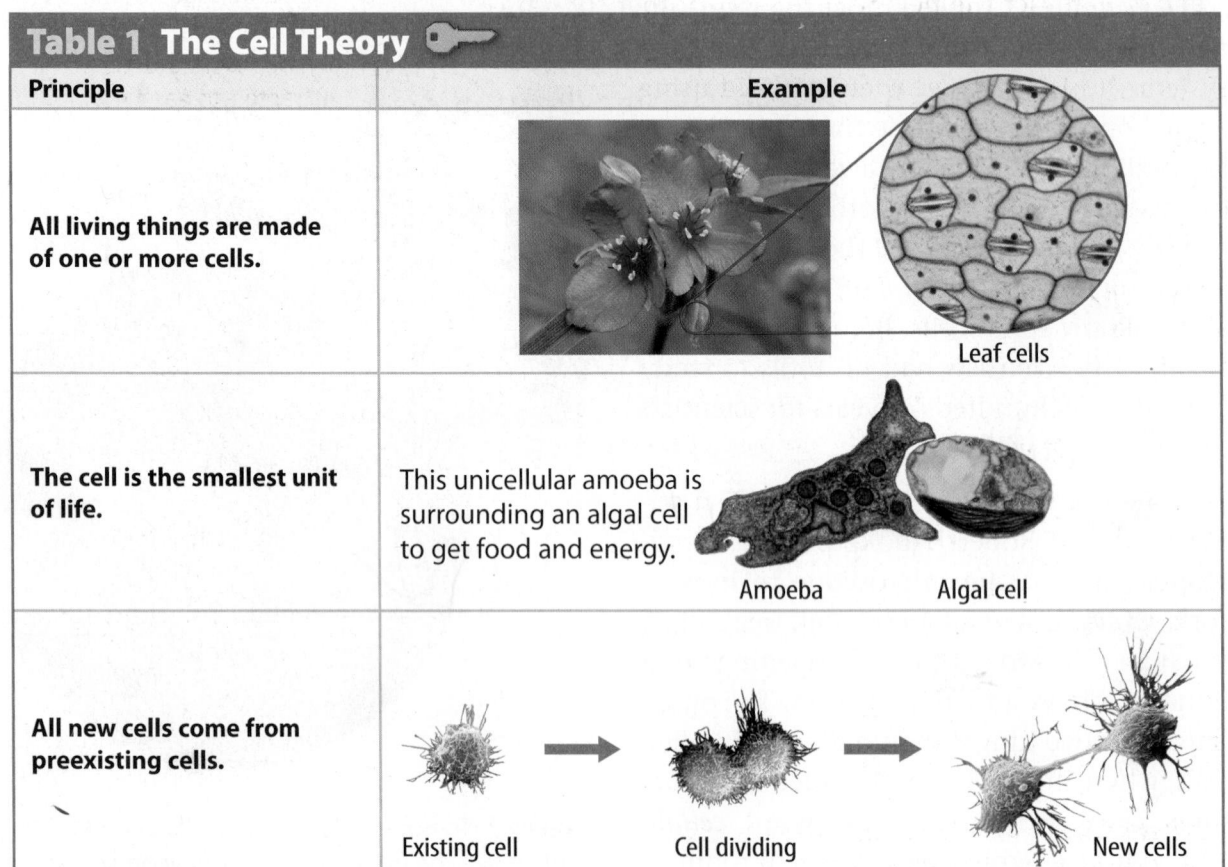

Table 1 The Cell Theory	
Principle	**Example**
All living things are made of one or more cells.	Leaf cells
The cell is the smallest unit of life.	This unicellular amoeba is surrounding an algal cell to get food and energy. Amoeba Algal cell
All new cells come from preexisting cells.	Existing cell Cell dividing New cells

Basic Cell Substances

Have you ever watched a train travel down a railroad track? The locomotive pulls train cars that are hooked together. Like a train, many of the substances in cells are made of smaller parts that are joined together. *These substances, called* **macromolecules,** *form by joining many small molecules together.* As you will read later in this lesson, macromolecules have many important roles in cells. But macromolecules cannot function without one of the most important substances in cells—water.

The Main Ingredient—Water

The main ingredient in any cell is water. It makes up more than 70 percent of a cell's volume and is essential for life. Why is water such an important molecule? In addition to making up a large part of the inside of cells, water also surrounds cells. The water surrounding your cells helps to insulate your body, which maintains homeostasis, or a stable internal environment.

The structure of a water molecule makes it ideal for dissolving many other substances. Substances must be in a liquid to move into and out of cells. A water molecule has two areas:

- An area that is more negative (–), called the negative end; this end can attract the positive part of another substance.

- An area that is more positive (+), called the positive end; this end can attract the negative part of another substance.

Examine **Figure 2** to see how the positive and negative ends of water molecules dissolve salt crystals.

WORD ORIGIN ·············

macromolecule
from Greek *makro–*, means "long"; and Latin *molecula*, means "mass"

Figure 2 The positive and negative ends of a water molecule attract the positive and negative parts of another substance, similar to the way magnets are attracted to each other.

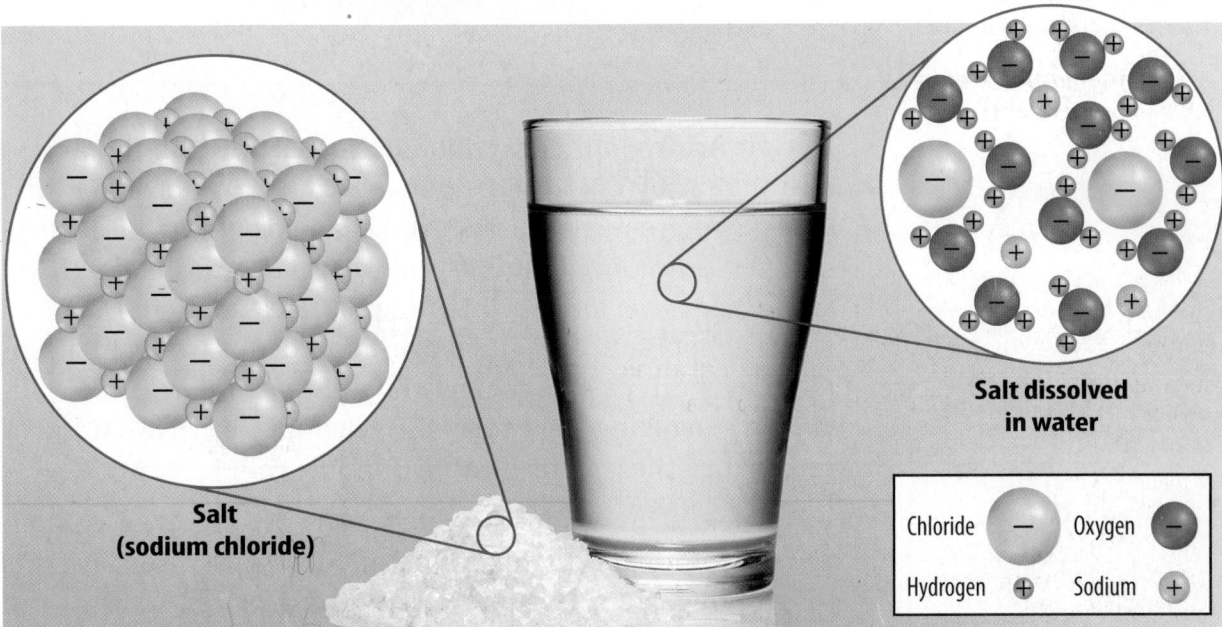

Salt (sodium chloride)

Salt dissolved in water

| Chloride | — | Oxygen | — |
| Hydrogen | + | Sodium | + |

🔵 **Visual Check** Which part of the salt crystal is attracted to the oxygen in the water molecule?

Macromolecules

Although water is essential for life, all cells contain other substances that enable them to function. Recall that macromolecules are large molecules that form when smaller molecules join together. As shown in **Figure 3,** there are four types of macromolecules in cells: nucleic acids, proteins, lipids, and carbohydrates. Each type of macromolecule has unique functions in a cell. These functions range from growth and communication to movement and storage.

Cell Macromolecules

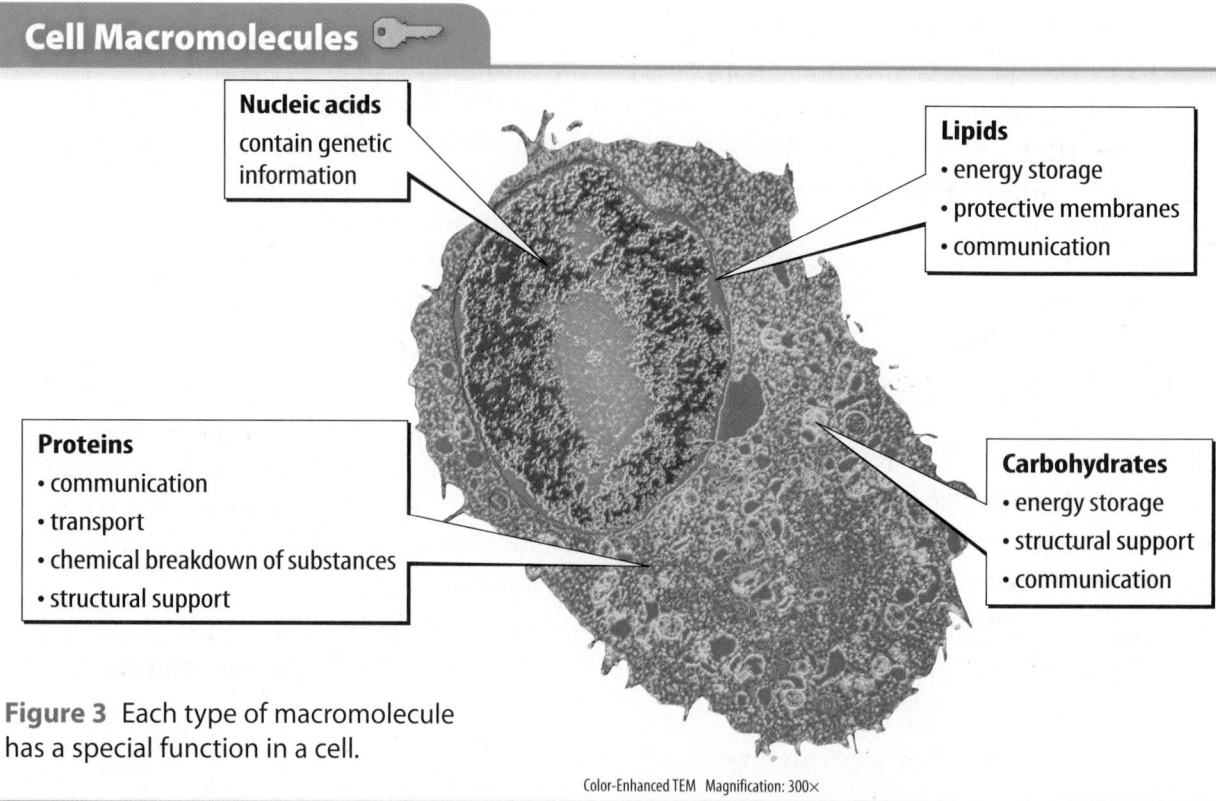

Nucleic acids
contain genetic information

Lipids
• energy storage
• protective membranes
• communication

Proteins
• communication
• transport
• chemical breakdown of substances
• structural support

Carbohydrates
• energy storage
• structural support
• communication

Figure 3 Each type of macromolecule has a special function in a cell.

Color-Enhanced TEM Magnification: 300×

FOLDABLES

Fold a sheet of paper to make a four-door book. Label it as shown. Use it to organize your notes on the macromolecules and their uses in a cell.

| Nucleic acids | Proteins |
| Lipids | Carbohydrates |

Nucleic Acids Both deoxyribonucleic (dee AHK sih ri boh noo klee ihk) acid (DNA) and ribonucleic (ri boh noo KLEE ihk) acid (RNA) are nucleic acids. **Nucleic acids** *are macromolecules that form when long chains of molecules called nucleotides* (NEW klee uh tidz) *join together.* The order of nucleotides in DNA and RNA is important. If you change the order of words in a sentence, you can change the meaning of the sentence. In a similar way, changing the order of nucleotides in DNA and RNA can change the genetic information in a cell.

Nucleic acids are important in cells because they contain genetic information. This information can pass from parents to offspring. DNA includes instructions for cell growth, cell reproduction, and cell processes that enable a cell to respond to its environment. DNA is used to make RNA. RNA is used to make proteins.

Proteins The macromolecules necessary for nearly everything cells do are proteins. **Proteins** *are long chains of amino acid molecules.* You just read that RNA is used to make proteins. RNA contains instructions for joining amino acids together.

Cells contain hundreds of proteins. Each protein has a unique function. Some proteins help cells communicate with each other. Other proteins transport substances around inside cells. Some proteins, such as amylase (AM uh lays) in saliva, help break down nutrients in food. Other proteins, such as keratin (KER uh tun)—a protein found in hair, horns, and feathers—provide structural support.

Lipids Another group of macromolecules found in cells is lipids. *A* **lipid** *is a large macromolecule that does not dissolve in water.* Because lipids do not mix with water, they play an important role as protective barriers in cells. They are also the major part of cell membranes. Lipids play roles in energy storage and in cell communication. Examples of lipids are cholesterol (kuh LES tuh rawl), phospholipids (fahs foh LIH pids), and vitamin A.

 Reading Check Why are lipids important to cells?

Carbohydrates *One sugar molecule, two sugar molecules, or a long chain of sugar molecules make up* **carbohydrates** (kar boh HI drayts). Carbohydrates store energy, provide structural support, and are needed for communication between cells. Sugars and starches are carbohydrates that store energy. Fruits contain sugars. Breads and pastas are mostly starch. The energy in sugars and starches can be released quickly through chemical reactions in cells. Cellulose is a carbohydrate in the cell walls in plants that provides structural support.

 Key Concept Check What basic substances make up a cell?

 **MiniLab**   **25 minutes**

How can you observe DNA?

Nucleic acids are macromolecules that are important in cells because they contain an organism's genetic information. In this lab, you will observe one type of nucleic acid, DNA, in onion root-tip cells using a compound light microscope.

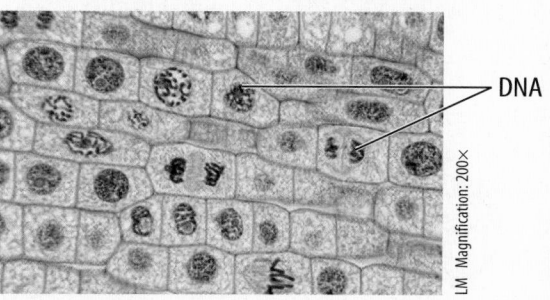

DNA

LM Magnification: 200×

1. Read and complete a lab safety form.
2. Obtain a **microscope** and a **slide** from your teacher. Use care and properly handle your microscope.
3. Observe the **onion root-tip cells** at the magnifications assigned by your teacher.
4. Determine the approximate number of cells in your field of view and the number of cells with visible DNA. Record these numbers in your Science Journal.

Analyze and Conclude

1. **Calculate** Using your data, find the percentage of cells with visible DNA that you saw in your microscope's field of view.

2. **Compare** your results with the results of other students. Are all the results the same? Explain.

3. **Create** a data table for the entire class that lists individual results.

4. **Calculate** the total percentage of cells with visible DNA at each magnification.

5. **Key Concept** Did looking at the cells at different magnifications change the percentage of cells with visible DNA? Explain.

Lesson 1 Review

Visual Summary

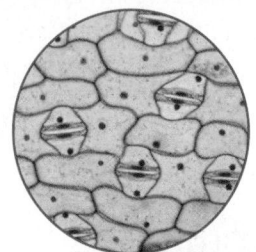

The cell theory summarizes the main principles for understanding that the cell is the basic unit of life.

Water is the main ingredient in every cell.

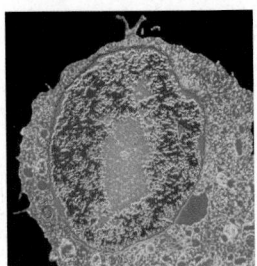

A nucleic acid, such as DNA, contains the genetic information for a cell.

FOLDABLES®

Use your lesson Foldable to review the lesson. Save your Foldable for the project at the end of the chapter.

What do you think NOW?

You first read the statements below at the beginning of the chapter.

1. Nonliving things have cells.

2. Cells are made mostly of water.

Did you change your mind about whether you agree or disagree with the statements? Rewrite any false statements to make them true.

Use Vocabulary

1 The _____ _____ states that the cell is the basic unit of all living things.

2 **Distinguish** between a carbohydrate and a lipid.

3 **Use the term** *nucleic acid* in a sentence.

Understand Key Concepts 🔑

4 Which macromolecule is made from amino acids?
- **A.** lipid
- **C.** carbohydrate
- **B.** protein
- **D.** nucleic acid

5 **Describe** how the invention of the microscope helped scientists understand cells.

6 **Compare** the functions of DNA and proteins in a cell.

Interpret Graphics

7 **Summarize** Copy and fill in the graphic organizer below to summarize the main principles of the cell theory.

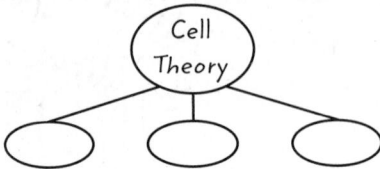

8 **Analyze** How does the structure of the water molecule shown below enable it to interact with other water molecules?

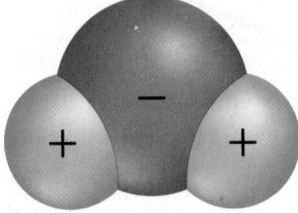

Critical Thinking

9 **Summarize** the functions of lipids in cells.

10 **Hypothesize** why carbohydrates are found in plant cell walls.

A Very Powerful Microscope

Using technology to look inside cells

If Robert Hooke had used an atomic force microscope (AFM), he would have observed more than just cells. He would have seen the macromolecules inside them! An AFM can scan objects that are only nanometers in size. A nanometer is one one-billionth of a meter. That's 100,000 times smaller than the width of a human hair. AFM technology has enabled scientists to better understand how cells function. It also has given them a three-dimensional look at the macromolecules that make life possible. This is how it works.

Photodiode

② The cantilever can bend up and down, similar to the way a diving board can bend, in response to pushing and pulling forces between the atoms in the tip and the atoms in the sample.

③ A laser beam senses the cantilever's up and down movements. A computer converts these movements into an image of the sample's surface.

① A probe moves across a sample's surface to identify the sample's features. The probe consists of a cantilever with a tiny, sharp tip. The tip is about 20 nm in diameter at its base.

It's Your Turn

RESEARCH NASA's Phoenix Mars Lander included an atomic force microscope. Find out what scientists discovered on Mars with this instrument.

The Cell

Reading Guide

Key Concepts 🔑
ESSENTIAL QUESTIONS

- How are prokaryotic cells and eukaryotic cells similar, and how are they different?

- What do the structures in a cell do?

Vocabulary
cell membrane p. 52

cell wall p. 52

cytoplasm p. 53

cytoskeleton p. 53

organelle p. 54

nucleus p. 55

chloroplast p. 57

g Multilingual eGlossary

▢ Video   BrainPOP®

Inquiry Hooked Together?

What do you think happens when one of the hooks in the photo above goes through one of the loops? The two sides fasten together. The shapes of the hooks and loops in the hook-and-loop tape are suited to their function—to hold the two pieces together.

Why do eggs have shells?

Bird eggs have different structures, such as a shell, a membrane, and a yolk. Each structure has a different function that helps keep the egg safe and assists in development of the baby bird inside of it.

1. Read and complete a lab safety form.
2. Place an **uncooked egg** in a bowl.
3. Feel the shell, and record your observations in your Science Journal.
4. Crack open the egg. Pour the contents into the bowl.
5. Observe the inside of the shell and the contents of the bowl. Record your observations in your Science Journal.

Think About This

1. What do you think is the role of the eggshell?

2. Are there any structures in the bowl that have the same function as the eggshell? Explain.

3. **Key Concept** What does the structure of the eggshell tell you about its function?

Cell Shape and Movement

You might recall from Lesson 1 that all living things are made up of one or more cells. As illustrated in **Figure 4,** cells come in many shapes and sizes. The size and shape of a cell relates to its job or function. For example, a human red blood cell cannot be seen without a microscope. Its small size and disk shape enable it to pass easily through the smallest blood vessels. The shape of a nerve cell enables it to send signals over long distances. Some plant cells are hollow and make up tubelike structures that carry materials throughout a plant.

The structures that make up a cell also have unique functions. Think about how the players on a football team perform different tasks to move the ball down the field. In a similar way, a cell is made of different structures that perform different functions that keep a cell alive. You will read about some of these structures in this lesson.

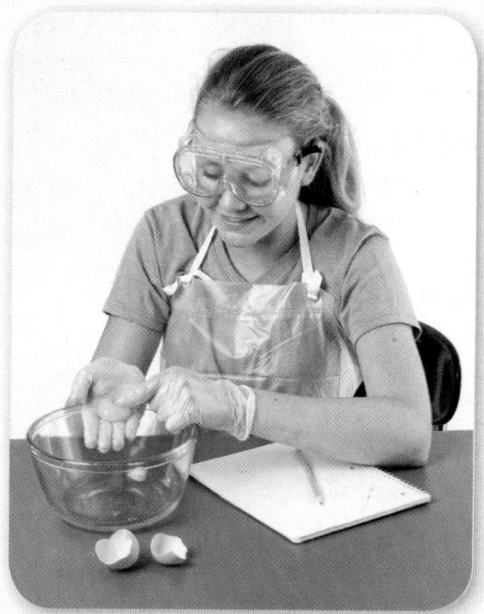

A nerve cell's projections can send signals over long distances.

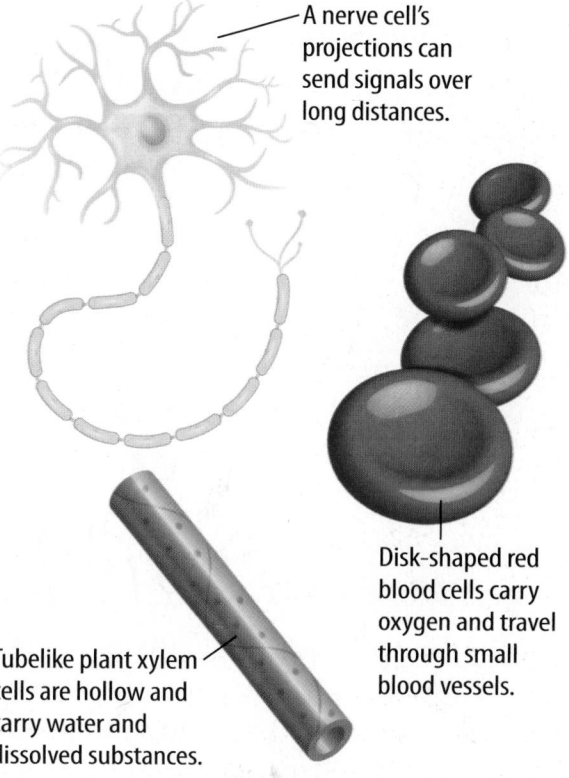

Disk-shaped red blood cells carry oxygen and travel through small blood vessels.

Tubelike plant xylem cells are hollow and carry water and dissolved substances.

Figure 4 The shape of a cell relates to the function it performs.

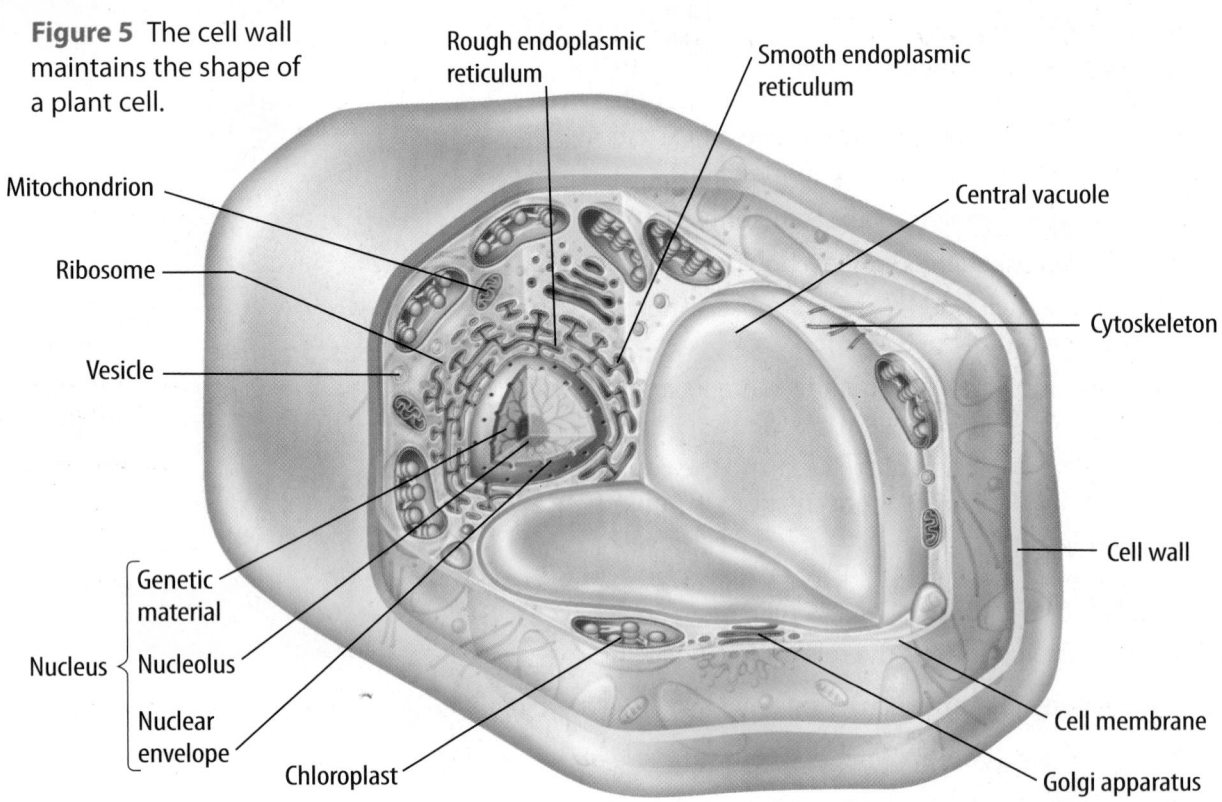

Figure 5 The cell wall maintains the shape of a plant cell.

Rough endoplasmic reticulum

Smooth endoplasmic reticulum

Mitochondrion

Ribosome

Vesicle

Central vacuole

Cytoskeleton

Cell wall

Genetic material

Nucleolus

Nucleus

Nuclear envelope

Chloroplast

Cell membrane

Golgi apparatus

ACADEMIC VOCABULARY ··

function
(noun) the purpose for which something is used

Cell Membrane

Although different types of cells perform different **functions,** all cells have some structures in common. As shown in **Figure 5** and **Figure 6,** every cell is surrounded by a protective covering called a membrane. *The* **cell membrane** *is a flexible covering that protects the inside of a cell from the environment outside a cell.* Cell membranes are mostly made of two different macromolecules—proteins and a type of lipid called phospholipids. Think again about a football team. The defensive line tries to stop the other team from moving forward with the football. In a similar way, a cell membrane protects the cell from the outside environment.

✓ **Reading Check** What are cell membranes made of?

Cell Wall

Every cell has a cell membrane, but some cells are also surrounded by a structure called the cell wall. Plant cells such as the one in **Figure 5,** fungal cells, bacteria, and some types of protists have cell walls. *A* **cell wall** *is a stiff structure outside the cell membrane.* A cell wall protects a cell from attack by viruses and other harmful organisms. In some plant cells and fungal cells, a cell wall helps maintain the cell's shape and gives structural support.

Figure 6 The cytoskeleton maintains the shape of an animal cell.

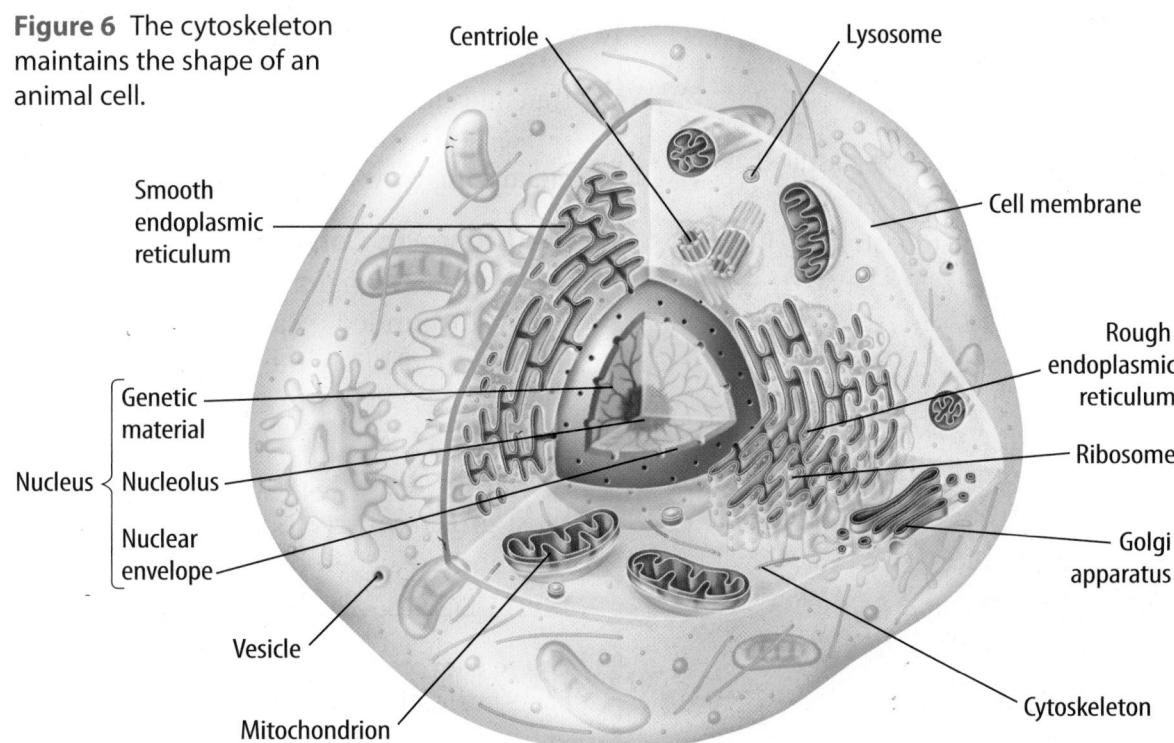

Centriole
Lysosome
Smooth endoplasmic reticulum
Cell membrane
Rough endoplasmic reticulum
Genetic material
Nucleus ⎰ Nucleolus
Nuclear envelope
Ribosome
Golgi apparatus
Vesicle
Cytoskeleton
Mitochondrion

🔘 **Visual Check** Compare this animal cell to the plant cell in **Figure 5.**

Cell Appendages

Arms, legs, claws, and antennae are all types of appendages. Cells can have appendages too. Cell appendages are often used for movement. Flagella (fluh JEH luh; singular, flagellum) are long, tail-like appendages that whip back and forth and move a cell. A cell can also have cilia (SIH lee uh; singular, cilium) like the ones shown in **Figure 7.** Cilia are short, hairlike structures. They can move a cell or move molecules away from a cell. A microscopic organism called a paramecium (pa ruh MEE shee um) moves around its watery environment using its cilia. The cilia in your windpipe move harmful substances away from your lungs.

Cytoplasm and the Cytoskeleton

In Lesson 1, you read that water is the main ingredient in a cell. Most of this water is in the **cytoplasm**, *a fluid inside a cell that contains salts and other molecules.* The cytoplasm also contains a cell's cytoskeleton. *The* **cytoskeleton** *is a network of threadlike proteins that are joined together.* The proteins form a framework inside a cell. This framework gives a cell its shape and helps it move. Cilia and flagella are made from the same proteins that make up the cytoskeleton.

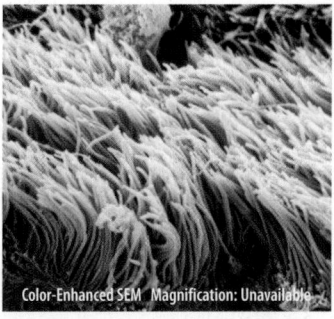

Color-Enhanced SEM Magnification: Unavailable

Figure 7 Lung cells have cilia that help move fluids and foreign materials.

WORD ORIGIN · · · · · · · · · · ·

cytoplasm
from Greek *kytos*, means "hollow vessel"; and *plasma*, means "something molded"

Inquiry MiniLab
25 minutes

How do eukaryotic and prokaryotic cells compare?

With the use of better microscopes, scientists discovered that cells can be classified as one of two types—prokaryotic or eukaryotic.

1. Read and complete a lab safety form.

2. Using different **craft items,** make a two-dimensional model of a eukaryotic cell.

3. In your cell model, include the number of cell structures assigned by your teacher.

4. Make each cell structure the correct shape, as shown in this lesson.

5. Make a label for each cell structure of your model.

Analyze and Conclude

1. **Describe** the nucleus of your cell.

2. **Classify** your cell as either a plant cell or an animal cell, and support your classification with evidence.

3. **Key Concept** Compare and contrast a prokaryotic cell, as shown in **Figure 8,** with your eukaryotic cell model.

Cell Types

Recall that the use of microscopes enabled scientists to discover cells. With more advanced microscopes, scientists discovered that all cells can be grouped into two types—prokaryotic (proh ka ree AH tihk) cells and eukaryotic (yew ker ee AH tihk) cells.

Prokaryotic Cells

The genetic material in a prokaryotic cell is not surrounded by a membrane, as shown in **Figure 8.** This is the most important feature of a prokaryotic cell. Prokaryotic cells also do not have many of the other cell parts that you will read about later in this lesson. Most prokaryotic cells are unicellular organisms and are called prokaryotes.

Figure 8 In prokaryotic cells, the genetic material floats freely in the cytoplasm.

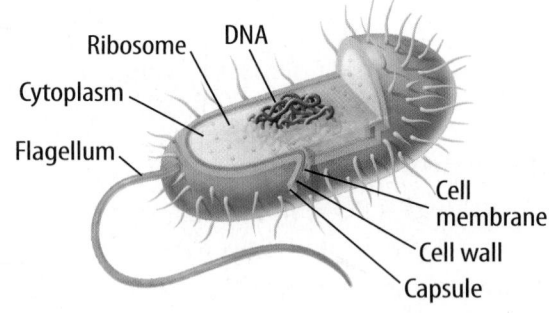

Ribosome
DNA
Cytoplasm
Flagellum
Cell membrane
Cell wall
Capsule

Eukaryotic Cells

Plants, animals, fungi, and protists are all made of eukaryotic cells, such as the ones shown in **Figure 5** and **Figure 6,** and are called eukaryotes. With few exceptions, each eukaryotic cell has genetic material that is surrounded by a membrane. Every eukaryotic cell also has *other structures, called* **organelles,** *which have specialized functions. Most organelles are surrounded by membranes.* Eukaryotic cells are usually larger than prokaryotic cells. About ten prokaryotic cells would fit inside one eukaryotic cell.

Key Concept Check How are prokaryotic cells and eukaryotic cells similar, and how are they different?

Cell Organelles

As you have just read, organelles are eukaryotic cell structures with specific functions. Organelles enable cells to carry out different functions at the same time. For example, cells can obtain energy from food, store information, make macromolecules, and get rid of waste materials all at the same time because different organelles perform the different tasks.

The Nucleus

The largest organelle inside most eukaryotic cells is the nucleus, shown in **Figure 9.** *The* **nucleus** *is the part of a eukaryotic cell that directs cell activities and contains genetic information stored in DNA.* DNA is organized into structures called chromosomes. The number of chromosomes in a nucleus is different for different species of organisms. For example, kangaroo cells contain six pairs of chromosomes. Most human cells contain 23 pairs of chromosomes.

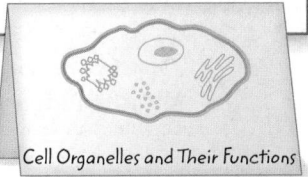
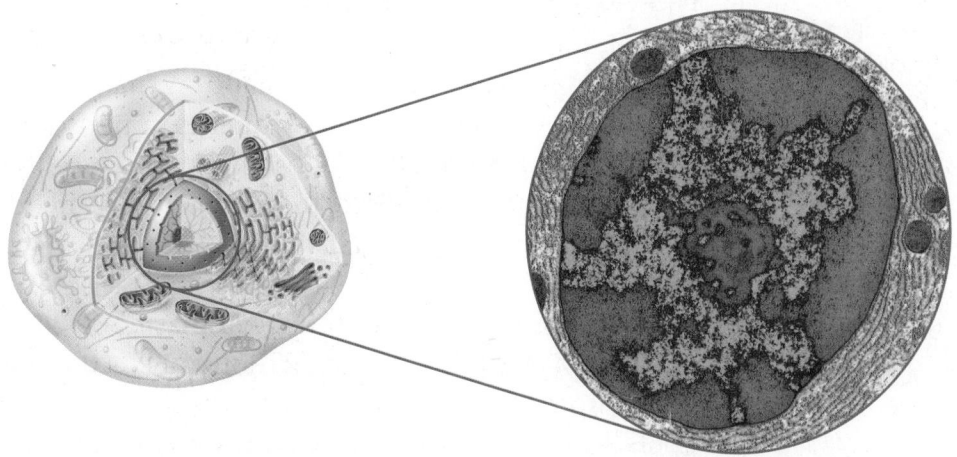

Nucleus
Color-Enhanced TEM Magnification: 15,500×

Figure 9 The nucleus directs cell activity and is surrounded by a membrane.

In addition to chromosomes, the nucleus contains proteins and an organelle called the nucleolus (new KLEE uh lus). The nucleolus is often seen as a large dark spot in the nucleus of a cell. The nucleolus makes ribosomes, organelles that are involved in the production of proteins. You will read about ribosomes later in this lesson.

Surrounding the nucleus are two membranes that form a structure called the nuclear **envelope.** The nuclear envelope contains many pores. Certain molecules, such as ribosomes and RNA, move into and out of the nucleus through these pores.

SCIENCE USE V. COMMON USE

envelope
Science Use an outer covering

Common Use a flat paper container for a letter

 Reading Check What is the nuclear envelope?

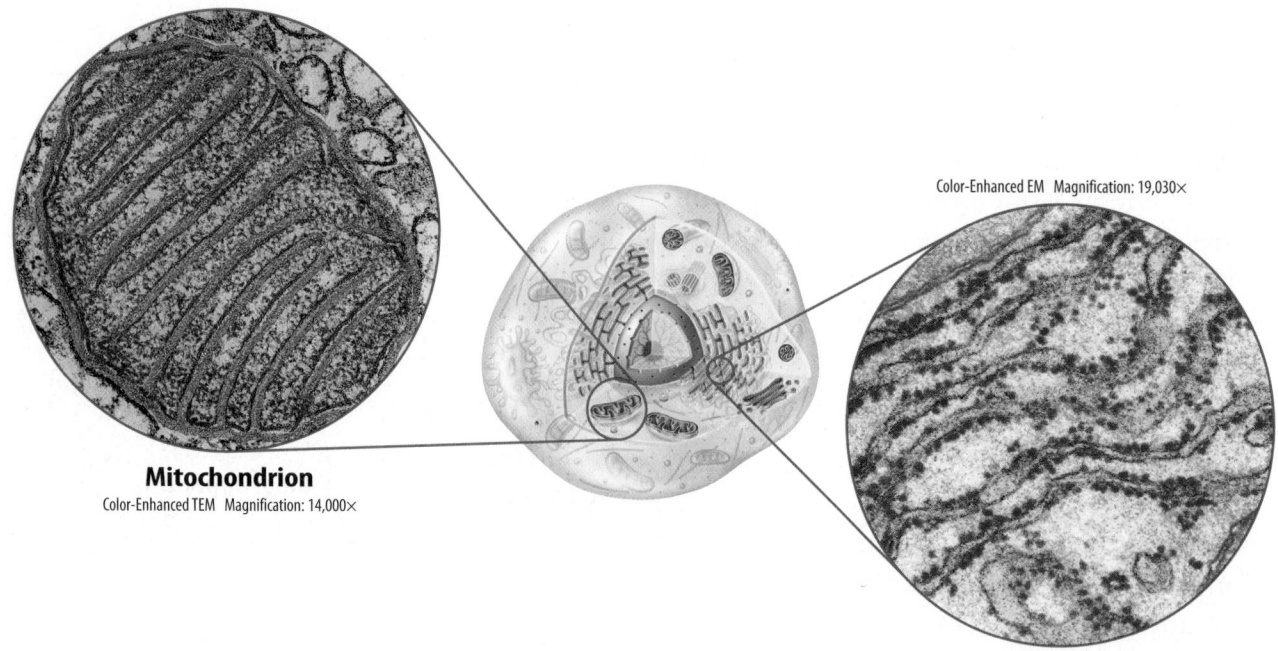

Mitochondrion
Color-Enhanced TEM Magnification: 14,000×

Color-Enhanced EM Magnification: 19,030×

Rough endoplasmic reticulum

Figure 10 The endoplasmic reticulum is made of many folded membranes. Mitochondria provide a cell with usable energy.

Manufacturing Molecules

You might recall from Lesson 1 that proteins are important molecules in cells. Proteins are made on small structures called ribosomes. Unlike other cell organelles, a ribosome is not surrounded by a membrane. Ribosomes are in a cell's cytoplasm. They also can be attached to a weblike organelle called the endoplasmic reticulum (en duh PLAZ mihk • rih TIHK yuh lum), or ER. As shown in **Figure 10,** the ER spreads from the nucleus throughout most of the cytoplasm. ER with ribosomes on its surface is called rough ER. Rough ER is the site of protein production. ER without ribosomes is called smooth ER. It makes lipids such as cholesterol. Smooth ER is important because it helps remove harmful substances from a cell.

 Reading Check Contrast smooth ER and rough ER.

Processing Energy

All living things require energy in order to survive. Cells process some energy in specialized organelles. Most eukaryotic cells contain hundreds of organelles called mitochondria (mi tuh KAHN dree uh; singular, mitochondrion), shown in **Figure 10.** Some cells in a human heart can contain a thousand mitochondria.

Like the nucleus, a mitochondrion is surrounded by two membranes. Energy is released during chemical reactions that occur in the mitochondria. This energy is stored in high-energy molecules called ATP—adenosine triphosphate (uh DEH nuh seen • tri FAHS fayt). ATP is the fuel for cellular processes such as growth, cell division, and material transport.

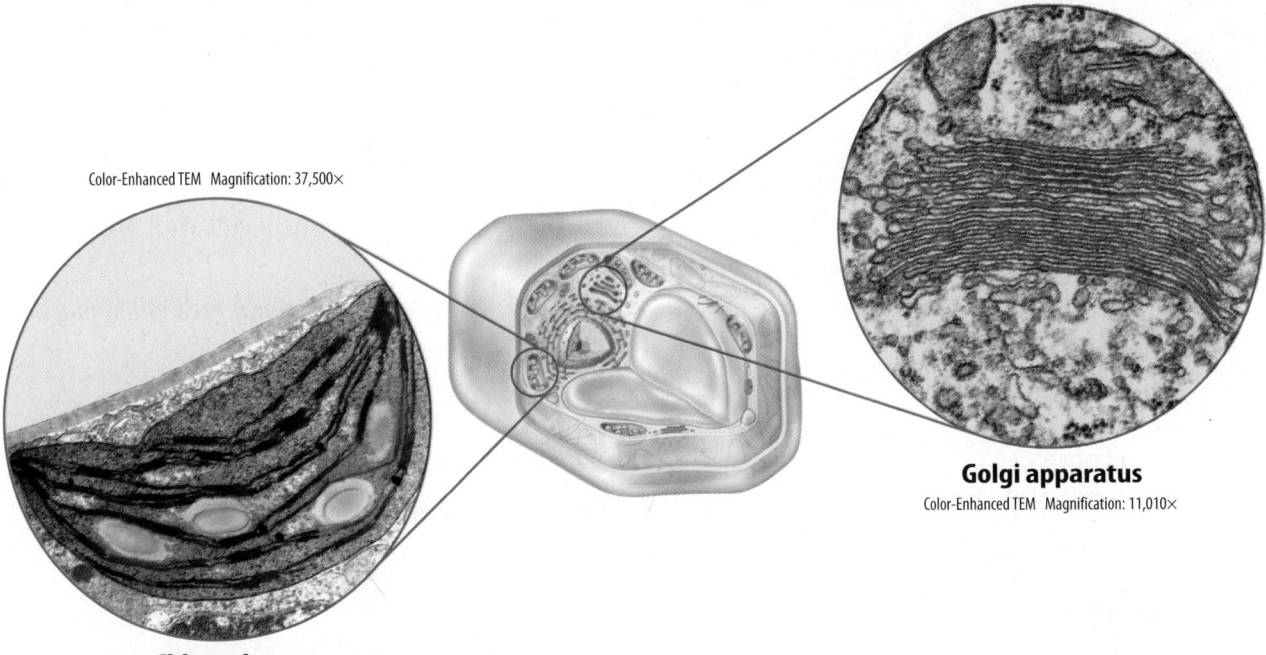

Color-Enhanced TEM Magnification: 37,500×

Golgi apparatus
Color-Enhanced TEM Magnification: 11,010×

Chloroplast

Plant cells and some protists, such as algae, also contain organelles called chloroplasts (KLOR uh plasts), shown in **Figure 11.** **Chloroplasts** *are membrane-bound organelles that use light energy and make food—a sugar called glucose—from water and carbon dioxide in a process known as photosynthesis* (foh toh SIHN thuh sus). The sugar contains stored chemical energy that can be released when a cell needs it. You will read more about photosynthesis in Lesson 4.

 Reading Check Which types of cells contain chloroplasts?

Processing, Transporting, and Storing Molecules

Near the ER is an organelle that looks like a stack of pancakes. This is the Golgi (GAWL jee) apparatus, shown in **Figure 11.** It prepares proteins for their specific jobs or functions. Then it packages the proteins into tiny, membrane-bound, ball-like structures called vesicles. Vesicles are organelles that transport substances from one area of a cell to another area of a cell. Some vesicles in an animal cell are called lysosomes. Lysosomes contain substances that help break down and recycle cellular components.

Some cells also have saclike structures called vacuoles (VA kyuh wohlz). Vacuoles are organelles that store food, water, and waste material. A typical plant cell usually has one large vacuole that stores water and other substances. Some animal cells have many small vacuoles.

 Key Concept Check What is the function of the Golgi apparatus?

Figure 11 Plant cells have chloroplasts that use light energy and make food. The Golgi apparatus packages materials into vesicles.

Lesson 2 Review

Visual Summary

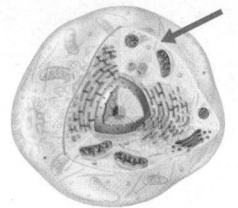

A cell is protected by a flexible covering called the cell membrane.

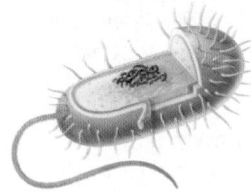

Cells can be grouped into two types—prokaryotic cells and eukaryotic cells.

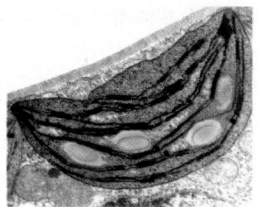

In a chloroplast, light energy is used for making sugars in a process called photosynthesis.

FOLDABLES

Use your lesson Foldable to review the lesson. Save your Foldable for the project at the end of the chapter.

What do you think NOW?

You first read the statements below at the beginning of the chapter.

3. Different organisms have cells with different structures.

4. All cells store genetic information in their nuclei.

Did you change your mind about whether you agree or disagree with the statements? Rewrite any false statements to make them true.

Use Vocabulary

1 **Distinguish** between the cell wall and the cell membrane.

2 **Use the terms** *mitochondria* and *chloroplasts* in a sentence.

3 **Define** *organelle* in your own words.

Understand Key Concepts

4 Which organelle is used to store water?
- **A.** chloroplast
- **B.** lysosome
- **C.** nucleus
- **D.** vacuole

5 **Explain** the role of the cytoskeleton.

6 **Draw** a prokaryotic cell and label its parts.

7 **Compare** the roles of the endoplasmic reticulum and the Golgi apparatus.

Interpret Graphics

8 **Explain** how the structure of the cells below relates to their function.

9 **Compare** Copy the table below and fill it in to compare the structures of a plant cell to the structures of an animal cell.

Structure	Plant Cell	Animal Cell
Cell membrane	yes	yes
Cell wall		
Mitochondrion		
Chloroplast		
Nucleus		
Vacuole		
Lysosome		

Critical Thinking

10 **Analyze** Why are most organelles surrounded by membranes?

11 **Compare** the features of eukaryotic and prokaryotic cells.

How are plant cells and animal cells similar and how are they different?

A light microscope enables you to observe many of the structures in cells. Increasing the magnification means you see a smaller portion of the object, but lets you see more detail. As you see more details, you can **compare and contrast** different cell types. How are they alike? How are they different?

Materials

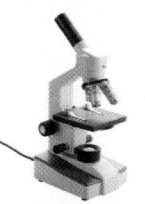

microscope

microscope slide and coverslip

forceps

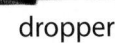

dropper

Elodea plant

Prepared slide of human cheek cells

Safety

Learn It

Observations can be analyzed by noting the similarities and differences between two or more objects that you observe. You **compare** objects by noting similarities. You **contrast** objects by looking for differences.

Try It

1. Read and complete a lab safety form.

2. Using forceps, make a wet-mount slide of a young leaf from the tip of an *Elodea* plant.

3. Use a microscope to observe the leaf on low power. Focus on the top layer of cells.

4. Switch to high power and focus on one cell. The large organelle in the center of the cell is the central vacuole. Moving around the central vacuole are green, disklike objects called chloroplasts. Try to find the nucleus. It looks like a clear ball.

5. Draw a diagram of an *Elodea* cell in your Science Journal. Label the cell wall, central vacuole, chloroplasts, cytoplasm, and nucleus. Return to low power and remove the slide. Properly dispose of the slide.

6. Observe the prepared slide of cheek cells under low power.

7. Switch to high power and focus on one cell. Draw a diagram of one cheek cell. Label the cell membrane, cytoplasm, and nucleus. Return to low power and remove the slide.

Apply It

8. Based on your diagrams, how do the shapes of the *Elodea* cell and cheek cell compare?

9. **Key Concept** Compare and contrast the cell structures in your two diagrams. Which structures did you observe in both cells? Which structures did you observe in only one of the cells?

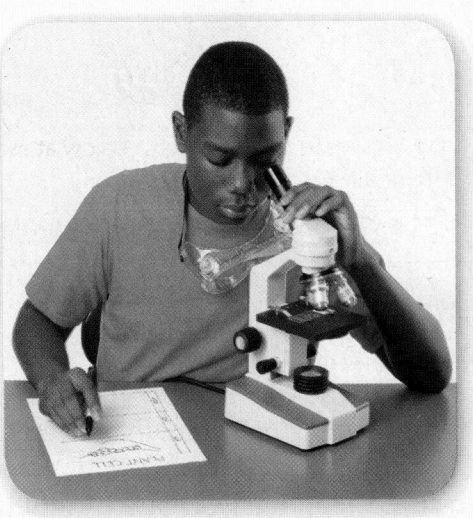

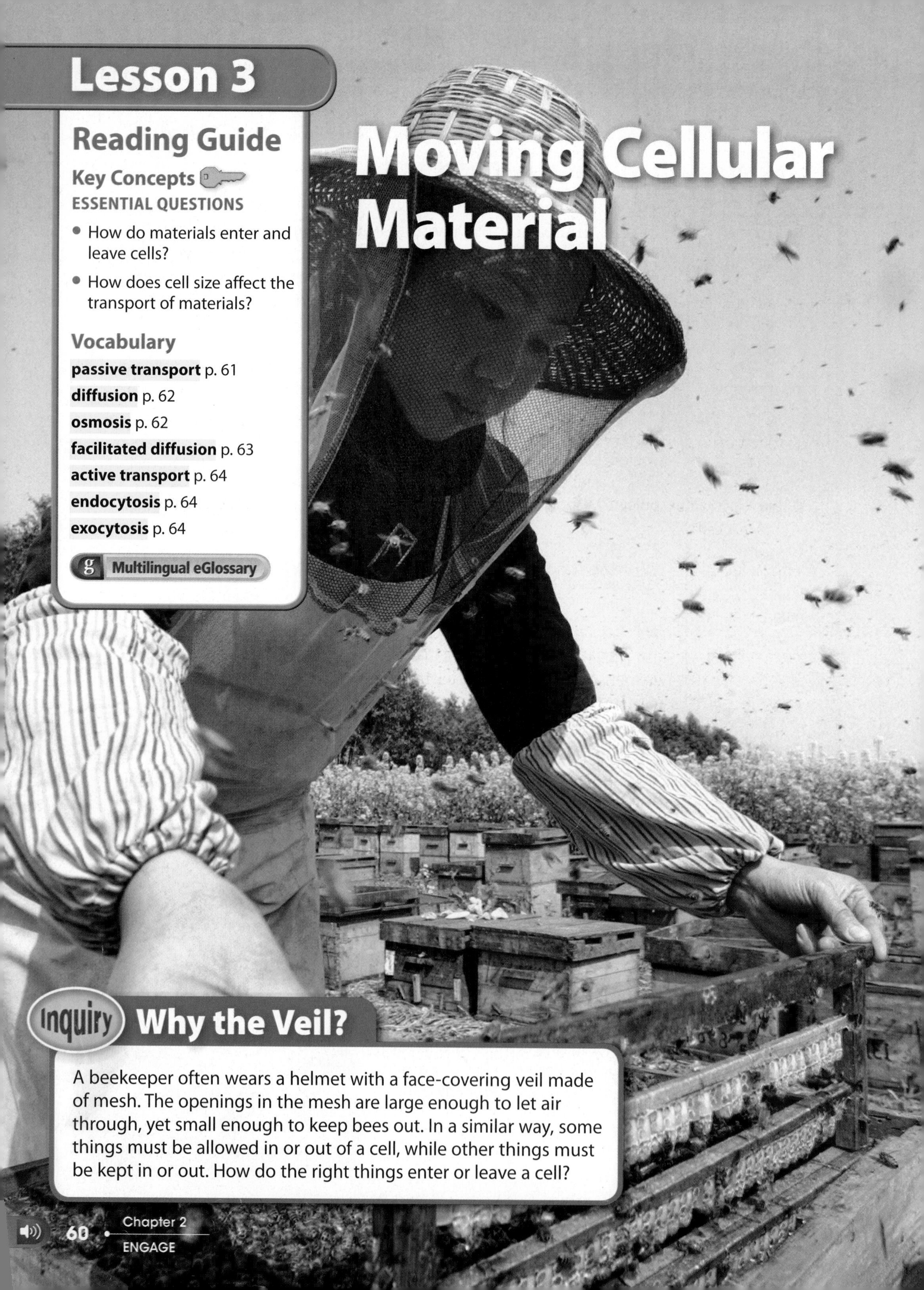

Lesson 3

Moving Cellular Material

Reading Guide

Key Concepts
ESSENTIAL QUESTIONS

- How do materials enter and leave cells?
- How does cell size affect the transport of materials?

Vocabulary

passive transport p. 61
diffusion p. 62
osmosis p. 62
facilitated diffusion p. 63
active transport p. 64
endocytosis p. 64
exocytosis p. 64

g Multilingual eGlossary

Inquiry Why the Veil?

A beekeeper often wears a helmet with a face-covering veil made of mesh. The openings in the mesh are large enough to let air through, yet small enough to keep bees out. In a similar way, some things must be allowed in or out of a cell, while other things must be kept in or out. How do the right things enter or leave a cell?

What does the cell membrane do?

All cells have a membrane around the outside of the cell. The cell membrane separates the inside of a cell from the environment outside a cell. What else might a cell membrane do?

① Read and complete a lab safety form.

② Place a square of **wire mesh** on top of a **beaker.**

③ Pour a small amount of **birdseed** on top of the wire mesh. Record your observations in your Science Journal.

Think About This

1. What part of a cell does the wire mesh represent?

2. What happened when you poured birdseed on the wire mesh?

3. 🔑 **Key Concept** How do you think the cell membrane affects materials that enter and leave a cell?

Passive Transport

Recall from Lesson 2 that membranes are the boundaries between cells and between organelles. Another important role of membranes is to control the movement of substances into and out of cells. A cell membrane is semipermeable. This means it allows only certain substances to enter or leave a cell. Substances can pass through a cell membrane by one of several different processes. The type of process depends on the physical and chemical properties of the substance passing through the membrane.

Small molecules, such as oxygen and carbon dioxide, pass through membranes by a process called passive transport. **Passive transport** *is the movement of substances through a cell membrane without using the cell's energy.* Passive transport depends on the amount of a substance on each side of a membrane. For example, suppose there are more molecules of oxygen outside a cell than inside it. Oxygen will move into that cell until the amount of oxygen is equal on both sides of the cell's membrane. Since oxygen is a small molecule, it passes through a cell membrane without using the cell's energy. The different types of passive transport are explained on the following pages.

✔️ **Reading Check** Describe a semipermeable membrane.

FOLDABLES

Fold a sheet of paper into a two-tab book. Label the tabs as shown. Use it to organize information about the different types of passive and active transport.

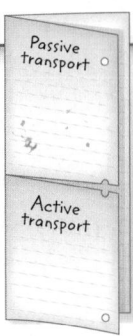

Diffusion

What happens when the concentration, or amount per unit of volume, of a substance is unequal on each side of a membrane? The molecules will move from the side with a higher concentration of that substance to the side with a lower concentration. **Diffusion** *is the movement of substances from an area of higher concentration to an area of lower concentration.*

Usually, diffusion continues through a membrane until the concentration of a substance is the same on both sides of the membrane. When this happens, a substance is in equilibrium. Compare the two diagrams in **Figure 12.** What happened to the red dye that was added to the water on one side of the membrane? Water and dye passed through the membrane in both directions until there were equal concentrations of water and dye on both sides of the membrane.

WORD ORIGIN ·············

diffusion
from Latin *diffusionem*, means "scatter, pour out"

Diffusion 🔑

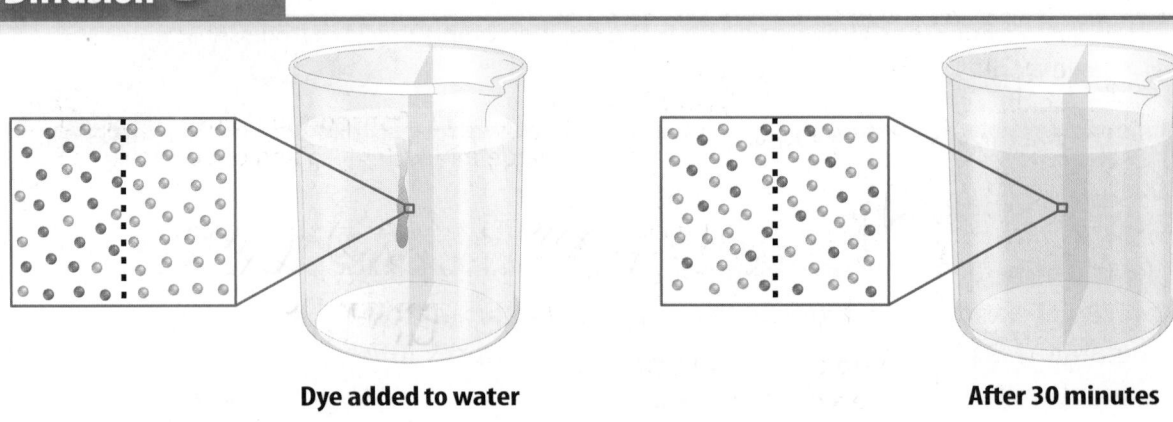

Dye added to water　　　　　　　**After 30 minutes**

✓ **Visual Check** What would the water in the beaker on the right look like if the membrane did not let anything through?

Figure 12 Over time, the concentration of dye on either side of the membrane becomes the same.

Osmosis—The Diffusion of Water

Diffusion refers to the movement of any small molecules from higher to lower concentrations. However, **osmosis** *is the diffusion of water molecules only through a membrane.* Semipermeable cell membranes also allow water to pass through them until equilibrium occurs. For example, the amount of water stored in the vacuoles of plant cells can decrease because of osmosis. That is because the concentration of water in the air surrounding the plant is less than the concentration of water inside the vacuoles of plant cells. Water will continue to diffuse into the air until the concentrations of water inside the plant's cells and in the air are equal. If the plant is not watered to replace the lost water, it will wilt and eventually die.

Facilitated Diffusion

Some molecules are too large or are chemically unable to travel through a membrane by diffusion. *When molecules pass through a cell membrane using special proteins called transport proteins, this is* **facilitated diffusion.** Like diffusion and osmosis, facilitated diffusion does not require a cell to use energy. As shown in **Figure 13,** a cell membrane has transport proteins. The two types of transport proteins are carrier proteins and channel proteins. Carrier proteins carry large molecules, such as the sugar molecule glucose, through the cell membrane. Channel proteins form pores through the membrane. Atomic particles, such as sodium ions and potassium ions, pass through the cell membrane by channel proteins.

 Reading Check How do materials move through the cell membrane in facilitated diffusion?

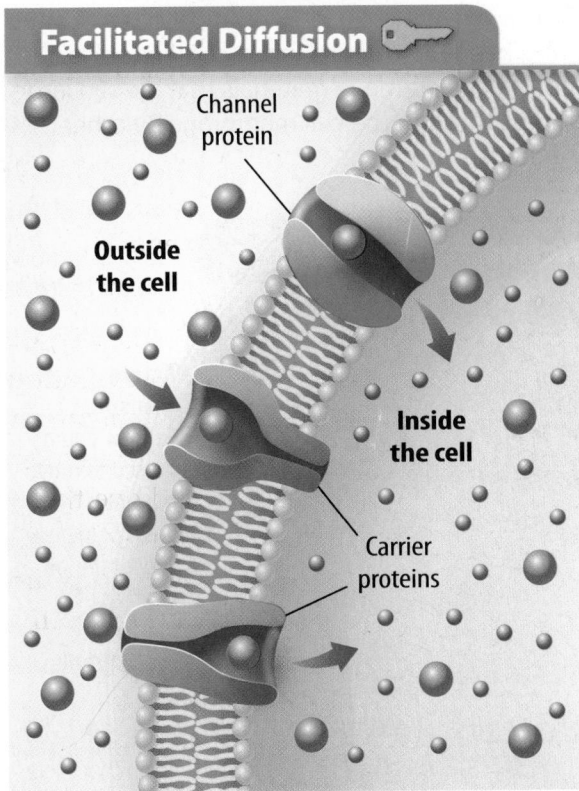

Facilitated Diffusion

Channel protein

Outside the cell

Inside the cell

Carrier proteins

Figure 13 Transport proteins are used to move large molecules into and out of a cell.

Inquiry **MiniLab** **20 minutes**

How is a balloon like a cell membrane?

Substances within a cell are constantly in motion. How can a balloon act like a cell membrane?

1. Read and complete a lab safety form.
2. Make a three-column table in your Science Journal to record your data. Label the first column *Balloon Number,* the second column *Substance,* and the third column *Supporting Evidence.*
3. Use your senses to identify what substance is in each of the **numbered balloons.**
4. Record what you think each substance is.
5. Record the evidence supporting your choice.

Analyze and Conclude

1. **List** the senses that were most useful in identifying the substances.

2. **Infer** if you could identify the substances if you were blindfolded. If so, how?

3. **Describe** how the substances moved, and explain why they moved this way.

4. **Key Concept** Explain how a balloon is like a cell membrane in terms of the movement of substances.

Figure 14 Active transport is most often used to bring needed nutrients into a cell. Endocytosis and exocytosis move materials that are too large to pass through the cell membrane by other methods.

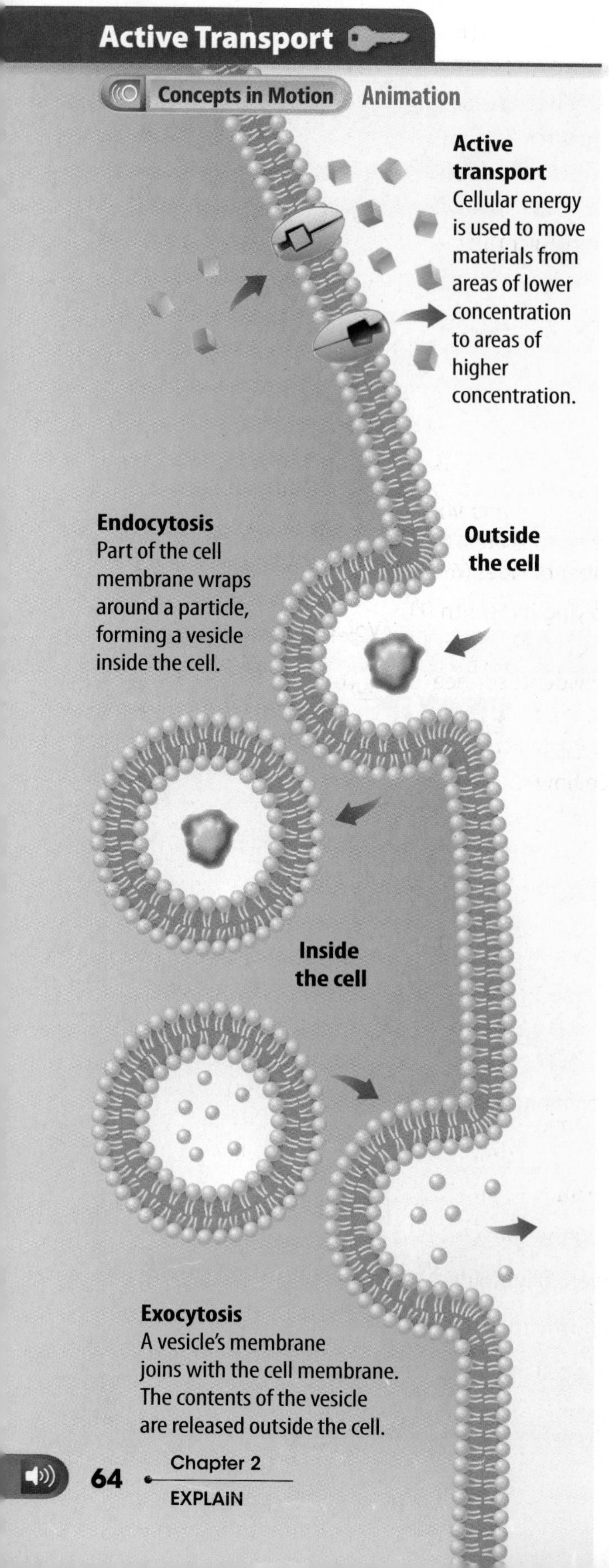

Active Transport
Concepts in Motion Animation
Active transport
Cellular energy is used to move materials from areas of lower concentration to areas of higher concentration.
Endocytosis
Part of the cell membrane wraps around a particle, forming a vesicle inside the cell.
Outside the cell
Inside the cell
Exocytosis
A vesicle's membrane joins with the cell membrane. The contents of the vesicle are released outside the cell.

Active Transport

Sometimes when cellular materials pass through membranes it requires a cell to use energy. **Active transport** *is the movement of substances through a cell membrane only by using the cell's energy.*

Recall that passive transport is the movement of substances from areas of higher concentration to areas of lower concentration. However, substances moving by active transport move from areas of lower concentration to areas of higher concentration, as shown in **Figure 14.**

Active transport is important for cells and organelles. Cells can take in needed nutrients from the environment through carrier proteins by using active transport. This occurs even when concentrations of these nutrients are lower in the environment than inside the cell. Some other molecules and waste materials also leave cells by active transport.

Endocytosis and Exocytosis

Some substances are too large to enter a cell membrane by diffusion or by using a transport protein. These substances can enter a cell by another process. **Endocytosis** (en duh si TOH sus), shown in **Figure 14,** *is the process during which a cell takes in a substance by surrounding it with the cell membrane.* Many different types of cells use endocytosis. For example, some cells take in bacteria and viruses using endocytosis.

Some substances are too large to leave a cell by diffusion or by using a transport protein. These substances can leave a cell another way. **Exocytosis** (ek soh si TOH sus), shown in **Figure 14,** *is the process during which a cell's vesicles release their contents outside the cell.* Proteins and other substances are removed from a cell through this process.

Key Concept Check How do materials enter and leave cells?

Cell Size and Transport

Recall that the movement of nutrients, waste material, and other substances into and out of a cell is important for survival. For this movement to happen, the area of the cell membrane must be large compared to its volume. The area of the cell membrane is the cell's surface area. The volume is the amount of space inside the cell. As a cell grows, both its volume and its surface area increase. The volume of a cell increases faster than its surface area. If a cell were to keep growing, it would need large amounts of nutrients and would produce large amounts of waste material. However, the surface area of the cell's membrane would be too small to move enough nutrients and wastes through it for the cell to survive.

 Key Concept Check How does cell size affect the transport of materials?

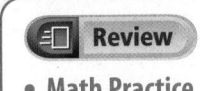 **Review**
- **Math Practice**
- **Personal Tutor**

Math Skills   Use Ratios

A ratio is a comparison of two numbers, such as surface area and volume. If a cell were cube-shaped, you would calculate surface area by multiplying its length (ℓ) by its width (w) by the number of sides (6).

You would calculate the volume of the cell by multiplying its length (ℓ) by its width (w) by its height (h).

To find the surface-area-to-volume ratio of the cell, divide its surface area by its volume.

In the table below, surface-area-to-volume ratios are calculated for cells that are 1 mm, 2 mm, and 4 mm per side. Notice how the ratios change as the cell's size increases.

Surface area $= \ell \times w \times 6$

Volume $= \ell \times w \times h$

$$\frac{\text{Surface area}}{\text{Volume}}$$

	1 mm 1 mm 1 mm	2 mm 2 mm 2 mm	4 mm 4 mm 4 mm
Length	1 mm	2 mm	4 mm
Width	1 mm	2 mm	4 mm
Height	1 mm	2 mm	4 mm
Number of sides	6	6	6
Surface area ($\ell \times w \times$ **no. of sides**)	1 mm $\times$ 1 mm $\times$ 6 $= 6$ mm^2	2 mm $\times$ 2 mm $\times$ 6 $= 24$ mm^2	4 mm $\times$ 4 mm $\times$ 6 $= 96$ mm^2
Volume ($\ell \times w \times h$)	1 mm $\times$ 1 mm $\times$ 1 mm $= 1$ mm^3	2 mm $\times$ 2 mm $\times$ 2 mm $= 8$ mm^3	4 mm $\times$ 4 mm $\times$ 4 mm $= 64$ mm^3
Surface-area-to-volume ratio	$\frac{6 \text{ mm}^2}{1 \text{ mm}^3} = \frac{6}{1}$ or 6:1	$\frac{24 \text{ mm}^2}{8 \text{ mm}^3} = \frac{3}{1}$ or 3:1	$\frac{96 \text{ mm}^2}{64 \text{ mm}^3} = \frac{1.5}{1}$ or 1.5:1

Practice

What is the surface-area-to-volume ratio of a cell whose six sides are 3 mm long?

Lesson 3 Review

Visual Summary

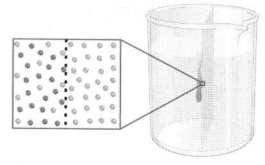

Small molecules can move from an area of higher concentration to an area of lower concentration by diffusion.

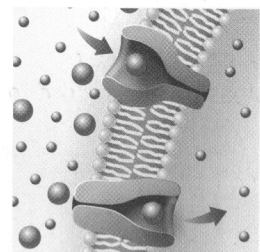

In facilitated diffusion, proteins transport larger molecules through a cell membrane.

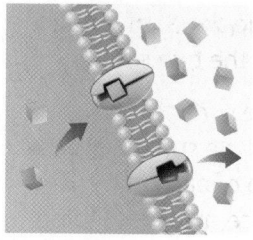

Some molecules move from areas of lower concentration to areas of higher concentration through active transport.

FOLDABLES

Use your lesson Foldable to review the lesson. Save your Foldable for the project at the end of the chapter.

What do you think NOW?

You first read the statements below at the beginning of the chapter.

5. Diffusion and osmosis are the same process.

6. Cells with large surface areas can transport more than cells with smaller surface areas.

Did you change your mind about whether you agree or disagree with the statements? Rewrite any false statements to make them true.

Use Vocabulary

1 **Use the term** *osmosis* in a sentence.

2 **Distinguish** between active transport and passive transport.

3 The process by which vesicles move substances out of a cell is _____.

Understand Key Concepts

4 **Explain** why energy is needed in active transport.

5 **Summarize** the function of endocytosis.

6 **Contrast** osmosis and diffusion.

7 What is limited by a cell's surface-area-to-volume ratio?
  A. cell shape   C. cell surface area
  B. cell size   D. cell volume

Interpret Graphics

8 **Identify** the process shown below, and explain how it works.

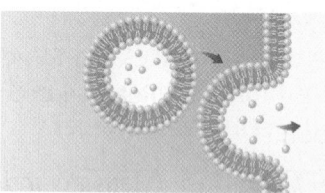

9 **Copy** and fill in the graphic organizer below to describe ways that cells transport substances.

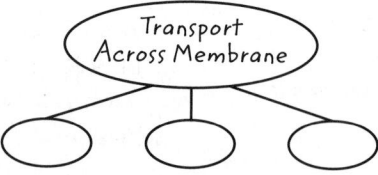

Critical Thinking

10 **Relate** the surface area of a cell to the transport of materials.

Math Skills

Review
— Math Practice —

11 **Calculate** the surface-area-to-volume ratio of a cube whose sides are 6 cm long.

How does an object's size affect the transport of materials?

Materials

hard-cooked eggs

metric ruler

blue food coloring

250-mL beaker

plastic spoon

plastic knife

paper towels

Safety

Nutrients, oxygen, and other materials enter and leave a cell through the cell membrane. Does the size of a cell affect the transport of these materials throughout the cell? In this lab, you will **analyze and conclude** how the size of a cube of egg white affects material transport.

Learn It

To **analyze** how an object's size affects material transport, you will need to calculate each object's surface-area-to-volume ratio. The following formulas are used to calculate surface area and volume of a cube.

surface area (mm²) = (length of 1 side)² × 6

volume (mm³) = (length of 1 side)³

To calculate the ratio of surface area to volume, divide surface area by volume.

Try It

1. Read and complete a lab safety form.

2. Measure and cut one large cube of egg white that is 20 mm on each side. Then, measure and cut one small cube of egg white that is 10 mm on each side.

3. Place 100 mL of water in a plastic cup. Add 10 drops of food coloring. Gently add the egg-white cubes, and soak overnight.

4. Remove the cubes from the cup with a plastic spoon and place them on a paper towel. Cut each cube in half.

5. Examine the inside surface of each cube. Measure and record in millimeters how deep the blue food coloring penetrated into each cube.

Apply It

6. How does the depth of the color compare on the two cubes?

7. Calculate the surface area, the volume, and the surface-area-to-volume ratio of each cube. How do the surface-area-to-volume ratios of the two cubes compare?

8. 🔑 **Key Concept** Would a cell with a small surface-area-to-volume ratio be able to transport nutrients and waste through the cell as efficiently as a cell with a large surface-area-to-volume ratio?

Reading Guide

Key Concepts
ESSENTIAL QUESTIONS

- How does a cell obtain energy?

- How do some cells make food molecules?

Vocabulary

cellular respiration p. 69

glycolysis p. 69

fermentation p. 70

photosynthesis p. 71

g Multilingual eGlossary

Cells and Energy

Inquiry Why are there bubbles?

Have you ever seen bubbles on a green plant in an aquarium? Where did the bubbles come from? Green plants use light energy and make sugars and oxygen.

What do you exhale?

Does the air you breathe in differ from the air you breathe out?

1. Read and complete a lab safety form.

2. Unwrap a **straw.** Use the straw to slowly blow into a small **cup** of **bromthymol blue.** Do not splash the liquid out of the cup.

3. In your Science Journal, record any changes in the solution.

Think About This

1. What changes did you observe in the solution?

2. What do you think caused the changes in the solution?

3. 🔑 **Key Concept** Why do you think the air you inhale differs from the air you exhale?

Cellular Respiration

When you are tired, you might eat something to give you energy. All living things, from one-celled organisms to humans, need energy to survive. Recall that cells process energy from food into the energy-storage compound ATP. **Cellular respiration** *is a series of chemical reactions that convert the energy in food molecules into a usable form of energy called ATP.* Cellular respiration is a complex process that occurs in two parts of a cell—the cytoplasm and the mitochondria.

Reactions in the Cytoplasm

The first step of cellular respiration, called glycolysis, occurs in the cytoplasm of all cells. **Glycolysis** *is a process by which glucose, a sugar, is broken down into smaller molecules.* As shown in **Figure 15,** glycolysis produces some ATP molecules. It also uses energy from other ATP molecules. You will read on the following page that more ATP is made during the second step of cellular respiration than during glycolysis.

Glycolysis 🔑

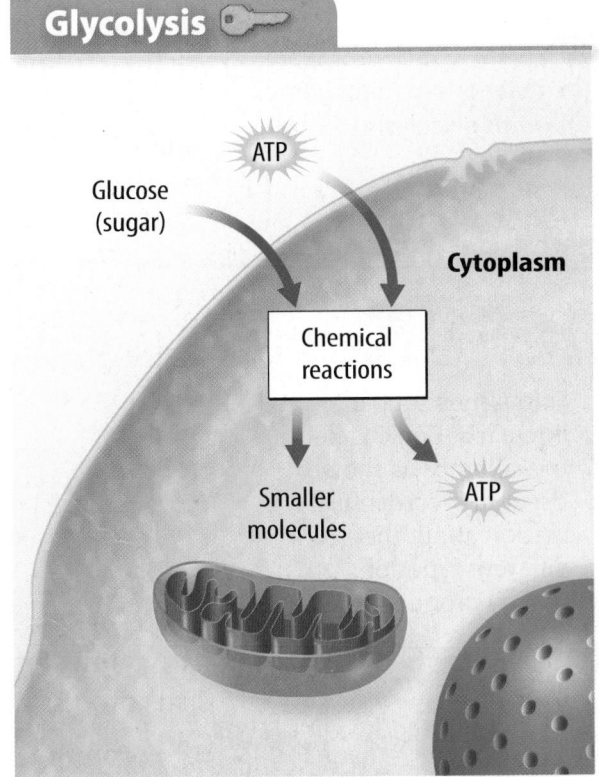

Figure 15 Glycolysis is the first step of cellular respiration.

✓ **Reading Check** What is produced during glycolysis?

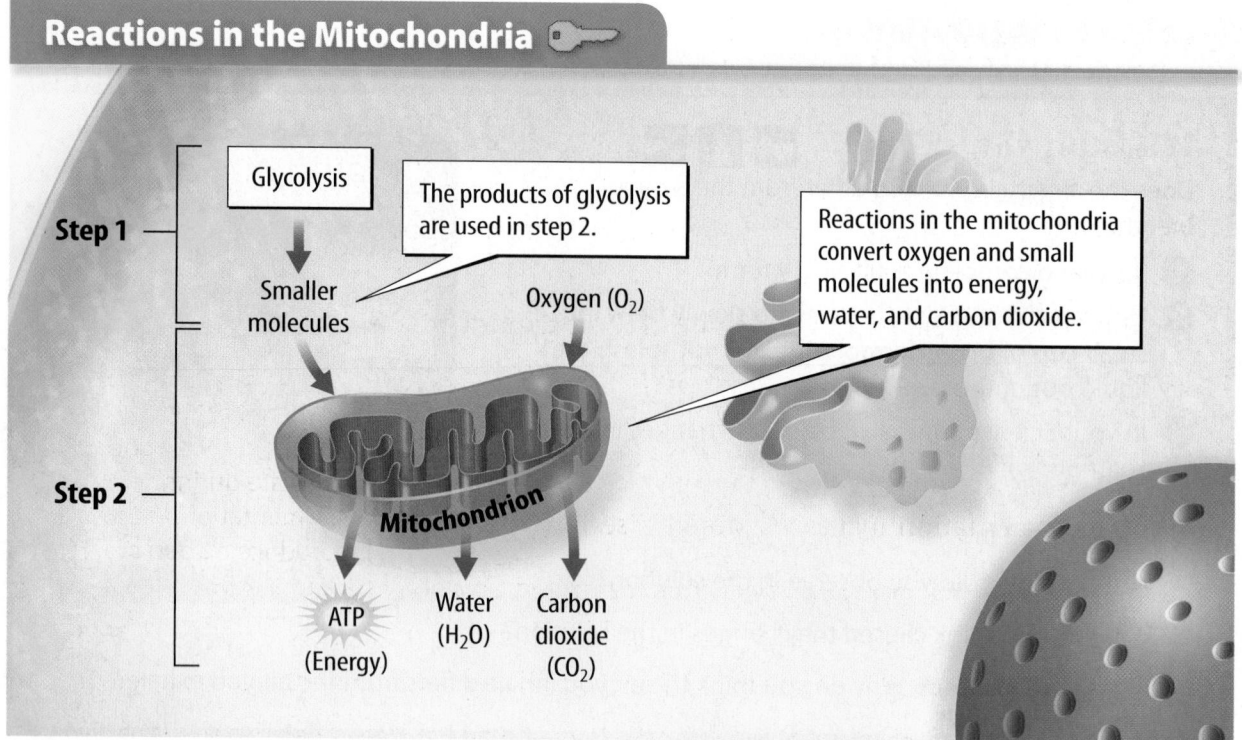

Glycolysis

Step 1

The products of glycolysis are used in step 2.

Smaller molecules

Oxygen (O_2)

Reactions in the mitochondria convert oxygen and small molecules into energy, water, and carbon dioxide.

Step 2

Mitochondrion

ATP (Energy)

Water (H_2O)

Carbon dioxide (CO_2)

Figure 16 After glycolysis, cellular respiration continues in the mitochondria.

✓ **Visual Check** Compare the reactions in mitochondria with glycolysis.

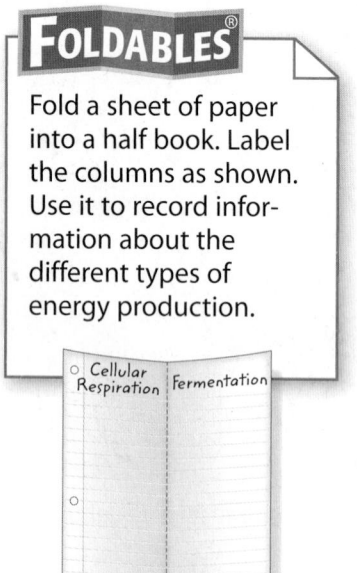

FOLDABLES®

Fold a sheet of paper into a half book. Label the columns as shown. Use it to record information about the different types of energy production.

Cellular Respiration | Fermentation

Reactions in the Mitochondria

The second step of cellular respiration occurs in the mitochondria of eukaryotic cells, as shown in **Figure 16.** This step of cellular respiration requires oxygen. The smaller molecules made from glucose during glycolysis are broken down. Large amounts of ATP—usable energy—are produced. Cells use ATP to power all cellular processes. Two waste products—water and carbon dioxide (CO_2)—are given off during this step.

The CO_2 released by cells as a waste product is used by plants and some unicellular organisms in another process called photosynthesis. You will read more about the chemical reactions that take place during photosynthesis in this lesson.

Fermentation

Have you ever felt out of breath after exercising? Sometimes when you exercise, your cells don't have enough oxygen to make ATP through cellular respiration. Then, chemical energy is obtained through a different process called fermentation. This process does not use oxygen.

Fermentation *is a reaction that eukaryotic and prokaryotic cells can use to obtain energy from food when oxygen levels are low.* Because no oxygen is used, fermentation makes less ATP than cellular respiration does. Fermentation occurs in a cell's cytoplasm, not in mitochondria.

🔑 **Key Concept Check** How does a cell obtain energy?

Types of Fermentation

One type of fermentation occurs when glucose is converted into ATP and a waste product called lactic acid, as illustrated in **Figure 17.** Some bacteria and fungi help produce cheese, yogurt, and sour cream using lactic-acid fermentation. Muscle cells in humans and other animals can use lactic-acid fermentation and obtain energy during exercise.

Some types of bacteria and yeast make ATP through a process called alcohol fermentation. However, instead of producing lactic acid, alcohol fermentation produces an alcohol called ethanol and CO_2, also illustrated in **Figure 17.** Some types of breads are made using yeast. The CO_2 produced by yeast during alcohol fermentation makes the dough rise.

Reading Check Compare lactic-acid fermentation and alcohol fermentation.

Figure 17 Your muscle cells produce lactic acid as a waste during fermentation. Yeast cells produce carbon dioxide and alcohol as wastes during fermentation.

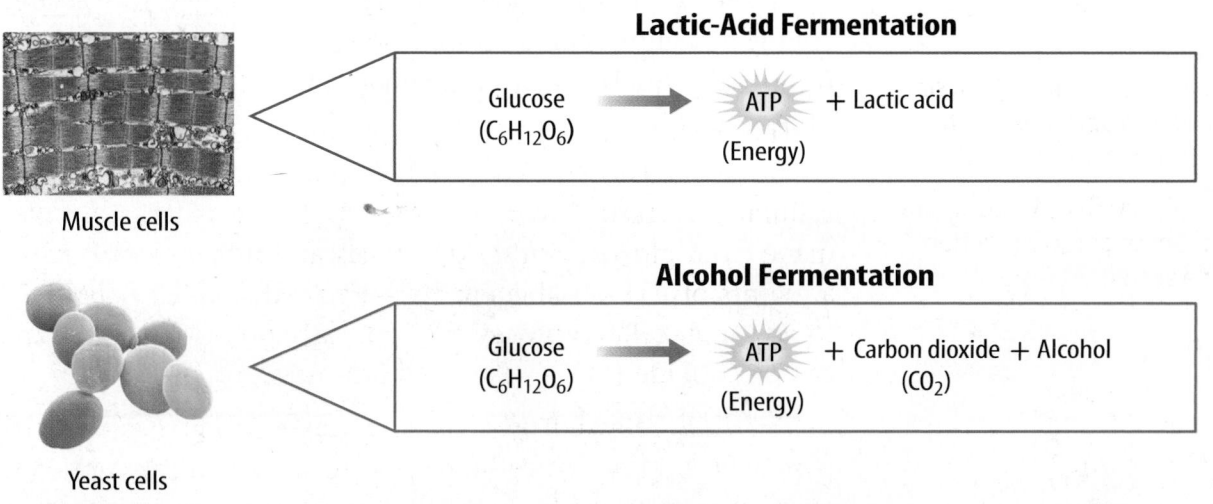

Lactic-Acid Fermentation

Muscle cells

Glucose ($C_6H_{12}O_6$) → ATP (Energy) + Lactic acid

Alcohol Fermentation

Yeast cells

Glucose ($C_6H_{12}O_6$) → ATP (Energy) + Carbon dioxide (CO_2) + Alcohol

Photosynthesis

Humans and other animals convert food energy into ATP through cellular respiration. However, plants and some unicellular organisms obtain energy from light. **Photosynthesis** *is a series of chemical reactions that convert light energy, water, and* CO_2 *into the food-energy molecule glucose and give off oxygen.*

Lights and Pigments

Photosynthesis requires light energy. In plants, pigments such as chlorophyll absorb light energy. When chlorophyll absorbs light, it absorbs all colors except green. Green light is reflected as the green color seen in leaves. However, plants contain many pigments that reflect other colors, such as yellow and red.

WORD ORIGIN · · · · · · · · · · · ·

photosynthesis
from Greek *photo*, means "light"; and *synthesis*, means "composition"

Reactions in Chloroplasts

The light energy absorbed by chlorophyll and other pigments powers the chemical reactions of photosynthesis. These reactions occur in chloroplasts, the organelles in plant cells that convert light energy to chemical energy in food. During photosynthesis, light energy, water, and carbon dioxide combine and make sugars. Photosynthesis also produces oxygen that is released into the atmosphere, as shown in **Figure 18.**

Key Concept Check How do some cells make food molecules?

Importance of Photosynthesis

Recall that photosynthesis uses light energy and CO_2 and makes food energy and releases oxygen. This food energy is stored in the form of glucose. When an organism, such as the bird in **Figure 18,** eats plant material, such as fruit, it takes in food energy. An organism's cells use the oxygen released during photosynthesis and convert the food energy into usable energy through cellular respiration. **Figure 18** illustrates the important relationship between cellular respiration and photosynthesis.

Figure 18 The relationship between cellular respiration and photosynthesis is important for life.

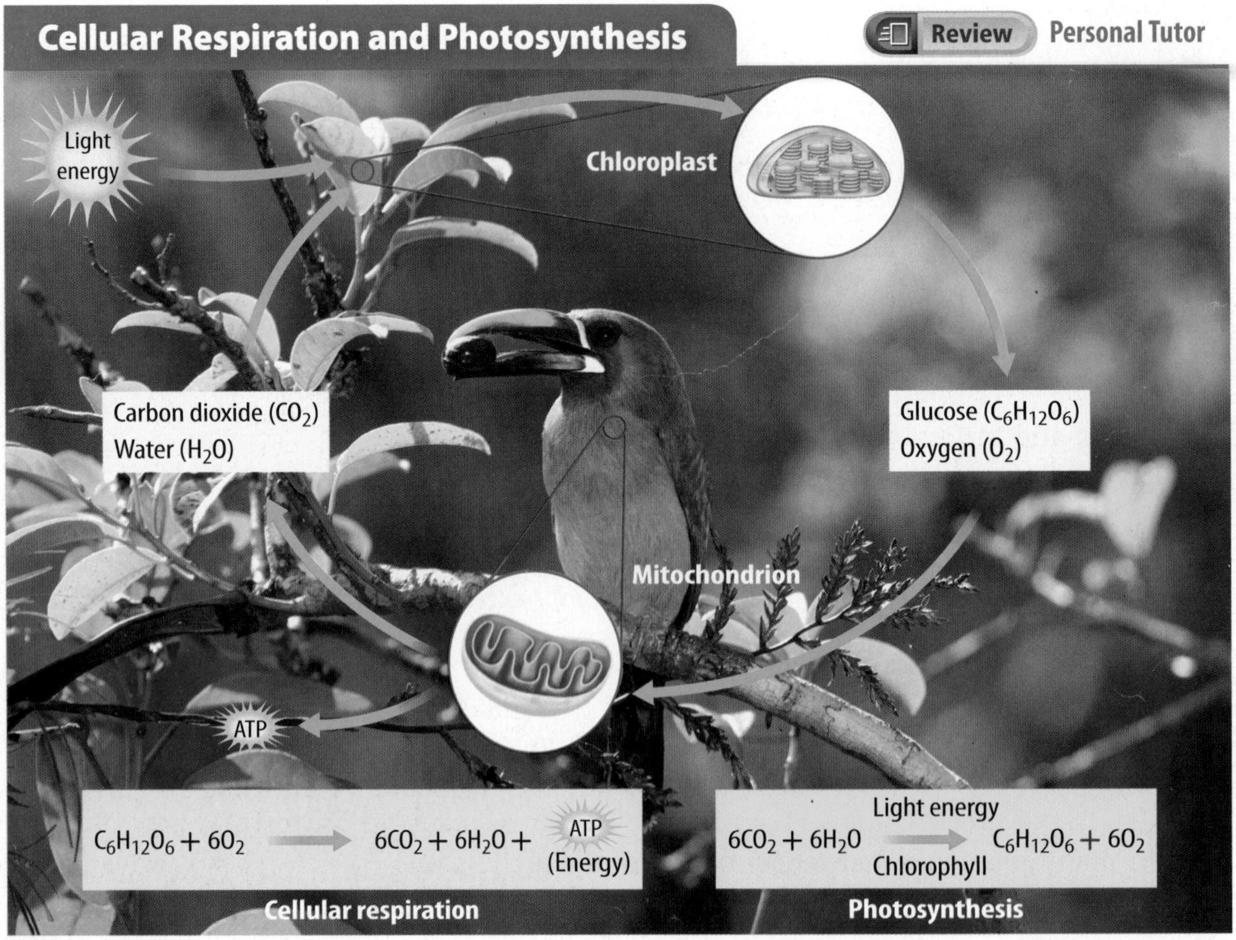

Cellular Respiration and Photosynthesis
Review
Personal Tutor
Light energy
Chloroplast
Carbon dioxide (CO_2)
Water (H_2O)
Glucose ($C_6H_{12}O_6$)
Oxygen (O_2)
Mitochondrion
ATP
$C_6H_{12}O_6 + 6O_2 \rightarrow 6CO_2 + 6H_2O +$ ATP (Energy)
Cellular respiration
$6CO_2 + 6H_2O \xrightarrow[\text{Chlorophyll}]{\text{Light energy}} C_6H_{12}O_6 + 6O_2$
Photosynthesis

Visual Summary

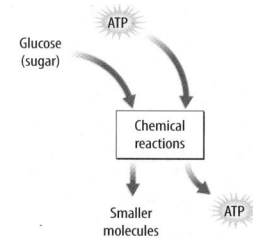

Glycolysis is the first step in cellular respiration.

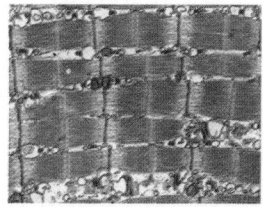

Fermentation provides cells, such as muscle cells, with energy when oxygen levels are low.

Light energy powers the chemical reactions of photosynthesis.

FOLDABLES

Use your lesson Foldable to review the lesson. Save your Foldable for the project at the end of the chapter.

What do you think NOW?

You first read the statements below at the beginning of the chapter.

7. ATP is the only form of energy found in cells.

8. Cellular respiration occurs only in lung cells.

Did you change your mind about whether you agree or disagree with the statements? Rewrite any false statements to make them true.

Use Vocabulary

1 **Define** *glycolysis* using your own words.

2 **Distinguish** between cellular respiration and fermentation.

3 A process used by plants to convert light energy into food energy is _____.

Understand Key Concepts

4 Which contains pigments that absorb light energy?
  A. chloroplast   C. nucleus
  B. mitochondrion D. vacuole

5 **Relate** mitochondria to cellular respiration.

6 **Describe** the role of chlorophyll in photosynthesis.

7 **Give an example** of how fermentation is used in the food industry.

Interpret Graphics

8 **Draw** a graphic organizer like the one below. Fill in the boxes with the substances used and produced during photosynthesis.

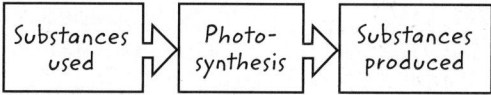

9 **Summarize** the steps of cellular respiration using the figure below.

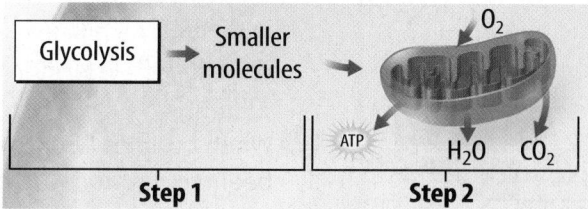

Critical Thinking

10 **Design** a concept map to show the relationship between cellular respiration in animals and photosynthesis in plants.

11 **Summarize** the roles of glucose and ATP in energy processing.

Photosynthesis and Light

Materials

test tube

Elodea

scissors

beaker

lamp

watch or clock

thermometer

Safety

You might think of photosynthesis as a process of give and take. Plant cells take in water and carbon dioxide, and, powered by light energy, make their own food. Plants give off oxygen as a waste product during photosynthesis. Can you determine how the intensity of light affects the rate of photosynthesis?

Ask a Question

How does the intensity of light affect photosynthesis?

Make Observations

1 Read and complete a lab safety form.

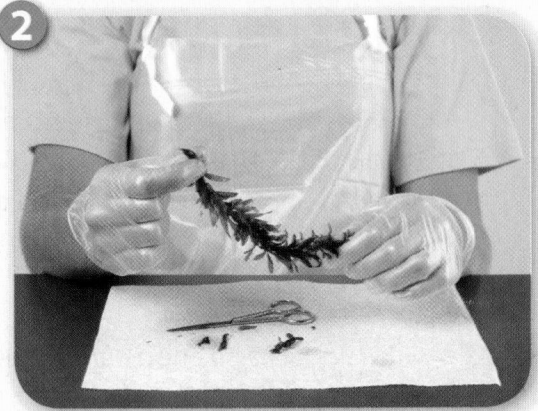

2 Cut the bottom end of an *Elodea* stem at an angle, and lightly crush the cut end. Place the *Elodea* in a test tube with the cut side at the top. Fill the test tube with water. Stand the test tube and a thermometer in a beaker filled with water. (The water in the beaker keeps the water in the test tube from getting too warm under the lamp.)

3 Place the beaker containing your test tube on a sheet of paper under a lamp. Measure the temperature of the water in the beaker. Record the temperature in your Science Journal.

4 When bubbles of oxygen begin to rise from the plant, start counting the number of bubbles per minute. Continue to record this data for 10 minutes.

5 Record the temperature of the water in the beaker at the end of the test.

6 Calculate the average number of bubbles produced per minute by your plant.

7 Compare your data with your classmates' data.

Form a Hypothesis

8 Use your data to form a hypothesis relating the amount of light to the rate of photosynthesis.

Test Your Hypothesis

9 Repeat the experiment, changing the light variable so that you are observing your plant's reaction to getting either more or less light. An increase or decrease in water temperature will indicate a change in the amount of light. Keep all other conditions the same.

10 Record your data in a table similar to the one shown at right, and calculate the average number of bubbles per minute.

Analyze and Conclude

11 **Use Variables** How does the amount of light affect photosynthesis? What is your evidence?

12 **The Big Idea** How do plant cells make food? What do they take in and what do they give off? What source of energy do they use?

Communicate Your Results

Compile all the class data on one graph to show the effects of varying amounts of light on the rate of photosynthesis.

Inquiry Extension

What other variables might affect the rate of photosynthesis? For example, how does different-colored light or a change in temperature affect the rate of photosynthesis? To investigate your question, design a controlled experiment.

Lab Tips

☑ To calculate the average number of bubbles per minute, add the total number of bubbles observed in 10 minutes, and then divide by 10.

Number of Bubbles per Minute

Time	Control	Less Light
1		
2		
3		
4		
5		
6		
7		
8		
9		
10		

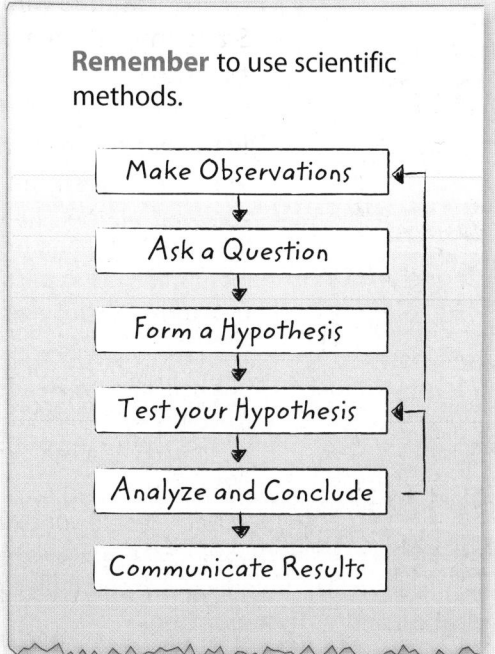

Remember to use scientific methods.

Make Observations
↓
Ask a Question
↓
Form a Hypothesis
↓
Test your Hypothesis
↓
Analyze and Conclude
↓
Communicate Results

 **THE BIG IDEA** **A cell is made up of structures that provide support and movement; process energy; and transport materials into, within, and out of a cell.**

 **Key Concepts Summary** | **Vocabulary**

Lesson 1: Cells and Life

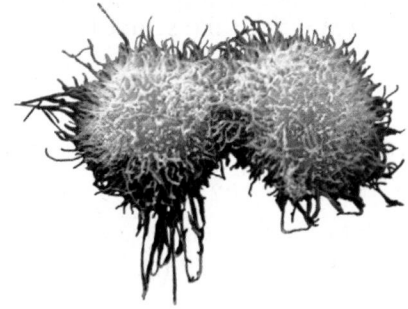

- The invention of the microscope led to discoveries about cells. In time, scientists used these discoveries to develop the **cell theory,** which explains how cells and living things are related.
- Cells are composed mainly of water, **proteins, nucleic acids, lipids,** and **carbohydrates.**

cell theory p. 44
macromolecule p. 45
nucleic acid p. 46
protein p. 47
lipid p. 47
carbohydrate p. 47

Lesson 2: The Cell

- Cell structures have specific functions, such as supporting a cell, moving a cell, controlling cell activities, processing energy, and transporting molecules.
- A prokaryotic cell lacks a nucleus and other **organelles,** while a eukaryotic cell has a nucleus and other organelles.

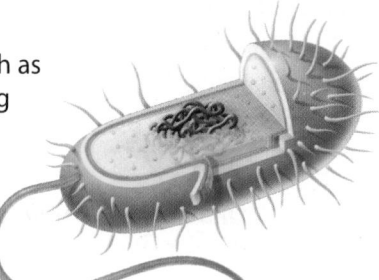

cell membrane p. 52
cell wall p. 52
cytoplasm p. 53
cytoskeleton p. 53
organelle p. 54
nucleus p. 55
chloroplast p. 57

Lesson 3: Moving Cellular Material

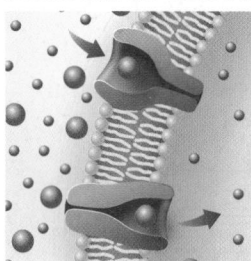

- Materials enter and leave a cell through the cell membrane using **passive transport** or **active transport, endocytosis,** and **exocytosis.**
- The ratio of surface area to volume limits the size of a cell. In a smaller cell, the high surface-area-to-volume ratio allows materials to move easily to all parts of a cell.

passive transport p. 61
diffusion p. 62
osmosis p. 62
facilitated diffusion p. 63
active transport p. 64
endocytosis p. 64
exocytosis p. 64

Lesson 4: Cells and Energy

- All living cells release energy from food molecules through **cellular respiration** and/or **fermentation.**
- Some cells make food molecules using light energy through the process of **photosynthesis.**

$$C_6H_{12}O_6 + 6O_2 \longrightarrow 6CO_2 + 6H_2O + \text{ATP (Energy)}$$

Cellular respiration

$$6CO_2 + 6H_2O \xrightarrow[\text{Chlorophyll}]{\text{Light energy}} C_6H_{12}O_6 + 6O_2$$

Photosynthesis

cellular respiration p. 69
glycolysis p. 69
fermentation p. 70
photosynthesis p. 71

FOLDABLES® Chapter Project

Assemble your lesson Foldables as shown to make a Chapter Project. Use the project to review what you have learned in this chapter.

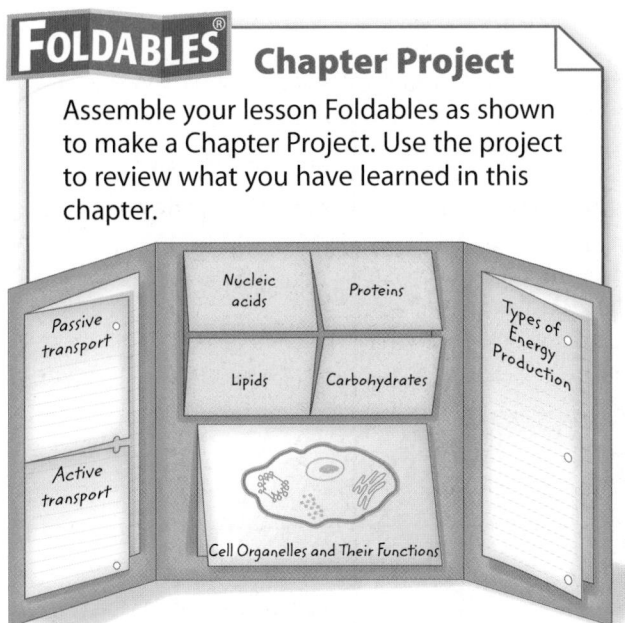

Use Vocabulary

1 Substances formed by joining smaller molecules together are called _____.

2 The _____ consists of proteins joined together to create fiberlike structures inside cells.

3 The movement of substances from an area of high concentration to an area of low concentration is called _____.

4 A process that uses oxygen to convert energy from food into ATP is _____ _____.

Link Vocabulary and Key Concepts

Concepts in Motion Interactive Concept Map

Copy this concept map, and then use vocabulary terms from the previous page to complete the concept map.

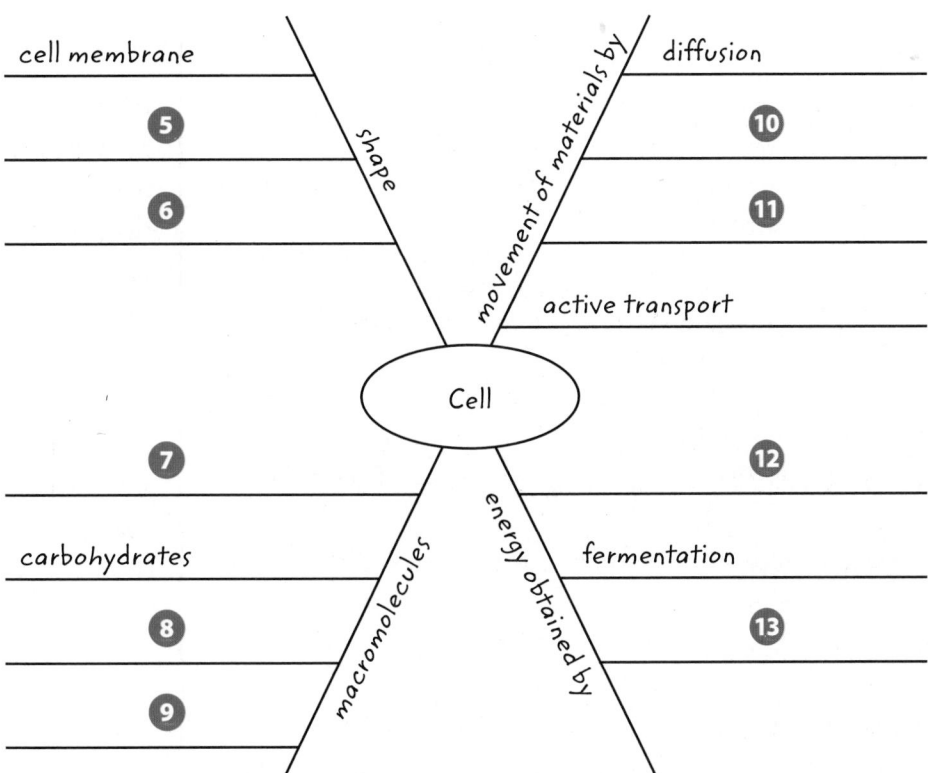

Understand Key Concepts

1 Cholesterol is which type of macromolecule?

A. carbohydrate
B. lipid
C. nucleic acid
D. protein

2 Genetic information is stored in which macromolecule?

A. DNA
B. glucose
C. lipid
D. starch

3 The arrow below is pointing to which cell part?

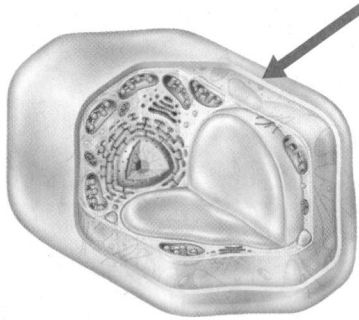

A. chloroplast
B. mitochondrion
C. cell membrane
D. cell wall

4 Which best describes vacuoles?

A. lipids
B. proteins
C. contained in mitochondria
D. storage compartments

5 Which is true of fermentation?

A. does not generate energy
B. does not require oxygen
C. occurs in mitochondria
D. produces lots of ATP

6 Which process eliminates substances from cells in vesicles?

A. endocytosis
B. exocytosis
C. osmosis
D. photosynthesis

7 Which cell shown below can send signals over long distances?

A.

B.

C.

D.

8 The figure below shows a cell. What is the arrow pointing to?

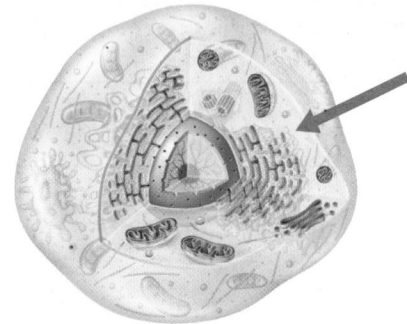

A. chloroplast
B. cytoplasm
C. mitochondrion
D. nucleus

Critical Thinking

9 **Evaluate** the importance of the microscope to biology.

10 **Summarize** the role of water in cells.

11 **Hypothesize** how new cells form from existing cells.

12 **Distinguish** between channel proteins and carrier proteins.

13 **Explain** osmosis.

14 **Infer** Why do cells need carrier proteins that transport glucose?

15 **Compare** the amounts of ATP generated in cellular respiration and fermentation.

16 **Assess** the role of fermentation in baking bread.

17 **Hypothesize** how air pollution like smog affects photosynthesis.

18 **Compare** prokaryotes and eukaryotes by copying and filling in the table below.

Structure	Prokaryote (yes or no)	Eukaryote (yes or no)
Cell membrane		
DNA		
Nucleus		
Endoplasmic reticulum		
Golgi apparatus		
Cell wall		

Writing in Science

19 **Write** a five-sentence paragraph relating the cytoskeleton to the walls of a building. Be sure to include a topic sentence and a concluding sentence in your paragraph.

REVIEW THE BIG IDEA

20 How do the structures and processes of a cell enable it to survive? As an example, explain how chloroplasts help plant cells.

21 The photo below shows a protozoan. What structures enable it to get food into its mouth?

Math Skills

Review

Math Practice

Use Ratios

22 A rectangular solid measures 4 cm long by 2 cm wide by 2 cm high. What is the surface-area-to-volume ratio of the solid?

23 At different times during its growth, a cell has the following surface areas and volumes:

Time	Surface area (μm)	Volume (μm)
1	6	1
2	24	8
3	54	27

What happens to the surface-area-to-volume ratio as the cell grows?

Standardized Test Practice

Record your answers on the answer sheet provided by your teacher or on a sheet of paper.

Multiple Choice

1 Which process do plant cells use to capture and store energy from sunlight?

   A endocytosis

   B fermentation

   C glycolysis

   D photosynthesis

Use the diagram below to answer question 2.

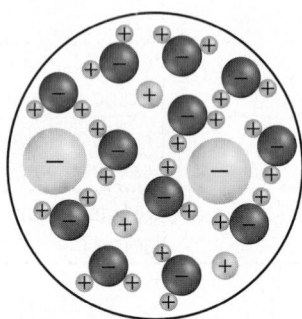

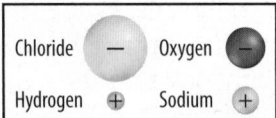

2 The diagram shows salt dissolved in water. What does it show about water molecules and chloride ions?

   A A water molecule consists of oxygen and chloride ions.

   B A water molecule is surrounded by several chloride ions.

   C A water molecule moves away from a chloride ion.

   D A water molecule points its positive end toward a chloride ion.

3 Which transport process requires the use of a cell's energy?

   A diffusion

   B osmosis

   C active transport

   D facilitated diffusion

4 Diffusion differs from active cell transport processes because it

   A forces large molecules from a cell.

   B keeps a cell's boundary intact.

   C moves substances into a cell.

   D needs none of a cell's energy.

Use the diagram below to answer questions 5 and 6.

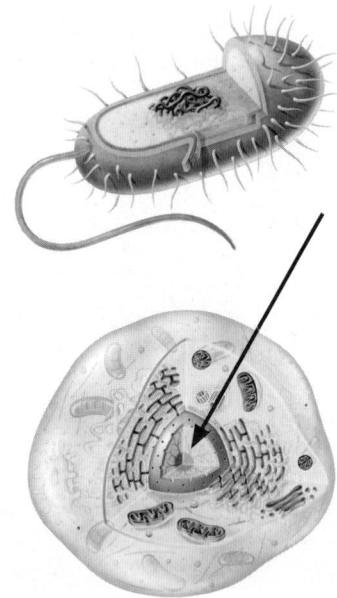

5 Which structure does the arrow point to in the eukaryotic cell?

   A cytoplasm

   B lysosome

   C nucleus

   D ribosome

6 Which feature does a typical prokaryotic cell have that is missing from some eukaryotic cells, like the one above?

   A cytoplasm

   B DNA

   C cell membrane

   D cell wall

✓ **Assessment**

Online Standardized Test Practice

7 Which explains why the ratio of cell surface area to volume affects the cell size? Cells with a high surface-to-volume ratio

   A consume energy efficiently.

   B produce waste products slowly.

   C suffer from diseases frequently.

   D transport substances effectively.

Use the diagram below to answer question 8.

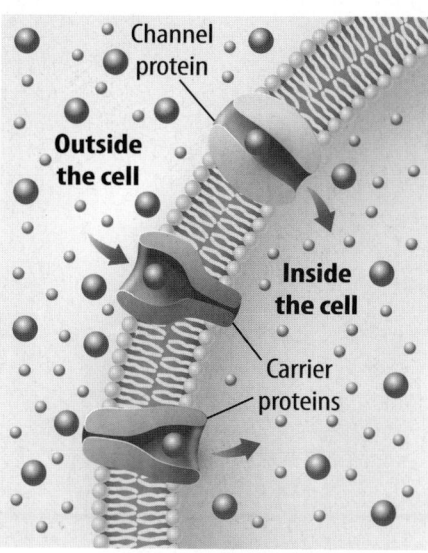

8 Which statement is NOT true of carrier proteins and channel proteins?

   A Carrier proteins change shape as they function but channel proteins do not.

   B Carrier proteins and channel proteins extend through the cell membrane.

   C Channel proteins move items inside a cell but carrier proteins do not.

   D Channel proteins and carrier proteins perform facilitated diffusion.

Constructed Response

9 Copy the table below and complete it using these terms: *cell membrane, cell wall, chloroplast, cytoplasm, cytoskeleton, nucleus.*

Cell Structure	Function
	Maintains the shape of an animal cell
	Controls the activities of a cell
	Traps energy from the Sun
	Controls the materials going in and out of a cell
	Holds the structures of a cell in a watery mix
	Maintains the shape of some plant cells

10 Name the kinds of organisms that have cells with cell walls. Name the kinds of organisms that have cells without cell walls. Briefly describe the benefits of cell walls for organisms.

11 Draw simple diagrams of an animal cell and a plant cell. Label the nucleus, the cytoplasm, the mitochondria, the cell membrane, the chloroplasts, the cell wall, and the central vacuole in the appropriate cells. Briefly describe the main differences between the two cells.

NEED EXTRA HELP?											
If You Missed Question...	1	2	3	4	5	6	7	8	9	10	11
Go to Lesson...	4	1	3	3	2	2	3	3	2	2	2

From a Cell to an Organism

THE BIG IDEA How can one cell become a multicellular organism?

Inquiry · What's happening inside?

From the outside, a chicken egg looks like a simple oval object. But big changes are taking place inside the egg. Over several weeks, the one cell in the egg will grow and divide and become a chick.

- How did the original cell change over time?
- What might have happened to the chick's cells as the chick grew?
- How can one cell become a multicellular chick?

Get Ready to Read

What do you think?

Before you read, decide if you agree or disagree with each of these statements. As you read this chapter, see if you change your mind about any of the statements.

1 Cell division produces two identical cells.

2 Cell division is important for growth.

3 At the end of the cell cycle, the original cell no longer exists.

4 Unicellular organisms do not have all the characteristics of life.

5 All the cells in a multicellular organism are the same.

6 Some organs work together as part of an organ system.

 **ConnectED** Your one-stop **online resource**

connectED.mcgraw-hill.com

Video

WebQuest

 Audio

Assessment

 Review

Concepts in Motion

 Inquiry

g Multilingual eGlossary

The Cell Cycle and Cell Division

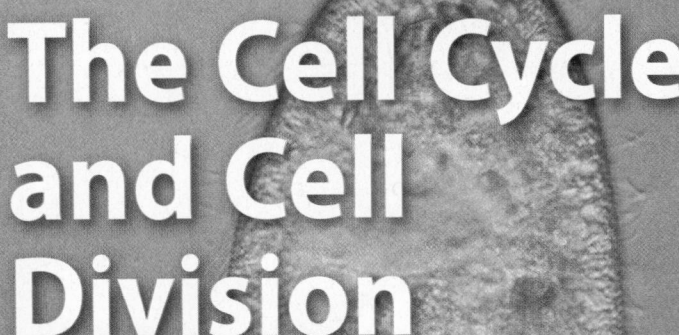

Reading Guide

Key Concepts 🔑
ESSENTIAL QUESTIONS

- What are the phases of the cell cycle?
- Why is the result of the cell cycle important?

Vocabulary

cell cycle p. 85

interphase p. 86

sister chromatid p. 88

centromere p. 88

mitosis p. 89

cytokinesis p. 89

daughter cell p. 89

g Multilingual eGlossary

📽 Video BrainPOP®

 **Time to Split?**

Unicellular organisms such as these reproduce when one cell divides into two new cells. The two cells are identical to each other. What do you think happened to the contents of the original cell before it divided?

Why isn't your cell like mine?

All living things are made of cells. Some are made of only one cell, while others are made of trillions of cells. Where do all those cells come from?

1. Read and complete a lab safety form.

2. Ask your team members to face away from you. Draw an animal cell on a sheet of **paper.** Include as many organelles as you can.

3. Use **scissors** to cut the cell drawing into equal halves. Fold each sheet of paper in half so the drawing cannot be seen.

4. Ask your team members to face you. Give each team member half of the cell drawing.

5. Have team members sit facing away from each other. Each person should use a **glue stick** to attach the cell half to one side of a sheet of paper. Then, each person should draw the missing cell half.

6. Compare the two new cells to your original cell.

Think About This

1. How did the new cells compare to the original cell?

2. 🔑 **Key Concept** What are some things that might be done in the early steps to produce two new cells that are more like the original cell?

The Cell Cycle

No matter where you live, you have probably noticed that the weather changes in a regular pattern each year. Some areas experience four seasons—winter, spring, summer, and fall. In other parts of the world, there are only two seasons—rainy and dry. As seasons change, temperature, precipitation, and the number of hours of sunlight vary in a regular cycle.

These changes can affect the life cycles of organisms such as trees. Notice how the tree in **Figure 1** changes with the seasons. Like changing seasons or the growth of trees, cells go through cycles. *Most cells in an organism go through a cycle of growth, development, and division called the* **cell cycle.** Through the cell cycle, organisms grow, develop, replace old or damaged cells, and produce new cells.

Figure 1 This maple tree changes in response to a seasonal cycle.

✓ **Visual Check** List the seasonal changes of this maple tree.

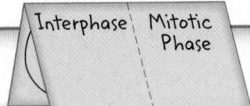

FOLDABLES

Make a folded book from a sheet of paper. Label the front *The Cell Cycle,* and label the inside of the book as shown. Open the book completely and use the full sheet to illustrate the cell cycle.

| Interphase | Mitotic Phase |

Phases of the Cell Cycle

There are two main phases in the cell cycle—interphase and the mitotic (mi TAH tihk) phase. **Interphase** *is the period during the cell cycle of a cell's growth and development.* A cell spends most of its life in interphase, as shown in **Figure 2.** During interphase, most cells go through three stages:

- rapid growth and replication, or copying, of the membrane-bound structures called organelles;
- copying of DNA, the genetic information in a cell; and
- preparation for cell division.

Interphase is followed by a shorter period of the cell cycle known as the mitotic phase. A cell reproduces during this phase. The mitotic phase has two stages, as illustrated in **Figure 2.** The nucleus divides in the first stage, and the cell's fluid, called the cytoplasm, divides in the second stage. The mitotic phase creates two new identical cells. At the end of this phase, the original cell no longer exists.

Key Concept Check What are the two main phases of the cell cycle?

The Cell Cycle

Figure 2 A cell spends most of its life growing and developing during interphase.

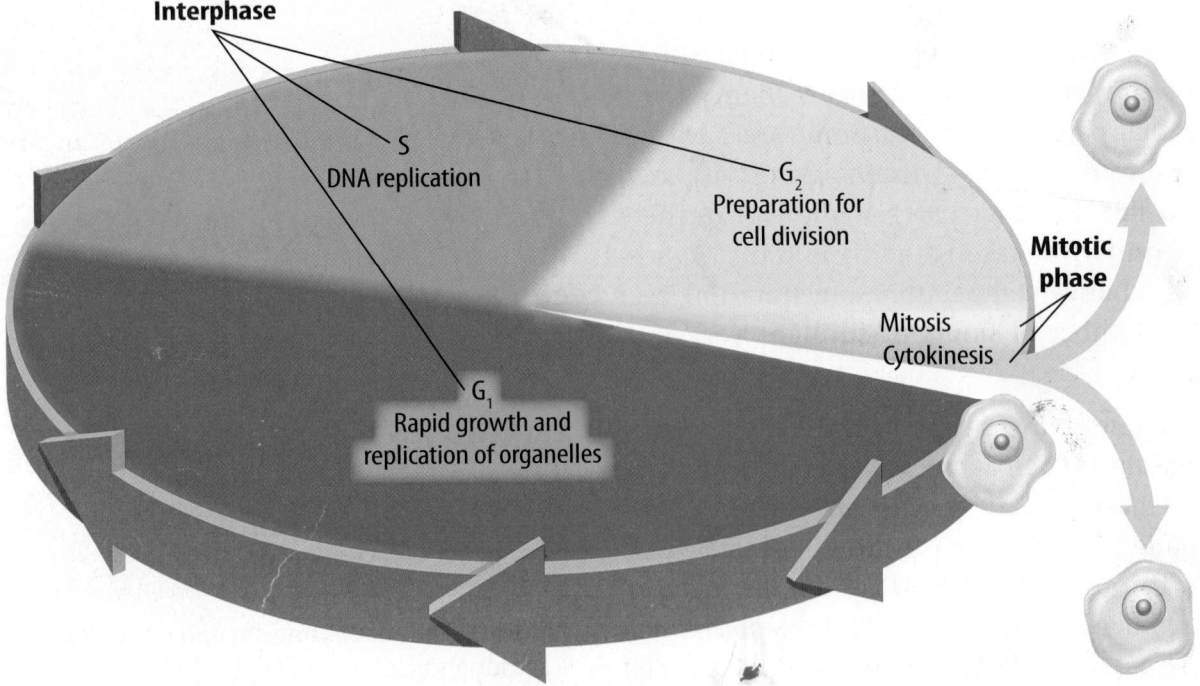

Visual Check Which stage of interphase is the longest?

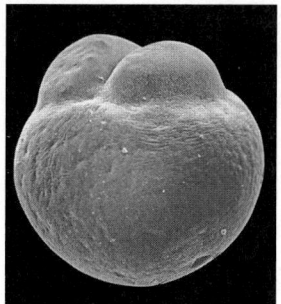
2-cell stage
SEM Magnification: 160×

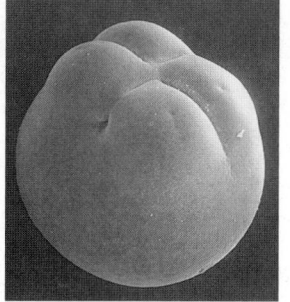
4-cell stage
SEM Magnification: 155×

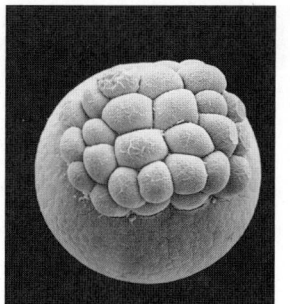
32-cell stage
SEM Magnification: 150×

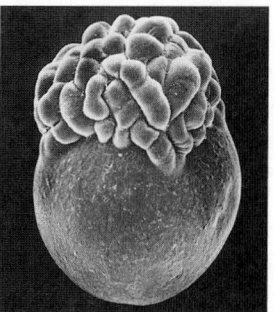
256-cell stage
SEM Magnification: 130×

Length of a Cell Cycle

The time it takes a cell to complete the cell cycle depends on the type of cell that is dividing. Recall that a **eukaryotic** cell has membrane-bound organelles, including a nucleus. For some eukaryotic cells, the cell cycle might last only eight minutes. For other cells, the cycle might take as long as one year. Most dividing human cells normally complete the cell cycle in about 24 hours. As illustrated in **Figure 3,** the cells of some organisms divide very quickly.

Interphase

As you have read, interphase makes up most of the cell cycle. Newly produced cells begin interphase with a period of rapid growth—the cell gets bigger. This is followed by cellular activities such as making proteins. Next, actively dividing cells make copies of their DNA and prepare for cell division. During interphase, the DNA is called chromatin (KROH muh tun). Chromatin is long, thin strands of DNA, as shown in **Figure 4.** When scientists dye a cell in interphase, the nucleus looks like a plate of spaghetti. This is because the nucleus contains many strands of chromatin tangled together.

▲ **Figure 3** The fertilized egg of a zebra fish divides into 256 cells in 2.5 hours.

Figure 4 During interphase, the nuclei of an animal cell and a plant cell contain long, thin strands of DNA called chromatin. ▼

Interphase

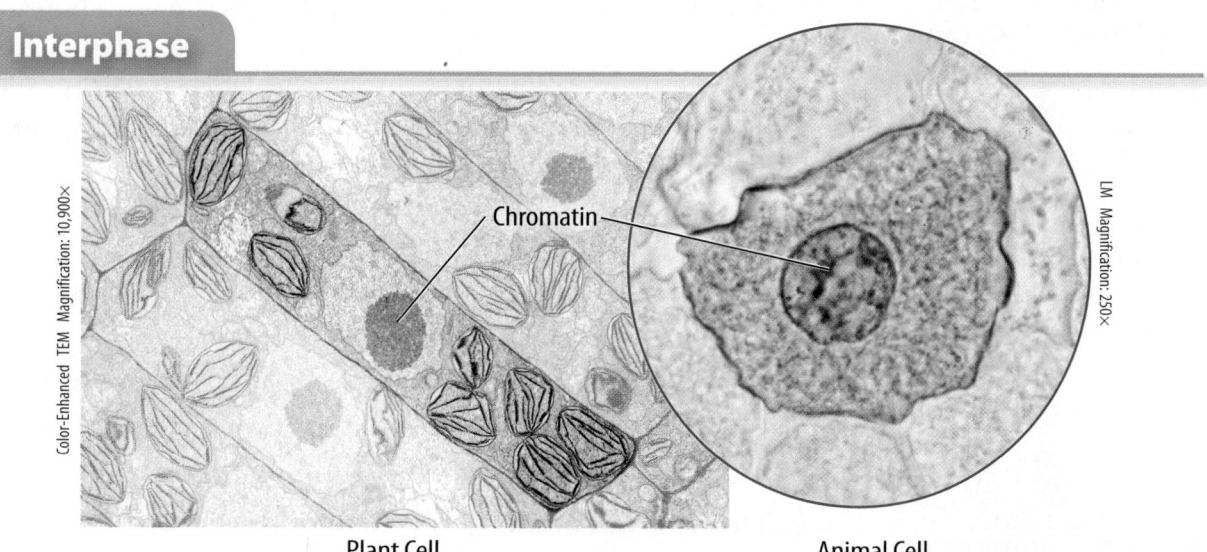

Color-Enhanced TEM Magnification: 10,900×

LM Magnification: 250×

Chromatin

Plant Cell

Animal Cell

(l)Dr. Richard Kessel & Dr. Gene Shih/Visuals Unlimited.

Table 1 Phases of the Cell Cycle 🔑 ⟨⟨◎ **Concepts in Motion** ⟩⟩ **Interactive Table**

Phase	Stage	Description
Interphase	G_1	growth and cellular functions; organelle replication
	S	growth and chromosome replication; organelle replication
	G_2	growth and cellular functions; organelle replication
Mitotic phase	mitosis	division of nucleus
	cytokinesis	division of cytoplasm

▲ **Table 1** The two phases of the cell cycle can each be divided into different stages.

Figure 5 The coiled DNA forms a duplicated chromosome made of two sister chromatids connected at the centromere. ▼

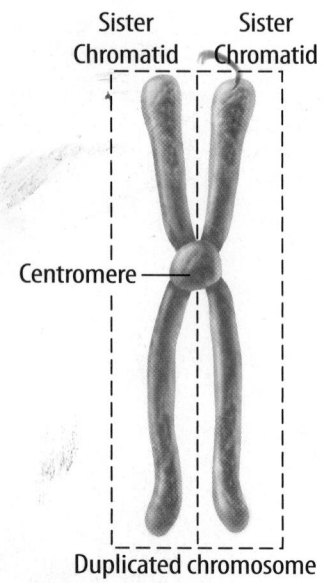

Sister Chromatid   Sister Chromatid

Centromere ——

Duplicated chromosome

Phases of Interphase

Scientists divide interphase into three stages, as shown in **Table 1.** Interphase begins with a period of rapid growth—the G_1 stage. This stage lasts longer than other stages of the cell cycle. During G_1, a cell grows and carries out its normal cell functions. For example, during G_1, cells that line your stomach make enzymes that help digest your food. Although most cells continue the cell cycle, some cells stop the cell cycle at this point. For example, mature nerve cells in your brain remain in G_1 and do not divide again.

During the second stage of interphase—the S stage—a cell continues to grow and copies its DNA. There are now identical strands of DNA. These identical strands of DNA ensure that each new cell gets a copy of the original cell's genetic information. Each strand of DNA coils up and forms a chromosome. Identical chromosomes join together. The cell's DNA is now arranged as pairs of identical chromosomes. Each pair is called a duplicated chromosome. *Two identical chromosomes, called* **sister chromatids,** *make up a duplicated chromosome,* as shown in **Figure 5.** Notice that the *sister chromatids are held together by a structure called the* **centromere.**

The final stage of interphase—the G_2 stage—is another period of growth and the final preparation for the mitotic phase. A cell uses energy copying DNA during the S stage. During G_2, the cell stores energy that will be used during the mitotic phase of the cell cycle.

✓ **Reading Check** Describe what happens in the G_2 phase.

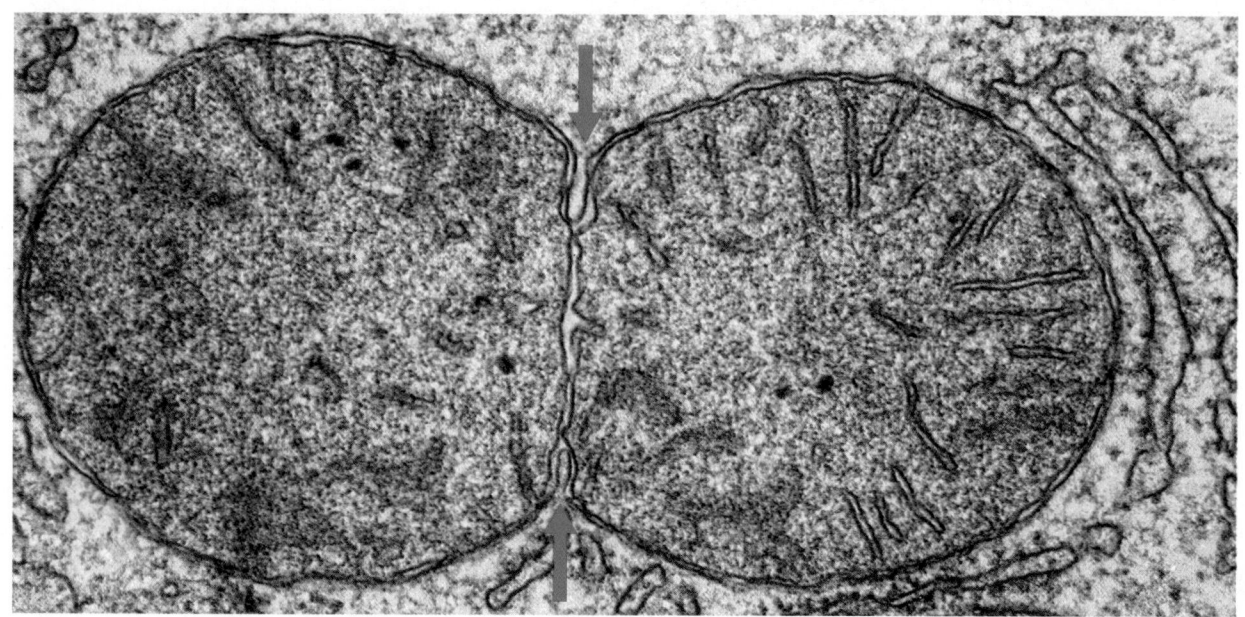

TEM Magnification: Unavailable

Organelle Replication

During cell division, the organelles in a cell are distributed between the two new cells. Before a cell divides, it makes a copy of each organelle. This enables the two new cells to function properly. Some organelles, such as the energy-processing mitochondria and chloroplasts, have their own DNA. These organelles can make copies of themselves on their own, as shown in **Figure 6.** A cell produces other organelles from materials such as proteins and lipids. A cell makes these materials using the information contained in the DNA inside the nucleus. Organelles are copied during all stages of interphase.

The Mitotic Phase

The mitotic phase of the cell cycle follows interphase. It consists of two stages: mitosis (mi TOH sus) and cytokinesis (si toh kuh NEE sus). *In* **mitosis,** *the nucleus and its contents divide. In* **cytokinesis,** *the cytoplasm and its contents divide.* **Daughter cells** *are the two new cells that result from mitosis and cytokinesis.*

During mitosis, the contents of the nucleus divide, forming two identical nuclei. The sister chromatids of the duplicated chromosomes separate from each other. This gives each daughter cell the same genetic information. For example, a cell that has ten duplicated chromosomes actually has 20 chromatids. When the cell divides, each daughter cell will have ten different chromatids. Chromatids are now called chromosomes.

In cytokinesis, the cytoplasm divides and forms the two new daughter cells. Organelles that were made during interphase are divided between the daughter cells.

Figure 6 This mitochondrion is in the final stage of dividing.

WORD ORIGIN · · · · · · · · · · ·

mitosis
from Greek *mitos*, means "warp thread"; and Latin *–osis*, means "process"

Phases of Mitosis

Like interphase, mitosis is a continuous process that scientists divide into different phases, as shown in **Figure 7.**

Prophase During the first phase of mitosis, called prophase, the copied chromatin coils together tightly. The coils form visible duplicated chromosomes. The nucleolus disappears, and the nuclear membrane breaks down. Structures called spindle fibers form in the cytoplasm.

Metaphase During metaphase, the spindle fibers pull and push the duplicated chromosomes to the middle of the cell. Notice in **Figure 7** that the chromosomes line up along the middle of the cell. This arrangement ensures that each new cell will receive one copy of each chromosome. Metaphase is the shortest phase in mitosis, but it must be completed successfully for the new cells to be identical.

Concepts in Motion Animation

Phases of Mitosis

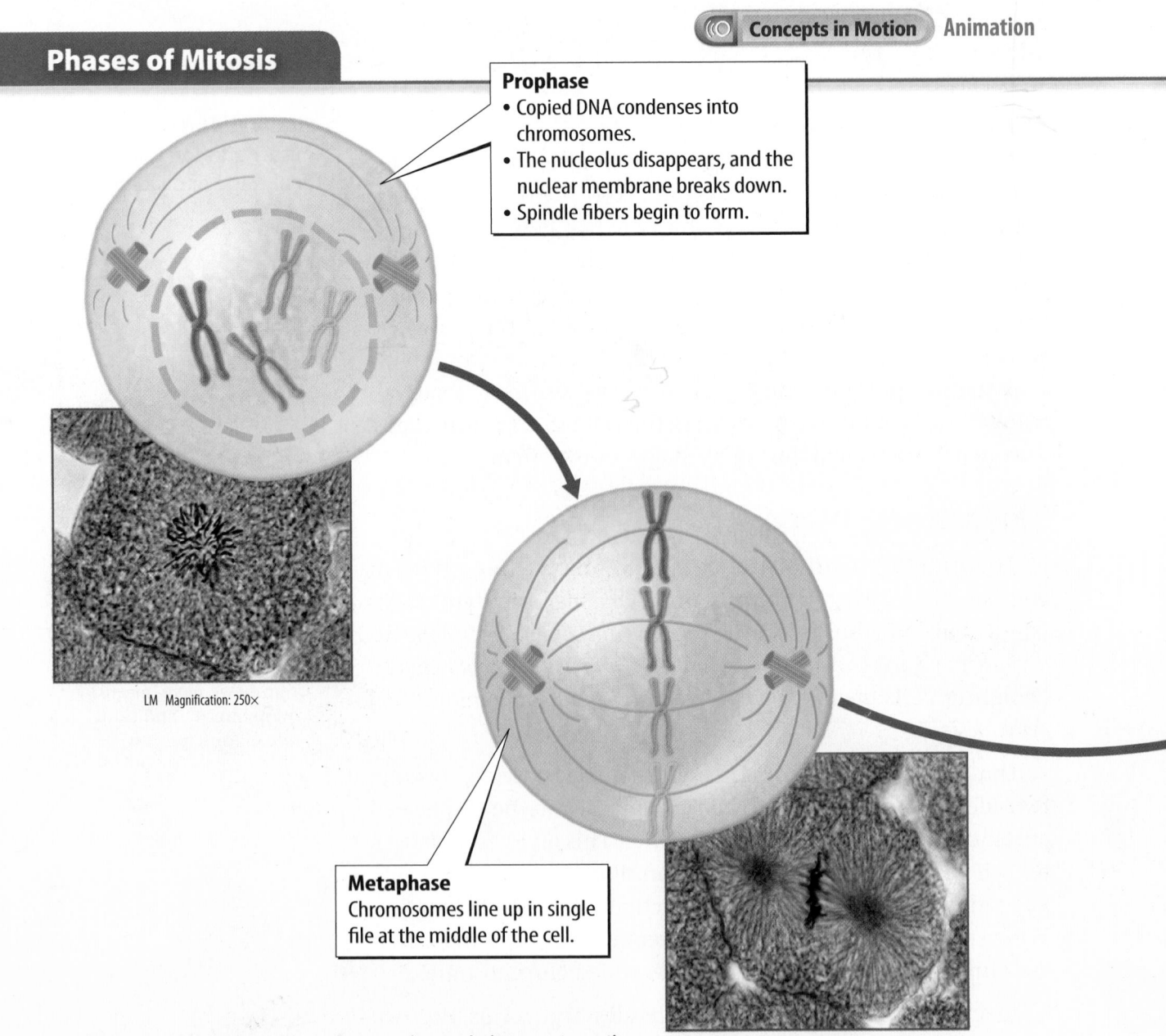

Prophase
- Copied DNA condenses into chromosomes.
- The nucleolus disappears, and the nuclear membrane breaks down.
- Spindle fibers begin to form.

LM Magnification: 250×

Metaphase
Chromosomes line up in single file at the middle of the cell.

LM Magnification: 250×

Figure 7 Mitosis begins when replicated chromatin coils together and ends when two identical nuclei are formed.

Anaphase In anaphase, the third stage of mitosis, the two sister chromatids in each chromosome separate from each other. The spindle fibers pull them in opposite directions. Once separated, the chromatids are now two identical single-stranded chromosomes. As they move to opposite sides of a cell, the cell begins to get longer. Anaphase is complete when the two identical sets of chromosomes are at opposite ends of a cell.

Telophase During telophase, the spindle fibers begin to disappear. Also, the chromosomes begin to uncoil. A nuclear membrane forms around each set of chromosomes at either end of the cell. This forms two new identical nuclei. Telophase is the final stage of mitosis. It is often described as the reverse of prophase because many of the processes that occur during prophase are reversed during telophase.

Reading Check What are the phases of mitosis?

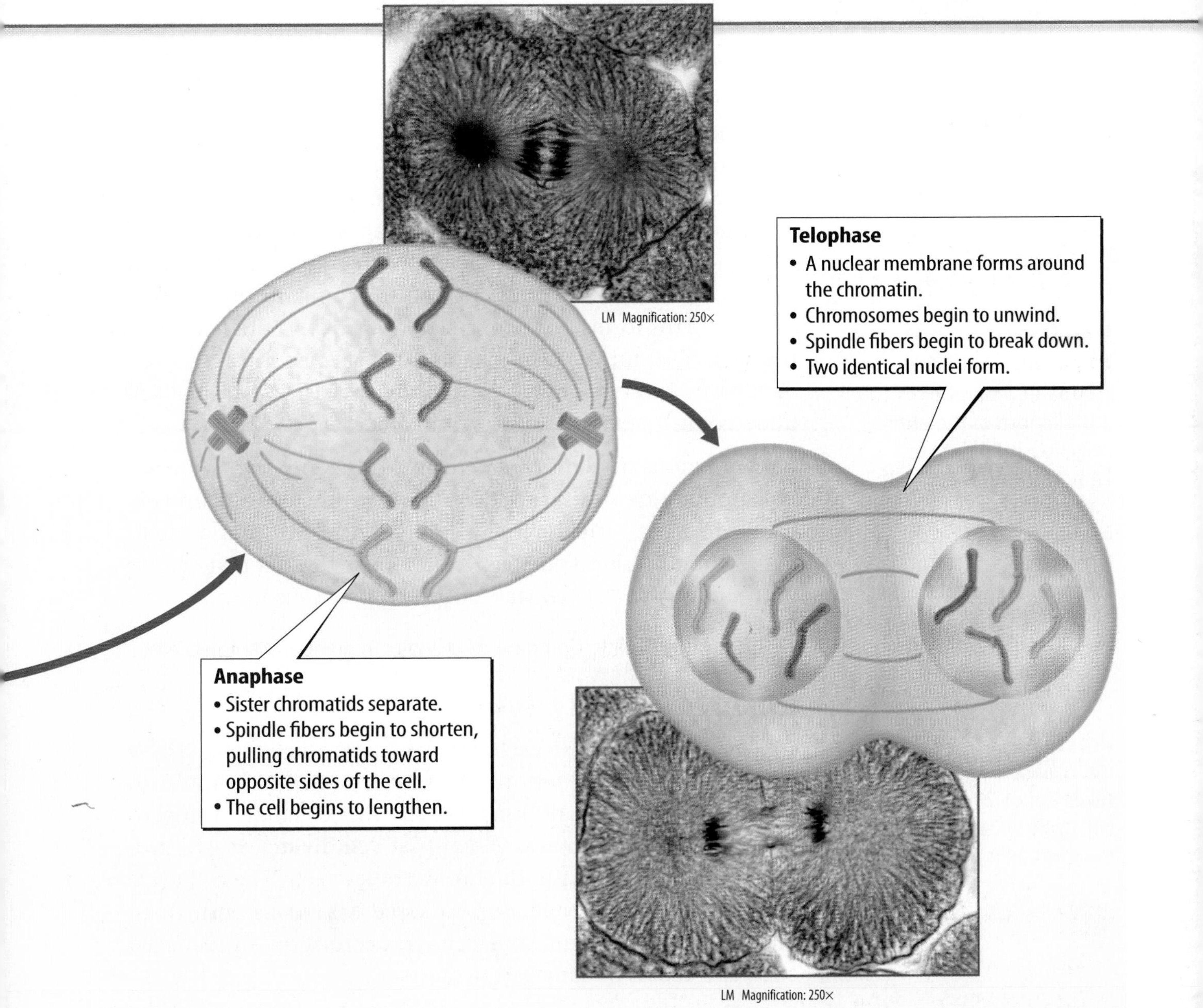

LM Magnification: 250×
Telophase
• A nuclear membrane forms around the chromatin.
• Chromosomes begin to unwind.
• Spindle fibers begin to break down.
• Two identical nuclei form.
Anaphase
• Sister chromatids separate.
• Spindle fibers begin to shorten, pulling chromatids toward opposite sides of the cell.
• The cell begins to lengthen.
LM Magnification: 250×

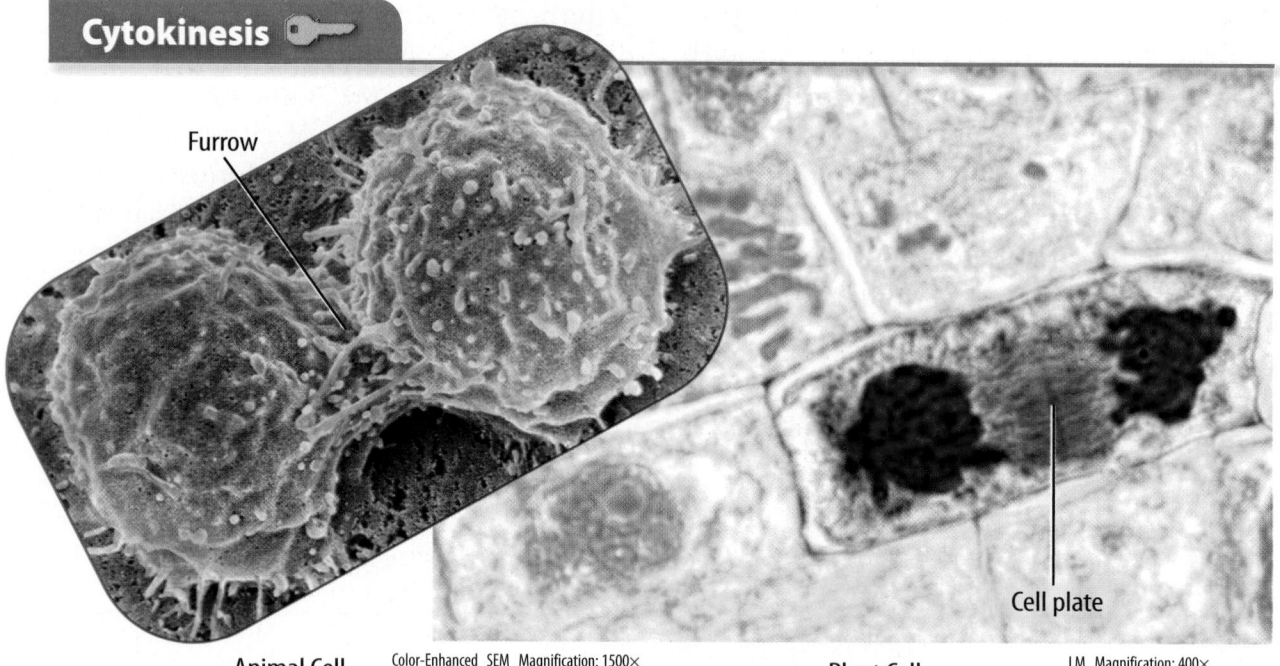

Furrow

Animal Cell

Color-Enhanced SEM Magnification: 1500×

Plant Cell

Cell plate

LM Magnification: 400×

Figure 8 Cytokinesis differs in animal cells and plant cells.

Math Skills

Use Percentages

A percentage is a ratio that compares a number to 100. If the length of the entire cell cycle is 24 hours, 24 hours equals 100%. If part of the cycle takes 6.0 hours, it can be expressed as 6.0 hours/ 24 hours. To calculate percentage, divide and multiply by 100. Add a percent sign.

$$\frac{6.0}{24} = 0.25 \times 100 = 25\%$$

Practice

Interphase in human cells takes about 23 hours. If the cell cycle is 24 hours, what percentage is interphase?

 Review

- **Math Practice**
- **Personal Tutor**

Dividing the Cell's Components

Following the last phase of mitosis, a cell's cytoplasm divides in a process called cytokinesis. The specific steps of cytokinesis differ depending on the type of cell that is dividing. In animal cells, the cell membrane contracts, or squeezes together, around the middle of the cell. Fibers around the center of the cell pull together. This forms a crease, called a furrow, in the middle of the cell. The furrow gets deeper and deeper until the cell membrane comes together and divides the cell. An animal cell undergoing cytokinesis is shown in **Figure 8.**

Cytokinesis in plants happens in a different way. As shown in **Figure 8,** a new cell wall forms in the middle of a plant cell. First, organelles called vesicles join together to form a membrane-bound disk called a cell plate. Then the cell plate grows outward toward the cell wall until two new cells form.

✓ **Reading Check** Compare cytokinesis in plant and animal cells.

Results of Cell Division

Recall that the cell cycle results in two new cells. These daughter cells are genetically identical to each other and to the original cell that no longer exists. For example, a human cell has 46 chromosomes. When that cell divides, it will produce two new cells with 46 chromosomes each. The cell cycle is important for reproduction in some organisms, growth in multicellular organisms, replacement of worn out or damaged cells, and repair of damaged tissues.

Reproduction

In some unicellular organisms, cell division is a form of reproduction. For example, an organism called a paramecium often reproduces by dividing into two new daughter cells or two new paramecia. Cell division is also important in other methods of reproduction in which the offspring are identical to the parent organism.

Growth

Cell division allows multicellular organisms, such as humans, to grow and develop from one cell (a fertilized egg). In humans, cell division begins about 24 hours after fertilization and continues rapidly during the first few years of life. It is likely that during the next few years you will go through another period of rapid growth and development. This happens because cells divide and increase in number as you grow and develop.

Replacement

Even after an organism is fully grown, cell division continues. It replaces cells that wear out or are damaged. The outermost layer of your skin is always rubbing or flaking off. A layer of cells below the skin's surface is constantly dividing. This produces millions of new cells daily to replace the ones that are rubbed off.

Repair

Cell division is also critical for repairing damage. When a bone breaks, cell division produces new bone cells that patch the broken pieces back together.

Not all damage can be repaired, however, because not all cells continue to divide. Recall that mature nerve cells stop the cell cycle in interphase. For this reason, injuries to nerve cells often cause permanent damage.

 Key Concept Check Why is the result of the cell cycle important?

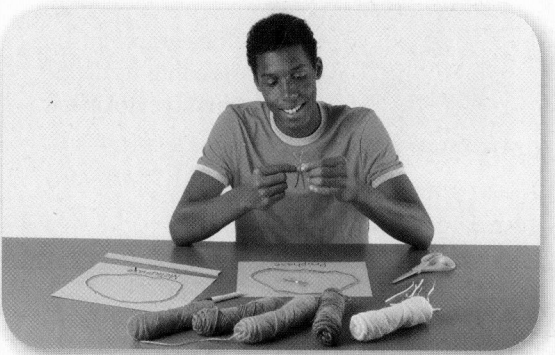

Visual Summary

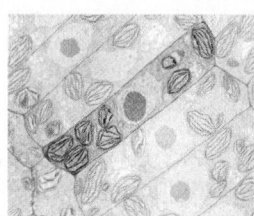

During interphase, most cells go through periods of rapid growth and replication of organelles, copying DNA, and preparation for cell division.

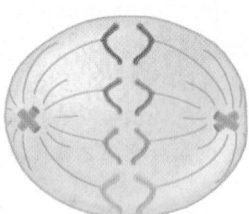

The nucleus and its contents divide during mitosis.

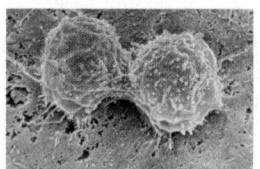

The cytoplasm and its contents divide during cytokinesis.

FOLDABLES

Use your lesson Foldable to review the lesson. Save your Foldable for the project at the end of the chapter.

What do you think NOW?

You first read the statements below at the beginning of the chapter.

1. Cell division produces two identical cells.

2. Cell division is important for growth.

3. At the end of the cell cycle, the original cell no longer exists.

Did you change your mind about whether you agree or disagree with the statements? Rewrite any false statements to make them true.

Use Vocabulary

1 **Distinguish** between mitosis and cytokinesis.

2 A duplicated chromosome is made of two _____.

3 **Use the term** *interphase* in a sentence.

Understand Key Concepts

4 Which is NOT part of mitosis?
   A. anaphase   C. prophase
   B. interphase   D. telophase

5 **Construct** a table to show the different phases of mitosis and what happens during each.

6 **Give three examples** of why the result of the cell cycle is important.

Interpret Graphics

7 **Identify** The animal cell on the right is in what phase of mitosis? Explain your answer.

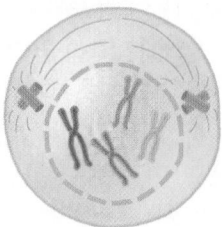

8 **Organize** Copy and fill in the graphic organizer below to show the results of cell division.

Results of cell division

Critical Thinking

9 **Predict** what might happen to a cell if it were unable to divide by mitosis.

Math Skills

Review
—— Math Practice ——

10 The mitotic phase of the human cell cycle takes approximately 1 hour. What percentage of the 24-hour cell cycle is the mitotic phase?

DNA Fingerprinting

▼ DNA

Solving Crimes One Strand at a Time

Every cell in your body has the same DNA in its nucleus. Unless you are an identical twin, your DNA is entirely unique. Identical twins have identical DNA because they begin as one cell that divides and separates. When your cells begin mitosis, they copy their DNA. Every new cell has the same DNA as the original cells. That is why DNA can be used to identify people. Just as no two people have the same fingerprints, your DNA belongs to you alone.

Using scientific methods to solve crimes is called forensics. DNA fingerprinting is now a basic tool in forensics. Samples collected from a crime scene can be compared to millions of samples previously collected and indexed in a computer.

Every day, everywhere you go, you leave a trail of DNA. It might be in skin cells. It might be in hair or in the saliva you used to lick an envelope. If you commit a crime, you will most likely leave DNA behind. An expert crime scene investigator will know how to collect that DNA.

DNA evidence can prove innocence as well. Investigators have reexamined DNA found at old crime scenes. Imprisoned persons have been proven not guilty through DNA fingerprinting methods that were not yet available when a crime was committed.

DNA fingerprinting can also be used to identify bodies that had previously been known only as a John or Jane Doe.

▼ The Federal Bureau of Investigation (FBI) has a nationwide index of DNA samples called CODIS (Combined DNA Index System).

It's Your Turn

DISCOVER Your cells contain organelles called mitochondria. They have their own DNA, called mitochondrial DNA. Your mitochondrial DNA is identical to your mother's mitochondrial DNA. Find out how this information is used.

Levels of Organization

Inquiry **Scales on Wings?**

This butterfly has a distinctive pattern of colors on its wings. The pattern is formed by clusters of tiny scales. In a similar way, multicellular organisms are made of many small parts working together.

How is a system organized?

The places people live are organized in a system. Do you live in or near a city? Cities contain things such as schools and stores that enable them to function on their own. Many cities together make up another level of organization.

1 Read and complete a lab safety form.

2 Using a **metric ruler** and **scissors,** measure and cut squares of **construction paper** that are 4 cm, 8 cm, 12 cm, 16 cm, and 20 cm on each side. Use a different color for each square.

3 Stack the squares from largest to smallest, and glue them together.

4 Cut apart the *City, Continent, Country, County,* and *State* labels your teacher gives you.

5 Use a **glue stick** to attach the *City* label to the smallest square. Sort the remaining labels from smallest to largest, and glue to the corresponding square.

Think About This

1. What is the largest level of organization a city belongs to?

2. Can any part of the system function without the others? Explain.

3. 🔑 **Key Concept** How do you think the system used to organize where people live is similar to how your body is organized?

Color-Enhanced SEM Magnification: 12×

Life's Organization

You might recall that all matter is made of atoms and that atoms combine and form molecules. Molecules make up cells. A large animal, such as a Komodo dragon, is not made of one cell. Instead, it is composed of trillions of cells working together. Its skin, shown in **Figure 9,** is made of many cells that are specialized for protection. The Komodo dragon has other types of cells, such as blood cells and nerve cells, that perform other functions. Cells work together in the Komodo dragon and enable it to function. In the same way, cells work together in you and in other multicellular organisms.

Recall that some organisms are made of only one cell. These unicellular organisms carry out all the activities necessary to survive, such as absorbing nutrients and getting rid of wastes. But no matter their sizes, all organisms are made of cells.

Figure 9 Skin cells are only one of the many kinds of cells that make up a Komodo dragon.

Figure 10 Unicellular organisms carry out life processes within one cell.

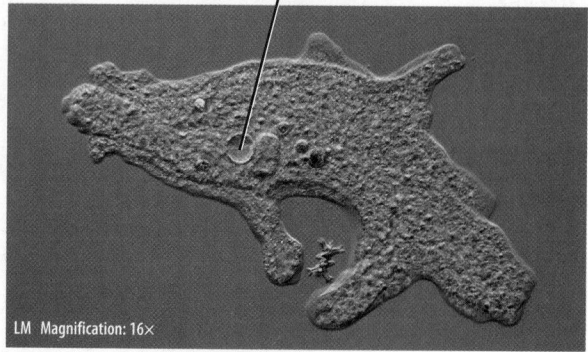

Contractile vacuole

LM Magnification: 16×

This unicellular amoeba captures a desmid for food.

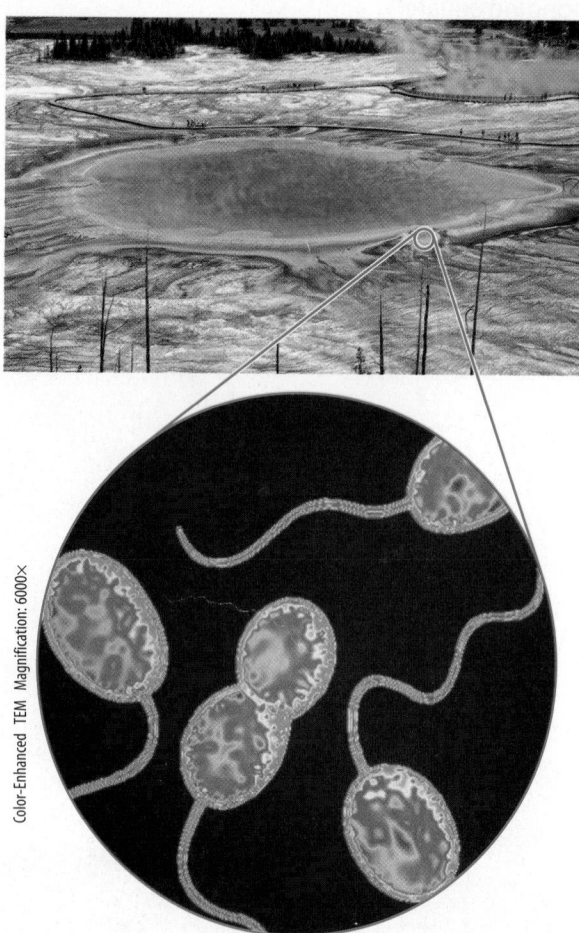

Color-Enhanced TEM Magnification: 6000×

These heat-loving bacteria are often found in hot springs as shown here. They get their energy to produce food from sulfur instead of from light like plants.

Unicellular Organisms

As you read on the previous page, some organisms have only one cell. Unicellular organisms do all the things needed for their survival within that one cell. For example, the amoeba in **Figure 10** is ingesting another unicellular organism, a type of green algae called a desmid, for food. Unicellular organisms also respond to their environment, get rid of waste, grow, and even reproduce on their own. Unicellular organisms include both prokaryotes and some eukaryotes.

Prokaryotes

Recall that a cell without a membrane-bound nucleus is a prokaryotic cell. In general, prokaryotic cells are smaller than eukaryotic cells and have fewer cell structures. A unicellular organism made of one prokaryotic cell is called a prokaryote. Some prokaryotes live in groups called colonies. Some can also live in extreme environments, as shown in **Figure 10.**

Eukaryotes

You might recall that a eukaryotic cell has a nucleus surrounded by a membrane and many other specialized organelles. For example, the amoeba shown in **Figure 10** has an organelle called a contractile vacuole. It functions like a bucket that is used to bail water out of a boat. A contractile vacuole collects excess water from the amoeba's cytoplasm. Then it pumps the water out of the amoeba. This prevents the amoeba from swelling and bursting.

A unicellular organism that is made of one eukaryotic cell is called a eukaryote. There are thousands of different unicellular eukaryotes, such as algae that grow on the inside of an aquarium and the fungus that causes athlete's foot.

 Reading Check Give an example of a unicellular eukaryotic organism.

Multicellular Organisms

Multicellular organisms are made of many eukaryotic cells working together, like the crew on an airplane. Each member of the crew, from the pilot to the mechanic, has a specific job that is important for the plane's operation. Similarly, each type of cell in a multicellular organism has a specific job that is important to the survival of the organism.

 Key Concept Check How do unicellular and multicellular organisms differ?

Cell Differentiation

As you read in the last lesson, all cells in a multicellular organism come from one cell—a fertilized egg. Cell division starts quickly after fertilization. The first cells made can become any type of cell, such as a muscle cell, a nerve cell, or a blood cell. *The process by which cells become different types of cells is called* **cell differentiation** (dihf uh ren shee AY shun).

You might recall that a cell's instructions are contained in its chromosomes. Also, nearly all the cells of an organism have identical sets of chromosomes. If an organism's cells have identical sets of instructions, how can cells be different? Different cell types use different parts of the instructions on the chromosomes. A few of the many different types of cells that can result from human cell differentiation are shown in **Figure 11.**

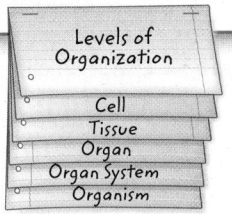
Figure 11 A fertilized egg produces cells that can differentiate into a variety of cell types.

Review   Personal Tutor

Cell Differentiation in Eukaryotes

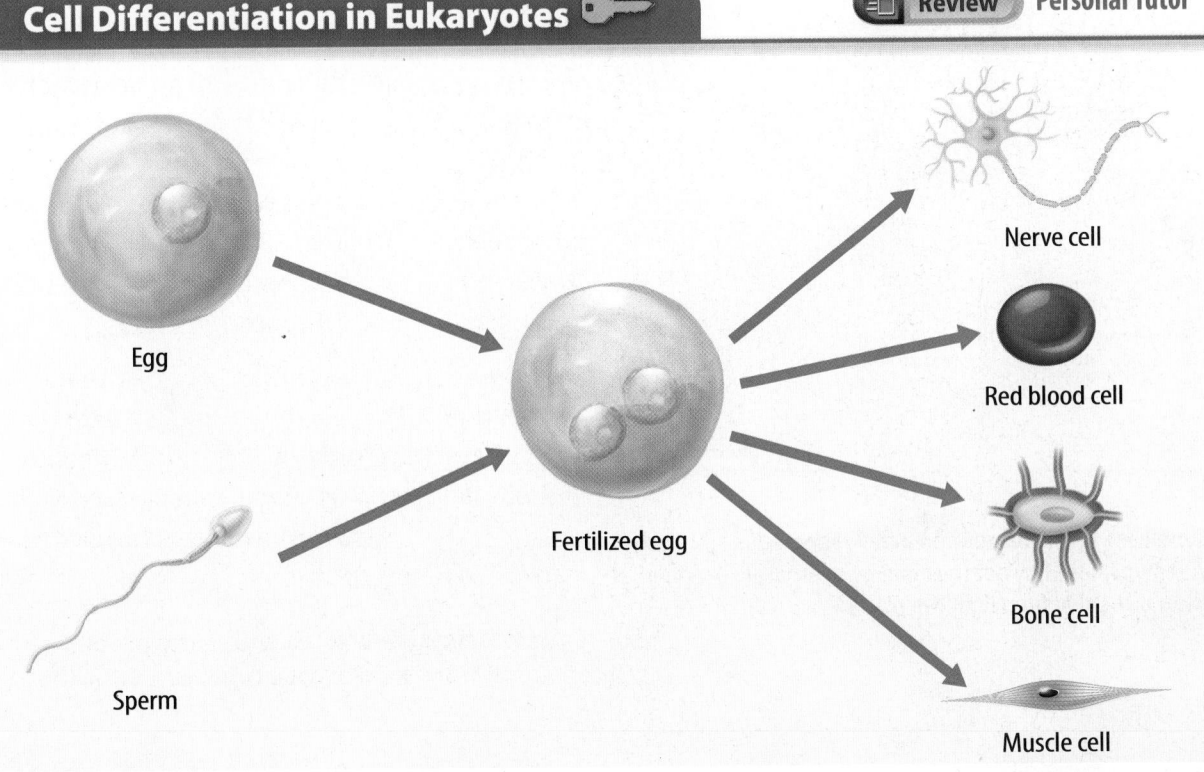

Egg

Sperm

Fertilized egg

Nerve cell

Red blood cell

Bone cell

Muscle cell

Animal Stem Cells Not all cells in a developing animal differentiate. **Stem cells** *are unspecialized cells that are able to develop into many different cell types.* There are many stem cells in embryos but fewer in adult organisms. Adult stem cells are important for the cell repair and replacement you read about in Lesson 1. For example, stem cells in your bone marrow can produce more than a dozen different types of blood cells. These replace ones that are damaged or worn out. Stem cells have also been discovered in skeletal muscles. These stem cells can produce new muscle cells when the fibers that make up the muscle are torn.

Plant Cells Plants also have unspecialized cells similar to animal stem cells. These cells are grouped in areas of a plant called meristems (MER uh stemz). Meristems are in different areas of a plant, including the tips of roots and stems, as shown in **Figure 12.** Cell division in meristems produces different types of plant cells with specialized structures and functions, such as transporting materials, making food, storing food, or protecting the plant. These cells might become parts of stems, leaves, flowers, or roots.

SCIENCE USE V. COMMON USE

fiber

Science Use a long muscle cell

Common Use a thread

Figure 12 Plant meristems produce cells that can become part of stems, leaves, flowers, or roots.

Stem meristem

Root meristem

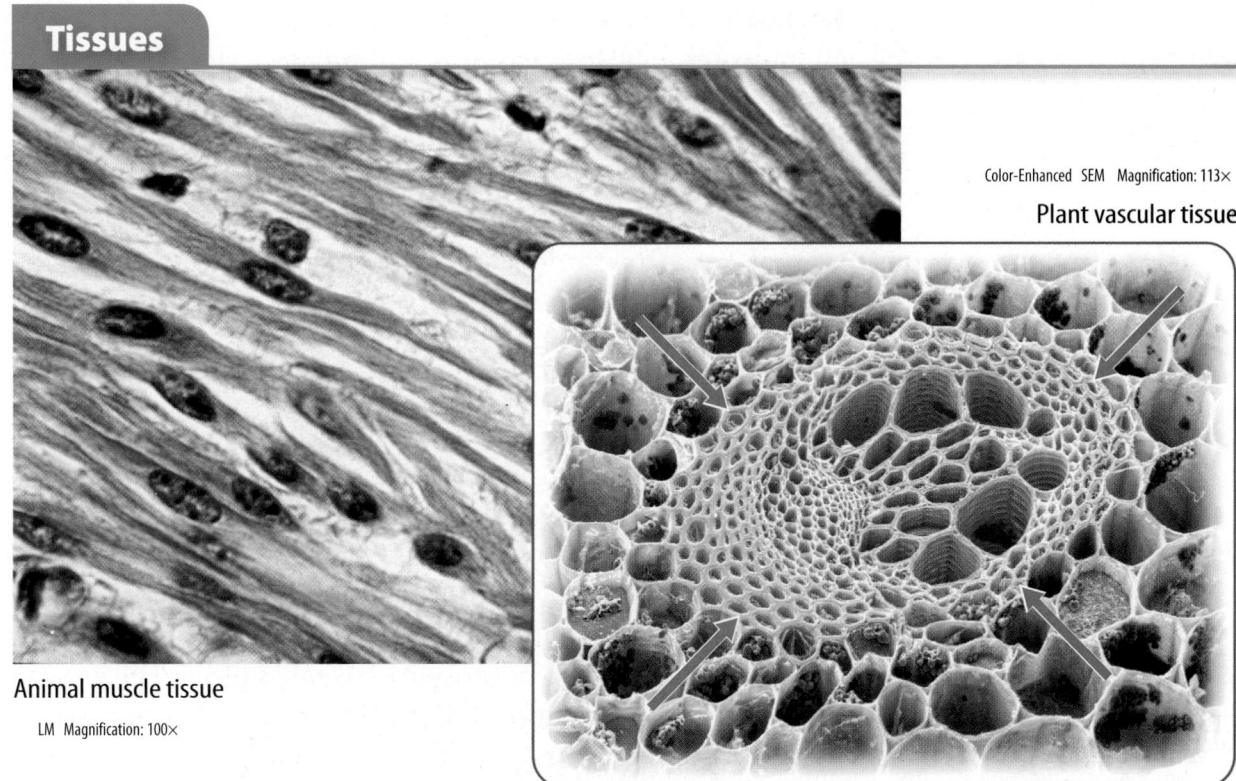

Color-Enhanced SEM Magnification: 113×

Plant vascular tissue

Animal muscle tissue

LM Magnification: 100×

Figure 13 Similar cells work together and form tissues such as this animal muscle tissue that contracts the stomach to help digestion. Plant vascular tissue, indicated by red arrows, moves water and nutrients throughout a plant.

Tissues

In multicellular organisms, similar types of cells are organized into groups. **Tissues** *are groups of similar types of cells that work together to carry out specific tasks.* Humans, like most other animals, have four main types of tissue—muscle, connective, nervous, and epithelial (eh puh THEE lee ul). For example, the animal tissue shown in **Figure 13** is smooth muscle tissue that is part of the stomach. Muscle tissue causes movement. Connective tissue provides structure and support and often connects other types of tissue together. Nervous tissue carries messages to and from the brain. Epithelial tissue forms the protective outer layer of the skin and the lining of major organs and internal body cavities.

Plants also have different types of tissues. The three main types of plant tissue are dermal, vascular (VAS kyuh lur), and ground tissue. Dermal tissue provides protection and helps reduce water loss. Vascular tissue, shown in **Figure 13,** transports water and nutrients from one part of a plant to another. Ground tissue provides storage and support and is where photosynthesis takes place.

✓ **Reading Check** Compare animal and plant tissues.

WORD ORIGIN · · · · · · · · · · ·

tissue
from Latin *texere,* means "weave"

Organs

Complex jobs in organisms require more than one type of tissue. **Organs** *are groups of different tissues working together to perform a particular job.* For example, your stomach is an organ specialized for breaking down food. It is made of all four types of tissue: muscle, epithelial, nervous, and connective. Each type of tissue performs a specific function necessary for the stomach to work properly. Layers of muscle tissue contract and break up pieces of food, epithelial tissue lines the stomach, nervous tissue sends signals to indicate the stomach is full, and connective tissue supports the stomach wall.

Plants also have organs. The leaves shown in **Figure 14** are organs specialized for photosynthesis. Each leaf is made of dermal, ground, and vascular tissues. Dermal tissue covers the outer surface of a leaf. The leaf is a vital organ because it contains ground tissue that produces food for the rest of the plant. Ground tissue is where photosynthesis takes place. The ground tissue is tightly packed on the top half of a leaf. The vascular tissue moves both the food produced by photosynthesis and water throughout the leaf and the rest of the plant.

 Reading Check List the tissues in a leaf organ.

Figure 14 A plant leaf is an organ made of several different tissues.

Visual Check Which plant tissue makes up the thinnest layer?

LM Magnification: 50×

Dermal tissue

Ground tissue

Vascular tissue

Organ Systems

Usually organs do not function alone. Instead, **organ systems** *are groups of different organs that work together to complete a series of tasks.* Human organ systems can be made of many different organs working together. For example, the human digestive system is made of many organs, including the stomach, the small intestine, the liver, and the large intestine. These organs and others all work together to break down food and take it into the body. Blood absorbs and transports nutrients from broken down food to cells throughout the body.

Plants have two major organ systems—the shoot system and the root system. The shoot system includes leaves, stems, and flowers. Food and water are transported throughout the plant by the shoot system. The root system anchors the plant and takes in water and nutrients.

Reading Check What are the major organ systems in plants?

Inquiry MiniLab 25 minutes

How do cells work together to make an organism?

In a multicellular organism, similar cells work together and make a tissue. A tissue can perform functions that individual cells cannot. Tissues are organized into organs, then organ systems, then organisms. How can you model the levels of organization in an organism?

1 Read and complete a lab safety form.

2 Your teacher will give you a **cardboard shape, macaroni,** and a **permanent marker.**

3 The macaroni represent cells. Use the marker to draw a small circle on each piece of macaroni. This represents the nucleus.

4 Arrange and **glue** enough macaroni on the blank side of the cardboard shape to cover it. Your group of similar cells represents a tissue.

5 One of the squares on the back of your shape is labeled *A, B, C,* or *D.* Find the group with a matching letter. Line up these squares, and use **tape** to connect the two tissues. This represents an organ.

6 Repeat step 4 with the squares labeled *E* or *F.* This represents an organ system.

7 Connect the organ systems by aligning the squares labeled *G* to represent an organism.

Analyze and Conclude

1. Each group had to work with other groups to make a model of an organism. Do cells, tissues, and organs need to work together in organisms? Explain.

2. 🔑 **Key Concept** How does your model show the levels of organization in living things?

Organisms

Multicellular organisms usually have many organ systems. These systems work together to carry out all the jobs needed for the survival of the organisms. For example, the cells in the leaves and the stems of a plant need water to live. They cannot absorb water directly. Water diffuses into the roots and is transported through the stem to the leaves by the transport system.

In the human body, there are many major organ systems. Each organ system depends on the others and cannot work alone. For example, the cells in the muscle tissue of the stomach cannot survive without oxygen. The stomach cannot get oxygen without working together with the respiratory and circulatory systems. **Figure 15** will help you review how organisms are organized.

Key Concept Check How does cell differentiation lead to the organization within a multicellular organism?

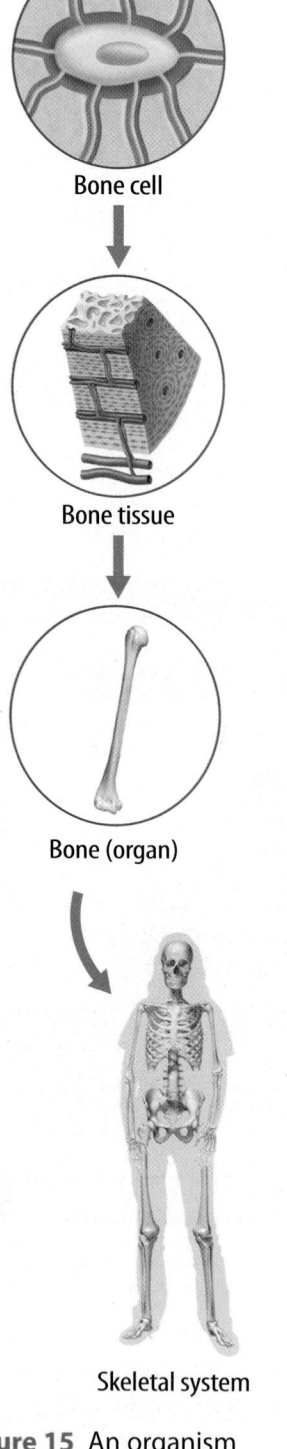

Bone cell

Bone tissue

Bone (organ)

Skeletal system

Figure 15 An organism is made of organ systems, organs, tissues, and cells that all function together and enable the organism's survival.

 Concepts in Motion Animation

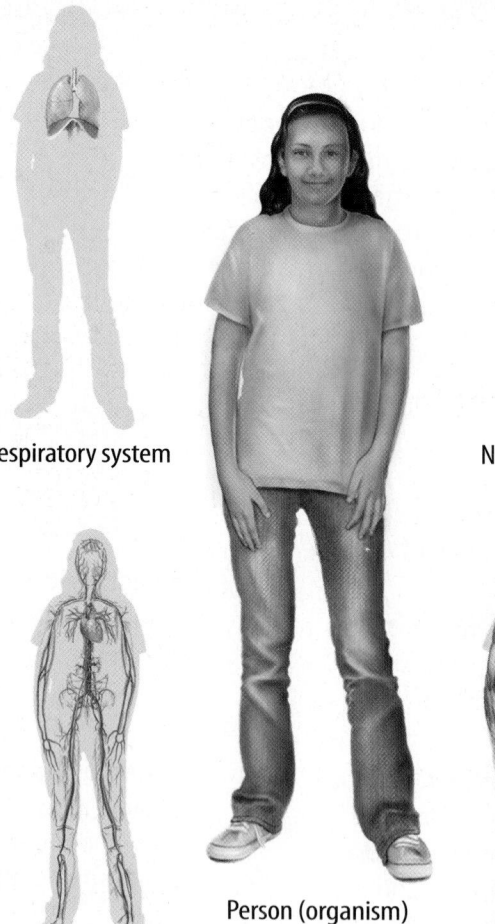

Respiratory system

Nervous system

Person (organism)

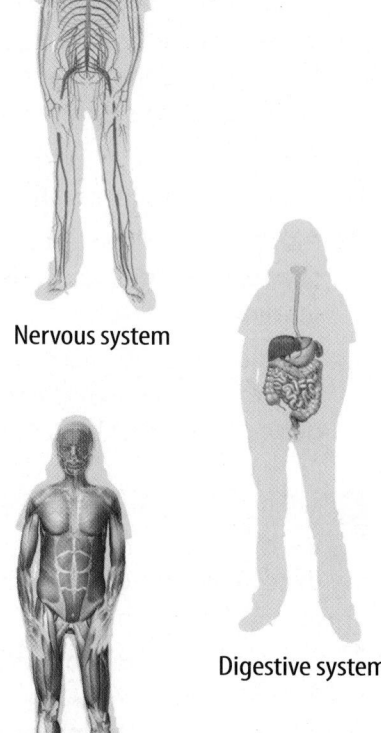

Digestive system

Circulatory system

Muscular system

Lesson 2 Review

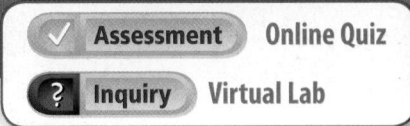
Visual Summary

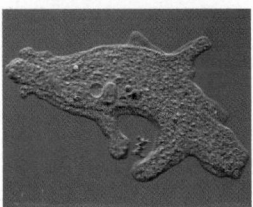

A unicellular organism carries out all the activities necessary for survival within one cell.

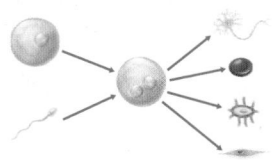

Cells become specialized in structure and function during cell differentiation.

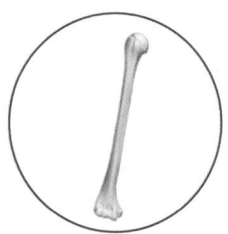

Organs are groups of different tissues that work together to perform a job.

FOLDABLES

Use your lesson Foldable to review the lesson. Save your Foldable for the project at the end of the chapter.

What do you think NOW?

You first read the statements below at the beginning of the chapter.

4. Unicellular organisms do not have all the characteristics of life.

5. All the cells in a multicellular organism are the same.

6. Some organs work together as part of an organ system.

Did you change your mind about whether you agree or disagree with the statements? Rewrite any false statements to make them true.

Use Vocabulary

1. **Define** *cell differentiation* in your own words.

2. **Distinguish** between an organ and an organ system.

Understand Key Concepts

3. **Explain** the difference between a unicellular organism and a multicellular organism.

4. **Describe** how cell differentiation produces different types of cells in animals.

5. Which is the correct sequence of the levels of organization?
   A. cell, organ, tissue, organ system, organism
   B. organism, organ, organ system, tissue, cell
   C. cell, tissue, organ, organ system, organism
   D. tissue, organ, organism, organ system, cell

Interpret Graphics

6. **Organize** Copy and fill in the table below to summarize the characteristics of unicellular and multicellular organisms.

Organism Characteristics	
Unicellular	Multicellular

Critical Thinking

7. **Predict** A mistake occurs during mitosis of a muscle stem cell. How might this affect muscle tissue?

8. **Compare** the functions of a cell to the functions of an organism, such as getting rid of wastes.

Cell Differentiation

Materials

cooked eggs

boiled chicken leg

forceps

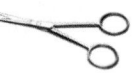

dissecting scissors

plastic knife

paper towels

Safety

It's pretty amazing that a whole chicken with wings, feet, beak, feathers, and internal organs can come from one cell, a fertilized egg. Shortly after fertilization, the cell begins to divide. The new cells in the developing embryo become specialized both in structure and function. The process by which cells become specialized is called cellular differentiation.

Question

How does a single cell become a multicellular organism?

Procedure

1. Read and complete a lab safety form.

2. Carefully examine the outside of your egg. Remove the shell.

3. Dissect the egg on a paper towel, cutting it in half from tip to rounded end. Examine the inside.

4. Record your observations in your Science Journal. Include a labeled drawing. Infer the function of each part.

5. Discard all your trash in the container provided.

6. Examine the outside of the chicken leg. Describe the skin and its functions.

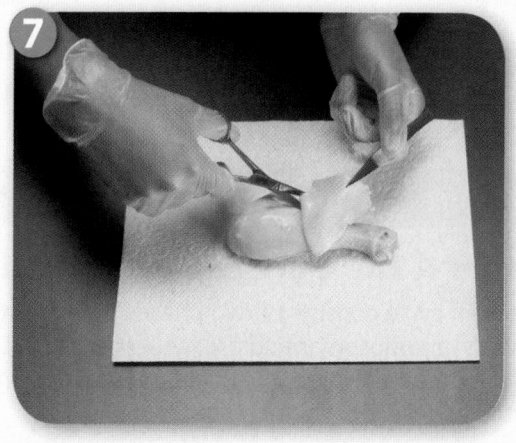

7 Carefully remove the skin using forceps and dissecting scissors. Put the skin in your discard container. Now you should see evidence of fat and muscles. You may also be able to see some blood vessels and tendons, but these are not always visible after cooking. Describe each part that you see and explain its function.

8 Peel back the muscles to reveal the bones. Tendons, ligaments, and cartilage holding the bones in place may also be evident.

9 Put all your trash in the discard container. Your teacher will give you instructions about cleaning up.

Analyze and Conclude

10  **The Big Idea** A single cell can become a multicellular organism through the process of cell differentiation. How do the organization of the egg and the chicken leg compare?

11 **Summarize** How many different types of cell differentiation did you observe in the chicken leg?

Communicate Your Results

Make a poster about how an egg transforms into a chicken through the process of cell differentiation.

 **Extension**

Examine a whole raw chicken or a raw chicken leg that is still attached to a thigh. You might be able to move the muscles in the legs or wings and see parts that were not visible in this lab. Be sure to wear gloves and to wash well with soap and water after touching the raw chicken.

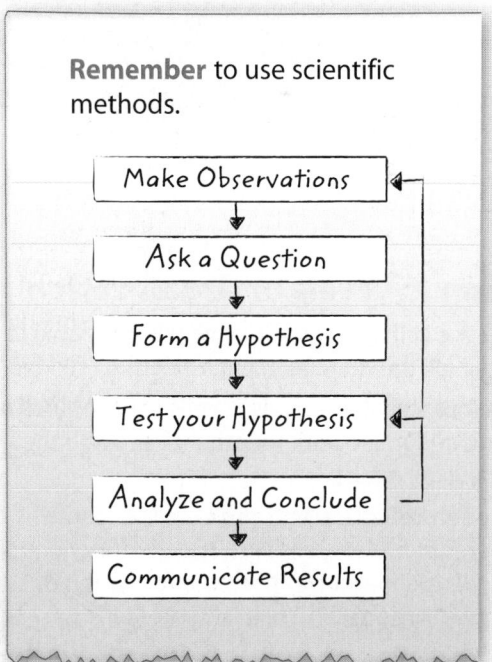

Remember to use scientific methods.

> Make Observations
>
> Ask a Question
>
> Form a Hypothesis
>
> Test your Hypothesis
>
> Analyze and Conclude
>
> Communicate Results

Lesson 2
EXTEND
107

 **THE BIG IDEA**

Through cell division, one cell can produce new cells to grow and develop into a multicellular organism.

Key Concepts Summary 🔑

Lesson 1: The Cell Cycle and Cell Division

- The **cell cycle** consists of two phases. During **interphase,** a cell grows and its chromosomes and organelles replicate. During the mitotic phase of the cell cycle, the nucleus divides during **mitosis,** and the cytoplasm divides during **cytokinesis.**

- The cell cycle results in two genetically identical **daughter cells.** The original parent cell no longer exists.

- The cell cycle is important for growth in multicellular organisms, reproduction in some organisms, replacement of worn-out cells, and repair of damaged cells.

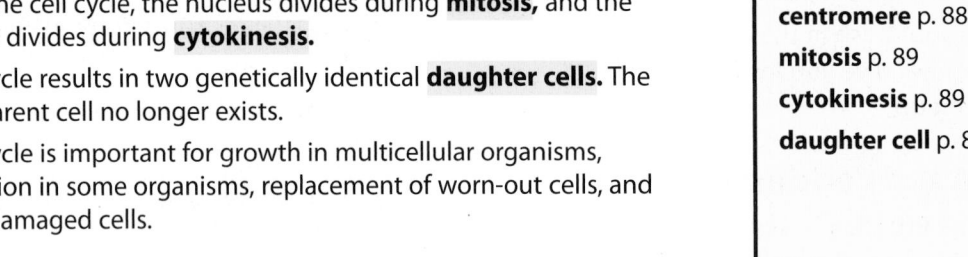

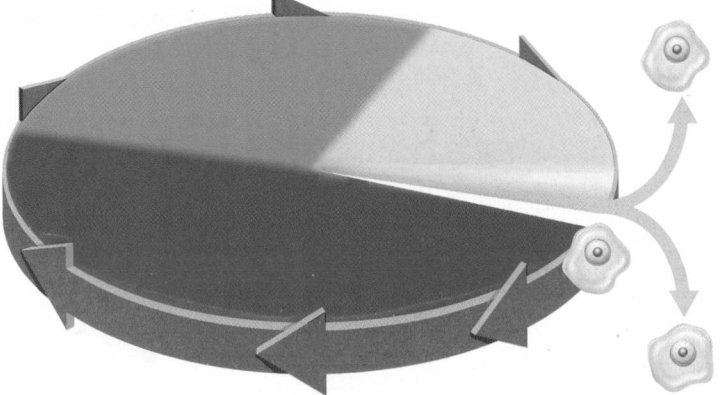

Vocabulary

cell cycle p. 85

interphase p. 86

sister chromatid p. 88

centromere p. 88

mitosis p. 89

cytokinesis p. 89

daughter cell p. 89

Lesson 2: Levels of Organization

- The one cell of a unicellular organism is able to obtain all the materials that it needs to survive.

- In a multicellular organism, cells cannot survive alone and must work together to provide the organism's needs.

- Through **cell differentiation,** cells become different types of cells with specific functions. Cell differentiation leads to the formation of **tissues, organs,** and **organ systems.**

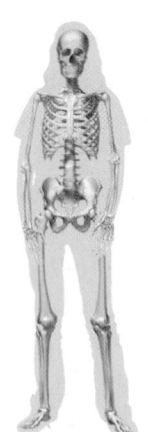

cell differentiation p. 99

stem cell p. 100

tissue p. 101

organ p. 102

organ system p. 103

Study Guide

Review
- Personal Tutor
- Vocabulary eGames
- Vocabulary eFlashcards

FOLDABLES® Chapter Project

Assemble your lesson Foldables as shown to make a Chapter Project. Use the project to review what you have learned in this chapter.

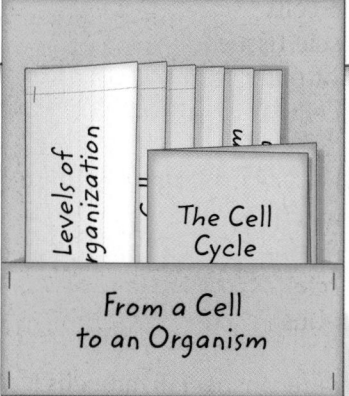

Levels of
The Cell Cycle
From a Cell to an Organism

Use Vocabulary

1. Use the term *sister chromatids* in a sentence.
2. Define the term *centromere* in your own words.
3. The new cells formed by mitosis are called ________.
4. Use the term *cell differentiation* in a sentence.
5. Define the term *stem cell* in your own words.
6. Organs are groups of ________ working together to perform a specific task.

Link Vocabulary and Key Concepts

Concepts in Motion Interactive Concept Map

Copy this concept map, and then use vocabulary terms from the previous page and from the chapter to complete the concept map.

Cell cycle
1st phase
2nd phase
leads to
7
Mitotic phase
10
1st stage
2nd stage
Cells work together to form
8
9
11
Other levels of organization include
12
13
14

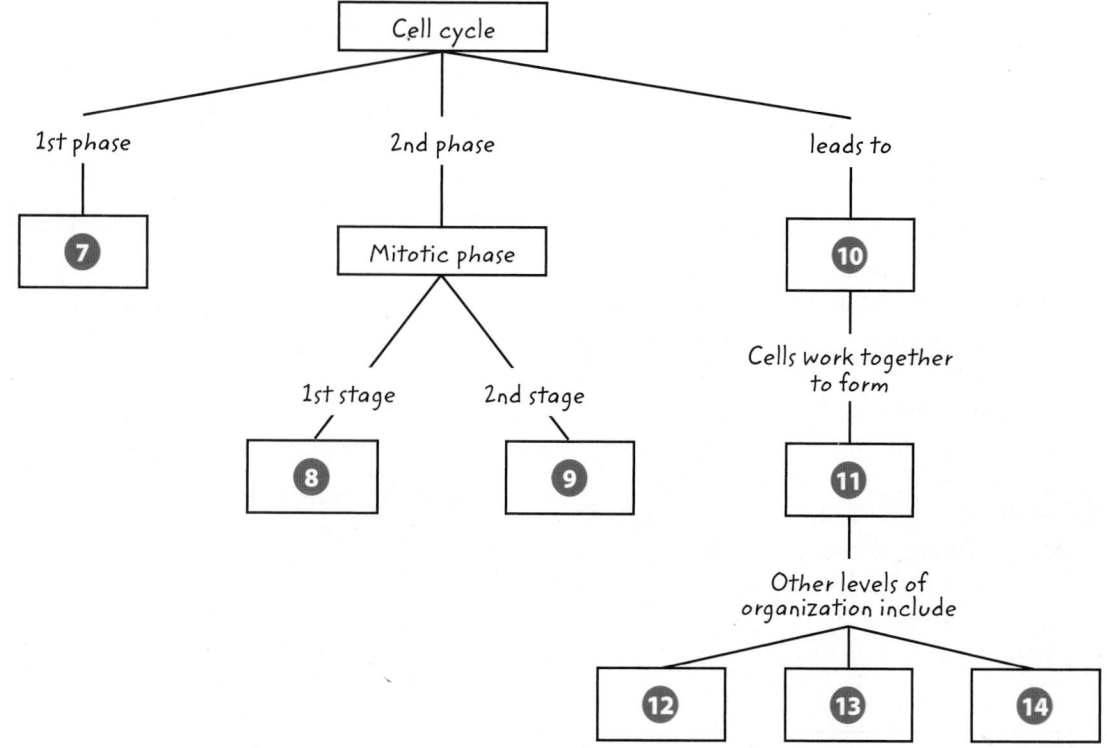

Chapter 3 Review

Understand Key Concepts

1 Chromosomes line up in the center of the cell during which phase?
- A. anaphase
- B. metaphase
- C. prophase
- D. telophase

2 Which stage of the cell cycle precedes cytokinesis?
- A. G_1
- B. G_2
- C. interphase
- D. mitosis

Use the figure below to answer questions 3 and 4.

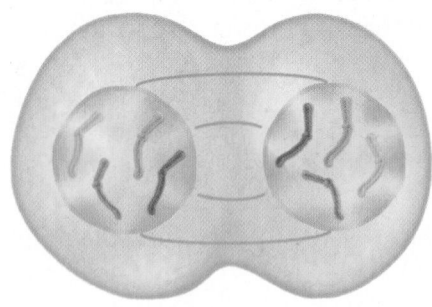

3 The figure represents which stage of mitosis?
- A. anaphase
- B. metaphase
- C. prophase
- D. telophase

4 What forms during this phase?
- A. centromere
- B. furrow
- C. sister chromatid
- D. two nuclei

5 What is the longest part of the cell cycle?
- A. anaphase
- B. cytokinesis
- C. interphase
- D. mitosis

6 A plant's root system is which level of organization?
- A. cell
- B. organ
- C. organ system
- D. tissue

7 Where is a meristem often found?
- A. liver cells
- B. muscle tissue
- C. tip of plant root
- D. unicellular organism

8 Which is NOT a type of human tissue?
- A. connective
- B. meristem
- C. muscle
- D. nervous

9 Which are unspecialized cells?
- A. blood cells
- B. muscle cells
- C. nerve cells
- D. stem cells

10 Which level of organization is shown in the figure below?
- A. cell
- B. organ
- C. organ system
- D. tissue

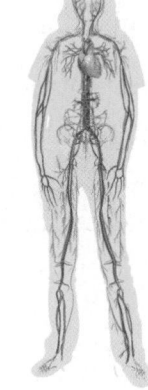

11 Which level of organization completes a series of tasks?
- A. cell
- B. organ
- C. organ system
- D. tissue

Why do offspring look different?

Unless you're an identical twin, you probably don't look exactly like any siblings you might have. You might have differences in physical characteristics such as eye color, hair color, ear shape, or height. Why are there differences in the offspring from the same parents?

1 Read and complete a lab safety form.

2 Open the **paper bag** labeled *Male Parent*, and, without looking, remove three **beads.** Record the bead colors in your Science Journal, and replace the beads.

3 Open the **paper bag** labeled *Female Parent,* and remove three **beads.** Record the bead colors, and replace the beads.

4 Repeat steps 2 and 3 for each member of the group.

5 After each member has recorded his or her bead colors, study the results. Each combination of male and female beads represents an offspring.

Think About This

1. Compare your group's offspring to another group's offspring. What similarities or differences do you observe?

2. What caused any differences you observed? Explain.

3. 🔑 **Key Concept** Why might this type of reproduction be beneficial to an organism?

What is sexual reproduction?

Have you ever seen a litter of kittens? One kitten might have orange fur like its mother. A second kitten might have gray fur like its father. Still another kitten might look like a combination of both parents. How is this possible?

The kittens look different because of sexual reproduction. **Sexual reproduction** *is a type of reproduction in which the genetic materials from two different cells combine, producing an offspring.* The cells that combine are called sex cells. Sex cells form in reproductive organs. *The female sex cell, an* **egg,** *forms in an ovary. The male sex cell, a* **sperm,** *forms in a testis. During a process called* **fertilization** (fur tuh luh ZAY shun), *an egg cell and a sperm cell join together.* This produces a new cell. *The new cell that forms from fertilization is called a* **zygote.** As shown in **Figure 1,** the zygote develops into a new organism.

Review Personal Tutor

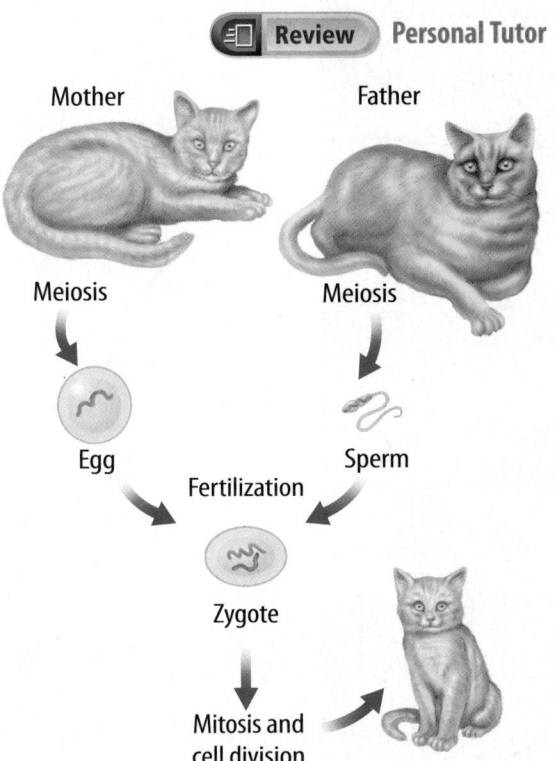

Figure 1 The zygote that forms during fertilization can become a multicellular organism.

Diploid Cells

Following fertilization, a zygote goes through mitosis and cell division. These processes produce nearly all the cells in a multicellular organism. Organisms that reproduce sexually form two kinds of cells—body cells and sex cells. In body cells of most organisms, similar chromosomes occur in pairs. **Diploid** *cells are cells that have pairs of chromosomes.*

Chromosomes

Pairs of chromosomes that have genes for the same traits arranged in the same order are called **homologous** (huh MAH luh gus) **chromosomes.** Because one chromosome is inherited from each parent, the chromosomes are not identical. For example, the kittens mentioned earlier in this lesson inherited a gene for orange fur color from their mother. They also inherited a gene for gray fur color from their father. So, some kittens might be orange, and some might be gray. Both genes for fur color are at the same place on homologous chromosomes, but they code for different colors.

Different organisms have different numbers of chromosomes. Recall that diploid cells have pairs of chromosomes. Notice in **Table 1** that human diploid cells have 23 pairs of chromosomes for a total of 46 chromosomes. A fruit fly diploid cell has 4 pairs of chromosomes, and a rice diploid cell has 12 pairs of chromosomes.

Table 1 An organism's chromosomes can be matched as pairs of chromosomes that have genes for the same traits.

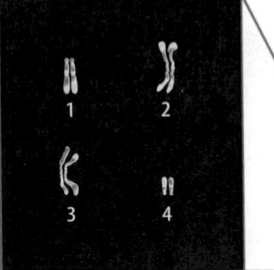

(○) **Concepts in Motion**   Interactive Table

Table 1 Chromosomes of Selected Organisms		
Organism	**Number of Chromosomes**	**Number of Homologous Pairs**
Fruit fly	8	4
Rice	24	12
Yeast	32	16
Cat	38	19
Human	46	23
Dog	78	39
Fern	1,260	630

Having the correct number of chromosomes is very important. If a zygote has too many or too few chromosomes, it will not develop properly. For example, a genetic condition called Down syndrome occurs when a person has an extra copy of chromosome 21. A person with Down syndrome can have short stature, heart defects, or mental disabilities.

Haploid Cells

Organisms that reproduce sexually also form egg and sperm cells, or sex cells. Sex cells have only one chromosome from each pair of chromosomes. **Haploid** *cells are cells that have only one chromosome from each pair.* Organisms produce sex cells using a special type of cell division called meiosis. *In* **meiosis,** *one diploid cell divides and makes four haploid sex cells.* Meiosis occurs only during the formation of sex cells.

✓ **Reading Check** How do diploid cells differ from haploid cells?

The Phases of Meiosis

Next, you will read about the phases of meiosis. Many of the phases might seem familiar to you because they also occur during mitosis. Recall that mitosis and cytokinesis involve one division of the nucleus and the cytoplasm. Meiosis involves two divisions of the nucleus and the cytoplasm. These divisions are called meiosis I and meiosis II. They result in four haploid cells—cells with half the number of chromosomes as the original cell. As you read about meiosis, think about how it produces sex cells with a reduced number of chromosomes.

WORD ORIGIN · · · · · · · · · · ·

haploid
from Greek *haploeides*, means "single"

FOLDABLES®

Make a shutter-fold book and label it as shown. Use it to describe and illustrate the phases of meiosis.

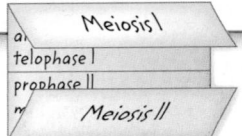

Inquiry MiniLab   **20 minutes**

How does one cell produce four cells? ✂

When a diploid cell goes through meiosis, it produces four haploid cells. How does this happen?

1. Read and complete a lab safety form.
2. Make a copy of the diagram by tracing circles around a **jar lid** on your **paper.** Label as shown.
3. Use **chenille craft wires** to make red and blue duplicated chromosomes 2.5 cm long and green and yellow duplicated chromosomes 1.5 cm long. Recall that a duplicated chromosome has two sister chromatids connected at the centromere.
4. Place the chromosomes in the diploid cell.
5. Move one long chromosome and one short chromosome into each of the middle cells.
6. Separate the two strands of the chromosomes, and place one strand into each of the haploid cells.

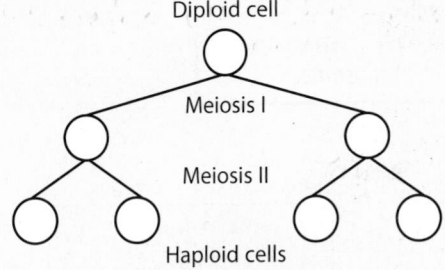

Diploid cell

Meiosis I

Meiosis II

Haploid cells

Analyze and Conclude

1. **Describe** What happened to the chromosomes during meiosis I? During meiosis II?

2. **Think Critically** Why are two haploid cells (sperm and egg) needed to form a zygote?

3. 🔑 **Key Concept** How does one cell form four cells during meiosis?

Phases of Meiosis I

A reproductive cell goes through interphase before beginning meiosis I, which is shown in **Figure 2**. During interphase, the reproductive cell grows and copies, or duplicates, its chromosomes. Each duplicated chromosome consists of two sister chromatids joined together by a centromere.

① **Prophase I** In the first phase of meiosis I, duplicated chromosomes condense and thicken. Homologous chromosomes come together and form pairs. The membrane surrounding the nucleus breaks apart, and the nucleolus disappears.

② **Metaphase I** Homologous chromosome pairs line up along the middle of the cell. A spindle fiber attaches to each chromosome.

③ **Anaphase I** Chromosome pairs separate and are pulled toward the opposite ends of the cell. Notice that the sister chromatids stay together.

④ **Telophase I** A nuclear membrane forms around each group of duplicated chromosomes. The cytoplasm divides through cytokinesis and two daughter cells form. Sister chromatids remain together.

Meiosis 🔑

(((O))) Concepts in Motion   Animation

Meiosis I

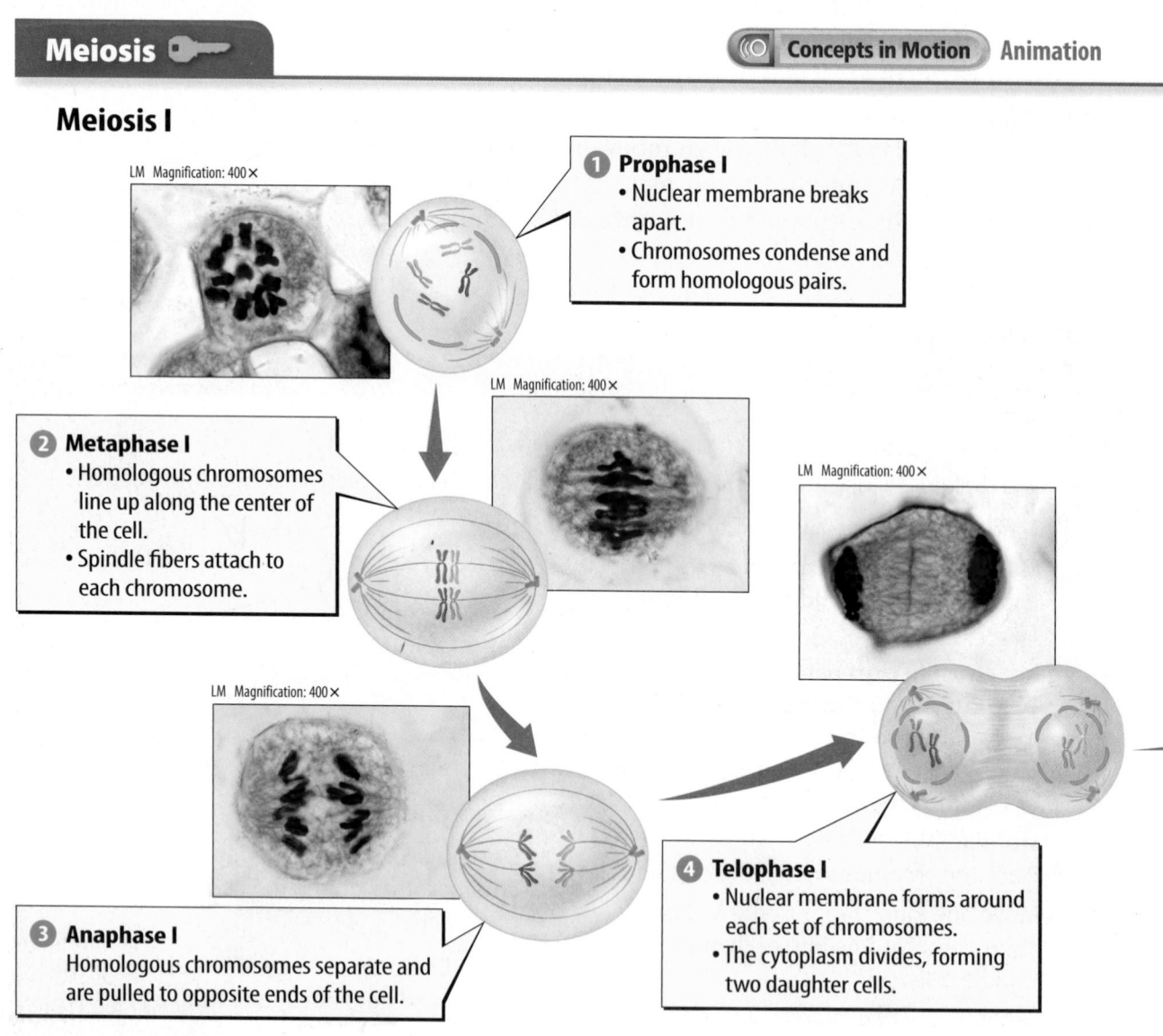

LM Magnification: 400×

① **Prophase I**
• Nuclear membrane breaks apart.
• Chromosomes condense and form homologous pairs.

LM Magnification: 400×

② **Metaphase I**
• Homologous chromosomes line up along the center of the cell.
• Spindle fibers attach to each chromosome.

LM Magnification: 400×

④ **Telophase I**
• Nuclear membrane forms around each set of chromosomes.
• The cytoplasm divides, forming two daughter cells.

LM Magnification: 400×

③ **Anaphase I**
Homologous chromosomes separate and are pulled to opposite ends of the cell.

Figure 2 Unlike mitosis, meiosis involves two divisions of the nucleus and the cytoplasm.

Phases of Meiosis II

After meiosis I, the two cells formed during this stage go through a second division of the nucleus and the cytoplasm. This process, shown in **Figure 2,** is called meiosis II.

5 Prophase II Chromosomes are not copied again before prophase II. They remain as condensed, thickened sister chromatids. The nuclear membrane breaks apart, and the nucleolus disappears in each cell.

6 Metaphase II The pairs of sister chromatids line up along the middle of the cell in single file.

7 Anaphase II The sister chromatids of each duplicated chromosome are pulled away from each other and move toward opposite ends of the cells.

8 Telophase II During the final phase of meiosis—telophase II—a nuclear membrane forms around each set of chromatids, which are again called chromosomes. The cytoplasm divides through cytokinesis, and four haploid cells form.

Key Concept Check List the phases of meiosis in order.

Meiosis II

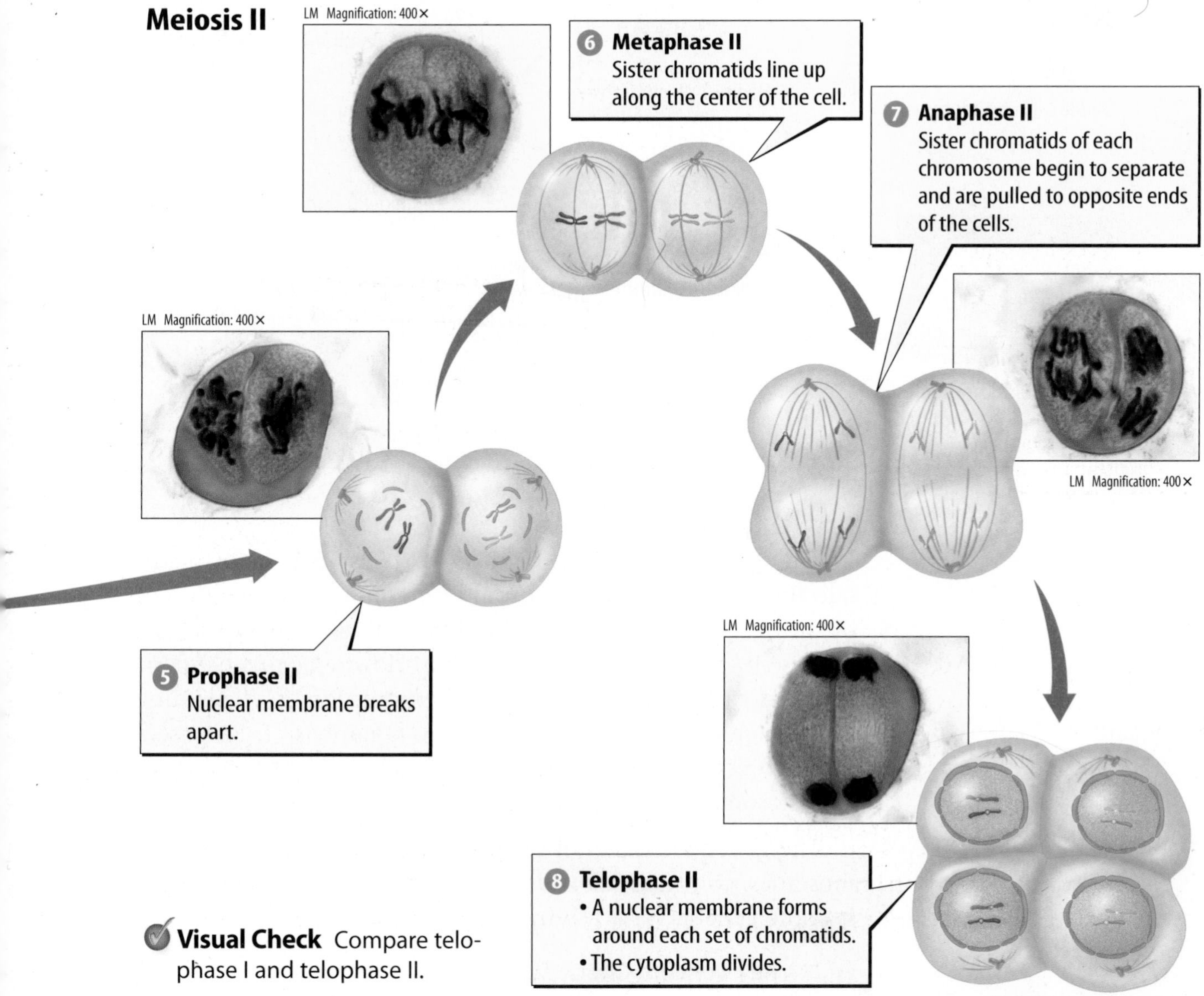
LM Magnification: 400×
6 Metaphase II
Sister chromatids line up along the center of the cell.
7 Anaphase II
Sister chromatids of each chromosome begin to separate and are pulled to opposite ends of the cells.
LM Magnification: 400×
LM Magnification: 400×
5 Prophase II
Nuclear membrane breaks apart.
LM Magnification: 400×
8 Telophase II
• A nuclear membrane forms around each set of chromatids.
• The cytoplasm divides.

Visual Check Compare telophase I and telophase II.

Why is meiosis important?

Meiosis forms sex cells with the correct haploid number of chromosomes. This maintains the correct diploid number of chromosomes in organisms when sex cells join. Meiosis also creates genetic variation by producing haploid cells.

Maintaining Diploid Cells

Recall that diploid cells have pairs of chromosomes. Meiosis helps to maintain diploid cells in offspring by making haploid sex cells. When haploid sex cells join together during fertilization, they make a diploid zygote, or fertilized egg. The zygote then divides by mitosis and cell division and creates a diploid organism. **Figure 3** illustrates how the diploid number is maintained in ducks.

Figure 3 Meiosis ensures that the chromosome number of a species stays the same from generation to generation.

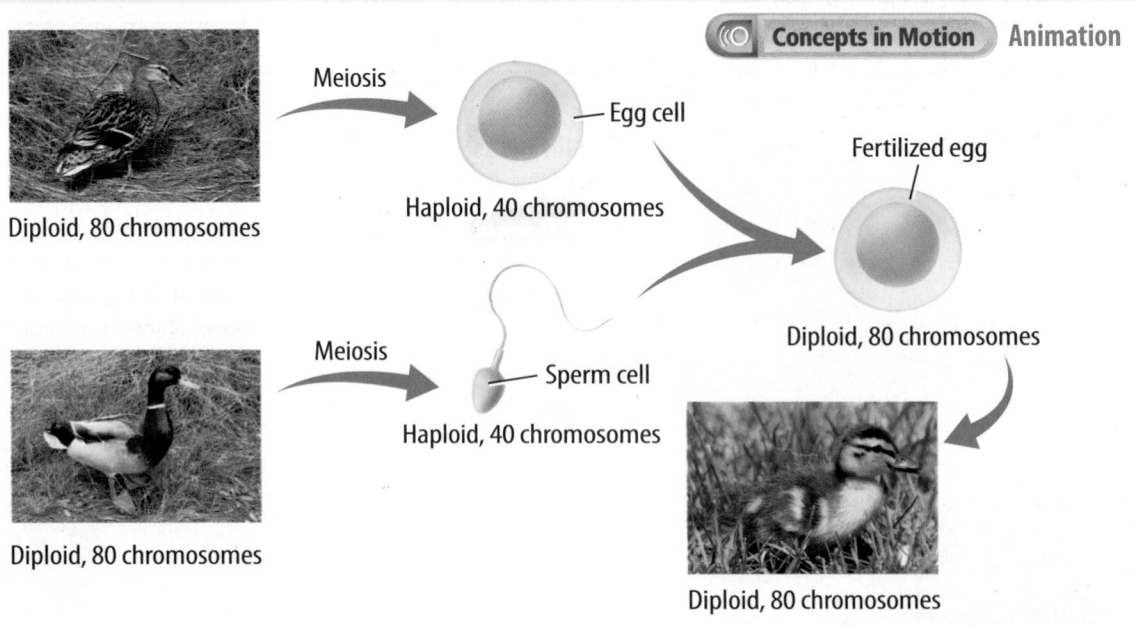

Concepts in Motion   Animation

Diploid, 80 chromosomes

Meiosis → Egg cell
Haploid, 40 chromosomes

Meiosis → Sperm cell
Haploid, 40 chromosomes

Diploid, 80 chromosomes

Fertilized egg
Diploid, 80 chromosomes

Diploid, 80 chromosomes

Creating Haploid Cells

The result of meiosis is haploid sex cells. This helps maintain the correct number of chromosomes in each generation of offspring. The formation of haploid cells also is important because it allows for genetic variation. How does this happen? Sex cells can have different sets of chromosomes, depending on how chromosomes line up during metaphase I. Because a cell only gets one chromosome from each pair of homologous chromosomes, the resulting sex cells can be different.

The genetic makeup of offspring is a combination of chromosomes from two sex cells. Variation in the sex cells results in more genetic variation in the next generation.

Key Concept Check Why is meiosis important?

How do mitosis and meiosis differ?

Sometimes, it's hard to remember the differences between mitosis and meiosis. Use **Table 2** to review these processes.

During mitosis and cell division, a body cell and its nucleus divide once and produce two identical cells. These processes are important for growth and repair or replacement of damaged tissue. Some organisms reproduce by these processes. The two daughter cells produced by mitosis and cell division have the same genetic information.

During meiosis, a reproductive cell and its nucleus divide twice and produce four cells—two pairs of identical haploid cells. Each cell has half the number of chromosomes as the original cell. Meiosis happens in the reproductive organs of multicellular organisms. Meiosis forms sex cells used for sexual reproduction.

 Reading Check How many cells are produced during mitosis? During meiosis?

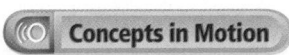 **Concepts in Motion** Interactive Table

Table 2 Comparison of Types of Cell Division

Characteristic	Meiosis	Mitosis and Cell Division
Number of chromosomes in parent cell	diploid	diploid
Type of parent cell	reproductive	body
Number of divisions of nucleus	2	1
Number of daughter cells produced	4	2
Chromosome number in daughter cells	haploid	diploid
Function	forms sperm and egg cells	growth, cell repair, some types of reproduction

Math Skills

Use Proportions

An equation that shows that two ratios are equivalent is a proportion. The ratios $\frac{1}{2}$ and $\frac{3}{6}$ are equivalent, so they can be written as $\frac{1}{2} = \frac{3}{6}$.

You can use proportions to figure out how many daughter cells will be produced during mitosis. If you know that one cell produces two daughter cells at the end of mitosis, you can use proportions to calculate how many daughter cells will be produced by eight cells undergoing mitosis.

Set up an equation of the two ratios. $\frac{1}{2} = \frac{8}{y}$

Cross-multiply. $1 \times y = 8 \times 2$

$1y = 16$

Divide each side by 1. $y = 16$

Practice

You know that one cell produces four daughter cells at the end of meiosis. How many daughter cells would be produced if eight sex cells undergo meiosis?

 **Review**
- Math Practice
- Personal Tutor

Advantages of Sexual Reproduction

Did you ever wonder why a brother and a sister might not look alike? The answer is sexual reproduction. The main advantage of sexual reproduction is that offspring inherit half their **DNA** from each parent. Offspring are not likely to inherit the same DNA from the same parents. Different DNA means that each offspring has a different set of traits. This results in genetic variation among the offspring.

 Key Concept Check Why is sexual reproduction beneficial?

Genetic Variation

As you just read, genetic variation exists among humans. You can look at your friends to see genetic variation. Genetic variation occurs in all organisms that reproduce sexually. Consider the plants shown in **Figure 4.** The plants are members of the same species, but they have different traits, such as the ability to resist disease.

Due to genetic variation, individuals within a population have slight differences. These differences might be an advantage if the environment changes. Some individuals might have traits that enable them to survive unusually harsh conditions such as a drought or severe cold. Other individuals might have traits that make them resistant to disease.

Genetic Variation 🔑

Disease-resistant cassava leaves

Cassava leaves with cassava mosaic disease

Figure 4 These plants belong to the same species. However, one is more disease-resistant than the other.

✓ **Visual Check** How does cassava mosaic disease affect cassava leaves?

Selective Breeding

Did you know that broccoli, kohlrabi, kale, and cabbage all descended from one type of mustard plant? It's true. More than 2,000 years ago farmers noticed that some mustard plants had different traits, such as larger leaves or bigger flower buds. The farmers started to choose which traits they wanted by selecting certain plants to reproduce and grow. For example, some farmers chose only the plants with the biggest flowers and stems and planted their seeds. Over time, the offspring of these plants became what we know today as broccoli, shown in **Figure 5.** This process is called selective breeding. Selective breeding has been used to develop many types of plants and animals with desirable traits. It is another example of the benefits of sexual reproduction.

Figure 5 The wild mustard is the common ancestor to all these plants.

Selective Breeding 🔑

Broccoli

Cabbage

Kale

Wild mustard

Kohlrabi

Disadvantages of Sexual Reproduction

Although sexual reproduction produces more genetic variation, it does have some disadvantages. Sexual reproduction takes time and energy. Organisms have to grow and develop until they are mature enough to produce sex cells. Then the organisms have to form sex cells—either eggs or sperm. Before they can reproduce, organisms usually have to find mates. Searching for a mate can take a long time and requires energy. The search for a mate might also expose individuals to predators, diseases, or harsh environmental conditions. In addition, sexual reproduction is limited by certain factors. For example, fertilization cannot take place during pregnancy, which can last as long as two years in some mammals.

✔ **Reading Check** What are the disadvantages of sexual reproduction?

Lesson 1 Review

Visual Summary

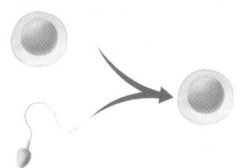

Fertilization occurs when an egg cell and a sperm cell join together.

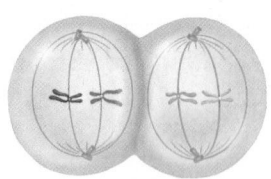

Organisms produce sex cells through meiosis.

Sexual reproduction results in genetic variation among individuals.

FOLDABLES

Use your lesson Foldable to review the lesson. Save your Foldable for the project at the end of the chapter.

What do you think NOW?

You first read the statements below at the beginning of the chapter.

1. Humans produce two types of cells: body cells and sex cells.

2. Environmental factors can cause variation among individuals.

3. Two parents always produce the best offspring.

Did you change your mind about whether you agree or disagree with the statements? Rewrite any false statements to make them true.

Use Vocabulary

1 **Use the terms** *egg*, *sperm*, and *zygote* in a sentence.

2 **Distinguish** between haploid and diploid.

3 **Define** *homologous chromosomes* in your own words.

Understand Key Concepts

4 **Define** sexual reproduction.

5 **Draw and label** the phases of meiosis.

6 Homologous chromosomes separate during which phase of meiosis?
   A. anaphase I   C. metaphase I
   B. anaphase II   D. metaphase II

Interpret Graphics

7 **Organize** Copy and fill in the graphic organizer below to sequence the phases of meiosis I and meiosis II.

Meiosis I   □▷□▷□▷□

Meiosis II □▷□▷□▷□

Critical Thinking

8 **Analyze** Why is the result of the stage of meiosis shown below an advantage for organisms that reproduce sexually?

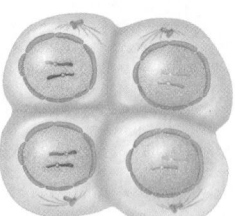

Math Skills ×÷  Review
——— Math Practice ———

9 If 15 cells undergo meiosis, how many daughter cells would be produced?

10 If each daughter cell from question 9 undergoes meiosis, how many total daughter cells will there be?

AMERICAN
MUSEUM OF
NATURAL
HISTORY

The Spider
Mating Dance

Meet Norman Platnick, a scientist studying spiders.

Norman Platnick is fascinated by all spider species—from the dwarf tarantula-like spiders of Panama to the blind spiders of New Zealand. These are just two of the over 1,400 species he's discovered worldwide.

How does Platnick identify new species? One way is the pedipalps. Every spider has two pedipalps, but they vary in shape and size among the over 40,000 species. Pedipalps look like legs but function more like antennae and mouthparts. Male spiders use their pedipalps to aid in reproduction.

Getting Ready When a male spider is ready to mate, he places a drop of sperm onto a sheet of silk he constructs. Then he dips his pedipalps into the drop to draw up the sperm.

Finding a Mate The male finds a female of the same species by touch or by sensing certain chemicals she releases.

Courting and Mating Males of some species court a female with a special dance. For other species, a male might present a female with a gift, such as a fly wrapped in silk. During mating, the male uses his pedipalps to transfer sperm to the female.

What happens to the male after mating? That depends on the species. Some are eaten by the female, while others move on to find new mates.

▲ Spiders reproduce sexually, so each offspring has a unique combination of genes from its parents. Over many generations, this genetic variation has led to the incredible diversity of spiders in the world today.

◀ Norman Platnick is an arachnologist (uh rak NAH luh just) at the American Museum of Natural History. Arachnologists are scientists who study spiders.

It's Your Turn

RESEARCH Select a species of spider and research its mating rituals. What does a male do to court a female? What is the role of the female? What happens to the spiderlings after they hatch? Use images to illustrate a report on your research.

Lesson 2

Reading Guide

Key Concepts 🔑
ESSENTIAL QUESTIONS

- What is asexual reproduction, and why is it beneficial?

- How do the types of asexual reproduction differ?

Vocabulary

asexual reproduction p. 129

fission p. 130

budding p. 131

regeneration p. 132

vegetative reproduction p. 133

cloning p. 134

g Multilingual eGlossary

Asexual Reproduction

Inquiry Plants on Plants?

Look closely at the edges of this plant's leaves. Tiny plants are growing there. This type of plant can reproduce without meiosis and fertilization.

How do yeast reproduce?

Some organisms can produce offspring without meiosis or fertilization. You can observe this process when you add sugar and warm water to dried yeast.

1. Read and complete a lab safety form.

2. Pour 125 mL of water into a **beaker.** The water should be at a temperature of 34°C.

3. Add 5 g of **sugar** and 5 g of **yeast** to the water. Stir slightly. Record your observations after 5 minutes in your Science Journal.

4. Using a **dropper,** put a drop of the yeast solution on a **microscope slide.** Place a **coverslip** over the drop.

5. View the yeast solution under a **microscope.** Draw what you see in your Science Journal.

Think About This

1. What evidence did you observe that yeast reproduce?

2. 🔑 **Key Concept** How do you think this process differs from sexual reproduction?

What is asexual reproduction?

Lunch is over and you are in a rush to get to class. You wrap up your half-eaten sandwich and toss it into your locker. A week goes by before you spot the sandwich in the corner of your locker. The surface of the bread is now covered with fuzzy mold—not very appetizing. How did that happen?

The mold on the sandwich is a type of fungus (FUN gus). A fungus releases enzymes that break down organic matter, such as food. It has structures that penetrate and anchor to food, much like roots anchor plants to soil. A fungus can multiply quickly in part because generally a fungus can reproduce either sexually or asexually. Recall that sexual reproduction involves two parent organisms and the processes of meiosis and fertilization. Offspring inherit half their DNA from each parent, resulting in genetic variation among the offspring.

In **asexual reproduction,** *one parent organism produces offspring without meiosis and fertilization.* Because the offspring inherit all their DNA from one parent, they are genetically identical to each other and to their parent.

🔑 **Key Concept Check** Describe asexual reproduction in your own words.

FOLDABLES

Fold a sheet of paper into a six-celled chart. Label the front "Asexual Reproduction," and label the chart inside as shown. Use it to compare types of asexual reproduction.

Fission	Mitotic cell division	Budding
Animal regeneration	Vegetative reproduction	Cloning

Types of Asexual Reproduction

There are many different types of organisms that reproduce by asexual reproduction. In addition to fungi, bacteria, protists, plants, and animals can reproduce asexually. In this lesson, you will learn how organisms reproduce asexually.

Fission

Recall that prokaryotes have a simpler cell structure than eukaryotes. A prokaryote's DNA is not contained in a nucleus. For this reason, mitosis does not occur and cell division in a prokaryote is a simpler process than in a eukaryote. *Cell division in prokaryotes that forms two genetically identical cells is known as* **fission.**

Fission begins when a prokaryote's DNA molecule is copied. Each copy attaches to the cell membrane. Then the cell begins to grow longer, pulling the two copies of DNA apart. At the same time, the cell membrane begins to pinch inward along the middle of the cell. Finally the cell splits and forms two new identical offspring. The original cell no longer exists.

As shown in **Figure 6,** *E. coli,* a common bacterium, divides through fission. Some bacteria can divide every 20 minutes. At that rate, 512 bacteria can be produced from one original bacterium in about three hours.

 Reading Check What advantage might asexual reproduction by fission have over sexual reproduction?

Fission 🔑

Figure 6 Bacteria can divide very rapidly through fission.

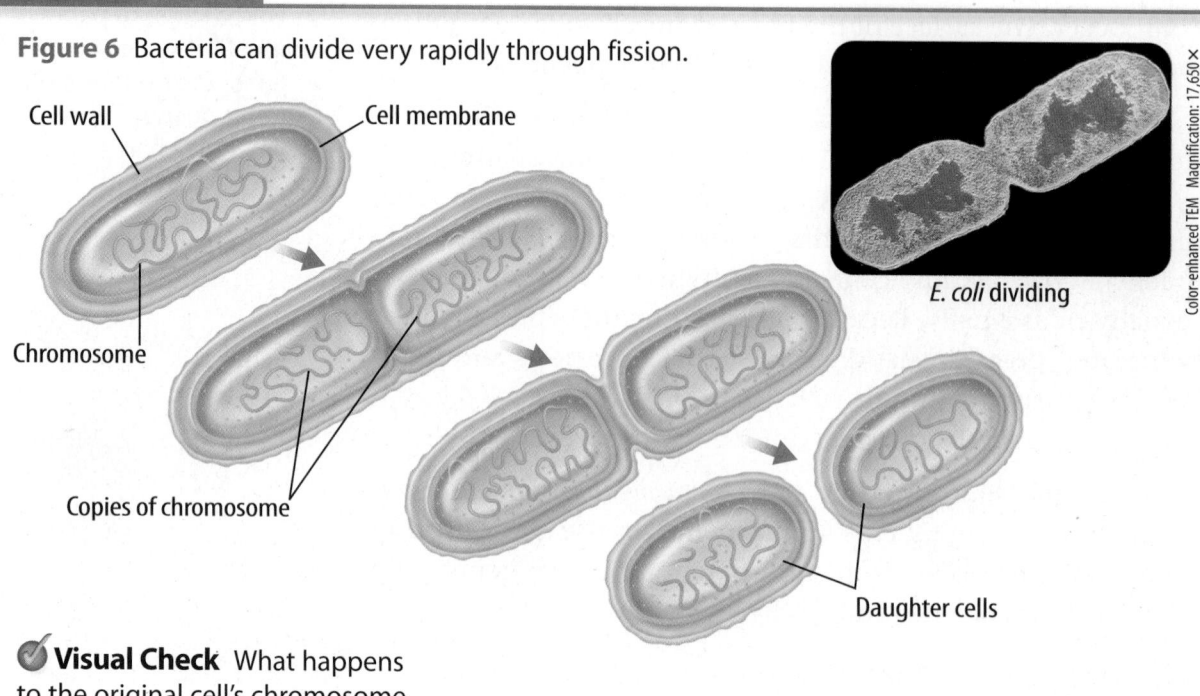

Cell wall

Cell membrane

Chromosome

Copies of chromosome

Daughter cells

E. coli dividing

Color-enhanced TEM Magnification: 17,650×

☑ **Visual Check** What happens to the original cell's chromosome during fission?

Mitotic Cell Division

Many unicellular eukaryotes reproduce by mitotic cell division. In this type of asexual reproduction, an organism forms two offspring through mitosis and cell division. In **Figure 7,** an amoeba's nucleus has divided by mitosis. Next, the cytoplasm and its contents divide through cytokinesis and two new amoebas form.

Budding

In **budding,** *a new organism grows by mitosis and cell division on the body of its parent.* The bud, or offspring, is genetically identical to its parent. When the bud becomes large enough, it can break from the parent and live on its own. In some cases, an offspring remains attached to its parent and starts to form a colony. **Figure 8** shows a hydra in the process of budding. The hydra is an example of a multicellular organism that can reproduce asexually. Unicellular eukaryotes, such as yeast, can also reproduce through budding, as you saw in the Launch Lab.

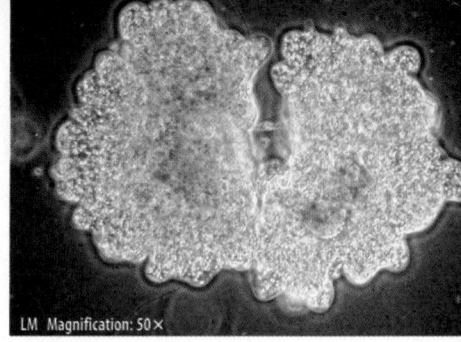
LM Magnification: 50×

▲ **Figure 7** During mitotic cell division, an amoeba divides its chromosomes and cell contents evenly between the daughter cells.

Budding 🔑

Figure 8 The hydra bud has the same genetic makeup as its parent.

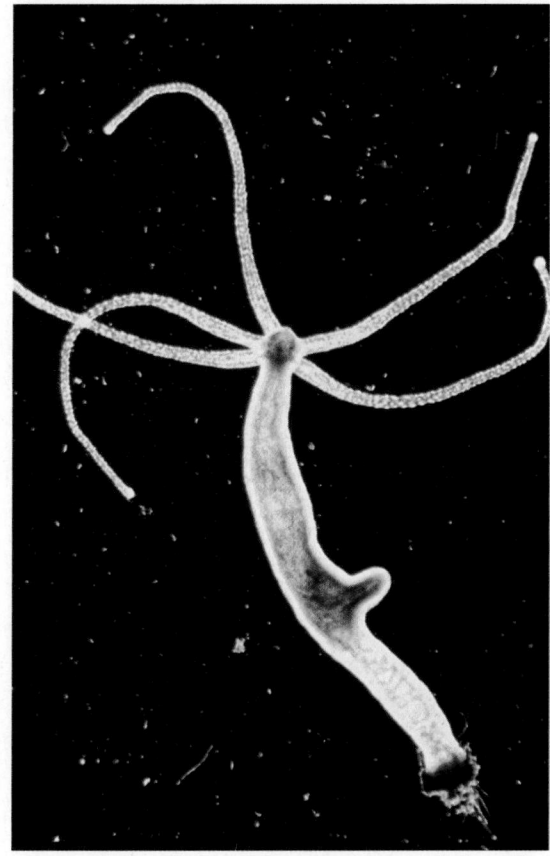

Bud forms.

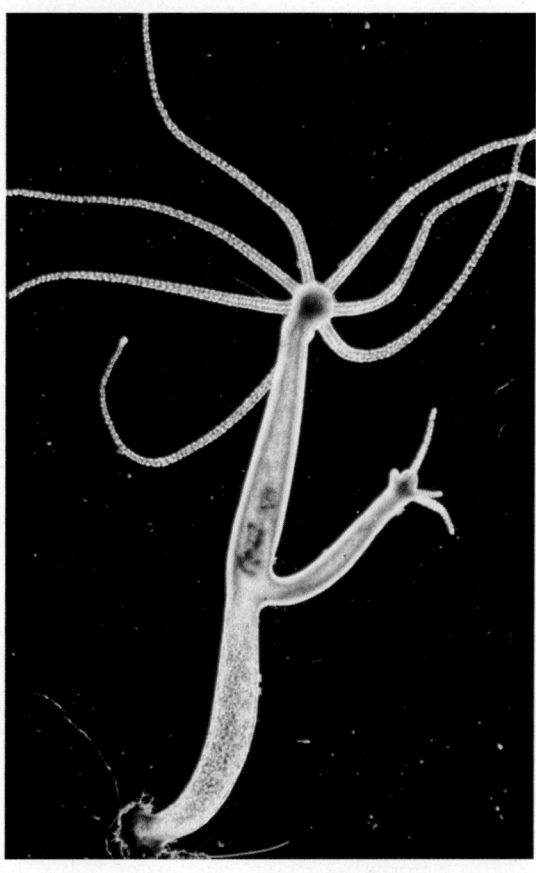

Bud develops a mouth and tentacles.

Figure 9 A planarian can reproduce through regeneration.

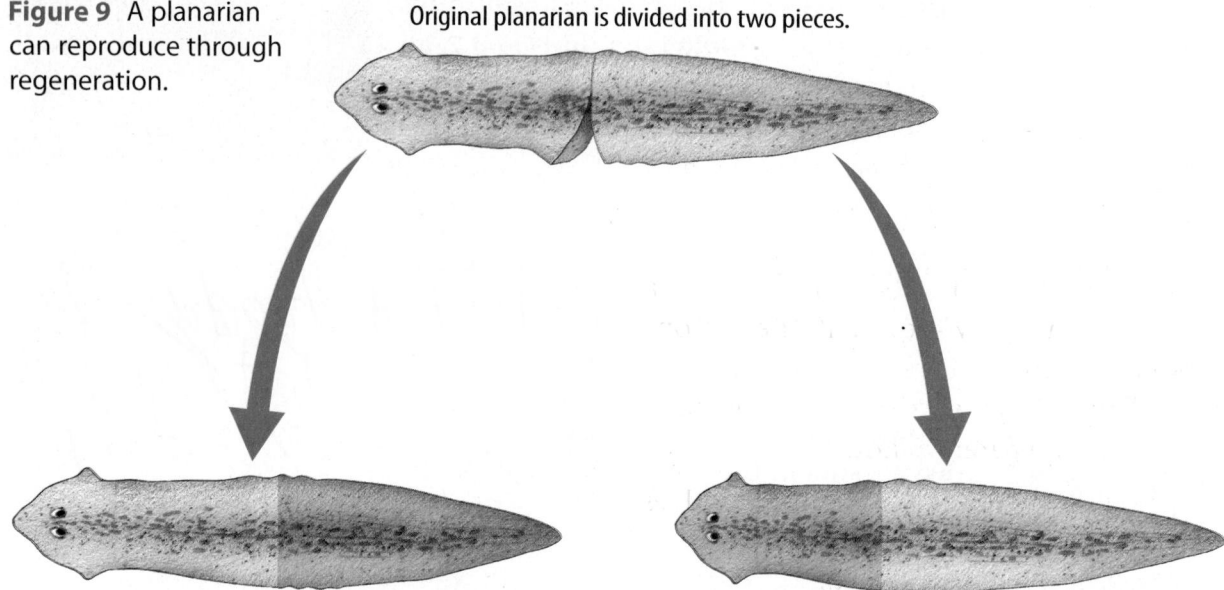

Original planarian is divided into two pieces.

The head end regenerates a new tail.

The tail end regenerates a new head.

Animal Regeneration

Another type of asexual reproduction, **regeneration**, *occurs when an offspring grows from a piece of its parent.* The ability to regenerate a new organism varies greatly among animals.

Producing New Organisms Some sea stars have five arms. If separated from the parent sea star, each arm has the potential to grow into a new organism. To regenerate a new sea star, the arm must contain a part of the central disk of the parent. If conditions are right, one five-armed sea star can produce as many as five new organisms.

Sea urchins, sea cucumbers, sponges, and planarians, such as the one shown in **Figure 9,** can also reproduce through regeneration. Notice that each piece of the original planarian becomes a new organism. As with all types of asexual reproduction, the offspring is genetically identical to the parent.

Reading Check What is true of all cases of asexual reproduction?

Producing New Parts When you hear the term *regeneration,* you might think about a salamander regrowing a lost tail or leg. Regeneration of damaged or lost body parts is common in many animals. Newts, tadpoles, crabs, hydra, and zebra fish are all able to regenerate body parts. Even humans are able to regenerate some damaged body parts, such as the skin and the liver. This type of regeneration, however, is not considered asexual reproduction. It does not produce a new organism.

ACADEMIC VOCABULARY

potential
(noun) possibility

Vegetative Reproduction

Plants can also reproduce asexually in a process similar to regeneration. **Vegetative reproduction** *is a form of asexual reproduction in which offspring grow from a part of a parent plant.* For example, the strawberry plants shown in **Figure 10** send out long horizontal stems called stolons. Wherever a stolon touches the ground, it can produce roots. Once the stolons have grown roots, a new plant can grow—even if the stolons have broken off the parent plant. Each new plant grown from a stolon is genetically identical to the parent plant.

Vegetative reproduction usually involves structures such as the roots, the stems, and the leaves of plants. In addition to strawberries, many other plants can reproduce by this method, including raspberries, potatoes, and geraniums.

Figure 10 The smaller plants were grown from stolons produced by the parent plant.

✓ **Visual Check** Which plants in the figure are the parent plants?

Inquiry) MiniLab

15 minutes

What parts of plants can grow?

You probably know that plants can grow from seeds. But you might be surprised to learn that other parts of plants can grow and produce a new plant.

1 Carefully examine the photos of vegetative reproduction.

2 Create a data chart in your Science Journal to record your observations. Identify which part of the plant (leaf, stem, etc.) would be used to grow a new plant.

Analyze and Conclude

1. **Explain** How is the vegetative reproduction you observed a kind of asexual reproduction?

2. **Infer** how farmers or gardeners might use vegetative reproduction.

3. 🔑 **Key Concept** Describe a method you might use to produce a new plant using vegetative reproduction.

Cloning

Fission, budding, and regeneration are all types of asexual reproduction that can produce genetically identical offspring in nature. In the past, the term *cloning* described any process that produced genetically identical offspring. Today, however, the word usually refers to a technique developed by scientists and performed in laboratories. **Cloning** *is a type of asexual reproduction performed in a laboratory that produces identical individuals from a cell or from a cluster of cells taken from a multicellular organism.* Farmers and scientists often use cloning to make copies of organisms or cells that have desirable traits, such as large flowers.

Plant Cloning Some plants can be cloned using a method called tissue culture, as shown in **Figure 11.** Tissue culture enables plant growers and scientists to make many copies of a plant with desirable traits, such as sweet fruit. Also, a greater number of plants can be produced more quickly than by vegetative reproduction.

Tissue culture also enables plant growers to reproduce plants that might have become infected with a disease. To clone such a plant, a scientist can use cells from a part of a plant where they are rapidly undergoing mitosis and cell division. This part of a plant is called a meristem. Cells in meristems are disease-free. Therefore, if a plant becomes infected with a disease, it can be cloned using meristem cells.

SCIENCE USE v. COMMON USE

culture
Science Use the process of growing living tissue in a laboratory

Common Use the social customs of a group of people

Figure 11 New carrot plants can be produced from cells of a carrot root using tissue culture techniques.

Plant Cloning

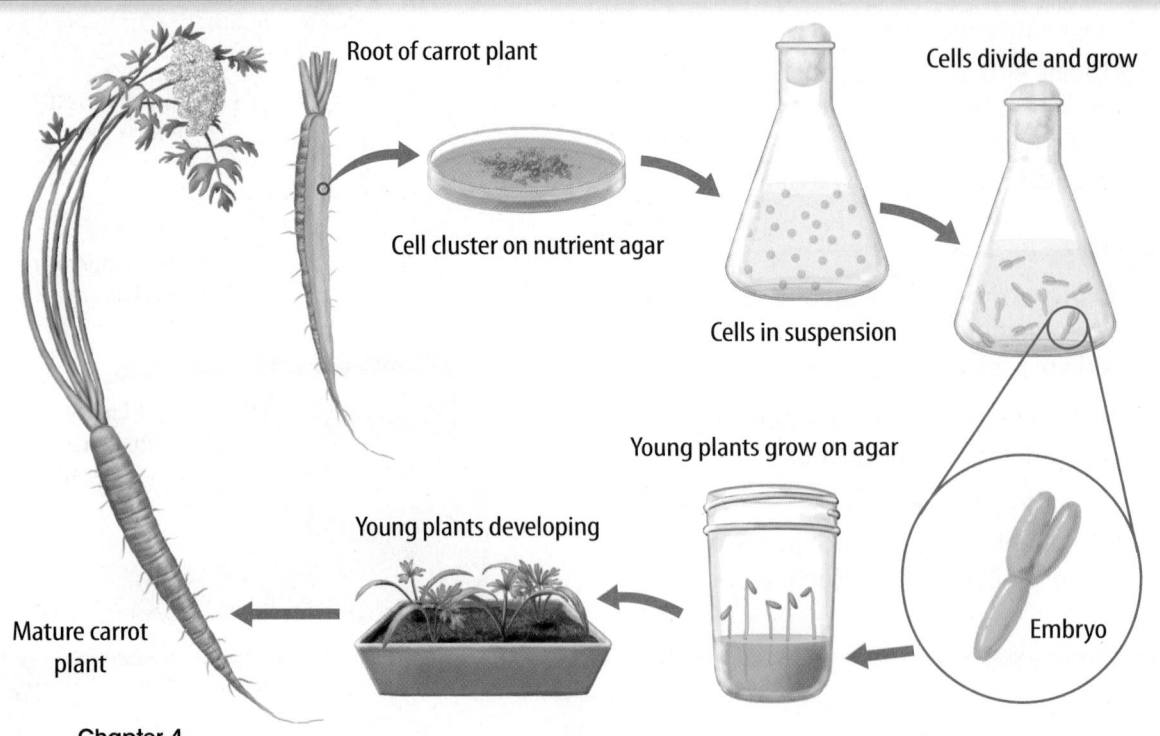

Root of carrot plant

Cell cluster on nutrient agar

Cells in suspension

Cells divide and grow

Young plants grow on agar

Young plants developing

Embryo

Mature carrot plant

Animal Cloning In addition to cloning plants, scientists have been able to clone many animals. Because all of a clone's chromosomes come from one parent (the donor of the nucleus), the clone is a genetic copy of its parent. The first mammal cloned was a sheep named Dolly. **Figure 12** illustrates how this was done.

Scientists are currently working to save some endangered species from extinction by cloning. Although cloning is an exciting advancement in science, some people are concerned about the high cost and the ethics of this technique. Ethical issues include the possibility of human cloning. You might be asked to consider issues like this during your lifetime.

Key Concept Check Compare and contrast the different types of asexual reproduction.

Figure 12 Scientists used two different sheep to produce the cloned sheep known as Dolly.

Animal Cloning

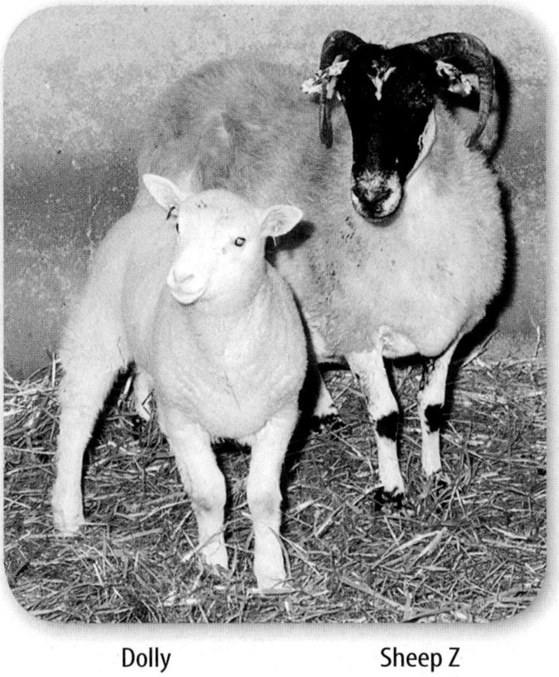
Dolly
Sheep Z

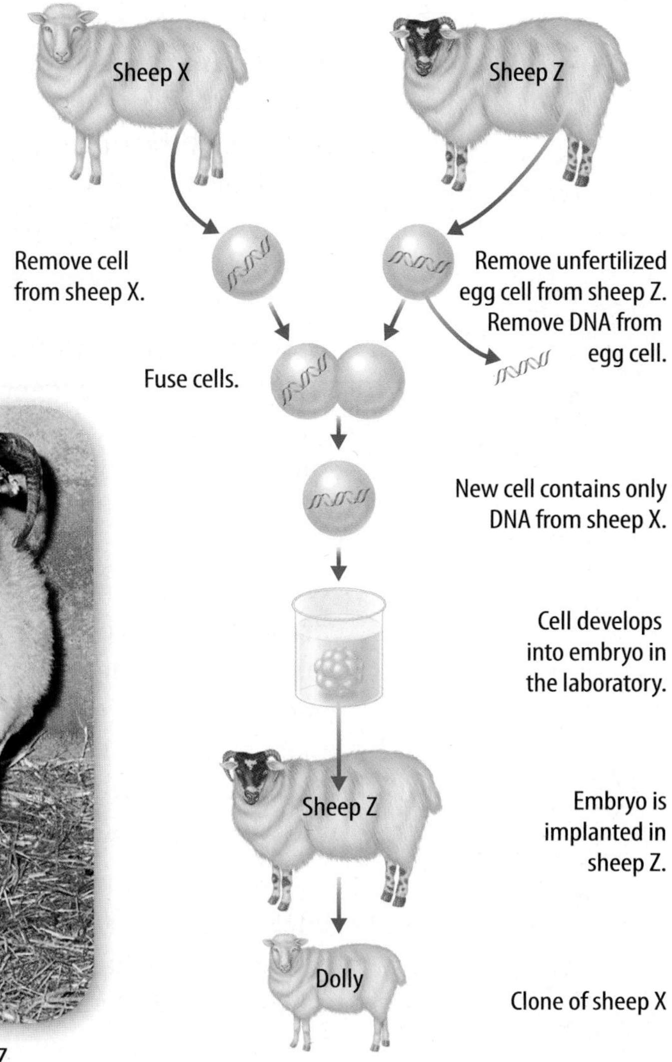
Sheep X
Sheep Z
Remove cell from sheep X.
Remove unfertilized egg cell from sheep Z. Remove DNA from egg cell.
Fuse cells.
New cell contains only DNA from sheep X.
Cell develops into embryo in the laboratory.
Sheep Z
Embryo is implanted in sheep Z.
Dolly
Clone of sheep X

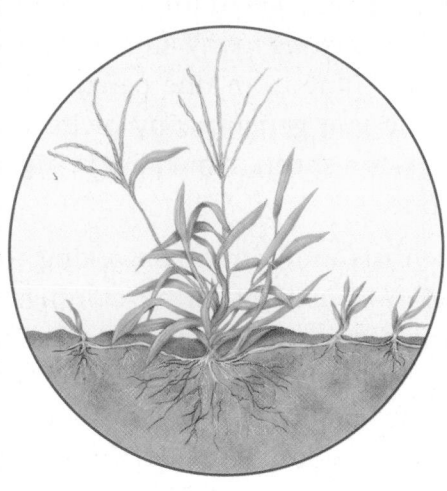

Figure 13 Crabgrass can spread quickly because it reproduces asexually.

Advantages of Asexual Reproduction

What are the advantages to organisms of reproducing asexually? Asexual reproduction enables organisms to reproduce without a mate. Recall that searching for a mate takes time and energy. Asexual reproduction also enables some organisms to rapidly produce a large number of offspring. For example, the crabgrass shown in **Figure 13** reproduces asexually by underground stems called stolons. This enables one plant to spread and colonize an area in a short period of time.

 Key Concept Check How is asexual reproduction beneficial?

Disadvantages of Asexual Reproduction

Although asexual reproduction usually enables organisms to reproduce quickly, it does have some disadvantages. Asexual reproduction produces offspring that are genetically identical to their parent. This results in little genetic variation within a population. Why is genetic variation important? Recall from Lesson 1 that genetic variation can give organisms a better chance of surviving if the environment changes. Think of the crabgrass. Imagine that all the crabgrass plants in a lawn are genetically identical to their parent plant. If a certain weed killer can kill the parent plant, then it can kill all the crabgrass plants in the lawn. This might be good for your lawn, but it is a disadvantage for the crabgrass.

Another disadvantage of asexual reproduction involves genetic changes, called mutations, that can occur. If an organism has a harmful mutation in its cells, the mutation will be passed to asexually reproduced offspring. This could affect the offspring's ability to survive.

Lesson 2 Review

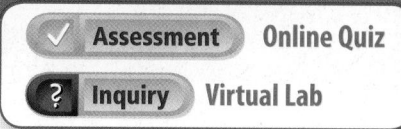

Visual Summary

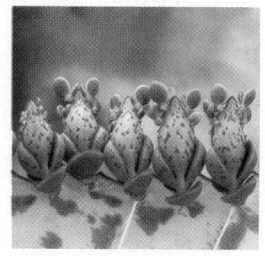

In asexual reproduction, offspring are produced without meiosis and fertilization.

Cloning is one type of asexual reproduction.

Asexual reproduction enables organisms to reproduce quickly.

FOLDABLES

Use your lesson Foldable to review the lesson. Save your Foldable for the project at the end of the chapter.

What do you think NOW?

You first read the statements below at the beginning of the chapter.

4. Cloning produces identical individuals from one cell.

5. All organisms have two parents.

6. Asexual reproduction occurs only in microorganisms.

Did you change your mind about whether you agree or disagree with the statements? Rewrite any false statements to make them true.

Use Vocabulary

1 In _____ _____, only one parent organism produces offspring.

2 **Define** the term *cloning* in your own words.

3 **Use the term** *regeneration* in a sentence.

Understand Key Concepts 🔑

4 **State** two reasons why asexual reproduction is beneficial.

5 Which is an example of asexual reproduction by regeneration?
- **A.** cloning sheep
- **B.** lizard regrowing a tail
- **C.** sea star arm producing a new organism
- **D.** strawberry plant producing stolons

6 **Construct** a chart that includes an example of each type of asexual reproduction.

Interpret Graphics

7 **Examine** the diagram below and write a short paragraph describing the process of tissue culture.

8 **Organize** Copy and fill in the graphic organizer below to list the different types of asexual reproduction that occur in multicellular organisms.

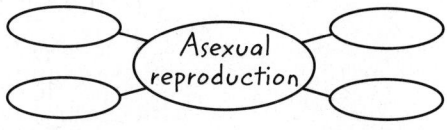

Asexual reproduction

Critical Thinking

9 **Justify** the use of cloning to save endangered animals.

Mitosis and Meiosis

Materials

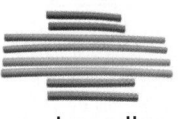

pool noodles

Safety

During cellular reproduction, many changes occur in the nucleus of cells involving the chromosomes. You could think about these changes as a set of choreographed moves like you would see in a dance. In this lab you will act out the moves that chromosomes make during mitosis and meiosis in order to understand the steps that occur when cells reproduce.

Ask a Question

How do chromosomes change and move during mitosis and meiosis?

Make Observations

1. Read and complete a lab safety form.

2. Form a cell nucleus with four chromosomes represented by students holding four different colors of pool noodles. Other students play the part of the nuclear membrane and form a circle around the chromosomes.

3. The chromosomes duplicate during interphase. Each chromosome is copied, creating a chromosome with two sister chromatids.

4. Perform mitosis.

   a. During prophase, the nuclear membrane breaks apart, and the nucleolus disappears.

   b. In metaphase, duplicated chromosomes align in the middle of the cell.

   c. The sister chromatids separate in anaphase.

   d. In telophase, the nuclear membrane reforms around two daughter cells.

5. Repeat steps 2 and 3. Perform meiosis.

   a. In prophase I, the nuclear membrane breaks apart, the nucleolus disappears, and homologous chromosomes pair up.

   b. In metaphase I, homologous chromosomes line up along the center of the cell.

   c. During anaphase I, the pairs of homologous chromosomes separate.

   d. In telophase I, the nuclear membrane reforms.

   e. Each daughter cell now performs meiosis II independently. In prophase II, the nuclear membrane breaks down, and the nucleolus disappears.

   f. During metaphase II, duplicated chromosomes align in the middle of the cell.

g. Sister chromatids separate in anaphase II.

h. In telophase II, the nuclear membrane reforms.

Form a Hypothesis

6 Use your observations to form a hypothesis about the results of an error in meiosis. For example, you might explain the results of an error during anaphase I.

Test your Hypothesis

7 Perform meiosis, incorporating the error you chose in step 6.

8 Compare the outcome to your hypothesis. Does your data support your hypothesis? If not, revise your hypothesis and repeat steps 6–8.

Analyze and Conclude

9 **Compare and Contrast** How are mitosis and meiosis I similar? How are they different?

10 **The Big Idea** What is the difference between the chromosomes in cells at the beginning and the end of mitosis? At the beginning and end of meiosis?

11 **Critique** How did performing cellular replications using pool noodles help you understand mitosis and meiosis?

Communicate Your Results

Create a chart of the changes and movements of chromosomes in each of the steps in meiosis and mitosis. Include colored drawings of chromosomes and remember to draw the cell membranes.

 **Extension**

Investigate some abnormalities that occur when mistakes are made during mitosis or meiosis. Draw a chart of the steps of reproduction showing how the mistake is made. Write a short description of the problems that result from the mistake.

5

Lab Tips

☑ Figure out where the boundaries of your cell are before you start.

☑ Review the phases of mitosis and meiosis before beginning to act out how the chromosomes move during each process.

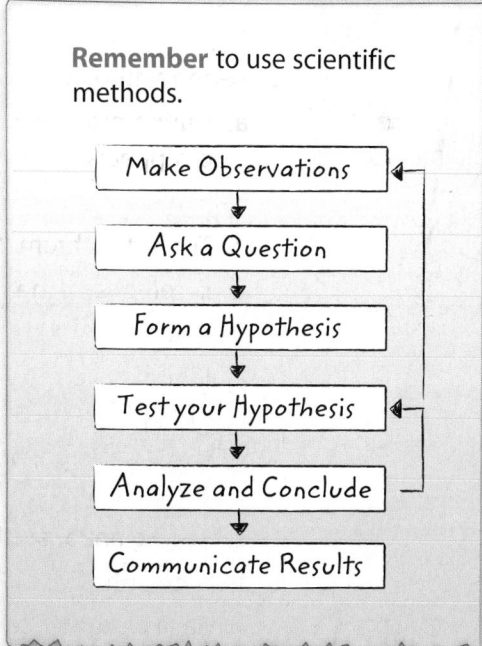

Remember to use scientific methods.

Make Observations

↓

Ask a Question

↓

Form a Hypothesis

↓

Test your Hypothesis

↓

Analyze and Conclude

↓

Communicate Results

Chapter 4 Study Guide

THE BIG IDEA Reproduction ensures the survival of species.

Key Concepts Summary

Lesson 1: Sexual Reproduction and Meiosis

- **Sexual reproduction** is the production of an offspring from the joining of a **sperm** and an **egg.**
- Division of the nucleus and cytokinesis happens twice in **meiosis.** Meiosis I separates homologous chromosomes. Meiosis II separates sister chromatids.
- Meiosis maintains the chromosome number of a species from one generation to the next.

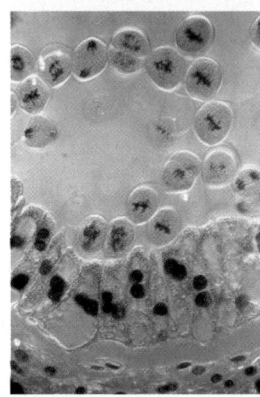

Lesson 2: Asexual Reproduction

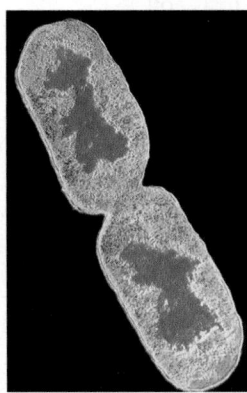

- **Asexual reproduction** is the production of offspring by one parent, which results in offspring that are genetically identical to the parent.
- Types of asexual reproduction include **fission,** mitotic cell division, **budding, regeneration, vegetative reproduction,** and **cloning.**
- Asexual reproduction can produce a large number of offspring in a short amount of time.

Vocabulary

sexual reproduction p. 117

egg p. 117

sperm p. 117

fertilization p. 117

zygote p. 117

diploid p. 118

homologous chromosomes p. 118

haploid p. 119

meiosis p. 119

asexual reproduction p. 129

fission p. 130

budding p. 131

regeneration p. 132

vegetative reproduction p. 133

cloning p. 134

FOLDABLES® Chapter Project

Assemble your lesson Foldables as shown to make a Chapter Project. Use the project to review what you have learned in this chapter.

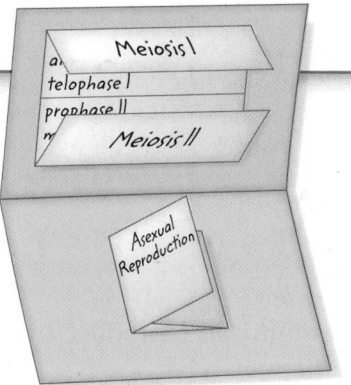

Use Vocabulary

1. Define meiosis in your own words.

2. Distinguish between an egg and a zygote.

3. Use the vocabulary words *haploid* and *diploid* in a sentence.

4. Cell division in prokaryotes is called _____.

5. Define the term *vegetative reproduction* in your own words.

6. Distinguish between regeneration and budding.

7. A type of reproduction in which the genetic materials from two different cells combine, producing an offspring, is called _____ _____.

Link Vocabulary and Key Concepts

Concepts in Motion Interactive Concept Map

Copy this concept map, and then use vocabulary terms from the previous page to complete the concept map.

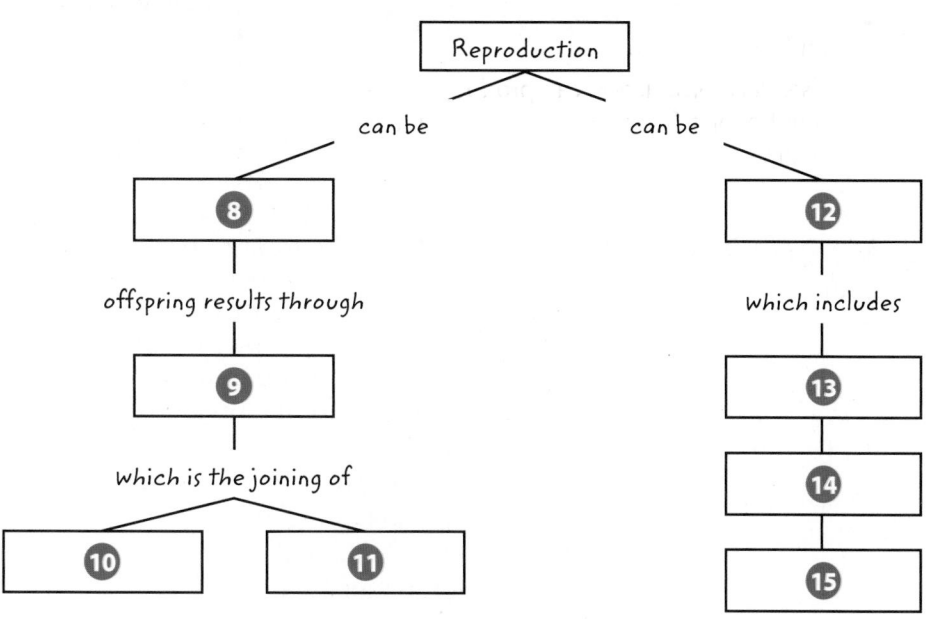

Understand Key Concepts

1 Which is an advantage of sexual reproduction?

A. Offspring are identical to the parents.
B. Offspring with genetic variation are produced.
C. Organisms don't have to search for a mate.
D. Reproduction is rapid.

2 Which describes cells that have only one copy of each chromosome?

A. diploid
B. haploid
C. homologous
D. zygote

Use the figure below to answer questions 3 and 4.

3 Which phase of meiosis I is shown in the diagram?

A. anaphase I
B. metaphase I
C. prophase I
D. telophase I

4 Which phase of meiosis I comes after the phase in the diagram?

A. anaphase I
B. metaphase I
C. prophase I
D. telophase I

5 Tissue culture is an example of which type of reproduction?

A. budding
B. cloning
C. fission
D. regeneration

6 Which type of asexual reproduction is shown in the figure below?

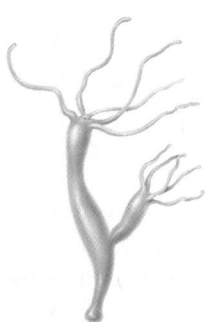

A. budding
B. cloning
C. fission
D. regeneration

7 A bacterium can reproduce by which method?

A. budding
B. cloning
C. fission
D. regeneration

8 Which statement best describes why genetic variation is beneficial to populations of organisms?

A. Individuals look different from one another.
B. Only one parent is needed to produce offspring.
C. Populations of the organism increase more rapidly.
D. Species can better survive environmental changes.

9 In which phase of meiosis II do sister chromatids line up along the center of the cell?

A. anaphase II
B. metaphase II
C. prophase II
D. telophase II

Critical Thinking

10 **Contrast** haploid cells and diploid cells.

11 **Model** Make a model of homologous chromosomes using materials of your choice.

12 **Form a hypothesis** about the effect of a mistake in separating homologous chromosomes during meiosis.

13 **Analyze** Crabgrass reproduces asexually by vegetative reproduction. Use the figure below to explain why this form of reproduction is an advantage for the crabgrass.

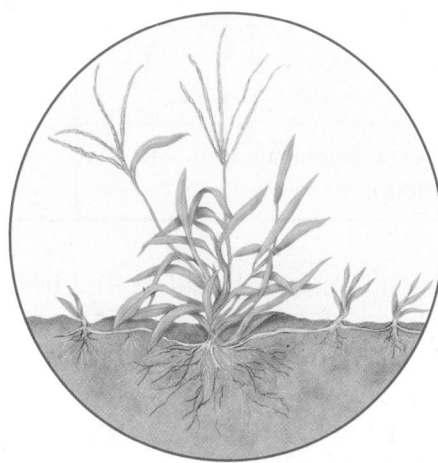

14 **Compare** budding and cloning.

15 **Create** a table showing the advantages and disadvantages of asexual reproduction.

16 **Compare and contrast** sexual reproduction and asexual reproduction.

Writing in Science

17 **Create** a plot for a short story that describes an environmental change and the importance of genetic variation in helping a species survive that change. Include characters, a setting, a climax, and an ending for your plot.

REVIEW THE BIG IDEA

18 Think of all the advantages of sexual and asexual reproduction. Use these ideas to summarize why organisms reproduce.

19 The baby penguin below has a mother and a father. Do all living things have two parents? Explain.

Math Skills ÷×+−

 **Review**
— Math Practice —

Use Proportions

20 During mitosis, the original cell produces two daughter cells. How many daughter cells will be produced if 250 mouse cells undergo mitosis?

21 During meiosis, the original reproductive cell produces four daughter cells. How many daughter cells will be produced if 250 mouse reproductive cells undergo meiosis?

22 Two reproductive cells undergo meiosis. Each daughter cell also undergoes meiosis. How many cells are produced when the daughter cells divide?

Record your answers on the answer sheet provided by your teacher or on a sheet of paper.

Multiple Choice

1 How do sea stars reproduce?

  A cloning

  B fission

  C animal regeneration

  D vegetative reproduction

Use the diagram below to answer questions 2 and 3.

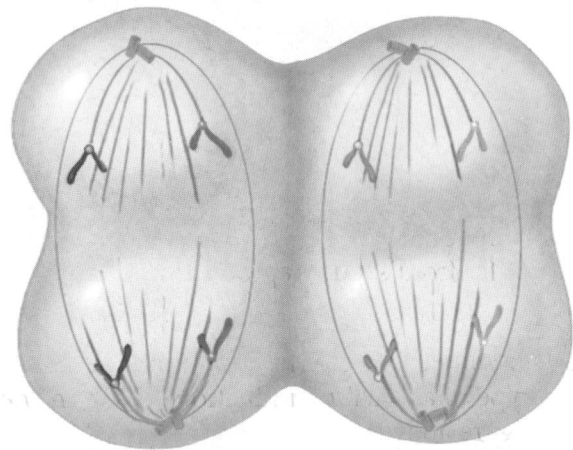

2 What stage of meiosis does the drawing illustrate?

  A anaphase I

  B anaphase II

  C prophase I

  D prophase II

3 Which stage takes place *before* the one in the diagram above?

  A metaphase I

  B metaphase II

  C telophase I

  D telophase II

4 What type of asexual reproduction includes stolons?

  A budding

  B cloning

  C animal regeneration

  D vegetative reproduction

Use the table below to answer question 5.

Comparison of Types of Cell Division		
Characteristic	**Meiosis**	**Mitosis**
Number of divisions of nucleus	2	A
Number of daughter cells produced	B	2

5 Which numbers should be inserted for A and B in the chart?

  A A=1 and B=2

  B A=1 and B=4

  C A=2 and B=2

  D A=2 and B=4

6 Which results in genetic variation?

  A cloning

  B fission

  C sexual reproduction

  D vegetative reproduction

7 Which is NOT true of homologous chromosomes?

  A The are identical.

  B They are in pairs.

  C They have genes for the same traits.

  D They have genes that are in the same order.

Use the figure below to answer question 8.

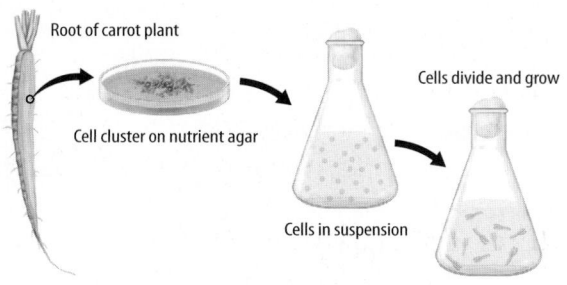

Root of carrot plant

Cell cluster on nutrient agar

Cells in suspension

Cells divide and grow

8 The figure illustrates the first four steps of which reproductive process?

   A animal cloning

   B regeneration

   C tissue culture

   D vegetative reproduction

9 If 12 reproductive cells undergo meiosis, how many daughter cells will result?

   A 12

   B 24

   C 48

   D 60

10 Which is NOT true of asexual reproduction?

   A Many offspring can be produced rapidly.

   B Offspring are different from the parents.

   C Offspring have no genetic variation.

   D Organisms can reproduce without a mate.

Constructed Response

Use the figure below to answer questions 11 and 12.

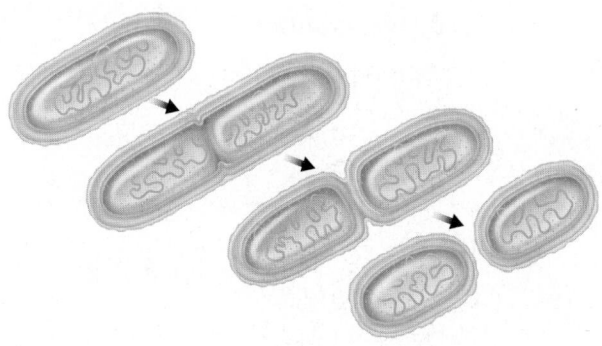

11 Identify the type of asexual reproduction shown in the figure above. How does it differ from sexual reproduction?

12 Compare and contrast budding with the type of asexual reproduction shown in the figure above.

13 What are some differences between the results of selectively breeding plants and cloning them?

14 Use the example of the wild mustard plant to describe the benefits of selective breeding.

15 What are the advantages and disadvantages of cloning animals?

NEED EXTRA HELP?															
If You Missed Question...	1	2	3	4	5	6	7	8	9	10	11	12	13	14	15
Go to Lesson...	2	1	1	2	1	1	1	2	1	2	1,2	2	1,2	1	2

Genetics

THE BIG IDEA

How are traits passed from parents to offspring?

Inquiry **How did this happen?**

The color of this fawn is caused by a genetic trait called albinism. Albinism is the absence of body pigment. Notice that the fawn's mother has brown fur, the normal fur color of an adult whitetail deer.

- Why do you think the fawn looks so different from its mother?
- What do you think determines the color of the offspring?
- How do you think traits are passed from generation to generation?

Get Ready to Read

What do you think?

Before you read, decide if you agree or disagree with each of these statements. As you read this chapter, see if you change your mind about any of the statements.

1 Like mixing paints, parents' traits always blend in their offspring.

2 If you look more like your mother than you look like your father, then you received more traits from your mother.

3 All inherited traits follow Mendel's patterns of inheritance.

4 Scientists have tools to predict the form of a trait an offspring might inherit.

5 New DNA is copied from existing DNA.

6 A change in the sequence of an organism's DNA always changes the organism's traits.

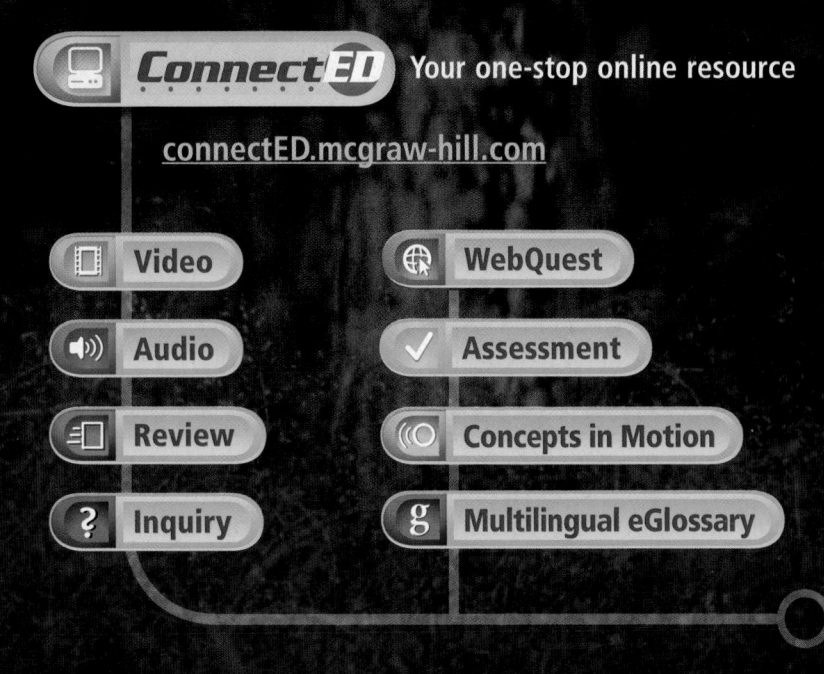

ConnectED Your one-stop online resource

connectED.mcgraw-hill.com

- Video
- Audio
- Review
- Inquiry
- WebQuest
- Assessment
- Concepts in Motion
- Multilingual eGlossary

Reading Guide

Key Concepts 🔑
ESSENTIAL QUESTIONS

- Why did Mendel perform cross-pollination experiments?

- What did Mendel conclude about inherited traits?

- How do dominant and recessive factors interact?

Vocabulary

heredity p. 149
genetics p. 149
dominant trait p. 155
recessive trait p. 155

g **Multilingual eGlossary**

□ **Video** **BrainPOP®**

Mendel and His Peas

Inquiry Same Species?

Have you ever seen a black ladybug? It is less common than the orange variety you might know, but both are the same species of beetle. So why do they look different? Believe it or not, a study of pea plants helped scientists explain these differences.

What makes you unique?

Traits such as eye color have many different types, but some traits have only two types. By a show of hands, determine how many students in your class have each type of trait below.

Student Traits		
Trait	Type 1	Type 2
Earlobes	Unattached	Attached
Thumbs	Curved	Straight
Interlacing fingers	Left thumb over right thumb	Right thumb over left thumb

Think About This

1. Why might some students have types of traits that others do not have?

2. If a person has dimples, do you think his or her offspring will have dimples? Explain.

3. **Key Concept** What do you think determines the types of traits you inherit?

Early Ideas About Heredity

Have you ever mixed two paint colors to make a new color? Long ago, people thought an organism's characteristics, or traits, mixed like colors of paint because offspring resembled both parents. This is known as blending inheritance.

Today, scientists know that **heredity** (huh REH duh tee)—*the passing of traits from parents to offspring*—is more complex. For example, you might have blue eyes but both of your parents have brown eyes. How does this happen? More than 150 years ago, Gregor Mendel, an Austrian monk, performed experiments that helped answer these questions and disprove the idea of blending inheritance. Because of his research, Mendel is known as the father of **genetics** (juh NEH tihks)—*the study of how traits are passed from parents to offspring.*

WORD ORIGIN

genetics
from Greek *genesis*, means "origin"

Mendel's Experimental Methods

During the 1850s, Mendel studied genetics by doing controlled breeding experiments with pea plants. Pea plants were ideal for genetic studies because

- they reproduce quickly. This enabled Mendel to grow many plants and collect a lot of data.

- they have easily observed traits, such as flower color and pea shape. This enabled Mendel to observe whether or not a trait was passed from one generation to the next.

- Mendel could control which pairs of plants reproduced. This enabled him to determine which traits came from which plant pairs.

Pollination in Pea Plants

To observe how a trait was inherited, Mendel controlled which plants pollinated other plants. Pollination occurs when pollen lands on the pistil of a flower. **Sperm** cells from the pollen then can fertilize **egg** cells in the pistil. Pollination in pea plants can occur in two ways. Self-pollination occurs when pollen from one plant lands on the pistil of a flower on the same plant, as shown in **Figure 1.** Cross-pollination occurs when pollen from one plant reaches the pistil of a flower on a different plant. Cross-pollination occurs naturally when wind, water, or animals such as bees carry pollen from one flower to another. Mendel allowed one group of flowers to self-pollinate. With another group, he cross-pollinated the plants himself.

Self-Pollination

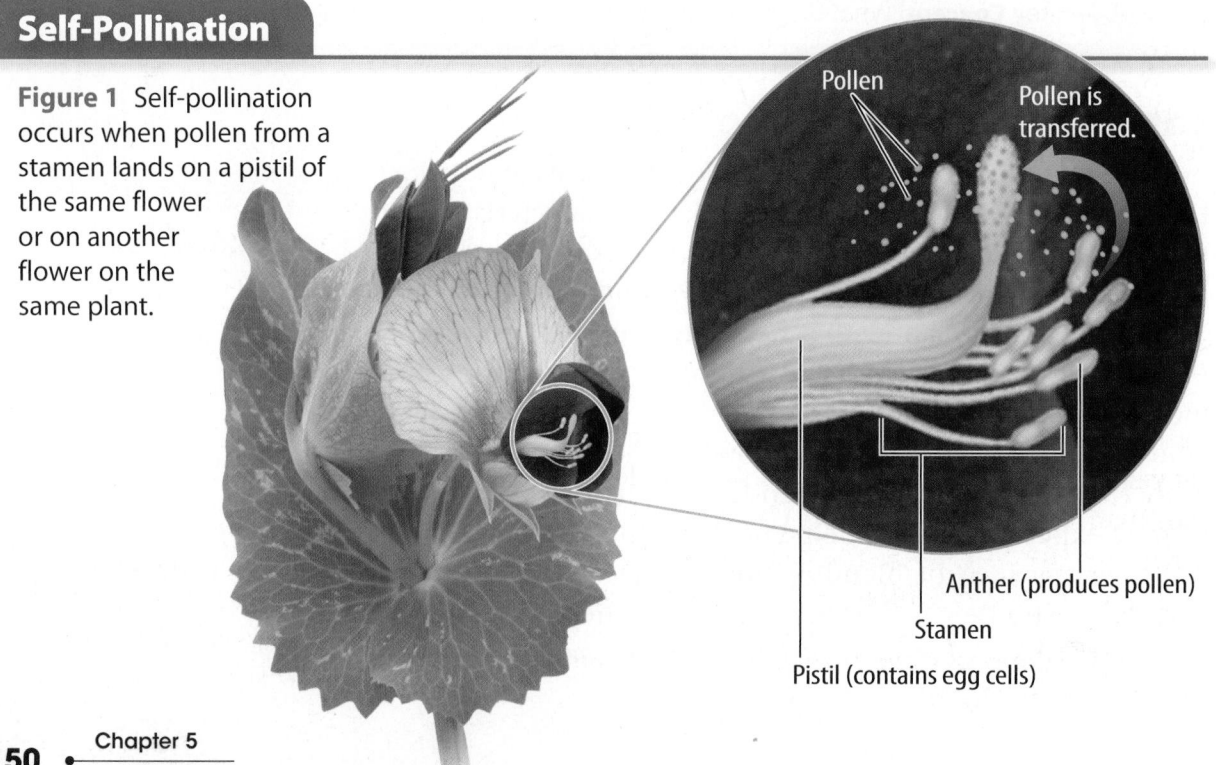

Figure 1 Self-pollination occurs when pollen from a stamen lands on a pistil of the same flower or on another flower on the same plant.

Pollen

Pollen is transferred.

Anther (produces pollen)

Stamen

Pistil (contains egg cells)

True-Breeding Plants

Mendel began his experiments with plants that were true-breeding for the trait he would test. When a true-breeding plant self-pollinates, it always produces offspring with traits that match the parent. For example, when a true-breeding pea plant with wrinkled seeds self-pollinates, it produces only plants with wrinkled seeds. In fact, plants with wrinkled seeds appear generation after generation.

Mendel's Cross-Pollination

By cross-pollinating plants himself, Mendel was able to select which plants pollinated other plants. **Figure 2** shows an example of a manual cross between a plant with white flowers and one with purple flowers.

Figure 2 Mendel removed the stamens of one flower and pollinated that flower with pollen from a flower of a different plant. In this way, he controlled pollination.

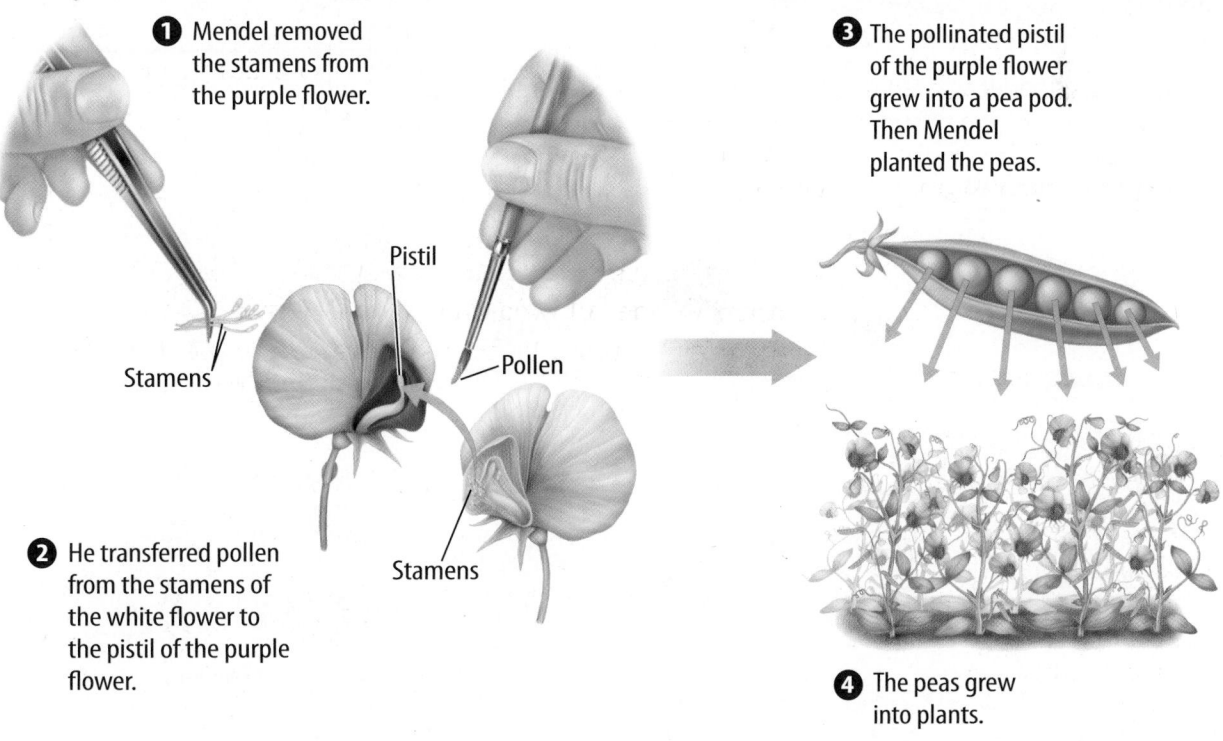

Cross-Pollination

❶ Mendel removed the stamens from the purple flower.

Stamens

Pistil

❷ He transferred pollen from the stamens of the white flower to the pistil of the purple flower.

Pollen

Stamens

❸ The pollinated pistil of the purple flower grew into a pea pod. Then Mendel planted the peas.

❹ The peas grew into plants.

Mendel cross-pollinated hundreds of plants for each set of traits, such as flower color—purple or white; seed color—green or yellow; and seed shape—round or wrinkled. With each cross-pollination, Mendel recorded the traits that appeared in the offspring. By testing such a large number of plants, Mendel was able to predict which crosses would produce which traits.

 Key Concept Check Why did Mendel perform cross-pollination experiments?

Mendel's Results

Once Mendel had enough true-breeding plants for a trait that he wanted to test, he cross-pollinated selected plants. His results are shown in **Figure 3.**

First-Generation Crosses

A cross between true-breeding plants with purple flowers produced plants with only purple flowers. A cross between true-breeding plants with white flowers produced plants with only white flowers. But something unexpected happened when Mendel crossed true-breeding plants with purple flowers and true-breeding plants with white flowers—all the offspring had purple flowers.

New Questions Raised

The results of the crosses between true-breeding plants with purple flowers and true-breeding plants with white flowers led to more questions for Mendel. Why did all the offspring always have purple flowers? Why were there no white flowers? Why didn't the cross produce offspring with pink flowers—a combination of the white and purple flower colors? Mendel carried out more experiments with pea plants to answer these questions.

✓ **Reading Check** Predict the offspring of a cross between two true-breeding pea plants with smooth seeds.

First-Generation Crosses

Figure 3 Mendel crossed three combinations of true-breeding plants and recorded the flower colors of the offspring.

Purple × Purple

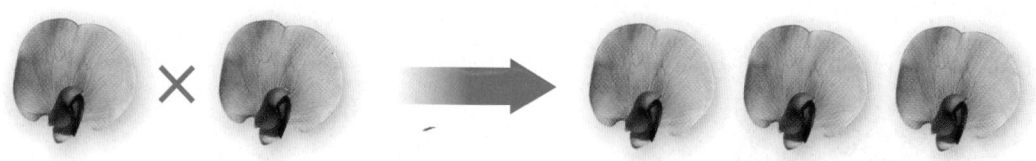

All purple flowers (true-breeding)

White × White

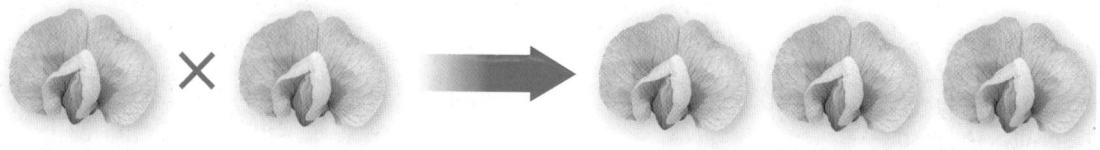

All white flowers (true-breeding)

Purple (true-breeding) × White (true-breeding)

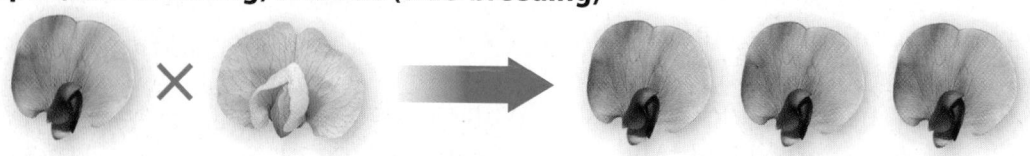

All purple flowers (hybrids)

✓ **Visual Check** Suppose you cross hundreds of true-breeding plants with purple flowers with hundreds of true-breeding plants with white flowers. Based on the results of this cross in the figure above, would any offspring produce white flowers? Explain.

Second-Generation (Hybrid) Crosses

The first-generation purple-flowering plants are called **hybrid** plants. This means they came from true-breeding parent plants with different forms of the same trait. Mendel wondered what would happen if he cross-pollinated two purple-flowering hybrid plants.

As shown in **Figure 4,** some of the offspring had white flowers, even though both parents had purple flowers. The results were similar each time Mendel cross-pollinated two hybrid plants. The trait that had disappeared in the first generation always reappeared in the second generation.

The same result happened when Mendel cross-pollinated pea plants for other traits. For example, he found that cross-pollinating a true-breeding yellow-seeded pea plant with a true-breeding green-seeded pea plant always produced yellow-seeded hybrids. A second-generation cross of two yellow-seeded hybrids always yielded plants with yellow seeds and plants with green seeds.

Reading Check What is a hybrid plant?

SCIENCE USE V. COMMON USE

hybrid

Science Use the offspring of two animals or plants with different forms of the same trait

Common Use having two types of components that perform the same function, such as a vehicle powered by both a gas engine and an electric motor

Second-Generation (Hybrid) Crosses

Purple (hybrid) × Purple (hybrid)

Purple and white offspring

Purple (hybrid) × Purple (hybrid)

Purple and white offspring

Figure 4 Mendel cross-pollinated first-generation hybrid offspring to produce second-generation offspring. In each case, the trait that had disappeared from the first generation reappeared in the second generation.

Table 1 When Mendel crossed two hybrids for a given trait, the trait that had disappeared then reappeared in a ratio of about 3:1.

Table 1   Results of Hybrid Crosses

Characteristic	Trait and Number of Offspring	Trait and Number of Offspring	Ratio
Flower color	Purple 705	White 224	3.15:1
Flower position	Axial (Side of stem) 651	Terminal (End of stem) 207	3.14:1
Seed color	Yellow 6,022	Green 2,001	3.01:1
Seed shape	Round 5,474	Wrinkled 1,850	2.96:1
Pod shape	Inflated (Smooth) 882	Constricted (Bumpy) 299	2.95:1
Pod color	Green 428	Yellow 152	2.82:1
Stem length	Long 787	Short 277	2.84:1

Math Skills

Use Ratios

A ratio is a comparison of two numbers or quantities by division. For example, the ratio comparing 6,022 yellow seeds to 2,001 green seeds can be written as follows:

6,022 to 2,001 or

6,022 : 2,001 or

$\frac{6,022}{2,001}$

To simplify the ratio, divide the first number by the second number.

$\frac{6,022}{2,001} = \frac{3}{1}$ or 3:1

Practice

There are 14 girls and 7 boys in a science class. Simplify the ratio.

▣ **Review**

- Math Practice
- Personal Tutor

More Hybrid Crosses

Mendel counted and recorded the traits of offspring from many experiments in which he cross-pollinated hybrid plants. Data from these experiments are shown in **Table 1.** He analyzed these data and noticed patterns. For example, from the data of crosses between hybrid plants with purple flowers, he found that the ratio of purple flowers to white flowers was about 3:1. This means purple-flowering pea plants grew from this cross three times more often than white-flowering pea plants grew from the cross. He calculated similar ratios for all seven traits he tested.

Mendel's Conclusions

After analyzing the results of his experiments, Mendel concluded that two genetic factors control each inherited trait. He also proposed that when organisms reproduce, each reproductive cell—sperm or egg—contributes one factor for each trait.

 Key Concept Check What did Mendel conclude about inherited traits?

Dominant and Recessive Traits

Recall that when Mendel cross-pollinated a true-breeding plant with purple flowers and a true-breeding plant with white flowers, the hybrid offspring had only purple flowers. Mendel hypothesized that the hybrid offspring had one genetic factor for purple flowers and one genetic factor for white flowers. But why were there no white flowers?

Mendel also hypothesized that the purple factor is the only factor seen or expressed because it blocks the white factor. *A genetic factor that blocks another genetic factor is called a* **dominant** (DAH muh nunt) **trait.** A dominant trait, such as purple pea flowers, is observed when offspring have either one or two dominant factors. *A genetic factor that is blocked by the presence of a dominant factor is called a* **recessive** (rih SE sihv) **trait.** A recessive trait, such as white pea flowers, is observed only when two recessive genetic factors are present in offspring.

From Parents to Second Generation

For the second generation, Mendel cross-pollinated two hybrids with purple flowers. About 75 percent of the second-generation plants had purple flowers. These plants had at least one dominant factor. Twenty-five percent of the second-generation plants had white flowers. These plants had the same two recessive factors.

 Key Concept Check How do dominant and recessive factors interact?

FOLDABLES

Make a vertical two-tab book and label it as shown. Use it to organize your notes on dominant and recessive factors.

Traits

| Dominant factors | Recessive factors |

---

inquiry MiniLab 20 minutes

Which is the dominant trait?

Imagine you are Gregor Mendel's lab assistant studying pea plant heredity. Mendel has crossed true-breeding plants with axial flowers and true-breeding plants with terminal flowers. Use the data below to determine which trait is dominant.

Pea Flower Location Results		
Generation	Axial (Number of Offspring)	Terminal (Number of Offspring)
First	794 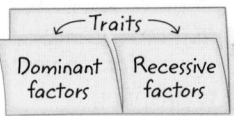	0
Second	651	207

Analyze and Conclude

1. **Determine** which trait is dominant and which trait is recessive. Support your answer with data.

2. **Key Concept** Analyze the first-generation data. What evidence do you have that one trait is dominant over the other?

Visual Summary

Genetics is the study of how traits are passed from parents to offspring.

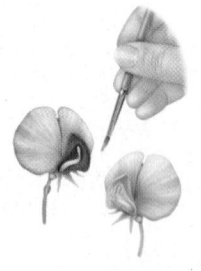

Mendel studied genetics by doing cross-breeding experiments with pea plants.

Purple
705

White
224

Mendel's experiments with pea plants showed that some traits are dominant and others are recessive.

FOLDABLES

Use your lesson Foldable to review the lesson. Save your Foldable for the project at the end of the chapter.

What do you think NOW?

You first read the statements below at the beginning of the chapter.

1. Like mixing paints, parents' traits always blend in their offspring.

2. If you look more like your mother than you look like your father, then you received more traits from your mother.

Did you change your mind about whether you agree or disagree with the statements? Rewrite any false statements to make them true.

Use Vocabulary

1 **Distinguish** between heredity and genetics.

2 **Define** the terms *dominant* and *recessive*.

3 **Use the term** *recessive* in a complete sentence.

Understand Key Concepts

4 A recessive trait is observed when an organism has _____ recessive genetic factor(s).

A. 0   C. 2
B. 1   D. 3

5 **Summarize** Mendel's conclusions about how traits pass from parents to offspring.

6 **Describe** how Mendel cross-pollinated pea plants.

Interpret Graphics

7 **Suppose** the two true-breeding plants shown below were crossed.

What color would the flowers of the offspring be? Explain.

Critical Thinking

8 **Design an experiment** to test for true-breeding plants.

9 **Examine** how Mendel's conclusions disprove blending inheritance.

Math Skills

Review
Math Practice

10 A cross between two pink camellia plants produced the following offspring: 7 plants with red flowers, 7 with white flowers, and 14 with pink flowers. What is the ratio of red to white to pink?

Pioneering
the Science of Genetics

One man's curiosity leads to a branch of science.

Gregor Mendel—monk, scientist, gardener, and beekeeper—was a keen observer of the world around him. Curious about how traits pass from one generation to the next, he grew and tested almost 30,000 pea plants. Today, Mendel is called the father of genetics. After Mendel published his findings, however, his "laws of heredity" were overlooked for several decades.

In 1900, three European scientists, working independently of one another, rediscovered Mendel's work and replicated his results. Then, other biologists quickly began to recognize the importance of Mendel's work.

Gregor Mendel ▶

1902: American physician Walter Sutton demonstrates that Mendel's laws of inheritance can be applied to chromosomes. He concludes that chromosomes contain a cell's hereditary material on genes.

1906: William Bateson, a United Kingdom scientist, coins the term *genetics*. He uses it to describe the study of inheritance and the science of biological inheritance.

1952: American geneticists Martha Chase and Alfred Hershey prove that DNA transmits inherited traits from one generation to the next.

1953: Francis Crick and James Watson determine the structure of the DNA molecule. Their work begins the field of molecular biology and leads to important scientific and medical research in genetics.

2003: The National Human Genome Research Institute (NHGRI) completes mapping and sequencing human DNA. Researchers and scientists are now trying to discover the genetic basis for human health and disease.

It's Your Turn

RESEARCH What are some genetic diseases? Report on how genome-based research might help cure these diseases in the future.

Lesson 2

Understanding Inheritance

Reading Guide

Key Concepts 🔑
ESSENTIAL QUESTIONS

- What determines the expression of traits?
- How can inheritance be modeled?
- How do some patterns of inheritance differ from Mendel's model?

Vocabulary

gene p. 160
allele p. 160
phenotype p. 160
genotype p. 160
homozygous p. 161
heterozygous p. 161
Punnett square p. 162
incomplete dominance p. 164
codominance p. 164
polygenic inheritance p. 165

g Multilingual eGlossary

▯ Video BrainPOP®

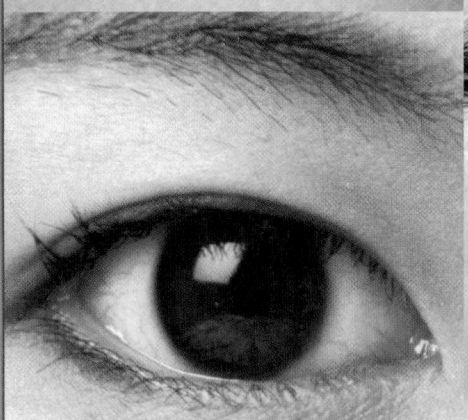

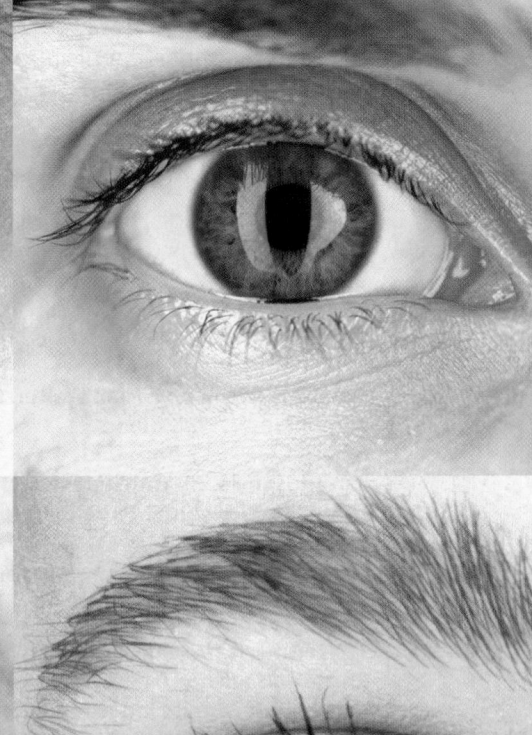

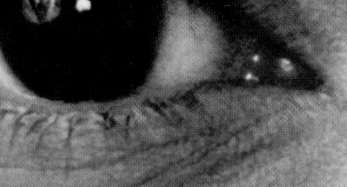

Inquiry Make the Connection

Physical traits, such as those shown in these eyes, can vary widely from person to person. Take a closer look at the eyes on this page. What traits can you identify among them? How do they differ?

What is the span of your hand?

Mendel discovered some traits have a simple pattern of inheritance—dominant or recessive. However, some traits, such as eye color, have more variation. Is human hand span a Mendelian trait?

1. Read and complete a lab safety form.

2. Use a **metric ruler** to measure the distance (in cm) between the tips of your thumb and little finger with your hand stretched out.

3. As a class, record everyone's name and hand span in a data table.

Think About This

1. What range of hand span measurements did you observe?

2. 🔑 **Key Concept** Do you think hand span is a simple Mendelian trait like pea plant flower color?

What controls traits?

Mendel concluded that two factors—one from each parent—control each trait. Mendel hypothesized that one factor came from the egg cell and one factor came from the sperm cell. What are these factors? How are they passed from parents to offspring?

Chromosomes

When other scientists studied the parts of a cell and combined Mendel's work with their work, these factors were more clearly understood. Scientists discovered that inside each cell is a nucleus that contains thread-like structures called chromosomes. Over time, scientists learned that chromosomes contain genetic information that controls traits. We now know that Mendel's "factors" are part of chromosomes and that each cell in offspring contains chromosomes from both parents. As shown in **Figure 5,** these chromosomes exist as pairs—one chromosome from each parent.

Figure 5 Humans have 23 pairs of chromosomes. Each pair has one chromosome from the father and one chromosome from the mother.

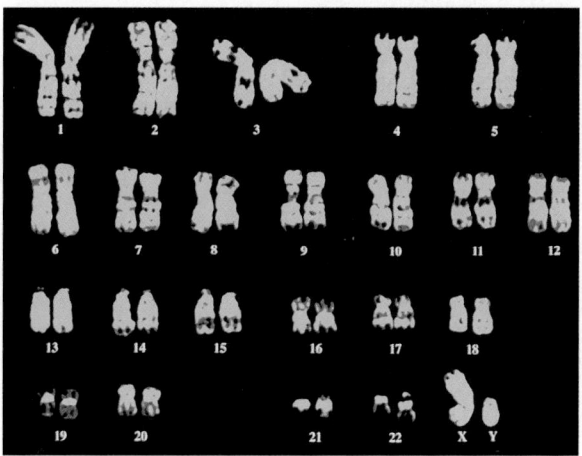

Genes and Alleles

Scientists have discovered that each chromosome can have information about hundreds or even thousands of traits. *A* **gene** *(JEEN) is a section on a chromosome that has genetic information for one trait.* For example, a gene of a pea plant might have information about flower color. Recall that an offspring inherits two genes (factors) for each trait—one from each parent. The genes can be the same or different, such as purple or white for pea flower color. *The different forms of a gene are called* **alleles** *(uh LEELs).* Pea plants can have two purple alleles, two white alleles, or one of each allele. In **Figure 6,** the chromosome pair has information about three traits—flower position, pod shape, and stem length.

Reading Check How many alleles controlled flower color in Mendel's experiments?

Genotype and Phenotype

Look again at the photo at the beginning of this lesson. What human trait can you observe? You might observe that eye color can be shades of blue or brown. *Geneticists call how a trait appears, or is expressed, the trait's* **phenotype** *(FEE nuh tipe).* What other phenotypes can you observe in the photo?

Mendel concluded that two alleles control the expression or phenotype of each trait. *The two alleles that control the phenotype of a trait are called the trait's* **genotype** *(JEE nuh tipe).* Although you cannot see an organism's genotype, you can make inferences about a genotype based on its phenotype. For example, you have already learned that a pea plant with white flowers has two recessive alleles for that trait. These two alleles are its genotype. The white flower is its phenotype.

WORD ORIGIN · · · · · · · · · ·

phenotype
from Greek *phainein,* means "to show"

Figure 6 The alleles for flower position are the same on both chromosomes. However, the chromosome pair has different alleles for pod shape and stem length.

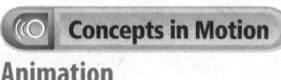

Concepts in Motion

Animation

Chromosome Pair

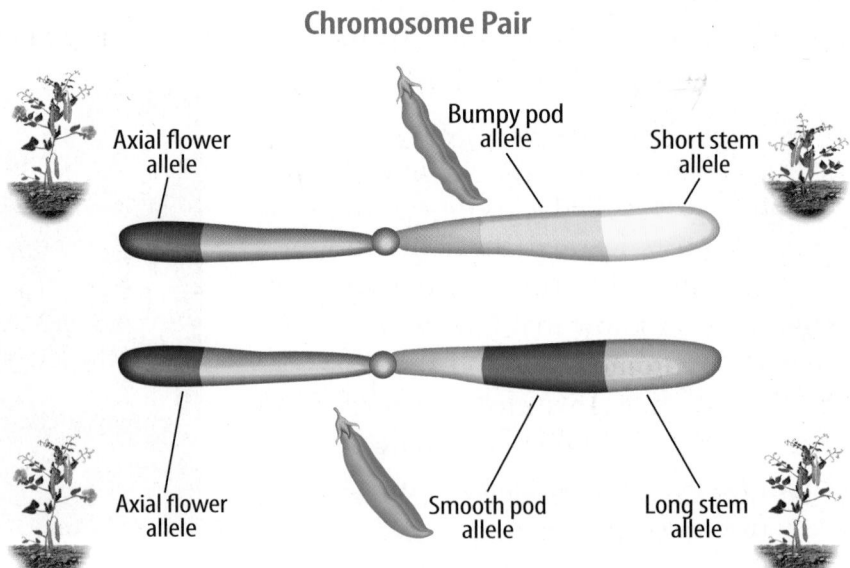

Axial flower allele

Bumpy pod allele

Short stem allele

Axial flower allele

Smooth pod allele

Long stem allele

Symbols for Genotypes Scientists use symbols to represent the alleles in a genotype. In genetics, uppercase letters represent dominant alleles and lowercase letters represent recessive alleles. **Table 2** shows the possible genotypes for both round and wrinkled seed phenotypes. Notice that the dominant allele, if present, is written first.

Table 2 Phenotype and Genotype	
Phenotypes (observed traits)	**Genotypes (alleles of a gene)**
Round	Homozygous dominant *(RR)*
	Heterozygous *(Rr)*
Wrinkled	Homozygous recessive *(rr)*

A round seed can have two genotypes—*RR* and *Rr*. Both genotypes have a round phenotype. Why does *Rr* result in round seeds? This is because the round allele *(R)* is dominant to the wrinkled allele *(r)*.

A wrinkled seed has the recessive genotype, *rr*. The wrinkled-seed phenotype is possible only when the same two recessive alleles *(rr)* are present in the genotype.

Homozygous and Heterozygous *When the two alleles of a gene are the same, its genotype is* **homozygous** *(hoh muh ZI gus). Both RR and rr are homozygous genotypes, as shown in* **Table 2.**

If the two alleles of a gene are different, its genotype is **heterozygous** *(he tuh roh ZI gus). Rr is a heterozygous genotype.*

 Key Concept Check How do alleles determine the expression of traits?

Inquiry MiniLab **20 minutes**

Can you infer genotype?

If you know that dragon traits are either dominant or recessive, can you use phenotypes of traits to infer genotypes?

1. Select one **trait card** from each of three **dragon trait bags.** Record the data in your Science Journal.

2. Draw a picture of your dragon based on your data. Label each trait *homozygous* or *heterozygous.*

3. Copy the table below in your Science Journal. For each of the three traits, place one check mark in the appropriate box.

Dragon Traits		
Phenotype	**Homozygous**	**Heterozygous**
Green body		
Red body		
Four legs		
Two legs		
Long wings		
Short wings		

4. Combine your data with your classmates' data.

Analyze and Conclude

1. **Describe** any patterns you find in the data table.

2. **Determine** which trait is dominant and which is recessive. Support your reasoning.

3. **Determine** the genotype(s) for each phenotype. Support your reasoning.

4. 🔑 **Key Concept** Decide whether you could have correctly determined your dragon's genotype without data from other dragons. Support your reasoning.

Figure 7 A Punnett square can be used to predict the possible genotypes of the offspring. Offspring from a cross between two heterozygous parents can have one of three genotypes.

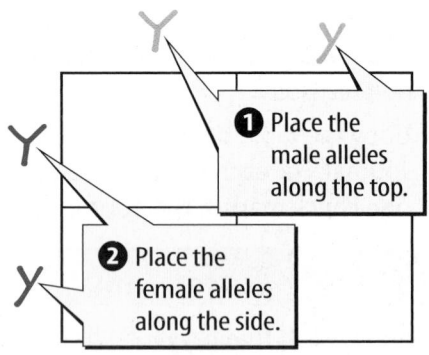

❶ Place the male alleles along the top.

❷ Place the female alleles along the side.

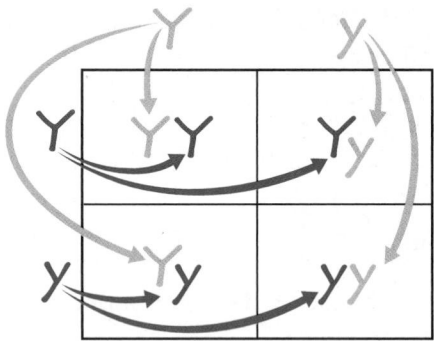

❸ Copy female alleles across each row. Copy male alleles down each column. Always list the dominant trait first.

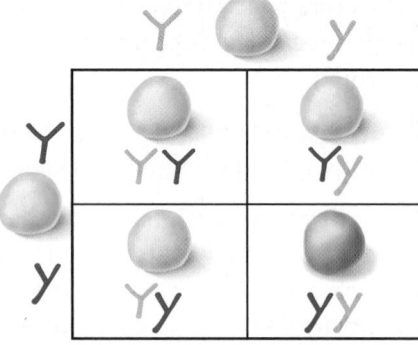

✔ **Visual Check** What phenotypes are possible for pea offspring of this cross?

Modeling Inheritance

Have you ever flipped a coin and guessed heads or tails? Because a coin has two sides, there are only two possible outcomes—heads or tails. You have a 50 percent chance of getting heads and a 50 percent chance of getting tails. The chance of getting an outcome can be represented by a ratio. The ratio of heads to tails is 50:50 or 1:1.

 **Reading Check** What does a ratio of 2:1 mean?

Plant breeders and animal breeders use a method for predicting how often traits will appear in offspring that does not require performing the crosses thousands of times. Two models—a Punnett square and a pedigree—can be used to predict and identify traits among genetically related individuals.

Punnett Squares

If the genotypes of the parents are known, then the different genotypes and phenotypes of the offspring can be predicted. *A* **Punnett square** *is a model used to predict possible genotypes and phenotypes of offspring.* Follow the steps in **Figure 7** to learn how to make a Punnett square.

Analyzing a Punnett Square

Figure 7 shows an example of a cross between two pea plants that are heterozygous for pea seed color—*Yy* and *Yy*. Yellow is the dominant allele—*Y*. Green is the recessive allele—*y*. The offspring can have one of three genotypes—*YY*, *Yy*, or *yy*. The ratio of genotypes is written as 1:2:1.

Because *YY* and *Yy* represent the same phenotype—yellow—the offspring can have one of only two phenotypes—yellow or green. The ratio of phenotypes is written 3:1. Therefore, about 75 percent of the offspring of the cross between two heterozygous pea plants will produce yellow seeds. About 25 percent of the plants will produce green seeds.

Using Ratios to Predict

Given a 3:1 ratio, you can expect that an offspring from heterozygous parents has a 3:1 chance of having yellow seeds. But you cannot expect that a group of four seeds will have three yellow seeds and one green seed. This is because one offspring does not affect the phenotype of another offspring. In a similar way, the outcome of one coin toss does not affect the outcome of other coin tosses.

However, if you counted large numbers of offspring from a particular cross, the overall ratio would be close to the ratio predicted by a Punnett square. Mendel did not use Punnett squares. However, by studying nearly 30,000 pea plants, his ratios nearly matched those that would have been predicted by a Punnett square for each cross.

Pedigrees

Another model that can show inherited traits is a pedigree. A pedigree shows phenotypes of genetically related family members. It can also help determine genotypes. In the pedigree in **Figure 8,** three offspring have a trait—attached earlobes—that the parents do not have. If these offspring received one allele for this trait from each parent, but neither parent displays the trait, the offspring must have received two recessive alleles.

 Key Concept Check How can inheritance be modeled?

Pedigree 🔑

Figure 8 In this pedigree, the parents and two offspring have unattached ear lobes—the dominant phenotype. Three offspring have attached ear lobes—the recessive phenotype.

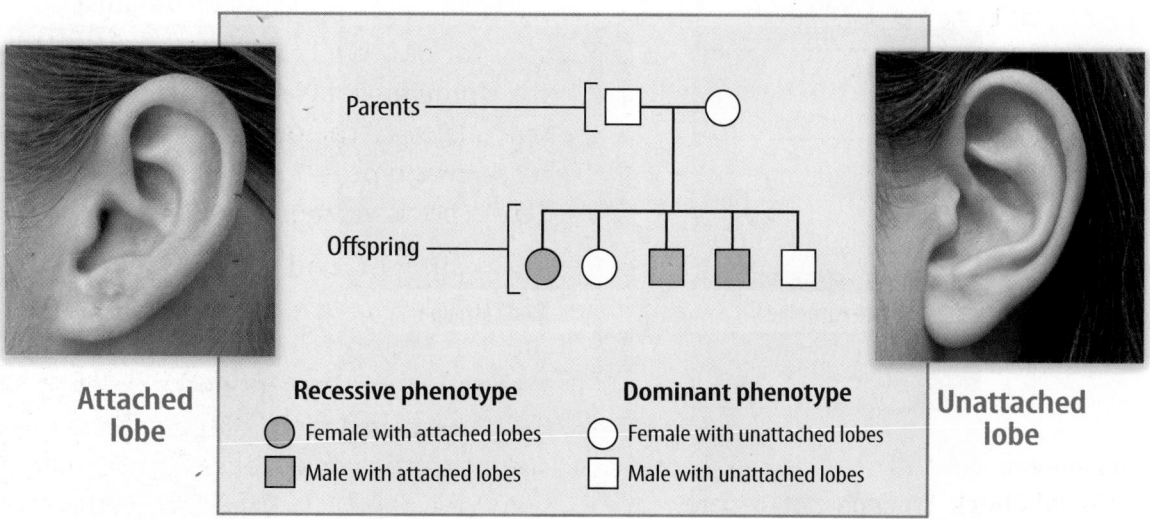

Attached lobe

Parents

Offspring

Recessive phenotype
- ● Female with attached lobes
- ■ Male with attached lobes

Dominant phenotype
- ○ Female with unattached lobes
- □ Male with unattached lobes

Unattached lobe

🔘 **Visual Check** If the genotype of the offspring with attached lobes is *uu,* what is the genotype of the parents? How can you tell?

Complex Patterns of Inheritance

By chance, Mendel studied traits only influenced by one gene with two alleles. However, we know now that some inherited traits have complex patterns of inheritance.

Types of Dominance

Recall that for pea plants, the presence of one dominant allele produces a dominant phenotype. However, not all allele pairs have a dominant-recessive interaction.

Incomplete Dominance Sometimes traits appear to be combinations of alleles. *Alleles show* **incomplete dominance** *when the offspring's phenotype is a combination of the parents' phenotypes.* For example, a pink camellia, as shown in **Figure 9,** results from incomplete dominance. A cross between a camellia plant with white flowers and a camellia plant with red flowers produces only camellia plants with pink flowers.

Codominance The coat color of some cows is an example of another type of interaction between two alleles. *When both alleles can be observed in a phenotype, this type of interaction is called* **codominance.** If a cow inherits the allele for white coat color from one parent and the allele for red coat color from the other parent, the cow will have both red and white hairs.

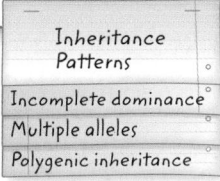
Types of Dominance 🔑

Figure 9 In incomplete dominance, neither parent's phenotype is visible in the offspring's phenotype. In codominance, both parents' phenotypes are visible separately in the offspring's phenotype.

	Parent	**Parent**	**Offspring**
Incomplete dominance	White camellia	× Red camellia	Pink camellia
Codominance	White coat color	× Red coat color	Roan coat color

Table 3 Human ABO Blood Types

Phenotype	Possible Genotypes
Type A	$I^A I^A$ or $I^A i$
Type B	$I^B I^B$ or $I^B i$
Type O	ii
Type AB	$I^A I^B$

Multiple Alleles

Unlike the genes in Mendel's pea plants, some genes have more than two alleles, or multiple alleles. Human ABO blood type is an example of a trait that is determined by multiple alleles. There are three different alleles for the ABO blood type—I^A, I^B, and i. The way the alleles combine results in one of four blood types—A, B, AB, or O. The I^A and I^B alleles are codominant to each other, but they both are dominant to the i allele. Even though there are multiple alleles, a person can inherit only two of these alleles—one from each parent, as shown in **Table 3**.

Polygenic Inheritance

Mendel **concluded** that each trait was determined by only one gene. However, we now know that a trait can be affected by more than one gene. **Polygenic inheritance** *occurs when multiple genes determine the phenotype of a trait.* Because several genes determine a trait, many alleles affect the phenotype even though each gene has only two alleles. Therefore, polygenic inheritance has many possible phenotypes.

Look again at the photo at the beginning of this lesson. Eye color in humans is an example of polygenic inheritance. There are also many phenotypes for height in humans, as shown in **Figure 10.** Other human characteristics determined by polygenic inheritance are weight and skin color.

 Key Concept Check How does polygenic inheritance differ from Mendel's model?

ACADEMIC VOCABULARY

conclude
(verb) to reach a logically necessary end by reasoning

Figure 10 The eighth graders in this class have different heights.

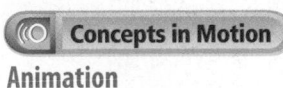 **Concepts in Motion**

Animation

Genes and the Environment

You read earlier in this lesson that an organism's genotype determines its phenotype. Scientists have learned that genes are not the only factors that can affect phenotypes. An organism's environment can also affect its phenotype. For example, the flower color of one type of hydrangea is determined by the soil in which the hydrangea plant grows. **Figure 11** shows that acidic soil produces blue flowers and basic, or alkaline, soil produces pink flowers. Other examples of environmental effects on phenotype are also shown in **Figure 11.**

For humans, healthful choices can also affect phenotype. Many genes affect a person's chances of having heart disease. However, what a person eats and the amount of exercise he or she gets can influence whether heart disease will develop.

✓ **Reading Check** What environmental factors affect phenotype?

Figure 11 Environmental factors, such as temperature and sunlight, can affect phenotype.

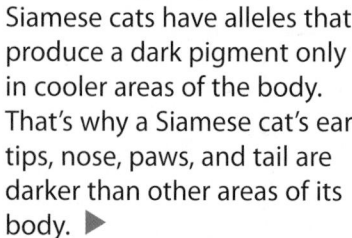

◀ These hydrangea plants are genetically identical. The plant grown in acidic soil produced blue flowers. The plant grown in alkaline soil produced pink flowers.

Siamese cats have alleles that produce a dark pigment only in cooler areas of the body. That's why a Siamese cat's ear tips, nose, paws, and tail are darker than other areas of its body. ▶

◀ The wing patterns of the map butterfly, *Araschnia levana,* depend on what time of year the adult develops. Adults that developed in the spring have more orange in their wings than those that developed in the summer.

Lesson 2 Review

✓ **Assessment** Online Quiz

? **Inquiry** Virtual Lab

Visual Summary

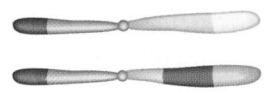

The genes for traits are located on chromosomes.

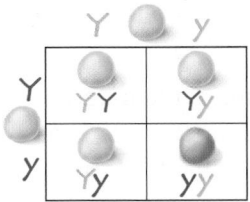

Geneticists use Punnett squares to predict the possible genotypes and phenotypes of offspring.

In polygenic inheritance, traits are determined by more than one gene and have many possible phenotypes.

FOLDABLES

Use your lesson Foldable to review the lesson. Save your Foldable for the project at the end of the chapter.

What do you think NOW?

You first read the statements below at the beginning of the chapter.

3. All inherited traits follow Mendel's patterns of inheritance.

4. Scientists have tools to predict the form of a trait an offspring might inherit.

Did you change your mind about whether you agree or disagree with the statements? Rewrite any false statements to make them true.

Use Vocabulary

1. **Use** the terms *phenotype* and *genotype* in a complete sentence.

2. **Contrast** homozygous and heterozygous.

3. **Define** *incomplete dominance* in your own words.

Understand Key Concepts

4. How many alleles control a Mendelian trait, such as pea seed color?
   - **A.** one
   - **B.** two
   - **C.** three
   - **D.** four

5. **Explain** where the alleles for a given trait are inherited from.

6. **Describe** how the genotypes *RR* and *Rr* result in the same phenotype.

7. **Summarize** how polygenic inheritance differs from Mendelian inheritance.

Interpret Graphics

8. **Analyze** this pedigree. If ■ represents a male with the homozygous recessive genotype (*aa*), what is the mother's genotype?

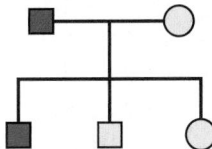

Critical Thinking

9. **Predict** the possible blood genotypes of a child, using the table below, if one parent is type O and the other parent is type A.

Phenotype	Genotype
Blood Type O	ii
Blood Type A	$I^A I^A$ or $I^A i$

How can you use Punnett squares to model inheritance?

Geneticists use models to explain how traits are inherited from one generation to the next. A simple model of Mendelian inheritance is a Punnett square. A Punnett square is a model of reproduction between two parents and the possible genotypes and phenotypes of the resulting offspring. It also models the probability that each genotype will occur.

Learn It

In science, a **model** is a representation of how something in the natural world works. A model is used to explain or predict a natural process. Maps, diagrams, three-dimensional representations, and mathematical formulas can all be used to help model nature.

Try It

1 Copy the Punnett square on this page in your Science Journal. Use it to complete a cross between a fruit fly with straight wings *(cc)* and a fruit fly with curly wings *(CC)*.

2 According to your Punnett square, which genotypes are possible in the offspring?

3 Using the information in your Punnett square, calculate the ratio of the dominant phenotype to the recessive phenotype in the offspring.

Apply It

4 Based on the information in your Punnett square, how many offspring will have curly wings? Straight wings?

5 If you switch the locations of the parent genotypes around the Punnett square, does it affect the potential genotypes of their offspring? Explain.

6 🔑 **Key Concept** Design and complete a Punnett square to model a cross between two fruit flies that are heterozygous for the curly wings *(Cc)*. What are the phenotypic ratios of the offspring?

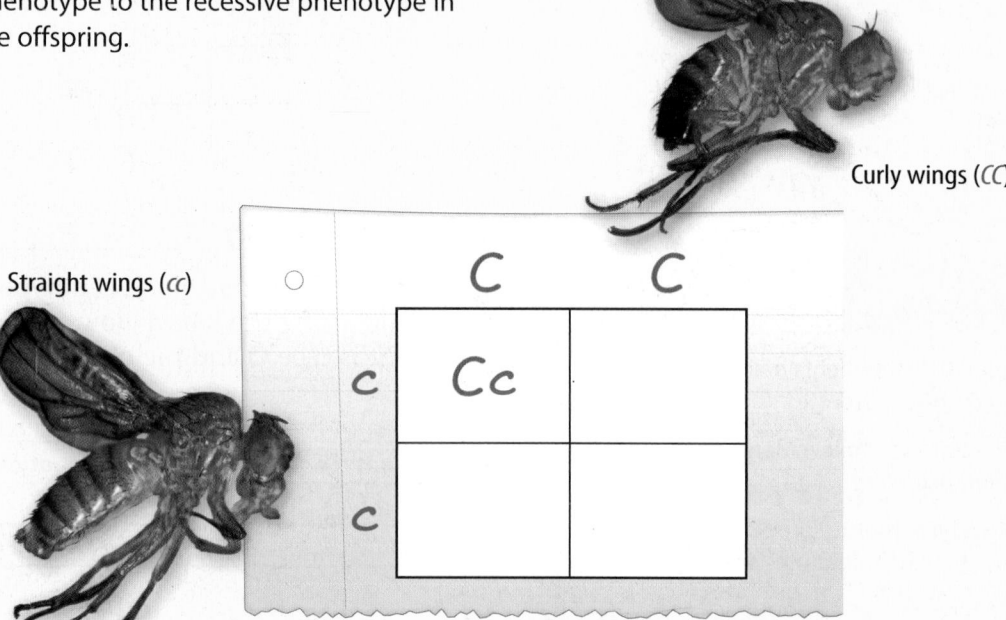

Magnification: 20×

Curly wings *(CC)*

Straight wings *(cc)*

	C	C
c	Cc	
c		

Lesson 3

DNA and Genetics

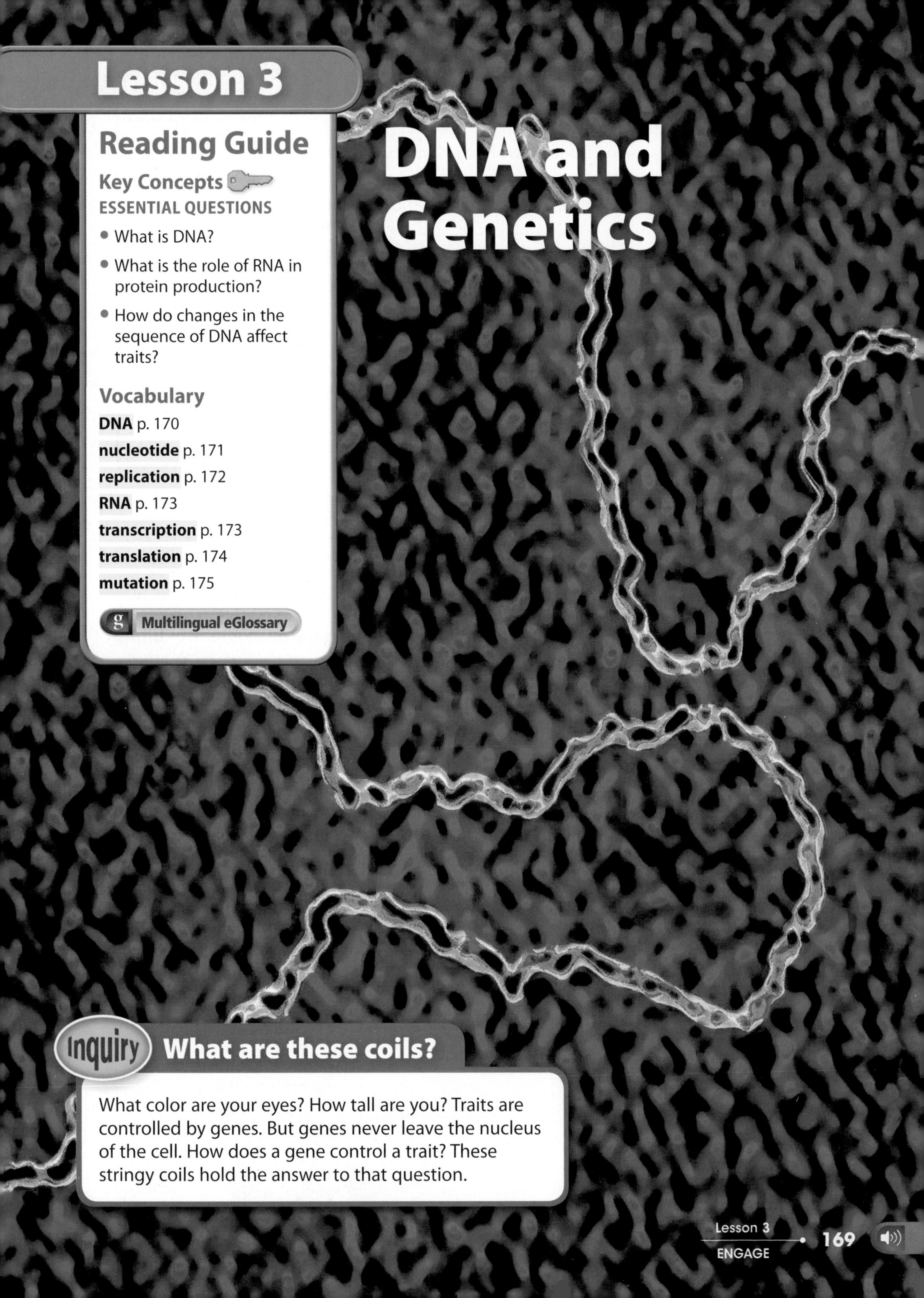

Reading Guide

Key Concepts
ESSENTIAL QUESTIONS

- What is DNA?
- What is the role of RNA in protein production?
- How do changes in the sequence of DNA affect traits?

Vocabulary

DNA p. 170
nucleotide p. 171
replication p. 172
RNA p. 173
transcription p. 173
translation p. 174
mutation p. 175

g Multilingual eGlossary

Inquiry What are these coils?

What color are your eyes? How tall are you? Traits are controlled by genes. But genes never leave the nucleus of the cell. How does a gene control a trait? These stringy coils hold the answer to that question.

How are codes used to determine traits?

Interpret this code to learn more about how an organism's body cells use codes to determine genetic traits.

1 Analyze the pattern of the simple code shown to the right. For example, ⟩⟨∟ = DOG

2 In your Science Journal, record the correct letters for the symbols in the code below.

⟩˅˅ ∧˨⟨⊡⊡⟩˩• ∟⊐˩ ∧⊐∫⌐◌∧∨⊓

∧⟨⟩˩ ∪⟨˨ ˅˅ ⟨˨∟˅˅◌∪⌐˩•

∟∫˅˩∟⊡∧ ⌐˅∟˩˩◌∨⊓

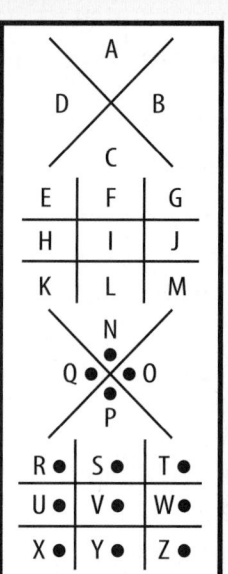

Think About This

1. What do all codes, such as Morse code and Braille, have in common?

2. What do you think might happen if there is a mistake in the code?

3. 🔑 **Key Concept** How do you think an organism's cells might use code to determine its traits?

The Structure of DNA

Have you ever put together a toy or a game for a child? If so, it probably came with directions. Cells put molecules together in much the same way you might assemble a toy. They follow a set of directions.

Genes provide directions for a cell to assemble molecules that express traits such as eye color or seed shape. Recall from Lesson 2 that a gene is a section of a chromosome. Chromosomes are made of proteins and deoxyribonucleic (dee AHK sih ri boh noo klee ihk) acid, or **DNA**—*an organism's genetic material.* A gene is a segment of DNA on a chromosome.

Cells and organisms contain millions of different molecules. Countless numbers of directions are needed to make all those molecules. How do all these directions fit on a few chromosomes? The information, or directions, needed for an organism to grow, maintain itself, and reproduce is contained in DNA. As shown in **Figure 12,** strands of DNA in a chromosome are tightly coiled, like a telephone cord or a coiled spring. This coiling allows more genes to fit in a small space.

🔑 **Key Concept Check** What is DNA?

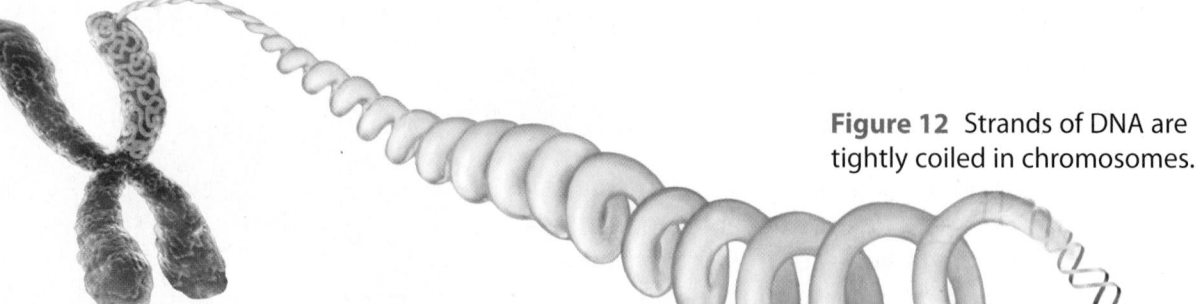

Figure 12 Strands of DNA are tightly coiled in chromosomes.

A Complex Molecule

What's the best way to fold clothes so they will fit into a drawer or a suitcase? Scientists asked a similar question about DNA. What is the shape of the DNA molecule, and how does it fit into a chromosome? The work of several scientists revealed that DNA is like a twisted zipper. This twisted zipper shape is called a double helix. A model of DNA's double helix structure is shown in **Figure 13.**

How did scientists make this discovery? Rosalind Franklin and Maurice Wilkins were two scientists in London who used X-rays to study DNA. Some of the X-ray data indicated that DNA has a helix shape.

American scientist James Watson visited Franklin and Wilkins and saw one of the DNA X-rays. Watson realized that the X-ray gave valuable clues about DNA's structure. Watson worked with an English scientist, Francis Crick, to build a model of DNA.

Watson and Crick based their work on information from Franklin's and Wilkins's X-rays. They also used chemical information about DNA discovered by another scientist, Erwin Chargaff. After several tries, Watson and Crick built a model that showed how the smaller molecules of DNA bond together and form a double helix.

Four Nucleotides Shape DNA

DNA's twisted-zipper shape is because of molecules called nucleotides. *A* **nucleotide** *is a molecule made of a nitrogen base, a sugar, and a phosphate group.* Sugar-phosphate groups form the sides of the DNA zipper. The nitrogen bases bond and form the teeth of the zipper. As shown in **Figure 13,** there are four nitrogen bases: adenine (A), cytosine (C), thymine (T), and guanine (G). A and T always bond together, and C and G always bond together.

 Reading Check What is a nucleotide?

Figure 13 A DNA double helix is made of two strands of DNA. Each strand is a chain of nucleotides.

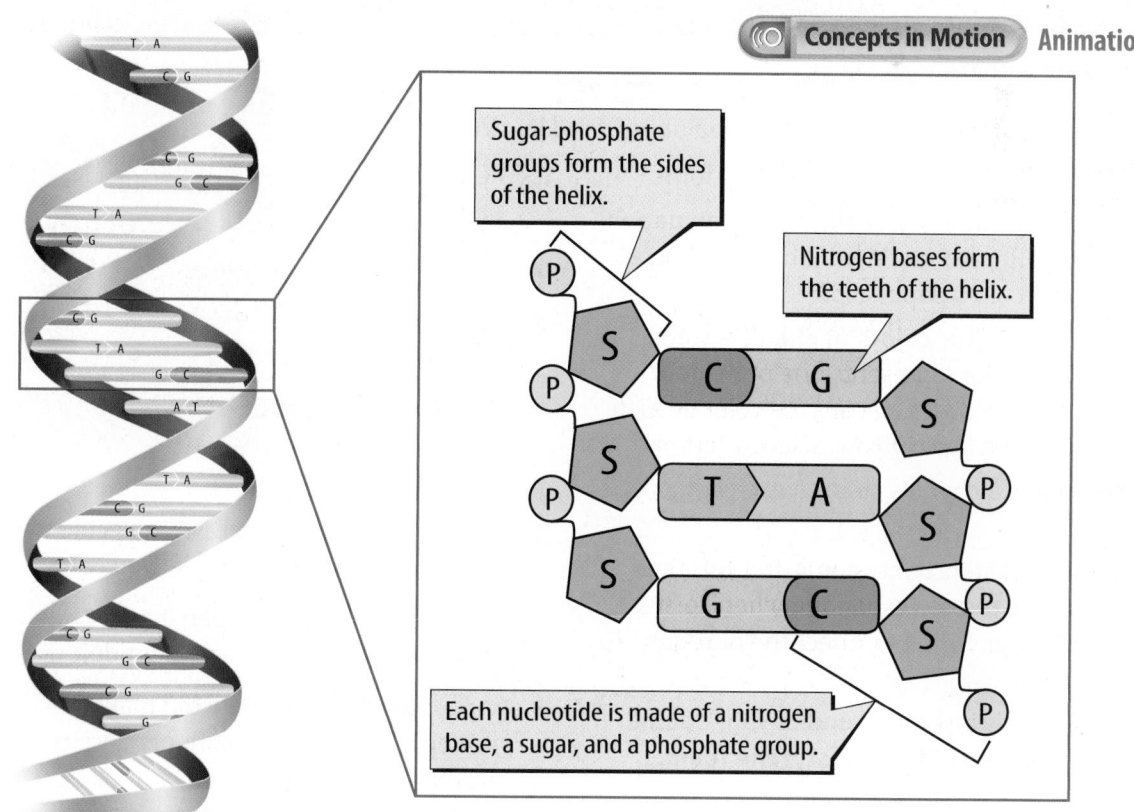

Concepts in Motion   Animation

Sugar-phosphate groups form the sides of the helix.

Nitrogen bases form the teeth of the helix.

Each nucleotide is made of a nitrogen base, a sugar, and a phosphate group.

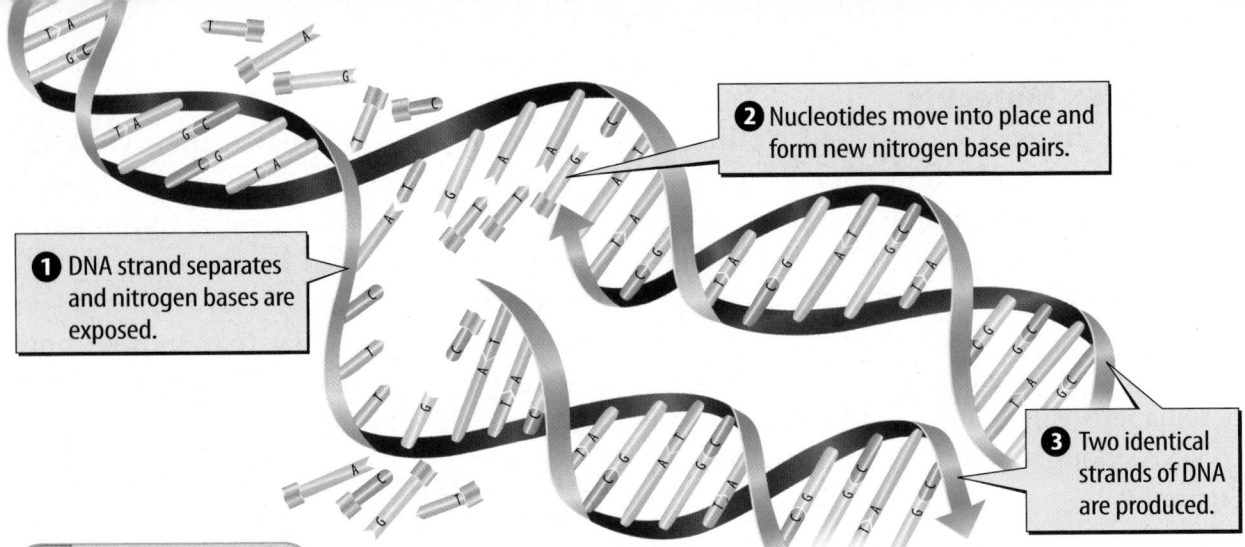

2 Nucleotides move into place and form new nitrogen base pairs.

1 DNA strand separates and nitrogen bases are exposed.

3 Two identical strands of DNA are produced.

Concepts in Motion

Animation

Figure 14 Before a cell divides, its DNA is replicated.

How DNA Replicates

Cells contain DNA in chromosomes. So, every time a cell divides, all chromosomes must be copied for the new cell. The new DNA is identical to existing DNA. *The process of copying a DNA molecule to make another DNA molecule is called* **replication.** You can follow the steps of DNA replication in **Figure 14.** First, the strands separate in many places, exposing individual bases. Then nucleotides are added to each exposed base. This produces two identical strands of DNA.

✓ **Reading Check** What is replication?

Inquiry MiniLab   **25 minutes**

How can you model DNA?

Making a model of DNA can help you understand its structure.

1. Read and complete a lab safety form.

2. Link a **small paper clip** to a **large paper clip.** Repeat four more times, making a chain of 10 paper clips.

3. Choose **four colors of chenille stems.** Each color represents one of the four nitrogen bases. Record the color of each nitrogen base in your Science Journal.

4. Attach a chenille stem to each large paper clip.

5. Repeat step 2 and step 4, but this time attach the corresponding chenille-stem nitrogen bases. Connect the nitrogen bases.

6. Securely insert one end of your double chain into a **block of styrene foam.**

7. Repeat step 6 with the other end of your chain.

8. Gently turn the blocks to form a double helix.

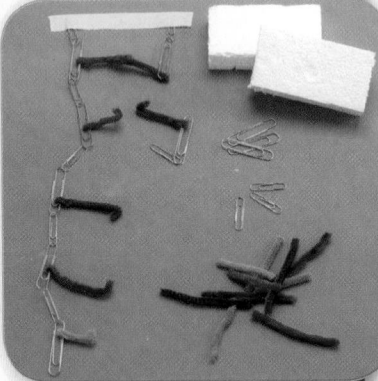

Analyze and Conclude

1. **Explain** which part of a DNA molecule is represented by each material you used.

2. **Predict** what might happen if a mistake were made in creating a nucleotide.

3. 🔑 **Key Concept** How did making a model of DNA help you understand its structure?

Making Proteins

Recall that proteins are important for every cellular process. The DNA of each cell carries a complete set of genes that provides instructions for making all the proteins a cell requires. Most genes contain instructions for making proteins. Some genes contain instructions for when and how quickly proteins are made.

Junk DNA

As you have learned, all genes are segments of DNA on a chromosome. However, you might be surprised to learn that most of your DNA is not part of any gene. For example, about 97 percent of the DNA on human chromosomes does not form genes. Segments of DNA that are not parts of genes are often called junk DNA. It is not yet known whether junk DNA segments have functions that are important to cells.

The Role of RNA in Making Proteins

How does a cell use the instructions in a gene to make proteins? Proteins are made with the help of ribonucleic acid **(RNA)**—*a type of nucleic acid that carries the code for making proteins from the nucleus to the cytoplasm.* RNA also carries amino acids around inside a cell and forms a part of ribosomes.

RNA, like DNA, is made of nucleotides. However, there are key differences between DNA and RNA. DNA is double-stranded, but RNA is single-stranded. RNA has the nitrogen base uracil (U) instead of thymine (T) and the sugar ribose instead of deoxyribose.

The first step in making a protein is to make mRNA from DNA. *The process of making mRNA from DNA is called* **transcription.** **Figure 15** shows how mRNA is transcribed from DNA.

Key Concept Check What is the role of RNA in protein production?

Transcription

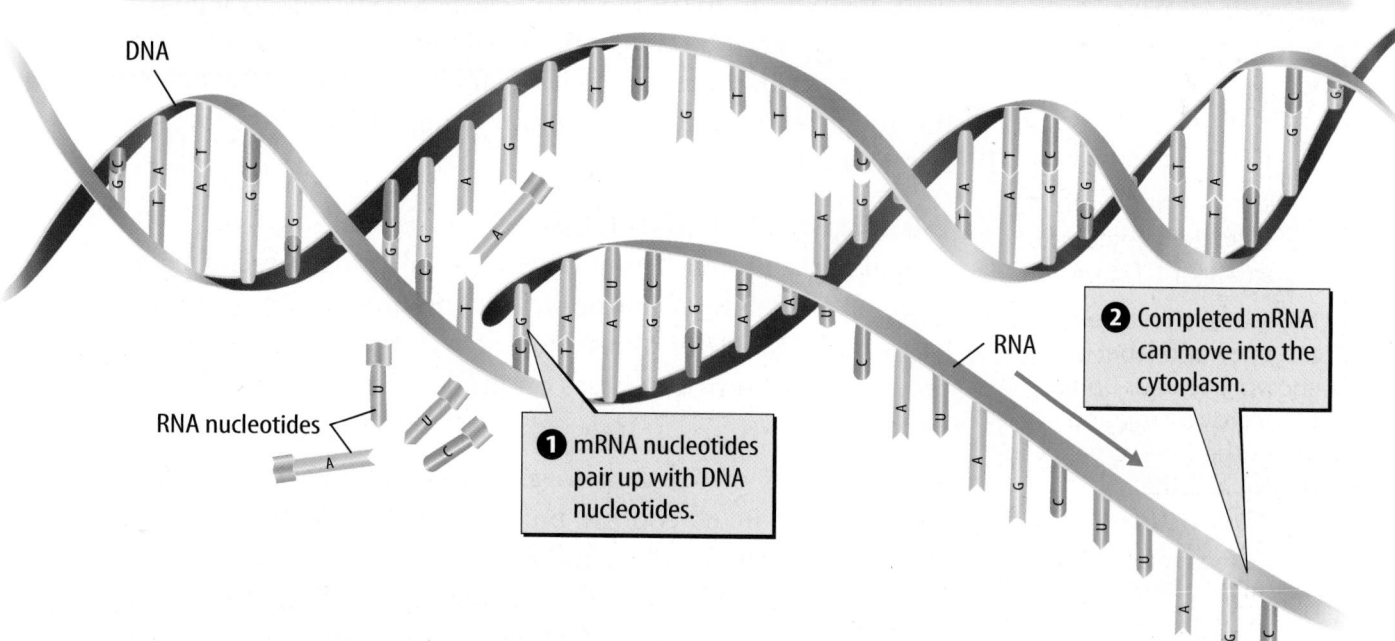

Figure 15 Transcription is the first step in making a protein. During transcription, the sequence of nitrogen bases on a gene determines the sequence of bases on mRNA.

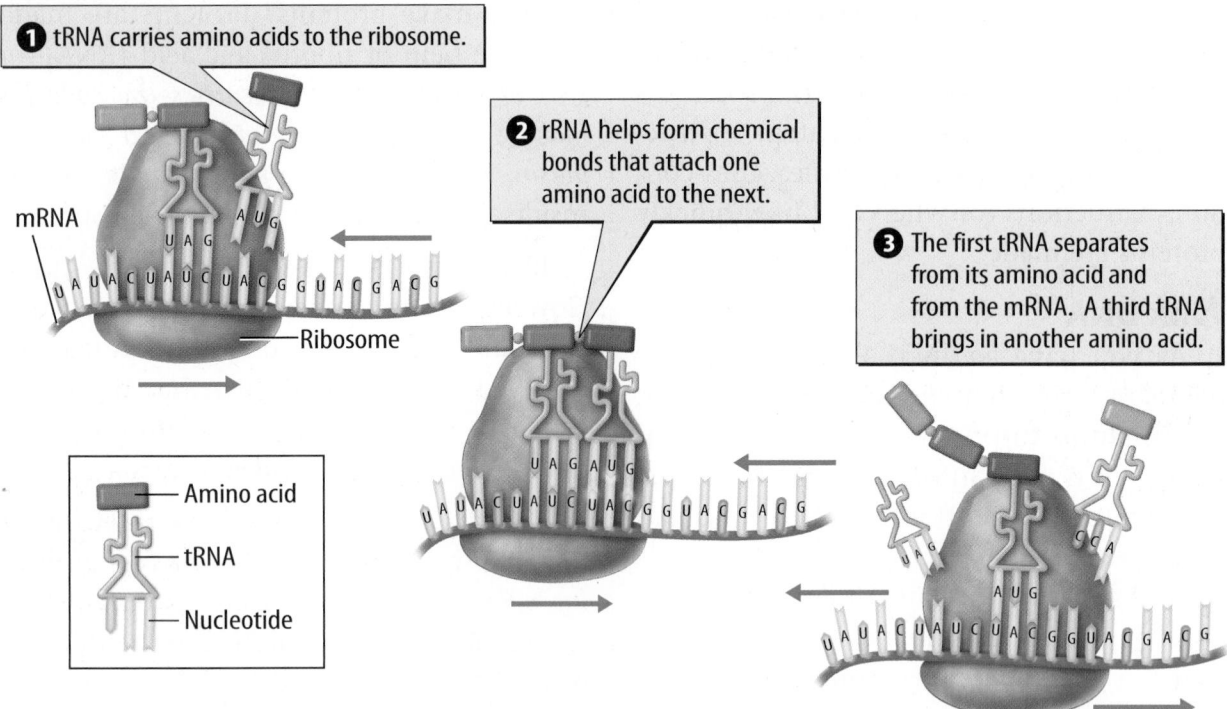

1 tRNA carries amino acids to the ribosome.

2 rRNA helps form chemical bonds that attach one amino acid to the next.

3 The first tRNA separates from its amino acid and from the mRNA. A third tRNA brings in another amino acid.

mRNA

Ribosome

Amino acid

tRNA

Nucleotide

Figure 16 A protein forms as mRNA moves through a ribosome. Different amino acid sequences make different proteins. A complete protein is a folded chain of amino acids.

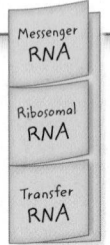

FOLDABLES®

Make a vertical three-tab book and label it as shown. Use your book to record information about the three types of RNA and their functions.

Messenger RNA

Ribosomal RNA

Transfer RNA

Three Types of RNA

On the previous page, you read about messenger RNA (mRNA). There are two other types of RNA, transfer RNA (tRNA) and ribosomal RNA (rRNA). **Figure 16** illustrates how the three work together to make proteins. *The process of making a protein from RNA is called* **translation.** Translation occurs in ribosomes. Recall that ribosomes are cell organelles that are attached to the rough endoplasmic reticulum (rough ER). Ribosomes are also in a cell's cytoplasm.

Translating the RNA Code

Making a protein from mRNA is like using a secret code. Proteins are made of amino acids. The order of the nitrogen bases in mRNA determines the order of the amino acids in a protein. Three nitrogen bases on mRNA form the code for one amino acid.

Each series of three nitrogen bases on mRNA is called a codon. There are 64 codons, but only 20 amino acids. Some of the codons code for the same amino acid. One of the codons codes for an amino acid that is the beginning of a protein. This codon signals that translation should start. Three of the codons do not code for any amino acid. Instead, they code for the end of the protein. They signal that translation should stop.

✓ **Reading Check** What is a codon?

Mutations

You have read that the sequence of nitrogen bases in DNA determines the sequence of nitrogen bases in mRNA, and that the mRNA sequence determines the sequence of amino acids in a protein. You might think these sequences always stay the same, but they can change. *A change in the nucleotide sequence of a gene is called a* **mutation.**

The 46 human chromosomes contain between 20,000 and 25,000 genes that are copied during DNA replication. Sometimes, mistakes can happen during replication. Most mistakes are corrected before replication is completed. A mistake that is not corrected can result in a mutation. Mutations can be triggered by exposure to X-rays, ultraviolet light, radioactive materials, and some kinds of chemicals.

Types of Mutations

There are several types of DNA mutations. Three types are shown in **Figure 17.** In a deletion mutation, one or more nitrogen bases are left out of the DNA sequence. In an insertion mutation, one or more nitrogen bases are added to the DNA. In a substitution mutation, one nitrogen base is replaced by a different nitrogen base.

Each type of mutation changes the sequence of nitrogen base pairs. This can cause a mutated gene to code for a different protein than a normal gene. Some mutated genes do not code for any protein. For example, a cell might lose the ability to make one of the proteins it needs.

WORD ORIGIN · · · · · · · · · · ·

mutation
from Latin *mutare,* means "to change"

Figure 17 Three types of mutations are substitution, insertion, and deletion.

Visual Check Which base pairs were omitted during replication in the deletion mutation?

Mutations 🔑

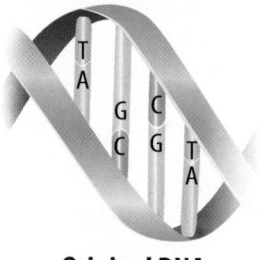

Original DNA sequence

Substitution
The C-G base pair has been replaced with a T-A pair.

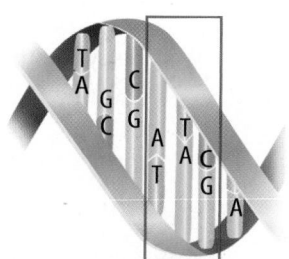

Insertion
Three base pairs have been added.

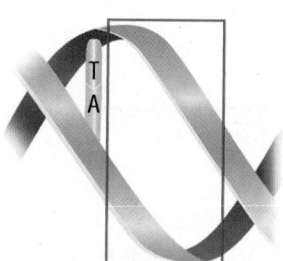

Deletion
Three base pairs have been removed. Other base pairs will move in to take their place.

Results of a Mutation

The effects of a mutation depend on where in the DNA sequence the mutation happens and the type of mutation. Proteins express traits. Because mutations can change proteins, they can cause traits to change. Some mutations in human DNA cause genetic disorders, such as those described in **Table 4.**

However, not all mutations have negative effects. Some mutations don't cause changes in proteins, so they don't affect traits. Other mutations might cause a trait to change in a way that benefits the organism.

 Key Concept Check How do changes in the sequence of DNA affect traits?

Scientists still have much to learn about genes and how they determine an organism's traits. Scientists are researching and experimenting to identify all genes that cause specific traits. With this knowledge, we might be one step closer to finding cures and treatments for genetic disorders.

Table 4 Genetic Disorders

Defective Gene or Chromosome	Disorder	Description
Chromosome 12, PAH gene	Phenylketonuria (PKU)	People with defective PAH genes cannot break down the amino acid phenylalanine. If phenylalanine builds up in the blood, it poisons nerve cells.
Chromosome 7, CFTR gene	Cystic fibrosis	In people with defective CFTR genes, salt cannot move in and out of cells normally. Mucus builds up outside cells. The mucus can block airways in lungs and affect digestion.
Chromosome 7, elastin gene	Williams syndrome	People with Williams syndrome are missing part of chromosome 7, including the elastin gene. The protein made from the elastin gene makes blood vessels strong and stretchy.
Chromosome 17, BRCA 1; Chromosome 13, BRCA 2	Breast cancer and ovarian cancer	A defect in BRCA1 and/or BRCA2 does not mean the person will have breast cancer or ovarian cancer. People with defective BRCA1 or BRCA2 genes have an increased risk of developing breast cancer and ovarian cancer.

Lesson 3 Review

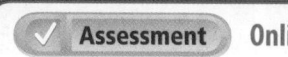

Visual Summary

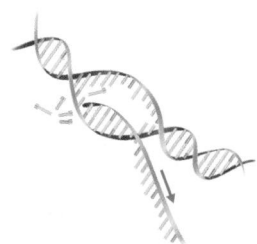

DNA is a complex molecule that contains the code for an organism's genetic information.

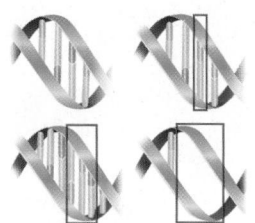

RNA carries the codes for making proteins.

An organism's nucleotide sequence can change through the deletion, insertion, or substitution of nitrogen bases.

FOLDABLES®

Use your lesson Foldable to review the lesson. Save your Foldable for the project at the end of the chapter.

What do you think NOW?

You first read the statements below at the beginning of the chapter.

5. Any condition present at birth is genetic.

6. A change in the sequence of an organism's DNA always changes the organism's traits.

Did you change your mind about whether you agree or disagree with the statements? Rewrite any false statements to make them true.

Use Vocabulary

1 **Distinguish** between transcription and translation.

2 **Use the terms** *DNA* and *nucleotide* in a sentence.

3 A change in the sequence of nitrogen bases in a gene is called a(n) _____.

Understand Key Concepts

4 Where does the process of transcription occur?
   A. cytoplasm   **C.** cell nucleus
   B. ribosomes   **D.** outside the cell

5 **Illustrate** Make a drawing that illustrates the process of translation.

6 **Distinguish** between the sides of the DNA double helix and the teeth of the DNA double helix.

Interpret Graphics

7 **Identify** The products of what process are shown in the figure below?

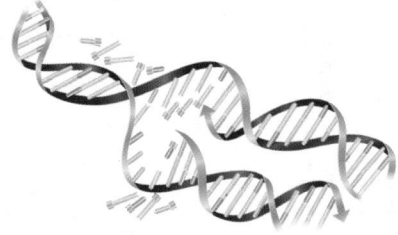

8 **Sequence** Draw a graphic organizer like the one below about important steps in making a protein, beginning with DNA and ending with protein.

Critical Thinking

9 **Hypothesize** What would happen if a cell were unable to make mRNA?

10 **Assess** What is the importance of DNA replication occurring without any mistakes?

Materials

gummy bears

calculator

paper bag

Safety

Gummy Bear Genetics

Imagine you are on a team of geneticists that is doing "cross-breeding experiments" with gummy bears. Unfortunately, the computer containing your data has crashed. All you have left are six gummy-bear litters that resulted from six sets of parents. But no one can remember which parents produced which litter. You know that gummy-bear traits have either Mendelian inheritance or incomplete dominance. Can you determine which parents produced each set of offspring and how gummy bear traits are inherited?

Ask a Question

What are the genotypes and phenotypes of the parents for each litter?

Make Observations

❶ Obtain a bag of gummy bears. Sort the bears by color (phenotype).

⚠ *Do not eat the gummy bears.*

❷ Count the number (frequency) of bears for each phenotype. Then, calculate the ratio of phenotypes for each litter.

❸ Combine data from your litter with those of your classmates using a data table like the one below.

❹ As a class, select a letter to represent the alleles for color. Record the possible genotypes for your bears in the class data table.

Gummy Bear Cross Data for Lab Group

Cross #	Phenotype Frequencies	Ratio	Possible Genotypes	Mode of Inheritance	Predicted Parental Genotypes
EXAMPLE	15 green/5 pink	3:1	GG or Gg/gg	Mendelian	Gg × Gg
1.					
2.					
3.					
4.					

Form a Hypothesis

5 Use the data to form a hypothesis about the probable genotypes and phenotypes of the parents of your litter and the probable type of inheritance.

Test Your Hypothesis

6 Design and complete a Punnett square using the predicted parental genotypes in your hypothesis.

7 Compare your litter's phenotype ratio with the ratio predicted by the Punnett square. Do your data support your hypothesis? If not, revise your hypothesis and repeat steps 5–7.

Analyze and Conclude

8 **Infer** What were the genotypes of the parents? The phenotypes? How do you know?

9 **THE BIG IDEA** **The Big Idea** Determine the probable modes of inheritance for each phenotype. Explain your reasoning.

10 **Graph** Using the data you collected, draw a bar graph that compares the phenotype frequency for each gummy bear phenotype.

Reminder

Using Ratios
- ☑ A ratio is a comparison of two numbers.
- ☑ A ratio of 15:5 can be reduced to 3:1.

Communicate Your Results

Create a video presentation of the results of your lab. Describe the question you investigated, the steps you took to answer the question, and the data that support your conclusions. Share your video with your classmates.

Inquiry **Extension**

Think of a question you have about genetics. For example, can you design a pedigree to trace a Mendelian trait in your family? To investigate your question, design a controlled experiment or an observational study.

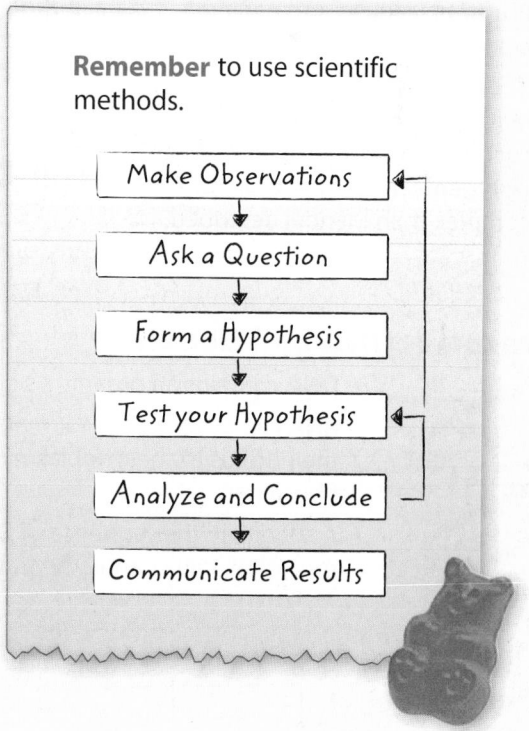

Remember to use scientific methods.

Make Observations
↓
Ask a Question
↓
Form a Hypothesis
↓
Test your Hypothesis
↓
Analyze and Conclude
↓
Communicate Results

Chapter 5 Study Guide

Inherited genes are the basis of an organism's traits.

Key Concepts Summary 🔑	Vocabulary
Lesson 1: Mendel and His Peas • Mendel performed cross-pollination experiments to track which traits were produced by specific parental crosses. • Mendel found that two genetic factors—one from a sperm cell and one from an egg cell—control each trait. • **Dominant** traits block the expression of **recessive** traits. Recessive traits are expressed only when two recessive factors are present. 	**heredity** p. 149 **genetics** p. 149 **dominant trait** p. 155 **recessive trait** p. 155
Lesson 2: Understanding Inheritance • **Phenotype** describes how a trait appears. • **Genotype** describes alleles that control a trait. • **Punnett squares** and pedigrees are tools to model patterns of inheritance. • Many patterns of inheritance, such as **codominance** and **polygenic inheritance,** are more complex than Mendel described. 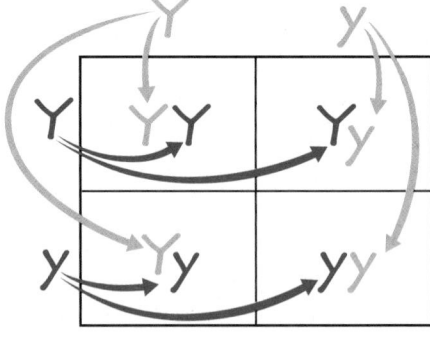	**gene** p. 160 **allele** p. 160 **phenotype** p. 160 **genotype** p. 160 **homozygous** p. 161 **heterozygous** p. 161 **Punnett square** p. 162 **incomplete dominance** p. 164 **codominance** p. 164 **polygenic inheritance** p. 165
Lesson 3: DNA and Genetics 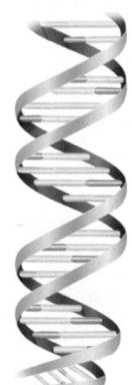 • **DNA** contains an organism's genetic information. • **RNA** carries the codes for making proteins from the nucleus to the cytoplasm. RNA also forms part of ribosomes. • A change in the sequence of DNA, called a **mutation,** can change the traits of an organism.	**DNA** p. 170 **nucleotide** p. 171 **replication** p. 172 **RNA** p. 173 **transcription** p. 173 **translation** p. 174 **mutation** p. 175

FOLDABLES® **Chapter Project**

Assemble your lesson Foldables as shown to make a Chapter Project. Use the project to review what you have learned in this chapter.

GENETICS

Traits
Recessive factors
Dominant factors

Inheritance Patterns
Incomplete dominance
Multiple alleles
Polygenic inheritance

Messenger RNA
Ribosomal RNA
Transfer RNA

Use Vocabulary

1 The study of how traits are passed from parents to offspring is called _____.

2 The passing of traits from parents to offspring is _____.

3 Human height, weight, and skin color are examples of characteristics determined by _____ _____.

4 A helpful device for predicting the ratios of possible genotypes is a(n) _____.

5 The code for a protein is called a(n) _____.

6 An error made during the copying of DNA is called a(n) _____.

Link Vocabulary and Key Concepts

🔊 **Concepts in Motion** **Interactive Concept Map**

Copy this concept map, and then use vocabulary terms from the previous page to complete the concept map.

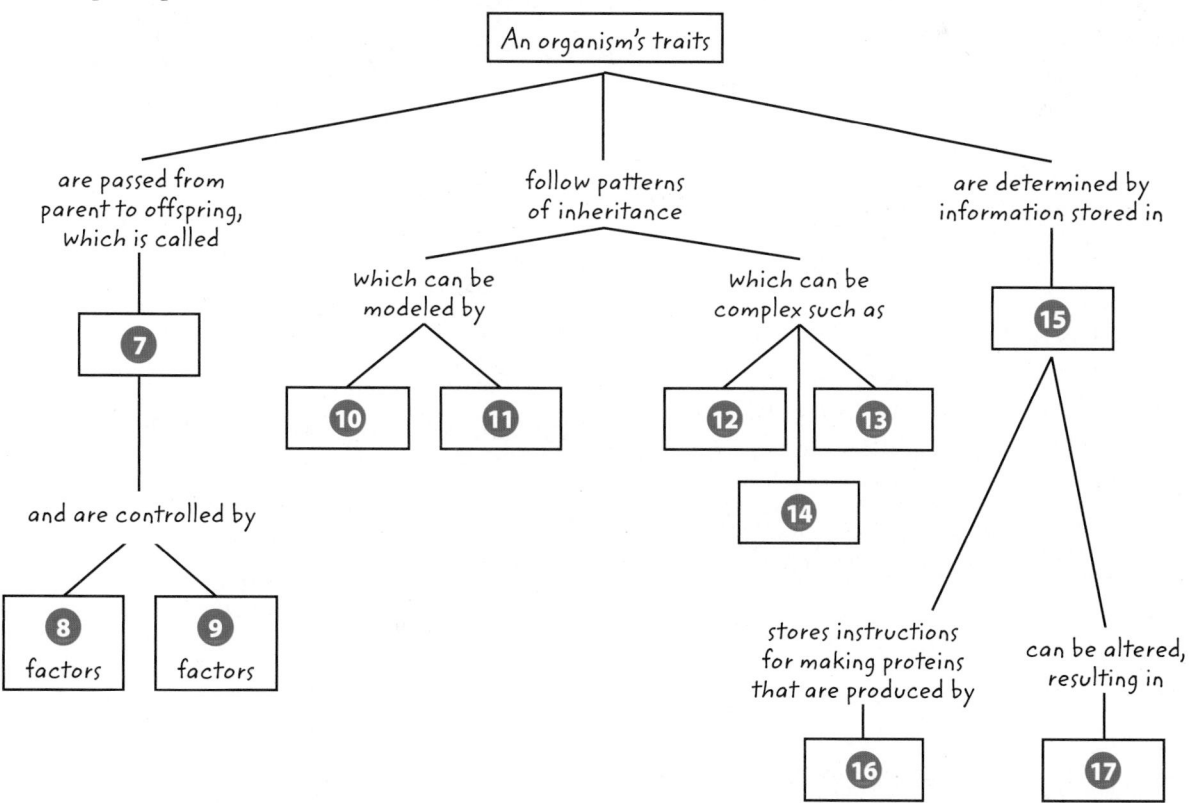

Understand Key Concepts 🔑

1 The process shown below was used by Mendel during his experiments.

What is the process called?

A. cross-pollination
B. segregation
C. asexual reproduction
D. blending inheritance

2 Which statement best describes Mendel's experiments?

A. He began with hybrid plants.
B. He controlled pollination.
C. He observed only one generation.
D. He used plants that reproduce slowly.

3 Before Mendel's discoveries, which statement describes how people believed traits were inherited?

A. Parental traits blend like colors of paint to produce offspring.
B. Parental traits have no effect on their offspring.
C. Traits from only the female parent are inherited by offspring.
D. Traits from only the male parent are inherited by offspring.

4 Which term describes the offspring of a first-generation cross between parents with different forms of a trait?

A. genotype
B. hybrid
C. phenotype
D. true-breeding

5 Which process makes a copy of a DNA molecule?

A. mutation
B. replication
C. transcription
D. translation

6 Which process uses the code on an RNA molecule to make a protein?

A. mutation
B. replication
C. transcription
D. translation

7 The Punnett square below shows a cross between a pea plant with yellow seeds and a pea plant with green seeds.

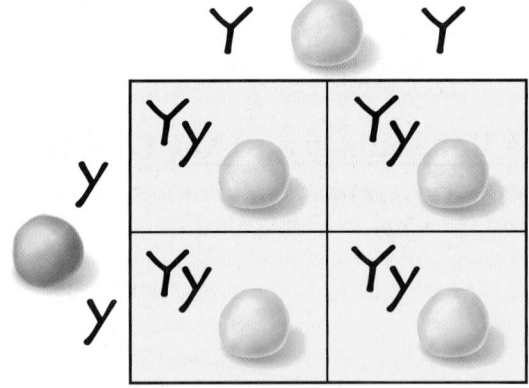

If mating produces 100 offspring, about how many will have yellow seeds?

A. 25
B. 50
C. 75
D. 100

8 Which term describes multiple genes affecting the phenotype of one trait?

A. codominance
B. blending inheritance
C. incomplete dominance
D. polygenic inheritance

Critical Thinking

9 **Compare** heterozygous genotype and homozygous genotype.

10 **Distinguish** between multiple alleles and polygenic inheritance.

11 **Give an example** of how the environment can affect an organism's phenotype.

12 **Predict** In pea plants, the allele for smooth pods is dominant to the allele for bumpy pods. Predict the genotype of a plant with bumpy pods. Can you predict the genotype of a plant with smooth pods? Explain.

13 **Interpret Graphics** In tomato plants, red fruit *(R)* is dominant to yellow fruit *(r)*. Interpret the Punnett square below, which shows a cross between a heterozygous red plant and a yellow plant. Include the possible genotypes and corresponding phenotypes.

	R	*r*
r	*Rr*	*rr*
r	*Rr*	*rr*

14 **Compare and contrast** characteristics of replication, transcription, translation, and mutation. Which of these processes takes place only in the nucleus of a cell? Which can take place in both the nucleus and the cytoplasm? How do you know?

Writing in Science

15 **Write** a paragraph contrasting the blending theory of inheritance with the current theory of inheritance. Include a main idea, supporting details, and a concluding sentence.

16 How are traits passed from generation to generation? Explain how dominant and recessive alleles interact to determine the expression of traits.

17 The photo below shows an albino offspring from a non-albino mother. If albinism is a recessive trait, what are the possible genotypes of the mother, the father, and the offspring?

Math Skills ✕ ÷ +

Review

Math Practice

Use Ratios

18 A cross between two heterozygous pea plants with yellow seeds produced 1,719 yellow seeds and 573 green seeds. What is the ratio of yellow to green seeds?

19 A cross between two heterozygous pea plants with smooth green pea pods produced 87 bumpy yellow pea pods, 261 smooth yellow pea pods, 261 bumpy green pea pods, and 783 smooth green pea pods. What is the ratio of bumpy yellow to smooth yellow to bumpy green to smooth green pea pods?

20 A jar contains three red, five green, two blue, and six yellow marbles. What is the ratio of red to green to blue to yellow marbles?

Standardized Test Practice

Record your answers on the answer sheet provided by your teacher or on a sheet of paper.

Multiple Choice

Use the diagram below to answer questions 1 and 2.

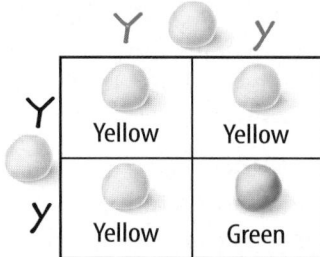

1 Which genotype belongs in the lower right square?

A YY

B Yy

C yY

D yy

2 What percentage of plants from this cross will produce yellow seeds?

A 25 percent

B 50 percent

C 75 percent

D 100 percent

3 When Mendel crossed a true-breeding plant with purple flowers and a true-breeding plant with white flowers, ALL off-spring had purple flowers. This is because white flowers are

A dominant.

B heterozygous.

C polygenic.

D recessive.

4 Which process copies an organism's DNA?

A mutation

B replication

C transcription

D translation

Use the chart below to answer question 5.

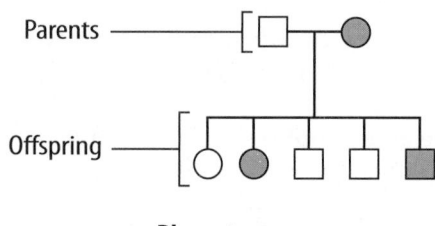

Phenotypes
○ Female, dominant ● Female, recessive
□ Male, dominant ■ Male, recessive

5 Based on the pedigree above, how many offspring from this cross had the recessive phenotype?

A 1

B 2

C 3

D 5

6 Which is NOT true of a hybrid?

A It has one recessive allele.

B It has pairs of chromosomes.

C Its genotype is homozygous.

D Its phenotype is dominant.

7 Alleles are different forms of a

A chromosome.

B gene.

C nucleotide.

D protein.

8 Which is true of an offspring with incomplete dominance?

A Both alleles can be observed in its phenotype.

B Every offspring shows the dominant phenotype.

C Multiple genes determine its phenotype.

D Offspring phenotype is a combination of the parents' phenotypes.

Use the diagrams below to answer question 9.

Before Replication

After Replication

9 The diagrams above show a segment of DNA before and after replication. Which occurred during replication?

   A deletion

   B insertion

   C substitution

   D translation

10 Which human characteristic is controlled by polygenic inheritance?

   A blood type

   B earlobe position

   C eye color

   D thumb shape

11 Mendel crossed a true-breeding plant with round seeds and a true-breeding plant with wrinkled seeds. Which was true of every offspring of this cross?

   A They had the recessive phenotype.

   B They showed a combination of traits.

   C They were homozygous.

   D They were hybrid plants.

Constructed Response

Use the diagram below to answer questions 12 and 13.

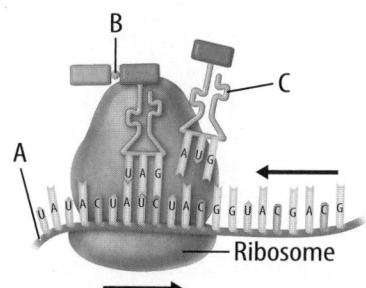

12 Describe what is happening in the phase of translation shown in the diagram.

13 What are the three types of RNA in the diagram? How do these types work together during translation?

14 What is the importance of translation in your body?

15 Mendel began his experiments with true-breeding plants. Why was this important?

16 How did Mendel's experimental methods help him develop his hypotheses on inheritance?

17 What environmental factors affect the phenotypes of organisms other than humans? Provide three examples from nature. What factor, other than genes, affects human phenotype? Give two examples. Why is knowledge of this non-genetic factor helpful?

NEED EXTRA HELP?																	
If You Missed Question...	1	2	3	4	5	6	7	8	9	10	11	12	13	14	15	16	17
Go to Lesson...	2	2	1	3	2	1,2	2	2	3	2	1	3	3	3	1	1	2

Chapter 6

The Environment and Change Over Time

THE BIG IDEA How do species adapt to changing environments over time?

Inquiry Swarm of Bees?

A type of orchid plant, called a bee orchid, produces this flower. You might have noticed that the flower looks like a bee.

- What is the advantage to the plant to have flowers that look like bees?

- How did the appearance of the flower develop over time?

- How do species adapt to changing environments over time?

Get Ready to Read

What do you think?

Before you read, decide if you agree or disagree with each of these statements. As you read this chapter, see if you change your mind about any of the statements.

1 Original tissues can be preserved as fossils.

2 Organisms become extinct only in mass extinction events.

3 Environmental change causes variations in populations.

4 Variations can lead to adaptations.

5 Living species contain no evidence that they are related to each other.

6 Plants and animals share similar genes.

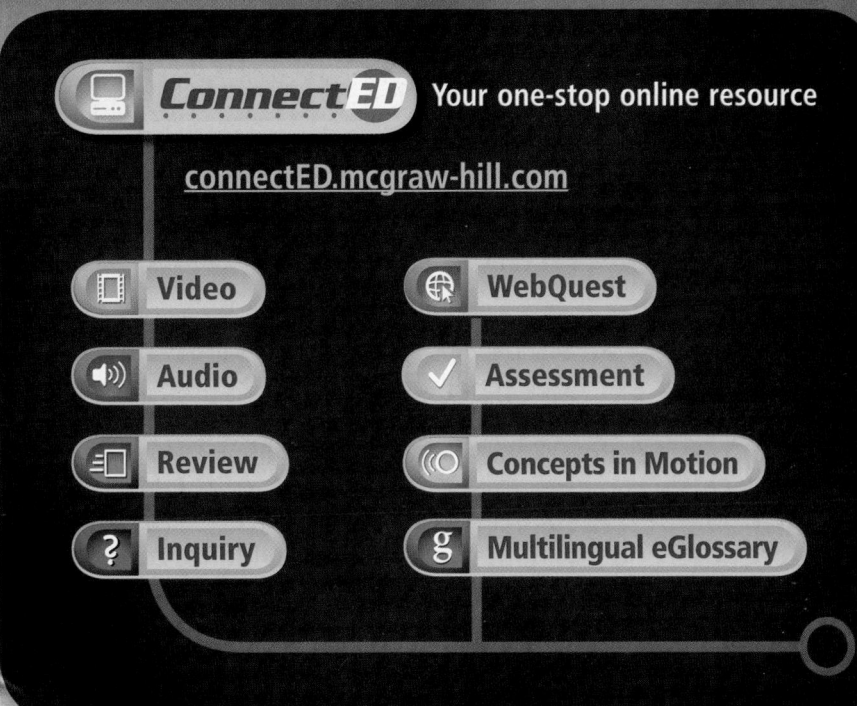

ConnectED Your one-stop online resource

connectED.mcgraw-hill.com

Video

WebQuest

Audio

Assessment

Review

Concepts in Motion

Inquiry

Multilingual eGlossary

Reading Guide

Key Concepts 🔑
ESSENTIAL QUESTIONS

- How do fossils form?
- How do scientists date fossils?
- How are fossils evidence of biological evolution?

Vocabulary

fossil record p. 189

mold p. 191

cast p. 191

trace fossil p. 191

geologic time scale p. 193

extinction p. 194

biological evolution p. 195

🄖 **Multilingual eGlossary**

🎞 **Video** **BrainPOP®**

Fossil Evidence of Evolution

Inquiry **What can be learned from fossils?**

When scientists find fossils, they use them as evidence to try to answer questions about past life on Earth. When did this organism live? What did this organism eat? How did it move or grow? How did this organism die? To what other organisms is this one related?

Molds and Casts

Sometimes when an organism dies, its shell or bone might make an impression in mud or sand. When the sediment hardens, so does the impression. *The impression of an organism in a rock is called a* **mold.** Sediments can later fill in the mold and harden to form a cast. *A* **cast** *is a fossil copy of an organism in a rock.* A single organism can form both a mold and a cast, as shown in **Table 1.** Molds and casts show only external features of organisms.

Trace Fossils

Evidence of an organism's movement or behavior—not just its physical structure—also can be preserved in rock. *A* **trace fossil** *is the preserved evidence of the activity of an organism.* For example, an organism might walk across mud. The tracks, such as the ones shown in **Table 1,** can fossilize if they are filled with sediment that hardens.

Original Material

In rare cases, the original tissues of an organism can be preserved. Examples of original-material fossils include mammoths frozen in ice and saber-toothed cats preserved in tar pits. Fossilized remains of ancient humans have been found in bogs. Most of these fossils are younger than 10,000 years old. However, the insect encased in amber in **Table 1** is millions of years old. Scientists also have found original tissue preserved in the bone of a dinosaur that lived 70 million years ago (mya).

Key Concept Check List the different ways fossils can form.

WORD ORIGIN

fossil
from Latin *fossilis*, means "to obtain by digging"

Molds and Casts	Trace Fossils	Original Material
When sediments hardened around this buried trilobite, a mold formed. Molds are usually of hard parts, such as shells or bone. If a mold is later filled with more sediments that harden, the mold can form a cast.	These footprints were made when a dinosaur walked across mud that later hardened. This trace fossil might provide evidence of the speed and weight of the dinosaur.	If original tissues of organisms are buried in the absence of oxygen for long periods of time, they can fossilize. The insect in this amber became stuck in tree sap that later hardened.

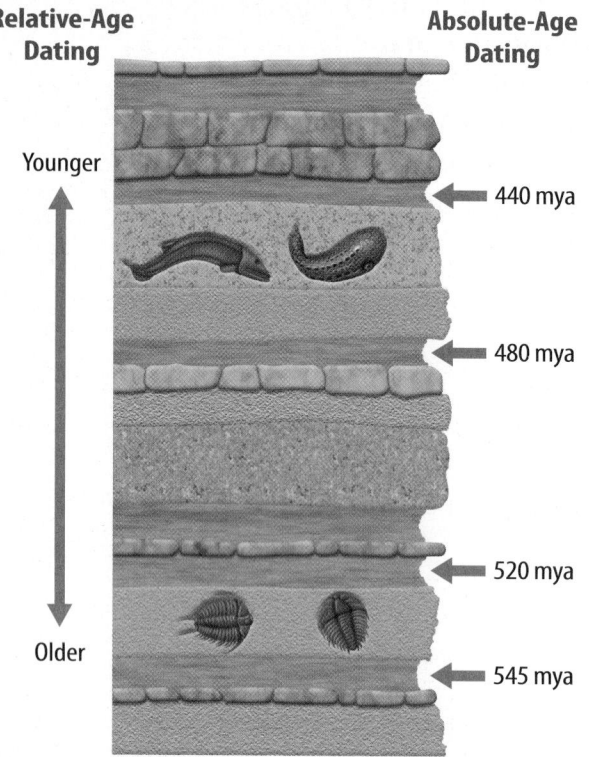

Younger

440 mya

480 mya

520 mya

Older

545 mya

Figure 2 If the age of the igneous layers is known, as shown above, it is possible to estimate the age of the sedimentary layers—and the fossils they contain—between them.

✓ **Visual Check** What is the estimated age of the trilobite fossils (bottom layer of fossils)?

REVIEW VOCABULARY

isotopes
atoms of the same element that have different numbers of neutrons

FOLDABLES®

Make a small shutter-fold book. Label it as shown. Under the left tab describe relative-age dating. Under the right tab describe absolute-age dating.

Relative-Age Dating

Absolute-Age Dating

Determining a Fossil's Age

Scientists cannot date most fossils directly. Instead, they date the rocks the fossils are embedded inside. Rocks erode or are recycled over time. However, scientists can determine ages for most of Earth's rocks.

Relative-Age Dating

How does your age compare to the ages of those around you? You might be younger than a brother but older than a sister. This is your relative age. Similarly, a rock is either older or younger than rocks nearby. In relative-age dating, scientists determine the relative order in which rock layers were deposited. In an undisturbed rock formation, they know that the bottom layers are oldest and the top layers are youngest, as shown in **Figure 2.** Relative-age dating helps scientists determine the relative order in which species have appeared on Earth over time.

 Key Concept Check How does relative-age dating help scientists learn about fossils?

Absolute-Age Dating

Absolute-age dating is more precise than relative-age dating. Scientists take advantage of radioactive decay, a natural clocklike process in rocks, to learn a rock's absolute age, or its age in years. In radioactive decay, unstable **isotopes** in rocks change into stable isotopes over time. Scientists measure the ratio of unstable isotopes to stable isotopes to find the age of a rock. This ratio is best measured in igneous rocks.

Igneous rocks form from volcanic magma. Magma is so hot that it is rare for parts of organisms in it to remain and form fossils. Most fossils form in sediments, which become sedimentary rock. To measure the age of sedimentary rock layers, scientists calculate the ages of igneous layers above and below them. In this way, they can estimate the ages of the fossils embedded within the sedimentary layers, as shown in **Figure 2.**

Fossils over Time

How old do you think Earth's oldest fossils are? You might be surprised to learn that evidence of microscopic, unicellular organisms has been found in rocks 3.4 billion years old. The oldest fossils visible to the unaided eye are about 565 million years old.

The Geologic Time Scale

It is hard to keep track of time that is millions and billions of years long. Scientists organize Earth's history into a time line called the geologic time scale. *The* **geologic time scale** *is a chart that divides Earth's history into different time units.* The longest time units in the geological time scale are eons. As shown in **Figure 3,** Earth's history is divided into four eons. Earth's most recent eon—the Phanerozoic (fa nuh ruh ZOH ihk) eon—is subdivided into three eras, also shown in **Figure 3.**

 Reading Check What is the geologic time scale?

Dividing Time

You might have noticed in **Figure 3** that neither eons nor eras are equal in length. When scientists began developing the geologic time scale in the 1800s, they did not have absolute-age dating methods. To mark time boundaries, they used fossils. Fossils provided an easy way to mark time. Scientists knew that different rock layers contained different types of fossils. Some of the fossils scientists use to mark the time boundaries are shown in **Figure 3.**

Often, a type of fossil found in one rock layer did not appear in layers above it. Even more surprising, entire collections of fossils in one layer were sometimes absent from layers above them. It seemed as if whole communities of organisms had suddenly disappeared.

 Reading Check What do scientists use to mark boundaries in the geologic time scale?

Review   Personal Tutor

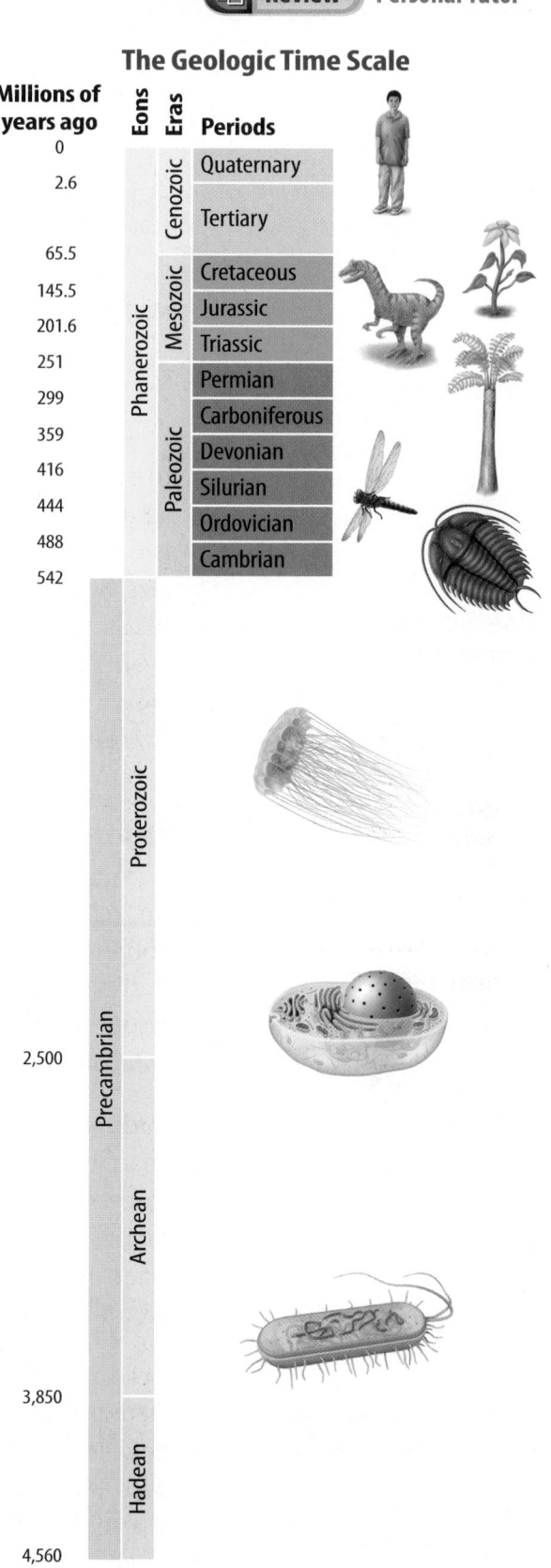

Figure 3 The Phanerozoic eon began about 540 million years ago and continues to the present day. It contains most of Earth's fossil record.

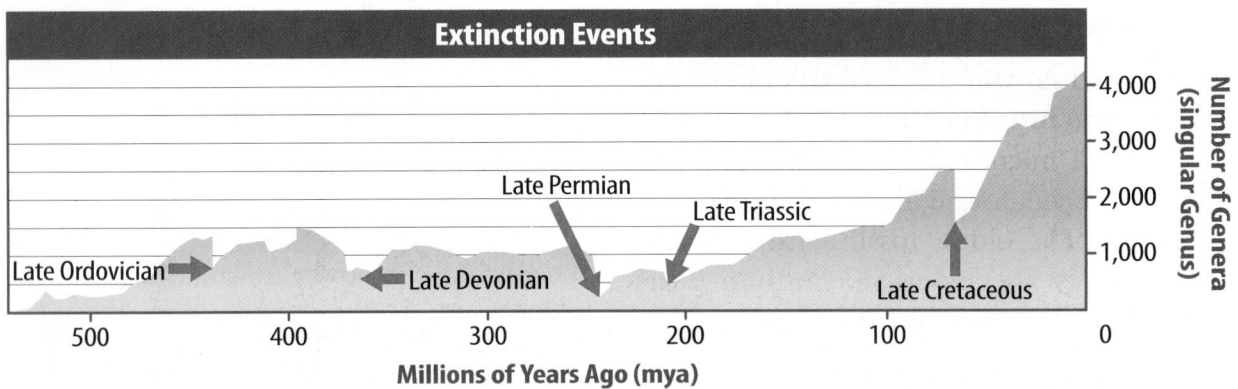

Extinction Events

Number of Genera (singular Genus)

4,000
3,000
2,000
1,000
0

Late Permian

Late Triassic

Late Ordovician

Late Devonian

Late Cretaceous

500   400   300   200   100   0

Millions of Years Ago (mya)

Figure 4 Arrows mark the five major extinction events of the Phanerozoic eon.

Math Skills

Use Scientific Notation

Numbers that refer to the ages of Earth's fossils are very large, so scientists use scientific notation to work with them. For example, mammals appeared on Earth about 200 mya or 200,000,000 years ago. Change this number to scientific notation using the following process.

Move the decimal point until only one nonzero digit remains on the left.

200,000,000 = 2.00000000

Count the number of places you moved the decimal point (8) and use that number as a power of ten.

$200{,}000{,}000 = 2.0 \times 10^8$ years.

Practice

The first vertebrates appeared on Earth about 490,000,000 years ago. Express this time in scientific notation.

 **Review**

- **Math Practice**
- **Personal Tutor**

Extinctions

Scientists now understand that sudden disappearances of fossils in rock layers are evidence of extinction (ihk STINGK shun) events. **Extinction** *occurs when the last individual organism of a species dies.* A mass extinction occurs when many species become extinct within a few million years or less. The fossil record contains evidence that five mass extinction events have occurred during the Phanerozoic eon, as shown in **Figure 4.** Extinctions also occur at other times, on smaller scales. Evidence from the fossil record suggests extinctions have been common throughout Earth's history.

Environmental Change

What causes extinctions? Populations of organisms depend on resources in their environment for food and shelter. Sometimes environments change. After a change happens, individual organisms of a species might not be able to find the resources they need to survive. When this happens, the organisms die, and the species becomes extinct.

Sudden Changes Extinctions can occur when environments change quickly. A volcanic eruption or a meteorite impact can throw ash and dust into the atmosphere, blocking sunlight for many years. This can affect global climate and food webs. Scientists hypothesize that the impact of a huge meteorite 65 million years ago contributed to the extinction of dinosaurs.

Gradual Changes Not all environmental change is sudden. Depending on the location, Earth's tectonic plates move between 1 and 15 cm each year. As plates move and collide with each other over time, mountains form and oceans develop. If a mountain range or an ocean isolates a species, the species might become extinct if it cannot find the resources it needs. Species also might become extinct if sea level changes.

Reading Check What is the relationship between extinction and environmental change?

Extinctions and Evolution

The fossil record contains clear evidence of the extinction of species over time. But it also contains evidence of the appearance of many new species. How do new species arise?

Many early scientists thought that each species appeared on Earth independently of every other species. However, as more fossils were discovered, patterns in the fossil record began to emerge. Many fossil species in nearby rock layers had similar body plans and similar structures. It appeared as if they were related. For example, the series of horse fossils in **Figure 5** suggests that the modern horse is related to other extinct species. These species changed over time in what appeared to be a sequence. Change over time is evolution. **Biological evolution** *is the change over time in populations of related organisms.* Charles Darwin developed a theory about how species evolve from other species. You will read about Darwin's theory in the next lesson.

 Key Concept Check How are fossils evidence of biological evolution?

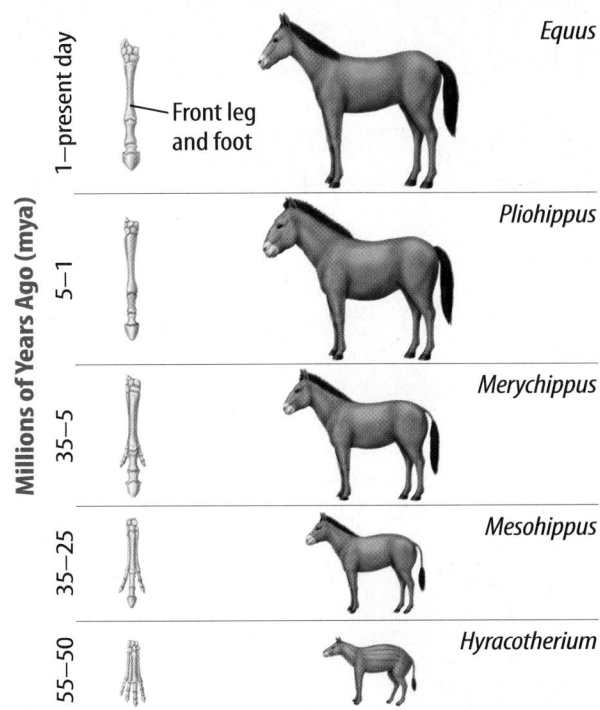

Figure 5 The fossil record is evidence that horses descended from organisms for which only fossils exist today.

Inquiry **MiniLab**   20 minutes

How do species change over time?

Over long time periods on Earth, certain individuals within populations of organisms were able to survive better than others.

1. Choose a species from the **Species I.D. Cards.**

2. On **chart paper,** draw six squares in a row and number them 1–6, respectively. Use **colored pencils** and **markers** to make a comic strip showing the ancestral and present-day forms of your species in frames 1 and 6.

3. Use information from the I.D. Card to show what you think would be the progression of changes in the species in frames 2–5.

4. In speech bubbles, explain how each change helped the species to survive.

Analyze and Conclude

1. **Infer** why a scientist would identify a fossil from the species in the first frame of your cartoon as the ancestral form of the present-day species.

2. **Key Concept** How would the fossils of the species at each stage provide evidence of biological change over time?

Lesson 1 Review

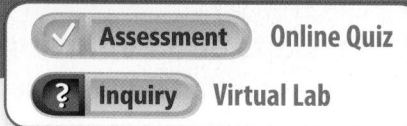
Visual Summary

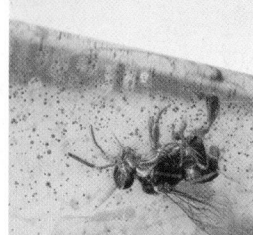

Fossils can consist of the hard parts or soft parts of organisms. Fossils can be an impression of an organism or consist of original tissues.

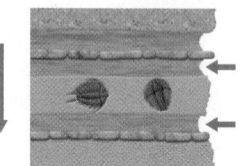

Scientists determine the age of a fossil through relative-age dating or absolute-age dating.

Scientists use fossils as evidence that species have changed over time.

FOLDABLES®

Use your lesson Foldable to review the lesson. Save your Foldable for the project at the end of the chapter.

What do you think NOW?

You first read the statements below at the beginning of the chapter.

1. Original tissues can be preserved as fossils.

2. Organisms become extinct only in mass extinction events.

Did you change your mind about whether you agree or disagree with the statements? Rewrite any false statements to make them true.

Use Vocabulary

1 All of the fossils ever found on Earth make up the _____.

2 When the last individual of a species dies, _____ occurs.

3 **Use the term** *biological evolution* in a sentence.

Understand Key Concepts 🗝

4 Which is the preserved evidence of the activity of an organism?
- **A.** cast
- **B.** mold
- **C.** fossil film
- **D.** trace fossil

5 **Explain** why the hard parts of organisms fossilize more often than soft parts.

6 **Draw and label** a diagram that shows how scientists date sedimentary rock layers.

Interpret Graphics

7 **Identify** Copy and fill in the table below to provide examples of changes that might lead to an extinction event.

Sudden changes	
Gradual changes	

Critical Thinking

8 **Infer** If the rock layers shown below have not been disturbed, what type of dating method would help you determine which layer is oldest? Explain.

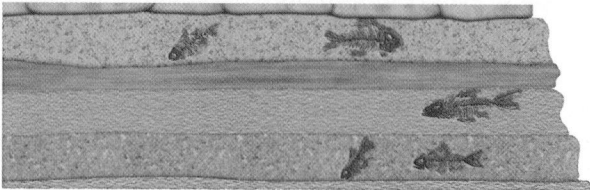

Math Skills ×÷+    Review

—— Math Practice ——

9 Dinosaurs disappeared from Earth about 65,000,000 years ago. Express this number in scientific notation.

Can you observe changes through time in collections of everyday objects?

Everyday objects that are invented, designed, and manufactured by humans often exhibit changes over time in both structure and function. How have these changes affected the efficiency and/or safety of some common items?

Materials

picture sets of items that have changed over time

Learn It

When scientists **observe** phenomena, they use their senses, such as sight, hearing, touch, and smell. They examine the entire object or situation first, then look carefully for details. After completing their observations, scientists use words or numbers to describe what they saw.

Try It

1 Working with your group members, choose a set of items that you wish to observe, such as telephones, bicycles, or automobiles.

2 Examine the pictures and observe how the item has changed over time.

3 Record your observations in your Science Journal.

4 Observe details of the structure and function of each of the items. Record your observations.

Apply It

5 **Present** your results in the form of an illustrated time line, a consumer magazine article, a role-play of a person-on-the-street interview, a television advertisement, or an idea of your own approved by your teacher.

6 🔑 **Key Concept** Identify how your product changed over time and in what ways the changes affected the efficiency and/or safety of the product.

Lesson 2

Reading Guide

Key Concepts 🔑
ESSENTIAL QUESTIONS

- Who was Charles Darwin?

- How does Darwin's theory of evolution by natural selection explain how species change over time?

- How are adaptations evidence of natural selection?

Vocabulary

naturalist p. 199

variation p. 201

natural selection p. 202

adaptation p. 203

camouflage p. 204

mimicry p. 204

selective breeding p. 205

 Multilingual eGlossary

 Video

What's Science Got to do With It?

Theory of Evolution by Natural Selection

inquiry **Are these exactly the same?**

Look closely at these zebras. Are they all exactly the same? How are they different? What accounts for these differences? How do the stripes help these organisms survive in their environment?

Are there variations within your class?

All populations contain variations in some characteristics of their members.

1. Read and complete a lab safety form.

2. Use a **meterstick** to measure the length from your elbow to the tip of your middle finger in centimeters. Record the measurement in your Science Journal.

3. Add your measurement to the class list.

4. Organize all of the measurements from shortest to longest.

5. Break the data into regular increments, such as 31–35 cm, 36–40 cm, and 41–45 cm. Count the number of measurements within each increment.

6. Construct a bar graph using the data. Label each axis and give your graph a title.

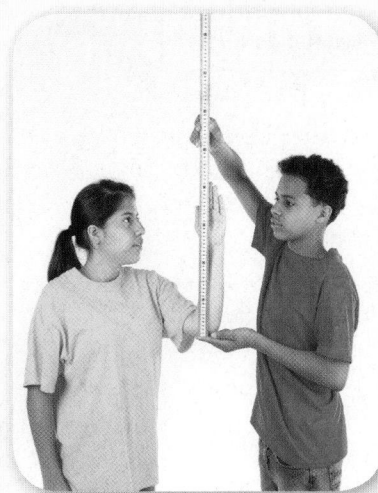

Think About This

1. What are the shortest and longest measurements?

2. How much do the shortest and longest lengths vary from each other?

3. 🔑 **Key Concept** Describe how your results provide evidence of variations within your classroom population.

Charles Darwin

How many species of birds can you name? You might think of robins, penguins, or even chickens. Scientists estimate that about 10,000 species of birds live on Earth today. Each bird species has similar characteristics. Each has wings, feathers, and a beak. Scientists hypothesize that all birds evolved from an earlier, or ancestral, population of birdlike organisms. As this population evolved into different species, birds became different sizes and colors. They developed different songs and eating habits, but all retained similar bird characteristics.

How do birds and other species evolve? One scientist who worked to answer this question was Charles Darwin. Darwin was an English naturalist who, in the mid-1800s, developed a theory of how evolution works. *A* **naturalist** *is a person who studies plants and animals by observing them.* Darwin spent many years observing plants and animals in their natural habitats before developing his theory. Recall that a theory is an explanation of the natural world that is well supported by evidence. Darwin was not the first to develop a theory of evolution, but his theory is the one best supported by evidence today.

🔑 **Key Concept Check** Who was Charles Darwin?

FOLDABLES

Make a small four-door shutterfold book. Use it to investigate the who, what, when, and where of Charles Darwin, the Galápagos Islands, and the theory of evolution by natural selection.

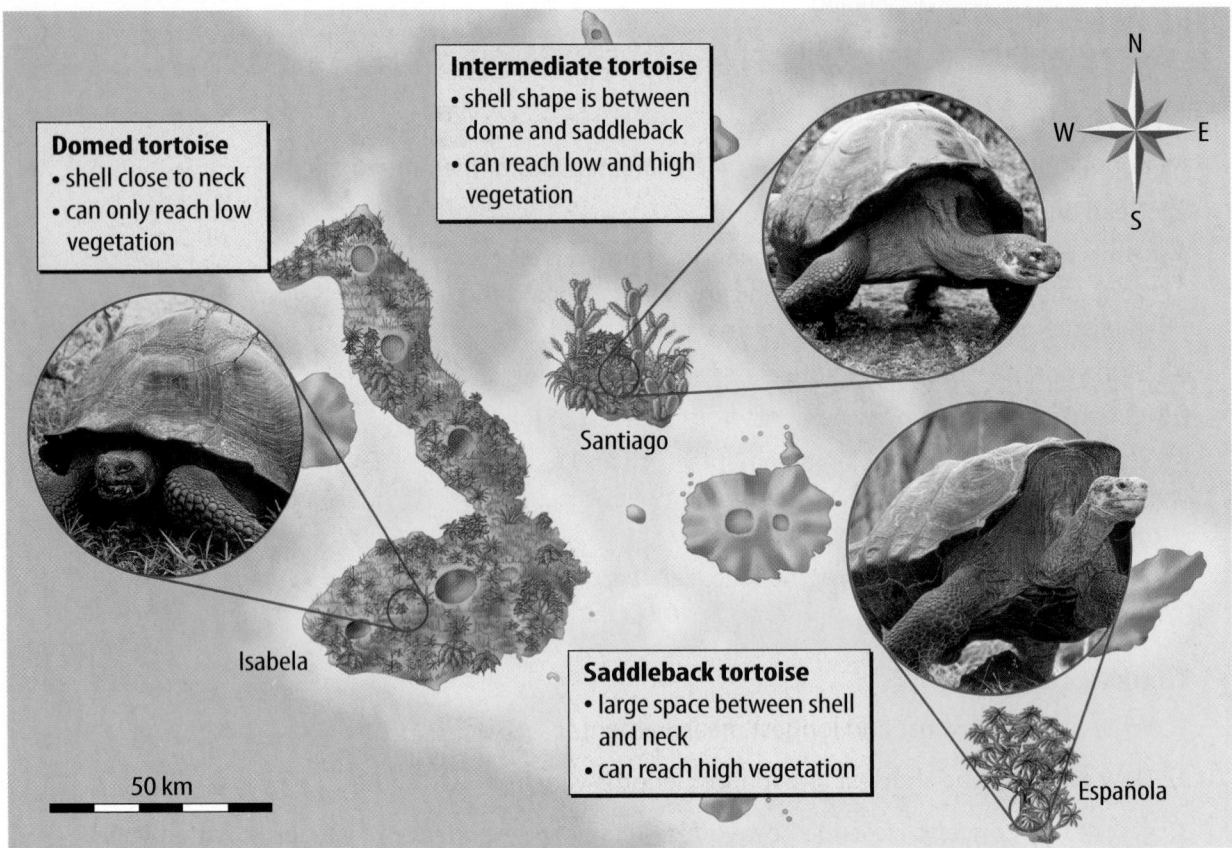

Domed tortoise
• shell close to neck
• can only reach low vegetation

Intermediate tortoise
• shell shape is between dome and saddleback
• can reach low and high vegetation

Santiago

Isabela

Saddleback tortoise
• large space between shell and neck
• can reach high vegetation

Española

50 km

N
W   E
S

Figure 6 Each island in the Galápagos has a different environment. Tortoises look different depending on which island environment they inhabit.

✓ **Visual Check** What type of vegetation do domed tortoises eat?

Voyage of the *Beagle*

Darwin served as a naturalist on the HMS *Beagle,* a survey ship of the British navy. During his voyage around the world, Darwin observed and collected many plants and animals.

The Galápagos Islands

Darwin was especially interested in the organisms he saw on the Galápagos (guh LAH puh gus) Islands. The islands, shown in **Figure 6,** are located 1,000 km off the South American coast in the Pacific Ocean. Darwin saw that each island had a slightly different environment. Some were dry. Some were more humid. Others had mixed environments.

Tortoises Giant tortoises lived on many of the islands. When a resident told him that the tortoises on each island looked different, as shown in **Figure 6,** Darwin became curious.

Mockingbirds and Finches Darwin also became curious about the variety of mockingbirds and finches he saw and collected on the islands. Like the tortoises, different types of mockingbirds and finches lived in different island environments. Later, he was surprised to learn that many of these varieties were different enough to be separate species.

✓ **Reading Check** What made Darwin become curious about the organisms that lived on the Galápagos Islands?

Darwin's Theory

Darwin realized there was a relationship between each species and the food sources of the island it lived on. Look again at **Figure 6.** You can see that tortoises with long necks lived on islands that had tall cacti. Their long necks enabled them to reach high to eat the cacti. The tortoises with short necks lived on islands that had plenty of short grass.

Common Ancestors

Darwin became **convinced** that all the tortoise species were related. He thought they all shared a common ancestor. He suspected that a storm had carried a small ancestral tortoise population to one of the islands from South America millions of years before. Eventually, the tortoises spread to the other islands. Their neck lengths and shell shapes changed to match their islands' food sources. How did this happen?

Variations

Darwin knew that individual members of a species exhibit slight differences, or variations. *A* **variation** *is a slight difference in an inherited trait of individual members of a species.* Even though the snail shells in **Figure 7** are not all exactly the same, they are all from snails of the same species. You can also see variations in the zebras in the photo at the beginning of this lesson. Variations arise naturally in populations. They occur in the offspring as a result of sexual reproduction. You might recall that variations are caused by random mutations, or changes, in genes. Mutations can lead to changes in phenotype. Recall that an organism's phenotype is all of the observable traits and characteristics of the organism. Genetic changes to phenotype can be passed on to future generations.

Figure 7 The variations among the shells of a species of tree snail occur naturally within the population.

✔ Visual Check Describe three variations among these snail shells.

Natural Selection

Darwin did not know about genes. But he realized that variations were the key to the puzzle of how populations of tortoises and other organisms evolved. Darwin understood that food is a limiting resource, which means that the food in each island environment could not support every tortoise that was born. Tortoises had to compete with each other for food. As the tortoises spread to the various islands, some were born with random variations in neck length. If a variation benefited a tortoise, allowing it to compete for food better than other tortoises, the tortoise lived longer. Because it lived longer, it reproduced more. It passed on its variations to its offspring.

This is Darwin's theory of evolution by natural selection. **Natural selection** *is the process by which populations of organisms with variations that help them survive in their environments live longer, compete better, and reproduce more than those that do not have the variations.* Natural selection explains how populations change as their environments change. It explains the process by which Galápagos tortoises became matched to their food sources, as illustrated in **Figure 8.** It also explains the diversity of the Galápagos finches and mockingbirds. Birds with beak variations that help them compete for food live longer and reproduce more.

Key Concept Check What role do variations have in the theory of evolution by natural selection?

Natural Selection

 **Review** **Personal Tutor**

① Reproduction
A population of tortoises produces many offspring that inherit its characteristics.

② Variation
A tortoise is born with a variation that makes its neck slightly longer.

③ Competition
Due to limited resources, not all offspring will survive. An offspring with a longer neck can eat more cacti than other tortoises. It lives longer and produces more offspring.

④ Selection
Over time, the variation is inherited by more and more offspring. Eventually, all tortoises have longer necks.

Figure 8 A beneficial variation in neck length spreads through a tortoise population by natural selection.

Adaptations

Natural selection explains how all species change over time as their environments change. Through natural selection, a helpful variation in one individual can be passed on to future members of a population. As time passes, more variations arise. The accumulation of many similar variations can lead to an adaptation (a dap TAY shun). *An* **adaptation** *is an inherited trait that increases an organism's chance of surviving and reproducing in its environment.* The long neck of certain species of tortoises is an adaptation to an environment with tall cacti.

 Key Concept Check How do variations lead to adaptations?

Types of Adaptations

Every species has many adaptations. Scientists classify adaptations into three categories: structural, behavioral, and functional. Structural adaptations involve color, shape, and other physical characteristics. The shape of a tortoise's neck is a structural adaptation. Behavioral adaptations involve the way an organism behaves or acts. Hunting at night and moving in herds are examples of behavioral adaptations. Functional adaptations involve internal body systems that affect **biochemistry.** A drop in body temperature during hibernation is an example of a functional adaptation. **Figure 9** illustrates examples of all three types of adaptations in the desert jackrabbit.

WORD ORIGIN · · · · · · · · · ·

adaptation
from Latin *adaptare*, means "to fit"

REVIEW VOCABULARY · · ·

biochemistry
the study of chemical processes in living organisms

Figure 9 The desert jackrabbit has structural, behavioral, and functional adaptations. These adaptations enable it to survive in its desert environment.

Structural adaptation The jackrabbit's powerful legs help it run fast to escape from predators.

Behavioral adaptation The jackrabbit stays still during the hottest part of the day, helping it conserve energy.

Functional adaptation The blood vessels in the jackrabbit's ears expand to enable the blood to cool before re-entering the body.

Seahorse

Caterpillar

Pelican

▲ Figure 10
Species evolve adaptations as they interact with their environments, which include other species.

Figure 11 This orchid and its moth pollinator have evolved so closely together that one cannot exist without the other. ▼

Environmental Interactions

Have you ever wanted to be invisible? Many species have evolved adaptations that make them nearly invisible. The sea-horse in **Figure 10** is the same color and has a texture similar to the coral it is resting on. This is a structural adaptation called camouflage (KAM uh flahj). **Camouflage** *is an adaptation that enables a species to blend in with its environment.*

Some species have adaptations that draw attention to them. The caterpillar in **Figure 10** resembles a snake. Predators see it and are scared away. *The resemblance of one species to another species is* **mimicry** (MIH mih kree). Camouflage and mimicry are adaptations that help species avoid being eaten. Many other adaptations help species eat. The pelican in **Figure 10** has a beak and mouth uniquely adapted to its food source—fish.

✓ **Reading Check** How do camouflage and mimicry differ?

Environments are complex. Species must adapt to an environment's living parts as well as to an environment's nonliving parts. Nonliving things include temperature, water, nutrients in soil, and climate. Deciduous trees shed their leaves due to changes in climate. Camouflage, mimicry, and mouth shape are adaptations mostly to an environment's living parts. An extreme example of two species adapting to each other is shown in **Figure 11**.

Living and nonliving factors are always changing. Even slight environmental changes affect how species adapt. If a species is unable to adapt, it becomes extinct. The fossil record contains many fossils of species unable to adapt to change.

Artificial Selection

Adaptations provide evidence of how closely Earth's species match their environments. This is exactly what Darwin's theory of evolution by natural selection predicted. Darwin provided many examples of adaptation in *On the Origin of Species,* the book he wrote to explain his theory. Darwin did not write this book until 20 years after he developed his theory. He spent those years collecting more evidence for his theory by studying barnacles, orchids, corals, and earthworms.

Darwin also had a hobby of breeding domestic pigeons. He selectively bred pigeons of different colors and shapes to produce new, fancy varieties. *The breeding of organisms for desired characteristics is called* **selective breeding.** Like many domestic plants and animals produced from selective breeding, pigeons look different from their ancestors, as shown in **Figure 12.** Darwin realized that changes caused by selective breeding were much like changes caused by natural selection. Instead of nature selecting variations, humans selected them. Darwin called this process artificial selection.

Artificial selection explains and supports Darwin's theory. As you will read in Lesson 3, other evidence also supports the idea that species evolve from other species.

Figure 12 The pouter pigeon (bottom left) and the fantail pigeon (bottom right) were derived from the wild rock pigeon (top).

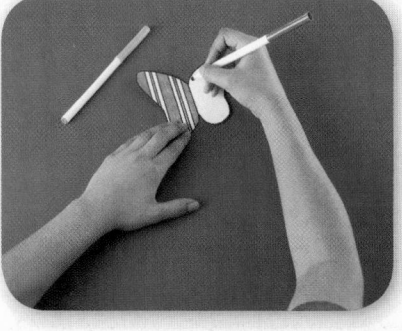

Lesson 2 Review

Visual Summary

Charles Darwin developed his theory of evolution partly by observing organisms in their natural environments.

Natural selection occurs when organisms with certain variations live longer, compete better, and reproduce more often than organisms that do not have the variations.

Adaptations occur when a beneficial variation is eventually inherited by all members of a population.

FOLDABLES

Use your lesson Foldable to review the lesson. Save your Foldable for the project at the end of the chapter.

What do you think NOW?

You first read the statements below at the beginning of the chapter.

3. Environmental change causes variations in populations.

4. Variations can lead to adaptations.

Did you change your mind about whether you agree or disagree with the statements? Rewrite any false statements to make them true.

Use Vocabulary

1. A person who studies plants and animals by observing them is a(n) _____.

2. Through _____, populations of organisms adapt to their environments.

3. Some species blend in to their environments through _____.

Understand Key Concepts

4. The observation that the Galápagos tortoises did not all live in the same environment helped Darwin
   A. develop his theory of adaptation.
   B. develop his theory of evolution.
   C. observe mimicry in nature.
   D. practice artificial selection.

5. **Assess** the importance of variations to natural selection.

6. **Compare and contrast** natural selection and artificial selection.

Interpret Graphics

7. **Explain** how the shape of the walking stick at right helps the insect survive in its environment.

8. **Sequence** Copy the graphic organizer below and sequence the steps by which a population of organisms changes by natural selection.

Critical Thinking

9. **Conclude** how Earth's birds developed their diversity through natural selection.

Peter and Rosemary Grant

Observing Natural Selection

Charles Darwin was a naturalist during the mid-1800s. Based on his observations of nature, he developed the theory of evolution by natural selection. Do scientists still work this way—drawing conclusions from observations? Is there information still to be learned about natural selection? The answer to both questions is yes.

Peter and Rosemary Grant are naturalists who have observed finches in the Galápagos Islands for more than 30 years. They have found that variations in the finches' food supply determine which birds will survive and reproduce. They have observed natural selection in action.

The Grants live on Daphne Major, an island in the Galápagos, for part of each year. They observe and take measurements to compare the size and shape of finches' beaks from year to year. They also examine the kinds of seeds and nuts available for the birds to eat. They use this information to relate changes in the birds' food supply to changes in the finch species' beaks.

The island's ecosystem is fragile, so the Grants take great care not to change the environment of Daphne Major as they observe the finches. They carefully plan their diet to avoid introducing new plant species to the island. They bring all the freshwater they need to drink, and they wash in the ocean. For the Grants, it's just part of the job. As naturalists, they try to observe without interfering with the habitat in which they are living.

▲ Peter and Rosemary Grant make observations and collect data in the field.

▲ This large ground finch is one of the kinds of birds studied by the Grants.

It's Your Turn

RESEARCH AND REPORT Find out more about careers in evolution, ecology, or population biology. What kind of work is done in the laboratory? What kind of work is done in the field? Write a report to explain your findings.

Reading Guide

Key Concepts 🔑
ESSENTIAL QUESTIONS

- What evidence from living species supports the theory that species descended from other species over time?

- How are Earth's organisms related?

Vocabulary

comparative anatomy p. 210

homologous structure p. 210

analogous structure p. 211

vestigial structure p. 211

embryology p. 212

g **Multilingual eGlossary**

Biological Evidence of Evolution

Inquiry Does this bird fly?

Some birds, such as the flightless cormorant above, have wings but cannot fly. Their wings are too small to support their bodies in flight. Why do they still have wings? What can scientists learn about the ancestors of present-day birds that have wings but do not fly?

How is the structure of a spoon related to its function?

Would you eat your morning cereal with a spoon that had holes in it? Is using a teaspoon the most efficient way to serve mashed potatoes and gravy to a large group of people? How about using an extra large spoon, or ladle, to eat soup from a small bowl?

1. Read and complete a lab safety form.

2. In a small group, examine your **set of spoons** and discuss your observations.

3. Sketch or describe the structure of each spoon in your Science Journal. Discuss the purpose that each spoon shape might serve.

4. Label the spoons in your Science Journal with their purposes.

Think About This

1. Describe the similarities and differences among the spoons.

2. If spoons were organisms, what do you think the ancestral spoon would look like?

3. 🔑 **Key Concept** Explain how three of the spoons have different structures and functions, even though they are related by their similarities.

Evidence for Evolution

Recall the sequence of horse fossils from Lesson 1. The sequence might have suggested to you that horses evolved in a straight line—that one species replaced another in a series of orderly steps. Evolution does not occur this way. The diagram in **Figure 13** shows a more realistic version of horse evolution, which looks more like a bush than a straight line. Different horse species were sometimes alive at the same time. They are related to each other because each descended from a common ancestor.

Living species that are closely related share a close common ancestor. The degree to which species are related depends on how closely in time they diverged, or split, from their common ancestor. Although the fossil record is incomplete, it contains many examples of fossil sequences showing close ancestral relationships. Living species show evidence of common ancestry, too.

Figure 13 The fossil record indicates that different species of horses often overlapped with each other.

✔️ **Visual Check** Which horse is the common ancestor to all horse species in this graph?

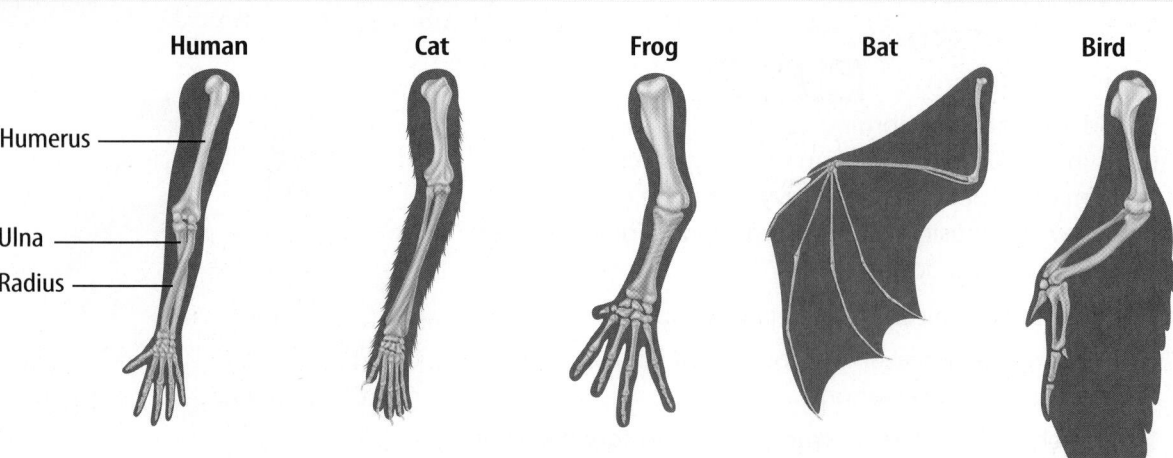

Human   Cat   Frog   Bat   Bird

Humerus

Ulna

Radius

Figure 14 The forelimbs of these species are different sizes, but their placement and structure suggest common ancestry.

Comparative Anatomy

Common ancestry is not difficult to see in many species. For example, it might seem easy to tell that robins, finches, and hawks evolved from a common ancestor. They all have similar features, such as feathers, wings, and beaks. The same is true for tigers, leopards, and house cats. But how are hawks related to cats? How are both hawks and cats related to frogs and bats? Observations of structural and functional similarities and differences in species that do not look alike are possible through comparative anatomy. **Comparative anatomy** *is the study of similarities and differences among structures of living species.*

Homologous Structures Humans, cats, frogs, bats, and birds look different and move in different ways. Humans use their arms for balance and their hands to grasp objects. Cats use their forelimbs to walk, run, and jump. Frogs use their forelimbs to jump. Bats and birds use their forelimbs as wings for flying. However, the forelimb bones of these species exhibit similar patterns, as shown in **Figure 14**. **Homologous** (huh MAH luh gus) **structures** *are body parts of organisms that are similar in structure and position but different in function.*

Homologous structures, such as the forelimbs of humans, cats, frogs, bats, and birds, suggest that these species are related. The more similar two structures are to each other, the more likely it is that the species have evolved from a recent common ancestor.

🔑 **Key Concept Check** How do homologous structures provide evidence for evolution?

Analogous Structures Can you think of a body part in two species that serves the same purpose but differs in structure? How about the wings of birds and flies? Both wings in **Figure 15** are used for flight. But bird wings are covered with feathers. Fly wings are covered with tiny hairs. *Body parts that perform a similar function but differ in structure are* **analogous** (uh NAH luh gus) **structures.** Differences in the structure of bird and fly wings indicate that birds and flies are not closely related.

Vestigial Structures

The bird in the photo at the beginning of this lesson has short, stubby wings. Yet it cannot fly. The bird's wings are an example of vestigial structures. **Vestigial** (veh STIH jee ul) **structures** *are body parts that have lost their original function through evolution.* The best explanation for vestigial structures is that the species with a vestigial structure is related to an ancestral species that used the structure for a specific purpose.

The whale shown in **Figure 16** has tiny pelvic bones inside its body. The presence of pelvic bones in whales suggests that whales descended from ancestors that used legs for walking on land. The fossil evidence supports this conclusion. Many fossils of whale ancestors show a gradual loss of legs over millions of years. They also show, at the same time, that whale ancestors became better adapted to their watery environments.

 Key Concept Check How are vestigial structures evidence of descent from ancestral species?

▲ **Figure 15** 🔑 Though used for the same function—flight—the wings of birds (top) and insects (bottom) are too different in structure to suggest close common ancestry.

Figure 16 🔑 Present-day whales have vestigial structures in the form of small pelvic bones. ▼

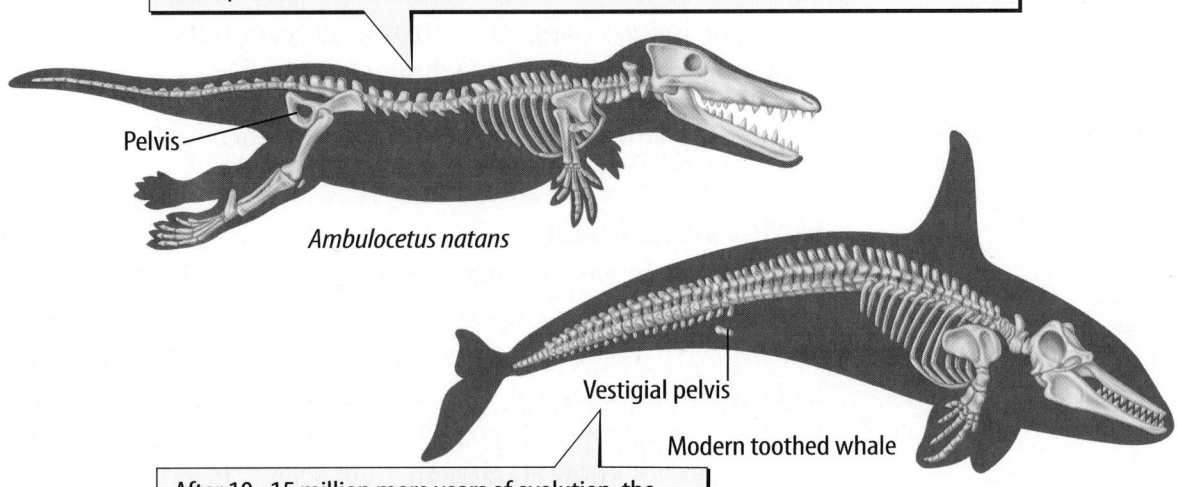

Between 50–40 million years ago, this mammal breathed air and walked clumsily on land. It spent a lot of time in water, but swimming was difficult because of its rear legs. Individuals born with variations that made their rear legs smaller lived longer and reproduced more. This mammal is an ancestor of modern whales.

Pelvis

Ambulocetus natans

Vestigial pelvis

Modern toothed whale

After 10–15 million more years of evolution, the ancestors of modern whales could not walk on land. They were adapted to an aquatic environment. Modern whales have two small vestigial pelvic bones that no longer support legs.

Pharyngeal pouches

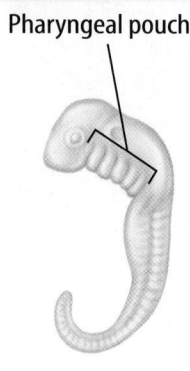

Fish

Pharyngeal pouches

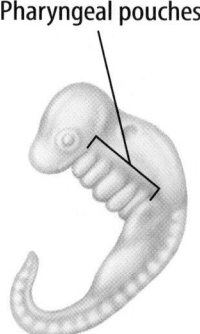

Reptile

Pharyngeal pouches

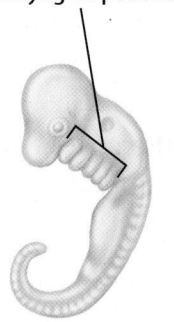

Bird

Pharyngeal pouches

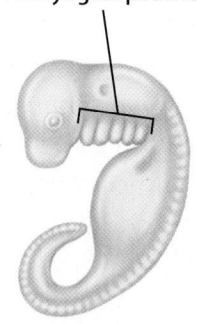

Human

Figure 17 All vertebrate embryos exhibit pharyngeal pouches at a certain stage of their development. These features, which develop into neck and face parts, suggest relatedness.

Word Origin

embryology
from Greek *embryon*, means "to swell" and from Greek *logia*, means "study of"

Developmental Biology

You have just read that studying the internal structures of organisms can help scientists learn more about how organisms are related. Studying the development of embryos can also provide scientists with evidence that certain species are related. *The science of the development of embryos from fertilization to birth is called* **embryology** (em bree AH luh jee).

Pharyngeal Pouches Embryos of different species often resemble each other at different stages of their development. For example, all vertebrate embryos have pharyngeal (fuh rihn JEE ul) pouches at one stage, as shown in **Figure 17.** This feature develops into different body parts in each vertebrate. Yet, in all vertebrates, each part is in the face or neck. For example, in reptiles, birds, and humans, part of the pharyngeal pouch develops into a gland in the neck that regulates calcium. In fish, the same part becomes the gills. One function of gills is to regulate calcium. The similarities in function and location of gills and glands suggest a strong evolutionary relationship between fish and other vertebrates.

 Key Concept Check How do pharyngeal pouches provide evidence of relationships among species?

Molecular Biology

Studies of fossils, comparative anatomy, and embryology provide support for Darwin's theory of evolution by natural selection. Molecular biology is the study of gene structure and function. Discoveries in molecular biology have confirmed and extended much of the data already collected about the theory of evolution. Darwin did not know about genes, but scientists today know that mutations in genes are the source of variations upon which natural selection acts. Genes provide powerful support for evolution.

✓ **Reading Check** What is molecular biology?

Comparing Sequences All organisms on Earth have genes. All genes are made of DNA, and all genes work in similar ways. This supports the idea that all organisms are related. Scientists can study relatedness of organisms by comparing genes and proteins among living species. For example, nearly all organisms contain a gene that codes for cytochrome *c*, a protein required for cellular respiration. Some species, such as humans and rhesus monkeys, have nearly identical cytochrome *c*. The more closely related two species are, the more similar their genes and proteins are.

 Key Concept Check How is molecular biology used to determine relationships among species?

Divergence Scientists have found that some stretches of shared DNA mutate at regular, predictable rates. Scientists use this "molecular clock" to estimate at what time in the past living species diverged from common ancestors. For example, as shown in **Figure 18,** molecular data indicate that whales and porpoises are more closely related to hippopotamuses than they are to any other living species.

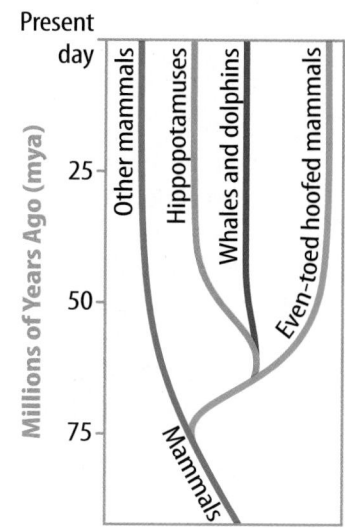

Figure 18 Whales and hippopotamuses share an ancestor that lived 50–60 mya.

Inquiry **MiniLab**

10 minutes

How related are organisms?

Proteins, such as cytochrome *c*, are made from combinations of just 20 amino acids. The graph below shows the number of amino acid differences in cytochrome *c* between humans and other organisms.

❶ Use the graph at right to answer the questions below.

Analyze and Conclude

1. **Identify** Which organism has the least difference in the number of amino acids in cytochrome *c* compared to humans? Which organism has the most difference?

2. **Infer** Which organisms do you think might be more closely related to each other: a dog and a turtle or a dog and a silkworm? Explain your answer.

3. **Key Concept** Notice the differences in the number of amino acids in cytochrome *c* between each organism and humans. How might these differences explain the relatedness of each organism to humans?

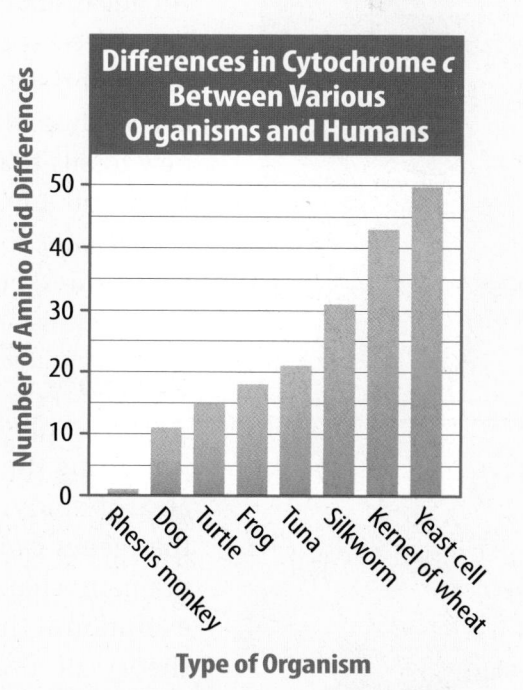

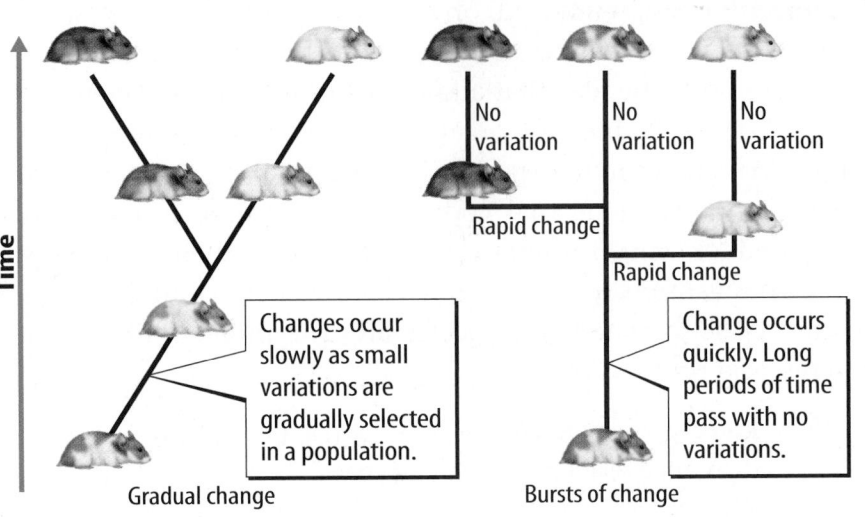

Figure 19 Many scientists think that natural selection produces new species slowly and steadily. Other scientists think species exist stably for long periods, then change occurs in short bursts. ▶

No variation

No variation

No variation

Rapid change

Rapid change

Changes occur slowly as small variations are gradually selected in a population.

Change occurs quickly. Long periods of time pass with no variations.

Gradual change

Bursts of change

Figure 20 *Tiktaalik* lived 385–359 mya. Like amphibians, it had wrists and lungs. Like fish, it had fins, gills, and scales. Scientists think it is an intermediate species linking fish and amphibians. ▼

The Study of Evolution Today

The theory of evolution by natural selection is the cornerstone of modern biology. Since Darwin published his theory, scientists have confirmed, refined, and extended Darwin's work. They have observed natural selection in hundreds of living species. Their studies of fossils, anatomy, embryology, and molecular biology have all provided evidence of relatedness among living and extinct species.

How New Species Form

New evidence supporting the theory of evolution by natural selection is discovered nearly every day. But scientists debate some of the details. **Figure 19** shows that scientists have different ideas about the rate at which natural selection produces new species—slowly and gradually or quickly, in bursts. The origin of a species is difficult to study on human time scales. It is also difficult to study in the incomplete fossil record. Yet, new fossils that have features of species that lived both before them and after them are discovered all the time. For example, the *Tiktaalik* fossil shown in **Figure 20** has both fish and amphibian features. Further fossil discoveries will help scientists study more details about the origin of new species.

Diversity

How evolution has produced Earth's wide diversity of organisms using the same basic building blocks—genes—is an active area of study in evolutionary biology. Scientists are finding that genes can be reorganized in simple ways and give rise to dramatic changes in organisms. Though scientists now study evolution at the molecular level, the basic principles of Darwin's theory of evolution by natural selection have remained unchanged for over 150 years.

Visual Summary

By comparing the anatomy of organisms and looking for homologous or analogous structures, scientists can determine if organisms had a common ancestor.

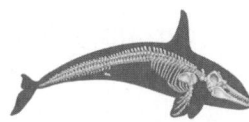

Some organisms have vestigial structures, suggesting that they descended from a species that used the structure for a purpose.

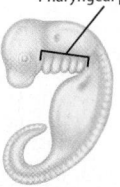

Pharyngeal pouches

Human

Scientists use evidence from developmental and molecular biology to help determine if organisms are related.

FOLDABLES

Use your lesson Foldable to review the lesson. Save your Foldable for the project at the end of the chapter.

What do you think NOW?

You first read the statements below at the beginning of the chapter.

5. Living species contain no evidence that they are related to each other.

6. Plants and animals share similar genes.

Did you change your mind about whether you agree or disagree with the statements? Rewrite any false statements to make them true.

Use Vocabulary

1. **Define** *embryology* in your own words.

2. **Distinguish** between a homologous structure and an analogous structure.

3. **Use the term** *vestigial structure* in a complete sentence.

Understand Key Concepts

4. Scientists use molecular biology to determine how two species are related by comparing the genes in one species to genes
   A. in extinct species. **C.** in related species.
   B. in human species. **D.** in related fossils.

5. **Discuss** how pharyngeal pouches provide evidence for biological evolution.

6. **Explain** Some blind cave salamanders have eyes. How might this be evidence that cave salamanders evolved from sighted ancestors?

Interpret Graphics

7. **Interpret** The wings of a flightless cormorant are an example of which type of structure?

8. **Assess** Copy and fill in the graphic organizer below to identify four areas of study that provide evidence for evolution.

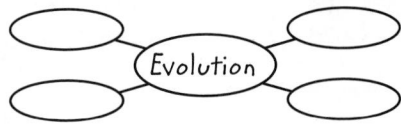

Evolution

Critical Thinking

9. **Predict** what a fossil that illustrates the evolution of a bird from a reptile might look like.

Model Adaptations in an Organism

Materials

clay

colored pencils

colored markers

toothpicks

construction paper

Also needed:
creative construction materials, glue, scissors

Safety

Conditions on our planet have changed since Earth formed over 4.5 billion years ago. Changes in the concentrations of gases in the atmosphere, temperature, and the amount of precipitation make Earth different today from when it first formed. Other events, such as volcanic eruptions, meteorite strikes, tsunamis, or wildfires, can drastically and rapidly change the conditions in certain environments. As you have read, Earth's fossil record provides evidence that, over millions of years, many organisms developed adaptations that enabled them to survive as Earth's environmental conditions changed.

Ask a Question

How do adaptations enable an organism to survive changes in the environment?

Make Observations

1 Read and complete a lab safety form.

2 Obtain Version 1.0 of the organism you will model from your teacher.

Volcanic eruption

3 Your teacher will describe Event 1 that has occurred on Earth while your organism is alive. Use markers and a piece of construction paper to design adaptations to your organism that would enable it to survive the changing conditions that result from Event 1. Label the adapted organism *Version 1.1.*

4 For each event that your teacher describes, design and draw the adaptations that would enable your organism to survive the changing conditions. Label each new organism *Version 1.X*, filling in the *X* with the appropriate version number.

5 Use the materials provided to make a model of the final version of your organism, showing all of the adaptations.

Predation

Form a Hypothesis

6 After reviewing and discussing all of the adaptations of your organism, formulate a hypothesis to explain how physical adaptations help an organism survive changes to the environment.

Test Your Hypothesis

7 Research evidence from the fossil record that shows one adaptation that developed and enabled an organism to survive over time under the conditions of one of the environmental events experienced by your model organism.

8 Record the information in your Science Journal.

Meteorite impact

Analyze and Conclude

9 **Compare** the adaptations that the different groups gave their organisms to survive each event described by your teacher. What kinds of different structures were created to help each organism survive?

10 **The Big Idea** Describe three variations in human populations that would enable some individuals to survive severe environmental changes.

Lab Tips

☑ Make sure you think of all of the implications of an environmental change event before you decide upon an adaptation.

☑ Decide upon your reasoning for the adaptation before putting the adaptation on your model.

Communicate Your Results

Present your completed organisms to the class and/or judges of "Ultimate Survivor." Explain the adaptations and the reasoning behind them in either an oral presentation or a demonstration, during which classmates and/or judges will review the models.

Inquiry **Extension**

Compare the organisms made by groups in your class to the organisms created by groups in other sections. Observe the differences in the adaptations of the organisms. In each section, the events were presented in a different order. How might this have affected the final appearance and characteristics of the different organisms?

Remember to use scientific methods.

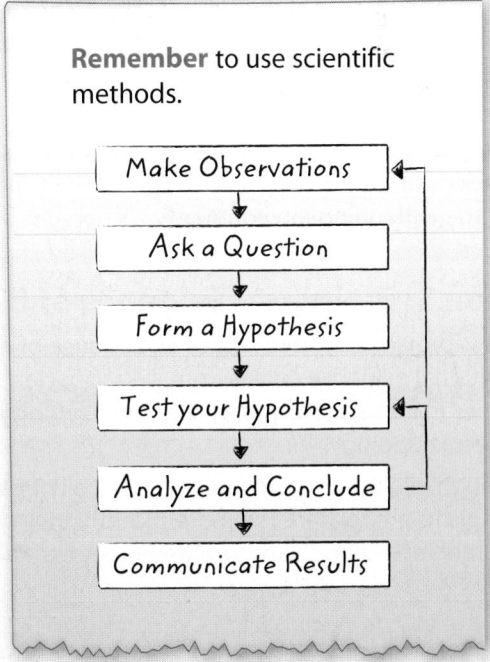

Make Observations
↓
Ask a Question
↓
Form a Hypothesis
↓
Test your Hypothesis
↓
Analyze and Conclude
↓
Communicate Results

 **THE BIG IDEA**

Through natural selection, species evolve as they adapt to Earth's changing environments.

Key Concepts Summary 🗝	Vocabulary
### Lesson 1: Fossil Evidence of Evolution • Fossils form in many ways, including mineral replacement, carbonization, and impressions in sediment. • Scientists can learn the ages of fossils by techniques of relative-age dating and absolute-age dating. • Though incomplete, the **fossil record** contains patterns suggesting the **biological evolution** of related species. 	**fossil record** p. 189 **mold** p. 191 **cast** p. 191 **trace fossil** p. 191 **geologic time scale** p. 193 **extinction** p. 194 **biological evolution** p. 195
### Lesson 2: Theory of Evolution by Natural Selection • The 19th century **naturalist** Charles Darwin developed a theory of evolution that is still studied today. • Darwin's theory of evolution by **natural selection** is the process by which populations with **variations** that help them survive in their environments live longer and reproduce more than those without beneficial variations. Over time, beneficial variations spread through populations, and new species that are adapted to their environments evolve. • **Camouflage, mimicry,** and other **adaptations** are evidence of the close relationships between species and their changing environments. 	**naturalist** p. 199 **variation** p. 201 **natural selection** p. 202 **adaptation** p. 203 **camouflage** p. 204 **mimicry** p. 204 **selective breeding** p. 205
### Lesson 3: Biological Evidence of Evolution • Fossils provide only one source of evidence of evolution. Additional evidence comes from living species, including studies in **comparative anatomy, embryology,** and molecular biology. • Through evolution by natural selection, all of Earth's organisms are related. The more recently they share a common ancestor, the more closely they are related. 	**comparative anatomy** p. 210 **homologous structure** p. 210 **analogous structure** p. 211 **vestigial structure** p. 211 **embryology** p. 212

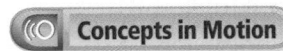
FOLDABLES® Chapter Project

Assemble your lesson Foldables as shown to make a Chapter Project. Use the project to review what you have learned in this chapter.

Use Vocabulary

Distinguish between the following terms.

1. *mold* and *cast*

2. *absolute-age dating* and *relative-age dating*

3. *extinction* and *biological evolution*

4. *variations* and *adaptations*

5. *camouflage* and *mimicry*

6. *natural selection* and *selective breeding*

7. *homologous structure* and *analogous structure*

8. *embryology* and *comparative anatomy*

9. *vestigial structure* and *homologous structure*

Link Vocabulary and Key Concepts

Concepts in Motion Interactive Concept Map

Copy this concept map, and then use vocabulary terms from the previous page to complete the concept map.

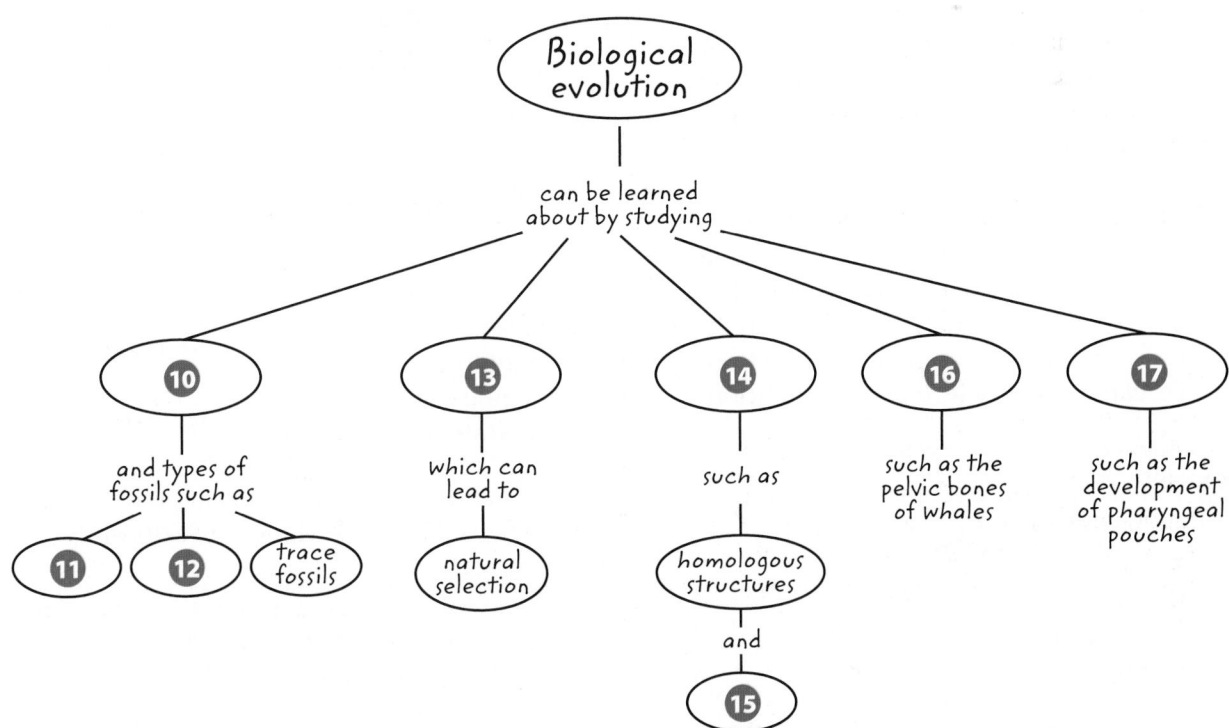

Understand Key Concepts

1 Why do scientists think the fossil record is incomplete?

A. Fossils decompose over time.

B. The formation of fossils is rare.

C. Only organisms with hard parts become fossils.

D. There are no fossils before the Phanerozoic eon.

2 What do the arrows on the graph below represent?

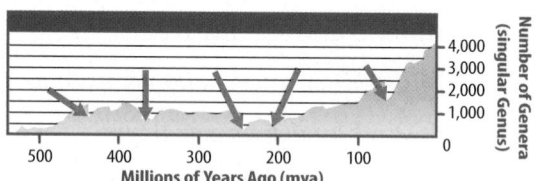

A. extinction events

B. meteorite impacts

C. changes in Earth's temperature

D. the evolution of a new species

3 What can scientists learn about fossils using techniques of absolute-age dating?

A. estimated ages of fossils in rock layers

B. precise ages of fossils in rock layers

C. causes of fossil disappearances in rock layers

D. structural similarities to other fossils in rock layers

4 Which is the sequence by which natural selection works?

A. selection → adaptation → variation

B. selection → variation → adaptation

C. variation → adaptation → selection

D. variation → selection → adaptation

5 Which type of fossil forms through carbonization?

A. cast

B. mold

C. fossil film

D. trace fossil

6 Which is the source of variations in a population of organisms?

A. changes in environment

B. changes in genes

C. the interaction of genes with an environment

D. the interaction of individuals with an environment

7 Which is an example of a functional adaptation?

A. a brightly colored butterfly

B. birds flying south in the fall

C. the spray of a skunk

D. thorns on a rose

8 Which is NOT an example of a vestigial structure?

A. eyes of a blind salamander

B. pelvic bones in a whale

C. thorns on a rose bush

D. wings on a flightless bird

9 Which do the images below represent?

Human

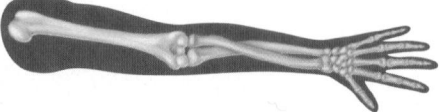

Cat

A. analogous structures

B. embryological structures

C. homologous structures

D. vestigial structures

10 Which is an example of a sudden change that could lead to the extinction of species?

A. a mountain range isolates a species

B. Earth's tectonic plates move

C. a volcano erupts

D. sea level changes

Critical Thinking

11 **Explain** the relationship between fossils and extinction events.

12 **Infer** In 2004, a fossil of an organism that had fins and gills, but also lungs and wrists, was discovered. What might this fossil suggest about evolution?

13 **Summarize** Darwin's theory of natural selection using the Galápagos tortoises or finches as an example.

14 **Assess** how the determination that Earth is 4.6 billion years provided support for the idea that all species evolved from a common ancestor.

15 **Describe** how cytochrome *c* provides evidence of evolution.

16 **Explain** why the discovery of genes was powerful support for Darwin's theory of natural selection.

17 **Interpret Graphics** The diagram below shows two different methods by which evolution by natural selection might proceed. Discuss how these two methods differ.

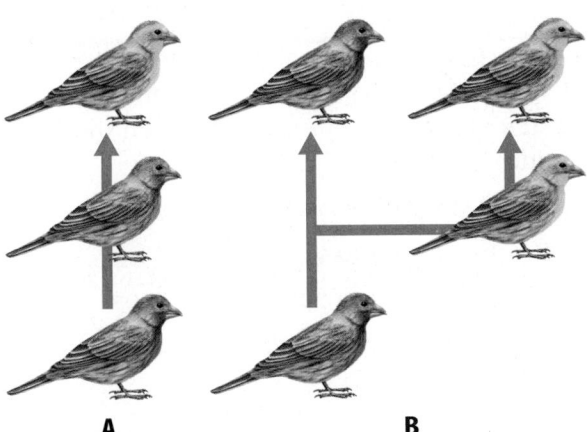

A   B

Writing in Science

18 **Write** a paragraph explaining how natural selection and selective breeding are related. Include a main idea, supporting details, and a concluding sentence.

REVIEW THE **BIG IDEA**

19 How do species adapt to changing environments over time? Explain how evidence from the fossil record and from living species suggests that Earth's species are related. List each type of evidence and provide an example of each.

20 The photo below shows an orchid that looks like a bee. How might this adaptation be evidence of evolution by natural selection?

Math Skills ×÷+

 **Review**
— Math Practice —

Use Scientific Notation

21 The earliest fossils appeared about 3,500,000,000 years ago. Express this number in scientific notation.

22 The oldest fossils visible to the unaided eye are about 565,000,000 years old. What is this time in scientific notation?

23 The oldest human fossils are about 1×10^4 years old. Express this as a whole number.

Record your answers on the answer sheet provided by your teacher or on a sheet of paper.

Multiple Choice

1 Which may form over time from the impression a bird feather makes in mud?

A cast

B mold

C fossil film

D trace fossil

2 Which is NOT one of the three main categories of adaptations?

A behavioral

B functional

C pharyngeal

D structural

Use the figure below to answer question 3.

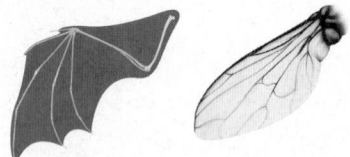

Bat wing   Insect wing

3 The figure shows the wings of a bat and an insect. Which term describes these structures?

A analogous

B developmental

C homologous

D vestigial

4 What is an adaptation?

A a body part that has lost its original function through evolution

B a characteristic that better equips an organism to survive in its environment

C a feature that appears briefly during early development

D a slight difference among the individuals in a species

5 What causes variations to arise in a population?

A changes in the environment

B competition for limited resources

C random mutations in genes

D rapid population increases

Use the image below to answer question 6.

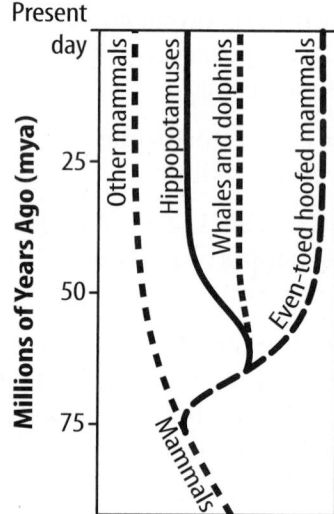

6 The image above shows that even-toed hoofed mammals and other mammals shared a common ancestor. When did this ancestor live?

A 25–35 million years ago

B 50–60 million years ago

C 60–75 million years ago

D 75 million years ago

7 Which term describes the method Darwin used that resulted in pigeons with desired traits?

A evolution

B mimicry

C natural selection

D selective breeding

Use the figure below to answer question 8.

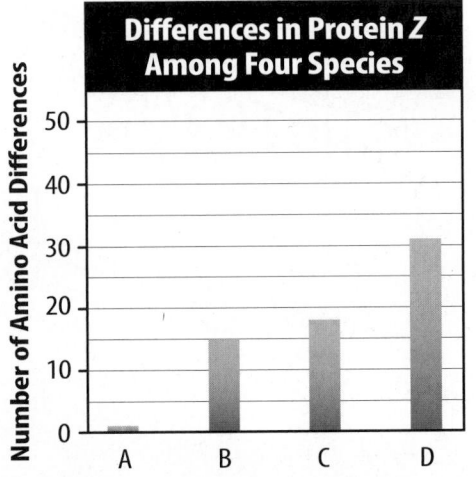

8 The chart shows that species B and C have the fewest amino acid differences for a protein among four species. What does this suggest about their evolutionary relationship?

  A They are more closely related to each other than to the other species.

  B They evolved at a faster rate when compared to the other species.

  C They share a developmental similarity not observed in the other species.

  D They do not share a common ancestor with the other species.

9 Which developmental similarity among all vertebrates is evidence that they share a common ancestor?

  A analogous structures

  B pharyngeal pouches

  C variation rates

  D vestigial structures

Constructed Response

Use the figure below to answer questions 10 and 11.

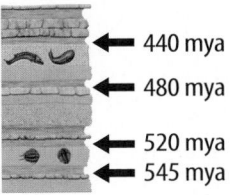

10 What is the approximate age of the fish fossils (top layer of fossils)? Express your answer as a range, and explain how you derived the answer.

11 What type of material or rock most likely forms the layer that contains the fossils? In your response, explain how these fossils formed.

12 Explain how a sudden and drastic environmental change might lead to the extinction of a species.

13 Darwin formulated his theory of evolution by natural selection based on the observation that food is a limiting resource. What did he mean by that? Use the Galápagos tortoises to explain your answer.

14 Explain how the fossil record provides evidence of biological evolution.

NEED EXTRA HELP?														
If You Missed Question...	1	2	3	4	5	6	7	8	9	10	11	12	13	14
Go to Lesson...	1	2	3	2	2	3	2	3	3	1	1	1	2	1

Unit 2

FROM BACTERIA TO PLANTS

1700 — **1800** — **1900**

1753
Swedish botanist Carl Linnaeus publishes *Species Plantarum*, a list of all plants known to him and the starting point of modern plant nomenclature.

1892
Russian botanist Dmitri Iwanowski discovers the first virus while studying tobacco mosaic disease. Iwanowski finds that the cause of the disease is small enough to pass through a filter made to trap all bacteria.

1930s
The development of commercial hybrid crops begins in the United States.

1983
Luc Montagnier's team at the Pasteur Institute in France isolates the retrovirus now called HIV.

Visit ConnectED for this unit's STEM activity.

2000

2002
Some scientists estimate that there are around 420,000 different species of plants on Earth.

2007
Researchers discover fungi that uses radioactivity as an energy source.

2008
While in the Bahamas, biologist Mikhail Matz discovers ocean-dwelling protists the size of grapes that leave complex trails in the sand. These trails resemble those found in Precambrian fossils and shed new light on the mystery of early animal development.

Inquiry

Technology

Some people wonder why governments have invested so much money to explore space. Why not solve problems here on Earth using that money? What did all of that money buy?

Technology is the practical application of science to commerce or industry. Science and technology depend on each other. Once scientists understand a scientific concept, they apply the science to new technologies. Today, many technologies originally developed for space are solving problems for people worldwide. For example, sensors designed to remotely measure the temperature of distant stars led to the development of the thermometer shown in **Figure 1.** When pointed toward the ear canal, the thermometer provides an accurate temperature reading in 2 seconds. The images in **Figure 2** show other technologies developed for space that are now used on Earth.

Figure 1 A technology originally developed to measure the temperature of stars now enables a parent to easily and quickly determine whether a child has a fever.

Figure 2 Medical professionals use technologies originally developed for space to help improve the health of patients.

To monitor the health of astronauts during space walks, space suits contain tiny sensors that measure astronauts' temperature, respiration, and cardiac activity. The technology that led to the development of these sensors is now used on Earth to monitor people's health. ▶

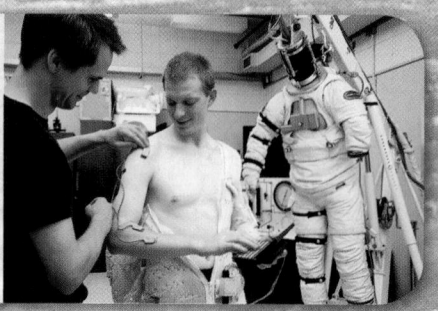

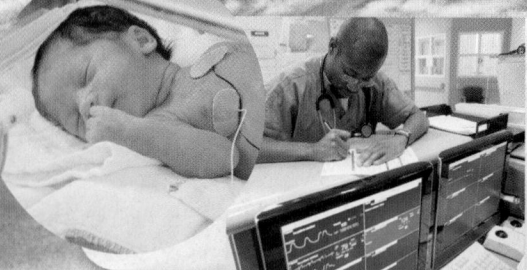

◀ Hospitals can monitor patients from a central nurses' station using electronics similar to those used in space suits. Sensors in infants' clothes can monitor a baby's breathing while the baby sleeps.

Doctors use sensors developed to study the effect of weightlessness on the muscles of astronauts to monitor repeated muscle movements that can lead to carpal tunnel syndrome in the workplace. ▶

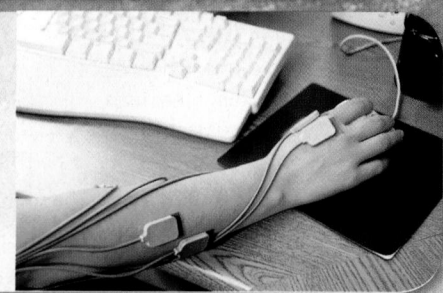

Space technology improves health worldwide.

Worldwide, people contribute to and benefit from space technologies. For example, a Canadian company produced robotic arms for the space shuttle. They collaborated with a medical school to develop instruments that enable surgeons to perform microscopic surgery on the brain. Chinese scientists developed a high-resolution X-ray imaging system for spacecraft. These X-rays are safer, faster, and more accurate than previous X-rays. Now, doctors can use the system to more accurately diagnose diseases. In addition, a Spanish company developed a navigation system for the blind based on space navigation technology.

Science and technology cannot solve all problems. But together, they help medical professionals keep people healthy and improve the quality of life for everyone on Earth.

Inquiry MiniLab
25 minutes

What can you invent from space technology?

Space technology may have more uses than are currently known. Your job is to think of a new use for a joystick.

1. Work with a partner to discuss ways in which technology used in space might be used to improve health. Consider various types of illnesses or medical conditions in which a person's abilities to do everyday tasks might be helped by space technology.

2. Select one idea and develop it. Draw pictures of your device to show how it will work.

Analyze and Conclude

1. **Explain** How does your invention improve the ability of medical professionals or the lives of people with medical conditions?

2. **Key Concept** Why is your device a space technology?

Surgeons use joysticks, similar to those used to control the Lunar Rover, to perform surgery on a patient who is thousands of miles away.

The temperature inside an astronaut's space suit can become extremely hot. So NASA developed a technology that circulates a cool fluid through tubes built into the suit.

Scientists applied this technology and developed a therapy for people with multiple sclerosis (MS). MS is a disease that slows the transfer of nerve signals from the brain. MS can affect the ability to think, speak, and control movement. Studies show that a slight decrease in body temperature can restore the transfer of some nerves signals. Therefore, scientists developed cooling suits for patients with MS based on NASA's cooling space suits.

Bacteria and Viruses

What are bacteria and viruses and why are they important?

Color-enhanced TEM Magnification: 63,000×

Inquiry Are robots attacking?

You might think this photo shows robots landing on another planet. Actually, this is a picture of viruses attacking a type of unicellular organism called a bacterium (plural, bacteria). Many viruses can attach to the surface of one bacterium.

- Do you think the bacterium is harmful? Are the viruses?
- What do you think happens after the viruses attach to the bacterium?
- What are viruses and bacteria and why are they important?

Get Ready to Read

What do you think?

Before you read, decide if you agree or disagree with each of these statements. As you read this chapter, see if you change your mind about any of the statements.

1 A bacterium does not have a nucleus.

2 Bacteria cannot move.

3 All bacteria cause diseases.

4 Bacteria are important for making many types of food.

5 Viruses are the smallest living organisms.

6 Viruses can replicate only inside an organism.

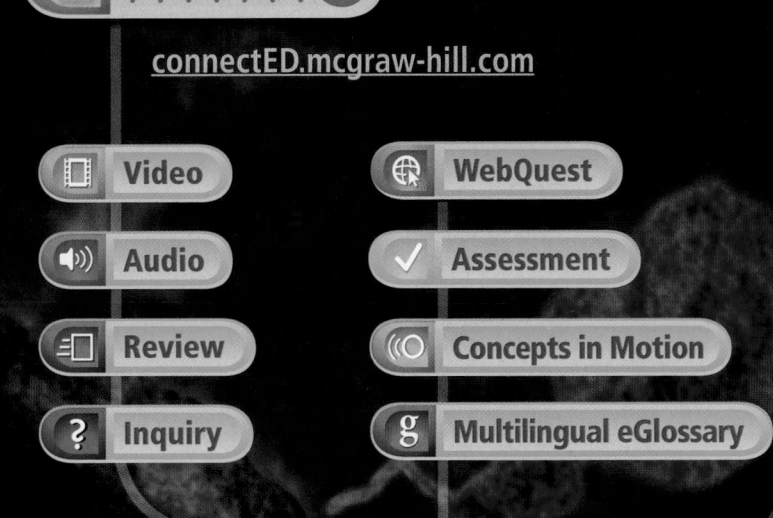

ConnectED Your one-stop online resource

connectED.mcgraw-hill.com

- Video
- WebQuest
- Audio
- Assessment
- Review
- Concepts in Motion
- Inquiry
- Multilingual eGlossary

Reading Guide

Key Concepts

ESSENTIAL QUESTIONS

- What are bacteria?

Vocabulary

bacterium p. 231

flagellum p. 234

fission p. 234

conjugation p. 234

endospore p. 235

[g] **Multilingual eGlossary**

[ ] **Video** **BrainPOP®**

What are bacteria?

Color-enhanced SEM Magnification: 560×

Inquiry How clean is this surface?

This photo shows a microscopic view of the point of a needle. The small orange things are bacteria. Bacteria are everywhere, even on surfaces that appear clean. Do you think bacteria are living or nonliving?

How small are bacteria?

Bacteria are tiny cells that can be difficult to see, even with a microscope. You might be surprised to learn that bacteria are found all around you, including in the air, on your skin, and in your body. One way of understanding how small bacteria are is to model their size.

1. Read and complete a lab safety form.

2. Examine the size of a **baseball** and a **2.5-gal. bucket.** Estimate how many baseballs you think would fit inside the bucket.

3. As a class, count how many baseballs it takes to fill the bucket.

Think About This

1. How much larger is the bucket than a baseball?

2. If your skin cells were the size of the bucket and bacteria were the size of the baseballs, how many bacterial cells would fit on a skin cell?

3. 🔑 **Key Concept** Why do you think you cannot see bacteria on your skin or on your desk?

Characteristics of Bacteria

Did you know that billions of tiny organisms too small to be seen surround you? These organisms, called bacteria, even live inside your body. **Bacteria** (singular, bacterium) *are microscopic prokaryotes.* You might recall that a prokaryote is a unicellular organism that does not have a nucleus or other membrane-bound organelles.

Bacteria live in almost every habitat on Earth, including the air, glaciers, the ocean floor, and in soil. A teaspoon of soil can contain between 100 million and 1 billion bacteria. Bacteria also live in or on almost every organism, both living and dead. Hundreds of species of bacteria live on your skin. In fact, your body contains more bacterial cells than human cells! The bacteria in your body outnumber human cells by 10 to 1.

🔑 **Key Concept Check** What are bacteria?

Other prokaryotes, called archaea (ar KEE uh; singular, archaean), are similar to bacteria and share many characteristics with them, including the lack of membrane-bound organelles. Archaea can live in places where few other organisms can survive, such as very warm areas or those with little oxygen. Both bacteria and archaea are important to life on Earth.

WORD ORIGIN · · · · · · · · · · · · ·

bacteria
from Greek *bakterion*, means "small staff" · · · · · · · · · · · · ·

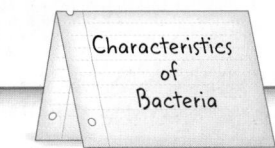

Make a folded book from a sheet of notebook paper. Label it as shown. Use your book to organize your notes on the characteristics of bacteria.

Characteristics of Bacteria

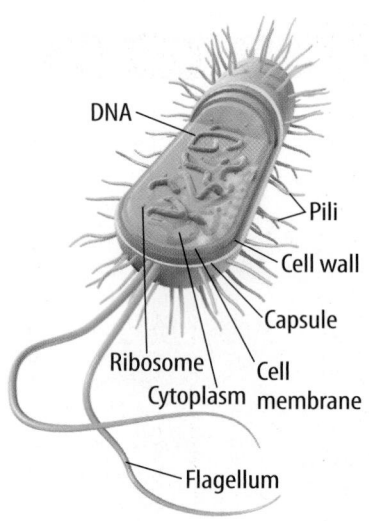

DNA
Pili
Cell wall
Capsule
Ribosome
Cell
Cytoplasm
membrane
Flagellum

▲ **Figure 1** Bacteria have a cell membrane and contain cytoplasm.

Structure of Bacteria

A typical bacterium, such as the one shown in **Figure 1,** consists of cytoplasm and DNA surrounded by a cell membrane and a cell wall. The cytoplasm also contains ribosomes. Most bacteria have DNA that is one coiled, circular chromosome. Many bacteria also have one or more small circular pieces of DNA called plasmids that are separate from its other DNA.

Some bacteria have specialized structures that help them survive. For example, the bacterium that causes pneumonia (noo MOH nyuh), an inflammation of the lungs, has a thick covering, or capsule, around its cell wall. The capsule protects the bacterium from drying out. It also prevents white blood cells from surrounding and antibiotics from entering it. Many bacteria have capsules with hairlike structures called pili (PI li) that help the bacteria stick to surfaces.

Size and Shapes of Bacteria

Bacteria are much smaller than plant or animal cells. Bacteria are generally only 1–5 micrometers (μm) (1 m = 1 million μm) wide, while an average eukaryotic cell is 10–100 μm wide. Scientists estimate that as many as 100 bacteria could be lined up across the head of a pin. As shown in **Figure 2,** bacteria generally have one of three basic shapes.

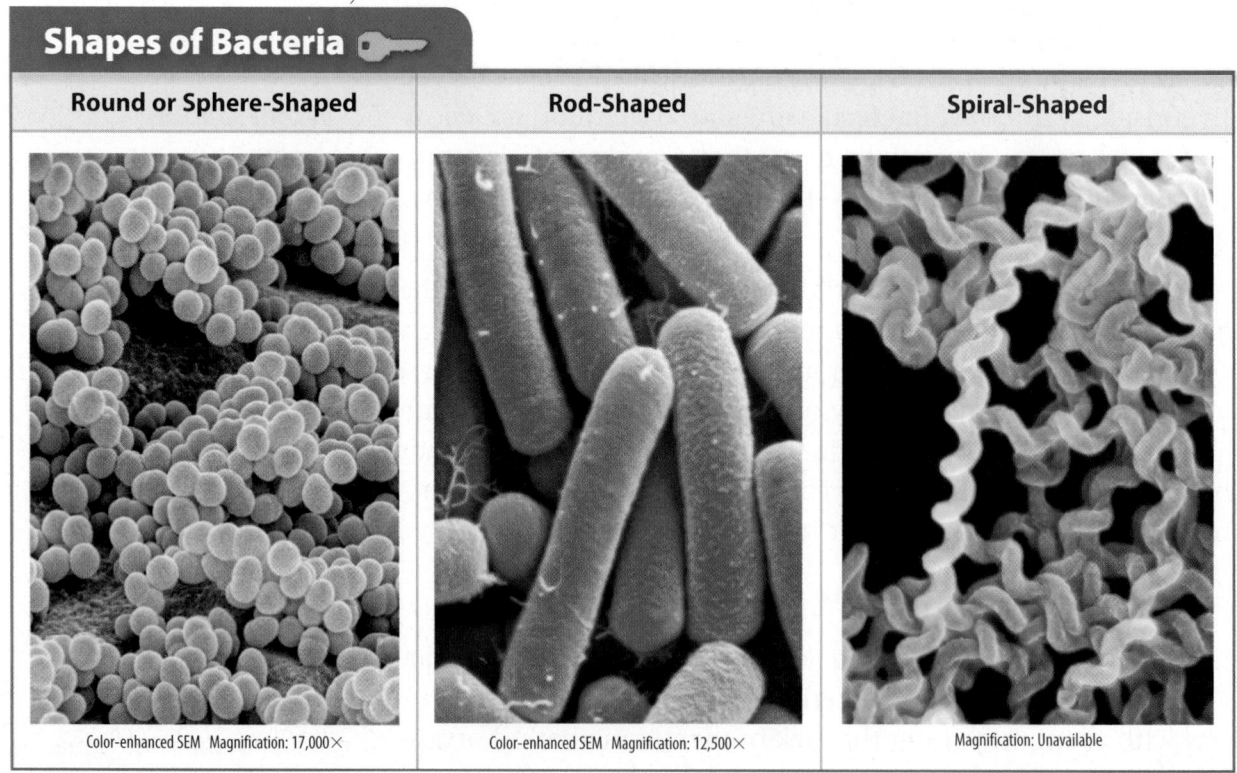

Shapes of Bacteria

Round or Sphere-Shaped	Rod-Shaped	Spiral-Shaped
Color-enhanced SEM Magnification: 17,000×	Color-enhanced SEM Magnification: 12,500×	Magnification: Unavailable

Figure 2 Bacteria are generally shaped like a sphere, a rod, or a spiral.

Visual Check What are the three basic shapes of bacteria?

How does a slime layer work?

Bacteria have a gelatinlike, protective coating called a slime layer on the outside of their cell walls. A slime layer can help a bacterium attach to surfaces or reduce water loss.

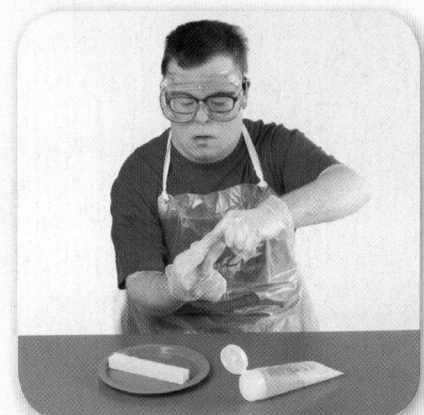

1. Read and complete a lab safety form.

2. Cut two 2-cm-wide strips from the long side of a **synthetic kitchen sponge**.

3. Soak both strips in **water**. Remove them from the water and squeeze out the excess water. Both strips should be damp.

4. Completely coat one strip with **hair-styling gel** to simulate a slime layer.

5. Place both strips on a **plate** and let them sit overnight.

Analyze and Conclude

1. **Describe** the appearance of the two strips in your Science Journal. How do they differ?

2. 🔑 **Key Concept** Explain how a slime layer might be beneficial to a bacterium when moving or finding food.

Obtaining Food and Energy

Bacteria live in many places. Because these environments are very different, bacteria obtain food in various ways. Some bacteria take in food and break it down and obtain energy. Many of these bacteria feed on dead organisms or organic waste, as shown in **Figure 3.** Others take in their nutrients from living hosts. For example, bacteria that cause tooth decay live in dental plaque on teeth and feed on sugars in the foods you eat and the beverages you drink.

Some bacteria make their own food. These bacteria use light energy and make food, like most plants do. These bacteria live where there is a lot of light, such as the surface of lakes and streams. Other bacteria use energy from chemical reactions and make their food. These bacteria live in places where there is no sunlight, such as the dark ocean floor.

🔑 **Key Concept Check** How do bacteria obtain food?

Most organisms, including humans, cannot survive without oxygen. However, certain bacteria do not need oxygen to survive. These bacteria are called anaerobic (a nuh ROH bihk) bacteria. Bacteria that need oxygen are called aerobic (er OH bihk) bacteria. Most bacteria in the environment are aerobic.

Figure 3 This banana is rotting because bacteria are breaking it down to use it for food.

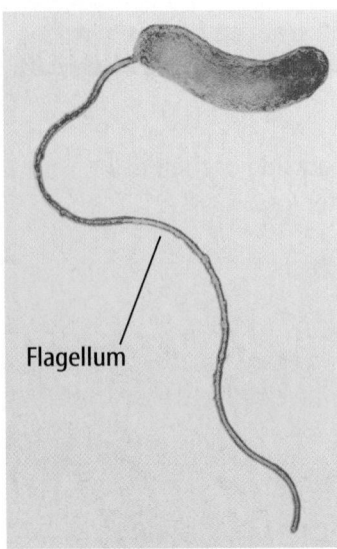

▲ **Figure 4** Some bacteria move using a flagellum.

Movement

Some bacteria are able to move around to find the resources that they need to survive. These bacteria have special structures for movement. *Many bacteria have long whiplike structures called* **flagella** (fluh JEH luh; singular, flagellum), *as shown in* **Figure 4.** Others twist or spiral as they move. Still other bacteria use their pili like grappling hooks or make threadlike structures that enable them to push away from a surface.

Reproduction

You might recall that organisms reproduce asexually or sexually. Bacteria reproduce asexually by fission. **Fission** *is cell division that forms two genetically identical cells.* Fission can occur quickly—as often as every 20 minutes under ideal conditions.

Bacteria produced by fission are identical to the parent cell. However, genetic variation can be increased by a process called conjugation, shown in **Figure 5.** *During* **conjugation** (kahn juh GAY shun), *two bacteria of the same species attach to each other and combine their genetic material.* DNA is transferred between the bacteria. This results in new combinations of genes, increasing genetic diversity. New organisms are not produced during conjugation, so the process is not considered reproduction.

✓ **Reading Check** How does conjugation increase the genetic diversity of bacteria?

Conjugation

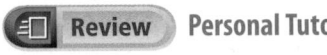 Review   Personal Tutor

Figure 5 Conjugation results in genetic diversity by transferring DNA between two bacteria cells.

✓ **Visual Check** What structure does the donor cell use to connect to the recipient cell?

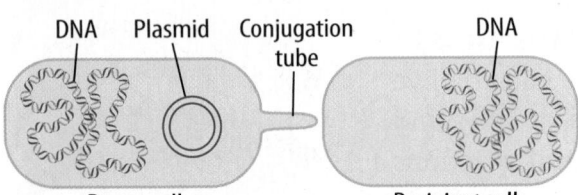

DNA   Plasmid   Conjugation tube   DNA

Donor cell   Recipient cell

❶ The donor cell and recipient cell both have circular chromosomal DNA. The donor cell also has DNA as a plasmid. The donor cell forms a conjugation tube and connects to the recipient cell.

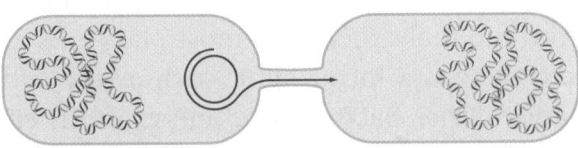

❷ The conjugation tube connects both cells. The plasmid splits in two and one plasmid strand moves through the conjugation tube into the recipient cell.

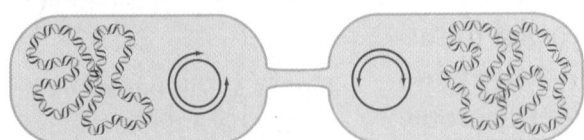

❸ The complimentary strands of the plasmids are completed in both bacteria.

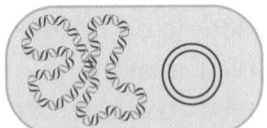 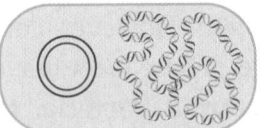

❹ With the new plasmids complete, the bacteria separate from each other. The recipient cell now contains plasmid DNA from the donor cell as well as its own chromosomal DNA.

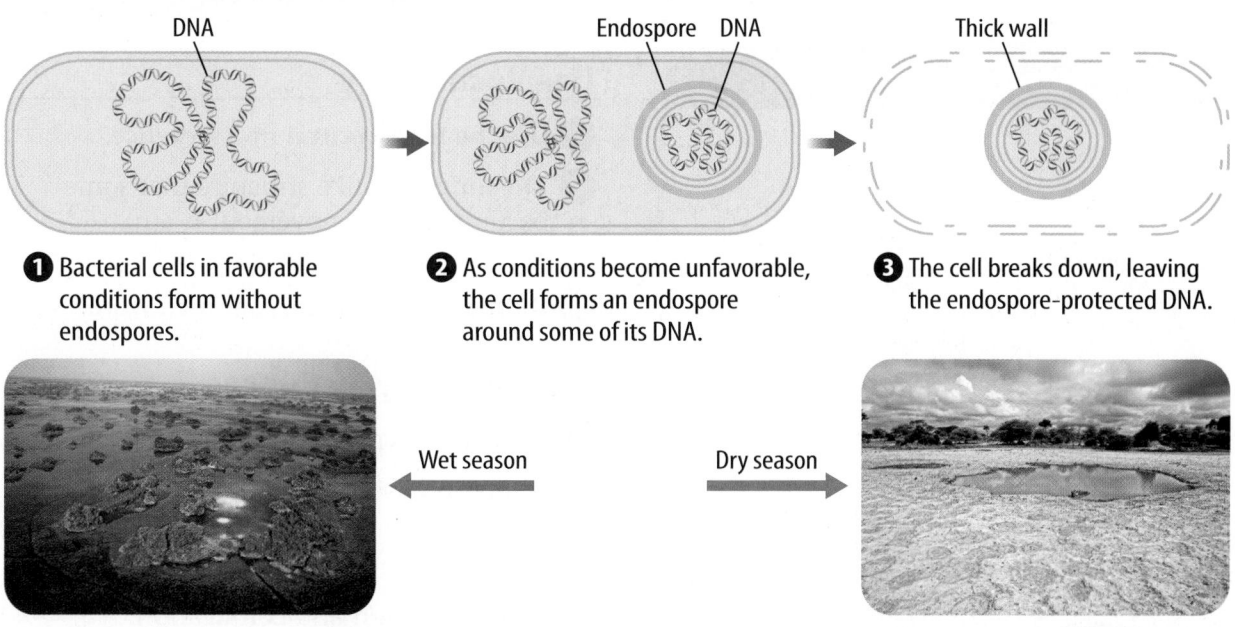

① Bacterial cells in favorable conditions form without endospores.

② As conditions become unfavorable, the cell forms an endospore around some of its DNA.

③ The cell breaks down, leaving the endospore-protected DNA.

Wet season → ← Dry season

Figure 6 An endospore protects a bacterium.

Endospores

Sometimes environmental conditions are unfavorable for the survival of bacteria. In these cases, some bacteria can form endospores. *An* **endospore** (EN doh spor) *forms when a bacterium builds a thick internal wall around its chromosome and part of the cytoplasm,* as shown in **Figure 6.** An endospore can protect a bacterium from intense heat, cold, or drought. It also enables a bacterium to remain dormant for months or even centuries. The ability to form endospores enables bacteria to survive extreme conditions that would normally kill them.

Archaea

Prokaryotes called archaea were once considered bacteria. Like a bacterium, an archaean has a cell wall and no nucleus or membrane-bound organelles. Its chromosome is also circular, like those in bacteria. However, there are some important differences between archaea and bacteria. The ribosomes of archaea more closely resemble the ribosomes of eukaryotes than those of bacteria. Archaea also contain molecules in their plasma membranes that are not found in any other known organisms. Archaea often live in extreme environments, such as hot springs and salt lakes. Some scientists refer to archaea as extremophiles (ik STREE muh filez)—a term that means "those that love extremes."

Math Skills

Use a Formula

Each time bacteria undergo fission, the population doubles. Use an equation to calculate how many bacteria there are: $n = x \times 2^f$ where n is the final number of bacteria, x is the starting number of bacteria, and f is the number of times that fission occurs.

Example: 100 bacteria undergo fission 3 times.

$f = 3$, so 2^f is 2 multiplied by itself 3 times. ($2 \times 2 \times 2 = 8$)

$n = 100 \times 8 = 800$ bacteria

Practice

How many bacteria would there be if 1 bacterium underwent fission 10 times?

 **Review**

• **Math Practice**
• **Personal Tutor**

Visual Summary

Bacteria are unicellu-lar prokaryotes.

Many bacteria feed on dead organic matter.

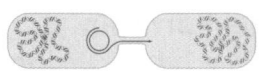

Bacteria can increase genetic diversity by sharing DNA through conjugation.

FOLDABLES®

Use your lesson Foldable to review the lesson. Save your Foldable for the project at the end of the chapter.

What do you think NOW?

You first read the statements below at the beginning of the chapter.

1. A bacterium does not have a nucleus.

2. Bacteria cannot move.

Did you change your mind about whether you agree or disagree with the statements? Rewrite any false statements to make them true.

Use Vocabulary

1 **Use the term** *bacteria* in a sentence.

2 The long whiplike structure that some bacteria use for movement is a(n) _____.

3 **Define** *conjugation* in your own words.

Understand Key Concepts

4 **Describe** a typical bacterium.

5 Which is NOT a common bacteria shape?
   A. rod   C. spiral
   B. sphere   D. square

6 **Contrast** fission and conjugation.

Interpret Graphics

7 **Identify** Copy and complete the table below to identify shapes of bacteria.

Bacterial Shapes	Illustration

Critical Thinking

8 **Describe** how a bacterium's small size could be an advantage or a disadvantage for its survival.

9 **Explain** how bacteria might find food and survive in an environment where few other organisms live.

10 **Analyze** how bacteria that can form endospores would have an advantage over bacteria that cannot form endospores.

Math Skills

Review
Math Practice

11 How many bacteria would there be if fission occurred 4 times with 1,000 bacteria?

Cooking Bacteria!

How Your Body Is Like Bleach

When it comes to killing germs, few things work as well as household bleach. How does bleach kill bacteria? Believe it or not, killing bacteria with bleach and boiling an egg involve similar processes.

▼ After cooking, egg proteins become a tangled mass.

Eggs are made mostly of proteins. Proteins are complex molecules in all plant and animal tissues. Proteins have specific functions that are dependent on the protein's shape. A protein's function changes if its shape is changed. When you cook an egg, the thermal energy transferred to the egg causes changes to the shape of the egg's proteins. Think of the firm texture of a cooked egg. When the egg's proteins are heated, they become a tangled mass.

▲ Before cooking, the proteins in eggs remain unfolded and change shape easily.

▼ Bacteria also contain proteins that change shape when exposed to heat.

A common ingredient in bleach is also found in your body's immune cells. ▶

Like eggs, bacteria also contain proteins. When bacteria are exposed to high temperatures, their proteins change shape, similar to those in a boiled egg. But what is the connection with bleach? Scientists have discovered that an ingredient in bleach, hypochlorite (hi puh KLOR ite), also causes proteins to change shape. The bacterial proteins that are affected by bleach are needed for the bacteria's growth. When the shape of those proteins changes, they no longer function properly, and the bacteria die.

Scientists also know now that your body's immune cells produce hypochlorite. Your body protects itself with the same chemical you can use to clean your kitchen!

It's Your Turn

RESEARCH AND REPORT A bacterial infection often causes inflammation, or a response to tissue damage that can include swelling and pain. Research and report on what causes inflammation.

Bacteria in Nature

Reading Guide

Key Concepts 🔑
ESSENTIAL QUESTIONS

- How can bacteria affect the environment?
- How can bacteria affect health?

Vocabulary

decomposition p. 240

nitrogen fixation p. 240

bioremediation p. 241

pathogen p. 242

antibiotic p. 242

pasteurization p. 243

 Multilingual eGlossary

 Video

What's Science Got to do With It?

Inquiry Why does this larva glow?

Some bacteria have the ability to glow in the dark. The moth larva shown on this page is filled with many such bacteria. These bacteria produce toxins that can slowly kill the animal. A chemical reaction within each bacterium makes the larva's body appear to glow.

How do bacteria affect the environment?

Bacteria are everywhere in your environment. They are in the water, in the air, and even in some foods.

1. Read and complete a lab safety form.
2. Carefully examine the contents of the two **bottles** provided by your teacher.
3. Record your observations in your Science Journal.

Think About This

1. Compare your observations of bottle A to those of bottle B. Which one appears to have more bacteria in it? Support your answer.

2. 🔑 **Key Concept** Based on your observations, how could bacteria affect the environment around you?

Beneficial Bacteria

When you hear about bacteria, you probably think about getting sick. However, only a fraction of all bacteria cause diseases. Most bacteria are beneficial. In fact, many organisms, including humans, depend on bacteria to survive. Some types of bacteria help with digestion and other body processes. For example, one type of bacteria in your intestines makes vitamin K, which helps your blood clot properly. Several others help break down food into smaller particles. Another type of bacteria called *Lactobacillus* lives in your intestines and prevents harmful bacteria from growing.

Animals benefit from bacteria as well. Without bacteria, some organisms, such as the cow pictured in **Figure 7,** wouldn't be able to digest the plants they eat. Bacteria and other microscopic organisms live in a large section of the cow's stomach called the rumen. The bacteria help break down a substance in grass called cellulose into smaller molecules that the cow can use.

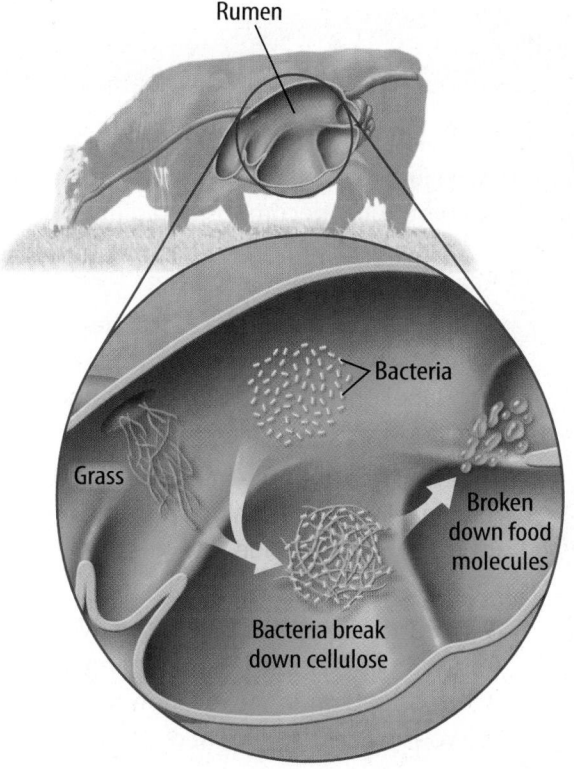

Rumen

Bacteria

Grass

Bacteria break down cellulose

Broken down food molecules

Figure 7 Cows get help digesting the cellulose in plants from the bacteria that live in their rumen— one of four stomach sections.

✓ **Visual Check** What role do bacteria play in a cow's digestion?

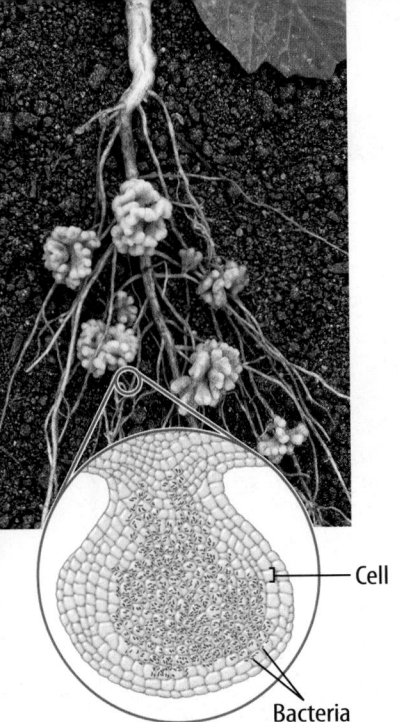

Cell

Bacteria

Figure 8 The roots of some plants have nodules that contain nitrogen-fixing bacteria.

Decomposition

What do you think would happen if organic waste such as food scraps and dead leaves never decayed? **Decomposition,** *the breaking down of dead organisms and organic waste,* is an important process in nature. When a tree dies, bacteria and other decomposing organisms feed on the dead organic matter. As decomposers break down the tree, they release molecules such as carbon and phosphorus into the soil that other organisms can then take in and use for life processes.

Nitrogen Fixation

Organisms use nitrogen to make proteins. Although about 78 percent of the atmosphere is nitrogen gas, it is in a form that plants and animals cannot use. Some plants can obtain nitrogen from bacteria. These plants have special structures called nodules, shown in **Figure 8,** on their roots. Bacteria in the nodules convert nitrogen from the atmosphere into a form usable to plants. **Nitrogen fixation** *is the conversion of atmospheric nitrogen into nitrogen compounds that are usable by living things.*

 Key Concept Check What are some ways that bacteria are beneficial to the environment?

Inquiry MiniLab 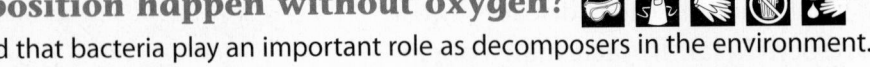 **20 minutes**

Can decomposition happen without oxygen?

You have just read that bacteria play an important role as decomposers in the environment. How do you think decomposition differs in aerobic and anaerobic environments?

1 Read and complete a lab safety form.

2 Obtain two **self-sealing plastic bags** from your teacher. Use a **permanent marker** and label one bag *Bag A* and the other *Bag B.*

3 Place a **slice of apple** in bag A. Seal the bag leaving as much air as possible inside of it. Set the bag aside.

4 Place **another slice of apple** in bag B. Carefully squeeze the bag to remove as much air as possible before sealing it. Place both bags in the location specified by your teacher and leave overnight.

5 The next lab day, observe both bags. Note the appearance of the apples. Record your observations in your Science Journal.

6 Carefully dispose of both bags according to your teacher's directions.

Analyze and Conclude

1. **Determine** which apple changed the most. How could you tell? List specific evidence to support your answer.

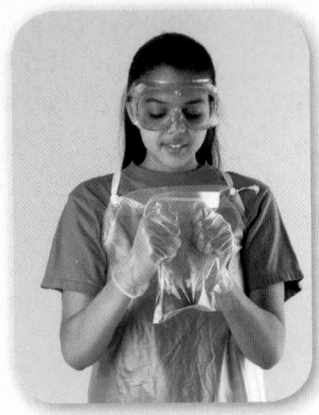

2. **Draw Conclusions** Does decomposition occur faster, slower, or not at all in environments without oxygen? Justify your answer.

3. **Key Concept** Summarize why bacteria are considered important decomposers.

Bioremediation

Can you imagine an organism that eats pollution? Some bacteria do just that. *The use of organisms, such as bacteria, to clean up environmental pollution is called* **bioremediation** (bi oh rih mee dee AY shun). These organisms often break down harmful substances, such as sewage, into less harmful material that can be used as landfill or fertilizers.

Bacteria are commonly used to clean up areas that have been contaminated by oil or harmful plastics. Some kinds of bacteria can even help clean up radioactive waste, such as uranium in the abandoned mine fields shown in **Figure 9.** In many cases, without using bacteria, the substances would take centuries to break down and would contaminate soils and water.

 Reading Check Why might using bacteria to clean up environmental spills be a good option?

FOLDABLES

Make a four-door book and label it as shown. Use it to summarize the ways bacteria are beneficial to the environment.

| Decomposition | Nitrogen Fixation |
| Bioremediation | Bacteria and Food |

Figure 9 These bacteria clean the environment by removing harmful uranium from the water.

Bacteria and Food

Would you like a side of bacteria with that sandwich? If you have eaten a pickle lately, you might have had some. Some pickles are made when the sugar in cucumbers is converted into an acid by a specific type of bacteria. Pickles are just one of the many food products made with the help of bacteria. Bacteria are used to make foods such as yogurt, cheese, buttermilk, vinegar, and soy sauce. Bacteria are even used in the production of chocolate. They help break down the covering of the cocoa bean during the process of making chocolate. Bacteria are responsible for giving chocolate some of its flavor.

WORD ORIGIN ·
  pathogen from Greek *pathos*, means "to suffer";
  and *gen*, means "to produce"

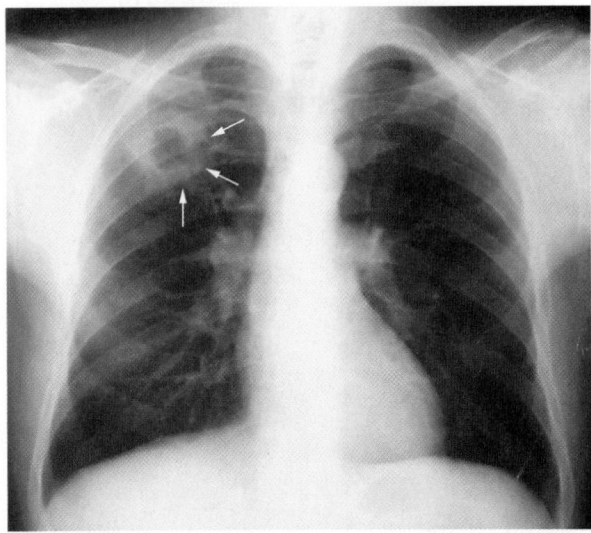

Figure 10 In an X-ray, the lungs of a person with tuberculosis may show pockets or scars where bacterial infection has begun.

 Visual Check How do you think the bacteria that made this person sick entered his or her body?

SCIENCE USE V. COMMON USE · · · · · · · · · · · · · ·

resistance
Science Use the capacity of an organism to defend itself against a disease

Common Use the act of opposing something

Harmful Bacteria

Of the 5,000 known species of bacteria, relatively few are considered **pathogens** (PA thuh junz)—*agents that cause disease.* Some pathogens normally live in your body, but cause illness only when your immune system is weakened. For example, the bacterium *Streptococcus pneumoniae* lives in the throats of most healthy people. However, it can cause pneumonia if a person's immune system is weakened. Other bacterial pathogens can enter your body through a cut, the air you breathe, or the food you eat. Once inside your body, they can reproduce and cause disease.

Key Concept Check Describe one way that bacteria can be harmful to health.

Bacterial Diseases

Bacteria can harm your body and cause disease in one of two ways. Some bacteria make you sick by damaging tissue. For example, the disease tuberculosis, shown in **Figure 10,** is caused by a bacterium that invades lung tissue and breaks it down for food. Other bacteria cause illness by releasing toxins. For example, the bacterium *Clostridium botulinum* can grow in improperly canned foods and produce toxins. If the contaminated food is eaten, the toxins can cause food poisoning, resulting in paralyzed limbs or even death.

Treating Bacterial Diseases Most bacterial diseases in humans can be treated with antibiotics. **Antibiotics** (an ti bi AH tihks) *are medicines that stop the growth and reproduction of bacteria.* Many antibiotics work by preventing bacteria from building cell walls. Others affect ribosomes in bacteria, interrupting the production of proteins.

Many types of bacteria have become **resistant** to antibiotics over time. Some diseases, such as tuberculosis, pneumonia, and meningitis, are now more difficult to treat.

Bacterial Resistance How do you think bacteria become resistant to antibiotics? This process, shown in **Figure 11,** can happen over a long or short period of time depending on how quickly the bacteria reproduce. Random mutations occur to a bacterium's DNA that enable it to survive or "resist" a specific antibiotic. If that antibiotic is used as a treatment, only the bacteria with the mutation will survive.

Over time, the resistant bacteria will reproduce and become more common. The antibiotic is no longer effective against that bacterium, and a different antibiotic must be used to fight the disease. Scientists are always working to develop more effective antibiotics to which bacteria have not developed resistances.

 Reading Check How do bacteria develop resistance to antibiotics?

Food Poisoning

All food, unless it has been treated or processed, contains bacteria. Over time these bacteria reproduce and begin breaking down the food, causing it to spoil. As you read on the previous page, eating food contaminated by some bacteria can cause food poisoning. By properly treating or processing food and killing bacteria before the food is stored or eaten, it is easier to avoid food poisoning and other illnesses.

Pasteurization (pas chuh ruh ZAY shun) *is a process of heating food to a temperature that kills most harmful bacteria.* Products such as milk, ice cream, yogurt, and fruit juice are usually pasteurized in factories before they are transported to grocery stores and sold to you. After pasteurization, foods are much safer to eat. Foods do not spoil as quickly once they have been pasteurized. Because of pasteurization, food poisoning is much less common today than it was in the past.

 Key Concept Check How does pasteurization affect human health?

Figure 11 A population of bacteria can develop resistance to antibiotics after being exposed to them over time.

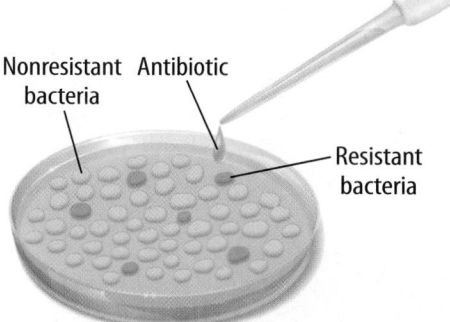

Nonresistant bacteria

Antibiotic

Resistant bacteria

❶ An antibiotic is added to a colony of bacteria. A few of the bacteria have mutations that enable them to resist the antibiotic.

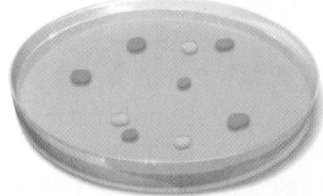

❷ The antibiotic kills most of the nonresistant bacteria. The resistant bacteria survive and reproduce, creating a growing colony of bacteria.

❸ Surviving bacteria are added to another plate containing more of the same antibiotic.

❹ The antibiotic now affects only a small percentage of the bacteria. The surviving bacteria continue to reproduce. Most of the bacteria are resistant to the antibiotic.

Lesson 2 Review

✓ Assessment Online Quiz
? Inquiry Virtual Lab

Visual Summary

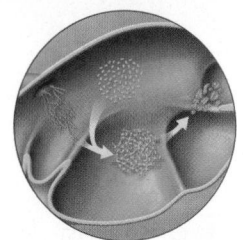

Bacteria can help some organisms, including humans and cows, digest food.

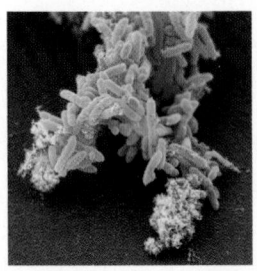

Bacteria can be used to remove harmful substances such as uranium.

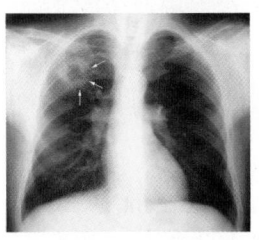

Some bacteria are pathogens, and cause diseases in humans and other organisms.

FOLDABLES

Use your lesson Foldable to review the lesson. Save your Foldable for the project at the end of the chapter.

What do you think NOW?

You first read the statements below at the beginning of the chapter.

3. All bacteria cause diseases.

4. Bacteria are important for making many types of food.

Did you change your mind about whether you agree or disagree with the statements? Rewrite any false statements to make them true.

Use Vocabulary

1. **Distinguish** between an antibiotic and a pathogen.

2. **Define** *bioremediation* using your own words.

3. **Use the term** *pasteurization* in a sentence.

Understand Key Concepts

4. Which of the following is NOT a beneficial use of bacteria?
   - **A.** bioremediation
   - **C.** food poisoning
   - **B.** decomposition
   - **D.** nitrogen fixation

5. **Compare** the benefits of nitrogen fixation and decomposition.

6. **Analyze** the importance of bacteria in food production.

Interpret Graphics

7. **Examine** the figure below and describe what would happen if bacteria were not present.

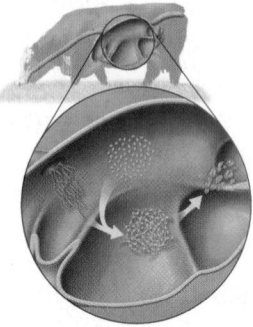

8. **Identify** Copy and complete the graphic organizer below to identify ways that bacteria can be beneficial.

Beneficial Bacteria

Critical Thinking

9. **Evaluate** the effect of all bacteria becoming resistant to antibiotics.

How do lab techniques affect an investigation?

Materials

petri dish

jar with samples

forceps

dissecting microscope

black light

Safety

Pathogens such as bacteria cover almost every surface. When you touch a surface, you transfer particles from that surface to your skin and then to other objects you touch. Your teacher has spread a substance that simulates bacteria on some surfaces in this lab. You will be divided into two groups. Each group will perform the same lab activity but will use slightly different laboratory techniques.

Learn It

In a laboratory it is important to be very careful to keep surfaces as free from contamination as possible. Scientists follow specific **lab techniques** very carefully to prevent contamination that could affect results.

Try It

1. Read and complete a lab safety form.

2. Put on a pair of gloves. Select a Petri dish from the stack. Open the Petri dish and follow the directions on the slip of paper.

3. Go to the station with the jar. Open the jar and use forceps to remove an item. Place the item in your Petri dish. Close the jar. Follow the directions again.

4. Take your Petri dish to the dissecting microscope and examine your object. Sketch the object in your Science Journal.

5. Observe the surfaces in your work area as your teacher shines a black light over them.

Apply It

6. What surfaces light up the most under the black light?

7. What do you see when you use the black light?

8. **Key Concept** What difference do you see in the lab areas used by the two groups? Based on your observations, how do you think this difference affects which techniques are used in labs and hospitals?

What are viruses?

Inquiry Painted Flowers?

The streaking patterns on the petals of these tulips are not painted on but are caused by a virus. Tulips with these patterns are prized for their beautiful appearance. How do you think a virus could cause this flower's pattern? Do you think all viruses are harmful?

Inquiry Launch Lab

10 minutes

How quickly do viruses replicate?

One characteristic that viruses share is the ability to produce many new viruses from just one virus. In this lab you can use grains of rice to model virus replication. Each grain of rice represents one virus.

Generation	First	Second	Third
Number of "viruses"			

1. Read and complete a lab safety form.
2. Copy the table above into your Science Journal.
3. Estimate the number of **grains of rice** in the **fishbowl** and record this number for the first generation.
4. One student will add the contents of his or her **cup** to the fishbowl. Estimate how many viruses are now in the fishbowl and record your estimate for the second generation.
5. The rest of the class will add the contents of their cups to the fishbowl. Estimate the number of viruses and record that number of viruses for the third generation.

Think About This

1. Recall that bacteria double every generation. How does the number of viruses produced in each generation compare with the number of bacteria produced in each generation?

2. 🔑 **Key Concept** How could the rate at which viruses are produced affect human health?

Characteristics of Viruses

Do chicken pox, mumps, measles, and polio sound familiar? You might have received shots to protect you from these diseases. You might have also received a shot to protect you from influenza, commonly known as the flu. What do these diseases have in common? They are caused by different viruses. *A* **virus** *is a strand of DNA or RNA surrounded by a layer of protein that can infect and replicate in a host cell.* If you have had a cold, you have been infected by a virus.

A virus does not have a cell wall, a nucleus, or any other organelles present in cells. The smallest viruses are between 20 and 100 times smaller than most bacteria. Recall that about 100 bacteria would fit across the head of a pin. Viruses can have different shapes, such as the crystal, cylinder, sphere, and bacteriophage (bak TIHR ee uh fayj) shapes shown in **Figure 12.**

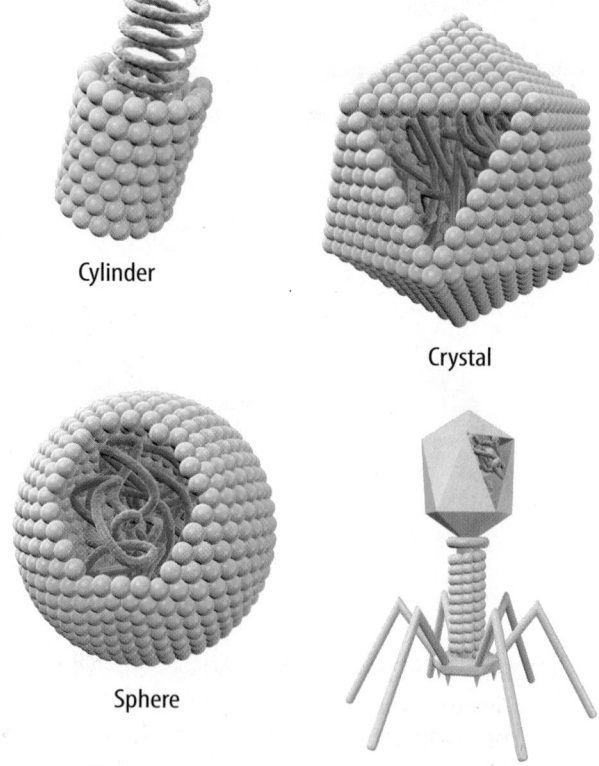

Cylinder

Crystal

Sphere

Bacteriophage

Figure 12 Viruses have a variety of shapes.

FOLDABLES®

Make a folded book from a sheet of paper. Label it as shown. Use it to organize your notes on the replication sequence of a virus.

Viral
Replication

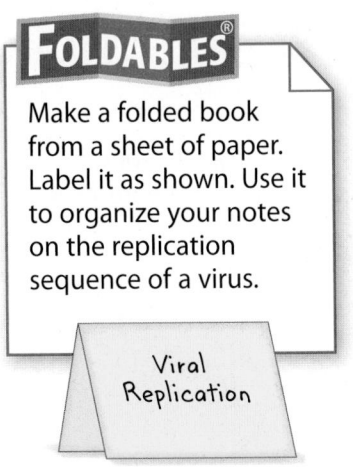

Dead or Alive?

Do you think that viruses are living things? Scientists do not consider viruses to be alive because they do not have all the characteristics of a living organism. Recall that living things are organized, respond to stimuli, use energy, grow, and reproduce. Viruses cannot do any of these things. A virus can make copies of itself in a process called replication, but it must rely on a living organism to do so.

Key Concept Check Are viruses alive? Explain why or why not.

Viruses and Organisms

Viruses must use organisms to carry on the processes that we usually associate with a living cell. Viruses have no organelles so they are not able to take in nutrients or use energy. They also cannot replicate without using the cellular parts of an organism. Viruses must be inside a cell to replicate. The living cell that a virus infects is called a host cell.

When a virus enters a cell, as shown in **Figure 13,** it can either be active or latent. Latent viruses go through an inactive stage. Their genetic material becomes part of the host cell's genetic material. For a period of time, the virus does not take over the cell to produce more viruses. In some cases, viruses have been known to be inactive for years and years. However, once it becomes active, a virus takes control of the host cell and replicates.

Figure 13 A virus infects a cell by inserting its DNA or RNA into the host cell. It then directs the host cell to make new viruses.

Visual Check What occurs when a virus becomes latent?

Viral Replication

Concepts in Motion Animation

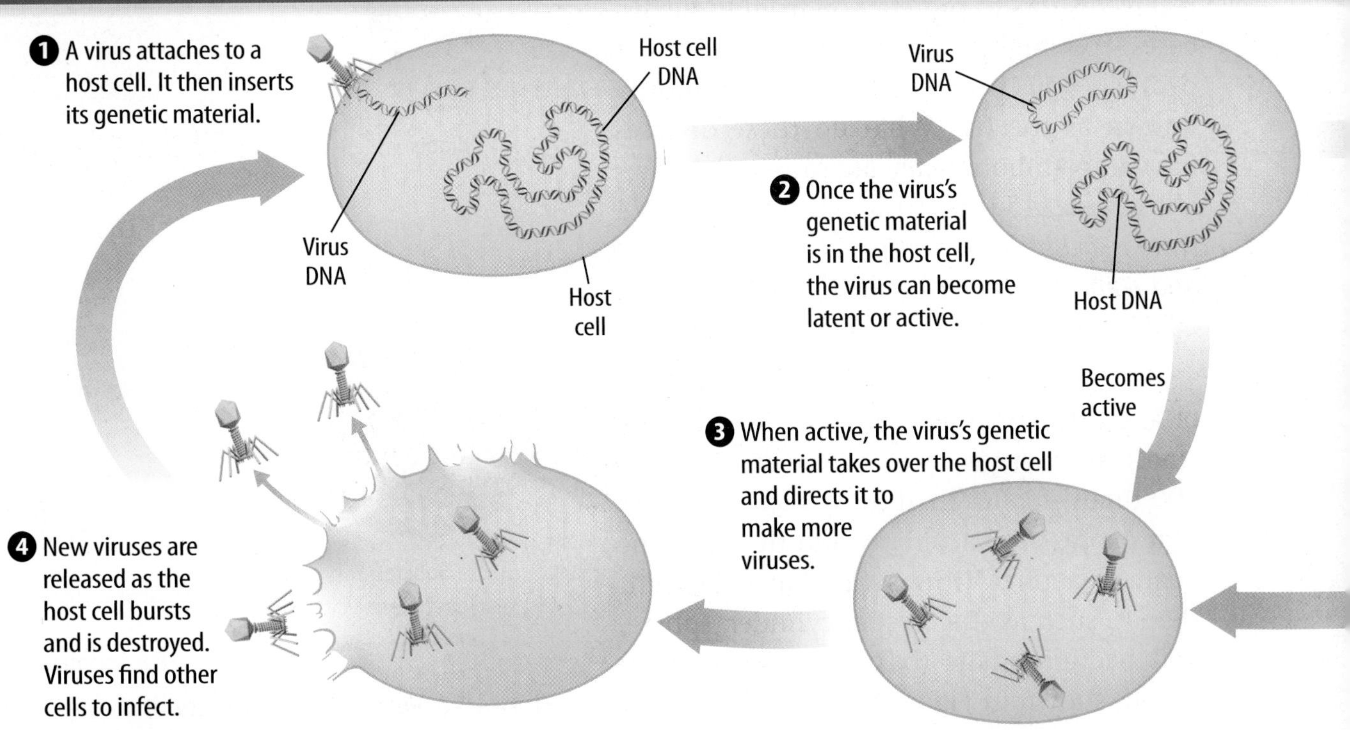

1 A virus attaches to a host cell. It then inserts its genetic material.
Host cell DNA
Virus DNA
Host cell
Virus DNA
2 Once the virus's genetic material is in the host cell, the virus can become latent or active.
Host DNA
Becomes active
3 When active, the virus's genetic material takes over the host cell and directs it to make more viruses.
4 New viruses are released as the host cell bursts and is destroyed. Viruses find other cells to infect.

Replication

As you read earlier, a virus can make copies of itself in a process called replication, shown in **Figure 13.** A virus cannot infect every cell. A virus can only attach to a host cell with specific molecules on its cell wall or cell membrane. These molecules enable the virus to attach to the host cell. This is similar to the way that only certain electrical plugs can fit into an outlet on a wall. After a virus attaches to the host cell, its DNA or RNA enters the host cell. Once inside, the virus either starts to replicate or becomes latent, also shown in **Figure 13.** After a virus becomes active and replicates in a host cell, it destroys the host cell. Copies of the virus are then released into the host organism, where they can infect other cells.

Mutations

As viruses replicate, their DNA or RNA frequently mutates, or changes. These **mutations** enable viruses to adjust to changes in their host cells. For example, the molecules on the outside of host cells change over time to prevent viruses from attaching to the cell. As viruses mutate, they are able to produce new ways to attach to host cells. These changes happen so rapidly that it can be difficult to cure or prevent viral diseases before they mutate again.

 Reading Check How does mutation enable viruses to continue causing disease?

REVIEW VOCABULARY

mutation
a change in genetic material

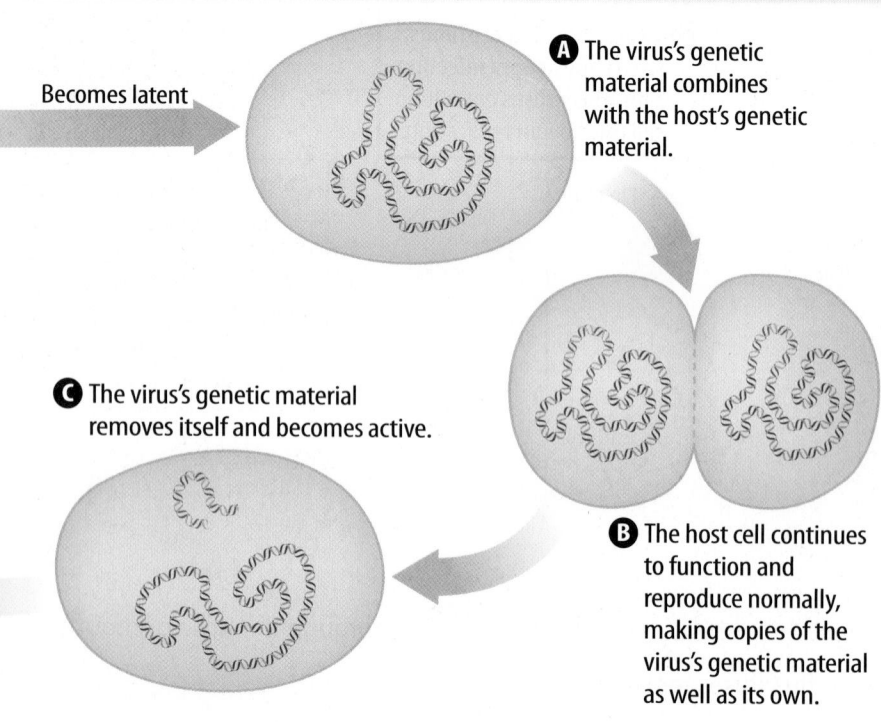

Becomes latent

A The virus's genetic material combines with the host's genetic material.

C The virus's genetic material removes itself and becomes active.

B The host cell continues to function and reproduce normally, making copies of the virus's genetic material as well as its own.

Viral Diseases

You might know that viruses cause many human diseases, such as chicken pox, influenza, some forms of pneumonia, and the common cold. But viruses also infect animals, causing diseases such as rabies and parvo. They can infect plants as well—in some cases causing millions of dollars of damage to crops. The tulips shown at the beginning of this lesson were infected with a virus that caused a streaked appearance on the petals. Most viruses attack and destroy specific cells. This destruction of cells causes the symptoms of the disease.

Some viruses cause symptoms soon after infection. Influenza viruses that cause the flu infect the cells lining your respiratory system, as shown in **Figure 14.** The viruses begin to replicate immediately. Flu symptoms, such as a runny nose and a scratchy throat, usually appear within 2–3 days.

Other viruses might not cause symptoms right away. These viruses are sometimes called latent viruses. Latent viruses continue replicating without damaging the host cell. HIV (human immunodeficiency virus) is one example of a latent virus that might not cause immediate symptoms.

HIV infects white blood cells, which are part of the immune system. Initially, infected cells can function normally, so an HIV-infected person might not appear sick. However, the virus can become active and destroy cells in the body's immune system, making it hard to fight other infections. It can often take a long time for symptoms to appear after infection. People infected with latent viruses might not know for many years that they have been infected.

Reading Check Why is HIV considered a latent virus?

The Flu 🔑

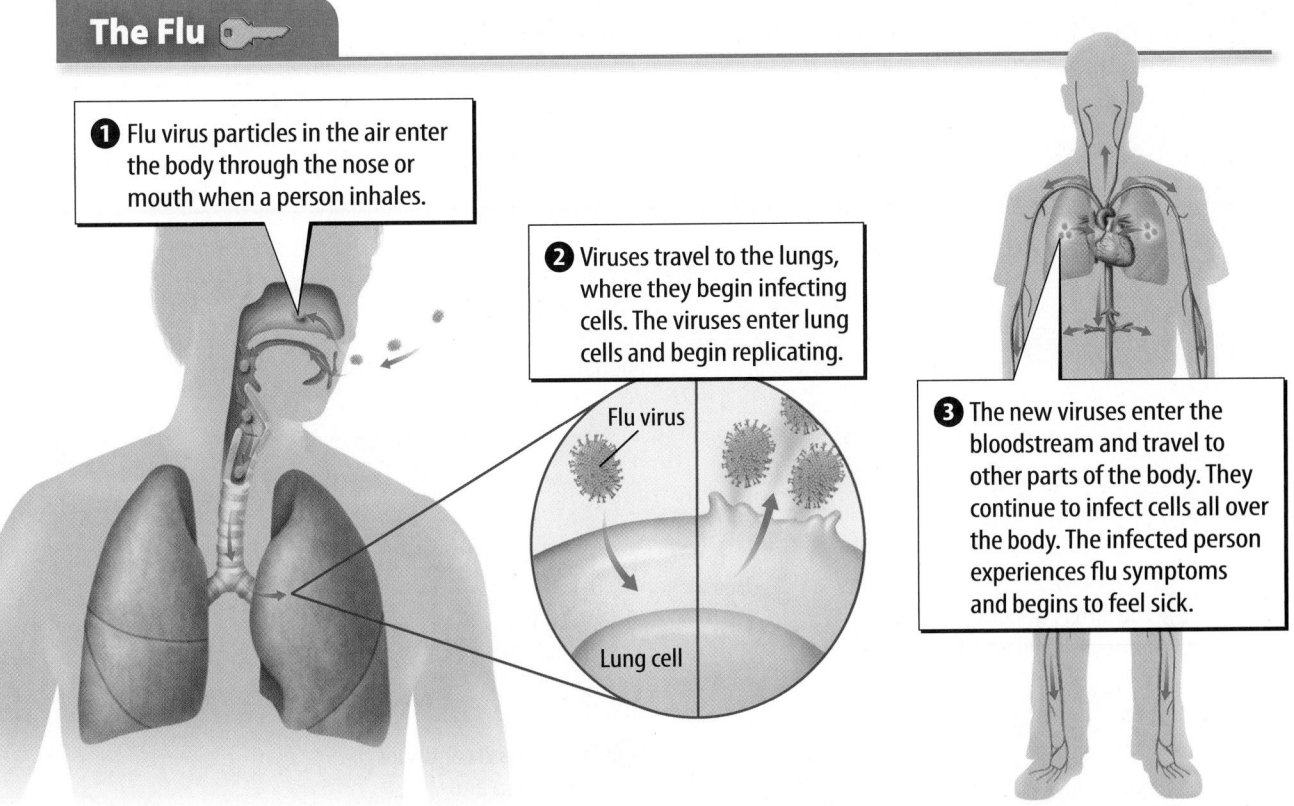

1 Flu virus particles in the air enter the body through the nose or mouth when a person inhales.

2 Viruses travel to the lungs, where they begin infecting cells. The viruses enter lung cells and begin replicating.

Flu virus

Lung cell

3 The new viruses enter the bloodstream and travel to other parts of the body. They continue to infect cells all over the body. The infected person experiences flu symptoms and begins to feel sick.

Figure 14 Viruses that infect the respiratory system usually enter through the nose or mouth.

Visual Check Where do flu viruses replicate?

Treating and Preventing Viral Diseases

Since viruses are constantly changing, viral diseases can be difficult to treat. Antibiotics work only against bacteria, not viruses. Antiviral medicines can be used to treat certain viral diseases or prevent infection. These medicines prevent the virus from entering a cell or stop the virus from replicating. Antiviral medicines are specific to each virus. Like bacteria, viruses can rapidly change and become resistant to medicines.

Health officials use many methods to prevent the spread of viral diseases. One of the best ways to prevent a viral infection is to limit contact with an infected human or animal. The most important way to prevent infections is to practice good hygiene, such as washing your hands.

Immunity

Has anyone you know ever had chicken pox? Did they get it more than once? Most people who became infected with chicken pox develop an immunity to the disease. This is an example of acquired **immunity.** When a virus infects a person, his or her body begins to make special proteins called antibodies. An **antibody** *is a protein that can attach to a pathogen and make it useless.* Antibodies bind to viruses and other pathogens and prevent them from attaching to a host cell, as shown in **Figure 15.** The antibodies also target viruses and signal the body to destroy them. These antibodies can multiply quickly if the same pathogen enters the body again, making it easier for the body to fight infection. Another type of immunity, called natural immunity, develops when a mother passes antibodies on to her unborn baby.

WORD ORIGIN

immunity
from Latin *immunis,* means "exempt, free"

Antibodies

Figure 15 Antibodies bind to pathogens and prevent them from attaching to cells.

Visual Check How does the antibody prevent the virus from attaching to the host cell?

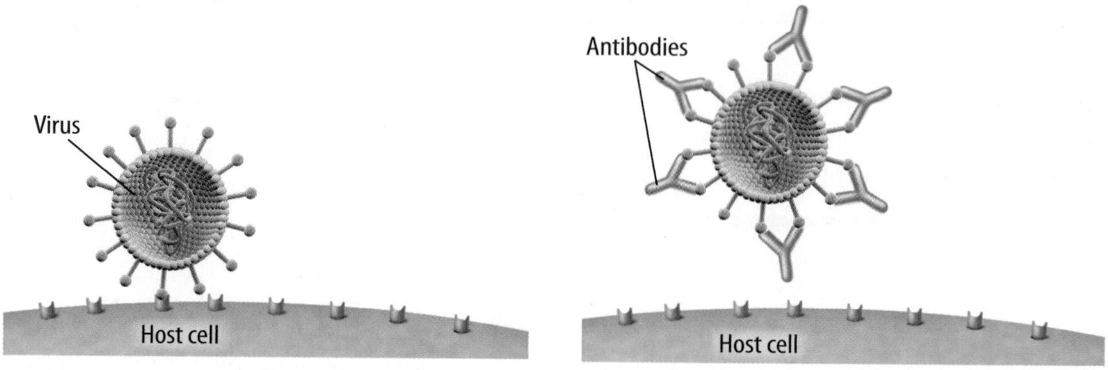
Virus
Host cell
Antibodies
Host cell

How do antibodies work?

When a virus infects a cell it binds to part of that cell called a receptor. The virus and the receptor fit together like puzzle pieces.

1. Read and complete a lab safety form.
2. Cut out two **virus shapes** and two **cell shapes.**
3. Using one virus shape and one cell shape, note how the virus fits against the receptor on the cell. **Tape** the virus and the cell together.
4. Cut out one **antibody shape.** Note how the virus shapes and the antibody shapes attach and tape them together.
5. Try to attach the virus shapes and the antibody shapes you just joined to the cell receptor.

Analyze and Conclude

1. **Observe** whether the virus or the joined virus and antibody were better able to attach to the cell.

2. **Key Concept** Explain how producing more antibodies would be beneficial during a viral infection.

Vaccines

One way to prevent viral diseases is through vaccination. *A* **vaccine** *is a mixture containing material from one or more deactivated pathogens, such as viruses.* When an organism is given a vaccine for a viral disease, the vaccine triggers the production of antibodies. This is similar to what would happen if the organism became infected with the virus normally. However, because the vaccine contains deactivated pathogens, the organism suffers only mild symptoms or none at all. After being vaccinated against a particular pathogen, the organism will not get as sick if exposed to the pathogen again.

Vaccines can prevent diseases in animals as well as humans. For example, pet owners and farmers get annual rabies vaccinations for their animals. This protects the animals from the disease. Humans are then protected from rabies.

Research with Viruses

Scientists are researching new ways to treat and prevent viral diseases in humans, animals, and plants. Scientists are also studying the link between viruses and cancer. Viruses can cause changes in a host's DNA or RNA, resulting in the formation of tumors or abnormal growth. Because viruses can change very quickly, scientists must always be working on new ways to treat and prevent viral diseases.

You might think that all viruses are harmful. However, scientists have also found beneficial uses for viruses. Viruses may be used to treat genetic disorders and cancer using gene transfer. Scientists use viruses to insert normal genetic information into a specific cell. Scientists hope that gene transfer will eventually be able to treat genetic disorders that are caused by one gene, such as cystic fibrosis or hemophilia.

Key Concept Check How do viruses affect human health?

Lesson 3 Review

Visual Summary

A virus is a strand of DNA or RNA surrounded by a layer of protein.

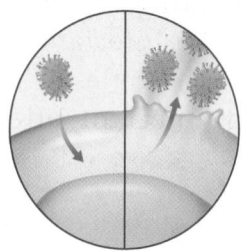

Viruses cause human diseases such as chicken pox and influenza.

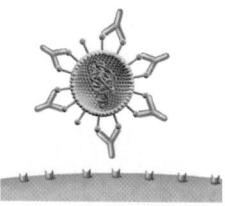

A person's body produces proteins called antibodies that prevent an infection by viruses.

FOLDABLES®

Use your lesson Foldable to review the lesson. Save your Foldable for the project at the end of the chapter.

What do you think NOW?

You first read the statements below at the beginning of the chapter.

5. Viruses are the smallest living organisms.

6. Viruses can replicate only inside an organism.

Did you change your mind about whether you agree or disagree with the statements? Rewrite any false statements to make them true.

Use Vocabulary

1 **List** the different shapes a virus can have.

2 **Describe** in your own words how a vaccine works.

3 **Use the term** *antibodies* in a sentence.

Understand Key Concepts

4 **Describe** the structure of a virus.

5 Which is made by the body to fight viruses?
  A. antibody
  B. bacteria
  C. bacteriophage
  D. proteins

6 **Classify** a virus as a living or nonliving thing. Explain your answer.

7 **Compare** a vaccine and an antibody.

Interpret Graphics

8 **Draw** a graphic organizer like the one below including the steps that occur when a virus infects a cell.

9 **Describe** what happens during this step of viral replication.

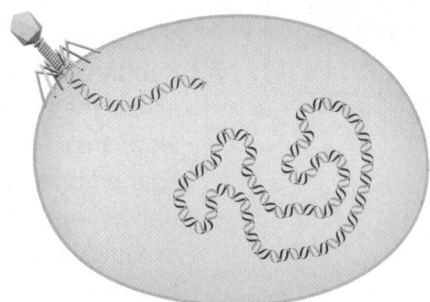

Critical Thinking

10 **Predict** the effect of preventing future mutations of the influenza virus.

11 **Evaluate** the importance of vaccines in keeping people healthy.

Materials

agar plates

cotton swabs

cellophane tape

permanent marker

hand sanitizer

Safety

Bacterial Growth and Disinfectants

Recall that pathogens such as bacteria and viruses are all around you. When studying pathogens, scientists often use agar plates to grow bacteria and other colonies. An agar plate is a Petri dish containing agar, a gel made from seaweed, and nutrients needed for bacteria to grow. When bacteria are transferred to an agar plate, they reproduce. After a few days, you can see colonies of bacteria. Disinfectants are chemicals that deactivate or kill pathogens such as bacteria. In this lab you will test how hand sanitizer, a common disinfectant, affects the growth of bacteria on agar plates.

Ask a Question

What effect does hand sanitizer have on bacterial growth?

Make Observations

1. Read and complete a lab safety form.

2. Set two agar plates on your desk or work area. Turn your agar plates upside down without opening them. With a permanent marker, label one plate *No Treatment* and the other *Disinfected*. Also write your name and the date on the plate. Turn the agar plates right side up.

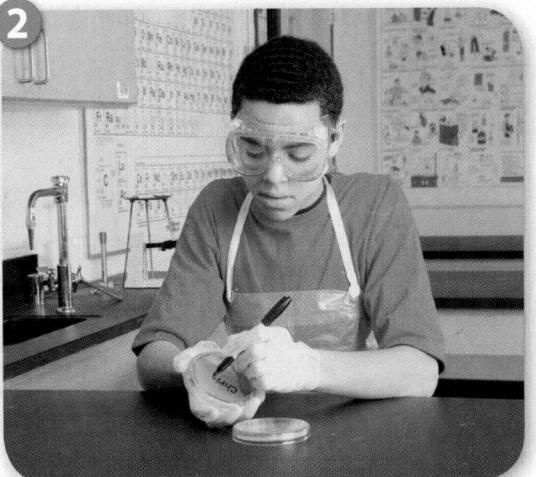

3. Rub the end of a cotton swab across the top of your desk or work area. Open the lid of the agar plate labeled *No Treatment* only enough to stick the swab in. Quickly make several S-shaped streaks on the agar. Close your plate and tape it shut.

4. Carefully clean the top of your desk or work area with hand sanitizer. Repeat step 3 using the agar plate labeled *Disinfected*.

5. Move your plates to an incubation area as directed by your teacher.

Form a Hypothesis

6 Using what you know about bacteria and disinfectants, write a hypothesis about how disinfectants affect the growth of bacteria. Make a prediction about how much bacterial growth you expect to see on your two agar plates.

Test Your Hypothesis

7 Check your agar plates after about three days. Record your observations in your Science Journal.

8 Compare the growth of bacteria on your two agar plates. Do your results support your hypothesis?

Analyze and Conclude

9 **Compare** Describe the differences in the amount of bacteria that grew on the two agar plates. Which plate had more?

10 What can you do to decrease the spread of bacteria in school and at home?

11 **Infer** Why didn't your experiment show any evidence of viral replication? How would you study the effect of disinfectants on viruses?

12 **The Big Idea** Why do doctors wash their hands or use hand sanitizer between appointments with different patients?

Communicate Your Results

Make a short video presentation about the results of your lab. Describe the question you investigated, the steps you took to answer your question, and the results that support your conclusions. Show your video to the class.

Inquiry Extension

Think about other situations in which cleanliness is important for preventing disease. Write a procedure in which you could test for bacteria as a comparison. Conduct your experiment and present your results to the class.

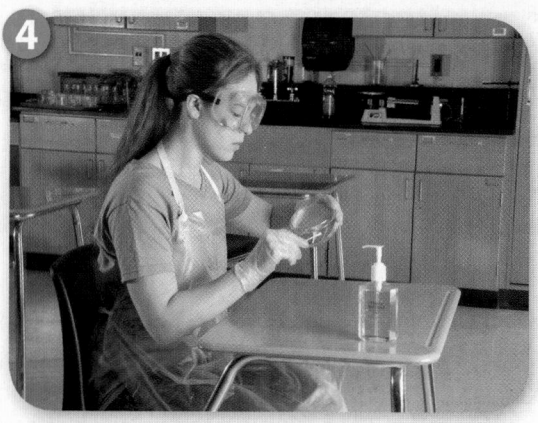

Lab Tips

☑ When streaking bacteria on your plates, use a steady, but light, pressure.

☑ After you disinfect your object, wait for the disinfectant to dry before testing the area.

Remember to use scientific methods.

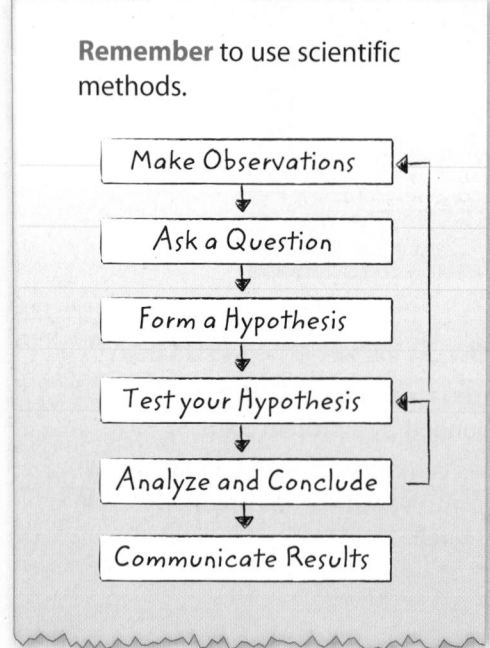

Make Observations → Ask a Question → Form a Hypothesis → Test your Hypothesis → Analyze and Conclude → Communicate Results

Chapter 7 Study Guide

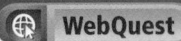

Bacteria are unicellular prokaryotes, and viruses are small pieces of DNA or RNA surrounded by protein. Both bacteria and viruses can cause harmful diseases or can be useful to humans.

Key Concepts Summary

Lesson 1: What are bacteria?

- **Bacteria** and archeans are unicellular organisms without nuclei. They have structures for movement, obtaining food, and reproduction.
- Bacteria exchange genetic information in a process called **conjugation.** They reproduce asexually by **fission.**

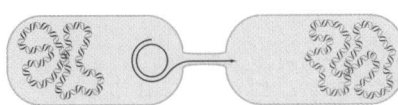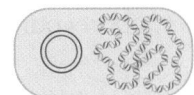

Lesson 2: Bacteria in Nature

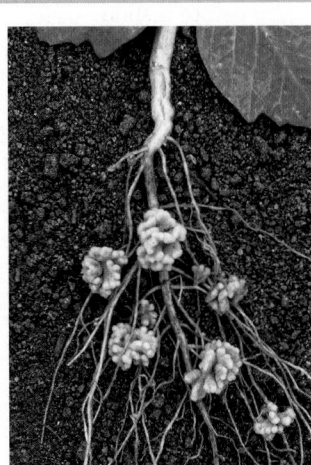

- Bacteria decompose materials, play a role in the nitrogen cycle, clean the environment, and are used in food.
- Some bacteria cause disease, while others are used to treat it.

Lesson 3: What are viruses?

- A **virus** is made up of DNA or RNA surrounded by a protein coat.
- Viruses can cause disease, can be made into **vaccines,** and are used in research.

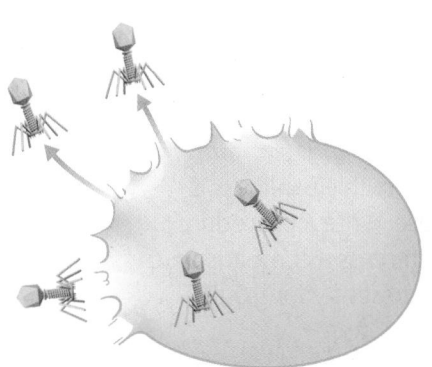

Vocabulary

bacterium p. 231
flagella p. 234
fission p. 234
conjugation p. 234
endospore p. 235

decomposition p. 240
nitrogen fixation p. 240
bioremediation p. 241
pathogen p. 242
antibiotic p. 242
pasteurization p. 243

virus p. 247
antibody p. 251
vaccine p. 252

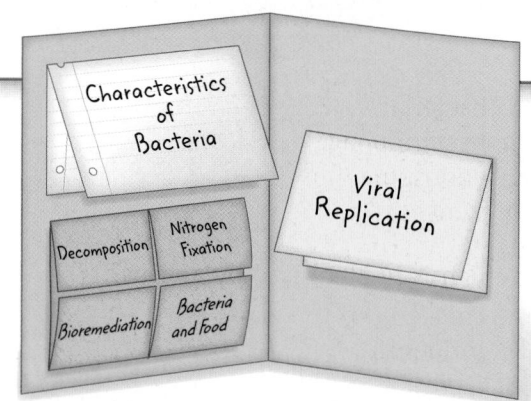
FOLDABLES® Chapter Project

Assemble your lesson Foldables as shown to make a Chapter Project. Use the project to review what you have learned in this chapter.

Characteristics of Bacteria

Decomposition | Nitrogen Fixation

Bioremediation | Bacteria and Food

Viral Replication

Use Vocabulary

1 Some bacteria have whiplike structures called _____ that are used for movement.

2 Your body produces proteins called _____ in response to infection by a virus.

3 Organisms that cause diseases are known as _____.

4 The process of killing bacteria in a food product by heating it is called _____ .

5 Bacteria can form a(n) _____ to survive when environmental conditions are severe.

6 A(n) _____ is made by using pieces of deactivated viruses or dead pathogens.

Link Vocabulary and Key Concepts

Concepts in Motion Interactive Concept Map

Copy this concept map, and then use vocabulary terms from the previous page and other terms from the chapter to complete the concept map.

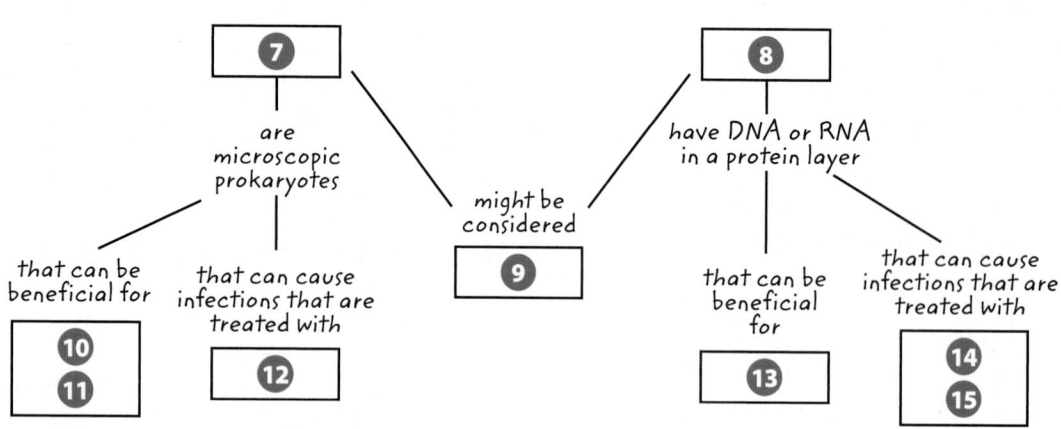

Chapter 7 Review

Understand Key Concepts

1 Which structure is NOT found in a bacterium?

A. chromosome
B. cytoplasm
C. nucleus
D. ribosome

2 Which structure helps a bacterium move?

A. capsule
B. endospore
C. flagellum
D. plasmid

3 What process is occurring in the illustration below?

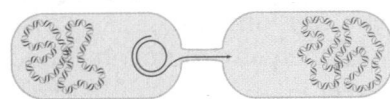

A. budding
B. conjugation
C. fission
D. replication

4 Which term describes how bacteria can be used to clean up environmental waste?

A. bioremediation
B. decomposition
C. pasteurization
D. nitrogen fixation

5 Which statement correctly describes pathogens?

A. They are always bacteria.
B. They are in your body only when you are sick.
C. They break down dead organisms.
D. They cause disease.

6 Which statement correctly describes antibiotics?

A. They can kill any kind of bacterium.
B. They help bacteria grow.
C. They stop the growth and reproduction of bacteria.
D. They treat all diseases.

7 What is shown below?

A. bacteria
B. bacteriophage
C. endospore
D. virus

8 Which is NOT caused by a virus?

A. chicken pox
B. influenza
C. rabies
D. tuberculosis

9 What do vaccines stimulate the production of?

A. antibodies
B. DNA or RNA
C. protein
D. ribosomes

10 Scientists hope to be able to use viruses for gene therapy because viruses can

A. become latent for long periods of time.
B. inject genetic material into host cells.
C. make proteins to attack cells.
D. transport themselves throughout the body.

11 Which statement correctly describes viruses?

A. All viruses are latent.
B. All viruses contain DNA.
C. Viruses are considered living things.
D. Viruses do not have organelles.

Critical Thinking

12 **Compare and contrast** bacteria and archaea.

13 **Evaluate** the importance of bacterial conjugation.

14 **Model** the life of a bacterium that performs nitrogen fixation in the soil.

15 **Contrast** asexual reproduction in bacteria and replication in viruses. What are some advantages and disadvantages of each?

16 **Organize** the effects of bacteria on health by copying and completing the table below.

Harmful Effects	Beneficial Effects

17 **Analyze** the importance of vaccines in preventing large outbreaks of influenza.

18 **Draw** and label a typical bacterium. Are the features you labeled beneficial for moving, for finding food, or for another purpose? Explain your answer.

19 **Explain** what happens during the process shown below. How does this process eventually create new strains of bacteria that are resistant to antibiotics?

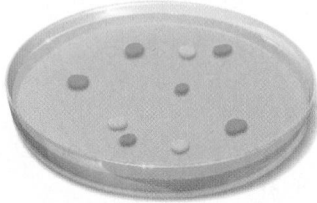

Writing in Science

20 **Summarize** an argument that you could use to encourage all the families in your neighborhood to make sure their pets are vaccinated against rabies.

REVIEW THE BIG IDEA

21 What are bacteria and viruses and why are they important? Include examples of how they are both beneficial and harmful to humans.

22 Describe what is happening in the photo below. Explain what is happening to both the bacterium and the virus.

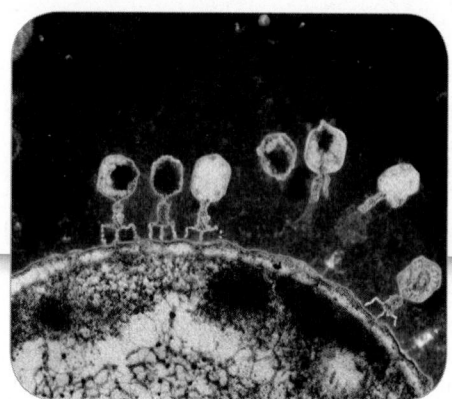

Math Skills

⊡ Review

— Math Practice —

Use a Formula

23 How many bacteria would there be if 100 bacteria underwent fission 8 times?

24 If each fission cycle takes 20 minutes, how many cycles would it take for 100 bacteria to divide into 100,000?

25 A strain of bacteria takes 30 minutes to undergo fission. Starting with 500 bacteria, how many would there be after 4 hours?

Standardized Test Practice

Record your answers on the answer sheet provided by your teacher or on a sheet of paper.

Multiple Choice

1 Which is NOT a characteristic of bacteria?

  A They are microscopic.

  B They are unicellular.

  C They can live in many environments.

  D They have a membrane-bound nucleus.

2 Which process increases genetic diversity in bacteria?

  A attachment to a host organism

  B division into two organisms

  C formation of an endospore

  D transfer of plasmid strands

Use the diagram below to answer questions 3 and 4.

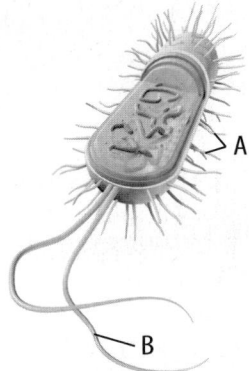

3 The diagram above illustrates a bacterium. What is the function of the structure labeled *A?*

  A attaching to surfaces

  B sensing surroundings

  C stinging prey

  D taking in nutrients

4 The structure labeled *B* helps a bacterium

  A move.

  B protect itself.

  C reproduce.

  D transfer DNA.

5 What beneficial vitamin do some human intestinal bacteria produce?

  A vitamin A

  B vitamin C

  C vitamin D

  D vitamin K

6 Which statement BEST explains why living organisms in an ecosystem depend on bacteria?

  A Bacteria help reduce the number of predators.

  B Bacteria kill weaker members of a species so only the stronger ones survive.

  C Bacteria protect organisms from harmful solar rays.

  D Bacteria release molecules into soil that are used by other organisms.

Use the diagram below to answer question 7.

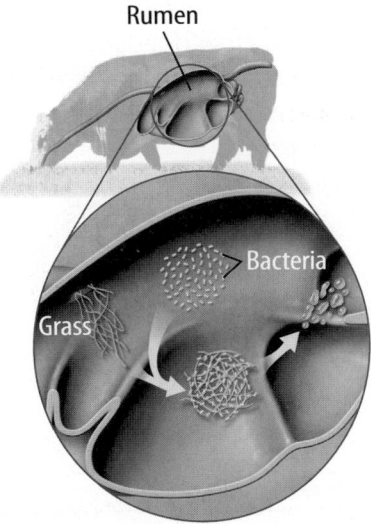

7 What role do bacteria play in the process shown above?

  A They break down cellulose.

  B They convert nitrogen in grass.

  C They prevent viruses from growing.

  D They remove harmful pollutants.

8 In which process do bacteria and other organisms clean up environmental pollution?

A bioremediation

B decomposition

C fixation

D pasteurization

Use the diagram below to answer question 9.

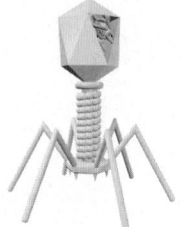

9 What is pictured in the diagram above?

A an antibody

B a bacteriophage

C a bacterium

D a plasmid

10 Which BEST explains how mutation benefits a virus?

A It enables the virus to adjust to changes in its host cell.

B It enables the virus to reproduce more quickly.

C It enables the virus to resist antibiotic therapy.

D It enables the virus to travel from host to host.

Constructed Response

Use the diagrams below to answer questions 11 and 12.

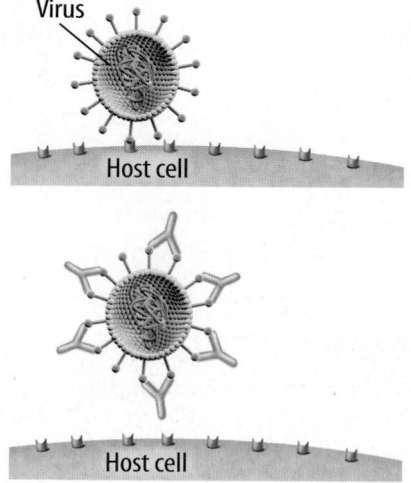

11 Describe how the virus attaches to the host cell in the figure at the top of the diagram.

12 What are the Y-shaped structures on the virus in the figure at the bottom of the diagram? Explain their interaction with the virus.

13 Why can viral infections be more difficult to treat than bacterial infections?

14 What are two methods you can use to prevent a viral infection?

15 What happens to the host cell when a latent virus goes through an inactive stage?

NEED EXTRA HELP?															
If You Missed Question...	1	2	3	4	5	6	7	8	9	10	11	12	13	14	15
Go to Lesson...	1	1	1	1	2	2	2	2	3	3	3	3	3	3	3

Chapter 8

Protists and Fungi

What are protists and fungi, and how do they affect an environment?

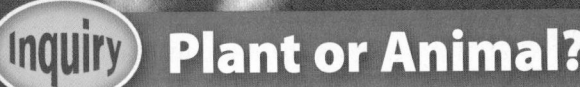

Inquiry | Plant or Animal?

These organisms are neither! Protists and fungi are two groups of living things that have characteristics similar to those of plants or animals.

- How is the organism pictured similar to a plant? An animal?

- How might this organism benefit its environment?

Get Ready to Read

What do you think?

Before you read, decide if you agree or disagree with each of these statements. As you read this chapter, see if you change your mind about any of the statements.

1 Protists are grouped together because they all look similar.

2 Some protists cause harm to other organisms.

3 Many protists make their own food.

4 Mushrooms and yeasts are two types of fungi.

5 Fungi are always helpful to plants.

6 Some fungi can be made into foods or medicines.

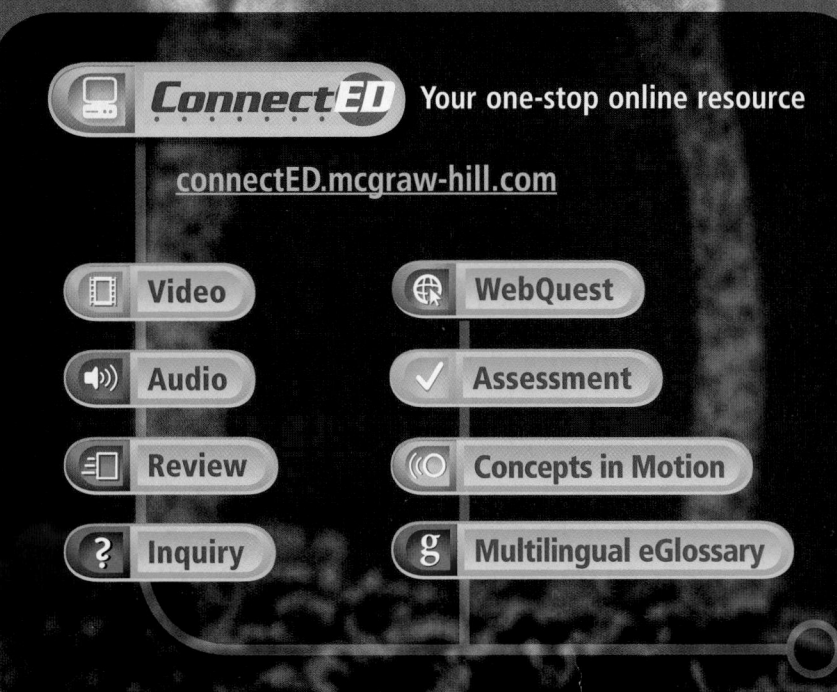

ConnectED Your one-stop online resource

connectED.mcgraw-hill.com

- Video
- Audio
- Review
- Inquiry
- WebQuest
- Assessment
- Concepts in Motion
- Multilingual eGlossary

Lesson 1

Reading Guide

Key Concepts
ESSENTIAL QUESTIONS

- What are the different types of protists and how do they compare?
- How are protists beneficial?

Vocabulary

protist p. 265

algae p. 266

diatom p. 267

protozoan p. 270

cilia p. 270

paramecium p. 270

amoeba p. 271

pseudopod p. 271

 Multilingual eGlossary

 Video BrainPOP®

What are protists?

 **Grabbing a Snack?**

The protist group includes diverse organisms. What is the larger organism doing in the photo? How is this organism similar to an animal?

How does a protist react to its environment?

Like other organisms, protists can react to their environment in many ways. One type of protist called *Euglena* has specialized structures to move, perform photosynthesis, and react to light.

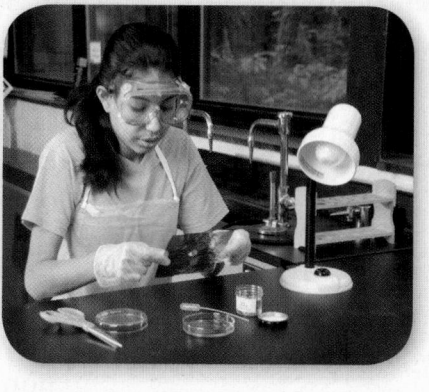

1. Read and complete a lab safety form.

2. Place a **Petri dish** containing a *Euglena* **culture** on a white piece of **paper.** Using a **hand lens,** observe the *Euglena.*

3. Carefully cut a hole the size of a dime in a piece of **aluminum foil.** Place the foil on top of the dish so that the hole is centered over the top. Shine the light from a **desk lamp** at the hole.

4. At the end of class, remove the foil and observe the *Euglena* again.

Think About This

1. Where were the *Euglena* in the dish at the beginning of class? At the end?

2. Why do you think this behavior is beneficial to *Euglena*?

3.  **Key Concept** What structures do you think help *Euglena* react to its environment?

What are protists?

When you see a living thing, one of the first questions you might have is whether it is a plant or an animal. You might recognize a dog as an animal because of its fur. You might know a flower is a plant because of its leaves. Besides appearance, organisms can also be classified by structures in their cells. For example, a plant cell has a cell wall made of cellulose and a membrane made of flexible fats. A plant cell often contains chloroplasts, organelles that carry out photosynthesis. An animal cell also has a membrane made of flexible fats but does not contain chloroplasts or have a cell wall. These characteristics make it easy to identify both types of cells. However, some organisms, such as the protist shown in **Figure 1,** cannot be classified as easily.

A **protist** *is a member of a group of eukaryotic organisms, which have a membrane-bound nucleus.* Members of the protist group share some characteristics with plants, animals, or organisms known as fungi. However, they are not classified as any of these groups. Although protists are classified together, they are diverse and have different adaptations for movement and for finding food.

✓ **Reading Check** What is a protist?

Figure 1 Many photosynthetic algae look like plants.

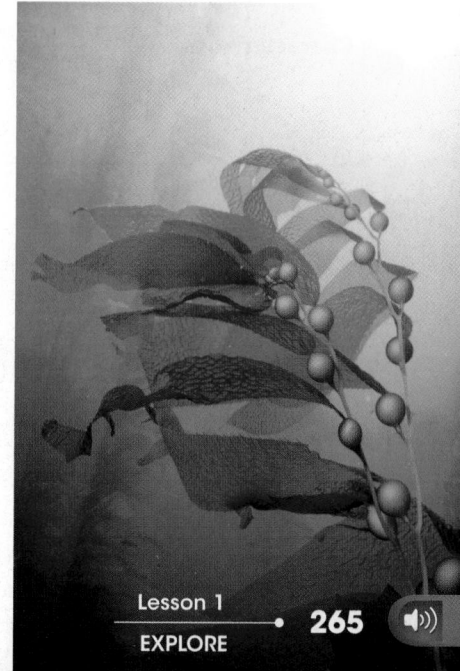

Reproduction of Protists

Most protists reproduce asexually. What does the offspring of asexual reproduction look like? It is an exact copy of the parent. Asexual reproduction can create new organisms quickly. However, many protists can also reproduce sexually. Offspring of sexual reproduction are genetically different from the parents. Sexual reproduction takes more time, but it creates new organisms with a variety of characteristics.

Classification of Protists

Scientists usually classify organisms according to their similarities. However, protists are a unique and diverse classification of organisms. Typically, a protist is any eukaryote that cannot be classified as a plant, an animal, or a fungus. However, protists might look and act very much like these other types of organisms. Scientists classify protists as plantlike, animal-like, or funguslike based on which group they most resemble, as shown in **Table 1.**

🔑 **Key Concept Check** What are the different types of protists?

 **Review** Personal Tutor

Table 1 Protists Classified into One of Three Groups 🔑

Classification	Plantlike	Animal-like	Funguslike
Example	algae	paramecium	slime mold
Characteristics	• make their own food • unicellular or multicellular	• eat other organisms for food • mostly microscopic and unicellular	• break down organic matter for food • mostly multicellular

Plantlike Protists

You might have seen brown, green, or red seaweed at the beach or in an aquarium. These seaweeds are algae (AL jee; singular, alga), one type of plantlike protist. Why might they be classified as plantlike? **Algae** *are plantlike protists that produce food through photosynthesis using light energy and carbon dioxide.* Most plantlike protists, however, are much smaller than the multicellular algae shown in **Table 1.** You can't see most algae without a microscope.

Diatoms

A type of microscopic plantlike protist with a hard outer wall is a **diatom** *(DI uh tahm).* Diatoms are so common that if you filled a cup with water from the surface of any lake or pond, you would probably collect thousands of them. Look at the unicellular diatoms shown at the top of **Figure 2.** A diatom can resemble colored glass. In fact, the cell walls of diatoms contain a large amount of silica, the main mineral in glass.

Dinoflagellates

Can you guess how the protist in the middle of **Figure 2** moves? This organism is a dinoflagellate (di noh FLA juh lat), a unicellular plantlike protist that has flagella—whiplike parts that enable the protist to move. The flagella beat back and forth, enabling the dinoflagellate to spin and turn. Some of these protists glow in the dark because of a chemical reaction that occurs when they are disturbed.

 Reading Check What purpose do flagella serve?

Euglenoids

Another type of plantlike protist also uses flagella to move but has a unique structure covering its body. A euglenoid (yew GLEE noyd), shown at the bottom of **Figure 2,** is a unicellular plantlike protist with a flagellum at one end of its body. Instead of a cell wall, euglenoids have a rigid, rubbery cell coat called a pellicle (PEL ih kul). Euglenoids have eyespots that detect light and determine where to move. Euglenoids swim quickly and can creep along the surface of water when it is too shallow to swim. These protists have chloroplasts and make their own food. If there is not enough light for making food, they can absorb nutrients from decaying matter in the water. Animals such as tadpoles and small fish eat euglenoids.

 Reading Check What characteristics do plantlike protists share with plants?

WORD ORIGIN

diatom
from Greek *diatomos,* means "cut in two"

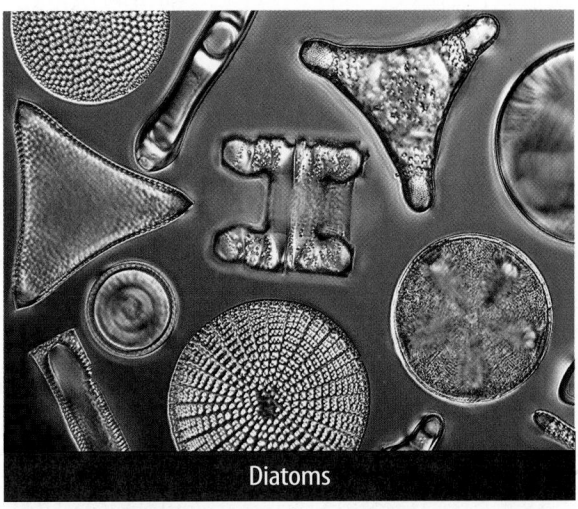
Diatoms

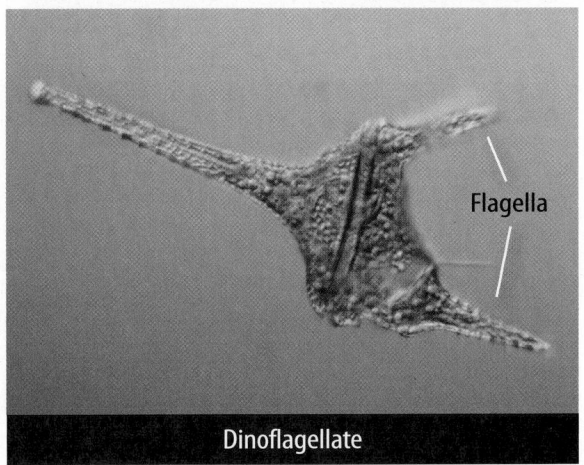
Flagella

Dinoflagellate

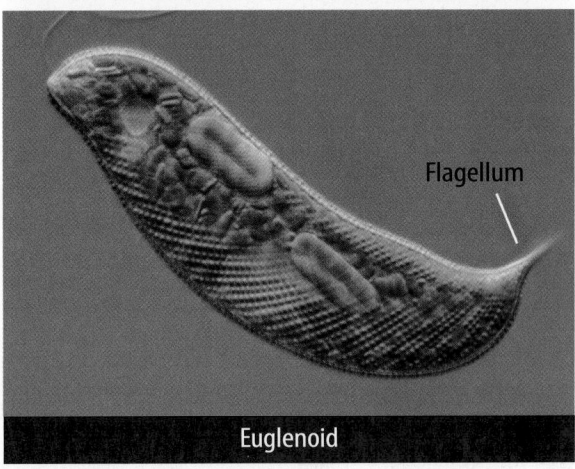
Flagellum

Euglenoid

Figure 2 All of these microscopic organisms are protists. The cell walls of diatoms contain silica. The dinoflagellate has two flagella that cause it to spin. The euglenoid has a flagellum and a rigid cell coat.

Algae

Recall that algae are photosynthetic plantlike protists. Some algae are big and multicellular, like the seaweeds in **Figure 3.** Other algae are unicellular and can be seen only with a microscope. Algae are classified as red, green, or brown, depending on the pigments they contain.

Some types of red and brown algae appear similar to plants. Unlike plants, these algae do not have a complex organ system for transporting water and nutrients. Instead of roots, they have holdfasts, structures that secrete a chemical-like glue that fastens them to the rocks.

One unusual green alga is volvox. In **Figure 3** you can see that many volvox cells come together to form a larger sphere. These cells move together as one group and beat their flagella in unison. Some cells produce parts necessary for sexual reproduction. The volvox cells in the front of the group have larger eyespots that sense light for photosynthesis. Do you think volvox should be considered unicellular or multicellular?

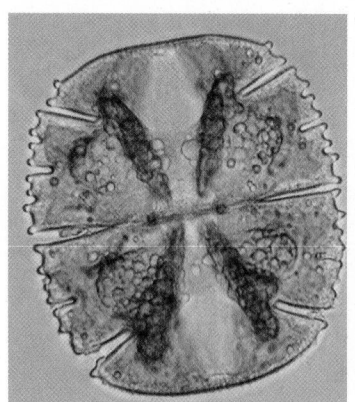

Unicellular Algae

Multicellular Algae

Figure 3 Volvox are unicellular green algae that join together to form a sphere. ▼

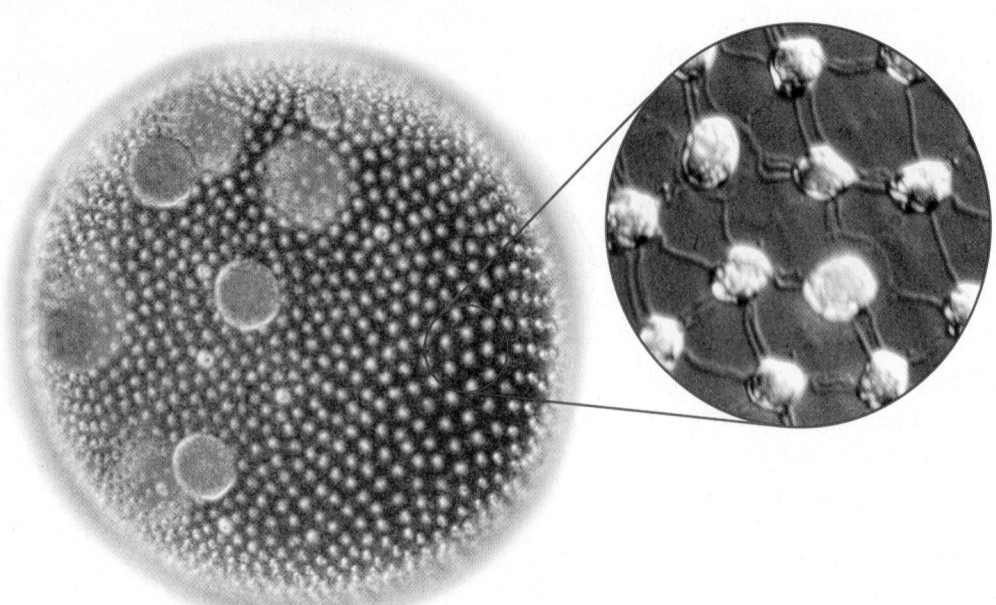

The Importance of Algae

Do you use algae in your everyday life? You might be surprised by all the materials you use that contain algae. You might be eating algae if you snack on ice cream, marshmallows, or pudding. Algae are a common ingredient in other everyday products, including toothpaste, lotions, fertilizers, and some swimming pool filters.

Algae and Ecosystems

Algae provide food for animals and animal-like protists. They also provide shelter for many aquatic organisms. In **Figure 4,** you can see that some brown algae grow tall. Thick groups of tall brown algae are called kelp forests. Sea otters and seals come to the kelp forest to eat smaller animals.

Key Concept Check How are algae beneficial to an ecosystem?

Do you think algae ever cause problems in an ecosystem? Algae and other photosynthetic protists can help remove pollution from the water. However, this pollution can be a food source for the algae, allowing the population of algae to increase quickly. The algae produce wastes that can poison other organisms. As shown in **Figure 5,** when the number of these protists increase, the water can appear red or brown. This is called a red tide or a harmful algal bloom (HAB).

Reading Check What causes a red tide?

Kelp Forest

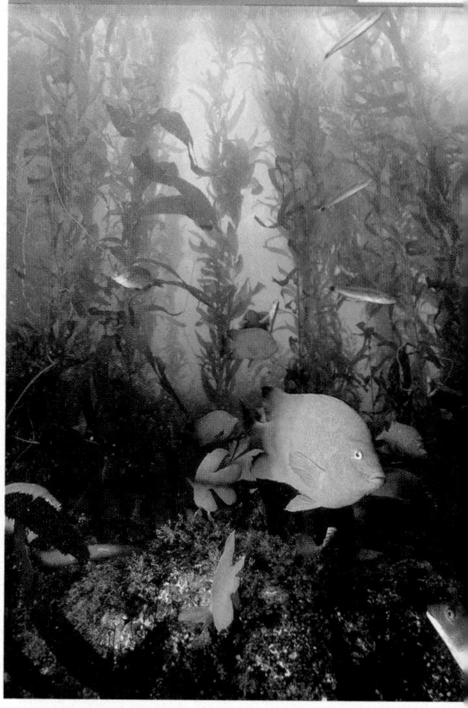

▲ **Figure 4** Brown algae can form thick kelp forests that are home to many animals and other protists.

Figure 5 Red tides can be harmful to aquatic organisms. ▼

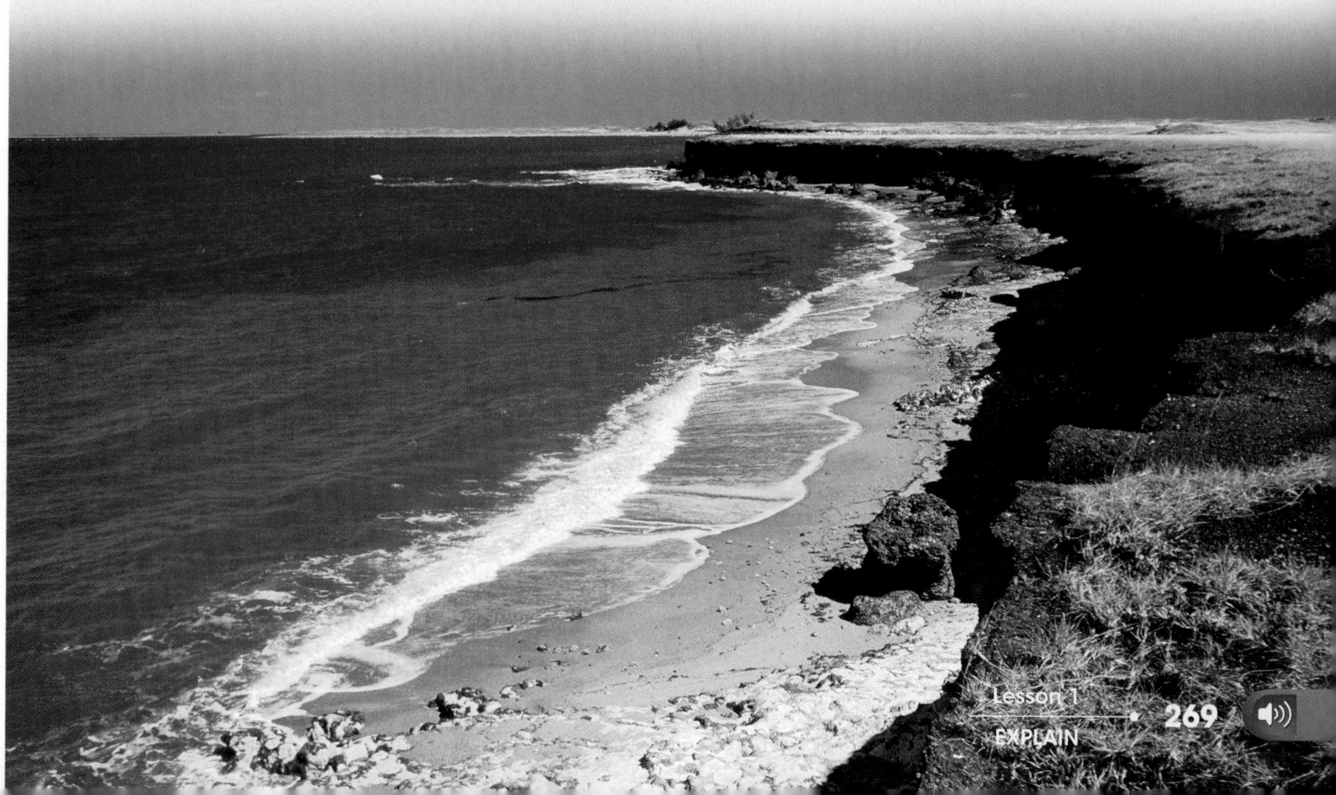

Animal-like Protists

Some protists are similar to plants, but others are more like animals. **Protozoans** (proh tuh ZOH unz) *are protists that resemble tiny animals.* Animal-like protists all share several characteristics. They do not have chloroplasts or make their own food. Protozoans are usually microscopic and all are unicellular. Most protozoans live in wet environments.

Ciliates

Cilia (SIH lee uh) *are short, hairlike structures that grow on the surface of some protists.* Protists that have these organelles are called ciliates. Cilia cover the surface of the cell. They can beat together and move the animal-like protist through the water.

✓ **Reading Check** What function do cilia perform?

A common protozoan with these cilia is the **paramecium** (pa ruh MEE see um; plural, paramecia)—*a protist with cilia and two types of nuclei.* One example of a paramecium is shown in **Figure 6.** A paramecium, like most ciliates, gets its food by forcing water into a groove in its side. The groove closes and a food vacuole, or storage area, forms within the cell. The food particles are digested and the extra water is forced back out. Ciliates reproduce asexually, but they can exchange some genetic material through a **process** called conjugation (kahn juh GAY shun). This results in more genetic variation.

ACADEMIC VOCABULARY

process
(noun) an event marked by gradual changes that lead toward a particular result

Paramecium

⊙ **Concepts in Motion** Animation

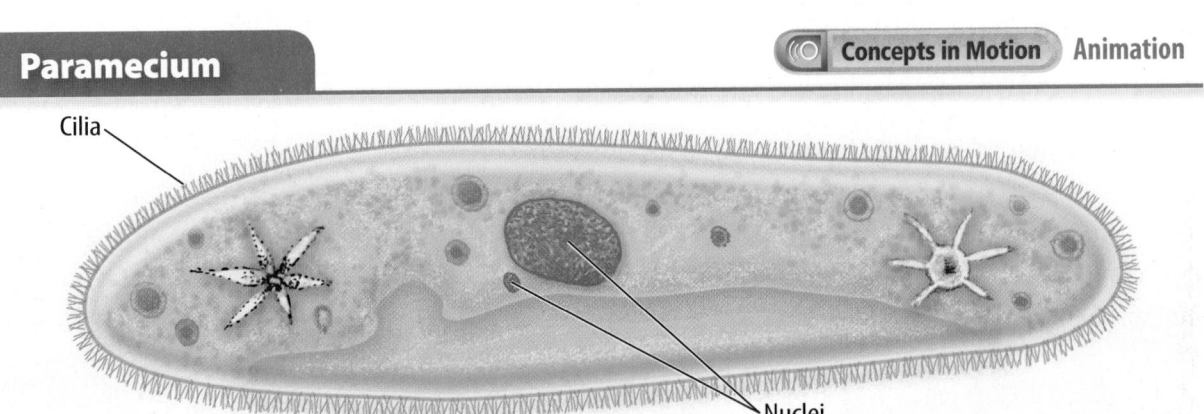

Cilia

Nuclei

Figure 6 A paramecium, like the one shown above, has two nuclei and is covered with hairlike structures called cilia.

Flagellates

Recall that dinoflagellates, a type of plant-like protist, use one or more flagella to move. A type of protozoan also has one or more flagella—a flagellate. However, a flagellate does not always spin when it moves.

Flagellates eat decaying matter including plants, animals, and other protists. Many flagellates live in the digestive system of animals and absorb nutrients from food eaten by them.

Sarcodines

Animal-like protists called sarcodines (SAR kuh dinez) have no specific shape. At rest, a sarcodine resembles a random cluster of cytoplasm, or cellular material. These animal-like protists can ooze into almost any shape as they slide over mud or rocks.

An **amoeba** (uh MEE buh) *is one common sarcodine with an unusual adaptation for movement and getting nutrients.* An amoeba moves by using a **pseudopod,** *a temporary "foot" that forms as the organism pushes part of its body outward.* It moves by first stretching out a pseudopod then oozing the rest of its body up into the pseudopod. This movement is shown in **Figure 7.**

Amoebas also use pseudopods to get nutrients. An amoeba surrounds a smaller organism or food particle with its pseudopod and then oozes around it. A food vacuole forms inside the pseudopod where the food is quickly digested. You can see an amoeba capturing its prey in the photo at the beginning of this lesson.

Some sarcodines get nutrients and energy from ingesting other organisms, while others make their own food. Some sarcodines even live in the digestive systems of humans and get nutrients and energy from the human's body.

Amoeba Movement

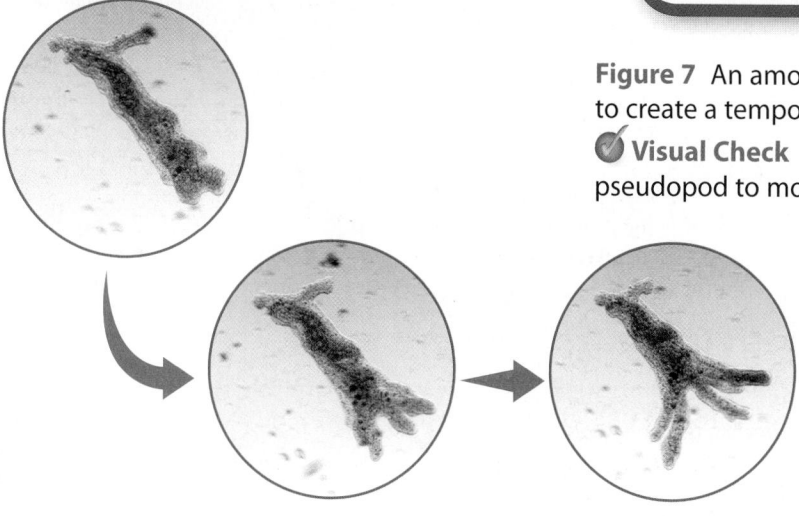

Lesson 1

271

EXPLAIN

 **MiniLab**   **15 minutes**

How can you model the movement of an amoeba?

The way an amoeba moves is so unusual that scientists use the term to describe a specific type of movement. Organisms that move by oozing are said to have "amoeboid" movement.

1. Read and complete a lab safety form.

2. Half-fill a **sock** with **dry beans.** Tie the end of the sock closed with a piece of **string.**

3. Place the sock on a flat surface and spread the beans evenly within the sock.

4. Demonstrate the organism's movement by pushing the beans forward in the sock until the sock moves.

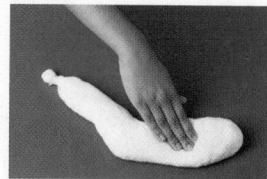

5. Model how amoebas capture their food by pushing the beans and sock around your finger.

Analyze and Conclude

1. **Explain** how amoebas capture their food.

2. **Formulate** models to demonstrate how other animal-like protists move.

3. 🔑 **Key Concept** How does an amoeba move like some animals?

Figure 7 An amoeba moves by extending its body to create a temporary "foot."

✓ **Visual Check** How does the amoeba use the pseudopod to move?

FOLDABLES®

Fold a sheet of paper to make a three-tab book. Label your book as shown. Use it to organize your notes about protozoans and how they move.

How Protozoans Move
Flagella
Cilia
Pseudopod

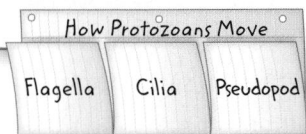

The Importance of Protozoans

Imagine living in a world without organisms that decompose other organisms. Plant material and dead animals would build up until the surface of Earth quickly became covered. Many protozoans are beneficial to an environment because they break down dead plant and animal matter. This decomposed matter is then recycled back into the environment and used by living organisms.

Some protozoans can cause disease by acting as parasites. These organisms can live inside a host organism and feed off it. Protozoan parasites are responsible for millions of human deaths every year.

One example of a disease caused by a protist is malaria. **Figure 8** illustrates how malaria develops and is spread to humans by mosquitoes. Protozoan parasites called plasmodia (singular, plasmodium) live and reproduce in red blood cells. Malaria kills more than one million people each year.

Key Concept Check In what ways are protists helpful and harmful to humans?

Plasmodium Life Cycle

Figure 8 A small parasitic protozoan called plasmodium causes malaria. It is transferred among humans by mosquitoes.

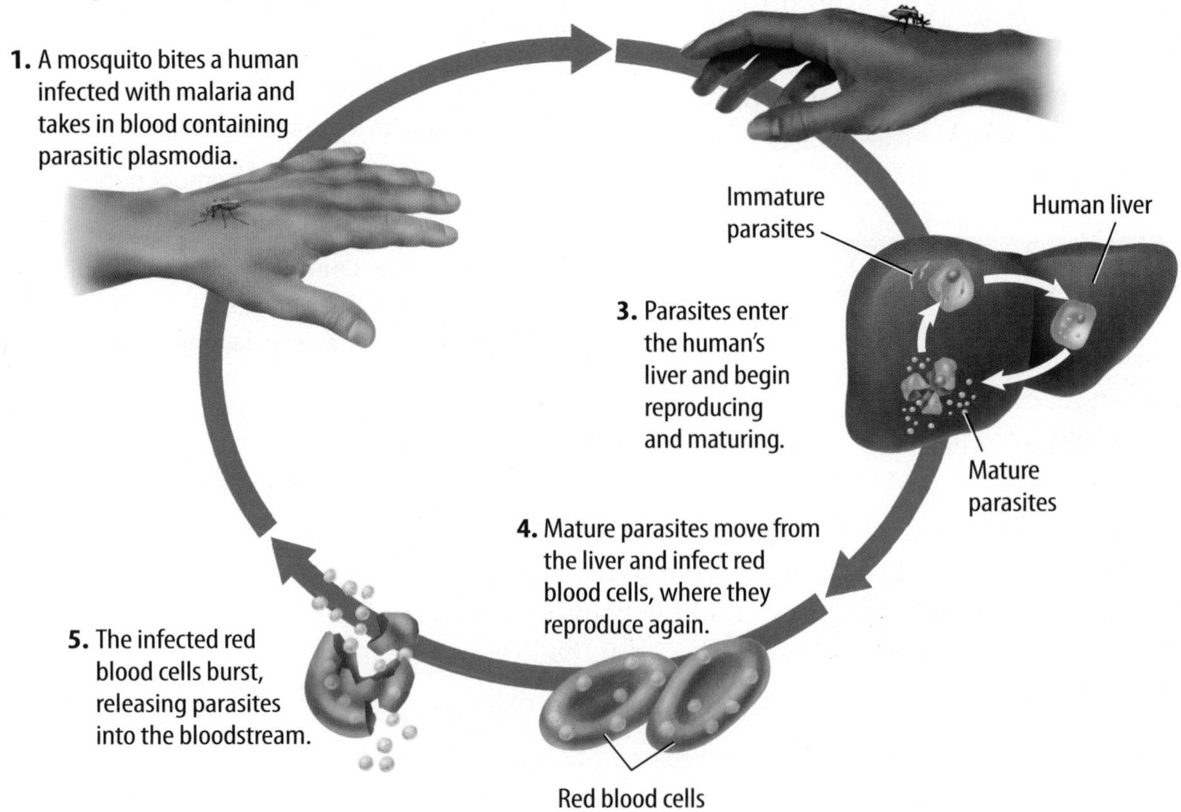

2. The mosquito transfers parasites to an uninfected human when it bites him or her.
1. A mosquito bites a human infected with malaria and takes in blood containing parasitic plasmodia.
Immature parasites
Human liver
3. Parasites enter the human's liver and begin reproducing and maturing.
Mature parasites
4. Mature parasites move from the liver and infect red blood cells, where they reproduce again.
5. The infected red blood cells burst, releasing parasites into the bloodstream.
Red blood cells

Funguslike Protists

In addition to plantlike and animal-like protists, there are funguslike protists. These protists share many characteristics with fungi. However, because of their differences from fungi, they are classified as protists.

Slime and Water Molds

Have you ever seen a strange organism like the one shown in **Figure 9?** These funguslike protists, called slime molds, look like they could have come from another planet. The body of the slime mold is composed of cell material and nuclei floating in a slimy mass. Most slime molds absorb nutrients from other organic matter in their environment.

A Funguslike Protist

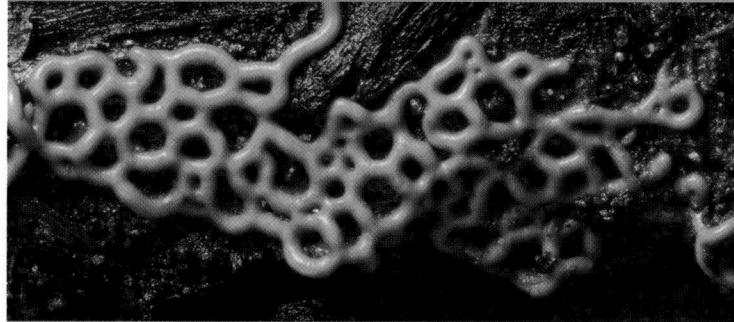

Figure 9 Slime molds come in a variety of colors and forms. These protists often live on the surfaces of plants.

A water mold is another kind of funguslike protist that lives as a parasite or feeds on dead organisms. Originally classified as fungi, water molds often cause diseases in plants.

Both slime molds and water molds reproduce sexually and asexually. The molds usually reproduce sexually when environmental conditions are harsh or unfavorable.

Importance of Funguslike Protists

Funguslike protists play a valuable role in the ecosystem. They break down dead plant and animal matter, making the nutrients from these dead organisms available for living organisms. While some slime molds and water molds are beneficial, many others can be very harmful.

Many funguslike protists attack and consume living plants. The Great Irish Potato Famine resulted from damage by a funguslike protist. In 1845 this water mold destroyed more than half of Ireland's potato crop. More than one million people starved as a result.

 Key Concept Check How are funguslike protists beneficial to an environment?

Lesson 1 Review

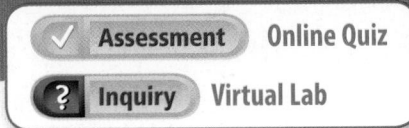
Visual Summary

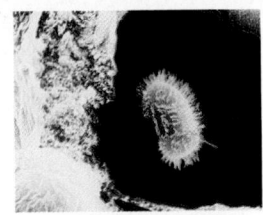

Protists are a diverse group of organisms that cannot be classified as plants, animals, or fungi.

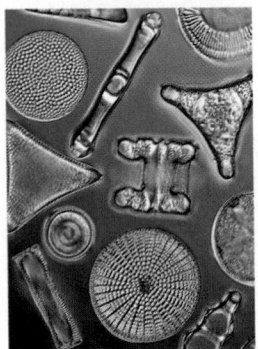

Protists are grouped according to the type of organisms they most resemble. Diatoms are one type of plantlike protist.

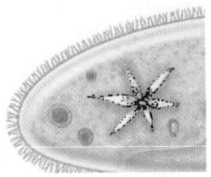

Some protists use hairlike structures called cilia to move.

FOLDABLES

Use your lesson Foldable to review the lesson. Save your Foldable for the project at the end of the chapter.

What do you think NOW?

You first read the statements below at the beginning of the chapter.

1. Protists are grouped together because they all look similar.

2. Some protists cause harm to other organisms.

3. Many protists make their own food.

Did you change your mind about whether you agree or disagree with the statements? Rewrite any false statements to make them true.

Use Vocabulary

1 **Distinguish** between cilia and flagella.

2 **Define** *pseudopod* in your own words or with a drawing.

Understand Key Concepts

3 **List** three groups of animal-like protists and three groups of plantlike protists.

4 **Describe** one example of how protists benefit humans.

5 Identify which protist causes red tides.
  A. algae   C. euglenoids
  B. diatoms   D. paramecia

Interpret Graphics

6 **Identify** Copy and fill in the graphic organizer with the three categories of protists.

7 The image below shows the plasmodium life cycle.

Explain in your own words how this disease can be spread among people.

Critical Thinking

8 **Formulate** a plan for deciding to classify a newly discovered protist.

The Benefits of Algae

Big Benefits from Tiny Organisms

▲ Processing plants, such as this one, are a major source of algae oil.

Algae are protists that can do more than just cover a pond as slimy scum. They release oxygen through photosynthesis. In fact, most of the oxygen in Earth's atmosphere comes from photosynthesis that occurs in algae, plants, and some bacteria. Algae are also food for many organisms, including humans. But algae can provide something else very valuable—oil.

A microalga is another type of protist that is very small and reproduces quickly. The total mass of some microalgae can double several times a day. More than half of their mass is fats, also called lipids, that store energy. One type of lipid, triglycerides, can be turned into diesel oil, gasoline, and jet fuel.

Microalgae can grow outdoors in ponds and produce 100 times more oil per acre than any other crop. They also can grow indoors under lights in photobioreactors. A photobioreactor is a tank filled with water and nutrients. Photosynthesis requires carbon dioxide. Instead of releasing carbon dioxide gas into the atmosphere, power plants can pump it into photobioreactors for microalgae to use. Also, microalgae can grow in water that is unsafe to drink. Using this technology, microalgae can grow in areas, such as deserts, where it is not ordinarily possible to grow other crops.

It's Your Turn

RESEARCH Protists, including algae, are important sources of food. Research five types of organisms that depend on protists for food. Make a display of your results to share with your class.

Lesson 2

Reading Guide

Key Concepts
ESSENTIAL QUESTIONS

- What are the different types of fungi and how do they compare?
- Why are fungi important?
- What are lichens?

Vocabulary

hyphae p. 277
mycelium p. 277
basidium p. 278
ascus p. 279
zygosporangia p. 279
mycorrhizae p. 282
lichen p. 284

Multilingual eGlossary

What are fungi?

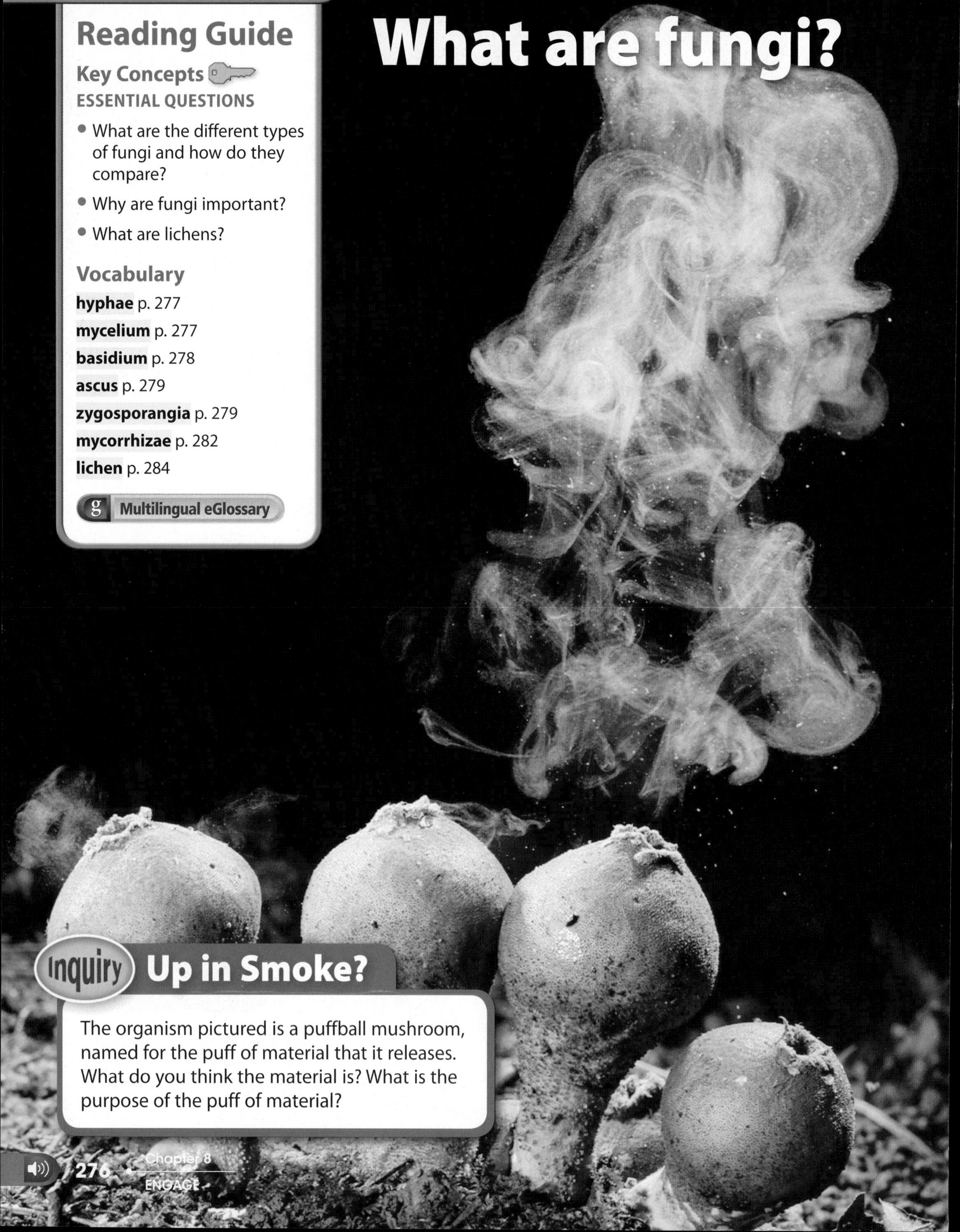

Inquiry Up in Smoke?

The organism pictured is a puffball mushroom, named for the puff of material that it releases. What do you think the material is? What is the purpose of the puff of material?

Is there a fungus among us?

The mold you see on food is fungi that are consuming and decomposing it. Fungi are also found as molds or mushrooms on wood, mulch, and other organic materials.

1. Read and complete a lab safety form.
2. Examine the different **samples of fungi** your teacher provides. Use a **magnifying lens** to observe similarities and differences among the samples.
3. Record your observations in your Science Journal. Include drawings of the different structures or characteristics you notice.

Think About This

1. What similarities did you see among the fungi samples?

2. Why do you think your teacher had the mold samples in closed containers?

3. 🔑 **Key Concept** In what ways do you think the fungi you observed are helpful or not helpful to people?

What are fungi?

What would you guess is the world's largest organism? A fungus in Oregon is the largest organism ever measured by scientists. It stretches almost 9 km². Fungi, like protists, are eukaryotes. Scientists estimate more than 1.5 million species of fungi exist.

Fungi form long, threadlike structures that grow into large tangles, usually underground. *These structures, which absorb minerals and water, are called* **hyphae** *(HI fee). The hyphae create a network called the* **mycelium** *(mi SEE lee um),* shown in **Figure 10.** The fruiting body of the mushroom, the part above ground, is also made of hyphae.

Fungi are heterotrophs, meaning they cannot make their own food. Some fungi are parasites, obtaining nutrients from living organisms. Fungi dissolve their food by releasing chemicals that decompose organic matter. Fungi then absorb the nutrients.

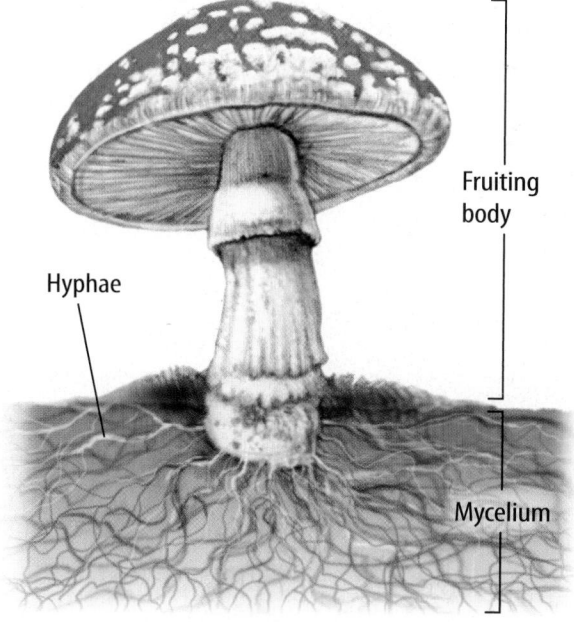

Figure 10 Mushrooms are common fungi. In the drawing, you can see mycelium, the network of hyphae. The hyphae release enzymes and absorb water and nutrients.

Types of Fungi

Scientists group fungi based on how they look and how they reproduce. Although fungi can reproduce sexually or asexually, almost all reproduce asexually by producing spores. Spores are small reproductive cells with a strong, protective outer covering. The spores can grow into new individuals.

The classification of fungi often changes as scientists learn more about them. Today, scientists recognize four groups of fungi: club fungi, sac fungi, zygote fungi, and imperfect fungi. As technology helps scientists understand more about fungi, the categories might change.

 Key Concept Check What are the four groups of fungi?

Club Fungi

When you think of fungi, you might think of a **mushroom.** Mushrooms belong to the group called club fungi. They are named for the clublike shape of their reproductive structures. However, the mushroom is just one part of the fungus. The part of the mushroom that grows above ground is a structure called a basidiocarp (bus SIH dee oh karp). Inside the basidiocarp are the **basidia** (buh SIH dee uh; singular, basidium), *reproductive structures that produce sexual spores.* Most of a club fungus is a network of hyphae that grows underground and absorbs nutrients.

 Reading Check Where does most of a club fungus grow?

Many club fungi are named for their various shapes and characteristics. Club fungi include puffballs like those at the beginning of the lesson, stinkhorns, and the bird's nest fungi shown in **Figure 11.** There is even a club fungus that glows in the dark due to a chemical reaction in its basidiocarp.

SCIENCE USE v. COMMON USE

mushroom
Science Use a type of club fungi

Common Use the part of a fungus above the ground

Figure 11 Club fungi, such as this bird's nest fungus, use basidiospores to reproduce.

Visual Check Which part of the fungus is club-shaped?

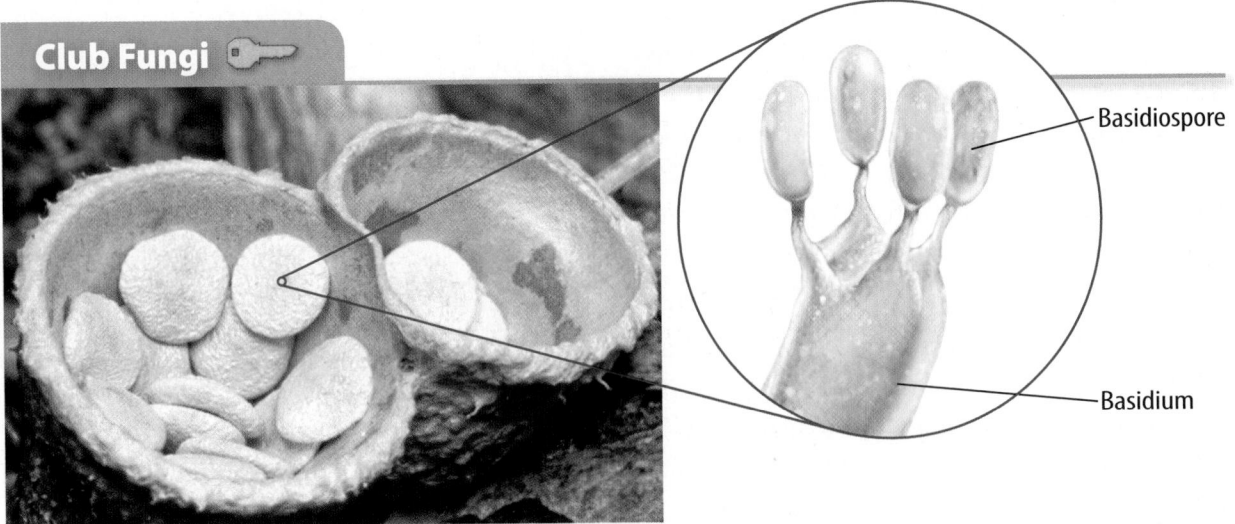

Club Fungi

Basidiospore

Basidium

Sac Fungi

Do you know what bread and a diaper rash have in common? A type of sac fungus causes bread dough to rise. A different sac fungus is responsible for a rash that babies can develop on damp skin under their diapers. Many sac fungi cause diseases in plants and animals. Other common sac fungi, such as truffles and morels, are harvested by people for food.

Like club fungi, sac fungi are named for their reproductive structures. *The **ascus** (AS kuhs; plural, asci) is the reproductive structure where spores develop on sac fungi.* The ascus often looks like the bottom of a tiny bag or sack. The spores from sac fungi are called ascospores (AS kuh sporz). Sac fungi can undergo both sexual and asexual reproduction. Many yeasts are sac fungi, including the common yeast used to make bread, as shown in **Figure 12**. When the yeast is mixed with water and warmed, the yeast cells become active. They begin cellular respiration and release carbon dioxide gas. This causes the bread dough to rise.

Zygote Fungi

Another type of fungus can cause bread to develop mold. Bread mold, like the type shown in **Figure 12**, is caused by a type of fungus called a zygote fungus. You might also find zygote fungi growing in moist areas, such as a damp basement or on a bathroom shower curtain.

The hyphae of a zygote fungus grow over materials, such as bread, dissolving the material and absorbing nutrients. *Tiny stalks called* **zygosporangia** *(zi guh spor AN jee uh) form when the fungus undergoes sexual reproduction.* The zygosporangia release spores called zygospores. These zygospores then fall on other materials where new zygote fungi might grow.

Reading Check How do sac and zygote fungi differ?

Figure 12 Some fungi can be used to make food, but other fungi can eat the food too.

Zygosporangia

FOLDABLES®

Fold a sheet of paper to make a four-door book. Label it as shown. Use your book to organize information about the characteristics of the different classifications of fungi.

Zygote fungi | Sac fungi

Club fungi | Imperfect fungi

Imperfect Fungi

How are itchy feet and blue cheese connected? They can both be caused by imperfect fungi. You might have had athlete's foot, an infection that causes flaking and itching in the skin of the feet. The imperfect fungus that causes athlete's foot grows and reproduces easily in the moist environment near a shower or in a sweaty shoe. The blue color you see in blue cheese comes from colonies of a different type of imperfect fungi. They are added to the milk or the curds during the cheese-making process.

Imperfect fungi are named because scientists have not observed a sexual, or "perfect," reproductive stage in their life cycle. Since fungi are classified according to the shape of their reproductive structures, these fungi are left out, or labeled "imperfect." Often after a species of imperfect fungi is studied, the sexual stage is observed. The fungi is then classified as a club, sac, or zygote fungus based on these observations.

 Reading Check Why are imperfect fungi classified that way?

Inquiry MiniLab　　　　　　　　　　　　　　**10 minutes**

What do fungal spores look like?

Have you ever seen spores from a mushroom? Some types of fungi reproduce by releasing these structures.

1 Read and complete a lab safety form.

2 Carefully remove the stem of your **mushroom.** Observe the gills, the soft structures on the underside of the cap.

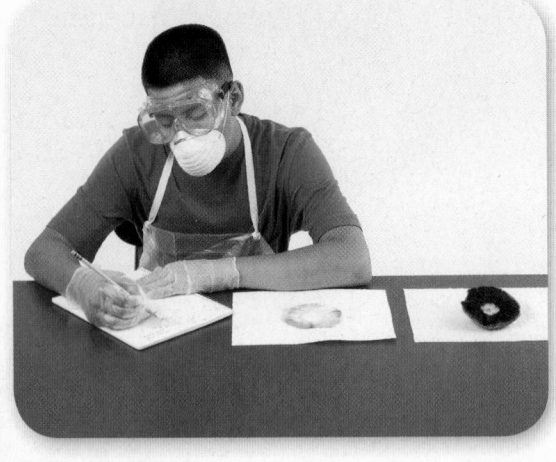

3 Gently place the mushroom cap with the gills down on a sheet of **unlined white paper.**

4 Let the mushroom cap sit undisturbed overnight. Remove it from the paper the next day.

Analyze and Conclude

1. **Describe** your results and sketch them in your Science Journal. What caused this result?

2. **Estimate** the number of mushrooms that could be produced from a single mushroom cap.

3. 🔑 **Key Concept** What type of fungi (club, sac, zygote, or imperfect) did you use to make the print?

Figure 13 Products such as bread, cheese, and medicines are made using fungi.

The Importance of Fungi

Do you like chocolate, carbonated sodas, cheese, or bread? If so, you might agree that fungi are beneficial to humans. Fungi are involved in the production of many foods and other products, as shown in **Figure 13.** Some fungi are used as a meat substitute because they are high in protein and low in cholesterol. Other fungi are used to make antibiotics.

Decomposers

Fungi help create food for people to eat, but they are also important because of the things they eat. As you read earlier, fungi are an important part of the environment because they break down dead plant and animal matter, as shown in **Figure 14.** Without fungi and other decomposers, dead plants and animals would pile up year after year. Fungi also help break down pollution, including pesticides, in soil. Without fungi to destroy it, pollution would build up in the environment.

Living things need nutrients. The nutrients available in the soil would eventually be used up if they were not replaced by decomposing plant and animal matter. Fungi help put these nutrients back into the soil for plants to use.

Figure 14 Fungi help decompose dead organic matter, such as this rabbit. ▼

May 8

October 6

Using Fractions

Under certain conditions, 100 percent of the cells in fungus A reproduce in 24 hours. The number of cells of fungus A doubles once each day.

Day 1 = 10,000 cells

Day 2 = 20,000 cells

Day 3 = 40,000 cells

Day 4 = 80,000 cells

When an antibiotic is added to the fungus, the growth is reduced by 50 percent. Only half the cells reproduce each day.

Day 2 = 15,000 cells

Day 3 = 22,500 cells

Day 4 = 33,750 cells

Practice

Without an antibiotic, how many cells of fungus A would there be on day 6?

Review

• **Math Practice**
• **Personal Tutor**

Fungi and Plant Roots

Plants benefit from fungi in other ways, too. Many fungi and plants grow together, helping each other. Recall that fungi take in minerals and water through the hyphae, or threadlike structures that grow on or under the surface. *The roots of the plants and the hyphae of the fungi weave together to form a structure called* **mycorrhiza** (mi kuh RI zuh; plural, micorrhizae).

Mycorrhizae can exchange molecules, as shown in **Figure 15.** As fungi break down decaying matter in the soil, they make nutrients available to the plant. They also increase water absorption by increasing the surface area of the plant's roots.

Fungi cannot photosynthesize, or make their own food using light energy. Instead, the fungi in mycorrhizae take in some of the sugars from the plant's photosynthesis. The plants benefit by receiving more nutrients and water. The fungi benefit and continue to grow by using plant sugars. Scientists suspect that most plants gain some benefit from mycorrhizae.

 Reading Check How do mycorrhizae benefit both the plant and the fungus?

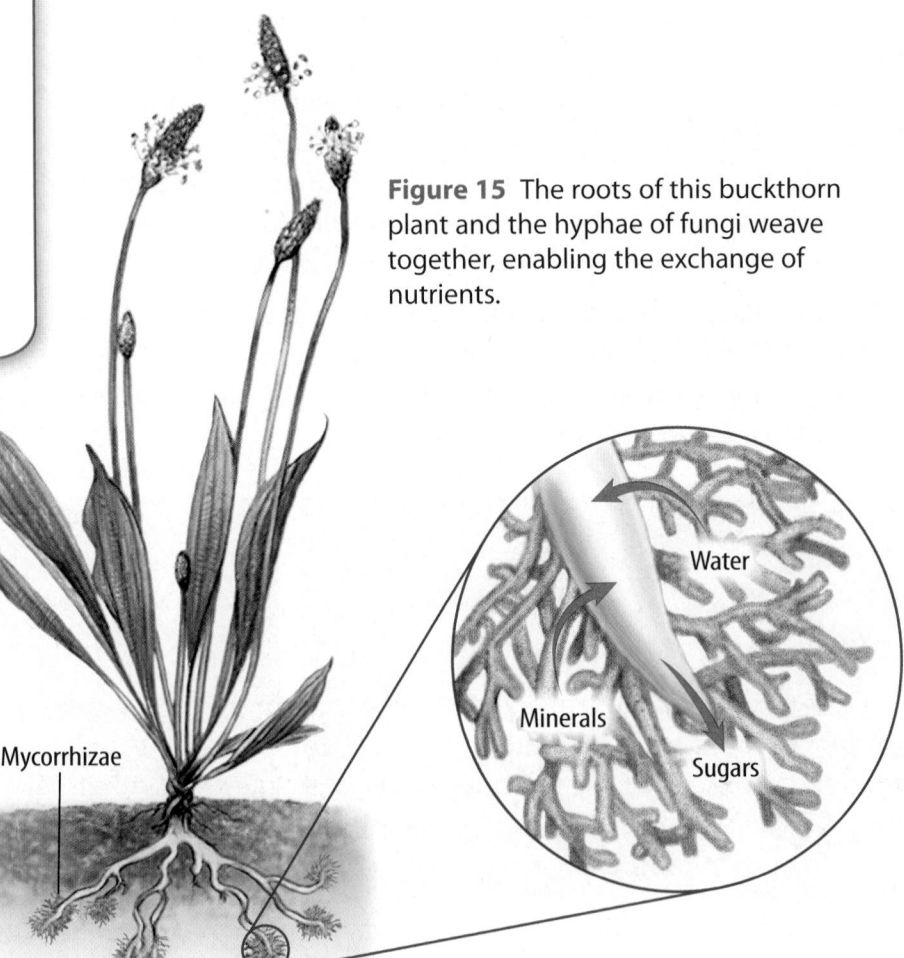

Figure 15 The roots of this buckthorn plant and the hyphae of fungi weave together, enabling the exchange of nutrients.

Mycorrhizae

Water

Minerals

Sugars

Health and Medicine

You might recall that many protists can be harmful to humans and the environment. This is true of fungi as well. A small number of people die every year after eating poisonous mushrooms or spoiled food containing harmful fungi.

You do not have to eat fungi for them to make you sick or uncomfortable. You already read that fungi cause athlete's foot rashes and diaper rashes. Some fungi cause allergies, pneumonia, and thrush. Thrush is a yeast infection that grows in the mouths of infants and people with weak immune systems.

Although fungi can cause disease, scientists also use them to make important medicines. Antibiotics, such as penicillin, are among the valuable medications made from fungi. An accident resulted in the discovery of penicillin. Alexander Fleming was studying bacteria in 1928 when spores of *Penicillium* fungus contaminated his experiment and killed the bacteria. After years of research, this fungus was used to make an antibiotic similar to the penicillin used today. **Figure 16** illustrates how penicillin affects bacterial growth.

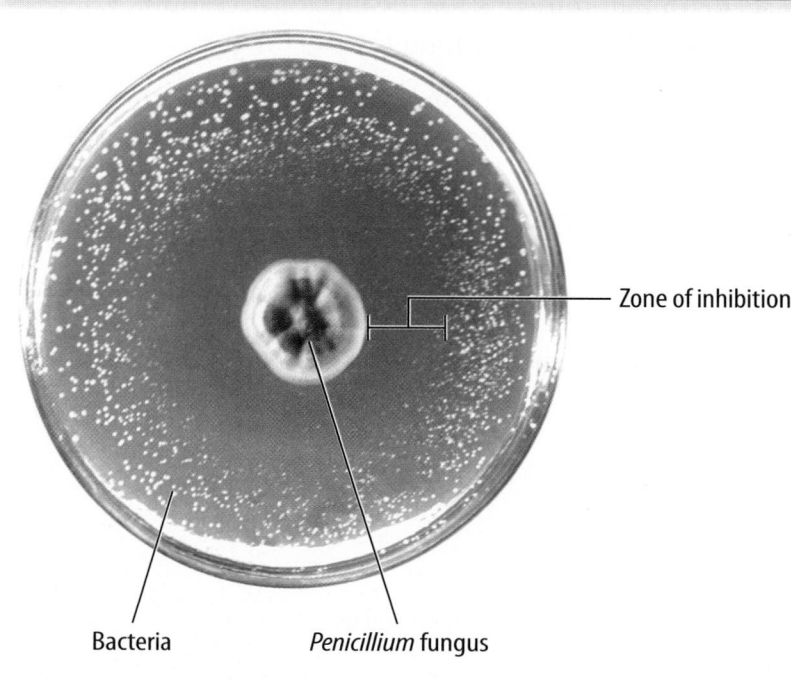

Zone of inhibition

Bacteria   *Penicillium* fungus

Figure 16 The *Penicillium* fungus that prevents bacteria from growing is used to make penicillin, an antibiotic medicine.

Visual Check How can you tell that the fungi are stopping the bacteria from growing?

Over time, some bacteria have become resistant to the many antibiotics used to fight illness. New antibiotics need to be developed to treat the same diseases. As new species of fungi are discovered and studied, scientists might find new sources of antibiotics and medicines.

 Key Concept Check Describe two ways that fungi are important to humans.

What are lichens?

Do you recall the photo at the beginning of the chapter? The structure pictured is a lichen. *A* **lichen** *(LI kun) is a structure formed when fungi and certain other photosynthetic organisms grow together.* Usually, a lichen consists of a sac fungus or club fungus that lives in a partnership with either a green alga or a photosynthetic bacterium. The fungus' hyphae grow in a layer around the algae cells.

Green algae and photosynthetic bacteria are autotrophs, which means they can make their own food using photosynthesis. Lichens are similar to mycorrhizae because both organisms benefit from the partnership. The fungus provides water and minerals while the bacterium or alga provides the sugars and oxygen from photosynthesis.

The Importance of Lichens

Imagine living on a sunny, rocky cliff like the one in **Figure 17.** Not many organisms could live there because there is little to eat. A lichen, however, is well suited to this harsh environment. The fungus can absorb water, help break down rocks, and obtain minerals for the alga or bacterium. They can photosynthesize and make food for the fungus.

Once lichens are established in an area, it becomes a better environment for other organisms. Many animals that live in harsh conditions survive by eating lichens. Plants benefit from lichens because the fungi help break down rocks and create soil. Plants can then grow in the soil, creating a food source for other organisms in the environment.

 Key Concept Check Which two organisms make up a lichen?

WORD ORIGIN

lichen
from Greek *leichen*, means "what eats around itself"

Figure 17 Lichens are structures made of photosynthetic organisms and fungi that can live in harsh conditions.

Lichen Structure

Fungal hyphae

Algal cell

284 Chapter 8
EXPLAIN

Lesson 2 Review

Visual Summary

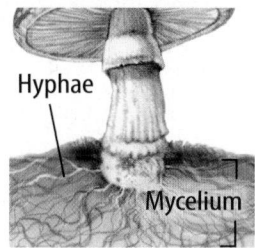

The body of a fungus is made up of thread-like hyphae that weave together to create a network of mycelium.

Hyphae

Mycelium

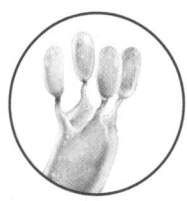

Club fungi produce sexual spores in the basidium.

A lichen is made of fungus and a photosynthetic bacterium or alga.

FOLDABLES®

Use your lesson Foldable to review the lesson. Save your Foldable for the project at the end of the chapter.

What do you think NOW?

You first read the statements below at the beginning of the chapter.

4. Mushrooms and yeasts are two types of fungi.

5. Fungi are always helpful to plants.

6. Some fungi can be made into foods or medicines.

Did you change your mind about whether you agree or disagree with the statements? Rewrite any false statements to make them true.

Use Vocabulary

1. **Distinguish** between a basidium and an ascus.

2. **Identify** the structure formed between fungal hyphae and plant roots.

3. **Define** *ascus* in your own words.

Understand Key Concepts

4. **List** the four groups of fungi.

5. **List** the two organisms that make up lichen.

6. Which disease is caused by a fungus?
   - **A.** athlete's foot
   - **B.** influenza
   - **C.** malaria
   - **D.** pneumonia

Interpret Graphics

7. Review the image below. Describe how this structure helps the fungus survive.

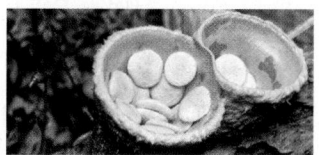

8. **Compare and Contrast** Create a table that compares and contrasts information about sac fungi and zygote fungi.

Sac Fungi	Zygote Fungi

Critical Thinking

9. **Design** a plan for using lichens to convert a harsh cliff environment into a habitat for small plants.

10. **Support** the claim that decomposition is important for the environment.

Math Skills

📲 Review
— Math Practice —

11. The number of cells in fungus X doubles every 2 hours. If you begin with 10 cells, how many would be present after 24 hours?

What does a lichen look like?

Materials

forceps

lichen sample

paper plate

plastic spoon

slide

dropper

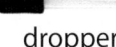

coverslip

microscope

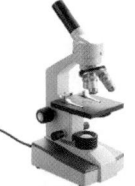

Safety

Lichens come in a wide variety of textures, colors, sizes, and shapes. A lichen is the partnership between a fungus and another organism—usually an alga but sometimes a photosynthetic bacterium. In this relationship, the alga or the bacterium provides the fungus with food through photosynthesis. The fungus provides the other organism with protection. Under magnification you might be able to see structures belonging to both organisms.

Question

What structures can you see in a lichen?

Procedure

1. Read and complete a lab safety form.

2. With your forceps, break off a tiny piece of lichen and place it on a paper plate. Grind the lichen very gently with the back of a plastic spoon until it is broken into small pieces.

3. Using the spoon, place the ground-up lichen into the well of a slide. Use the dropper to add a few drops of water and then place the coverslip over the well.

4. Observe the lichen under the microscope and make a drawing of your observations in your Science Journal.

5. Label the parts of the lichen you observe. Were you able to see any green algal cells? Where are the hyphae? How is the fungus different in color, shape, and texture?

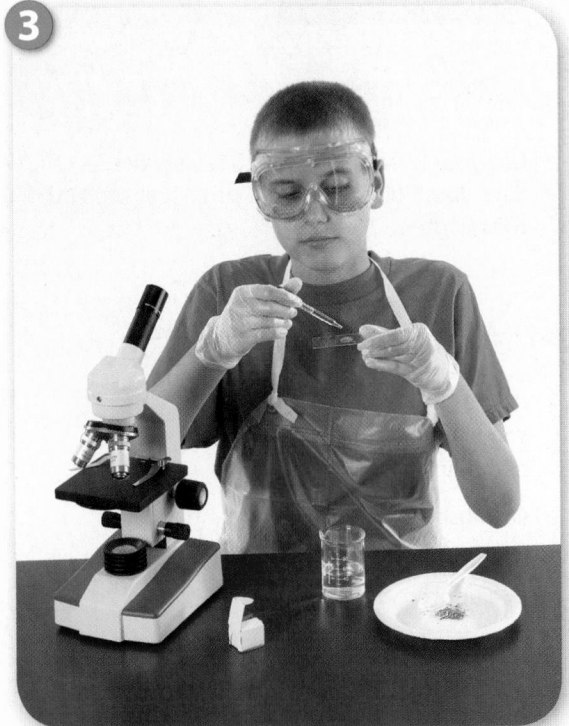

6. Review the structures of the different protists and fungi you have studied so far.

7. Based on your observations from this dissection and your research, determine the ways in which the structures in lichens are similar to and different from those of other organisms.

Analyze and Conclude

8. **Compare** Did you see more fungal structures or algal structures in the slide?

9. **Infer** Based on your observations, do you think a lichen should be classified as a protist, a fungus, neither, or both?

10.  **The Big Idea** How do the structures of the algae and fungus benefit each other in a lichen?

Communicate Your Results

Create a poster to represent the data obtained from your investigation. Describe how you used your data to determine the classification of a lichen. Use drawings and photos to support your findings.

Inquiry Extension

Think of a question about lichen that you might investigate through further observation. Your question might focus on the life cycle of lichen, the best growing conditions, or the lichen as an indicator of air quality. Develop and conduct an experiment to explore your question.

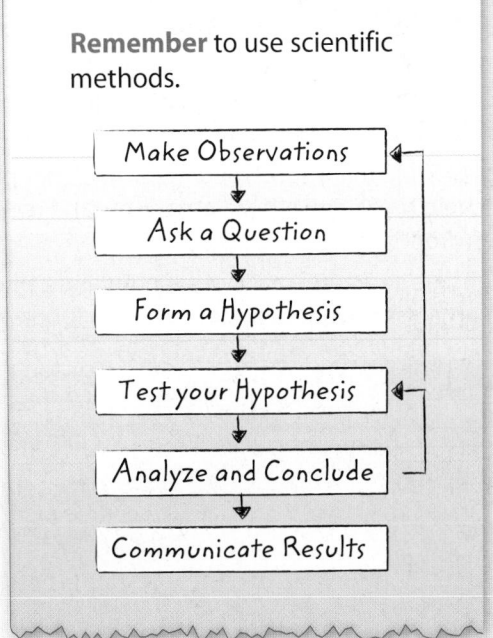

Lab Tips

☑ Look for differences in the structures you observe. Try to match the characteristics of these structures to those of protists or fungi.

☑ Begin observing the samples under low magnification first, and then increase as you identify structures.

Remember to use scientific methods.

Make Observations
↓
Ask a Question
↓
Form a Hypothesis
↓
Test your Hypothesis
↓
Analyze and Conclude
↓
Communicate Results

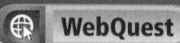 **WebQuest**

 **THE BIG IDEA** Protists and fungi are diverse groups of organisms. They are classified as neither plant nor animal and serve many functions in the ecosystem.

Key Concepts Summary 🔑

Vocabulary

Lesson 1: What are protists?

- Scientists divide **protists** into three groups based on the type of organisms they most resemble. There are plantlike, animal-like, and funguslike protists.
- Protists are beneficial to humans in many ways. They are used to create many of the useful products you depend on. They also help decompose dead organisms and return nutrients to the environment.

Vocabulary

protist p. 265
algae p. 266
diatom p. 267
protozoan p. 270
cilia p. 270
paramecium p. 270
amoeba p. 271
pseudopod p. 271

Plantlike	Animal-like	Funguslike

Lesson 2: What are fungi?

- Scientists divide fungi into four groups, based on the type of structures they use for sexual reproduction. The four groups are club fungi, sac fungi, zygote fungi, and imperfect fungi.
- Fungi provide many foods and medicines that people use. In addition, fungi help break down dead organisms and recycle the nutrients into the environment.
- **Lichens** are structures made of a fungus and a photosynthetic organism. Both organisms work together to obtain food, water, and nutrients.

hyphae p. 277
mycelium p. 277
basidium p. 278
ascus p. 279
zygosporangia p. 279
mycorrhizae p. 282
lichen p. 284

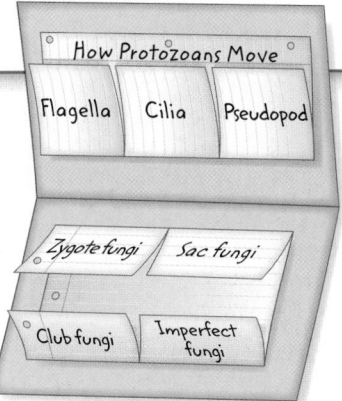
FOLDABLES® Chapter Project

Assemble your lesson Foldables as shown to make a Chapter Project. Use the project to review what you have learned in this chapter.

How Protozoans Move

Flagella   Cilia   Pseudopod

Zygote fungi   Sac fungi

Club fungi   Imperfect fungi

Use Vocabulary

1 A protist that resembles a tiny animal is called a(n) _____.

2 A fungus and the roots of a plant form a structure called _____ that benefits both organisms.

3 The _____ is a saclike structure on a fungus that produces spores.

4 A(n) _____ is a microscopic, plantlike protist that can resemble glass or gems.

5 Short structures that cover the outside of some protists and help them move are called _____.

6 Fungi grow by extending threadlike body structures called _____.

Link Vocabulary and Key Concepts

Concepts in Motion Interactive Concept Map

Copy this concept map, and then use vocabulary terms from the previous page and other terms from this chapter to complete the concept map.

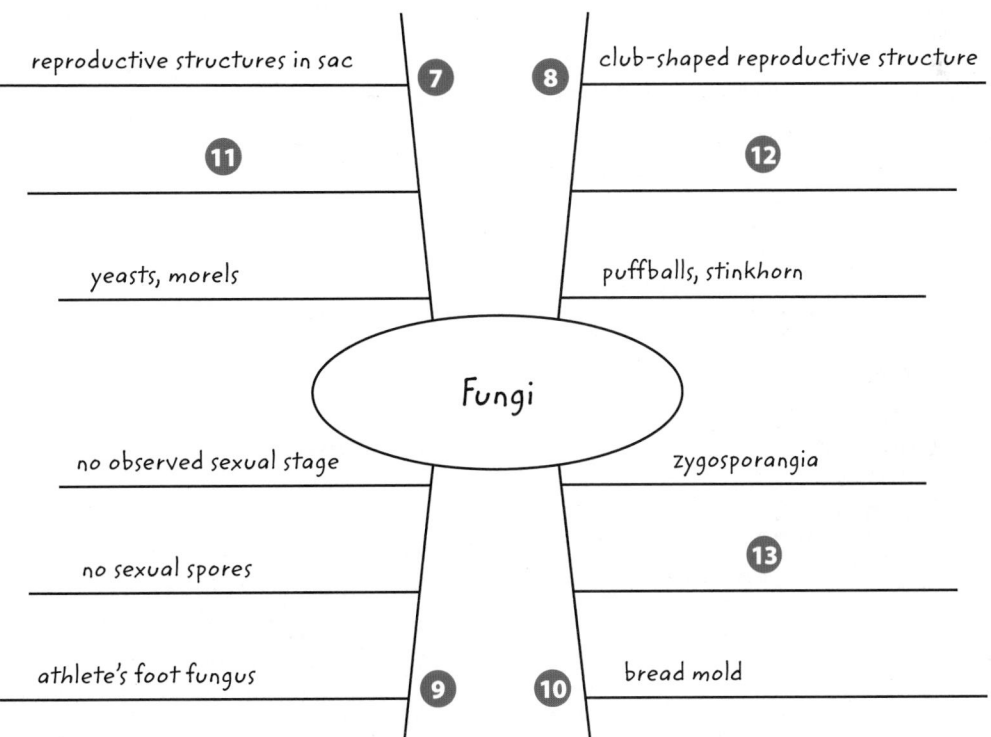

reproductive structures in sac **7**

8 club-shaped reproductive structure

11

12

yeasts, morels

puffballs, stinkhorn

Fungi

no observed sexual stage

zygosporangia

no sexual spores

13

athlete's foot fungus **9**

10 bread mold

Understand Key Concepts

1 Which organism causes red tides when found in large numbers?

A. algae
B. amoebas
C. ciliates
D. diatoms

2 Protists are a diverse group of organisms divided into what three categories?

A. animal-like, plantlike, protozoanlike
B. euglenoid, slime-mold, diatoms
C. plantlike, animal-like, and funguslike
D. green algae, red algae, and kelp

3 Which type of protist is commonly used in ice cream, toothpaste, soups, and body lotions?

A. algae
B. amoebas
C. ciliates
D. diatoms

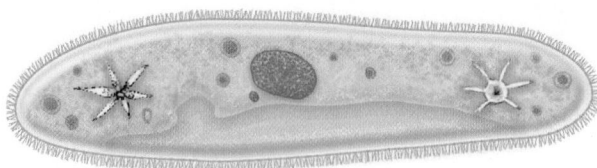

4 The organism in the figure above is a

A. ciliate.
B. diatom.
C. dinoflagellate.
D. kelp.

5 The main function of the hairlike structures surrounding the organism above is

A. decomposition.
B. movement.
C. photosynthesis.
D. reproduction.

6 What type of fungus is bread mold?

A. club
B. imperfect
C. sac
D. zygote

7 Which type of fungus is shown below?

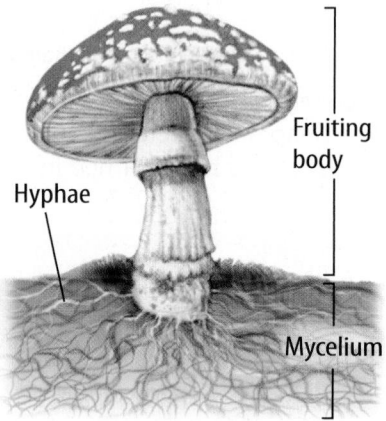

A. club fungus
B. sac fungus
C. zygote fungus
D. imperfect fungus

8 Lichens often consist of

A. plants and animals helping each other.
B. animals and fungi helping each other.
C. protozoans living as parasites on animals.
D. fungi and green algae helping each other.

9 An example of a disease caused by a fungus is

A. athlete's foot.
B. malaria.
C. red tide.
D. the common cold.

10 Sac fungi can be

A. capable of both asexual and sexual reproduction.
B. capable of making their own food.
C. protists.
D. unicellular plants.

11 Which is not a common use of fungi?

A. a predator in forest ecosystems
B. decomposing plant and animal material
C. killing bacteria
D. serving as a food source for other organisms

Critical Thinking

12 **Compare and contrast** plantlike protists with funguslike protists.

13 **Draw** a diagram to show how a parasitic protist can be transferred from one mammal to another and cause malaria. Imagine you are a doctor in an area where malaria is common. How could you prevent the spread of this disease?

14 **Evaluate** Imagine you are asked to justify removing kelp from an area of the ocean. Based on your knowledge of plantlike protists, what benefits or problems would you consider before you decide if the algae should be removed?

15 **Describe** Complete the table below with characteristics of the different types of animal-like protists.

	Number of nuclei	Method of eating	Method of movement
Ciliates			
Flagellates			
Sarcodines			

16 **Explain** how the movement of an amoeba differs from the movement of a dinoflagellate.

17 **List** several products you have used or seen that were made using fungi.

18 **Evaluate** how Alexander Fleming's experiments helped determine the importance of fungi to medicine.

Writing in Science

19 **Design** a brochure for a tour in which people could see several different types of lichens and fungi. What locations would be included and which organisms would people be likely to observe?

REVIEW

20 Explain how decomposers such as protists and fungi play an important role in the environment.

21 What is the organism shown below and how does it affect the environment?

Math Skills

Review

Math Practice

Calculating Growth

22 The number of cells of Fungus Q doubles every three hours. If you begin with 1,000 cells, how many will there be after 12 hours?

23 Scientists want to know if an antibiotic is effective in treating a fungal infection. They start with two colonies of 100 cells each. The table shows what happens during the first two days.

	Day 2 Number of Cells	Day 3 Number of Cells
Untreated fungus	400	1600
Antibiotic A	200	300

a. How long does it take the untreated fungus to double?

b. What effect does the antibiotic have on the growth rate of the fungus?

Standardized Test Practice

Record your answers on the answer sheet provided by your teacher or on a sheet of paper.

Multiple Choice

1 Which often live on decaying leaves in a forest?

  A diatoms

  B dinoflagellates

  C sarcodines

  D slime molds

Use the diagram below to answer question 2.

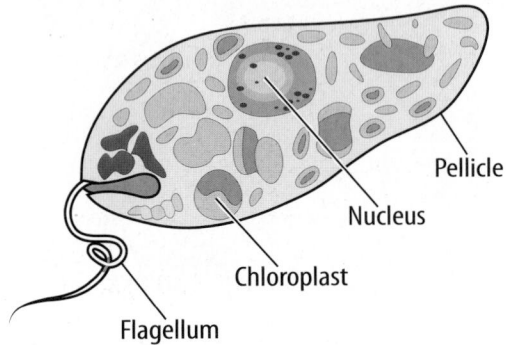

2 This organism has plant and animal characteristics. Which characteristic makes the organism plantlike?

  A chloroplast

  B flagellum

  C nucleus

  D pellicle

3 Which statement is false?

  A Fungi cause bread to rise.

  B Fungi cause dead organisms to decay.

  C Fungi are sources of antibiotics.

  D Fungi use sunlight and produce food.

4 Which protists have cell walls that look like glass?

  A algae

  B diatoms

  C dinoflagellates

  D euglenoids

Use the diagram below to answer question 5.

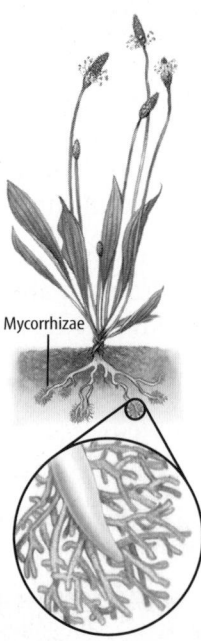

5 What does the plant give the fungus that surrounds its roots?

  A antibiotics

  B minerals

  C sugars

  D water

Use the diagram below to answer question 6.

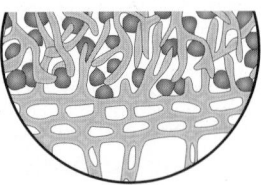

Lichen

6 Which organisms, combined with green algae, form this structure?

  A bacteria

  B fungi

  C plants

  D protozoans

7 Suppose a pond contains no living or decaying organisms. Which could be added to the pond to act as producers?

   A algae

   B ciliates

   C sarcodines

   D water molds

Use the diagram below to answer questions 8 and 9.

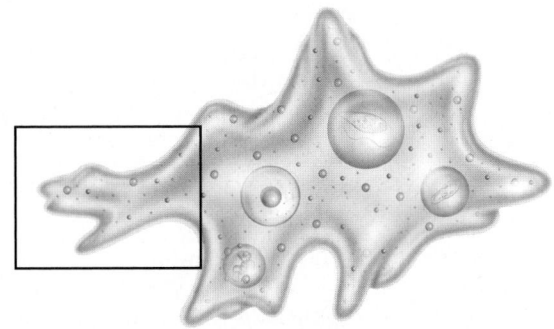

8 What is the function of the boxed area of this microscopic organism?

   A cellular respiration

   B defense

   C locomotion

   D photosynthesis

9 To which group does this organism belong?

   A animal-like protists

   B animals

   C fungi

   D funguslike protists

Constructed Response

Use the diagram below to answer question 10.

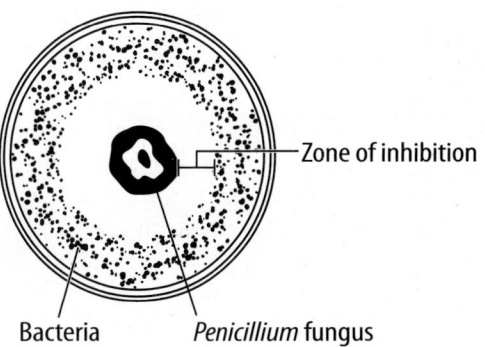

Zone of inhibition

Bacteria   *Penicillium* fungus

10 What is the interaction between the fungus and the bacteria?

11 Copy and complete the table below.

Group of Protists	Beneficial Effects	Harmful Effects
Plantlike		
Animal-like		
Funguslike		

12 For one of the groups of protists you listed in the table in question 11, explain why their beneficial effects are important to other organisms.

13 Identify two ways protists might reproduce. Describe the offspring that result from each method. What is an advantage of each method?

NEED EXTRA HELP?													
If You Missed Question...	1	2	3	4	5	6	7	8	9	10	11	12	13
Go to Lesson...	1	1	2	1	2	2	1	1	1	2	1,2	1,2	1

Plant Diversity

THE BIG IDEA

Why are plants in so many different environments on Earth?

Inquiry **Why so many plants?**

There are many different kinds of plants growing here! What plant characteristics do you think enable such a wide variety of plants to grow in one place?

● Where else do plants grow?

● How are those plants different from the plants growing in this environment? How are they similar?

Get Ready to Read

What do you think?

Before you read, decide if you agree or disagree with each of these statements. As you read this chapter, see if you change your mind about any of the statements.

1 All plants produce flowers and seeds.

2 Humans depend on plants for their survival.

3 Some plants move water only by diffusion.

4 Mosses can grow only in moist, shady places.

5 Some mosses and gymnosperms are used for commercial purposes.

6 All plants grow, flower, and produce seeds in one growing season.

Connect ED Your one-stop online resource

connectED.mcgraw-hill.com

Video

WebQuest

Audio

Assessment

Review

Concepts in Motion

Inquiry

Multilingual eGlossary

Reading Guide

Key Concepts 🔑
ESSENTIAL QUESTIONS

- What characteristics are common to all plants?

- What adaptations have enabled plant species to survive Earth's changing environments?

- How are plants classified?

Vocabulary

producer p. 298

cuticle p. 299

cellulose p. 299

vascular tissue p. 300

g **Multilingual eGlossary**

What is a plant?

Inquiry Why So Successful?

This plant cell has parts animal cells don't have. How do you think those cellular parts help plants live? What other parts do plants have that enable them to be successful in so many diverse environments on Earth?

What is a plant?

A plant often is described as a living thing that makes its own food, has leaves and stems, and is green in color. Even with the many different types of plants on Earth, this description often holds true. Or does it?

1 Examine the photos in the table below.

1	2	3	4	5	6

2 Number from 1 to 6 in your Science Journal. Next to each number write *yes* if you think the photo is of a plant or *no* if you think the photo is not of a plant.

Think About This

1. Which photos do you think are plants? Explain your choices.

2. Visualize each object without the background, and decide if you want to make changes in your list.

3. **Key Concept** What characteristics are common to each plant in these pictures?

Characteristics of Plants

You might not think about plants often, but they are an important part of life on Earth. As you read this lesson, look for the characteristics that make plants so important to other organisms.

Cell Structure

Plants are made of eukaryotic cells. Recall that eukaryotic cells have membrane-bound organelles. Some of a plant cell's organelles are shown in **Figure 1.** A plant cell differs from an animal cell because it contains chloroplasts and a cell wall. Chloroplasts convert light energy to chemical energy. The cell wall provides support and protection. A mature plant cell also has one or two vacuoles that store a watery liquid called sap.

Reading Check Describe the structure of a plant cell.

Concepts in Motion Animation

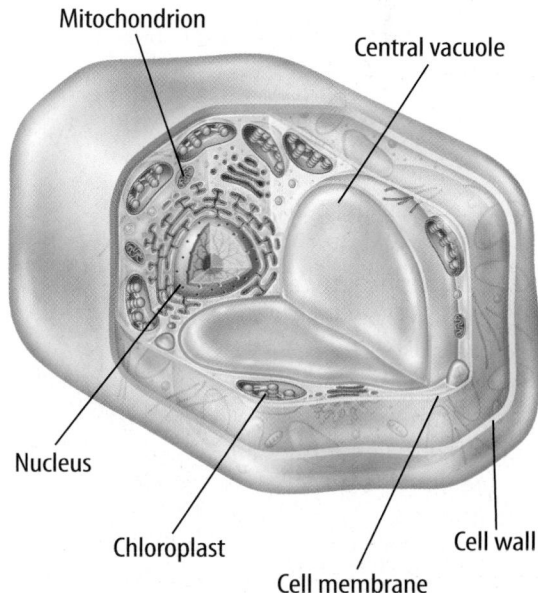

Mitochondrion

Central vacuole

Nucleus

Chloroplast

Cell membrane

Cell wall

Figure 1  Plant cells and animal cells have many of the same organelles.

Figure 2 Some plants, such as the reproductive stage of some ferns, are microscopic. Other plants, such as redwood trees, are huge.

WORD ORIGIN ·

producer
from Latin *producer*, means "lead or bring forth, draw out"
· ·

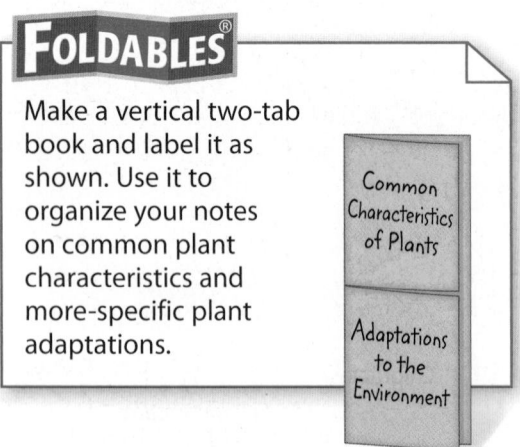

FOLDABLES®

Make a vertical two-tab book and label it as shown. Use it to organize your notes on common plant characteristics and more-specific plant adaptations.

Common Characteristics of Plants

Adaptations to the Environment

Multicellular

Plants are multicellular. This means they are made of many cells. The cells carry out specialized functions and work together to keep the plant alive. As shown in **Figure 2**, some plants are microscopic while others are some of the largest organisms on Earth.

Producers

Organisms that use an outside energy source, such as the Sun, to make their own food are called **producers.** Plants are producers. They make their own food, a simple sugar called glucose, during a process called photosynthesis. All other organisms rely on producers, either directly or indirectly, for their sources of food.

Key Concept Check What characteristics are common to all plants?

Plant Adaptations

Millions of years ago, there were no land plants. Scientists hypothesize that present-day land plants and green algae evolved from a common ancestor. They base their hypothesis on chemical similarities between green algae and plants. Some of the pigments in green algae and land plants are the same kind. There also are DNA similarities between these two groups of organisms.

The first land plants probably lived in moist areas. Life on land would have provided some advantages to plants. There would have been plenty of sunlight for photosynthesis to occur. The air that surrounded those plants would have been a mixture of gases, including carbon dioxide—another thing needed for photosynthesis. As land plants became more abundant, the amount of oxygen in the atmosphere increased because oxygen is a product of photosynthesis.

Plant species also had to adapt to survive without being surrounded by water. Many of the characteristics we now see in plants are adaptations to life on land.

Protection

One advantage to life on land is a constant supply of air that contains carbon dioxide. As you just read, carbon dioxide is needed for photosynthesis. Many plants have a *waxy, protective layer on their leaves, stems, and flowers called the* **cuticle.** It is made of a waxy substance that is secreted by the cells. Its waxy nature slows the evaporation of water from a plant's surface. This covering also provides some protection from insects that might harm a plant's tissues.

 Reading Check How does a plant's cuticle protect it?

Support

The water that surrounds aquatic plants supports them. Land plants must provide their own support. Like all cells, a plant cell has a cell membrane. Recall that a rigid cell wall surrounds the cell membrane in a plant cell. The cell wall provides support and is made of cellulose. **Cellulose** *is an organic compound made of chains of glucose molecules.* Many land plants also produce a chemical compound called lignin (LIG nun). Lignin strengthens cellulose and makes it more rigid. The piece of wood shown in **Figure 3** is mostly made of cellulose and lignin.

Figure 3 🔑 The combined strength of all of a plant's cell walls provides support for the plant.

Inquiry MiniLab **30 minutes**

How does water loss from a leaf relate to the thickness of the cuticle?

Plants need water for structural support and nutrients. Land plants developed a thickened layer of waxy material on their leaves, called a cuticle, that prevented water loss. The thickness of the cuticle varies from one plant type to another.

1. Read and complete a lab safety form.
2. In your Science Journal, make a table like the one below.

Leaf	Mass (mg) Day 1	Mass (mg) Day 2	Difference in Mass	% Decrease
1				
2				
3				
4				

3. Choose **leaves from four different plants.** Use a **balance** to determine the mass, in milligrams, of each leaf. Record the data in your table.
4. Lay each leaf on a **small tray,** making sure that none of the leaves touch other leaves. Leave them undisturbed overnight.
5. Measure the mass of each leaf again the following day. Record the data.
6. Calculate the difference in mass from day 1 to day 2. Calculate the percent difference.

Analyze and Conclude

1. **Analyze** Did you observe any changes in the initial and final masses of the leaves? Explain.

2. **Compare** the thickness of the leaves and determine which type(s) lost the least amount of water.

3. 🔑 **Key Concept** Consider the structure of the leaf that lost the least amount of water. Why do you think this adaptation is helpful?

Transporting Materials

In order for a plant to survive, water and nutrients must move throughout its tissues. In some plants such as mosses, these materials can move from cell to cell by the processes of osmosis and diffusion. This means that water and other materials dissolved in water move from areas of a plant where they are more concentrated to areas where they are less concentrated. However, other plants such as grasses and trees have specialized tissues called vascular tissue. **Vascular tissue** *is composed of tubelike cells that* transport *water and nutrients in some plants.* Vascular tissue can carry materials throughout a plant—great distances if necessary, up to hundreds of meters. You will read more about vascular tissues in Lesson 3 of this chapter.

ACADEMIC VOCABULARY

transport
(verb) to carry somebody or something

Reproduction

Water carries the reproductive cells of aquatic plants from plant to plant. How do you think land plants reproduce without water? Land plants evolved other strategies for reproduction. Some plants have water-resistant seeds or spores that are part of their reproductive process. Seeds and spores move throughout environments in different ways. These include animals and environmental factors such as wind and water. Several methods of seed dispersal are shown in **Figure 4**.

Key Concept Check What adaptations of plants have enabled them to survive Earth's changing environments?

Adaptations for Seed Dispersal

Figure 4 Plants have developed different methods of dispersing their seeds.

Coconut seeds float in water.

Wind carries milkweed seeds.

Burrs, which contain seeds, cling to clothes, fur, or feathers.

Liverwort

Pine Tree

Moss

Magnolia

Plant Classification

You might recall that kingdoms such as the animal kingdom consist of smaller groups called phyla. Members of the plant kingdom are organized into groups called divisions instead of phyla. Like all organisms, each plant has a two-word scientific name. For example, the scientific name for a red oak is *Quercus rubra*.

 Key Concept Check How are plants classified?

Seedless Plants

Liverworts and mosses, such as the ones shown in **Figure 5,** reproduce by structures called spores. Plants that reproduce by spores often are called seedless plants. Seedless plants do not have flowers. Some seedless plants do not have vascular tissue and are called nonvascular plants. Others, such as ferns, have vascular tissue and are called vascular plants. Seedless plants are classified into several divisions.

Seed Plants

Most of the plants you see around you, such as pine trees, grasses, petunias, and oak trees, are seed plants. Almost all the plants we use for food are seed plants. Some seed plants have flowers that produce fruit with one or more seeds. Others, such as pine trees, produce their seeds in cones. Each seed has tissues that surround, nourish, and protect the tiny plant embryo inside it. It is thought that all present-day plants originated from a common ancestor, an ancient green algae, as shown in **Figure 6** on the next two pages.

Figure 5 Liverworts and mosses reproduce by producing spores. Both pine and magnolia trees produce seeds.

Visual Check How are the pine tree and the magnolia tree alike? How are they different?

Classification of Plants 🔑

Ferns are vascular plants, but fern reproduction includes spores.

Hornworts often grow in fields or along roads.

Mosses are the most abundant nonvascular plants. Mosses generally grow in shady, moist places.

Club mosses are spore-producing vascular plants.

Nonvascular Plants

Vascular Plants

Liverworts grow in almost every habitat on Earth.

Ancient green algae are thought to be the ancestors of land plants as well as present-day green algae.

Figure 6 This tree represents the evolutionary relationships among plant divisions.

✓ **Visual Check** What type of plant is thought to be the ancestor of land plants?

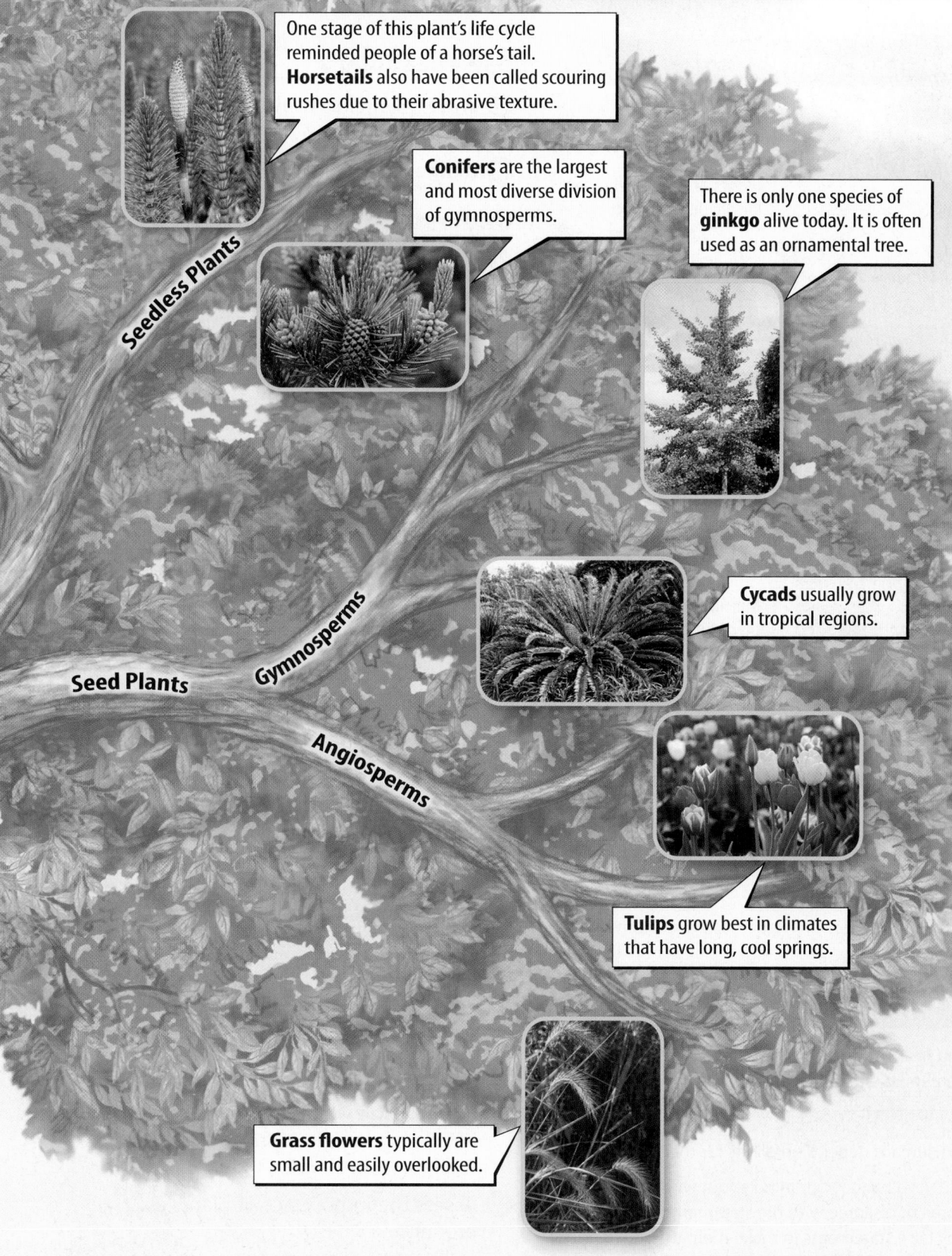

One stage of this plant's life cycle reminded people of a horse's tail. **Horsetails** also have been called scouring rushes due to their abrasive texture.

Conifers are the largest and most diverse division of gymnosperms.

There is only one species of **ginkgo** alive today. It is often used as an ornamental tree.

Seedless Plants

Cycads usually grow in tropical regions.

Gymnosperms

Seed Plants

Angiosperms

Tulips grow best in climates that have long, cool springs.

Grass flowers typically are small and easily overlooked.

Lesson 1 Review

Visual Summary

Plants are multicellular producers.

Water carries the reproductive cells of aquatic plants from plant to plant. Land plants evolved different reproductive strategies to ensure their survival.

Members of the plant kingdom are classified into groups called divisions.

FOLDABLES

Use your lesson Foldable to review the lesson. Save your Foldable for the project at the end of the chapter.

What do you think NOW?

You first read the statements below at the beginning of the chapter.

1. All plants produce flowers and seeds.

2. Humans depend on plants for their survival.

Did you change your mind about whether you agree or disagree with the statements? Rewrite any false statements to make them true.

Use Vocabulary

1. **Write** a sentence using the term *vascular tissue*.

2. **Define** *cellulose* in your own words.

Understand Key Concepts

3. Which structure helps support plant cells?
   A. cell wall
   B. chloroplast
   C. mitochondria
   D. ribosome

4. **List** the common characteristics of plants.

5. **Describe** an example of a plant adaptation that helps plants survive on land.

6. **Distinguish** between seedless and seed plants.

Interpret Graphics

7. **Examine** the diagram below and list the cell structures that identify it as a plant cell.

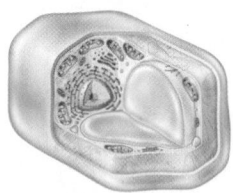

8. **Organize** Copy and fill in the graphic organizer below. In the center oval write *Adaptations to Life on Land*. Fill in the other ovals with plant adaptations.

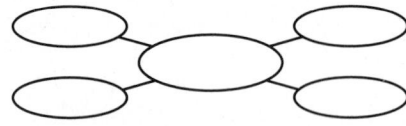

Critical Thinking

9. **Hypothesize** which of the adaptations to life on land might be missing in a plant that grows in shallow water.

10. **Assess** the importance of plants as producers.

Trees in the Sea

HOW NATURE WORKS

AMERICAN MUSEUM of NATURAL HISTORY

How can a plant survive in salt water?

Mangrove forests thrive along warm coastlines. Birds perch in the treetops, while young fish and other animals hide among the widespread underwater roots. These amazing trees can survive where others cannot—in salt water. Salt water kills most plants. It causes freshwater to diffuse out of plant cells, and they collapse. In addition, most plants would not survive with their roots under water because they cannot absorb oxygen from water. But mangrove trees have special traits that help them survive along the ocean's edge.

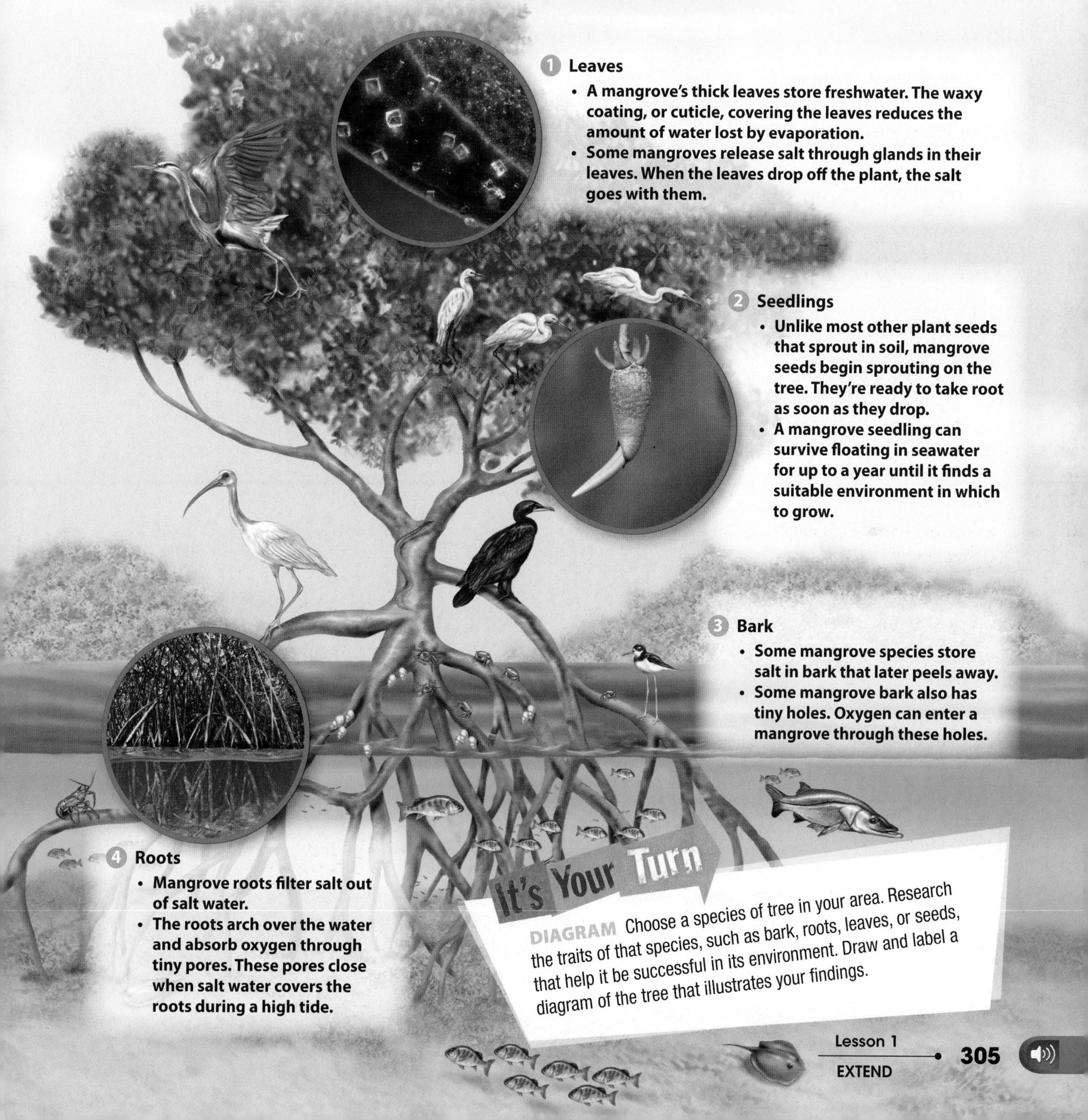

1 Leaves

- **A mangrove's thick leaves store freshwater. The waxy coating, or cuticle, covering the leaves reduces the amount of water lost by evaporation.**
- **Some mangroves release salt through glands in their leaves. When the leaves drop off the plant, the salt goes with them.**

2 Seedlings

- **Unlike most other plant seeds that sprout in soil, mangrove seeds begin sprouting on the tree. They're ready to take root as soon as they drop.**
- **A mangrove seedling can survive floating in seawater for up to a year until it finds a suitable environment in which to grow.**

3 Bark

- **Some mangrove species store salt in bark that later peels away.**
- **Some mangrove bark also has tiny holes. Oxygen can enter a mangrove through these holes.**

4 Roots

- **Mangrove roots filter salt out of salt water.**
- **The roots arch over the water and absorb oxygen through tiny pores. These pores close when salt water covers the roots during a high tide.**

It's Your Turn

DIAGRAM Choose a species of tree in your area. Research the traits of that species, such as bark, roots, leaves, or seeds, that help it be successful in its environment. Draw and label a diagram of the tree that illustrates your findings.

Lesson 2

Reading Guide

Key Concepts
ESSENTIAL QUESTIONS

How are nonvascular and vascular seedless plants alike, and how are they different?

Vocabulary

rhizoid p. 307

frond p. 309

Multilingual eGlossary

Seedless Plants

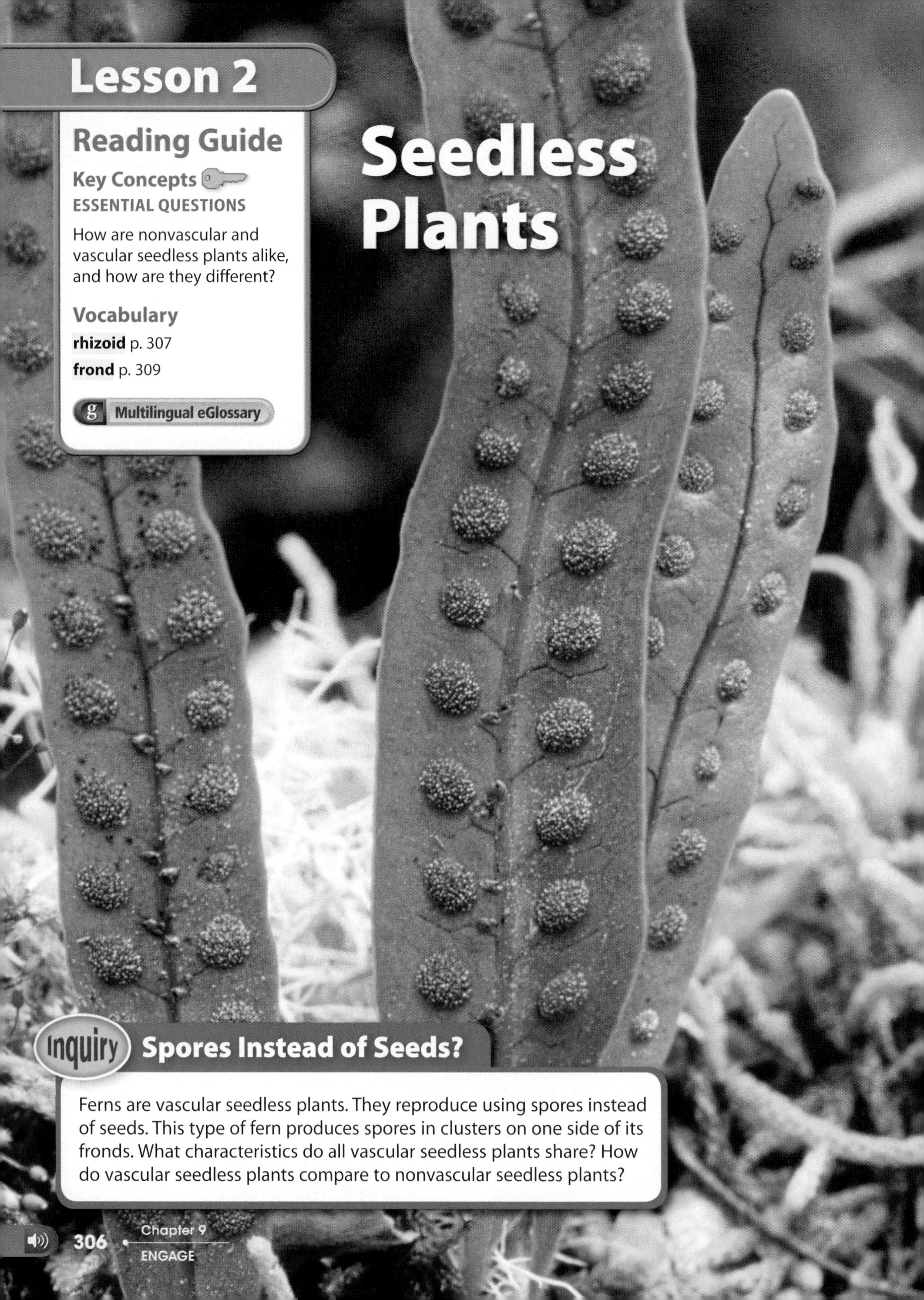

Inquiry Spores Instead of Seeds?

Ferns are vascular seedless plants. They reproduce using spores instead of seeds. This type of fern produces spores in clusters on one side of its fronds. What characteristics do all vascular seedless plants share? How do vascular seedless plants compare to nonvascular seedless plants?

Which holds more water?

Peat moss is the common name of approximately 300 different types of mosses. The partially decomposed remains of these moss plants form peat moss. Some potting soils contain peat moss.

1. Read and complete a lab safety form.
2. Fill a **250-mL beaker** with **potting soil** to about 3 cm from the top.
3. In a **tub,** mix equal parts **peat moss** and potting soil. Fill a second 250-mL beaker to the same level with this mixture.
4. Pour 30 mL of water into each beaker. Examine the beakers after 5 minutes and record your observations in your Science Journal.
5. After another 5 minutes, place each beaker on its side in an **aluminum pie pan.** Record your observations.

Think About This

1. How quickly did each soil mixture absorb the water?
2. What happened when you placed the beakers on their sides in the pie pans?
3. 🔑 **Key Concept** Why do you think peat moss is added to potting soil? How might this benefit plants?

Nonvascular Seedless Plants

If someone asked you to make a list of plants, your list might include plants such as your favorite flowers or trees that grow near your home. You probably would not include any nonvascular seedless plants on your list.

Many scientists refer to all nonvascular seedless plants as bryophytes (BRI uh fites). These plants usually are small. Because they lack tubelike structures, called vascular tissue, that transport water and nutrients, the bryophytes usually live in moist environments. Materials move from cell to cell by diffusion and *osmosis.*

Because bryophytes do not have vascular tissue, they do not have roots, stems, or leaves. They have rootlike structures called rhizoids, shown in **Figure 7. Rhizoids** *are structures that anchor a nonvascular seedless plant to a surface.* Rhizoids can be unicellular—consisting of only one cell—or they can be multicellular. The photosynthetic tissue of bryophytes is often only one cell layer thick. This layer does not have a cuticle, which most other plants have. Reproduction is by spores and requires water. Mosses, liverworts, and hornworts are bryophytes.

✔ **Reading Check** What characteristics are common in bryophytes?

Figure 7 🔑 Rhizoids anchor bryophytes to a surface, such as soil, rocks, and the bark of trees.

⊘ **Visual Check** How is the structure of rhizoids well-suited to the function of rhizoids?

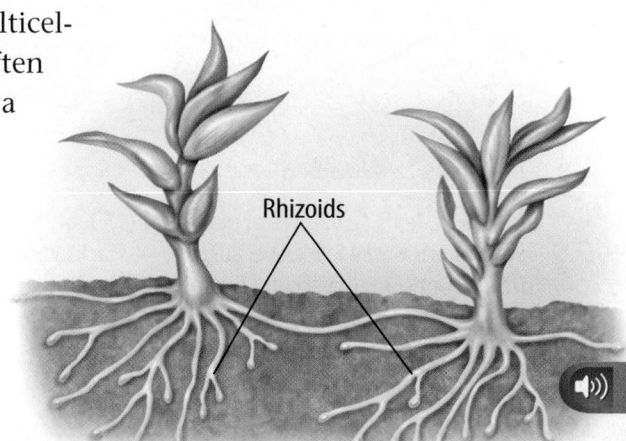

Rhizoids

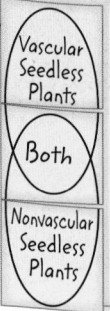
Mosses

You might be familiar with the most common bryophytes—the mosses. These small, green plants grow in forests, in parks, and sometimes even in the cracks of sidewalks. Mosses usually grow in shady, damp environments, but they are able to survive periods of dryness. As shown in **Figure 8,** mosses have leaf-like structures that grow on a stemlike structure called a stalk. They have multicellular rhizoids.

Mosses play an important role in the ecosystem. They are often the first plants to grow in barren areas or after a natural disturbance such as a fire or a mudslide. The ability of mosses to retain large amounts of water makes peat moss a useful additive for potting soil, as you discovered in the Launch Lab. This moss has been used to enrich soil and as a heating source.

Liverworts

Hundreds of years ago, people thought that this plant could be used to treat liver diseases. Liverwort also gets its name from its appearance—it resembles the flattened lobes of a liver. The rhizoids of liverworts are unicellular. The two common forms of liverworts are leafy and thallose (THA los) liverworts, as shown in **Figure 8.**

Hornworts

The long, hornlike reproductive structures shown in **Figure 8** give this group of plants its name. These reproductive structures produce spores. Hornworts are only about 2.5 cm in diameter. One unusual characteristic of hornworts is that each of its photosynthetic cells has only one chloroplast.

Figure 8 Mosses, liverworts, and hornworts all lack vascular tissue.

Nonvascular Seedless Plants 🔑

The green, leafy structures of mosses are not considered leaves because they do not contain vascular tissue.

A leafy liverwort, on the left, also lacks vascular tissue. The lobes of a thallose liverwort, on the right, can be as thin as one cell layer thick.

Until hornworts produce their reproductive structures, or "horns," they can easily be mistaken for liverworts.

Vascular Seedless Plants

Over 90 percent of plant species are vascular plants. Unlike nonvascular plants, they contain vascular tissue in their stems, roots, and leaves. Because vascular plants contain tubelike structures that transport water and nutrients, these plants generally are larger than nonvascular plants. However, present-day vascular seedless plants are smaller than their ancient ancestors. These ancient plants grew as tall as trees. Much of the fossil fuels that we use today came from the remains of these ancient plants.

Ferns

The **fronds,** *or leaves of ferns,* make up most of a fern. Ferns range in size from a few centimeters to several meters tall, such as the one in **Figure 9.** They grow in a variety of habitats, including damp, swampy areas and dry, rocky cliffs. Ferns often are houseplants or grow in gardens. Some people consider young fronds, also called fiddleheads, a gourmet treat.

Club Mosses

Unlike mosses, club mosses have roots, stems, and leaves. Club mosses, shown in **Figure 10,** are small plants that rarely grow taller than 50 cm. The stems often grow along the ground. The leaves are scalelike. The spores of club mosses make a fine powder that is so flammable that it has been used to make fireworks!

Horsetails

As shown in **Figure 11,** horsetails have small leaves growing in circles around the stems. Horsetail stems are hollow, and the tissues contain silica, a mineral in sand, that makes them abrasive. They once were used for scrubbing pots. Horsetails can be grown in water gardens but tend to spread rapidly.

 Key Concept Check How are nonvascular and vascular seedless plants alike? How are they different?

▲ **Figure 9** Tree ferns, such as this one, once were the dominant plants on Earth.

▲ **Figure 10** Club mosses reproduce by producing spores in two or three cylindrical, yellow-green colored cones.

▲ **Figure 11** The hollow stem of a horsetail is its main photosynthetic structure.

Lesson 2 Review

Visual Summary

Many scientists refer to all nonvascular seedless plants as bryophytes.

Because vascular plants contain tube-like structures that transport water and nutrients, these plants usually are larger than nonvascular plants.

Humans use both vascular and nonvascular plants for many purposes.

FOLDABLES®

Use your lesson Foldable to review the lesson. Save your Foldable for the project at the end of the chapter.

What do you think NOW?

You first read the statements below at the beginning of the chapter.

3. Some plants move water only by diffusion.

4. Mosses can grow only in moist, shady places.

Did you change your mind about whether you agree or disagree with the statements? Rewrite any false statements to make them true.

Use Vocabulary

1 **Write** a sentence using the term *rhizoid*.

Understand Key Concepts

2 Which does NOT belong with the others?
   A. club moss   C. horsetail
   B. fern   D. liverwort

3 **List** the different types of bryophytes.

Interpret Graphics

4 **Examine** the picture of the club moss below, and explain why some people call club mosses "ground pine."

5 **Organize** Copy and fill in the table below to summarize the different types of vascular and nonvascular seedless plants.

Types of Seedless Plants	
Vascular	Nonvascular

Critical Thinking

6 **Predict** how well moss plants would grow in the desert. Explain your reasoning.

7 **Compare and contrast** nonvascular and vascular seedless plants.

How do differences in plant structures reflect their environments?

Materials

cactus plant

rain forest plant

Safety

Plants with the same structures can appear to be very different from each other. Often the same structures serve different purposes, depending on the environment in which the plant lives. You can compare and contrast the same structures on two different plants to learn about their needs in different environments.

Learn It

Comparing and contrasting allows you to learn more about things than observing them separately. Noting the similarities and differences of these plants can help you learn which features are adaptations to a specific environment.

Try It

1. Read and complete a lab safety form.

2. Observe a cactus plant and a rain forest plant in your classroom.

⚠ Take care touching and handling the cactus plant.

3. Compare and contrast the leaves of both plants. Describe the leaves of each plant in a table. Hint: The spines of the cactus plant are modified leaves, while the green, thick parts are stems.

4. Observe the pictures of the desert environment and the rain forest environment. Think about how the leaves of both plants might have a different function in each environment. Fill out the next row of the table with your thoughts and descriptions.

5. Compare and contrast the stems. Describe the stems of each plant in your table.

6. Think about how the stems of both plants might have a different function in each environment. Fill out the next row of the table with your thoughts and descriptions.

Rain forest

Desert

Apply It

7. **Describe** which parts of each plant capture energy from sunlight.

8. **Analyze** how the availability of sunlight in each environment might affect the size and number of light-capturing structures on both plants.

9. **Infer** how both plants store water differently based on the differences in their structures.

10. 🔑 **Key Concept** Which plant structures were similar in both environments? Explain why these structures were so similar.

Lesson 3

Reading Guide

Key Concepts
ESSENTIAL QUESTIONS

- What characteristics are common to seed plants?
- How do other organisms depend on seed plants?
- How are gymnosperms and angiosperms alike, and how are they different?
- What adaptations of flowering plants enable them to survive in diverse environments?

Vocabulary

cambium p. 314
xylem p. 314
phloem p. 315
stoma p. 317

g Multilingual eGlossary

Video BrainPOP®

Seed Plants

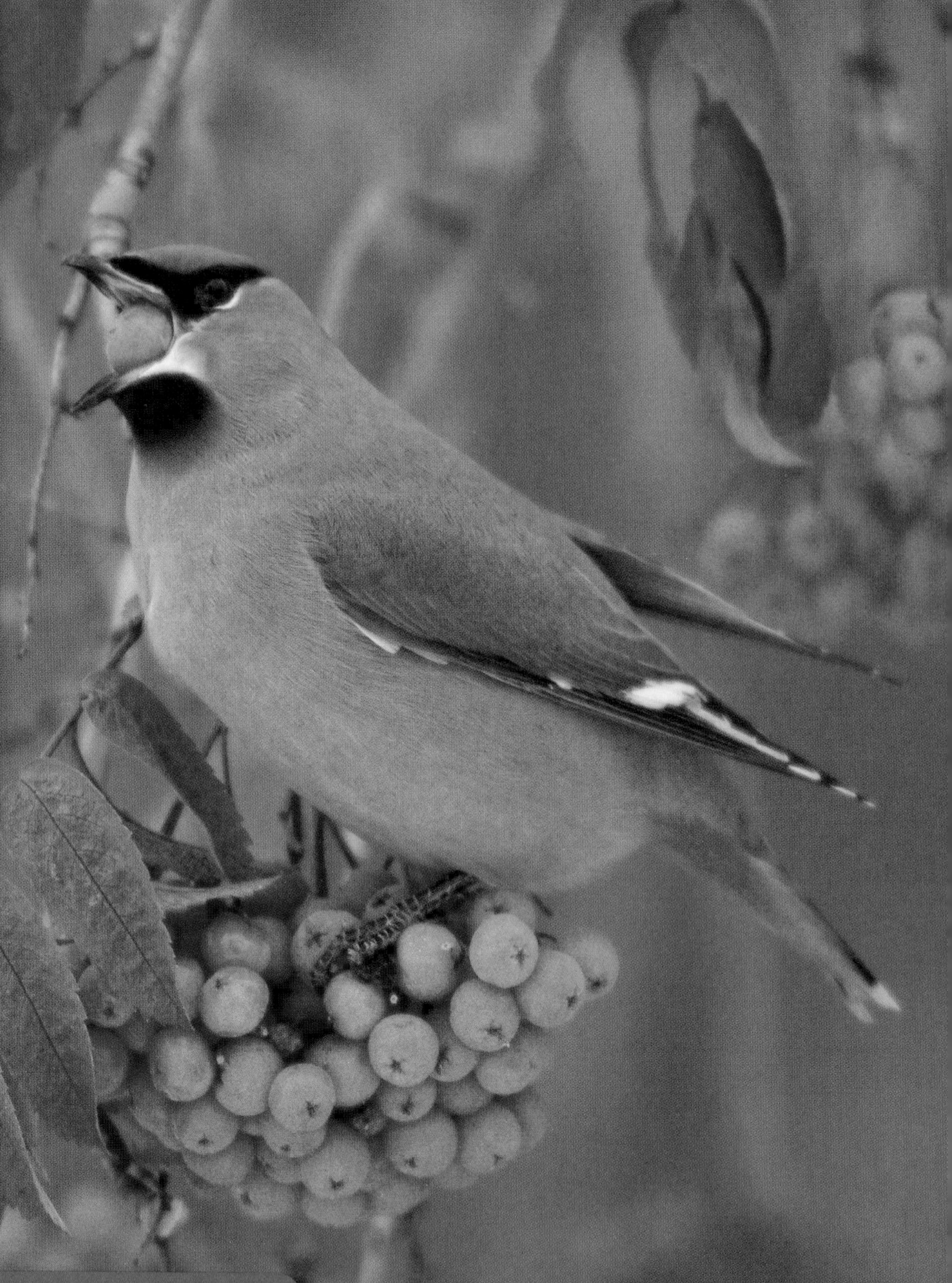

Inquiry A Great Relationship?

The berry the bird is eating has seeds in it. The bird depends on the tree for food—the berries. The tree helps the bird live. How do you think the bird is helping the tree live and be successful in its environment? What other adaptations might help seed plants be successful in different environments?

What characteristics do seeds have in common?

Seed plants have two characteristics in common: they have vascular tissue and seeds for reproduction. Do seeds also have common characteristics?

1. Read and complete a lab safety form.
2. Examine the **several types of seeds** on your **tray.**
3. In your Science Journal, make a grid of 2-cm by 2-cm squares to classify the seeds. Choose your own criteria to classify the seeds; for example, color, texture, size, or other special characteristics.
4. Label the columns and rows of your grid with the characteristics you chose.
5. Place the seeds on the section(s) of your grid where they belong based on the criteria you have chosen to classify them.

Think About This

1. Explain why you placed some of the seed samples in the same square.

2. Could some of the seeds have been placed in more than one square? Elaborate.

3. **Key Concept** Do any of the seeds share common characteristics? Explain.

Characteristics of Seed Plants

Have you ever eaten corn, beans, peanuts, peas, or pine nuts, such as the ones shown in **Figure 12?** They are all examples of edible seeds. Recall that a seed contains a tiny plant embryo and nutrition for the embryo to begin growing. There are more than 300,000 species of seed plants on Earth.

Seed plants are organized into two groups—cone-bearing seed plants, or gymnosperms (JIHM nuh spurmz) and flowering seed plants, or angiosperms (AN gee uh spurmz). All seed plants have vascular tissue that transports water and nutrients throughout the plant. This means they also have roots, stems, and leaves. You will read more about the characteristics of seed plants in this lesson.

 Key Concept Check What characteristics do all seed plants have in common?

Corn kernels
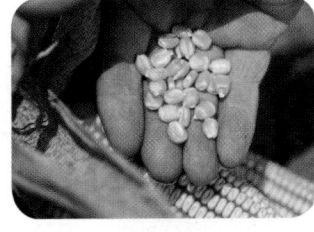

Peas

Pine nuts

Peanuts

Beans

Figure 12 Of the major plant parts, seeds are the most important source of human food.

Vascular Tissue

All seed plants contain vascular **tissues** in their roots, stems, and leaves. This tissue transports water and nutrients throughout a plant. The two types of vascular tissue are xylem (ZI lum) and phloem (FLOH em). *The* **cambium** *is a layer of tissue that produces new vascular tissue and grows between xylem and phloem.* How do xylem and phloem differ? Keep reading to find out.

 Reading Check What are the two types of vascular tissue? In what structures of a vascular plant would such tissues be?

Xylem *One type of vascular tissue—***xylem***— carries water and dissolved nutrients from the roots to the stem and the leaves.* Due to the thickened cell walls of some xylem cells, this tissue also provides support for a plant.

Two kinds of xylem cells are tracheids (TRAY kee udz) and vessel elements. All vascular plants have xylem that is composed of tracheids. As shown in **Figure 13,** tracheid cells are long and narrow with tapered ends. The tracheid cells grow end-to-end and form a strawlike tube. Water can flow from one cell to another, passing through openings or pits in the end wall of each cell. Tracheid cells die at maturity, leaving a hollow tube. This enables water to flow freely through them.

In addition to tracheids, xylem in flowering plants includes a type of cell called a vessel element. The diameter of a vessel element is greater than that of a tracheid. The end walls of vessel elements have large openings where water can pass through, as shown in **Figure 13.** In some vessel elements, the end walls are completely open. Vessel elements are more efficient at transporting water than tracheids are.

 Reading Check Why can water and dissolved nutrients flow so freely through xylem?

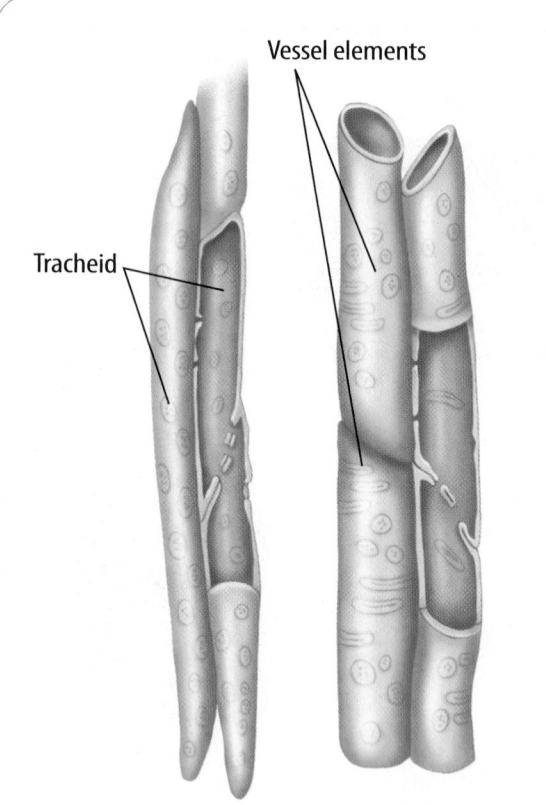

Vessel elements

Tracheid

Figure 13 The cell walls between individual vessel elements have larger openings than the cell walls between tracheids.

Phloem *Another type of vascular tissue—***phloem***—carries dissolved sugars throughout a plant.* It is composed of two types of cells—sieve-tube elements and companion cells.

Sieve-tube elements are specialized phloem cells. These long, thin cells are stacked end-to-end and form long tubes. The end walls have holes in them, as shown in **Figure 14.** The cytoplasm of a sieve-tube element lacks many organelles, including a nucleus, mitochondria, and ribosomes.

Each sieve-tube element has a companion cell next to it that contains a nucleus. A companion cell helps control the functions of the sieve-tube element.

Reading Check List and describe the function of each of the two types of vascular tissue in plants.

Roots

Even though the roots of most plants are never seen, they are vital to a plant's survival. Roots anchor a plant, either in soil or onto another plant or an object such as a rock. All roots help a plant stay upright. Some plants have roots that spread out in all directions several meters from a plant's stem.

All root systems, such as the one shown in **Figure 15,** help a plant absorb water and other substances from the soil.

Plants such as radishes and carrots store food in their roots. This food can be used to grow new plant tissues after a dry period or a cold season. Sugar stored in the roots of sugar maple trees over the winter is converted to maple sap in the spring. Farmers drain some of the sap from these trees and boil it to make maple syrup.

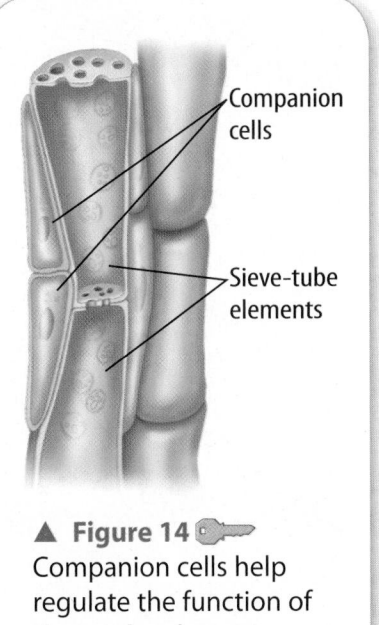

▲ **Figure 14** 🔑
Companion cells help regulate the function of sieve-tube elements.

Figure 15 🔑 Roots help anchor a plant and absorb water and minerals from the soil. ▼

Figure 16 🔑 An herbaceous stem supports the black-eyed Susan flower. A woody stem supports this tree.

Stems

The part of a plant that connects its roots to its leaves is the stem. In plants such as the tree in **Figure 16,** the stem is obvious. Other plants, such as the potato and the iris, have underground stems that are often mistaken for roots.

Stems support branches and leaves. Their vascular tissues transport water, minerals, and food. Xylem carries water and minerals from the roots to the leaves. The sugar produced during photosynthesis flows through a stem's phloem to all parts of a plant. Another important function of stems is the production of new cells for growth, but only certain regions of a stem produce new cells.

Plant stems usually are classified as either herbaceous or woody. Woody stems, such as the one shown in **Figure 16,** are stiff and typically not green. Trees and shrubs have woody stems. Herbaceous stems usually are soft and green, as also shown in **Figure 16.**

✔ **Reading Check** What is the importance of a stem to a plant?

Inquiry **MiniLab**

25 minutes

How can you determine the stems, roots, and leaves of plants?

When the environment changes, the functions of a plant's roots, stems, and leaves do not change. Instead, the structure of one or more of these parts will change in the species over time and adapt to the change in the environment.

1. Read and complete a lab safety form.

2. Examine the **four plants** on your **lab tray.** Gently remove a root, a stem, and a leaf from each plant.

3. Classify the roots into groups based on their characteristics. Do the same with the stems and the leaves. Record your classifications in your Science Journal.

4. In your Science Journal, describe some characteristics of roots, stems, and leaves that you observed in each of the plant parts.

Analyze and Conclude

1. **Describe** how you classified the roots, the stems, and the leaves.

2. **Analyze** any unusual characteristics you observed in any of the plant parts that might be an adaptation. Explain your reasoning.

3. 🔑 **Key Concept** What characteristics were common to all the plants you examined?

Leaves

Leaves come in many shapes and sizes. Most leaves have an important function in common—they are the major site of photosynthesis for the plant. By capturing light energy and converting it to chemical energy, leaves provide the plant's food.

As shown in **Figure 17,** most leaves are made of layers of cells. The top and bottom layers of a leaf are made of epidermal (eh puh DUR mul) tissue. Epidermal cell walls are transparent, and light passes through them easily. These cells produce a waxy outer layer called the cuticle. The cuticle helps reduce the amount of water that evaporates from a leaf. *Most leaves have small openings in the epidermis called* **stomata** (STOH muh tuh; singular, stoma). When the stomata open, carbon dioxide, oxygen, and water vapor can pass through them. Two guard cells surround each stoma and control its size.

Below the upper epidermis are rows of tightly packed cells called palisade (pa luh SAYD) mesophyll (MEH zuh fil) cells. Photosynthesis mainly occurs in these cells. Under the palisade mesophyll cells is the spongy mesophyll layer. The arrangement of these cells enables gases to diffuse throughout a leaf. A leaf's xylem and phloem transport materials throughout the leaf.

Angiosperm and gymnosperm leaves each have some unique characteristics. An angiosperm leaf tends to be flat with a broad surface area. A gymnosperm leaf is usually needlelike or scalelike and often has a thick cuticle. Because gymnosperms often grow in drier areas, these characteristics help conserve water.

Figure 17 The structure of a leaf is well suited to its function of photosynthesis.

Visual Check Describe the location and appearance of the stomata. What role do they play in photosynthesis?

Leaf Anatomy

Concepts in Motion Animation

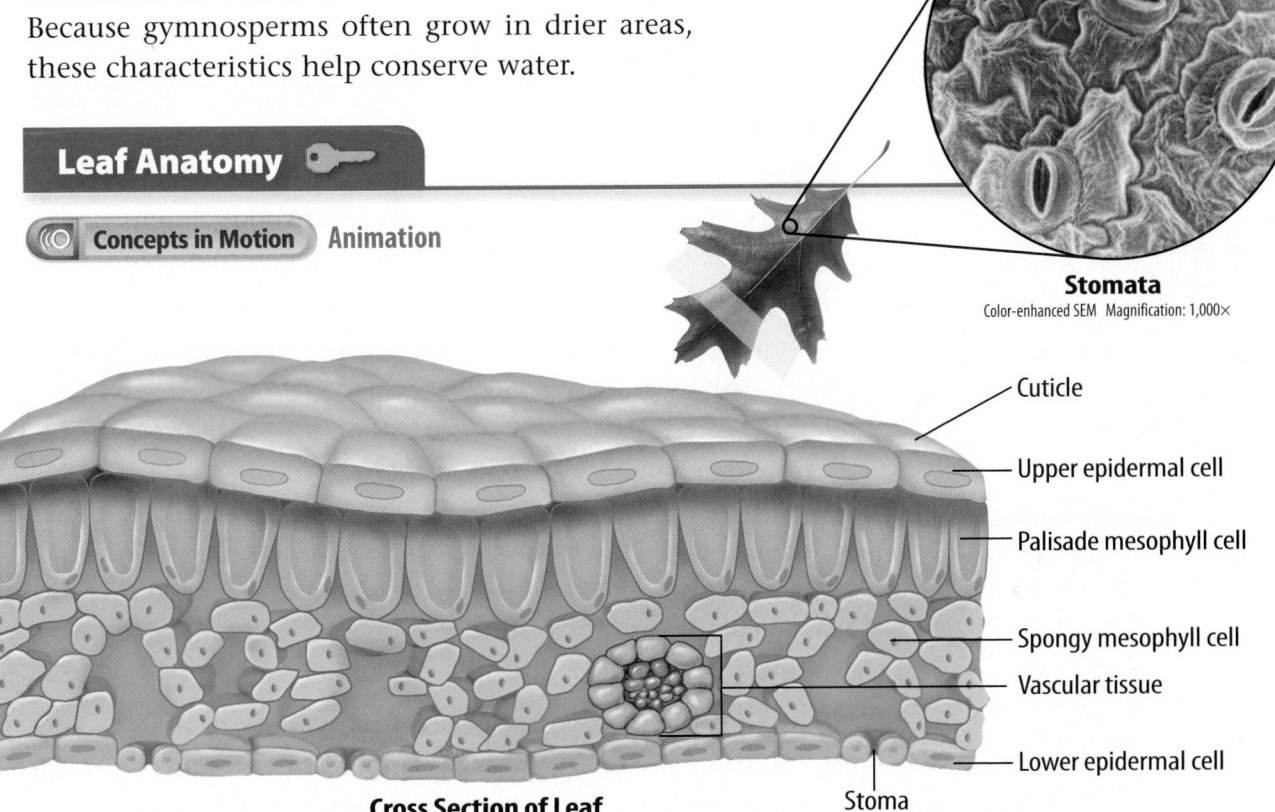

Stomata
Color-enhanced SEM Magnification: 1,000×

Cuticle

Upper epidermal cell

Palisade mesophyll cell

Spongy mesophyll cell

Vascular tissue

Lower epidermal cell

Cross Section of Leaf

Stoma

Types of Gymnosperms 🔑

▲ Gnetophyte

Conifer ▶

◀ Ginkgo

Cycad ▼

Figure 18 Gymnosperms are a diverse group of plants, and all produce seeds without surrounding fruits.

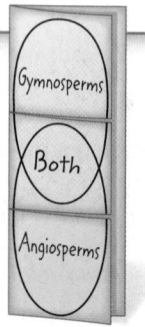

FOLDABLES®

Make a three-tab Venn book, and label it as shown. Use it to compare and contrast seed plants.

Gymnosperms
Both
Angiosperms

Gymnosperms

In gymnosperms, seeds are produced in a cone. This group includes the oldest plant (the bristlecone pine at 4,900 years old), the tallest plant (the coast redwood that can grow to 115 m), and perhaps Earth's largest organism (the sequoia). Conifers, such as spruces, pines, and redwoods, might be the most familiar gymnosperms to you. However, there are several other types of gymnosperms, as shown in **Figure 18.**

Conifers grow on all the world's continents except Antarctica. Cycads usually grow in tropical regions. Although cycads might resemble ferns, they are seed plants. DNA evidence indicates that they are closely related to other gymnosperms. One gymnosperm group has only one species—ginkgo. Ginkgoes have broad leaves and are popular as an ornamental tree in urban areas. The gnetophytes (NEE tuh fites), another type of cone-bearing plant, are an unusual and diverse group of gymnosperms, as shown in **Figure 18.**

Humans rely on gymnosperms for a variety of uses, including building materials; paper production; medicines; and as ornamental plants in gardens, along streets, and in parks.

Angiosperms

There are more than 260,000 species of flowering plants, or angiosperms. Angiosperms began to flourish about 80 million years ago. They grow in a variety of habitats, from deserts to the tundra. Anytime you have stopped to smell a flower, you have enjoyed an angiosperm. Almost all of the food eaten by humans comes from angiosperms or from animals that eat angiosperms. Grains, vegetables, herbs, and spices are just a few examples of foods that come from angiosperms. Many other items, such as clothing, medicines, and building materials, also come from these plants.

 Key Concept Check How do other organisms depend on seed plants?

Flowers

Angiosperms produce seeds that are part of a fruit. This fruit grows from parts of a flower. All angiosperms produce flowers. Some flowers, such as tulips and roses, are beautiful and showy. You also might be familiar with other flowers, such as dandelions, because you have seen them growing in your neighborhood. However, some plants produce flowers that you might never have noticed. Grass flowers are tiny and not easily seen, as shown in **Figure 19.**

 Key Concept Check How are angiosperms and gymnosperms alike, and how are they different?

Types of Angiosperms

Tulips

Grass

Beans

Figure 19 All angiosperms have flowers that contain reproductive organs. After pollination and fertilization, seeds are produced within a flower.

Table 1 Monocots v. Dicots

Monocots	Dicots
Leaves	
narrow with parallel veins	veins are branched
Flowers	
flower parts in multiples of three	flower parts in multiples of four or five
Stems	
vascular tissue in bundles scattered throughout the stem	vascular tissue in bundles in rings
Seeds	
one cotyledon	two cotyledons

Table 1 Monocots and dicots differ in leaf, flower, stem, and seed structure.

Visual Check How are the leaves, flowers, stems, and seeds of monocots different from those of dicots?

Annuals, Biennials, and Perennials

Plants that grow, flower, and produce seeds in one growing season are called annuals. After one growing season, the plant dies. Examples include tomatoes, beans, pansies, and many common weeds.

Biennials complete their life cycles in two growing seasons. During the first year, the plant grows roots, stems, and leaves. The part of the plant that is above ground might become dormant during the winter months. In the second growing season, the plant produces new stems and leaves. It also flowers and produces seeds during this second growing season. After flowering and producing seeds, the plant dies. Carrots, beets, and foxglove are all biennials.

Perennial plants can live for more than two growing seasons. Trees and shrubs are perennials. The leaves and stems of some herbaceous perennial plants die in the winter. Stored food in the roots is used each spring for new growth.

 Reading Check How do the growing seasons of an annual, a biennial, and a perennial differ? Give an example of each type of plant.

Monocots and Dicots

Flowering plants traditionally have been organized into two groups—monocots and dicots. These groups are based on the number of leaves in early development, or cotyledons (kah tuh LEE dunz), in a seed. Researchers have learned that dicots can be organized further into two groups based on the structure of their pollen. However, because these two groups of dicots share many characteristics, we will continue to refer to them just as dicots. Look carefully at **Table 1** to learn some of the differences between monocots and dicots.

 Key Concept Check What adaptations of flowering plants enable them to survive in diverse environments?

Lesson 3 Review

Visual Summary

Angiosperms are flowering plants.

Seed plants have many adaptations that enable them to survive in diverse environments.

Seed plants have many uses.

FOLDABLES

Use your lesson Foldable to review the lesson. Save your Foldable for the project at the end of the chapter.

What do you think NOW?

You first read the statements below at the beginning of the chapter.

5. Some mosses and gymnosperms are used for commercial purposes.

6. All plants grow, flower, and produce seeds in one growing season.

Did you change your mind about whether you agree or disagree with the statements? Rewrite any false statements to make them true.

Use Vocabulary

1 The tissue that produces new xylem and phloem cells is the _____.

2 **Write** a sentence using the terms *xylem* and *phloem*.

3 **Define** *stomata* in your own words.

Understand Key Concepts 🔑

4 Which cells carry on most of a plant's photosynthesis?
   A. guard cells
   B. xylem cells
   C. palisade mesophyll cells
   D. spongy mesophyll cells

5 **Evaluate** the importance of the guard cells that surround the stomata.

6 **Contrast** gymnosperms with angiosperms.

7 **Distinguish** between a woody stem and an herbaceous stem.

Interpret Graphics

8 **Organize** Copy and fill in the table below to describe the function of each plant structure.

Structure	Function
Roots	
Stem	
Leaves	

Critical Thinking

9 **Explain** why the placement of the cells in the figure at right is so critical to the function of the phloem.

Math Skills ×÷+   Review
— Math Practice —

10 There are 300,000 species of seed plants. There are 9,000 species of grasses. What percentage of seed plants are grass species?

Materials

computer with Internet access

Compare and Contrast Extreme Plants

Over time, plant species have developed adaptations to many environments. As you examine the types of plants that live in extreme environments, you can compare and contrast the features plants have developed that enable them to be successful in such environments.

Arctic

Ask a Question

How are plants able to live in extreme environments?

Make Observations

1. Read and complete a lab safety form.

2. Observe the environments shown in the pictures to the right. Choose one of the environments. In your Science Journal, write a description of the environment and an explanation of why you think it might be difficult for plants to grow in that environment.

3. Select one plant from the list of those living in the environment you chose to investigate.

Hot springs

Form a Hypothesis

4. After writing a description of the environment you chose, form a hypothesis explaining how a plant might be able to survive in the extreme environment.

Saltwater marsh

Test Your Hypothesis

5. Research the environment and the plant you selected. Copy the table provided. Fill out the table with as many details as you can find. As you fill in details on your plant, fill in the other half of the table with information about a common plant in your area. This will allow you to compare and contrast an extreme environment and plant with a familiar environment and plant.

6. While you research, look for photographs or illustrations of the plant you are investigating. Pay particular attention to graphics that show the unique features of your plant or illustrate how it survives in its extreme environment.

	Plant in an extreme environment	Common plant in your home environment
Name of plant		
Environment the plant lives in		
Challenges the plant face in its environment		
Resources plant needs to survive		
Plant's specialized structures to live in its environment		
Plant's method of reproduction		

Analyze and Conclude

7 **Summarize** the differences between the plant that lives in the extreme environment and the plant that lives in your familiar environment. How do these differences enable the plant living in the extreme environment to thrive in its environment?

8 **Analyze** Why is the extreme environment you studied difficult for other plants to live in? How do these conditions create an opportunity for the extreme plant?

9 **Infer** How well do you think the extreme plant would grow if you tried to grow it in your familiar environment instead of the extreme environment? Explain.

10 **The Big Idea** Why are plants found in so many different environments, including extreme environments?

Communicate Your Results

Collect images of the plant and the extreme environment you researched. Create two side-by-side pages that illustrate how your plant survives in its environment. Use call-out boxes to point out the special features and structures of the plant that ensure the plant's survival.

 **Extension**

Research other plants that fill interesting niches. For example, many conifers have developed resistance to forest fires and produce seed cones that are dependent on heat from a forest fire to germinate and grow.

Lab Tips

☑ Focus on key features and structures that plants use to respond to the environment for survival when you do your research.

Remember to use scientific methods.

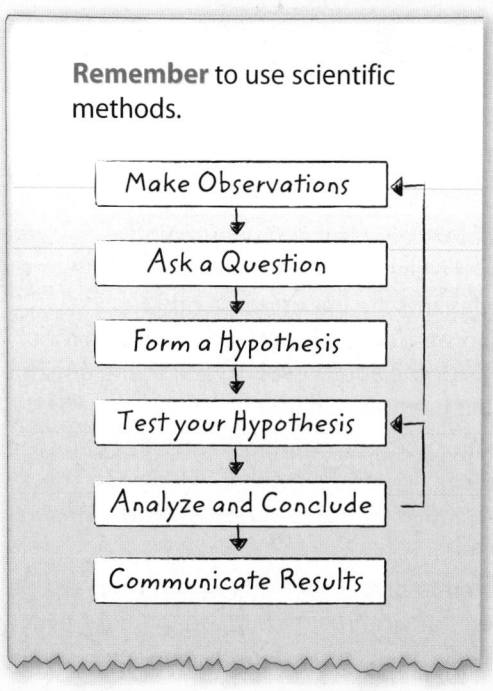

Make Observations → Ask a Question → Form a Hypothesis → Test your Hypothesis → Analyze and Conclude → Communicate Results

Chapter 9 Study Guide

Different plant species have different adaptations that enable them to survive in most of the environments on Earth.

Key Concepts Summary 🔑

Vocabulary

Lesson 1: What is a plant?

- Plants are multicellular **producers** composed of eukaryotic cells with cell walls composed of **cellulose.** Many plant cells have chloroplasts.

- Plants have developed adaptations, such as a cell wall for support, a **cuticle** to prevent water loss and to provide protection from insects, **vascular tissue** to transport materials, and numerous reproductive strategies, to survive in Earth's changing environments.

- Members of the plant kingdom are classified into groups called divisions, which are equivalent to phyla in other kingdoms. Plants have two-word scientific names.

producer p. 298
cuticle p. 299
cellulose p. 299
vascular tissue p. 300

Lesson 2: Seedless Plants

- Vascular and nonvascular seedless plants are multicellular producers composed of eukaryotic cells. Nonvascular seedless plants usually are smaller than vascular seedless plants, lack vascular tissue, and have **rhizoids** instead of roots to anchor them.

rhizoid p. 307
frond p. 309

Lesson 3: Seed Plants

- All seed plants make seeds and reproduce. Seed plants have leaves, stems, roots, and vascular tissue—**xylem** and **phloem.**

- Seed plants are important to other organisms for various reasons including for food, for the addition of oxygen to the environment, and for commercial uses.

- Gymnosperms and angiosperms are both seed plants. Angiosperms produce flowers, gymnosperms do not. The seeds of angiosperms are surrounded by fruit. The seeds of gymnosperms are not surrounded by fruit.

- Flowering plants have adaptations that enable them to survive in diverse environments. Such adaptations include leaves, stems, vascular tissue, roots, flowers, and seeds protected by a fruit.

cambium p. 314
xylem p. 314
phloem p. 315
stoma p. 317

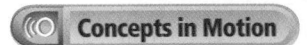
FOLDABLES® Chapter Project

Assemble your lesson Foldables as shown to make a Chapter Project. Use the project to review what you have learned in this chapter.

Use Vocabulary

1 Distinguish between xylem and phloem.

2 The openings in leaves that allow gases to pass into and out of the leaf are _____.

3 Define the term *rhizoid* in your own words.

4 The tissue that produces new xylem and phloem cells is the _____.

5 Write a sentence using the term *cuticle*.

6 Use the term *vascular tissue* in a sentence.

Link Vocabulary and Key Concepts

Concepts in Motion Interactive Concept Map

Copy this concept map, and then use vocabulary terms from the previous page to complete the concept map.

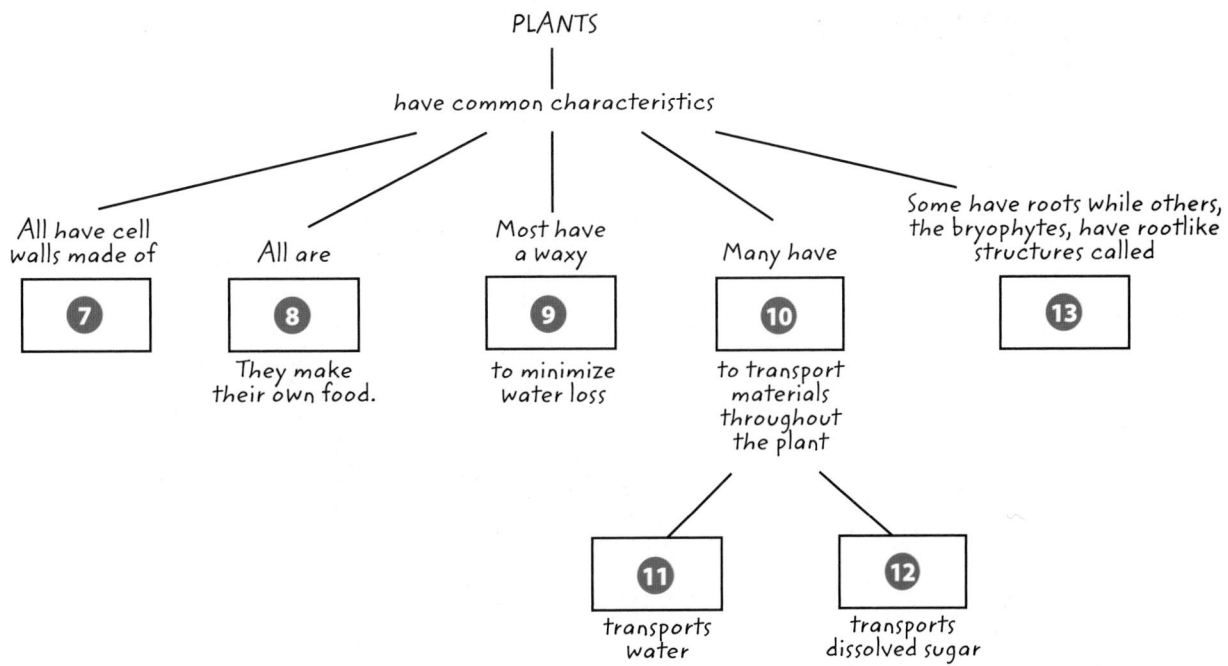

Chapter 9 Review

Understand Key Concepts

1 Guard cells control the size of the opening of the
  A. cambium.
  B. cotyledon.
  C. stomata.
  D. xylem.

2 The major function of leaves is to
  A. anchor the plant.
  B. perform photosynthesis.
  C. shade the tree.
  D. support the stem.

3 Which is an angiosperm?
  A. fern
  B. moss
  C. pine
  D. tulip

4 Which does the plant below NOT have?

  A. chloroplasts
  B. rhizoids
  C. cell walls
  D. vascular tissue

5 Which is the plant part responsible for anchoring the plant in soil?
  A. flower
  B. leaf
  C. root
  D. stem

6 Which are vascular plants?
  A. ferns
  B. hornworts
  C. liverworts
  D. mosses

7 Only members of the plant kingdom are organized into
  A. categories.
  B. divisions.
  C. groups.
  D. phyla.

8 Which is composed of cellulose?
  A. chloroplasts
  B. cytoplasm
  C. plant cell membrane
  D. plant cell wall

9 What is the function of the stomata?
  A. to perform photosynthesis
  B. to produce sugar
  C. to allow water into the leaf
  D. to enable gases to enter and leave

10 Which are produced by angiosperms but not by gymnosperms?
  A. cones
  B. flowers
  C. leaves
  D. seeds

11 The leaflike structures of mosses do NOT contain
  A. chloroplasts.
  B. water.
  C. photosynthetic cells.
  D. vascular tissue.

12 What is the function of the structure shown below?

  A. control gas exchange
  B. perform photosynthesis
  C. transport sugar
  D. transport water

Critical Thinking

13 **Choose** one of the adaptations that plants have for living on land, and explain its significance.

14 **Suggest** an environment where plants would not need a cuticle.

15 **Design** a new division of plants. Describe them and their environment.

16 **Suggest** additional uses for peat moss.

17 **Construct** a table to organize information about vascular seedless plants.

18 **Evaluate** the lack of cuticle in moss plants.

19 **Explain** the advantage of fruit production in angiosperms.

20 **Predict** the impact of a disease that killed all gymnosperms. Explain your reasoning.

21 **Explain** how the structure of a leaf as shown in the figure below is appropriate for its role in photosynthesis.

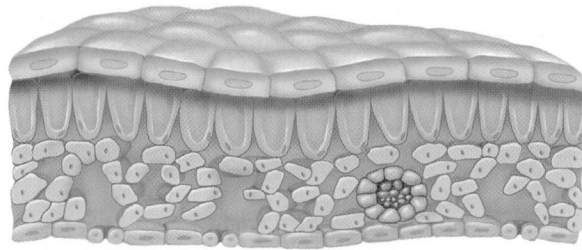

Writing in Science

22 **Write** a short story about a hiker's thoughts as he or she comes across different plants such as mosses, liverworts, ferns, horsetails, gymnosperms, and angiosperms.

REVIEW THE BIG IDEA

23 Write a brief description of two different environments. Now describe how plant adaptations would help the plants survive in each of your environments.

24 What structures enable the plants in the photo below to live in this environment?

Math Skills

Review — **Math Practice**

Use Percentages

25 Some scientists estimate the total number of species of organisms on Earth to be about 14,000,000. If there are 300,000 species of seed plants, what percentage of Earth's species are seed plants?

26 Of the 1,090 species of gymnosperms, there is only one species of ginkgo. What percentage of gymnosperm species are ginkgoes?

27 Of the 1,090 species of gymnosperms, 90 species are gnetophytes. What percentage of gymnosperm species are gnetophytes?

Standardized Test Practice

Record your answers on the answer sheet provided by your teacher or on a sheet of paper.

Multiple Choice

1 Which is NOT a characteristic of all plants?

  A They are multicellular.

  B They have vascular tissue.

  C They make their own food.

  D They undergo photosynthesis.

2 Which are seedless nonvascular plants?

  A conifers

  B grasses

  C mosses

  D tulips

Use the diagram below to answer question 3.

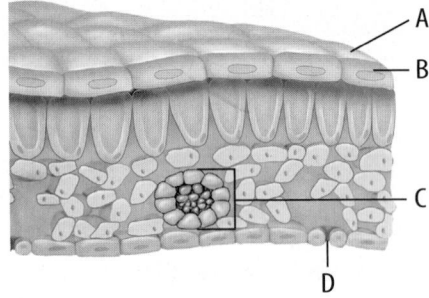

3 Which feature in the figure is a plant adaptation to life on land and reduces water loss through evaporation?

  A A

  B B

  C C

  D D

4 Which are NOT common to all seed plants?

  A cell walls

  B flowers

  C roots

  D vascular tissues

5 Which feature do scientists use to classify angiosperms as monocots or dicots?

  A embryonic leaves

  B flower shapes

  C seed numbers

  D xylem cells

Use the image below to answer question 6.

6 Which plants form seeds in structures such as the one shown in the figure?

  A biennials

  B conifers

  C maples

  D roses

7 Which plants provide most of the food humans eat?

  A angiosperms

  B gymnosperms

  C seedless nonvascular plants

  D seedless vascular plants

8 Which structures are in plant cells but are not in animal cells?

  A cell membranes and vacuoles

  B cell walls and chloroplasts

  C chloroplasts and mitochondria

  D vacuoles and mitochondria

Use the figure below to answer question 9.

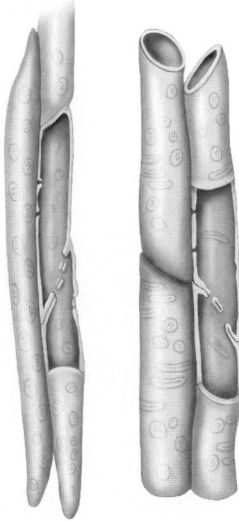

9 What type of plant tissue contains the cells shown in the figure?

    A cambium

    B mesophyll

    C phloem

    D xylem

10 An unknown plant is a few centimeters tall when fully grown. It lives only in moist areas and reproduces with spores. How would you classify this plant?

    A nonvascular seed plant

    B nonvascular seedless plant

    C vascular seedless plant

    D vascular seed plant

Constructed Response

Use the figure below to answer questions 11 and 12.

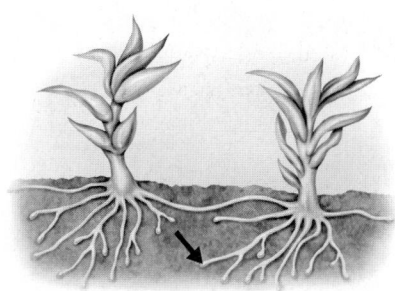

11 The above diagram shows a seedless non-vascular plant. Identify the structure marked with an arrow, and explain its function.

12 Which structure in vascular plants performs a similar function?

13 Some angiosperms can store food in their roots. How does this adaptation help them to survive diverse environmental conditions? Give an example of a plant that has this adaptation.

14 How do the leaves of gymnosperms differ from the leaves of angiosperms?

15 Describe the role of vascular tissue in enabling a plant to adapt to its environment.

NEED EXTRA HELP?															
If You Missed Question...	1	2	3	4	5	6	7	8	9	10	11	12	13	14	15
Go to Lesson...	1	2	1	3	1	3	3	1	3	1&2	2	2&3	3	3	1

Chapter 10

Plant Processes and Reproduction

THE BIG IDEA

What processes enable plants to survive and reproduce?

Inquiry Holding on for Dear Life?

The tendril of this *Omphalea* (om FAL ee uh) vine grows around a branch in a tropical rain forest.

- How do you think growing around another plant might help the *Omphalea* plant survive?

- Can you think of any other processes that enable plants to survive and reproduce?

Get Ready to Read

What do you think?

Before you read, decide if you agree or disagree with each of these statements. As you read this chapter, see if you change your mind about any of the statements.

1 Plants do not carry on cellular respiration.

2 Plants are the only organisms that carry on photosynthesis.

3 Plants do not produce hormones.

4 Plants can respond to their environments.

5 Seeds contain tiny plant embryos.

6 Flowers are needed for plant reproduction.

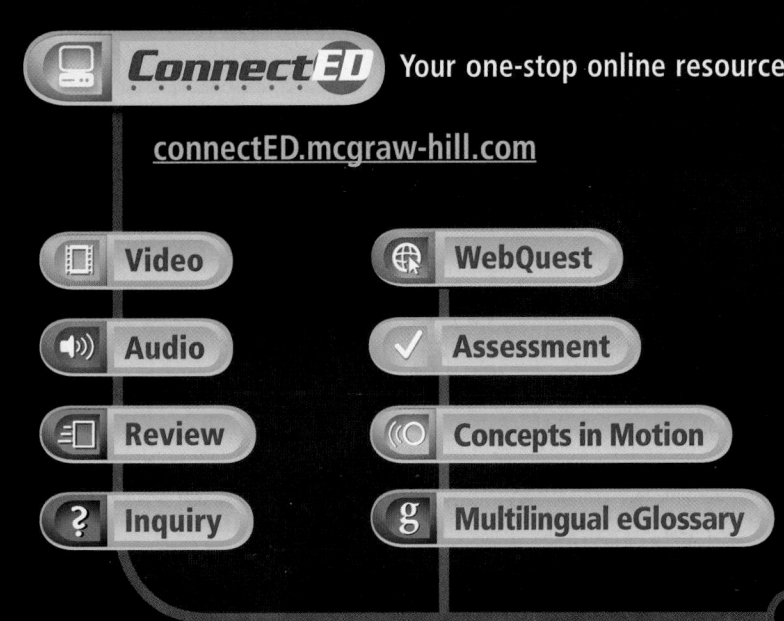

ConnectED Your one-stop online resource

connectED.mcgraw-hill.com

- Video
- Audio
- Review
- Inquiry
- WebQuest
- Assessment
- Concepts in Motion
- Multilingual eGlossary

Energy Processing in Plants

Reading Guide

Key Concepts 🔑
ESSENTIAL QUESTIONS

- How do materials move through plants?
- How do plants perform photosynthesis?
- What is cellular respiration?
- What is the relationship between photosynthesis and cellular respiration?

Vocabulary
photosynthesis p. 334
cellular respiration p. 336

g Multilingual eGlossary

Inquiry All Leaf Cells?

You are looking at a magnified cross section of a leaf. As you can see, the cells in the middle of the leaf are different from the cells on the edges. What do you think this might have to do with the cellular processes a leaf carries out that enable a plant's survival?

How can you show the movement of materials inside a plant?

Most parts of plants need water. They also need a system to move water throughout the plant so cells can use it for plant processes.

1. Read and complete a lab safety form.

2. Gently pull two stalks from the base of a bunch of **celery.** Leave one stalk complete. Use a **paring knife** to carefully cut directly across the bottom of the second stalk.

3. Put 100 mL of water into each of two **beakers.** Place 3–4 drops of **blue food coloring** into the water. Place one celery stalk in each beaker.

4. After 20 min, observe the celery near the bottom of each stalk. Observe again after 24 h. Record your observations in your Science Journal.

Think About This

1. What happened in each celery stalk?

2. **Key Concept** What did the colored water do? Why do you think this occurred?

Materials for Plant Processes

Food, water, and oxygen are three things you need to survive. Some of your organ systems process these materials, and others transport them throughout your body. Like you, plants need food, water, and oxygen to survive. Unlike you, plants do not take in food. Most of them make their own.

Moving Materials Inside Plants

You might recall reading about xylem (ZI lum) and phloem (FLOH em)—the vascular tissue in most plants. These tissues transport materials throughout a plant.

After water enters a plant's roots, it moves into xylem. Water then flows inside xylem to all parts of a plant. Without enough water, plant cells wilt, as shown in **Figure 1.**

Most plants make their own food—a liquid sugar. The liquid sugar moves out of food-making cells, enters phloem, and flows to all plant cells. Cells break down the sugar and release energy. Some plant cells can store food.

Plants require oxygen and carbon dioxide to make food. Like you, plants produce water vapor as a waste product. Carbon dioxide, oxygen, and water vapor pass into and out of a plant through tiny openings in leaves.

Key Concept Check How do materials move through plants?

Figure 1 This plant wilted due to lack of water in the soil.

Make a shutterfold book, leaving a 2-cm space between the tabs. Label it as shown. Use the book as a diagram of leaf structure.

Upper Epidermis

Mesophyll Cells

Lower Epidermis

WORD ORIGIN

photosynthesis
from Greek *photo-*, means "light"; and *synthesis*, means "composition"

Figure 2 Photosynthesis occurs inside the chloroplasts of mesophyll cells in most leaves.

Photosynthesis

Plants need food, but they cannot eat as people do. They make their own food, and leaves are the major food-producing organs of plants. This means that leaves are the sites of photosynthesis (foh toh SIHN thuh sus). **Photosynthesis** *is a series of chemical reactions that convert light energy, water, and carbon dioxide into the food-energy molecule glucose and give off oxygen.* The structure of a leaf is well-suited to its role in photosynthesis.

Leaves and Photosynthesis

As shown in **Figure 2**, leaves have many types of cells. The cells that make up the top and bottom layers of a leaf are flat, irregularly shaped cells called epidermal (eh puh DUR mul) cells. On the bottom epidermal layer of most leaves are small openings called stomata (STOH muh tuh). Carbon dioxide, water vapor, and oxygen pass through stomata. Epidermal cells can produce a waxy covering called the cuticle.

Most photosynthesis occurs in two types of mesophyll (ME zuh fil) cells inside a leaf. These cells contain chloroplasts, the organelle where photosynthesis occurs. Near the top surface of the leaf are palisade mesophyll cells. They are packed together. This arrangement exposes the most cells to light. Spongy mesophyll cells have open spaces between them. Gases needed for photosynthesis flow through the spaces between the cells.

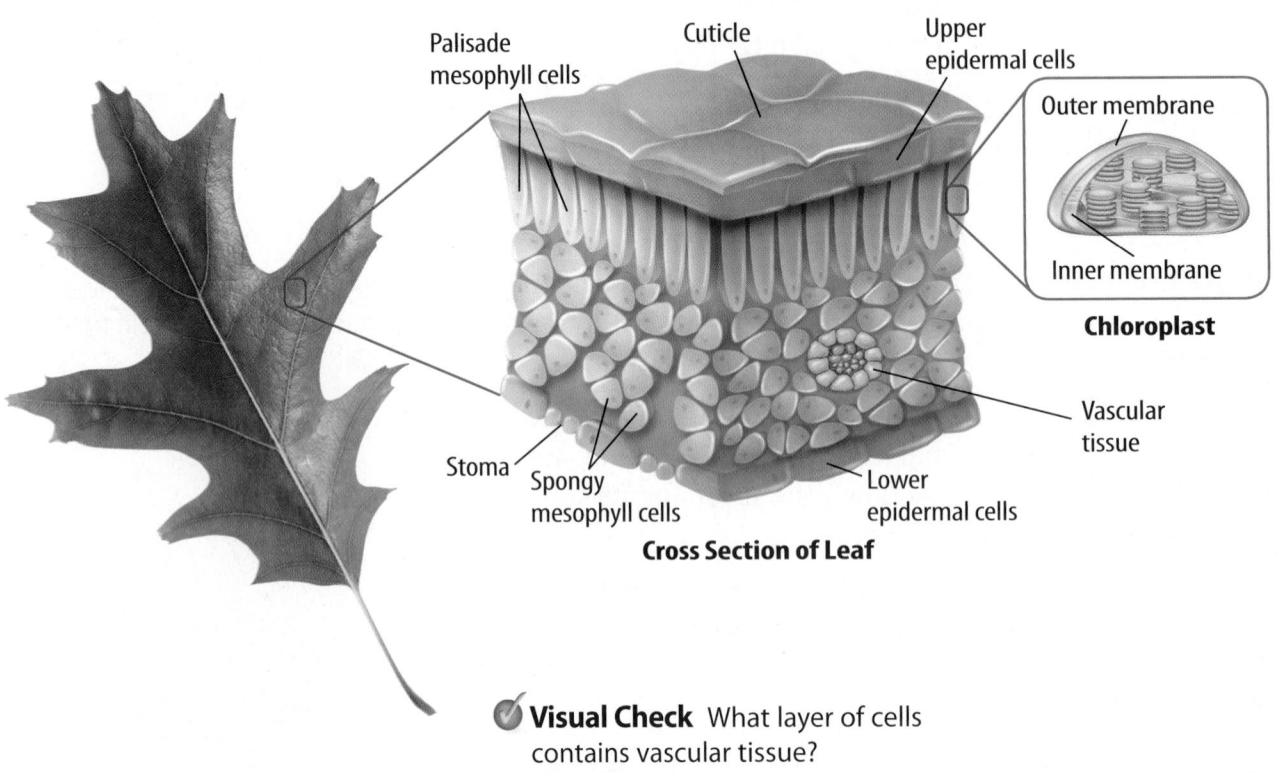

Cuticle · Upper epidermal cells · Palisade mesophyll cells · Outer membrane · Inner membrane · **Chloroplast** · Vascular tissue · Stoma · Spongy mesophyll cells · Lower epidermal cells

Cross Section of Leaf

Visual Check What layer of cells contains vascular tissue?

Capturing Light Energy

As you read about the steps of photosynthesis, refer to **Figure 3** to help you understand the process. In the first step of photosynthesis, plants capture the energy in light. This occurs in chloroplasts. Chloroplasts contain plant pigments. Pigments are chemicals that can absorb and reflect light. Chlorophyll, the most common plant pigment, is necessary for photosynthesis. Most plants appear green because chlorophyll reflects green light. Chlorophyll absorbs other colors of light. This light energy is used during photosynthesis.

Once chlorophyll traps and stores light energy, this energy can be transferred to other molecules. During photosynthesis, water molecules are split apart. This releases oxygen into the atmosphere, as shown in **Figure 3**.

 Reading Check How do plants capture light energy?

Making Sugars

Sugars are made in the second step of photosynthesis. This step can occur without light. In chloroplasts, carbon dioxide from the air is converted into sugars by using the energy stored and trapped by chlorophyll. Carbon dioxide combines with hydrogen atoms from the splitting of water molecules and forms sugar molecules. Plants can use this sugar as an energy source or can store it. Potatoes and carrots are examples of plant structures where excess sugar is stored.

 Key Concept Check What are the two steps of photosynthesis?

Why is photosynthesis important?

Try to imagine a world without plants. How would humans or other animals get the oxygen that they need? Plants help maintain the atmosphere you breathe. Photosynthesis produces most of the oxygen in the atmosphere.

Photosynthesis 🔑

Figure 3 Photosynthesis is a series of complex chemical processes. The first step is capturing light energy. In the second step, that energy is used for making glucose, a type of sugar.

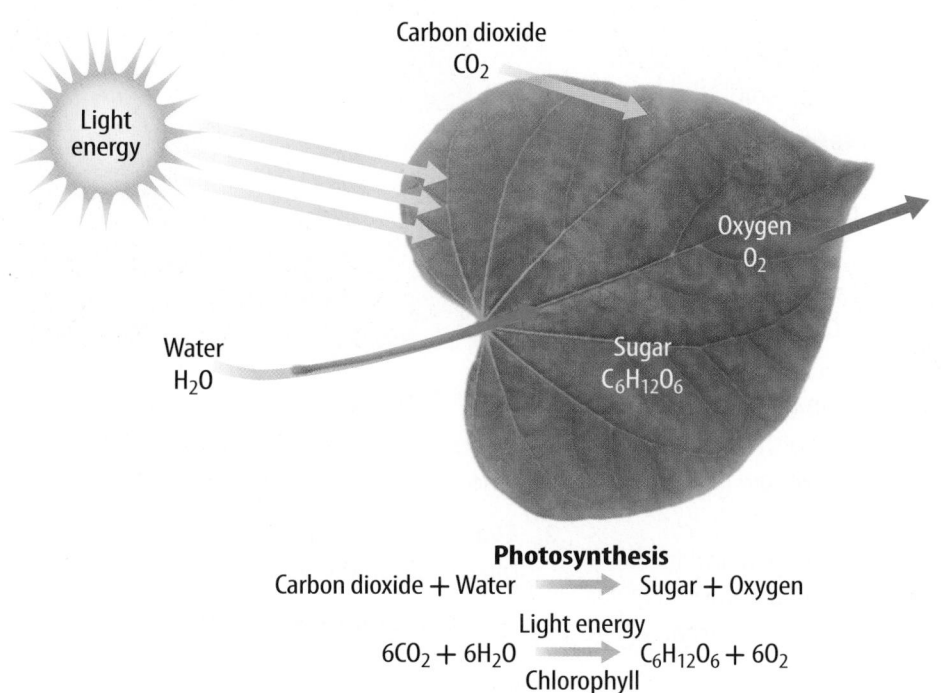

Photosynthesis

Carbon dioxide + Water $\longrightarrow$ Sugar + Oxygen

$$6CO_2 + 6H_2O \xrightarrow[\text{Chlorophyll}]{\text{Light energy}} C_6H_{12}O_6 + 6O_2$$

Cellular Respiration

ACADEMIC VOCABULARY

energy
(*noun*) usable power

All organisms require **energy** to survive. Energy is in the chemical bonds in food molecules. A process called cellular respiration releases energy. **Cellular respiration** *is a series of chemical reactions that convert the energy in food molecules into a usable form of energy called ATP.*

Releasing Energy from Sugars

Glucose molecules break down during cellular respiration. Much of the energy released during this process is used to make ATP, an energy storage molecule. This process requires oxygen, produces water and carbon dioxide as waste products, and occurs in the cytoplasm and mitochondria of cells.

Why is cellular respiration important?

If your body did not break down the food you eat through cellular respiration, you would not have energy to do anything. Plants produce sugar, but without cellular respiration, plants could not grow, reproduce, or repair tissues.

 Key Concept Check What is cellular respiration?

---

inquiry MiniLab   **20 minutes**

Can you observe plant processes?

Plants perform both photosynthesis and cellular respiration. Can you observe both processes in radish seedlings?

1. Read and complete a lab safety form.

2. Put **potting soil** in the bottom of a **small, self-sealing plastic bag** so that the soil is 3–4 cm deep. Dampen the soil.

3. Drop several **radish seeds** into the bag and close the top, but leave a small opening so air can still get into the bag.

4. Place the bag upright in a place that has a **light source.** Each group should use a different light source. Observe for 4–5 days.

5. Carefully place an open container of **bromthymol blue (0.004%) solution** upright in the bag next to the seedlings. Bromthymol blue turns yellow in the presence of carbon dioxide.

6. Seal the bag. Observe the bag and its contents the next day. Record your observations in your Science Journal.

Analyze and Conclude

1. **Describe** the differences in seedling samples among groups. Why are there differences?

2. **Evaluate** What change in the bromthymol blue solution did you observe? Why?

3. **Key Concept** Explain what processes occurred in the seedlings.

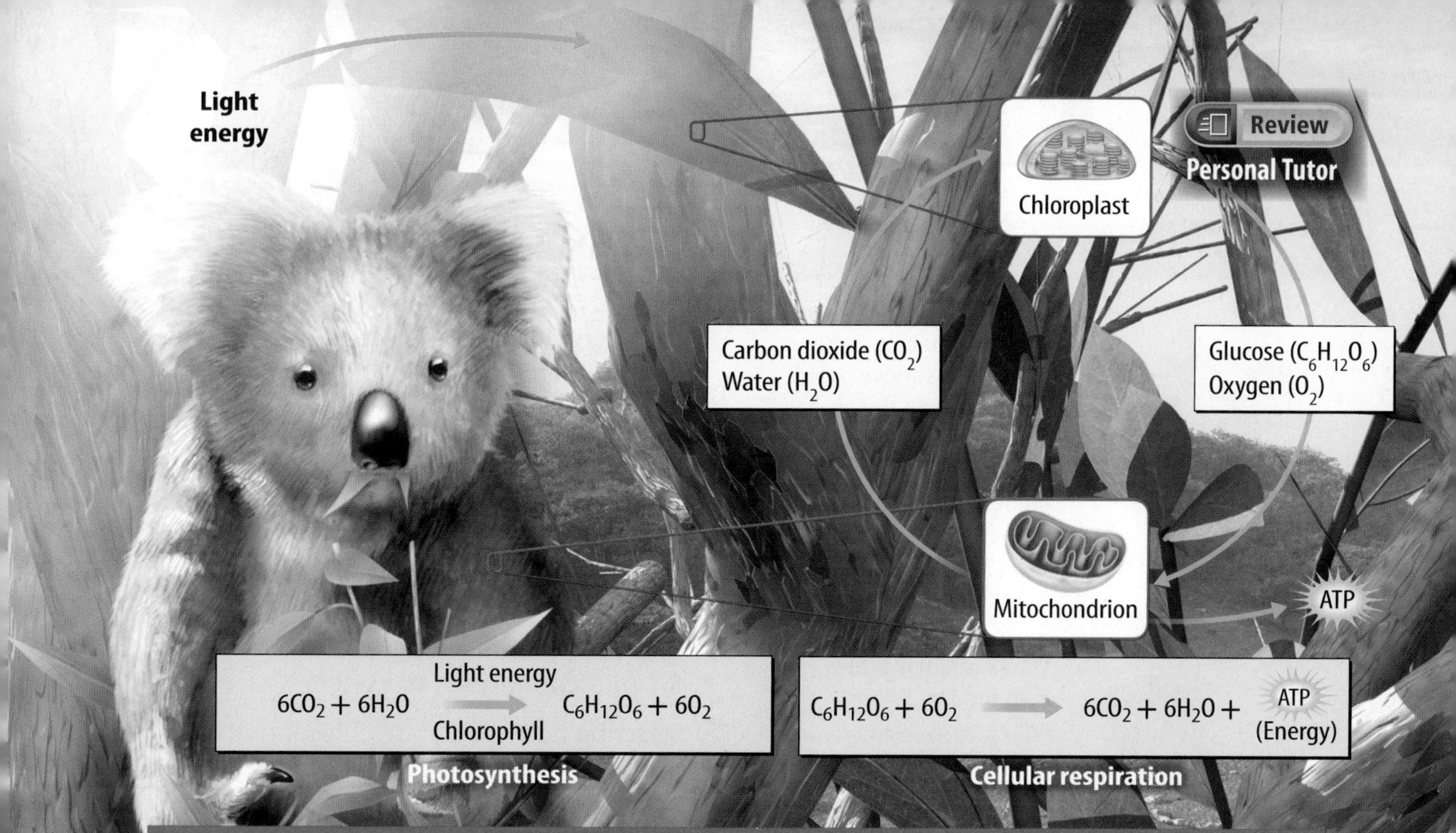

Light energy
Chloroplast
Review
Personal Tutor
Carbon dioxide (CO_2)
Water (H_2O)
Glucose ($C_6H_{12}O_6$)
Oxygen (O_2)
Mitochondrion
ATP
$6CO_2 + 6H_2O \xrightarrow[\text{Chlorophyll}]{\text{Light energy}} C_6H_{12}O_6 + 6O_2$
Photosynthesis
$C_6H_{12}O_6 + 6O_2 \rightarrow 6CO_2 + 6H_2O +$ ATP (Energy)
Cellular respiration

Photosynthesis v. Cellular Respiration

Concepts in Motion
Interactive Table

Process	Photosynthesis	Cellular Respiration
Reactants	light energy, CO_2, H_2O	glucose [sugar], O_2
Products	glucose, O_2	CO_2, H_2O, ATP
Organelle in which it occurs	chloroplasts	mitochondria
Type of organism	photosynthetic organisms including plants and algae	most organisms including plants and animals

Comparing Photosynthesis and Cellular Respiration

Photosynthesis requires light energy and the reactants—substances that react with one another during the process—carbon dioxide and water. Oxygen and the energy-rich molecule glucose are the products, or end substances, of photosynthesis. Most plants, some protists, and some bacteria carry on photosynthesis.

Cellular respiration requires the reactants glucose and oxygen, produces carbon dioxide and water, and releases energy in the form of ATP. Most organisms carry on cellular respiration. Photosynthesis and cellular respiration are interrelated, as shown in **Figure 4.** Life on Earth depends on a balance of these two processes.

Key Concept Check How are photosynthesis and cellular respiration alike, and how are they different?

Figure 4 The relationship between cellular respiration and photosynthesis is important for life.

Visual Check What are the reactants of cellular respiration? What are the products?

Lesson 1 Review

Visual Summary

Materials that a plant requires to survive move through the plant in the vascular tissue, xylem and phloem.

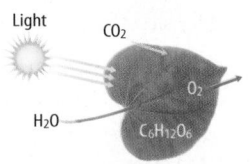

Plants can make their own food by using light energy, water, and carbon dioxide.

The products of photosynthesis are the reactants for cellular respiration.

FOLDABLES

Use your lesson Foldable to review the lesson. Save your Foldable for the project at the end of the chapter.

What do you think NOW?

You first read the statements below at the beginning of the chapter.

1. Plants do not carry on cellular respiration.

2. Plants are the only organisms that carry on photosynthesis.

Did you change your mind about whether you agree or disagree with the statements? Rewrite any false statements to make them true.

Use Vocabulary

1 A series of chemical reactions that convert the energy in food molecules into a usable form of energy, called ATP, is called _____.

2 **Define** *photosynthesis* in your own words.

Understand Key Concepts

3 Which structure moves water through plants?
  A. chloroplast   C. nucleus
  B. mitochondrion D. xylem

4 **Describe** how plants use chlorophyll for photosynthesis.

5 **Summarize** the process of cellular respiration.

Interpret Graphics

6 **Explain** how the structure shown below is organized for its role in photosynthesis.

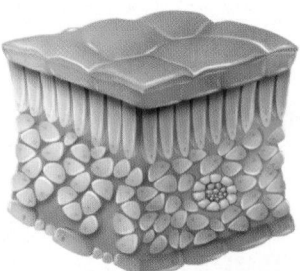

7 **Compare and Contrast** Copy and fill in the table below to compare and contrast photosynthesis and cellular respiration.

Process	Similarities	Differences

Critical Thinking

8 **Predict** the effect of a plant disease that destroys all of the chloroplasts in a plant.

9 **Evaluate** why plants perform cellular respiration.

Deforestation and Carbon Dioxide
in the Atmosphere

How does carbon dioxide affect climate?

What do you think when you hear the words *greenhouse gases?* Many people picture pollution from automobiles or factory smokestacks. It might be surprising to learn that cutting down forests affects the amount of one of the greenhouse gases in the atmosphere—carbon dioxide.

Deforestation is the term used to describe the destruction of forests. Deforestation happens because people cut down forests to use the land for other purposes, such as agriculture or building sites, or to use the trees for fuel or building materials.

Trees, like most plants, carry out photosynthesis and make their own food. Carbon dioxide from the atmosphere is one of the raw materials, or reactants, of photosynthesis. When deforestation occurs, trees are unable to remove carbon dioxide from the atmosphere. As a result, the level of carbon dioxide in the atmosphere increases.

Trees affect the amount of atmospheric carbon dioxide in other ways. Large amounts of carbon are stored in the molecules that make up trees. When trees are burned or left to rot, much of this stored carbon is released as carbon dioxide. This increases the amount of carbon dioxide in the atmosphere.

Carbon dioxide in the atmosphere has an impact on climate. Greenhouse gases, such as carbon dioxide, increase the amount of the Sun's energy that is absorbed by the atmosphere. They also reduce the ability of heat to escape back into space. So, when levels of carbon dioxide in the atmosphere increase, more heat is trapped in Earth's atmosphere. This can lead to climate change.

▲ These cattle are grazing on land that was once part of a forest in Brazil.

▲ In a process called slash-and-burn, forest trees are cut down and burned to clear land for agriculture.

It's Your Turn

RESEARCH AND REPORT How can we lower the rate of deforestation? What are some actions you can take that could help slow the rate of deforestation? Research to find out how you can make a difference. Make a poster to share what you learn.

Plant Responses

Reading Guide

Key Concepts 🔑
ESSENTIAL QUESTIONS

- How do plants respond to environmental stimuli?

- How do plants respond to chemical stimuli?

Vocabulary

stimulus p. 341

tropism p. 342

photoperiodism p. 344

plant hormone p. 345

 Multilingual eGlossary

 Video **BrainPOP®**

Inquiry **A Meat-Eating Plant?**

Venus flytraps have leaves that look like jaws. The leaves close only when a stimulus, such as a fly, brushes against tiny, sensitive hairs on the surface of the leaves. To what other stimuli do you think plants might respond?

How do plants respond to stimuli?

Plants use light energy and make their own food during photosynthesis. How else do plants respond to light in their environment?

1. Read and complete a lab safety form.
2. Choose a **pot of young radish seedlings.**
3. Place **toothpicks** parallel to a few of the seedlings in the pot in the direction of growth.
4. Place the pot near a **light source**, such as a gooseneck lamp or next to a window. The light source should be to one side of the pot, not directly above the plants.
5. Check the position of the seedlings in relation to the toothpicks after 30 minutes. Record your observations in your Science Journal.
6. Observe the seedlings when you come to class the next day. Record your observations.

Think About This

1. What happened to the position of the seedlings after the first 30 minutes? What is your evidence of change?

2. What happened to the position of the seedlings after a day?

3. 🔑 **Key Concept** Why do you think the position of the seedlings changed?

Stimuli and Plant Responses

Have you ever been in a dark room when someone suddenly turned on the light? You might have reacted by quickly shutting or covering your eyes. **Stimuli** (STIM yuh li; singular, stimulus) *are any changes in an organism's environment that cause a response.*

Often a plant's response to stimuli might be so slow that it is hard to see it happen. The response might occur gradually over a period of hours or days. Light is a stimulus. A plant responds to light by growing toward it, as shown in **Figure 5.** This response occurs over several hours.

In some cases, the response to a stimulus is quick, such as the Venus flytrap's response to touch. When stimulated by an insect's touch, the two sides of the trap snap shut immediately, trapping the insect inside.

✓ **Reading Check** Why is it sometimes hard to see a plant's response to a stimulus?

Figure 5 The light is the stimulus, and the seedlings have responded by growing toward the light.

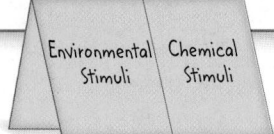
WORD ORIGIN ············

tropism
from Greek *tropos*, means
"turn" or "turning"

Environmental Stimuli

When it is cold outside, you probably wear a sweatshirt or a coat. Plants cannot put on warm clothes, but they do respond to their environments in a variety of ways. You might have seen trees flower in the spring or drop their leaves in the fall. Both are plant responses to environmental stimuli.

Growth Responses

Plants respond to a number of different environmental stimuli. These include light, touch, and gravity. *A* **tropism** (TROH pih zum) *is a response that results in plant growth toward or away from a stimulus.* When the growth is toward a stimulus, the tropism is called positive. A plant bending toward light is a positive tropism. Growth away from a stimulus is considered negative. A plant's stem growing upward against gravity is a negative tropism.

Light The growth of a plant toward or away from light is a tropism called phototropism. A plant has a light-sensing chemical that helps it detect light. Leaves and stems tend to grow in the direction of light, as shown in **Figure 6.** This response maximizes the amount of light the plant's leaves receive. Roots generally grow away from light. This usually means that the roots grow down into the soil and help anchor the plant.

Reading Check How is phototropism beneficial to a plant?

Response to Light

Figure 6 As a plant's leaves turn toward the light, the amount of light that the leaves can absorb increases.

Touch The response of a plant to touch is called a thigmotropism (thihg MAH truh pih zum). You might have seen vines growing up the side of a building or a fence. This happens because the plant has special structures that respond to touch. These structures, called tendrils, can wrap around or cling to objects, as shown in **Figure 7.** A tendril wrapping around an object is an example of positive thigmotropism. Roots display negative thigmotropism. They grow away from objects in soil, enabling them to follow the easiest path through the soil.

Gravity The response of a plant to gravity is called gravitropism. Stems grow away from gravity, while roots grow toward gravity. The seedlings in **Figure 8** are exhibiting both responses. No matter how a seed lands on soil, when it starts to grow, its roots grow down into the soil. The stem grows up. This happens even when a seed is grown in a dark chamber, indicating that these responses can occur independently of light.

 Key Concept Check What types of environmental stimuli do plants respond to? Give three examples.

Response to Touch

▲ **Figure 7** The tendrils of the vine respond to touch and coil around the blade of grass.

Response to Gravity

Figure 8 Both of these plant stems are growing away from gravity. The upward growth of a plant's stem is negative gravitropism, and the downward growth of its roots is positive gravitropism.

Visual Check How is the plant on the left responding to the pot begin placed on its side?

Flowering Responses

You might think all plants respond to light, but in some plants, flowering is actually a response to darkness! **Photoperiodism** *is a plant's response to the number of hours of darkness in its environment.* Scientists once hypothesized that photoperiodism was a response to light. Therefore, these flowering responses are called long-day, short-day, and day-neutral and relate to the number of hours of daylight in a plant's environment.

Long-Day Plants Plants that flower when exposed to less than 10–12 hours of darkness are called long-day plants. The carnations shown in **Figure 9** are examples of long-day plants. This plant usually produces flowers in summer, when the number of hours of daylight is greater than the number of hours of darkness.

Short-Day Plants Short-day plants require 12 or more hours of darkness for flowering to begin. An example of a short-day plant is the poinsettia, shown in **Figure 9.** Poinsettias tend to flower in late summer or early fall when the number of hours of daylight is decreasing and the number of hours of darkness is increasing.

Day-Neutral Plants The flowering of some plants doesn't seem to be affected by the number of hours of darkness. Day-neutral plants flower when they reach maturity and the environmental conditions are right. Plants such as the roses in **Figure 9** are day-neutral plants.

 Reading Check How is the flowering of day-neutral plants affected by exposure to hours of darkness?

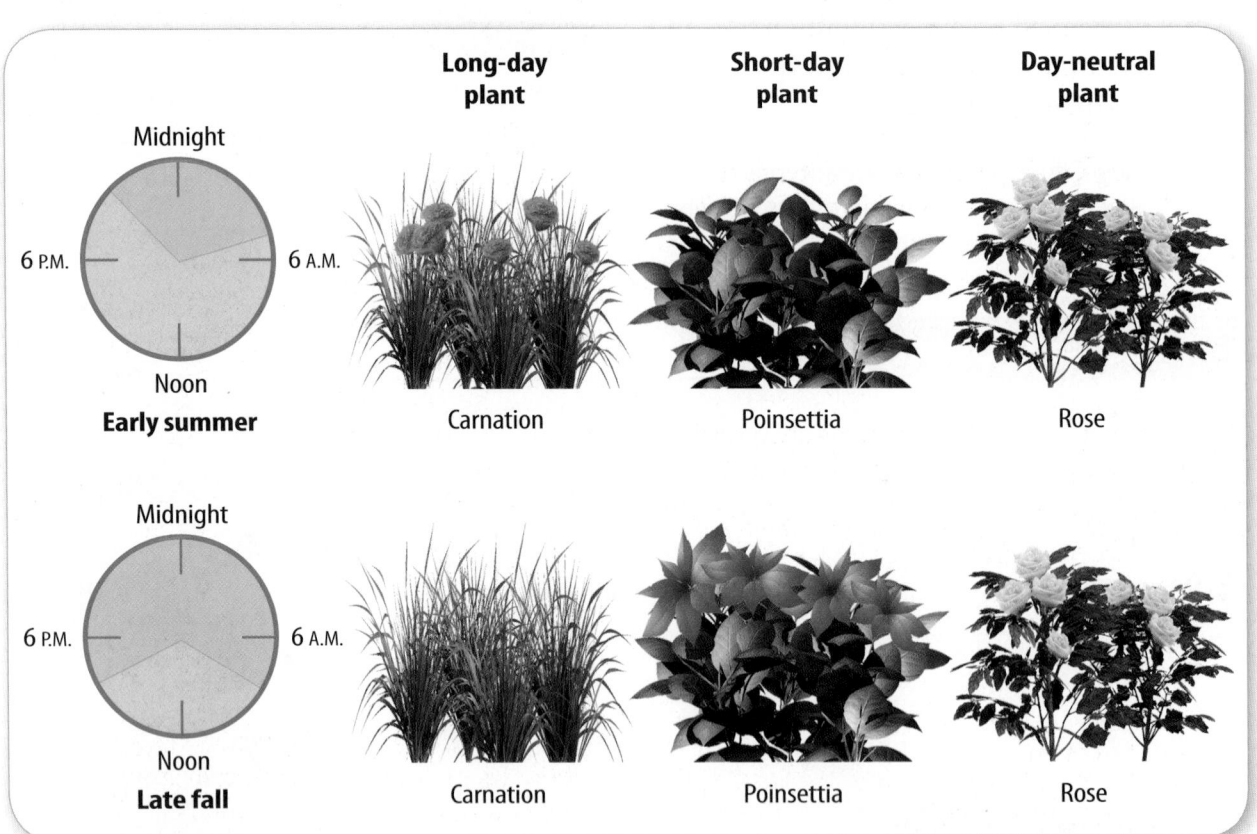

Figure 9 The number of hours of darkness controls flowering in many plants. Long-day plants flower when there are more hours of daylight than darkness, and short-day plants flower when there are more hours of darkness than daylight.

Visual Check What time of year receives more darkness, and what type of plant produces flowers during that season?

Chemical Stimuli

Plants respond to chemical stimuli as well as environmental stimuli. **Plant hormones** *are substances that act as chemical messengers within plants.* These chemicals are produced in tiny amounts. They are called messengers because they usually are produced in one part of a plant and affect another part of that plant.

Auxins

One of the first plant hormones discovered was auxin (AWK sun). There are many different kinds of auxins. Auxins generally cause increased plant growth. They are responsible for phototropism, the growth of a plant toward light. Auxins concentrate on the dark side of a plant's stem, and these cells grow longer. This causes the stem of the plant to grow toward the light, as shown in **Figure 10.**

Ethylene

The plant hormone ethylene helps stimulate the ripening of fruit. Ethylene is a gas that can be produced by fruits, seeds, flowers, and leaves. You might have heard someone say that one rotten apple spoils the whole barrel. This is based on the fact that rotting fruits release ethylene. This can cause other fruits nearby to ripen and possibly rot. Ethylene also can cause plants to drop their leaves.

 Key Concept Check How do plants respond to the chemical stimuli, or hormones, auxin and ethylene?

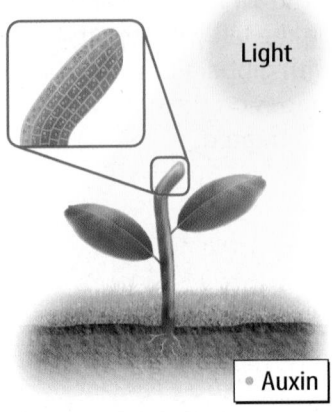
Light
• Auxin

Figure 10 🔑 Auxin on the left side of the seedling causes more growth and makes the seedling bend to the right.

Inquiry MiniLab   **20 minutes**

When will plants flower?

Did you ever think plants could have strategies so that they can germinate, live, grow, reproduce, and continue their species? Photoperiodism is one such strategy.

1 In your Science Journal, copy the table below to classify plants based on their photoperiodisms.

2 Choose 8–10 **pictures of flowers.** Record their names in your table. Use the clues on the back of each photo to determine the correct photoperiodism of each plant.

Analyze and Conclude

1. Interpret Data Based on your table, which plants would flower during the summer?

2. Explain why some plants flower at the same time every year.

3. Infer what might happen if short-day plants were placed under light for an hour or two at night.

4. 🔑 **Key Concept** Why would photoperiodism be an important strategy for flowering plants?

Plant	Season	Short-Day	Long-Day	Day-Neutral

Figure 11 The grapes on the left were treated with gibberellins, and the grapes on the right were not treated.

Gibberellins and Cytokinins

Rapidly growing areas of a plant, such as roots and stems, produce gibberellins (jih buh REL unz). These hormones increase the rate of cell division and cell elongation. This results in increased growth of stems and leaves. Gibberellins also can be applied to the outside of plants. As shown in **Figure 11**, applying gibberellins to plants can have a dramatic effect.

Root tips produce most of the cytokinins (si tuh KI nunz), another type of hormone. Xylem carries cytokinins to other parts of a plant. Cytokinins increase the rate of cell division, and in some plants, cytokinins slow the aging process of flowers and fruits.

Summary of Plant Hormones

Plants produce many different hormones. The hormones you have just read about are groups of similar compounds. Often, two or more hormones interact and produce a plant response. Scientists are still discovering new information about plant hormones.

Humans and Plant Responses

Humans depend on plants for food, fuel, shelter, and clothing. Humans make plants more productive using plant hormones. Some crops now are easier to grow because humans understand how they respond to hormones. As you study **Figure 12** on the next page, make a list of all the ways humans can benefit from understanding and using plant responses.

✓ **Reading Check** How are humans dependent on plants?

Figure 12 Understanding how plants respond to hormones can benefit people in many ways.

The cutting on the left has been treated with synthetic auxins, which encourage cuttings to root.

By choosing seeds that produce climbing cucumbers, farmers grow plants that are easier to pick. The cucumbers grow faster and bigger because they get more light.

Removing the apical bud of a plant suppresses auxin causing the plant to grow out instead of up, producing a fuller plant.

Bananas can be picked and shipped while still green and then be treated with ethylene to cause them to ripen.

The use of cytokinins helps scientists and horticulturists grow hundreds of identical plants.

Lesson 2 Review

Visual Summary

Plants respond to stimuli in their environments in many ways.

Carnation

Photoperiodism occurs in long-day plants and short-day plants. Day-neutral plants are not affected by the number of hours of darkness.

Light

Auxin

Plant hormones are internal chemical stimuli that produce different responses in plants.

FOLDABLES

Use your lesson Foldable to review the lesson. Save your Foldable for the project at the end of the chapter.

What do you think NOW?

You first read the statements below at the beginning of the chapter.

3. Plants do not produce hormones.

4. Plants can respond to their environments.

Did you change your mind about whether you agree or disagree with the statements? Rewrite any false statements to make them true.

Use Vocabulary

❶ **Define** *plant hormone* in your own words.

❷ The response of an organism to the number of hours of darkness in its environment is called _____.

❸ **Distinguish** between *stimuli* and *tropism*.

Understand Key Concepts

❹ **Describe** an example of a plant responding to environmental stimuli.

❺ **Distinguish** between a long-day plant and a short-day plant.

❻ **Compare** the effect of auxins and gibberellins on plant cells.

❼ Which is NOT likely to cause a plant response?
   A. changing the amount of daylight
   B. moving plants away from each other
   C. treating with plant hormones
   D. turning a plant on its side

Interpret Graphics

❽ **Identify** Copy the table below and list the plant hormones mentioned in this lesson. Describe the effect of each on plants.

Hormone	Effect on Plants

Critical Thinking

❾ **Infer** why the plant shown to the right is growing at an angle.

Math Skills ✗÷+

Review
—— Math Practice ——

❿ When sprayed with gibberellins, the diameter of mature grapes increased from 1.0 cm to 1.75 cm. What was the percent increase in size?

What happens to seeds if you change the intensity of light?

Seeds require light, water, gases, and soil to germinate, grow into seedlings, and then grow into mature plants. Different types of seeds require different amounts of each of these factors. What happens if one of these factors is changed?

Materials

plastic tub

potting soil

fast-growing grass seeds

sun shields

light source

metric ruler

mister bottle with water

Safety

Learn It

In any experiment, it is important to keep everything the same except for the item you are testing. The one factor you change, or **manipulate,** is called the independent **variable.** Your experiment should also have a control. The control is an individual instance or experimental subject for which the independent **variable** is not changed.

Try It

1 Read and complete a lab safety form.

2 Fill the plastic tub with potting soil. Water the soil, and then add more soil. Level it to about 1–2 cm from the top. Spread the grass seeds evenly across the soil. Cover the seeds with a thin layer of soil.

3 Obtain the precut shields of vellum, plastic needlepoint grid, and cardboard. These will be used to change the intensity of light coming onto the soil.

4 Cover the soil with the shields by laying them next to each other. Leave one section of soil uncovered.

5 Place the tub on a windowsill or under a growing light.

6 Keep the soil damp, not wet, with a mister. Water gently so the seeds stay in position.

7 Design a table to record observations in your Science Journal. Include columns for day, growth pattern, height, and random sampling counts. Begin observations when seedlings first emerge. Observe seedlings for 3–5 days.

Apply It

8 **Identify** the variables and the controls used in this investigation.

9 **Analyze** the data you collected through your observations. Which light intensity appeared to bring about the fullest, tallest growth?

10 **Draw conclusions** about what would happen if you put one section of seeds in total darkness. Would it germinate? If you changed the light intensity immediately after the seeds germinated, would it survive?

11 🔑 **Key Concept** Does the amount of light affect the germination and growth of grass seeds? Explain.

Lesson 3

Reading Guide

Key Concepts 🔑
ESSENTIAL QUESTIONS

- What is the alternation of generations in plants?
- How do seedless plants reproduce?
- How do seed plants reproduce?

Vocabulary

alternation of generations p. 352

spore p. 352

pollen grain p. 354

pollination p. 354

ovule p. 354

embryo p. 354

seed p. 354

stamen p. 356

pistil p. 356

ovary p. 356

fruit p. 357

g Multilingual eGlossary

Plant Reproduction

Inquiry A Bee's-Eye View?

Bees can see ultraviolet (UV) light. We see a dandelion as yellow. Because of a bee's ability to see UV light, a bee sees a dandelion like the one above. Why do you think bees see flowers differently than we do? Why do some plants produce flowers while others do not?

Launch Lab

15 minutes

How can you identify fruits?

Flowering plants grow from seeds that they produce. Animals depend on flowering plants for food. The function of the fruit is to disperse the seeds for plant reproduction.

1. Read and complete a lab safety form.

2. Make a two-column table in your Science Journal. Label the columns *Fruits* and *Not Fruits*.

3. Examine a collection of **food items.** Determine whether each item is a fruit. Record your observations in your table.

4. Place each food item on a piece of **plastic wrap.** Use a **plastic or paring knife** to cut the items in half.

5. Examine the inside of each food item. Record your observations.

Think About This

1. What observations did you make about the insides of the food items? Would you reclassify any food item based on your observations? Explain.

2. How can the number of seeds or how they are placed in the fruit help with seed dispersal?

3. 🔑 **Key Concept** What role do you think a fruit has in a flowering plant's reproduction?

Asexual Reproduction Versus Sexual Reproduction

In early spring, you might see cars or sidewalks covered with a thick, yellow dust. Where did it come from? It probably came from plants that are reproducing. As in all living things, reproduction is part of the life cycles of plants.

Plants can reproduce either asexually, sexually, or both ways. Asexual reproduction occurs when a portion of a plant develops into a separate new plant. This new plant is genetically identical to the original, or parent, plant. Some plants, such as irises and daylilies, can use their underground stems for asexual reproduction. Other plants, such as the houseleeks, or hens and chicks, in **Figure 13,** reproduce asexually using horizontal stems called stolons. One advantage of asexual reproduction is that just one parent organism can produce offspring. However, sexual reproduction in plants usually requires two parent organisms. Sexual reproduction occurs when a plant's sperm combines with a plant's egg. A resulting zygote can grow into a plant. This new plant is a genetic combination of its parents.

Figure 13 Hens and chicks can reproduce without seeds, or asexually. New "chicks" can grow from the stolons on the main "hen" plant.

✓ **Reading Check** How are sexual and asexual reproduction different in plants?

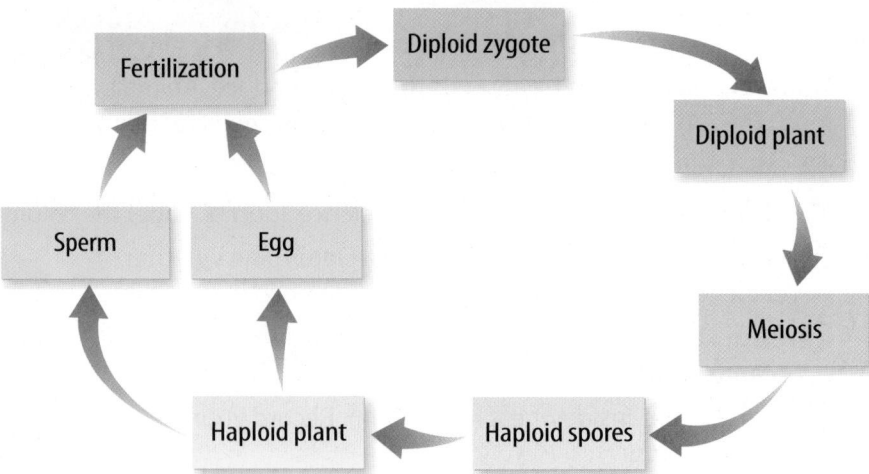

Figure 14 The life cycle of all plants includes an alternation of generations. The diploid generation begins with fertilization. The haploid generation begins with meiosis.

Alternation of Generations

Your body is made of two types of cells—haploid cells and diploid cells. Most of your cells are diploid. The only human haploid cells are sperm and eggs. As a result, you will live your entire life as a diploid organism. To put it another way, your life cycle includes only a diploid stage. That isn't true for all organisms. Some organisms, including plants, have two life stages called **generations.** One generation is almost all diploid cells. The other generation has only haploid cells. **Alternation of generations** *occurs when the life cycle of an organism alternates between diploid and haploid generations,* as shown in **Figure 14.**

 Key Concept Check What is alternation of generations in plants?

The Diploid Generation

When you look at a tree or a flower, you're seeing part of the plant's diploid generation. Meiosis occurs in certain cells in the reproductive structures of a diploid plant. *The daughter cells produced from haploid structures are called* **spores.** Spores grow by mitosis and cell division and form the haploid generation of a plant.

The Haploid Generation

In most plants, the haploid generation is tiny and lives surrounded by special tissues of the diploid plant. In other plants, the haploid generation lives on its own. Certain reproductive cells of the haploid generation produce haploid sperm or eggs by mitosis and cell division. Fertilization takes place when a sperm and an egg fuse and form a diploid zygote. Through mitosis and cell division, the zygote grows into the diploid generation of a plant.

Reproduction in Seedless Plants

Not all plants grow from seeds. The first land plants to inhabit Earth probably were seedless plants—plants that grow from haploid spores, not from seeds. The mosses and ferns in **Figure 15** are examples of seedless plants found on Earth today.

Life Cycle of a Moss

The life cycle of a moss is typical for some seedless plants. The tiny, green moss plants that carpet rocks, bark, and soil in moist areas are haploid plants. These plants grow by **mitosis** and cell division from haploid spores produced by the diploid generation. They have male structures that produce sperm and female structures that produce eggs. Fertilization results in a diploid zygote that grows by mitosis and cell division into the diploid generation of moss, such as the one shown in **Figure 15.** A diploid moss is tiny and not easily seen.

Review Vocabulary

mitosis
the process during which a nucleus and its contents divide

Life Cycle of a Fern

An alternation of generations is also seen in the life cycle of a fern. The diploid generations are the green leafy plants often seen in forests. These plants produce haploid spores. The spores grow into tiny plants. The haploid plants produce eggs and sperm that can unite and form the diploid generations.

Key Concept Check How do seedless plants such as mosses and ferns reproduce?

Figure 15 Mosses and ferns usually grow in moist environments. Sperm must swim through a film of water to reach an egg.

Reproduction in Seedless Plants

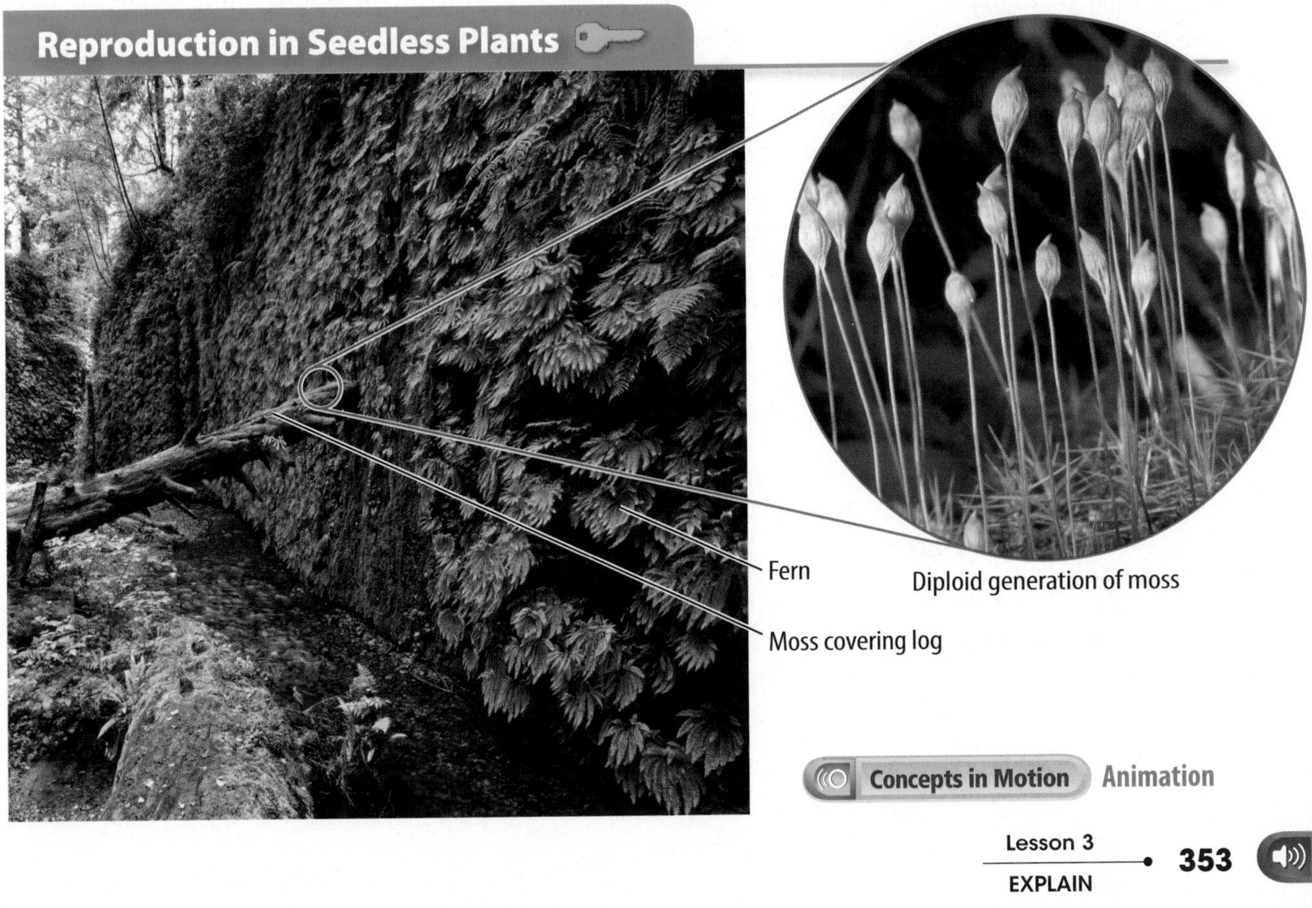

Fern
Diploid generation of moss
Moss covering log

Concepts in Motion Animation

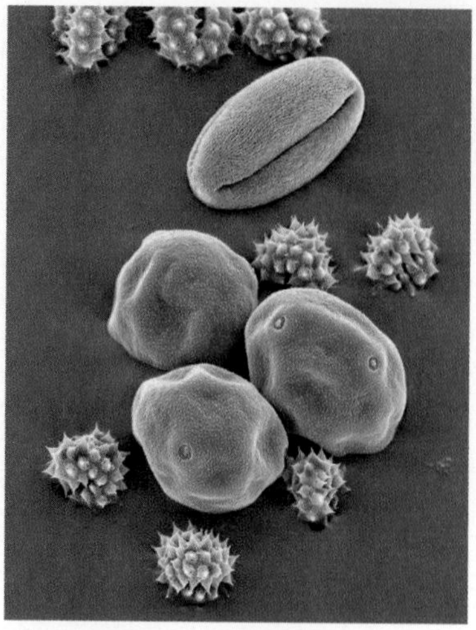

Color-enhanced SEM Magnification: 1,100×

▲ **Figure 16** Pollen grains of one type of plant are different from those of any other type of plant.

Visual Check How many different types of pollen are visible in **Figure 16?**

How do seed plants reproduce?

Most land plants that cover Earth grow from seeds. There are two groups of seed plants—flowerless seed plants and flowering seed plants.

Unlike seedless plants, the haploid generation of a seed plant is within diploid tissue. Separate diploid male and diploid female reproductive structures produce haploid sperm and haploid eggs that join during fertilization.

The Role of Pollen Grains

A **pollen** (PAH lun) **grain** *forms from tissue in a male reproductive structure of a seed plant.* Each pollen grain contains nutrients and has a hard, protective outer covering, as shown in **Figure 16.** Pollen grains produce sperm cells. Wind, animals, gravity, or water currents can carry pollen grains to female reproductive structures.

Plants cannot move and find a mate as most animals can. Do you recall reading about the yellow dust at the beginning of this lesson? That dust is pollen grains. Male reproductive structures produce a vast number of pollen grains. **Pollination** (pah luh NAY shun) *occurs when pollen grains land on a female reproductive structure of a plant that is the same species as the pollen grains.*

FOLDABLES®

Make a two-tab book and label it as shown. Use it to record information about reproduction in flowerless and flowering plants.

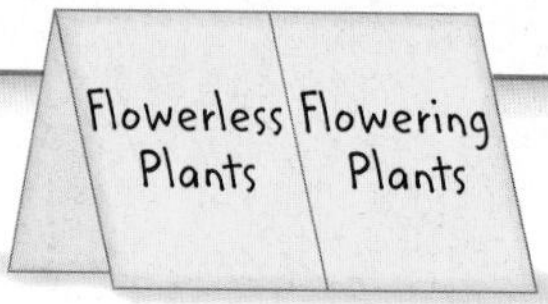

Flowerless Plants
Flowering Plants

The Role of Ovules and Seeds

The female reproductive structure of a seed plant where the haploid egg develops is called the **ovule.** Following pollination, sperm enter the ovule and fertilization occurs. A zygote forms and develops into an **embryo,** *an immature diploid plant that develops from the zygote.* As shown in **Figure 17,** *an embryo, its food supply, and a protective covering make up a* **seed.** A seed's food supply provides the embryo with nourishment for its early growth.

Key Concept Check How do seed plants reproduce?

Figure 17 A seed contains a diploid plant embryo and a food supply protected by a hard outer covering.

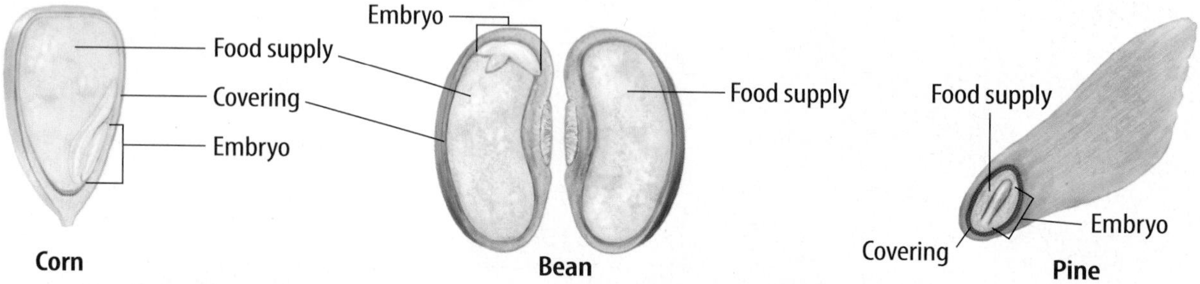

Food supply
Covering
Embryo
Corn
Embryo
Food supply
Bean
Food supply
Embryo
Covering
Pine

Reproduction in Flowerless Seed Plants

Flowerless seed plants are also known as gymnosperms (JIHM nuh spurmz). The word *gymnosperm* means "naked seed," and gymnosperm seeds are not surrounded by a fruit. The most common gymnosperms are conifers. Conifers, such as pines, firs, cypresses, redwoods, and yews, are trees and shrubs with needlelike or scalelike leaves. Most conifers are evergreens, which means they have leaves all year long. Conifers can live for many years. Bristlecone pines, such as the one shown in **Figure 18,** are among the oldest living trees on Earth.

Life Cycle of a Gymnosperm The life cycle of a gymnosperm, shown in **Figure 19,** includes an alternation of generations. Cones are the male and female reproductive structures of conifers. They contain the haploid generation. Male cones are small, papery structures that produce pollen grains. Female cones can be woody, berrylike, or soft, and they produce eggs. A zygote forms when a sperm from a male cone fertilizes an egg. The zygote is the beginning of the diploid generation. Seeds form as part of the female cone.

 Reading Check Where is the haploid generation of conifers contained?

▲ **Figure 18** Seeds form at the base of each scale on a female cone.

Female cones

Male cones

Reproduction in Flowerless Seed Plants 🔑

Concepts in Motion   Animation

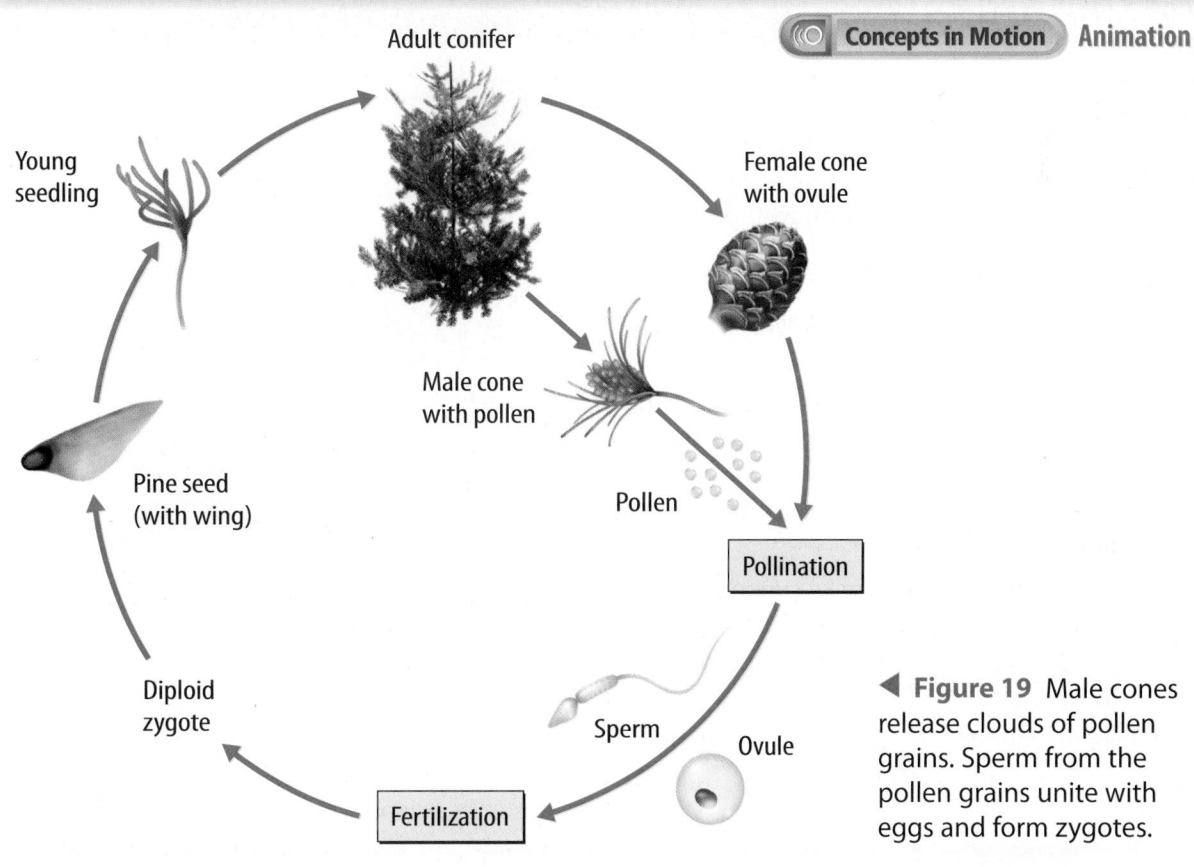

Adult conifer

Young seedling

Female cone with ovule

Male cone with pollen

Pine seed (with wing)

Pollen

Pollination

Diploid zygote

Sperm

Ovule

Fertilization

◀ **Figure 19** Male cones release clouds of pollen grains. Sperm from the pollen grains unite with eggs and form zygotes.

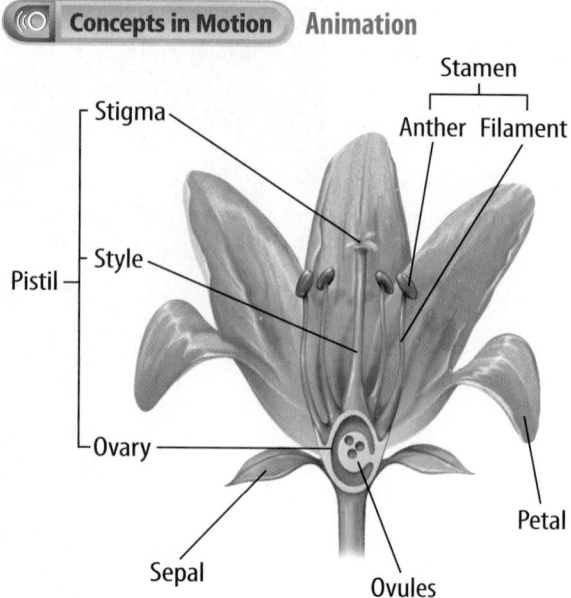

Figure 20 Typical flowers have both male and female structures.

Reproduction in Flowering Seed Plants

Most plants you see around you are angiosperms, or flowering plants. Fruits and vegetables come from angiosperms. Many animals depend on angiosperms for food.

The Flower Reproduction of an angiosperm begins in a flower. Most flowers have male and female reproductive structures, as shown in **Figure 20.**

The male reproductive organ of a flower is the **stamen.** Pollen grains form at the tip of the stamen in the anther. The filament supports the anther and connects it to the base of the flower. *The female reproductive organ of a flower is the* **pistil.** Pollen can land at the tip of the pistil, or stigma. The stigma is at the top of a long tube called the style. *At the base of the style is the* **ovary,** *which contains one or more ovules.* Recall that each ovule eventually will contain a haploid egg and might become a seed if fertilized.

Inquiry MiniLab

30 minutes

How can you model a flower?

Imagine that you have just discovered a new species of flowering plant. No one has ever seen this flower before, but it has all the basic flower parts.

1. Read and complete a lab safety form.
2. In your Science Journal, list all the parts your flower has as an angiosperm.
3. Make a large 3-dimensional model of your new flower using **chenille stems, tissue paper, construction paper, tag board, pom poms, plastic beads, scissors,** and **glue.**
4. Check your model to make sure each flower part is in the correct proportion and shows how it interacts with other flower parts.
5. Name your flower. Create a key to identify each part and its function.

Analyze and Conclude

1. **Analyze** Why do flowers have colorful petals and strong scents?
2. **Infer** Why does the end of the stigma feel sticky?
3. **Key Concept** Could your flower be self-pollinating? Explain.

Life Cycle of an Angiosperm A typical life cycle for an angiosperm is shown in **Figure 21.** Pollen grains travel by wind, gravity, water, or animal from the anther to the stigma, where pollination occurs. A pollen tube grows from the pollen grain into the stigma, down the style, to the ovary at the base of the pistil. Sperm develop from a haploid cell in the pollen tube. When the pollen tube enters an ovule, fertilization takes place.

As you read earlier, the zygote that results from fertilization develops into an embryo. Each ovule and its embryo will become a seed. *The ovary, and sometimes other parts of the flower, will develop into a* **fruit** *that contains one or more seeds.* The seeds can grow into new, genetically related plants that produce flowers, and the cycle repeats.

✓ **Reading Check** Do sperm develop before or after pollination?

Reproduction in Flowering Seed Plants 🔑

Concepts in Motion
Animation

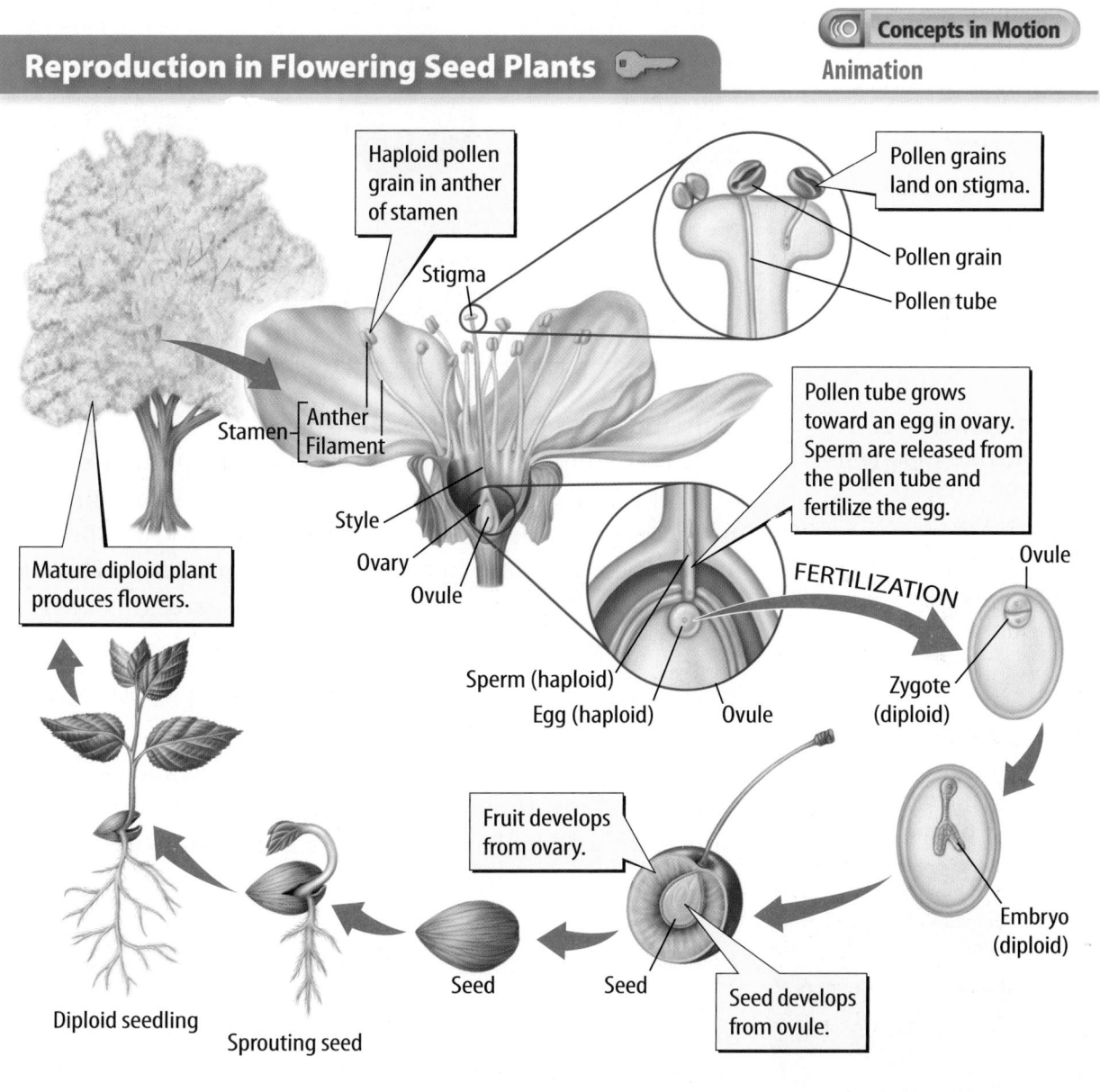

Haploid pollen grain in anther of stamen

Stigma

Pollen grains land on stigma.

Pollen grain

Pollen tube

Stamen — Anther / Filament

Style

Ovary

Ovule

Pollen tube grows toward an egg in ovary. Sperm are released from the pollen tube and fertilize the egg.

FERTILIZATION

Ovule

Sperm (haploid)

Egg (haploid)

Ovule

Zygote (diploid)

Mature diploid plant produces flowers.

Embryo (diploid)

Fruit develops from ovary.

Seed

Seed

Seed develops from ovule.

Diploid seedling

Sprouting seed

Figure 21 During the life cycle of a flowering plant, the haploid generation grows and develops inside the diploid plant.

✓ **Visual Check** How does sperm in a pollen grain reach an egg in the ovule?

Table 1 Flowers, Fruits, and Seeds of Common Plants

Plant	Flower	Fruit	Seed
Pea			
Corn			
Strawberry			
Dandelion			

Table 1 Flowers, fruits, and seeds are important for reproduction in angiosperms.

✅ **Visual Check** Which of these fruits has seeds on the outside?

Figure 22 The seeds will be excreted by the mouse and might grow into new blackberry bushes.

Fruit and Seed Dispersal Fruits and seeds, such as those in **Table 1,** are important sources of food for people and animals. In most cases, seeds of flowering plants are inside fruits. Pods are the fruits of a pea plant. The peas inside a pod are the seeds. An ear of corn is made up of many fruits, or kernels. The main part of each kernel is the seed. Strawberries have tiny seeds on the outside of the fruit.

✅ **Reading Check** Where are the seeds of flowering plants usually found?

We usually think of fruits as juicy and edible, such as oranges or watermelons. However, some fruits are hard, dry, and not particularly edible. For example, each parachutelike structure of a dandelion is a dry fruit.

Fruits help protect seeds and disperse them. Some fruits, such as those of a dandelion, are light and float on air currents, which helps to scatter the seeds. Also, when an animal eats a fruit, the fruit's seeds can pass through the animal's digestive system with little or no damage to the seed. Imagine what happens when an animal, such as the mouse shown in **Figure 22,** eats blackberries. The animal digests the juicy fruit and deposits the seeds with its wastes. By this time, the animal might have traveled some distance away from the blackberry bush. This means the animal helped to disperse the seeds away from the blackberry bush.

Lesson 3 Review

Visual Summary

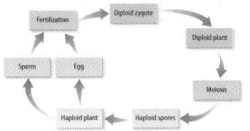

The life cycle of a plant includes an alternation of generations.

Seedless plants, such as ferns and mosses, grow from haploid spores.

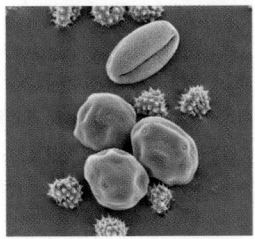

In seed plants, pollination occurs when pollen grains land on the female reproductive structure of a plant of the same species.

FOLDABLES®

Use your lesson Foldable to review the lesson. Save your Foldable for the project at the end of the chapter.

What do you think NOW?

You first read the statements below at the beginning of the chapter.

5. Seeds contain tiny plant embryos.

6. Flowers are needed for plant reproduction.

Did you change your mind about whether you agree or disagree with the statements? Rewrite any false statements to make them true.

Use Vocabulary

1 The daughter cells produced from haploid structures are called _____.

2 **Distinguish** between an ovule and an ovary.

3 **Define** *pollination* in your own words.

Understand Key Concepts

4 Which is NOT part of the alternation of generations life cycle in plants?
- **A.** anther
- **B.** diploid
- **C.** haploid
- **D.** spore

5 **Contrast** the haploid generation of a moss with that of a fern.

6 **Describe** how a pollen tube carries sperm to the ovule in a flower.

7 **Give an example** of a flowerless seed plant.

Interpret Graphics

8 **Examine** the figure below and describe the function of each part of the seed.

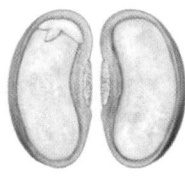

9 **Identify** Copy and fill in the graphic organizer below to identify the female parts of a flower.

Critical Thinking

10 **Create** a picture to show the life cycle of a fern.

11 **Evaluate** the advantages of fruit production in plant reproduction.

Design a Stimulating Environment for Plants

Plants usually respond to stimuli in the environment by growing. The response to light is phototropism; plants grow toward the light. The growth response of gravitropism is a little more complicated; stems grow away from the direction of gravity (negative gravitropism), and roots grow in the direction of gravity (positive gravitropism). Thigmotropism is a plant response to touch.

Ask a Question

You have explored tropisms in other labs in this chapter. What questions would you like to answer more thoroughly, or what outcomes would you like to double-check? Do you have another approach in mind to investigate one of the tropisms? Ask a question that you would like to investigate further. Make sure it is testable; think about the variables and equipment you would need.

Make Observations

1. Read and complete a lab safety form.

2. Examine your quad of plants and decide which tropism you want to explore.

3. Make a plan and write it in your Science Journal.

4. Have your teacher approve your plan for your investigation.

5. Choose materials from those provided by your teacher for a simple lab setup.

6. Decide the criteria you will use to show the outcomes you expect.

7. Set up your lab according to your plan.

Form a Hypothesis

8. After observing your plants and lab setup, formulate a hypothesis about the relationship between your selected tropism and a plant's growth. Make a prediction about how the tropism will affect your plants.

Test Your Hypothesis

9 Make any necessary modifications to your setup so your procedure will move toward your expected outcome.

10 Make a data table like the one to the right in your Science Journal.

11 Make your observations as directed by your procedure, and record them in your table.

Analyze and Conclude

12 **Compare** the position of the parts of your plant at the beginning and end of your study. Check to see if the change is easily visible and measurable; try not to jump to conclusions.

13 **Consider** the possible causes of the changes. Determine if it was changing the variable that brought about the effect. Explain.

14 **Relate** how the tropism you modeled could enable plants to meet their needs and survive.

15 **The Big Idea** What might happen if the stimulus you provided for the plant was enlarged, minimized, or eliminated?

Communicate Your Results

Prepare a drama to present your findings. Group members or volunteers from the class can wear pictures or signs to indicate their roles. Begin with students role-playing a healthy plant. Add the role of the stimulus, and be sure to identify the tropism and show results in the plant(s).

Inquiry Extension

Phototropism is one of the plant responses to stimuli that you have been able to explore easily by changing the position of the light source or the position of the plants in relation to the light source. What might happen if you changed the light source itself? What if you put a colored plastic sheet between the light and the plant? Would a red filter cause the same response as a green filter? What if you used different plants? For example, some mustard seeds are fast-germinating. Would these respond the same way as the other plants?

Time Period	[Variable observed] of Plant			
	1	2	3	4
Day 0 prior to tropism				
Day 1				
Day 2				
Day 3				

Lab Tips

☑ Discuss the possible materials you will use with your lab partner. Remember that the materials should help you learn more about the tropism you selected.

☑ Be creative when deciding how to test the tropism you selected.

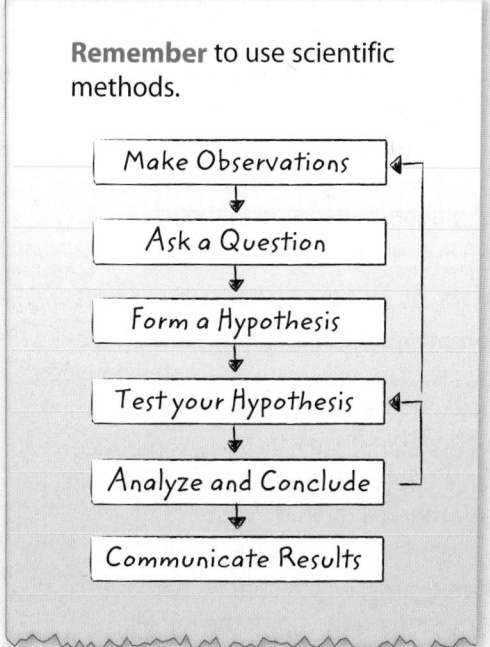

Remember to use scientific methods.

Make Observations → Ask a Question → Form a Hypothesis → Test your Hypothesis → Analyze and Conclude → Communicate Results

Plants transform light energy into chemical energy, respond to stimuli and maintain homeostasis, and reproduce with and without seeds.

Key Concepts Summary 🔑

Vocabulary	

Lesson 1: Energy Processing in Plants

- The vascular tissue in most plants, xylem and phloem, move materials throughout plants.

- In **photosynthesis,** plants convert light energy, water, and carbon dioxide into the food-energy molecule glucose through a series of chemical reactions. The process gives off oxygen.

- **Cellular respiration** is a series of chemical reactions that convert the energy in food molecules into a usable form of energy called ATP.

- Photosynthesis and cellular respiration can be considered opposite processes of each other.

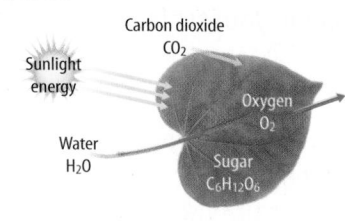

Carbon dioxide CO_2
Sunlight energy
Oxygen O_2
Water H_2O
Sugar $C_6H_{12}O_6$

Vocabulary

photosynthesis p. 334
cellular respiration p. 336

Lesson 2: Plant Responses

- Although plants cannot move from one place to another, they do respond to **stimuli,** or changes in their environments. Plants respond to stimuli in different ways.

- **Tropisms** are growth responses toward or away from stimuli such as light, touch, and gravity. **Photoperiodism** is a plant's response to the number of hours of darkness in its environment.

- Plants respond to chemical stimuli, or **plant hormones,** such as auxins, ethylene, gibberellins, and cytokinins. Different hormones have different effects on plants.

stimulus p. 341
tropism p. 342
photoperiodism p. 344
plant hormone p. 345

Lesson 3: Plant Reproduction

- **Alternation of generations** is when the life cycle of an organism alternates between diploid and haploid generations.

- Seedless plants, such as ferns, reproduce when a haploid sperm fertilizes a haploid egg, forming a diploid zygote.

- Seed plants reproduce when **pollen grains,** which contain haploid sperm, land on the tip of the female reproductive organ. At the base of this organ is the **ovary,** which usually contains one or more **ovules.** Each ovule eventually will contain a haploid egg. If the sperm fertilizes the egg, an **embryo** will form within a **seed.**

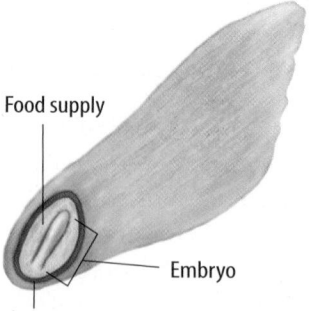

Food supply
Embryo
Covering

alternation of generations p. 352
spore p. 352
pollen grain p. 354
pollination p. 354
ovule p. 354
embryo p. 354
seed p. 354
stamen p. 356
pistil p. 356
ovary p. 356
fruit p. 357

FOLDABLES® Chapter Project

Assemble your lesson Foldables as shown to make a Chapter Project. Use the project to review what you have learned in this chapter.

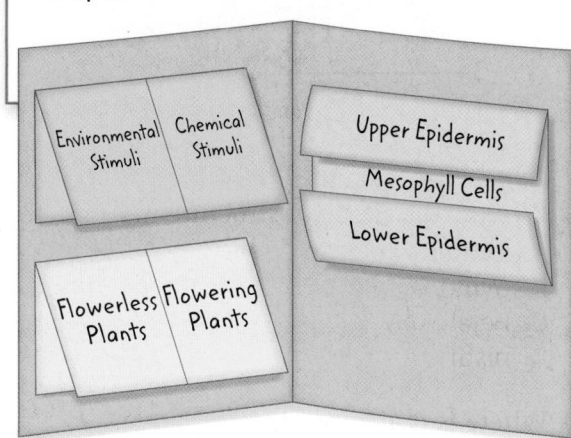

Environmental Stimuli | Chemical Stimuli

Upper Epidermis
Mesophyll Cells
Lower Epidermis

Flowerless Plants | Flowering Plants

Use Vocabulary

1 Long-day and short-day plants are examples of plants that respond to _____.

2 The process that uses oxygen and produces carbon dioxide is _____.

3 A(n) _____ forms from tissue in a male reproductive structure of a seed plant.

4 A(n) _____ develops from an ovary and surrounding tissue.

5 Sperm travel down the _____ inside the stigma of a flower to reach the ovary.

Link Vocabulary and Key Concepts

Concepts in Motion Interactive Concept Map

Copy this concept map, and then use vocabulary terms from the previous page to complete the concept map.

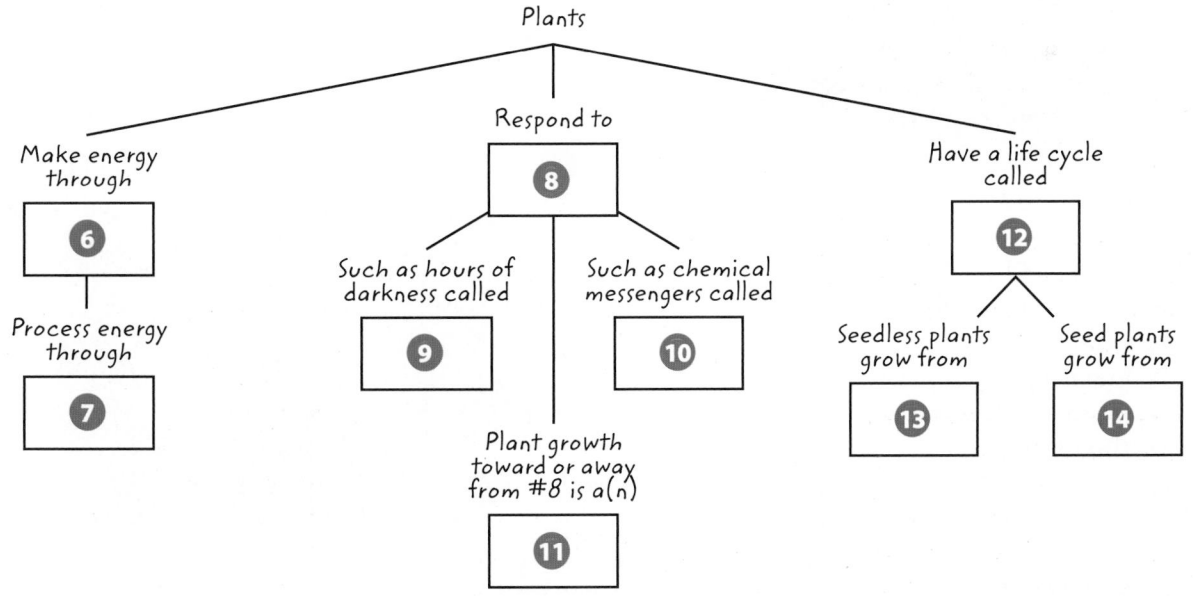

Plants

Make energy through
6

Process energy through
7

Respond to
8

Such as hours of darkness called
9

Such as chemical messengers called
10

Plant growth toward or away from #8 is a(n)
11

Have a life cycle called
12

Seedless plants grow from
13

Seed plants grow from
14

Understand Key Concepts

1 Which material travels from the roots to the leaves through the xylem?

A. oxygen
B. sugar
C. sunlight
D. water

2 Which organelle is the site of photosynthesis?

A. chloroplast
B. mitochondria
C. nucleus
D. ribosome

3 Which is a product of cellular respiration?

A. ATP
B. light
C. oxygen
D. sugar

Use the image below to answer questions 4 and 5.

4 What type of plant-growth response is shown in the photo above?

A. flowering
B. gravitropism
C. photoperiodism
D. thigmotropism

5 Which stimulus is responsible for this type of growth?

A. gravity
B. light
C. nutrients
D. touch

Use the image below to answer questions 6–8.

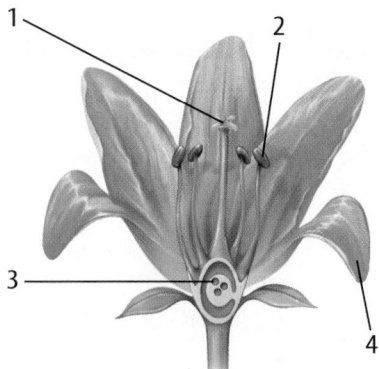

6 What is the name of structure number 3?

A. anther
B. ovule
C. petal
D. pistil

7 Where is pollen produced?

A. 1
B. 2
C. 3
D. 4

8 What part of a flower becomes a seed?

A. 1
B. 2
C. 3
D. 4

9 What plant is shown in the figure below?

A. diploid fern
B. diploid moss
C. haploid fern
D. haploid moss

Critical Thinking

10 **Infer** which came first—photosynthesis or cellular respiration.

11 **Assess** the importance of material transport in plants.

12 **Construct** a table to compare the reactants and products of photosynthesis and cellular respiration.

13 **Evaluate** the internal structure of a leaf as a location for photosynthesis.

14 **Assess** the need for plants to respond to their environment.

15 **Predict** what would happen if a short-day plant were exposed to more hours of daylight.

16 **Critique** the saying "one rotten apple spoils the whole barrel."

17 **Infer** from the photo below where the light source is in relation to the plant.

18 **Evaluate** the importance of fruit production in flowering plants.

19 **Predict** the effect of cold temperature killing all the flowers on fruit trees.

Writing in Science

20 **Write** a five-sentence paragraph about the importance of plants in your life. Include a main idea, supporting details, and a concluding sentence.

REVIEW  THE B|G IDEA

21 Make a list of the plant processes you learned about in this chapter. How do these processes help a plant survive and reproduce?

22 How does the process shown below help a plant survive?

Math Skills ×÷+

 **Review**

—Math Practice—

Use Percentages

23 Without treatment with gibberellins, 500 out of 1,000 grass seeds germinated. When sprayed with gibberellins, 875 of the seeds germinated. What was the percentage increase?

24 A bunch of bananas ripens (turns from green to yellow) in 42 hours. When the bananas are placed in a bag with an apple, which releases ethylene, the bananas ripen in 21 hours. What is the percentage change in ripening time?

Standardized Test Practice

Record your answers on the answer sheet provided by your teacher or on a sheet of paper.

Multiple Choice

1 Which structure transports sugars throughout a plant?

  A epidermis

  B phloem

  C stomata

  D xylem

2 What is one similarity between plants and animals?

  A Both plants and animals carry on cellular respiration.

  B Both plants and animals carry on photosynthesis.

  C Both plants and animals have chloroplasts.

  D Both plants and animals use xylem and phloem to transport materials.

Use the diagram below to answer question 3.

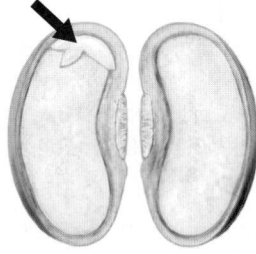

3 Look at the structure that is marked with an arrow in the image above. What will this structure become?

  A a diploid moss

  B a diploid seed plant

  C a haploid fern

  D a haploid flowerless seed plant

4 Which two plant hormones increase the rate of cell division?

  A auxins and cytokinins

  B cytokinins and giberellins

  C ethylene and auxins

  D giberellin and ethylene

5 Which is a product of photosynthesis?

  A carbon dioxide

  B glucose

  C light

  D water

Use the image below to answer question 6.

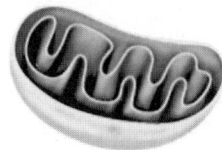

6 Which cellular process occurs within the organelle shown above?

  A photosynthesis

  B cellular respiration

  C transport of phloem

  D transport of xylem

7 Which plant has a diploid stage that is difficult to see?

  A conifer

  B cherry tree

  C dandelion

  D moss

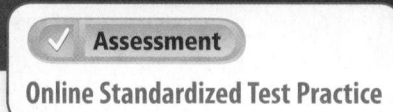
8 How is cellular respiration related to photosynthesis?

   A Animals produce sugars through cellular respiration that are broken down by plants through photosynthesis.

   B Animals use cellular respiration while plants use photosynthesis.

   C Cellular respiration produces sugars, which are stored through photosynthesis.

   D Photosynthesis produces sugars, which are broken down in cellular respiration.

Use the diagram below to answer question 9.

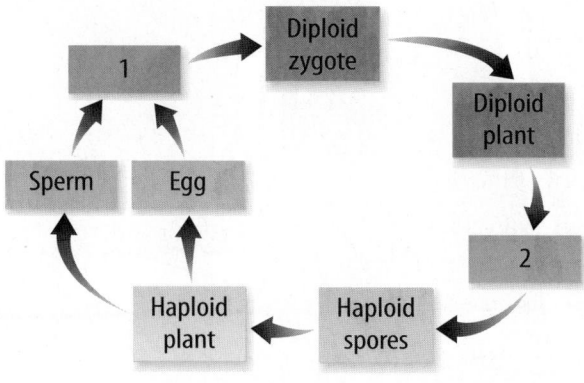

9 Which process occurs at the stage marked *2* on the plant life cycle diagram above?

   A asexual reproduction

   B fertilization

   C meiosis

   D mitosis

Constructed Response

Use the figure below to answer questions 10 and 11.

10 Describe what is happening in the image above. In your response, identify the environmental stimulus and the plant growth response.

11 Which plant hormone is involved in the growth response shown in the drawing above? Explain how this hormone causes the growth response.

12 Fruit distributors might use technologies to remove ethylene from the area where fruits are stored. How does this practice affect the fruit? Explain your answer.

13 Plants might reproduce both sexually and asexually. How are these two forms of reproduction similar? How are they different?

NEED EXTRA HELP?													
If You Missed Question...	1	2	3	4	5	6	7	8	9	10	11	12	13
Go to Lesson...	1	1	3	2	1	1	3	1	3	2	2	2	3

Unit 3

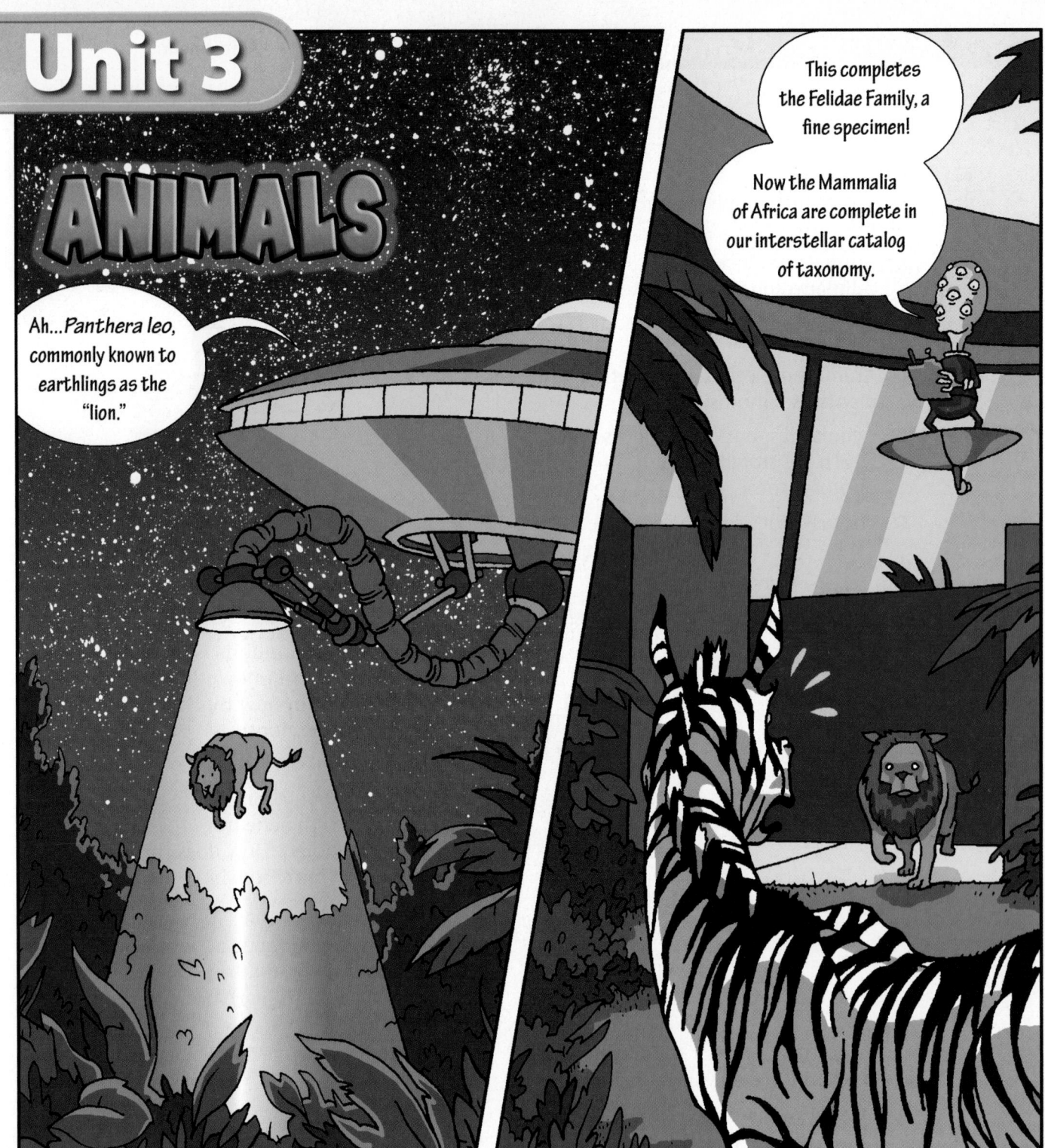

350–341 B.C.
Greek philosopher Aristotle classifies organisms by grouping 500 species of animals into eight classes.

1735
Carl Linnaeus classifies nature within a hierarchy and divides life into three kingdoms: mineral, vegetable, and animal. He uses five ranks: class, order, genus, species and variety. Linnaeus's classification is the basis of modern biological classification.

1859
Charles Darwin publishes *On the Origin of Species,* in which he explains his theory of natural selection.

1866
German biologist Ernst Haeckel coins the term *ecology.*

The comic panels contain the following dialogue:

"Oh my snortex!"

"Perhaps further studies of animal behavior are necessary before I proceed with my specimen collecting and storage."

1950

1969
American ecologist Robert Whittaker is the first to propose a five-kingdom taxonomic classification of the world's biota. The five kingdoms are Animalia, Plantae, Fungi, Protista and Monera.

1973
Konrad Lorenz, Niko Tinbergen, and Karl von Frisch are jointly awarded the Nobel Prize for their studies in animal behavior.

2000

1990
Carl Woese introduces the three-domain system that groups cellular life-forms into Archaea, Bacteria, and Eukaryote domains.

? Inquiry
Visit ConnectED for this unit's **STEM** activity.

Graphs

Polar bears are one of the largest land mammals. They hunt for food on ice packs that stretch across the Arctic Ocean. Recently, ice in the Arctic has not been as thick as it has been in the past. In addition, the ice does not cover as much area as it used to, making it difficult for polar bears to hunt. Scientists collect data about how these changes in the ice affect polar bear populations. One well-studied population of polar bears is on Wrangel Island, Russia, shown in **Figure 1.** Scientists collect and study data on polar bears to draw conclusions and make predictions about a possible polar bear extinction. Scientists often use graphs to better understand data. A **graph** is a type of chart that shows relationships between variables. Scientists use graphs to visually organize and summarize data. You can use different types of graphs to present different kinds of data.

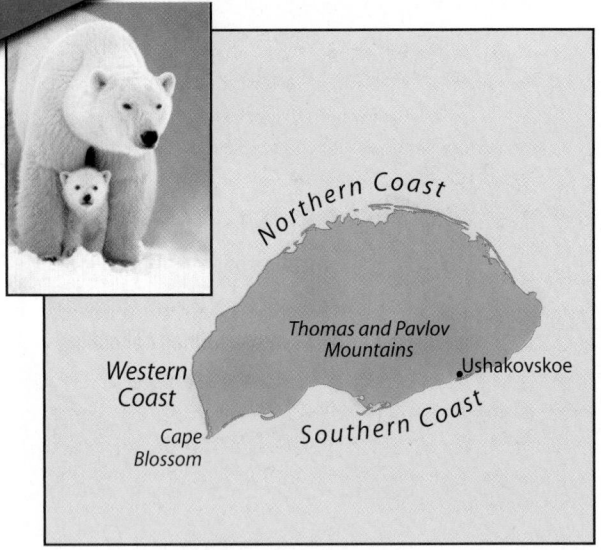

Figure 1 Scientists collect data about polar bears on Wrangel Island, Russia.

Types of Graphs

Bar Graphs

The horizontal *x*-axis on a bar graph often contains categories rather than measurements. The heights of the bars show the measured quantity. For example, the *x*-axis on this bar graph contains different locations on Wrangel Island. The heights of the bars show how many bears researchers observed. The different colors show the age categories of polar bears. Where were ten adult polar bears observed?

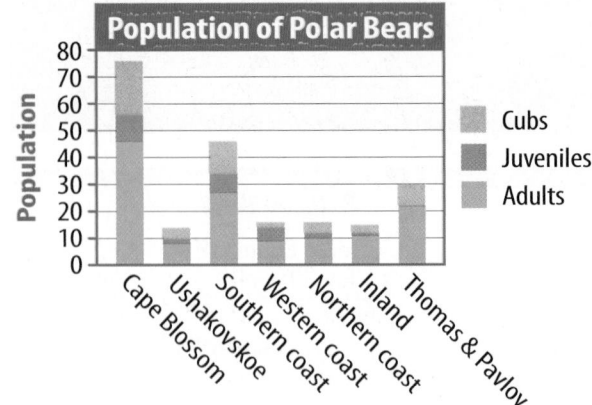

Circle Graphs

A circle graph usually illustrates the percentage of each category of data as it relates to the whole. This circle graph shows the percentage of different age categories of polar bears on Wrangel Island. Adults, shown by the blue color, make up the largest percentage of the total population. This circle graph contains similar data to the bar graph but presents it in a different way. What percentage of the total polar bear population are cubs?

Age Distribution of Polar Bears

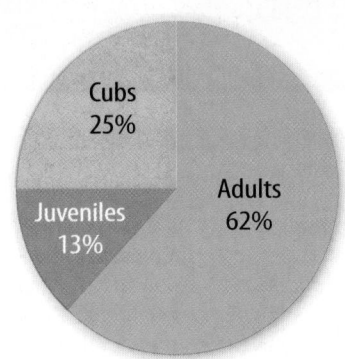

What can graphs tell you about polar bears?

A colleague gives you some data she collected about polar bears on Wrangel Island. She observed the condition of bears near Cape Blossom and classified the bears as starving, average, or healthy. She also recorded the age category of each bear. What can you learn by graphing these data?

1 Make a bar graph of the number of bears in each category that are starving, in average condition, or healthy.

2 Add the numbers of starving bears. Add the total number of bears. Divide the number of starving

	Starving	Average	Healthy
Adult	3	11	14
Juvenile	4	33	13
Cub	3	12	6

bears by the total number of bears and multiply by 100 to calculate the percentage of starving bears. Repeat the calculations to find the percentages of average-condition and healthy bears. Make a circle graph showing the different conditions of the bears. For more information on how to make circle graphs, go to the Science Skill Handbook in the back of your book.

Analyze and Conclude

1. **Analyze** On your bar graph, indicate how you can tell which age category of bears is the healthiest.

2. **Determine** What group of bears do you think left the most walrus carcasses? Explain.

Line Graphs

A line graph helps you analyze how a change in one variable affects another variable. Scientists on Wrangel Island counted all the polar bears on the island each year for 10 years. They plotted each year of the survey on the horizontal x-axis and the bear population on the vertical y-axis. The population decreased between years 2 and 4. It increased between years 6 and 8. How did the population change during the last three years of the survey?

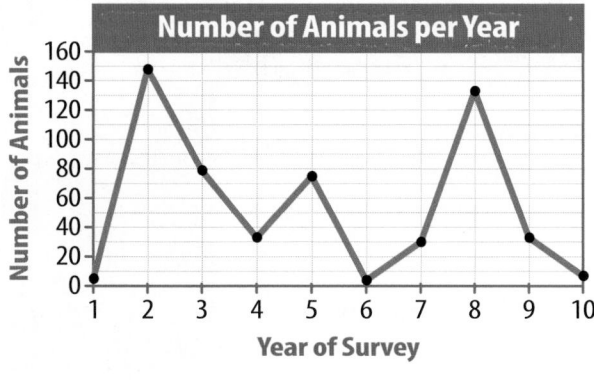

Double Line Graphs

You can use a double line graph to compare relationships of two sets of data. The blue line represents the population of polar bears. The orange line represents the number of walrus carcasses found on Wrangel Island. You can see that the blue and orange lines follow a similar pattern. This tells scientists that these two sets of data are related. Walruses are an important food source for polar bears on the island.

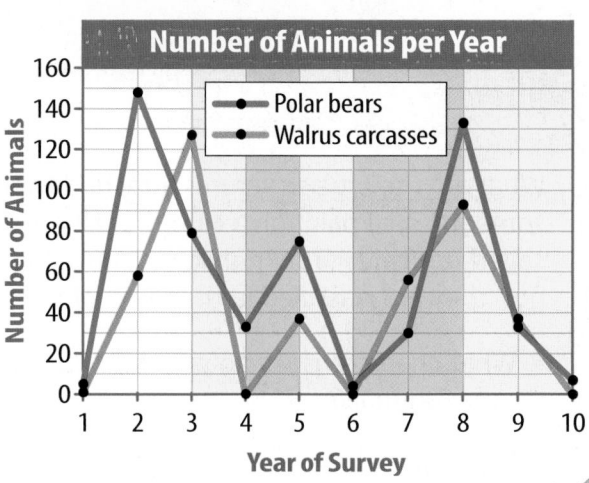

Chapter 11

Animal Diversity

THE BIG IDEA

What are the major groups of animals, and how do they differ?

Inquiry **Are these animals?**

What are the blue structures attached to these underwater rocks? Did someone spill paint on a clump of algae? This is a colony of animals called tunicates (TEW nuh kayts), also known as sea squirts. Believe it or not, they are classified in the same phylum as humans.

- What characteristics do you think tunicates have in common with other animals?

- How do tunicates differ from other animals?

Get Ready to Read

What do you think?

Before you read, decide if you agree or disagree with each of these statements. As you read this chapter, see if you change your mind about any of the statements.

1. All animals digest food.

2. Corals and jellyfish belong to the same phylum.

3. Most animals have backbones.

4. All worms belong to the same phylum.

5. All chordates have backbones.

6. Reptiles have three-chambered hearts.

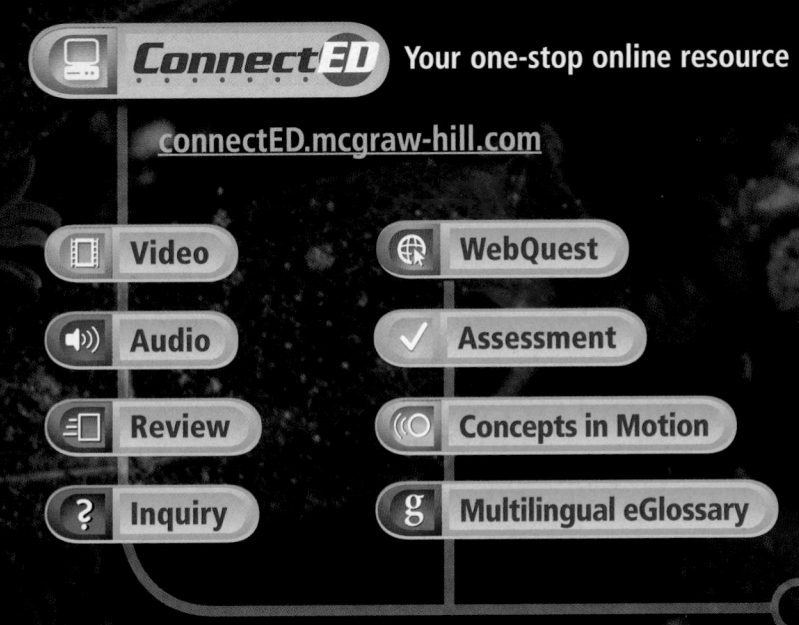

ConnectED Your one-stop online resource

connectED.mcgraw-hill.com

- Video
- Audio
- Review
- Inquiry
- WebQuest
- Assessment
- Concepts in Motion
- Multilingual eGlossary

Lesson 1

Reading Guide

Key Concepts
ESSENTIAL QUESTIONS

- What characteristics do all animals have?
- How are animals classified?

Vocabulary

vertebrate p. 376

invertebrate p. 376

radial symmetry p. 377

bilateral symmetry p. 377

asymmetry p. 377

g Multilingual eGlossary

What defines an animal?

Inquiry A Pair of Leaves?

What kind of organism is shown in this photo? Although they might look like leaves, they are butterflies, a type of animal. What makes leaves and butterflies different? All animals share some characteristics that leaves do not.

What does an animal look like?

Have you ever seen an animal that looks like a vase? How about an animal that looks just like a twig? There are even some animals that look like alien spaceships. The forms that animals take are almost as varied as your imagination.

1. Look at a **photograph of an animal.** Without showing the picture to your partner, describe the animal in as much detail as possible.

2. Have your partner draw the animal using your description as a guide.

3. Compare the drawing to the photograph.

Think About This

1. Could someone looking at the drawing identify it as the same animal in the photograph? Why or why not?

2. **Key Concept** What characteristics do you think you and the animal you described have in common?

Animal Characteristics

When you look at an animal, what do you expect to see? Would you expect every animal to have legs and eyes? Ants and birds have legs, but the snake in **Figure 1** does not. Snails, spiders, and many other animals have eyes, but jellyfish do not. Although animals have many traits that make them unique, all animals have certain characteristics in common. Members of the Kingdom Animalia have the following characteristics:

• Animals are multicellular and eukaryotes.

• Animal cells are specialized for different functions, such as digestion, reproduction, vision, or taste.

• Animals have a protein, called collagen (KAHL uh juhn), that surrounds the cells and helps them keep their shape.

• Animals get energy for life processes by eating other organisms.

• Animals, such as the snake in **Figure 1,** digest their food.

In addition to the characteristics above, most animals reproduce sexually and are capable of movement at some point in their lives.

Figure 1 The snake began digesting its prey even before it finished swallowing.

Key Concept Check What characteristics do all animals have?

Animal Classification

Scientists have described and named more than 1.5 million species of animals. Every year, thousands more are added to that number. Many scientists estimate that Earth is home to millions of animal species that no one has discovered—at least, not yet. What might happen if you discovered an animal no one else had ever seen? How would you begin to classify it?

Vertebrates and Invertebrates

You could start classifying an animal by finding out if the animal has a backbone. Animals can be grouped into two large categories: vertebrates (VUR tuh brayts) and invertebrates (ihn VUR tuh brayts). *A* **vertebrate** *is an animal with a backbone.* Fish, humans, and the lizard shown in **Figure 2** are examples of vertebrates. *An* **invertebrate** *is an animal that does not have a backbone.* Worms, spiders, snails, crayfish, and insects are examples of invertebrates. Invertebrates make up most of the animal kingdom—about 95 percent.

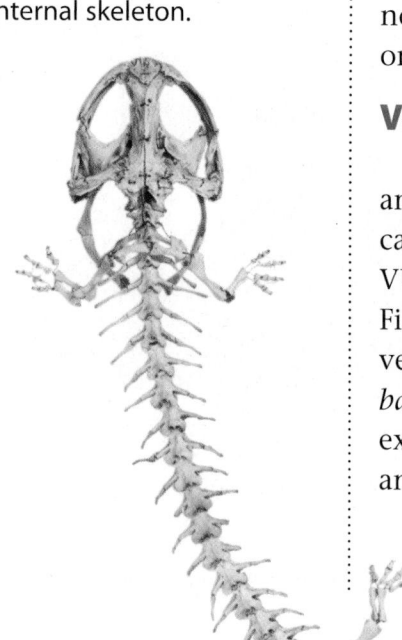

Figure 2 A backbone, or spine, is part of a vertebrate's internal skeleton.

✓ **Reading Check** What is the difference between a vertebrate and an invertebrate?

Inquiry MiniLab

15 minutes

What is this animal?

Biologists use many characteristics to classify animals. A dichotomous key helps you identify animals based on differences in characteristics. Use the dichotomous key to identify different animals.

1 Obtain a set of **animal pictures.** Follow the dichotomous key at right to identify each animal in the set.

Analyze and Conclude

1. **Observe** How many steps were there in the dichotomous key? How many organisms did you identify? What is the relationship between the number of steps in the dichotomous key and the number of animals identified?

2. **Explain** Were you uncertain about the identification of any animal? How did you decide on its identification?

1a. has a backbone	puffer fish
1b. does not have a backbone	go to step 2
2a. has bilateral symmetry	nudibranch
2b. has radial symmetry	go to step 3
3a. has spines	go to step 4
3b. does not have spines	ctenophore
4a. spherical shape	sea urchin
4b. cylindrical shape	sea cucumber

3. 🔑 **Key Concept** What characteristics did you use to classify each organism?

Figure 3 Animals can be classified as having radial symmetry, bilateral symmetry, or asymmetry.

✓ **Visual Check** What kind of symmetry does a bird have?

Radial symmetry

Bilateral symmetry

Asymmetry

Symmetry

Another step you could take to classify an animal is to determine what kind of symmetry it has. As shown in **Figure 3,** symmetry describes an organism's body plan. Symmetry can help identify the phylum to which an animal belongs.

An animal with **radial symmetry** *can be divided into two parts that are nearly mirror images of each other anywhere through its central axis.* A radial animal has a top and a bottom but no head or tail. It can be divided along more than one plane and still have two nearly identical halves. Examples include jellyfish, sea stars, and sea anemones.

An animal with **bilateral symmetry** *can be divided into two parts that are nearly mirror images of each other.* Examples include birds, mammals, reptiles, worms, and insects.

An animal with **asymmetry** *cannot be divided into any two parts that are nearly mirror images of each other.* An asymmetrical animal, such as the sponge in **Figure 3,** does not have a symmetrical body plan.

✓ **Reading Check** What is bilateral symmetry?

WORD ORIGIN ··········

bilateral
from Latin *bi-*, means "two" and *latus*, means "side"

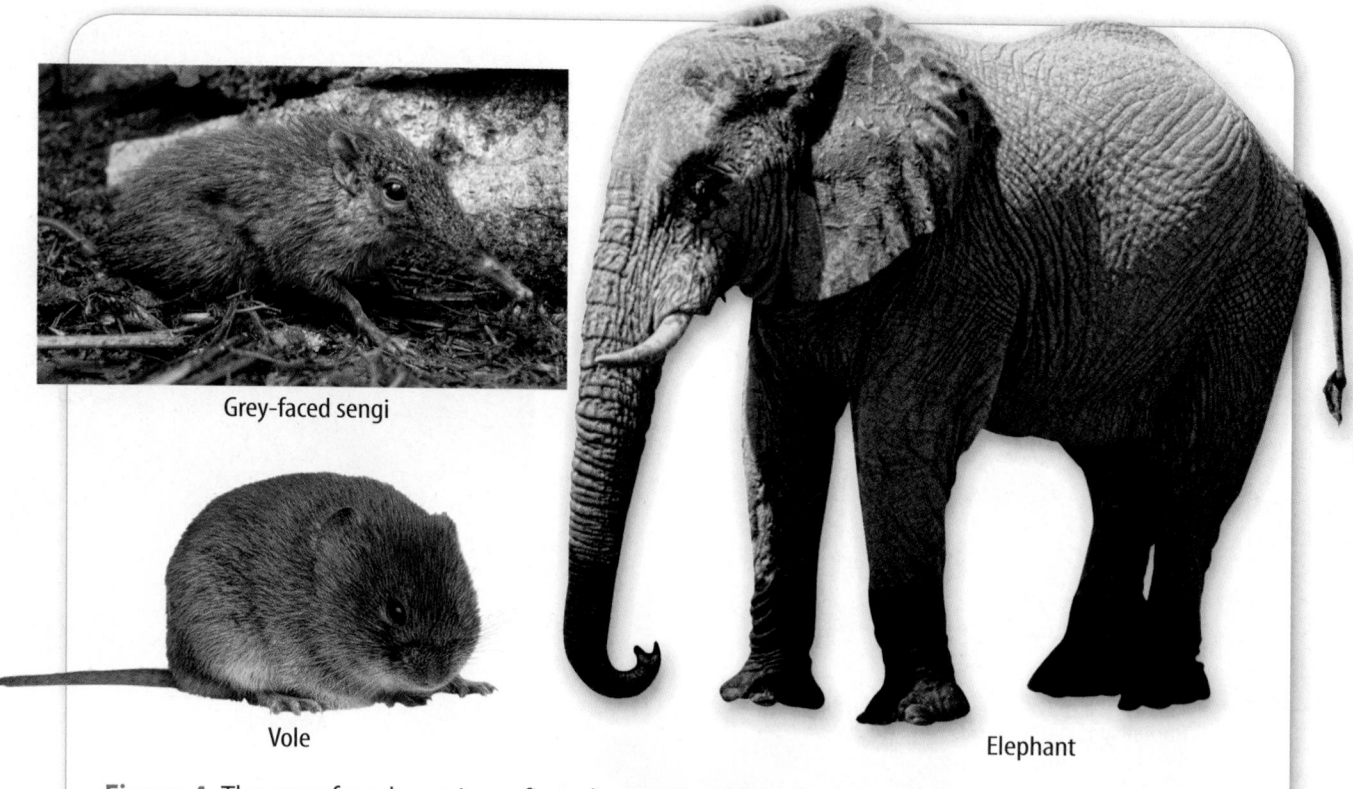

Grey-faced sengi

Vole

Elephant

Figure 4 The grey-faced sengi was first observed in Africa in 2006. Sengis look like voles, but molecular evidence shows that they are more closely related to elephants.

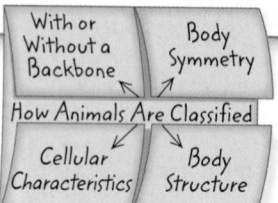

FOLDABLES®

Make a small horizontal four-door book. Leave a 1-cm space between the tabs. Draw arrows and label the book as shown. Use it to record your notes about the classification of animals.

Molecular Classification

Molecules such as DNA, RNA, and proteins in an animal's cells also can be used for classification. For example, scientists can compare the DNA from two animals to determine if they are related. The more similar the DNA, the more closely the animals are related.

Molecular classification has led to new discoveries about relationships among species. Scientists used to classify the grey-faced sengi shown in **Figure 4** as a close relative of shrews and voles. Recently, molecular evidence has shown that sengis are more closely related to elephants and aardvarks.

Key Concept Check How are animals classified?

Major Phyla

Scientists classify the members of the animal kingdom into as many as 35 phyla (singular, phylum). The nine major phyla, shown in **Figure 5,** contain 95–99 percent of all animal species. Animals belonging to the same phylum have similar body structures and other characteristics. For example, all sponges (the phylum Porifera [puh RIH fuh ruh]) have asymmetry, and their cells do not form tissues. Only one animal phylum, Chordata (kor DAH tuh), contains vertebrates, also shown in **Figure 5.** The other major phyla contain only invertebrates.

Phylum Annelida
(earthworms, leeches, marine worms)

Phylum Arthropoda
(insects, spiders, shrimp, crabs)

Phylum Chordata
(tunicates, lancelets, vertebrates)

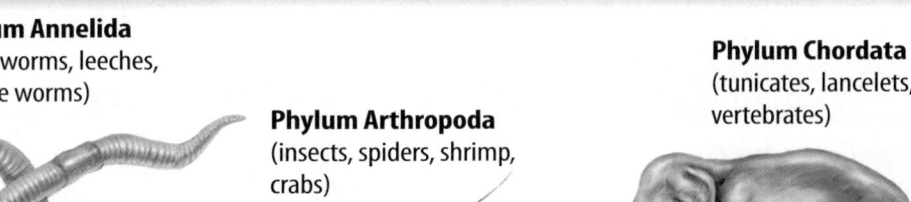

Phylum Mollusca
(snails, slugs, clams, mussels, octopi, squid)

Phylum Echinodermata
(sea stars, sea urchins, sea cucumbers)

Phylum Nematoda
(roundworms)

Phylum Platyhelminthes
(flatworms)

Phylum Cnidaria
(jellyfish, sea anemones, corals)

KINGDOM ANIMALIA
(classified according to body plan)

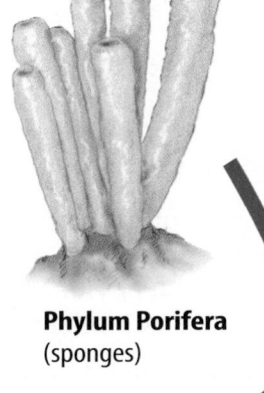

Phylum Porifera
(sponges)

Figure 5 Most animals can be classified in one of nine major phyla.

Visual Check What are the major phyla of animals?

Lesson 1 Review

Visual Summary

All animals share a series of characteristics.

Animals can be classified in several ways.

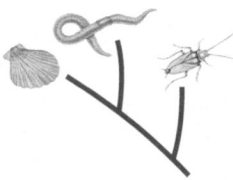

Animal classifications are always changing based on advanced technology.

FOLDABLES

Use your lesson Foldable to review the lesson. Save your Foldable for the project at the end of the chapter.

What do you think NOW?

You first read the statements below at the beginning of the chapter.

1. All animals digest food.

2. Corals and jellyfish belong to the same phylum.

Did you change your mind about whether you agree or disagree with the statements? Rewrite any false statements to make them true.

Use Vocabulary

1. **Define** *asymmetry*.

2. **Distinguish** between vertebrate and invertebrate animals.

3. **Compare and contrast** radial symmetry and bilateral symmetry.

Understand Key Concepts

4. **List** the characteristics that all animals have in common.

5. Which characteristic applies to a horse?
   A. asymmetry
   B. invertebrate
   C. spherical
   D. vertebrate

Interpret Graphics

6. **Classify** each object below as having bilateral symmetry, radial symmetry, or asymmetry.

7. **Summarize Information** Copy the graphic organizer below, and use it to summarize the ways animals can be separated into groups.

Critical Thinking

8. **Develop** a series of instructions that could be used to determine if an animal should be classified in the phylum Arthropoda, Echinodermata, or Chordata.

9. **Analyze** how the classification of the grey-faced sengi changed over time. How might technological advances change how other animals are classified?

A Family Tree for Bats

Meet Nancy Simmons, a taxonomist who identifies bats.

When most people are going to bed, taxonomist Nancy Simmons is going to work. She's off to capture bats in a dense rain forest of South America. Because bats are most active at night, she and her team from the American Museum of Natural History work from dusk until dawn. They must capture, identify, and release the bats while it's dark.

Taxonomists study animals to see how they are related to each other and use that information to classify them. To classify a bat, Simmons carefully examines its body. She looks at characteristics such as wing size, fur color, and the shape of the bat's teeth. These characteristics help her classify each bat into a family or a group that shares physical features and behaviors.

In 1999 Dr. Simmons added a new member to the bat family tree. In the rain forest in Peru, her team discovered a species they named *Micronycteris matses,* the Matses' big-eared bat. Like other species in its genus, *M. matses* is small with large round ears, a long snout, and a fold of skin on its nose called a nose-leaf. *M. matses* is unique, however, because of its combination of dark brown fur, medium body size, small bottom front teeth, and short fur around its ears.

Dr. Simmons is looking for links between *M. matses* and other bat species. She compares their bodies, behavior, and even their DNA. Her goal is to create a family tree for all bats. With over a thousand species of bats worldwide, Dr. Simmons has plenty of work still to do.

All Kinds of Bats

Bats live on every continent except Antarctica, in areas ranging from tropical rain forests to chilly mountaintops. They also have an amazing variety of shapes and sizes. With over 1,100 species, bats make up one-fifth of the world's mammals.

Simmons holds a bat that she caught in her net.

▲ This species is the largest in the New World—it weighs about 150 g.

It's Your Turn

RESEARCH Investigate a species of bat in your area. Record where it lives in the environment and its characteristics, such as wingspan, fur color, and weight. With a partner, compare your bats. What do they have in common? What is different?

Lesson 2

Reading Guide

Key Concepts
ESSENTIAL QUESTIONS

- What are the characteristics of invertebrates?
- How do the invertebrate phyla differ?

Vocabulary

exoskeleton p. 387

appendage p. 387

 Multilingual eGlossary

Video **BrainPOP®**

Invertebrate Phyla

Inquiry **How did it get there?**

This octopus is alive and got inside the bottle by slowly pushing its soft, flexible body inside. Like many invertebrates, an octopus does not have a skeleton made of bone or other hard structures.

What does an invertebrate look like?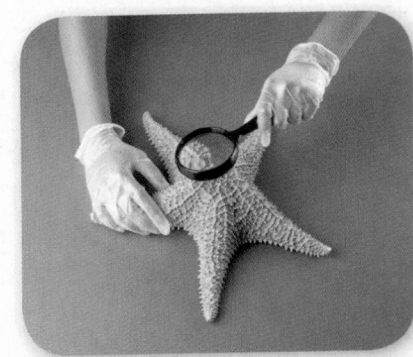

Some invertebrates have features that are similar to yours, such as eyes and legs. Others have little in common with you. What do you see when you look at invertebrates close-up?

1 Read and complete a lab safety form.

2 Examine a **collection of invertebrates,** and record your observations in your Science Journal.

3 Use a **magnifying lens** to further examine the invertebrates. Record any additional observations.

4 Make a Venn diagram in your Science Journal to compare similarities and contrast differences among the invertebrates.

Think About This

1. Which two invertebrates were the most dissimilar? Why?

2. Did you see any details using a magnifying lens that you missed by looking just with your eyes?

3. **Key Concept** What characteristics do you think all the invertebrates you looked at have in common?

Characteristics of Invertebrates

Can you imagine living without a backbone? Most animals do just that. As you have read, invertebrates are animals that lack a backbone. In most cases, invertebrates have no **internal** structures to help support their bodies. They also tend to be smaller and move more slowly than vertebrates. As shown in **Figure 6,** over 95 percent of all animal species that have been recorded are invertebrates.

You probably could recognize a jellyfish or a clam if you saw one. What about an anemone or a sea cucumber? Invertebrates are a diverse group. Their physical characteristics range from the simple structures of sponges and jellyfish to the more complex bodies of worms, snails, and insects. Each invertebrate phylum contains animals with similar body plans and physical characteristics.

Key Concept Check What are the characteristics of invertebrates?

ACADEMIC VOCABULARY

internal
(adjective) existing inside something

Invertebrate and Vertebrate Species

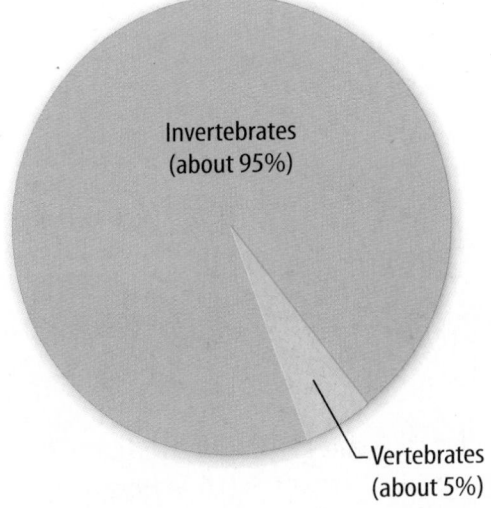

Invertebrates (about 95%)

Vertebrates (about 5%)

Figure 6 Invertebrates make up more than 95 percent of all living species on Earth.

Sponges and Cnidarians

The simplest of the invertebrates are the sponges, which belong to the phylum Porifera. All sponges share several characteristics.

All sponges are asymmetrical and have no tissues, organs, or organ systems. Their cells are specialized for capturing food, digestion, and reproduction. Other cells provide support inside the layers of the sponge. All sponges live in water, and most species live in ocean environments.

The phylum Cnidaria (ni DAR ee uh) includes jellyfish, sea anemones, hydras, and corals. Cnidarians, such as the sea anemone shown in **Figure 7,** differ from all other animals based on their unique characteristics.

Cnidarians have no organs or organ systems, but, unlike sponges, they have radial symmetry. They have a single body opening surrounded by tentacles. Simple tissues, including muscles, nerves, and digestive tissue, enable cnidarians to survive by moving, reacting to stimuli, and digesting food. They have specialized cells, called nematocysts (NE mah toh sihsts), that are used for defense and capturing food. Similar to sponges, most species of cnidarians live in ocean environments, and all live in water.

✓ **Reading Check** What characteristics do poriferans and cnidarians share?

Figure 7 The tentacles of all cnidarians contain stinging structures for capturing food and defending against predators.

Cnidarians have a single body opening surrounded by tentacles.

Cnidarians are radially symmetrical.

Nematocyst

Flatworms and Roundworms

Flatworms are invertebrates that belong to the phylum Platyhelminthes (pla tih hel MIHN theez). All flatworms, including the tapeworm shown in **Figure 8,** have bilateral symmetry with nerve, muscle, and digestive tissues and a simple brain. They have soft and flattened bodies that are usually only a few cells thick. The digestive system of a flatworm has only one opening: a mouth.

Flatworms live in moist environments. Most, like tapeworms, are parasites that live in or on the bodies of other organisms and rely on them for food. Others are free-living, and many live in oceans or other marine environments.

 Reading Check What characteristics do all flatworms share?

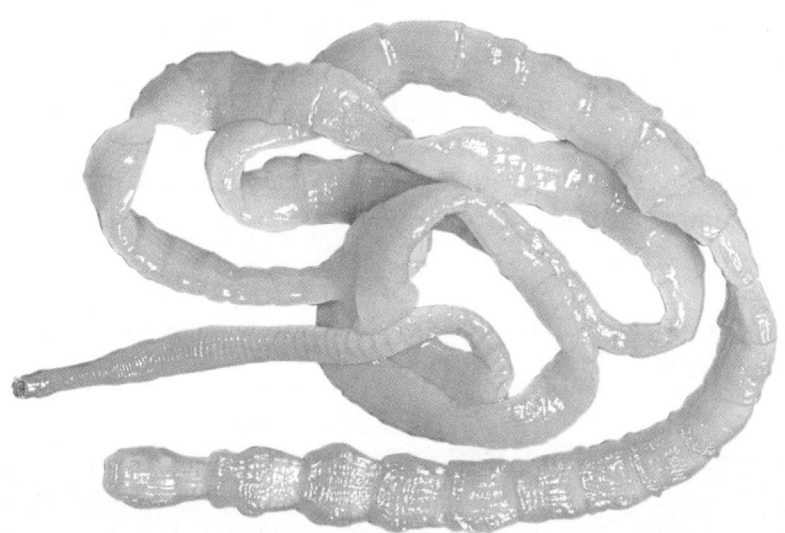

◀ **Figure 8** Most flatworm species, including this tapeworm, are parasites. They depend on other organisms for food and a place to live.

Visual Check How would you describe a flatworm's body?

Roundworms, also called nematodes, belong to the phylum Nematoda (ne muh TOH duh). Roundworms, like flatworms, have bilateral symmetry with nerve, muscle, and digestive tissues and a simple brain. However, unlike flatworms, their bodies are round and covered with a stiff outer covering called a cuticle. A roundworm's digestive system has two openings: a mouth and an anus. Food enters the mouth and is digested as it travels to the anus where wastes are excreted.

Roundworms live in moist environments. Some species are parasites that live in animals' digestive systems. Free-living roundworms such as the one pictured in **Figure 9** eat material such as fecal matter and dead organisms.

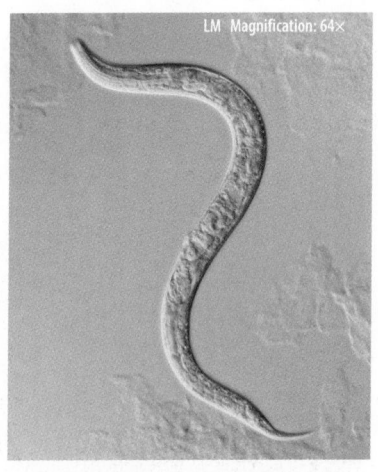

LM Magnification: 64×

▲ **Figure 9** Roundworms are narrow and tapered at both ends. Most species are less than 1 mm long.

Reading Check How do flatworms and roundworms differ?

Mollusks and Annelids

The phylum Mollusca (mah LUS kuh) includes snails, slugs, clams, mussels, octopi, and squid. All mollusks, including the snail shown in **Figure 10,** have bilateral symmetry. Their bodies are soft, and some species have hard shells that protect their bodies. You might have seen a slug slithering along the ground after a rainstorm. Slugs are one type of mollusk without a shell.

Mollusks have digestive systems with two openings. A body cavity contains the heart, the stomach, and other organs. The mollusk circulatory system contains blood, but no blood vessels. Their nervous systems include eyes and other sensory organs as well as simple brains. Members of this phylum must remain wet and live in water or moist environments.

The phylum Annelida includes earthworms, leeches, and marine worms. Annelid worms, including the one shown in **Figure 11,** have bilateral symmetry and soft bodies. Their bodies consist of repeating segments covered with a thin cuticle. Their digestive systems have two openings. Annelids have circulatory systems that are made up of blood vessels that carry blood throughout the body. Their nervous systems include a simple brain. Annelids live in water or moist environments such as soil.

Reading Check What do mollusks and segmented worms have in common?

▲ **Figure 10** Snails have shells that protect their bodies.

Figure 11 One characteristic that distinguishes annelids from other worms is their segments. ▼

Visual Check How does this annelid differ from an earthworm?

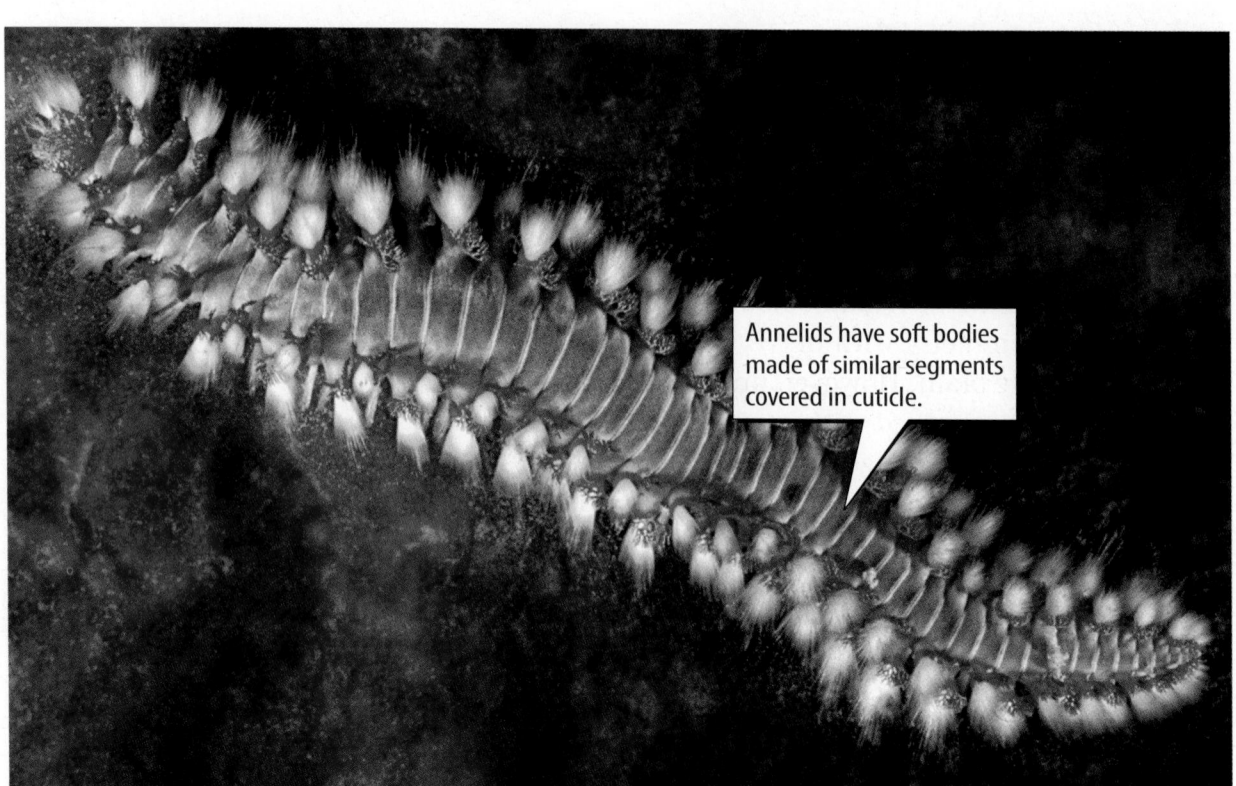

Annelids have soft bodies made of similar segments covered in cuticle.

Arthropods

The phylum Arthropoda includes insects, spiders, shrimp, crabs, and their relatives. More species belong to this phylum than all the other animal phyla combined. There are more than 1 million identified species of arthropods.

All arthropods have bilateral symmetry. They also have **exoskeletons**—*thick, hard outer coverings that protect and support animals' bodies.* Arthropods have several pairs of jointed appendages. *An* **appendage** *is a structure, such as a leg or an arm, that extends from the central part of the body.* The body parts of arthropods are segmented and specialized for different functions such as flying and eating. Unlike many of the other animals you have read about so far, arthropods live in almost every environment on Earth.

 Reading Check What do exoskeletons do?

Insects

The largest order of arthropods is the insects, which includes the stag beetle shown in **Figure 12.** All insect species have three pairs of jointed legs, three body segments, a pair of antennae, and a pair of compound eyes. Many species also have one or two pairs of wings.

There are 16 major groups of insects. However, most insect species belong to one of five groups. Beetles form the largest group of insects. About 40 percent of all known species of insects are beetles.

WORD ORIGIN · · · · · · · · · · ·

appendage
from Latin *appendere*, means "to cause to hang from"

Figure 12 🔑 A stag beetle has characteristics common to all insect species.

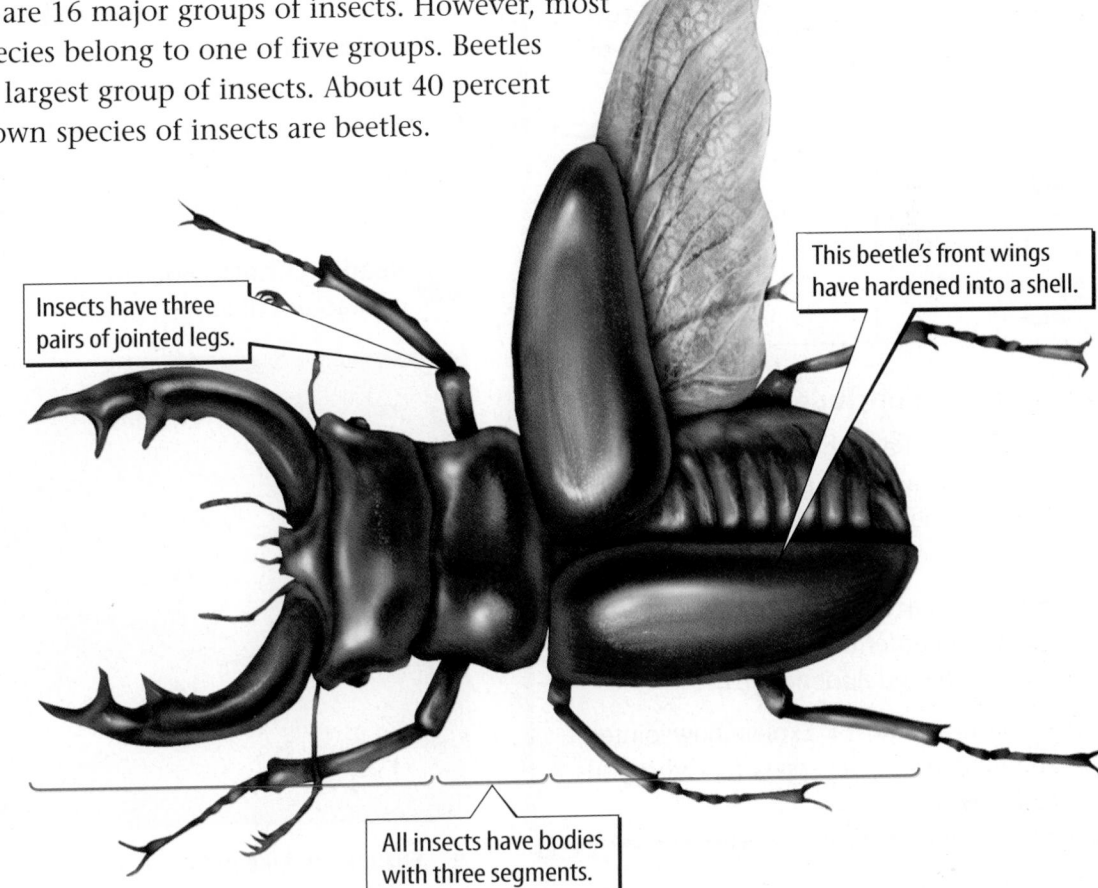

Insects have three pairs of jointed legs.

This beetle's front wings have hardened into a shell.

All insects have bodies with three segments.

How does your arm move?

Both arthropods and mammals have jointed appendages. Try doing some simple tasks without bending your appendages to understand how useful jointed appendages are.

1. Using **newspaper** and **masking tape,** wrap your partner's arms at the elbow so he or she cannot bend them.

2. Ask your partner to perform the tasks in the data table below. Record your observations and your partner's experiences.

Task	Completed? (yes/no)	How was behavior changed?
Walk 5 m.		
Take a drink of water.		
Lay down on the ground and then stand up.		

Analyze and Conclude

1. **Summarize** Rank the tasks in order from hardest to easiest to perform without jointed appendages. What made the tasks harder to perform?

2. **Infer** What activities that you must perform in order to survive are impossible without jointed appendages?

3. **Key Concept** Explain how jointed appendages are necessary for arthropods to survive.

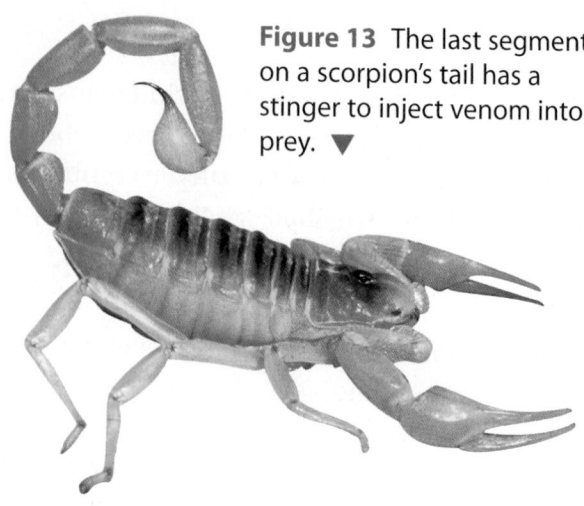

Figure 13 The last segment on a scorpion's tail has a stinger to inject venom into prey. ▼

Arachnids

Spiders, ticks, and scorpions, such as the one shown in **Figure 13,** are arachnids (uh RAK nudz). All arachnids have four pairs of jointed legs and two body segments. They do not have antennae or wings.

Crustaceans

Crabs, shrimp, lobsters, and their close relatives are crustaceans (krus TAY shunz). All crustaceans have one or two pairs of antennae. They also have jointed appendages in the mouth area that are specialized for biting and crushing food. Many people like to eat crustaceans, including lobsters and crabs, such as the one shown in **Figure 14.**

Reading Check How do arachnids and crustaceans differ?

▲ **Figure 14** Like most crustaceans, this crab's eyes are on stalks.

Echinoderms

The phylum Echinodermata (ih kin uh DUR muh tuh) includes sea stars, sea cucumbers, and sea urchins, such as the one shown in **Figure 15**. *Echinoderm* (ih KI nuh durm) means "spiny skin." Echinoderms have some unique features that are not in any of the other invertebrate phyla. They also are more closely related to vertebrates than to any other phyla.

All echinoderms have radial symmetry. Unlike any other phyla, echinoderms have hard plates embedded in the skin that support the body. Thousands of small, muscular, fluid-filled tubes, called tube feet, enable them to move and feed. They also have complete digestive systems including a mouth and an anus. Echinoderms live only in oceans. However, some can survive out of the water for short periods during low tides.

 Key Concept Check How do the invertebrate phyla differ?

Figure 15 Sea urchins are one type of echinoderm.

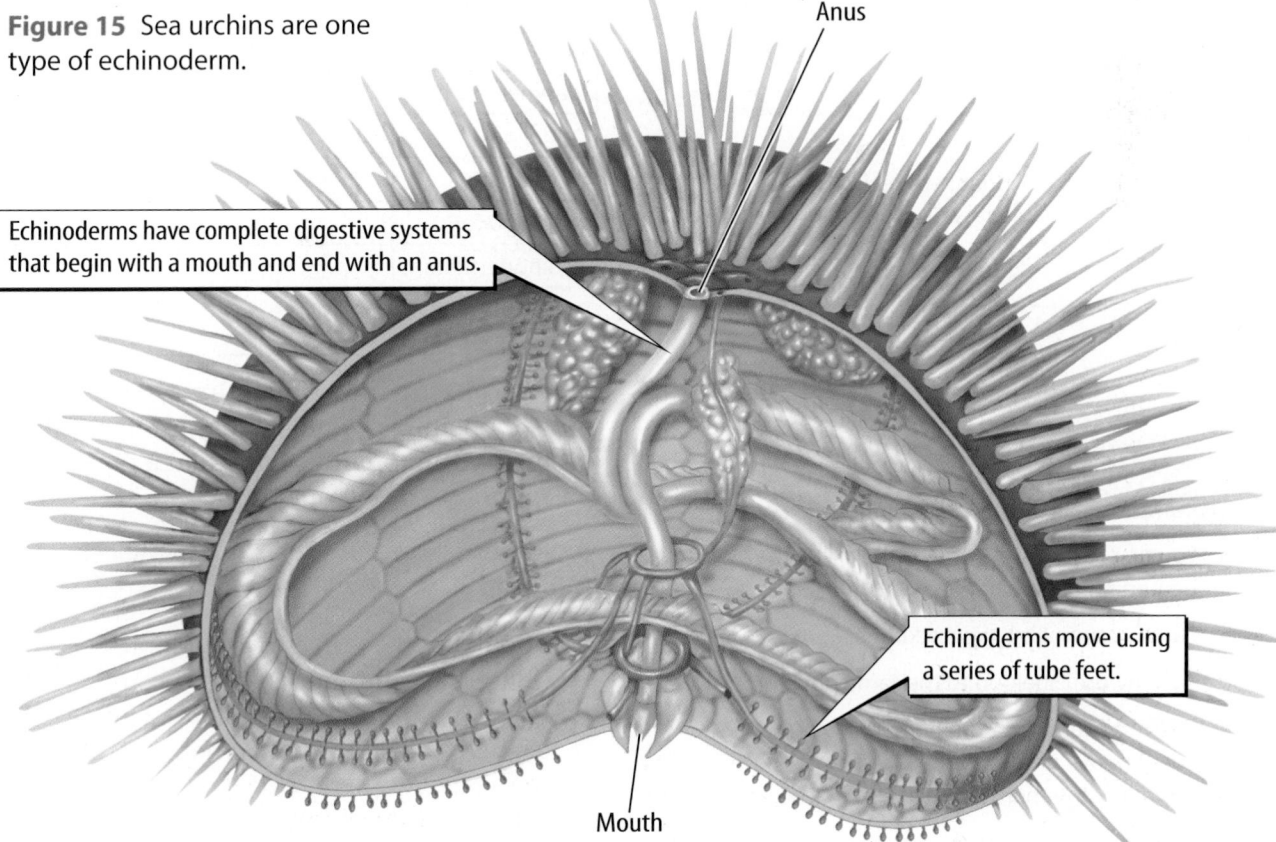

Anus

Echinoderms have complete digestive systems that begin with a mouth and end with an anus.

Echinoderms move using a series of tube feet.

Mouth

Lesson 2 Review

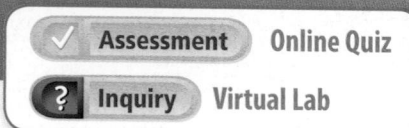
Visual Summary

Most invertebrates have no internal structures that support their bodies.

There are more arthropods than members of any other phyla.

The largest order of arthropods is the insects.

FOLDABLES

Use your lesson Foldable to review the lesson. Save your Foldable for the project at the end of the chapter.

What do you think NOW?

You first read the statements below at the beginning of the chapter.

3. Most animals have backbones.

4. All worms belong to the same phylum.

Did you change your mind about whether you agree or disagree with the statements? Rewrite any false statements to make them true.

Use Vocabulary

1. **Define** *exoskeleton*.

2. **Distinguish** between the phylum Platyhelminthes and the phylum Nematoda.

3. **Use the term** *appendage* in a sentence.

Understand Key Concepts

4. Which phylum contains asymmetrical invertebrates that have no tissues?
   - **A.** Annelida
   - **B.** Cnidaria
   - **C.** Echinodermata
   - **D.** Porifera

5. **Describe** the characteristics of the phylum that contains invertebrates with wings.

Interpret Graphics

6. **Summarize Information** Copy the table below, and fill in the features common to the members of each invertebrate phylum.

Phylum	Characteristics	Example
Porifera		
Cnidaria		
Platyhelminthes		
Annelida		
Nematoda		
Arthropoda		
Echinodermata		

Critical Thinking

7. **Hypothesize** how a digestive system with two openings would enable an organism to absorb more nutrients than a digestive system with one opening.

Math Skills ×÷+ Review
— Math Practice —

8. About 11,000 species of Lepidoptera (butterflies and moths) have been identified in the United States. Only 679 of them are butterflies. What percentage of the Lepidoptera species in the United States are butterflies?

How do you build a dichotomous key?

Materials

invertebrates

magnifying lens

Safety

A dichotomous key helps you classify animals based on their characteristics. *Dichotomous* means "divided in two parts." Each step of the key has two choices. You choose the one that applies to the animal you are studying, and it directs you to the next set of choices. By picking the best choices for an animal's characteristics, you can classify animals in a list of possibilities.

Learn It

Sorting objects into groups based on common features is called **classifying.** When classifying, first observe the objects being classified. Then select one feature that is shared by some, but not all, of the objects. Place all the members that share a feature into a subgroup. You can classify members into smaller and smaller subgroups based on characteristics.

Try It

1. Read and complete a lab safety form.

2. Study your invertebrate collection. You may want to use a magnifying lens. Step 1 of your dichotomous key is to divide your collection into two groups based on a characteristic. Make a table like the one shown below.

Step	Characteristic	"Go to"/ Identity
1.	legs present	step 2
	legs absent	step 3

3. Now think about the subgroup of animals that have the characteristic in step 1. Divide these animals into two smaller subgroups based on another characteristic. Enter this choice in step 2 of your dichotomous key.

4. Suppose only one animal in your collection falls into a subgroup. Place the identity of the animal in the right column of the table.

Step	Characteristic	"Go to"/ Identity
1.	legs present	step 2
	legs absent	step 3
2.	wings present	step 4
	wings absent	pavement ant (*Tetramorium caespitum*)

5. Repeat steps 3–5 until the animals are each in their own subgroup and the dichotomous key leads you to the identity of each animal.

Apply It

6. **Identify** Remove the labels from your animal collection. Trade your collection and your dichotomous key with a classmate. Identify all the animals in your classmate's collection using his or her key. Check your answers.

7. 🔑 **Key Concept** What characteristics did all the animals you identified have in common?

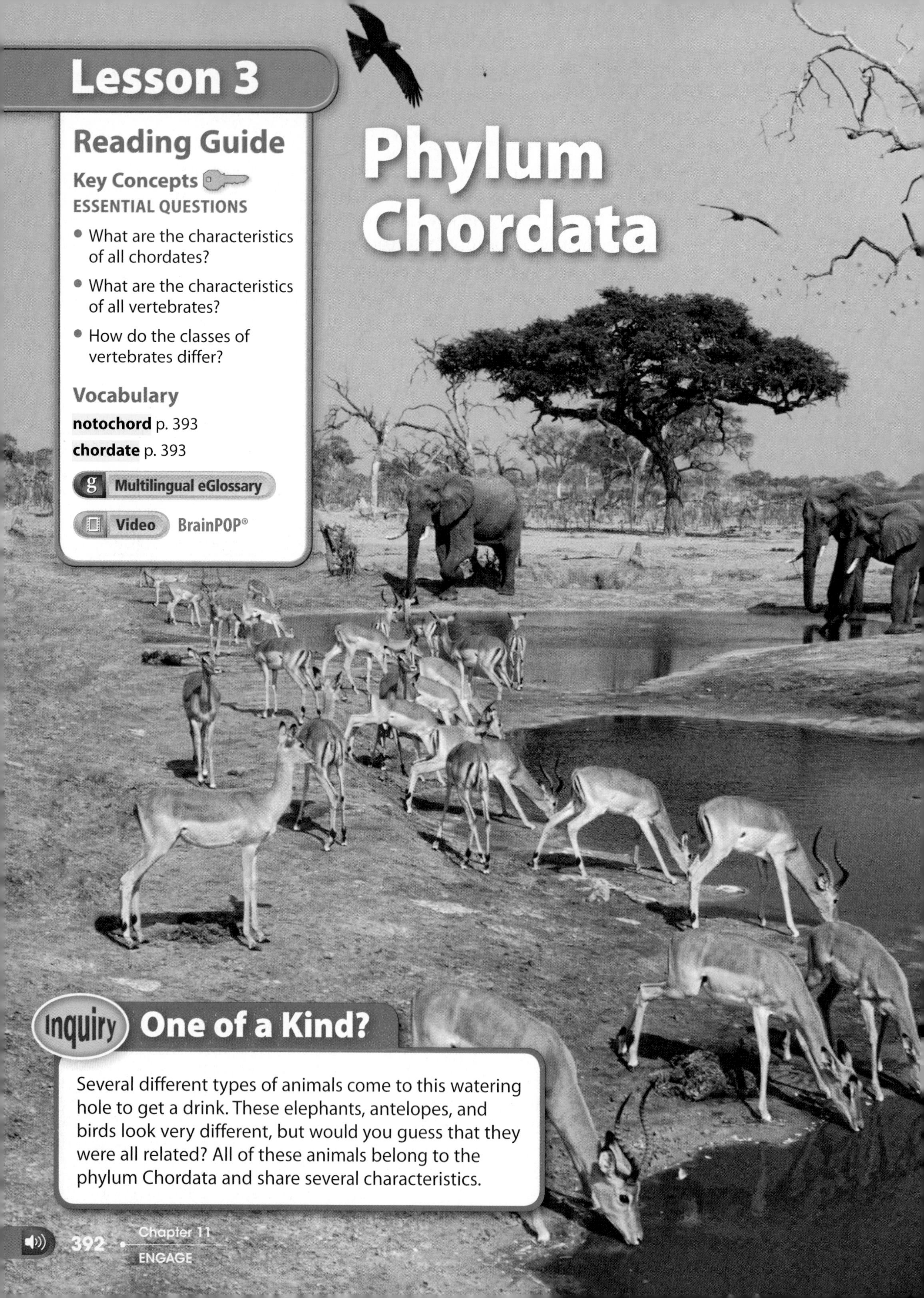

Lesson 3

Phylum Chordata

Reading Guide

Key Concepts
ESSENTIAL QUESTIONS

- What are the characteristics of all chordates?
- What are the characteristics of all vertebrates?
- How do the classes of vertebrates differ?

Vocabulary

notochord p. 393
chordate p. 393

g Multilingual eGlossary

Video BrainPOP®

Inquiry One of a Kind?

Several different types of animals come to this watering hole to get a drink. These elephants, antelopes, and birds look very different, but would you guess that they were all related? All of these animals belong to the phylum Chordata and share several characteristics.

How can you model a backbone?

All vertebrates have backbones. Most backbones are made out of a stack of short bones called vertebrae. Some vertebrae are shaped like discs with holes in the center. The largest structure passing through the center of the stack of vertebrae is the spinal cord. Between each of the vertebrae are padlike structures, called discs, that cushion the bones. Try building a model of a backbone.

1. Read and complete a lab safety form.
2. Obtain **pasta wheels, circular gummy candies,** and a **chenille stem.** ⚠ Do not eat the lab materials.
3. Assemble the materials to make a model of a backbone.
4. Gently bend and move your model backbone. Observe how the parts move and interact with each other.

Think About This

1. When you bend your model backbone, how are the vertebrae, the discs, and the spinal cord affected?

2. When you compress your model backbone, how are the vertebrae, the discs, and the spinal cord affected?

3. **Key Concept** How do you think the structure of the backbone provides advantages to the body plan of vertebrates?

Characteristics of Chordates

Recall that one way to classify an animal is to check for a backbone and that animals with backbones are called vertebrates. Another way to classify animals is to look for the four characteristics of a chordate (KOR dayt). *A* **chordate** *is an animal that has a notochord, a nerve cord, a tail, and structures called pharyngeal* (fer IN jee ul) *pouches at some point in its life.* In vertebrates, these characteristics are present only during embryonic development. *A* **notochord** *is a flexible, rod-shaped structure that supports the body of a developing chordate.* The nerve cord develops into the central nervous system. The pharyngeal pouches are between the mouth and the digestive system.

Most chordates are vertebrates, but the chordates also include two groups of invertebrates: tunicates and lancelets (LAN sluhts), shown in **Figure 16.** Invertebrate chordates are rarely more than a few centimeters long and live in salt water. In vertebrate chordates, such as humans, the notochord develops into a backbone during the growth of an embryo.

Key Concept Check What are the characteristics of chordates?

Figure 16 Lancelets can swim but spend most of their lives almost completely buried in sand.

A lancelet is one type of invertebrate that has a notochord.

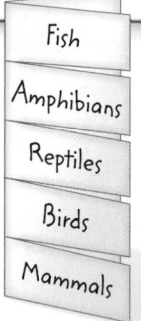
Characteristics of Vertebrates

Recall that all vertebrates have a backbone, also called a spinal column or spine. The backbone is a series of structures that surround and protect the nerve cord, or spinal cord. The spinal cord connects all the nerves in the body to the brain. Bones that form a backbone are called vertebrae (VUR tuh bray). If you gently touch the back of your neck, the bones you feel are some of your vertebrae.

Vertebrates have well-developed organ systems. All vertebrates have digestive systems with two openings, circulatory systems that move blood through the body, and nervous systems that include brains. The five major groups of vertebrates are fish, amphibians, reptiles, birds, and mammals.

Key Concept Check What are the characteristics of all vertebrates?

Fish

Most fish spend their entire lives in water. They have two important characteristics in common: gills for absorbing oxygen gas from water and paired fins for swimming. Fish are grouped into one of three classes.

Hagfish and lampreys lack jaws and are in a group called jawless fish. Sharks, such as the one shown in **Figure 17,** skates, and rays are cartilaginous fish. They have skeletons made of a tough, fibrous tissue called cartilage (KAR tuh lihj). Both jawless and cartilaginous fish have internal structures made of cartilage.

Trout, guppies, perch, tuna, mackerel, and thousands of other species do not have cartilaginous skeletons. Instead, they have bones and are grouped together as bony fish.

Figure 17 Like all fish, sharks have gills and fins.

Structures called gills enable fish to absorb oxygen from the water.

Amphibians

Frogs, toads, and salamanders belong to the class Amphibia, as shown in **Figure 18.** Most **amphibians** spend part of their lives in water and part on land. Their bodies change as they grow older. In many species, the young have different body forms than the adults do.

Amphibians have skeletons made of bone and have legs for movement. Their skin is smooth and moist, and their hearts have three chambers. Amphibians lay eggs that do not have hard protective coverings, or shells. Their eggs must be laid in moist environments, such as ponds. Young live in water and have gills; most adults develop lungs and live on land.

Reading Check How do amphibians differ from fish?

WORD ORIGIN

amphibian
from Greek *amphi-*, means "of both kinds" and *bios*, means "life"

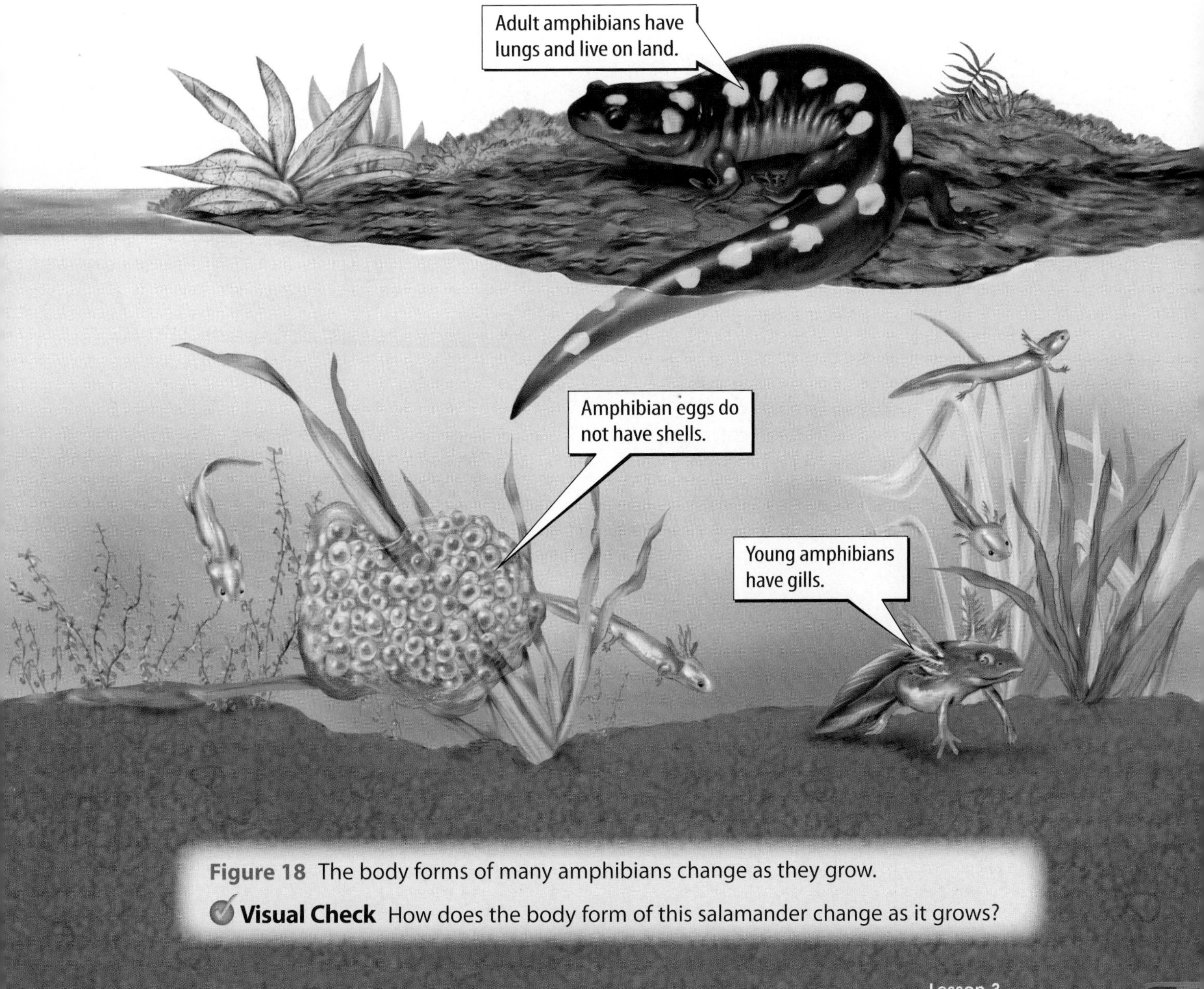
Adult amphibians have lungs and live on land.
Amphibian eggs do not have shells.
Young amphibians have gills.

Figure 18 The body forms of many amphibians change as they grow.

Visual Check How does the body form of this salamander change as it grows?

Science Use v. Common Use

scale

Science Use small, flat plate that forms part of an animal's external covering

Common Use an instrument for measuring the mass of an object

Reptiles

Lizards, snakes, turtles, crocodiles, and alligators belong to the class Reptilia. A leopard gecko, one example of this class, is shown in **Figure 19.**

All reptiles share several characteristics. Their skin is waterproof and covered in **scales.** Like amphibians, most reptiles have three-chambered hearts. Unlike amphibians, lizards and other reptiles have lungs throughout their lives.

Most reptiles lay fluid-filled eggs with leathery shells. Unlike amphibian eggs, reptile eggs are laid on land rather than in water. Young reptiles do not change form as they mature into adult reptiles.

Reading Check How do reptiles differ from amphibians?

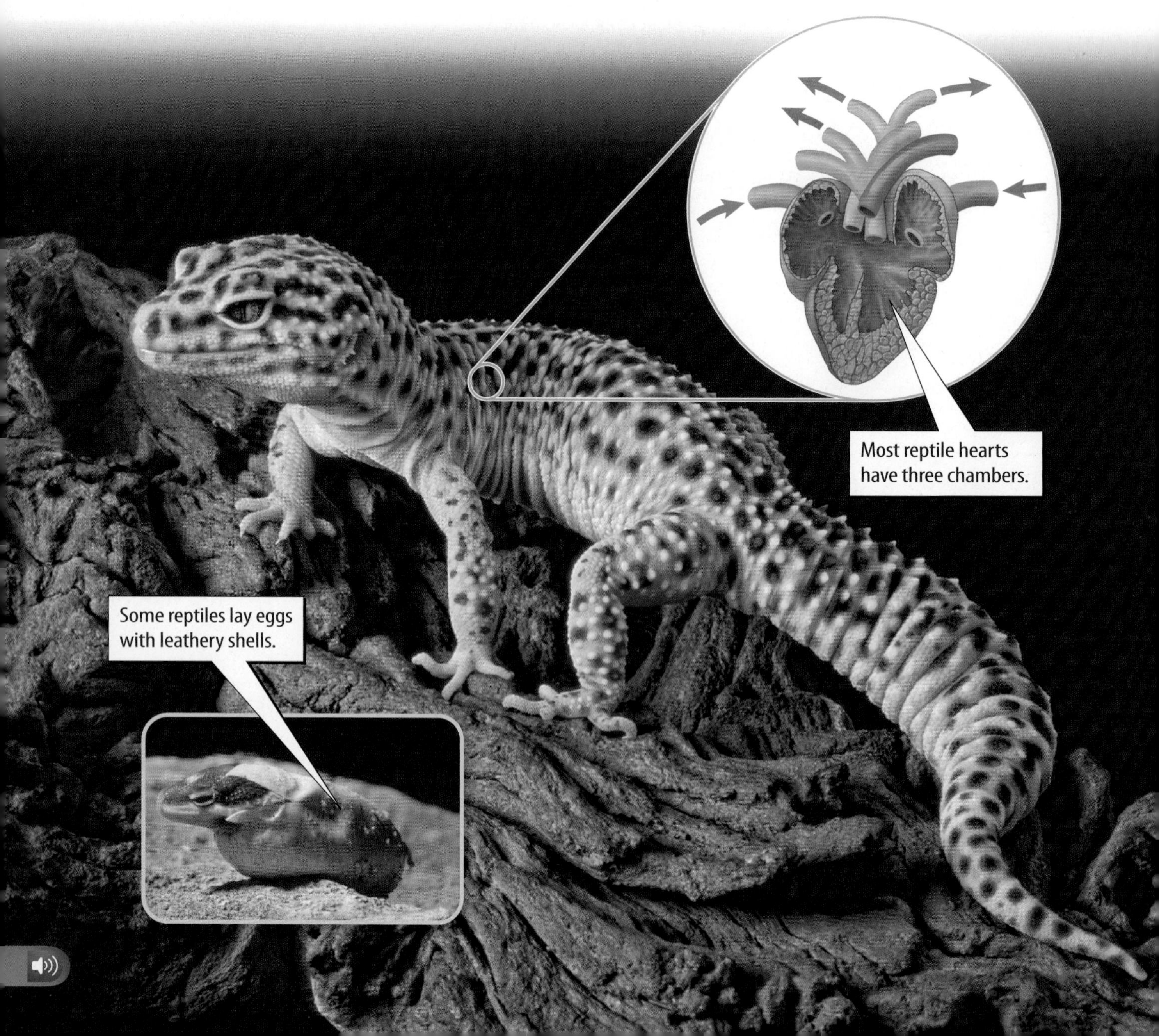
Most reptile hearts have three chambers.
Some reptiles lay eggs with leathery shells.

Figure 19 This lizard has a three-chambered heart and lays fluid-filled eggs.

Birds

All birds, including the owl shown in **Figure 20**, are in the class Aves. Many birds make nests to hold their eggs, and many have unique calls or songs.

Birds have lightweight bones. Their skin is covered with feathers and scales. Birds also have two legs and two wings. Many birds can fly, and they have stiff feathers that enable them to move through the air. Birds that spend a lot of time in the water have oil glands that help water roll off their feathers.

Birds have beaks and do not chew their food. Instead, their digestive systems include gizzards, organs that help grind food into smaller pieces. Their circulatory systems include four-chambered hearts. Birds also lay fluid-filled eggs with hard shells and feed and care for their young.

Reading Check How do birds differ from reptiles?

Figure 20 All birds have several characteristics in common, including lightweight bones and four-chambered hearts.

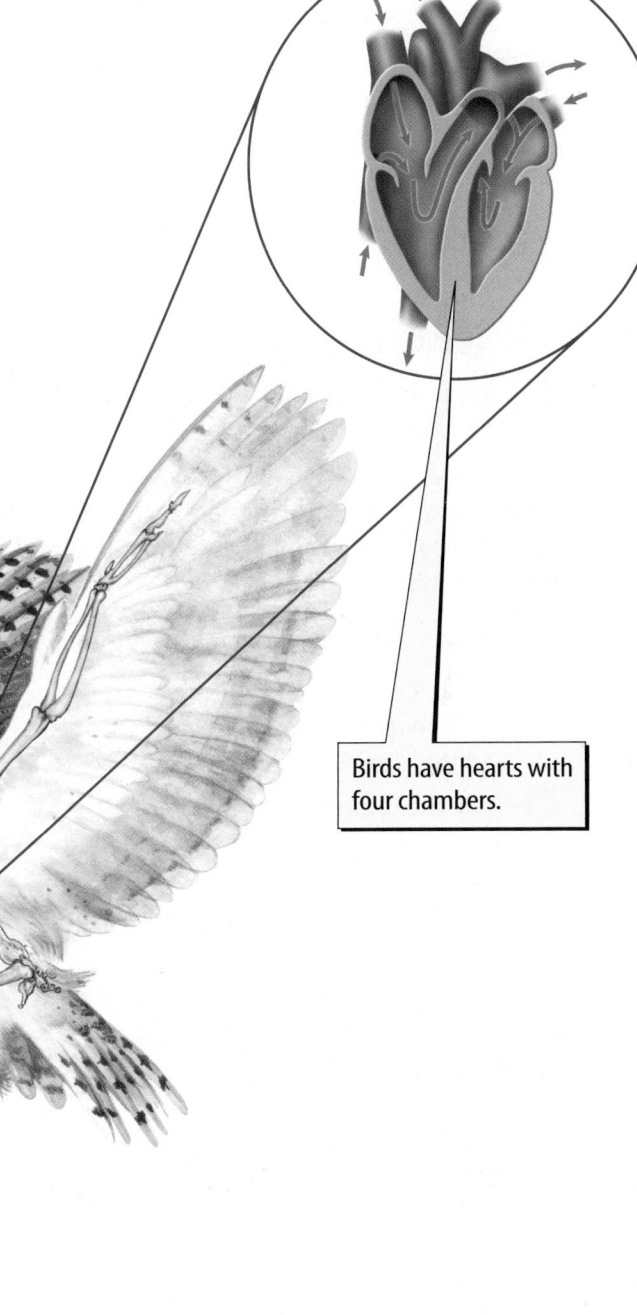

Birds have lightweight bones that help enable most of them to fly.

Birds have hearts with four chambers.

Figure 21 Mammals have hair or fur and mammary glands.

Mammals

Dogs, cats, goats, rats, seals, whales, and humans are among the many vertebrates belonging to the class Mammalia. All mammals have hair or fur covering their bodies. As shown in **Figure 21,** they tear and chew their food using teeth. Mammals have complete digestive systems, which include a mouth and an anus, and a complex nervous system including a brain.

The most notable characteristic of mammals, however, is the presence of mammary glands. These glands produce milk that feeds young mammals. Although many mammals have live young, a few species, including the duck-billed platypus, lay eggs.

Key Concept Check How do the classes of vertebrates differ?

---

inquiry MiniLab   **15 minutes**

Whose bones are these?

The skeletons of vertebrates are made up of bones. Bones have different characteristics depending on the animal in which they are found and their function in the body. Observe bones from different animals.

1. Read and complete a lab safety form.
2. Obtain a collection of **bones.**
3. Examine the shape, the texture, the mass, and the size of the bones.
4. Copy the table below in your Science Journal. Record your observations in the table. Add extra columns if you notice other characteristics you would like to record.

Analyze and Conclude

1. **Compare** What traits did all the bones you observed share?

2. **Contrast** What was the biggest difference among the bones you observed?

3. **Key Concept** Use your observations to identify bones from two different classes of vertebrates.

Bone	Shape	Texture	Mass	Size	Other Observations
1					
2					
3					
4					

Visual Summary

Most chordates are vertebrates.

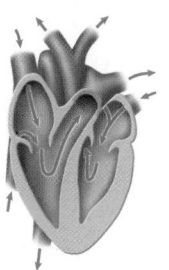

Vertebrates have well-developed organ systems including digestive systems with two openings, circulatory systems that move blood through the body, and nervous systems including brains.

Mammals produce milk to feed their young.

FOLDABLES

Use your lesson Foldable to review the lesson. Save your Foldable for the project at the end of the chapter.

What do you think NOW?

You first read the statements below at the beginning of the chapter.

5. All chordates have backbones.

6. Reptiles have three-chambered hearts.

Did you change your mind about whether you agree or disagree with the statements? Rewrite any false statements to make them true.

Use Vocabulary

1 **Distinguish** between reptiles and amphibians.

2 **Define** *notochord*.

Understand Key Concepts

3 Which characteristic is common to all chordates?
- **A.** bones
- **B.** fur
- **C.** lungs
- **D.** notochord

4 **List** the characteristics common to all fish.

5 **Compare and contrast** birds and mammals.

Interpret Graphics

6 **Summarize Information** Copy the table below, and fill in the features of each type of chordate.

Type of Animal	Characteristics	Example Animals
Invertebrate chordates		
Vertebrate chordates		

7 **Analyze** To which class of vertebrates does the animal below belong? How do you know?

Critical Thinking

8 **Assess** Why does a backbone make vertebrates better adapted for life on land than invertebrates? Explain your answer.

9 **Infer** What is the advantage of having bones that protect the central nerve cord?

Design Your Own Phylum

Materials

markers

colored pencils

In this chapter, you have learned that different types of animals have different characteristics. Some animals have radial symmetry. Others have bilateral symmetry. Still others have no symmetry at all. Vertebrates have backbones. Invertebrates do not. Your task is to design a new phylum of alien animals that has never before been described. What are the characteristics of the animals in your phylum? Remember that animals must perform tasks in order to survive, such as capturing food and reproducing. What characteristics enable the animals in your phylum to survive?

Question

What characteristics enable you to identify animals in your new phylum? What different characteristics do animals in your phylum have?

Procedure

1 Read and complete a lab safety form.

2 Spend time thinking about your phylum. In your Science Journal, write down characteristics that are common to all the animals in your phylum. Try writing a list of structures animals must have and functions that animals must perform as a guide for creating your phylum's characteristics. Create a name for your phylum.

3 Create five different species of animals in your phylum. Write a list of characteristics for each of these animals that make them different from each other. Name each animal.

4 On five separate pieces of paper, draw each of your animals to the best of your ability.

5 Build a dichotomous key that someone could use to identify the animals in your phylum.

6 Trade pictures of animals and dichotomous keys with a classmate. Using your classmate's dichotomous key, identify each of the animals in the drawings.

7 **Analyze** Show your classmate your identifications. Were your answers correct? If not, make modifications to your identifications. Record your changes in your Science Journal.

Analyze and Conclude

8 **Compare** your phylum with your classmate's phylum. What characteristics did the two phyla share? Name some characteristics that were different.

9 **Evaluate** What types of characteristics were the most useful for identifying animals? What types were the hardest to use?

10 **The Big Idea** If your new phylum was included in Kingdom Animalia, where would it go? Why would it be placed in that location?

Communicate Your Results

Suppose that you are a zoologist, and you have discovered animals in your new phylum. Prepare a press release describing your phylum. Use your pictures to illustrate the characteristics of the animals you discovered. Explain where you found your animals, how they survive in the wild, and any other information that makes your phylum interesting.

 **Extension**

Try building physical models of the animals in your phylum. Use wood, wire, clay, paint, and other sculpting materials.

6

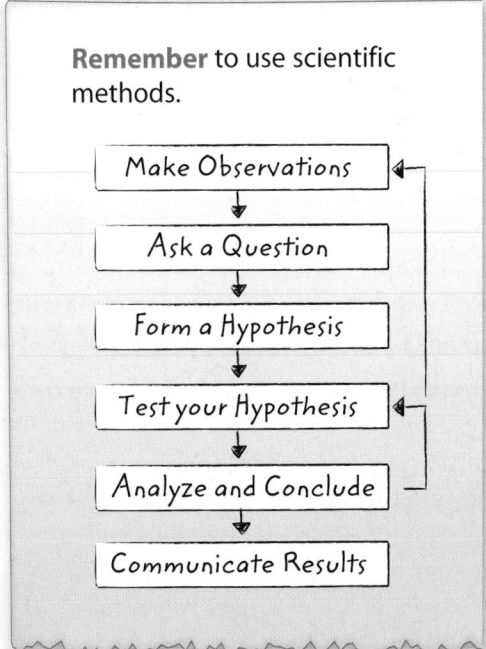

Lab Tips

☑ Try thinking about the environment where you would find your phylum to help you think of characteristics that enable it to live there.

☑ Think about the animals that might have been ancestors to phyla that exist today. What predators might the animals in your phylum have?

Remember to use scientific methods.

Make Observations

↓

Ask a Question

↓

Form a Hypothesis

↓

Test your Hypothesis

↓

Analyze and Conclude

↓

Communicate Results

WebQuest

THE BIG IDEA

The major groups of animals include sponges, cnidarians, flatworms, roundworms, mollusks, segmented worms, arthropods, and chordates. They differ based on body structures and types of reproduction.

Key Concepts Summary 🔑

	Vocabulary

Lesson 1: What defines an animal?

- Animals are eukaryotic, multicellular organisms that eat other organisms, digest food, and have collagen to support cells. Most animals reproduce sexually and can move.
- Animals can be classified based on the presence of a backbone; body symmetry; the characteristics of proteins, DNA, and other molecules that make up their cells; and the kinds of body structures they possess.

vertebrate p. 376
invertebrate p. 376
radial symmetry p. 377
bilateral symmetry p. 377
asymmetry p. 377

Lesson 2: Invertebrate Phyla

- Invertebrates have no backbone or internal skeleton, and they tend to be smaller and slower-moving than vertebrates.
- Invertebrates differ based on symmetry, presence or absence of certain types of specialized body structures, and presence or absence of specific internal organs and organ systems.

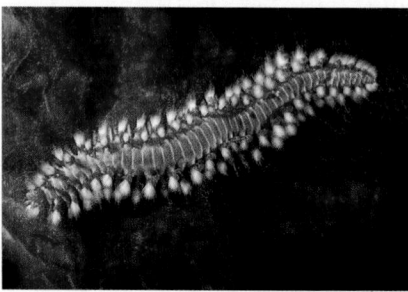

exoskeleton p. 387
appendage p. 387

Lesson 3: Phylum Chordata

- All **chordates** have a **notochord**, a nerve cord, pharyngeal pouches, and a tail at some time during their development.
- All vertebrates have a backbone and well-developed organs and organ systems.
- The classes of vertebrates differ based on presence or absence of characteristics such as gills, fins, scales, legs, wings, fur, and eggs.

notochord p. 393
chordate p. 393

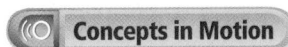
FOLDABLES® Chapter Project

Assemble your lesson Foldables as shown to make a Chapter Project. Use the project to review what you have learned in this chapter.

Use Vocabulary

Write the vocabulary term that best matches each phrase.

1 body plan that can be divided into two nearly equal parts anywhere through its central axis

2 body plan that cannot be divided into two nearly equal parts

3 structure that develops into a backbone in vertebrates

4 a structure such as a leg or an arm

5 two sides that are nearly mirror images of each other

6 a thick, hard covering on arthropods

Link Vocabulary and Key Concepts

Concepts in Motion Interactive Concept Map

Copy this concept map, and then use vocabulary terms from the previous page to complete the concept map.

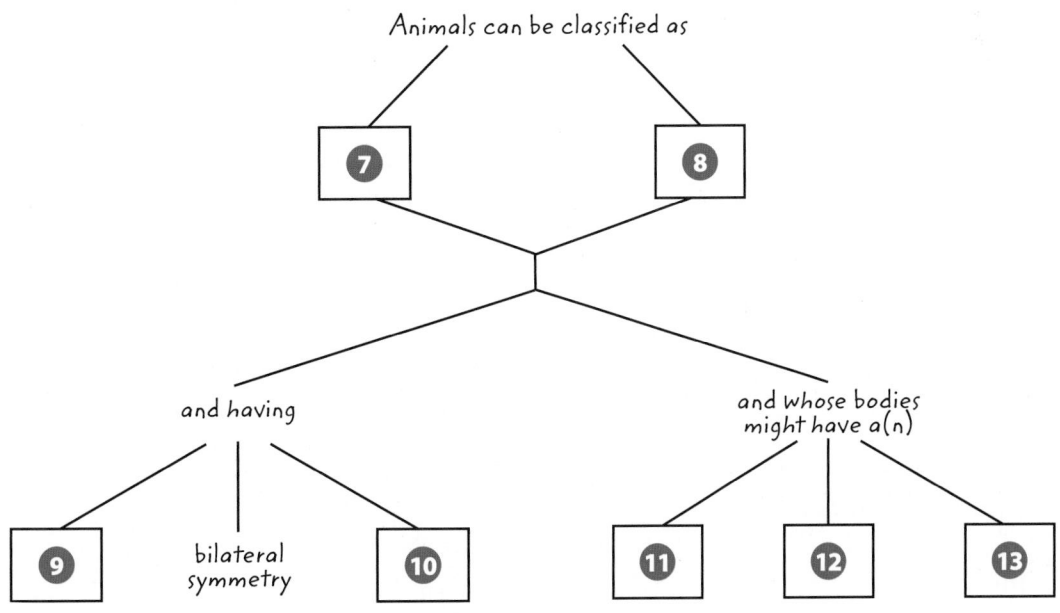

Understand Key Concepts

1 Which characteristic does NOT apply to animals?

A. collagen
B. photosynthesis
C. digestive system
D. eukaryotic cell

2 What characteristic applies to the animal shown below?

A. asymmetry
B. vertebrate
C. bilateral symmetry
D. radial symmetry

3 Which characteristic separates the animal kingdom into two categories?

A. backbone
B. DNA
C. notochord
D. symmetry

4 Which characteristics do all cnidarians have in common?

A. free swimming, radial symmetry
B. radial symmetry, attached to rocks
C. tentacles, bilateral symmetry
D. tentacles, stinging cells

5 Which characteristic is NOT shared by both flatworms and nematodes?

A. bilateral symmetry
B. a simple brain
C. live in moist environments
D. two openings in digestive system

6 To which phylum does the animal below belong?

A. Annelida
B. Mollusca
C. Nematoda
D. Platyhelminthes

Use the figure below to answer questions 7 and 8.

7 What characteristic distinguishes the animal shown above from a fish?

A. bones
B. notochord
C. nerve cord
D. no gills

8 To which phylum does this animal belong?

A. Annelida
B. Cnidaria
C. Chordata
D. Mollusca

Critical Thinking

9 Create a table that compares the three types of symmetry in the animal kingdom.

10 Analyze Why is digestion important to animals, but not to plants?

11 Infer Animals have cells specialized for different functions. Why is this feature an advantage for survival in a multicellular organism?

12 Analyze Explain how you could determine whether the animals shown below are from the same phylum or different phyla.

 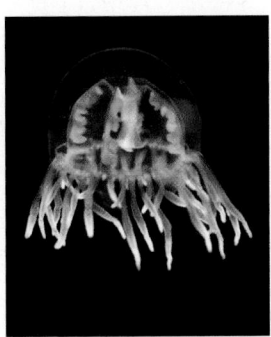

13 Evaluate Why are sponges, cnidarians, flatworms, and roundworms limited to life in water or moist environments?

14 Compare What characteristics do fish and lancelets have in common? How are they different?

15 Infer Why do most vertebrates have appendages such as fins, wings, and legs, whereas most invertebrates do not?

Writing in Science

16 Write a paragraph giving two ways a scuba diver could tell the difference between a sea anemone and a sea slug during an ocean dive.

REVIEW THE **BIG IDEA**

17 In what ways does a body with an internal skeleton have an advantage over a body with no internal or external support?

18 What are the major groups of animals, and how do they differ?

Math Skills

Review
Math Practice

Use Percentages

19 Worldwide, there are about 300,000 species of Lepidoptera, of which an estimated 14,500 are butterflies. What percentage of Lepidoptera species are butterflies?

20 Of the estimated 1.2 million species of invertebrates, about 40,000 are crustaceans. What percentage of invertebrates are crustaceans?

21 Of the estimated 1.2 million species of invertebrates, about 950,000 are insects. What percentage of invertebrates are insects?

Record your answers on the answer sheet provided by your teacher or on a sheet of paper.

Multiple Choice

1 Which is a characteristic of all vertebrates?

A digestive system with one opening

B offspring hatch from eggs

C respiratory system with lungs

D spinal cord enclosed in bones

Use the figure below to answer question 2.

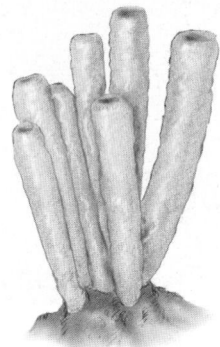

2 Which is true of the animal shown above?

A It has bilateral symmetry.

B It has radial symmetry.

C It is an invertebrate.

D It is a vertebrate.

3 Which animals make up Phylum Chordata?

A insects, spiders, and crabs

B mussels, octopuses, and squids

C snails, slugs, and clams

D vertebrates, lancelets, and tunicates

4 Which is a characteristic of all invertebrates?

A backbone absent

B exoskeleton present

C symmetry absent

D tube feet present

5 Which is NOT a characteristic of all animals?

A digesting food

B eating other organisms

C having specialized cells

D moving around

Use the figure below to answer question 6.

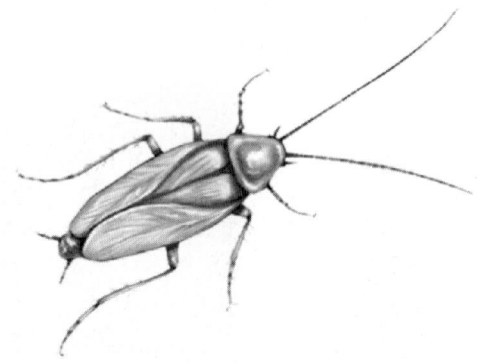

6 The animal in the figure above is classified in which phylum?

A Arthropoda

B Chordata

C Echinodermata

D Mollusca

7 Which animal has radial symmetry?

A flatworm

B jellyfish

C octopus

D sponge

Use the figure below to answer questions 8 and 9.

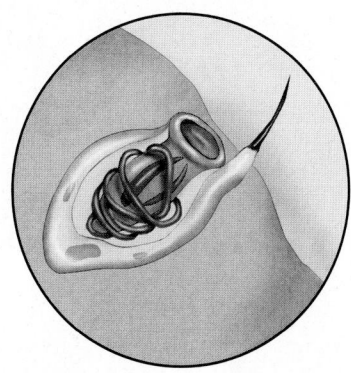

8 Which animals contain the structure shown in the figure?

  A bees and wasps

  B jellyfish and corals

  C octopuses and squids

  D sea stars and sea urchins

9 How do animals use the structure shown in the figure?

  A for breathing

  B for feeding

  C for mating

  D for seeing

10 Which class of vertebrates feeds milk to its young?

  A amphibians

  B fish

  C mammals

  D reptiles

Constructed Response

Use the figure below to answer questions 11 and 12.

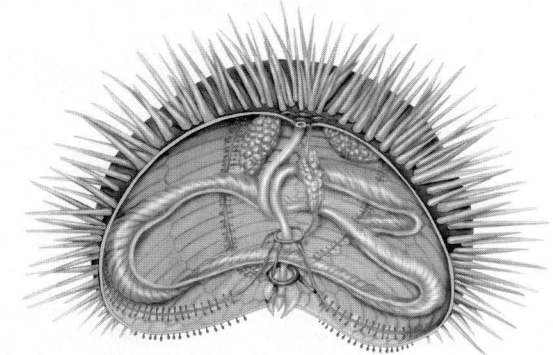

11 Identify the phylum of the animal shown in the figure. What type of animal is it? Give examples of other animals in this phylum.

12 Use the figure above to describe at least three characteristics typical of the phylum represented.

13 Which adaptations enable birds and reptiles to live on land while fish and amphibians must live in or near water for at least part of their life cycles?

14 List the four characteristics of all chordates. Explain the relationship of each characteristic to an adult human.

NEED EXTRA HELP?														
If You Missed Question...	1	2	3	4	5	6	7	8	9	10	11	12	13	14
Go to Lesson...	3	1	1	2	1	1	1	2	2	3	2	2	3	3

Animal Structure and Function

THE BIG IDEA

Why do animals have different structures that perform similar functions?

Inquiry **Feathers for Hearing?**

The feathers around this great gray owl's eyes enable it to hear better. The feathers form discs around the eyes that funnel sounds toward the owl's ears.

- What other functions do you think feathers have for an owl?

- What other structures might enable the owl to survive?

- Why do animals have different structures that perform similar functions?

Get Ready to Read

What do you think?

Before you read, decide if you agree or disagree with each of these statements. As you read this chapter, see if you change your mind about any of the statements.

1 All animals on Earth have internal skeletons.

2 All animals that live in the water move using fins.

3 Earthworms have an open circulatory system that transports blood and other substances throughout the body.

4 Gills and lungs are different structures that perform the same function.

5 The shape of an animal's teeth depends on its diet.

6 Excretion is used only by animals that live on land.

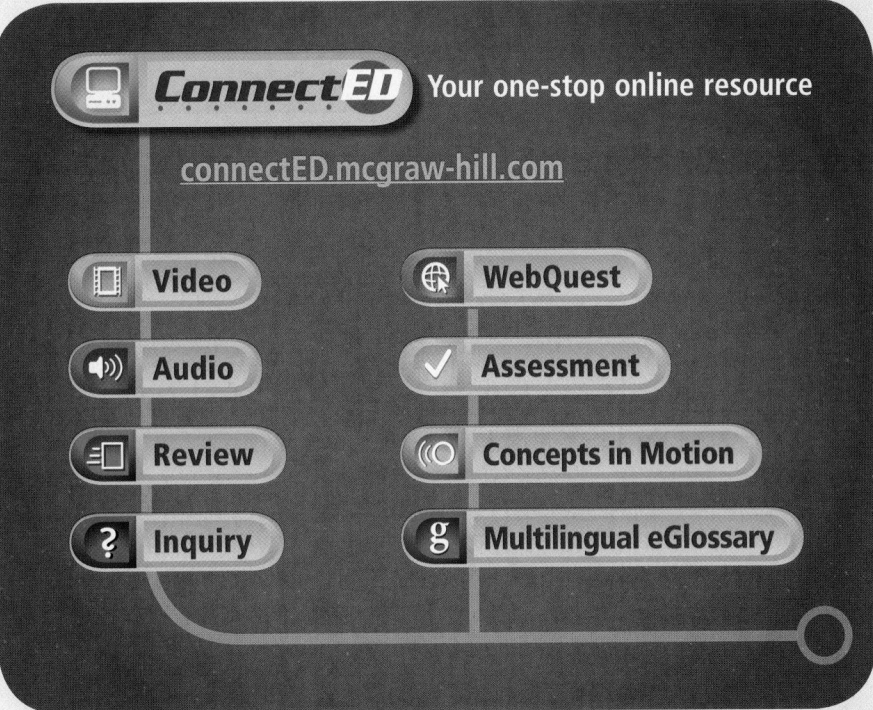

ConnectED Your one-stop online resource

connectED.mcgraw-hill.com

- Video
- Audio
- Review
- Inquiry
- WebQuest
- Assessment
- Concepts in Motion
- Multilingual eGlossary

Lesson 1

Reading Guide

Key Concepts
ESSENTIAL QUESTIONS

- How are the types of support alike, and how are they different?
- How do the types of control compare and contrast?
- How do the types of movement compare and contrast?

Vocabulary

hydrostatic skeleton p. 412
coelom p. 412
nerve net p. 414
undulation p. 416

g Multilingual eGlossary

Video Science Video

Support, Control, and Movement

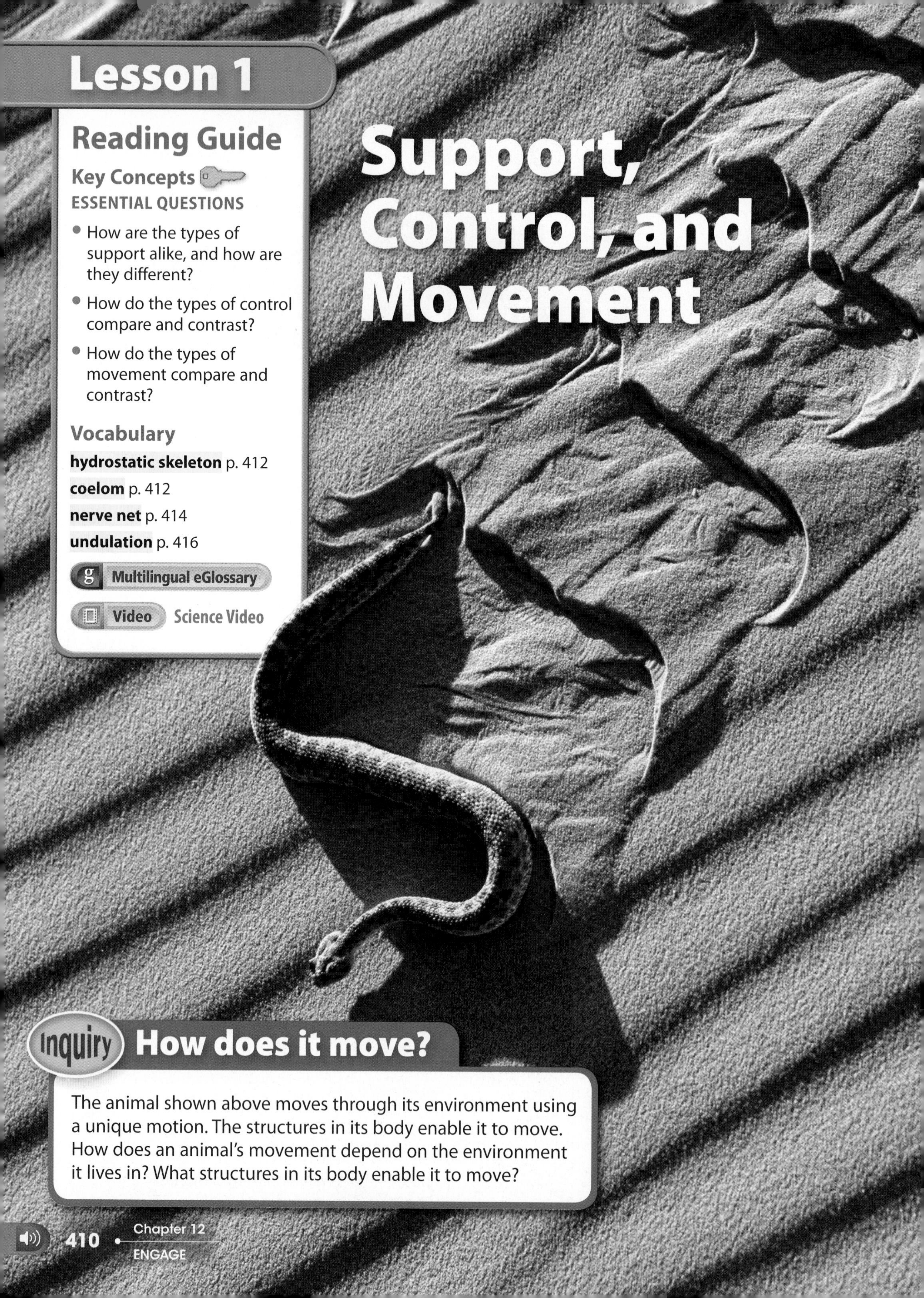

Inquiry How does it move?

The animal shown above moves through its environment using a unique motion. The structures in its body enable it to move. How does an animal's movement depend on the environment it lives in? What structures in its body enable it to move?

How does an earthworm move?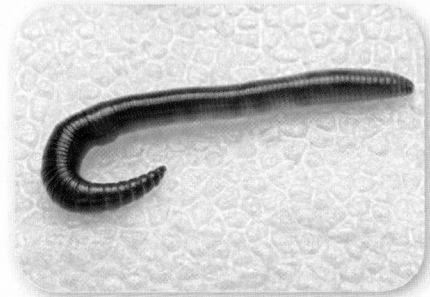

You move by using your muscles and skeleton. However, an earthworm does not have a skeleton. How is an earthworm able to move?

1. Read and complete a lab safety form.

2. Place a **paper towel** in the bottom of a **plastic container.** Add water to the paper towel until it is damp, but not dripping wet.

3. Place an **earthworm** on the surface of the paper towel and observe the earthworm for several minutes.

4. Pay particular attention to what happens when the earthworm moves. Note the changes in the earthworm's body and the motion that enables it to move.

Think About This

1. How do you think the body of an earthworm has structure even though it has no skeleton?

2. Describe how the shape and length of the different segments of the earthworm change to cause it to move.

3. 🔑 **Key Concept** How do you think the structure and movement of an earthworm is different from that of animals with skeletons?

The Importance of Support, Control, and Movement

Think about the different environments where animals live. Some animals live their entire lives in water. Others live only on land. Regardless of their environments, all animals have the same basic needs: food, water, and oxygen. However, in order to survive in different habitats, animals have different structures with similar functions.

Fish and birds live in dramatically different environments. However, both use structures to obtain oxygen from their environments. In a similar way, animals have different structures for support, control, and movement. Without these, animals, such as the goats in **Figure 1,** could not obtain the things they need to survive. In this lesson you will read about how animals in different habitats use different structures to provide support and control for their bodies and to move around.

Figure 1 These goats have pads between their hooves that enable them to climb trees and reach food.

Structures for Support

As you have just read, organisms have structures to provide support, control, and movement. What structures provide support? Most animals are invertebrates, or animals without backbones. Animals with backbones, such as humans, are called vertebrates. Vertebrate and invertebrate animals have different types of structures that provide support.

FOLDABLES®

Make a vertical three-tab book. Label it as shown. Use it to organize your notes about support structures.

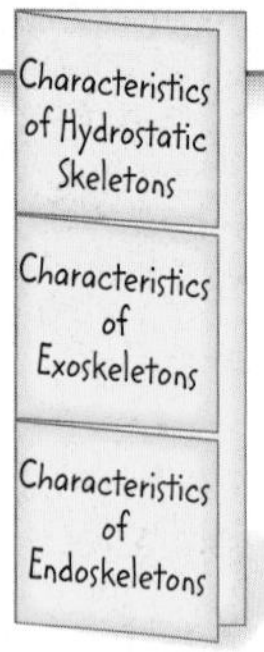

Characteristics of Hydrostatic Skeletons
Characteristics of Exoskeletons
Characteristics of Endoskeletons

Hydrostatic Skeletons

Filling a balloon with water gives it shape. This is because the force of the water against the surface of the balloon gives the balloon structure. Just as the water in a balloon provides structure, many organisms use internal fluids to provide support. *A* **hydrostatic skeleton** *is a fluid-filled internal cavity surrounded by muscle tissue. The fluid-filled cavity is called the* **coelom** (SEE lum). Muscles that surround the coelom help some organisms move by pushing the fluid in different directions. Earthworms, such as the one shown in **Figure 2,** jellyfish, and sea anemones (uh NE muh neez) are organisms that have hydrostatic skeletons. Organisms with hydrostatic skeletons do not have bones or other hard structures that provide support.

Reading Check What type of skeleton do jellyfish have?

Hydrostatic Skeletons

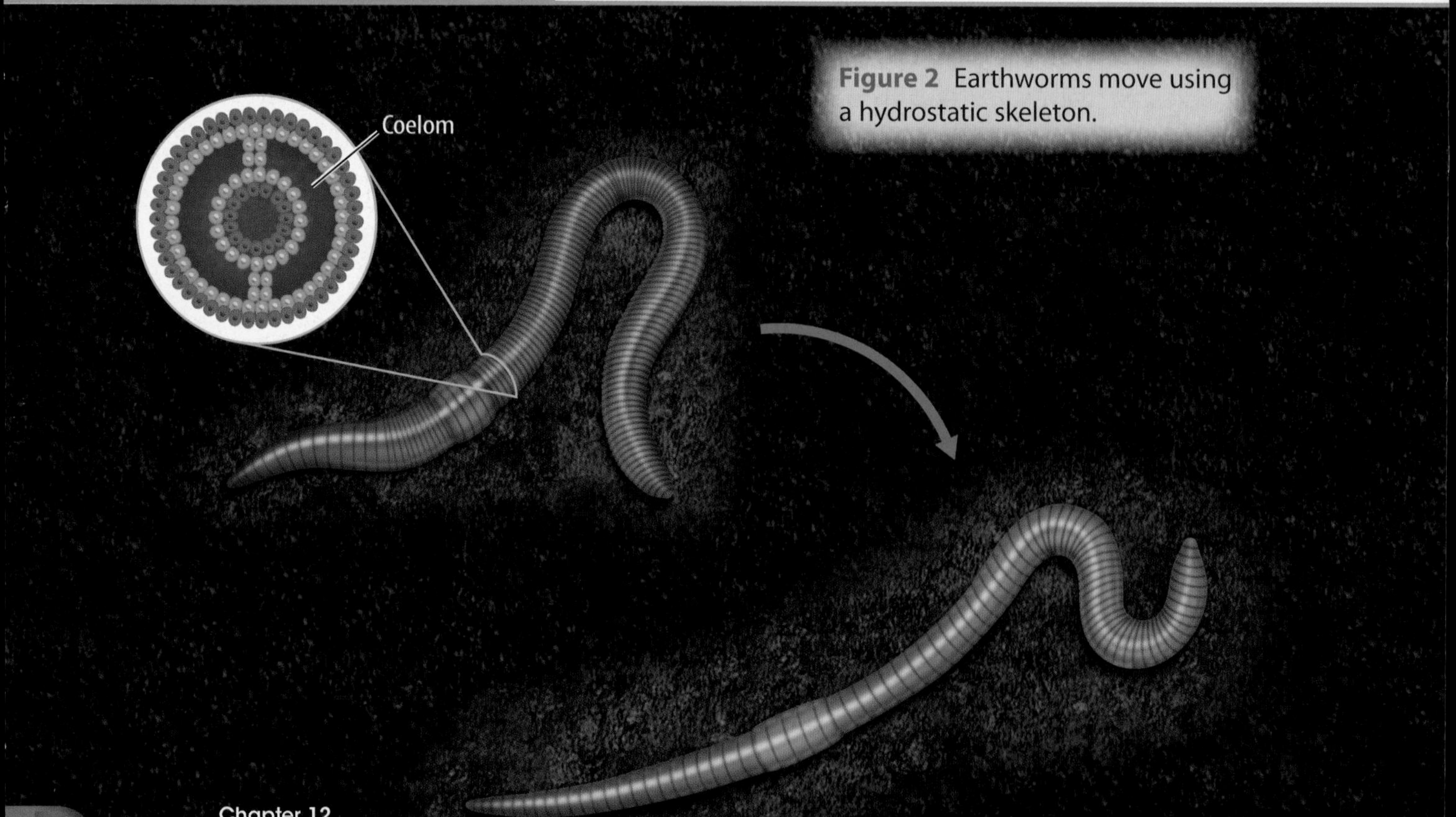

Coelom

Figure 2 Earthworms move using a hydrostatic skeleton.

Exoskeletons

Some organisms get support from structures on the outside of the body. Hard outer coverings, called exoskeletons, provide support and protection for many invertebrates. A hard exoskeleton protects internal tissues from predators or damage. Exoskeletons are sometimes called shells in species such as crabs and snails. In some species, such as the lobster shown in **Figure 3,** the exoskeleton does not grow as the animal grows. It must be shed when it gets too small, leaving the animal defenseless until the new exoskeleton forms and hardens.

Endoskeletons

Peaches have a soft, fleshy exterior that covers a hard seed. The bodies of many animals are similar in that they also have a covering over hard internal structures. These internal support structures in animals such as fish, birds, and mammals are called endoskeletons. Most endoskeletons, such as the one shown in **Figure 3,** are made of bone. Some, for example the endoskeletons of sharks, are made of cartilage. An endoskeleton protects internal organs and provides the organism with structure and support. Tortoises and turtles are unique because they have both endoskeletons and exoskeletons. The endoskeleton protects the organs and the hard exoskeleton shell protects the animal from predators.

🔑 **Key Concept Check** How are the types of support alike, and how are they different?

Figure 3 Most organisms get support from either exoskeletons or endoskeletons.

🔎 **Visual Check** How do the support structures of the squirrel and the lobster differ?

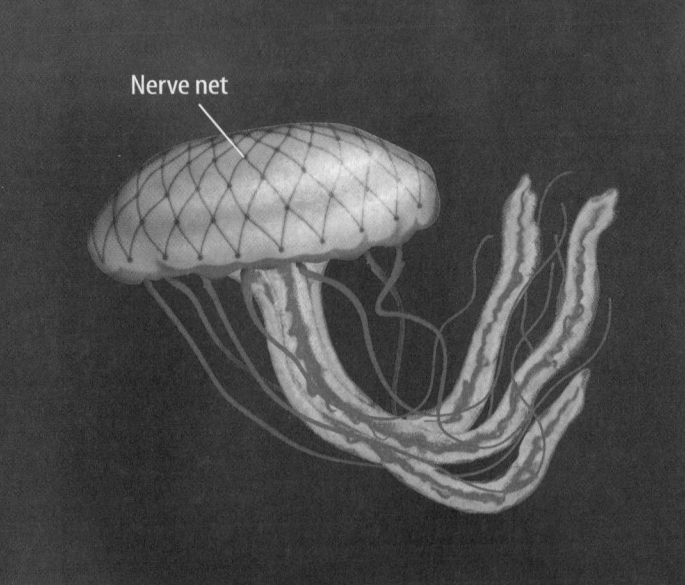

Nerve net

Figure 4 The nerve net of this jellyfish enables it to respond to its environment.

Structures for Control

All animals react to changes in their environments. Just as different animals have different structures for support, they also have different control systems. These control systems, called nervous systems, help protect animals from harm and help animals move and find food.

Nerve Nets

Animals with radial symmetry and no brain have nerve nets with a central ring that control their bodies. *A* **nerve net** *is a netlike control system that sends signals to and from all parts of the body.* Signals sent through the nerve net and ring cause an organism's muscle cells to contract. These contractions help the animal move. Cnidarians (nih DAYR ee unz) such as jellyfish and sea anemones have nerve nets that sense physical contact and detect food. Nerve nets and rings help the jellyfish shown in **Figure 4** move and capture prey.

Inquiry **MiniLab**   **10 minutes**

How do nerve nets and nerve cords function?

Animals use different types of systems to sense the environment and react. Animals that do not have a brain use nerve nets to send signals throughout their bodies. Animals with brains use a nerve cord.

1 Read and complete a lab safety form.

2 One of your classmates will use a **stopwatch** to time the procedure.

3 Use **segments of string** to connect to your classmates in the shape of a nerve net. When you have formed the structure, close your eyes and bow your head.

4 When you receive the signal, gently tug on the next student's nerve-cell string. When you feel a tug on your string, raise your head, open your eyes, and tug the ends of the string connected to the people next to you.

5 Form a nerve-cord structure and repeat the activity. Record the results of your activities in your Science Journal.

Analyze and Conclude

1. **Assess** which nerve structure took longer to reach the final student.

2. **Key Concept** Describe one advantage and one disadvantage of using each type of structure to convey information.

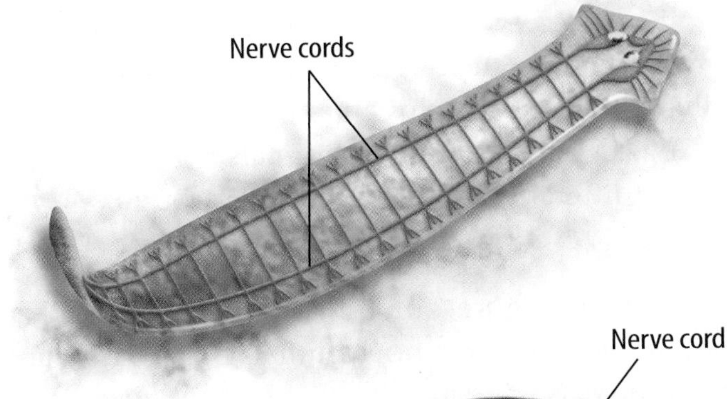

Nerve cords

Figure 5 Animals with brains or brainlike structures, such as this zebra and planarian, have nerve cords.

✔️ **Visual Check** How do the nerve structures of the zebra and the planarian differ?

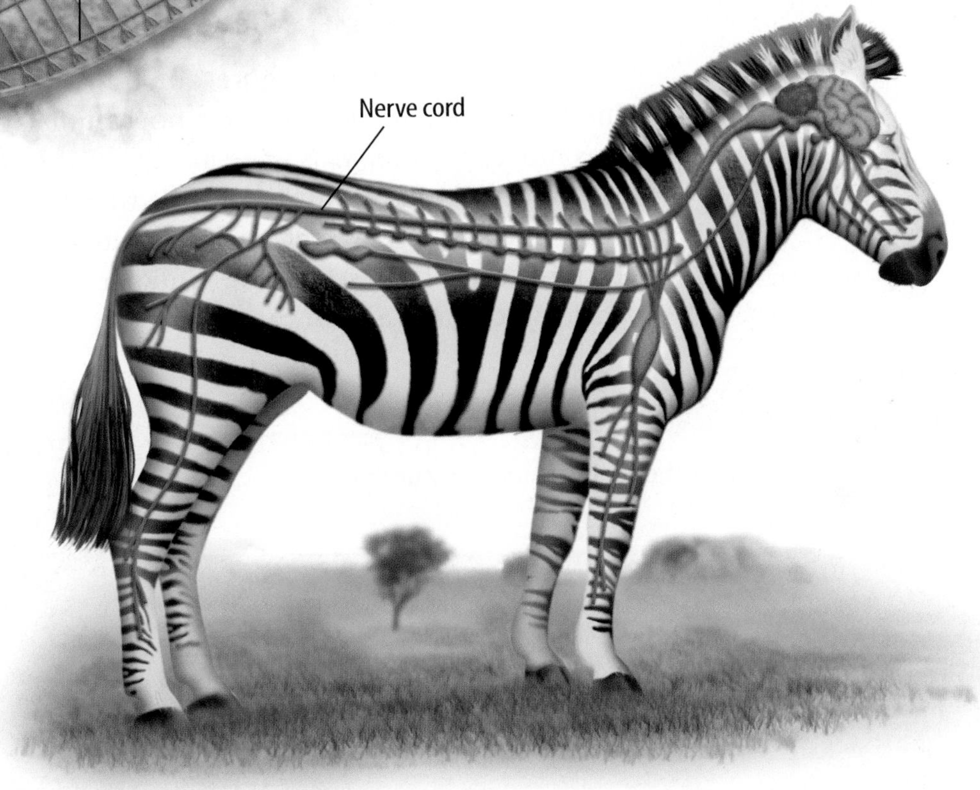

Nerve cord

Nerve Cords

Animals with bilateral symmetry have brains or brainlike structures to detect and respond to their environments. An animal with a brain or a brainlike structure has a nerve cord, as shown in **Figure 5**. An animal with a nerve cord usually has many **neurons** that detect changes in its external environment. Signals detected by neurons are sent to the nerve cord, which might initiate a reflex response, and then to the brain for processing. Just as a telephone wire transmits signals between two buildings, the nerve cord enables signals to move between neurons and the brain. In vertebrates, nerve cords are also called spinal cords.

🔑 **Key Concept Check** How do the types of control compare and contrast?

REVIEW VOCABULARY

neuron
basic functioning unit of the nervous system

Types of Movement

All animals move at some point in their lives. Some animals, such as birds or tigers, move around throughout most of their lives. Other animals, such as sponges, move during only part of their lives. Movement helps an animal obtain food and escape from danger. Because different animals live in different habitats, they use different structures to move around.

Undulate Motion

It might be easy to figure out how an animal with legs moves around. But do you know how animals that do not have legs move? *Some animals move in a wavelike motion called* **undulation** (un juh LAY shun). Animals that move by undulation, such as snakes, fishes, and the eel in **Figure 6,** use their muscles to push their bodies forward. Undulation is used by animals that live on land and in the water.

Undulation 🔑

Figure 6 Snakes, eels, and other animals move by undulating their bodies.

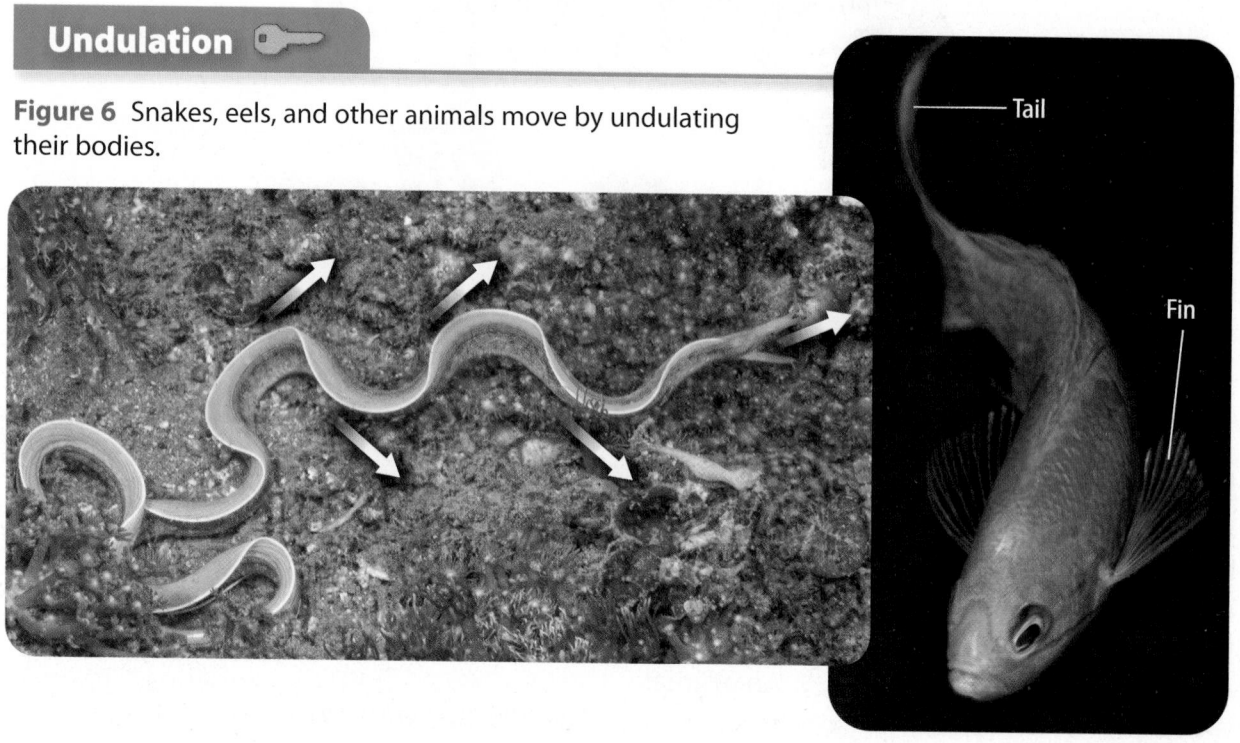

Tail

Fin

Swimming

Many animals that live in water move by swimming. Some animals, such as the fish shown in **Figure 6,** use their fins and tails to move through water. Other animals, such as octopuses, take in water and then push the water out forcefully to move forward in a process called jet propulsion. You might already know that many organisms, such as humans and dogs, also can swim by moving their arms and legs, even though they do not live in water.

Walking

Most animals that live on land move by walking. The body's weight rests on two, four, six, or eight legs and shifts when the legs move. Some animals, such as rabbits and frogs, also are capable of jumping using their limbs.

Flying

Many animals move through the air by flying. Birds, some insects, and bats all use wings to move around. Wings, such as those shown in **Figure 7,** are a type of limb. By moving their wings, animals can lift their bodies and keep them in the air. Animals that have wings also have legs that are used to move around on land.

Wings are not the only structures that enable animals to move through the air. Some animals can glide or move through the air without flapping their limbs. Some species of fish have large fins that are used to glide short distances to escape predators. Some squirrels, marsupials, and even snakes can glide. They launch themselves from a high point and glide down by flattening their bodies or stretching out tissues to form a structure similar to a parachute.

Key Concept Check How do the types of movement compare and contrast?

Figure 7 Many birds move by flying, while a flying squirrel has the ability to glide.

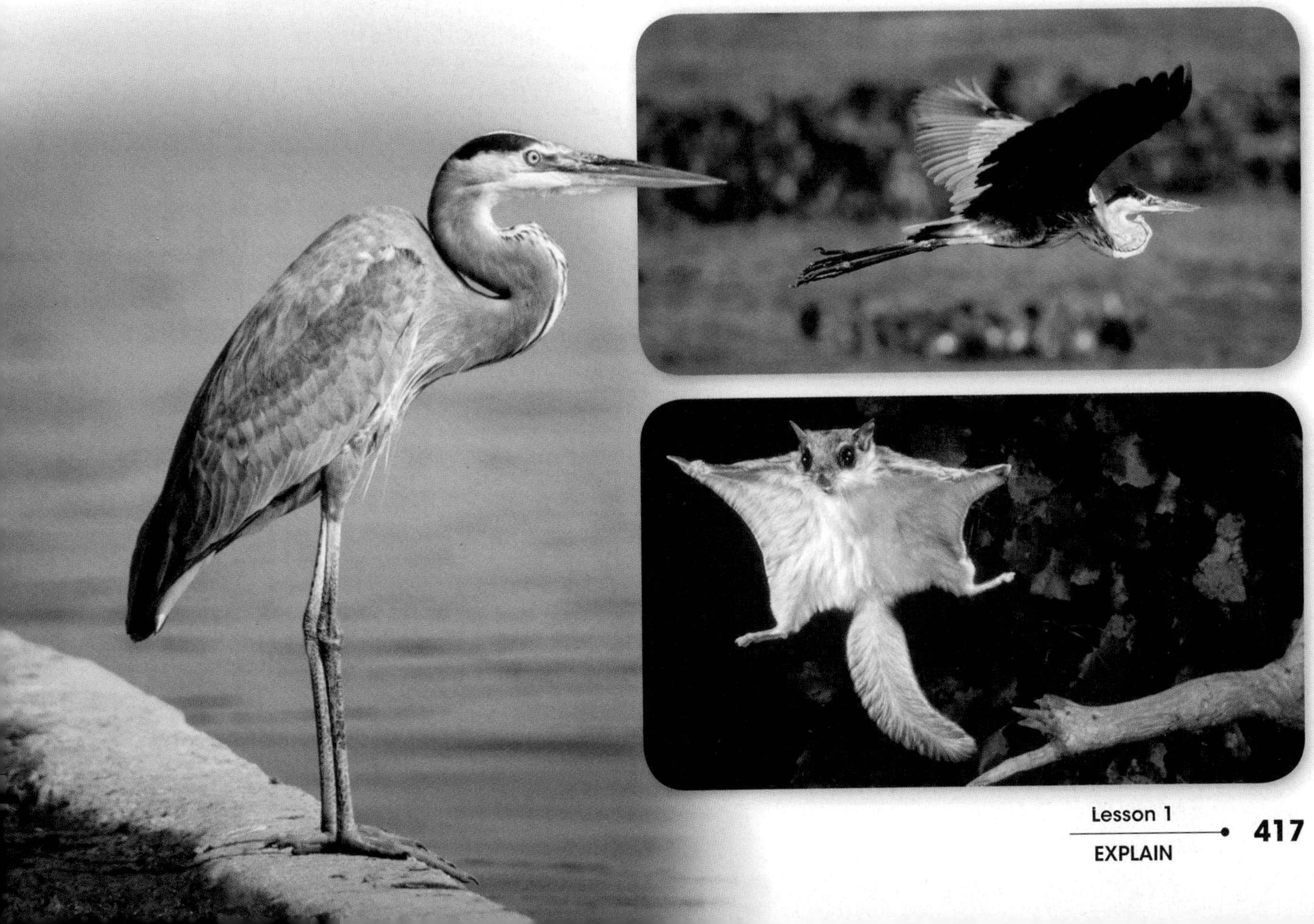

Lesson 1 Review

Assessment Online Quiz
Inquiry Virtual Lab

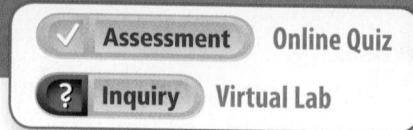

Visual Summary

Animals have different structures for support, control, and movement.

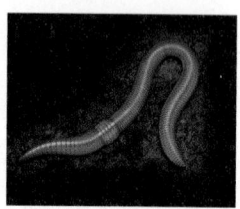

Some animals have hydrostatic skeletons.

Most animals with wings move by flying.

FOLDABLES®

Use your lesson Foldable to review the lesson. Save your Foldable for the project at the end of the chapter.

What do you think NOW?

You first read the statements below at the beginning of the chapter.

1. All animals on Earth have internal skeletons.
2. All animals that live in the water move using fins.

Did you change your mind about whether you agree or disagree with the statements? Rewrite any false statements to make them true.

Use Vocabulary

1. **Use the terms** *hydrostatic skeleton* and *coelom* in a sentence.
2. **Define** *endoskeleton* in your own words.
3. Eels contract their muscles and move forward by a process called ________.

Understand Key Concepts

4. Which is used by a jellyfish to sense and respond to changes in the environment?
   A. coelom
   B. undulation
   C. nerve cord
   D. nerve net
5. **Explain** how a turtle's support system enables it to survive.

Interpret Graphics

6. **Analyze** how the control system shown below helps cnidarians respond to changes and capture prey.

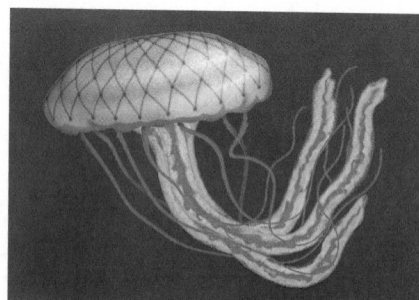

7. **Organize Information** Copy and fill in the table below to describe how animals move in their habitats.

Type of Movement	Type of Limb	Habitat
Undulation		
Swimming	fins	
Walking		land
Flying		

Critical Thinking

8. **Relate** a bird's limbs to its ability to walk and fly.
9. **Assess** the role of the coelom in providing earthworms with support.

Jet Propulsion

The Secret of a Squid's Speed

A squid swims slowly along the ocean floor, flapping its delicate fins. Suddenly, it spots a shark approaching. In a flash, the squid darts away and is gone. When a squid has to move fast, its fins can't get the job done. It uses jet propulsion.

Think of what happens when you let go of a balloon as you're blowing it up. Air rushes out of the balloon in one direction, launching it in the opposite direction. This movement is an example of jet propulsion. Cephalopods (SE fuh luh podz) , animals such as squids, jellyfishes, and octopuses, use jet propulsion to move quickly through the ocean. However, they shoot water out of their bodies instead of air.

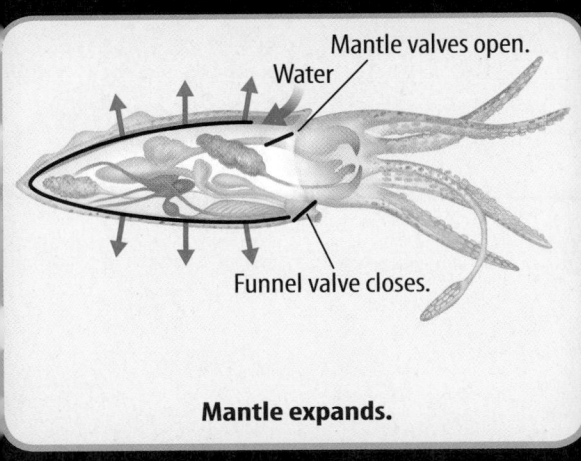

Mantle valves open.
Water
Funnel valve closes.
Mantle expands.

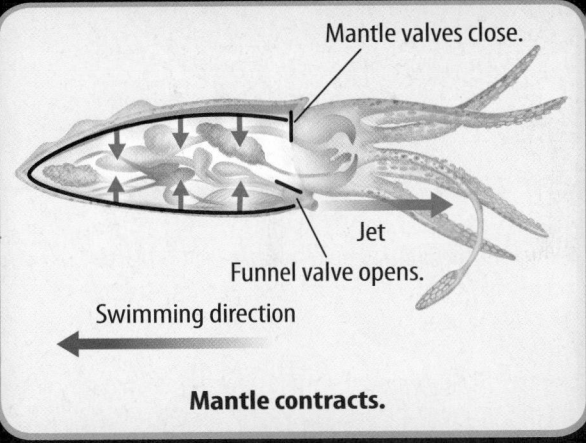

Mantle valves close.
Jet
Funnel valve opens.
Swimming direction
Mantle contracts.

(A) A squid opens its mantle valves, drawing in water. Then the mantle valves close so the water can't escape.

(B) The squid contracts its mantle, opens its funnel valve, and shoots out water through the funnel. This propels the squid through the water in the opposite direction. A squid can change directions by bending its funnel the other way.

AMERICAN
MUSEUM ŏf
NATURAL
HISTORY

It's Your Turn

DIAGRAM Work with a partner to research another animal that uses jet propulsion. Then draw and label a diagram that you can use to explain your findings to the class.

Circulation and Gas Exchange

Reading Guide

Key Concepts 🔑
ESSENTIAL QUESTIONS

- How do the types of gas exchange differ?
- What are the differences between open and closed circulatory systems?

Vocabulary
diffusion p. 422

spiracle p. 422

gills p. 423

open circulatory system p. 424

closed circulatory system p. 425

g Multilingual eGlossary

Inquiry Underground Tunnels?

The large, orange structure might look like the entrance to an underground system of tunnels, but it is part of an insect! Tiny holes such as this enable some organisms to exchange gases directly with the environment.

Which system is faster?

In some animals, blood surrounds organs. In other animals, blood is carried through vessels. Which system can transport oxygen and nutrients more efficiently?

1. Read and complete a lab safety form.

2. Fill a **large plastic bowl** with water. Center a **coin** on the bottom of the bowl as a target. Place three **marbles** around the inside bottom of the bowl.

3. Have your partner time you with a **stopwatch.** Use a **turkey baster** to move each of the marbles onto the target by pushing water behind each marble. Do not touch any of the marbles directly. Stop timing when all marbles have touched the target.

4. Remove water from the bowl until it is 1/3 full. Center the coin on the bottom of the bowl. Place the three marbles in a small **beaker** of water.

5. Take a length of **plastic tubing** and aim one end at the target in the water. Have your partner start timing you. Pour the marbles and water from the beaker into the other end of the tube so that the marbles flow through the tube and strike the target in the bowl. Stop timing when the third marble touches the target.

Think About This

1. Which system was able to deliver the marbles to the target faster? Why do you think one system is faster than the other?

2. What materials are represented by the marbles? What is represented by the target?

3. 🔑 **Key Concept** Which system do you think might work best for slow-moving animals? For fast-moving animals? Explain your reasoning.

The Importance of Gas Exchange and Circulation

All cells need nutrients and oxygen to survive. Recall that animals obtain nutrients and oxygen from their environment. Organisms must take in these substances and get them to each cell. Structures in animal bodies transport the substances to all cells. They also help remove wastes such as carbon dioxide from the body. You might recall that most of an animal cell is made of water. In addition to nutrients, oxygen, and wastes, water also is transported throughout the body.

As with support, control, and movement, different animals use different structures to exchange gases and move substances throughout the body. The type of system used depends on the animal's habitat. In this lesson, you will read about the different structures that animals have that help cells exchange gases and get nutrients and oxygen.

FOLDABLES

Make a vertical book. Label it as shown. Use it to organize your notes about gas exchange and circulatory systems.

Gas Exchange Systems | Circulatory Systems

How do the surface areas of different respiratory systems compare?

The respiratory systems of animals need a large surface area to perform gas exchange. Which system has the most surface area?

1 Read and complete a lab safety form.

2 Use **paper** and **scissors** to create a model of gills and a model of book lungs. Calculate the surface areas of the completed models. Record the data in your Science Journal.

3 Create a model of the alveoli in a lung. Wrap paper around **marbles** to model alveoli. Use **rubber bands** or **string** to hold the paper around the marbles. Calculate the surface area of the model.

4 When your models are completed, unfold each of them and measure the surface area of each model. Record the data in your Science Journal.

Analyze and Conclude

1. **Compare and contrast** the surface area of each model before and after you unfolded it. How does it differ?

2. **Analyze** how folding affects the structures of the respiratory system in terms of size and surface area.

3. 🔑 **Key Concept** Infer why the amount of surface area might be important in determining the respiratory rates of organisms.

Gas Exchange

All animals must take in oxygen and eliminate carbon dioxide to survive. Oxygen must enter the body so the cells and tissues are able to use it for life processes. However, different animals use various structures to perform gas exchange.

Diffusion

The basic process of gas exchange requires no structures at all and is called diffusion. **Diffusion** *is the movement of substances from an area of higher concentration to an area of lower concentration.* In simple animals such as sponges, whose bodies are only a few cell layers thick, no special gas exchange structures are needed. Diffusion occurs through all parts of the body. Oxygen passes directly into cells from the environment. In a similar manner, waste gases leave cells and enter the environment. Other animals use specialized structures in addition to diffusion.

✓ **Reading Check** What is diffusion?

Spiracles

Some organisms exchange gases through the sides of their bodies. **Spiracles** *are tiny holes on the surface of an organism where oxygen enters the body and carbon dioxide leaves the body.* Insects such as beetles and arachnids such as spiders have spiracles. Although beetles and spiders both have spiracles, they use different tissues to transport oxygen throughout the body. Beetles have structures called tracheal (TRAY kee ul) tubes, and spiders have folded structures called book lungs to take in oxygen.

Tracheal tubes, such as the ones shown in **Figure 8,** are hoselike structures that branch into smaller tubes. Much as a river branches off into smaller streams, smaller branches of tracheal tubes help oxygen get to more places in the body. In contrast, book lungs are stacks of folded wall-like structures. Although tracheal tubes and book lungs look different, they are both used for gas exchange.

Structures for Gas Exchange 🔑

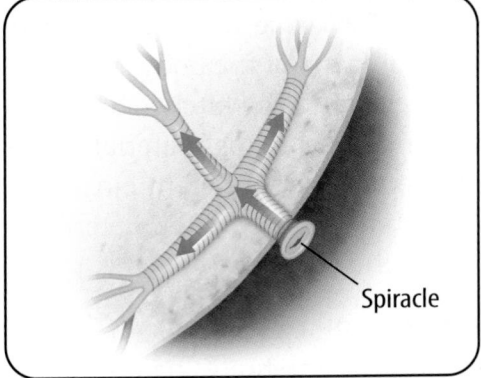

Tracheal tubes

Gills

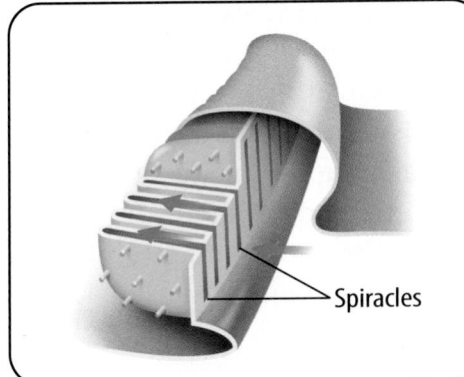

Book lungs

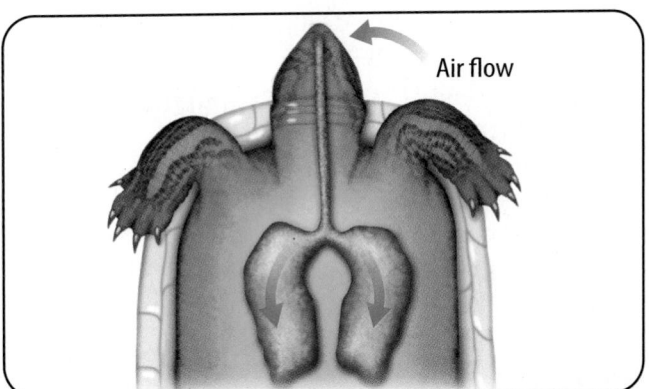

Lungs

Gills

Most animals that live in the water have gills for gas exchange. **Gills** *are organs that enable oxygen to diffuse into an animal's body and carbon dioxide to diffuse out.* In aquatic animals such as the fish shown in **Figure 8,** water enters the mouth to get to the gills. Oxygen in the water is taken in by gill filaments and then transported to the rest of the body. Gills also remove carbon dioxide from the body. Like other organs in the body, gills are surrounded by capillaries that help transport oxygen and carbon dioxide to and from cells.

Lungs

Many animals that live on land, including the turtle in **Figure 8,** and some types of fish and snails have lungs for gas exchange. Lungs are baglike organs that can be filled with air. Once the lungs fill with air, oxygen diffuses into the capillaries within the lungs' tissues and carbon dioxide diffuses out of the animal's body. Recall that capillaries transport oxygen to other cells in the body through the circulatory system.

🔑 **Key Concept Check** How do the organs used for gas exchange differ?

Figure 8 Spiracles, tracheal tubes, gills, and lungs are all used for gas exchange.

✓ **Visual Check** What structures for gas exchange involve spiracles?

WORD ORIGIN ··············

diffusion
from Latin *diffundere,* means "to scatter"

Lesson 2

423

EXPLAIN

Circulation

You have just read about how gases are **exchanged** between animals and the environment. After an animal takes in oxygen, the oxygen has to travel to all parts of the body. Much like pipes in a house help transport water to the kitchen and bathrooms, an animal's circulatory system helps materials move through the body. Different animals have different circulatory systems. The type of circulatory system used often determines how quickly blood moves through the animal.

Open Circulatory Systems

Snails, insects, and many other invertebrates have open circulatory systems. *An* **open circulatory system** *is a system that transports blood and other fluids into open spaces that surround organs in the body.* In an open circulatory system, such as the circulatory system of a bee shown in **Figure 9,** oxygen and nutrients in blood can enter all tissues and cells directly. Carbon dioxide and other wastes are taken up by blood surrounding the organs and removed from the body. Muscles help move blood through the body. It can take a long time for blood to move through an open circulatory system.

Figure 9 Open circulatory systems transport blood into open spaces in the body. Closed circulatory systems transport blood through vessels.

Open and Closed Circulatory Systems 🔑

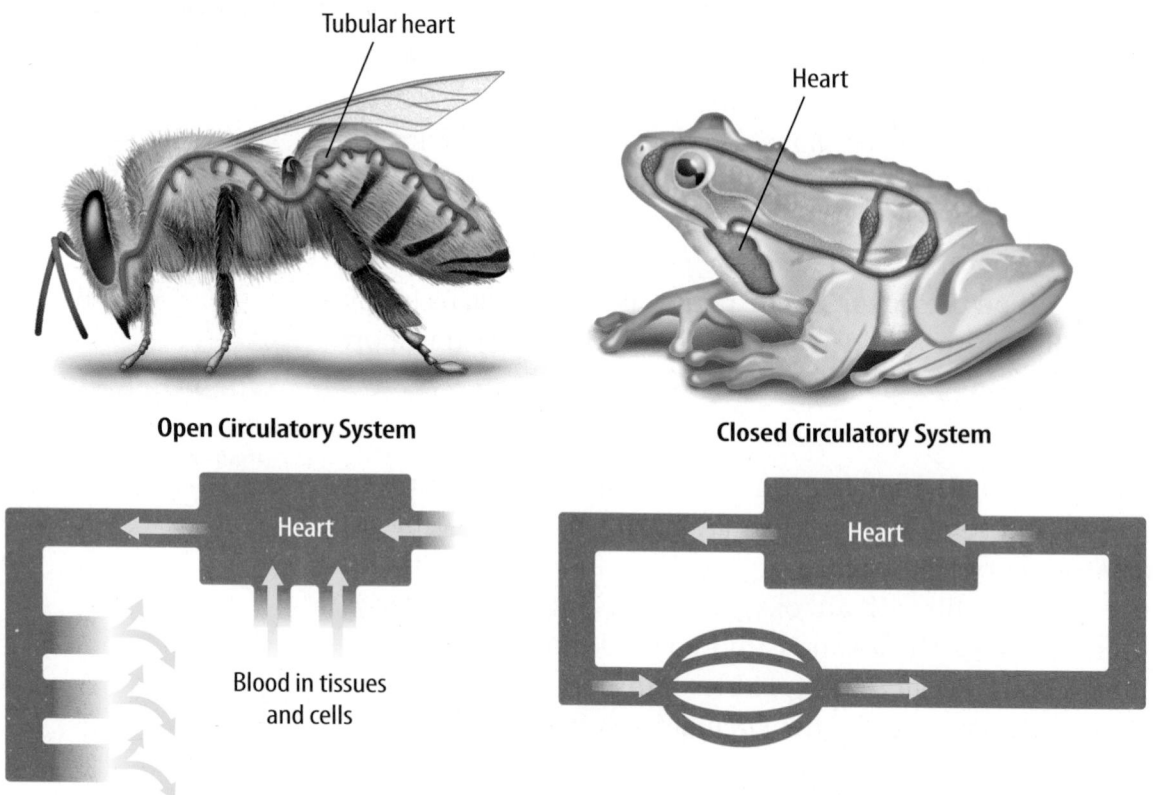

Open Circulatory System

Closed Circulatory System

Closed Circulatory Systems

Some animals, such as the tree frog shown in **Figure 9**, transport materials through another system called a closed circulatory system. *A* **closed circulatory system** *is a system that transports materials through blood using vessels.* Vessels help animals with closed circulatory systems move blood and other substances through the body faster than an open circulatory system.

As in an open circulatory system, muscles help blood move in a closed circulatory system. However, in a closed circulatory system, the muscles surround the blood vessels. These muscles contract and push blood through the vessels. They also can change the amount of blood flow. A closed circulatory system keeps plasma and red blood cells that carry oxygen separated from other fluids and structures in the body. Small blood vessels called capillaries surround organs and help oxygen and nutrients move from the circulatory system to cells in organs.

 Key Concept Check What are the differences between open and closed circulatory systems?

Chambered Hearts

Different animals have hearts with different numbers of compartments called chambers, as shown in **Figure 10**. Fish have hearts with two chambers, whereas amphibian hearts consist of three chambers. Birds and mammals such as cats, dogs, and humans have hearts with four chambers. Almost all animals with three- or four-chambered hearts have lungs.

Figure 10 Animals can have hearts with two, three, or four chambers.

 Visual Check How would you describe an amphibian's circulatory system?

Math Skills

Use Proportions

A proportion is an equation with two ratios that are equivalent. Use proportions to solve problems such as the following: Veins hold about 55 percent of the body's blood. What is an organism's blood volume if the veins hold 2.6 L?

Set up the proportion.

$$\frac{55\%}{2.6\ L} = \frac{100\%}{x\ L}$$

Cross multiply.

$$55x = 260$$

Divide both sides by 55.

$$\frac{55x}{55} = \frac{260}{55} = 4.7\ L$$
$$x = 4.7\ L$$

Practice

If a normal, complete heart cycle takes 0.8 s, how many cycles would the heart make in one day?

📖 **Review**

- **Math Practice**
- **Personal Tutor**

 **Concepts in Motion** Animation

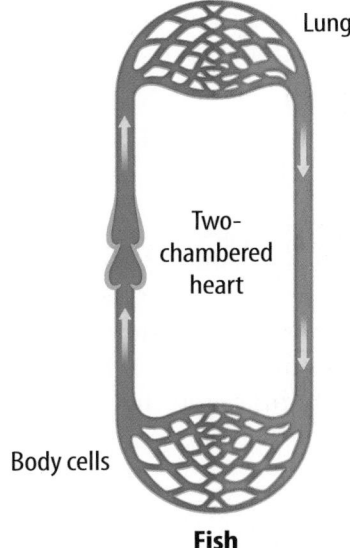

Lungs

Two-chambered heart

Body cells

Fish

Lungs

Three-chambered heart

Body cells

Amphibians and most reptiles

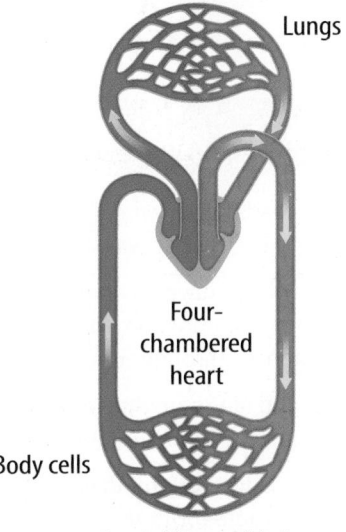

Lungs

Four-chambered heart

Body cells

Crocodilians, birds and mammals

Lesson 2 Review

Visual Summary

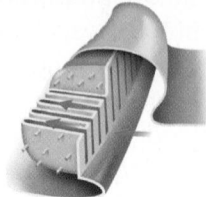

Animals have different structures for gas exchange and circulation.

Animals can have open or closed circulatory systems.

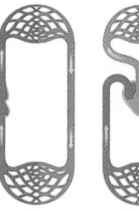

Different animals have a different number of chambers in their hearts.

FOLDABLES

Use your lesson Foldable to review the lesson. Save your Foldable for the project at the end of the chapter.

What do you think NOW?

You first read the statements below at the beginning of the chapter.

3. Earthworms have an open circulatory system that transports blood and other substances throughout the body.

4. Gills and lungs are different structures that perform the same function.

Did you change your mind about whether you agree or disagree with the statements? Rewrite any false statements to make them true.

Use Vocabulary

1 **Use the term** *spiracles* in a sentence.

2 **Distinguish** between an open circulatory system and a closed circulatory system.

3 Aquatic animals use _____ to obtain oxygen from their environment.

Understand Key Concepts

4 Which process helps oxygen move from the outside to the inside of cells?
  A. absorption   C. diffusion
  B. circulation   D. undulation

5 **Compare** the roles of book lungs and tracheal tubes in gas exchange.

6 **Infer** how the number of chambers in an animal's heart relates to its habitat.

Interpret Graphics

7 **Identify** Copy and fill in the graphic organizer below with the ways animals exchange gases with their environment.

Critical Thinking

8 **Hypothesize** how blood moves faster in a closed circulatory system when compared to an open circulatory system.

9 **Relate** the structures of gills and lungs to their roles in gas exchange.

Math Skills

Review
—— Math Practice ——

10 In one experiment, the heart rate of a mollusk at rest was measured at 0.3 cycles/s. How many times did the mollusk's heart beat in 1 min?

How do you determine what environment an animal lives in?

Materials

index cards

Safety

Animals have different structures and functions in order to survive in their environments. The combination of these different structures and functions makes animals unique from each other. How can you recognize the characteristics that determine the environments in which animals live and survive?

Learn It

Classifying is the process of grouping objects or living organisms based on common features. Scientists classify animals according to the structures and functions they share.

Try It

1. Label one blank index card for each of the characteristics listed in the categories below.

2. Shuffle the cards and spread them facedown on top of your desk.

3. Label four more index cards as follows: *Earthworm, Spider, Wolf,* and *Fish.* Shuffle these cards and place them facedown in a pile next to the cards you spread out.

4. Taking turns with your partner, choose one of the cards from the animal deck. Next, choose one of the cards spread out on the table and turn it over. If the characteristic you turned over applies to your animal, turn over another card and see if the second characteristic applies to your animal. If the characteristic does not apply to your animal, turn the card over, return it to the deck, and end your turn.

5. The object of the game is to select two cards in a row that apply to your animal. Each time you select a card, you must decide if it applies to your animal. If it does, select another card.

6. Score 1 point each time you can successfully select and turn over two cards that apply to the animal card you selected. Continue playing until all of the cards have been used.

Apply It

7. **Record** the matches you made between characteristics and animals. Which matches did you complete?

8. **Describe** how some characteristics help animals compete better to find food or shelter.

9. 🔑 **Key Concept** Analyze the types of physical characteristics that make an animal best suited for a terrestrial or an aquatic environment. Explain how the different methods of gas exchange might be linked to these environments or other characteristics.

Support Systems	Gas Exchange Systems	Circulatory Systems	Environments
Hydrostatic skeleton	book lungs	open circulatory system	aquatic environment
Exoskeleton	gills	closed circulatory system	terrestrial environment
Endoskeleton	lungs		
	diffusion		

Digestion and Excretion

Reading Guide

Key Concepts
ESSENTIAL QUESTIONS

- How are an animal's structures for feeding and digestion related to its diet?

- How do the excretory structures of aquatic and terrestrial animals differ?

Vocabulary

crop p. 432

gizzard p. 432

absorption p. 433

g Multilingual eGlossary

Inquiry **What is it doing?**

This caterpillar is chewing food—one step in the processes of digestion and excretion. Animals perform these processes to get the energy they need to live.

What does it eat?

Humans and animals use several types of teeth to eat. Can you tell what an animal eats by looking at its teeth?

1 Incisors are teeth with a sharp edge in the shape of a wedge. Canines are pointy teeth. Molars have a large rough surface. Look at the photo of these teeth and answer the questions below.

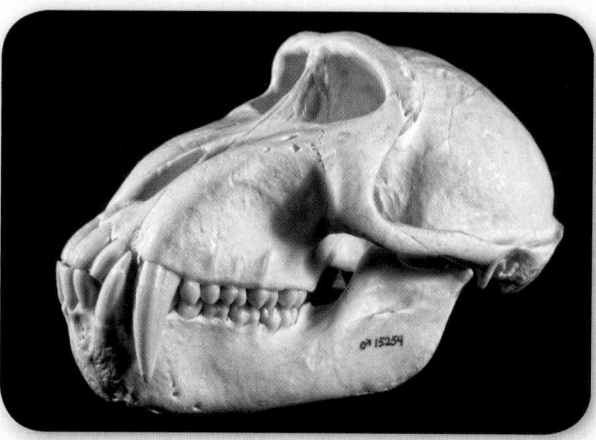

Think About This

1. Which tooth do you think would be useful for cutting off the stem of a plant?

2. Which tooth might be helpful for tearing into flesh?

3. Which tooth might be used to grind up plants and meat?

4. 🔑 **Key Concept** Which type of teeth do you think is used by humans? Why?

The Importance of Digestion and Excretion

You read in the first lesson that animals need nutrients to survive. Nutrients are obtained from food through digestion—the process of breaking down food into molecules that cells can absorb and use. After all nutrients are taken in, waste products not used by the body are removed by excretion. Excretion is important for survival because it removes harmful substances from the body. Just as different animals have different structures for gas exchange, they also have different structures to obtain and process nutrients and to remove wastes.

Digestion

Animals have different structures for digestion, depending on what type of food they eat. For example, an animal that eats only seeds has a different set of structures from an animal that eats only meat. The first step of digestion usually happens when food is chewed, as shown in **Figure 11.** The food is further broken down by the digestive system in various ways, depending on the animal's diet. As you will read in this lesson, different animals use different structures to obtain and break down food.

 Reading Check How do animals obtain nutrients?

Figure 11 The structures that this cow uses for digestion are good at breaking down grass and other plant matter.

Structures for Feeding

For many animals, the first step in feeding is obtaining food. As with other functions of the body, animals use different structures to find and chew their food. You often can tell what type of diet an animal eats by looking at the structures that it has for feeding.

Teeth Many animals have teeth, one type of structure used for feeding. Different types of teeth are used to process different diets, as shown in **Figure 12.**

Animals that eat plants often have wide teeth used for chewing grass and other plants. Some have a few sharp teeth used to cut through twigs. Animals that eat insects have teeth with sharp points that are used for chewing.

Animals that eat only meat have several types of teeth. As shown in **Figure 12,** teeth in the front of the mouth are used for biting and holding food. Teeth in the rear of the mouth are pointed and used to cut up food. Animals that eat both plants and meat have sharp teeth that are used for cutting up food and wide, flat teeth that are used for grinding up food.

Figure 12 🔑 The shape of an animal's teeth depends on its diet.

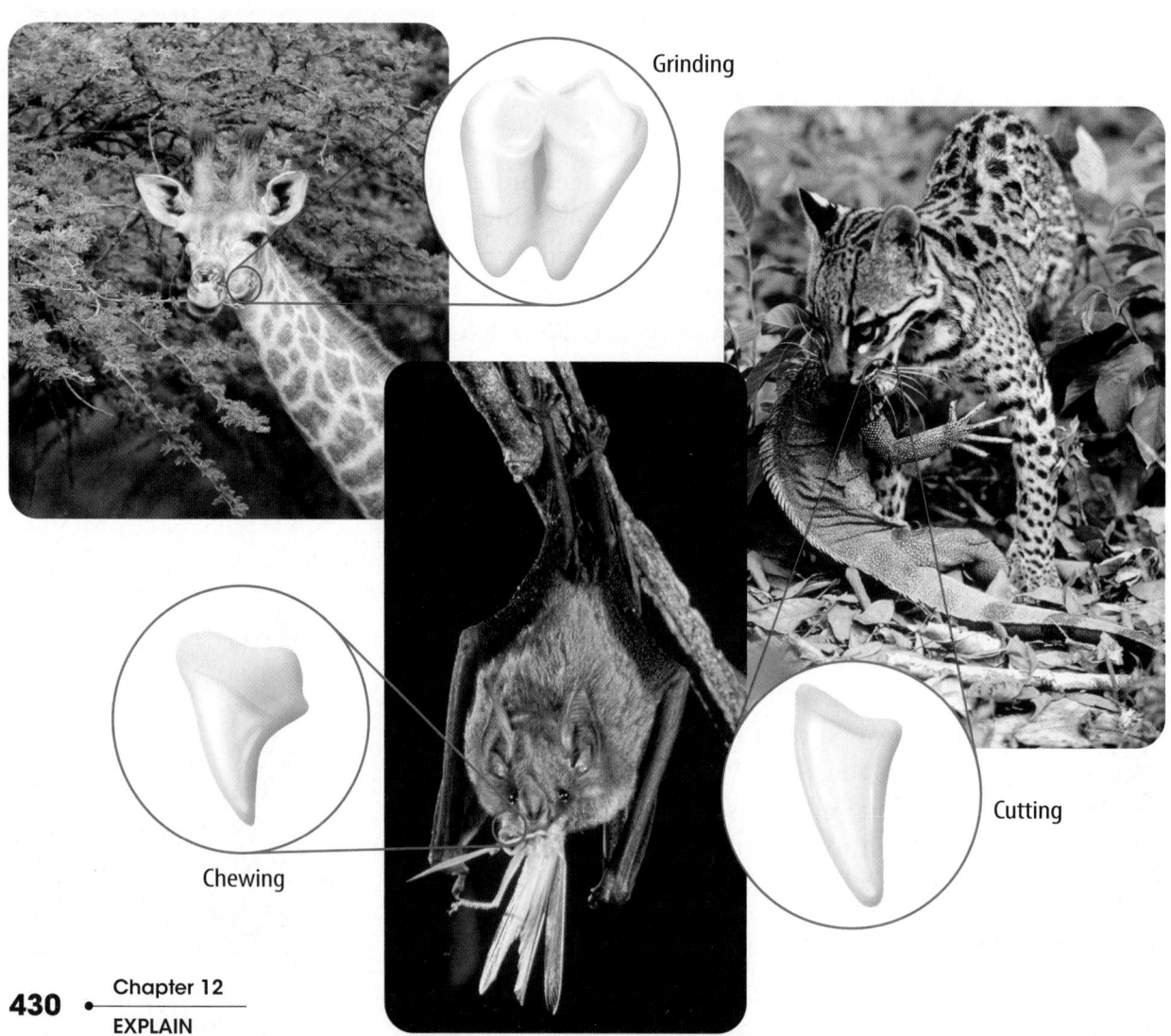

Grinding

Cutting

Chewing

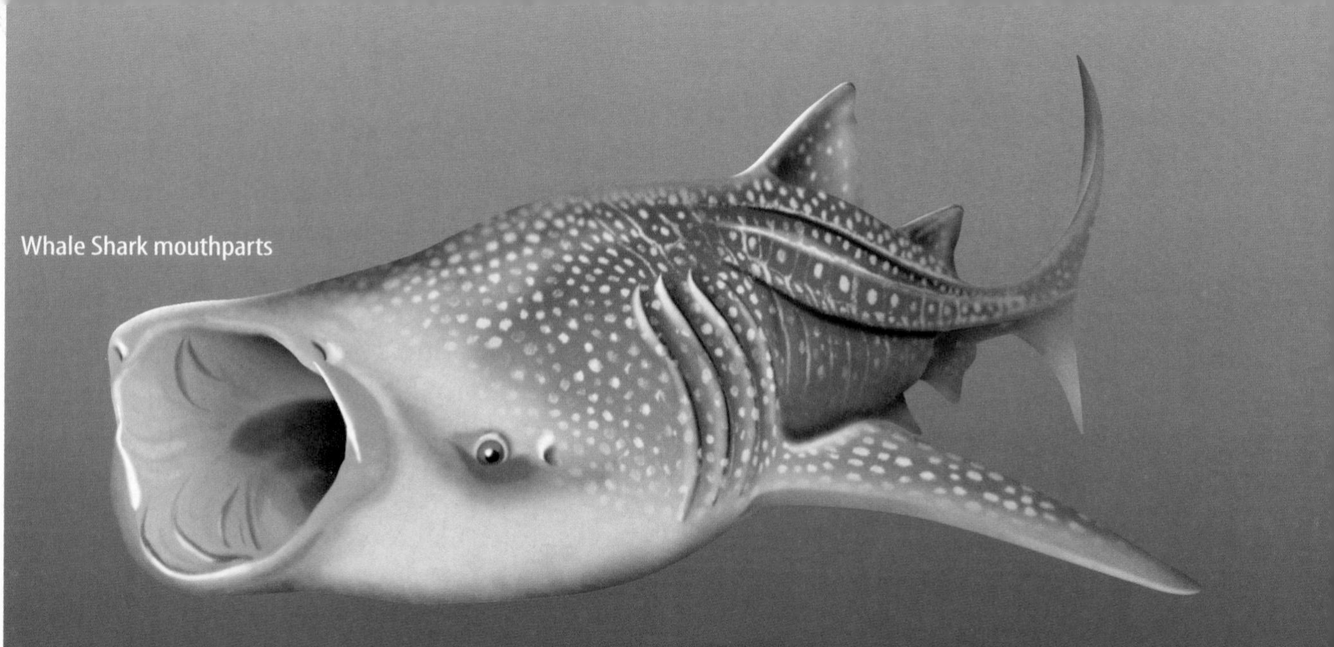
Whale Shark mouthparts

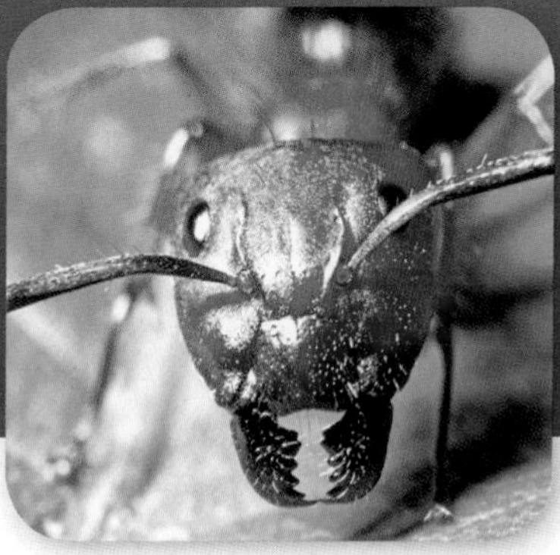
Ant mouthparts

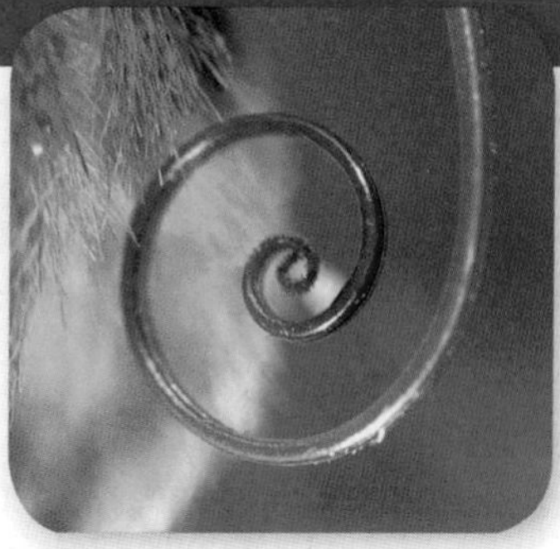
Moth mouthparts

Figure 13 Whale sharks and some insects have specialized mouthparts for feeding.

Visual Check How do mouthparts differ among the shark, the ant, and the moth?

Filter Feeding Animals that take in food suspended in water have structures for filter feeding. They take in the water with the food, push the water out through a filtering structure, then eat the organisms that remain.

Some animals, such as certain whales, take a mouthful of water and push it out through baleen (bay LEEN). Baleen is a material similar to the bristles of a broom that filter out tiny organisms in the water. Certain types of sharks and fish filter food through their gills, such as the whale shark shown in **Figure 13.** Some animals, such as clams, filter feed without moving. They filter food from the water that moves around them. However, many filter feeders move around to find food. When flamingoes filter feed, they eat shrimp that is filtered through their beak from the water they take in.

Mouthparts Some animals, particularly insects, have specialized mouthparts for eating. Butterflies and moths use a long, tubelike mouthpart, shown in **Figure 13,** to get nectar from flowers. Ants and certain beetles have crushing jaws for ripping plant and animal matter.

Key Concept Check How are an animal's feeding structures related to its diet?

Structures for Digestion

After food is broken down into smaller parts by chewing, it breaks into even smaller components during digestion. Most animals have organs that form a specialized system for digestion. For example, many animals have stomachs and intestines that are used to digest food. The structures of the stomach and the intestine depend on the animal's diet. For example, animals such as cows and sheep that eat a lot of plant material have stomachs with several chambers. In each of these chambers, the tough plant material is processed so the animal can digest it.

Crops Some animals store their food in a crop before digesting it. *A* **crop** *is a specialized structure in the digestive system where ingested material is stored.* Many birds and insects have crops. Leeches, snails, and earthworms also have crops where they store undigested food. The crop in a leech can store blood and expands up to five times its body size.

Gizzards Animals without teeth that eat hard foods such as seeds sometimes have structures called gizzards. *A* **gizzard** *is a muscular pouch similar to a stomach that is used to grind food.* Some animals with gizzards, including certain birds, swallow rocks with their food. The rocks help break up the food.

SCIENCE USE v. COMMON USE

crop

Science Use a digestive system structure where material is stored

Common Use a plant or animal product that can be grown or harvested

Inquiry MiniLab

10 minutes

How do gizzards help birds eat?

Some birds use gizzards to grind food into smaller pieces. Gizzards are small pouches that store food. The bird fills its gizzard with small stones that create the grinding action.

1. Read and complete a lab safety form.
2. Place 20 **sunflower seeds in the shell** in a **small, self-sealing plastic freezer bag.**
3. Fill another freezer bag about one-quarter full with **small stones.** Add 20 sunflower seeds in the shell.
4. Seal both bags and knead the contents of each bag for several minutes with your hands.
5. Open the bags and observe the condition of the seeds. Record your observations in your Science Journal.

Analyze and Conclude

1. **Compare and contrast** the condition of the sunflower seeds in the bag with stones to the sunflower seeds in the bag without stones.

2. **Analyze** how you think having a gizzard could be an advantage to a bird.

3. **Key Concept** Infer how the structure and function of the gizzard relates to the type of food that a bird can eat.

Lesson 3 Review

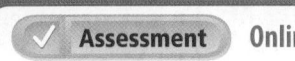

Visual Summary

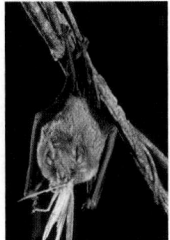

Animals have different structures for digestion and excretion.

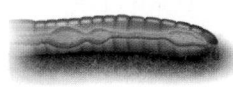

Some organisms have structures that enable them to store food.

The type of waste an animal excretes depends on its environment.

FOLDABLES®

Use your lesson Foldable to review the lesson. Save your Foldable for the project at the end of the chapter.

What do you think NOW?

You first read the statements below at the beginning of the chapter.

5. The shape of an animal's teeth depends on its diet.

6. Excretion is used only by animals that live on land.

Did you change your mind about whether you agree or disagree with the statements? Rewrite any false statements to make them true.

Use Vocabulary

1 Nutrients are taken into the body by the process of _____.

2 **Define** *gizzard* in your own words.

3 Flamingoes and leeches have storage compartments for food called _____.

Understand Key Concepts

4 Which process moves nutrients from the digestive system into the circulatory system?
   A. absorption   C. excretion
   B. diffusion   D. undulation

5 **Compare** the roles of gills and lungs in excreting carbon dioxide.

6 **Explain** the role of gizzards in digestion.

Interpret Graphics

7 **Explain** the function of the system of structures shown below.

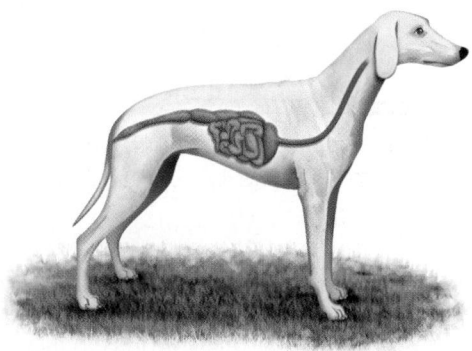

8 **Summarize** Copy and fill in the graphic organizer below with the names of materials that animals excrete.

Wastes

Critical Thinking

9 **Relate** the shape of an animal's teeth to its diet.

10 **Assess** the role of kidneys in aquatic and terrestrial animals.

Materials

craft materials

Safety

Design an Alien Animal

You have read that animals have a variety of structures and functions in order to survive. The type of structures that a particular animal has depends on the environment where it lives. Your task is to imagine a unique environment on another planet. Be creative and describe the alien planet in detail. Then use what you know about animal structures and functions to imagine what life-forms live on the planet. The life-forms you design must be able to survive in the unique environmental conditions of the planet you described.

Question

How do specialized structures and abilities help animals survive in specific environments? What animal characteristics would you expect to find in different environments?

Procedure

1. Read and complete a lab safety form.

2. In your Science Journal, write a description of an imaginary alien planet. Be creative in describing your planet. Write down as many details as you can think of, including:

- Is the planet dry, or covered with water?

- What temperatures are experienced on your planet?

- What sources of food are present?

3. Include drawings along with your descriptions. Use labels to add detailed information to the environments you create.

4. Think about how the different animal species you studied have changed over time to live in different environments. Write a statement about the relationship between a species' characteristics and its environment. Predict how the environments you have created will affect organisms on your planet.

Alien Structure and Function	
Structure	Function in Environment
Fins	
Claws	

5 Design several animals that will inhabit your alien planet. Create a data card for each animal that includes a picture of the animal. Add a chart like the one on the previous page to each data card that describes the structures of the animal and the functions of the structures. Include detailed drawings and/or descriptions of the body systems of each animal.

6 Use the information you've gathered to create a three-dimensional model, or diorama, that illustrates your environment and the animals you have described.

Analyze and Conclude

7 **Explain** For what environmental conditions has your organism developed structures?

8 **Analyze** How have some organisms gained an advantage over other organisms on the planet?

9 **Compare and Contrast** How are the animals on your planet similar to and different from each other in terms of control, support, movement, gas exchange, feeding, digestion, and excretion? How do these characteristics help them maintain homeostasis?

10 **The Big Idea** Why do the animals on your alien planet have different structures, even though they all live on the same planet?

Communicate Your Results

Share your diorama with the rest of the class. Compare your planet's environment and life-forms with the ones your classmates created. What similarities and differences do you notice?

 **Inquiry** **Extension**

Pair up with another student. Choose an organism from your partner's planet to bring to your planet. Write a prediction of what would happen. Would the new organism survive? How would the species adapt to the new environment? What organisms would it compete with? Would it threaten the survival of other organisms upon its arrival?

Lab Tips

☑ Consider your animal's environment when determining its diet.

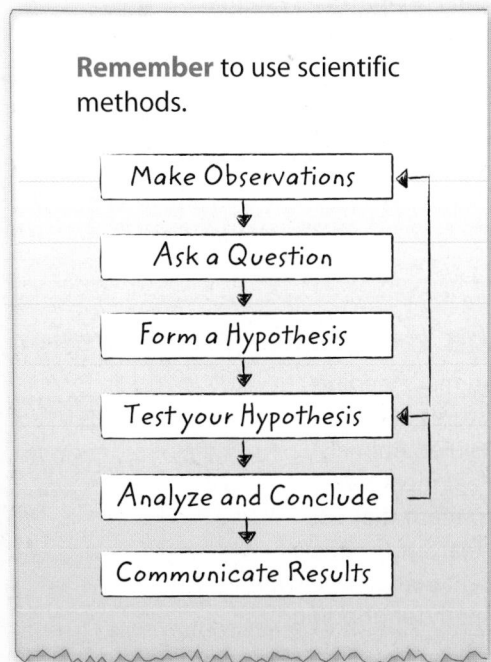

Remember to use scientific methods.

Make Observations
↓
Ask a Question
↓
Form a Hypothesis
↓
Test your Hypothesis
↓
Analyze and Conclude
↓
Communicate Results

Chapter 12 Study Guide

Animals have different structures that perform similar functions which enable them to survive in different environments.

Key Concepts Summary 🔑	Vocabulary
Lesson 1: Support, Control, and Movement • Support structures give internal organs protection. Endoskeletons are made of bone or cartilage. Exoskeletons form shells made of minerals. 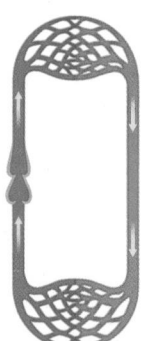 • **Nerve nets** detect changes in the environment over a large area without a brain. Nerve cords sense the environment, send the information to the brain for processing, and transmit the response to neurons. • Animals have different structures that enable them to move through their habitats.	**hydrostatic skeleton** p. 412 **coelum** p. 412 **nerve net** p. 414 **undulation** p. 416
Lesson 2: Circulation and Gas Exchange • Gas exchange occurs through **gills** in aquatic animals and through lungs or **spiracles** in terrestrial animals. • In **open circulatory systems**, blood surrounds all organs in the body. **Closed circulatory systems** use blood vessels to transport substances throughout the body. 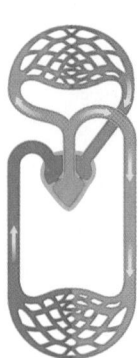	**diffusion** p. 422 **spiracle** p. 422 **gills** p. 423 **open circulatory system** p. 424 **closed circulatory system** p. 425
Lesson 3: Digestion and Excretion • An animal's feeding structures depend on its diet. Animals that eat meat have sharp teeth that cut and tear, and animals that eat plants have wide, flat teeth for grinding.  • Aquatic animals use kidneys to excrete large amounts of water and ammonia. Terrestrial animals use kidneys to excrete smaller amounts of water and either urea or uric acid. Aquatic animals excrete carbon dioxide through gills, and terrestrial animals excrete carbon dioxide through the lungs or spiracles.	**crop** p. 432 **gizzard** p. 432 **absorption** p. 433

FOLDABLES® Chapter Project

Assemble your lesson Foldables as shown to make a Chapter Project. Use the project to review what you have learned in this chapter.

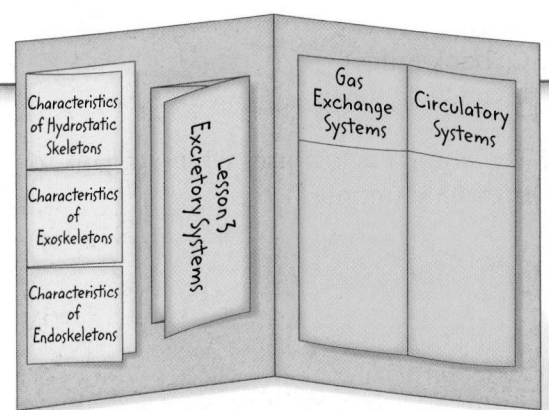

Use Vocabulary

1 Use the term *coelom* in a sentence.

2 Some animals store food in structures called _____.

3 Tiny openings on the surface of some animals that are used to take in oxygen are _____.

4 Define the term *crop* in your own words.

5 Snakes and eels move by _____.

6 Define the term *diffusion* in your own words.

Link Vocabulary and Key Concepts

Concepts in Motion   Interactive Concept Map

Copy this concept map, and then use vocabulary terms from the previous page to complete the concept map.

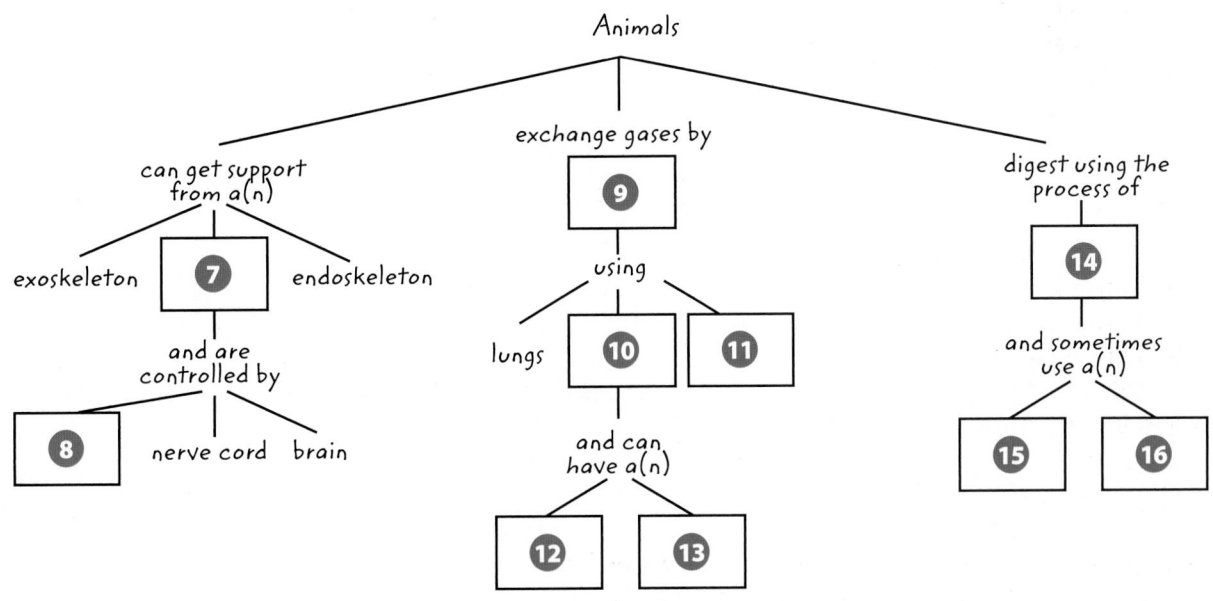

Understand Key Concepts

1 Which is NOT used to provide an animal with structural support?

A. endoskeleton
B. exoskeleton
C. hydrostatic skeleton
D. nerve net

2 The fluid-filled sac in an earthworm is called a(n)

A. coelom.
B. endoskeleton.
C. nerve cord.
D. nerve net.

3 The animal pictured below has which type of support system?

A. endoskeleton
B. exoskeleton
C. hydrostatic skeleton
D. no skeleton

4 Animals with _____ do not have brains.

A. endoskeletons
B. gills
C. nerve cords
D. nerve nets

5 Which structure is used for food storage?

A. crop
B. gizzard
C. kidney
D. stomach

6 Capillaries are found in animals with

A. coeloms.
B. spiracles.
C. closed circulatory systems.
D. open circulatory systems.

7 Which is NOT used for gas exchange?

A. crops
B. gills
C. book lungs
D. tracheal tubes

8 The animal below uses which organs to excrete ammonia?

A. gills
B. intestines
C. kidneys
D. lungs

9 Which is NOT used by aquatic animals to move through the water?

A. fin
B. gill
C. tail
D. wing

10 What is the basic process of gas exchange?

A. absorption
B. circulation
C. diffusion
D. excretion

Critical Thinking

11 **Describe** how the structure of cnidarians helps them respond to stimuli from all directions.

12 **Compare** the roles of endoskeletons and exoskeletons in providing animals with protection.

13 **Assess** the role of undulation in helping animals without appendages move.

14 **Relate** the structure of an animal's circulatory system to the rate at which blood moves throughout its body.

15 **Relate** the structure an organism uses for gas exchange to its habitat.

16 **Describe** how diffusion helps animals exchange gases.

17 **Relate** an animal's habitat to the amount of water it excretes.

18 **Hypothesize** how the structure pictured below helps an animal obtain nutrients without having to eat more food.

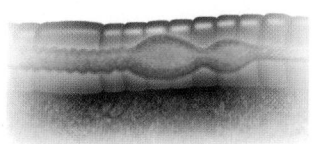

19 **Compare** the structure of teeth in animals that eat plants and animals that eat other animals.

Writing in Science

20 **Write** a five-sentence paragraph that describes how spiracles work together with book lungs and tracheal tubes to obtain oxygen. Be sure to include a topic sentence and a concluding sentence in your paragraph.

REVIEW THE BIG IDEA

21 Why do animals have different structures that perform similar functions? Compare and contrast some structures that appear different but perform the same function.

22 The owl shown below has various structures that enable it to survive. Compare these structures with an animal that lives in a different environment. List the similarities and differences.

Math Skills

 **Review**

Math Practice

Use Proportions

23 Birds and mammals have four-chambered hearts. Out of a sample with 52,750 species of animals, 9,600 are birds and 5,500 are mammals. What percentage of animals in the sample have four-chambered hearts?

24 The average human heart beats about 3 billion times during a lifetime. If the average heart rate is 70 beats/min, what is the average life span, in years, for the human heart? [Hint: 525,600 min = 1 y]

Standardized Test Practice

Record your answers on the answer sheet provided by your teacher or on a sheet of paper.

Multiple Choice

1 Which term describes a protective support structure found on the outside of certain organisms?

  A endoskeleton

  B exoskeleton

  C cartilage skeleton

  D hydrostatic skeleton

Use the figure below to answer question 2.

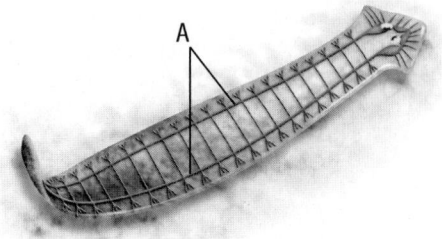

2 What parts are labeled with the letter *A* in the figure?

  A bones

  B intestines

  C nerve cords

  D nerve nets

3 How do the excretory structures of fish compare with those of birds?

  A Birds excrete feces and fish do not.

  B Birds have gizzards and fish have crops.

  C Fish have gills and birds have lungs.

  D Fish have kidneys and birds do not.

4 Which animal moves by undulation?

  A a seagull

  B a snake

  C a squid

  D a squirrel

5 What is the function of a crop?

  A exchange gases

  B protect organs

  C store food

  D transport material

Use the figure below to answer question 6.

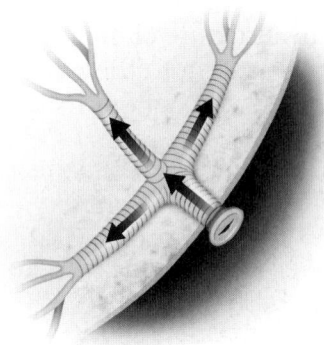

6 Which gas exchange structure is shown?

  A a gill

  B a lung

  C a book lung

  D a tracheal tube

7 How do terrestrial animals excrete carbon dioxide?

  A through gills

  B through inhalation

  C through lungs

  D through undulation

8 Which animal has a nerve net that controls its body?

  A a dog

  B a python

  C a flying squirrel

  D a sea anemone

Use the figure below to answer question 9.

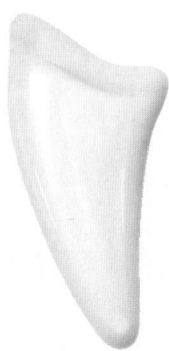

9 A biologist in the field finds a large animal tooth like the one shown. Which describes how a tooth of this shape and size was most likely used?

   A to bite into large prey

   B to chew insects

   C to eat grass

   D to eat leaves from trees

10 What gives a hydrostatic skeleton support?

   A bones

   B cartilage

   C coelom

   D shell

Constructed Response

Use the diagrams below to answer questions 11 and 12.

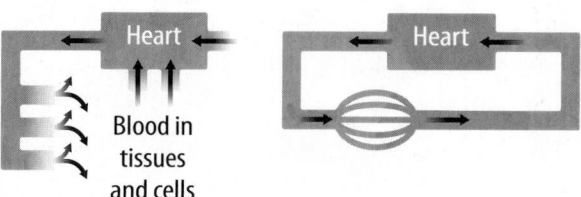

11 Which type of circulatory system would be more efficient in moving blood through the body? Explain your answer.

12 An open circulatory system allows oxygen and nutrients to enter all tissues and cells directly. A closed circulatory system allows blood to be moved through the body faster. Which system would enable an animal to process energy faster? Explain your answer.

13 Explain how a book lung differs from the lung of a turtle.

14 Give an example of an animal that has the ability to move by two different means.

NEED EXTRA HELP?														
If You Missed Question...	1	2	3	4	5	6	7	8	9	10	11	12	13	14
Go to Lesson...	1	1	3	1	3	2	3	1	3	1	2	2	2	1

Animal Behavior and Reproduction

THE BIG IDEA How do animals communicate, interact, and reproduce?

Inquiry **What are they doing?**

This female chimpanzee is showing its offspring how to use a stick to find termites.

- How might this behavior be beneficial to the young chimpanzee?

- What other types of behaviors do animals have?

- In what ways might animals communicate, interact, and find mates?

Get Ready to Read

What do you think?

Before you read, decide if you agree or disagree with each of these statements. As you read this chapter, see if you change your mind about any of the statements.

1 Animals react to their environments.

2 All animal behavior is instinctive.

3 Some animals give off light to communicate with each other.

4 Animals always fight to protect their territories.

5 During sexual reproduction, a sperm cell and an egg cell join.

6 Some animals develop inside the mother.

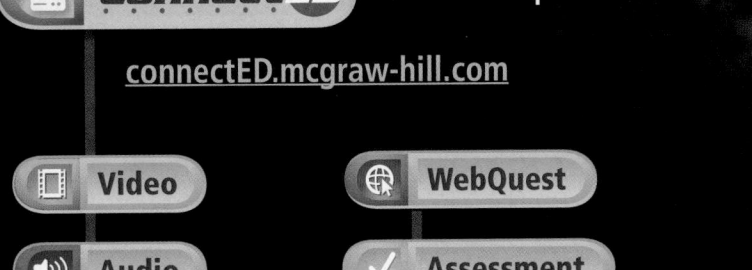

ConnectED Your one-stop online resource

connectED.mcgraw-hill.com

▤ Video	⊕ WebQuest
◀)) Audio	✓ Assessment
▤ Review	((◎ Concepts in Motion
? Inquiry	g Multilingual eGlossary

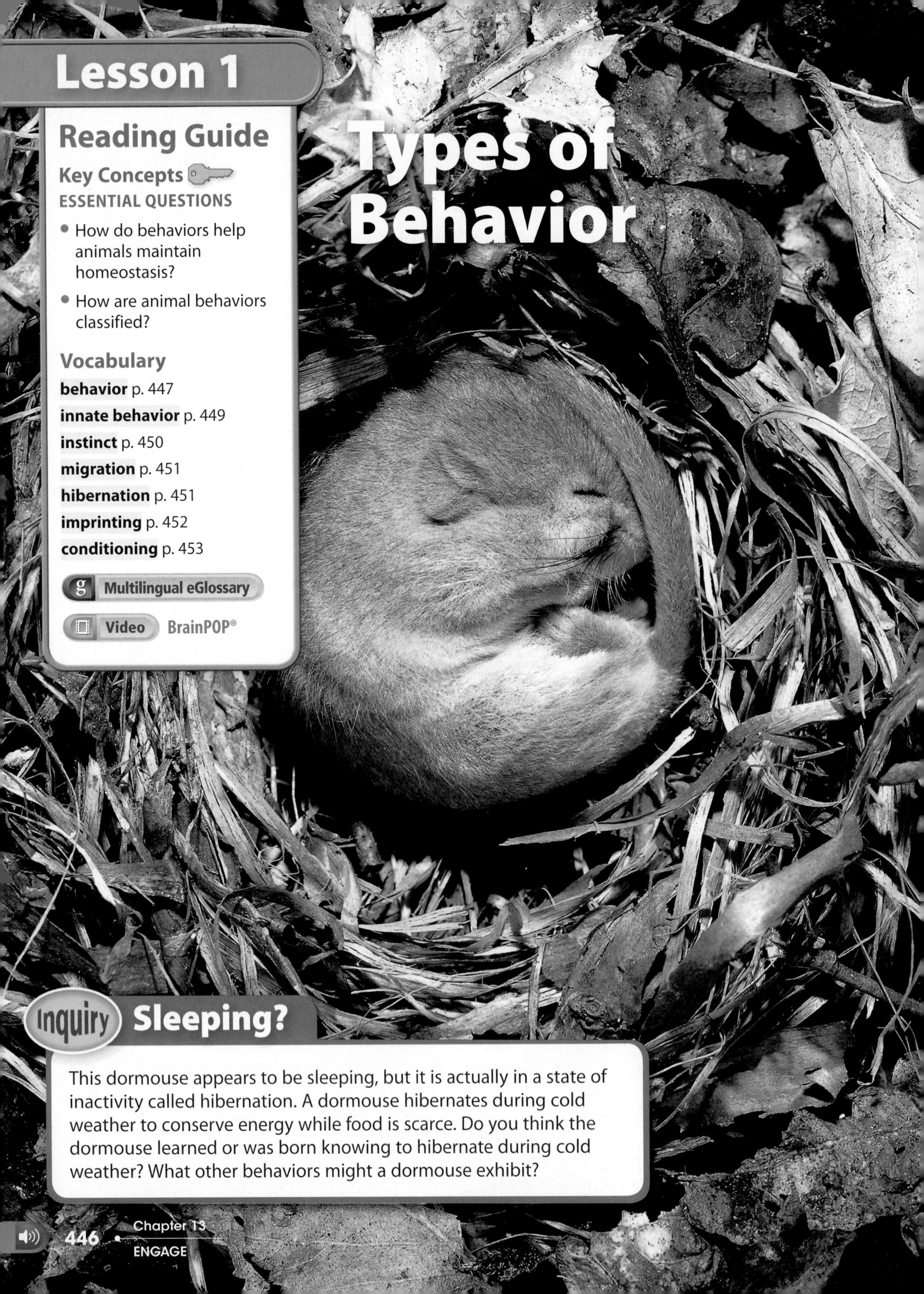

Lesson 1

Types of Behavior

Reading Guide

Key Concepts
ESSENTIAL QUESTIONS

- How do behaviors help animals maintain homeostasis?
- How are animal behaviors classified?

Vocabulary

behavior p. 447
innate behavior p. 449
instinct p. 450
migration p. 451
hibernation p. 451
imprinting p. 452
conditioning p. 453

g Multilingual eGlossary

Video BrainPOP®

Inquiry Sleeping?

This dormouse appears to be sleeping, but it is actually in a state of inactivity called hibernation. A dormouse hibernates during cold weather to conserve energy while food is scarce. Do you think the dormouse learned or was born knowing to hibernate during cold weather? What other behaviors might a dormouse exhibit?

What happens when you touch a pill bug?

Pill bugs are arthropods that live under leaf litter and rocks. They have a special behavior that helps them defend themselves against other animals that might eat them.

1. Read and complete a lab safety form.

2. Obtain a **pill bug** and gently place it in a **petri dish** for observation. Study the pill bug without touching it, and draw it in your Science Journal.

3. Use a **cotton swab** to gently touch the pill bug, and observe it again. Draw the pill bug's reaction.

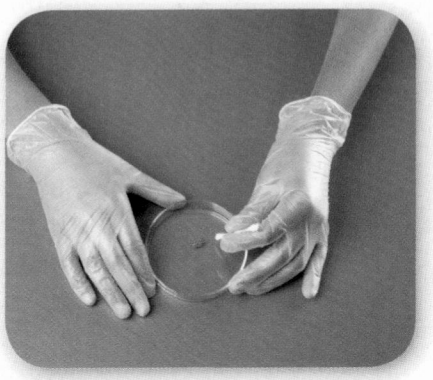

Think About This

1. How did the pill bug react when you touched its back?

2. What stimulus did you provide that was different from the pill bug's natural environment?

3. **Key Concept** What other stimuli do you think might affect the pill bug?

What is a behavior?

Have you ever watched a dog sniff the ground while it was out for a walk? Or have you seen a dog, such as the one in **Figure 1**, working with law enforcement and sniffing luggage at an airport? Why does a dog do this? Dogs receive information about their surroundings by sniffing. Dogs have a much more developed sense of smell than humans do. A dog's nose has about 220 million scent receptors, but a human's nose has only about 5 million.

The act of sniffing is a common dog behavior. *A* **behavior** *is the way an organism reacts to other organisms or to its environment.* Behaviors might be carried out by individual animals, such as a dog sniffing, or by groups of animals of the same species, such as a flock of birds flying together. Recall that organisms' bodies work to maintain a steady internal state called **homeostasis.** Behaviors are a way to maintain homeostasis when the environment changes.

 Key Concept Check How do behaviors help animals maintain homeostasis?

Figure 1 A dog's sniffing behavior helps it get information about its surroundings.

REVIEW VOCABULARY

homeostasis
an organism's ability to maintain steady internal conditions when outside conditions change

REVIEW VOCABULARY
stimulus
a change in an organism's
environment that causes
a response

Stimuli and Responses

When an animal carries out a behavior, it is reacting to a **stimulus** (STIHM yuh lus; plural, stimuli), or change. A stimulus can be external, such as the weather getting warmer, or internal, such as hunger. Scents coming from the pavement or a tree are external stimuli for a dog. The dog's response to the stimuli is sniffing.

Stimuli

Stimuli can come in many forms and result in different behaviors. Changes in the external environment, such as a temperature change or a rainstorm, can affect an animal's behavior. Hunger, thirst, illness, and other changes in an animal's internal environment are stimuli, too.

Responses to Change

Animals respond to changes and maintain homeostasis in different ways. For example, when the weather gets cooler, an organism might respond with a specific behavior. Birds, which must keep their bodies at the same temperature year-round, fluff their feathers and retain more thermal energy, as shown in **Figure 2.** The cooler weather is the stimulus, and the bird's feather fluffing is a response.

Animals also respond to internal stimuli, such as illnesses. If an animal is sick, its body might respond with a fever. The fever increases body temperature and might help the animal fight a disease. Vomiting is another response to an internal stimulus. A dog that ate something from the garbage might vomit to get the material out of its body. This behavior helps the dog maintain homeostasis by removing something that could cause an illness.

 Reading Check Explain how vomiting can maintain homeostasis.

Figure 2 🔑 During warm weather, a bird's feathers are close to its body. When a bird fluffs its feathers during cold weather, it traps a layer of air around its body. The air helps keep the bird warm.

Figure 3 Some animals, such as antelope, respond to threatening situations by running away.

Stress

Have you ever seen an animal run away when a human got too close? The human caused the animal to become stressed, and the animal reacted by running away. Some animals, such as the antelope shown in **Figure 3,** will almost always run away if they feel threatened. When an animal identifies a danger, its body prepares to either fight or run away from the perceived threat. This behavior is called the fight-or-flight response.

Not all animals have the same reaction and run away from dangerous situations. A wild male horse might attack another male in the same area to protect its herd. Some animals, such as rats, will run from danger but will fight if cornered.

Innate Behaviors

As you have read, behaviors are responses to some type of stimulus. An animal's behaviors are a combination of those that are learned and those that are inherited and not linked to past experiences. *A behavior that is inherited rather than learned is called an* **innate behavior.**

An innate behavior happens automatically the first time an animal responds to a certain stimulus. For example, when tadpoles hatch, they already know how to swim. They do not learn how to do so by watching other tadpoles. Tadpoles can swim away from danger and find food as soon as they hatch.

Animals with short life spans have mostly innate behaviors. Animals such as insects rely on behaviors that they do not have to learn. They are able to find food and mates and avoid danger early in their lives. Insect innate behaviors include a cricket's ability to chirp and a moth's attraction to light. These types of behaviors enable animals to survive without learning from another animal.

FOLDABLES®

Make a small, horizontal four-door shutterfold book. Leave a 2-cm space between the tabs so the inside shows. Draw arrows, and label the tabs as shown. Use your book to compare and contrast animal behaviors.

Internal Environment
External Environment
Animal Behaviors
Innate
Learned

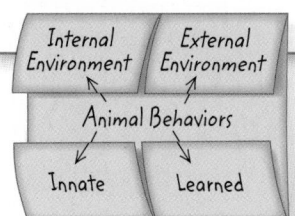

▲ **Figure 4** This armadillo has a reflex that causes it to jump when startled.

 **Review** **Personal Tutor**

Reflexes

Have you ever noticed what happens to the pupils in your eyes when you go into a dimly lit room? After a short period of time, they get larger. This happens without you thinking about it. This is an example of the simplest type of innate behavior, called a reflex. A reflex is an automatic response that does not involve a message from the brain.

Animals have reflexes, too. For example, an armadillo will jump straight upward about 1 m when startled, as shown in **Figure 4.** By jumping, the armadillo might be able to startle predators and escape.

Instincts

Reflexes happen quickly and involve one behavior. Some innate behaviors involve a number of steps performed in a specific order. *A complex pattern of innate behaviors is called an* **instinct** (IHN stingt). Finding food, running away from danger, and grooming are some behaviors that are instincts in many animals.

Instincts, such as web spinning in spiders, might take hours or days to complete and are usually made up of many behaviors. The feeding behavior of an egg-eating snake is shown in **Figure 5.** The snake's pattern of behavior is an instinct.

✓ **Reading Check** Explain the difference between reflexes and instincts.

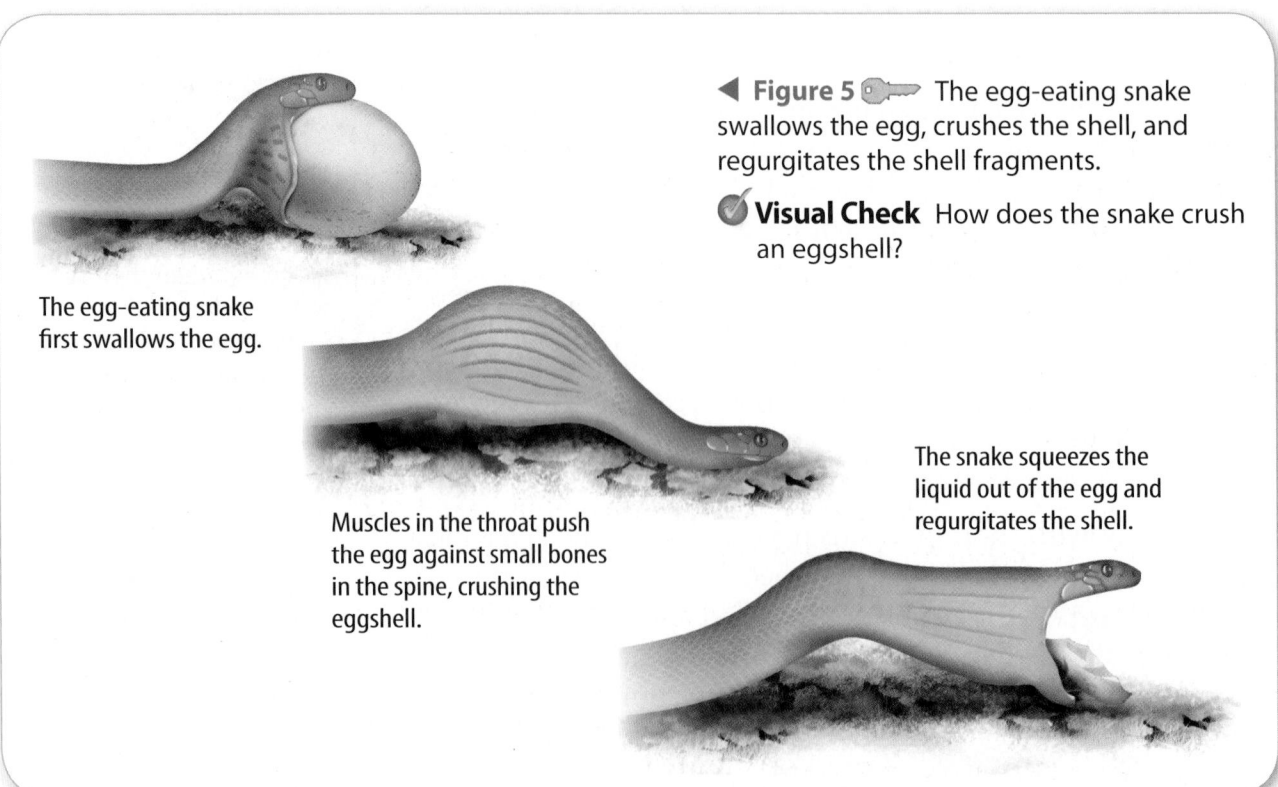

◀ **Figure 5** The egg-eating snake swallows the egg, crushes the shell, and regurgitates the shell fragments.

◉ **Visual Check** How does the snake crush an eggshell?

The egg-eating snake first swallows the egg.

Muscles in the throat push the egg against small bones in the spine, crushing the eggshell.

The snake squeezes the liquid out of the egg and regurgitates the shell.

Behavior Patterns

Many animal behaviors change in response to the change of seasons. In warm weather, there is plenty of food and water, and animals have no difficulty keeping warm. As the weather becomes cooler, food and water supplies might decrease, and animals might have difficulty surviving.

Migration Some animals move to warmer places during cooler weather. *This instinctive, seasonal movement of animals from one place to another is called* **migration.** Animals migrate to find food and water when the weather becomes too hot or too cold, or to return to specific breeding locations. Many birds, such as the ruby-throated hummingbird shown in **Figure 6,** fly many kilometers to warmer climates where they can find food.

Figure 6 🔑 Ruby-throated hummingbirds fly from New England to Louisiana. They then fly nonstop for about 805 km to the Yucatan Peninsula and Central and South America.

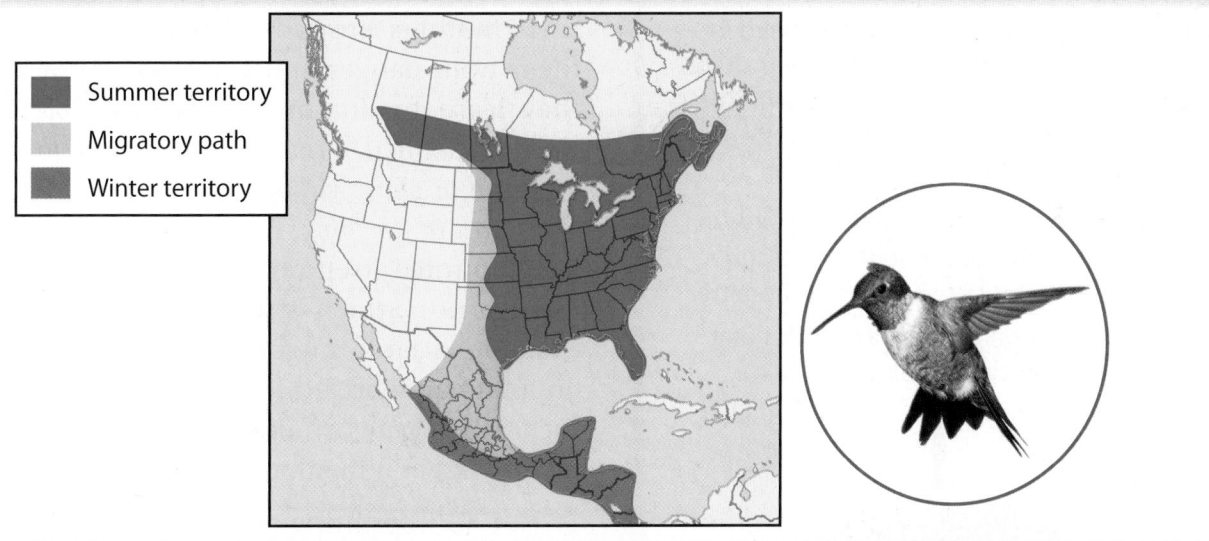

Summer territory
Migratory path
Winter territory

Hibernation Other animals do not migrate when temperatures get colder. Some animals, such as snowy owls and snowshoe hares, have feathers or fur that keep them warm in the winter. Other animals respond to cold temperatures and limited food supplies by hibernating. **Hibernation** *is a response in which an animal's body temperature, activity, heart rate, and breathing rate decrease during periods of cold weather.*

Chipmunks, some bat species, and prairie dogs are just a few types of animals that hibernate. Hibernating animals live on the fat that was stored in their bodies before hibernation. In some hibernating rodents, up to 50 percent of their body weight is fat.

Reptiles and other animals whose internal temperatures change with the environment do not hibernate. Rather, they enter a hibernationlike state. In dry, hot areas such as deserts, many animals also decrease their activity. This period of inactivity is called estivation (es tuh VAY shun).

WORD ORIGIN · · · · · · · · · · · ·

hibernation
from Latin *hibernare*, means "the action of passing the winter"

You have probably heard about service dogs that help humans by opening doors or turning on light switches. How are these dogs able to do such amazing things? Dogs and all other mammals, birds, reptiles, amphibians, and fish learn. This means that these animals develop new behaviors through experience or practice. Invertebrates, such as mollusks, insects, and arthropods, also can learn, but most of their behaviors are innate, or inherited.

Imprinting

Young birds and mammals usually follow their mothers around. This helps protect them from danger and find food. How do they learn to do this? **Imprinting** *occurs when an animal forms an attachment to an organism or place within a specific time period after birth or hatching.* Once a young animal has imprinted itself on an organism, it will usually not attach itself to another. For example, a lamb might become imprinted on a human who fed it from a bottle. Once the lamb matures, it might have a hard time identifying as a member of a flock of sheep.

Not all imprinting occurs on organisms. Turtles do not imprint on other turtles. Female sea turtles return to the beach where they were born to lay their eggs. These turtles have imprinted on the beach.

Trial and Error

Some behaviors, such as a child learning to button a shirt, take many tries before they are performed correctly. The child might try several buttoning techniques before finding one that works. This type of learning, called trial and error, happens in animals as well. For example, a monkey presented with food in a box might try to open the box many ways before succeeding. The next time it encounters a similar box, it will remember how to open the box without retrying the techniques that did not work.

▲ **Figure 7** 🔑 Some fish learn through conditioning to come to the surface of the water when they are hungry.

🔘 **Visual Check** What is the stimulus that the fish are responding to?

Conditioning

Another way that animals might learn new behaviors is through conditioning. *In* **conditioning**, *behavior is modified so that a response to one stimulus becomes associated with a different stimulus.* As shown in **Figure 7,** some fish learn to come to the surface of the water when a hand is held over the water. They have learned that the hand often holds food. Through conditioning, some birds learn to avoid stinging wasps and monarch butterflies, which have a bad taste.

Cognitive Behavior

Thinking, reasoning, and solving problems are cognitive behaviors. Humans use cognitive behavior to solve problems and plan for the future. Scientists have done experiments with animals such as primates, dolphins, elephants, and ravens that suggest they also might use cognitive behaviors. For example, studies done with ravens showed the birds could figure out how to get meat by pulling a string attached to the food. Other animals appear to show cognitive behaviors such as using tools to get food. For example, sea otters use rocks to crack the shells of clams and mussels, as shown in **Figure 8.**

🔑 **Key Concept Check** How are animal behaviors classified?

Figure 8 🔑 Scientists have observed otters using what appears to be cognitive behavior. ▼

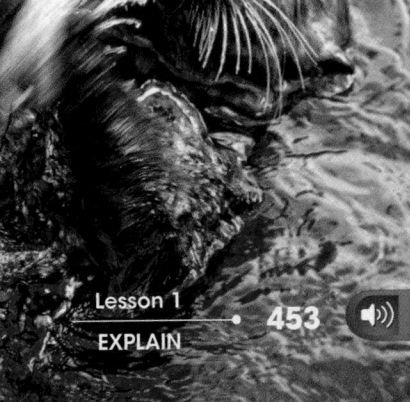

Visual Summary

Animals react to stimuli with behaviors.

Behaviors can be either innate or learned.

Many animals have complex patterns of innate behaviors.

FOLDABLES®

Use your lesson Foldable to review the lesson. Save your Foldable for the project at the end of the chapter.

What do you think NOW?

You first read the statements below at the beginning of the chapter.

1. Animals react to their environments.

2. All animal behavior is instinctive.

Did you change your mind about whether you agree or disagree with the statements? Rewrite any false statements to make them true.

Use Vocabulary

1. **Define** *innate behavior* in your own words.

2. **Use the term** *migration* in a sentence.

3. **Distinguish** between conditioning and cognitive behavior.

Understand Key Concepts

4. Which is a learned behavior?
   - **A.** conditioning
   - **B.** instinct
   - **C.** migration
   - **D.** reflexes

5. **Classify** the following behaviors as innate or learned: birds flying to warmer climates for winter, a mussel closing its shell, a duckling following its mother, a spider spinning a web.

6. **Compare** learning by trial and error and conditioning.

Interpret Graphics

7. **Explain** Use the image below to explain how conditioning works in animals.

8. **Identify** Copy and fill in the table below with examples of the types of behavior.

Innate Behavior	Learned Behavior

Critical Thinking

9. **Design an experiment** to determine if a goldfish can learn by conditioning.

Can the color or surface of an area determine how a mealworm will move?

Animal behaviors help maintain homeostasis, a steady internal state. An example of this is finding an environment that meets all the needs for living and survival, such as food, water, or shelter. If an animal is put in an environment that is not familiar and does not meet its needs, it will seek a more suitable environment.

Materials

mealworms

marker

metric ruler

string

Also needed:
surface materials

Safety

Learn It

In science experiments, the one factor you change is called the independent variable. The factor that changes as a result is the dependent variable. An experimental subject for which the independent variable is not changed is the control. By **manipulating variables,** you can get more accurate results from experiments.

Try It

1. Read and complete a lab safety form.

2. Choose four different surfaces for testing movement of a mealworm. In your Science Journal, make a table like the one below to record your observations.

3. Carefully place worm 1 on the first surface, and leave it for 30 s. Trace the path of the worm as it moves across the surface. Use the string to follow the path it travels, then place the string on a ruler to measure the distance in centimeters.

4. Repeat step 3 two more times with the same worm.

5. Repeat steps 3 and 4 on different surfaces for worms 2, 3, and 4.

Apply It

6. **Identify** the independent variable and the dependent variable. What factor enabled the mealworm to move the farthest? Explain.

7. **Summarize** Change another independent variable, such as putting one surface on an upward slant, putting flour, sand, or soil on one surface, or placing a transparent cover over the color of the surface. Summarize the outcomes from changing this independent variable.

8. 🔑 **Key Concept** What did the mealworms do to try to regain a balance with their environment after being moved from the container? What behavior is this?

Worm	Trial	Surface	Distance (cm)
1	1		
1	2		
1	3		
2	1		
2	2		
2	3		
3	1		

Lesson 2

Reading Guide

Key Concepts 🗝
ESSENTIAL QUESTIONS

- How do animals communicate?
- How do animals interact in societies?

Vocabulary

bioluminescence p. 458

pheromone p. 459

society p. 460

territory p. 461

aggression p. 461

g Multilingual eGlossary

Interacting with Others

Inquiry Fighting or Playing?

These red foxes appear to be fighting, but they are actually playing in the snow. All animals have ways to communicate and interact with other members of their species. They also have ways of communicating and interacting with other species.

How are you feeling?

Although they do not use words, animals still can communicate. Many use sounds, such as chirping or singing, but some use only body language and facial expressions to communicate with other animals. Some animals even communicate changes in mood, all without words.

1 Brainstorm several emotions with your group, and write them in your Science Journal.

2 Decide which emotion you could demonstrate using just your facial expression and/or body language without props or touching anyone.

3 Take turns communicating your emotion and guessing which one each person is trying to show.

Think About This

1. What was your emotion, and how did you communicate it?

2. How do you think animals might communicate that same emotion?

3. **Key Concept** Why do you think animals might need to communicate with other animals?

Communication

In the last lesson, you read about behaviors in individual animals. Animals have distinct behaviors in groups as well. Have you ever noticed a swarm of ants around a piece of food that has fallen on the sidewalk, as shown in **Figure 9?** How do you think the ants knew where to go? A foraging ant discovered the food and left a trail of chemicals for the other ants to follow. This and other types of communication are important for animal group behavior.

Animals use communication for many reasons, such as protection, locating other members of their groups, warning others of danger, and finding mates. Animals communicate using sound, light, chemicals, and body language. An animal might communicate with other animals of the same species, or it might communicate with different species in the same area.

Key Concept Check How do animals communicate?

FOLDABLES

Make a vertical two-tab book. Label it as shown. Use it to record what you learn about animal communication and animal societies.

Animal Communication

Animal Societies

 Figure 9 Ants follow the trail of another ant from their colony to find food.

 **Concepts in Motion** Animation

How can you demonstrate sound communication?

Sometimes in the evening or during a walk in the woods, you hear a distinctive sound from an animal. It might be a bird with an unusual call, a cricket chirping, or a bullfrog croaking in a pond nearby. All of these sounds are forms of communication that enable animals to find each other.

1. Pull a **sound card** from the pile of cards, and wait until everyone is ready.

2. If your sound card directs you to make a sound, begin to make the sound as directed on the card. Continue to make the sound intermittently until your partner recognizes your call. If your sound card directs you to listen for a sound, listen carefully and find the student who is making the sound described on your card.

Analyze and Conclude

1. **Explain** what made it possible for you to distinguish your partner from others who were also making sounds.

2. **Infer** What might happen if another person used a pattern or sound that was similar to the one you were listening for?

3. 🔑 **Key Concept** What other ways, besides sound, do animals in the wild use to find others of the same kind? Why do animals need to find others?

Sound

Many animals, such as birds, amphibians, reptiles, and mammals, communicate with sound. Dolphins make a wide variety of sounds, including whistles and grunts. Each sound has a different meaning to the other dolphins, such as excitement, play, or warning of danger. Although many animals make calls, some animals, such as the ruffed grouse, produce sound in other ways. The male grouse makes a drumming noise to attract a mate by using its wings to beat the air. Many insects, such as cicadas and crickets, also produce sounds to attract mates.

Figure 10 🔑 Male fireflies move quickly, leaving a trail of flashes.

Light

To communicate in the dark, some animals use bioluminescence (BI oh lew muh NE sunts). **Bioluminescence** *is the ability of certain living things to give off light.* Chemical reactions in the animal's body produce the light. You might have seen fireflies, such as the one in **Figure 10,** as they blink out a code to attract females in the area. However, most animals that use bioluminescence live in the ocean. In the dimly lit zone of the ocean, up to 90 percent of fish and crustaceans are thought to use bioluminescence. Some fish use bioluminescence to lure prey into their mouths. Others have pockets of bioluminescent bacteria in their cheeks, which help the fish attract mates.

Chemicals

Many animals produce chemicals, called pheromones (FER uh mohnz), to communicate. *A **pheromone** is a chemical that is produced by one animal and influences the behavior of another animal of the same species.* When released to the environment, pheromones can signal the presence of danger, food, mates, or even communicate the borders of a territory. Some flying animals, such as some moths, release pheromones into the air that attract mates. Other animals, such as male dogs, mark surfaces with pheromones that identify their territory to other dogs. Recall the ants that you read about in the beginning of this lesson. Ants leave a trail of one type of pheromone that leads other ants to food. They produce different pheromones that warn other ants of danger.

 Reading Check Summarize how animals use pheromones.

Body Language

Can you tell what mood a person is in by looking at his or her face or body position? The person is using body language to communicate his or her mood. Animals also communicate with body language. Animals such as wolves communicate excitement, aggression, and other moods through facial expressions, as shown in **Figure 11**. Some parrots bob their heads when they are content and crouch with their heads down when they are sick or stressed. This body language can make it easier for an animal to communicate with other members of its species.

WORD ORIGIN ············

pheromone
from Greek *pherein*, means "to carry"

Figure 11 Wolves communicate their moods through facial expressions and body language.

Visual Check If a wolf has narrowed eyes and ears laid back, what mood is it communicating?

Wolf Body Language 🗝

Aggression:
- ears forward
- narrowed or staring eyes
- body tense and upright

Playfulness:
- ears relaxed
- wide open eyes
- relaxed body

Fear:
- ears laid back
- narrowed eyes
- body crouched low

Figure 12 🔑 In this hyena society, one adult member watches for danger while other group members feed.

SCIENCE USE V. COMMON USE · ·

submission

Science Use the condition of being humble or compliant

Common Use something presented to another for review

Societies and Behaviors

Have you ever seen a flock of birds flying together? Animals live in groups for many reasons, such as for protection and obtaining food. *A* **society** *is a group of animals of the same species living and working together in an organized way.* Animal societies are sometimes highly structured with specific roles for its members, such as that of the spotted hyenas shown in **Figure 12.** Spotted hyenas live in large groups of up to 90 members. The members work together to hunt and defend their kill. Other animal societies are less organized, and each member might serve different roles. Some species of animals group together closely only at certain times of the year, such as for breeding or migration.

Dominance and Submission

Spotted hyena societies are organized by dominance. This means that the members are organized according to their social status relative to the other animals. The animal with the highest social status, the dominant animal, has power over the ones below it. Animals with a lower relative status to a dominant animal are **submissive** to that animal. In a spotted hyena society, females are most dominant, then cubs, and then males. Dominance also is important in groups of other animals, such as wolves, chickens, and some primates.

Dominance also might help reduce fighting among animals living in a society. For example, hyenas rarely hurt each other while fighting with other members of their society. Less dominant members usually submit to, or stop fighting, more dominant ones. Sometimes a submissive animal might mimic the behavior of a young animal and show that they are not a threat. For example, submissive wolves roll over or crouch, and less dominant hens move out of the way of the dominant hen.

Territorial Behaviors

Animals might set up and defend an area for feeding, mating, and raising young called a **territory.** Some insects and most vertebrates have a territory. Animals might identify their territories by making noises, physically changing the territory by scraping bark off trees, or by marking the area with pheromones, urine, or feces.

Animals defend the borders of their territory from other members of their species. If the borders are crossed, the animal, such as the cat shown in **Figure 13,** first might attempt to scare or intimidate the invading animal. If the animal does not leave, the defender might use aggression. **Aggression** *is a forceful behavior used to dominate or control another animal.* When animals fight another member of the same species, they usually do not try to cause serious harm to the other animal. For example, giraffes have the ability to kick fiercely, and they use this ability to defend against predators such as lions. These attacks can be deadly. However, when two male giraffes show aggression towards each other, they push at each other with their necks. This behavior is common and rarely fatal.

Courtship

Animals have specialized behaviors that help them find and attract a mate. They often compete with others of the same species for a mate. Some animals, such as female gypsy moths, release pheromones that attract males. Other animals, such as frogs and birds, use mating songs that gain the attention of mates. Some male birds bring the female a gift of food, such as a male tern bringing a fish to a female. Male fiddler crabs wave their enlarged claws and skitter across the ocean floor in the hopes of getting a female fiddler crab's attention. Male bowerbirds, such as the one shown in **Figure 14,** build elaborate nests using brightly colored objects during courtship.

 Key Concept Check How do animals interact in societies?

▲ **Figure 13** When a cat puffs up its fur, it appears more threatening to intruders.

◀ **Figure 14** Male bowerbirds use shiny or brightly colored objects while building nests in an attempt to attract a mate.

Lesson 2 Review

Visual Summary

Animals communicate in many ways, including with sound, light, chemicals, and body language.

Some animals live in societies that are highly structured.

Societal behaviors include dominance, submission, territorial behaviors, and courtship behaviors.

FOLDABLES

Use your lesson Foldable to review the lesson. Save your Foldable for the project at the end of the chapter.

What do you think NOW?

You first read the statements below at the beginning of the chapter.

3. Some animals give off light to communicate with each other.

4. Animals always fight to protect their territories.

Did you change your mind about whether you agree or disagree with the statements? Rewrite any false statements to make them true.

Use Vocabulary

1 Some animals use _____ to communicate in the dark.

2 **Define** *society* in your own words.

3 **Use the term** *territory* in a complete sentence.

Understand Key Concepts

4 Which form of communication includes pheromones?
- **A.** chemicals
- **B.** light
- **C.** body language
- **D.** facial expressions

5 **Compare** dominance and submission.

6 **Infer** why light communication is common in marine environments.

Interpret Graphics

7 **Identify** the form of animal communication in the figure below. Explain what is happening.

8 **Identify** Copy and fill in the graphic organizer below to identify the forms of animal communication.

Communication

Critical Thinking

9 **Hypothesize** what form of communication might be used by animals living in a noisy environment.

Courtship
Displays

A "Superb" Way to Find a Mate

What kind of animal do you think this is? Although it might look like a cartoon character, these are pictures of a male superb bird of paradise during a courtship display.

A courtship display is a series of specialized behaviors that help an animal attract a mate. It can include movements, sounds, and/or chemical communication. In its courtship display, the male superb bird of paradise transforms itself, as shown in the following sequence.

1 This pose is the beginning of the courtship display. At this stage, the bird sometimes moves its wings to make a clicking sound.

2 In this part of the courtship display, the feathers on the top of the bird's head are displayed, and the blue feathers on the bird's chest are extended outward.

3 The bird then extends the feathers on its head outward and around the head to form a rounded shape. Body feathers are extended as well. The bird appears as a black oval with a bright blue shape in the middle. The small blue spots are not the bird's eyes; they are spots on its feathers. In this stage of the display, the male bird hops around the female.

It's Your Turn

REPORT Research another animal's courtship display. Draw diagrams to show the different appearances and behaviors that are part of the display. Share your research with your class.

▲ Male superb bird of paradise

Reading Guide

Key Concepts
ESSENTIAL QUESTIONS

- What are the roles of male and female reproductive organs?
- How do the two types of fertilization differ?
- What are the different types of animal development?

Vocabulary

sexual reproduction p. 465

testis p. 466

ovary p. 466

fertilization p. 466

zygote p. 466

metamorphosis p. 470

 Multilingual eGlossary

 Video

- BrainPOP®
- What's Science Got to do With It?

Animal Reproduction and Development

Inquiry Leaving Home?

You probably know that caterpillars turn into butterflies. This butterfly is emerging from its chrysalis (KRIH suh lus). Why do you think the different life stages of this animal look so different? What other types of animal development are there?

Launch Lab

15 minutes

How is development similar in different animals?

No matter what the life span is of any animal, it starts with birth and develops to maturity, which is called adulthood. No matter the size of the animal, you might be able to see some similarities in the young animals.

1. Examine the pictures of young animals and adults in the table.
2. In your Science Journal, note some similarities between each baby and the adult counterpart.
3. Find one thing the young have in common and one thing the adults have in common.

Think About This

1. What similarities were you able to find between young animals and adults?

2. What similar characteristics were you able to identify in the babies as a group?

3. 🔑 **Key Concept** What do you think was the most obvious characteristic related to development in all the animals pictured? Explain.

Sexual Reproduction

Have you ever found a cluster of tiny, beadlike structures on the underside of a leaf? They might be eggs laid by a butterfly, a ladybug, or some other insect. Eggs are an important part of the life **cycle** of many animals. *In* **sexual reproduction,** *the genetic material from two different cells—a sperm and an egg—combine, producing an offspring.* Most animals reproduce sexually, although some can reproduce asexually, without a sperm and egg joining.

Male and female animals of the same species often look different from each other. It's easy to tell the difference between the male and the female shown in **Figure 15.** In mammals and birds, males are often larger or more colorful than females.

ACADEMIC VOCABULARY

cycle
(noun) a series of events that regularly recur and lead back to the starting point

Figure 15 A lion has a ruff of fur around his neck and is larger than the lioness.

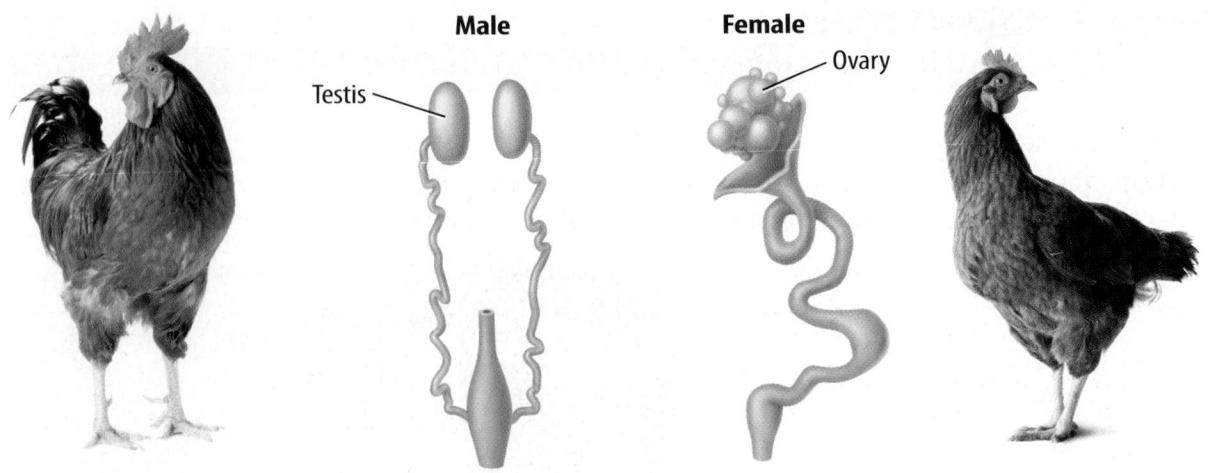

Male

Testis

Female

Ovary

Figure 16 Testes of male animals produce sperm cells. Ovaries of female animals produce egg cells.

Math Skills

Use Ratios

A ratio can be used to compare data about sperm and eggs. For example, the head of a human sperm cell averages 5 μm. (A μm, or micron, is one-millionth of a meter.) If the tail of the sperm cell measures 50 μm, what is the ratio of tail to head?

Set up the two numbers as a ratio by writing them in any of the following forms:

50 to 5; 50:5; $\frac{50}{5}$

Reduce the numbers to their lowest form.

Divide each side by 5. The ratio is 10 to 1 or 10:1 or $\frac{10}{1}$

Practice

A fruit fly sperm cell is about 1.8 mm in length. What is the ratio of a human sperm cell to a fly sperm cell?

Review

- Math Practice
- Personal Tutor

Male Reproductive Organs

The reproductive system of an animal includes specialized reproductive organs that produce sperm or eggs. The reproductive systems of male and female chickens are shown in **Figure 16.** Male animals have **testes** (TES teez; singular, testis), *the male reproductive organs that produce sperm.* Sperm are reproductive cells with tails that enable them to swim through fluid to reach an egg cell. Most male animals have two testes located inside the body cavity.

Female Reproductive Organs

Female animals have **ovaries,** (OH va reez) *the female reproductive organs that produce egg cells.* Most female animals have two ovaries except female birds, such as the chicken in **Figure 16,** which have only one ovary. Egg cells are larger than sperm and cannot move on their own.

Key Concept Check What are the functions of male and female reproductive organs?

Fertilization

Sexual reproduction requires **fertilization**—*the joining of an egg cell with a sperm cell.* Half of the genetic material is in a sperm cell. The other half is in an egg cell. *When a sperm cell fertilizes an egg cell, the new cell that forms is called a* **zygote** (ZI goht). The zygote develops into a new organism and contains the genetic material from both the sperm cell and the egg cell.

Not all animals fertilize their eggs in the same way. The eggs of some animals are fertilized inside the mother's body, and some are fertilized outside the body. Next, you will read about both types of fertilization and how organisms develop.

Internal Fertilization When fertilization occurs inside the body of an animal, it is called internal fertilization. For many animals, the male has a specialized structure that can deposit sperm in or near the female's reproductive system. The sperm swim to the egg or eggs. Earthworms, spiders, insects, reptiles, birds, and mammals have internal fertilization.

Internal fertilization ensures that an embryo, which develops from a fertilized egg, or zygote, is protected and nourished until it leaves the female's body. This increases the chance that an embryo will survive, develop into an adult, and reproduce.

External Fertilization A female frog, such as the one shown in **Figure 17,** deposits unfertilized eggs under water. A male frog releases its sperm above the eggs as the female lays them. Fertilization that occurs outside the body of an animal is called external fertilization. When a sperm reaches an egg, fertilization takes place. Animals that reproduce using external fertilization include jellyfish, clams, sea urchins, sea stars, many species of fish, and amphibians.

Most animals that reproduce using external fertilization do not care for the fertilized eggs or for the newly hatched young. As a result, eggs and young are exposed to predators and other dangers in the environment, reducing their chances of surviving. Successful reproduction of animals with external fertilization requires that a large number of eggs be produced to ensure that at least a few offspring will survive to become adults.

 Key Concept Check How do the two types of fertilization differ?

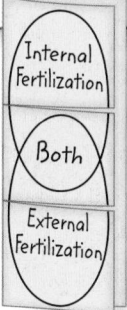

Internal Fertilization

Both

External Fertilization

Figure 17 For organisms that have external fertilization, mating behaviors help make certain that eggs are fertilized as soon as possible after they leave the female's body.

Development

The zygote produced by fertilization is only the beginning of an animal's development. The zygote grows by mitosis and cell divisions and becomes an embryo—the next stage in an animal's development. A growing embryo needs nourishment and protection from predators and other dangers in the environment. Different animals have different ways of supplying the needs of an embryo. In some animals, the embryo develops outside the mother's body. In others, the embryo develops inside the mother.

External Development

The grass snake in **Figure 18** is an example of an animal whose embryos develop outside the mother. Animals that develop outside the mother usually are protected inside an egg. In most instances, one embryo develops inside each egg. Most eggs contain a yolk that provides food for the developing embryo. A covering surrounds the egg. The covering protects the embryo, helps keep it moist, and discourages predators. Eggs laid by lizards, snakes, and other reptiles have a tough, leathery covering, as shown in **Figure 18.** A tough jellylike substance usually surrounds eggs laid under water, such as those laid by frogs. Bird eggs have a hard covering called a shell.

Figure 18 This grass snake protects its eggs while the embryos develop.

Internal Development

The embryos of some animals, including most mammals, develop inside the mother. These embryos get nourishment from the mother. An organ or tissue transfers nourishment from the mother to the embryo. Other embryos, such as those of some snakes, insects, and fish, develop in an egg with a yolk while inside the mother. For these animals, the yolk, not the mother, provides nourishment for the developing young. The young hatch from the eggs while they are inside the mother and then leave the mother's body.

 Reading Check Where does a snake embryo get nourishment if it develops inside its mother?

Gestation

The length of time between fertilization and birth of an animal is called the gestation (jeh STAY shun) period. Gestation period varies from species to species and usually relates to the size of an animal—the smaller the animal, the shorter its gestation period. For example, the gestation period for a mouse is about 21 days, for a human is about 266 days, and for an elephant is about 600 days. The gestation period for a kangaroo is 35 days. A kangaroo is only about 2.5 cm long at birth, as shown in **Figure 19**. Most of its development occurs in a pouch on the mother's body.

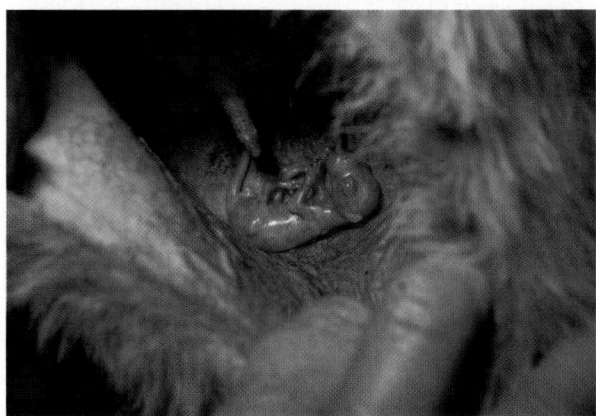

Figure 19 A newborn kangaroo crawls into a pouch on the mother's body. It feeds and grows inside the pouch until it is large enough to live on its own.

Is it possible to select which animal will have the largest newborn if you know the gestation period?

If you looked at pictures of newborn animals and compared them to a set of pictures of the animal mothers, you would probably say that the larger baby had a larger mother. What do you think you would find if you compared the gestation period of these animals?

1. Analyze the data in the table below.

2. As you are making comparisons using the data, see if you recognize any numbers that seem unusual. Record these in your Science Journal.

3. Graph your data on a line graph.

Animal	Gestation Period in Days (average)	Newborn Weight in kg (average)
Meadow mouse	18	0.0008
Guinea pig	68	0.1
Porcupine	105	0.2
Giant panda	135	0.2
Squirrel monkey	150	0.1
Ribbon seal	330	10.5
Bactrian camel	406	40
Giraffe	435	70
Elephant	660	113

Analyze and Conclude

1. **Identify** the animal(s) that had a gestation period or newborn weight that did not follow a logical pattern.

2. **Explain** how the discrepancy was shown on the graph.

3. **Key Concept** Can you make a comparison between the size of an animal, the length of the gestation period, and the weight of the newborn?

Metamorphosis

Some animals, including amphibians and many animals without backbones, go through more than one phase of development. **Metamorphosis** (me tuh MOR fuh sihs) *is a developmental process in which the form of the body changes as an animal grows from an egg to an adult.*

Word Origin

metamorphosis
from Greek *meta*, means "change"; and *morphe*, means "form"

The metamorphosis of a ladybug and the metamorphosis of a frog are shown in **Figure 20.** During its development, the ladybug goes from egg to larva to pupa to adult. The tadpole is the larval stage of a frog. Larva and adult forms often have different lifestyles. The larva of the frog lives only in water. The adult frog can live on land or in water.

Key Concept Check What are the different types of animal development?

Concepts in Motion Animation

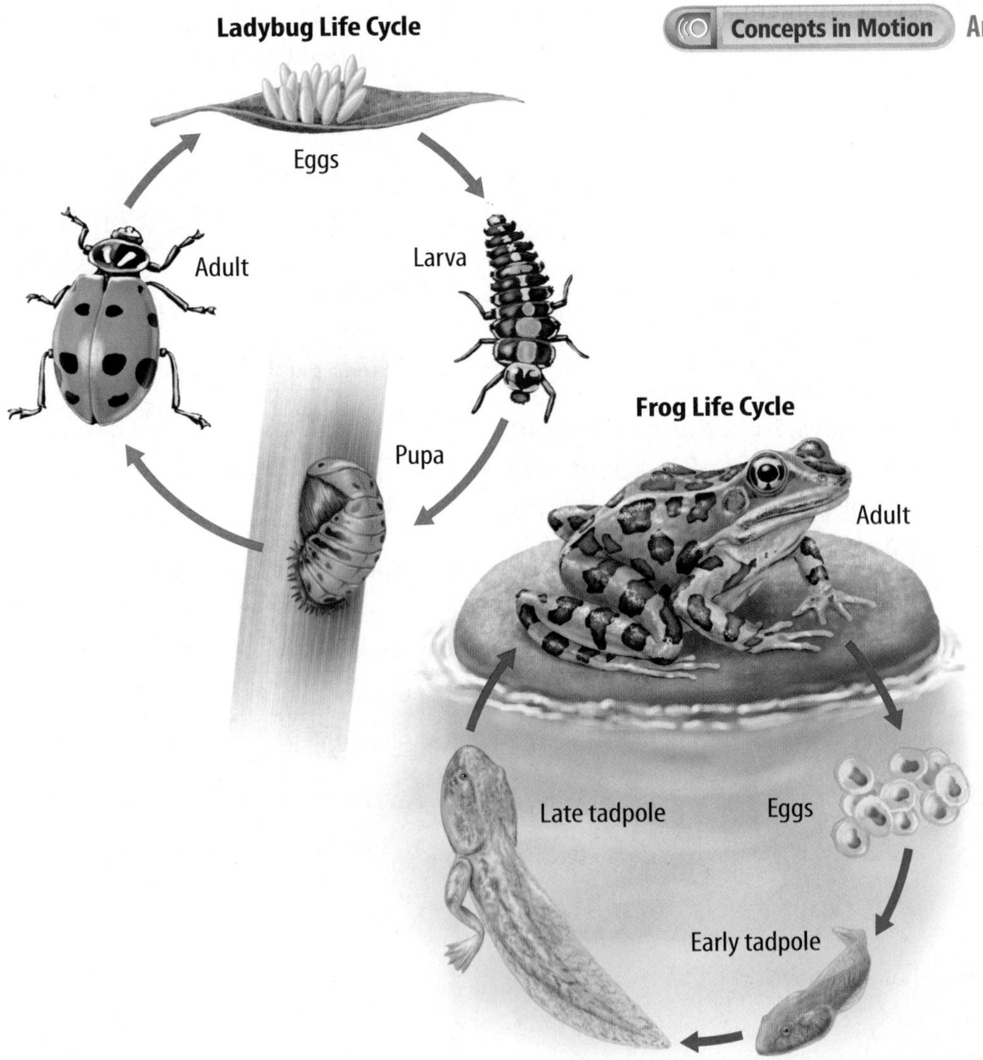
Ladybug Life Cycle
Eggs
Larva
Pupa
Adult
Frog Life Cycle
Adult
Eggs
Early tadpole
Late tadpole

Figure 20 A ladybug larva hatches from the egg, changes to a pupa, then the pupa changes into an adult. A tadpole hatches from an egg. It grows legs and loses its tail as it develops into an adult frog.

Visual Check Which developmental stage is not in a frog life cycle?

Visual Summary

Most animals reproduce sexually, and male and female animals often look different.

Fertilization can be internal or external.

Some animals have internal development, and others have external development.

FOLDABLES®

Use your lesson Foldable to review the lesson. Save your Foldable for the project at the end of the chapter.

What do you think NOW?

You first read the statements below at the beginning of the chapter.

5. During sexual reproduction, a sperm cell and an egg cell join.

6. Some animals develop inside the mother.

Did you change your mind about whether you agree or disagree with the statements? Rewrite any false statements to make them true.

Use Vocabulary

1 **Distinguish** between testes and ovaries.

2 **Define** *metamorphosis* in your own words.

3 The production of offspring by joining of a sperm and an egg is called _____.

Understand Key Concepts

4 Which are the reproductive cells that form in female animals?
   A. eggs   **C.** sperm
   B. ovaries   **D.** testes

5 **Infer** why snake eggs have leathery shells.

6 **Contrast** the survival of offspring from species with internal or external fertilization.

Interpret Graphics

7 **Explain** Use the image below to explain the benefits of external fertilization in frogs.

8 **Sequence** Copy and fill in the graphic organizer below to sequence the stages of metamorphosis in a ladybug.

Critical Thinking

9 **Hypothesize** why large animals have a longer period of gestation than small animals.

Math Skills

Review — Math Practice

10 A human egg cell has a diameter of about 120 μm. If a human sperm cell measures 5 μm, what is the ratio of the size of the egg cell to the size of the sperm cell?

Materials

rectangular plastic container with lid

construction paper

earthworms

gooseneck lamp

paper towels

sand

dark soil

Safety

What changes an earthworm's behavior?

Have you ever seen an earthworm on the ground after it rains? Earthworms favor moist conditions and often are found in gardens or forest soil. They move to more favorable conditions when their environment becomes unsuitable.

Ask a Question

Think about ways you could investigate an earthworm without hurting the worm. Develop a question based on your thoughts. If you want to be sure your question is testable, consider the variables, constants, and equipment that would be involved.

Make Observations

1. Read and complete a lab safety form.
2. Observe the earthworms in your container, and think about their needs.
3. In your Science Journal, write down some ideas you could easily explore about earthworm behavior.
4. Discuss your ideas with your group, and choose one idea. Identify your variables and your control.
5. Ask your teacher for approval of your plan and any materials that you might need that are not available already.
6. Set up the lab materials according to your plan.

Form a Hypothesis

7 After you have looked over your plan and lab setup, discuss what you think you will find out about the earthworm in response to the stimulus you chose. Form a hypothesis to explain the relationship between the change in the environment and the earthworm's behavior.

Test Your Hypothesis

8 Make adjustments, if necessary, to your lab setup and get one or more worms from your container.

9 Decide how you are going to record your observations, and create a table in your Science Journal.

10 Follow your plan and record your observations.

Analyze and Conclude

11 **Compare** the behavior of the earthworm before and after you applied the stimulus.

12 **Interpret** any unexpected responses during one or more trials.

13 **Infer** from your data if the earthworm learned to change its behavior because of repeated trials.

14 **The Big Idea** What do you think would happen if a worm in a natural environment encountered the change you designed?

Communicate Your Results

Draw a comic strip depicting your question, your hypothesis, and the results. Share your comic strip with the class.

 **Extension**

Observe both mealworms and earthworms under the same conditions. Predict which worms would get used to the new environment faster.

10

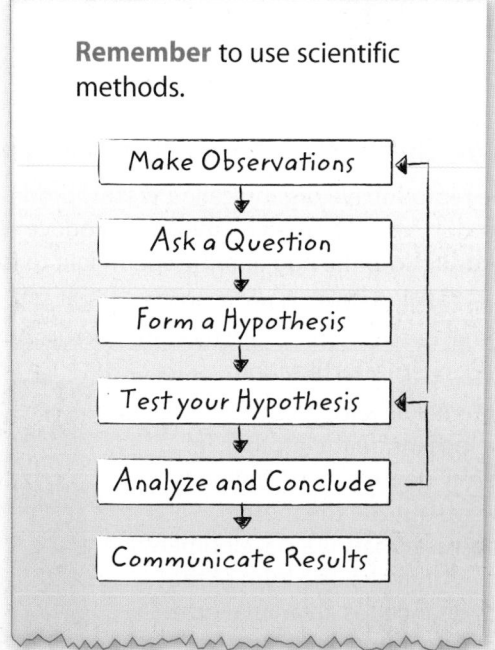

Remember to use scientific methods.

> Make Observations
> ↓
> Ask a Question
> ↓
> Form a Hypothesis
> ↓
> Test your Hypothesis
> ↓
> Analyze and Conclude
> ↓
> Communicate Results

Chapter 13 Study Guide

Animals communicate using sound, light, chemicals, and body language. Societies and social behaviors help them interact with each other. Courtship behaviors help animals find mates. Most animals use sexual reproduction.

Key Concepts Summary 🔑

Vocabulary

Lesson 1: Types of Behavior

- Animal **behaviors** help maintain homeostasis by reacting to stimuli in their internal and external environments.
- Animal behaviors can be **innate** or learned.

behavior p. 447

innate behavior p. 449

instinct p. 450

migration p. 451

hibernation p. 451

imprinting p. 452

conditioning p. 453

Lesson 2: Interacting with Others

- Animals use sound, light, chemicals, and body language to communicate.
- Animals live and work together in **societies.** They might exhibit dominance, submission, territorial behaviors, and courtship.

bioluminescence p. 458

pheromone p. 459

society p. 460

territory p. 461

aggression p. 461

Lesson 3: Animal Reproduction and Development

- Male reproductive organs, called **testes,** produce sperm. Female reproductive organs, called **ovaries,** produce eggs. In **sexual reproduction,** the egg and the sperm join to form a new organism.
- When **fertilization** occurs inside the body of an animal, it is called internal fertilization. Fertilization that occurs outside the body is called external fertilization.
- In internal development, the embryo develops inside the mother. In external development, embryos develop outside the mother. **Metamorphosis** is a developmental process in which the form of the body changes as an animal grows from an egg to an adult.

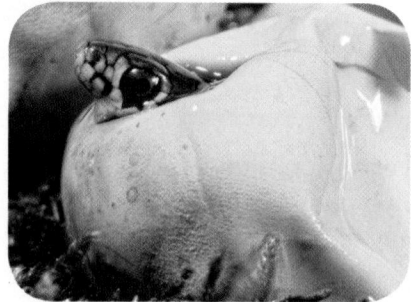

sexual reproduction p. 465

testis p. 466

ovary p. 466

fertilization p. 466

zygote p. 466

metamorphosis p. 470

FOLDABLES® Chapter Project

Assemble your lesson Foldables as shown to make a Chapter Project. Use the project to review what you have learned in this chapter.

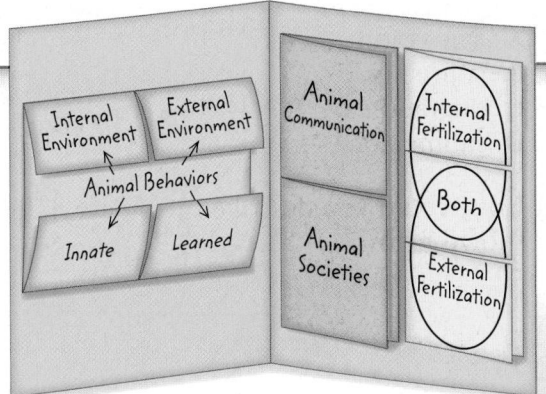

Use Vocabulary

❶ The way an organism reacts to other organisms is _____.

❷ Define the term *hibernation* in your own words.

❸ In chemical communication, an animal might use a(n) _____.

❹ Use the word *aggression* in a complete sentence.

❺ The joining of a sperm cell and an egg cell is called _____.

❻ Use the word *zygote* in a sentence.

Link Vocabulary and Key Concepts   🔘 Concepts in Motion Interactive Concept Map

Copy this concept map, and then use vocabulary terms from the previous page and other terms from the chapter to complete the concept map.

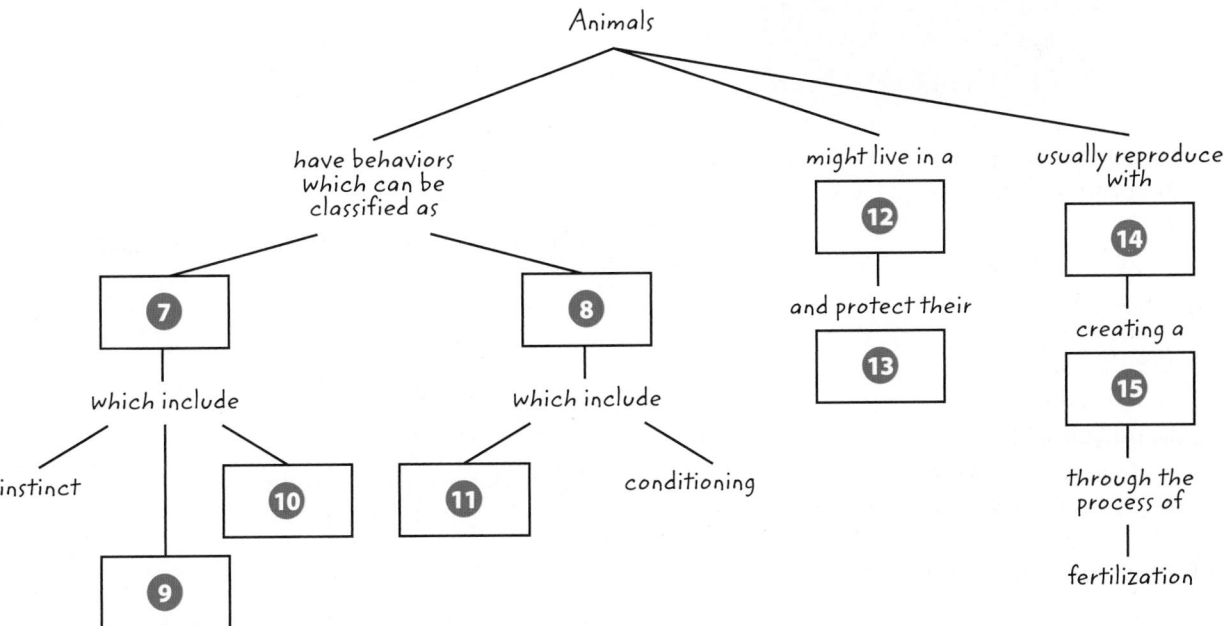

Chapter 13 Review

Understand Key Concepts 🔑

1. Which is a reflex?
   A. a bird building a nest
   B. pulling a string to get food
   C. pupils getting smaller in dim light
   D. tying your shoelaces

2. Which animal does NOT hibernate?
   A. bat
   B. chipmunk
   C. snake
   D. squirrel

3. Which type of animal behavior is shown in the figure below?

   A. conditioning
   B. imprinting
   C. instinct
   D. reflex

4. Which is a learned response that uses reasoning from past experiences?
   A. conditioning
   B. imprinting
   C. cognitive behavior
   D. trial and error

5. Body language is an example of
   A. communication.
   B. conditioning.
   C. migration.
   D. societies.

6. Which type of behavior is shown in the figure below?

   A. aggression
   B. courtship
   C. migration
   D. submission

7. How would you describe the organ system shown below?

   A. asexual
   B. embryo
   C. female
   D. male

8. What is the length of time between fertilization and birth called?
   A. external development
   B. gestation period
   C. metamorphosis
   D. zygote

9. What are the reproductive cells that form in male animals?
   A. eggs
   B. ovaries
   C. sperm
   D. testes

Critical Thinking

10 **Formulate** a question to ask a scientist who investigated cognitive behavior in ravens.

11 **Summarize** how animals respond to change.

12 **Develop** a plan of communication for an animal that lives in darkness.

13 **Hypothesize** how the bird shown below might attract more mates.

14 **Research** one example of body language for a tree-dwelling mammal.

15 **Hypothesize** why most frog species enter water to reproduce.

16 **Compare** the number of eggs produced by animals that reproduce by external fertilization with the number of eggs produced by animals that reproduce by internal fertilization.

17 **Consider** why mammals do not develop by metamorphosis.

Writing in Science

18 **Write** a five-sentence paragraph comparing internal and external fertilization. Be sure to include a topic sentence and a concluding sentence in your paragraph.

REVIEW THE BIG IDEA

19 How do animals communicate, interact, and reproduce?

20 What type of behavior is illustrated in the photo below?

Math Skills

Review — Math Practice

Use Ratios

21 In one species of trout, the egg cell has a diameter of 5 mm. The circumference of the cell is 15.7 mm. What is the ratio of the circumference to the diameter of the cell?

22 A chinook salmon has an average body length of 70 cm. If the sperm cell measures 55 μm, what is the ratio of the length of the salmon's body to the length of the sperm cell? [Hint: 1 cm = 10,000 μm]

23 A sperm cell contains genetic material with a mass of 1.26 picogram (pg) [1 pg = one-trillionth of a gram]. After the sperm fertilizes an egg, the zygote contains 2.52 pg of genetic material. What is the ratio of genetic material from the egg and the sperm cells? [Hint: Subtract the genetic material of the sperm from the total to get the egg's contribution.]

Record your answers on the answer sheet provided by your teacher or on a sheet of paper.

Multiple Choice

1 Which is NOT one of the ways that animals communicate?

   A They make chemicals.

   B They migrate long distances.

   C They use light.

   D They use sound.

2 A wolf rolls onto its back, exposing its belly to its pack mates. Which behavior does this show?

   A aggression

   B courtship

   C dominance

   D submission

Use the figure below to answer question 3.

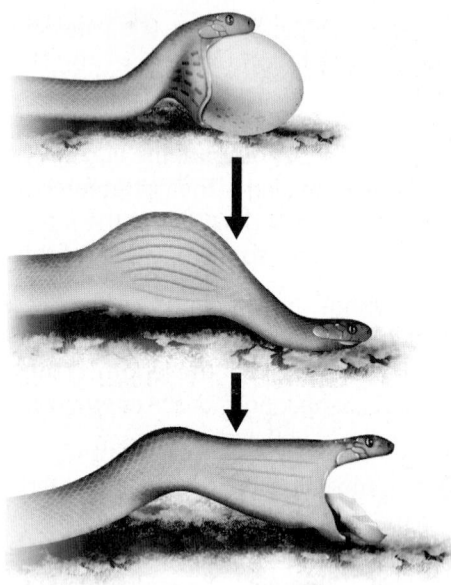

3 Which term describes the behavior shown in the figure?

   A conditioning

   B imprinting

   C instinct

   D reflex

Use the figure below to answer question 4.

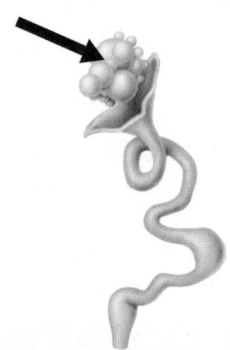

4 Which are produced in the structure shown in the figure?

   A embryos

   B zygotes

   C egg cells

   D sperm cells

5 Which is true of external fertilization?

   A It happens outside the female body.

   B It involves a small number of eggs.

   C It occurs only in the spring months.

   D It requires extended parental care.

6 When a baby kangaroo is born, it crawls into its mother's pouch. Which type of behavior is this?

   A cognitive behavior

   B imprinting

   C innate behavior

   D trial and error

7 A turtle perches on a log in the sun. How does this behavior help the turtle maintain homeostasis?

   A It attracts suitable mates.

   B It frightens potential predators.

   C It maintains body temperature.

   D It protects newborn offspring.

Use the figure below to answer questions 8 and 9.

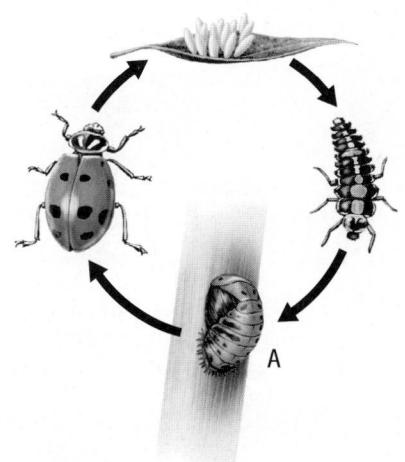

8 Which stage of development is marked *A* in the figure?

  A adult

  B larva

  C pupa

  D zygote

9 Which process occurs at the stage marked *A* in the figure?

  A fertilization

  B imprinting

  C hibernation

  D metamorphosis

10 Which is the result of fertilization?

  A egg

  B embryo

  C sperm

  D zygote

Constructed Response

Use the figure below to answer questions 11 and 12.

11 Describe the behavior shown in the figure. Give an example of a stimulus that could cause the behavior shown.

12 Explain how the behavior shown in the figure is an example of the flight-or-fight response.

13 Describe how animals use chemicals as a territorial behavior.

14 A shopping mall was constructed where a forest once grew. Many of the animals living in the area moved to another wooded area. Is this movement of animals an example of migration? Why or why not?

NEED EXTRA HELP?														
If You Missed Question...	1	2	3	4	5	6	7	8	9	10	11	12	13	14
Go to Lesson...	2	2	1	1	3	1	1	3	3	3	1	1	2	1

Human Body Systems

1818
The first well-documented case of a person-to-person blood transfusion is performed. British obstetrician James Blundell transfuses 4 oz. of blood from a man to his wife who had just given birth.

1823
German surgeon Christian Bünger performs the first autograft, replacing skin on a man's nose with some from his thigh.

1905
Dr. Eduard Zirm performs the first successful cornea transplant on patient Alois Glogar.

1954
The first successful organ transplant between living relatives (a kidney transplant between twins) is completed by Dr. Joseph Murray and Dr. David Hume in Boston.

1967
The first successful liver and heart transplants are completed. Dr. Thomas Starzl performs the liver transplant in Denver, Colorado. Dr. Christiaan Barnard performs the heart transplant in Cape Town, South Africa.

1960   1980   2000

1968
The Uniform Anatomical Gift Act establishes the Uniform Donor Card as a legal document that allows anyone 18 years of age or older to legally donate their organs upon death.

1984
The National Organ Transplant Act (NOTA) establishes a nationwide computer registry, authorizes financial support for organ procurement organizations, and prohibits the buying or selling of organs in the United States.

2001
Due to widespread use of advanced surgical techniques and higher success rates for surgeries, the number of living donors passes the number of deceased donors.

? Inquiry
Visit ConnectED for this unit's **STEM** activity.

Nature of SCIENCE

Systems

A **system** is a collection of parts that influence or interact with one another. For example, the human body is a large system made up of many smaller subsystems, such as the ones shown in **Figure 1.**

Like the human body system, complex systems often contain smaller, or less complex, subsystems. The parts of each subsystem interact among themselves, as well as with other subsystems. Each subsystem has a different purpose, but they interact to keep the larger system working properly.

Parts of a System

Systems and subsystems often attempt to achieve a goal. For example, the nervous system, a subsystem of the human body system, regulates your body temperature, as shown in **Figure 2.** Systems and subsystems often are described in terms of their input, processing, and output.

Input is the matter, energy, or information that enters a system. When you exercise, one input to your nervous system is thermal energy. The input, or thermal energy, is detected by special brain and skin cells called receptors.

Processing is the changing of the input to achieve a goal. The hypothalamus processes the input from receptors. It sends electrical signals, carried by the nerves, to other parts of the body. The signals tell the body it is warmer than it should be.

Output is the material, energy, or information that leaves a system. Outputs from the nervous system include sweat, goose bumps, and shivers, all of which can change body temperature.

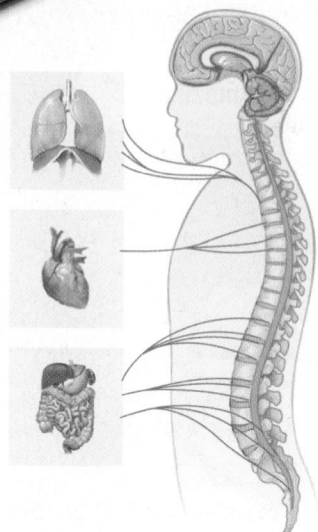

▲ **Figure 1** The nervous system, the respiratory system, the circulatory system, and the digestive system are subsystems of a larger system—the human body.

Figure 2 The nervous system is responsible for regulating body temperature. ▼

Input: Thermal energy released by contracting muscles is detected by receptors.

Processing: Signals from receptors are sent to the brain. The brain then signals glands in the skin to produce sweat.

Hypothalamus

Brain

Nervous signals sent throughout body

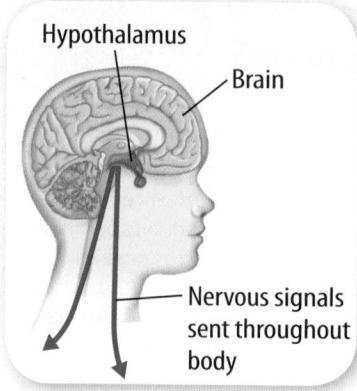

Output: Sweat forms on the skin. Then, it cools the body as it evaporates.

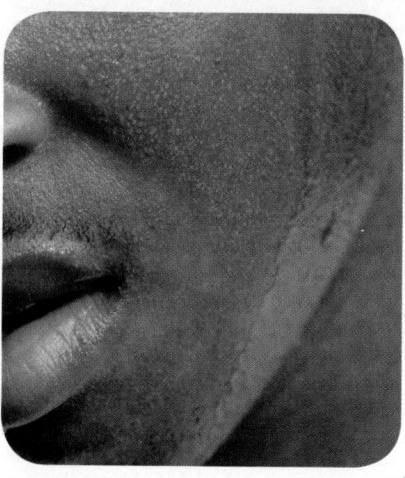

Figure 3 After a hard race, decreasing levels of carbon dioxide in a rower's blood act as feedback to the nervous system. This feedback signals the rower's brain to restore her breathing to a normal rate.

Feedback in Systems

Many systems use feedback, or information, to monitor and regulate input, process, and output. For example, when you exercise, as shown in **Figure 3,** your muscles produce carbon dioxide as a waste product. Receptors detect this input—high levels of carbon dioxide in your blood. The brain processes this information and signals your nervous system to increase breathing. When you breathe harder and faster, you take in more oxygen and the levels of carbon dioxide in your blood decrease. Once this change is detected by receptors, your brain signals your nervous system to return to normal breathing.

Cooperation, Order, and Change

Body subsystems work together in specific ways to regulate temperature, remove waste from your blood, and respond to other changes in your body. A failure in one subsystem affects other subsystems. For example, if a bad cold causes your lungs to become congested, your respiratory system cannot efficiently exchange oxygen for carbon dioxide. Therefore, muscle cells no longer receive enough oxygen to function normally. As a result, you easily become tired and have trouble catching your breath when you exercise.

Systems Thinking

Thinking in terms of systems might change the way you make choices. For example, some people think that if they reduce the amount they eat, they will lose weight. However, protein is necessary for your muscular system to function properly. Without an input of protein, muscle tissues begin to break down. Someone who does not eat enough protein might not lose weight because they become weak and tired and stop exercising. Thinking about the interactions of the systems and subsystems in your body can lead to decisions that help you achieve long-term goals.

Chapter 14

Structure and Movement

THE BIG IDEA How do bones, muscles, and skin help maintain the body's homeostasis?

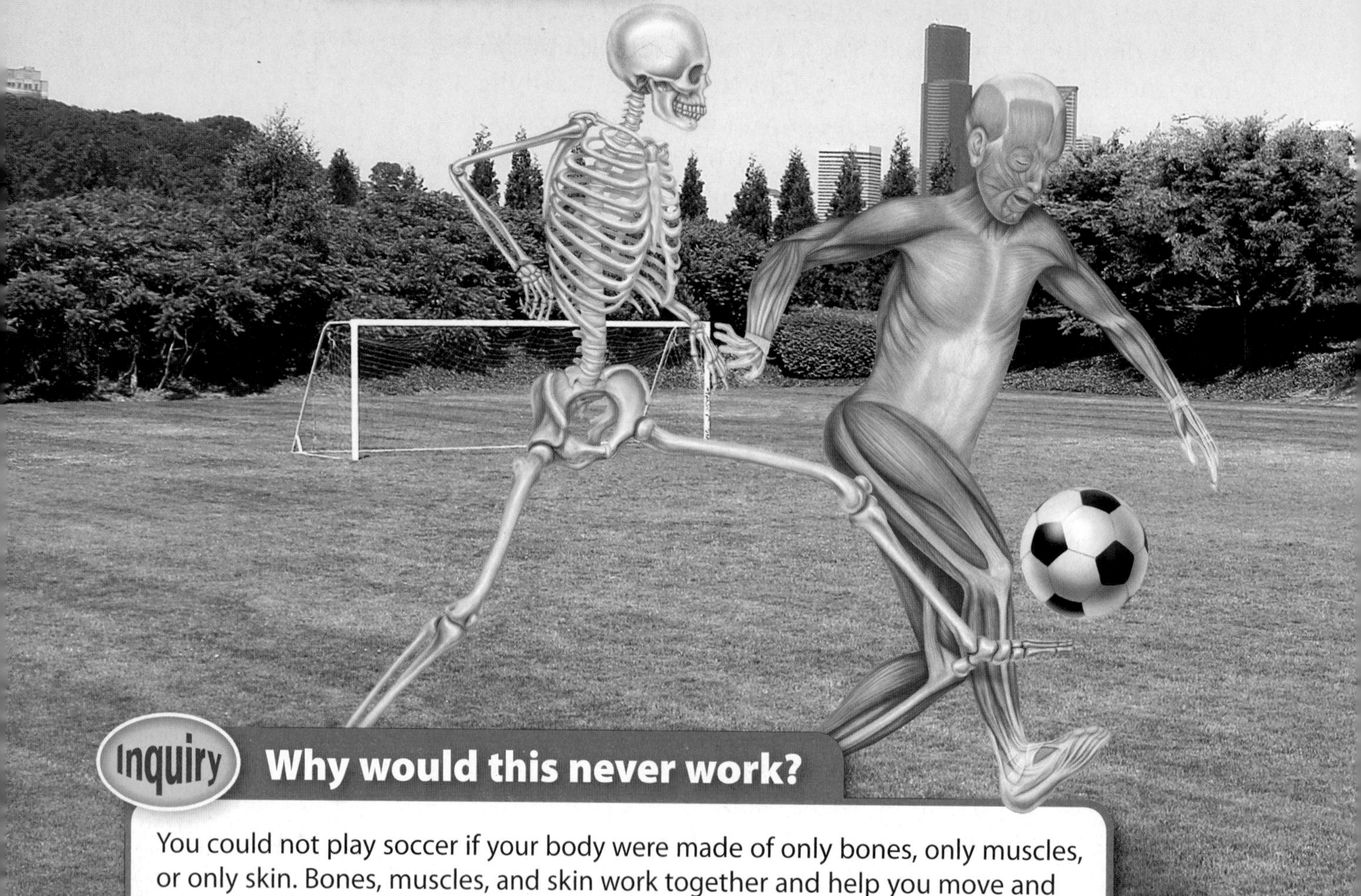

Inquiry Why would this never work?

You could not play soccer if your body were made of only bones, only muscles, or only skin. Bones, muscles, and skin work together and help you move and carry out processes you need in order to live.

- What would happen to your body if you had no skin? No muscles?
- What functions do you think bones, muscles, and skin have?
- How do bones, muscles, and skin work together to help your body function?

Get Ready to Read

What do you think?

Before you read, decide if you agree or disagree with each of these statements. As you read this chapter, see if you change your mind about any of the statements.

1 Bones protect internal organs.

2 Bones do not change during a person's lifetime.

3 The same type of muscle that moves bones also pumps blood through the heart.

4 Muscles cannot push bones.

5 Skin helps regulate body temperature.

6 Skin is made of two layers of tissue.

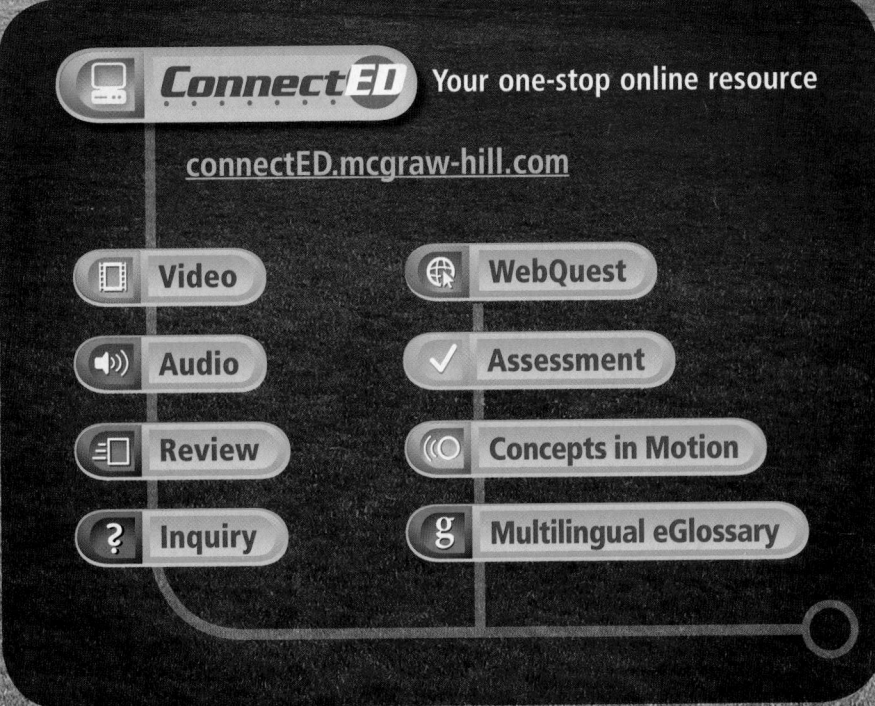

ConnectED Your one-stop online resource

connectED.mcgraw-hill.com

Video	WebQuest
Audio	Assessment
Review	Concepts in Motion
Inquiry	Multilingual eGlossary

Reading Guide

Key Concepts
ESSENTIAL QUESTIONS

- What does the skeletal system do?

- How do the parts of the skeletal system work together?

- How does the skeletal system interact with other body systems?

Vocabulary

skeletal system p. 487

cartilage p. 490

periosteum p. 490

joint p. 491

ligament p. 491

arthritis p. 492

osteoporosis p. 492

g **Multilingual eGlossary**

Video **BrainPOP®**

The Skeletal System

Inquiry How do bones move so easily?

Bones work like mechanical joints, enabling you to turn, pivot, twist, and bend. However, they don't do this alone. Other parts of your skeletal system work with the bones and help you move.

How are bones used for support?

If you have ever watched the construction of a building, you might have seen a wood or steel frame being used to provide support. In a similar way, bones support your body and the organs inside it.

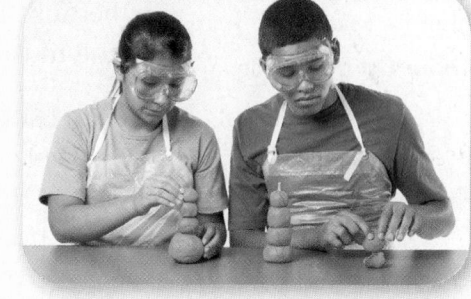

1. Read and complete a lab safety form.

2. Using pieces of **clay,** try to build a tower taller than your partner's. One person should use a **wooden dowel** to support his or her tower.

3. Measure and record the height of both towers. Find the class average for the height of towers with and without dowels.

Think About This

1. Were towers with or without dowels generally higher?

2. 🔑 **Key Concept** What do you think your body would be like if you had no bones?

Functions of the Skeletal System

Squeeze your hands and arms. The hard parts you feel are parts of your skeleton. When you think of your skeleton, you might think of bones, like those shown in **Figure 1.** These bones support your body and help you move. Your skeleton is part of your skeletal system and contains more than 200 bones. *The **skeletal system** contains bones as well as other structures that connect and protect the bones and that support other functions in the body.* In this lesson, you will learn how all parts of the skeletal system work together.

Support

Can you imagine trying to stack jiggling blocks of gelatin 1 m high? You would probably have a hard time because gelatin does not have any support structures inside it. Without bones, your body would be similar to gelatin. Bones provide support. They help you sit up, stand, and raise your arm over your head to ask a question.

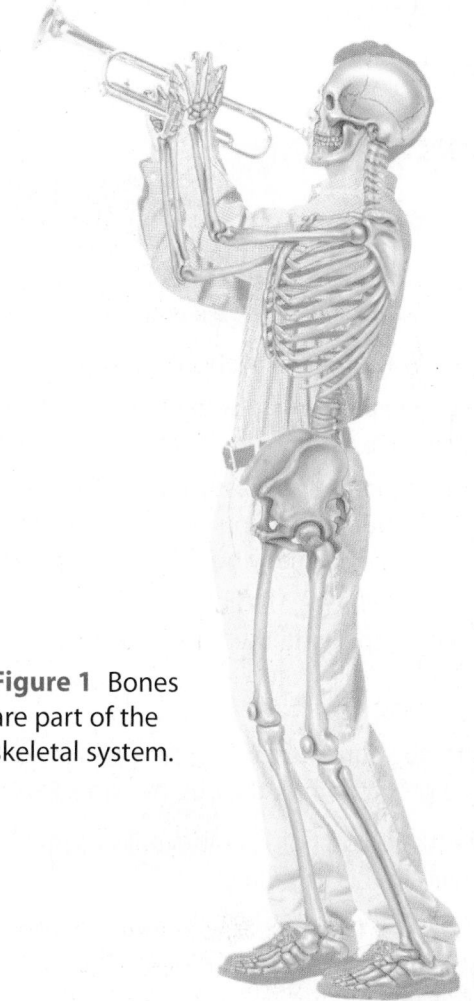

Figure 1 Bones are part of the skeletal system.

✔ **Reading Check** How do bones act as a support system?

Movement

The skeletal system enables different parts of the body to move in different ways, like when a person kicks a soccer ball, as shown in the beginning of this chapter. Bones can move because they are attached to muscles. The skeletal system and the muscular system work together and move your body.

Protection

Feel your head and then feel your stomach. Your stomach is softer than your head. The hard, rigid structure you feel in your head is your skull, shown in **Figure 2.** It protects the soft, fragile **tissue** of your brain from damage. Other bones protect the spinal cord, heart, lungs, and other internal organs.

Production and Storage

Another function of bones is to produce and store materials needed by your body. Red blood cells are produced inside your bones. Bones store fat and calcium. Calcium is needed for strong bones and for many cellular processes. When the body needs calcium, it is released from bones into the blood.

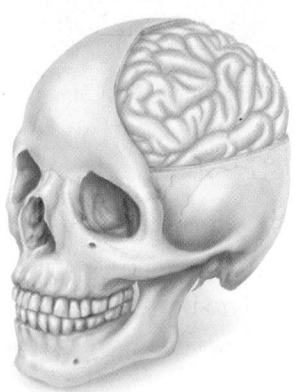

Figure 2 The skull protects the soft tissue of the brain.

Key Concept Check What are the major functions of the skeletal system?

---

inquiry MiniLab   **15 minutes**

How does the skeleton protect organs?

The hard bones of your skeleton protect some of the soft tissues and organs of your body.

1 Read and complete a lab safety form.

2 Place one piece of **bubble wrap** in a **plastic bag** and another piece of bubble wrap in a **plastic jar.**

3 Firmly squeeze the plastic bag for five seconds, popping as many bubbles as you can. Remove the bubble wrap and count how many bubbles are popped. Record the data in your Science Journal.

4 Repeat step 3 with the bubble wrap in the plastic jar.

Analyze and Conclude

1. **Analyze** your data to determine which container provided more protection for the bubble wrap. Explain your answer.

2. **Infer** which part of your skeletal system the plastic jar models in this experiment.

3. **Key Concept** How does the skeleton provide protection for internal organs?

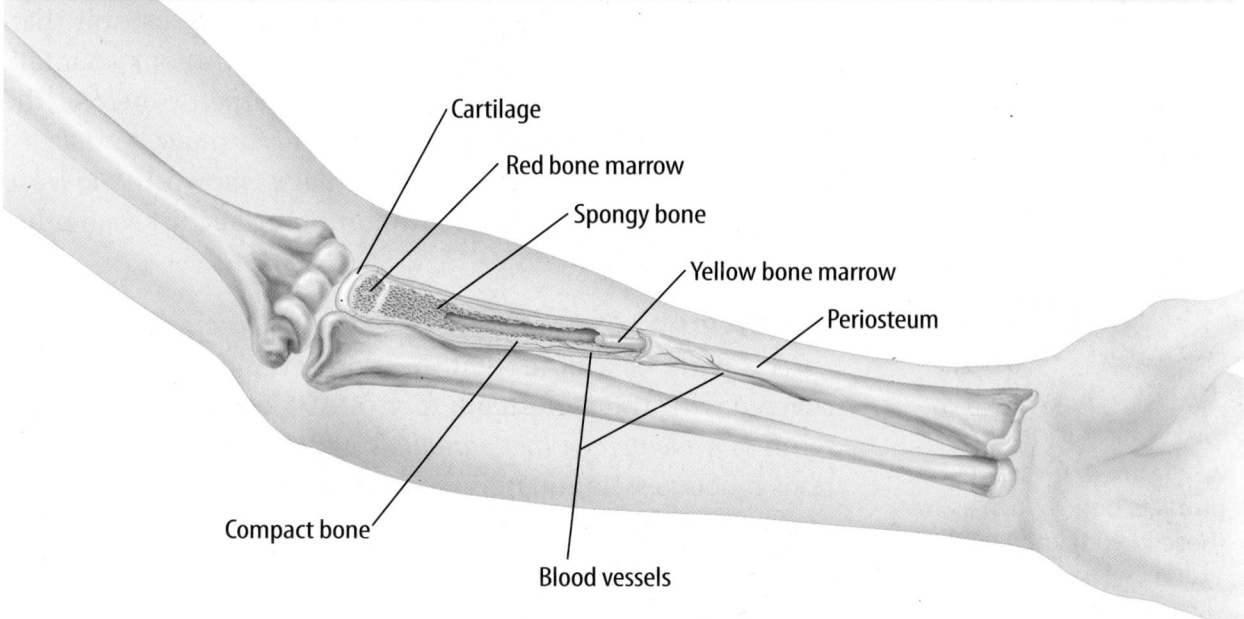

Cartilage

Red bone marrow

Spongy bone

Yellow bone marrow

Periosteum

Compact bone

Blood vessels

Structure of Bones

A bone is an organ composed of living tissue. There are two main types of bone tissue: compact and spongy. A bone also contains other types of tissue, as you can see in the arm bone shown in **Figure 3.**

Compact Bone Tissue

The hard, outer portions of bones are made of compact bone tissue. Compact bone tissue is a dense web of fibers. A long bone, like the arm bone shown in **Figure 3,** is made mostly of compact bone tissue. However, in its ends, a long bone contains a different kind of tissue called spongy bone tissue.

Spongy Bone Tissue

The small holes in spongy bone tissue make it look like a sponge. Because of these holes, spongy bone is less dense than compact bone. A short bone, like one in your wrist, is mostly spongy bone tissue.

Bone Marrow

The insides of most bones contain a soft tissue called bone marrow (MER oh). There are two types of bone marrow. Red bone marrow is the tissue where red blood cells are made. It is found in the spongy ends of long bones and in some flat bones, such as the ribs. Yellow bone marrow stores fat and is found inside the longest part of long bones.

 Reading Check What is the difference between red bone marrow and yellow bone marrow?

Figure 3 A bone contains many types of tissue.

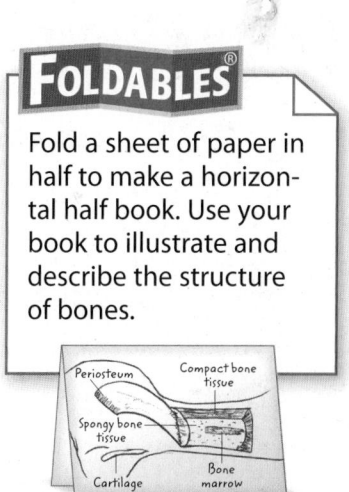

FOLDABLES®

Fold a sheet of paper in half to make a horizontal half book. Use your book to illustrate and describe the structure of bones.

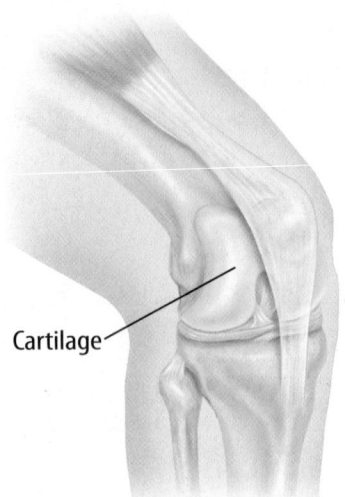

▲ **Figure 4** Cartilage protects bones, such as those in your knee joint.

WORD ORIGIN · · · · · · · · · · ·

ligament
from Latin *ligare*, means
"to bind, tie"

Figure 5 Bone gradually replaces cartilage as children grow. ▼

Cartilage

Have you ever fallen on a hard floor made of tiles or concrete? Falling on a hard surface is usually more painful than falling on a soft surface like a carpet, which cushions your fall. A special tissue in your body acts like a carpet to protect the skeletal system. **Cartilage** (KAR tuh lihj) *is a strong, flexible tissue that covers the ends of bones.* Cartilage, shown in **Figure 4,** prevents the surfaces of bones from rubbing against each other and reduces friction.

Periosteum

The parts of a bone that are not covered in cartilage are covered with the periosteum (per ee AHS tee um). *The* **periosteum** *is a membrane that surrounds bone.* This thin tissue contains blood vessels and nerves as well as cells that produce new bone tissue. Periosteum nourishes bones and helps them function and grow properly, as well as heal after injury.

Formation of Bones

Before you were born, your skeleton was made mostly of cartilage. During your infancy and childhood, the cartilage was gradually replaced by bone, as shown in **Figure 5.** The long bones in children and young teens have regions of bone growth that produce new bone cells. These regions are called growth plates. A growth plate produces cartilage that is then replaced by bone tissue. A growth plate, shown in **Figure 5,** is the weakest part of an adolescent bone. Growth continues until adulthood, when most of the cartilage has turned to bone.

Bone Development

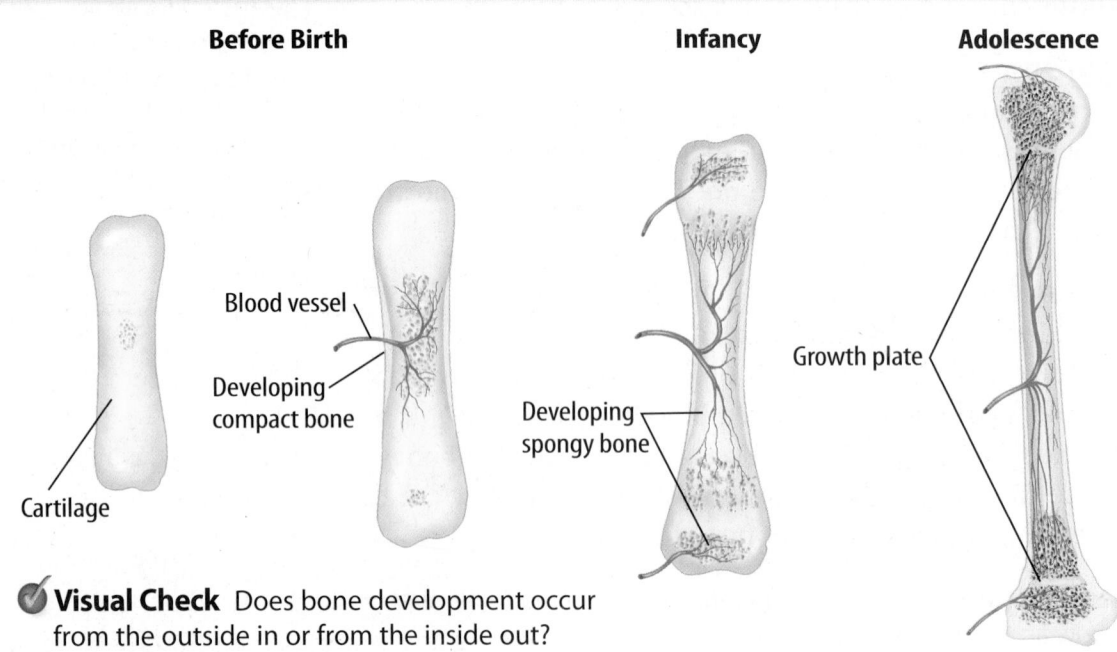

Before Birth

Infancy

Adolescence

Blood vessel

Developing compact bone

Cartilage

Developing spongy bone

Growth plate

Visual Check Does bone development occur from the outside in or from the inside out?

Joints

Your bones do not function independently. They work together at places called joints. *A* **joint** *is where two or more bones meet.* Joints provide flexibility and enable the skeleton to move. *Bones are connected to other bones by tissues called* **ligaments** (LIH guh munts). When the bones in joints move, ligaments stretch and keep the bones from shifting away from each other.

Ligaments connect bones at joints, but they do not protect bones. As you read earlier, cartilage protects the ends of bones, reducing friction between them so the bones move easily. Your skeletal system contains two types of joints—immovable joints and movable joints.

Immovable Joints

Some parts of your skeleton are made of bones that connect but do not move. These are immovable joints. Your skull contains several immovable joints.

Movable Joints

You are able to move your hand or bend your body because of movable joints. The body's movable joints allow for a wide range of motion. Three main types of movable joints and the ligaments that hold them together are shown in **Table 1**.

🔑 **Key Concept Check** How do ligaments and cartilage help the skeletal system function?

Table 1 Types of Movable Joints	Concepts in Motion — Interactive Table	
Joint	**Description**	**Example**
Ball and socket	allows bones to move and rotate in nearly all directions	hips and shoulders
Hinge	allows bones to move back and forth in a single direction	fingers, elbows, knees
Pivot	allows bones to rotate	neck, lower arm below the elbow

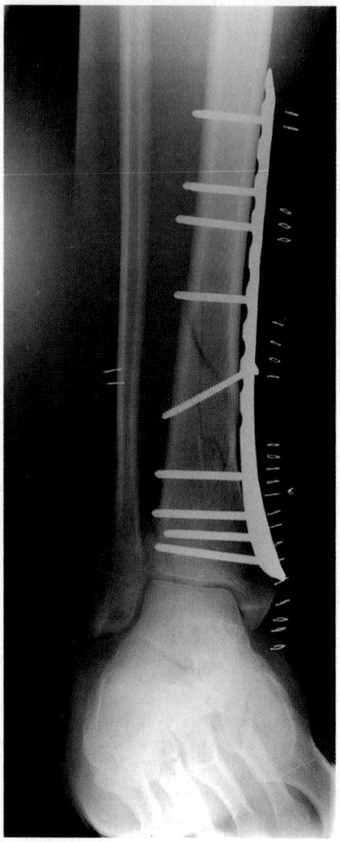

Bone Injuries and Diseases

Because bones are made of living tissues, they are at risk of injury and disease. A wooden board is hard and strong, but if enough pressure is applied to it, the board will break. The same is true for bones.

Broken Bones

A break in a bone is called a fracture (FRAK chur). Broken bones are able to repair themselves, but it is a slow process. A broken bone must be held together while it heals, just as you hold two glued objects together while the glue dries. Often, a person wears a cast to keep broken bones in place. Sometimes metal plates and screws like those in **Figure 6** hold bones together while they heal.

Arthritis

You are able to move because your skeleton bends and rotates at joints. If the joints become irritated, it can be painful to move. **Arthritis** (ar THRI tus) *is a disease in which joints become irritated or inflamed, such as when cartilage in joints is damaged or wears away.* Arthritis is most common in adults, but it can also affect children.

Osteoporosis

Another common bone disease is **osteoporosis** (ahs tee oh puh ROH sus), *which causes bones to weaken and become brittle.* Anyone can develop osteoporosis, but it is most common in women over the age of 50. Osteoporosis can change a person's skeleton and cause fractures, as shown in **Figure 7.**

▲ **Figure 6** This X-ray was taken after screws and plates were placed in the bone to hold it together.

Osteoporosis

Figure 7 Osteoporosis can weaken the skeletal system over time.

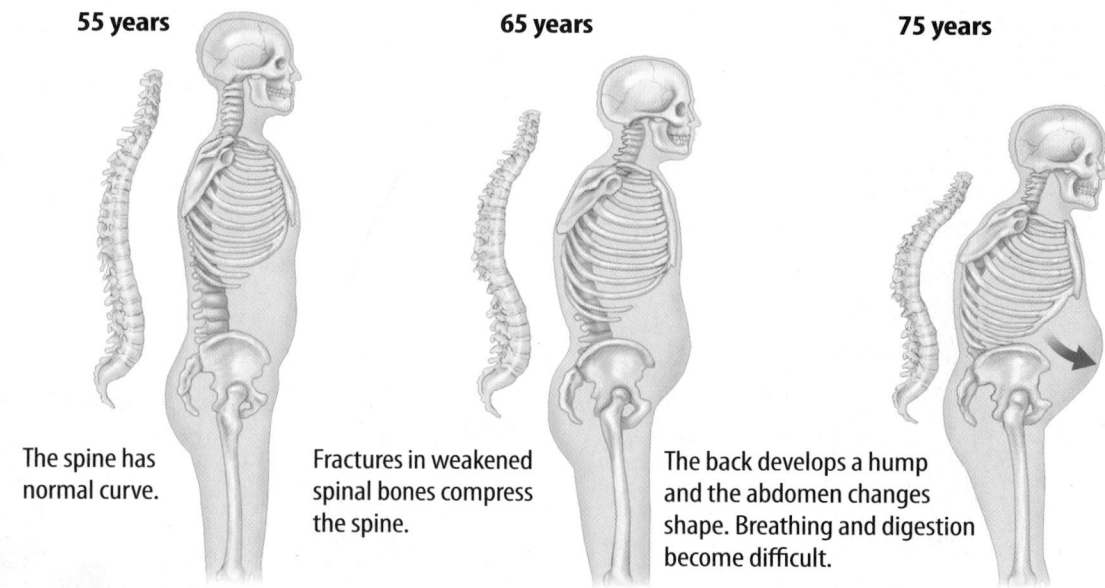

55 years

The spine has normal curve.

65 years

Fractures in weakened spinal bones compress the spine.

75 years

The back develops a hump and the abdomen changes shape. Breathing and digestion become difficult.

| Running and walking build bone in your hips, legs, and feet. | Playing tennis is one way to build bone strength in your arms, wrists, and shoulders. | Weight-bearing exercise is beneficial to many bones. |

Figure 8 Exercises that place weight on bones or work bones against gravity help keep the skeletal system healthy.

Healthy Bones

One of the best ways to keep bones healthy is to exercise. Certain types of exercise, such as those shown in **Figure 8,** place weight on bones. This strengthens bones and builds new bone tissue. Without exercise, bones weaken and lose mass.

A balanced diet also keeps bones healthy. Bones especially need calcium and vitamin D. Calcium makes bones strong. It is also necessary for cellular processes in blood, nerve, and muscle cells. If you do not have enough calcium in your diet, your body will use the calcium stored in your bones. If your body uses too much of the stored calcium, your bones can become weak. Vitamin D is also important because it helps the body use calcium.

The Skeletal System and Homeostasis

You might recall that homeostasis is an organism's ability to maintain a stable internal environment. Homeostasis requires that all body systems function properly together. Because bones supply calcium to your nerves, muscles, and heart, a healthy skeletal system is important in maintaining your body's homeostasis.

Bones also help you respond to unpleasant stimuli, such as a mosquito bite. Working together with muscles, bones enable you to move away from unpleasant stimuli or danger, or even swat a mosquito.

 Key Concept Check How does the skeletal system help the body maintain homeostasis?

REVIEW VOCABULARY

homeostasis
the ability of an organism to maintain a stable internal environment

Lesson 1 Review

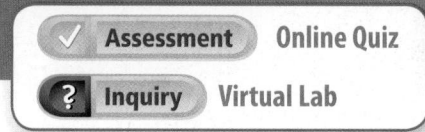
Visual Summary

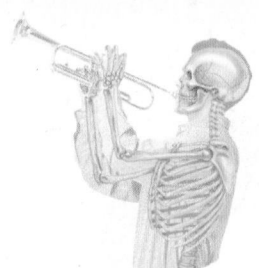

The skeletal system consists of all the bones, ligaments, and cartilage in the body.

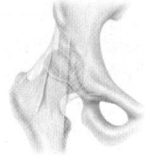

Joints provide flexibility and enable the skeleton to move.

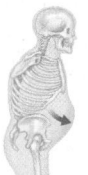

Osteoporosis is a disease that causes bones to weaken and become brittle.

FOLDABLES

Use your lesson Foldable to review the lesson. Save your Foldable for the project at the end of the chapter.

What do you think NOW?

You first read the statements below at the beginning of the chapter.

1. Bones protect internal organs.

2. Bones do not change during a person's lifetime.

Did you change your mind about whether you agree or disagree with the statements? Rewrite any false statements to make them true.

Use Vocabulary

1 Strong, flexible tissue that covers the ends of bones is called _____.

2 Bones connect to other bones at _____.

3 A person with _____ has irritated joints.

Understand Key Concepts

4 Which is NOT a part of the periosteum?
  A. blood vessels   **C.** bone marrow
  B. bone cells   **D.** nerves

5 **Distinguish** between cartilage and ligaments.

6 **Give** an example of how the skeletal system interacts with the nervous system.

Interpret Graphics

7 **Determine** the type of joint shown in the figure below.

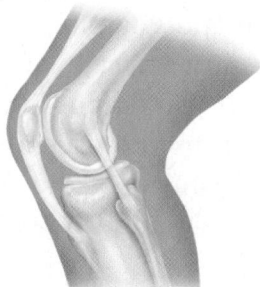

8 **Organize** Copy the graphic organizer below and, in the ovals, list the four major functions of the skeletal system.

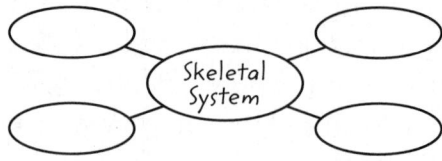

Skeletal System

Critical Thinking

9 **Summarize** how bones help the body maintain homeostasis.

10 **Evaluate** why it is better for an adult's skull to have immovable joints and not movable joints.

A Bionic Arm

How brains control mechanical arms

Imagine what your arms would be like without muscles. They would simply swing from your shoulders like pendulums. You would not be able to control them. For many years prosthetic, or artificial, arms looked real, but they didn't work like real arms. Recently scientists have developed a bionic, or mechanical, arm. Signals from the patient's brain control it.

1 Doctors perform surgery and attach nerves that were once part of the damaged arm to chest muscles. These nerves sent signals to the patient's arm muscles.

Nerves

Electrodes

Chest muscles

Computer

2 When the patient's brain sends signals to move the arm or the hand, the signals travel from the brain to the chest muscles.

3 Electronic sensors in the bionic arm's harness detect the chest muscle moving. The sensors send corresponding signals down the bionic arm.

4 A computer processes the signals from the harness and moves the arm and hand. These movements are similar to those of a biological arm and hand.

It's Your Turn

RESEARCH AND REPORT In science-fiction films, some characters have bionic body parts such as ears and eyes. Are any other bionic body parts in development? Summarize your findings in a paragraph.

Reading Guide

Key Concepts 🔑
ESSENTIAL QUESTIONS

- What does the muscular system do?
- How do types of muscle differ?
- How does the muscular system interact with other body systems?

Vocabulary

muscle p. 497

skeletal muscle p. 499

voluntary muscle p. 499

cardiac muscle p. 500

involuntary muscle p. 500

smooth muscle p. 500

 Multilingual eGlossary

 Video

- Science Video
- What's Science Got to do With It?

The Muscular System

 **How can she do that?**

This person is a contortionist (kun TOR shuh nist)—someone who can bend and flex his or her body in unusual ways. The contortionist pictured here is able to stay in this position because her muscular system can hold her body in place.

Can you control all your muscles?

Can you feel your heart beating? Your body contains many muscles that you can control by thinking about them. However, not all types of muscle are controllable.

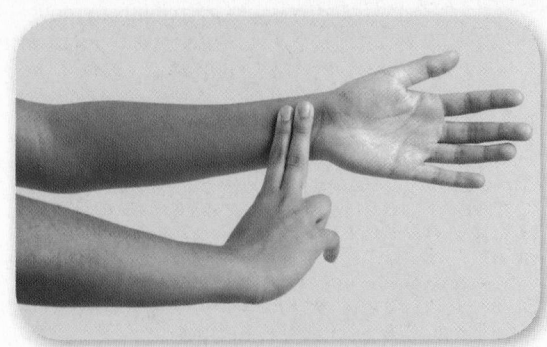

1 Shake hands with another student. Did you have to think about this action?

2 Rest your index and middle fingers on the thumb side of your wrist until you can feel your pulse. Can you change the speed of your pulse by thinking about it?

Think About This

1. Make a list of the muscles in your body that you can consciously control. What are their functions?

2. ⚷ **Key Concept** Think of other muscles in your body, besides your heart, that work without you thinking about them. How do the functions of these muscles differ from the ones you consciously control?

Functions of the Muscular System

What comes to mind when you think of muscles? Maybe you think about the muscles in your arms or legs that enable you to carry books or run fast. Movement is an important function of the muscular system. But muscles are also important for protection, stability, and maintaining body temperature.

Although muscles have different functions, all muscle tissues are made of cells that contract. *A* **muscle** *is made of strong tissue that can contract in an orderly way.* When a muscle contracts, the cells of the muscle become shorter, as shown in **Figure 9.** When the muscle relaxes, the cells return to their original length.

Movement

Many of your muscles are attached to bone and enable your skeleton to move. Bones move when these muscles contract. This movement can be fast, such as when you run, or slow, like when you stretch.

You also have many muscles in your body that are not attached to bones. The contractions in these muscles cause blood and food to move throughout your body. They also cause your heart to beat and the hair on your arms to stand on end when you get goose bumps.

⚷ **Key Concept Check** What is one major function of the muscular system?

Figure 9 A muscle cell works by contracting and relaxing.

Relaxed

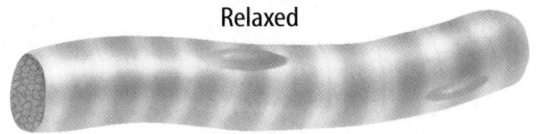

Contracted

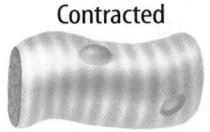

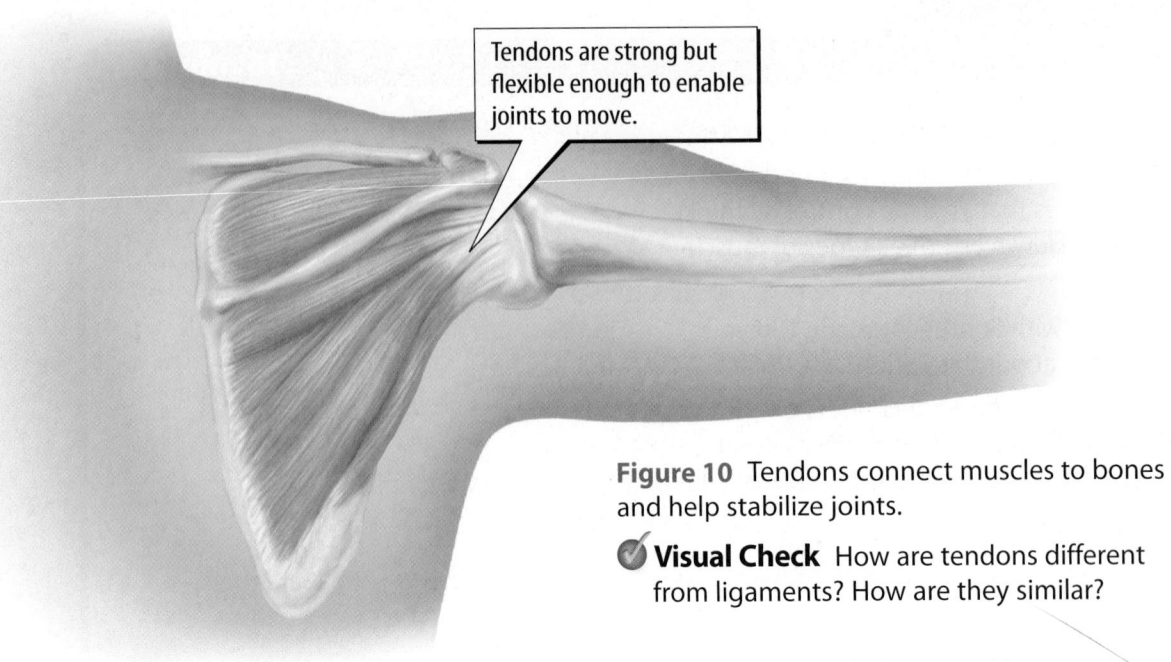

Tendons are strong but flexible enough to enable joints to move.

Figure 10 Tendons connect muscles to bones and help stabilize joints.

✅ **Visual Check** How are tendons different from ligaments? How are they similar?

Figure 11 Muscles cover the skeleton. ▼

Stability

Muscles that are attached to bones support your body and help you balance. If your body becomes unstable, such as when you trip and lose your balance, your muscles pull in different directions and you regain your balance.

Tendons attach muscles to bones, as shown in **Figure 10.** Look at the back of your hand and move your fingers. Do you see cordlike structures moving under your skin? These are tendons. You can feel the Achilles tendon above either of your heels. Tendons work with muscles and keep joints in place when your body moves. Tendons also help hold your body in a proper posture, or shape.

Protection

Muscles protect your body. As shown in **Figure 11,** muscles cover most of your skeleton. Muscles also cover most of the organs inside your body. Muscles are like a layer of padding. They surround your abdomen, chest, and back and protect your internal organs.

Temperature Regulation

Have you ever been in a cold environment and started shivering? Shivering is when muscles contract rapidly and change chemical energy to thermal energy. The thermal energy helps raise your body's temperature. This is important because a human's body temperature must stay around 37°C in order for the body to function properly. Muscles also change chemical energy to thermal energy during exercise. This is why you feel warm after physical activity.

Types of Muscles

Your body has three different types of muscles: skeletal, cardiac, and smooth. Each of these muscle tissues is specialized for a different function.

Skeletal Muscle

The type of muscle that attaches to bones is **skeletal muscle.** Skeletal muscles, as shown in **Figure 12,** are also called **voluntary muscles,** *which are muscles that you can consciously control.* Have you ever played with a puppet on a string? You controlled how the puppet moved. In a similar way, you control how skeletal muscles move. The contractions of skeletal muscles can be quick and powerful, such as when you run fast. However, contracting these muscles for long periods of time can exhaust or cramp them.

How Skeletal Muscles Work Skeletal muscles work by pulling on bones. Because muscles cannot push bones, they must work in pairs. **Figure 12** illustrates how an arm's biceps (BI seps) and triceps (TRI seps) muscles work as a pair.

✓ **Reading Check** Why must skeletal muscles work in pairs?

Changes in Skeletal Muscles Your skeletal muscles can change throughout your lifetime. If you exercise, your muscle cells increase in size and the entire muscle becomes larger and stronger.

FOLDABLES

Fold a sheet of paper into thirds to make a tri-fold book. Use it to organize your notes on the three types of muscle tissue.

Skeletal muscle

Cardiac muscle

Smooth muscle

Concepts in Motion **Animation**

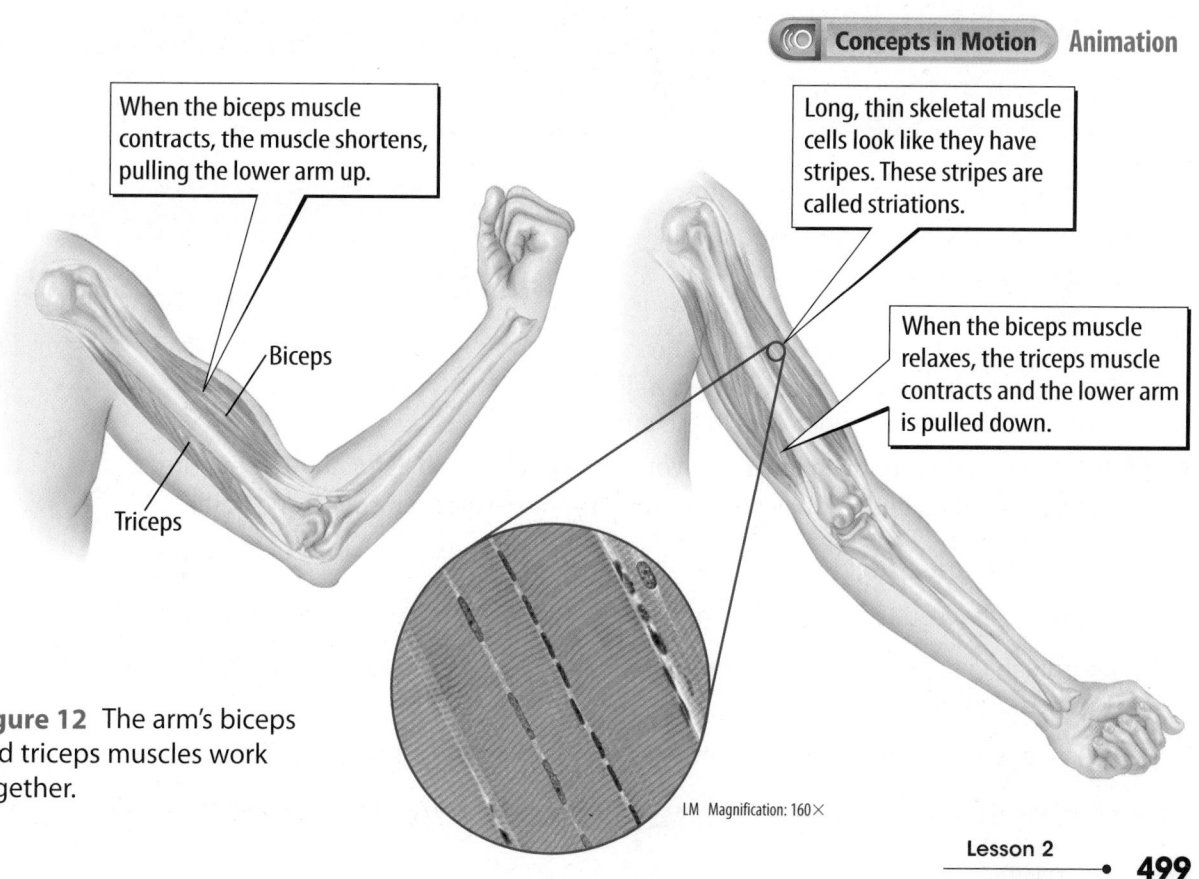

When the biceps muscle contracts, the muscle shortens, pulling the lower arm up.

Long, thin skeletal muscle cells look like they have stripes. These stripes are called striations.

When the biceps muscle relaxes, the triceps muscle contracts and the lower arm is pulled down.

Biceps

Triceps

LM Magnification: 160×

Figure 12 The arm's biceps and triceps muscles work together.

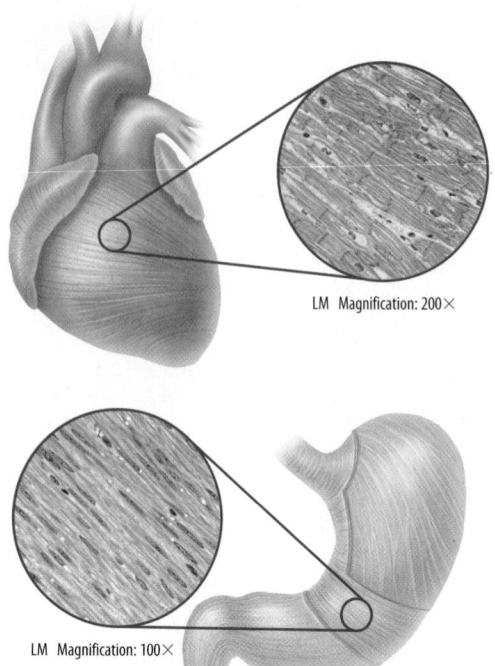

LM Magnification: 200✕

LM Magnification: 100✕

Figure 13 The heart is made of cardiac muscle. The stomach is lined with three layers of smooth muscle.

Cardiac Muscle

Your heart is made of **cardiac** (KAR dee ak) **muscles,** *which are found only in the heart.* A cardiac muscle is a type of **involuntary muscle,** *which is muscle you cannot consciously control.* When cardiac muscles contract and relax, they pump blood through your heart and through vessels throughout your body. Cardiac muscle cells, shown in **Figure 13,** have branches with discs at the ends. The discs send signals to other cardiac cells and they all contract at nearly the same time.

Smooth Muscle

Blood vessels and many organs, such as the stomach shown in **Figure 13,** are lined with smooth muscles. **Smooth muscles** *are involuntary muscles named for their smooth appearance.* Contraction of smooth muscles helps move material through the body, such as food in the stomach, and controls the movement of blood through vessels.

Key Concept Check What are the three types of muscles?

Inquiry MiniLab   **20 minutes**

How strong are your hand muscles?

Have you ever done hand exercises? Do your hand muscles tire?

1. Read and complete a lab safety form.
2. Copy the data table to the right in your Science Journal.
3. Choose a partner. While your partner keeps time with a **stopwatch,** count how many times you can squeeze a **tennis ball** in one minute. Record your data in the table.

	Number of Squeezes	
Student Name	First Minute	Second Minute

4. Immediately count how many times you can squeeze the ball for another minute. Again record your data in the table. Switch roles so your partner can collect the data.

Analyze and Conclude

1. **Compare** the results from the first minute to the second minute for both partners.

2. **Design** an experiment to determine whether daily practice would increase the number of squeezes per minute.

3. **Key Concept** Evaluate the importance of doing exercises to keep muscles strong.

Healthy Muscles

Recall that a good diet keeps your bones healthy. Your muscles benefit from a healthy diet, too. All muscles require energy to contract. This energy comes from the food you eat. Eating a diet full of nutrients such as protein, fiber, and potassium can help keep muscles strong.

Exercise also helps keep muscles healthy. Muscle cells decrease in size and strength without exercise, as shown in **Figure 14.** Decreased muscle strength can increase the risk of heart disease and bone injuries. It can also make joints less stable.

WORD ORIGIN

cardiac
from Greek *kardia*, means "heart"

Figure 14 Muscles lose size, strength, and mobility if they are not exercised.

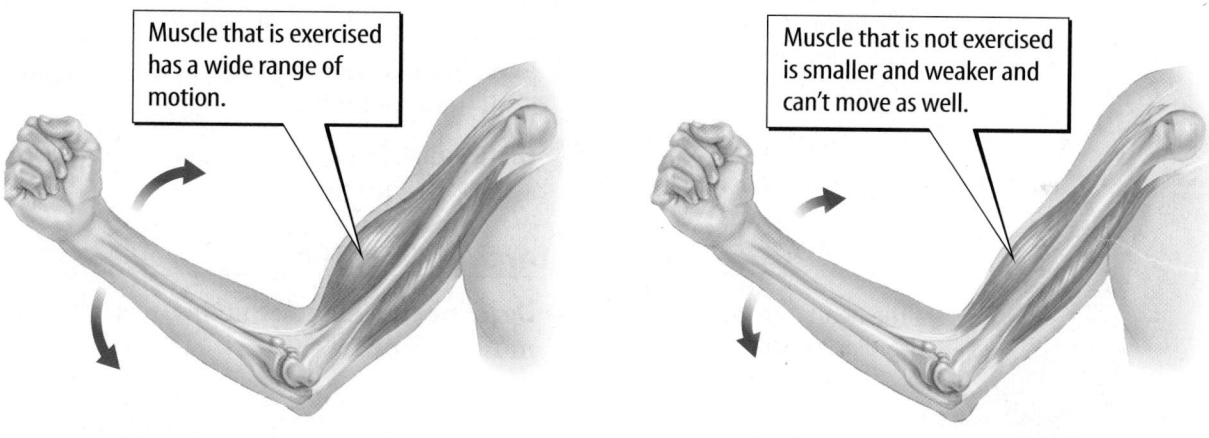

Muscle that is exercised has a wide range of motion.

Muscle that is not exercised is smaller and weaker and can't move as well.

The Muscular System and Homeostasis

There are many ways the muscular system helps your body maintain homeostasis. You are probably sitting in a room where the temperature is somewhere between 21°C and 27°C. However, your body temperature is around 37°C. Your body must stay at this temperature to function well. As you have read, muscle contractions **convert** chemical energy to thermal energy and keep your body warm.

When you exercise, your cells need more oxygen and release more waste, such as carbon dioxide. The cardiac muscles of your heart help maintain homeostasis by contracting more often. When it contracts faster, the heart pumps more blood, and more oxygen is carried to the cells.

ACADEMIC VOCABULARY

convert
(verb) to change something into a different form

 Key Concept Check How do muscles help maintain homeostasis in the body?

Lesson 2 Review

Visual Summary

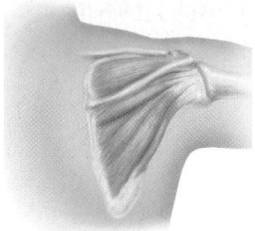

Your muscular system is made of different types of muscles. Skeletal muscles attach to bone and are muscles you can control.

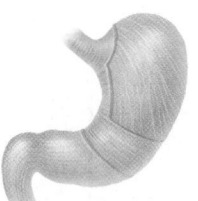

Smooth muscles line blood vessels and many internal organs.

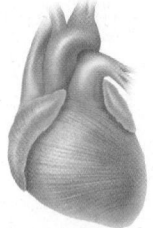

The heart is made of cardiac muscle.

FOLDABLES®

Use your lesson Foldable to review the lesson. Save your Foldable for the project at the end of the chapter.

What do you think NOW?

You first read the statements below at the beginning of the chapter.

3. The same type of muscle that moves bones also pumps blood through the heart.

4. Muscles cannot push bones.

Did you change your mind about whether you agree or disagree with the statements? Rewrite any false statements to make them true.

Use Vocabulary

1 Muscle that pumps blood through the body is called _____.

2 A person is unable to control the contractions of _____.

3 Strong tissue that contracts is called _____.

Understand Key Concepts

4 Which is a voluntary muscle?
   A. biceps   **C.** blood vessel
   B. stomach   **D.** small intestine

5 **Explain** how the muscular system regulates body temperature.

6 **Distinguish** between a cardiac muscle and a smooth muscle.

Interpret Graphics

7 **Describe** the relationship between the two muscles shown.

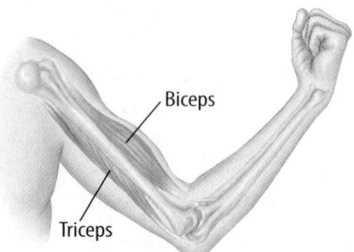

Biceps

Triceps

8 **Identify** Copy and fill in the graphic organizer below to identify three functions of the muscular system.

Muscle functions

Critical Thinking

9 **Predict** what would happen if the smooth muscles in a person's body could not contract.

10 **Assess** the importance of exercise for muscle health.

How do the three types of muscle cells compare?

Materials

compound microscope

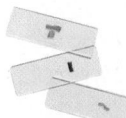

muscle cell slides

Safety

As you have read in this chapter, there are three types of muscle cells. Skeletal muscle cells are voluntary muscle cells and can be controlled. Smooth and cardiac muscle cells are involuntary muscle cells. An organism does not need to think about their movement. These three types of muscle cells have different characteristics and functions in the body. In this activity, you will examine cells of each type and observe their similarities and differences.

Learn It

Scientists can learn a great deal about organisms or objects through **observation.** A scientist might note the characteristics that several things have in common. He or she might also observe characteristics that make something unique. Observations help scientists classify things and understand how they function.

Try It

1 Read and complete a lab safety form.

2 Copy the table below into your Science Journal.

3 Place a prepared slide of skeletal muscle cells on the stage of a compound light microscope.

4 In your table, describe the cells' shape and color. Note any differences among them.

5 Locate the nucleus in one of the cells. Where is it in the cell? Do any cells have more than one nucleus?

6 Describe the arrangement of the cells in the tissue. Do they have a pattern or are they randomly arranged?

7 Repeat steps 3 through 6 for the prepared cardiac muscle and smooth muscle slides.

Apply It

8 **Compare and Contrast** How do the characteristics of each cell type differ?

9 🔑 **Key Concept** Based on your observations and on what you have read, what characteristics of each cell type might relate to its function?

Observations of Three Types of Muscle Cells			
Cell Characteristics	Skeletal	Smooth	Cardiac
Shape			
Nucleus location			
Arrangement patterns			

Lesson 3

The Skin

Reading Guide

Key Concepts 🔑
ESSENTIAL QUESTIONS

- What does the skin do?
- How do the three layers of skin differ?
- How does the skin interact with other body systems?

Vocabulary

integumentary system p. 505
epidermis p. 507
melanin p. 507
dermis p. 507
bruise p. 508

g **Multilingual eGlossary**

Color-enhanced SEM   Magnification: unknown

Inquiry   What is this?

You might think this is a picture of a landscape on another planet. However, this image shows what your skin looks like under a microscope. Your skin sheds its top layer of cells constantly as new cells are made to take their place.

Launch Lab

5 minutes

How does your skin protect your body?

Your skin is your body's first line of defense. When you touch something with your fingers you can instantly tell if it is hot or cold. Are all parts of your body equally sensitive?

1. Read and complete a lab safety form.
2. Touch the back of your hand with an **ice cube** in a **plastic bag.**
3. Now do the same to the back of your knee.

Analyze and Conclude

1. Which area was more sensitive to cold?

2. How do you think the skin senses temperature?

3. 🔑 **Key Concept** How does sensitivity to temperature protect the body?

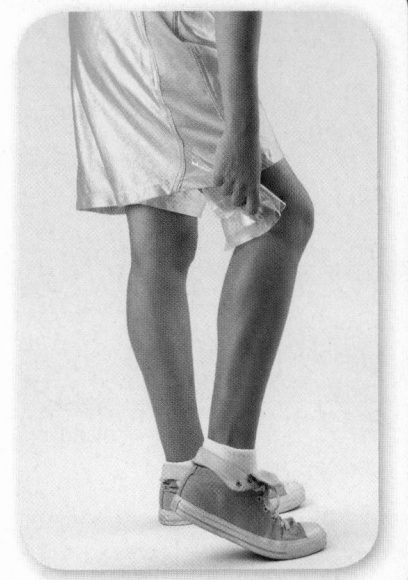

Functions of the Skin

Touch your fingertips, your arm, and your face. The soft tissue you feel is the outermost layer of your skin. Skin is the largest organ of your body. It is part of the **integumentary** (ihn teh gyuh MEN tuh ree) **system,** *which includes all the external coverings of the body, including the skin, nails, and hair.* Most parts of the integumentary system are shown in **Figure 15.** Like bones and muscles, skin serves many different functions in your body.

Protection

When you look at yourself in a mirror, you cannot see the bones, muscles, or other parts of your skeletal and muscular systems. Instead, you see your skin. Skin covers your bones and muscles and protects them from the external environment. It keeps your body from drying out in sunlight and wind. Skin also protects the cells and tissues under the skin from damage. Skin is the first line of defense against dirt, bacteria, viruses, and other substances that might enter your body.

✔ **Reading Check** What would happen to your body if you had no skin?

WORD ORIGIN ·

integumentary
from Latin *integere*, means "to cover"

· ·

Figure 15 The integumentary system includes skin, nails, and hair.

Figure 16 During exercise, sweat evaporates and blood vessels enlarge. This releases thermal energy.

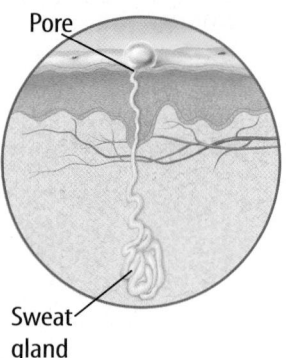

Pore

Sweat gland

Sensory Response

Close your eyes, and feel the surface of your desk and the objects on top. Even with your eyes closed, you can tell the difference between the desk, a book, paper, and pencils. This is because your skin has special cells called sensory receptors that detect texture. Sensory receptors also detect temperature and sense pain. The more sensory receptors there are in an area of skin, the more sensitive it is.

Temperature Regulation

Skin helps control body temperature. When you exercise, sweat comes from tiny holes, or pores, on the skin's surface, as shown in **Figure 16.** Sweating is one way skin lowers your body temperature. As sweat evaporates, excess thermal energy leaves the body and the skin cools.

Another way that skin lowers body temperature is by releasing thermal energy from blood vessels. Has your face ever turned red while exercising? The girl in **Figure 16** has a red face because the blood vessels near the skin's surface dilated, or enlarged. This increases the surface area of the blood vessels and releases more thermal energy.

Key Concept Check How does skin regulate body temperature?

Production of Vitamin D

If your skin is exposed to sunlight, it can make vitamin D. Your body needs vitamin D to help it absorb calcium and phosphorous and to promote the growth of bones. Your skin is not the only source of vitamin D. Vitamin D is usually added to milk and is found naturally in certain types of fish.

Elimination

Normal cellular processes produce waste products. The skin helps to eliminate these wastes. Water, salts, and other waste products are removed through the pores. This occurs all the time, but you might only notice it when you sweat during exercise.

Inquiry MiniLab 10 minutes

Why are you sweating?

You might think that you sweat only when you exercise, but your body also sweats when you are at rest.

1. Read and complete a lab safety form.

2. Wipe your hands dry on a **paper towel.**

3. Place your non-writing hand in a **one-quart plastic bag.** With a partner's help, tape it around your wrist.

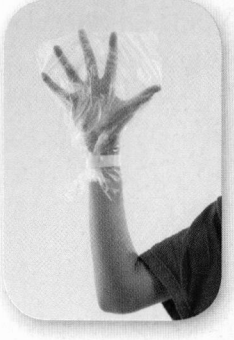

4. Observe the inside of the bag after 5 minutes. Record your observations in your Science Journal.

5. Observe the inside of the bag again after 10 minutes. Record your observations.

Analyze and Conclude

1. **Describe** what happened to the inside of the bag after 10 minutes.

2. **Explain** what might have caused this change.

3. **Key Concept** How does skin help regulate body temperature?

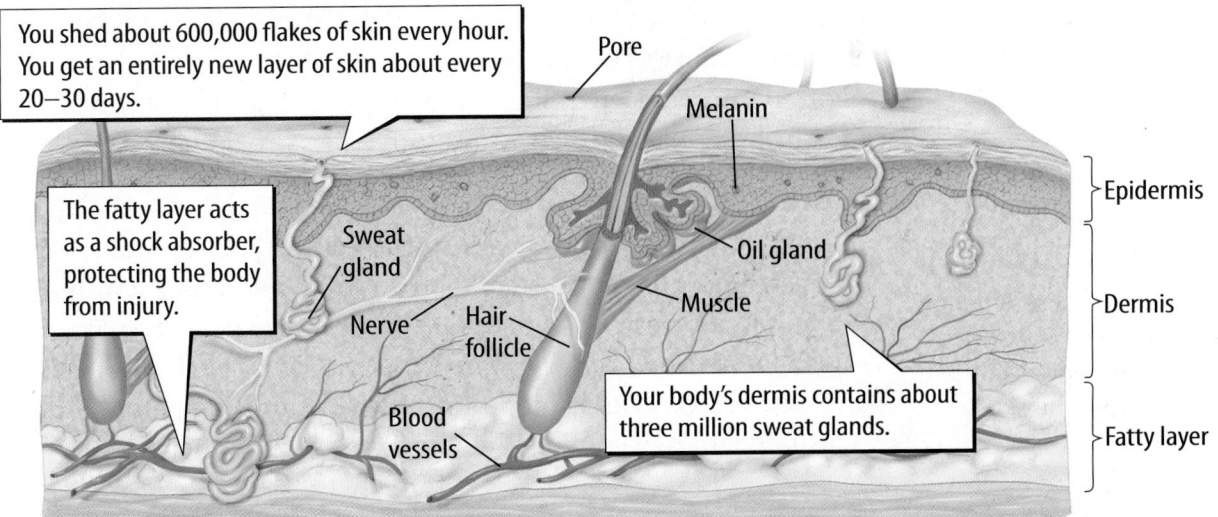

You shed about 600,000 flakes of skin every hour. You get an entirely new layer of skin about every 20–30 days.

Pore

Melanin

Epidermis

The fatty layer acts as a shock absorber, protecting the body from injury.

Sweat gland

Oil gland

Dermis

Nerve Hair follicle

Muscle

Blood vessels

Your body's dermis contains about three million sweat glands.

Fatty layer

Figure 17 Skin has three layers, each with different functions.

Structures of the Skin

The skin that you see and feel on your body is the outermost layer of skin. Below it are two other layers of skin. These layers, shown in **Figure 17,** differ in structure and function.

Epidermis

The **epidermis** (eh puh DUR mus) *is the outermost layer of skin and the only layer in direct contact with the outside environment.* The epidermis is tough but thin. The epidermis on your eyelids is thinner than a sheet of paper. Cells of the epidermis are constantly shed and replaced by new cells.

One important function of the epidermis is the production of melanin (MEH luh nun). **Melanin** *is a pigment that protects the body by absorbing some of the Sun's damaging ultraviolet rays.*

Dermis

Below the epidermis is the dermis. *The **dermis** is a thick layer of skin that gives skin strength, nourishment, and flexibility.* The dermis contains sweat glands, blood vessels, nerves, hair follicles, and muscles, as shown in **Figure 17.** When the muscles in the dermis contract, you get goose bumps.

Fatty Layer

The innermost layer of skin insulates the body, acts as a protective padding, and stores energy. This layer is sometimes called the fatty layer. It can be very thin or very thick, depending on its location on the body.

Key Concept Check How do the skin's three layers differ?

Math Skills

Using Proportions

The ratios $\frac{5}{1}$ and $\frac{25}{5}$ are equivalent, so they can be written as the proportion $\frac{5}{1} = \frac{25}{5}$. When ratios form a proportion, the cross products are equal. In the above proportion, $5 \times 5 = 25 \times 1$. You can use cross products to find a missing term. For example, if each 1 cm^2 of skin contains 300 pores, how many pores are there in 5 cm^2 of skin?

$$\frac{1 \text{ cm}^2}{300 \text{ pores}} = \frac{5 \text{ cm}^2}{n \text{ pores}}$$

$$1 \times n = 300 \times 5;$$
$$n = 1500 \text{ pores}$$

Practice

The palm of the hand has about 500 sweat glands per 1 cm^2. How many sweat glands would there be on a palm measuring 7 cm by 8 cm?

📖 Review

- **Math Practice**
- **Personal Tutor**

Skin Injuries and Repair

You have probably fallen down and injured your knees or other parts of your body. You might also have damaged your skin. Because skin is exposed to the outside environment, it is often injured. Depending on the type and severity of the injury, your body has different ways to repair skin.

Bruises

Have you ever bumped into the edge of a table and noticed later that your skin turned red or purple and blue? You probably had a bruise. A **bruise** is an injury where blood vessels in the skin are broken, but the skin is not cut or opened. The broken blood vessels release blood into the surrounding tissue. Bruises usually change color as they heal, as shown in **Figure 18**.

Figure 18 Bruises change color as they heal due to chemical changes in the blood under the skin's surface.

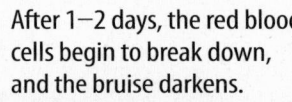
A new bruise is red because blood pools under the skin.

After 1–2 days, the red blood cells begin to break down, and the bruise darkens.

After 5–10 days, the bruise turns greenish-yellow. After about 2 weeks, it fades away.

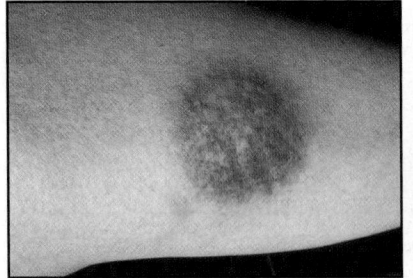
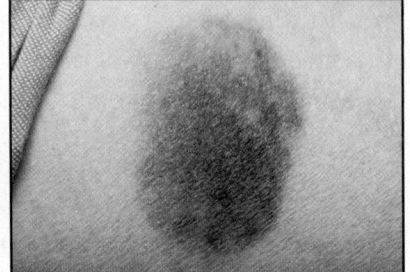
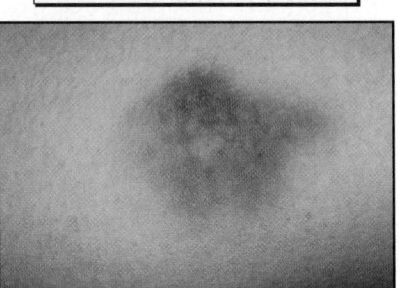

Cuts

When you break one or more layers of skin, it is called a cut. Cuts often cut blood vessels, too. The released blood will usually thicken and form a scab over the cut. The scab prevents dirt and other outside substances from entering the body. Skin heals by producing new skin cells that eventually repair the cut. Some cuts are too large to heal naturally. If that happens, stitches might be needed to close the cut while it heals.

Burns

Have you ever injured your skin by contact with hot water or hot food? If so, then you had a burn. You might think that burns only occur from touching hot objects. However, burns can also be caused by touching extremely cold objects, chemicals, radiation (such as sunlight), electricity, or friction (rubbing). **Table 2** describes the three degrees, or levels, of burns.

Reading Check What can cause your skin to burn?

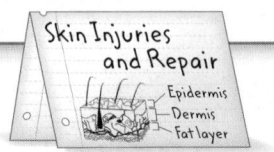

Table 2 Degrees of Burns

Burn	Symptoms	Damage
First-degree burn	Damages top layer of skin Symptoms: pain, redness, swelling Usually heals in 5–7 days without scarring	
Second-degree burn	Damages top two layers of skin Symptoms: pain, redness, swelling, blistering Usually heals in 2–6 weeks with some scarring	
Third-degree burn	Damages all three layers of skin and sometimes the tissue below skin Symptoms: black or white charred skin, may be temporarily numb due to damaged nerves Heals over months with scarring; might require surgery	

Table 2 Burns are classified by the depth of damage to the skin. There are three different degrees, or levels, of burns.

Visual Check If swelling and blisters appear on the surface of a burned area of skin, what degree burn would it be?

▲ **Figure 19** Protecting your skin from sunlight is important for maintaining skin health.

Healthy Skin

Just as diet and exercise are important to healthy skeletal and muscular systems, good life choices can keep your skin functioning well.

One important thing you can do for your skin is protect it from sunlight. The ultraviolet rays in sunlight can cause permanent damage to the skin, including wrinkles, dry skin, and skin cancer. Like the person in **Figure 19,** you can protect your skin by using sunscreen. You can also wear protective clothing and avoid outdoor activities during the middle of the day.

Another way to keep your skin healthy is to eat a balanced diet. You can also apply lotion to your skin to help keep it moist and use gentle soaps to clean it.

The Skin and Homeostasis

Skin helps your body maintain homeostasis in many ways. You read that the skin can make vitamin D and that it protects the body from outside substances. These functions of the skin help regulate the body's internal environment.

The skin also works with other body systems to maintain homeostasis. You read earlier how the skin and the circulatory system help cool the body when it becomes overheated. If the body becomes cold, blood vessels constrict, or narrow, reducing thermal energy loss. As you can see in **Figure 20,** the skin also works with the nervous and muscular systems to help the body react to stimuli.

Key Concept Check How does the skin interact with other body systems to help maintain homeostasis?

Figure 20 The skin, the nervous system, and the muscular system work together to maintain homeostasis. ▼

Reaction to Stimuli

Review   Personal Tutor

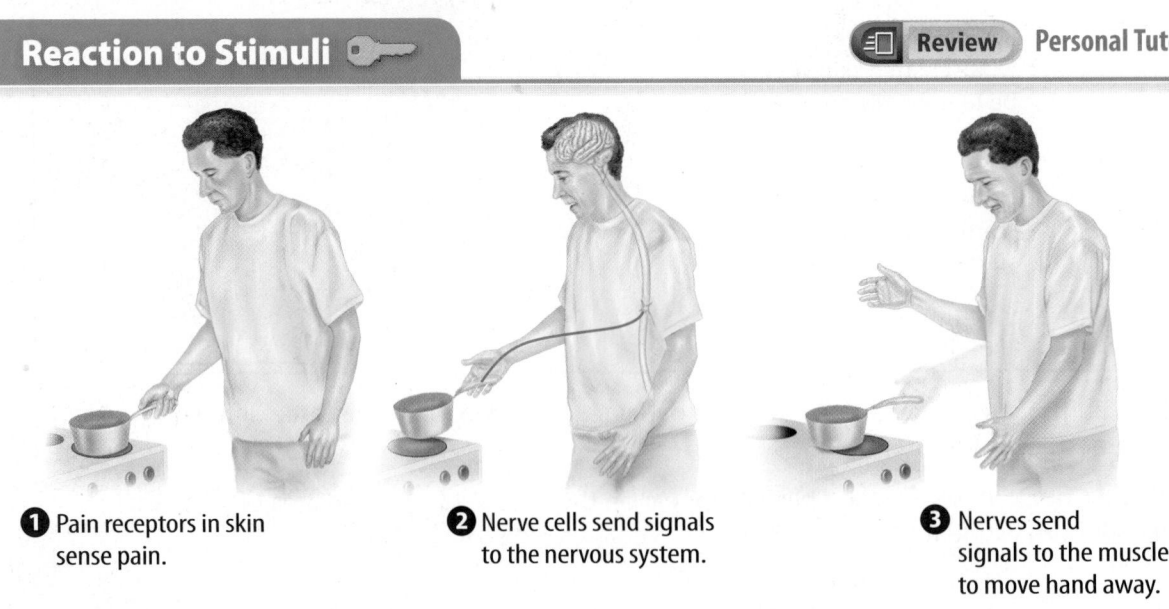

❶ Pain receptors in skin sense pain.

❷ Nerve cells send signals to the nervous system.

❸ Nerves send signals to the muscles to move hand away.

Visual Summary

The integumentary system consists of all the external coverings of the body.

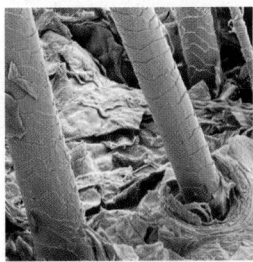

The epidermis is the outermost layer of skin.

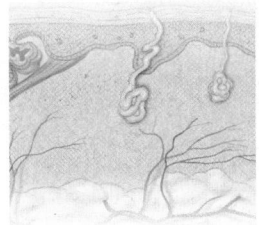

The dermis is the layer of skin that contains sweat glands, blood vessels, nerves, hair follicles, and muscles.

FOLDABLES®

Use your lesson Foldable to review the lesson. Save your Foldable for the project at the end of the chapter.

What do you think NOW?

You first read the statements below at the beginning of the chapter.

5. Skin helps regulate body temperature.

6. Skin is made of two layers of tissue.

Did you change your mind about whether you agree or disagree with the statements? Rewrite any false statements to make them true.

Use Vocabulary

1 A pigment that absorbs ultraviolet rays is called _____.

2 The _____ is the layer that nourishes the skin.

Understand Key Concepts

3 Which is the innermost layer of skin?
- **A.** dermis
- **B.** epidermis
- **C.** fatty layer
- **D.** melanin

4 **Give** an example of how the skin regulates body temperature.

5 **Compare** the dermis and epidermis. Explain the function of each.

Interpret Graphics

6 **Estimate** the age of the bruise shown on the right.

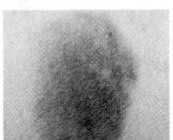

7 **Organize Information** Copy and fill in the table below with details about the three degrees of burns.

First-degree burn	
Second-degree burn	
Third-degree burn	

Critical Thinking

8 **Evaluate** the importance of your skin to your homeostasis.

Math Skills

Review
——— Math Practice ———

9 The palms of the hands and soles of the feet have the highest concentration of sweat glands—about 500/cm². How many sweat glands would there be on the sole of a foot measuring 10 cm × 27 cm?

Materials

dissecting scissors

paper towel

forceps

dissection tray

chicken wing

Safety

Dissect a Chicken Wing

A chicken wing has many structures similar to those of a human arm. As in humans, these structures perform different functions. How do these structures work together? How are they like your arm?

Question

How do the skin, muscles, and bones of a chicken help support the chicken, enable it to move, and regulate its internal environment?

Procedure

1. Read and complete a lab safety form.

2. Obtain a boiled chicken wing and pat it dry with a paper towel. Flex the wing at its joints and notice what happens.

3. Insert the scissors under the skin at the large end and cut the skin down the length of the wing. Look at the underside of the skin. Does it look any different from the outside?

4. Carefully peel the skin off the wing. Identify the muscles—the pink or white tissues between the skin and the bone.

5. Examine the outer surface of the muscles. Identify the tendons, which are shiny white tissues at either end of the muscles. Carefully cut one of the tendons and pull the muscle back.

6. Remove enough muscle from the wing to expose a bone. Look for veins and arteries, which are thin, dark, rubbery tissues.

7. Examine the surface of the bone, including the ends and the middle. Try to separate it from another bone. Look for cartilage and ligaments holding the bones together. Try to identify the type of joint you see.

Analyze and Conclude

8 **Describe** how the wing changed when you bent and then released it. Why do you think this happened?

9 **Think Critically** Compare the joints of the chicken wing to joints in your own arm and shoulder.

10 **The Big Idea** Explain how the different parts of the chicken wing work together and how they help the chicken maintain its homeostasis.

Communicate Your Results

Prepare a poster illustrating the observations that you made as you dissected the chicken wing. Include a diagram of the chicken wing and label the structures that you identified.

 **Extension**

How do the structure and function of chicken wings differ from those of human arms? Design an experiment that would help you determine what structures human arms and chicken wings do not share, and how the functions of each of these structures differ. Include your hypothesis, any materials you will use, and any safety guidelines that should be observed.

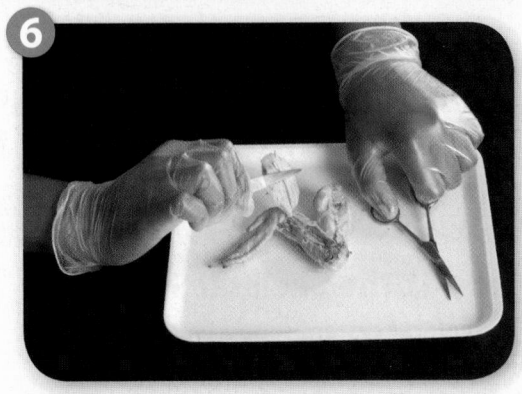
6

Lab Tips

☑ As you dissect, look for evidence of injuries or abnormalities the chicken might have. Share your observations with your classmates.

☑ Cut skin and other tissues only with the chicken wing resting in the dissection pan.

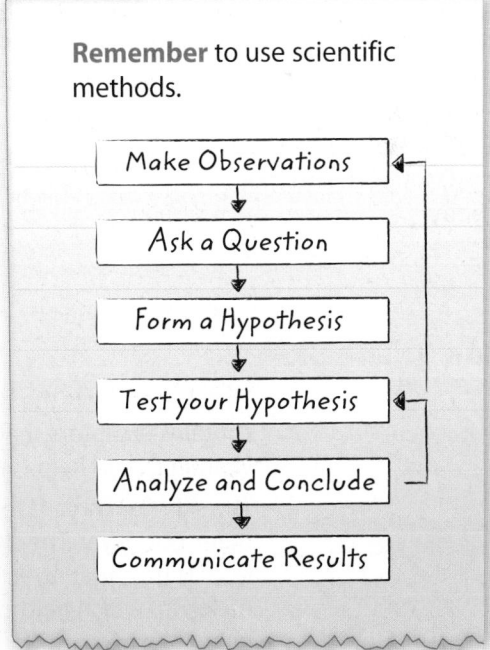

Remember to use scientific methods.

- Make Observations
- Ask a Question
- Form a Hypothesis
- Test your Hypothesis
- Analyze and Conclude
- Communicate Results

Chapter 14 Study Guide

THE BIG IDEA — The skeletal system, the muscular system, and the skin work together to move, support, and protect the body and maintain its homeostasis.

Key Concepts Summary 🔑

| Vocabulary |

Lesson 1: The Skeletal System

- The **skeletal system** supports the body, helps it move, and protects internal organs. Bones store fat and calcium and make red blood cells.

- Bones are protected by **cartilage** and are connected to other bones by **ligaments** at **joints.**

- The skeletal system works with the muscular system and the skin to protect and support the body and enable it to move.

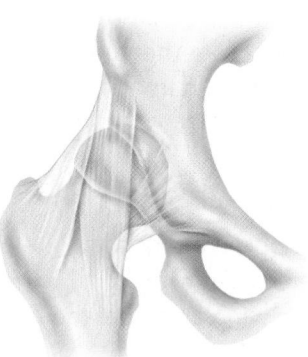

Vocabulary

skeletal system p. 487

cartilage p. 490

periosteum p. 490

joint p. 491

ligament p. 491

arthritis p. 492

osteoporosis p. 492

Lesson 2: The Muscular System

- **Muscles** support and stabilize the skeleton, enable bones and organs to move, protect the body, and regulate temperature.

- You can consciously control **skeletal,** or **voluntary, muscles.** You cannot consciously control **involuntary muscles,** which include the **cardiac muscle** that pumps blood and the **smooth muscles** that move food and blood.

- The muscular system interacts with other body systems to protect, support, and move the body.

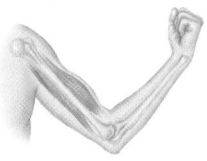 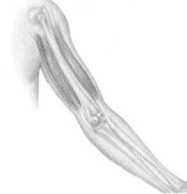

muscle p. 497

skeletal muscle p. 499

voluntary muscle p. 499

cardiac muscle p. 500

involuntary muscle p. 500

smooth muscle p. 500

Lesson 3: The Skin

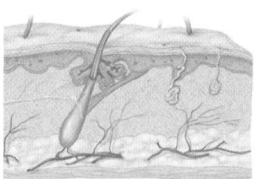

- The skin protects the body, regulates temperature, contains receptors that respond to stimuli, makes vitamin D, and helps eliminate waste.

- The skin has three layers. The **epidermis** is the outermost layer. The **dermis** is below, and the fat layer is the inner layer. The epidermis produces **melanin,** which help protect the body from ultraviolet rays.

- The skin works together with the skeletal and muscular systems to protect and support the body.

integumentary system p. 505

epidermis p. 507

melanin p. 507

dermis p. 507

bruise p. 508

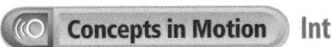
FOLDABLES® Chapter Project

Assemble your lesson Foldables as shown to make a Chapter Project. Use the project to review what you have learned in this chapter.

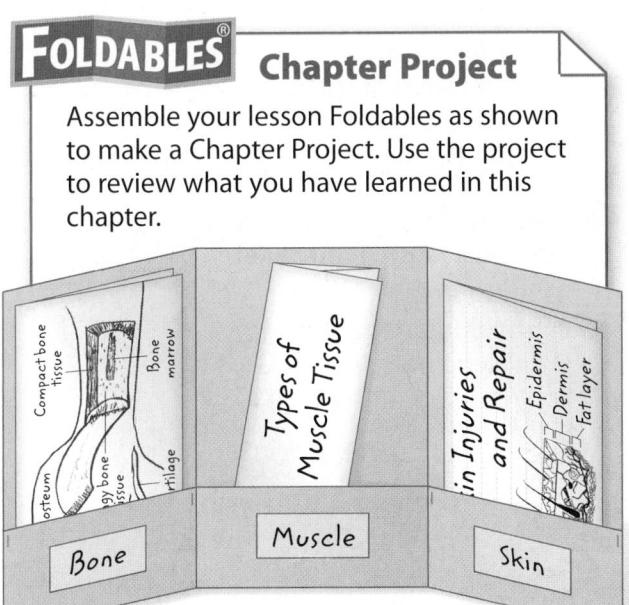

Use Vocabulary

Explain the differences and similarities between the vocabulary words in each of the following sets.

1 arthritis, osteoporosis

2 ligament, joint

3 cartilage, periosteum

4 skeletal muscle, cardiac muscle

5 voluntary muscle, involuntary muscle

6 skeletal system, muscular system

7 epidermis, dermis

8 integumentary system, muscular system

9 cut, bruise

Link Vocabulary and Key Concepts

Concepts in Motion Interactive Concept Map

Copy this concept map, and then use vocabulary terms from the previous page and other terms from the chapter to complete the concept map.

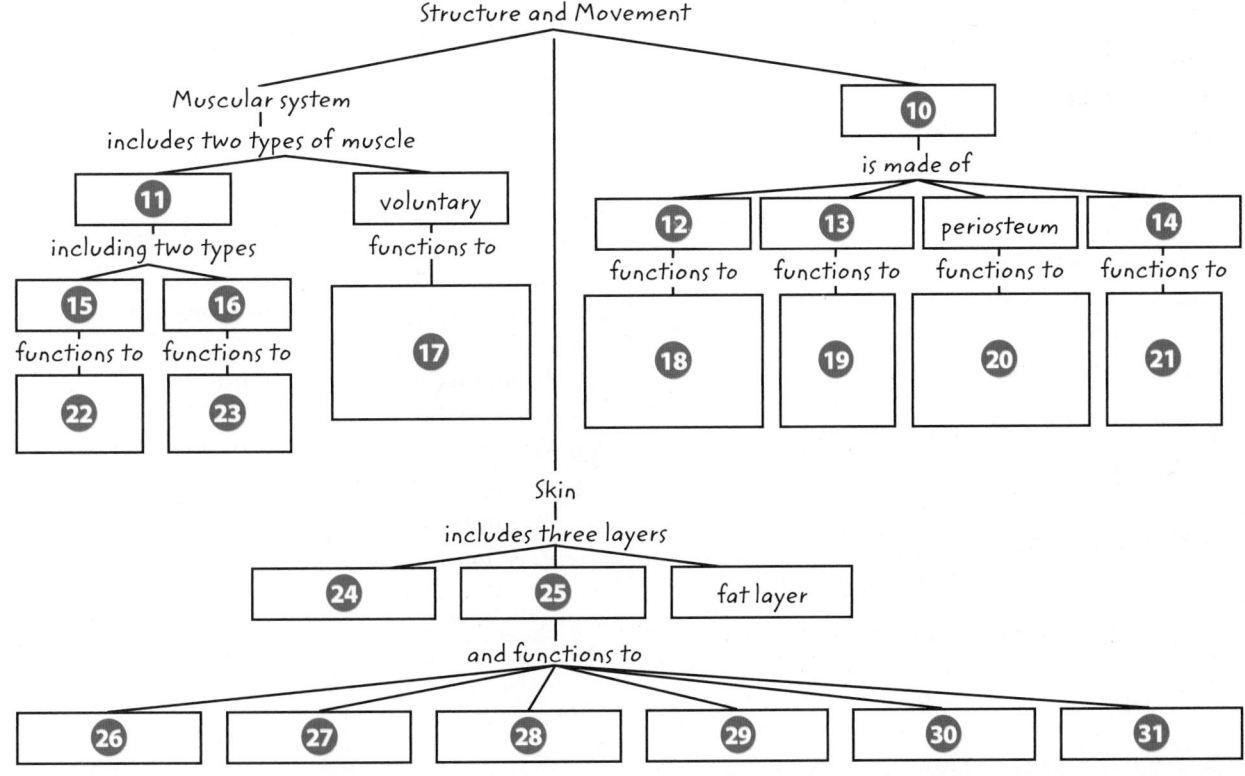

Understand Key Concepts

1 What is the arrow pointing to in the figure below?

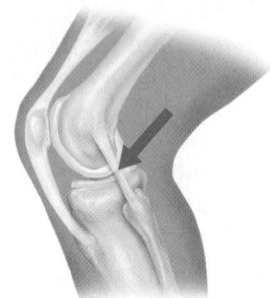

A. cartilage
B. ligament
C. periosteum
D. tendon

2 Which is NOT produced or stored inside bones?

A. calcium
B. fat
C. melanin
D. red blood cells

3 Which organ is NOT protected by the skeletal system?

A. brain
B. heart
C. lungs
D. skin

4 Which prevents bones from rubbing against each other?

A. cartilage
B. compact bone
C. ligament
D. spongy bone

5 What happens to a muscle when it contracts?

A. The muscle lengthens.
B. The muscle pushes on a bone.
C. The muscle pushes on another muscle.
D. The muscle shortens.

6 Which type of muscle is responsible for movement of the arms and legs?

A. cardiac muscle
B. involuntary muscle
C. skeletal muscle
D. smooth muscle

7 A contraction of what type of muscle is not consciously controlled?

A. arm muscle
B. involuntary muscle
C. skeletal muscle
D. voluntary muscle

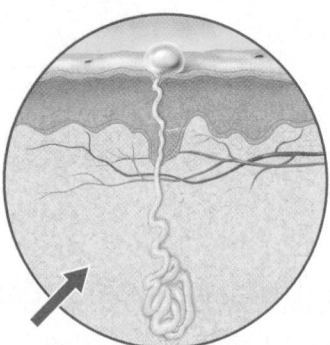

8 To which layer of skin is the arrow in the figure above pointing?

A. dermis
B. epidermis
C. fat layer
D. melanin

9 What is one function of sweating?

A. allows the body to move
B. enables calcium to be absorbed
C. increases body temperature
D. lowers body temperature

10 Which vitamin is made in the skin?

A. vitamin A
B. vitamin B
C. vitamin C
D. vitamin D

Critical Thinking

11 **Explain** how the muscular system and the skin regulate body temperature.

12 **Compare** spongy bone and compact bone.

13 **Assess** the importance of calcium in your diet, including the consequences of not getting enough.

14 **Give an example** of how the skeletal system maintains homeostasis.

15 **Predict** how your daily life would change if your skin contained no melanin.

16 **Discuss** why muscles must work in pairs.

17 **Evaluate** how the skin's ability to continually produce new skin cells helps protect your body.

18 **Identify** the kind of joint shown below. Give an example of where it is found in the body and what type of movement it enables the body to do. Record what structures you can identify and what system they belong to.

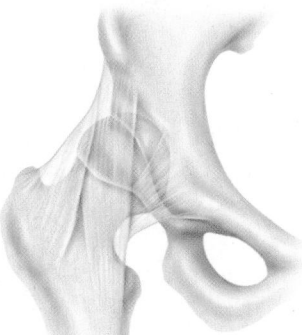

Writing in Science

19 **Write** a paragraph about how bones grow, starting before birth. Hypothesize why children and teens are in greater danger of breaking a bone than adults. Include a main idea, supporting details and examples, and a concluding sentence.

REVIEW THE BIG IDEA

20 How do the skeletal system, the muscular system, and the skin help the body maintain homeostasis? Explain how each system works independently to maintain homeostasis, and give an example of how two of them work together.

21 The photo below shows two soccer players—one using just muscles, the other using just bones. Explain why this would not be possible in real life.

Math Skills

Review

— Math Practice —

Use Proportions

22 A particular person produces about 95 mg of sweat per minute. How much sweat will the person produce in 1 hour?

23 There is approximately 1.8 m² of skin on the average human body. (1 m² =10,000 cm²)

A. What is the surface area of the human body in cm²?

B. If the body averages 277 sweat glands per square centimeter, about how many sweat glands would the human body contain?

Record your answers on the answer sheet provided by your teacher or on a sheet of paper.

Multiple Choice

1 Which is part of the integumentary system?

   A fingernail

   B lung

   C muscle

   D nerve

Use the diagram below to answer question 2.

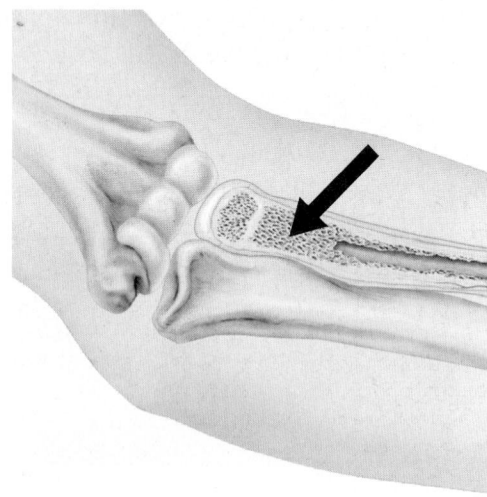

2 What does the arrow in the figure point to?

   A cartilage

   B compact bone

   C spongy bone

   D yellow marrow

3 Which does NOT help to control a person's body temperature?

   A contracting muscles rapidly

   B enlarging blood vessels

   C producing melanin

   D sweating through pores

4 Which is a characteristic of skeletal muscles?

   A They are involuntary.

   B They are smooth muscle.

   C They contain discs.

   D They have striations.

5 Where is cardiac muscle?

   A heart

   B legs

   C lungs

   D stomach

Use the diagram below to answer question 6.

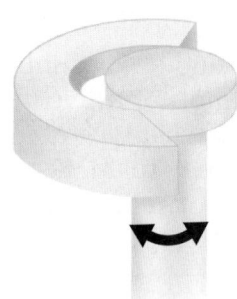

6 Where is this type of joint in the human body?

   A finger

   B knee

   C neck

   D shoulder

Use the figure below to answer questions 7 and 8.

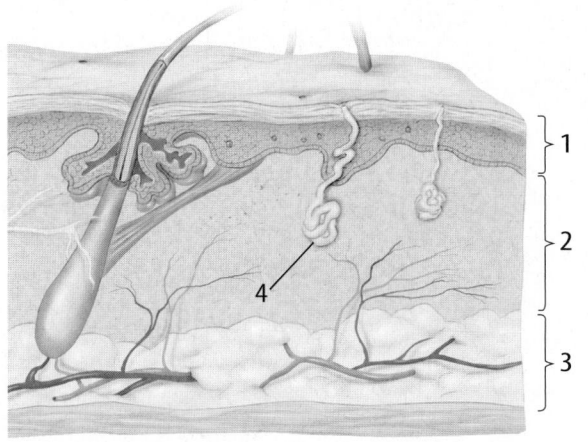

7 Where is melanin produced?

   A 1

   B 2

   C 3

   D 4

8 Which area gives the skin strength, flexibility, and nourishment?

   A 1

   B 2

   C 3

   D 4

9 Which bone material stores fat?

   A cartilage

   B compact bone

   C spongy bone

   D yellow bone marrow

Constructed Response

Use the image below to answer questions 10–13.

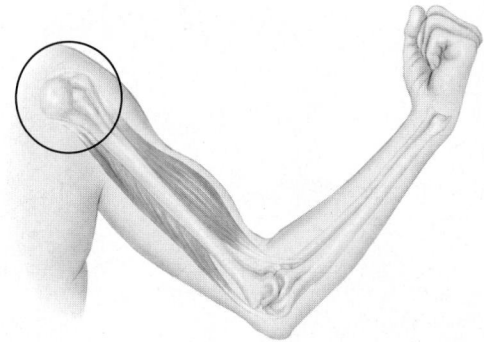

10 What joint type is circled in the diagram? What other area of the body contains the same kind of joint?

11 How do ligaments and tendons function in this type of joint?

12 What kind of muscle is attached to the joint shown? Explain your answer. How does this type of muscle differ from the muscle in a person's stomach?

13 How are the functions of muscle and skin similar? Explain how each performs these functions.

NEED EXTRA HELP?													
If You Missed Question...	1	2	3	4	5	6	7	8	9	10	11	12	13
Go to Lesson...	3	1	2, 3	2	2	1	3	3	1	1	1, 2	2	2, 3

Digestion and Excretion

THE BIG IDEA

How do the digestive and excretory systems help maintain the body's homeostasis?

Inquiry **Why So Long?**

This image shows parts of the digestive system. The small intestine is the structure that looks like a tangled-up rope. The small intestine can be up to 6 m long.

- Why do you think the small intestine is so long?

- What do you think the function of the small intestine is?

- How might the digestive system help your body maintain homeostasis?

Get Ready to Read

What do you think?

Before you read, decide if you agree or disagree with each of these statements. As you read this chapter, see if you change your mind about any of the statements.

1. An activity such as sleeping does not require energy.

2. All fats in food should be avoided.

3. Digestion begins in the mouth.

4. Energy from food stays in the digestive system.

5. Several human body systems work together to eliminate wastes.

6. Blood contains waste products that must be removed from the body.

 **ConnectED** Your one-stop online resource

connectED.mcgraw-hill.com

Video

Audio

Review

Inquiry

WebQuest

Assessment

Concepts in Motion

Multilingual eGlossary

Nutrition

Reading Guide

Key Concepts 🔑
ESSENTIAL QUESTIONS

- Why do you eat?
- Why does your body need each of the six groups of nutrients?
- Why is eating a balanced diet important?

Vocabulary

Calorie p. 523
protein p. 524
carbohydrate p. 524
fat p. 525
vitamin p. 525
mineral p. 525

 **Multilingual eGlossary**

▢ **Video** Science Video

Inquiry Time for Lunch?

This photo shows fried moth larvae on a banana leaf. It might not look appetizing, but it contains nutrients your body needs for energy and growth. Nutrients are in many different foods, from a cheeseburger to a fried insect.

How much energy is in an almond? 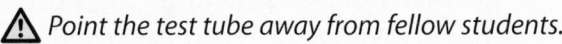 Food allergy

Food contains energy. Is there enough energy in an almond to boil water?

1 Read and complete a lab safety form.

2 Place a small amount of **clay** in a **shallow baking dish.** Straighten a **metal paper clip.** Insert one end into an unshelled **almond.** Anchor the other end in the clay.

3 Place a **25-mL test tube** in a **test-tube clamp.** Add 10 mL of **water** to the test tube.

4 Have your partner light the almond with a **long wooden match** until the almond starts burning on its own.

5 Gently swirl the test tube at an angle over the flame until the almond completely burns. Record your observations in your Science Journal.

⚠ *Point the test tube away from fellow students.*

Think About This

1. What happened to the water? Why did this happen?

2. 🔑 **Key Concept** What do you think happens to your body when you eat an almond?

Why do you eat?

How do you decide what to eat or when to eat? Although you can survive for weeks without food, you might become hungry within hours of your last meal. Hunger is your body's way of telling you that it needs food. Why does your body need food? Food provides your body with the energy and nutrients it needs to survive.

Energy

Every activity you do, such as riding a bike or even sleeping, requires energy. Your digestive system processes food and releases energy that is used for cellular processes and all activities that you do.

The amount of energy in food is measured in Calories. *A* **Calorie** *(Cal) is the amount of energy it takes to raise the temperature of 1 kg of water by 1°C.* How much energy do foods contain? Each food is different. One grape contains 2 Cal, but a slice of cheese pizza has 220 Cal. All foods give your body energy to use.

The amount of energy a person needs depends on several factors, such as weight, age, activity level, and gender. For example, a person with a mass of 68 kg usually burns more Calories than a person with a mass of 45 kg. Playing soccer requires more energy than playing a video game. How does the food you eat supply you with energy? The energy comes from nutrients.

Nutrients

Food is made of nutrients—substances that provide energy and materials for cell development, growth, and repair. The types and amounts of nutrients a person needs depend on age, gender, and activity level. Toddlers need more fat in their diets than older children do. Women need more calcium and iron than men do. Active people need more protein. Next, you'll read about the six groups of nutrients and their roles in maintaining your health.

✔ **Key Concept Check** Why do you eat?

WORD ORIGIN

protein
from Greek *proteios*, means "the first quality"

Groups of Nutrients

The six groups of nutrients are proteins, carbohydrates, fats, vitamins, minerals, and water. Each nutrient has a different function in the body. To be healthy, you need foods from each group every day.

Proteins

Most of the tissues in your body are made of proteins. *A* **protein** *is a large molecule that is made of amino acids and contains carbon, hydrogen, oxygen, nitrogen, and sometimes sulfur.* Proteins have many functions, such as relaying signals between cells, protecting against disease, providing support to cells, and speeding up chemical reactions. All of these functions are needed to maintain homeostasis, or the regulation of an organism's internal condition regardless of changes in its environment.

Combinations of 20 different amino acids make up the proteins in your body. Your cells can make more than half of these amino acids. The remaining amino acids must come from the foods that you eat. Some foods that are good sources of protein are shown in **Figure 1**.

 Reading Check How does your body obtain amino acids that cannot be made in cells?

Carbohydrates

What do pasta, bread, and potatoes have in common? They are all foods that have high levels of carbohydrates (kar boh HI drayts). **Carbohydrates** *are molecules made of carbon, hydrogen, and oxygen atoms and are usually the body's major source of energy.* They are commonly in one of three forms— starches, sugars, or fibers. All of them are made of sugar molecules that are linked together like a chain. It is best to eat foods that contain carbohydrates from whole grains because they are easier to digest. Also shown in **Figure 1** are some foods that are high in carbohydrates.

Figure 1 Good sources of protein include red meat, eggs, beans, and peanuts. Good sources of carbohydrates include red beans, fruits, and vegetables.

Proteins

Carbohydrates

Visual Check Describe a lunch that is high in proteins and carbohydrates.

Fats

You might think that fats in food are bad for you. But, you need a certain amount of fat in your diet and on your body to stay healthy. **Fats,** *also called lipids, provide energy and help your body absorb vitamins.* They are a major part of cell membranes. Body fat helps to insulate against cold temperatures. Most people get plenty of fat in their diet, so deficiencies in fats are rare. But too much fat in your diet can lead to health problems. Only about 25–35 percent of the Calories you consume should be fats.

Fats are often classified as either saturated or unsaturated. A diet high in saturated fats can increase levels of cholesterol, which can increase the risk of heart disease. Most of the fat in your diet should come from unsaturated fats, such as those shown in **Figure 2.**

Vitamins

Has anyone ever told you to eat certain foods because you need vitamins? **Vitamins** *are nutrients that are needed in small amounts for growth, regulation of body functions, and prevention of some diseases.* You can obtain most of the vitamins you need by eating a well-balanced diet. If you do not consume enough of one or more vitamins, then you might develop symptoms of vitamin deficiency. The symptoms depend on which vitamin you are lacking. **Table 1** lists some vitamins people need in their diet.

 Reading Check Why do you need vitamins in your diet?

Minerals

In addition to vitamins, you also need other nutrients called minerals. **Minerals** *are inorganic nutrients—nutrients that do not contain carbon—that help the body regulate many chemical reactions.* Similar to vitamins, if you do not consume enough of certain minerals, you might develop a mineral deficiency. **Table 1** also lists some minerals that you need in your diet.

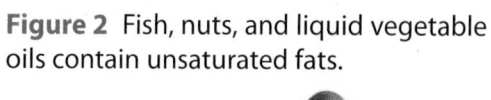

Figure 2 Fish, nuts, and liquid vegetable oils contain unsaturated fats.

Fats

((o)) Concepts in Motion Interactive Table

Table 1 Vitamins and Minerals

Vitamin	Good Sources	Health Benefit
Vitamin B₂ (riboflavin)	milk, meats, vegetables	helps release energy from nutrients
Vitamin C	oranges, broccoli, tomatoes, cabbage	growth and repair of body tissues
Vitamin A	carrots, milk, sweet potatoes, broccoli	enhances night vision, helps maintain skin and bones
Mineral	**Good Sources**	**Health Benefit**
Calcium	milk, spinach, green beans	builds strong bones and teeth
Iron	meat, eggs, green beans	helps carry oxygen throughout the body
Zinc	meat, fish, wheat/grains	aids protein formation

Table 1 Vitamins and minerals are essential for maintaining a healthy body.

Visual Check What foods are good sources of vitamin A?

Lesson 1

EXPLAIN

525

Water

You might recall that your body is mostly water. You need water for chemical reactions to occur in your body. Your body takes in water when you eat or drink. However, you lose water when you sweat, urinate, and breathe. To stay healthy, it is important to replace the water that your body loses. If you exercise, live in a warm area, or become sick, your body loses more water. When lost water is not replaced, you might become dehydrated. Symptoms of dehydration include thirst, headache, weakness, dizziness, and little or no urination.

Key Concept Check Why does your body need nutrients?

Healthful Eating

Imagine walking through a grocery store. Each aisle in the store contains hundreds of different foods. With so many choices, it's difficult to choose foods that are part of a healthful diet. Healthful eaters need to be smart shoppers. They make grocery lists beforehand and buy products that are high in nutrients. Nutritious foods come from the major food groups, which include grains, vegetables, fruits, oils, milk products, and meats and beans.

Inquiry MiniLab

25 minutes

What nutrients are in foods?

Food provides your body with nutrients and Calories. Each nutrient is important and has its own function in the body.

1. Using the materials provided by your teacher, search for foods that contain a high amount of your assigned nutrient.

2. Find the number of items for your nutrient that your teacher has assigned.

3. Once you have found the appropriate number of items, form a group with other students who were assigned the same nutrient.

4. As a group, make a chart listing your food items. Show the amount of your assigned nutrient present in each item. Share your chart with the class.

Analyze and Conclude

1. **Classify** the foods studied by all groups according to their nutrient value. Which foods were high in proteins? Fats? Carbohydrates?

2. **Explain** the function each nutrient has in the body.

3. **Key Concept** Describe what might happen if your body did not get enough of a particular nutrient.

Table 2 Daily Recommended Amounts of Each Food Group for 9–13-Year-Olds

Food Group	Daily Amount males, 9–13 years old	Daily Amount females, 9–13 years old	Examples of Foods
Grains	6-ounce equivalents	5-ounce equivalents	whole-wheat flour, rye bread, brown rice
Vegetables	2 1/2 cups	2 cups	broccoli, spinach, carrots
Fruits	1 1/2 cups	1 1/2 cups	apples, strawberries, oranges
Fats	5 teaspoons or less	5 teaspoons or less	canola oil, olive oil, avocados
Milk	3 cups	3 cups	milk, cheese, yogurt
Meat and beans	5 ounces or less	5 ounces or less	fish, beans, lean beef, lean chicken

A Balanced Diet

A healthful diet includes carbohydrates, proteins, fats, vitamins, minerals, and water. But how do you know how much of each food group you should eat? **Table 2** lists the daily recommended amounts of each food group for 9–13-year-olds.

The nutrient-rich foods that you choose might be different from the nutrient-rich foods eaten by people in China, Kenya, or Mexico. People usually eat foods that are grown and produced regionally. Regardless of where you live, eating a balanced diet ensures that your body has the nutrients it needs to function.

Key Concept Check Why is eating a balanced diet important?

Food Labels

What foods would you buy to follow the recommended guidelines in **Table 2**? Most grocery stores sell many varieties of bread, milk, meat, and other types of food. How would you know what nutrients these foods contain? You can look at food labels, such as the one in **Figure 3**. Food labels help you determine the amount of protein, carbohydrates, fats, and other substances in food.

 **Review**   **Personal Tutor**

Figure 3 A food label lists a food's nutrients per serving, not per container.

Visual Check List the nutrients in this food product.

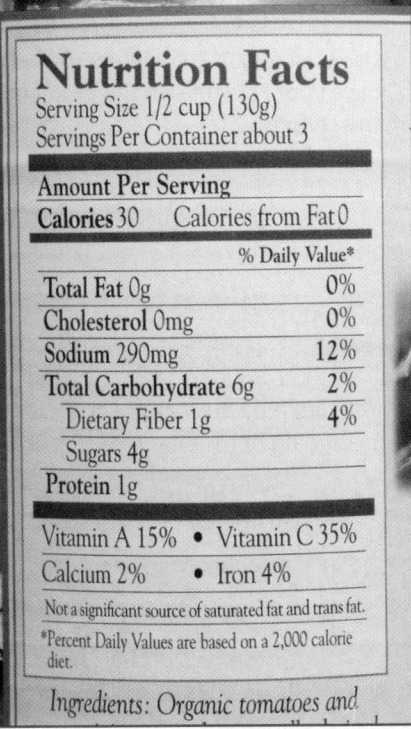

Nutrition Facts
Serving Size 1/2 cup (130g)
Servings Per Container about 3

Amount Per Serving

Calories 30   Calories from Fat 0

	% Daily Value*
Total Fat 0g	0%
Cholesterol 0mg	0%
Sodium 290mg	12%
Total Carbohydrate 6g	2%
Dietary Fiber 1g	4%
Sugars 4g	
Protein 1g	

Vitamin A 15% • Vitamin C 35%
Calcium 2% • Iron 4%

Not a significant source of saturated fat and trans fat.

*Percent Daily Values are based on a 2,000 calorie diet.

Ingredients: Organic tomatoes and

Lesson 1 Review

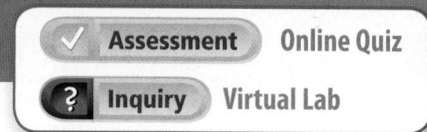

Visual Summary

People eat food to obtain the energy their bodies need to function.

Proteins are one of the six groups of nutrients.

Evaluating food labels can help you eat a balanced diet.

FOLDABLES®

Use your lesson Foldable to review the lesson. Save your Foldable for the project at the end of the chapter.

What do you think NOW?

You first read the statements below at the beginning of the chapter.

1. An activity such as sleeping does not require energy.

2. All fats in food should be avoided.

Did you change your mind about whether you agree or disagree with the statements? Rewrite any false statements to make them true.

Use Vocabulary

1 Nutrients made of long chains of amino acids are _____.

2 The major source of energy in your diet comes from _____.

3 The amount of energy in food is measured in _____.

Understand Key Concepts

4 **Explain** why it is important to consume vitamins.

5 Which nutrient helps your body absorb vitamins?
- **A.** carbohydrate
- **B.** fat
- **C.** mineral
- **D.** protein

6 **Give an example** of when you might need to drink more water than usual.

Interpret Graphics

7 **Calculate** How many grams of carbohydrates are in three servings of this food?

Sodium 290mg	12%
Total Carbohydrate 6g	2%
Dietary Fiber 1g	4%
Sugars 4g	
Protein 1g	

8 **Summarize** Copy and fill in the graphic organizer below to identify the six groups of nutrients.

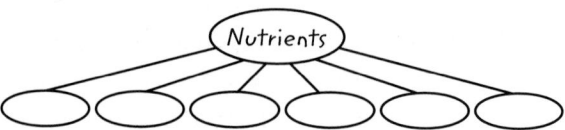

Critical Thinking

9 **Plan** a meal that contains a food from each of the six food groups.

10 **Analyze** One serving of a certain food contains 370 Cal, 170 Cal from fat, and 12 g of saturated fat (60% of the daily value). Is this food a good choice for a healthful lifestyle? Why or why not?

How do foods compare?

Materials

brown paper
grocery bag

permanent
marker

food samples

small plastic
cup

metric ruler

Safety

As you have learned, not all foods are alike. Knowing about different types of nutrients will help you make good food choices. Foods with a lot of fat often taste good but might not be healthful for you in large amounts. It is important to be able to identify foods with different fat contents in order to have a balanced diet. How do these different foods compare?

Learn It

Observations can be analyzed by noting the similarities and differences between two or more objects or events that you observe. You **compare** objects or events by seeing how they are similar. You **contrast** objects or events by looking for differences.

Try It

1. Read and complete a lab safety form.

2. Create a data table like the one below in your Science Journal.

3. Use a permanent marker and a plastic cup to draw seven circles on a large piece of a brown paper grocery bag.

4. Obtain one each of the seven food items your teacher has provided. Label each circle with the name of the food to be tested.

5. Place one piece of the labeled food in each circle.

6. Allow the foods to sit for 30 minutes.

7. Remove the foods and properly dispose of them. Record in the table whether the food left a greasy mark, a wet mark, or no mark. Also record the diameter of the mark.

8. Dispose of the used grocery bag as directed by your teacher.

Apply It

9. **Compare and contrast** the marks produced by the foods. Describe both their appearances and their sizes.

10. **Infer** Which items left a greasy mark on the paper bag? How are these foods alike?

11. 🔑 **Key Concept** Why is it important to eat a variety of foods every day?

Product	Type of Mark	Diameter (cm)

Reading Guide

Key Concepts 🔑
ESSENTIAL QUESTIONS

- What does the digestive system do?
- How do the parts of the digestive system work together?
- How does the digestive system interact with other systems?

Vocabulary

digestion p. 531
mechanical digestion p. 532
chemical digestion p. 532
enzyme p. 532
esophagus p. 534
peristalsis p. 534
chyme p. 535
villi p. 536

g Multilingual eGlossary

📹 Video BrainPOP®

The Digestive System

Inquiry Under the Sea?

These colorful projections look like something you might see on the ocean floor, but they are found in your body. They line the walls of the small intestine, which is part of your digestive system. What do you think these projections do?

Which dissolves faster?

Has anyone ever told you to take small bites and chew your food thoroughly? The size of chewed food particles can affect how quickly food is digested. Similarly, the size of a sugar particle can affect how fast it dissolves in water.

1. Read and complete a lab safety form.

2. Add the contents of one serving package of **granulated sugar** to a **500-mL beaker** containing 300 mL of **warm water.**

3. Gently stir the contents of the beaker with a **plastic spoon.** Have your partner use a **stopwatch** to time how long it takes the sugar to dissolve. Record the time in your Science Journal.

4. Add a **sugar cube** to another **500-mL beaker** containing 300 mL of warm water.

5. Repeat step 3.

Think About This

1. Which dissolved faster—the granulated sugar or the sugar cube?

2. Why do you think particle size affects the rate at which sugar dissolves?

3. 🔑 **Key Concept** How might food particle size affect how quickly food is digested?

Functions of the Digestive System

Suppose you ate a cheeseburger and a pear for lunch. What happens to the food after it is eaten?

As soon as the food enters your mouth, it begins its journey through your digestive system. No matter what you eat, your food goes through four steps—ingestion, digestion, absorption, and elimination. All four steps happen in the organs and tissues of the digestive system in the following order:

- Food is ingested. Ingestion is the act of eating, or putting food in your mouth.

- Food is digested. **Digestion** *is the mechanical and chemical breakdown of food into small particles and molecules that your body can absorb and use.*

- Nutrients and water in the food are absorbed, or taken in, by cells. Absorption occurs when the cells of the digestive system take in small molecules of digested food.

- Undigested food is eliminated. Elimination is the removal of undigested food and other wastes from your body.

🔑 **Key Concept Check** What does the digestive system do?

WORD ORIGIN ···········
digestion
from Latin *digestus*, means "to separate, divide" ··············

Types of Digestion

Before your body can absorb nutrients from food, the food must be broken down into small molecules by digestion. There are two types of digestion—mechanical and chemical. *In* **mechanical digestion,** *food is physically broken into smaller pieces.* Mechanical digestion happens when you chew, mash, and grind food with your teeth and tongue. Smaller pieces of food are easier to swallow and have more surface area, which helps with chemical digestion. *In* **chemical digestion,** *chemical reactions break down pieces of food into small molecules.*

Enzymes

Chemical digestion cannot occur without substances called enzymes (EN zimez). **Enzymes** *are proteins that help break down larger molecules into smaller molecules. Enzymes also speed up, or catalyze, the rate of* **chemical reactions.** Without enzymes, some chemical reactions would be too slow or would not occur at all.

There are many kinds of enzymes. Each one is specialized to help break down a specific molecule at a specific location.

 Reading Check What are enzymes?

Inquiry MiniLab | **20 minutes**

How can you model digestion?

Your saliva contains enzymes to help with digestion. You can use radishes to model the effect saliva has on food. Radishes and saliva contain the same enzyme.

1. Read and complete a lab safety form.
2. Place a small amount of **cooked rice** into two **100-mL beakers.**
3. Add a small amount of **grated radish** to one beaker and stir well with a **plastic spoon.**
4. Let the rice sit for 5 minutes.
5. Use a **dropper** to add three drops of **iodine tincture solution** to the rice in each beaker. Record the color of the rice in your Science Journal.

Analyze and Conclude

1. **Compare** the colors of the rice in the two beakers after the iodine was added.

2. **Infer** Iodine reacts with starches. Starches are made up of sugar molecules. Infer what happened to the starches in the rice when an enzyme was added.

3. 🔑 **Key Concept** Summarize the role enzymes play in digestion.

The Role of Enzymes in Digestion

Nutrients in food are made of different molecules, such as carbohydrates, proteins, and fats. Many of these molecules are too large for your body to use. But, because these molecules are made of long chains of smaller molecules joined together, they can be broken down into smaller pieces.

The digestive system produces enzymes that are specialized to help break down each type of food molecule. For example, the enzyme amylase helps break down carbohydrates. The enzymes pepsin and papain help break down proteins. Fats are broken down with the help of the enzyme lipase. **Figure 4** illustrates how an enzyme helps break down food molecules into smaller pieces.

Notice in **Figure 4** that the food molecule breaks apart, but the enzyme itself does not change. Therefore, the enzyme can immediately be used to break down another food molecule.

 Reading Check What happens to an enzyme after it helps break down a food molecule?

Organs of the Digestive System

In order for your body to use the nutrients in the foods you eat, the nutrients must pass through your digestive system. Your digestive system has two parts: the digestive tract and the other organs that help the body break down and absorb food. These organs include the tongue, salivary glands, liver, gallbladder, and pancreas.

The digestive tract extends from the mouth to the anus. It has different organs connected by tubelike structures. Each of these organs is specialized for a certain function.

Recall the cheeseburger and pear mentioned at the beginning of this lesson. Where do you think digestion of this food begins?

 **Concepts in Motion** Animation

Figure 4 An enzyme helps break down food molecules into smaller pieces.

Step 1
An enzyme attaches to a food particle.

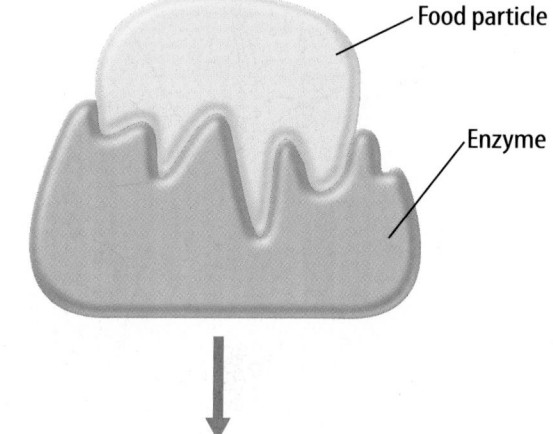

Food particle

Enzyme

Step 2
The enzyme speeds up a chemical reaction that breaks down the food particle.

Step 3
The enzyme releases the broken-down food particle.

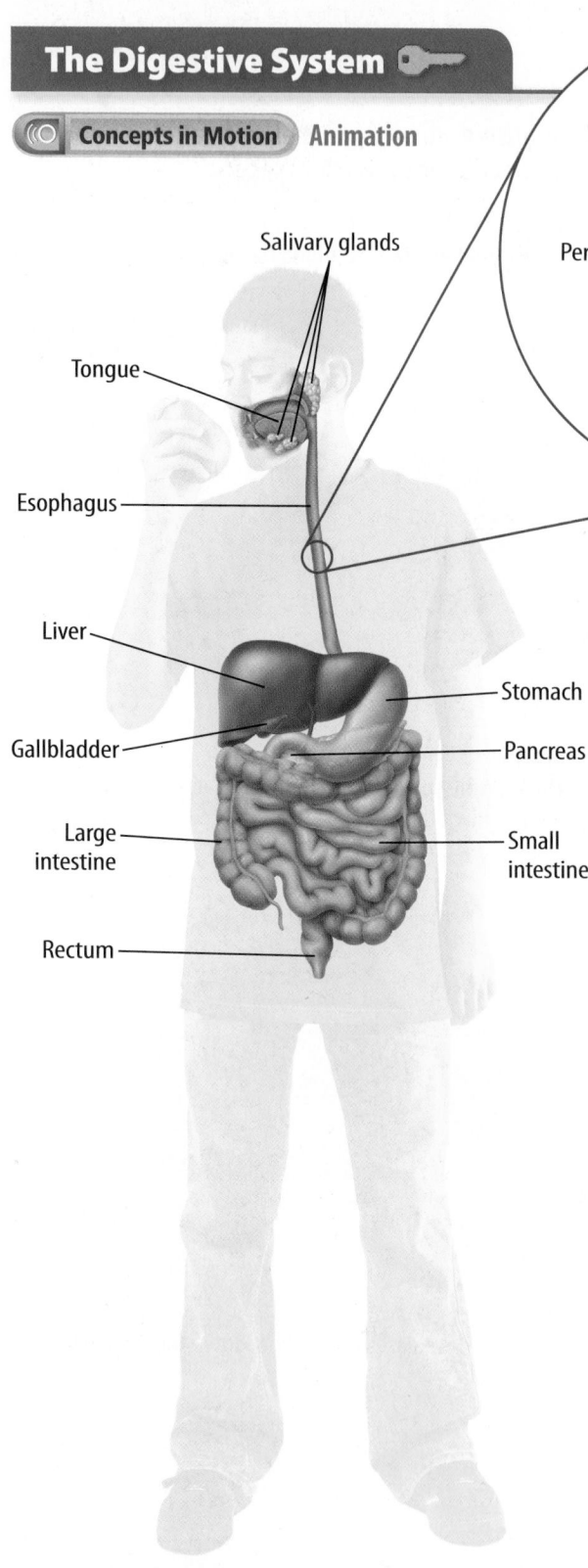

Salivary glands

Peristalsis

Tongue

Esophagus

Liver

Stomach

Gallbladder

Pancreas

Large intestine

Small intestine

Rectum

Figure 5 The digestive system includes the organs of the digestive tract, as well as other organs such as the tongue, salivary glands, liver, gallbladder, and pancreas.

Visual Check Which organ connects the mouth to the stomach?

The Mouth

You can follow the path food takes through your digestive tract in **Figure 5.** Mechanical digestion of food, such as a pear or a cheeseburger, begins in your mouth. Your teeth and tongue mechanically digest food as you chew. But even before chewing begins, your mouth prepares for digestion.

Your salivary (SA luh ver ee) glands produce saliva (suh LI vuh) at the very thought of food. They produce more than 1 L of saliva every day. Saliva contains an enzyme that helps break down carbohydrates, such as those found in a hamburger bun. Saliva also contains substances that neutralize acidic foods. It also contains a slippery substance that makes food easier to swallow.

The Esophagus

After you swallow a bite of your food, it enters your esophagus (ih SAH fuh gus). *The* **esophagus** *is a muscular tube that connects the mouth to the stomach. Food moves through the esophagus and the rest of the digestive tract by waves of muscle contractions, called* **peristalsis** (per uh STAHL sus).

Peristalsis is similar to squeezing a tube of toothpaste. When you squeeze the bottom of the tube, toothpaste is forced toward the top of the tube. As muscles in the esophagus contract and relax, partially digested food is pushed down the esophagus and into the stomach.

The Stomach

Once your partially digested food leaves the esophagus, it enters the stomach. The stomach is a large, hollow organ. One function of the stomach is to temporarily store food. This allows you to go many hours between meals. The stomach is like a balloon that can stretch when filled. An adult stomach can hold about 2 L of food and liquids.

 Reading Check Why is the stomach's ability to store food beneficial?

Another function of the stomach is to aid in chemical digestion. As shown in **Figure 6,** the walls of the stomach are folded. These folds enable the stomach to expand and hold large amounts of food. In addition, the cells in these folds produce chemicals that help break down proteins. For example, the stomach contains an acidic fluid called gastric juice. Gastric juice makes the stomach acidic. Acid helps break down some of the structures that hold plant and animal cells together, like the cells in hamburger meat, lettuce, tomatoes, and pears. Gastric juice also contains pepsin, an enzyme that helps break down proteins in foods into amino acids. Food and gastric juices mix as muscles in the stomach contract through peristalsis. As food mixes with gastric juice in the stomach, it forms *a thin, watery liquid called* chyme (KIME).

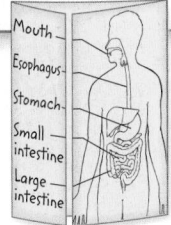
Figure 6 The stomach temporarily stores food and aids in chemical digestion.

Visual Check Where does food go after it leaves the stomach?

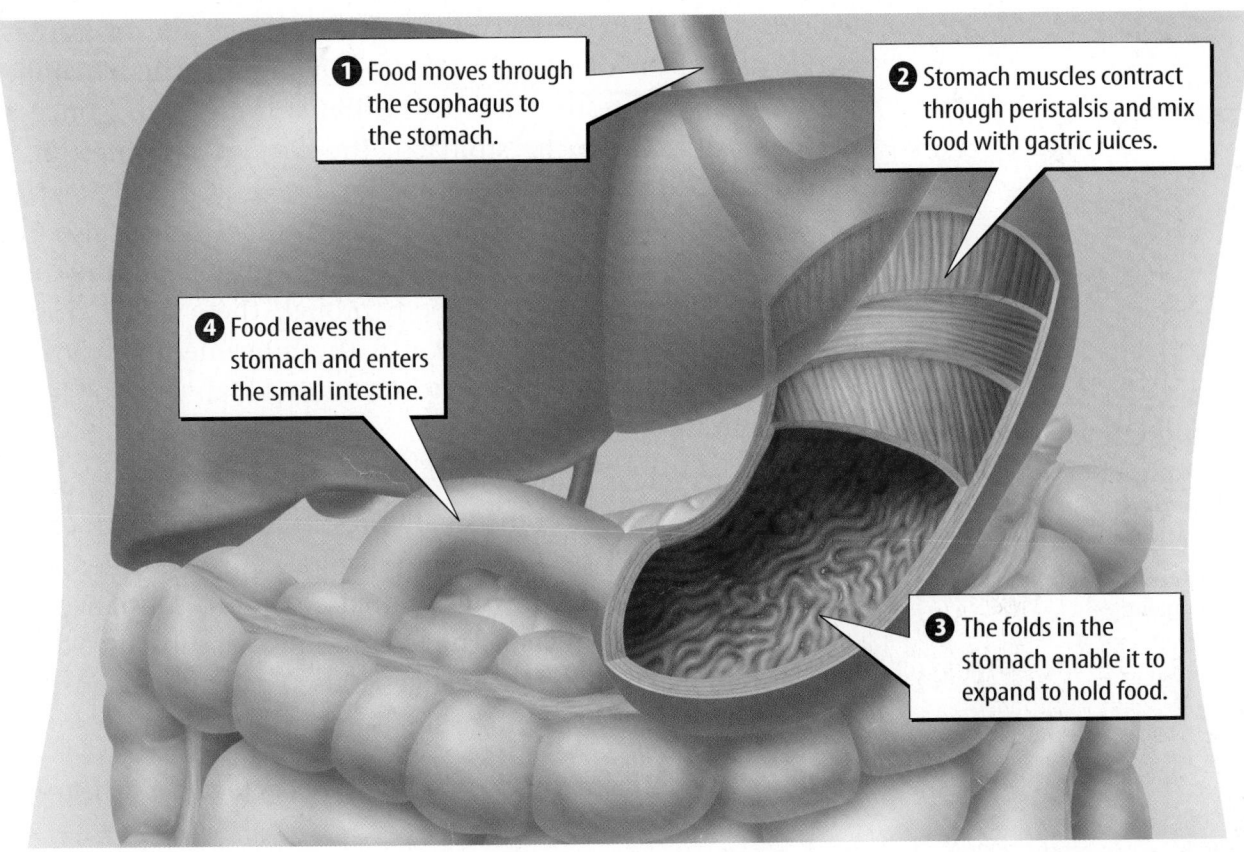

❶ Food moves through the esophagus to the stomach.

❷ Stomach muscles contract through peristalsis and mix food with gastric juices.

❹ Food leaves the stomach and enters the small intestine.

❸ The folds in the stomach enable it to expand to hold food.

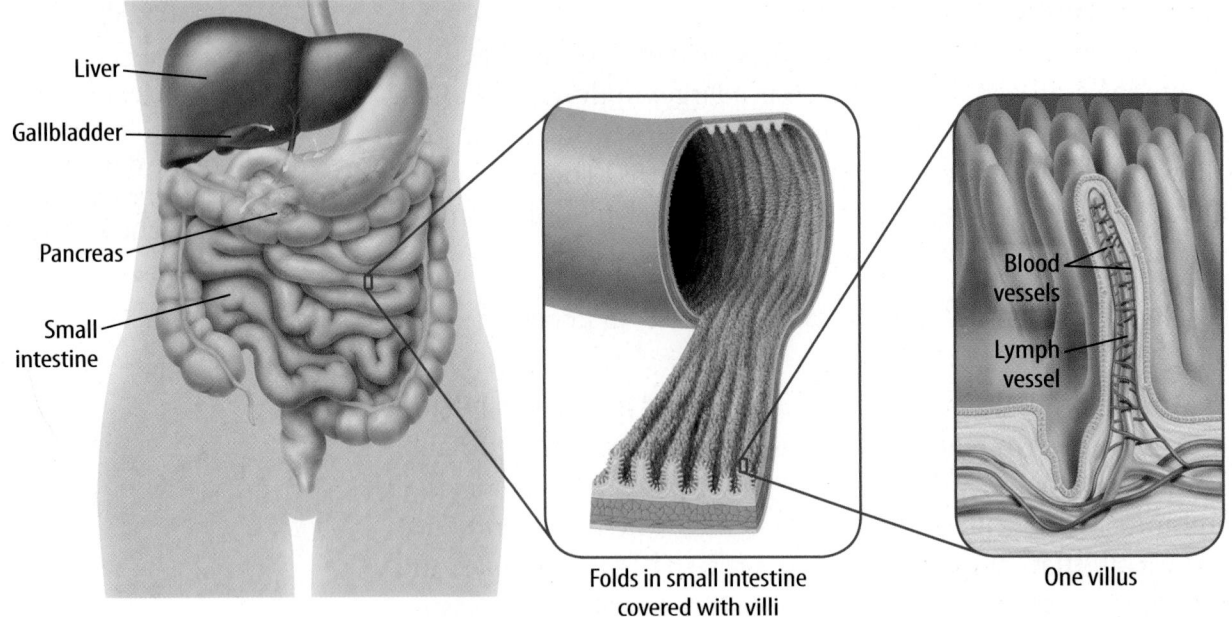

Liver

Gallbladder

Pancreas

Small intestine

Folds in small intestine covered with villi

Blood vessels

Lymph vessel

One villus

Figure 7 The walls of the small intestine are covered with villi that help move nutrients into the blood.

The Small Intestine

Chemical digestion of your cheeseburger and pear begins in the mouth and stomach. But most chemical digestion occurs in the small intestine. The small intestine is a long tube connected to the stomach. It is where chemical digestion and nutrient absorption occur. The small intestine is named for its small diameter—about 2.5 cm. It is about 7 m long.

Chemical digestion of proteins, carbohydrates, nucleic acids, and fats takes place in the first part of the small intestine, called the duodenum (doo uh DEE num). The remainder of the small intestine absorbs nutrients from food. Notice in **Figure 8** that, like the stomach, the wall of the intestine is folded. *The folds of the small intestine are covered with fingerlike projections called* **villi** (VIH li) (singular, villus). Notice also that each villus contains small blood vessels. Nutrients in the small intestine diffuse into the blood through these blood vessels. You might recall that diffusion is the movement of particles from an area of higher concentration to an area of lower concentration.

The pancreas and the liver, shown in **Figure 7,** produce **substances** that enter the small intestine and help with chemical digestion. The pancreas produces an enzyme called amylase that helps break down carbohydrates and a substance that neutralizes stomach acid. The liver produces a substance called bile. Bile makes it easier to digest fats. The gallbladder stores bile until it is needed in the small intestine.

Key Concept Check What organs work together to help with chemical digestion?

Figure 8 The bacteria shown here live in the large intestine. Without them, your food would not be digested well.

 Visual Check Cocci bacteria are spherical, bacilli bacteria are rod-shaped, and spirilla bacteria are spiral-shaped. Which type of bacteria is shown in the photo?

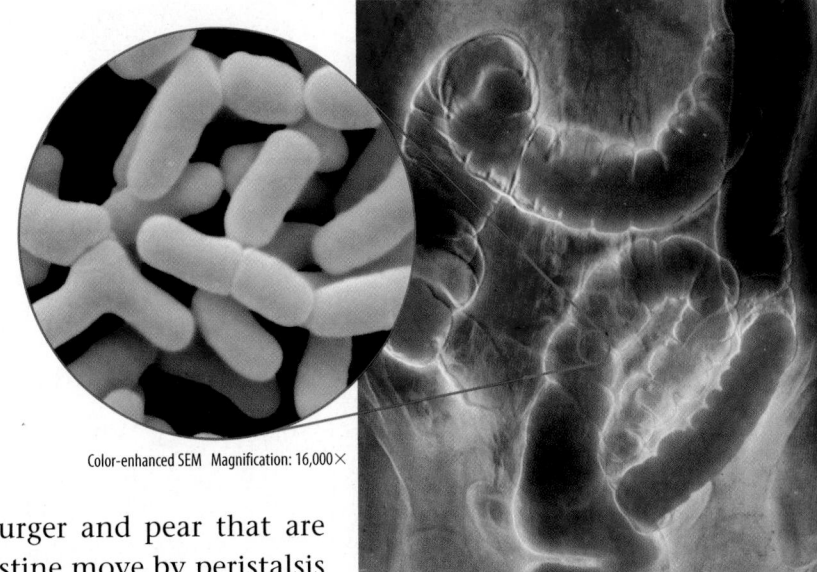

Color-enhanced SEM Magnification: 16,000×

The Large Intestine

The parts of your cheeseburger and pear that are not absorbed in the small intestine move by peristalsis into the large intestine, also called the colon. The large intestine, shown in **Figure 8,** has a larger diameter (about 5 cm) than the small intestine. However, at about 1.5 m long, it is much shorter than the small intestine.

Most of the water in ingested foods and liquids is absorbed in the small intestine. As food travels through the large intestine, even more water is absorbed. Materials that pass through the large intestine are the waste products of digestion. The waste products become more solid as excess water is absorbed. Peristalsis continues to force the remaining semisolid waste material into the last section of the large intestine, called the rectum. Muscles in the rectum and anus control the release of this semisolid waste, called feces (FEE seez).

Bacteria and Digestion

You might think that all bacteria are harmful. However, some bacteria have an important role in the digestive system. Bacteria, such as the ones shown in **Figure 8,** digest food and produce important vitamins and amino acids. Bacteria in the intestines are essential for proper digestion.

The Digestive System and Homeostasis

Recall that nutrients from food are absorbed in the small intestine. The digestive system must be functioning properly for this absorption to occur. These nutrients are necessary for other body systems to maintain homeostasis. For example, the blood in the circulatory system absorbs the products of digestion. The blood carries the nutrients to all other body systems, providing them with materials that contain energy.

 Key Concept Check What might happen to other body systems if the digestive system did not function properly?

Visual Summary

Enzymes in the digestive system break down food so nutrients can be absorbed by your body.

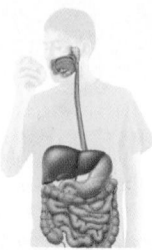

Food moves through the digestive tract by waves of peristalsis.

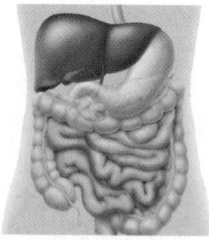

The liver and the pancreas produce substances that help with chemical digestion.

FOLDABLES

Use your lesson Foldable to review the lesson. Save your Foldable for the project at the end of the chapter.

What do you think NOW?

You first read the statements below at the beginning of the chapter.

3. Digestion begins in the mouth.

4. Energy from food stays in the digestive system.

Did you change your mind about whether you agree or disagree with the statements? Rewrite any false statements to make them true.

Use Vocabulary

1 **Define** *enzyme* in your own words.

2 **Distinguish** between absorption and digestion.

Understand Key Concepts

3 Where is the first place digestion occurs?
- **A.** mouth
- **C.** large intestine
- **B.** stomach
- **D.** small intestine

4 **Compare** the functions of the stomach and the small intestine.

5 **Give an example** of how the digestive system affects other body systems.

Interpret Graphics

6 **Explain** How do structures like the one to the right affect digestion?

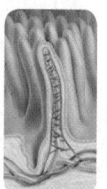

7 **Organize Information** Copy and fill in the graphic organizer below to show how food moves through the digestive tract.

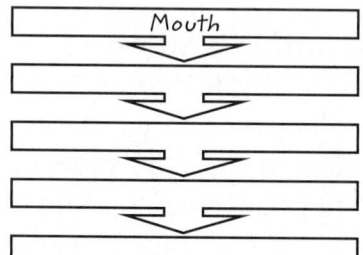

Mouth

Critical Thinking

8 **Infer** what would happen if food passed more quickly than normal through the digestive system.

Math Skills

Review

—— Math Practice ——

9 If the total length of the intestines is 8.5 m and the large intestine is 1.5 m long, what percentage of the intestines is made up of the small intestine?

Are digestive bacteria related to obesity?

SCIENCE & SOCIETY

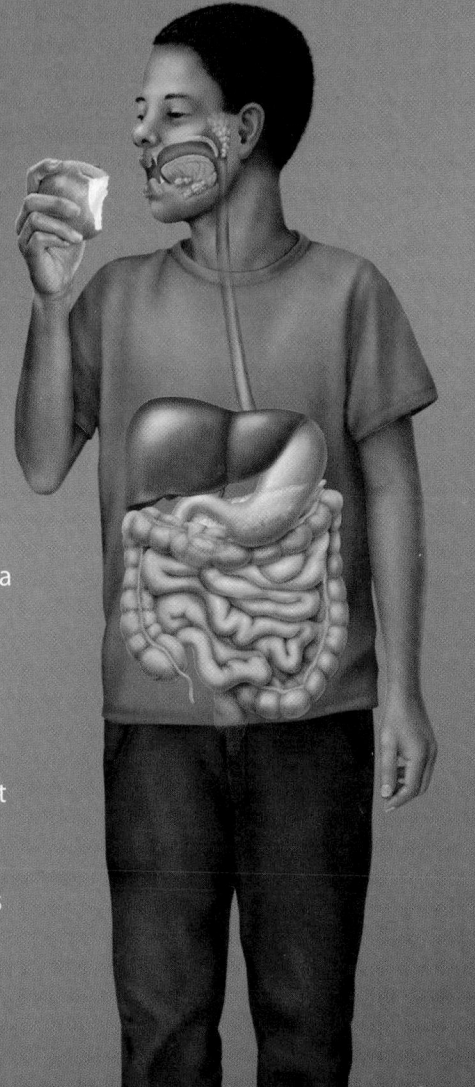

Bacteria percentages might affect your health.

The worldwide rate of obesity greatly concerns medical and health professionals. New research reveals a possible link between bacteria in the human digestive tract and the risk of being overweight.

Your digestive system is home to between 10 and 100 trillion bacteria. That's ten times the number of cells in your body! Certain bacteria are necessary, however, for the digestion of food. Without "friendly" bacteria, you could eat all you wanted, but the food would pass through your intestines mostly undigested.

Recent studies suggest there might be a link between the bacteria in the human digestive tract and obesity. Some people have a type of bacteria that causes them to absorb more calories than normal from their food. They gain more weight than people with a different type of bacteria. In general, obese humans have a lower percentage of a group of bacteria called Bacteroidetes (BAK-tear-oid-dee-teez) and more of a group of bacteria called Firmicutes (fir-MIC-cu-teez). It is not clear whether Firmicutes bacteria make people obese, or whether obese people have more of this type of bacteria. But evidence supports the idea that changing the bacteria in someone's intestines and stomach—by means of diet or medications—might be an important weapon in the fight against obesity.

Additional research is needed to understand any link between digestive bacteria and obesity. But it is an exciting possibility that managing the bacteria in the digestive tract could be a new way to improve human health.

It's Your Turn

RESEARCH Find out more about the role of bacteria in human health. Research how the bacteria in your digestive tract help to regulate your immune system.

The Excretory System

Reading Guide

Key Concepts

ESSENTIAL QUESTIONS

- What does the excretory system do?
- How do the parts of the excretory system work together?
- How does the excretory system interact with other body systems?

Vocabulary

excretory system p. 541

kidney p. 543

nephron p. 543

urine p. 543

ureter p. 545

bladder p. 545

urethra p. 545

g Multilingual eGlossary

Inquiry **A Sweaty Job?**

Did you know that these are the ridges on a fingertip? The circular openings along the ridges are sweat glands. The sweat from these glands can leave a mark, or fingerprint, on objects that you touch. Why does sweat, or any material, leave your body?

What happens when you breathe out?

Look again at the photo of the fingertip on the previous page. The sweat glands in your skin are one way substances leave your body. Do substances also leave your body when you breathe out?

1. Read and complete a lab safety form.

2. Take a deep breath and hold it.

3. Breathe out through your mouth into a **plastic bag.** Leave a small opening to allow some of the air to leave the bag as you blow into it.

4. Remove the bag from around your mouth. Let the air escape from the bag, but do not push the sides of the bag together.

5. Using the same plastic bag, repeat steps 2–4 three more times.

6. Observe the contents of the bag. Record your observations in your Science Journal.

Think About This

1. Did the plastic bag look different after you breathed into it? Explain.

2. What do you think was in the plastic bag at the end of the activity?

3.  **Key Concept** Based on your observations, do you think the respiratory system is part of the excretory system? Explain.

Functions of the Excretory System

You have read about the nutrients in food that are necessary to maintain health. You have also read how the digestive system processes that food. However, your body doesn't use all the food that you ingest. The unused food parts are waste products. What happens to the wastes? They are processed by the excretory system. *The* **excretory system** *collects and eliminates wastes from the body and regulates the level of fluid in the body.*

Collection and Elimination

Your home probably has several places where waste is collected. You might have a trash can in the kitchen and another one in the bathroom. The furnace has an air filter that removes and collects dust from the air. Similarly, your body also collects wastes. The digestive system collects waste products in the intestines. The circulatory system collects waste products in the blood.

When the trash cans in your home fill up, you must take the trash outside. The same is true of the waste in your body. If waste is not removed, or eliminated, from your body, it could become toxic and damage your organs. You'll read about the different body systems that eliminate waste later in this lesson.

Regulation of Liquids

Another function of the excretory system is to regulate the level of fluids in the body. You might recall that water is an essential nutrient for your body. Some of the water in your body is lost when waste is eliminated. The excretory system controls how much water leaves the body through elimination. This ensures that neither too little nor too much water is lost.

 Key Concept Check What does the excretory system do?

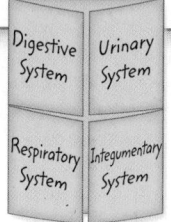

Figure 9 Several body systems make up the excretory system.

✓ **Visual Check** What substances are eliminated by the body systems shown below?

Types of Excretion

Your body excretes, or eliminates, different substances from different body systems. The excretory system is made of four body systems.

- The digestive system collects and removes undigested solids from the foods you eat.

- The urinary system processes, transports, collects, and removes liquid waste from the body.

- The respiratory system removes carbon dioxide and water vapor from the body.

- The integumentary system, which includes the skin, secretes excess salt and water through sweat glands.

Figure 9 illustrates the body systems that make up the excretory system and identifies the substances they excrete. You read previously about how the organs of the digestive system, the respiratory system, and the integumentary system eliminate waste products from the body. In this lesson, you will read about the organs of the urinary system and their roles in eliminating waste from the body.

✓ **Reading Check** What body systems make up the excretory system?

The Excretory System 🔑

Urinary system
Removes liquid wastes

Integumentary system
Removes excess salt and water

Digestive system
Removes undigested food

Respiratory system
Removes carbon dioxide and water

Organs of the Urinary System

The urinary system produces, stores, and removes liquid waste from the body and helps maintain homeostasis. The organs of the urinary system are shown in **Figure 10.** They include two kidneys, two ureters, the bladder, and the urethra. These organs work together to process, transport, collect, and excrete liquid waste.

 Reading Check What is the function of the urinary system?

The Kidneys

The bean-shaped organ that filters, or removes, wastes from blood is the **kidney.** You have two kidneys, one on each side of your body. They are near the back wall of your abdomen, above your waist, and below your rib cage. Each kidney is about the size of your fist. Kidneys are dark red in color because of the large volume of blood that passes through them.

The kidneys have several functions. This lesson will focus on the role of the kidneys in the urinary system. However, the kidneys also produce hormones that stimulate the production of red blood cells. In addition, they control blood pressure and help control calcium levels in the body.

The kidneys contain blood vessels and nephrons (NEH frahnz). **Nephrons** *are networks of capillaries and small tubes, or tubules, where filtration of blood occurs.* Each kidney contains about one million nephrons.

Blood contains waste products, salts, and sometimes toxins from cells that need to be removed from the body. These products are filtered from the blood as it passes through the kidneys. *When blood is filtered, a fluid called* **urine** *is produced.* The kidneys filter the blood and produce urine in two stages. You will read about this two-stage filtration process on the next page.

The Urinary System

Figure 10 Most functions of the urinary system occur in the kidneys. The kidneys connect to the ureters, then the bladder, and finally the urethra.

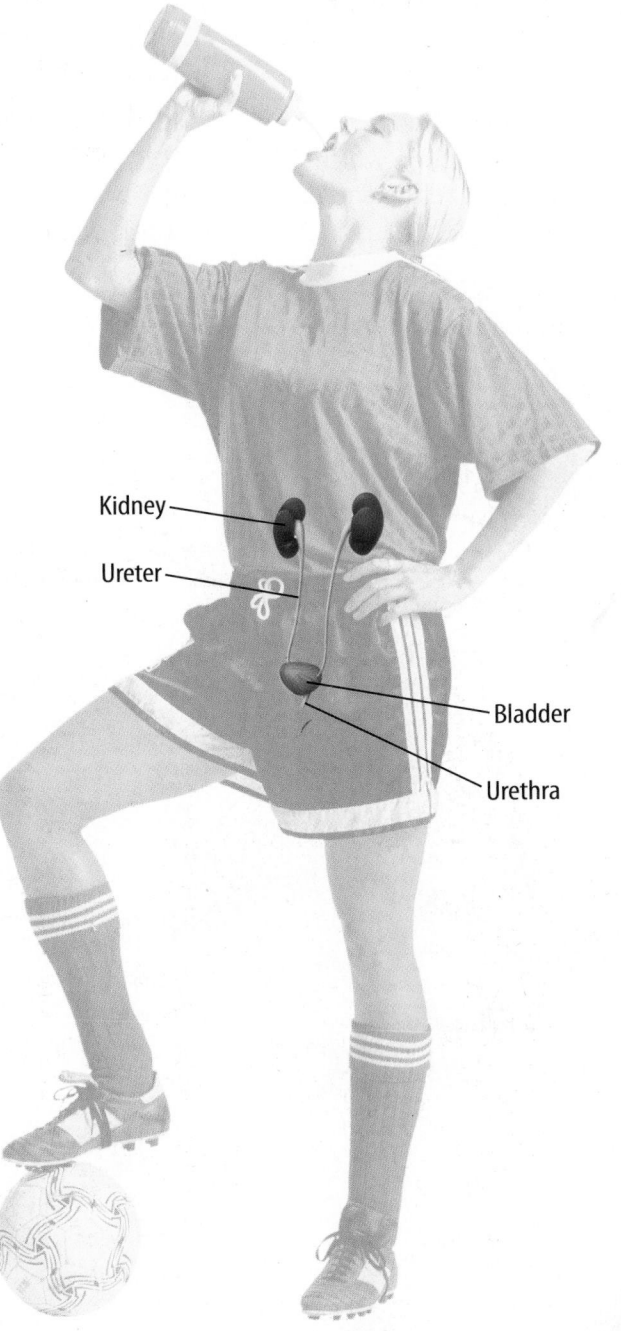

Kidney

Ureter

Bladder

Urethra

WORD ORIGIN ············

nephron
from Greek *nephros*, means "kidney"
·················

First Filtration Blood is constantly circulating and filtering through the kidneys. In one day, the kidneys filter about 180 L of blood plasma, or the liquid part of blood. That's enough liquid to fill 90 2-L bottles. Your body contains about 3 L of blood plasma. This means your entire blood supply is filtered by your kidneys about 60 times each day. As shown in **Figure 11,** the first filtration occurs in clusters of capillaries in the nephrons. These clusters of capillaries filter water, sugar, salt, and wastes out of the blood.

Second Filtration If all of the liquid from the first filtration were excreted, your body would quickly dehydrate and important nutrients would be lost. To regain some of this water, the kidneys filter the liquid collected in the first filtration again. As shown in **Figure 11,** the second filtration occurs in small tubes in the nephrons. During the second filtration, up to 99 percent of the water and nutrients from the first filtration are separated out and reabsorbed into the blood. The remaining liquid and waste products form urine. On average, an adult excretes about 1.5 L of urine per day.

Figure 11 The kidneys produce urine in two stages.

🔵 **Visual Check** Urine passes through which structure before entering the ureter?

((◎ **Concepts in Motion**   Animation

Filtration in the Kidneys

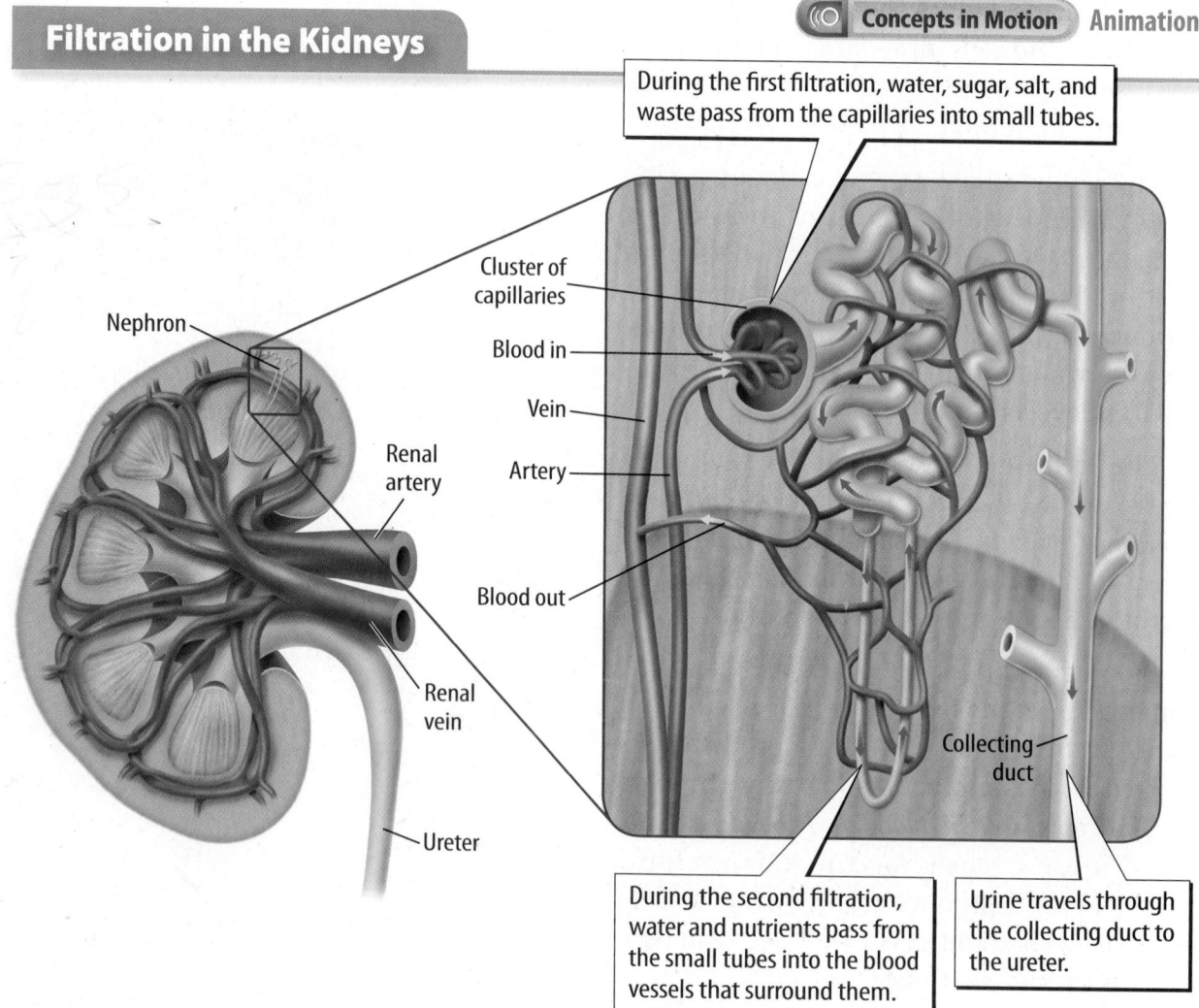

During the first filtration, water, sugar, salt, and waste pass from the capillaries into small tubes.

Nephron

Cluster of capillaries

Blood in

Vein

Artery

Blood out

Renal artery

Renal vein

Ureter

Collecting duct

During the second filtration, water and nutrients pass from the small tubes into the blood vessels that surround them.

Urine travels through the collecting duct to the ureter.

The Ureters, Bladder, and Urethra

Do you remember the trash can you read about earlier in this lesson? What would happen if you put garbage in the trash can but never emptied the trash can? The garbage would pile up. After a while, there would be too much garbage for the trash can to hold. To keep this from happening, you must empty the trash from the trash can. In a similar way, the urine produced by your body cannot stay in the kidney. *Urine leaves each kidney through a tube called the* **ureter** (YOO ruh tur). Refer back to **Figure 10** to see the locations of the ureter and other organs of the urinary system.

Both ureters drain into the bladder. *The* **bladder** *is a muscular sac that holds urine until the urine is excreted.* The bladder expands and contracts like a balloon when filled or emptied. An adult bladder can hold about 0.5 L of urine.

Urine leaves the bladder through a tube called the **urethra** (yoo REE thruh). The urethra contains circular muscles called sphincters (SFINGK turz) that control the release of urine.

WORD ORIGIN · · · · · · · · · · ·

ureter
from Greek *ourethra*, means
"passage for urine"

 Key Concept Check How do the ureters, bladder, and urethra work together to excrete urine?

Inquiry) MiniLab   **30 minutes**

How can you model the function of a kidney?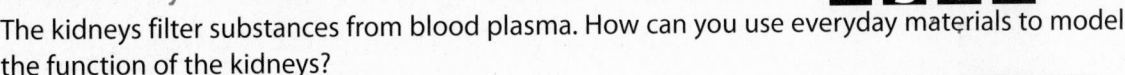

The kidneys filter substances from blood plasma. How can you use everyday materials to model the function of the kidneys?

1. Read and complete a lab safety form.
2. Label three **plastic cups** *1, 2,* and *3.*
3. Mix a small amount of **fine gravel** and **sand** with **water** in cup 1.
4. Place a small piece of **wire screen** in a **funnel,** and place the funnel in cup 2.
5. Carefully pour the sand-water-gravel mixture into the funnel. Let it drain. Record your observations in your Science Journal.
6. Remove the screen. Replace it with a piece of **filter paper.** Place the funnel in cup 3.
7. Carefully pour the contents of cup 2 into the funnel. Let it drain. Record your observations.

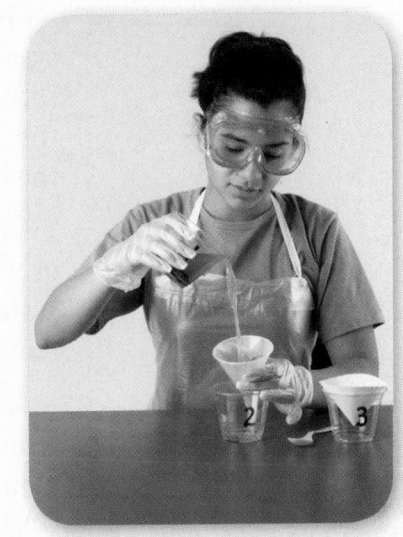

Analyze and Conclude

1. **Describe** what happened during each filtration.

2. **Key Concept** Summarize how your filtration systems model the function of the kidneys.

Table 3 Urinary Disorders

Concepts in Motion   Interactive Table

Urinary Disorder	Description	Possible Causes
Kidney disease	The nephrons are damaged and the ability of the kidneys to filter blood is reduced. However, a person can have the beginning stages of kidney disease and experience no symptoms.	diabetes, high blood pressure, poisons, trauma
Urinary tract infection	Infections usually occur in the bladder or urethra, but infections can also occur in the kidney and ureters. Symptoms can include burning during urination, small and frequent urination, and blood in urine.	bacteria in the urinary system
Kidney stones	Kidney stones are solid substances that form in the kidney. The most common type is made of calcium. Stones that pass through the urinary system can be very painful.	calcium buildup in the kidney
Bladder control problems	The bladder releases urine involuntarily. Occurs in women more often than men.	urinary tract infections, muscle weakness, prostate enlargement

Urinary Disorders

A urinary disorder is an illness that affects one or more organs of the urinary system. Some urinary disorders are described in **Table 3.** Several of these disorders are relatively common. Urinary tract infections, for example, are a leading cause of doctor visits, second only to respiratory infections.

The Excretory System and Homeostasis

You have already read about some of the ways the excretory system helps to maintain homeostasis. For example, the excretory system filters wastes from the blood. The blood is part of the circulatory system. If wastes were allowed to build up in the circulatory system, they would become toxic.

Another example of maintaining homeostasis is the removal of wastes from the digestive system. Similar to the circulatory system, wastes would damage your body if they were not removed from the digestive system by the excretory system.

The excretory system also interacts with the nervous system. The hypothalamus is an **area** of the brain that helps to maintain homeostasis. One function of the hypothalamus is to control the secretion of some hormones. One such hormone causes the tubules in the kidney to absorb more water from the blood. This helps the body to regulate fluid levels. Water is retained in the blood instead of being excreted in the urine.

ACADEMIC VOCABULARY

area
(noun) a part of something that has a particular function

Key Concept Check How does the excretory system interact with the nervous system?

Lesson 3 Review

Visual Summary

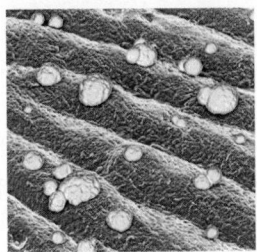

The excretory system collects and eliminates wastes from the body and regulates the level of fluid in the body.

The respiratory system is one of the body systems that make up the excretory system.

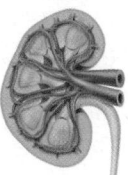

The organs of the urinary system process, transport, collect, and excrete waste.

FOLDABLES

Use your lesson Foldable to review the lesson. Save your Foldable for the project at the end of the chapter.

What do you think NOW?

You first read the statements below at the beginning of the chapter.

5. Several human body systems work together to eliminate wastes.

6. Blood contains waste products that must be removed from the body.

Did you change your mind about whether you agree or disagree with the statements? Rewrite any false statements to make them true.

Use Vocabulary

1 **Define** the word *nephron* in your own words.

2 **Distinguish** between ureter and urethra.

3 **Use the term** *bladder* in a sentence.

Understand Key Concepts

4 The kidneys filter wastes from the
   A. blood.   C. lungs.
   B. intestine.   D. skin.

5 **Construct** a diagram of the urinary system showing the production and flow of urine.

6 **Distinguish** between the excretory functions of the respiratory system and the integumentary system.

Interpret Graphics

7 **Identify** the function of the highlighted portion of the diagram to the right.

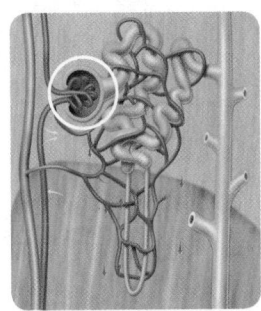

8 **Organize Information** Copy and fill in the table below with details about each organ of the urinary system.

Organ	Structure and Function

Critical Thinking

9 **Hypothesize** What might happen if urine did not go through a second filtration?

10 **Evaluate** the role of the hypothalamus in maintaining the level of fluid in the body.

Model Digestion from Start to Finish

Materials

graham crackers

banana

resealable plastic bag (1 quart size)

nylon hose

nylon netting

funnel

Also needed: scissors, water, paper towel, paper cup, newspaper.

Safety

Recall from Lesson 2 that all food goes through four steps: ingestion, digestion, absorption, and elimination. These steps happen in the digestive system. Your task is to model the four steps with the materials provided by your teacher. Before you create your model, think about all the digestive processes and plan each step. Will you model mechanical or chemical digestion or both?

Question

How does food change during the process of digestion? What are the steps in digestion?

Procedure

1. Read and complete a lab safety form.

2. In your Science Journal, make a chart like the one shown here that includes the parts of the digestive system. Record the functions of each part.

3. Using the materials provided by your teacher, design a model to show the steps in digestion. Begin with chewing and end with excretion.

4. Your teacher must approve your design before you test your model.

5. Pass food through your model.

6. Compare the food at the beginning and the end of digestion.

7. Dispose of the materials as directed by your teacher.

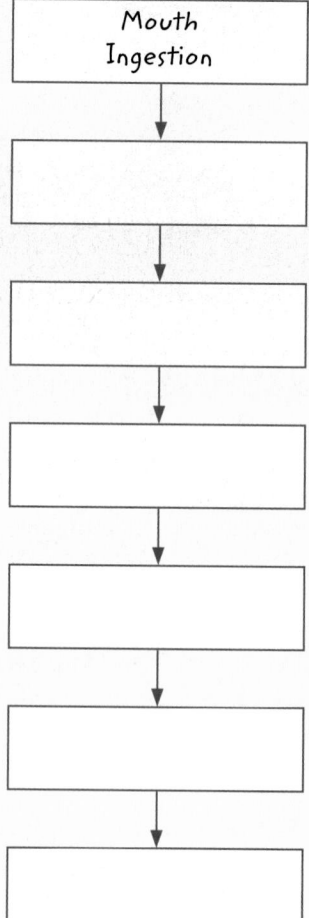

Mouth
Ingestion

8 Copy and complete the chart at right. Then, compare your model to the four steps as outlined in the text. Does your model include everything? Is there another way to model some of the steps?

9 Make modifications to your model. Record your revisions in your Science Journal.

Part of the Digestive System	Function	Part of the Model	Comparison
Mouth	Ingestion		

Analyze and Conclude

10 **Analyze** Is there a structure or function in digestion that was not included in your model? Did you model mechanical or chemical digestion or both?

11 **Contrast** How did the food change in your model? How does food change in the digestive process?

12  **The Big Idea** How does the digestive system maintain homeostasis in a healthy body?

Communicate Your Results

Share your results with the class. Discuss your chart with those of other groups. Demonstrate to the class how you modeled the digestive system.

Inquiry **Extension**

How might your model change if you were modeling a disease of the digestive system, such as an inability to produce saliva?

Lab Tips

☑ This lab might be messy, so work on several layers of newspaper.

☑ Be careful not to cut large holes in bags or cups; small holes work better.

☑ Never eat anything during a lab exercise.

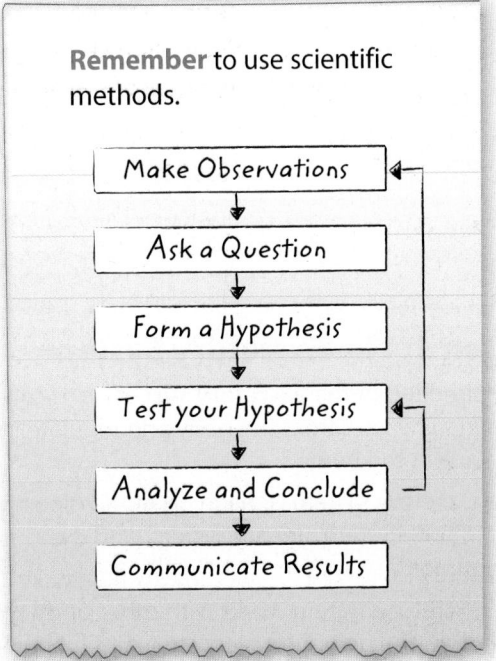

Remember to use scientific methods.

Make Observations → Ask a Question → Form a Hypothesis → Test your Hypothesis → Analyze and Conclude → Communicate Results

 **THE BIG IDEA** The digestive and excretory systems move materials through the body and remove waste. The digestive system also absorbs nutrients.

Key Concepts Summary

Vocabulary

Lesson 1: Nutrition

- People eat food to obtain the energy their bodies need to function. The amount of energy in food is measured in **Calories.**

- The types and amounts of nutrients a person needs depend on age, gender, and activity level.

- The six groups of nutrients are **proteins, carbohydrates, fats, vitamins, minerals,** and water.

- A balanced diet provides nutrients and energy for a healthful lifestyle.

Calorie p. 523
protein p. 524
carbohydrate p. 524
fat p. 525
vitamin p. 525
mineral p. 525

Lesson 2: The Digestive System

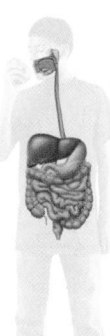

- The function of the digestive system is to break down food and absorb nutrients for the body.

- Organs of the digestive system include the mouth, **esophagus,** stomach, small intestine, and large intestine.

- The digestive system interacts with other body systems to maintain the body's internal balance.

digestion p. 531
mechanical digestion p. 532
chemical digestion p. 532
enzyme p. 532
esophagus p. 534
peristalsis p. 534
chyme p. 535
villi p. 536

Lesson 3: The Excretory System

- The function of the **excretory system** is to collect and eliminate wastes from the body and regulate the level of fluids in the body.

- The excretory system is made up of the digestive system, respiratory system, urinary system, and the integumentary system.

- The excretory system works with other body systems, including the nervous system, to maintain homeostasis.

excretory system p. 541
kidney p. 543
nephron p. 543
urine p. 543
ureter p. 545
bladder p. 545
urethra p. 545

FOLDABLES® Chapter Project

Assemble your lesson Foldables as shown to make a Chapter Project. Use the project to review what you have learned in this chapter.

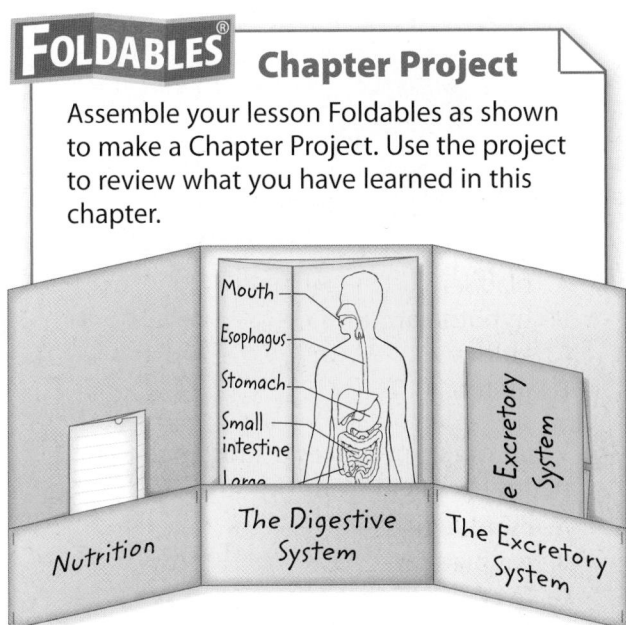

Mouth
Esophagus
Stomach
Small intestine
Large

The Excretory System

Nutrition

The Digestive System

The Excretory System

Use Vocabulary

1. About 25–35 percent of your total daily _____ should be from fats.

2. One type of nutrient, _____, is made of long chains of sugars.

3. Food moves down the esophagus by _____.

4. The breakdown of food into small particles and molecules is called _____.

5. A tube that connects a kidney to the bladder is called a(n) _____.

6. Urine is stored in the _____.

Link Vocabulary and Key Concepts

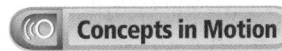 Concepts in Motion Interactive Concept Map

Copy this concept map, and then use vocabulary terms from the previous page to complete the concept map.

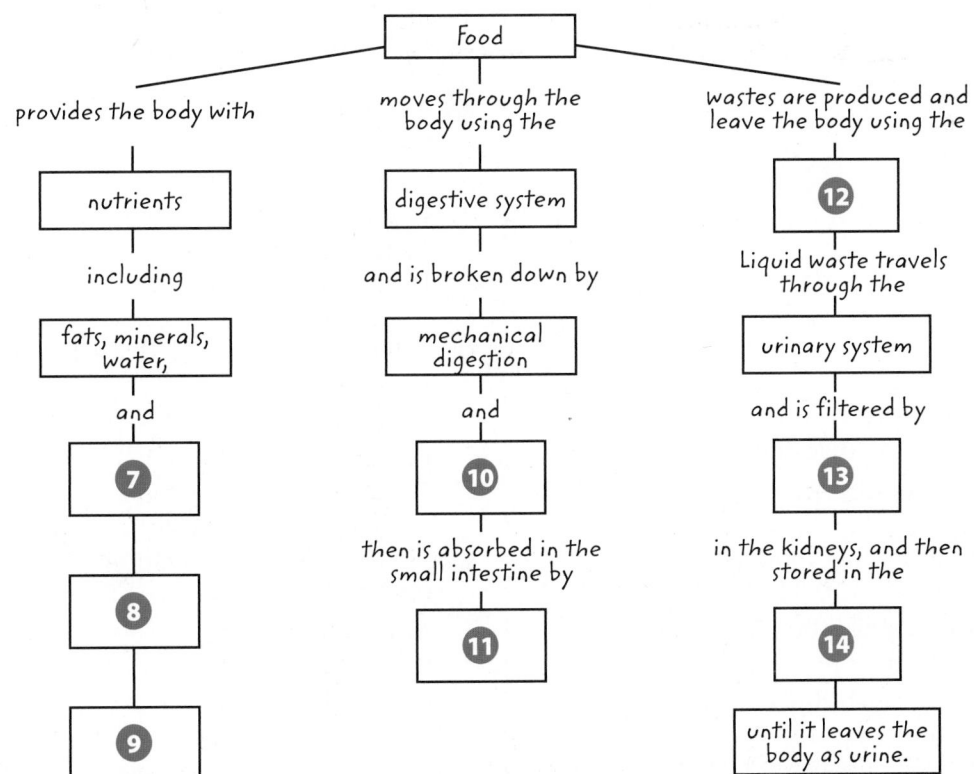

Food

provides the body with

nutrients

including

fats, minerals, water,

and

7

8

9

moves through the body using the

digestive system

and is broken down by

mechanical digestion

and

10

then is absorbed in the small intestine by

11

wastes are produced and leave the body using the

12

Liquid waste travels through the

urinary system

and is filtered by

13

in the kidneys, and then stored in the

14

until it leaves the body as urine.

Chapter 15 Review

Understand Key Concepts

1 What are proteins made of?
- A. amino acids
- B. minerals
- C. sugars
- D. vitamins

2 Which would be considered a grain?
- A. black beans
- B. brown rice
- C. canola oil
- D. lean chicken

3 What is the main source of energy for your body?
- A. carbohydrates
- B. minerals
- C. proteins
- D. water

4 Look at the diagram below. Where does most absorption of nutrients occur?

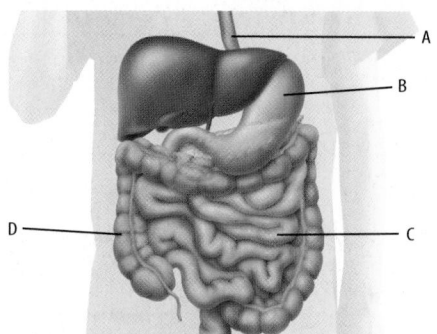

- A. A
- B. B
- C. C
- D. D

5 What is the correct order for how food is processed in the digestive system?
- A. absorption, digestion, ingestion, elimination
- B. elimination, ingestion, absorption, digestion
- C. ingestion, absorption, digestion, elimination
- D. ingestion, digestion, absorption, elimination

6 What organ is shown below?

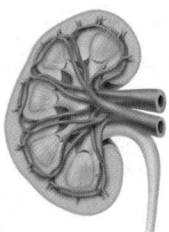

- A. bladder
- B. hypothalamus
- C. kidney
- D. ureter

7 What organ produces a substance that neutralizes acid from the stomach?
- A. esophagus
- B. gallbladder
- C. liver
- D. pancreas

8 What fluid produced in the mouth contains digestive enzymes?
- A. bile
- B. blood
- C. chyme
- D. saliva

9 Carbon dioxide is eliminated by which body system?
- A. digestive system
- B. integumentary system
- C. respiratory system
- D. urinary system

10 What is produced by the urinary system?
- A. blood
- B. feces
- C. perspiration
- D. urine

11 The bladder is most similar to which object?
- A. a balloon
- B. a tube
- C. a folded paper
- D. a rigid container

Critical Thinking

12 **Distinguish** between minerals and vitamins.

13 **Hypothesize** why a child might have different nutritional needs than an adult over the age of 60.

14 **Select** Study the nutrient information below. Select the snack that would be a better choice as part of a healthful lifestyle. Explain your choice.

Nutrient Information	Tortilla Chips	
	Fried	Baked
Calories	150	110
Calories from fat	60	5
Total fat (g)	7	1
Saturated fat (g)	1	0
Sodium (mg)	135	200
Total carbohydrate (g)	22	24
Sugars	3	0
Protein	3	2

15 **Differentiate** Suppose your teacher showed you a diagram of a small intestine and a diagram of a large intestine. How might you distinguish between them?

16 **Hypothesize** How might digestion be affected if a person swallowed his or her food without first chewing it?

17 **Critique** the following statement: "Bacteria are harmful and should not be in the digestive system."

18 **Compare** the excretions of the urinary system and the digestive system.

Writing in Science

19 **Create** a commercial to encourage people to eat a healthful amount from each food group. Include a setting and dialogue for your commercial.

REVIEW THE BIG IDEA

20 Give examples of how the digestive system and excretory system help to maintain homeostasis.

21 What is the function of the small intestine?

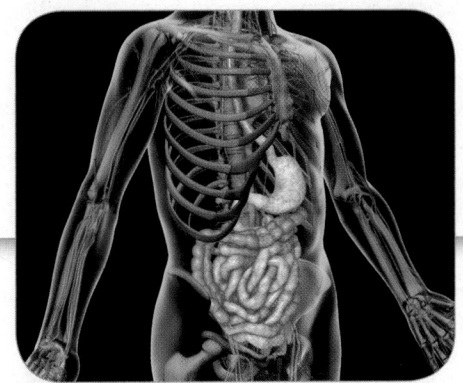

Math Skills

Math Practice

Use Percentages

Use the table below to answer questions 22–24.

Location of food	Time in location (hrs)
Stomach	4
Small intestine	6
Large intestine	24

22 What percentage of the total digestive time does food spend in the stomach?

23 What percentage of the total digestive time does food spend in the large intestine?

24 What percentage of the total digestive time does food spend in the stomach and the small intestine combined?

Record your answers on the answer sheet provided by your teacher or on a sheet of paper.

Multiple Choice

1 Which process depends on enzymes?

   A chemical digestion

   B elimination

   C mechanical digestion

   D respiration

Use the diagram below to answer question 2.

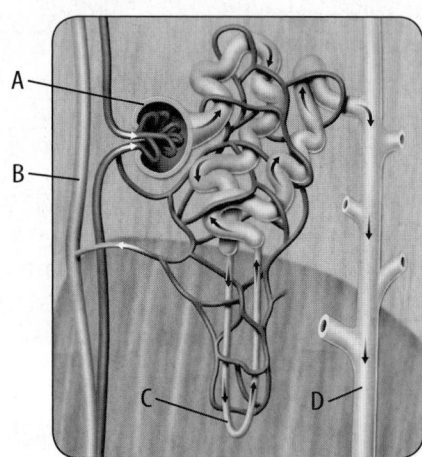

2 Where does the first filtration process occur in the nephron shown above?

   A A

   B B

   C C

   D D

3 Which factor does NOT influence how much energy a person needs?

   A age

   B gender

   C height

   D weight

Use the diagram below to answer questions 4 and 5.

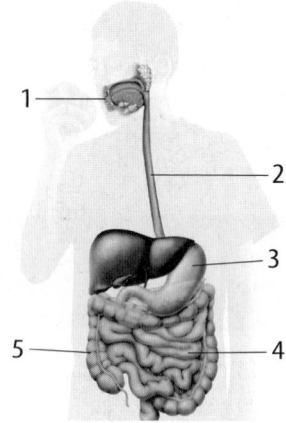

4 In which part of the system pictured above does chemical digestion begin?

   A 1

   B 2

   C 3

   D 4

5 In the diagram above, from which organ are nutrients absorbed into the bloodstream?

   A 2

   B 3

   C 4

   D 5

6 What is a main function of the excretory system?

   A fight diseases

   B move limbs

   C pump blood

   D remove wastes

7 Which part of the brain works with the urinary system to help maintain homeostasis?

A cerebellum

B cerebrum

C hypothalamus

D medulla

Use the diagram below to answer question 8.

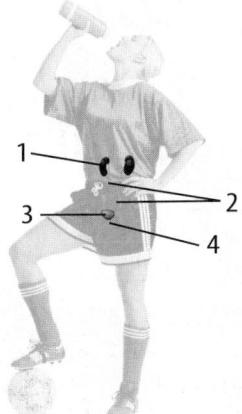

8 In the diagram above, where is urine produced?

A 1

B 2

C 3

D 4

9 Which system works with the digestive system to carry nutrients to the cells of the body?

A circulatory

B excretory

C lymphatic

D respiratory

Constructed Response

Use the table below to answer questions 10 and 11.

Nutrient	Example of Food
Carbohydrates	
Fats	
Minerals	
Proteins	
Vitamins	
Water	

10 In the table above, the six main groups of nutrients are provided. What is an example of a food that contains each nutrient? What is the function of each nutrient in the body?

11 Explain how the nutrients in the table above are related to eating a balanced diet.

Use the table below to answer question 12.

Process	Description
Ingestion	
Digestion	
Absorption	
Elimination	

12 When a person eats food, the food undergoes four processes in the digestive system. Briefly describe each process provided in the table above.

NEED EXTRA HELP?												
If You Missed Question...	1	2	3	4	5	6	7	8	9	10	11	12
Go to Lesson...	2	3	1	2	2	3	3	3	2	1	1	2

Chapter 16

Respiration and Circulation

THE BIG IDEA

How do the respiratory and circulatory systems help maintain the body's homeostasis?

Inquiry **What makes the bubbles?**

Scuba divers use special equipment to breathe under water. Notice the hose that runs from the air tank to the device in the diver's mouth. When she breathes in, air from the tank moves into her lungs.

- Why does the diver need air while she's under water?
- Why do bubbles form when the diver breathes out?
- How do you think your respiratory system helps your body maintain homeostasis?

Get Ready to Read

What do you think?

Before you read, decide if you agree or disagree with each of these statements. As you read this chapter, see if you change your mind about any of the statements.

1. Breathing and respiration are the same.

2. Lungs are the only parts of the body that use oxygen.

3. There are four chambers in a human heart.

4. Blood travels in both directions in veins.

5. All blood cells are red.

6. Blood plasma is just water.

7. Lymph nodes are only in the neck.

8. The lymphatic system helps fight infections to maintain a healthy body.

ConnectED Your one-stop online resource

connectED.mcgraw-hill.com

- Video
- WebQuest
- Audio
- Assessment
- Review
- Concepts in Motion
- Inquiry
- Multilingual eGlossary

The Respiratory System

Reading Guide

Key Concepts 🔑
ESSENTIAL QUESTIONS

- What does the respiratory system do?
- How do the parts of the respiratory system work together?
- How does the respiratory system interact with other body systems?

Vocabulary

breathing p. 559

pharynx p. 560

larynx p. 560

trachea p. 560

bronchi p. 561

lungs p. 561

alveoli p. 561

diaphragm p. 562

 Multilingual eGlossary

 Video **BrainPOP®**

Inquiry Cleaning Up?

The hairlike structures shown here are called cilia (SIH lee uh). They move together in wavelike motions. Cilia line the air passages in your nose, throat, and lungs. The round particles on top of the cilia are bits of dust and other things that can block or irritate airways. What do you think these cilia are doing?

How much air is in a breath?

Do your lungs empty completely every time you breathe out? You can use a balloon to find out.

1. Read and complete a lab safety form.

2. Place your hands on your ribs as you breathe in and out. Record your observations in your Science Journal.

3. Breathe in normally. Breathe out normally into a **balloon.** Twist and hold the end of the balloon.

4. Have your partner use a **metric tape measure** to measure around the balloon at its widest point. Record the measurement. Let the air out of the balloon.

5. Breathe in normally again. Breathe out as much air as you can into the balloon. Twist and hold the end. Repeat step 4.

6. Switch roles with your partner, and repeat steps 2–5 using a different balloon.

Think About This

1. Was there a difference in the two measurements? Why do you think this happened?

2. 🔑 **Key Concept** How do your lungs interact with the bones and muscles of your chest?

Functions of the Respiratory System

If you've ever held your breath, you probably took deep breaths afterward. That's your body's way of getting the oxygen it needs. **Breathing** *is the movement of air into and out of the lungs.* Breathing enables your respiratory system to take in oxygen and to eliminate carbon dioxide.

Taking in Oxygen

Think about the plumbing pipes that bring water into a house. Your respiratory system is similar. It is a system of organs that brings oxygen into your body. Oxygen is so important for life that your brain will tell your body to breathe even if you try not to. Why is oxygen so important? Every cell in your body needs oxygen for a series of chemical reactions called **cellular respiration.** During cellular respiration, oxygen and sugars react. This reaction releases energy a cell can use.

Eliminating Carbon Dioxide

The plumbing in a house also includes pipes that take away wastewater. In a similar way, your respiratory system removes carbon dioxide and other waste gases from your body. If waste gases are not removed, cells cannot function.

🔑 **Key Concept Check** What does the respiratory system do?

REVIEW VOCABULARY

cellular respiration
a series of chemical reactions that transform the energy in food molecules to usable energy

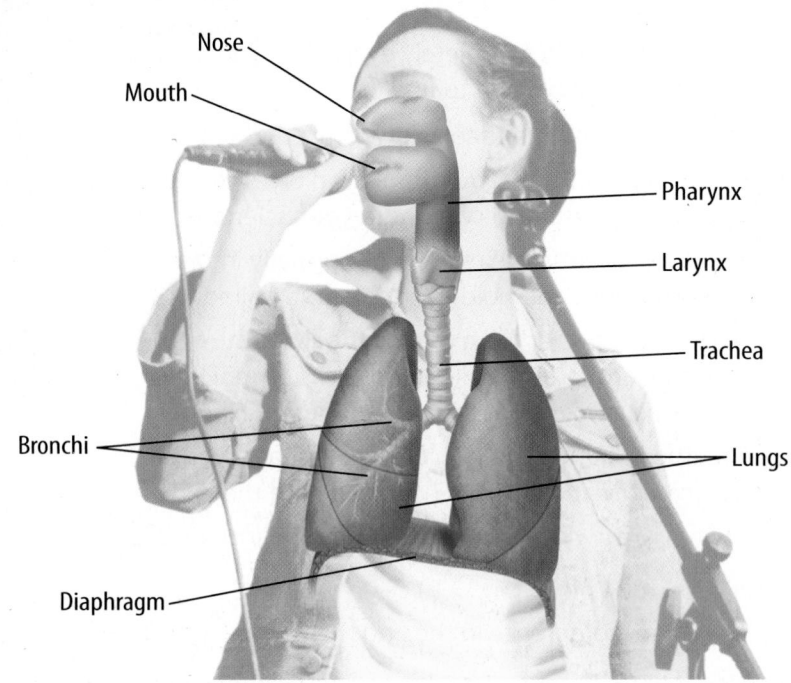

Figure 1 Air moves into and out of the lungs through the respiratory system.

🔘 **Visual Check** Which part of the respiratory system contains bronchi?

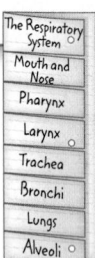
Organs of the Respiratory System

Follow the path of oxygen through the respiratory system in **Figure 1.** Air enters through the mouth and the nose. In the nose, the air is warmed and moistened. Hairs and sticky mucus in the nose help trap dust and dirt from the air. Cilia line the nose and most other airways in the respiratory system. Wavelike motions of the cilia carry trapped particles away from your lungs. The cilia help prevent harmful particles from getting very far into your respiratory system.

 Key Concept Check What function do cilia have in the respiratory system?

Pharynx

Air passes from the nose and mouth into the throat. *The* **pharynx** *(FER ingks) is a tubelike passageway at the top of the throat that receives air, food, and liquids from the mouth or nose.* The epiglottis (eh puh GLAH tus) is a flap of tissue at the lower end of the pharynx. It keeps food and liquids from entering the rest of the respiratory system.

Larynx and Trachea

Air passes from the pharynx into a triangle-shaped area called the voice box or **larynx** *(LER ingks).* Two thick folds of tissue in the larynx—the vocal cords—vibrate and make sounds as air passes over them. Air then enters the **trachea** (TRAY kee uh), *a tube that is held open by C-shaped rings of cartilage.*

Bronchi and Lungs

The trachea branches into two narrower tubes called **bronchi** (BRAHN ki) *(singular, bronchus) that lead into the lungs.* **Lungs** *are the main organs of the respiratory system.* Inside the lungs, the bronchi continue to branch into smaller and narrower tubes called bronchioles.

Alveoli

In the lungs, the bronchioles end in *microscopic sacs, or pouches, called* **alveoli** (al VEE uh li; singular, alveolus), *where gas exchange occurs.* During gas exchange, oxygen from the air you breathe moves into the blood, and carbon dioxide from your blood moves into the alveoli.

Alveoli look like bunches of grapes at the ends of the bronchioles. Like tiny balloons, the alveoli fill with air when you breathe in. They contract and expel air when you breathe out. Notice in **Figure 2** how blood vessels surround an alveolus.

The walls of alveoli are only one cell thick. The thin walls and the large surface areas of the alveoli enable a high rate of gas exchange. If you could spread out all the alveoli in your lungs onto a flat surface, they would cover an area bigger than most classrooms. Every time you breathe, your alveoli enable your body to take in billions of molecules of oxygen and get rid of billions of molecules of carbon dioxide.

✓ **Reading Check** What gases are exchanged in the alveoli?

WORD ORIGIN

alveoli
from Latin *alveus*, means "cavity"

Figure 2 Red blood cells drop off carbon dioxide and pick up oxygen as they move through the small blood vessels that surround each alveolus.

✓ **Visual Check** How many layers of cells form the walls of the alveolus shown in this figure?

Gas Exchange 🔑

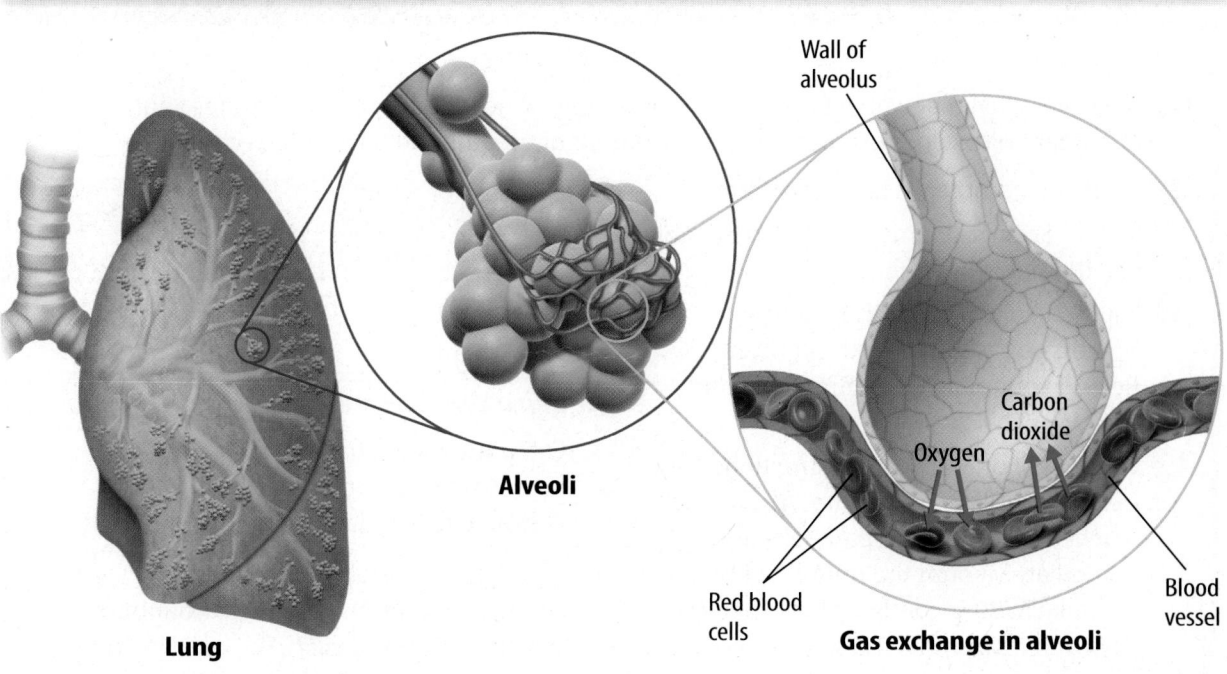

Wall of alveolus

Alveoli

Carbon dioxide

Oxygen

Red blood cells

Blood vessel

Lung

Gas exchange in alveoli

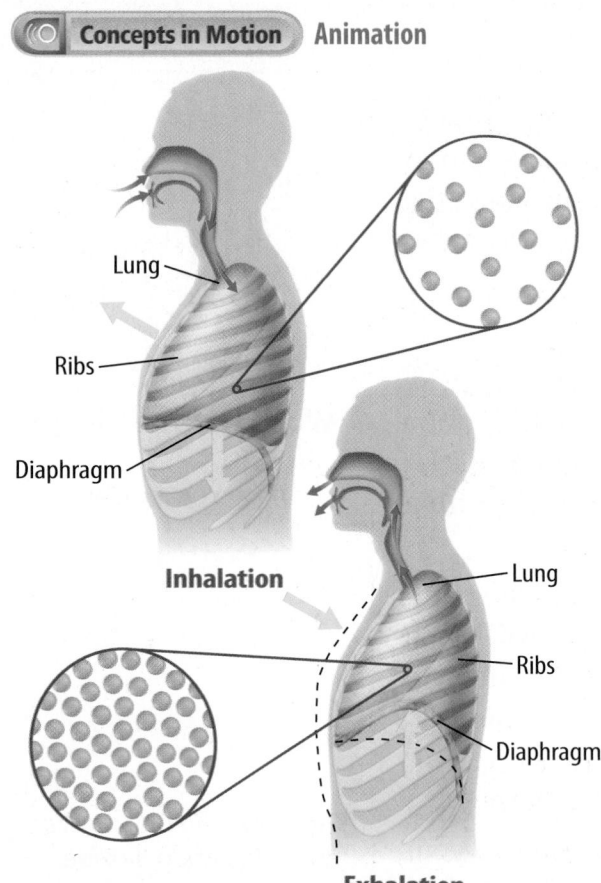

Inhalation

Exhalation

Figure 3 Your diaphragm contracts and moves down when you inhale. The chest cavity gets larger, and air rushes in to equalize the air pressure inside and outside the body. Your diaphragm relaxes and moves up as you exhale. Air rushes out to equalize air pressure.

Breathing and Air Pressure

How does your body know when to breathe? When high levels of carbon dioxide build up in your blood, the nervous system signals your body to breathe out, or exhale. After each exhalation, you breathe in, or inhale. How does this happen?

Below the lungs is a large muscle called the **diaphragm** *(DI uh fram) that contracts and relaxes and moves air in and out of the lungs.* The movement of your diaphragm causes changes in the air pressure inside your chest, as shown in **Figure 3.** Breathing occurs because of these changes in air pressure.

During inhalation, the diaphragm contracts and moves down, enlarging the space around the lungs. The increased space reduces air pressure in the chest. Air rushes into your lungs until the pressure inside your chest equals the air pressure outside it.

During exhalation, the diaphragm relaxes and moves up, reducing the space around the lungs. Air pressure in the chest increases. Waste gases rush out of your lungs.

Inquiry MiniLab   **20 minutes**

How does exercise affect breathing rate?

If you've ever played or watched a sport, you probably noticed that exercise changes your breathing rate. How does exercise affect the number of breaths you take in 30 seconds?

1. Read and complete a lab safety form.

2. In your Science Journal, create a data table like the one shown.

3. For 30 seconds, count the number of breaths you take while sitting quietly. Record your data. Repeat for two more trials.

4. Following your teacher's instructions, exercise briskly for 1 minute. When your teacher tells you to stop exercising, immediately count the number of breaths you take in 30 seconds. Record your data. Repeat for two more trials.

Activity	Number of Breaths		
	Trial 1	Trial 2	Trial 3
Sitting			
Exercising			

Analyze and Conclude

1. **Calculate** individual and class averages. How does your average breathing rate compare to the class average?

2. 🔑 **Key Concept** How does the change in breathing rate help your body maintain homeostasis?

Respiratory Health

If you've ever had a cold, allergies, or asthma, you know what it's like to have a respiratory illness. A sore throat or a stuffed-up head makes breathing uncomfortable. Some respiratory illnesses make breathing difficult and can even become life-threatening. Common respiratory illnesses and their causes are listed in **Table 1.**

The best way to maintain good respiratory health is to stay away from irritants and air pollution. Don't smoke, and avoid secondhand smoke. On days when air quality is poor or pollen counts are high, it might be best to spend more time indoors.

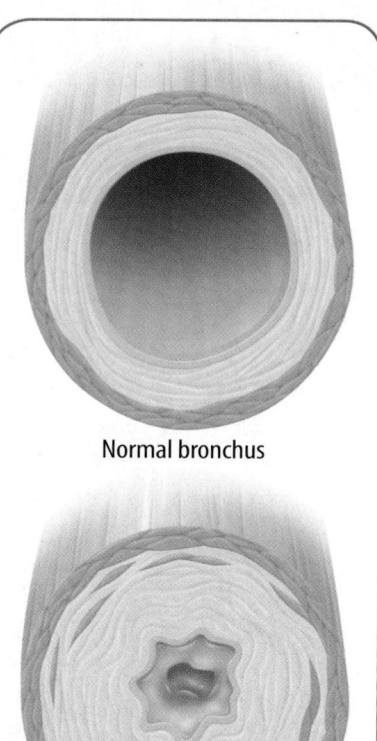

Normal bronchus

Bronchitis

Concepts in Motion   Interactive Table

Table 1 Respiratory Illnesses		
Illness	**Causes**	**Symptoms**
Colds, flu	viruses	congestion, runny nose, watery eyes, coughing, sneezing
Bronchitis (brahn KI tus)	viruses, bacteria	coughing and fatigue due to mucus blocking the bronchi and bronchioles slows air movement
Pneumonia (noo MOH nyuh)	viruses, bacteria	difficulty breathing due to fluid in the alveoli that slows gas exchange
Asthma (AZ muh)	dust, smoke, pollen, pollution	difficulty breathing due to swollen airways and increased mucus
Emphysema (em fuh SEE muh)	smoking	coughing, fatigue, loss of appetite, and weight loss due to destruction of alveoli
Lung cancer	smoking	coughing, difficulty breathing, and chest pain

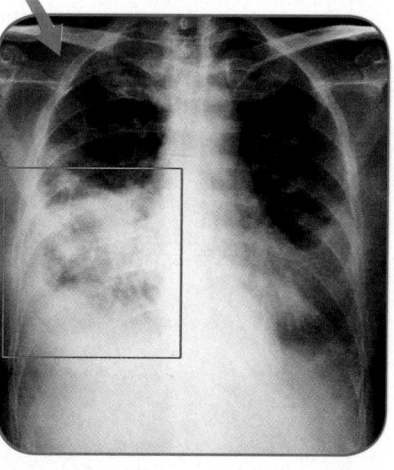

Pneumonia

The Respiratory System and Homeostasis

As you've read in this lesson, the muscular system interacts with the respiratory system so you can breathe. This interaction brings oxygen into your lungs and removes carbon dioxide from your lungs. In the next lesson, you'll read how the circulatory and respiratory systems work together to bring oxygen to body cells and remove carbon dioxide. All these systems help maintain homeostasis.

 Key Concept Check How do the respiratory and muscular systems work together to maintain your body's homeostasis?

Lesson 1 Review

Visual Summary

Air enters the body through the nose and mouth. It passes through the pharynx, larynx, and trachea on its way into the lungs.

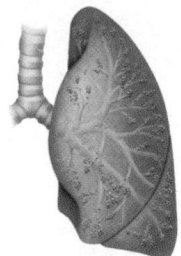

Inside the lungs, air moves through bronchi and bronchioles to the alveoli, where gas exchange takes place.

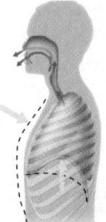

Breathing results from air pressure changes inside the chest that are created by the movement of the diaphragm muscle.

FOLDABLES

Use your lesson Foldable to review the lesson. Save your Foldable for the project at the end of the chapter.

What do you think NOW?

You first read the statements below at the beginning of the chapter.

1. Breathing and respiration are the same.

2. Lungs are the only parts of the body that use oxygen.

Did you change your mind about whether you agree or disagree with the statements? Rewrite any false statements to make them true.

Use Vocabulary

1 The trachea branches into two narrower airways called _____.

2 Capillaries surround the _____, where gas exchange occurs.

3 **Distinguish** between breathing and respiration.

Understand Key Concepts

4 **Explain** how the nose helps to clean air as the air enters the respiratory system.

5 **Describe** the functions of the respiratory system.

6 Which body system helps the respiratory system bring oxygen into the body?
- **A.** circulatory
- **B.** digestive
- **C.** excretory
- **D.** muscular

Interpret Graphics

7 **Explain** how oxygen moves into and out of the structures shown to the right.

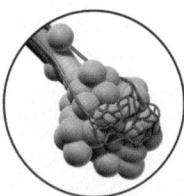

8 **Compare** Copy and fill in the Venn diagram below to explain the similarities and differences between the trachea and the bronchi.

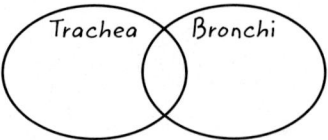

Critical Thinking

9 **Compose** a letter explaining why a friend of the family should stop smoking. Focus on the health reasons.

10 **Justify** Imagine that you answered a question in class by saying the contraction of the diaphragm causes a person to inhale. Another student disagrees. Justify your answer using words and a drawing.

How can a model show the physics of breathing?

Materials

1-L plastic drink bottle

1 small balloon

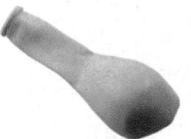

1 large balloon

duct tape

scissors

Safety

Air flows from areas of higher pressure to areas of lower pressure. This physics principle explains how air gets into and out of your lungs. Can this principle be observed in a model of the lungs?

Learn It

In science, a **model** is a representation of how something in the natural world works. A model can be used to explain or predict a natural process.

Try It

1. Read and complete a lab safety form.

2. Cut off the bottom one-third of a 1-liter clear, plastic drink bottle.

3. Blow into a small balloon two or three times to stretch it. Have your partner hold on to the bottle. Place the balloon inside the top of the bottle. Stretch the opened end of the balloon over the opening of the bottle.

4. Blow into a large balloon two or three times to stretch it. Tie a knot in the open end of the balloon. Cut off the tip of the opposite end of the balloon. Stretch the cut end of the balloon over the cut end of the bottle. Secure the balloon to the bottle with duct tape.

5. Pull down on the knotted end of the large balloon and then slowly release it. Observe what happens as you do this several times. Record your observations in your Science Journal.

Apply It

6. **Make a diagram** of your model. Label the parts representing the chest cavity, mouth and nose, diaphragm, and lungs.

7. **Describe** what happens to the volume inside the bottle when the large balloon is pulled downward.

8. On your diagram, label the areas of higher and lower pressure when you pull down on the large balloon. Label the areas of higher and lower pressure when the large balloon is released.

9. 🔑 **Key Concept** Use your model and air pressure diagram to explain how air gets into your lungs when you inhale.

Lesson 2

Reading Guide

Key Concepts 🔑
ESSENTIAL QUESTIONS

- What does the circulatory system do?
- How do parts of the circulatory system work together?
- How does the circulatory system interact with other body systems?

Vocabulary

atrium p. 568

ventricle p. 568

artery p. 570

capillary p. 570

vein p. 570

systemic circulation p. 571

coronary circulation p. 571

pulmonary circulation p. 571

atherosclerosis p. 572

🄖 **Multilingual eGlossary**

▢ **Video** BrainPOP®

The Circulatory System

Inquiry Where To?

How does food get from where it's grown to your dinner table? Food and most other products that people need are transported on roads and highways. Believe it or not, the vessels that carry blood through your body share similarities with roads and highways.

How fast does your heart beat?

Have you ever felt your heartbeat speed up when you're exercising or when you're watching a scary movie? You can take your own pulse to find out how many times your heart beats every minute.

1. Read and complete a lab safety form.
2. Sit quietly for 1 minute.
3. Feel your pulse by placing the middle and index fingers of one hand on an artery in your neck or an artery in your wrist.
4. While sitting quietly, count the number of heartbeats you feel in 30 seconds. Multiply this number by two to calculate your pulse. Record your data in your Science Journal.
5. Jog in place for 1 minute.
6. Immediately repeat step 4.

Think About This

1. How did your pulse after exercising compare to your resting pulse?

2. 🔑 **Key Concept** Why do you think your pulse changed when you exercised?

Functions of the Circulatory System

Have you ever looked at a road map of the United States? A complex network of highways and roads crisscrosses the country. This road network is important for transporting people and materials from place to place. In a similar way, your circulatory system is important for transporting materials from one part of your body to another.

Transportation

Trucks haul food, fuel, and other products from factories and farms to markets and businesses around the country. Your circulatory system is like the network of roads, and your blood cells are like the vehicles that travel on those roads. Blood carries food, water, oxygen, and other materials through your circulatory system to your body's cells and tissues.

Elimination

Blood also carries away waste materials, just as garbage trucks haul away trash. As blood travels through the circulatory system, it picks up carbon dioxide produced during cellular respiration. It also picks up wastes produced by all the other chemical reactions that take place inside cells.

🔑 **Key Concept Check** What does the circulatory system do?

FOLDABLES

Make a horizontal two-tab book from a sheet of notebook paper. Label the front *The Circulatory System,* and label the inside as shown. Use it to organize your notes on the functions of the circulatory system and the organs associated with those functions.

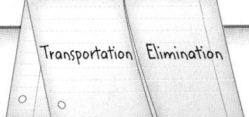

Transportation | Elimination

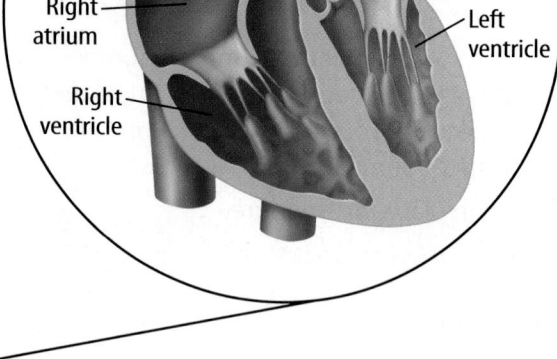

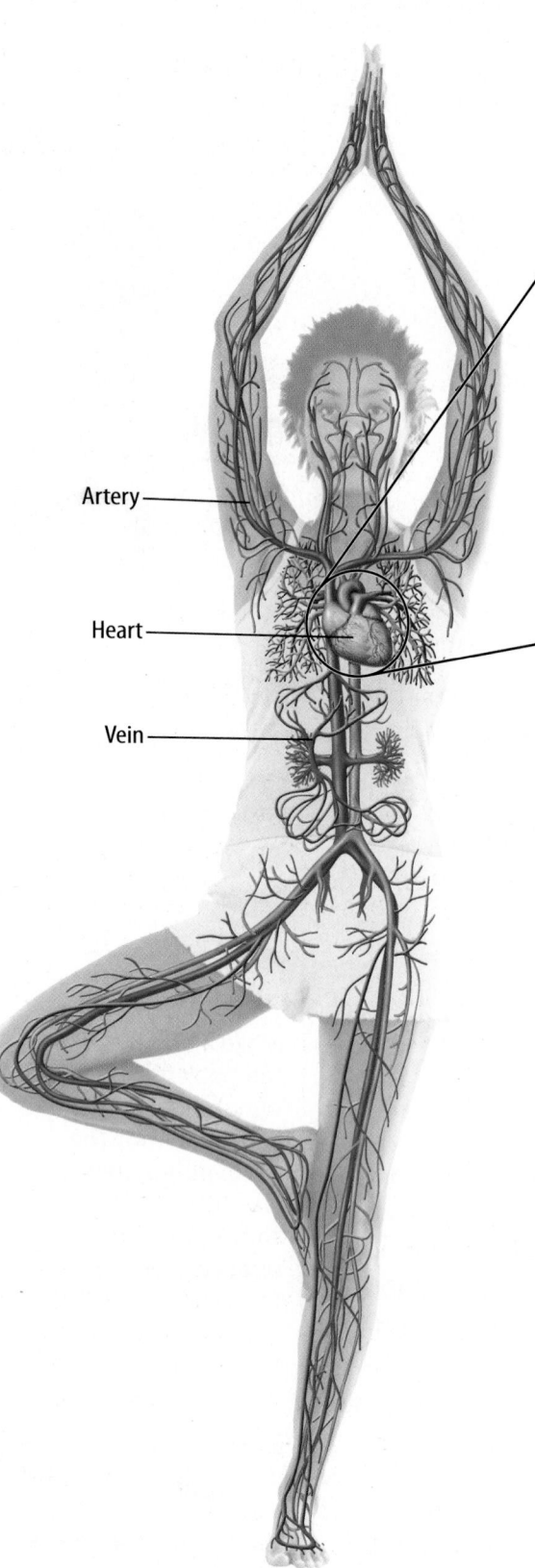

Figure 4 Your heart muscle is about the size of your fist. It acts as a pump that pushes blood through your circulatory system.

Circulatory System Organs

Highways connect and intersect and provide routes for traffic. **Figure 4** illustrates how your circulatory (SUR kyuh luh tor ee) system is similar. It provides routes for blood to flow through your body. Just as every vehicle on a highway is powered by its engine, your heart powers the flow of blood through your circulatory system.

The Heart

Your heart is always at work. The heart is a muscle that pushes blood through the circulatory system, as shown in **Figure 5.** On average, a human heart beats 70 to 75 times per minute, every minute of your life. It slows when you sleep. It speeds up when you exercise or are frightened.

 Reading Check What does the heart do?

Look again at **Figure 4.** Notice that your heart has four chambers, two upper and two lower. *Blood enters the upper two chambers of the heart, called the* **atria** (AY tree uh; singular, atrium). *Blood leaves through the lower two chambers of the heart, called the* **ventricles** (VEN trih kulz).

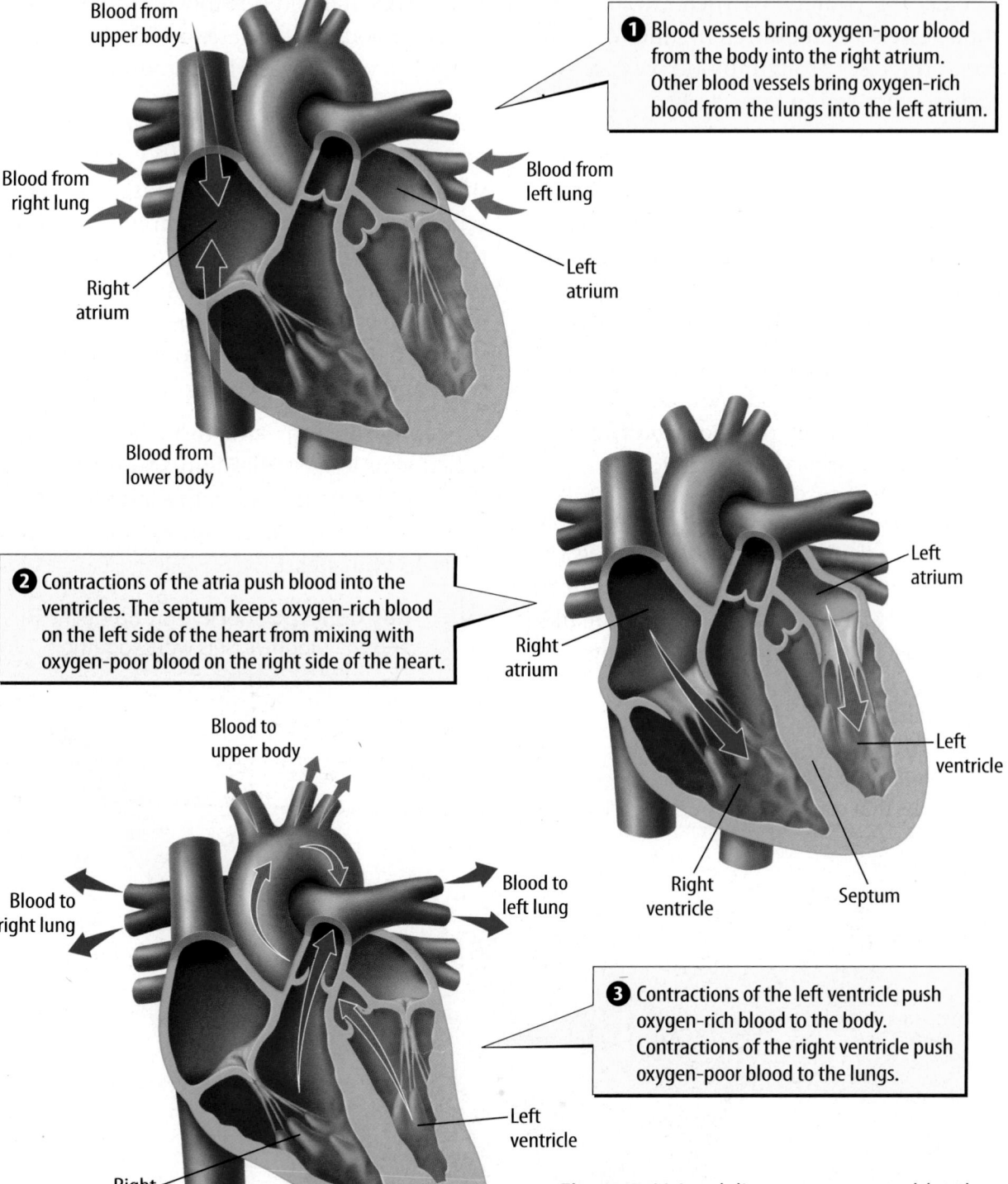

Blood from upper body

❶ Blood vessels bring oxygen-poor blood from the body into the right atrium. Other blood vessels bring oxygen-rich blood from the lungs into the left atrium.

Blood from right lung

Blood from left lung

Right atrium

Left atrium

Blood from lower body

❷ Contractions of the atria push blood into the ventricles. The septum keeps oxygen-rich blood on the left side of the heart from mixing with oxygen-poor blood on the right side of the heart.

Left atrium

Right atrium

Left ventricle

Blood to upper body

Right ventricle

Septum

Blood to right lung

Blood to left lung

❸ Contractions of the left ventricle push oxygen-rich blood to the body. Contractions of the right ventricle push oxygen-poor blood to the lungs.

Left ventricle

Right ventricle

Blood to lower body

Figure 5 Veins deliver oxygen-poor blood from the body to the heart. The heart pumps this blood to the lungs, where it is resupplied with oxygen. The oxygen-rich blood then travels back to the heart and is pumped to the rest of the body.

✅ **Visual Check** What structure in the heart separates oxygen-poor blood from oxygen-rich blood?

Blood Vessels

If the circulatory system is like a network of roads for your body, then the different blood vessels are like different kinds of roads. Blood travels through blood vessels and reaches every cell in your body.

Arteries As shown in **Figure 6,** *a vessel that takes blood away from the heart is an* **artery.** Blood pressure in arteries is high because arteries are near the pumping action of the heart. Artery walls are thick and can withstand the high pressure of flowing blood.

The aorta is the largest artery. It carries a large volume of blood, just like freeways carry a high volume of traffic. Arteries branch into smaller vessels called arterioles.

Capillaries Notice in Figure 6 that arterioles branch into **capillaries,** *tiny blood vessels that deliver supplies to individual cells and take away waste materials.* Capillaries are the smallest blood vessels in the circulatory system.

Many capillary walls are only one cell thick. This makes it possible for molecules of oxygen, food, water, wastes, and other materials to move between blood and body cells.

Veins *A vessel that brings blood toward the heart is a* **vein.** The pressure in veins is lower than in arteries. This is because capillaries separate veins from the pumping action of the heart. Because there is less pressure in veins, there is a greater chance that blood could flow backward. Veins have one-way valves that prevent blood from moving backward and keep it moving toward the heart.

Capillaries join and form larger vessels called venules. Venules join and form veins. The inferior vena cava is the largest vein. It carries blood from the lower half of your body to your heart.

Key Concept Check How do the heart and the blood vessels work together?

Figure 6 Arteries branch into arterioles and capillaries and bring oxygen-rich blood to cells. Capillaries combine to form venules and veins that carry oxygen-poor blood back to the heart. ▼

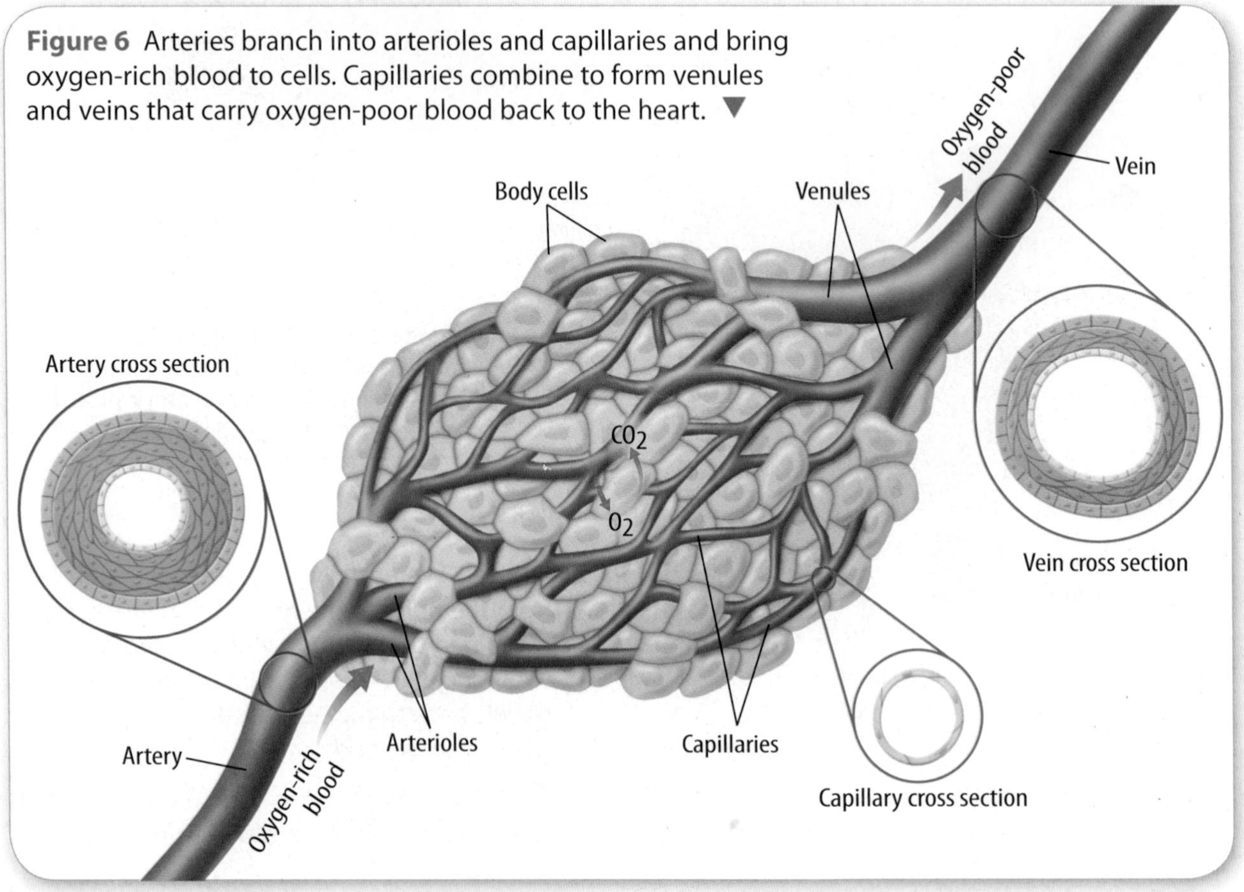
Oxygen-poor blood
Vein
Body cells
Venules
Artery cross section
CO_2
O_2
Vein cross section
Artery
Oxygen-rich blood
Arterioles
Capillaries
Capillary cross section

Types of Circulation

Your circulatory system is one large system that circulates blood throughout your entire body. However, when scientists and medical professionals discuss the circulatory system, they name three different types of circulation. One type supplies blood to the body. A second type supplies blood to the heart. A third type carries blood to and from the lungs.

Systemic Circulation

Blood leaves your heart through the aorta and travels to your arms, your toes, your head, and all other parts of your body, as shown by the orange vessels in **Figure 7.** **Systemic circulation** *is the network of vessels that carry blood from the heart to the body and from the body back to the heart.*

Coronary Circulation

You might think the cells of the heart get oxygen and nutrients from the blood that travels through the heart. However, the heart is a thick organ made up of many layers of cells. As a result, most heart cells don't come into contact with the blood inside the heart. *A network of arteries and veins called the* **coronary circulation** *supplies blood to all the cells of the heart.* Some of these vessels are on the outside of the heart, as shown in **Figure 7.**

 Reading Check What does coronary circulation do?

Pulmonary Circulation

The purple part of the circulation shown in **Figure 7** illustrates how blood moves back and forth between the heart and the lungs. *The network of vessels that carries blood to and from the lungs is called* **pulmonary circulation.** Pulmonary circulation carries oxygen-poor blood from the heart to the lungs. It also carries oxygen-rich blood from the lungs back to the heart. Blood that enters the heart from the lungs is then pushed to the rest of the body.

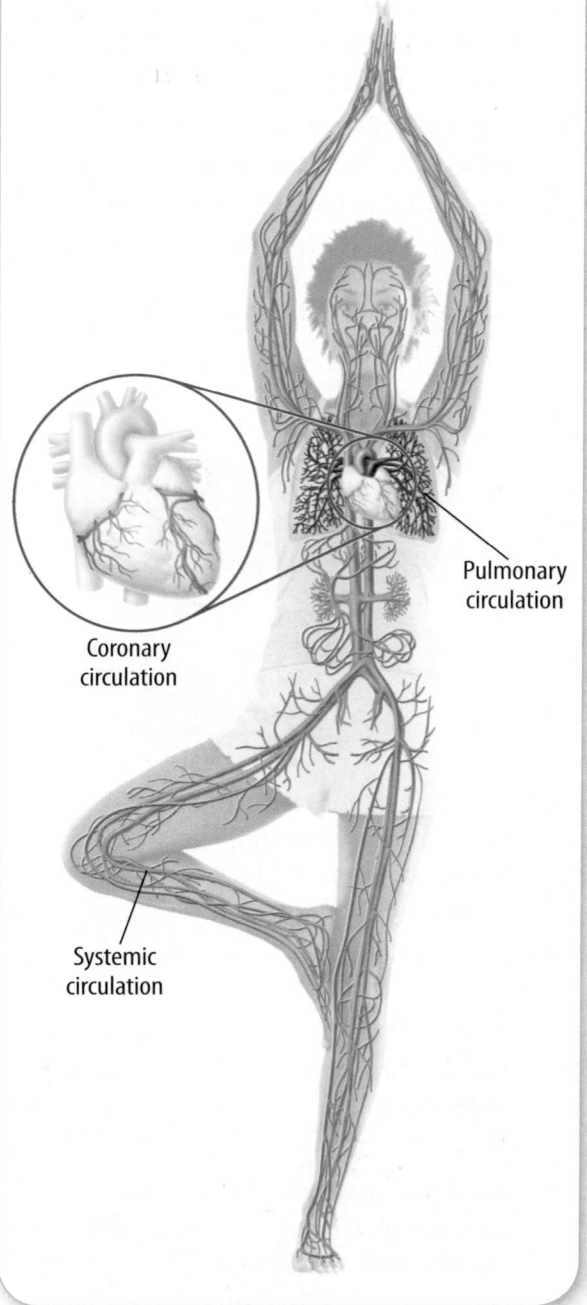

Figure 7 Coronary circulation, shown in green, provides oxygen to heart cells. Pulmonary circulation, shown in purple, supplies blood with oxygen and removes carbon dioxide. Systemic circulation, shown in orange, supplies the rest of the body with oxygen and nutrients and removes wastes.

Pulmonary circulation

Coronary circulation

Systemic circulation

WORD ORIGIN · · · · · · · · · · · · · · · · · · ·

pulmonary
from Latin *pulmonarius*, means "of the lungs"

How can you model atherosclerosis?

Atherosclerosis is the buildup of fatty deposits in arteries. You can model atherosclerosis to see how it affects blood flow.

1 Read and complete a lab safety form.

2 Fit the end of a **funnel** into a piece of **plastic tubing.** Place the end of the tubing into a **beaker.**

3 Have your partner measure 10 mL of **water** into a **graduated cylinder.**

4 Pour the water into the funnel while your partner uses a **stopwatch** to time how long it takes the water to move through the tubing. Record the data in your Science Journal.

5 Fill the open end of the tubing with a small amount of **modeling clay.** Use a **toothpick** to make a hole in the center of the clay.

6 Repeat steps 3 and 4.

Analyze and Conclude

1. **Describe** any differences in the flow rate of water with and without clay in the tubes.

2. **Identify** which parts of your model represent blood, blood vessels, and fatty deposits of atherosclerosis.

3. 🔑 **Key Concept** Explain how the presence of fatty deposits could affect the function of the circulatory system.

Circulatory System Health

Good health depends on a healthy circulatory system. Your heart muscle must be strong enough to push blood through all the blood vessels in your body. Your blood vessels must be flexible so that the volume of blood flowing through them can change. The valves in your heart and veins must work properly to keep blood from flowing in the wrong direction.

Circulatory diseases are illnesses that occur when some part of the circulatory system stops working properly. About one-third of all adults in the United States have some form of circulatory disease. Nearly 2,400 people die from it every day.

Hypertension

When the ventricles of the heart contract, they push blood into the arteries. When this happens, the arteries bulge a little. The bulging of an artery is what you feel when you check your pulse. The bulge happens because blood presses against the sides of the artery. That pressure is called blood pressure.

Have you ever had your blood pressure measured? Normal blood pressure is considered to be 120 mm Hg (millimeters of mercury) or less during the contraction of the ventricles. It is 80 mm Hg or less after the contraction. Normal blood pressure can be written as 120/80 mm Hg. Blood pressure higher than 140/90 mm Hg is known as hypertension, or high blood pressure. Hypertension can lead to weakened and less flexible artery walls.

Atherosclerosis

The buildup of fatty material within the walls of arteries is called **atherosclerosis** (a thuh roh skluh ROH sus). Fat deposits can interfere with the artery's blood flow. If a deposit breaks loose, it can flow to and block a narrower artery. A blockage in the heart can cause a heart attack. A blockage in a blood vessel in the brain can cause a stroke.

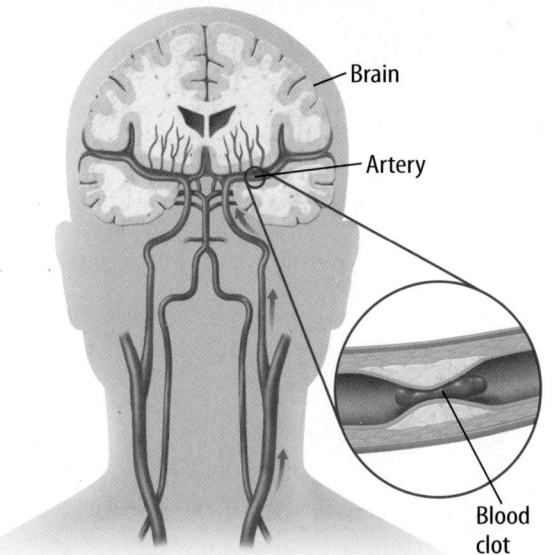

Brain

Artery

Blood clot

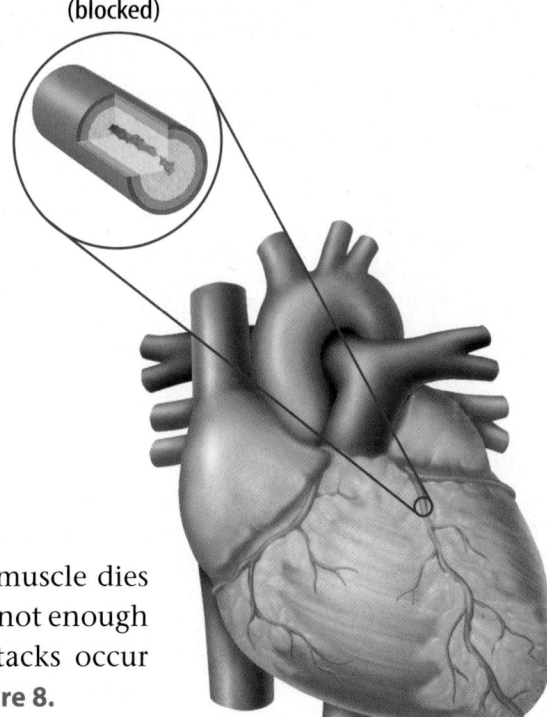

Diseased (blocked)

Heart Attacks, Strokes, and Heart Failure

A heart attack happens when part of the heart muscle dies or is damaged. A heart attack is usually caused when not enough oxygen reaches cells in the heart. Most heart attacks occur when a coronary vessel is blocked, as shown in **Figure 8.**

A stroke happens when part of the brain dies or is damaged. Most strokes are caused when not enough oxygen reaches cells in the brain. A stroke might occur if a blood clot blocks a blood vessel in the brain, also shown in **Figure 8.**

Heart failure occurs when the heart is not working efficiently. It can result from a previous heart attack, a problem with heart valves, or diseases that damage the heart.

Preventing Circulatory System Disorders

Some risk factors for circulatory system diseases cannot be avoided. For example, if one of your parents has a circulatory disease, you might have inherited a slightly higher risk of developing a similar disease. However, most risk **factors** can be controlled by making good life choices, like eating a healthful diet, controlling weight, exercising, and not smoking.

The Circulatory System and Homeostasis

The circulatory system is closely connected with other body systems. Once oxygen enters your body, the respiratory system interacts with the circulatory system and transports oxygen to your body's cells. It also transports nutrients from the digestive system and hormones from the endocrine system. The nervous system regulates your heartbeat. Later in this chapter, you'll read how the circulatory and skeletal systems work together.

Figure 8 Most heart attacks occur when a vessel of the coronary circulation is blocked. Most strokes occur when a blood clot blocks a vessel in the brain.

ACADEMIC VOCABULARY

factor
(***noun***) something that helps produce a result

 Key Concept Check How do the circulatory system and the respiratory system work together to maintain homeostasis?

Visual Summary

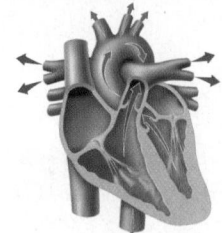

The contractions of the heart push blood through the circulatory system.

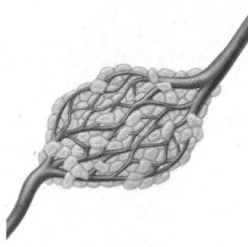

Arteries and veins carry blood throughout the body. Materials move between blood and cells through capillary walls.

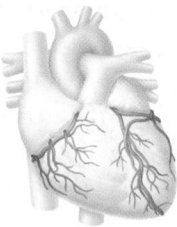

Coronary circulation supplies blood to heart cells.

FOLDABLES

Use your lesson Foldable to review the lesson. Save your Foldable for the project at the end of the chapter.

What do you think NOW?

You first read the statements below at the beginning of the chapter.

3. There are four chambers in a human heart.

4. Blood travels in both directions in veins.

Did you change your mind about whether you agree or disagree with the statements? Rewrite any false statements to make them true.

Use Vocabulary

1. The narrow blood vessels where gas exchange occurs are _____.

2. The two lower chambers of the heart are _____.

3. **Distinguish** between veins and arteries.

Understand Key Concepts 🔑

4. **Explain** how blood keeps flowing continuously through the body.

5. **Illustrate** at least five parts of the heart and the main blood vessels that enter and leave the heart.

6. A blockage of blood vessels in the brain can cause
   A. a heart attack.   C. heart failure.
   B. a stroke.   D. hypertension.

Interpret Graphics

7. **Identify** the artery and the vein in the figure below. Explain your answer.

8. **Summarize** Copy and fill in the graphic organizer below to identify the three types of circulation.

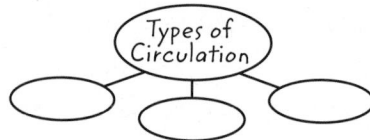

Critical Thinking

9. **Design** a daily schedule that includes at least three lifestyle choices that can help you avoid circulatory system disorders.

10. **Justify** A physician has a patient, age 42, whose blood pressure averages 141/89 mm Hg. Why might the physician recommend healthful life choices to the patient?

How strong is your heart muscle?

Materials

plastic basin

turkey baster bulb

stopwatch

Safety

Your heart is a muscle that beats about 75 times every minute. With each beat, it pushes about 60 mL of blood into your arteries. Heart muscle cells differ from skeletal muscle cells. Heart muscle cells have about 35 percent more mitochondria than skeletal muscle cells do. More mitochondria means that a heart cell can obtain more energy from the nutrients it receives. Can you use the skeletal muscles in your hand to pump liquid as fast as your heart pumps blood—without getting tired?

Learn It

To **infer** means to reach a conclusion based on facts. Your heart beats continuously to keep blood flowing through your body. Modeling the function of the heart can help you infer how hard your heart works.

Try It

1. Read and complete a lab safety form.

2. Fill a plastic basin with enough water to cover your fist.

3. Remove the bulb from a turkey baster. Hold the bulb in your fist and submerge it completely in the water. Move slowly to avoid spilling water.

4. Aim the opening of the bulb toward the side of the basin. Let the bulb fill with water.

5. Squeeze the bulb repeatedly as quickly as you can to simulate the beating of your heart.

6. Have a partner count the number of times you squeeze the bulb. Have another partner time the experiment.

7. Continue the squeezing action for as long as you can, but not more than 3 minutes. Record the number of squeezes and the time in your Science Journal.

8. Repeat steps 3–7 for all the students in your group.

Apply It

9. **Describe** how your hand felt at the end of the experiment.

10. **Compare** how tired your hand muscles got with how tired you think your heart muscle is after the same number of beats.

11. **Calculate** Suppose a man who lives to the age of 80 has an average heart rate of 75 beats per minute. About how many times would his heart beat in his lifetime?

12. **Key Concept** Infer which type of muscle, heart or skeletal, is able to perform more consistently without tiring.

Lesson 3

Reading Guide

Key Concepts
ESSENTIAL QUESTIONS

- What does the blood do?
- How do the parts of the blood differ?

Vocabulary

platelet p. 579

plasma p. 579

Rh factor p. 581

g **Multilingual eGlossary**

Blood

Inquiry Working Hard?

You might have noticed that the cheeks of some people turn bright red during vigorous exercise. Why does this happen? The red color comes from blood flowing near the surface of the skin. It helps release excess thermal energy from the body. What else does your blood do?

What do blood cells look like?

Like every tissue in your body, blood is a tissue made of different cells. Take a look in the microscope to see the different types of blood cells.

1 Read and complete a lab safety form.

2 Observe a **prepared blood smear slide** under low power on a **microscope.**

3 Switch to high power, and observe the different cell types on the slide. In your Science Journal, draw one example of each type of cell you see.

4 Return to low power, and remove the slide.

Think About This

1. How many kinds of cells did you observe? How did their appearances differ?

2. **Key Concept** Why do you think there are different kinds of blood cells?

Functions of Blood

Have you ever had an injury that caused bleeding? Blood is a red liquid, slightly thicker than water. At the end of Lesson 2 you read that your circulatory system works closely with all your other body systems to maintain homeostasis. Blood is the link that connects the circulatory system with all other body systems. Blood transports substances throughout your body, helps protect your body against infection, and helps regulate your body's temperature.

Transportation

Blood transports many different substances throughout your body. You've read that blood carries oxygen to and carbon dioxide from the lungs. Blood also picks up nutrients in the small intestine and carries them to all body cells. It transports hormones produced by the endocrine system. Blood also carries waste products to the excretory system. Most of the substances carried in blood are dissolved in the liquid part of blood.

Protection

Some blood cells fight infection. They help protect you from harmful organisms, such as bacteria, viruses, fungi, and parasites. Blood also contains materials that help repair torn blood vessels and heal wounds. These materials help protect the body from losing too much blood.

Temperature Regulation

Blood helps your body maintain a steady temperature of about 37°C. When your body temperature rises, blood vessels near the surface of your skin widen. This increases blood flow to your skin's surface and releases more thermal energy to the air. Your body cools down. When your body temperature lowers, the vessels at your skin's surface get narrower. This decreases blood flow to the surface of your skin and reduces the amount of thermal energy that is lost to the air. Your body warms up.

 Key Concept Check What does the blood do?

Parts of Blood

Blood is considered a tissue because it is made up of different kinds of cells that work together. As shown in **Figure 9,** blood consists of four main parts: red blood cells, white blood cells, platelets, and plasma. Most adults have about 70 mL of blood per kilogram of body weight. An average adult has about five to six liters of blood.

Red Blood Cells

Every cubic millimeter of your blood contains four to six million red blood cells, or erythrocytes (ih RIHTH ruh sites). Red blood cells contain hemoglobin (HEE muh gloh bun), iron-rich protein molecules. In the alveoli of the lungs, oxygen binds to the hemoglobin in red blood cells. The hemoglobin releases the oxygen when red blood cells enter the capillaries and come into close contact with body cells.

How would you describe the shape of the red blood cells in **Figure 9?** Some people describe them as a doughnut without a hole. This flattened disk shape gives them more surface area. This means red blood cells can carry more oxygen than if they were round like a ball. Your body produces new red blood cells all the time because they wear out in a few months.

White Blood Cells

Your blood also contains several kinds of white blood cells, or leukocytes (LEW kuh sites), shown in **Figure 9.** All white blood cells protect your body from illness and infection. Some attack viruses, bacteria, fungi, and parasites that might invade your body. Most white blood cells last only a few days and are constantly replaced. You have far fewer white blood cells—5,000 to 10,000 per cubic millimeter—than red blood cells.

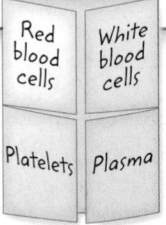
Figure 9 Blood flows through blood vessels. It is made of liquid plasma, red blood cells, white blood cells, and platelets.

Parts of Blood 🔑

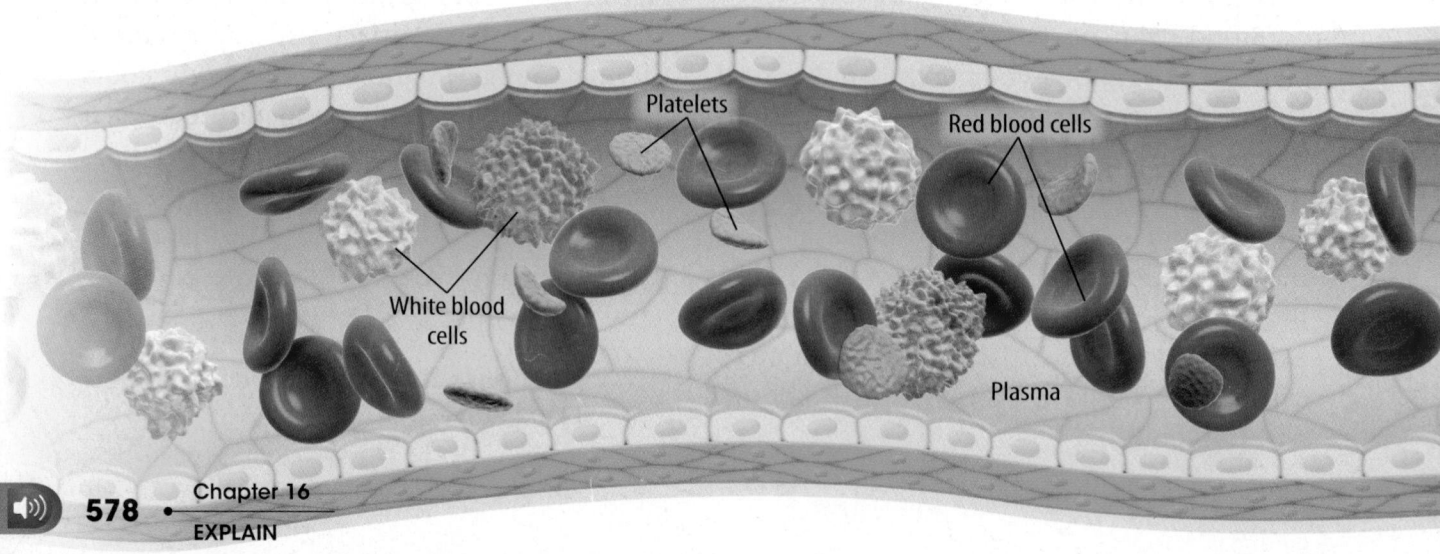

Platelets

Red blood cells

White blood cells

Plasma

Platelets

What happens if you get a cut? The cut bleeds for a short time, and then the blood clots, as shown in **Figure 10**. **Platelets** *are small, irregularly shaped pieces of cells that plug wounds and stop bleeding.* Platelets produce proteins that help strengthen the plug. Without platelets, blood would not stop flowing. Your blood contains 150,000 to 440,000 platelets per cubic millimeter.

Plasma

The yellowish, liquid part of blood, called **plasma,** *transports blood cells.* Plasma is 90 percent water, which helps thin the blood. This enables it to travel through small blood vessels. Many molecules are dissolved in plasma. They include salts, vitamins, sugars, minerals, proteins, and cellular wastes.

Plasma also plays an important role in regulating the activities of cells in your body. For example, plasma carries chemical messengers that control the amounts of salts and glucose that enter cells.

 Key Concept Check How do the parts of blood differ?

Figure 10 When a blood vessel breaks, platelets rush to the wound. They cause the formation of a threadlike protein that makes a net. A blood clot forms as blood cells are trapped in the net.

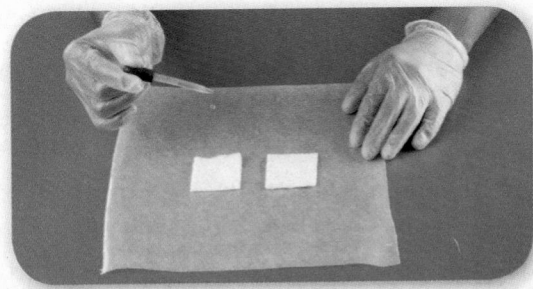 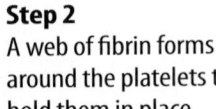
How a Blood Clot Forms

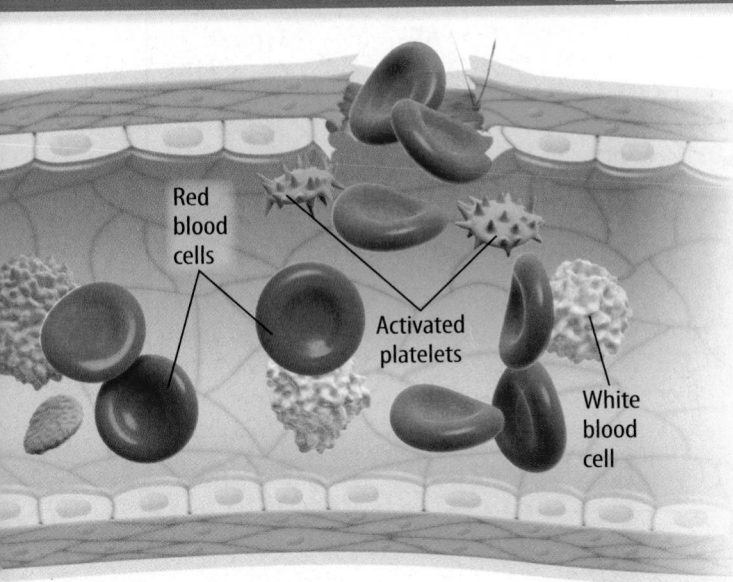

Red blood cells

Activated platelets

White blood cell

Step 1 Platelets rush to the tear and form a plug to stop the bleeding.	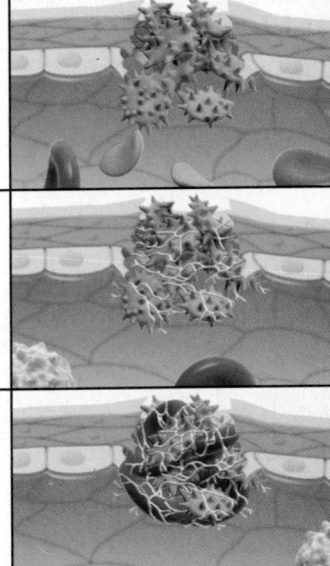
Step 2 A web of fibrin forms around the platelets to hold them in place.	
Step 3 More platelets and red blood cells are caught in the fibrin web, forming a blood clot.	

Blood Types

Do you know anyone who donates blood? Donated blood is used to help people who have lost too much blood from an injury or surgery and need a transfusion. A blood transfusion is the transfer of blood from one person to another. Even though your blood has the same four parts as everyone else's—red cells, white cells, platelets, and plasma—you can't receive blood from just anyone. Why? Because different people have different blood types.

WORD ORIGIN

plasma
from Greek *plassein*, means "to mold"

The ABO System

You inherited your blood type from your parents. Blood type refers to the type of proteins, or antigens, on red blood cells. The four human blood types are A, B, AB, and O. Type A blood cells have the A antigen. Type B cells have the B antigen. Type AB has both A and B antigens. Type O has no antigens.

Why is blood type important? Any time a blood transfusion brings foreign antigens to someone's blood, the red blood cells will clump together and lose their ability to function. Clumps form because of clumping proteins in blood plasma. As shown in **Table 2,** people with types A, B, and O blood have clumping proteins in their plasma. For example, a person with type A blood has anti-B clumping proteins. If given type B blood, his or her anti-B proteins would attack the type B antigens and cause the type B red blood cells to clump together.

Type AB blood has no clumping proteins. People with AB blood are known as "universal recipients" because they can receive transfusions of any blood type. Type O blood has clumping proteins that attack both A and B antigens. People with type O blood are known as "universal donors" because they can donate blood to anyone.

Table 2 People with blood types A, B, and O have clumping proteins in their plasma. These proteins determine what blood type a person can safely receive in a blood transfusion.

Table 2 Human Blood Types
Concepts in Motion Interactive Table

Blood Type	Type A	Type B	Type AB	Type O
Antigens on red blood cells				
Percentage of US population with this blood type	42	10	4	44
Clumping proteins in plasma	Anti-B	Anti-A	None	Anti-A and anti-B
Blood type(s) that can be RECEIVED in a transfusion	A or O	B or O	A or B or AB or O	O only
This blood type can DONATE TO these blood types	A or AB	B or AB	AB only	A or B or AB or O

The Rh Factor

Another protein found on red blood cells is a chemical marker called the **Rh factor.** People with blood cells that have this protein are Rh positive. People who do not have it are Rh negative. If Rh positive blood is mixed with Rh negative blood, clumping can result. Blood types usually have a plus (+) sign or a minus (–) sign to indicate whether a person is Rh positive or negative. For example, a person with an A+ blood type has red cells with A antigens and the Rh factor. Someone with O– blood has no antigens and no Rh factor.

 Reading Check What kinds of antigens are found in AB+ blood?

Blood Disorders

Some medical conditions disrupt the normal functions of blood. People with hemophilia lack a protein needed to clot blood. A person who has hemophilia bleeds at the same rate as other people, but the bleeding does not stop as quickly.

People suffering from anemia have low numbers of red blood cells or have red blood cells that do not contain enough hemoglobin. As a result, the blood might not carry as much oxygen as the body needs.

Bone marrow, the soft tissue in the center of bones, produces red blood cells. Cancer of the bone marrow is called leukemia. This kind of cancer can slow or prevent blood cell formation. Leukemia can lead to anemia and a damaged immune system.

People who inherit sickle-cell disease have red blood cells shaped like crescents, as shown in **Figure 11.** Sickle-shaped cells do not move through blood vessels as easily as normal disk-shaped cells. Sickle cells can prevent oxygen from reaching tissues and cause sickle-cell anemia.

Math Skills

Use Percentages

If percentages refer to the same factor, they can be added or subtracted. For example, you could add the percentages of people with each of the four blood types:

42% + 10% + 4% + 44% = 100%

You could also subtract to find what percentage of people do not have type O blood:

100% – 44% = 56%

Practice

Forty-four percent of people have type O blood. If 7 percent of people have type O blood and are Rh negative, what percent has type O Rh positive blood?

 **Review**

- **Math Practice**
- **Personal Tutor**

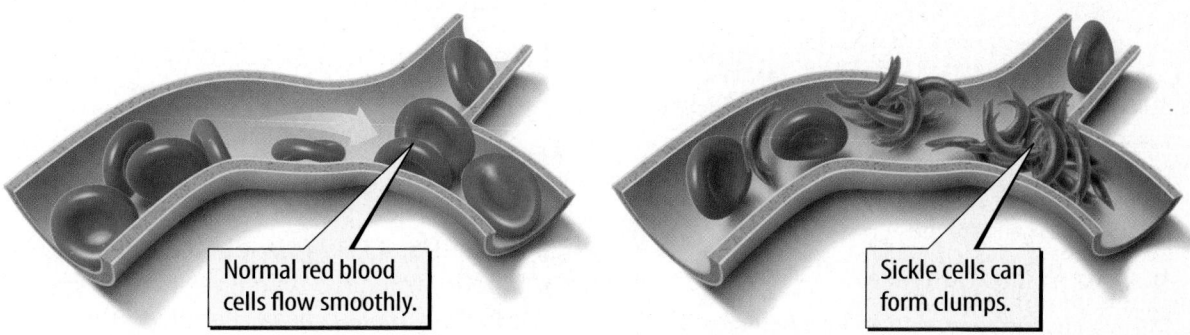

Normal red blood cells flow smoothly.

Sickle cells can form clumps.

Figure 11 The crescent-shaped red blood cells in sickle-cell disorder form clumps that can block blood vessels.

Lesson 3 Review

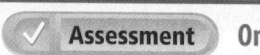

Visual Summary

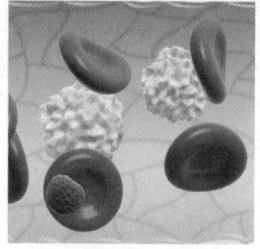

Red blood cells contain hemoglobin and carry oxygen. White blood cells help fight disease.

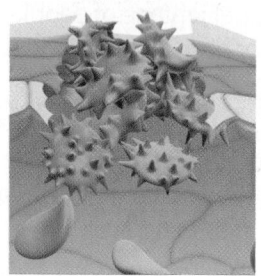

Platelets are pieces of cells that aid in blood clotting.

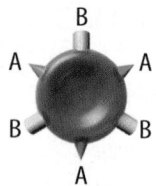

Blood type is determined by antigens on the surface of red blood cells and clumping proteins in blood plasma.

FOLDABLES

Use your lesson Foldable to review the lesson. Save your Foldable for the project at the end of the chapter.

What do you think NOW?

You first read the statements below at the beginning of the chapter.

5. All blood cells are red.

6. Blood plasma is just water.

Did you change your mind about whether you agree or disagree with the statements? Rewrite any false statements to make them true.

Use Vocabulary

1 **Identify** the yellowish liquid part of blood.

2 **Distinguish** between plasma and platelets.

3 **Define** the term *Rh factor* using your own words.

Understand Key Concepts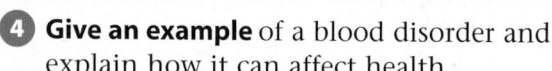

4 **Give an example** of a blood disorder and explain how it can affect health.

5 Which part of the blood carries dissolved molecules such as glucose and salt?
   A. plasma
   B. platelets
   C. red blood cells
   D. white blood cells

Interpret Graphics

6 What blood type is shown below? What blood type(s) can a person with this blood type receive in a transfusion?

7 **Organize Information** Copy the table below and list the parts of blood and their functions.

Part of Blood	Functions

Critical Thinking

8 **Design** a model to show how blood can help regulate body temperature.

Math Skills

—— Math Practice ——

9 In the US, 42% of people have type A blood, 10% have type B, 4% have type AB, and 44% have type O. People with type B and type AB blood can receive type B blood. What percentage of people can receive transfusions of type B blood?

Very Special Blood Cells

Horseshoe crabs, living relatives of extinct trilobites, have been gathering on beaches for 350 million years. They usually become food for fish and birds. Yet someday your life might depend on horseshoe crabs—or at least on their blood. Unlike human blood, horseshoe crab blood contains only one type of blood cell. If bacteria enter the crab's bloodstream from an open wound, blood cells secrete a clotting factor. This secretion closes the wound, and the blood cells engulf the bacteria. When scientists saw that horseshoe crab blood turned to a gel in the presence of harmful bacteria, they realized its value. Today, medical professionals use an extract made from horseshoe crab blood to screen all intravenous medicines for bacteria. A quart of this special blood costs about $15,000!

The horseshoe crab blood can do even more. Another component of the blood can stop the human immunodeficiency virus (HIV) from replicating, or making copies of itself. Part of horseshoe crab blood can act as an antibiotic. Scientists also are using horseshoe crab blood in the development of a hand-held instrument that helps to diagnose human illnesses. The instrument uses enzymes from the blood as illness detectors.

▲ Technicians remove only a small portion of the crabs' blood. After this procedure, the crabs are returned to the ocean. Their blood cell levels return to normal in a couple of weeks.

It's Your Turn

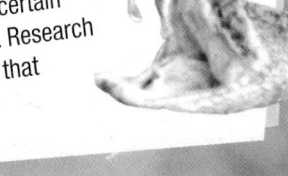

REPORT Medical professionals use certain types of snake venom to treat strokes. Research to find other unusual animal products that have medical uses.

The Lymphatic System

Reading Guide

Key Concepts
ESSENTIAL QUESTIONS

- What does the lymphatic system do?
- How do the parts of the lymphatic system work together?
- How does the lymphatic system interact with other body systems?

Vocabulary

lymphatic system p. 585
lymph p. 586
lymph node p. 586
thymus p. 587
spleen p. 587

g Multilingual eGlossary

Inquiry Healthy or Not?

Do you know anyone who has had his or her tonsils removed? Tonsils are clusters of lymph tissue that help the body fight off disease. Why do tonsils sometimes get swollen and inflamed, like the ones shown here? Knowing how the lymphatic system works will help you answer that question.

Launch Lab

How can you model a lymph node?

Fluid surrounds your body cells. Body cells absorb materials from and release materials into this fluid. Some of the fluid drains into vessels and then drains into spongy structures called lymph nodes. What happens in the lymph nodes?

1. Read and complete a lab safety form.

2. Observe a **liquid** provided by your teacher. Record the observations in your Science Journal.

3. Use a **rubber band** to attach a square of **cheesecloth** to a **plastic drinking straw.** Hold the straw upright over a **paper plate.**

4. Use a **plastic dropper** to squeeze about 1 mL of the liquid into the open end of the straw.

5. Allow the liquid to drain from the cheesecloth and onto the plate. Observe the liquid. Record the observations in your Science Journal.

Think About This

1. What differences did you observe in the liquid after it passed through the cheesecloth?

2. 🔑 **Key Concept** What do you think the function of the lymph nodes might be?

Functions of the Lymphatic System

At times when you were sick, you might have noticed small, swollen structures under your jaw on each side of your neck. These structures can become swollen when they're working to fight off an infection in your body.

*The **lymphatic system** is part of the immune system and helps destroy microorganisms that enter the body.* The lymphatic system works closely with the circulatory system. Both systems move liquids through the body, and both contain white blood cells. However, their functions are different. There are four main functions of the lymphatic system.

- It absorbs some of the tissue fluid that collects around cells.

- It absorbs fats from the digestive system and transports them to the circulatory system.

- It filters dead cells, viruses, bacteria, and other unneeded particles from tissue fluid and then returns the tissue fluid to the circulatory system.

- It helps fight off illness and infections and includes structures in which white blood cells develop.

✓ **Key Concept Check** What does the lymphatic system do?

FOLDABLES

Fold a sheet of paper into an eight-page book. Use it to organize your notes about the parts of the lymphatic system and their functions.

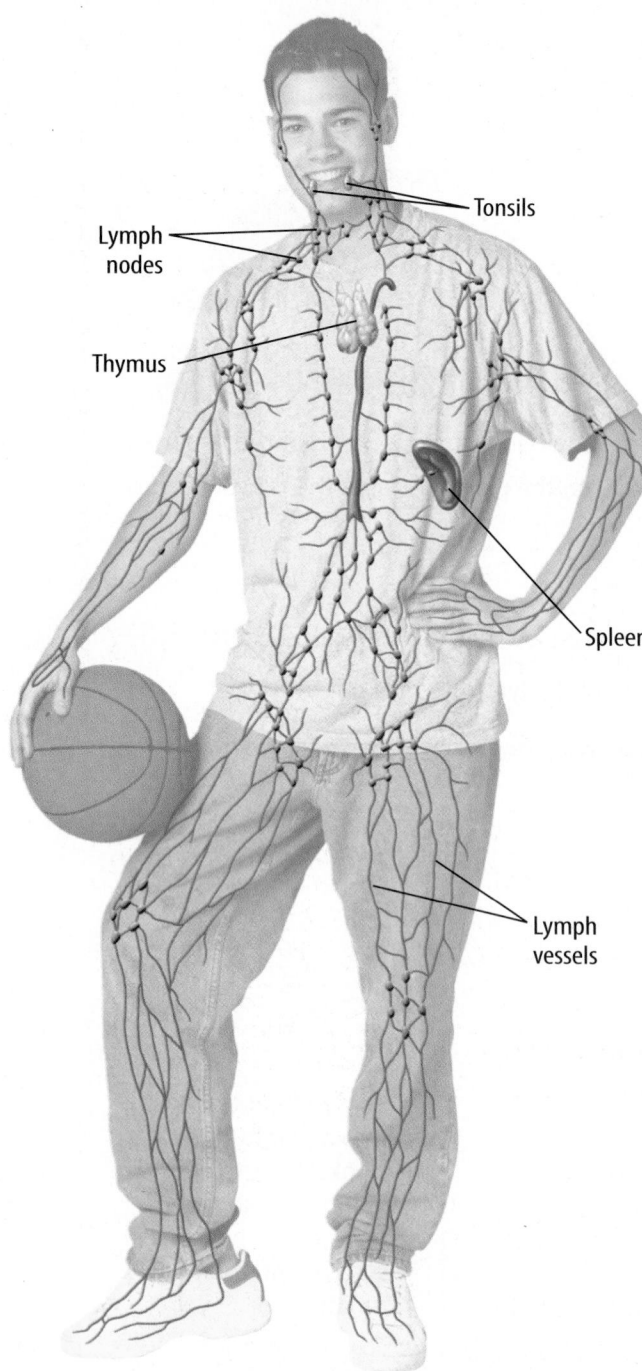

Tonsils

Lymph
nodes

Thymus

Spleen

Lymph
vessels

Figure 12 The lymphatic system is a network of vessels and organs. Vessels transport lymph. When it reaches the area beneath the collarbone, it re-enters the circulatory system.

Visual Check What organs of the lymphatic system are in the throat?

Parts of the Lymphatic System

The lymphatic system, shown in **Figure 12**, includes lymph vessels and the fluid they carry. It also includes several other structures.

Lymph

Water, white blood cells, and dissolved materials such as salts and glucose leak out of capillary walls and into the spaces that surround tissue cells. This fluid is called tissue fluid. Cells absorb the materials they need from tissue fluid and release wastes into it. About 90 percent of the tissue fluid is reabsorbed by the capillaries. *About 10 percent of the tissue fluid is absorbed by the lymph vessels and is called* **lymph.**

Reading Check What is lymph?

Lymph Vessels

The lymphatic system forms a network of lymph vessels that look similar to the circulatory system's network of blood vessels. Lymph vessels absorb and transport lymph. The lymph is pushed through the lymph vessels by contractions of the muscles you use to move your body. Lymph is not pumped through the lymph vessels by the heart.

Lymph Nodes

Lymph vessels include *clusters of small, spongy structures called* **lymph nodes** *that filter particles from lymph.* Bacteria, viruses, fungi, and pieces of dead cells are trapped and removed from the lymph as it flows through a lymph node. Lymph nodes also store white blood cells that attack and destroy the trapped particles.

Large groups of lymph nodes are in the neck, the groin, and the armpits. When you have an infection, your body increases its production of white blood cells that fight the infection. Many of these white blood cells gather in your lymph nodes and cause the nodes to swell. The swelling disappears when the infection is gone.

How strong is your heart muscle?

Materials

plastic basin

turkey baster bulb

stopwatch

Safety

Your heart is a muscle that beats about 75 times every minute. With each beat, it pushes about 60 mL of blood into your arteries. Heart muscle cells differ from skeletal muscle cells. Heart muscle cells have about 35 percent more mitochondria than skeletal muscle cells do. More mitochondria means that a heart cell can obtain more energy from the nutrients it receives. Can you use the skeletal muscles in your hand to pump liquid as fast as your heart pumps blood—without getting tired?

Learn It

To **infer** means to reach a conclusion based on facts. Your heart beats continuously to keep blood flowing through your body. Modeling the function of the heart can help you infer how hard your heart works.

Try It

1. Read and complete a lab safety form.

2. Fill a plastic basin with enough water to cover your fist.

3. Remove the bulb from a turkey baster. Hold the bulb in your fist and submerge it completely in the water. Move slowly to avoid spilling water.

4. Aim the opening of the bulb toward the side of the basin. Let the bulb fill with water.

5. Squeeze the bulb repeatedly as quickly as you can to simulate the beating of your heart.

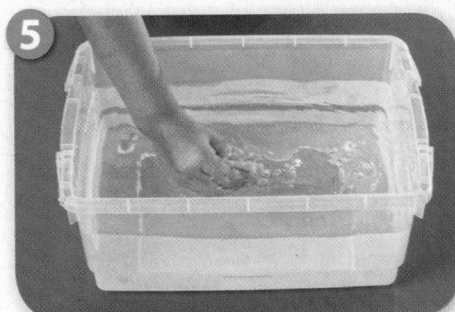

6. Have a partner count the number of times you squeeze the bulb. Have another partner time the experiment.

7. Continue the squeezing action for as long as you can, but not more than 3 minutes. Record the number of squeezes and the time in your Science Journal.

8. Repeat steps 3–7 for all the students in your group.

Apply It

9. **Describe** how your hand felt at the end of the experiment.

10. **Compare** how tired your hand muscles got with how tired you think your heart muscle is after the same number of beats.

11. **Calculate** Suppose a man who lives to the age of 80 has an average heart rate of 75 beats per minute. About how many times would his heart beat in his lifetime?

12. 🔑 **Key Concept** Infer which type of muscle, heart or skeletal, is able to perform more consistently without tiring.

Lesson 3

Reading Guide

Key Concepts
ESSENTIAL QUESTIONS

- What does the blood do?
- How do the parts of the blood differ?

Vocabulary

platelet p. 579

plasma p. 579

Rh factor p. 581

g Multilingual eGlossary

Blood

Inquiry Working Hard?

You might have noticed that the cheeks of some people turn bright red during vigorous exercise. Why does this happen? The red color comes from blood flowing near the surface of the skin. It helps release excess thermal energy from the body. What else does your blood do?

What do blood cells look like?

Like every tissue in your body, blood is a tissue made of different cells. Take a look in the microscope to see the different types of blood cells.

1. Read and complete a lab safety form.
2. Observe a **prepared blood smear slide** under low power on a **microscope.**
3. Switch to high power, and observe the different cell types on the slide. In your Science Journal, draw one example of each type of cell you see.
4. Return to low power, and remove the slide.

Think About This

1. How many kinds of cells did you observe? How did their appearances differ?

2. **Key Concept** Why do you think there are different kinds of blood cells?

Functions of Blood

Have you ever had an injury that caused bleeding? Blood is a red liquid, slightly thicker than water. At the end of Lesson 2 you read that your circulatory system works closely with all your other body systems to maintain homeostasis. Blood is the link that connects the circulatory system with all other body systems. Blood transports substances throughout your body, helps protect your body against infection, and helps regulate your body's temperature.

Transportation

Blood transports many different substances throughout your body. You've read that blood carries oxygen to and carbon dioxide from the lungs. Blood also picks up nutrients in the small intestine and carries them to all body cells. It transports hormones produced by the endocrine system. Blood also carries waste products to the excretory system. Most of the substances carried in blood are dissolved in the liquid part of blood.

Protection

Some blood cells fight infection. They help protect you from harmful organisms, such as bacteria, viruses, fungi, and parasites. Blood also contains materials that help repair torn blood vessels and heal wounds. These materials help protect the body from losing too much blood.

Temperature Regulation

Blood helps your body maintain a steady temperature of about 37°C. When your body temperature rises, blood vessels near the surface of your skin widen. This increases blood flow to your skin's surface and releases more thermal energy to the air. Your body cools down. When your body temperature lowers, the vessels at your skin's surface get narrower. This decreases blood flow to the surface of your skin and reduces the amount of thermal energy that is lost to the air. Your body warms up.

 Key Concept Check What does the blood do?

Parts of Blood

Blood is considered a tissue because it is made up of different kinds of cells that work together. As shown in **Figure 9**, blood consists of four main parts: red blood cells, white blood cells, platelets, and plasma. Most adults have about 70 mL of blood per kilogram of body weight. An average adult has about five to six liters of blood.

Red Blood Cells

Every cubic millimeter of your blood contains four to six million red blood cells, or erythrocytes (ih RIHTH ruh sites). Red blood cells contain hemoglobin (HEE muh gloh bun), iron-rich protein molecules. In the alveoli of the lungs, oxygen binds to the hemoglobin in red blood cells. The hemoglobin releases the oxygen when red blood cells enter the capillaries and come into close contact with body cells.

How would you describe the shape of the red blood cells in **Figure 9?** Some people describe them as a doughnut without a hole. This flattened disk shape gives them more surface area. This means red blood cells can carry more oxygen than if they were round like a ball. Your body produces new red blood cells all the time because they wear out in a few months.

White Blood Cells

Your blood also contains several kinds of white blood cells, or leukocytes (LEW kuh sites), shown in **Figure 9.** All white blood cells protect your body from illness and infection. Some attack viruses, bacteria, fungi, and parasites that might invade your body. Most white blood cells last only a few days and are constantly replaced. You have far fewer white blood cells—5,000 to 10,000 per cubic millimeter—than red blood cells.

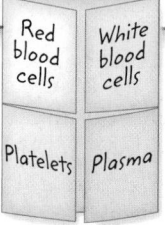
Figure 9 Blood flows through blood vessels. It is made of liquid plasma, red blood cells, white blood cells, and platelets.

Parts of Blood 🔑

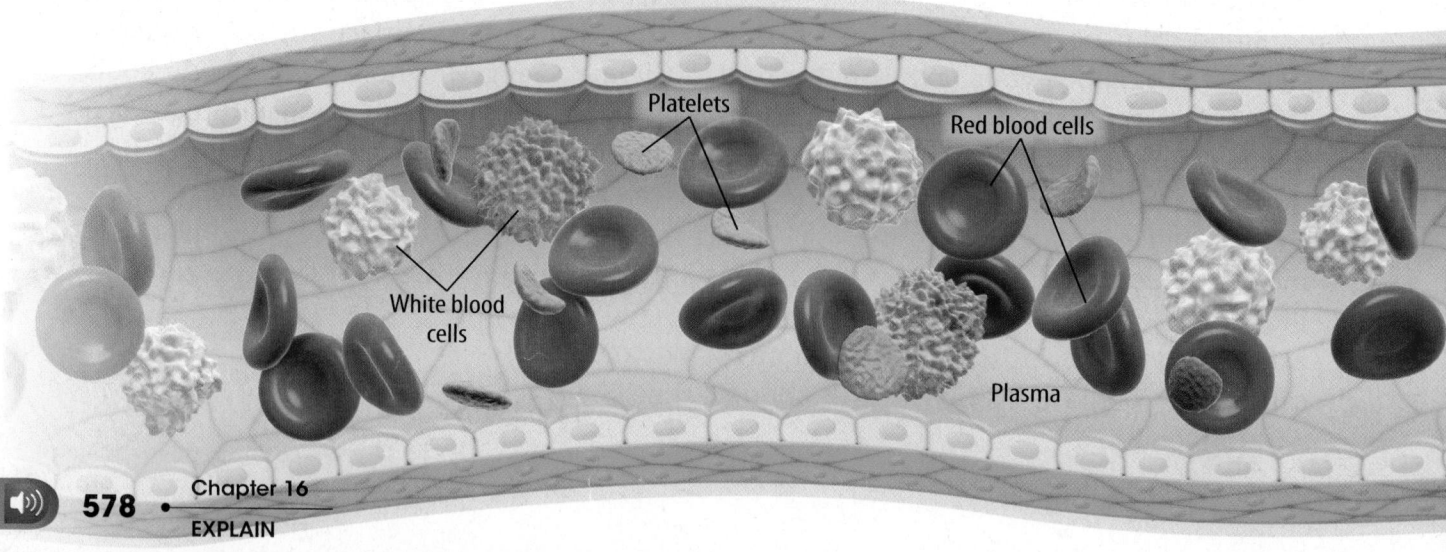

Platelets

Red blood cells

White blood cells

Plasma

Platelets

What happens if you get a cut? The cut bleeds for a short time, and then the blood clots, as shown in **Figure 10**. **Platelets** *are small, irregularly shaped pieces of cells that plug wounds and stop bleeding.* Platelets produce proteins that help strengthen the plug. Without platelets, blood would not stop flowing. Your blood contains 150,000 to 440,000 platelets per cubic millimeter.

Plasma

The yellowish, liquid part of blood, called **plasma,** *transports blood cells.* Plasma is 90 percent water, which helps thin the blood. This enables it to travel through small blood vessels. Many molecules are dissolved in plasma. They include salts, vitamins, sugars, minerals, proteins, and cellular wastes.

Plasma also plays an important role in regulating the activities of cells in your body. For example, plasma carries chemical messengers that control the amounts of salts and glucose that enter cells.

 Key Concept Check How do the parts of blood differ?

Figure 10 When a blood vessel breaks, platelets rush to the wound. They cause the formation of a threadlike protein that makes a net. A blood clot forms as blood cells are trapped in the net.

Inquiry MiniLab  **20 minutes**

How does a cut heal?

How does a scab help a cut stop bleeding? Use gauze and liquid bandage to find out.

1. Read and complete a lab safety form.

2. Place two 5-cm square pieces of **gauze** side by side on a piece of **waxed paper.**

3. Make a 2-cm circle of **liquid bandage** in the center of one piece of gauze. Allow it to dry for 5 minutes.

4. Use a **plastic dropper** to place a drop of **water** in the center of each piece of gauze.

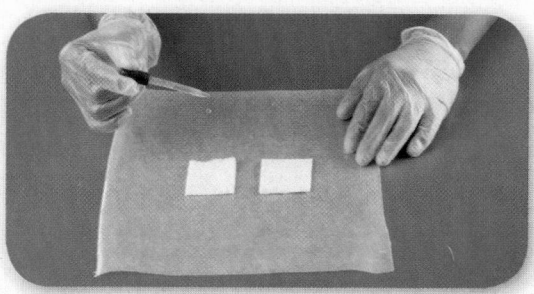

Analyze and Conclude

1. **Compare** what happened to the drop of water on each piece of gauze.

2. **Identify** which piece of gauze best models a scab. Explain why you think so.

3. **Key Concept** Explain how blood helps heal cuts in the skin.

How a Blood Clot Forms

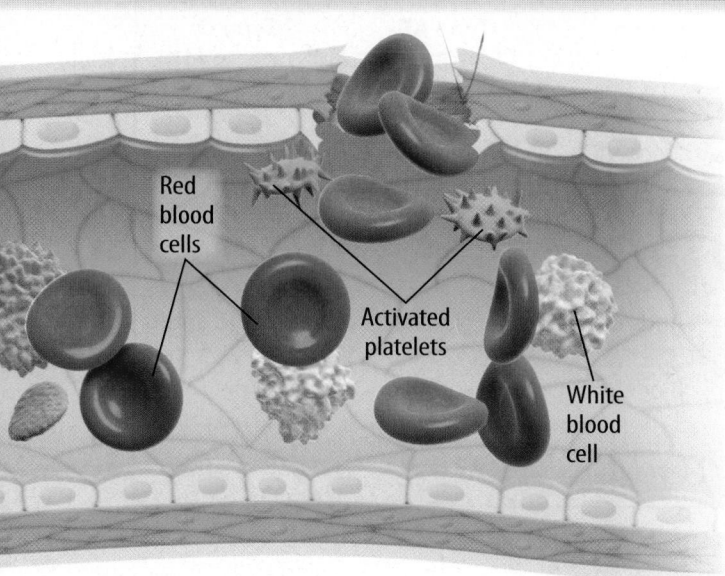

Red blood cells

Activated platelets

White blood cell

Step 1
Platelets rush to the tear and form a plug to stop the bleeding.

Step 2
A web of fibrin forms around the platelets to hold them in place.

Step 3
More platelets and red blood cells are caught in the fibrin web, forming a blood clot.

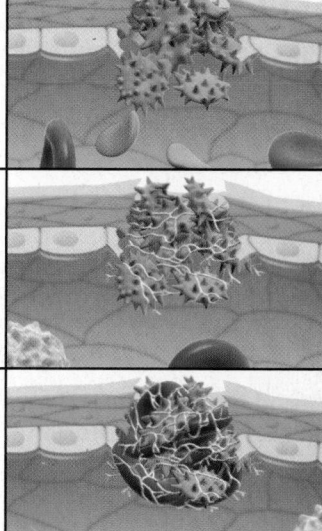

How can you model a lymph node?

Fluid surrounds your body cells. Body cells absorb materials from and release materials into this fluid. Some of the fluid drains into vessels and then drains into spongy structures called lymph nodes. What happens in the lymph nodes?

1 Read and complete a lab safety form.

2 Observe a **liquid** provided by your teacher. Record the observations in your Science Journal.

3 Use a **rubber band** to attach a square of **cheesecloth** to a **plastic drinking straw.** Hold the straw upright over a **paper plate.**

4 Use a **plastic dropper** to squeeze about 1 mL of the liquid into the open end of the straw.

5 Allow the liquid to drain from the cheesecloth and onto the plate. Observe the liquid. Record the observations in your Science Journal.

Think About This

1. What differences did you observe in the liquid after it passed through the cheesecloth?

2. **Key Concept** What do you think the function of the lymph nodes might be?

Functions of the Lymphatic System

At times when you were sick, you might have noticed small, swollen structures under your jaw on each side of your neck. These structures can become swollen when they're working to fight off an infection in your body.

The **lymphatic system** *is part of the immune system and helps destroy microorganisms that enter the body.* The lymphatic system works closely with the circulatory system. Both systems move liquids through the body, and both contain white blood cells. However, their functions are different. There are four main functions of the lymphatic system.

• It absorbs some of the tissue fluid that collects around cells.

• It absorbs fats from the digestive system and transports them to the circulatory system.

• It filters dead cells, viruses, bacteria, and other unneeded particles from tissue fluid and then returns the tissue fluid to the circulatory system.

• It helps fight off illness and infections and includes structures in which white blood cells develop.

Key Concept Check What does the lymphatic system do?

FOLDABLES

Fold a sheet of paper into an eight-page book. Use it to organize your notes about the parts of the lymphatic system and their functions.

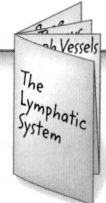

Bone Marrow and Thymus

Lymphocytes (LIHM fuh sites) are white blood cells that destroy pathogens—infection-causing microorganisms such as viruses and bacteria. Bone marrow is the spongy center of bones where red and white blood cells, including lymphocytes, form. Lymphocytes include B cells and T cells. As shown in **Figure 13,** B cells mature in the bone marrow, and T cells mature in the thymus gland.

The **thymus** *is the organ of the lymphatic system in which T cells complete their development.* After immature T cells move from the bone marrow to the thymus, they develop the ability to recognize and destroy body cells that have been infected by microorganisms. Mature B cells and T cells move into the lymph and blood to help fight infection.

 Key Concept Check How do bone marrow and the thymus work together?

Spleen

You read earlier that the life of a red blood cell is only a few months. *The* **spleen** *is an organ of the lymphatic system that recycles worn-out red blood cells and produces and stores lymphocytes.* The spleen also stores blood and platelets. If a person is injured and loses a lot of blood, the spleen can release stored blood and platelets into the circulatory system.

WORD ORIGIN

lymph
from Latin *lympha,* means "water"

Figure 13 Lymphocytes attack and destroy disease-causing microorganisms. B cells mature in the bone marrow. T cells mature in the thymus.

Where Lymphocytes Mature

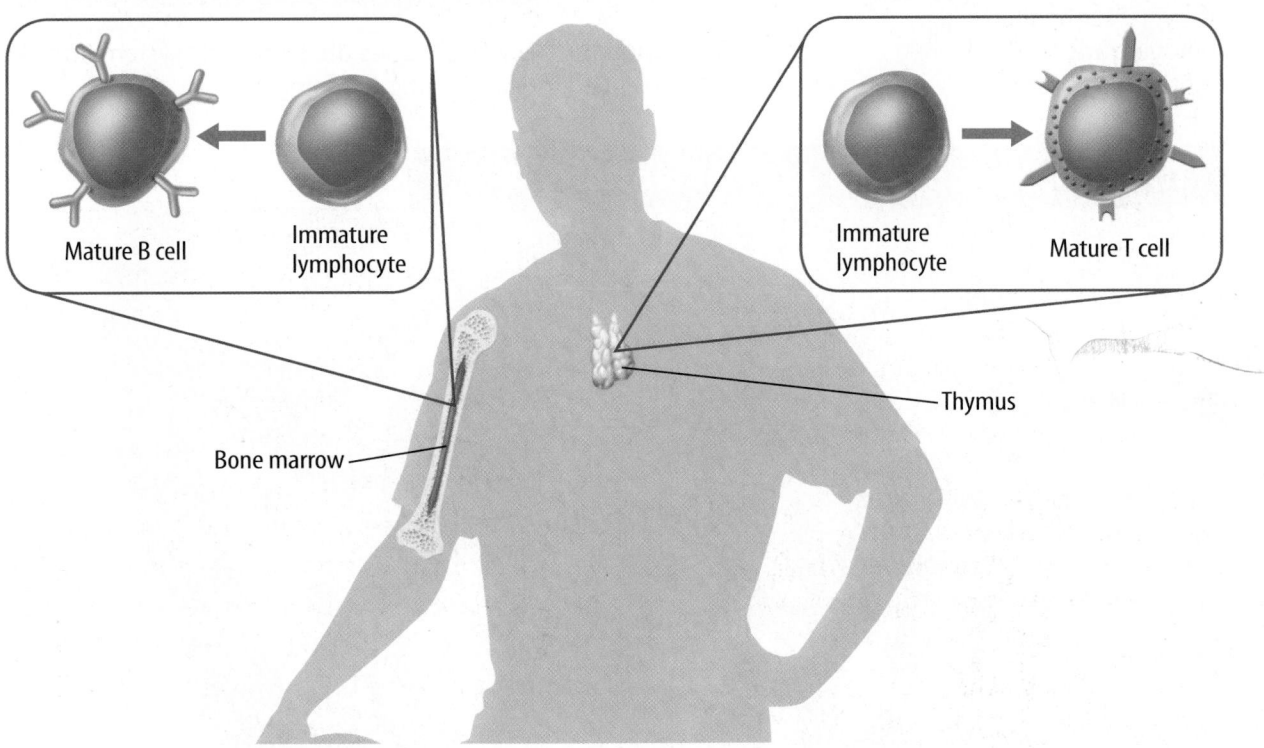

Mature B cell

Immature lymphocyte

Immature lymphocyte

Mature T cell

Thymus

Bone marrow

Tonsils

Your tonsils are clusters of lymph tissue on the sides of your throat. They help protect your body from infection by trapping and destroying bacteria and other pathogens that enter your nose and mouth. However, you can live without tonsils.

Lymph Diseases and Disorders

Damage to the lymphatic system from injury or surgery can prevent tissue fluid from draining into lymph **vessels.** As a result, tissue fluid can build up around cells and cause swelling. Recall that the action of your body muscles pushes lymph through the lymph vessels. Inactivity can also cause lymph buildup and swelling.

Do you recall the swollen tonsils shown at the beginning of this lesson? If the cells of your tonsils become infected, you have tonsillitis—an inflammation of the tonsils.

The uncontrolled production of white blood cells is a type of cancer called lymphoma. Cancer of the lymph nodes is a related disease called Hodgkin's lymphoma.

The Lymphatic System and Homeostasis

The lymphatic system helps maintain your body's homeostasis by regulating fluid buildup around cells, as shown in **Figure 14.** It supports the circulatory system by cleaning fluids and replacing them in the bloodstream. It also supports overall health by helping to fight infection throughout the body.

 Key Concept Check How does the lymphatic system interact with the circulatory and immune systems?

SCIENCE USE v. COMMON USE

vessel
Science Use a tube through which a body fluid travels

Common Use a container for holding something

Figure 14 The lymphatic system helps maintain the body's homeostasis by preventing the buildup of excess tissue fluid, removing wastes, and fighting infection.

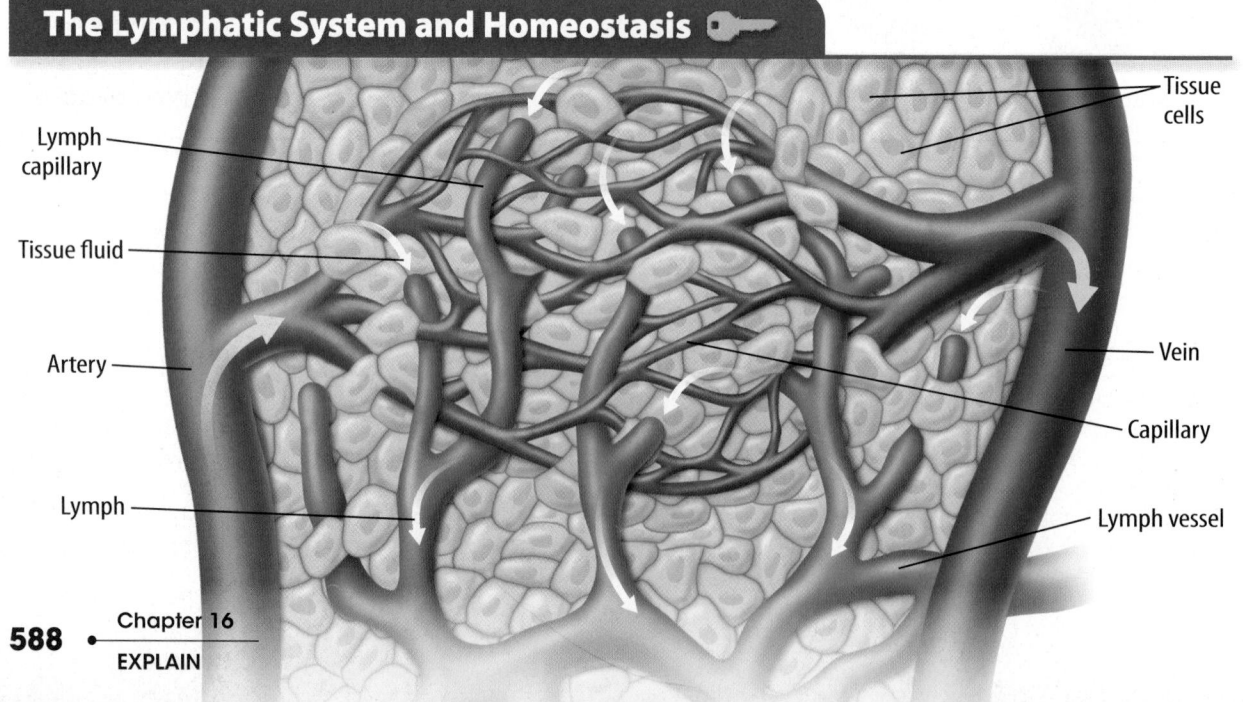

The Lymphatic System and Homeostasis

Lymph capillary

Tissue fluid

Artery

Lymph

Tissue cells

Vein

Capillary

Lymph vessel

Lesson 4 Review

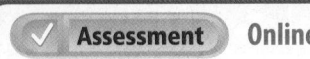

Visual Summary

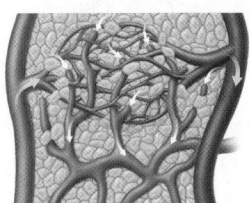

Tissue fluid that drains into the lymph vessels becomes lymph.

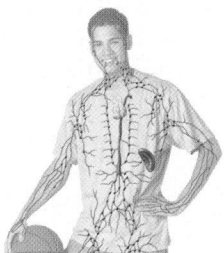

The lymphatic system consists of lymph nodes, lymph vessels, lymph, and several other organs.

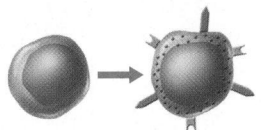

The lymphatic system cleans lymph, fights infection, and includes structures in which white blood cells develop.

FOLDABLES®

Use your lesson Foldable to review the lesson. Save your Foldable for the project at the end of the chapter.

What do you think NOW?

You first read the statements below at the beginning of the chapter.

7. Lymph nodes are only in the neck.

8. The lymphatic system helps fight infections to maintain a healthy body.

Did you change your mind about whether you agree or disagree with the statements? Rewrite any false statements to make them true.

Use Vocabulary

1 **Define** the term *lymph*.

2 **Distinguish** between the spleen and the thymus.

3 Clusters of small, spongy structures that filter particles from lymph are called _____ _____.

Understand Key Concepts

4 **Describe** the function of the lymph nodes.

5 **Distinguish** between lymph and tissue fluid.

6 The lymphatic system cleans fluid for which system?
   A. circulatory   C. immune
   B. digestive   D. respiratory

Interpret Graphics

7 **Identify** the structures of the lymphatic system shown in the figure below.

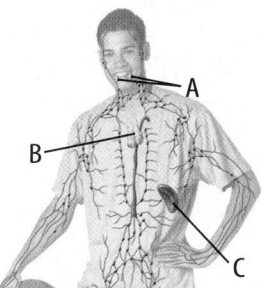

8 **Summarize** Copy and fill in the graphic organizer below to identify the functions of the lymphatic system.

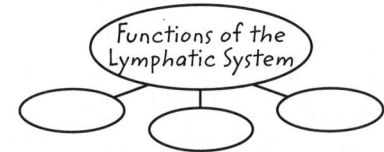

Critical Thinking

9 **Synthesis** Design a three-dimensional model of the lymphatic system.

10 **Evaluate** In what ways are the circulatory and lymphatic systems similar? In what ways are they different?

Materials

Model of blood

Paper plates

Safety

Using a Blood Count to Evaluate Health

You are a physician who uses blood test results to help evaluate the health of your patients. One of the most common blood tests is a complete blood count, or CBC. A CBC measures the number of red blood cells, white blood cells, and platelets in a small sample of a person's blood. As a physician, you can use the results of a CBC to tell whether your patient is healthy or might have health problems.

Ask a Question

What do the results of a CBC tell you about your patient's health status?

Make Observations

1 Read and complete a lab safety form.

2 Obtain a bag of beans representing a blood sample from a healthy patient. This is your control sample. Red beans represent red blood cells, white beans represent white blood cells, and lentils represent platelets.

⚠ *Do not put beans or lentils in your mouth.*

3 In your Science Journal, make a data table like the one below to record your data.

4 Count the number of each type of blood cell in the sample. Calculate the percentage of each type of blood cell in your sample. Record your data.

Form a Hypothesis

5 After looking at the data you collected, form a hypothesis about the relationship between the percentages of blood cell types and the health of a patient.

Patient Number	Red Blood Cells		White Blood Cells		Platelets	
	Number	Percent	Number	Percent	Number	Percent
Control						

Test Your Hypothesis

6 Select blood samples from three other patients.

7 Repeat step 4 for each sample.

Analyze and Conclude

8 **Analyze** the CBC results for each patient. Based on the data from your healthy control patient, explain whether each patient is healthy.

9 **Conclude** Use information from the table below to conclude whether each of your patients is probably healthy or might have a health problem.

Lab **TIPS**

☑ Calculate percentages by taking the number of one type of blood cell and dividing it by the total number of all blood cell types. Then multiply by 100.

☑ Some of the white beans might be different sizes.

Type of Blood Cell	Normal Levels	Illnesses Associated with High Levels	Illnesses Associated with Low Levels
Red (RBCs)	94%	Smoking Lung disease	Anemia
White (WBCs)	1%	Infection Leukemia	Infection Leukemia
Platelets	5%	Chronic inflammation Bone marrow problems	Weak immune system

10 **The Big Idea** How do changes in the circulatory system affect homeostasis?

Communicate Your Results

Write a medical report explaining the results of each patient's CBC test and the conclusions you reached as their physician.

 **Inquiry** **Extension**

Think of some other blood-related diseases you could model with the materials used in this lab. Are there some diseases that would not be easy to model with these materials?

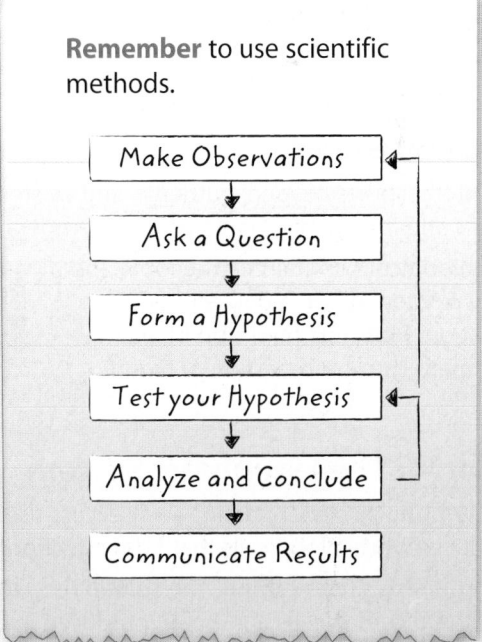

Remember to use scientific methods.

Make Observations

↓

Ask a Question

↓

Form a Hypothesis

↓

Test your Hypothesis

↓

Analyze and Conclude

↓

Communicate Results

 **THE BIG IDEA**

The respiratory and circulatory systems move materials through the body and remove wastes.

Key Concepts Summary 🗝	Vocabulary

Lesson 1: The Respiratory System

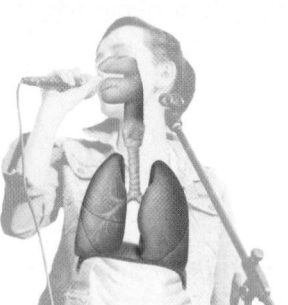

- The respiratory system provides the body with oxygen and removes carbon dioxide.
- In the **lungs,** oxygen is carried by the **bronchi** and the bronchioles to the **alveoli.**
- The respiratory system works with the circulatory and muscular systems to maintain homeostasis.

breathing p. 559
pharynx p. 560
larynx p. 560
trachea p. 560
bronchi p. 561
lungs p. 561
alveoli p. 561
diaphragm p. 562

Lesson 2: The Circulatory System

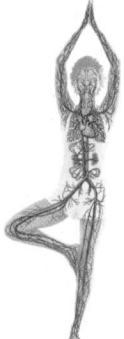

- The circulatory system moves materials throughout the body.
- **Arteries** carry blood away from the heart. **Capillaries** allow the exchange of materials between blood and body cells. **Veins** return blood to the heart.
- The circulatory system works with the respiratory, digestive, nervous, and endocrine systems to maintain homeostasis.

atrium p. 568
ventricle p. 568
artery p. 570
capillary p. 570
vein p. 570
systemic circulation p. 571
coronary circulation p. 571
pulmonary circulation p. 571
atherosclerosis p. 572

Lesson 3: Blood

- Blood transports oxygen, nutrients, and wastes; protects against illness and injury; and regulates body temperature.
- Red blood cells contain hemoglobin and carry oxygen. White blood cells fight infection. **Platelets** help stop bleeding. **Plasma** is the liquid portion of blood.

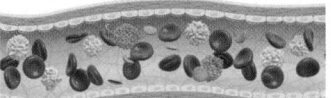

platelet p. 579
plasma p. 579
Rh factor p. 581

Lesson 4: The Lymphatic System

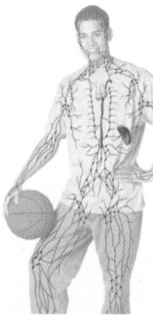

- The **lymphatic system** drains away excess tissue fluid and produces white blood cells that fight infection.
- **Lymph nodes** filter **lymph.** The **spleen** recycles worn-out red blood cells. B cells and T cells produced in the bone marrow fight disease-causing organisms. T cells mature in the **thymus.**
- The lymphatic system works together with the circulatory system to regulate the amount of fluid between cells.

lymphatic system p. 585
lymph p. 586
lymph node p. 586
thymus p. 587
spleen p. 587

FOLDABLES® Chapter Project

Assemble your lesson Foldables as shown to make a Chapter Project. Use the project to review what you have learned in this chapter.

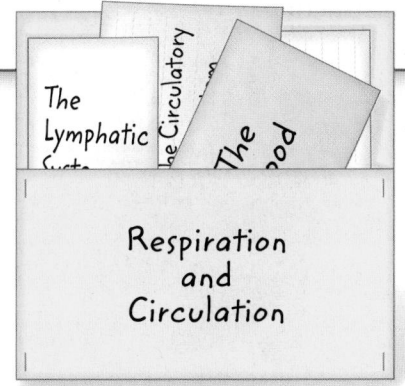

Use Vocabulary

1 The large muscle that contracts and relaxes to move gases into and out of the lungs is the _____.

2 A respiratory infection in which the bronchi swell is _____.

3 The smallest blood vessels are _____.

4 The two lower chambers of the heart are called _____.

5 Small, irregularly shaped pieces of cells in blood are _____.

6 The organ that holds a reserve supply of blood and produces white blood cells is the _____.

Link Vocabulary and Key Concepts   🔘 Concepts in Motion Interactive Concept Map

Copy this concept map, and then use vocabulary terms from the previous page to complete the concept map.

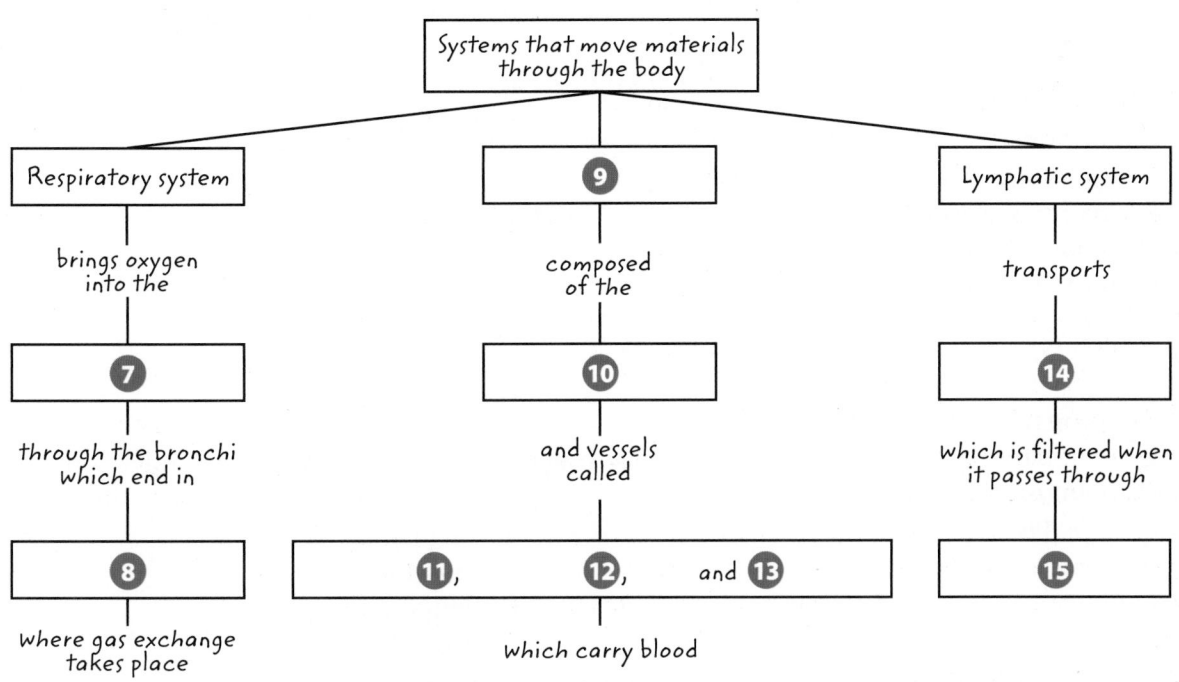

Chapter 16 Review

Understand Key Concepts 🗝

1 Which process takes place in the structure shown below?

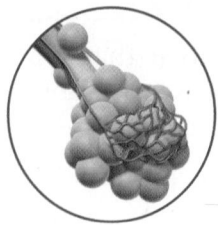

A. breathing
B. immunity
C. blood clotting
D. gas exchange

2 Which structure is held open by rings of cartilage?

A. alveolus
B. larynx
C. pharynx
D. trachea

3 What happens to the diaphragm during inhalation?

A. It contracts and moves down.
B. It contracts and moves up.
C. It relaxes and moves down.
D. It relaxes and moves up.

4 Which term describes the main function of pulmonary circulation?

A. fight infection
B. oxygenate blood
C. produce T cells
D. stop bleeding

5 Which type of circulation supplies oxygen to the cells of the heart?

A. coronary
B. lymphatic
C. pulmonary
D. systemic

6 Which organ keeps blood flowing through the body?

A. heart
B. lungs
C. spleen
D. thymus

7 The arrow in the diagram below points to which structure?

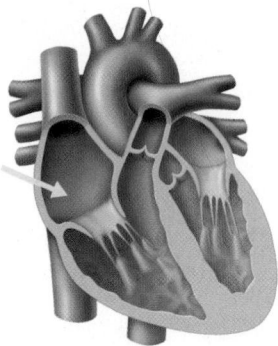

A. aorta
B. atrium
C. vein
D. ventricle

8 Which part of the blood helps defend the body from a virus infection?

A. plasma
B. platelets
C. red blood cells
D. white blood cells

9 What is the primary role of hemoglobin in blood?

A. attract platelets
B. blood typing
C. carry oxygen
D. fight parasites

10 Which body system filters infection-causing organisms from tissue fluids?

A. circulatory
B. immune
C. lymphatic
D. respiratory

Critical Thinking

11 **Illustrate** the path of air from the nose into the lungs.

12 **Compare** the structures and functions of the circulatory and lymphatic systems.

13 **Give an example** of a life choice that can harm the health of both the respiratory and circulatory systems.

14 **Interpret Graphics** The arrow below points to one of the chambers of the heart. Where does blood entering this chamber come from? Where does it go when it leaves this chamber? Is the blood oxygen-rich or oxygen-poor?

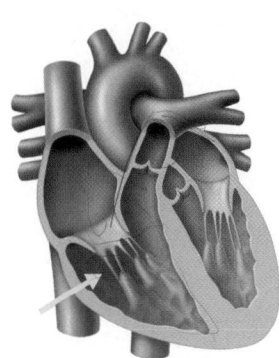

15 **Determine** A person with type AB blood regularly donates blood as a community service. Determine the blood type(s) that can receive this blood in a transfusion.

16 **Synthesis** Design a brochure for a tour through the lymphatic system. Include all the structures of the lymphatic system.

Writing in Science

17 **Write** a paragraph comparing the functions of the alveoli, the capillaries, and the lymph nodes. Your paragraph should have a topic sentence, supporting details, and a concluding sentence.

REVIEW THE BIG IDEA

18 How does oxygen reach the cells of the body? Explain how the respiratory and circulatory systems work together to supply cells with the materials they need.

19 The photo below shows bubbles of gas exhaled by a diver who is breathing from an air tank. Why is it important that the bubbles be released into the water rather than going back into the air tank?

Math Skills

Review
Math Practice

Use Percentages

The table below shows the percentages of the total population in the US with different blood types and with Rh– blood. Use the table to answer questions 20–22.

Blood type	A	B	AB	O
Percent with blood type	42	10	4	44
Percent who are Rh–	6	2	1	7

20 What percentage of people has Rh+ blood?

21 What percentage of the total population has AB+ blood?

22 What percentage of people could donate blood to a person with O+ blood?

Record your answers on the answer sheet provided by your teacher or on a sheet of paper.

Multiple Choice

1 Where in the human body does gas exchange occur?

  A alveoli

  B bronchi

  C pharynx

  D trachea

Use the diagram below to answer question 2.

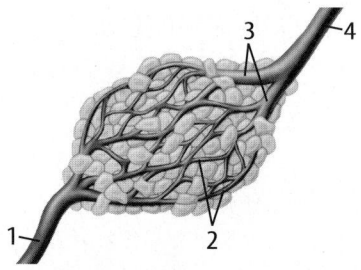

2 Which numbered blood vessel in the diagram above could be the aorta?

  A 1

  B 2

  C 3

  D 4

3 Which blood component stops the bleeding after a cut?

  A plasma

  B platelets

  C red blood cells

  D white blood cells

4 Which shows the general path of blood from the time it leaves the heart until it returns?

  A arteries → capillaries → veins

  B arteries → veins → capillaries

  C capillaries → arteries → veins

  D veins → capillaries → arteries

Use the diagram below to answer question 5.

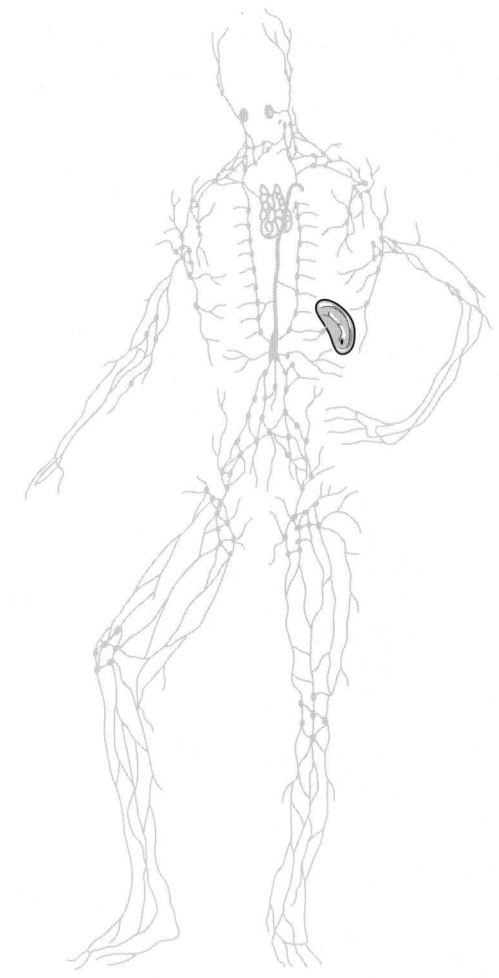

5 Which organ is highlighted in the diagram above?

  A heart

  B lung

  C spleen

  D stomach

6 Which blood type can be donated to all humans?

  A type A

  B type AB

  C type B

  D type O

7 Which is a function of the lymphatic system?

   A circulate blood

   B digest food

   C fight infection

   D transport gas

Use the diagram below to answer question 8.

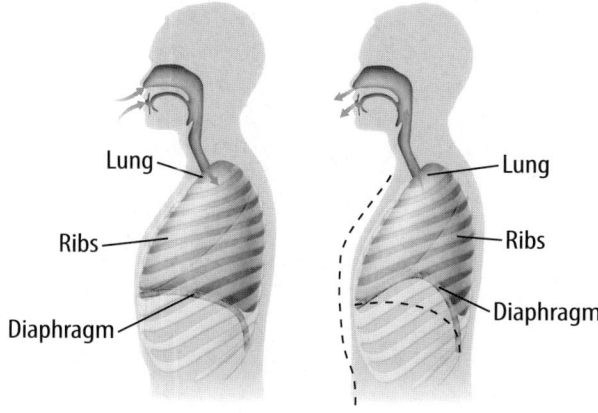

8 What process do the dotted lines in the diagram represent?

   A gas exchange

   B diaphragm contraction

   C muscle expansion

   D weight increase

9 Which contracts to move lymph through the lymphatic system?

   A heart

   B stomach

   C body muscle

   D heart muscle

Constructed Response

Use the diagram below to answer questions 10 and 11.

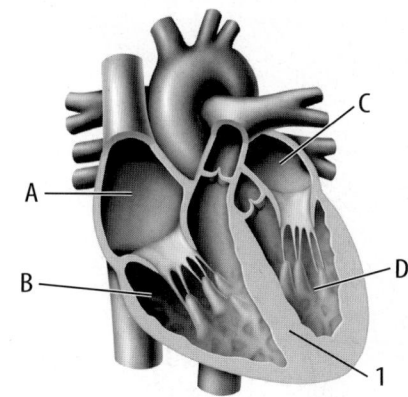

10 The four main chambers of the heart are represented by letters in the diagram above. Identify each chamber. What is the structure in the heart represented by the number 1? Describe its function.

11 Use the labels in the diagram to describe in a paragraph the path of blood through the heart.

12 Describe the three types of circulation in the human body.

13 Which organs of the respiratory system help keep dirt and food from entering the lungs? Describe how each functions to protect the lungs.

14 How does your body know when to breathe? How and why does air pressure change in your body as you breathe?

NEED EXTRA HELP?														
If You Missed Question...	1	2	3	4	5	6	7	8	9	10	11	12	13	14
Go to Lesson...	1	2	3	2	4	3	4	1	4	2	2	2	1	1

Immunity and Disease

THE BIG IDEA

How does the immune system help maintain the body's homeostasis?

Inquiry What is going on?

Your immune system protects your body against invaders. Notice the two small brown-yellow cells on the large green cell.

- Why might the small cells be attacking the large cell?

- How does your immune system help your body maintain homeostasis?

Get Ready to Read

What do you think?

Before you read, decide if you agree or disagree with each of these statements. As you read this chapter, see if you change your mind about any of the statements.

1 Some diseases are infectious, and others are noninfectious.

2 Cancer is an infectious disease.

3 The immune system helps keep the body healthy.

4 All immune responses are specific to the invading germs.

5 Exercise and sleep can help keep you healthy.

6 Chemicals make you sick and should not be used.

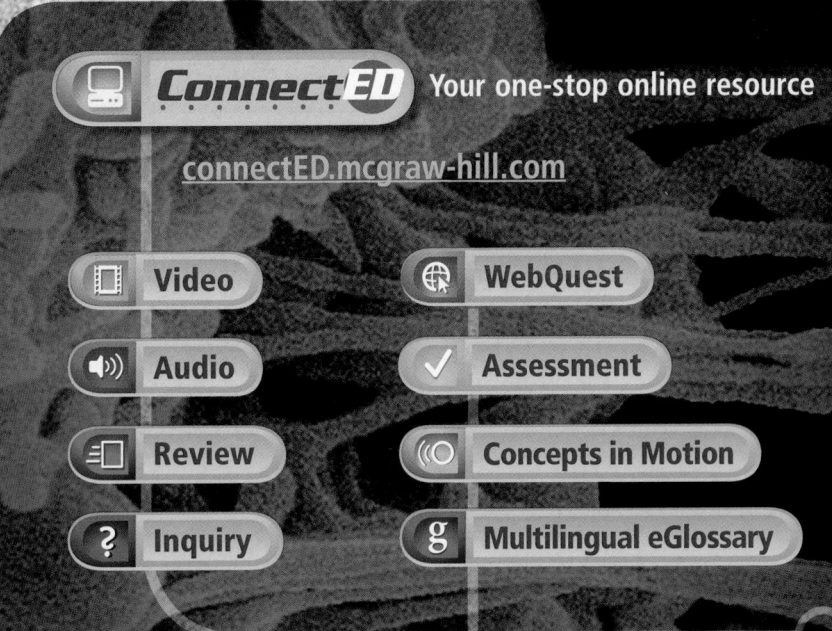

ConnectED Your one-stop online resource

connectED.mcgraw-hill.com

▣ Video

⊕ WebQuest

◀⬤ Audio

✓ Assessment

▤ Review

⦿ Concepts in Motion

? Inquiry

g Multilingual eGlossary

Diseases

Reading Guide

Key Concepts
ESSENTIAL QUESTIONS

- Why do we get diseases?
- How do the two types of diseases differ?

Vocabulary
pathogen p. 601
pasteurization p. 603
infectious disease p. 605
vector p. 605
noninfectious disease p. 606
cancer p. 607

g Multilingual eGlossary

Video BrainPOP®

Inquiry A Bull's-Eye?

Have you ever seen a bull's-eye on someone's skin? It is a rash caused by Lyme disease. The disease is spread by a tick like the one shown here.

Which well is contaminated?

Imagine that you live in a town with four wells. You get your water regularly from one well, but sometimes you also drink water from another well. People are getting sick. Some suspect the water in one well is causing the sickness. Which well is contaminated?

1. Take an **envelope** from your assigned well. Do not look inside the envelope.

2. Write your name on the envelope, and then pass it to another person from any well. You should also receive a different envelope from another person.

3. Repeat step 2.

4. Write your name on the third envelope and open it. If there is an "X" on the card inside, the three people who signed the envelope drank from the contaminated well and are sick. As a class, compile the results in a table.

Think About This

1. Which well was contaminated? How could you tell?

2. 🔑 **Key Concept** What do you think you might do to stop the sickness from spreading?

Disease Through History

Imagine you are sick, and your doctor suggests scraping your skull with a rock until a hole is created, as shown in **Figure 1.** The doctor tells you that the hole in your skull will allow the cause of your illness to escape. Today you might think this was strange. But thousands of years ago, this was an accepted treatment for disease.

Today we know that many diseases are caused by bacteria and viruses. *Disease-causing agents, such as bacteria and viruses, are called* **pathogens.** Pathogens have always caused illnesses, but only in the last few hundred years has the relationship between pathogens and diseases been understood.

Before then little was known about disease and immunity, and superstitions were common. Today we know the hole-in-the-head treatment would be painful and would create an opportunity for even more pathogens to enter the body.

WORD ORIGIN ·

pathogen
from Greek *pathos*, means "disease"

· ·

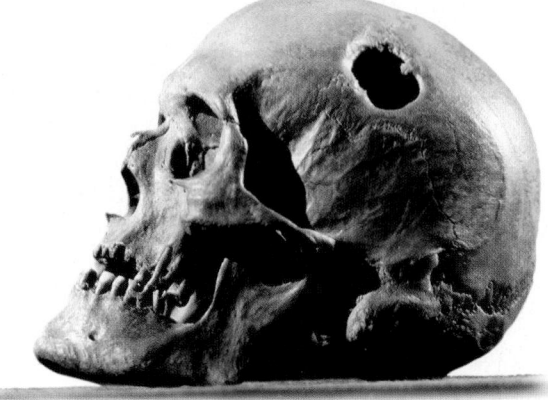

Figure 1 Archaeologists have found skulls with smooth holes made while the patient was alive. Bone growth around the hole in this skull shows that the patient lived after the procedure.

Early Research on Diseases

Despite limited technology and equipment, doctors in the eighteenth and nineteenth centuries learned a lot about the causes and treatments of diseases. The research and experiments performed by a few scientists saved many lives.

First Vaccination

In 1796 a doctor in England named Edward Jenner developed the first vaccination—a procedure that helps the body defend itself against disease. Jenner knew that women who milked cows often developed a mild disease called cowpox. However, these women were resistant to the deadly disease smallpox. He made a cut in the arm of a young boy and inserted pus from a cowpox sore. Two weeks later, he infected the boy with smallpox, but the boy did not develop smallpox. Although the smallpox vaccination saved many lives, scientists did not understand why or how it worked.

Connecting Disease with a Source

In the mid-1800s people realized there was a connection between pathogens and disease. During this period, many people in London were dying from cholera, a bacterial disease of the intestinal tract. Dr. John Snow mapped outbreaks of the disease, as shown in **Figure 2.** He tracked the origin of one outbreak to a water pump. He had the pump closed, and new cases of cholera decreased immediately. John Snow thought a microscopic organism that he saw in the water—the cholera bacteria shown in **Figure 2**—caused the disease. Not everyone agreed, but people were beginning to think pathogens existed.

Figure 2 John Snow mapped the outbreak of cholera and realized the origin was the water from a specific pump.

⊘ **Visual Check** How did Snow use his map to identify the source of the cholera outbreak?

John Snow

LM Magnification: Unavailable

- • Cholera death
- ■ Water pump
- ☆ Contaminated water pump

Cholera bacteria

LM Magnification: Unavailable

The Development of Microscopes

One of the reasons people were slow to accept the idea of pathogens was because they could not see them. The development of microscopes changed that. In the late 1600s, Dutch merchant Anton van Leeuwenhoek (LAY vun hook) made one of the first microscopes. He discovered bacteria in pond water, as illustrated in **Figure 3.** However, van Leeuwenhoek did not share how he made the lenses, so bacteria were not observed again until the nineteenth century.

Connecting Bacteria to Infections

When scientists first realized bacteria were present in wounds, they thought the wounds caused the bacteria to appear. When Louis Pasteur began doing experiments in the mid-1800s, he realized that this idea was backward. Instead, bacteria from outside the body caused the tissue in the wound to decay. Pasteur discovered that he could kill bacteria in boiling liquids. **Pasteurization** *is the process in which a food is heated to a temperature that kills most harmful bacteria.* It is based on the work of Pasteur.

Joseph Lister used Pasteur's discoveries to make surgery safer for patients. He found that carbolic acid killed bacteria. He developed a misting system to spray carbolic acid throughout an operating room during surgery. Infection and death from surgeries decreased greatly. In the late 1800s, doctors improved on Lister's idea. They used carbolic acid to sterilize tools before surgery and steam to sterilize the linens and clothes.

✅ **Reading Check** How did Lister make surgery safer?

Figure 3 Anton van Leeuwenhoek made many scientific discoveries using simple microscopes he designed. He named the moving organisms he saw in pond water *animalcules.* Today they are called bacteria and protozoa.

① The bacterium must be found in all organisms suffering from the disease, but not in healthy organisms.

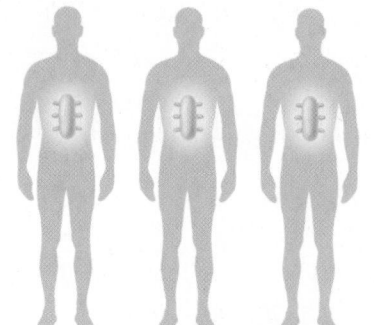

② The bacterium must reproduce in the lab.

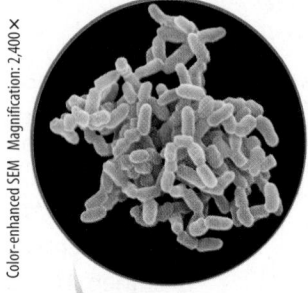

Color-enhanced SEM Magnification: 2,400×

③ A sample of the newly grown pathogen must cause the illness when injected into a healthy animal.

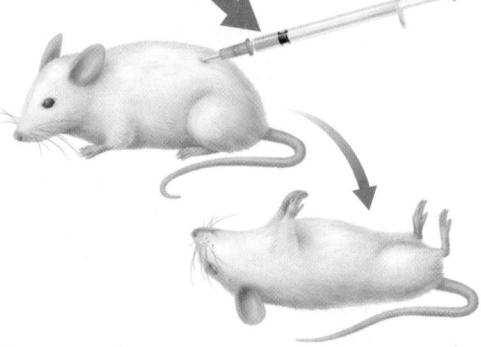

④ When the suspected pathogen is removed from the infected animal and grown in the lab, it must be identical to the original pathogen.

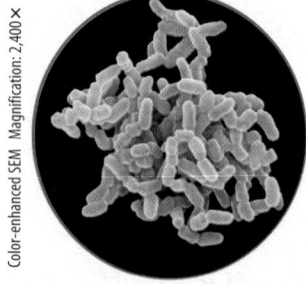

Color-enhanced SEM Magnification: 2,400×

Figure 4 Koch developed a procedure to determine if a bacterium caused an illness.

Discovering Disease Organisms

Despite the research on bacteria in wounds, most people did not think bacteria could make a healthy person sick. In 1867, Robert Koch was one of the first scientists to argue that bacteria could cause illness in an animal as large as a cow. He developed a set of rules to determine if specific bacteria caused an illness. Koch's rules are illustrated in **Figure 4.** The research based on these rules convinced most scientists that some bacteria were disease-causing pathogens. Although the roles of pathogens in disease are not as simple as Koch thought, current understandings are based on his findings.

Reading Check What are Koch's rules?

Bacteria are not the only pathogens that cause disease—viruses are others. However, they are so small that many years passed before scientists understood that viruses could be pathogens too. Some fungi and protists can also cause diseases. Some of the diseases in humans caused by different pathogens include the following:

- Viruses cause the flu, colds, chickenpox, and AIDS.

- Bacteria cause ear infections, strep throat, pneumonia, meningitis, whooping cough, and syphilis, a sexually transmitted disease.

- Fungi cause athlete's foot, ringworm, and yeast infections.

- Protists cause malaria, African sleeping sickness, and dysentery.

Pathogens can be transmitted through food and water and carried by insects. They also can be passed directly among people by physical contact, sneezing, coughing, or exchange of bodily fluids. Some pathogens, such as the bacterium that causes syphilis, require a host to reproduce.

Types of Diseases

Have you ever heard anyone say they "caught" a cold? The common cold is contagious. This means that the pathogens that cause the common cold can be passed from person to person. Not all diseases are caused by pathogens. Your inherited traits are responsible for some diseases. Others can be caused by external factors, such as your environment and the choices you make about diet, exercise, and sleep.

 Key Concept Check Why do we get diseases?

Infectious Diseases

Diseases caused by pathogens that can be transmitted from one person to another are **infectious diseases.** The way this happens can vary depending on the pathogen.

Flu and cold viruses can pass to others through direct contact, such as shaking hands. The human immunodeficiency virus (HIV) can pass through the exchange of blood or bodily fluids. HIV causes acquired immunodeficiency syndrome (AIDS), a disease that attacks the body system that fights pathogens.

The protist that causes malaria is transferred by a **vector,** *a disease-carrying organism that does not develop the disease.* The vector for malaria is a certain type of mosquito. The mosquito bites an animal that has the protist in its bloodstream. Then the pathogen enters the saliva of the mosquito but the mosquito does not develop malaria. When the mosquito bites another animal, the pathogen moves into that animal's blood.

Inquiry MiniLab · **20 minutes**

How does an infectious disease spread through a population?

Imagine that one of the students in your class has a new disease, similar to a mild case of the flu. You can model the spread of this disease to indicate infection.

1. Read and complete a lab safety form.
2. Obtain a **cup** of **clear liquid** from your teacher.
3. Partner with another student in round 1. Pour the contents of your cup into his or her cup. Your partner should then pour the contents of his or her cup into your empty cup. Pour half the contents of your cup into your partner's cup.
4. Repeat step 3 three more times with a different partner in each round.
5. Your teacher will add an **indicator** to your cup. If your liquid changes color, you are infected.

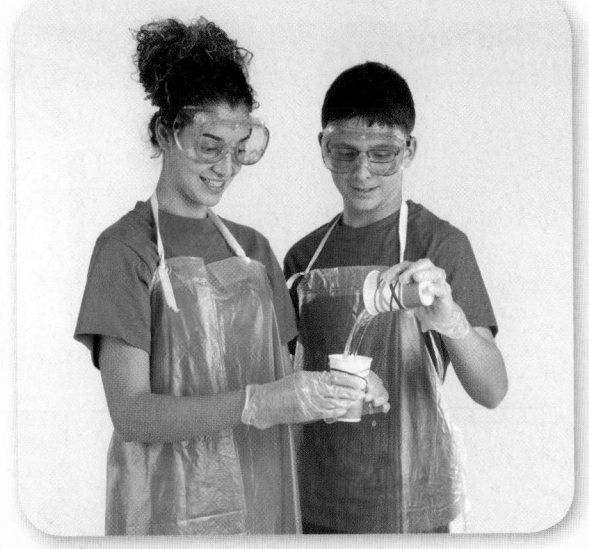

Analyze and Conclude

1. **Determine** how many students were infected in each round.

2. **Key Concept** Describe the pattern of how the number of infected persons changes as an infection progresses.

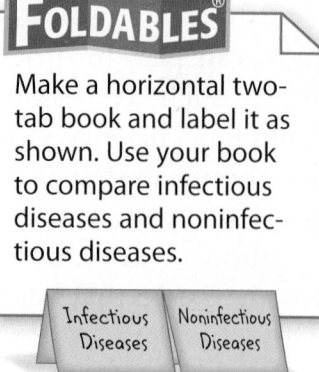
Noninfectious Diseases

A disease that cannot pass from person to person is a **noninfectious disease.** For example, you cannot catch lung cancer from another person. Pathogens do not directly cause noninfectious diseases. Two common causes of noninfectious diseases include:

- genetics, or traits inherited in your DNA from your biological parents, and

- environmental conditions, including lifestyle choices.

In many cases of noninfectious disease, a person has a genetic trait for a disease that environmental conditions make worse. It is the combination of genetics and environment that causes the disease to develop.

Childhood Diseases Noninfectious diseases that affect children are primarily due to genetics. One genetic disease is cystic fibrosis. It causes the body to produce mucus thicker than normal. This affects breathing and other body functions. Children with cystic fibrosis inherit a form of the gene that causes this disorder. It is a recessive trait, which means a person must inherit the gene from each parent, as shown in **Figure 5.** The parents might not have the disease, but they each must carry at least one gene form, or allele (uh LEEL), for cystic fibrosis. Like many genetic disorders in children, environmental conditions can make the disease worse. A poor diet, air pollution, and lack of exercise can make the symptoms of cystic fibrosis worse.

Figure 5 Diseases caused by genetic disorders are inherited.

✓ **Visual Check** How many children inherited a gene for cystic fibrosis?

Inheritance of Cystic Fibrosis 🔑

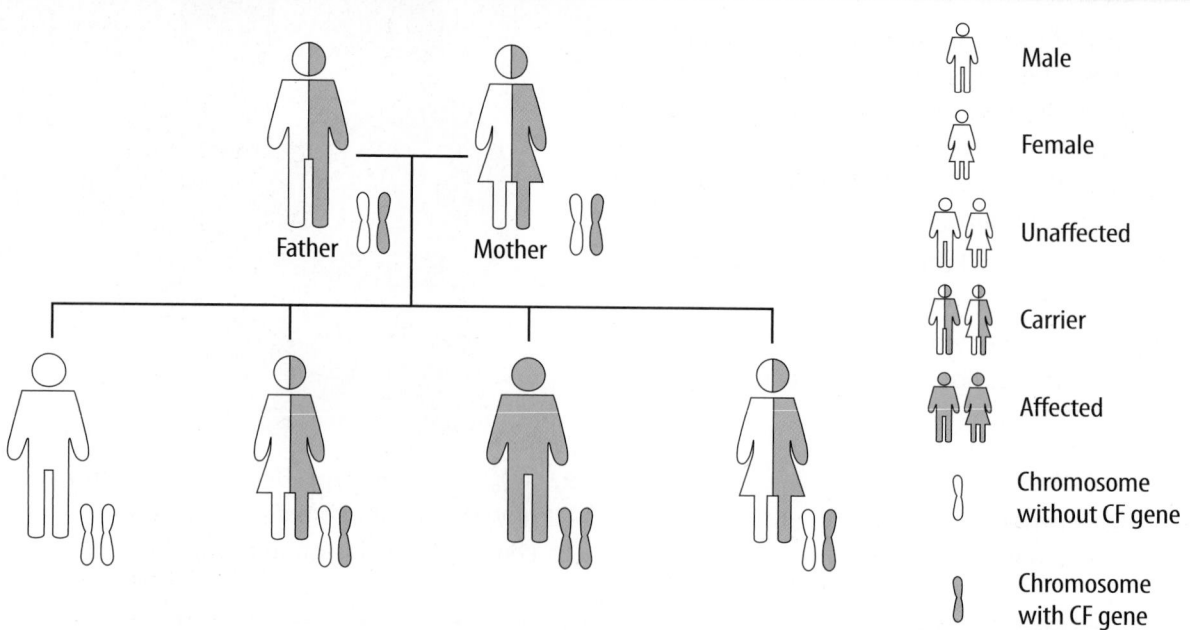

Other Diseases Many noninfectious diseases that affect adults are due primarily to environmental causes and life choices. For example, an unhealthful diet, obesity, a lack of regular exercise, and smoking cause most cases of heart disease. Osteoporosis is a disease in which bones become weak and less dense. People inherit a tendency to develop osteoporosis. However, years of poor lifestyle choices such as an unhealthful diet, lack of calcium and **vitamin** D, smoking, and a lack of exercise can all lead to weakened bones. There is also a type of diabetes that develops in adults that is strongly linked to environmental conditions, although there might also be a genetic link.

 Reading Check List some causes of noninfectious diseases.

Cancer Tumors form when cells reproduce uncontrollably. **Cancer** *is a disease in which cells reproduce uncontrollably without the usual signals to stop.* For example, lung-cancer tumors form in the lungs and interfere with normal lung function. In **Figure 6,** notice the color difference of the lung that has not been functioning properly due to cancer. People can inherit forms of genes that make them more likely to develop lung cancer. However, if they are not exposed to such environmental conditions as poor air quality, or they do not smoke, they might not develop lung cancer.

Key Concept Check How do infectious and noninfectious diseases differ?

REVIEW VOCABULARY

vitamin
nutrient needed for growth, regulation of body functions, and prevention of some diseases

Figure 6 Cancer cells in the lung form tumors and interfere with normal functioning.

Visual Check Identify the differences between the healthy lungs and the diseased lungs.

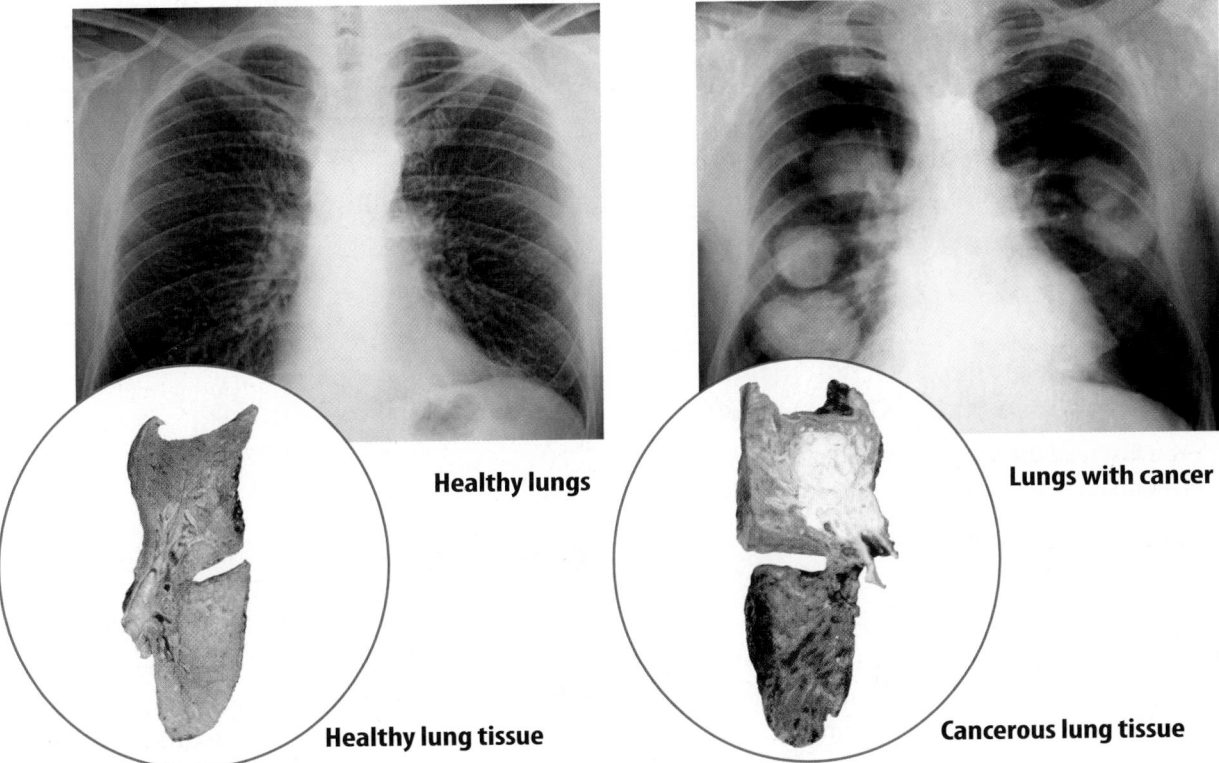

Healthy lungs

Healthy lung tissue

Lungs with cancer

Cancerous lung tissue

Visual Summary

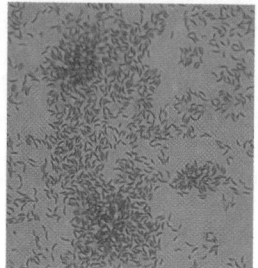

How a disease spreads depends on the pathogen. Some pathogens can be transmitted by a vector, such as a tick or a mosquito.

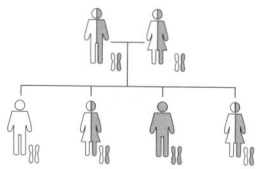

The two common causes of noninfectious diseases are environmental conditions and genetics.

People might inherit forms of genes that make them more likely to develop cancer.

FOLDABLES®

Use your lesson Foldable to review the lesson. Save your Foldable for the project at the end of the chapter.

What do you think NOW?

You first read the statements below at the beginning of the chapter.

1. Some diseases are infectious, and others are noninfectious.

2. Cancer is an infectious disease.

Did you change your mind about whether you agree or disagree with the statements? Rewrite any false statements to make them true.

Use Vocabulary

1 **Define** the term *pathogen* in your own words.

2 The process of boiling a liquid to kill bacteria and sealing it so bacteria cannot enter is called _____.

3 A host that transmits a pathogen but does not develop the disease is called a(n) _____.

Understand Key Concepts

4 **List** two main causes of disease.

5 Which is NOT a pathogen?
   A. bacterium   C. vector
   B. fungus   D. virus

Interpret Graphics

6 **Summarize** Copy and fill in the table below using these terms: *viruses, bacteria, unhealthful diet, smoking, protists, gene forms, fungus.*

Heredity	Environmental Conditions	Pathogens

7 **Explain** the illustration below using one of Koch's rules.

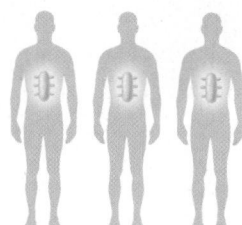

Critical Thinking

8 **Design** a plan to determine the source of a pathogen found in food.

9 **Support** the claim that genetics and environmental conditions can both contribute to a disease.

How would you prepare a work area for procedures that require aseptic techniques?

Aseptic techniques are methods used to prevent microbial contamination. Hospitals use aseptic techniques to reduce the risk of infection by microorganisms during surgery. Although their procedures might be less stringent than in an operating room, microbiologists also use aseptic techniques to prevent their work from becoming contaminated by unwanted microorganisms.

Materials

bleach

spray bottle

paper towels

black light

Safety

Learn It

You can practice aseptic **techniques** by disinfecting a bench top or desk. You will use a smooth, nonporous surface because rough surfaces are hard to clean and they provide many surfaces for microorganisms to grow.

Try It

1. Read and complete a lab safety form.

2. Thoroughly wash your hands. Then, wearing disposable gloves, prepare a bleach solution according to your teacher's directions. Place the solution in a spray bottle.

3. Spray the entire work area and wipe it with a paper towel. Instead of drying the area with another paper towel, let it air dry. After disinfecting, do not recontaminate the area by touching or leaning over it.

4. Test the effectiveness of your cleaning procedure by using a black light. The invisible test solution your teacher applied will glow under the black light. In your Science Journal, draw a diagram to indicate the areas you missed.

5. Reclean the work area and check the effectiveness of your cleaning procedure again.

6. Thoroughly wash your hands after the activity.

3

Apply It

7. Some people think polished granite countertops are better for food preparation than rough tiles. Explain why this might be so.

8. **Propose** an argument to defend this statement: Hand washing is an essential part of aseptic techniques.

9. **Key Concept** How do aseptic techniques reduce the risk of infection and disease?

Preparing a Work Area for Aseptic Procedures
Wash your hands.
Choose an area with a smooth, dry surface.
Thoroughly disinfect the entire area.
Do not recontaminate.

The Immune System

Reading Guide

Key Concepts 🔑
ESSENTIAL QUESTIONS

- What does the immune system do?
- How do the parts of the immune system work together?
- How does the immune system interact with other body systems?

Vocabulary

inflammation p. 615

antigen p. 616

antibody p. 616

B cell p. 616

T cell p. 616

allergy p. 616

immunity p. 617

active immunity p. 617

vaccination p. 617

passive immunity p. 617

g Multilingual eGlossary

🎞 Video

- BrainPOP®
- What's Science Got to do With It?

Inquiry Mysterious Blobs?

The large yellow blobs you see are bacteria. The bacteria grew after a human hand touched the red agar plate. With all that bacteria on your hand, what keeps you from getting sick? How does the body protect itself?

Can you escape the pox?

The loffpox disease is an imaginary disease. How might it affect you?

1. Your teacher will give you one of **three cards**: *healthy, in poor health,* or *pox.* Only one person will be given the *pox* card. Do not tell anyone which card you receive.

2. As you stand in a circle looking at each other, the person with the *pox* card will wink at the other students. If he or she winks at you and you have an *in poor health* card, you have caught the disease and you must sit down. If you have a *healthy* card, you do not catch the disease and you remain standing. However, if the person with the *pox* card winks at you a second time, you must sit down.

Think About This

1. Who is left standing?

2. 🔑 **Key Concept** How does a person's state of health affect the pox disease? Why do you think it took the pox more than one wink to infect a healthy person?

Functions of the Immune System

Your body is constantly exposed to different pathogens. In Lesson 1 you read that disease-causing agents, such as bacteria and viruses, are pathogens. Pathogens also include fungi and protists. Pathogens are in the air, on objects, and in water. Like a spacesuit protects an astronaut, your immune system works to protect your body. There are many barriers to keep pathogens from entering your body.

Sometimes pathogens get past your body's initial barriers. When this happens, your immune system also has defenses to stop any pathogens that get past the barriers. For example, there are cells in your body that can destroy the pathogens. The immune system interacts with other body systems and helps keep you healthy, even as the environment outside your body changes.

🔑 **Key Concept Check** What does the immune system do?

You can improve the effectiveness of these prevention methods by making healthful choices every day. Choices such as eating healthful food, getting enough sleep, exercising regularly, and using sunscreen support your immune system. As you read about the parts of the immune system, consider how the choices you make every day could affect how well your immune system functions.

FOLDABLES

Fold two sheets of paper into a layered book. Label it as shown. Use it to organize information about the immune system's lines of defense.

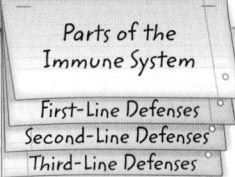

Parts of the Immune System
First-Line Defenses
Second-Line Defenses
Third-Line Defenses

How do different layers of your skin protect your body?

Your skin has three layers. The top layer, called the epidermis, is thin but tough. It helps prevent harmful microorganisms from getting into the tissues and provides physical protection. The middle layer, called the dermis, is the thickest layer. It provides strength and elasticity. The bottom layer, called the subcutaneous layer, insulates against heat and cold and helps cushion the skin. In this activity, you will build a model of skin.

1 Read and complete a lab safety form.

2 Start with a sheet of **cardboard** or **cardstock paper** as the base. **Glue** a piece of **cotton batting** to the base.

3 Glue a **sponge** onto the cotton batting.

4 Glue a piece of **vinyl** to the sponge.

5 Test your skin model with a drop of **water** containing **food coloring.** Record your observations in your Science Journal.

6 Use **scissors** to make a small cut in the top layer of your model. Repeat step 5.

Analyze and Conclude

1. **Identify** Which skin layer does the vinyl represent? The sponge? The cotton batting?

2. **Key Concept** Relate the results of the water and food coloring test to what would happen with real skin.

Parts of the Immune System

Different parts of your body work together to keep pathogens from making you sick. The integumentary system (skin), the respiratory system, the circulatory system, the digestive system, and the nervous system all work with the immune system and protect you against disease.

First-Line Defenses

Keeping germs from reaching the parts of your body where they can make you sick is the function of first-line defenses. Skin, hair, mucus, and acids are first-line defenses. They are effective against many types of pathogens. An immune defense that protects against more than one type of pathogen is a nonspecific defense.

Skin Often, the first nonspecific defense that protects you from pathogens is your skin, as shown in **Figure 7.** Your skin keeps dirt and germs from entering your body. Sweat and acids from skin cells kill some bacteria. Natural oils make skin waterproof so you can easily wash it.

You encounter pathogens every day, but your skin stops most of them from entering your body. Pathogens, such as cold and flu viruses, can survive for short periods on objects such as doorknobs or telephones. When you touch these objects, the pathogens can be transferred to your hand. If they reach your mouth, nose, eyes, or a cut, they can enter your body. Washing your hands often with soap and water easily removes most pathogens from your skin.

Your skin protects you from other dangers. It forms a chemical called melanin that protects you from the Sun's ultraviolet (UV) rays. Nerve endings in your skin can help you sense the warmth of a stove or the sharpness of a pin to protect you from injury.

Reading Check Why is your skin considered a first-line defense?

Respiratory System You can inhale pathogens from the air through your nose or mouth. The hairs in your nose help protect you by trapping dirt and pathogens. This keeps them from reaching the rest of your respiratory system. Small hairlike structures called cilia, shown in **Figure 7,** also trap pathogens and move them up and out of the upper respiratory system. If pathogens get past the cilia, they might encounter mucus. Mucus traps pathogens and enables your respiratory system to remove them by coughing, sneezing, or swallowing.

Digestive System Pathogens can enter your digestive system on or in the food you eat. The digestive system is effective at stopping bacteria from making you seriously ill.

The stomach, also shown in **Figure 7,** contains strong acids. Stomach acids destroy many pathogens. Like the mucus in the respiratory system, mucus in the digestive system traps disease-causing bacteria and viruses, too.

Sometimes when you feel nauseated, it is actually your immune system clearing your body of pathogens. When disease-causing bacteria are not destroyed by stomach acids, your digestive system can reverse the usual direction of muscle contractions, and you vomit. Other times, muscle contractions speed up, and pathogens are removed through diarrhea.

✔ **Reading Check** List ways the digestive system helps defend against pathogens.

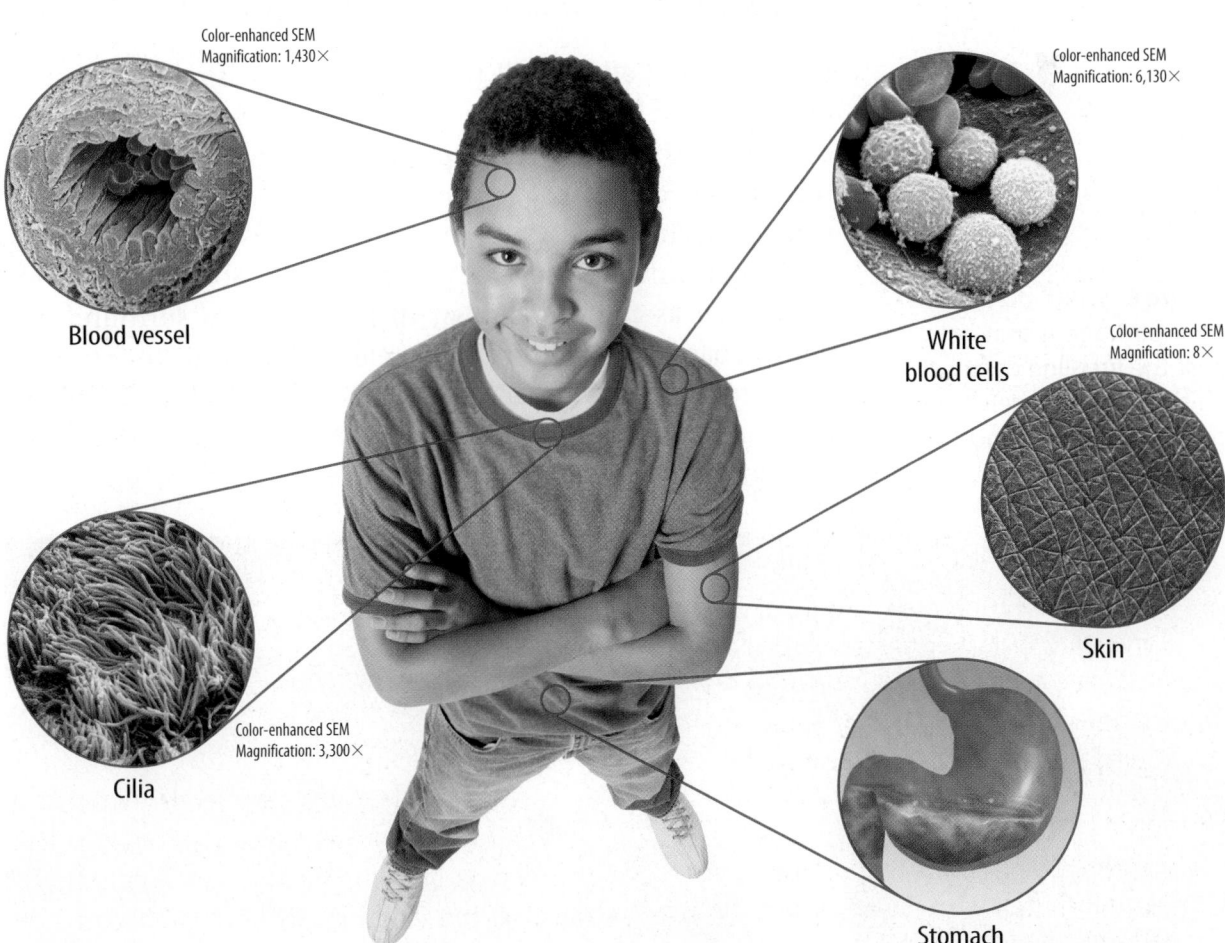

Color-enhanced SEM
Magnification: 1,430×

Blood vessel

Color-enhanced SEM
Magnification: 6,130×

White
blood cells

Color-enhanced SEM
Magnification: 8×

Skin

Color-enhanced SEM
Magnification: 3,300×

Cilia

Stomach

Figure 7 The skin, the respiratory system, the digestive system, and the circulatory system all support the immune system to provide the first line of protection against disease-causing pathogens. Blood vessels and white blood cells throughout the body help protect from pathogens.

✔ **Visual Check** How does the respiratory system trap pathogens?

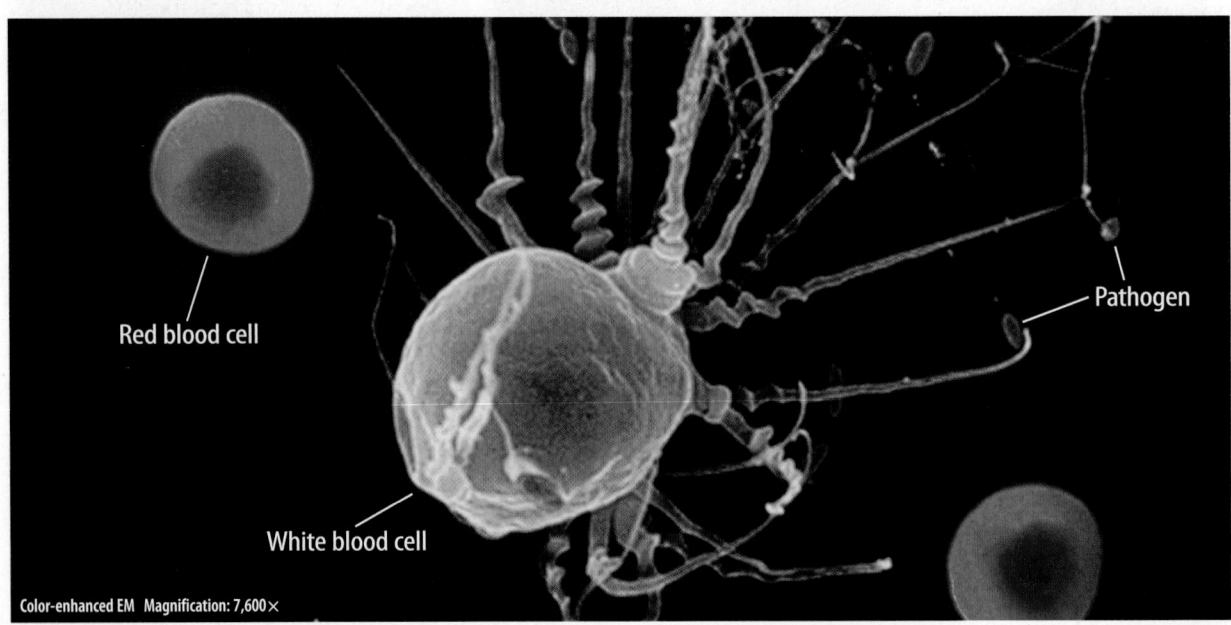

Circulatory System and Nervous System Your circulatory system also protects you from pathogens. Pathogens can be moved through the circulatory system to organs that fight infection. The nervous system and the circulatory system also work together and increase the body's temperature to fight pathogens more effectively. Certain foreign substances trigger the brain to increase body temperature. When this *occurs,* blood vessels narrow and a fever develops. Many pathogens cannot survive at this higher temperature. For those that do survive, the fever brings another line of defense. The fever also stimulates white blood cells, which are part of the second-line defenses against pathogens.

Second-Line Defenses

Sometimes pathogens get past the defenses of the skin, the respiratory system, the digestive system, and the circulatory system. When they do, the next line of defense goes into action. Like the first-line defense, second-line defenses are nonspecific, fighting against any type of pathogen.

White Blood Cells Recall that the spongy tissue in the center of your bones is called bone marrow. This is where white blood cells form. These cells attack pathogens. White blood cells flow through the circulatory system. However, they do most of their work attacking pathogens in the fluid outside blood vessels. They fight infection several different ways. Some white blood cells, such as the one shown in **Figure 8,** can surround and destroy bacteria directly. Others release chemicals that make it easier to kill the pathogens. Another type of white blood cell produces proteins that destroy viruses and other foreign substances that get past the first-line defenses.

ACADEMIC VOCABULARY

occur
(verb) to come into existence

Figure 8 White blood cells fight pathogens that get past the first-line defenses. This white blood cell can digest pathogens and damaged cells.

Red blood cell

White blood cell

Pathogen

Color-enhanced EM Magnification: 7,600×

The Inflammatory Response 🔑

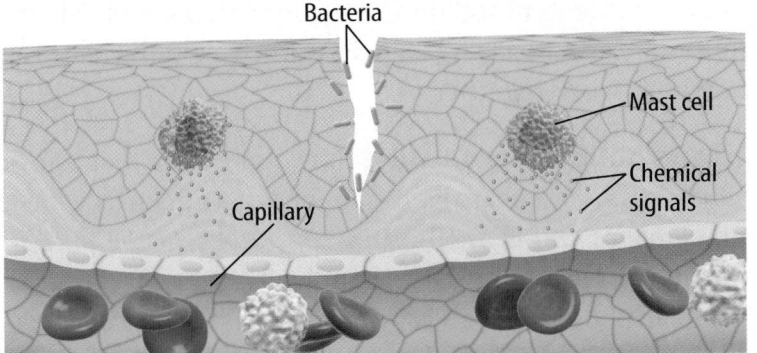

Bacteria
Mast cell
Chemical signals
Capillary

❶ When skin is torn or cut, the damaged tissue triggers the inflammatory response. Special cells called mast cells release chemical signals into the surrounding tissue.

❷ Some chemical signals attract more white blood cells to the area. Other chemical signals cause the capillary to dilate. White blood cells and plasma leak into the tissue, causing swelling.

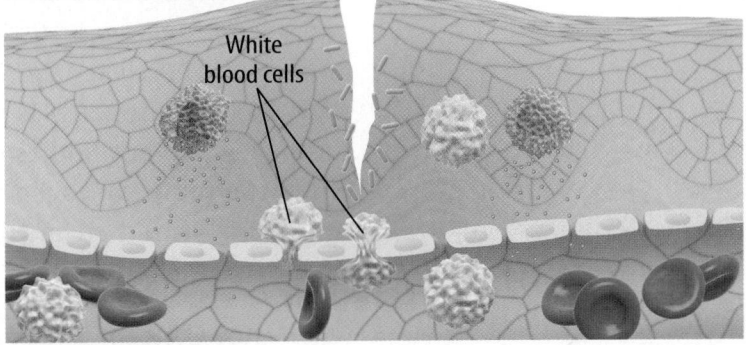

White blood cells

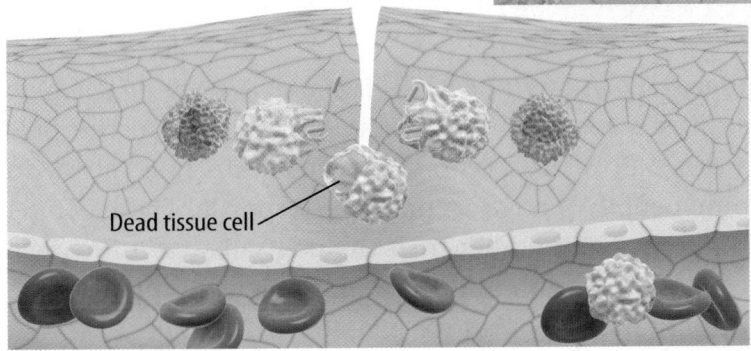

Dead tissue cell

❸ The white blood cells surround and take in the bacteria and any dead cells. As the tissue heals, the white blood cells and the plasma flow back into the capillary, and swelling decreases. The area returns to normal.

Inflammatory Response When you have an injury, your body produces an inflammatory response, causing inflammation. **Inflammation** *is a process that causes the area to become red and swollen.* If the injury is to the surface of the skin, you can observe the inflammatory response, as shown in **Figure 9**. First, damaged cells release a protein that signals the capillaries to dilate, or widen. Blood flow to the area increases and the injury site becomes red and warmer than the surrounding area. Second, plasma and white blood cells leak into the area, causing swelling. Third, the white blood cells break down damaged cells and destroy any bacteria that might have entered the wound. The inflammatory response cleans the area of the injury and keeps the infection from spreading. The inflammation enables the damaged tissue to heal.

✅ **Reading Check** Explain the inflammatory response.

Figure 9 Inflammation is another nonspecific response to pathogens.

WORD ORIGIN ············

inflammation
from Latin *inflammare*, means "to set on fire"

Third-Line Defenses

If first- and second-line defenses do not destroy all invading pathogens, another type of immune response occurs. Third-line defenses are specific to foreign substances. Often the three lines of defense work together.

Antigens and Antibodies *An* **antigen** *is a substance that causes an immune response.* An antigen can be on the surface of a pathogen. *Proteins called* **antibodies** *can attach to the antigen and make it useless.* Certain white blood cells, called B cells and T cells, form antibodies. **B cells** *form and mature in the bone marrow and secrete antibodies into the blood.* **T cells** *form in the bone marrow and mature in the thymus gland. They produce a protein antibody that becomes part of a cell membrane.* Antibodies match with specific antigens, as shown in **Figure 10.** Once your body has developed antibodies to an antigen, it can respond rapidly when the same pathogen invades your body again. This information is stored in antibodies on white blood cells called memory B cells.

 Key Concept Check How do the parts of the immune system work together?

An **allergy** *is an overly sensitive immune response to common antigens.* Most people do not produce antibodies to the proteins in dog saliva. However, the antigens in dog saliva do cause some people to have an immune response. These people have an allergy. Their bodies treat the dog saliva as if it were a pathogen. Inflammation and increased mucus production are common immune responses for people with allergies.

Figure 10 Antibodies are produced as a result of a specific immune response to particular antigens on pathogens.

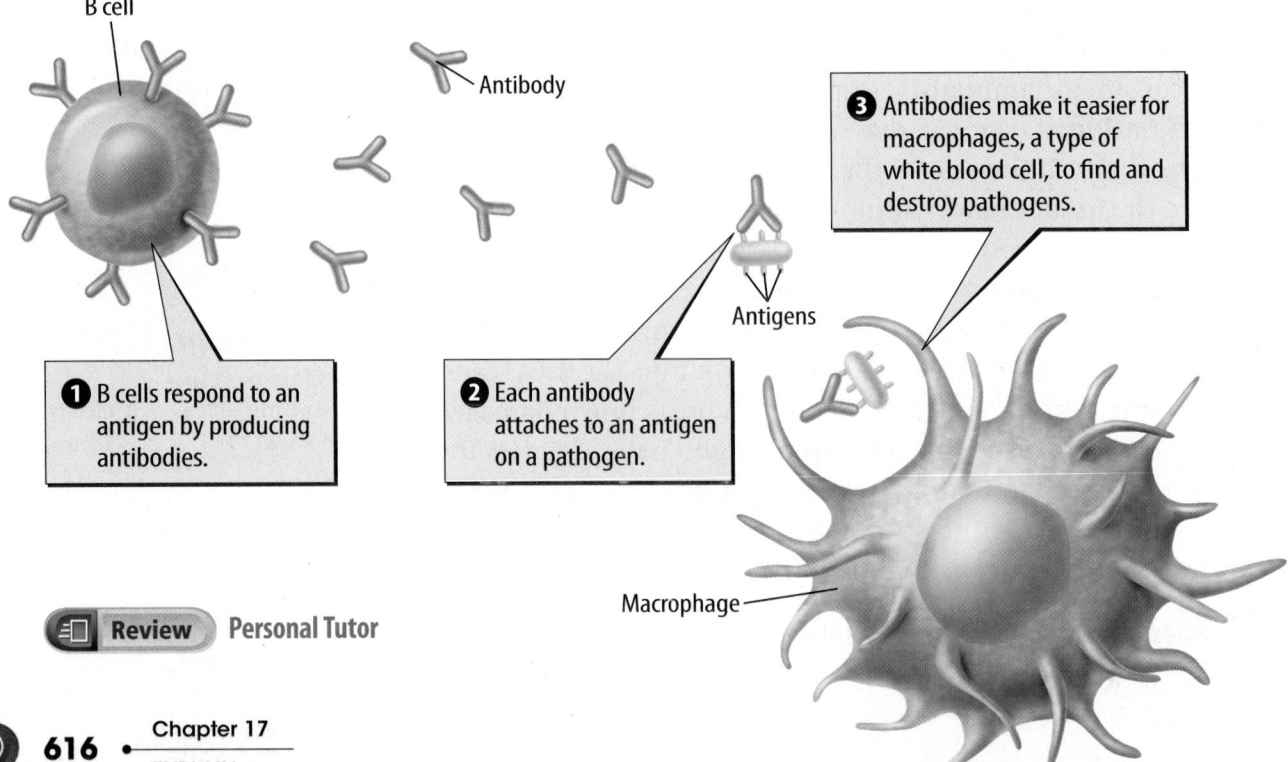

B cell

Antibody

❸ Antibodies make it easier for macrophages, a type of white blood cell, to find and destroy pathogens.

Antigens

❶ B cells respond to an antigen by producing antibodies.

❷ Each antibody attaches to an antigen on a pathogen.

Macrophage

Review **Personal Tutor**

Immunity

The resistance to specific pathogens is **immunity.** There are two types of immunity—active immunity and passive immunity.

Active Immunity *Your body produces antibodies in response to an antigen in* **active immunity.** Your body recognizes the antigen, and the matching antibodies respond quickly. You can develop active immunity through illness or infection. After an illness or an infection is over, antibodies remain in your body. Because of this, you usually get certain diseases, such as chicken pox, only once. However, you can catch a cold many times because many different cold viruses cause similar symptoms.

You can also develop antibodies if you are exposed to an antigen through a vaccination. *A* **vaccination** *is weakened or dead pathogens placed in the body, usually by injection or by mouth.* A vaccination causes the body to develop specific antibodies that can rapidly fight a pathogen's antigens when exposed to them. **Table 1** lists the effects of vaccinations on the average annual number of cases of some diseases.

Passive Immunity You can also become resistant to specific antigens through passive immunity. **Passive immunity** *is the introduction of antibodies that were produced outside the body.* A fetus can get antibodies from its mother. Injections of some antibodies are available for adults. Passive immunity is temporary—the body does not continue to make these antibodies.

The Immune System and Homeostasis

You are exposed to many different pathogens every day. The immune system works to maintain your body's homeostasis. Body systems, including the circulatory system and respiratory system, work together and protect against invaders.

 Key Concept Check How does the immune system interact with other body systems?

Table 1 Effects of Vaccinations		 Concepts in Motion Interactive Table	
Disease	**Cases Before Vaccination (annual average in the United States)**	**Year Vaccination Was Developed**	**Cases After Vaccination (annual average in the United States)**
Tetanus	1,300	1927	34
Polio	18,000	1955/1962	8
Measles	425,000	1963	90
Mumps	200,000	1967	610
Rubella	48,000	1970	345

Lesson 2 Review

Visual Summary

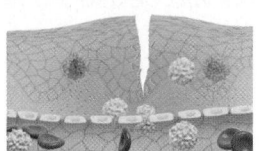

Inflammation may cause an injury to become warmer than the surrounding area due to increased blood flow to the area.

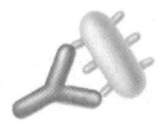

Antibodies produced by the white blood cells match with specific antigens, like a lock and key.

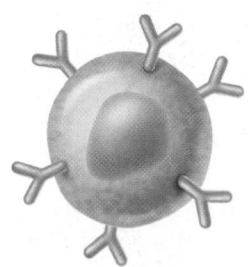

Immunity can be developed through different processes. If you have immunity to a particular pathogen, you will experience little or no effect from exposure to that pathogen.

FOLDABLES

Use your lesson Foldable to review the lesson. Save your Foldable for the project at the end of the chapter.

What do you think NOW?

You first read the statements below at the beginning of the chapter.

3. The immune system helps keep the body healthy.

4. All immune responses are specific to the invading germs.

Did you change your mind about whether you agree or disagree with the statements? Rewrite any false statements to make them true.

Use Vocabulary

1 **Distinguish** between active immunity and passive immunity.

2 The _____ response includes swelling and heat near injured tissue.

3 **Define** the term *vaccination* in your own words.

Understand Key Concepts

4 **List** three body systems that work with the immune system to form first-line defenses.

5 Which is a first-line defense?
   A. antibody   **C.** inflammation
   B. hormone   **D.** skin

6 **Explain** why antibodies are considered specific responses to pathogens.

Interpret Graphics

7 **Summarize** Copy and fill in the graphic organizer below to summarize the steps in the inflammatory response.

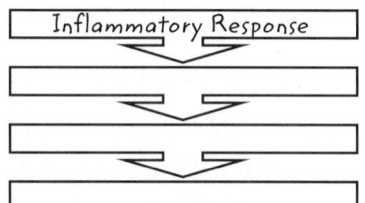

Critical Thinking

8 **Predict** what might happen to a person who had very few of the type of cell shown at right.

Math Skills

Review
— Math Practice —

9 The number of diphtheria cases fell from 175,000 cases before the vaccine to one case after the vaccine was developed. What percent change does this represent?

The Victory over Chicken Pox

Vaccines are helping win the war against viruses.

Until recently, having chicken pox was just a part of growing up. The disease commonly occurs in children, usually before the age of 15.

Chicken pox is highly contagious, passing easily from person to person. The chicken pox virus, varicella-zoster, produces a rash of red spots and small blisters that can appear all over the body. The fluid-filled blisters crust over and become very itchy. Within a few days, the spots and blisters disappear. It takes about one week for the disease to run its course.

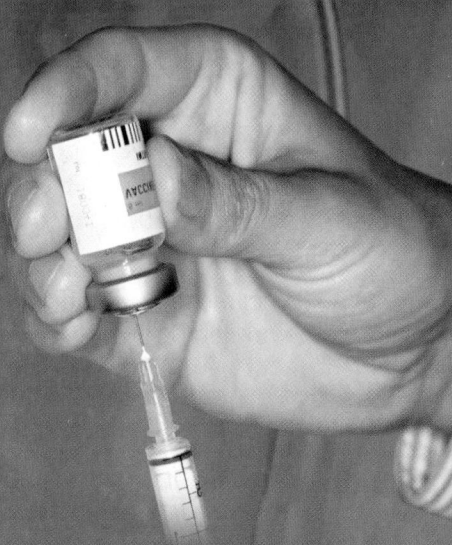

▲ The chicken pox vaccine is 80 to 90 percent effective in preventing the disease.

◀ The chicken pox rash usually appears on the face, chest, and back.

Chicken pox is contagious beginning 1–2 days before the rash appears until all the blisters form scabs. During this period, the virus can be spread through direct contact with the sores or through the air. Those who have not had chicken pox can become infected easily.

In 1995, a chicken pox vaccine was introduced in the United States, and the number of cases of chicken pox reported each year has declined sharply. It is estimated that almost 80 percent of young children develop immunity after one dose of vaccine. Over 90 percent of older children and adults develop immunity after the second dose.

◀ Varicella-zoster virus

It's Your Turn

REPORT Identify three diseases that were common 50 years ago but are not common today due to vaccines. Write a report about the diseases, when vaccines were developed against them, and how the incidences of the diseases changed.

Staying Healthy

Reading Guide

Key Concepts
ESSENTIAL QUESTIONS

- How can healthful habits and healthful choices affect diseases?

- How do sanitation practices affect human health?

- How can chemicals affect the human body?

Vocabulary

antibiotic p. 624

chemotherapy p. 624

g **Multilingual eGlossary**

Inquiry Why Wash?

Why do surgeons wash their hands before an operation even though they wear gloves? Can hand washing keep you healthy?

Where might bacteria be?

The people who work in the cafeteria in your school probably wear aprons, hairnets, and gloves. They might also wash dishes and wipe the counters with a bleach solution to kill bacteria. Why do they take such precautions?

1 Read and complete a lab safety form.

2 Go to your assigned station where surfaces, **utensils,** and **other objects** representing cookware have been coated with a "bacterial" solution of invisible **fluorescent detergent.**

3 Using a **cloth** and a **cleaning solution containing bleach,** clean the objects at your station as well as you can in 5 minutes.

⚠ Be careful with the bleach solution; it will stain your clothes.

4 When you are finished, your teacher will examine your station with a **black light,** which will show any remaining "bacteria."

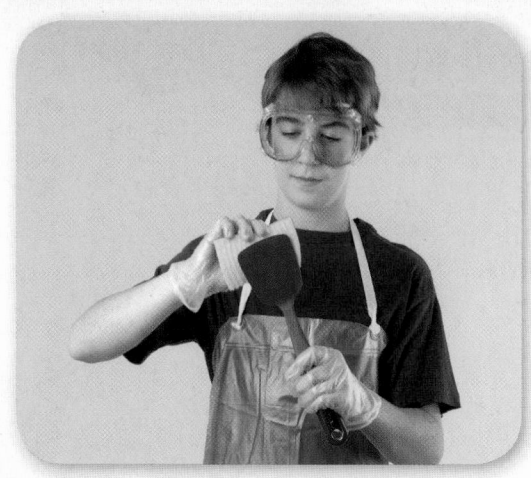

Think About This

1. How well did you clean your station? Did you miss any bacteria?

2. How could you change your cleaning methods to clean all surfaces and objects of bacteria?

3. 🔑 **Key Concept** Why do you think it is important to keep a kitchen clean, especially in a school or a restaurant?

Healthful Habits

Imagine you are sitting in class, and the person next to you sneezes. Fortunately, she covers her nose and mouth with her hand. After sneezing, she picks up a pencil. Just then, you realize you need to borrow a pencil. She hands you her pencil. Will you get her cold? What could you do to make that less likely?

Pathogens passed from person to person make infectious diseases such as colds and flu very common. Personal hygiene can limit the spread of these pathogens. For example, good hygiene includes using a tissue or handkerchief when you sneeze and then washing your hands. This lessens the chance you will spread your germs to others. Good hygiene can protect you from getting an infectious disease, too.

Pathogens are less likely to get past your first-line defenses if you wash your hands before you eat and avoid putting objects, such as pencils, in your mouth. Why do you think surgeons scrub their hands, as shown in the lesson opener photo, even though they wear gloves during surgical procedures?

FOLDABLES

Make a vertical half-book from a sheet of paper. Use it to record information about habits and choices that can help you stay healthy.

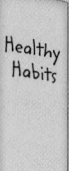

Healthy Habits

Figure 11 You can make healthful choices when planning for a day at the beach.

 Visual Check Identify the healthful choices.

Healthful Choices

In addition to good personal hygiene, other everyday choices, like those shown in **Figure 11,** can help keep you healthy. Choices that affect environmental conditions can also protect you from many infectious and noninfectious diseases.

Diet Think about the foods you ate this week. If you eat a healthful diet, your immune system can react more efficiently against pathogens. A healthful diet can even protect you against noninfectious diseases such as osteoporosis and heart disease. A healthful diet, a healthful weight, and regular exercise have been linked with overall disease prevention.

Reading Check How can a healthful diet protect against disease?

Sun Protection Skin cancer is a noninfectious disease. The ultraviolet (UV) rays from the Sun damage skin **cells** and can cause them to reproduce uncontrollably. Sunscreen blocks the UV rays and limits the damage from sunlight. Wearing a hat, long sleeves, pants, and sunglasses also helps protect you against UV damage.

Alcohol and Tobacco Lung cancer is one of the most deadly cancers. Most cases of lung cancer are related to smoking or working in environments with poor air quality. Many other cancers are related to excessive drinking of alcohol and to smoking. Healthful choices include not smoking or chewing tobacco and limiting or avoiding alcoholic beverages.

 Key Concept Check How can healthful habits and healthful choices affect diseases?

SCIENCE USE v. COMMON USE

cell

Science Use the basic unit of life

Common Use a room in a monastery or prison

Health and Sanitation

Improved cleanliness in schools, hospitals, and public areas has increased overall health in our communities. In the mid-1800s, hospitals were dirty, overcrowded places. Patients were rarely bathed, and linens were rarely washed. Pathogens caused infections in most patients. One nurse, Florence Nightingale, is credited with improving cleanliness in hospitals. She understood there was a connection between cleanliness and health.

Food Preparation

Improved sanitation in food preparation has also led to better health. Employees must wash their hands regularly, as indicated in **Figure 12,** and keep equipment clean. Inspections are performed regularly to catch problems early and protect consumers from most pathogens.

Waste Management

In the mid-1300s, there were no plumbing or sewer systems. People in European cities often dumped their personal waste and garbage in the streets. Today modern landfills and sewer systems keep our streets and households much cleaner. This cleanliness slows the spread of infectious diseases.

Figure 12 Sanitation has improved health by reducing exposure to pathogens.

 Key Concept Check How do sanitation practices affect human health?

Inquiry **MiniLab**   **20 minutes**

How clean are your hands?

Washing your hands properly can keep you from getting sick or spreading illnesses. How clean are your hands after you wash them?

1. Read and complete a lab safety form.

2. Have your partner thoroughly cover both of your hands, including your wrists and under your fingernails, with **washable paint.** Let your hands dry for 2 minutes.

3. Hold your hands over a **sink.** Have your partner put a drop of **liquid soap** on one of your hands and turn on the **warm water.** Have your partner cover your eyes with a **bandana.**

4. Wash your hands for 20 seconds. Have your partner remove the bandana from your eyes. Have him or her draw your hands on a **sheet of paper** and record any areas that still have paint.

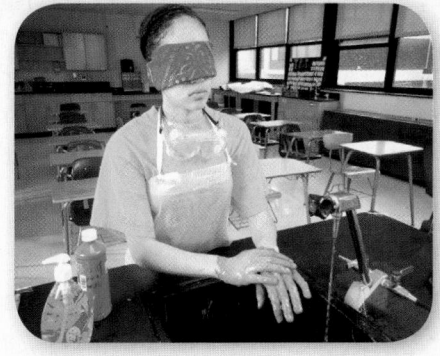

5. Wash any remaining paint from your hands.

6. Switch roles and repeat steps 2–5.

Analyze and Conclude

1. **Describe** how well you washed your hands.

2. **Key Concept** Explain why hand washing is important to keep from getting sick or spreading disease.

Figure 13 Many chemicals are beneficial to our health.

Health and Chemicals

Chemicals, like those shown in **Figure 13,** can be beneficial for people. Some chemicals, such as the ones in sunscreen that block UV rays, protect us from noninfectious diseases. Chemicals used to make vitamin supplements improve nutrition, which helps the immune system fight disease.

Other chemicals are used in medicines. **Antibiotics** *are medicines that stop the growth and reproduction of bacteria.* Chemicals are also used to destroy cancer cells. *These medicines, used in a type of treatment called* **chemotherapy,** *kill the cells that are reproducing uncontrollably.*

These and many other chemicals, such as paints and pesticides, might make lives easier. But if they are not disposed of properly, they can harm our health. Some people choose to use chemicals that are harmful to health. For instance, more than 50 of the chemicals in cigarettes have been linked to cancer.

WORD ORIGIN ···········

antibiotic
anti–, means "against"; and Greek *biotikos,* means "fit for life"

Health and the Environment

Some chemicals that are harmful to our health, such as lead, are in our environment. Before 1978, lead was used in many paints. If the dried paint flaked, it released lead into the air. Inhaling lead-contaminated air can cause noninfectious kidney and nervous system diseases.

Some objects containing harmful chemicals are safe until the object is broken. For example, when ceiling and floor tiles containing asbestos are broken, asbestos fibers are released. People who are often exposed to such chemicals might develop cancer.

Key Concept Check How can chemicals affect the human body?

Visual Summary

Developing healthful habits and making healthful choices is one of the best ways you can stay healthy.

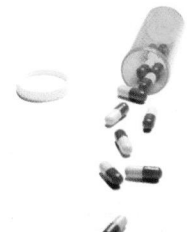

Chemicals are used in medicines such as antibiotics. These may be used for common bacterial infections, such as strep throat or ear infections.

Life choices, such as whether or not you eat a healthful diet, can influence the development and severity of diseases.

FOLDABLES

Use your lesson Foldable to review the lesson. Save your Foldable for the project at the end of the chapter.

What do you think NOW?

You first read the statements below at the beginning of the chapter.

5. Exercise and sleep can help keep you healthy.

6. Chemicals make you sick and should not be used.

Did you change your mind about whether you agree or disagree with the statements? Rewrite any false statements to make them true.

Use Vocabulary

1 A treatment that uses chemicals to kill cancer cells is called _____.

2 Medicines that kill bacteria are called _____.

Understand Key Concepts

3 **List** two healthful life choices.

4 Which chemical can be harmful to your health?
- **A.** antibiotic
- **C.** sunscreen
- **B.** asbestos
- **D.** vitamin

Interpret Graphics

5 **Examine** the photo on the right and identify the healthful practices you see.

6 **Create** a table like the one below. In the first column, list four chemicals or materials containing chemicals. In the second column, indicate whether the chemical is beneficial or harmful. In the third column, describe how the chemical benefits or harms people.

Chemical	Beneficial or Harmful?	How?

Critical Thinking

7 **Justify** Imagine you are Florence Nightingale. Justify your plan to increase cleanliness in hospitals.

8 **Evaluate** your personal hygiene in your daily routine. What could you do to limit your exposure to pathogens?

Materials

rotting apple

fresh apples (4)

potato peeler

cotton swabs

rubbing alcohol

self-sealing plastic bags (5)

camera

Also needed: labels, paper towels

Safety

Can one bad apple spoil the bunch?

Just like your skin protects the tissue underneath from infection, an apple's skin protects the inside of the apple from infection by harmful organisms.

Question

How is an apple's skin like your skin?

Procedure

1. Read and complete a lab safety form.

2. Use aseptic techniques to prepare your work area. Wash your hands, thoroughly disinfect the entire work area, and do not recontaminate. Put on gloves.

3. Label the plastic bags 1 through 5. Take a picture of a fresh apple. Place the apple in bag 1.

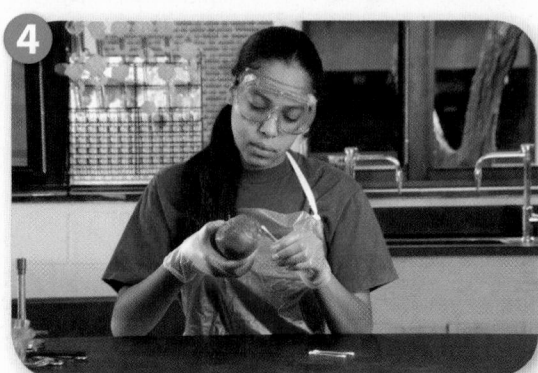

4. Insert a cotton swab into the decayed tissue from the rotting apple. Spread the tissue on a fresh apple and let it dry. Take a picture of the apple. Place the apple in bag 2.

5. Use the end of a potato peeler to carefully make two holes about 2 cm in diameter in the peels of the remaining three apples. Take a picture of one apple with holes. Place the apple in bag 3.

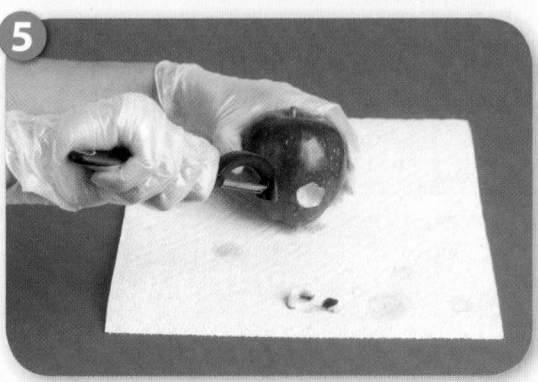

6. Insert a cotton swab into the decayed tissue of the rotten apple and then into one hole in one of the remaining apples. Repeat for the remaining holes in the last two apples. Take a picture of one apple. Place the apple in bag 4.

7 Use a cotton swab to disinfect the holes in the last apple with rubbing alcohol. Take a picture of the disinfected apple. Place the apple in bag 5.

8 Seal all bags and put them in a dark place.

9 After 3 days, note the condition of each apple. Do not open the plastic bags. In your Science Journal, record your observations in a data table like the one shown at right. Take a picture of each apple.

10 After 7 days, repeat step 9.

Analyze and Conclude

11 **Describe** How does each apple look at the start of this activity, after 3 days, and after 7 days?

12 **Explain** What are the differences in the conditions of the apples?

13 **The Big Idea** Relate what you have learned about rotting in apples to how the immune system protects humans from infection and helps maintain homeostasis.

Communicate Your Results

Display your data on a poster. Include the photos of each of the apples at the beginning of the activity, after 3 days, and after 7 days.

Inquiry Extension

There are other factors that contribute to apples rotting besides infection by microorganisms. How can you tell if the rotting in this case was caused by microorganisms or other factors? Propose a study using microscope observations that might help establish the role of microorganisms in rotting fruit.

Apple Observations		
Condition	Day 3	Day 7
Fresh, no decay		
Fresh with decay		
Holes, no decay		
Holes with decay		
Holes with decay and rubbing alcohol		

Lab Tips

☑ Remember that hand washing is an important part of aseptic techniques.

☑ Use good aseptic techniques to prepare your work area prior to this lab.

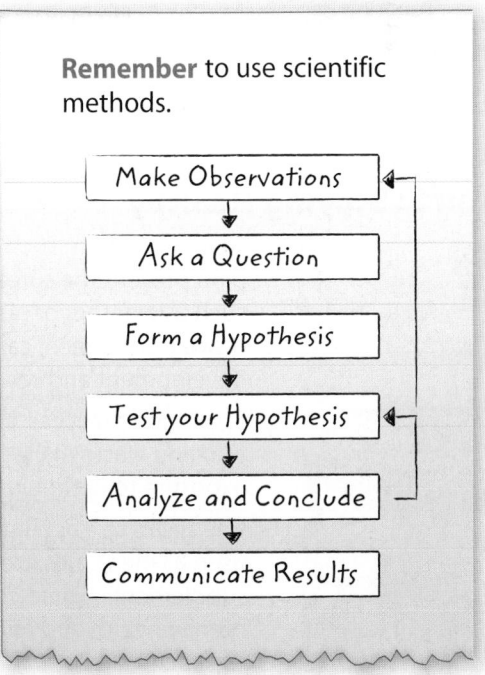

Remember to use scientific methods.

Make Observations

↓

Ask a Question

↓

Form a Hypothesis

↓

Test your Hypothesis

↓

Analyze and Conclude

↓

Communicate Results

Chapter 17 Study Guide

THE BIG IDEA The immune system protects the body against infections and diseases.

Key Concepts Summary 🔑

	Vocabulary

Lesson 1: Diseases

- Diseases can result from infection by **pathogens,** heredity, or the environment.
- **Infectious diseases** are caused by pathogens and are spread from an infected organism or the environment to another organism. **Noninfectious diseases** are not caused by pathogens and are not spread from one organism to another.

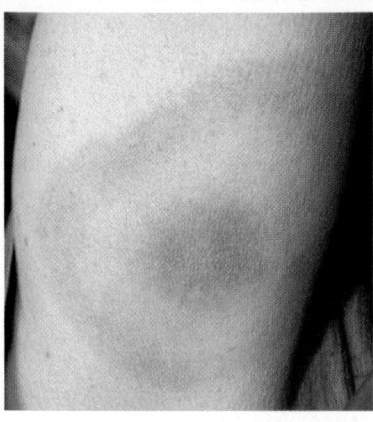

pathogen p. 601
pasteurization p. 603
infectious disease p. 605
vector p. 605
noninfectious disease p. 606
cancer p. 607

Lesson 2: The Immune System

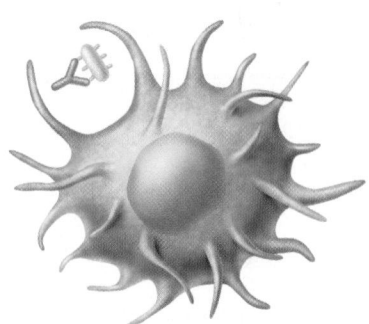

- The immune system protects against and defends the body from disease.
- Your body has first-line, second-line, and third-line defenses against pathogens.
- The immune system works with other body systems, including the circulatory system, the respiratory system, and the digestive system, to protect against invaders.

inflammation p. 615
antigen p. 616
antibody p. 616
B cell p. 616
T cell p. 616
allergy p. 616
immunity p. 617
active immunity p. 617
vaccination p. 617
passive immunity p. 617

Lesson 3: Staying Healthy

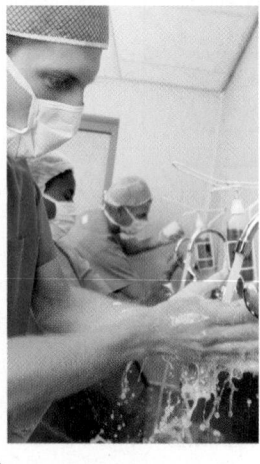

- Healthful habits, such as hand washing, can help prevent the spread of disease. Life choices, such as whether or not you eat a healthful diet or wear sunscreen, can influence the development and severity of diseases.
- Sanitation practices, such as safe food preparation and waste management, limit human exposure to pathogens and toxic substances.
- Chemicals can benefit human health when used as medicines, treatments for disease, and supplements. Some chemicals are harmful to human health and might cause diseases such as cancer.

antibiotic p. 624
chemotherapy p. 624

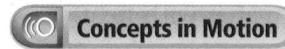
FOLDABLES® **Chapter Project**

Assemble your lesson Foldables as shown to make a Chapter Project. Use the project to review what you have learned in this chapter.

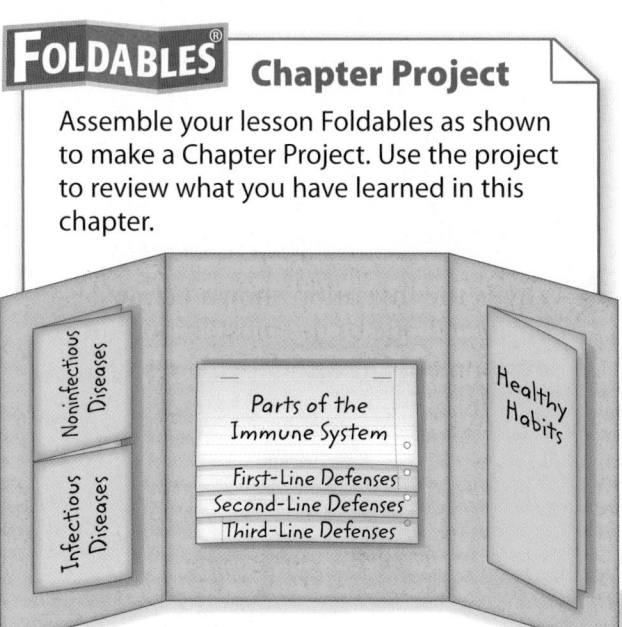

Use Vocabulary

1 A disease in which cells multiply uncontrollably is called _____.

2 Use the term *vector* in a sentence.

3 Define *pasteurization* in your own words.

4 Distinguish between antibodies and antigens.

5 In your own words, define *immunity*.

6 An overly sensitive immune response to common antigens is a(n) _____.

7 Use the term *antibiotics* in a sentence.

8 Differentiate between antibiotics and chemotherapy.

Link Vocabulary and Key Concepts

Concepts in Motion Interactive Concept Map

Copy this concept map, and then use vocabulary terms from the previous page to complete the concept map.

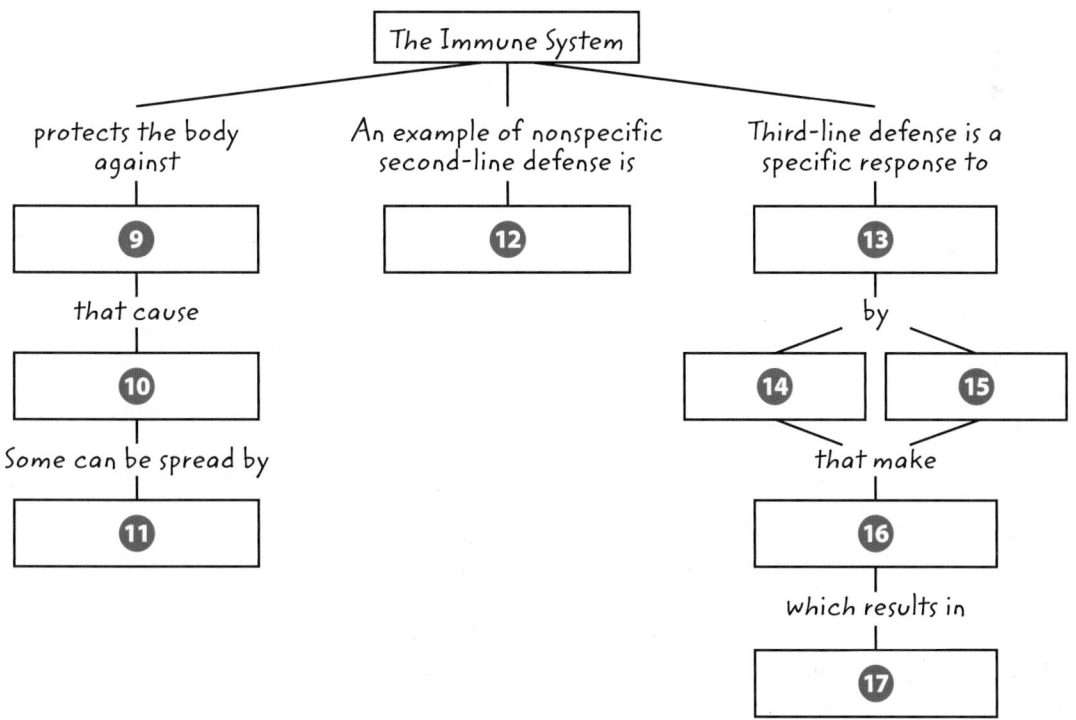

Understand Key Concepts 🔑

1 Which part of the blood plays the most direct role in fighting pathogens?

A. plasma
B. platelets
C. red blood cells
D. white blood cells

2 What is illustrated below?

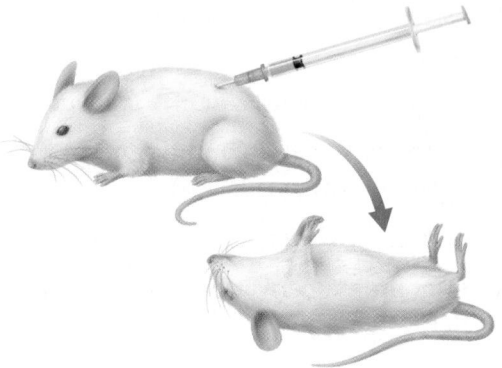

A. Bacteria can be treated with heat.
B. Bacteria do not infect other animals.
C. Bacteria cause disease in healthy animals.
D. One type of bacteria causes several different diseases.

3 Which has NOT led to improved health?

A. cleaner hospitals
B. lead paint
C. better waste management
D. cleaner food preparation tools

4 Which chemical might be helpful to the human body?

A. asbestos
B. antibiotic
C. lead
D. pesticide

5 Which is NOT part of the nonspecific, first-line defenses against pathogens?

A. antibody
B. cilia
C. mucus
D. skin

6 Inflammation is a common response to pathogens. Which would NOT be a common part of the inflammatory response at the site of an injury?

A. bruising
B. reddening
C. swelling
D. warmth

7 Why is the invention shown below considered one of the most important developments in early disease research?

A. It showed people how to pasteurize liquids.
B. It showed people that vaccines were effective.
C. It showed people that microorganisms existed outside of wounds.
D. It showed people that some diseases had a genetic component.

8 Which is NOT a healthful lifestyle choice?

A. exercising regularly
B. smoking cigarettes
C. using sunscreen
D. washing hands

9 Which is true about John Snow's research?

A. He developed the first vaccine.
B. He invented the first microscope.
C. He made surgery safer for patients.
D. He mapped a cholera outbreak.

10 Which is caused by a virus?

A. chicken pox
B. malaria
C. pneumonia
D. ringworm

Critical Thinking

11 **Compose** a letter to explain the causes and symptoms of cystic fibrosis to a friend of the family who is concerned about his or her child developing cystic fibrosis.

12 **Role-Play** Choose the most important researcher from among John Snow, Joseph Lister, Robert Koch, and Edward Jenner. Defend your choice.

13 **Evaluate** the following statement, using the data in the table below to support your conclusion: Every person has not been vaccinated for common diseases, such as tetanus, polio, measles, mumps, and rubella.

Effects of Vaccinations		
Disease	Rate Before Vaccination	Rate After Vaccination Developed
Tetanus	1,300	34
Polio	18,000	8
Measles	425,000	90
Mumps	200,000	610
Rubella	48,000	345

14 **Categorize** these parts of the immune system as first-line, second-line, or third-line defenses: cilia, white blood cells, antibodies, skin, mucus, inflammation.

15 **Plan and implement** a survey to determine when and how often the students in your class wash their hands.

16 **Design and create** a poster to remind the students in your school to make healthful life choices.

Writing in Science

17 **Write** a paragraph analyzing the differences in the causes of most childhood non-infectious diseases compared to other noninfectious diseases.

REVIEW THE BIG IDEA

18 Explain how the immune system helps the body maintain homeostasis.

19 The photo below shows a cancer cell being attacked by T cells. How does your immune system react when it detects an invader?

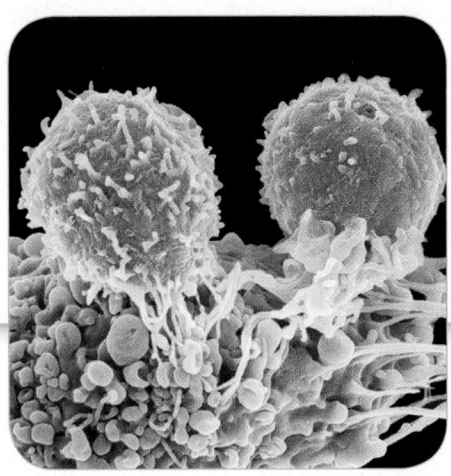

Math Skills

Math Practice

Use Percentages

20 The average annual number of rubella cases before the vaccine was developed was 48,000. There were 345 cases after the vaccine was developed. What percent change does this represent?

21 The average annual number of cases before vaccines were developed was 425,000 for measles and 200,000 for mumps. After the vaccines were developed, there were 90 cases of measles and 610 cases of mumps. Which vaccine was most effective in reducing cases of the disease?

Standardized Test Practice

Record your answers on the answer sheet provided by your teacher or on a sheet of paper.

Multiple Choice

1 Which would a doctor *exclude* as the cause of her patient's noninfectious disease?

  A environmental conditions

  B inherited traits

  C lifestyle choices

  D transmitted pathogens

Use the diagram below to answer question 2.

Immune Response

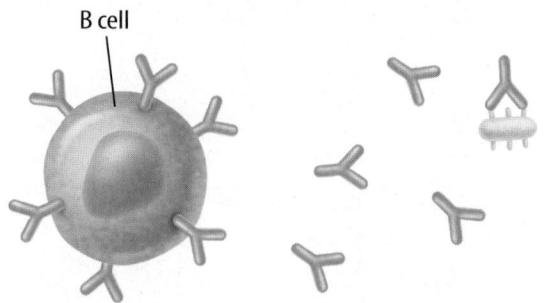

2 What are the Y-shaped objects in the diagram?

  A antibodies

  B antigens

  C bacteria

  D pathogens

3 Which first-line defense systems use acids to kill pathogens?

  A circulatory and respiratory

  B digestive and integumentary

  C nervous and circulatory

  D respiratory and digestive

4 Which is directly linked to increased risk of skin cancer in humans?

  A acid rain

  B asbestos insulation

  C sunlight exposure

  D water pollution

Use the diagram below to answer question 5.

Stage 1 - The Inflammatory Response

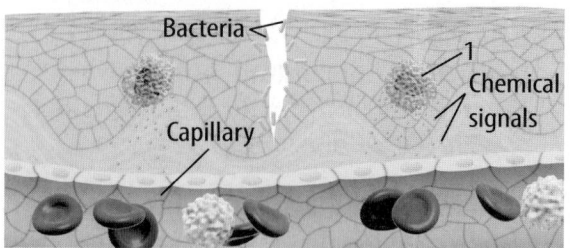

5 Which does *1* in the diagram represent?

  A host cell

  B mast cell

  C sheath cell

  D stem cell

6 In stage 2 of the inflammatory response, white blood cells and plasma leak into the area. What happens as a result?

  A bacteria destruction

  B capillary dilation

  C protein release

  D tissue swelling

7 How does sanitation improve health?

  A aids white blood cell production

  B increases vitamin absorption

  C reduces pathogen exposure

  D stimulates blood circulation

8 How do vitamin supplements contribute to health?

  A They block UV rays.

  B They improve nutrition.

  C They kill bacteria.

  D They kill cancer cells.

Use the table below to answer question 9.

Bacteria are present in ALL organisms with the disease but NOT in healthy organisms.
Bacteria must reproduce in the lab.
Sample of bacteria must cause disease in healthy animals.
Lab-grown pathogen is identical to original.

9 Which scientist developed the rules in the table above?

A Koch

B Lister

C Pasteur

D Snow

10 What kills bacteria in the pasteurization process?

A antiseptic

B heat

C isolation

D pressure

11 What is a disease-carrying organism that does NOT develop the disease?

A antigen

B B cell

C T cell

D vector

Constructed Response

Use the diagram below to answer questions 12 and 13.

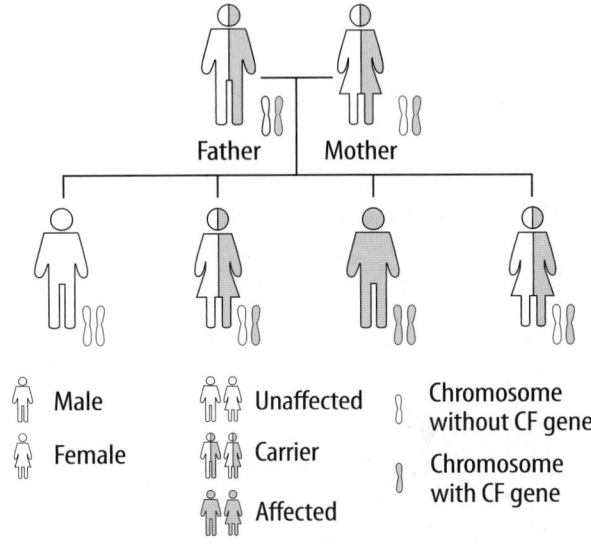

12 Based on the diagram above, why is cystic fibrosis a noninfectious disease? Use the terms *allele* and *recessive trait* to describe how someone contracts this disease.

13 Why might the parents in the diagram above be unaware that their children could contract cystic fibrosis? Suppose the parents had only one child. Will that child have cystic fibrosis? Explain.

14 List three sanitation practices. How do they promote health?

15 Explain the difference between active and passive immunity. How do vaccinations contribute to human immunity?

NEED EXTRA HELP?															
If You Missed Question...	1	2	3	4	5	6	7	8	9	10	11	12	13	14	15
Go to Lesson...	1	2	2	3	2	2	3	3	1	1	1	1	1	3	2

Control and Coordination

THE BIG IDEA

How do the nervous and endocrine systems help maintain the body's homeostasis?

Inquiry How does she do it?

This softball player must be able to sense activity and react quickly. The batter quickly swings the bat as the ball speeds toward her.

- How will this softball player react to try to hit the ball thrown toward her?

- What is happening in her brain and body to prepare for the action?

- How are these activities essential for survival in daily life?

Get Ready to Read

What do you think?

Before you read, decide if you agree or disagree with each of these statements. As you read this chapter, see if you change your mind about any of the statements.

1. The nervous system contains two parts—the central nervous system and the peripheral nervous system.

2. The autonomic nervous system controls voluntary functions.

3. A human has five senses that detect his or her environment.

4. The senses of smell and hearing work together.

5. Positive feedback systems in humans help maintain homeostasis.

6. Endocrine glands secrete hormones.

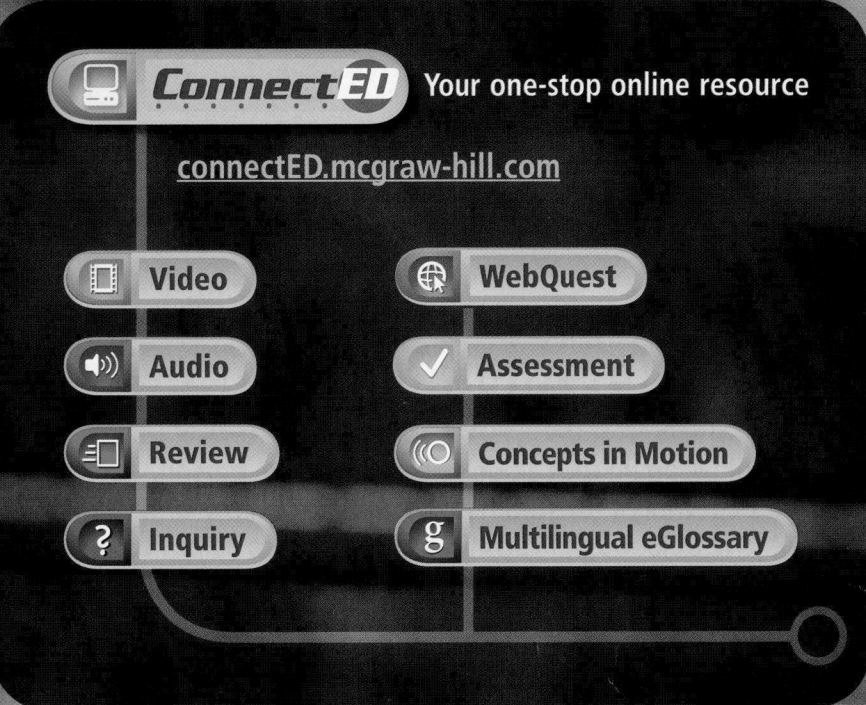

ConnectED Your one-stop online resource

connectED.mcgraw-hill.com

- Video
- WebQuest
- Audio
- Assessment
- Review
- Concepts in Motion
- Inquiry
- Multilingual eGlossary

The Nervous System

Reading Guide

Key Concepts 🔑
ESSENTIAL QUESTIONS

- What does the nervous system do?
- How do the parts of the nervous system work together?
- How does the nervous system interact with other body systems?

Vocabulary

nervous system p. 637

stimulus p. 638

neuron p. 639

synapse p. 639

central nervous system p. 640

cerebrum p. 640

cerebellum p. 640

brain stem p. 641

spinal cord p. 641

peripheral nervous system p. 641

reflex p. 642

ⓖ **Multilingual eGlossary**

Inquiry What is memory?

These brain scan images all belong to the same person. Activity occurring in the brain is colored red, yellow, and orange. The person being scanned was asked to listen to and memorize words as the scans were taking place. What might the scans tell you about how the brain is working as the person hears different words?

Can you make your eyes blink or dilate?

Are you telling your body to breathe right now? Many functions the human body performs are not under your control. These functions, such as your heart beating, are usually important to your survival. Can you always control your muscles?

1. Sit facing a partner. Take turns trying to blink your eyes. Record your observations in your Science Journal.

2. Face your partner again. Try to make your pupils dilate, or get bigger. Record your observations.

3. Cover your eyes with your hand for 30 seconds. Make sure to completely block the light from your eyes.

4. Have your partner look at your eyes as you take your hand away. Record the observation in your Science Journal.

5. Repeat steps 3 and 4 using a **mirror** to observe your own eyes when you open them. Record what you observe.

Think About This

1. Why do you think it might be important that you do not need to think about blinking or breathing, even though you can make yourself do those actions?

2. 🔑 **Key Concept** What do you think the purpose of dilating the eye might be? Why might it be helpful to not have to think about dilating your eyes?

Functions of the Nervous System

Have you ever had goose bumps form on your arms when you were cold? These bumps form because muscle cells in your skin respond to the cold temperature. As the muscle cells contract, or shorten, bumps form, and the hairs on your arms rise up. The hairs trap air, which helps to insulate the skin. This helps you feel warmer. How did the muscle cells know to contract? When you first felt the cold, a message was sent to your brain. After the message was processed, the brain sent a message to your skin's muscle cells, and goose bumps formed.

The part of an organism that gathers, processes, and responds to information is called the **nervous system.** Your nervous system receives information from your five senses—vision, hearing, smell, taste, and touch. You will read more about the five senses in Lesson 2.

The nervous system functions very quickly. It can receive information, process it, and respond in less than one second. In fact, signals received by the nervous system can travel as fast as some airplanes. This is around 400 km/h.

Make a horizontal three-tab book and label it as shown. Use the book to organize your notes about the functions of the nervous system.

| Gathering Information | Responding to Stimuli | Maintaining Homeostasis |

The Nervous System

Figure 1 The goalie gathers information about the puck and responds by moving to block it from entering the goal. His body maintains homeostasis when his heart rate and breathing return to normal.

✓**Visual Check** What is the stimulus that the goalie is reacting to?

WORD ORIGIN · · · · · · · · · ·

stimulus
from Latin *stimulare*, means "goad, urge"
· · · · · · · · · · · · · · · ·

Gathering Information

Have you ever seen a goalie react quickly to block a hockey puck from entering the goal? The sight of an object, such as the approaching puck in **Figure 1,** is a stimulus (STIHM yuh lus) (plural, stimuli). *A* **stimulus** *is a change in an organism's environment that causes a response.* The goalie's nervous system gathers and interprets the sight of the puck approaching and causes his body to react by raising his arm to block the shot.

Responding to Stimuli

How would you react if you saw the puck approaching the goal in **Figure 1?** Some people might move quickly to block the shot, while others might turn away to avoid being hit. These reactions are ways that the nervous system enables people to respond to a stimulus from the environment. Since the nervous system receives many stimuli at the same time, the type of response depends on how the information is processed.

Maintaining Homeostasis

Think again about the event shown in **Figure 1.** While responding to the stimuli of the approaching puck, the goalie's nervous system causes his heart and breathing rates to increase. This helps make his reaction time faster. People continually react to changes in their environments. Their nervous systems help maintain homeostasis, or the regulation of their internal environments. For example, the goalie's nervous system must signal his heart and breathing to slow down to restore homeostasis once he has blocked the shot.

🔑 **Key Concept Check** What are some of the tasks performed by the nervous system?

Neurons

The basic functioning units of the nervous system are called nerve cells, or **neurons** (NOO rahnz). Neurons help different parts of your body communicate with each other. Without looking down, how do you know whether you are walking on sand or pavement? Neurons in your feet connect to other neurons that send information to your brain about the surface. As shown in **Figure 2**, neurons have three parts—dendrites (DEN drites), a cell body, and an axon (AK sahn). A dendrite receives information from another neuron or from another cell in your body. A cell body processes information. An axon sends information out to another neuron or cell in your body.

Types of Neurons

There are three types of neurons that work together. They send and receive information throughout your body. Sensory neurons send information about your environment to your brain or spinal cord. Motor neurons send information from your brain or spinal cord to tissues and organs in your body. Interneurons connect sensory and motor neurons, much like a bridge connects two different areas of land.

Synapses

The gap between two neurons is called a **synapse** (SIH naps), as shown in **Figure 2.** Most neurons communicate across synapses by releasing chemicals. The chemicals carry information from the axon of one neuron to a dendrite of another neuron. This is similar to the way a baton is passed between runners in a relay race. Most synapses are between an axon of one neuron and a dendrite of another neuron. Information is usually transmitted in only one direction.

Figure 2 Information travels through the nervous system when chemical signals are released by the axon of one neuron and received by a dendrite on another neuron.

Neurons and Synapses

Concepts in Motion Animation

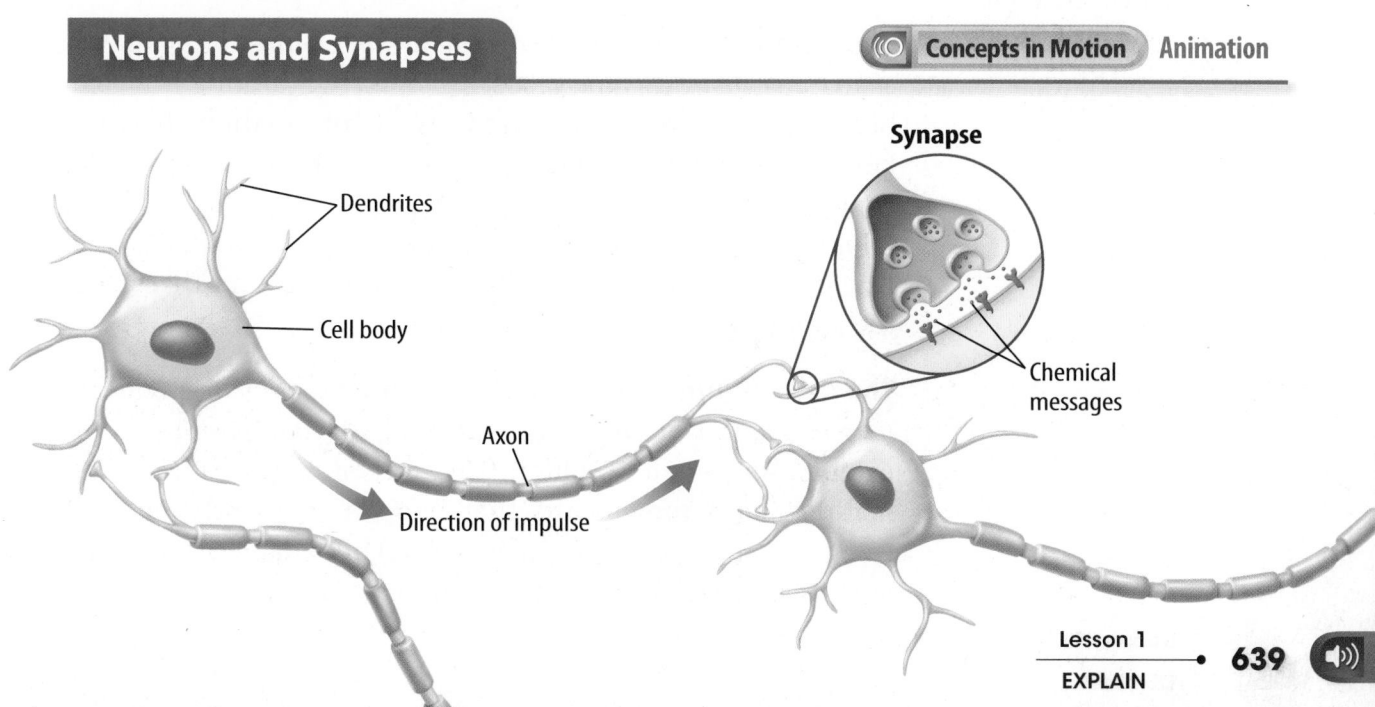

Synapse

Dendrites

Cell body

Axon

Direction of impulse

Chemical messages

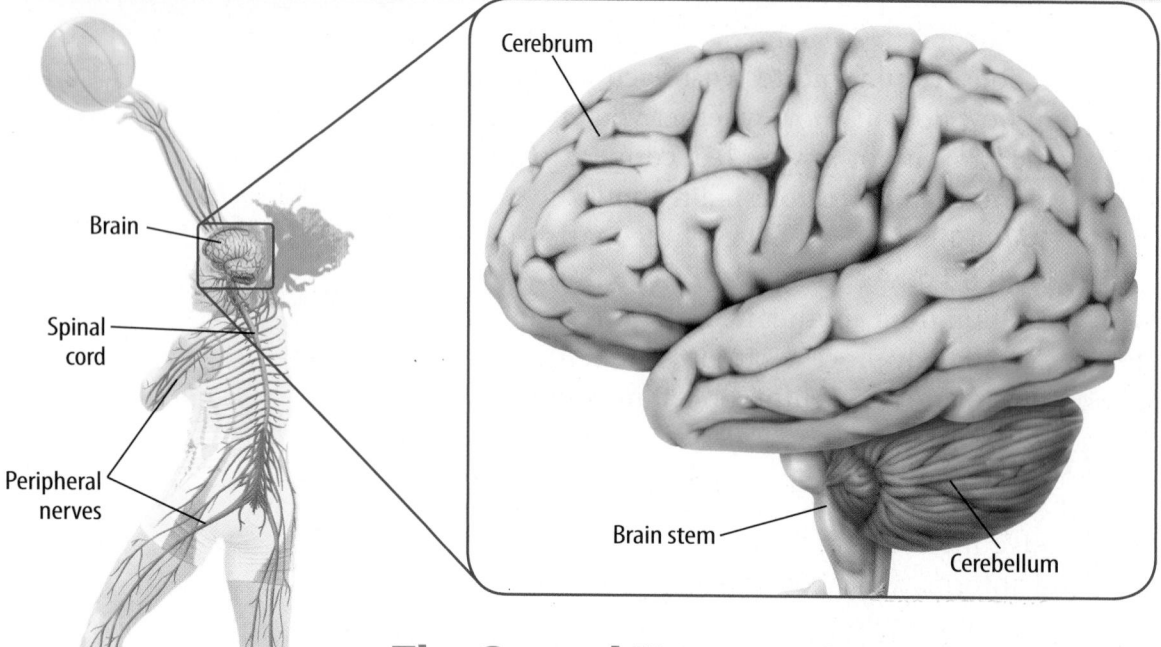

Brain

Spinal cord

Peripheral nerves

Cerebrum

Brain stem

Cerebellum

■ Central nervous system (CNS)
■ Peripheral nervous system (PNS)

Figure 3 The nervous system consists of the central nervous system (CNS) and the peripheral nervous system (PNS). The brain is part of the CNS and has three main parts with specialized functions.

The Central Nervous System

As shown in **Figure 3,** your nervous system has two parts—the central nervous system and the peripheral (puh RIH frul) nervous system. You will read about the peripheral nervous system later in this lesson. *The* **central nervous system** (CNS) *is made up of the brain and the spinal cord.* The CNS receives, processes, stores, and transfers information.

The Brain

Much like a general is the commander of an army, the brain is the control center of your body. Your brain receives information, processes it, and sends out a response. The brain also stores some information as memories.

The Cerebrum *The part of the brain that controls memory, language, and thought is the* **cerebrum** (suh REE brum). The cerebrum also processes touch and visual information. It is the largest and most complex part of the brain. As shown in **Figure 3,** the surface of the cerebrum has many folds. These folds enable a large number of neurons to fit into a small space. If you could unfold the cerebrum, you would find that it has the surface area of a large pillowcase.

The Cerebellum *The part of the brain that coordinates voluntary muscle movement and regulates balance and posture is the* **cerebellum** (ser uh BEH lum). The cerebellum also stores information about movements that happen frequently, such as tying a shoe or pedaling a bicycle. This enables you to do repetitive things faster and with more accuracy.

The Brain Stem Some functions, such as digestion and the beating of your heart, are involuntary—they happen without your controlling them. *The area of the brain that controls involuntary functions is the* **brain stem**, shown in **Figure 4.** It also controls sneezing, coughing, and swallowing. It connects the brain to the spinal cord.

The Spinal Cord

The **spinal cord,** shown in **Figure 4,** *is a tubelike structure of neurons.* The neurons extend to other areas of the body. This enables information to be sent out and received by the brain. The spinal cord is like an information highway. Just like cars travel on a highway from one city to another, neurons in the spinal cord send information back and forth between the brain and other body parts. Bones called vertebrae protect the spinal cord.

 Reading Check What are the two parts of the central nervous system?

The Peripheral Nervous System

Recall that the nervous system is made of both the CNS and the peripheral nervous system. *The* **peripheral nervous system** (PNS), shown in **Figure 3,** *has sensory neurons and motor neurons that transmit information between the CNS and the rest of the body.*

Like the CNS, the PNS also has two parts—the somatic system and the autonomic system. The somatic system controls skeletal muscles. Neurons of the somatic system communicate between the CNS and skeletal muscles and cause voluntary movements, such as picking up a book. The autonomic system controls smooth muscles and cardiac muscles. It regulates involuntary actions, such as dilating blood vessels and the beating of your heart.

 Key Concept Check How do the PNS and the CNS interact?

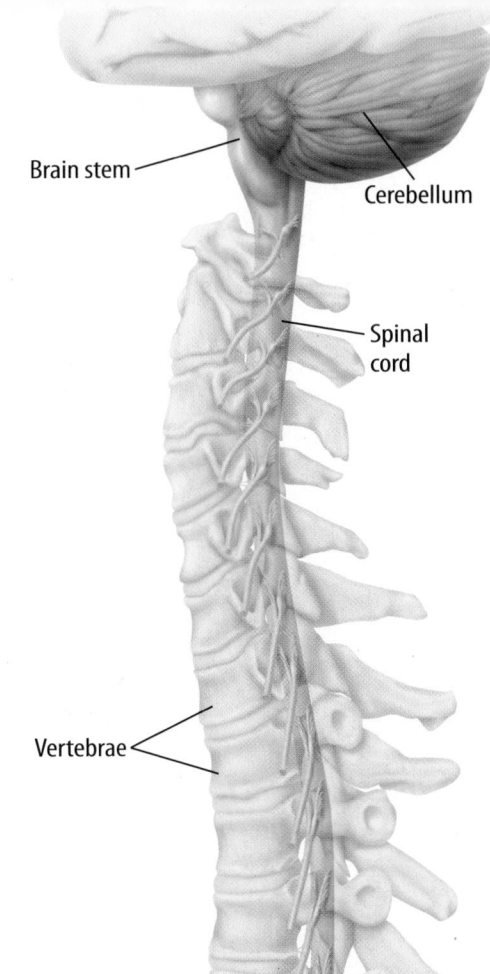

Figure 4 The spinal cord relays information between the brain and the PNS.

Labels: Brain stem, Cerebellum, Spinal cord, Vertebrae

Math Skills

Use Proportions

A nerve impulse from your hand travels at about 119 m/s. How long does it take the signal from your hand to reach your spinal cord if the distance is 0.40 m? You can use proportions to solve the problem.

Set up a proportion. $\dfrac{119 \text{ m}}{1 \text{ s}} = \dfrac{0.40 \text{ m}}{y \text{ s}}$

Cross multiply. $119 \text{ m} \times y \text{ s} = 0.40 \text{ m} \times 1 \text{ s}$

Solve for the y by dividing both sides by 119 m. $y = \dfrac{0.40 \text{ m·s}}{119 \text{ m}}$

$y = 0.003 \text{ s}$

Practice

One giraffe neuron has an axon 4.6 m long that extends from its toe to the base of its neck. How long will it take a nerve impulse to travel this distance at a speed of 75 m/s?

Nervous System Health

A healthy nervous system is necessary for maintaining homeostasis. The nervous system can be damaged by infections and diseases. The most common way the nervous system is damaged is by **physical** injuries.

ACADEMIC VOCABULARY

physical
(adjective) relating to material things

Physical Injuries

Falling, being in an automobile accident, and being hurt while participating in sports are some of the ways that you can injure and harm the nervous system. The injured nerves can no longer send and receive signals. This stops communication between the CNS and the PNS. When this happens, paralysis can occur. Paralysis is the loss of muscle function and sometimes a loss of feeling.

Preventing Injuries

Imagine that you are walking barefoot and you step on a sharp object. Without thinking, you quickly lift your foot. You do not think about moving your foot, it just happens. *An automatic movement in response to a stimulus is called a* **reflex.** Reflexes are fast because, in most cases, the information goes only to the spinal cord, not to the brain, as shown in **Figure 5.** This fast response protects us from injuries because it takes less time to move away from harm. A reflex often occurs before the brain knows that the body was in danger. However, once nerve signals reach the brain after the response, you feel pain.

Figure 5 A reflex enables you to respond to stimuli quickly.

 Reading Check Why are reflexes fast?

The Path of a Reflex

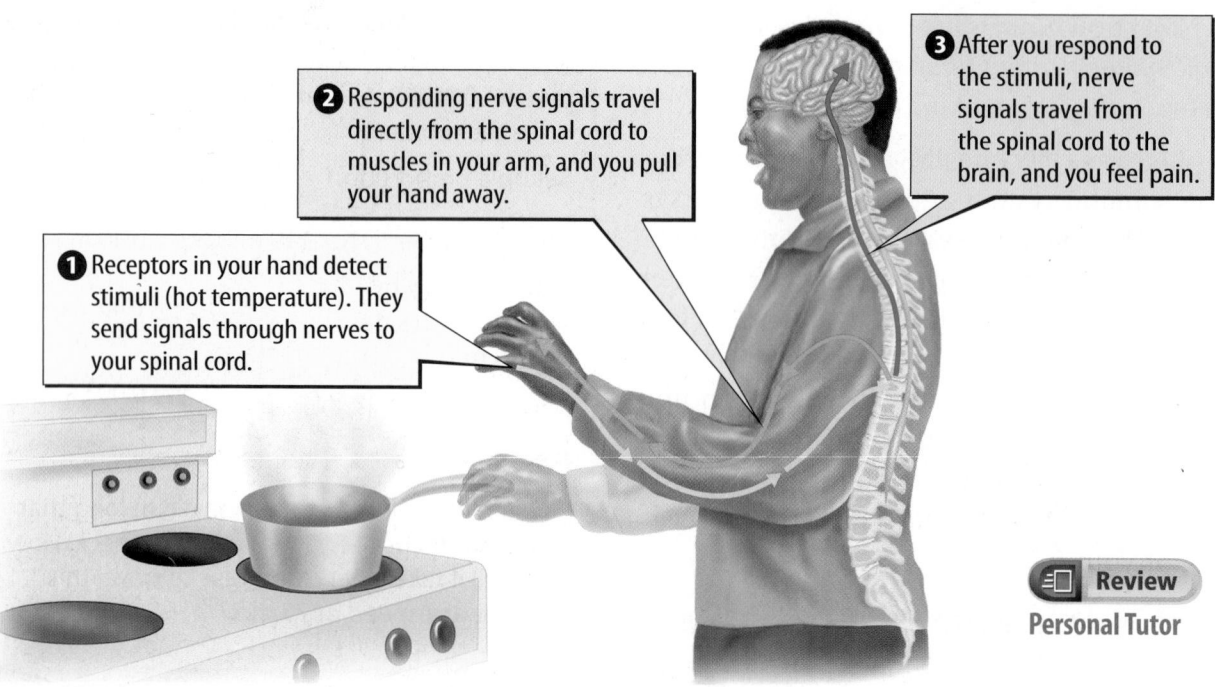

❷ Responding nerve signals travel directly from the spinal cord to muscles in your arm, and you pull your hand away.

❸ After you respond to the stimuli, nerve signals travel from the spinal cord to the brain, and you feel pain.

❶ Receptors in your hand detect stimuli (hot temperature). They send signals through nerves to your spinal cord.

Review
Personal Tutor

Drugs

In addition to physical injuries, the nervous system can also be affected by substances you take into your body. Drugs are chemicals that affect the body's functions. Many drugs affect the nervous system by either speeding up or slowing down the communication between neurons.

Some pain medicines slow down this communication so much that they stop pain stimuli from reaching the brain. A drug that slows down the communication between neurons is called a depressant. Some people avoid drinking beverages that contain caffeine in the evening because it keeps them awake. Caffeine speeds up the communication between neurons. A drug that speeds up neuron communication is called a stimulant.

The Nervous System and Homeostasis

Why do you shiver when you get cold? It's because your nervous system senses the cold temperature and signals your muscles to contract rapidly in order to warm your body. Your body maintains homeostasis by receiving information from your environment and responding to it. The nervous system is vital to sensing changes in your environment. The nervous system signals other systems, such as the digestive, endocrine, and circulatory systems, to make adjustments when needed.

 Key Concept Check Give an example of how the nervous system works with another body system to maintain homeostasis.

Inquiry MiniLab
20 minutes

How quickly can you improve your reaction time?

During a baseball game, a batter has less than one second to see the pitch, decide to try to hit the ball, and aim his swing. Through practice, he can improve his reaction time, which improves his performance. Can you improve your reaction time in just five trials?

1. Read and complete a lab safety form.
2. In your Science Journal, design a data sheet for five trials.
3. Hold a **metric ruler** vertically from the top. Have your partner position his or her open index finger and thumb just below the bottom edge of the ruler without touching it.
4. With the ruler slightly above the catcher's fingers, release the ruler without warning. Your partner should try to catch the ruler as quickly as possible by closing his or her thumb and index finger together. Record the distance the ruler fell.
5. Repeat steps 3 and 4 for four more trials.
6. Switch places with your partner, and repeat steps 3–5. Then create a graph to show the results for your five trials.
7. Record your results on a class data sheet.

Analyze and Conclude

1. **Determine** the mean, median, mode, and range for your results and the class results.

2. **Predict** what factors might affect reaction time for this activity.

3. **Key Concept** How is the ability of your nervous system to react quickly helpful to your survival?

Lesson 1 Review

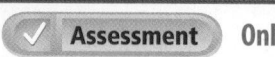

Visual Summary

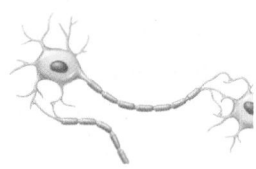

The nervous system gathers and interprets stimuli using a system of neurons that connect throughout the body.

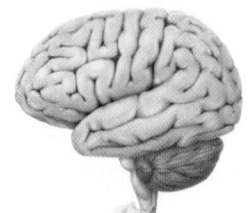

The central nervous system receives, processes, stores, and transfers information.

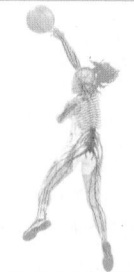

The peripheral nervous system is made up of the neurons that transmit information between the CNS and the rest of the body.

FOLDABLES®

Use your lesson Foldable to review the lesson. Save your Foldable for the project at the end of the chapter.

What do you think NOW?

You first read the statements below at the beginning of the chapter.

1. The nervous system contains two parts—the central nervous system and the peripheral nervous system.

2. The autonomic nervous system controls voluntary functions.

Did you change your mind about whether you agree or disagree with the statements? Rewrite any false statements to make them true.

Use Vocabulary

1 **List** the parts of the central nervous system.

2 **Distinguish** between a neuron and a synapse.

3 **Use the terms** *autonomic* and *somatic* in a sentence.

Understand Key Concepts

4 Which causes an organism to react?
  A. CNS   C. stimulus
  B. PNS   D. synapse

5 **Compare** the functions of the three parts of the brain.

6 **Explain** how a spinal cord injury may prevent movement.

Interpret Graphics

7 **Summarize** Copy and fill in the graphic organizer below to summarize how the nervous system receives, processes, and responds to a stimulus.

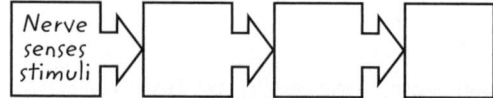

Critical Thinking

8 **Describe** Look at the synapse shown below. Describe the path of a signal from one neuron to another.

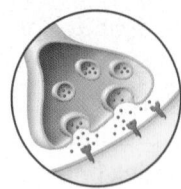

Math Skills
— Math Practice —

9 The longest axon in a whale can be 18.2 m long. If it takes 0.26 s for a signal to travel the length of this axon, how fast is the nerve impulse traveling in m/s?

How does the nervous system respond to a stimulus?

Neuroscientists can model how information moves between neurons in the body. The chemicals that send messages between neurons are too small to see, so a neuroscientist might make a model that shows how the messages are transmitted.

Learn It

A **model** is a representation of how something functions. It might be an object, a drawing, a calculation, a diagram, or something else that explains and describes how things work. Scientists often model biological activities in order to better understand them.

Try It

1 Read and complete a lab safety form.

2 Form groups of five. Stand in a line with the four other students so that you can reach the hand of the person next to you. Do not move or talk. The student at the front of the line represents the neurons in the fish's head and eyes. The student at the end of the line represents the neurons in the fish's tail. Only the fish's tail—the last student in line—can make the fish swim.

3 Imagine that your fish sees a tasty shrimp in the water. In order to eat the shrimp, the head must pass a message to the tail telling it to swim toward the shrimp. The student that represents neurons in the fish's head should send the message to the tail by squeezing the hand of the next student in line.

4 Continue passing the message between neurons (students). When the student representing neurons in the tail gets the message, this student should move forward. Observe how long it takes for the message to reach the tail and make the fish swim toward the shrimp.

Apply It

5 Take one student out of the middle of the line, leaving a gap. Now imagine that the fish sees a shark that wants to eat it. What happens when the head sends a message to the tail to swim away from the shark? What happens to the fish?

6 Take two more students out of the middle of the line, making the line only two cells long—the fish's head and tail. Stand so that the head and tail are next to one another and hold hands. Now how long does it take to send a message to swim away from the shark? Why does the message move more quickly?

7 **Key Concept** What type of neuron does the student at the fish's head represent? What type of neuron does the student at the fish's tail represent? When students squeeze hands to pass messages down the line of neurons, what function are they modeling?

The Senses

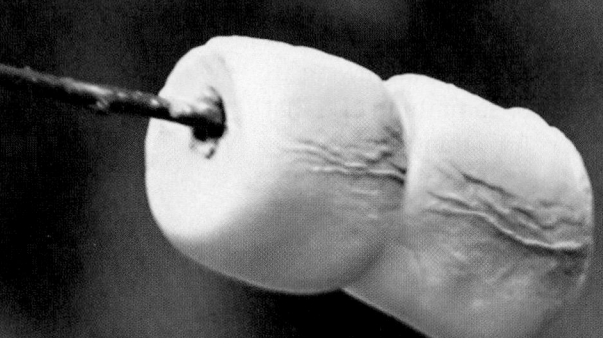

Reading Guide

Key Concepts
ESSENTIAL QUESTIONS

- How do you learn about your environment?
- What is the role of the senses in maintaining homeostasis?

Vocabulary

sensory system p. 647

receptor p. 647

retina p. 648

eardrum p. 650

g Multilingual eGlossary

▢ Video

- BrainPOP®
- What's Science Got to do With It?

Inquiry **Using All Five Senses?**

Have you ever toasted marshmallows over a campfire? What did you see? What smells did you experience? What sounds did you hear? Which sensations did you feel? What tastes do you remember? How do these things together make up a campfire experience?

Does your nose help you taste food?

Sometimes you might hold your nose when you don't want to taste something you're eating. Does this really work? Your senses all function because of nervous impulses that send information. Are your senses of taste and smell connected?

1. Read and complete a lab safety form.

2. Hold your nose closed while your teacher walks around and places a **food cube** on your **plate**.

3. While still holding your nose, place the food cube in your mouth and chew it.

4. In your Science Journal, write down what the food tasted like to you and what you think the food is.

5. Repeat steps 2–4 with a different food cube. Record your observations.

6. Let go of your nose and chew another sample of both food cubes. Record your observations.

Think About This

1. What did the two food cubes taste like when you held your nose?

2. What did the two food cubes taste like when you were not holding your nose?

3. **Key Concept** How do both senses together affect your ability to learn about your environment?

You and Your Environment

Recall from Lesson 1 that your nervous system enables your body to receive information about your environment, process the information, and react to it. Your nervous system is constantly responding to many different types of stimuli. However, your body has to receive a stimulus before it can respond to one. How does this happen?

The **sensory system** *is the part of your nervous system that detects or senses the environment.* A human uses five senses—vision, hearing, smell, taste, and touch—to detect his or her environment. What senses might you use around a campfire, like the one in the photo on the opposite page? You might see the flames of the campfire, hear the crackle of the wood burning, smell the smoke, feel the warmth of the fire, and taste the cooked marshmallows. *All parts of the sensory system have special structures called* **receptors** *that detect stimuli.* Each of the five senses uses different receptors.

WORD ORIGIN ·············

sensory
from Latin *sentire*, means
"to perceive, feel"

Key Concept Check Describe one way your senses help you to learn about the environment.

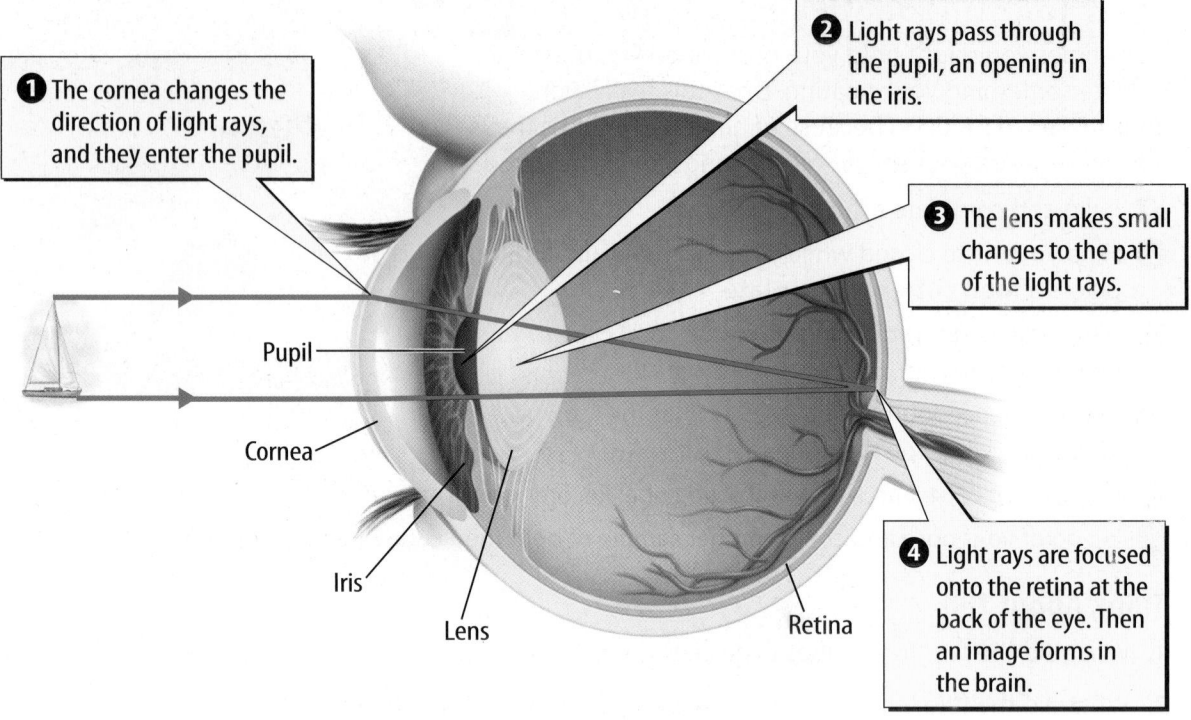

❶ The cornea changes the direction of light rays, and they enter the pupil.

❷ Light rays pass through the pupil, an opening in the iris.

❸ The lens makes small changes to the path of the light rays.

❹ Light rays are focused onto the retina at the back of the eye. Then an image forms in the brain.

Pupil

Cornea

Iris

Lens

Retina

Figure 6 Your eyes contain photoreceptors that receive and interpret light signals from the environment.

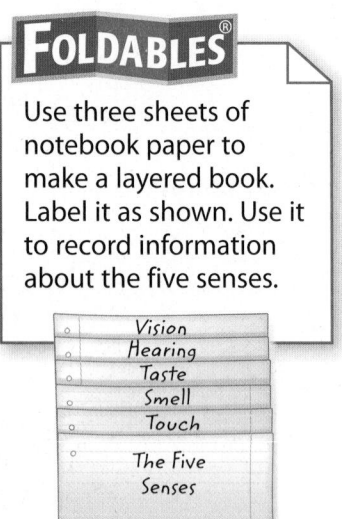

Use three sheets of notebook paper to make a layered book. Label it as shown. Use it to record information about the five senses.

Vision
Hearing
Taste
Smell
Touch
The Five Senses

Vision

Have you ever wondered how your eyes work? Your sense of vision lets you see things that are close, such as the words on this page, and objects that are far away, such as a star in the night sky. The visual system uses photoreceptors in the eye to detect light and create vision.

The Parts of the Eye

As shown in **Figure 6,** light enters the eye through the cornea (KOR nee uh), a thin membrane that protects the eye and changes the direction of light rays. The colored part of your eye is the iris (I rus). After light passes through the cornea, it goes through an opening formed by the iris called the pupil. The iris controls the amount of light that enters the eye by changing the size of the pupil. In bright light, the iris constricts, making the pupil smaller and letting in less light. In dim light, the iris relaxes, making the pupil larger and letting in more light. Light then travels through a clear structure called the lens. As shown in **Figure 6,** the lens works with the cornea and focuses light. *The* **retina** *(RET nuh) is an area at the back of the eye that has two types of cells—rod cells and cone cells—with photoreceptors.* Rod cells detect shapes and low levels of light. They are important for night vision. Cone cells detect color and function best in bright light.

How You See

In order to see, light that enters your eyes has to be detected by the **rods** and cones in the retina. The rods and cones detect information about the colors and shapes of objects from the light that enters the eyes. The retina then sends that information as electric signals through the optic nerve to the brain. The brain uses the information and creates a picture of what you are seeing.

Focusing Light

The lens and the cornea work together and change the direction of the light that enters the eye. As shown in **Figure 6,** both the lens and the cornea are curved. These curved shapes change the direction of light and focus it onto the retina. Why do some people need glasses to see well? If corneas or lenses are not curved exactly right, the eyes will have trouble focusing images, as shown in **Figure 7.** If a person's eyes are longer than normal, the person is nearsighted and has trouble seeing images that are far away. If a person's eyes are shorter than normal, the person is farsighted and has trouble seeing images that are close up. Glasses or contacts are used to correct vision problems by correctly focusing the light on the retina.

 Reading Check Which parts of vision are rods and cones responsible for?

Figure 7 The lens and the cornea focus light. Vision problems occur when they are not curved correctly.

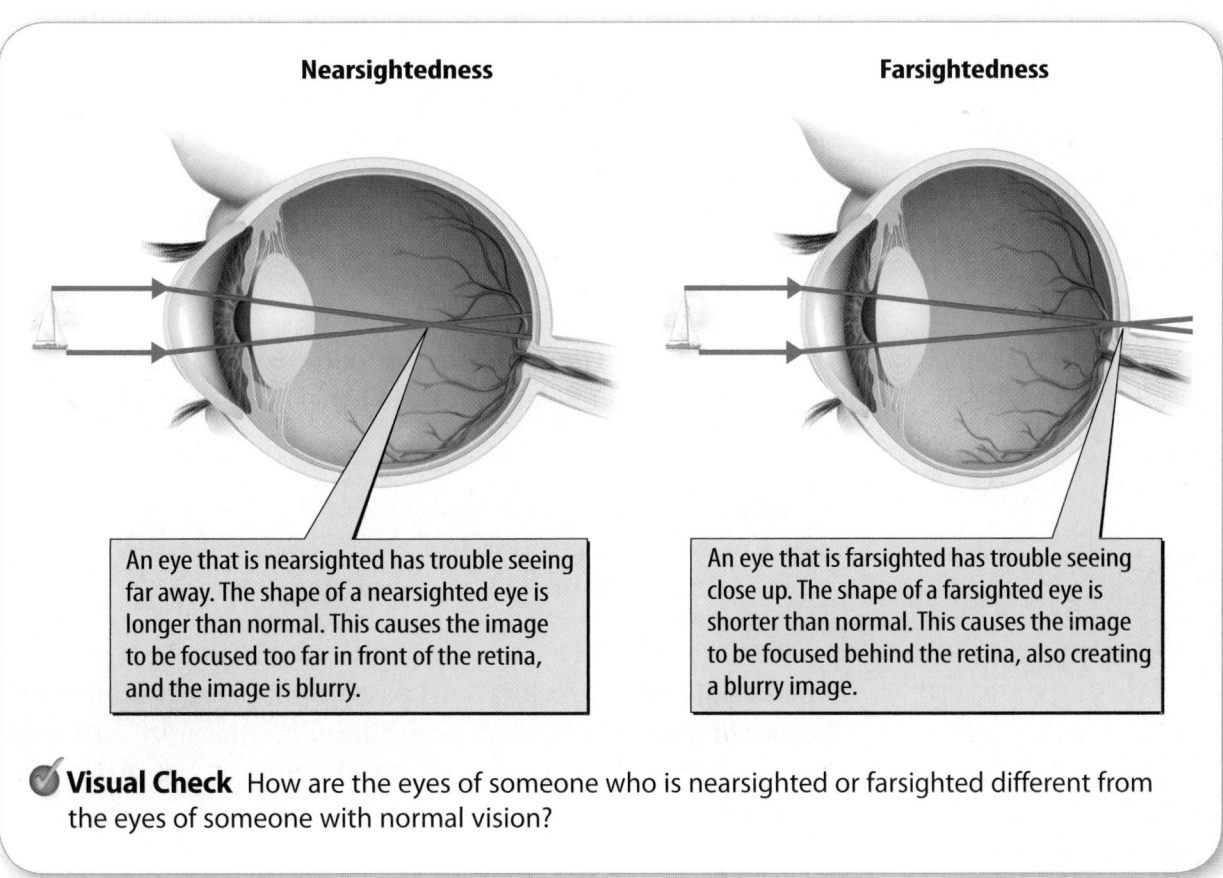

Nearsightedness

Farsightedness

An eye that is nearsighted has trouble seeing far away. The shape of a nearsighted eye is longer than normal. This causes the image to be focused too far in front of the retina, and the image is blurry.

An eye that is farsighted has trouble seeing close up. The shape of a farsighted eye is shorter than normal. This causes the image to be focused behind the retina, also creating a blurry image.

Visual Check How are the eyes of someone who is nearsighted or farsighted different from the eyes of someone with normal vision?

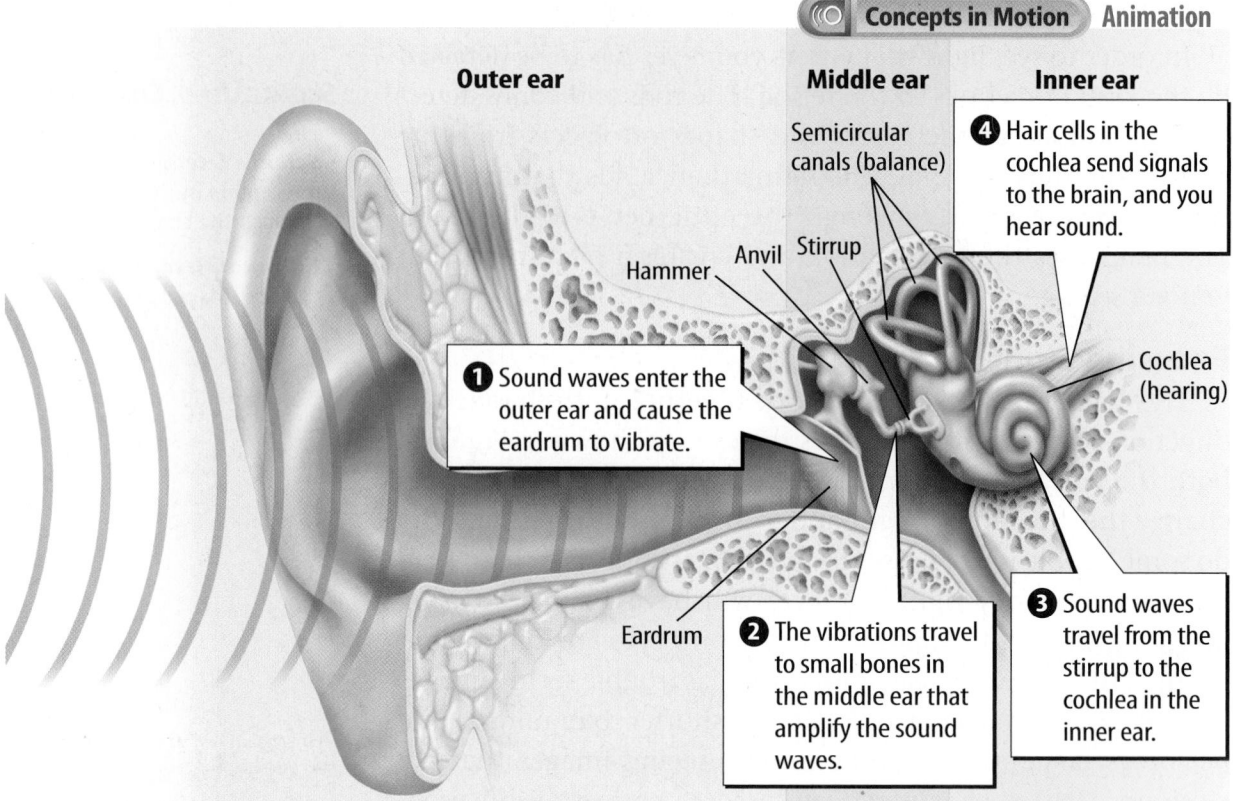

Outer ear

Middle ear   **Inner ear**

Semicircular
canals (balance)

❹ Hair cells in the
cochlea send signals
to the brain, and you
hear sound.

Anvil Stirrup

Hammer

❶ Sound waves enter the
outer ear and cause the
eardrum to vibrate.

Cochlea
(hearing)

Eardrum

❷ The vibrations travel
to small bones in
the middle ear that
amplify the sound
waves.

❸ Sound waves
travel from the
stirrup to the
cochlea in the
inner ear.

Figure 8 Scientists have identified three specialized regions in the human ear.

REVIEW VOCABULARY

wave
a disturbance in a material that transfers energy without transferring matter

Hearing

How do you hear the sounds around you? The vibration of matter creates sound **waves** that travel through air and other substances. Sound waves that enter the ear are detected by auditory (AW duh tor ee) receptors. As waves travel within the ear, they are amplified, or increased, and move hair cells. The hair cells send information about the sound waves to the brain. The brain processes information about the loudness and tone of the sound, and you hear.

The Parts of the Ear

As shown in **Figure 8,** human ears have three areas—the outer ear, the middle ear, and the inner ear—each with a special function.

The Outer Ear The outer ear includes the parts of the ear that you can see. It collects sound waves that make the eardrum vibrate. *The **eardrum** is a thin membrane between the outer ear and the inner ear.*

The Middle Ear The vibrations pass from the eardrum to small bones in the middle ear—the hammer, the anvil, and the stirrup. The movement of these bones amplifies the sound waves.

The Inner Ear The part of the ear that detects sound is the inner ear. The inner ear converts sound waves into messages that are sent to the brain. The structure shown in **Figure 8** that looks like a snail shell is called the cochlea (KOHK lee ah). The cochlea is filled with fluid. When sound waves reach the cochlea, they make the fluid vibrate. The liquid in the cochlea moves much like the way that hot chocolate moves in a cup when you blow on it. The moving fluid bends hair cells, which send messages to the brain for processing.

Reading Check What are the three areas of the ear?

The Ear and Balance

In addition to detecting sound waves, the inner ear has another function. Parts of the inner ear, called the semicircular canals, help maintain balance. Like the cochlea, the semicircular canals contain fluid and hair cells. Whenever you move your head, the fluid moves, which moves the hair cells, as shown in **Figure 9.** Information about the movement of the hair cells is sent to the brain. The brain then signals muscles to move your head and body in order to maintain your balance.

Figure 9 Fluid in your inner ear helps maintain your balance by sensing changes in the position of your head.

The Ear and Balance

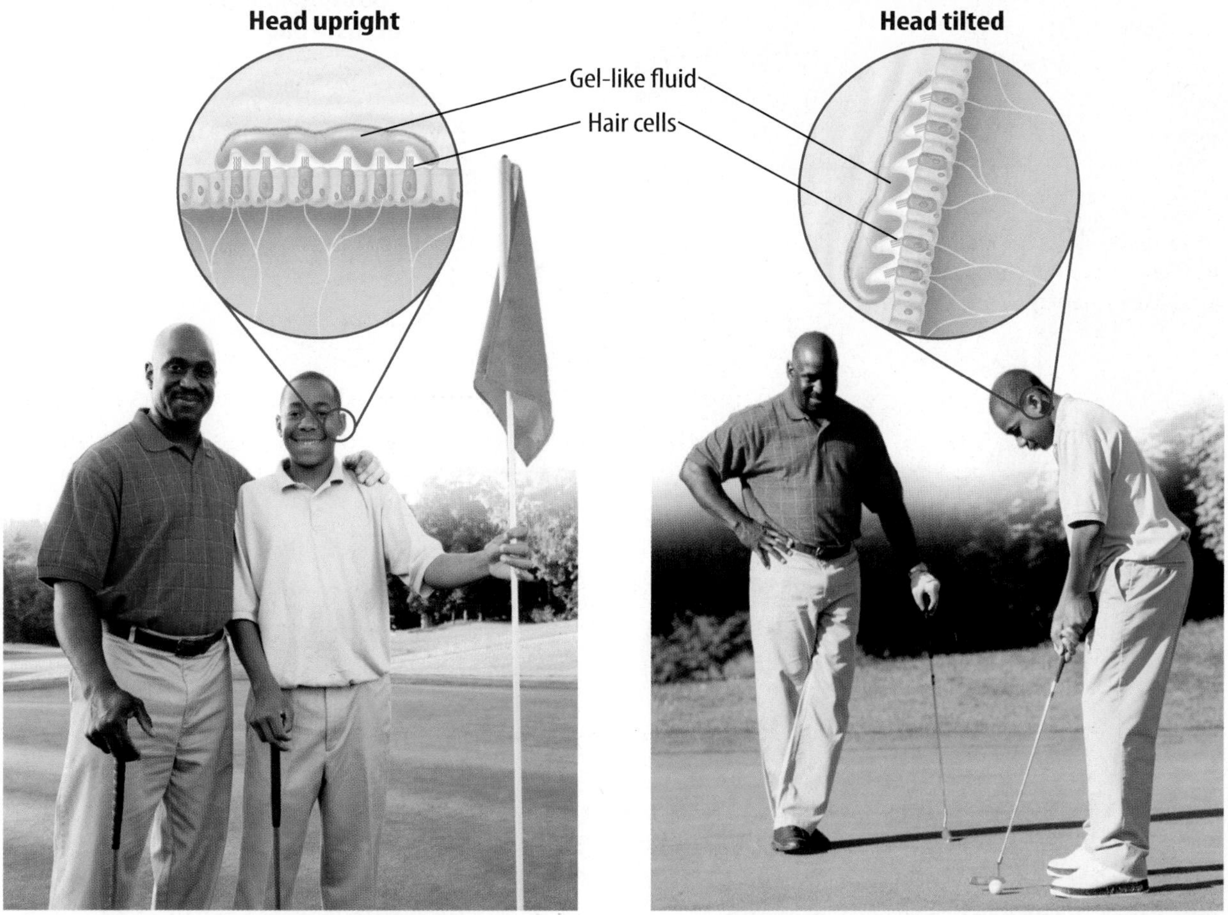
Head upright
Head tilted
Gel-like fluid
Hair cells

Smell

How are you able to distinguish between the citrus aroma of an orange and the sulfur odor of rotten eggs? Humans have hundreds of different receptors for detecting odors. Some dogs have over 1,000 different odor receptors and can be used to track things by smell. Odors are molecules that are detected by chemical receptors, called chemoreceptors (kee moh rih SEP turz), in your nose. These receptors send messages to the brain. The brain then processes the information about the odor. A smell might make you feel hungry, or it could trigger a strong memory or feeling.

Taste

The sense of taste also relies on chemoreceptors. Chemoreceptors on your tongue detect chemicals in foods and drinks. The receptors then send messages to the brain for processing. Chemoreceptors on the tongue are called taste buds. Taste buds, such as the ones shown in **Figure 10,** can detect five different tastes: bitter, salty, sour, sweet, and a taste called umami (oo MAH mee). Umami is the taste of MSG (monosodium glutamate), a substance often used in processed foods. **Figure 10** illustrates how the chemoreceptors in your nose and mouth work together to help you taste foods.

Taste and Smell 🔑

Figure 10 Taste and smell stimuli are both detected by chemoreceptors. Chemoreceptors detect chemicals in the substances you eat and drink and in the odors you breathe.

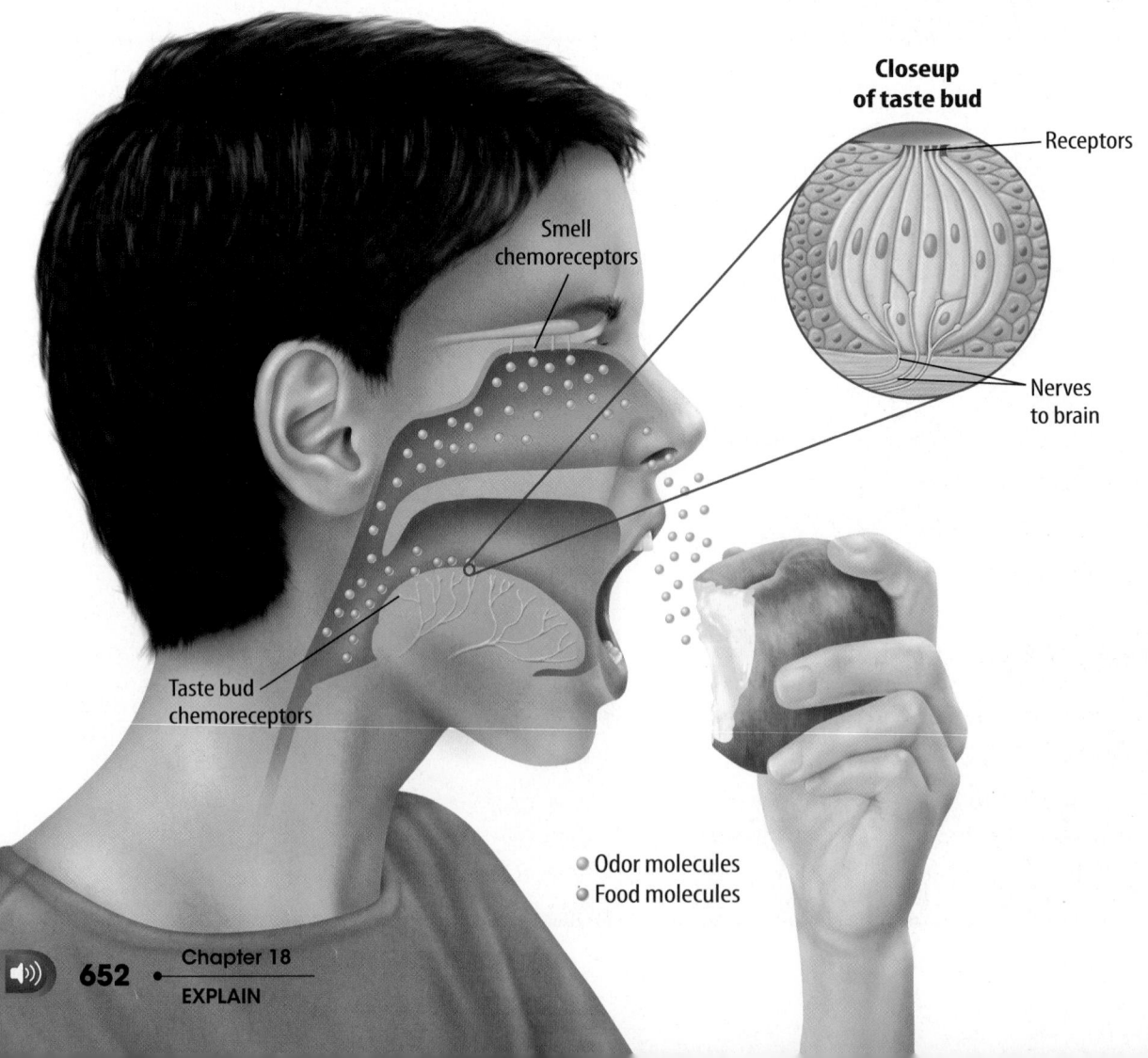

Closeup of taste bud

Receptors

Nerves to brain

Smell chemoreceptors

Taste bud chemoreceptors

● Odor molecules
● Food molecules

Touch

Like all the other senses, the sense of touch also uses special receptors that detect the environment. Touch receptors in your skin can detect temperature, pain, and pressure. For example, skin receptors can detect the difference between a light tap and a poke. These receptors are all over your body. Some areas, such as the palms of your hands and the soles of your feet, have lots of receptors. The middle of your back has fewer receptors. Just like the other four senses, touch receptors send messages to the brain for processing.

The Senses and Homeostasis

Gathering information about the environment is important for your survival. The five senses collect information about the environment and send it to your nervous system. Your brain is then able to respond and activate your body to maintain homeostasis. Whether it is sensing temperature changes, finding food and water, avoiding harmful environments, or detecting other important stimuli, your senses are the vital first step.

Key Concept Check Why are senses important in maintaining homeostasis?

Inquiry MiniLab

20 minutes

What area of your skin is most sensitive?

Your skin has millions of nerve endings. Although this might not be a surprise, you might not realize that different areas of the body are more sensitive to touch and pain than other areas. Which regions of the skin are most sensitive to touch? How does the sense of touch help maintain homeostasis?

1. Read and complete a lab safety form.

2. In your Science Journal, design a data sheet to include experimental results for both you and your partner. You will record the sensitivity of the following eight areas of the body: fingertip, back of hand, elbow, toes, top of foot, knee, back of neck, and nose.

3. Blindfold your partner with a **clean tube sock or scarf**. Lightly touch one of the areas of your partner's skin with a **thin, washable marker.** Leave a small, colored mark where you touched your partner's skin.

4. Using a **different colored marker,** have your partner try to touch the same point that was previously marked by your pen.

5. Test all eight areas of the body.

6. Use a **metric tape measure** to determine the distance from the point you marked to the point your partner touched.

7. Record your results and your partner's results in your data table. Graph both sets of results from least distance to greatest distance between the actual point of touch and the guessed point of touch. Label your graph.

Analyze and Conclude

1. **Calculate and analyze** what part of your body has the least distance between the actual point and the guessed point. Which body part has the greatest distance?

2. **Compare** the results for both you and your partner. Predict the results for all class members.

3. **Key Concept** Analyze how the sensitivity of different areas of your skin help you maintain homeostasis.

Lesson 2 Review

Visual Summary

The sensory system is part of the nervous system. It uses receptors in five senses and collects information about the environment.

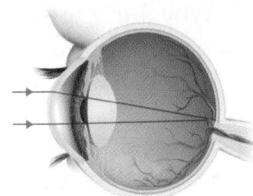

Your eyes detect light as it passes through the cornea, the pupil, and the lens, and then to the retina.

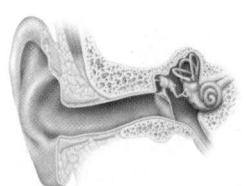

The eardrum is a structure between the outer and middle ear. It vibrates in the presence of sound waves.

FOLDABLES®

Use your lesson Foldable to review the lesson. Save your Foldable for the project at the end of the chapter.

What do you think NOW?

You first read the statements below at the beginning of the chapter.

3. A human has five senses that detect his or her environment.

4. The senses of smell and hearing work together.

Did you change your mind about whether you agree or disagree with the statements? Rewrite any false statements to make them true.

Use Vocabulary

1. **Name** the part of the ear that collects sound waves from the environment.

2. **Define** the term *receptor* using your own words.

3. **Use the word** *retina* in a sentence.

Understand Key Concepts

4. Which is NOT a sensory system?
   A. digestion   C. smell
   B. hearing   D. vision

5. **Explain** the relationship between the five senses and homeostasis.

6. **Contrast** the different types of stimuli that can be detected by touch receptors.

Interpret Graphics

7. **Evaluate** the relationship between the senses of smell and taste using the figure at right as a guide.

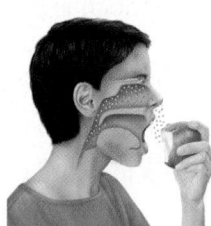

8. **Organize** Copy and fill in the table below to organize information about the five senses.

Sense	Stimulus

Critical Thinking

9. **Examine** why it might be difficult to taste food when you have a cold.

10. **Infer** how an ear infection might lead to problems with balance.

Night Vision Goggles

Would you like to be able to see in the dark?

You might already know that vision begins with light entering your eyes. What happens when it is dark? If there is no light available to enter your eyes, how can any device make it possible to see?

Even when it is dark, there is light all around you. Although you can't see it, almost everything gives off, or emits, infrared light. Objects also reflect some infrared light, in the same way that they reflect visible light. Night vision goggles work by collecting that infrared light and converting it to visible light.

3 The electrons speed up and are multiplied in the image intensifier tube.

4 The electrons strike a phosphor screen, a screen coated with phosphorescent material. The phosphor screen converts the electrons back into photons, forming an image that can be seen through the ocular lens.

1 Infrared light enters the objective lens.

2 Infrared photons, or particles of light, enter the photocathode. This structure converts the pattern of infrared photons into a pattern of electrons.

It's Your Turn

REPORT How can owls see more clearly in dim light than humans can? Research rods and cones in the eye and what they have to do with vision. Use what you discover to make a "How It Works" diagram about rods and cones in the eye.

The Endocrine System

Reading Guide

Key Concepts 🔑
ESSENTIAL QUESTIONS

- What does the endocrine system do?
- How does the endocrine system interact with other body systems?

Vocabulary

endocrine system p. 657

hormone p. 657

negative feedback p. 660

positive feedback p. 660

g Multilingual eGlossary

Inquiry Blue Butterfly?

This image might look like a blue and green butterfly, but it is actually an image of a person's butterfly-shaped thyroid gland. The image was taken after a dose of radioactive material was given to the patient. The radioactive material collected in thyroid tissue.

What makes your heart race?

Have you ever felt your heart start to race? Maybe something startled you or you were nervous or frightened. Usually this sensation lasts only for a few minutes. What causes your heart to pound so fast at times?

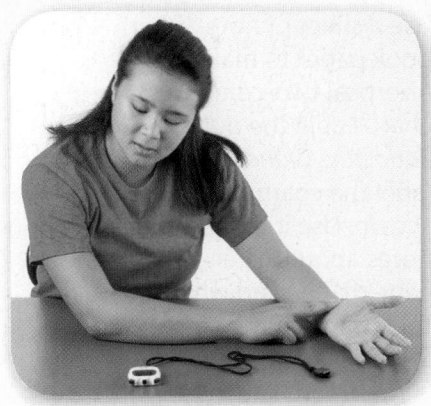

1 Read and complete a lab safety form.

2 Find your pulse by holding your first and second fingers of one hand on the inside of the wrist of your other hand. Count heartbeats for 15 seconds. Record this number in your Science Journal. Multiply this number by four to find your average heartbeats per minute.

3 Your teacher will attempt to startle you. Immediately afterward, count your heartbeats again for 15 seconds and multiply by 4.

4 Wait five minutes. Calculate your heartbeats per minute again.

Think About This

1. What changes did you note in your heart rate after your teacher startled you?

2. What happened to your heartbeat when you checked five minutes later?

3. 🔑 **Key Concept** Why do you think your heart reacted to the noise even though you knew it was coming? Why do you think this change occurred?

Functions of the Endocrine System

Like the nervous system, your body sends messages using another system called the endocrine (EN duh krun) system. *The **endocrine system** consists of groups of organs and tissues that release chemical messages into the bloodstream.*

Endocrine tissues that secrete chemical molecules are called endocrine glands. The thyroid gland on the previous page is one of the glands in the endocrine system. The chemical messages sent by the endocrine system are called hormones. *A **hormone** is a chemical that is produced by an endocrine gland in one part of an organism and is carried in the bloodstream to another part of the organism.*

The messages sent by the endocrine system are transmitted less rapidly than messages sent by the nervous system. The chemical messages usually are sent to more cells and last longer than the messages sent by the nervous system. For example, a message from the nervous system might cause a body movement. A message from the endocrine system might cause your body to grow taller over a period of time.

🔑 **Key Concept Check** What does the endocrine system do?

WORD ORIGIN · · · · · · · · · ·

hormone
from Greek *hormon*, means "that which sets in motion"

Endocrine Glands and Their Hormones

Hormones move from endocrine glands to other parts of the body in the bloodstream. Hormones affect the functions of organs and tissues by carrying messages to specific cells called target cells. Hormones recognize their target cells because the target cells have certain receptor proteins on or inside them. The hormone recognizes the receptor proteins and attaches to them. A hormone is like a key that wanders around and tries locks until it finds one that it fits and unlocks it. Once a hormone finds its target cell, it binds to a receptor protein and delivers its chemical message. The target cell responds by taking a specific action.

Figure 11 illustrates the path that a hormone takes from its production in an endocrine gland until it finds and delivers its message to the target cell. There are many different hormones with various purposes that are produced and distributed throughout your body. The endocrine glands and the hormones they produce are shown in **Figure 12.**

The Path of a Hormone

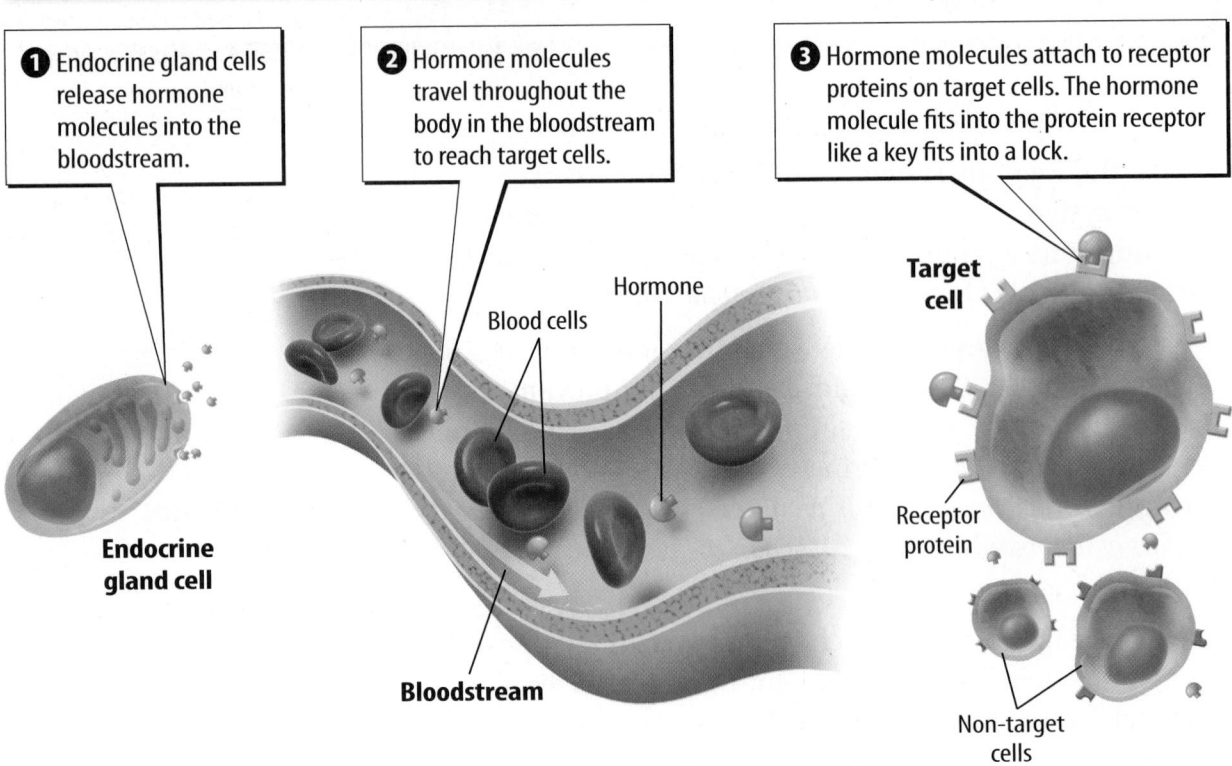

❶ Endocrine gland cells release hormone molecules into the bloodstream.

❷ Hormone molecules travel throughout the body in the bloodstream to reach target cells.

❸ Hormone molecules attach to receptor proteins on target cells. The hormone molecule fits into the protein receptor like a key fits into a lock.

Hormone

Blood cells

Target cell

Endocrine gland cell

Receptor protein

Bloodstream

Non-target cells

Figure 11 Hormones move through the bloodstream until they encounter the specific cells they are targeted to affect.

✔ Visual Check Why doesn't the green hormone molecule attach to non-target cells?

The **pituitary gland** secretes many different hormones. Hormones secreted by the pituitary gland regulate different body functions and control other endocrine glands. In addition, the pituitary gland secretes growth hormone, which causes the body to grow.

The **hypothalamus** receives information from the nervous system and controls the activity of the pituitary gland.

The four **parathyroid glands** regulate the amount of calcium released into the blood. This activity helps maintain your bones, muscles, and nerve cells.

The **thyroid gland** controls how the body uses energy. It causes your metabolism to speed up or slow down when necessary.

The **thymus gland** signals the immune system to produce cells to fight infections.

The two **adrenal glands** release hormones that enable the body to respond to stress and react quickly.

The **pancreas** secretes insulin and glucagon. They regulate the level of sugars in the blood.

Two **ovaries** in females release estrogen and produce egg cells for reproduction.

Two **testes** in males release testosterone and produce sperm cells for reproduction.

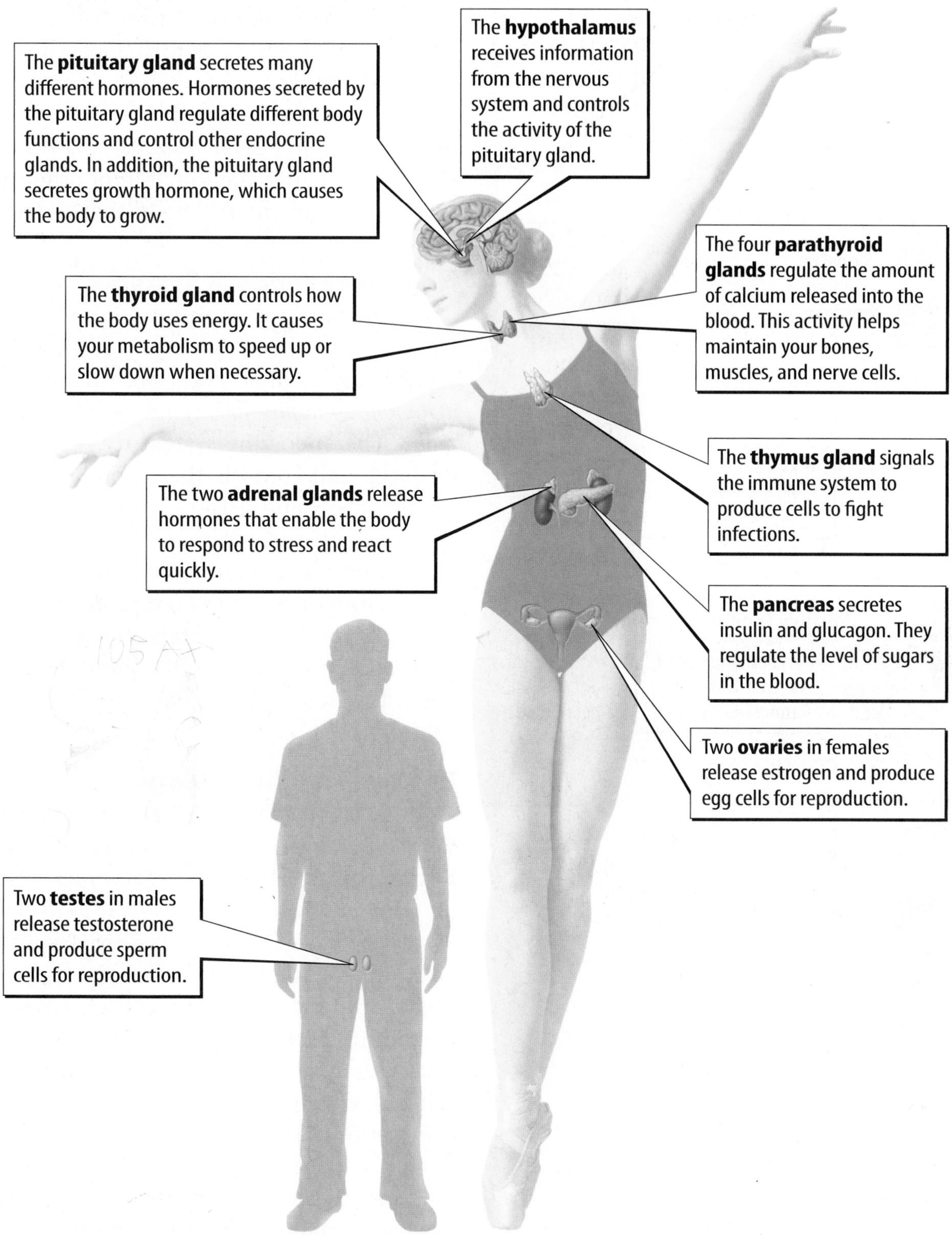

Figure 12 The endocrine system is made up of different glands that secrete hormones to maintain homeostasis in the body.

✅ **Visual Check** Which endocrine gland affects metabolism?

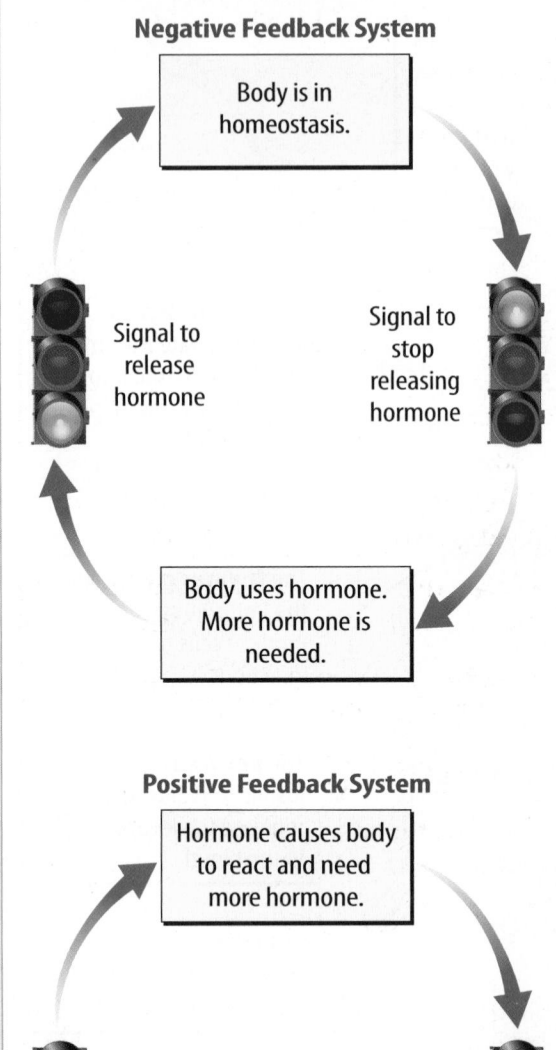

Negative Feedback System

Body is in homeostasis.

Signal to stop releasing hormone

Body uses hormone. More hormone is needed.

Signal to release hormone

Positive Feedback System

Hormone causes body to react and need more hormone.

Signal to release hormone

Signal to release hormone

Hormone causes body to react and need more hormone.

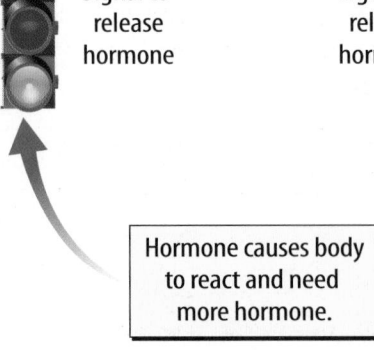

Figure 13 Negative feedback systems are used to maintain homeostasis while positive feedback systems increase the production of hormones.

Visual Check How do positive and negative feedback systems work?

The Endocrine System and Homeostasis

You might recall from Lesson 1 that your nervous system responds to changes in your environment and maintains homeostasis. Glands also help maintain homeostasis by releasing hormones in response to stimuli. Hormones change the function of other tissues and organs in the body that regulate internal conditions.

Negative Feedback Systems

Organisms can maintain homeostasis using negative feedback systems. **Negative feedback** *is a control system where the effect of a hormone inhibits further release of the hormone.* The endocrine system uses negative feedback and controls the amount of hormone that a gland releases. This is similar to the way a thermostat in a house monitors temperature. The thermostat signals the furnace to turn on when the temperature in the house drops below a preset temperature. After the house warms to the preset temperature, the thermostat signals the furnace to shut off.

Positive Feedback Systems

Whereas negative feedback helps maintain homeostasis, positive feedback does not. **Positive feedback** *is a control system in which the effect of a hormone causes more of the hormone to be released.* Because positive feedback does not help maintain homeostasis, your body uses fewer positive feedback systems. Childbirth is one example of a positive feedback system. Labor begins when a hormone called oxytocin is released. Oxytocin causes contractions. The contractions cause more oxytocin to be released. **Figure 13** shows how both negative feedback systems and positive feedback systems work within the endocrine system.

 Key Concept Check How do other body systems work with the endocrine system to maintain homeostasis?

Lesson 3 Review

Visual Summary

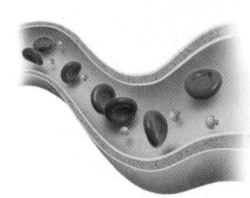

The endocrine system is made up of glands that secrete chemical hormones. They send messages throughout the body and maintain homeostasis.

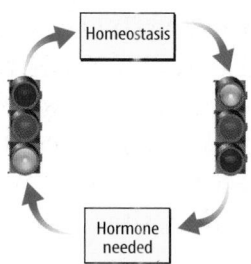

Negative feedback systems maintain homeostasis by inhibiting the release of a hormone as part of the effect of that hormone.

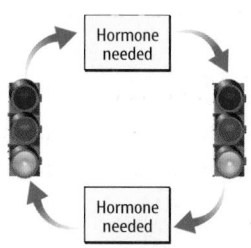

Positive feedback systems increase the effects caused by a hormone by signaling more of that hormone to be released.

FOLDABLES

Use your lesson Foldable to review the lesson. Save your Foldable for the project at the end of the chapter.

What do you think NOW?

You first read the statements below at the beginning of the chapter.

5. Positive feedback systems in humans help maintain homeostasis.

6. Endocrine glands secrete hormones.

Did you change your mind about whether you agree or disagree with the statements? Rewrite any false statements to make them true.

Use Vocabulary

1 **Define** the phrase *endocrine system*.

2 **Distinguish** between negative feedback and positive feedback.

3 **Describe** the function of a hormone using your own words.

Understand Key Concepts

4 Hormones travel to other parts of the body using the _____ system.
   A. circulatory   C. nervous
   B. digestive   D. skeletal

5 **Explain** the relationship between the nervous system and the endocrine system.

6 **Relate** negative feedback systems to maintaining homeostasis.

Interpret Graphics

7 **Describe** the function of the endocrine gland shown below.

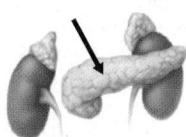

8 **Explain** Copy the graphic organizer below. Fill in information about the role of oxytocin in the positive feedback system of childbirth.

Critical Thinking

9 **Predict** what might happen if negative feedback did not function correctly in one of the endocrine glands.

10 **Explain** why doctors often check the activity of the thyroid glands of a person who is feeling tired and sluggish frequently.

Modeling a Negative Feedback Cycle

Materials

creative
construction
materials

Safety

The activity of cells and chemicals in your body is important. However, cells and molecules are so small that it is helpful to use models to simulate their activities. Cells use the process of negative feedback to maintain homeostasis. This happens when hormones are released and deliver a chemical message to specific target cells. The message directs the cells to take a specific action to cause an effect in the body. It also signals the other cells to stop producing the hormone. You will use materials to model the cells, hormones, and receptor sites that make up the pathway in a negative feedback cycle. Your model should show how some hormones use receptor sites to identify target cells and avoid the wrong cells.

Question

How do specific hormones find and enter the proper cells to cause an effect?

Procedure

1. Read and complete a lab safety form.
2. Review the diagram of the negative feedback cycle and the list of hormones.
3. Observe the working model your teacher demonstrates for the class. How do the hormone and the cell interact to ensure that the hormone is delivered to the proper cell to cause the necessary effect?

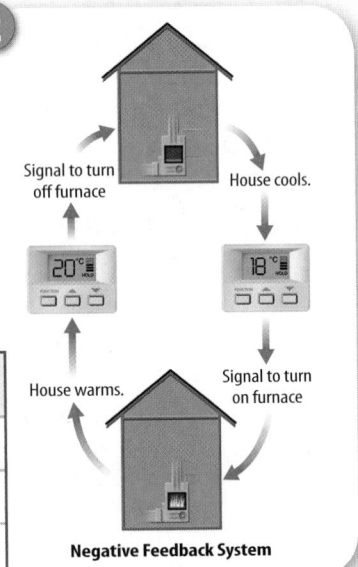

Signal to turn off furnace

House cools.

House warms.

Signal to turn on furnace

Negative Feedback System

Endocrine gland	Hormone
Adrenal glands	Adrenaline
Hypothalamus	Oxytocin
Ovaries	Estrogen
Pancreas	Insulin
Parathyroid glands	Parathyroid hormone
Pituitary gland	Growth hormone
Testes	Testosterone
Thyroid gland	Thyroxine

4 Form small groups. Your teacher will hand out an assortment of materials to each group.

5 Choose one of the hormone examples and create a working model that demonstrates the pathway that the hormone and the target cells undergo as part of negative feedback.

6 Label the parts of your model with the following tags: *hormone, hormone receptor, target cell*.

Analyze and Conclude

7 **Think Critically** How does your model demonstrate the delivery of hormones to the proper cells in order to cause an effect?

8 **The Big Idea** How does the activity you modeled interact with other systems in the body to maintain homeostasis?

Communicate Your Results

Draw a diagram of your model on the chalkboard in the form of a negative feedback cycle. Then demonstrate your model, showing how it follows the process of the negative feedback pathway.

Inquiry Extension

Imagine that the different models built in your class all make up different hormones and cells in the endocrine system. What will happen if you attempt to use the hormone model from another group to activate your cell? Take turns trying the hormone models from other groups with your cell model. Describe the results and what they mean.

5

Lab Tips

☑ Remember that your model is meant to represent the functions of the negative feedback system. It is not meant to resemble the appearance of the things it represents.

☑ The putty can be used to attach some of the parts together.

Remember to use scientific methods.

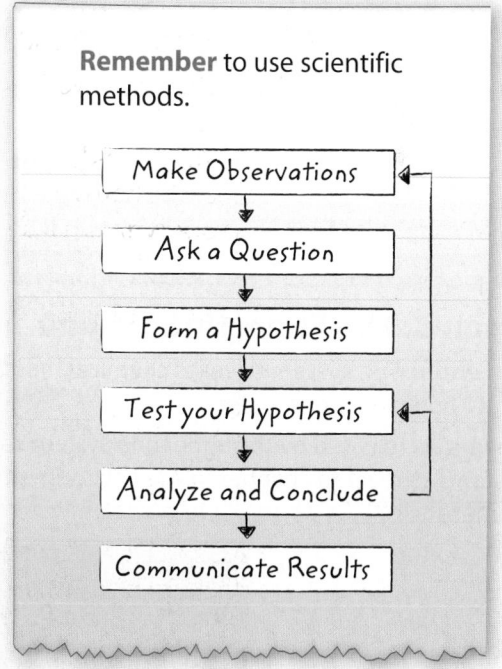

Make Observations

Ask a Question

Form a Hypothesis

Test your Hypothesis

Analyze and Conclude

Communicate Results

Chapter 18 Study Guide

The nervous and endocrine systems work to sense the environment and coordinate body functions.

Key Concepts Summary 🗝

Lesson 1: The Nervous System

- The **nervous system** gathers information from the environment, processes it, and signals the body to respond.

- The nervous system is made up of the **central nervous system** and **peripheral nervous system.** The peripheral nervous system gathers and transmits information to and from the central nervous system, which processes the information.

- The nervous system helps other body systems maintain homeostasis by responding to the environment.

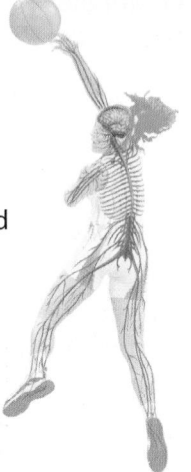

Vocabulary

nervous system p. 637
stimulus p. 638
neuron p. 639
synapse p. 639
central nervous system
    p. 640
cerebrum p. 640
cerebellum p. 640
brain stem p. 641
spinal cord p. 641
peripheral nervous system
    p. 641
reflex p. 642

Lesson 2: The Senses

- The **sensory system** provides information about the environment.

- The senses help maintain homeostasis by gathering information about changes in the environment so the body can respond.

sensory system p. 647
receptor p. 647
retina p. 648
eardrum p. 650

Lesson 3: The Endocrine System

- The **endocrine system** releases chemical messages that control or affect body functions.

- Chemicals released by the endocrine system cause other body systems to react to changes in the environment to maintain homeostasis.

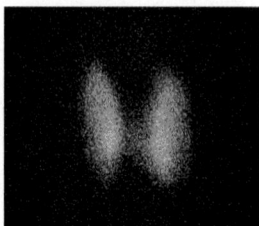

endocrine system p. 657
hormone p. 657
negative feedback p. 660
positive feedback p. 660

FOLDABLES® Chapter Project

Assemble your lesson Foldables as shown to make a Chapter Project. Use the project to review what you have learned in this chapter.

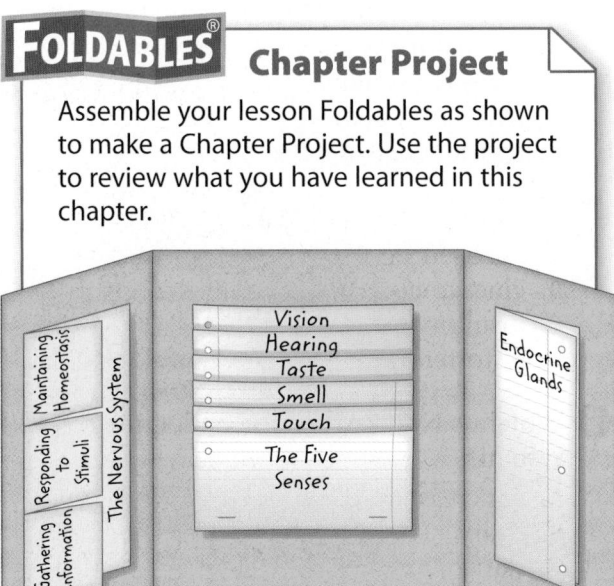

Use Vocabulary

1 The _____ nervous system is made up of the somatic and autonomic systems.

2 Voluntary muscle movement and coordination is managed by the _____ part of the brain.

3 The _____ in the eye contains photoreceptors.

4 The fluid-filled structure in the inner ear that helps maintain balance is the _____.

5 Chemicals produced by endocrine glands are called _____.

6 The effect of a hormone on a _____ feedback system is to cause it to release more of the hormone.

Link Vocabulary and Key Concepts

((○)) **Concepts in Motion** Interactive Concept Map

Copy this concept map, and then use vocabulary terms from the previous page to complete the concept map.

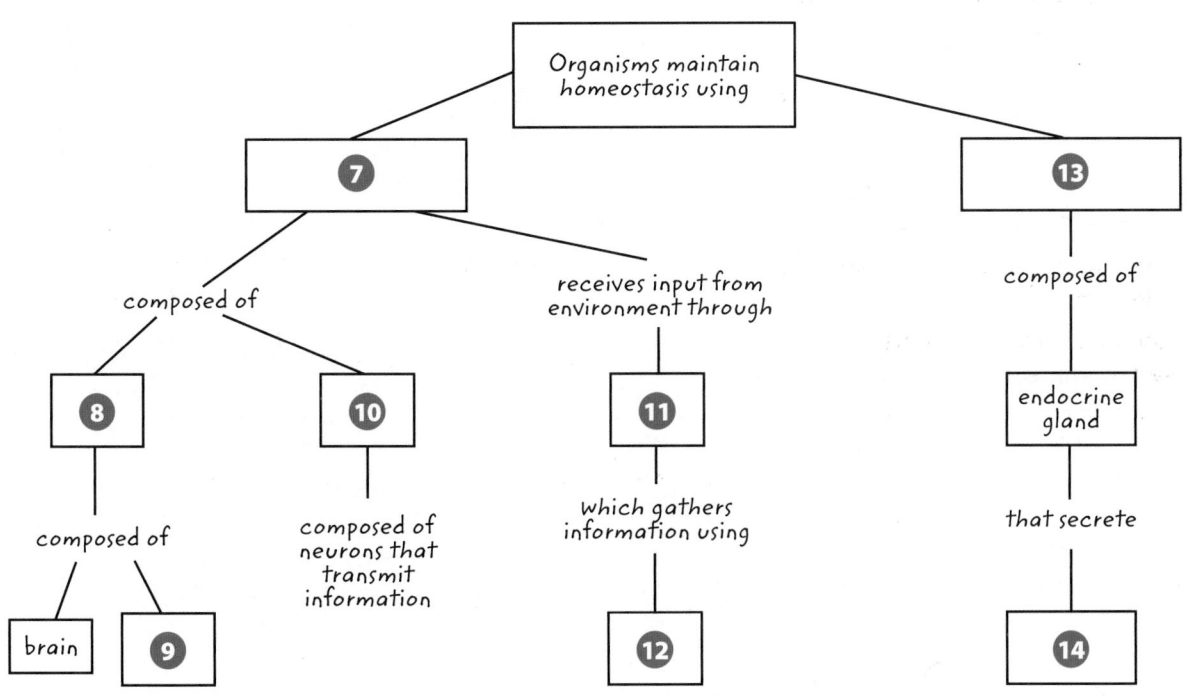

Understand Key Concepts 🗝️

1 Which part of the brain controls language, memory, and thought?

A. brain stem
B. cerebellum
C. cerebrum
D. spinal cord

2 Which is NOT a part of the CNS?

A. brain stem
B. cerebellum
C. somatic system
D. spinal cord

3 What is the gap between the two neurons shown below?

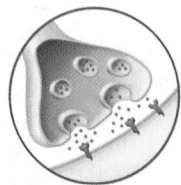

A. motor
B. reflex
C. stimulus
D. synapse

4 Which is NOT a part of the eye?

A. cochlea
B. cornea
C. pupil
D. retina

5 Which senses work together and determine how a person perceives flavor?

A. smell and taste
B. taste and hearing
C. taste and touch
D. vision and taste

6 Which part of the eye focuses light?

A. iris
B. lens
C. pupil
D. retina

7 Which system transports hormones to other parts of the body?

A. circulatory system
B. digestive system
C. nervous system
D. reproductive system

8 Which hormone do ovaries release?

A. estrogen
B. glucagon
C. insulin
D. testosterone

9 Which is NOT part of the endocrine system?

A. pancreas
B. ovary
C. skin
D. thymus

10 Which system is illustrated by the diagram below?

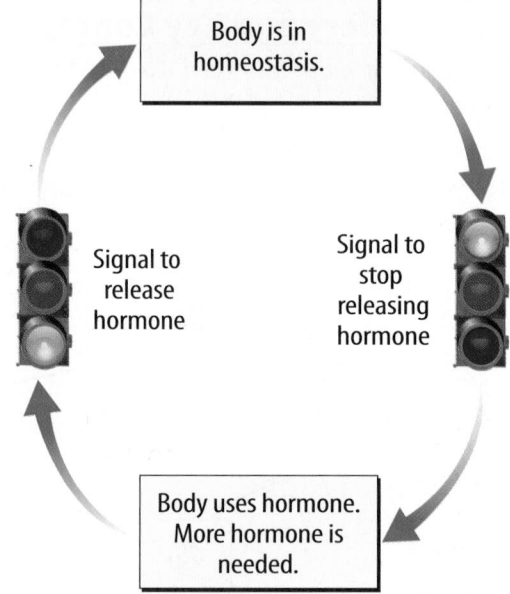

A. autonomic system
B. reflex system
C. negative feedback system
D. positive feedback system

Critical Thinking

11 **Describe** how reflexes prevent injuries.

12 **Compare and contrast** the somatic nervous system and the autonomic nervous system.

13 **Investigate** the effect of a spinal cord injury on the function of the nervous system.

14 **Relate** how receptors in the nose take part in sensing food.

15 **Determine** Is the vision problem shown in the figure below nearsightedness or farsightedness? Explain your answer.

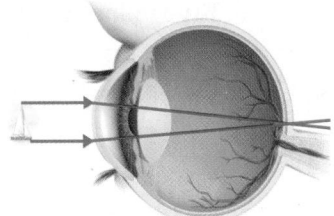

16 **Infer** why people sometimes feel sick when traveling on a boat.

17 **Evaluate** how negative feedback systems control the amount of hormone released by a gland.

18 **Infer** why positive feedback systems are not used to maintain homeostasis.

19 **Assess** why reflexes are controlled by the nervous system and not the endocrine system.

20 **Evaluate** how the endocrine system works with the circulatory system to maintain the body's homeostasis.

Writing in Science

21 **Write** a paragraph that describes a time when your nervous system helped you to survive. Describe what likely occurred in your body, including the use of your senses and the endocrine system during the event.

REVIEW THE BIG IDEA

22 **Describe** the relationship between the nervous system and the endocrine system in the body. Include some examples of how they maintain homeostasis.

23 **Explain** what is most likely happening in the nervous system and the endocrine system of the batter shown below. Describe how these activities help her accomplish her goal of hitting the ball.

Math Skills ✕⁄÷

— Math Practice —

Use Proportions

Use the information below to answer questions 24 and 25.

A person's nerve axon from a toe to the spine is 1.1 m long. The nerve impulse that signals touch travels about 76.2 m/s.

24 How long does it take the nerve impulse for touch to travel from the toe to the spine?

25 Pain impulses travel more slowly—about 0.61 m/s. How long would it take the pain impulse to travel from the toe to the spine?

26 A reflex nerve impulse travels 100 m/s from a fingertip touching a hot object to the spine. The distance is 0.5 m. If a signal from the spine telling the finger to move travels back at the same speed, how long will it take the person to react?

Standardized Test Practice

Record your answers on the answer sheet provided by your teacher or on a sheet of paper.

Multiple Choice

Use the diagram below to answer question 1.

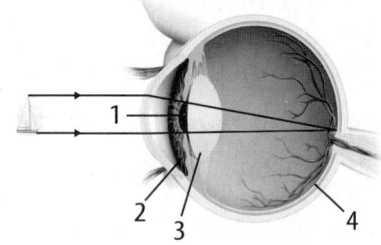

1 Which numbered structure focuses the light on the retina?

  A 1

  B 2

  C 3

  D 4

2 A doctor sees a patient who has a loss of balance from an illness. The doctor thinks the receptors for balance might be injured. Where are they located?

  A inner ear

  B middle ear

  C nasal cavity

  D spinal cord

3 Which statement about the nervous system is false?

  A It gathers information.

  B It maintains homeostais.

  C It responds to stimuli.

  D It transports hormones.

4 Which relies on chemoreceptors?

  A hearing

  B sight

  C taste

  D touch

Use the graph below to answer question 5.

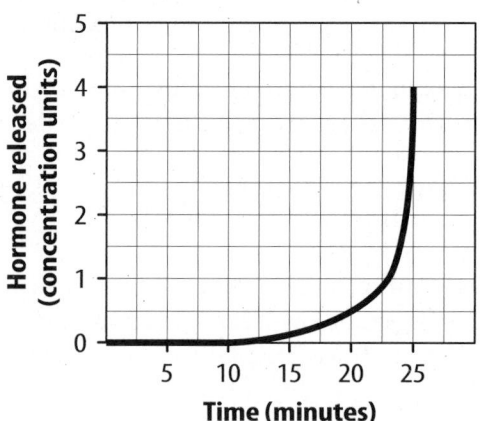

5 Which is likely to produce a curve similar to the one above?

  A a reflex

  B a synapse

  C negative feedback

  D positive feedback

6 Which system releases chemical messages to the bloodstream?

  A circulatory

  B digestive

  C endocrine

  D skeletal

7 Why does the nervous system tell the body to shiver?

  A to imprint a memory on the brain

  B to maintain homeostasis

  C to slow neuron communication

  D to stop PNS–CNS communication

Use the diagram below to answer question 8.

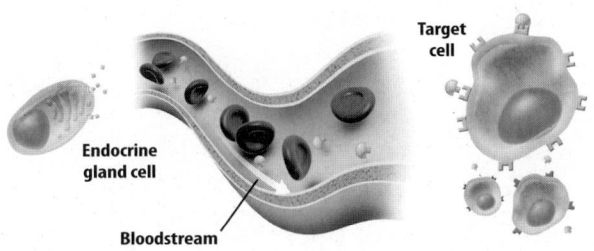

Target cell

Endocrine gland cell

Bloodstream

8 What is the path of a hormone as illustrated above?

A bloodstream → endocrine cell → target cell

B endocrine cell → bloodstream → target cell

C endocrine cell → target cell → bloodstream

D target cell → bloodstream → endocrine cell

9 What is the primary function of the senses?

A choosing pleasant scents, sounds, tastes, and textures

B gathering information about the environment

C making each organism slightly different from others

D providing ideas for organisms to communicate

Constructed Response

Use the table below to answer questions 10 and 11.

Part	Description
Neuron	
Synapse	
CNS	
PNS	

10 Briefly describe the parts of the nervous system listed in the table. Explain what the abbreviations *CNS* and *PNS* represent.

11 Using an example, such as a pain reflex, explain how the parts of the nervous system provided in the table above work together.

Use the table below to answer question 12.

Sense	Organ and Function

12 List the five human senses. Then identify each sensory organ and describe its function.

NEED EXTRA HELP?												
If You Missed Question...	1	2	3	4	5	6	7	8	9	10	11	12
Go to Lesson...	2	2	1	2	3	3	1	3	2	1	1	2

Reproduction and Development

THE BIG IDEA

What are the stages of human reproduction and development?

Strands of Hair?

The things in this photograph that look like strands of hair are male reproductive cells called sperm. They are covering a female reproductive cell called an egg.

- What do you think the sperm are doing?

- What stage of human reproduction do you think this is?

Get Ready to Read

What do you think?

Before you read, decide if you agree or disagree with each of these statements. As you read this chapter, see if you change your mind about any of the statements.

1 Reproduction ensures that a species survives.

2 The male reproductive system has internal and external parts.

3 The menstrual cycle occurs in males and females.

4 Eggs are fertilized in the ovary.

5 Lead is a nutrient that helps a fetus develop.

6 Puberty occurs during adolescence.

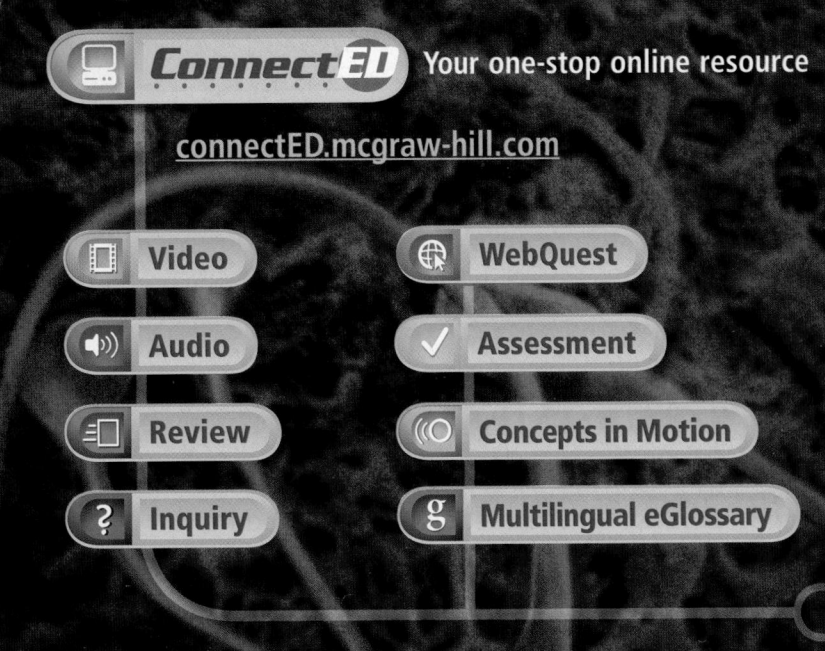

ConnectED Your one-stop online resource

connectED.mcgraw-hill.com

- Video
- WebQuest
- Audio
- Assessment
- Review
- Concepts in Motion
- Inquiry
- Multilingual eGlossary

The Reproductive System

Reading Guide

Key Concepts 🔑
ESSENTIAL QUESTIONS

- What does the reproductive system do?
- How do the parts of the male reproductive system work together?
- How do the parts of the female reproductive system work together?
- How does the reproductive system interact with other body systems?

Vocabulary

sperm p. 673

egg p. 673

testis p. 674

semen p. 674

penis p. 674

ovary p. 676

vagina p. 676

menstrual cycle p. 678

ovulation p. 678

fertilization p. 679

g Multilingual eGlossary

Inquiry A Red Ball?

The round object is a human egg being released from the ovary. Are eggs released often? What is shown here is part of the reproductive process in the human female. In this lesson, you will learn about the process.

How do male and female gametes compare?

At some point in their lives, except in rare instances, humans will all make sex cells, or gametes. Males produce sperm, and females produce eggs. When a sperm cell and an egg cell unite, fertilization occurs.

1. Read and complete a lab safety form.
2. Obtain a **microscope** and **prepared slides of sperm cells and egg cells.** Carefully handle the microscope according to your teacher's instructions.
3. Observe the slides under the magnification power specified by your teacher.
4. Sketch a sperm cell and an egg cell in your Science Journal.

Think About This

1. Compare and contrast the appearance of an egg cell and the appearance of a sperm cell.

2. **Key Concept** Why do you think there is a difference in the appearance of the male and female reproductive cells?

Functions of the Reproductive System

You have read about many of the organ systems that enable you to grow and respond to changes in the environment. Organ systems such as the nervous system, the skeletal system, the circulatory system, and the digestive system are all important for an individual's survival. But what organ system ensures that the human species survives?

A reproductive system is a group of tissues and organs. It enables the male and female reproductive cells to join and form new offspring. Like other animals, human males produce **sperm,** *the male reproductive cells,* and human females produce **eggs,** *the female reproductive cells.*

During reproduction, a sperm joins with an egg, as shown in **Figure 1.** This usually happens inside a female's reproductive system. Once joined, part of the female's reproductive system nourishes the developing human. In order to understand how humans develop, we must first learn the parts of the male and female reproductive systems.

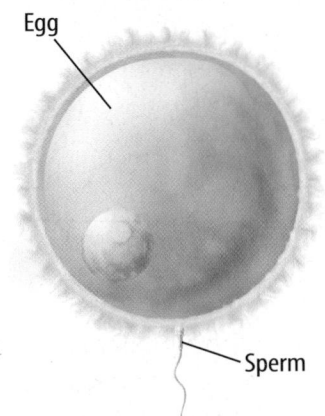

Figure 1 When a sperm cell combines with an egg cell, development of a new human being begins.

Egg

Sperm

 Key Concept Check What does the reproductive system do?

The Male Reproductive System

The main function of the male reproductive system is to produce and transport sperm to the female reproductive system. As shown in **Figure 2,** there are many parts of the male reproductive system, each with a unique function. *The* **testis** (TES tihs; plural, testes) *is the male reproductive organ that produces sperm.* A male's two testes are inside an external saclike **structure** called the scrotum (SKROH tum). Sperm development can occur only at a temperature that is lower than normal body temperature. Because the scrotum is outside the male's body, it is at a temperature slightly lower than normal body temperature.

Once sperm develop, they move to a tube called the sperm duct and are stored. During storage, sperm mature and develop the ability to swim. As mature sperm move through the remainder of the male reproductive system, they mix with fluids produced by several glands. *This mixture of sperm and fluids is called* **semen** (SEE mun). Semen also contains nutrients that provide sperm with energy. Semen leaves the body through the penis. *The* **penis** *is a tubelike structure that delivers sperm to the female reproductive system.* The path of sperm is shown in **Figure 3.**

✓ **Reading Check** What does semen contain?

SCIENCE USE V. COMMON USE

structure
Science Use cells and tissues arranged in a definite pattern

Common Use a building

Figure 2 The male reproductive system has many parts, each with a unique function.

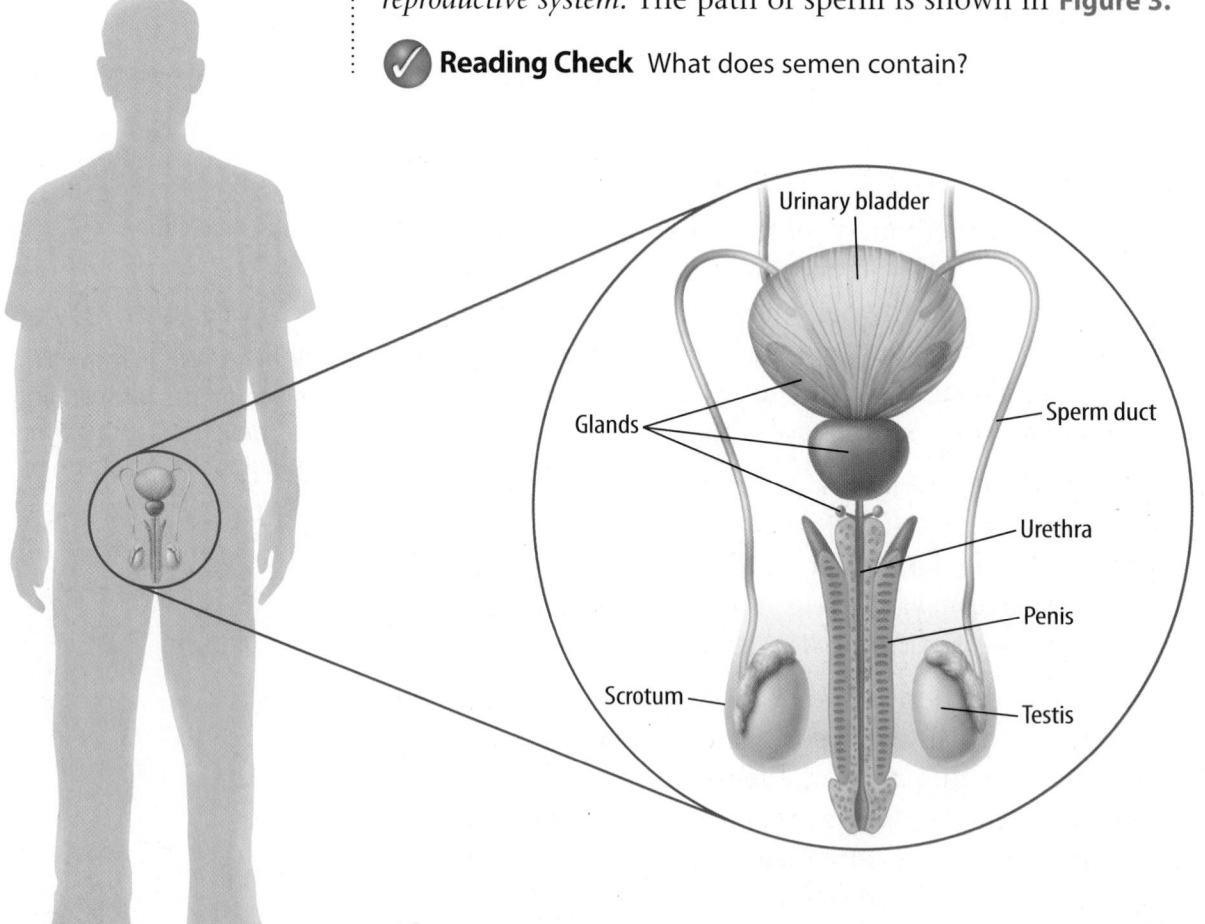

- Urinary bladder
- Glands
- Sperm duct
- Urethra
- Penis
- Scrotum
- Testis

✓ **Visual Check** How many different glands are shown in the male reproductive system?

Sperm

Now that you have learned about the parts of the male reproductive system, let's take a closer look at sperm. When mature, sperm can join with an egg. As illustrated in **Figure 3,** a mature sperm cell has three main parts—a head, a midpiece, and a tail. The head contains DNA and substances that help the sperm join with an egg. The midpiece contains organelles called mitochondria. Recall that mitochondria are the cell organelles that process food molecules and release energy. This energy enables movement of a sperm's tail. The tail is a long, slender structure that whips back and forth and moves the sperm. Although semen contains millions of sperm, only one sperm joins with an egg.

 Key Concept Check How do the parts of the male reproductive system work together?

Male Reproductive System

Figure 3 Mature sperm leave the body through the penis.

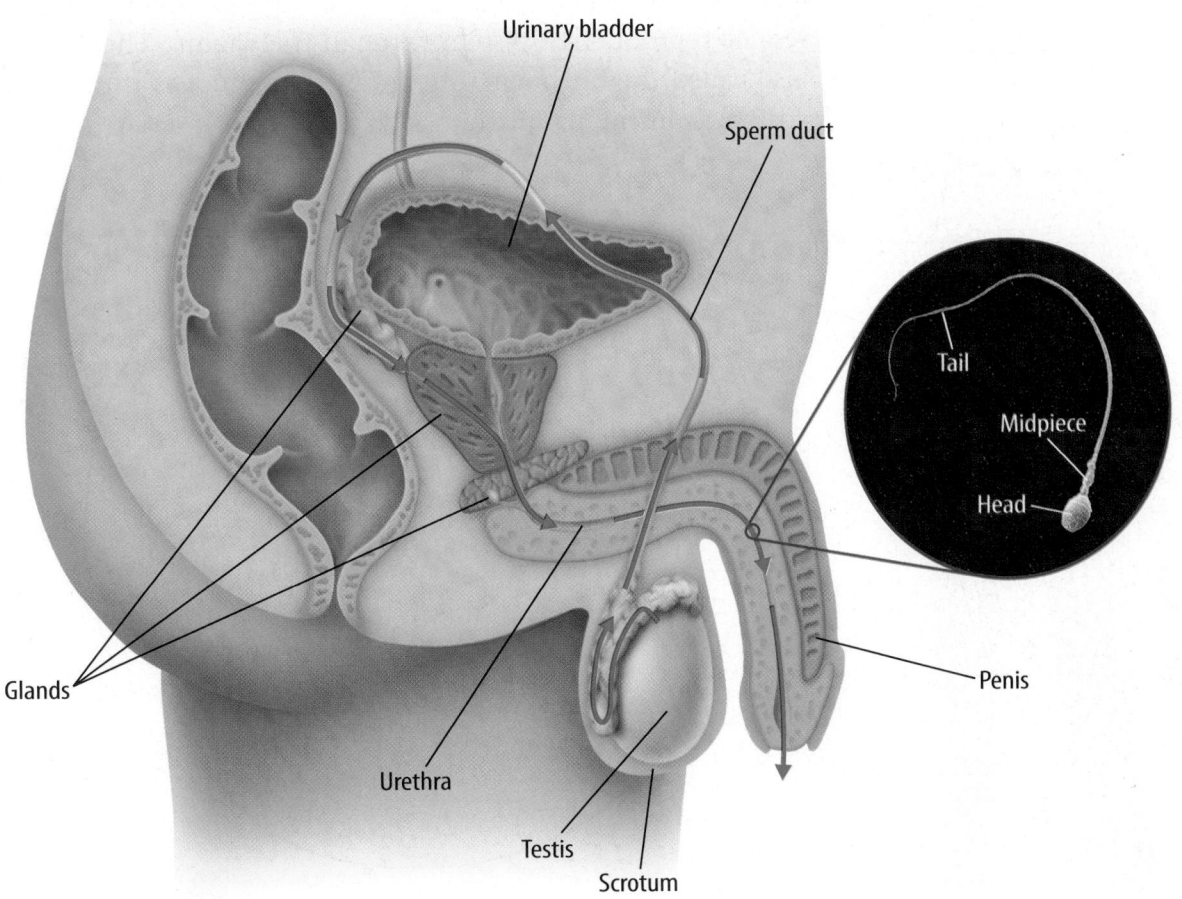

The Female Reproductive System

As shown in **Figure 4,** the female reproductive system also has many structures, each with a unique function. Recall from **Figure 2** that the male reproductive system has both internal and external parts. In contrast, all the parts of the female reproductive system are inside the body.

Recall that both the male and female reproductive systems produce reproductive cells. Males produce sperm, and females produce immature eggs called oocytes (OH uh sites). *An* **ovary** (OH vah ree) *is an organ where oocytes are stored and mature.* A mature oocyte is called an egg, or ovum (plural, ova). Just as males have two testes, females have two ovaries.

About once a month, an ovary releases an egg. After an egg is released, it enters the fallopian (fuh LOH pee un) tube. Short, hairlike structures called cilia move the egg through the fallopian tube toward the uterus. If the egg is fertilized by a sperm, the uterus provides a nourishing environment for a fertilized egg's development. You will read more about how humans develop in Lesson 2.

The part of the female reproductive system that connects the uterus to the outside of the body is the **vagina.** Sperm enter the female reproductive system through the vagina. The vagina is also called the birth canal because a baby moves through this structure during its birth.

WORD ORIGIN · · · · · · · · · · · ·

ovary
from Latin *ovum*, means "egg"

Figure 4 The female reproductive system has many parts, each with a unique function.

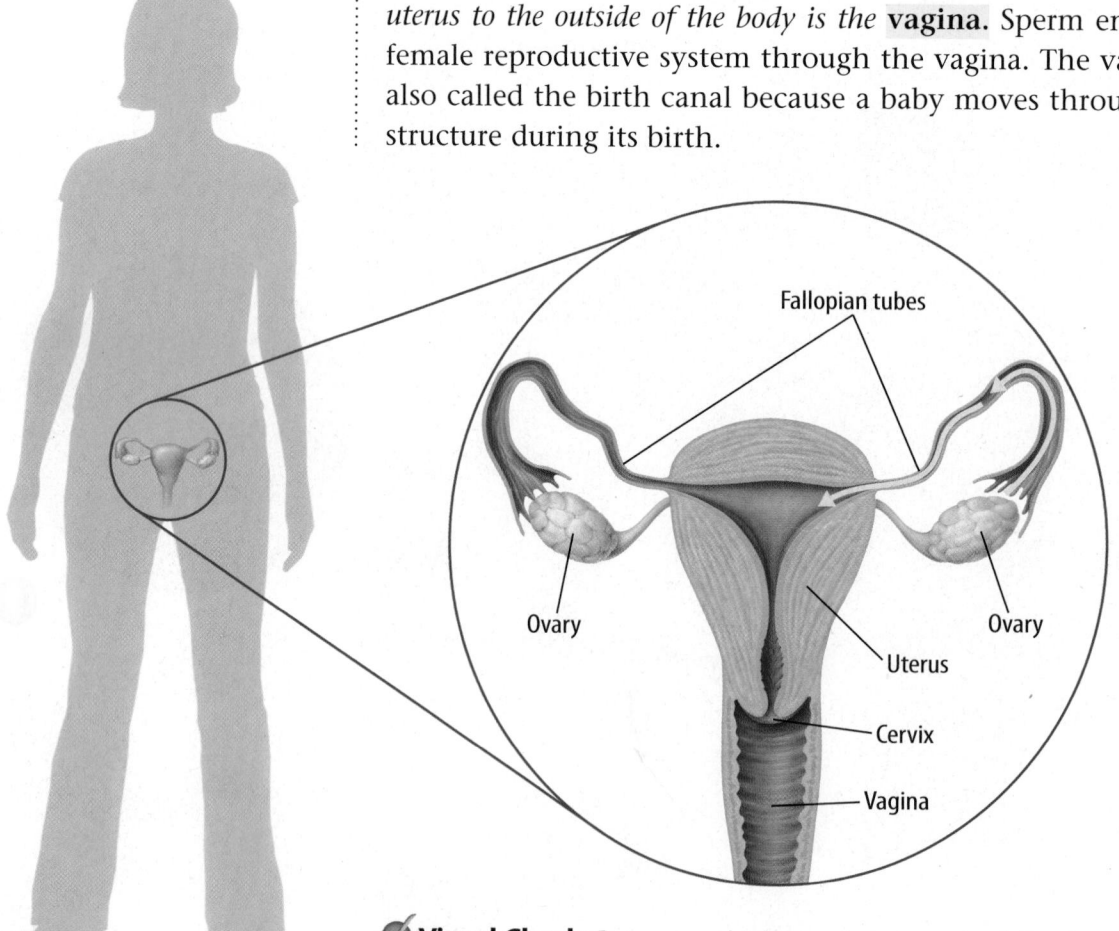

Fallopian tubes

Ovary

Ovary

Uterus

Cervix

Vagina

Visual Check Between which structures are the fallopian tubes located?

The Egg

Unlike sperm, which are long and slender when mature, eggs are large and round when mature. In fact, an egg is about 2,000 times larger than a sperm. Like sperm, eggs contain DNA. However, unlike sperm, an egg is filled with substances that provide it with nourishment. Another important difference between males and females is that a male releases millions of sperm in semen, but a female usually releases only one egg at a time. As shown in **Figure 5,** each oocyte in an ovary is surrounded by follicle cells. The follicle cells release hormones that help the oocytes develop into eggs. The changes that occur as oocytes develop and the release of an egg are also shown in **Figure 5.**

Reading Check How do mature sperm and eggs differ?

Female Reproductive System

Figure 5 A follicle increases in size as it prepares to release an egg.

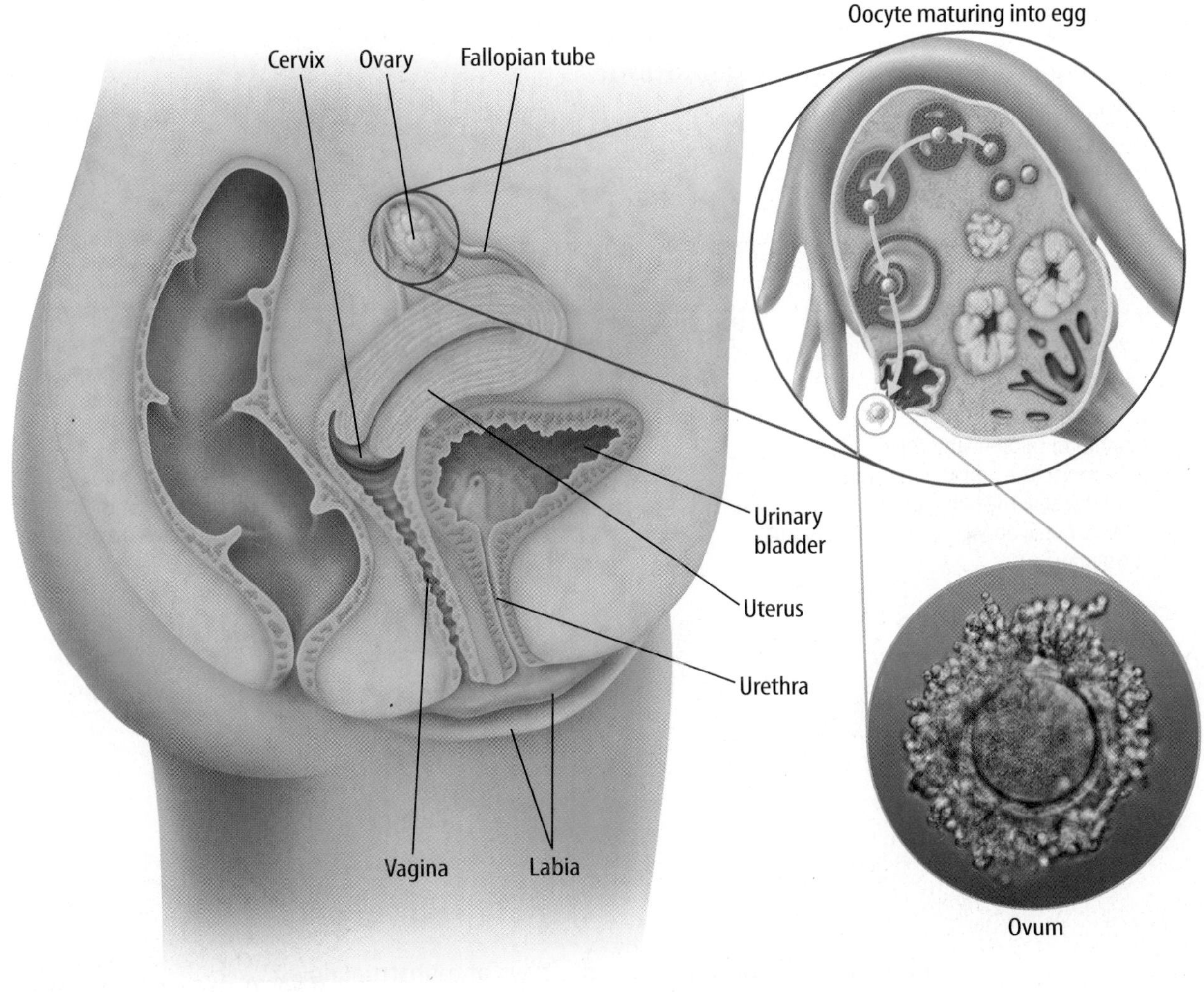

Oocyte maturing into egg
Cervix
Ovary
Fallopian tube
Urinary bladder
Uterus
Urethra
Vagina
Labia
Ovum

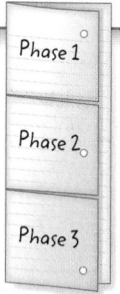

FOLDABLES®

Make a three-tab book from a sheet of notebook paper. Label it as shown. Use it to organize information about the phases of the menstrual cycle.

Phase 1

Phase 2

Phase 3

The Menstrual Cycle

A female usually releases one egg at a time. Because the function of the reproductive system is to produce a new human, an egg is released only when the uterus is prepared to nourish it. *The ovaries and the uterus go through reproductive-related changes called the* **menstrual** (MEN stroo ul) **cycle.** The menstrual cycle is caused by chemical signals called hormones. One menstrual cycle is about 28 days long and can be divided into three phases. It is called a cycle because the phases repeat in the same order and in about the same amount of time.

Phase 1 The menstrual cycle begins with a process called menstruation (men stroo WAY shun). During menstruation, tissue, fluid, and blood cells pass from the uterus through the vagina and are removed from the body. Menstruation usually lasts about five days.

Phase 2 In the next phase of the menstrual cycle, the tissue lining the uterus thickens, as shown in **Figure 6.** In the ovary, several oocytes begin maturing at the same time. After about a week, usually only one egg survives. *Near the end of this phase, hormones cause an egg to be released from the ovary in a process called* **ovulation.**

Figure 6 The tissue lining the uterus changes in thickness during the menstrual cycle.

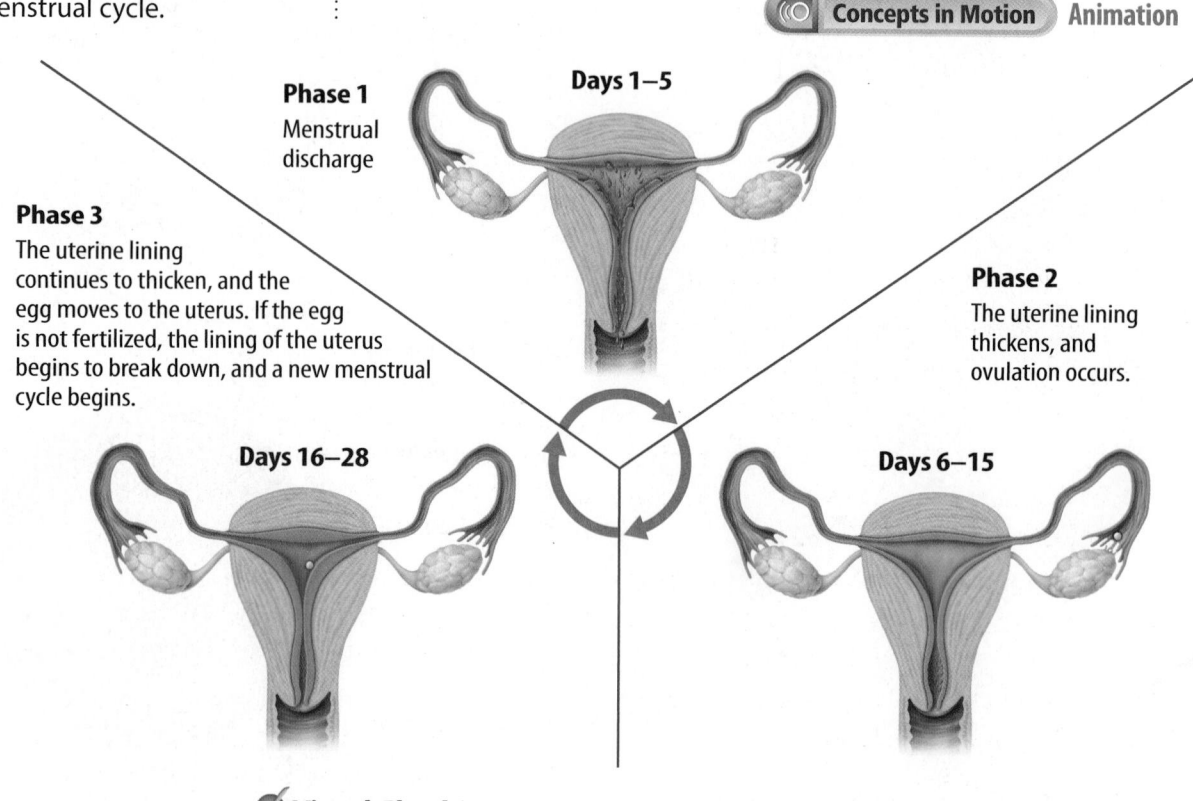

Concepts in Motion Animation

Phase 1
Menstrual discharge

Days 1–5

Phase 3
The uterine lining continues to thicken, and the egg moves to the uterus. If the egg is not fertilized, the lining of the uterus begins to break down, and a new menstrual cycle begins.

Days 16–28

Phase 2
The uterine lining thickens, and ovulation occurs.

Days 6–15

Visual Check Which are the days of menstrual flow?

Phase 3 During phase 3, the tissue that lines the uterus continues to thicken. *If sperm are present, the egg might join with a sperm in a process called* **fertilization.**

The tissue lining the uterus is called the endometrium (en doh MEE tree um). The endometrium provides a fertilized egg with nutrients and oxygen during its early development. If fertilization does not occur, the endometrium breaks down and the menstrual cycle repeats itself.

 Key Concept Check How do the parts of the female reproductive system work together?

Menopause When females get older, the reproductive system stops releasing eggs. When this happens, a woman reaches menopause—a time when the menstrual cycle stops. Menopause occurs because a woman's ovaries produce fewer hormones. There are not enough hormones to cause oocyte maturation and ovulation. Menopause usually happens between the ages of 45 and 55.

The Reproductive System and Homeostasis

Although the reproductive system does not help the body maintain homeostasis, reproduction is essential to ensure the survival of the human species. The reproductive systems of both males and females are controlled by the endocrine system.

Recall that hormones produced by the endocrine system cause the menstrual cycle. These hormones act by positive and negative feedback mechanisms and control when oocytes mature. Hormones also control sperm maturation in the male reproductive system. The reproductive system and the endocrine system work together and control when sperm and eggs mature.

 Key Concept Check How do body systems interact with the reproductive system?

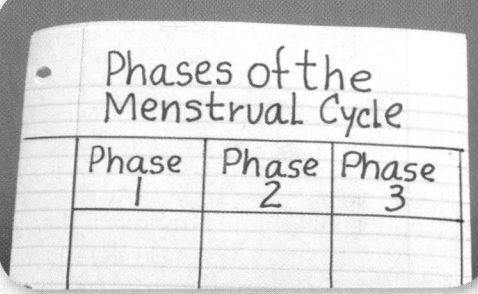

Lesson 1 Review

✓ **Assessment**   Online Quiz

Visual Summary

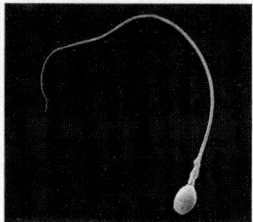

Sperm are male reproductive cells.

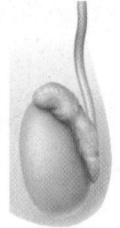

The testes produce sperm and are inside the scrotum.

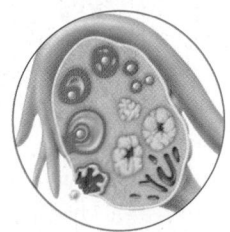

The ovary is the female reproductive organ where oocytes are stored and mature into eggs.

FOLDABLES

Use your lesson Foldable to review the lesson. Save your Foldable for the project at the end of the chapter.

What do you think NOW?

You first read the statements below at the beginning of the chapter.

1. Reproduction ensures that a species survives.

2. The male reproductive system has internal and external parts.

3. The menstrual cycle occurs in males and females.

Did you change your mind about whether you agree or disagree with the statements? Rewrite any false statements to make them true.

Use Vocabulary

1 **Use the terms** *testes* and *sperm* in a sentence.

2 **Distinguish** between ovulation and menstruation.

3 Cyclic changes in the uterus and ovaries of the female reproductive system are called the _____ _____.

Understand Key Concepts

4 Which is a mixture of sperm, nutrients, and fluids?
   A. oocyte   C. penis
   B. ovum   D. semen

5 **Explain** why the scrotum is outside of the body.

6 **Compare** the structure of an egg to the structure of a sperm.

Interpret Graphics

7 **Summarize** Copy and fill in the table below to list the parts and functions of the male reproductive system.

Part	Function

8 **Identify** the phase of the menstrual cycle shown below. Explain your choice.

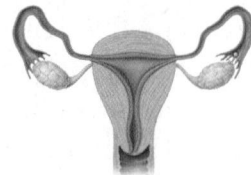

Critical Thinking

9 **Relate** the structures of the female reproductive system to their functions.

10 **Assess** the role of hormones in the function of the reproductive system.

A Medical Breakthrough

Scientific research provides help for infertile couples.

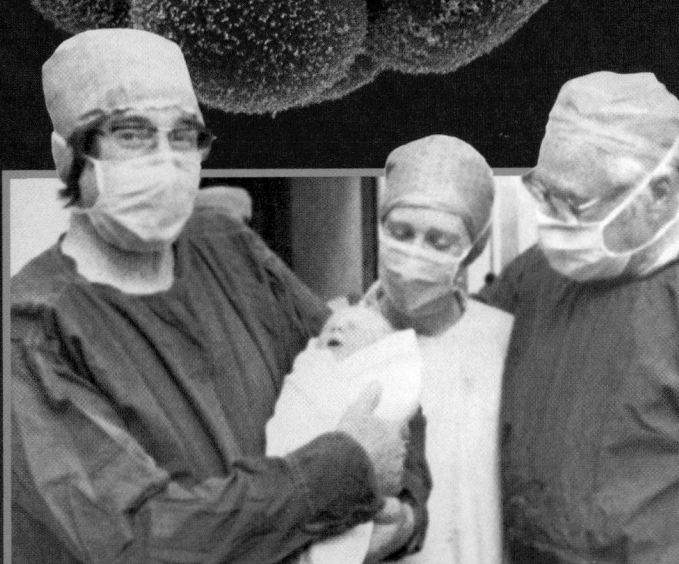

Have you heard the term "test-tube baby"? Can a baby really come from a test tube? Three decades ago, two British scientists answered that question. Patrick Steptoe, an obstetrician and gynecologist, and Robert Edwards, a biologist and physiologist, developed a procedure that helped a British woman overcome infertility, or the inability to become pregnant. As a result of this procedure, the world's first test-tube baby, Louise Joy Brown, was born on July 25, 1978.

Prior to meeting, Steptoe and Edwards worked separately on human infertility. Steptoe developed a process called laparoscopy. Laparoscopy uses a narrow, tubelike instrument fitted with a fiber-optic light and a lens. This enables a doctor to examine a woman's ovaries, fallopian tubes, and uterus through a small incision in her abdomen. Edwards researched the fertilization of human eggs outside the body under laboratory conditions. As a team, Steptoe and Edwards developed a procedure now known as in vitro fertilization (IVF). In IVF, a doctor uses laparoscopy to remove mature eggs from a woman's ovaries. The eggs are fertilized in a Petri dish (the test tube) and grow into zygotes. A doctor transfers the zygotes into a woman's uterus, where they can continue to develop.

▲ Dr. Steptoe (right) looks on as Dr. Edwards holds the world's first test-tube baby.

Steptoe and Edwards worked for ten years to perfect their procedure. The successful implantation and pregnancy achieved through IVF opened new doors for infertile couples. By 2006, it was estimated that as many as 3 million babies had been born using IVF since the birth of Louise Joy Brown in 1978.

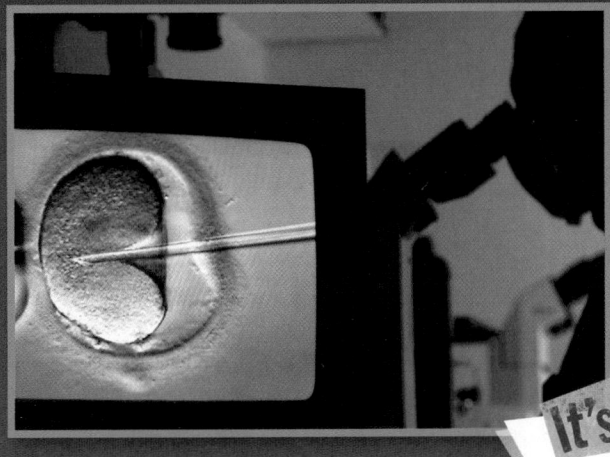

▲ A doctor performs IVF by injecting a sperm cell into an egg cell.

It's Your Turn

REPORT How long has in vitro fertilization been practiced in the United States? What is its success rate? Research these questions and write a short report.

Lesson 2

Reading Guide

Key Concepts

ESSENTIAL QUESTIONS

- What happens during fertilization of a human egg?
- What are the major stages in the development of an embryo and a fetus?
- How do the life stages differ after birth?

Vocabulary

zygote p. 684

pregnancy p. 685

placenta p. 685

umbilical cord p. 685

embryo p. 686

fetus p. 686

cervix p. 688

puberty p. 690

 Multilingual eGlossary

 Video BrainPOP®

Human Growth and Development

Inquiry When's my birthday?

This developing human is 12 weeks old. How did it develop from one cell? In this lesson, you will learn about development before and after birth.

How does a fetus develop in the uterus?

Just as humans have several stages of development after birth, scientists have given names to the developmental stages from fertilization to birth.

1. Observe the copy of a **sonogram** provided by your teacher.

2. Match the numbered structures on the sonogram to the **list of body parts** that your teacher has given you. Record your answers in your Science Journal.

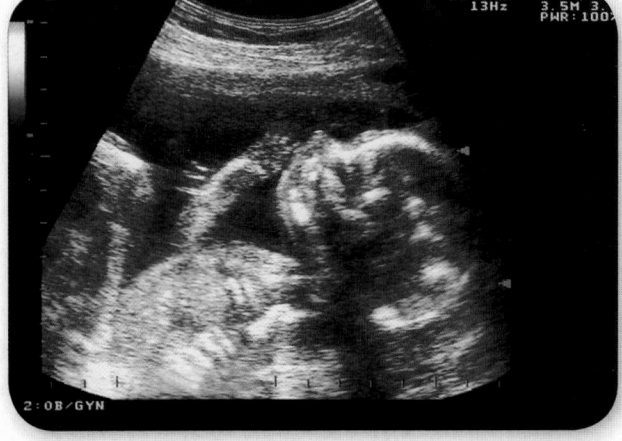

Think About This

1. What were the most difficult structures to identify? Why?

2. What questions do you have about fetal development?

3. 🔑 **Key Concept** How do you think the stages of development after birth compare to the stages of development before birth?

Stages of Development

Have you ever been to a large family gathering? If you have, you might recall seeing people of every age. As shown in **Figure 7**, there probably were babies, children, teens, and adults.

As you might have noticed at the family gathering, people go through stages of development—infancy, childhood, adolescence (a duh LES unts), and adulthood. These stages are based on major developments that take place during each stage. In infancy there is rapid development of the nervous and muscular systems. During childhood, the abilities to speak, read, write, and reason develop. Adolescence is when a person becomes physically able to reproduce. Adulthood is the last stage—when growth of the muscular and skeletal systems stops.

Just as a human has several stages of development after he or she is born, the time before birth is divided into stages, beginning with fertilization.

Figure 7 People at this family reunion are in different stages of development. Humans grow and develop after birth.

Fertilization

If sperm enter the vagina, they can travel to the uterus and up into the fallopian tubes. The fallopian tubes are thin tubes that connect the uterus to the ovaries. Although millions of sperm are released into the vagina, most die before reaching the fallopian tubes.

A sperm contains substances that help its cell membrane join with the cell membrane of an egg. Once a sperm enters an egg, the egg's cell membrane changes rapidly. These changes ensure that only one male reproductive cell and one female reproductive cell combine to create a new human. When the nucleus of the sperm joins with the nucleus of the egg, fertilization is complete, as shown in **Figure 8**.

Figure 8 Sperm travel through the uterus and fallopian tubes to fertilize an egg. Eggs are fertilized in the fallopian tube.

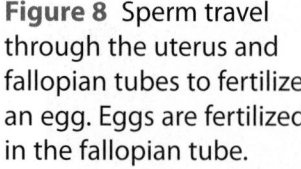 **Key Concept Check** What happens during fertilization?

 Concepts in Motion Animation

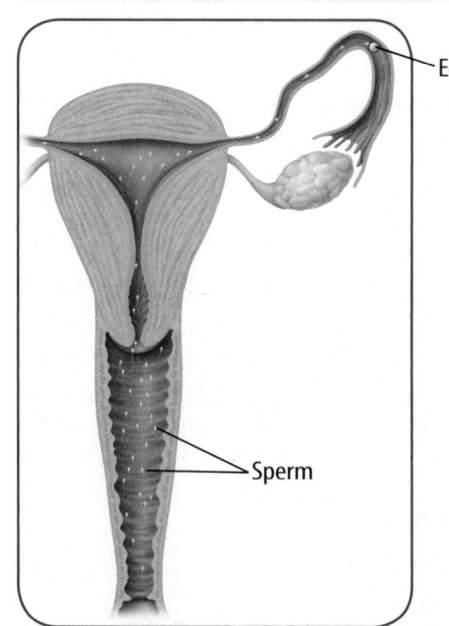

Fertilization

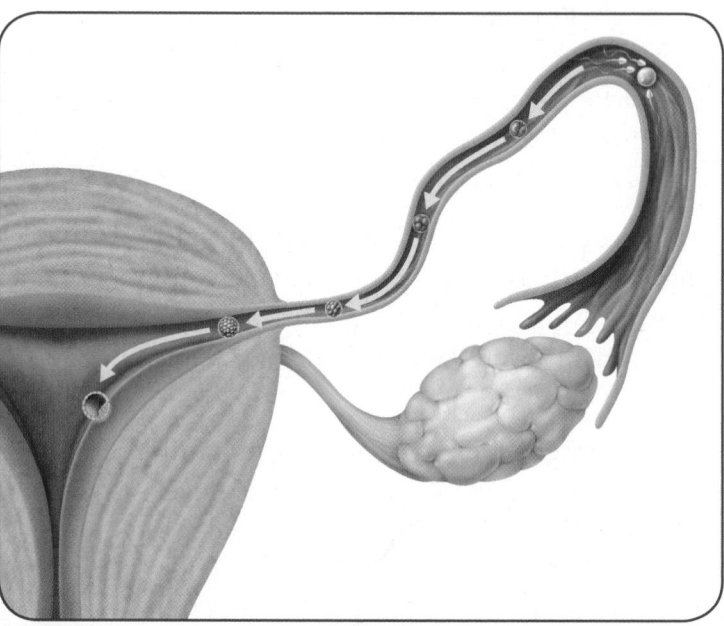

Implantation

Zygote Formation

A fertilized egg is called a **zygote** (ZI goht). Human zygotes contain 46 chromosomes of DNA—23 chromosomes from the sperm cell and 23 chromosomes from the egg cell. This means a zygote is a diploid cell. You might recall that reproductive cells form during meiosis and are haploid cells—they contain half the number of chromosomes of a diploid cell.

The zygote moves through the fallopian tube to the uterus. As it moves toward the uterus, the zygote undergoes mitosis and cell division many times, developing into a ball of cells.

REVIEW VOCABULARY

meiosis
the process in which one diploid cell divides to form four haploid cells

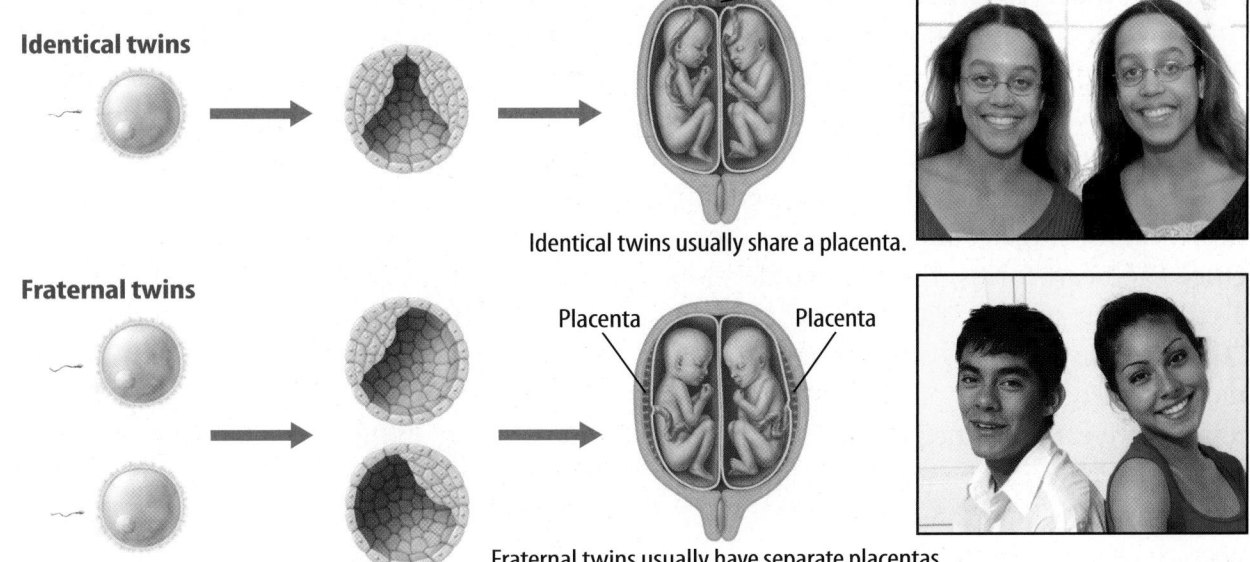

Identical twins

Identical twins usually share a placenta.

Fraternal twins

Placenta   Placenta

Fraternal twins usually have separate placentas.

Multiple Births

A zygote is now a ball of cells with a group of cells on the inside. This group of cells, called the inner cell mass, can develop into a baby. Sometimes the inner cell mass divides in two. When one zygote contains two inner cell masses, as shown in **Figure 9,** identical twins can develop. Identical twins are always of the same gender and usually look very similar. Multiple births can also occur when more than one egg is released and each is fertilized by a different sperm. This results in fraternal twins, also shown in **Figure 9.** Unlike identical twins, fraternal twins can be different genders.

Development Before Birth

Recall that the tissue lining the uterus, the endometrium, thickens during the menstrual cycle. About seven days after fertilization, the zygote enters the uterus and attaches to the thickened endometrium. As shown in **Figure 8,** this process is called implantation. After implantation, a zygote can develop into a baby in about nine months. *The period of development from fertilized egg to birth is called* **pregnancy.**

After attaching to the uterus, *the outer cells of the zygote and cells from the uterus form an organ called the* **placenta** (pluh SEN tuh). *The outer zygote cells also form a rope-like structure, called the* **umbilical** (um BIH lih kul) **cord,** *which attaches the developing offspring to the placenta.* The developing offspring and the mother exchange materials through the umbilical cord. Nutrients and oxygen from the mother pass to the developing offspring and waste and carbon dioxide are removed from it.

Figure 9 Each inner cell mass can develop into a baby.

Math Skills

Use Percentages

In 2005, 32.2 sets of twins were born for every 1,000 births in the United States. You can express this rate as 32.2/1,000. To convert this to a percentage, first convert the fraction to a decimal:

$$\frac{32.2}{1,000} = 0.0322$$

Multiply the decimal by 100 and add a percent sign.

$$0.0322 \times 100 = 3.22\%$$

Practice

In 2005, there were 161.8 multiple births per 100,000 live births. What percent of live births were multiples?

Review

• **Math Practice**
• **Personal Tutor**

From Zygote to Embryo

From the time the zygote attaches to the uterus until the end of the eighth week of pregnancy, it is called an **embryo.** During this time, cells divide, grow, and gain unique functions. As shown in **Figure 10,** the brain, heart, limbs, fingers, and toes start to form. Once the heart forms, the embryo develops a circulatory system. The embryo can now take in more nutrients and oxygen from its mother through the placenta. Bones and reproductive tissues begin to develop. The ears and eyelids can be seen. By eight weeks, the embryo is about 2.5 cm long.

Reading Check What changes take place in the embryo?

From Embryo to Fetus

During the time between nine weeks and birth, the developing offspring is called a **fetus.** Organ systems begin to function, and the fetus continues to grow in size, as shown in **Figure 10.** The fetus is now able to move its arms and legs. The heartbeat can be heard with a medical instrument called a stethoscope (STEH thuh skohp). During the remaining time until birth, the fetus grows rapidly. The bones fully develop but are still soft, and the lungs mature. The fetus can respond to sounds from outside the uterus, such as its mother's voice.

Key Concept Check What are the major stages in the development of a fetus?

Review Personal Tutor

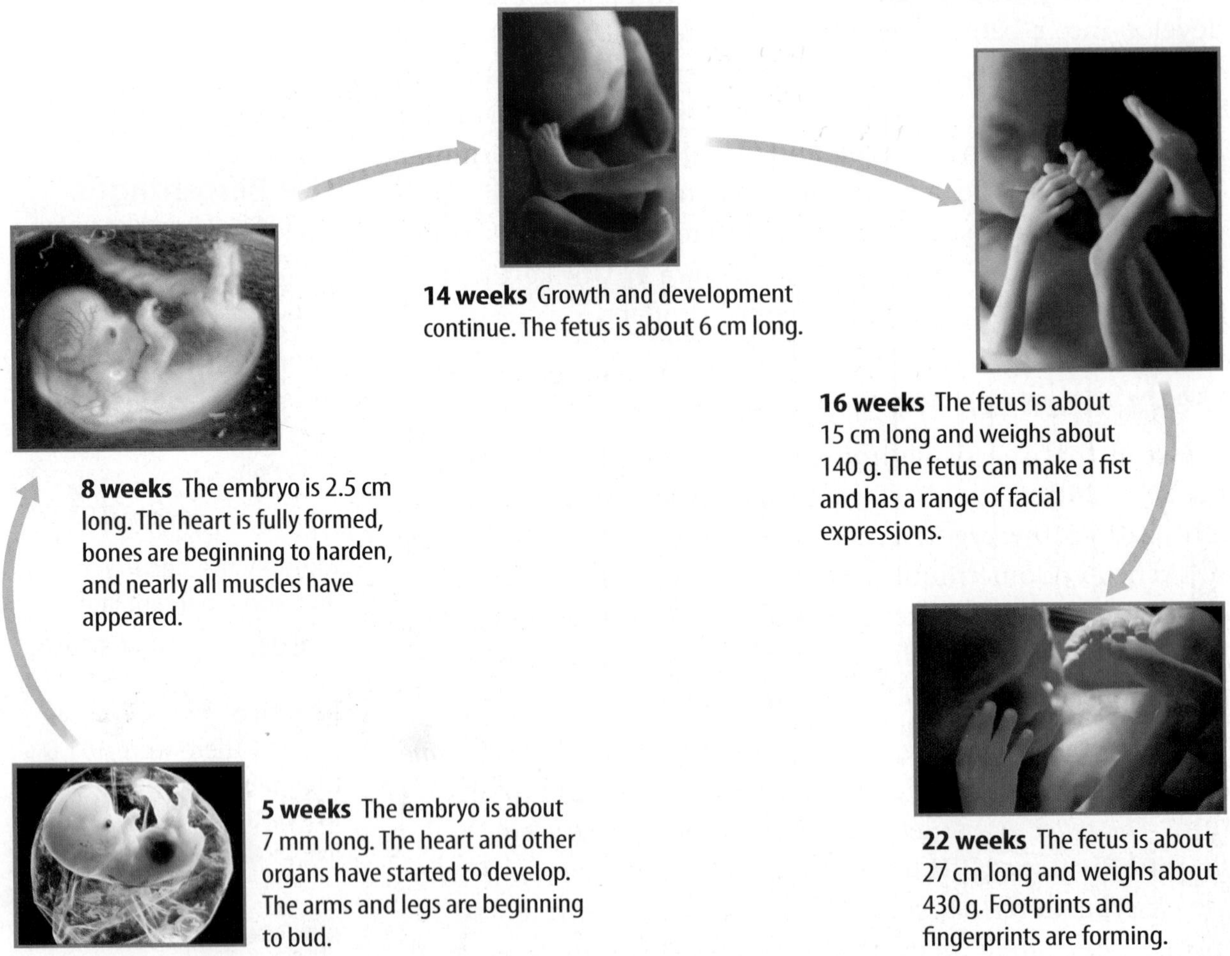

5 weeks The embryo is about 7 mm long. The heart and other organs have started to develop. The arms and legs are beginning to bud.

8 weeks The embryo is 2.5 cm long. The heart is fully formed, bones are beginning to harden, and nearly all muscles have appeared.

14 weeks Growth and development continue. The fetus is about 6 cm long.

16 weeks The fetus is about 15 cm long and weighs about 140 g. The fetus can make a fist and has a range of facial expressions.

22 weeks The fetus is about 27 cm long and weighs about 430 g. Footprints and fingerprints are forming.

Figure 10 As an embryo develops into a fetus, it grows in size and organ systems form.

Visual Check What features do you recognize in the developing human?

Fetal Health

Because a fetus receives all nutrients from its mother, the fetus's growth and development depends on the food, water, and other nutrients that its mother eats and drinks. Other factors in a pregnant woman's environment, such as cigarette smoke or chemicals, can also affect the growth and development of her fetus.

Nutrition It is important that a pregnant woman takes in enough protein and vitamins to provide her fetus with the nutrients it needs to grow and develop. Nutrients such as vitamin D, folic acid, and zinc are needed for fetal development of bones and the nervous system. Protein is needed for making all of the new cells as the fetus grows.

Environmental Factors A fetus is protected from many environmental factors because it develops in a woman's uterus. However, the mother's exposure to substances such as chemicals and smoke can harm her fetus. Heavy metals such as lead and mercury can also affect its growth and development.

Drugs and Alcohol When a woman drinks alcohol during pregnancy, the developing fetus can be harmed. This is because her fetus also takes in the alcohol through the placenta. When a fetus is exposed to alcohol, the baby that develops can be born with fetal alcohol syndrome, as shown in **Figure 11**. Fetal alcohol syndrome is a group of lifelong problems that include growth problems, vision and hearing problems, and delayed mental development. Drugs such as cocaine and the nicotine in tobacco can also have harmful effects on a developing fetus if a woman uses them during pregnancy.

ACADEMIC VOCABULARY

affect
(verb) to influence or alter an outcome

Figure 11 When a fetus is exposed to alcohol, many problems can occur. Some parts of the brain in the fetus with fetal alcohol syndrome are smaller than normal. This can cause learning and behavior problems.

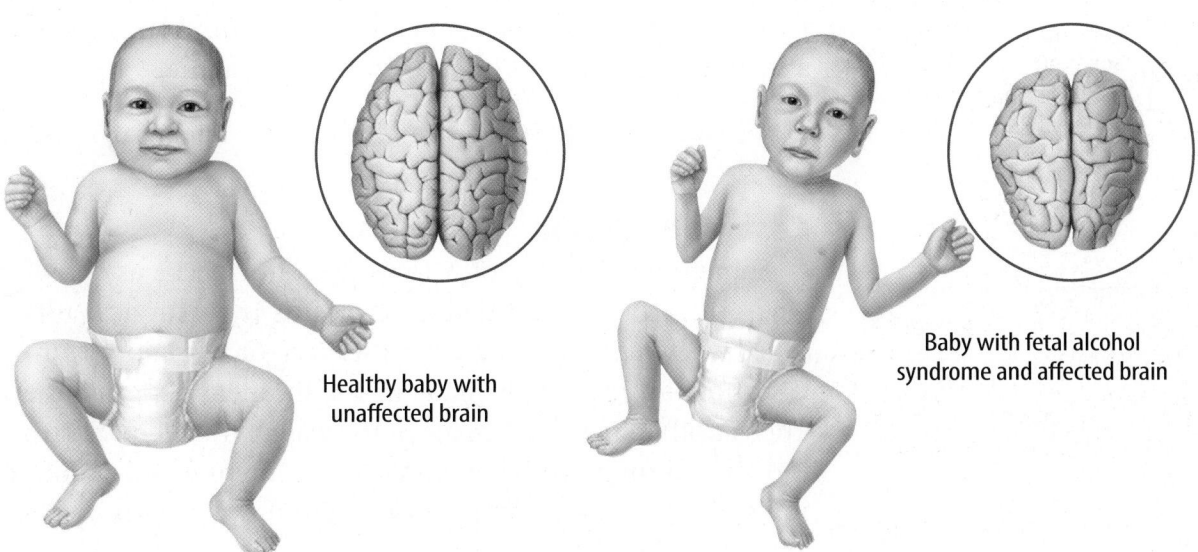

Healthy baby with unaffected brain

Baby with fetal alcohol syndrome and affected brain

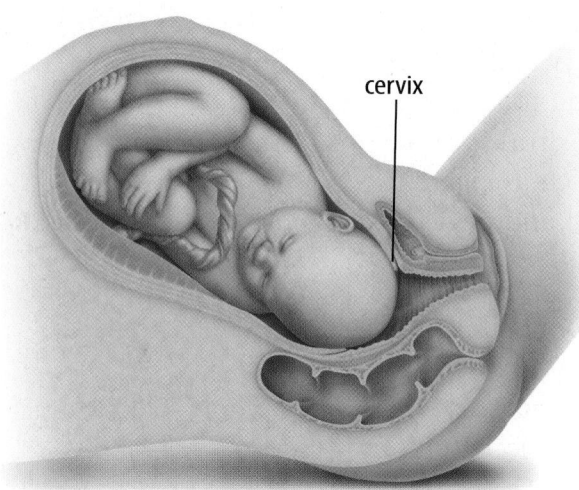

cervix

Stage 1 As the fetus moves into the birth canal, the opening to the uterus widens.

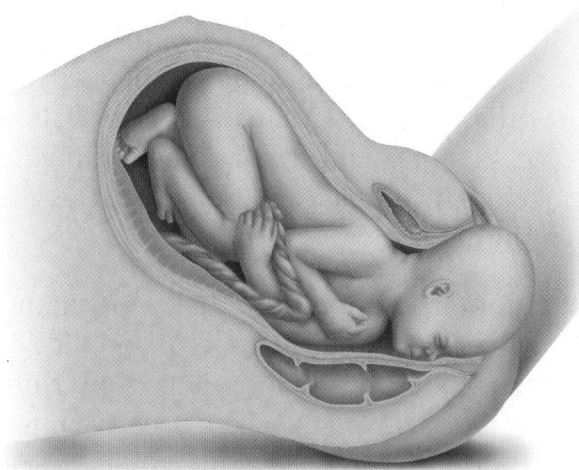

Stage 2 Muscle contractions help push the fetus out through the birth canal.

Figure 12 During birth, the head of the fetus moves toward the cervix. The fetus is delivered after the cervix opens.

WORD ORIGIN · · · · · · · · · · · ·

cervix
Latin, means "neck"
· · · · · · · · · · · · · · ·

Birth

A fetus leaves its mother's body and enters the world through a process called birth, as shown in **Figure 12.** Like the menstrual cycle, the birth of a fetus requires hormones. Hormones cause changes in the female reproductive system. These changes, called labor, help a fetus leave the uterus.

Labor and Delivery

Labor begins when hormones that are released by the endocrine system cause muscles in the uterus to contract. Also, *a small structure between the uterus and the vagina, called the* **cervix** (SUR vihks), begins to open. As more hormones are released, muscles in the uterus continue to contract faster and more strongly. As shown in **Figure 12,** the cervix opens wider to enable the fetus to leave the body. The contractions push a fetus into the vagina and out of the woman's body. After the fetus is delivered, the placenta breaks away from the uterus and also exits the woman's body through the vagina.

 Reading Check Summarize what happens during labor and delivery.

Cesarean Section

Sometimes delivery of a fetus does not occur as shown in **Figure 12.** Doctors can deliver the fetus by a surgical process called a cesarean (suh ZER ee un) section, or C-section. During a C-section, an incision is made in the mother's abdominal wall. Then another incision is made in the wall of the uterus. The baby is delivered through the openings in the uterine and abdominal walls. C-sections are often performed to prevent harm to a fetus and its mother.

Infancy

Once a baby is born, it stops depending directly on its mother for nutrients and oxygen and starts to function on its own. For the first time, the baby uses its own respiratory system and digestive system. The first two years of a newborn's life are called infancy. During infancy, the brain continues to develop, teeth form, and bones grow and get harder. As shown in **Figure 13,** an infant grows in size and learns to crawl, sit, walk, and speak. Organ systems continue to develop and mature, and the infant begins to eat solid food.

Childhood

The period following infancy is called childhood. During this time, the brain continues to grow and develop and thinking improves. Muscle strength increases, and arms and legs grow longer.

FOLDABLES®

Make a four-tab book from a sheet of notebook paper. Use it to organize your notes on the changes that occur during the stages of human development after birth.

Infancy
Childhood
Adolescence
Adulthood

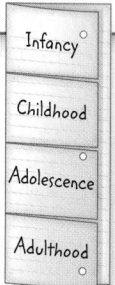

Milestones in Infancy
Walks without support
Stands without support
Walks with support
Crawls
Stands with support
Sits without support
Rolls over
Lifts head
Stages of motor development
0 1 2 3 4 5 6 7 8 9 10 11 12 13 14 15 16 17 18
Age (months)

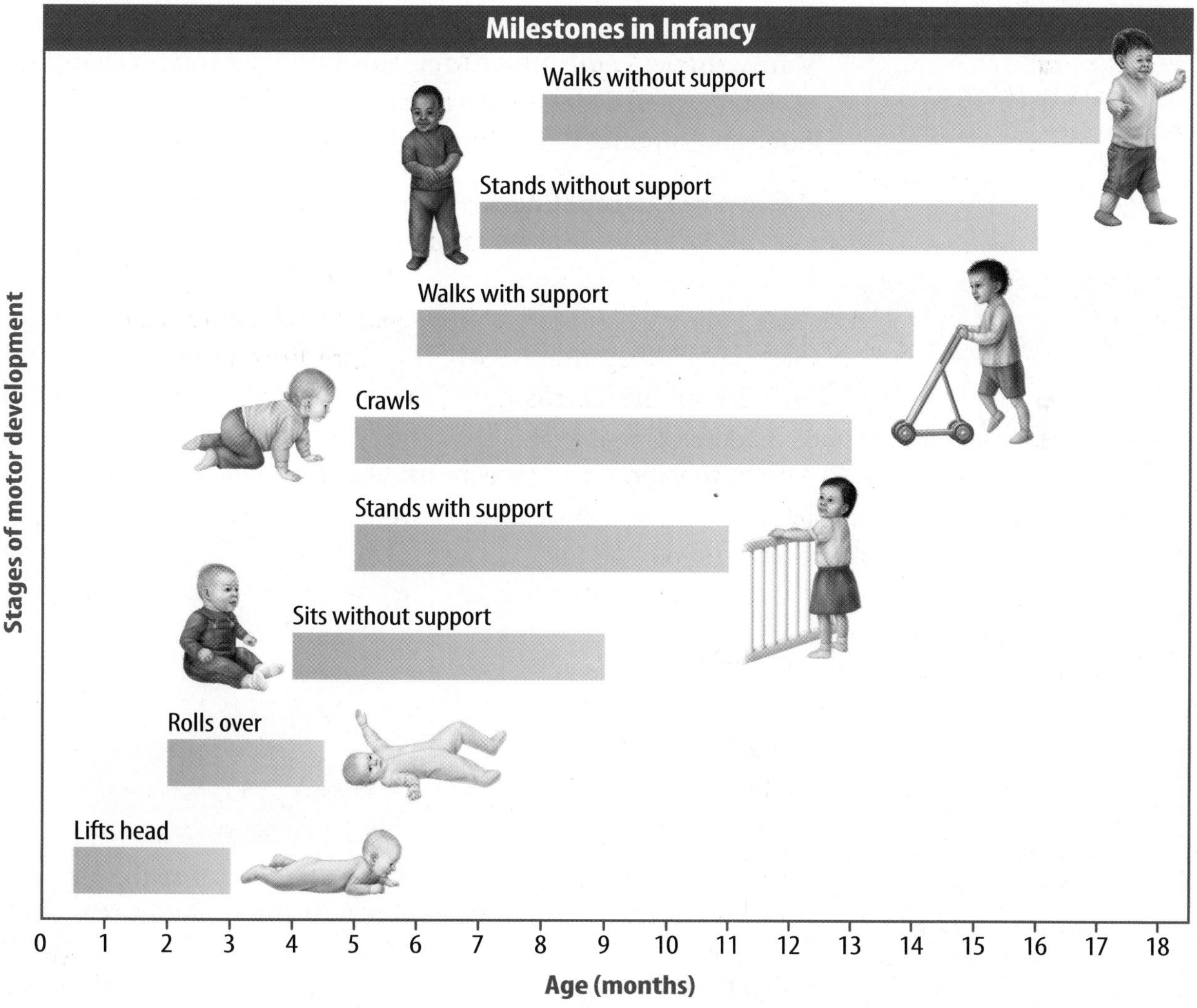

Figure 13 During infancy, infants begin to move around independently.

Visual Check At what age do infants sit without support?

Figure 14 Many physical changes take place between adolescence and older adulthood.

Visual Check What changes can you identify in this photo?

Adolescence

Following childhood is a period of growth called adolescence. Both males and females grow taller as muscles and bones continue to grow. *During adolescence, the reproductive system matures in a process called* **puberty** (PYEW bur tee). Just as hormones are important for the menstrual cycle and for birth, hormones cause the changes that occur during puberty. In males, the voice deepens, muscles increase in size, and facial, pubic, and underarm hair grow. In females, breasts develop, pubic and underarm hair appear, and fatty tissue is added to the buttocks and thighs.

Adulthood and Aging

At the end of adolescence, a person enters adulthood, which continues through old age, as shown in **Figure 14.** Although adults will not grow taller, physical changes in body mass can still occur. Aging is the process of changes in the body over time. Hair can turn white or gray and stop growing, and the skin wrinkles. As humans get older, the sensory system and skeletal system decrease in function. Vision and hearing decline, bones become weaker, and the digestive system slows down.

Key Concept Check How do the life stages after birth differ?

---

inquiry MiniLab   25 minutes

How do life stages after birth differ?

People go through several stages of development after birth—infancy, childhood, adolescence, and adulthood. These stages are based on major developments that take place during those years.

1. Read the information on the small **construction-paper shape** given to you by your teacher.
2. Discuss with other students in your group when exactly in a person's lifetime the event on your paper occurs. Decide where the paper should be placed on the "Human Life Continuum."
3. When your teacher calls upon your group, place the paper in the appropriate spot on the Human Life Continuum.

Analyze and Conclude

1. Where do the most events fall on the Human Life Continuum? Explain why this is so.

2. Where do the fewest events fall on the Human Life Continuum? Explain why this is so.

3. **Key Concept** Summarize how the life stages after birth differ from one another.

Lesson 2 Review

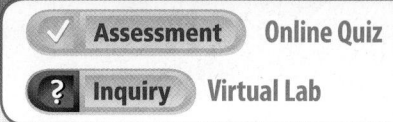
Visual Summary

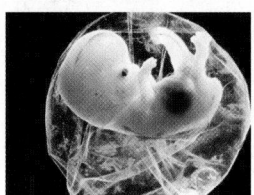

The developing zygote is called an embryo after it attaches to the uterus and until the end of the eighth week of pregnancy.

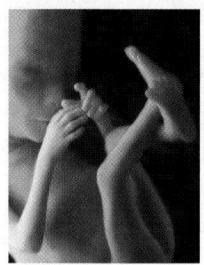

From the ninth week of pregnancy until birth, the developing embryo is called a fetus.

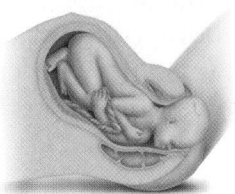

During labor, the fetus leaves the uterus through the cervix, a structure between the uterus and the vagina.

FOLDABLES

Use your lesson Foldable to review the lesson. Save your Foldable for the project at the end of the chapter.

What do you think NOW?

You first read the statements below at the beginning of the chapter.

4. Eggs are fertilized in the ovary.

5. Lead is a nutrient that helps a fetus develop.

6. Puberty occurs during adolescence.

Did you change your mind about whether you agree or disagree with the statements? Rewrite any false statements to make them true.

Use Vocabulary

1 **Distinguish** between zygote and embryo.

2 **Define** *umbilical cord* in your own words.

3 **Use the term** *puberty* in a sentence.

Understand Key Concepts

4 **Describe** the changes in the cervix and the uterus during birth.

5 **Compare** the functions of the placenta and the umbilical cord.

6 Which does not happen during aging?
  A. Hair turns white.
  B. Skin wrinkles.
  C. An individual grows taller.
  D. Vision and hearing decline.

Interpret Graphics

7 **Summarize** Copy and fill in the graphic organizer below to summarize the stages of development after an egg is fertilized and before birth.

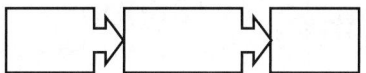

Critical Thinking

8 **Explain** why a developing human can be harmed during the stage of development shown in the figure below.

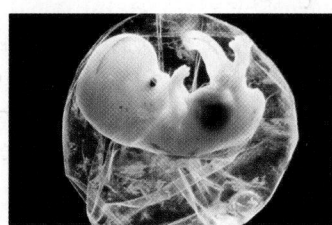

Math Skills

📘 **Review**
— **Math Practice** —

9 In 1990, 12 births out of 1,000 live births resulted in fraternal twins, and 4 births out of 1,000 live births resulted in identical twins. What percent of live births were fraternal twins? Identical twins?

Materials

index cards

construction paper

small plastic bag of pictures

markers

Educating Extraterrestrials About Human Development

Imagine you are an astronaut whose ship has landed on a faraway planet. Upon stepping out of your spaceship, you meet a friendly mob of aliens. They all look very similar. They are all approximately the same height, their arms and legs are all the same length, and their body shapes and proportions are all the same. You are surprised to find out that the aliens differ drastically in ages. They are very curious about you and your crew because you don't look alike. The aliens ask you and your crew to educate them on the human race, specifically how humans develop after birth.

Question

How do the bodies of humans change as they develop from infancy to adulthood?

Procedure

1 Using knowledge about yourself, as well as observations of other humans, make four sketches of yourself for the aliens to see. Sketch yourself in each of the following stages of development—infancy, childhood, adolescence, adulthood—making note of any obvious physical characteristics of that stage. Be sure to think about physical characteristics of each stage, such as length of the extremities, head size in relation to body size, muscle mass, body shape, and any other physical changes you have observed to happen in each stage of development (e.g., losing teeth, acne, gray hair).

2 Obtain the copies of pictures from your teacher. Place the photographs in the correct chronological order from infancy through childhood and adolescence and into adulthood. Compare and contrast the physical traits you observe in each of the photos.

Analyze and Conclude

3 **Compare and contrast** the physical characteristics of an infant and an adult.

4 **Compare and contrast** the physical characteristics of a child and an adolescent.

5 **The Big Idea** Explain how human bodies change as we go through the stages of development from infancy to adulthood. Describe the trends seen in body shape, extremity length, muscle mass, body proportions, and any other details you wish to include.

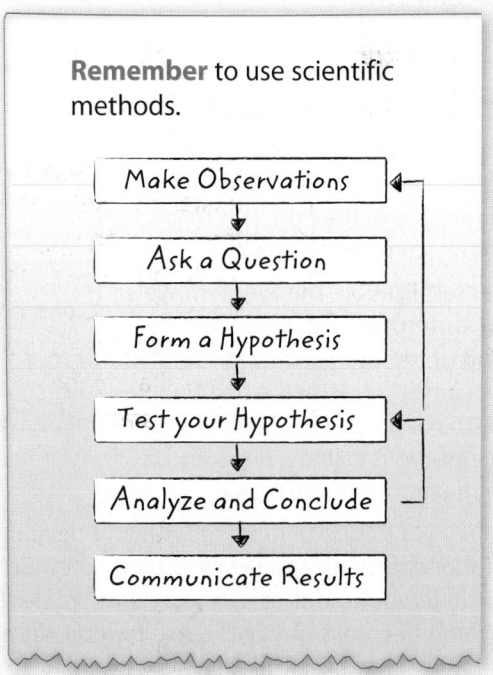

Communicate Your Results

Record a newscast or write a newspaper article detailing your expedition. Be sure to include information regarding where you went, who you encountered there, and what you taught them about your species.

 **Extension**

Think of a question you have regarding a specific stage of development. Design a controlled experiment or an observational study to investigate your question.

Remember to use scientific methods.

Make Observations

↓

Ask a Question

↓

Form a Hypothesis

↓

Test your Hypothesis

↓

Analyze and Conclude

↓

Communicate Results

Chapter 19 Study Guide

THE BIG IDEA

Human reproduction and development begin when a sperm and an egg join. After fertilization, the zygote develops into an embryo and then a fetus. Human development continues after birth.

Key Concepts Summary 🔑

Lesson 1: The Reproductive System

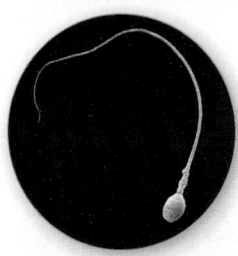

- The main function of the reproductive system is to ensure that the species survives. The male and female reproductive systems enable **sperm** and **egg** to join.
- The parts of the male reproductive system work together and produce and transport sperm to the female reproductive system.
- The parts of the female reproductive system work together and produce oocytes, provide a suitable environment for **fertilization** to occur, and nourish the developing offspring.
- The endocrine system interacts with the **testes** and **ovaries** and produces hormones that control and aid in sexual development.

Lesson 2: Human Growth and Development

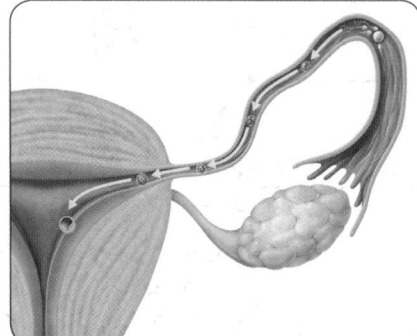

- After a sperm enters an egg, the nucleus of the sperm joins with the nucleus of the egg. This forms a fertilized egg, or **zygote.**
- After fertilization, the zygote travels to the uterus and attaches to the lining of the uterus. It is now known as an **embryo.** After the first two months of pregnancy, the developing embryo is called a **fetus** and it can move its arms and legs.
- Infancy is a period of rapid growth and development. During childhood, growth and development continue at a less rapid pace than in infancy. Adolescence is a period of development during which a person becomes physically able to reproduce. During adulthood, a person reaches his or her peak physical development, and then continues to change as aging occurs.

Vocabulary

sperm p. 673

egg p. 673

testis p. 674

semen p. 674

penis p. 674

ovary p. 676

vagina p. 676

menstrual cycle p. 678

ovulation p. 678

fertilization p. 678

zygote p. 684

pregnancy p. 685

placenta p. 685

umbilical cord p. 685

embryo p. 686

fetus p. 686

cervix p. 688

puberty p. 690

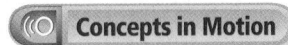
FOLDABLES® Chapter Project

Assemble your lesson Foldables as shown to make a Chapter Project. Use the project to review what you have learned in this chapter.

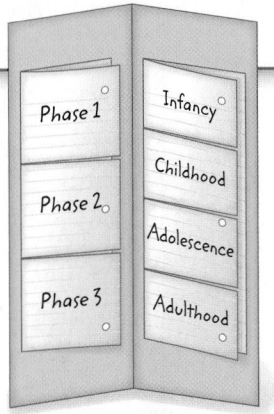

Use Vocabulary

Distinguish between the vocabulary words in each pair.

1 sperm and egg

2 ovulation and menstruation

3 uterus and ovary

Determine if each statement is true or false.

4 The umbilical cord attaches the developing offspring to the uterus.

5 Puberty occurs during childhood.

6 A human zygote contains 23 chromosomes.

Link Vocabulary and Key Concepts

Concepts in Motion Interactive Concept Map

Copy this concept map, and then use vocabulary terms from the previous page to complete the concept map.

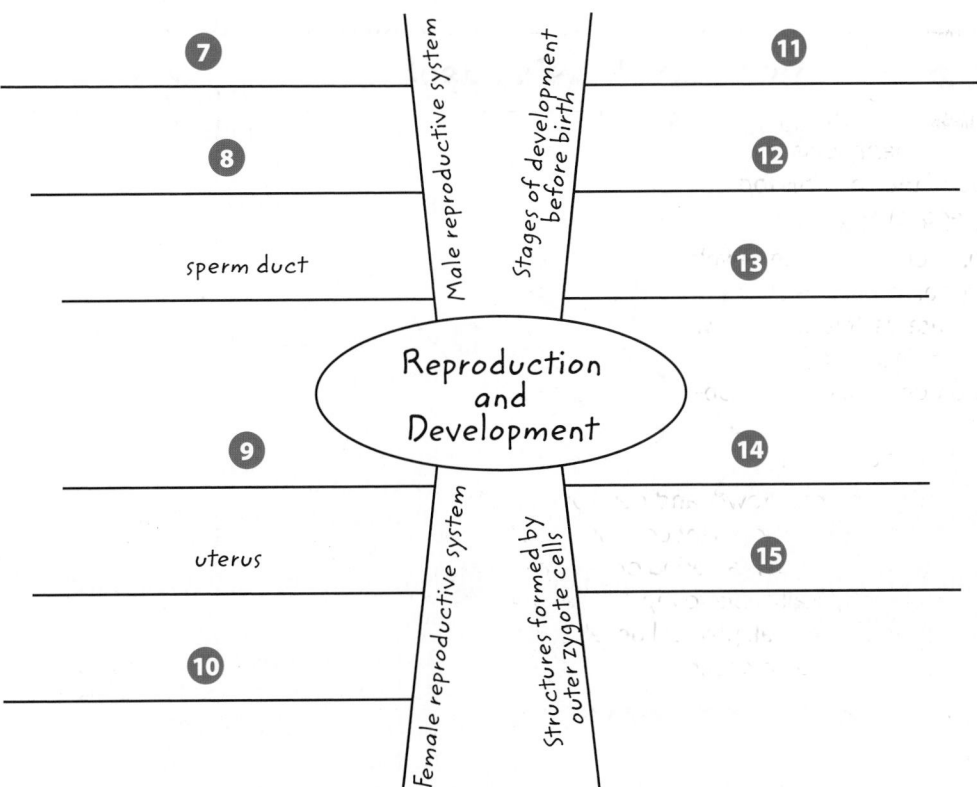

Understand Key Concepts

1 Which part of the male reproductive system in the figure below produces sperm?

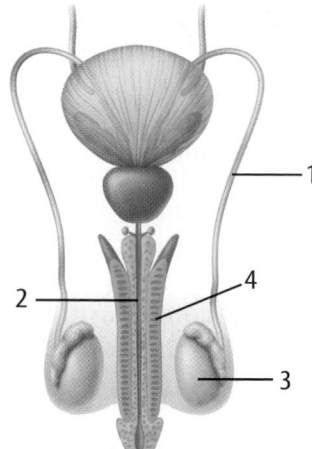

A. 1
B. 2
C. 3
D. 4

2 Which is NOT a part of sperm?

A. egg
B. head
C. midpiece
D. tail

3 Where do fertilized eggs develop?

A. ovary
B. scrotum
C. uterus
D. vagina

4 What happens to the menstrual cycle during menopause?

A. It begins.
B. It stops.
C. It gets faster.
D. It gets longer.

5 Which causes changes in male and female reproductive systems?

A. eggs
B. hormones
C. oocytes
D. sperm

6 How many diploid cells make up a zygote immediately following fertilization?

A. 0
B. 1
C. 2
D. 4

7 Fertilization of an egg takes place in which of the structures in the figure below?

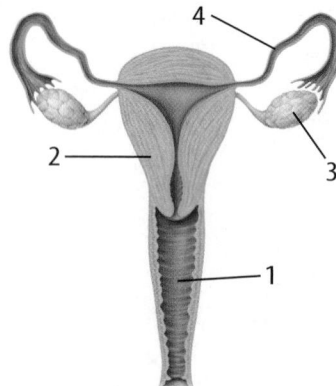

A. 1
B. 2
C. 3
D. 4

8 Which widens during delivery so the fetus can leave the uterus?

A. cervix
B. fallopian tube
C. ovary
D. uterus

9 Puberty occurs during which stage of development?

A. adolescence
B. adulthood
C. childhood
D. infancy

10 How is a fetus delivered during a cesarean section?

A. by hormones
B. by surgery
C. through the cervix
D. through the vagina

 ✓ **Assessment**
Online Test Practice

Critical Thinking

11 **Infer** why semen contains millions of sperm.

12 **Compare** the parts of the male reproductive system to the parts of the female reproductive system.

13 **Infer** What would happen to sperm in a man whose testes were located inside his body instead of in the scrotum?

14 **Explain** why sperm and eggs contain only 23 chromosomes.

15 **Interpret** what is happening in the illustration below.

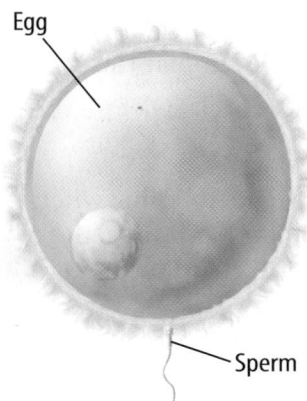

Egg

Sperm

16 **Predict** how not having enough hormones affects puberty.

17 **Assess** the effect on the development of a fetus if a pregnant woman does not take in enough nutrients.

18 **Form** a hypothesis that explains why hormones are necessary for childbirth.

Writing in Science

19 **Write** a paragraph describing the changes in the uterus that lead to menstruation. Include a main idea, supporting details, and a concluding sentence.

REVIEW THE BIG IDEA

20 What are the stages in human reproduction and development? Explain the stages before and after birth.

21 The photo below shows an egg with many sperm on its surface. What changes occur in the egg to ensure that only one sperm fertilizes the egg? Why?

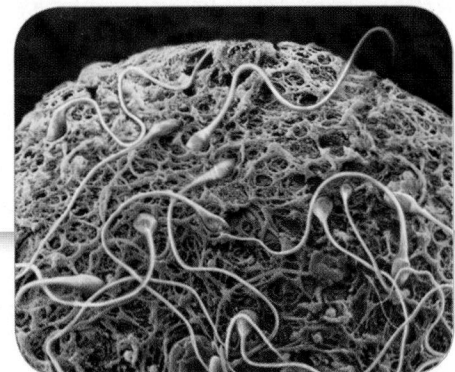

Math Skills

 **Review**
Math Practice

Use Percentages

22 Women who are themselves fraternal twins give birth to about 200 sets of twins in every 2,000 births. What is the probability of a fraternal twin having twins?

23 Women who are themselves identical twins give birth to about 12 sets of twins in every 2,000 births. What is the probability of an identical twin having twins?

24 The Yoruba people in West Africa have the highest rate of twin births in the world. About 23 sets of twins are born per 500 live births. What is the probability of a Yoruba woman having twins?

Standardized Test Practice

Record your answers on the answer sheet provided by your teacher or on a sheet of paper.

Multiple Choice

1 Which body system works with the reproductive system to determine when sperm and eggs mature?

  A circulatory

  B endocrine

  C lymphatic

  D nervous

Use the diagram below to answer question 2.

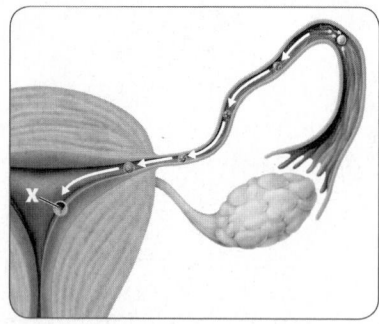

2 What takes place at the location marked *X* in the diagram above?

  A fertilization

  B implantation

  C menstruation

  D ovulation

3 How many chromosomes does each human zygote contain?

  A 1

  B 2

  C 23

  D 46

4 Which statement about fraternal twins is false?

  A They can resemble each other.

  B They must be different genders.

  C They result from multiple eggs.

  D They result from multiple sperm.

Use the table below to answer questions 5 and 6.

Milestone	Earliest Age	Latest Age
Rolls over	2 months	$4\frac{1}{2}$ months
Sits without support	4 months	9 months
Crawls	5 months	13 months
Stands alone	7 months	16 months
Walks alone	8 months	17 months

5 Which can be inferred from the above chart?

  A Age brings more independence.

  B All babies crawl before walking.

  C Infants develop at the same rate.

  D Muscles develop before the brain.

6 A parent wants to know when her baby might exhibit a certain skill. When is her baby most likely to begin crawling?

  A 4–9 months

  B 5–13 months

  C 7–16 months

  D 8–17 months

7 How are sperm and eggs similar?

  A Both are large and round when they mature.

  B Both are released one at a time.

  C Both contain DNA.

  D Both contain substances that nourish them.

8 Through which does nourishment pass directly to a fetus?

  A intestine

  B stomach

  C fallopian tube

  D umbilical cord

9 In which developmental stage do humans become physically capable of reproduction?

A adolescence

B adulthood

C childhood

D infancy

Use the diagram below to answer questions 10 and 11.

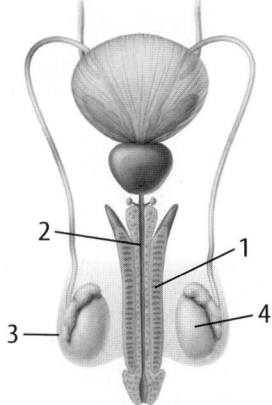

10 Which structure in the above diagram produces male reproductive cells?

A 1

B 2

C 3

D 4

11 Which structure in the diagram regulates temperature for sperm development?

A 1

B 2

C 3

D 4

Constructed Response

Use the diagram below to answer questions 12 and 13.

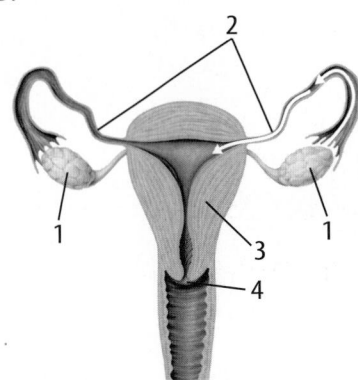

12 Name the numbered parts in the above diagram of the female reproductive system. Explain their functions.

13 What happens to a fertilized egg when it reaches the organ labeled 3 in the diagram above?

Use the table below to answer question 14.

Stage	Description
Fertilization	
Zygote	
Embryo	
Fetus	
Birth	

14 Complete the table above to describe the early stages of human development.

NEED EXTRA HELP?														
If You Missed Question...	1	2	3	4	5	6	7	8	9	10	11	12	13	14
Go to Lesson...	1	2	2	2	2	2	1	2	2	1	1	1	2	2

Unit 5

INTERACTIONS OF LIFE

ALONG THE WAY, I VISITED A TEMPERATE FOREST. IT WAS NOT VERY HOT OR COLD. IT WAS JUST RIGHT.

I WAVED GOODBYE TO MY FRIENDS IN THE HOT AFRICAN GRASSLAND AND MIGRATED NORTH FOR THE SUMMER...

1850   1875   1900

1849
The U.S. Department of Interior is established and is responsible for the management and conservation of most federal land.

1872
The world's first national park, Yellowstone, is created.

1892
The Sierra Club is founded in San Francisco by John Muir. It goes on to be the oldest and largest grassroots environmental organization in the United States.

1915
Congress passes a bill establishing Rocky Mountain National Park in Colorado.

1920
Congress passes the Federal Water Power Act. This act creates a Federal Power Commission with authority over waterways, and the construction and use of water-power projects.

THEN, I RESTED FOR A FEW DAYS IN A COLD, RAINY, MOUNTAIN FOREST IN ASIA. I SAW BEAUTIFUL BAMBOO TREES AND GIANT PANDAS.

I SAID "HI" TO MY FRIENDS IN THE ARCTIC CIRCLE BEFORE HEADING HOME TO THE ALASKAN TUNDRA. NEXT FALL IT'S BACK TO AFRICA FOR THE WINTER.

1950

2000

1955
The Air Pollution Control Act is the first of several United States Clean Air Acts to control air pollution on a national level.

1990
The Clean Air Act Amendments propose emissions trading and add provisions for reducing acid rain, ozone depletion, and toxic air pollution. They also establish a national permits program.

2006
The documentary *An Inconvenient Truth* is released to educate about global warming. The film's popularity raises international awareness of the cause.

? Inquiry

Visit ConnectED for this unit's **STEM** activity.

History and Science

Nearly 50,000 years ago, a group of hunter-gatherers might have roamed through the forest searching for food among the lush plants. The plants and animals that lived in that environment provided the nutritional needs of these people. Humans adapted to the nutrients that the wild foods contained.

Many of the foods you eat today are very different from those eaten by hunter-gatherers. **Table 1** shows how some of these changes occurred.

Table 1 How Science Has Changed Foods			
	What?	**Advantages**	**Disadvantages**
	Gathering Wild Foods— Foods found in nature were the diet of humans until farming began around 12,000 years ago.	Wild foods provided all the nutrients needed by the human body.	Finding wild foods is not reliable. People moved from place to place in search of food. Sometimes they didn't find food, so they went hungry or starved.
	Farming—People grew seeds from the plants they ate. Tribes settled on land near where they grew crops. If soil conditions were not ideal, farmers learned to add water or animal manure to improve plant growth.	Farming allowed more food to be grown in less space. Over time, people learned to breed plants for larger size or greater disease resistance.	Sometimes, farming changed the nutrient content of foods. People began to suffer from nutrient deficiencies and were prone to disease.
	Hybridizing Plants— Gregor Mendel fertilized one plant with the genetic material from another, producing a hybrid. A hybrid is the offspring of two genetically different organisms.	Hybridization produced new plant foods that combined the best qualities of two plants. The variety of plants available for food increased.	Hybrid crops are prone to disease because of their genetic similarity. Seeds from hybrids do not always grow into plants that produce food of the same quality as the hybrid.
	Genetically Modified (GM) Foods—Scientists remove or replace genes to improve a plant. For example, removing the gene that controls flowering in spinach results in more leaves.	GM plants can increase crop yields, nutrient content, insect resistance, and shelf-life of foods. The lettuce shown here has been modified to produce insulin.	Inserted genes might spread to other plants, producing "superweeds." Allergies to GM foods might increase. The long-term effect on humans is unknown.

A Matter of Taste

In early history, food was eaten raw, just as it was found in nature. Cooking food probably occurred by accident. Someone might have accidentally dropped a root into a fire. When people ate the burnt root, it might have tasted better or been easier to chew. This possibly led to cooking more foods. Over many generations, and with the influence of different cultures and their various ways to prepare food, the taste buds of people changed. People no longer enjoy as many raw foods.

Today, the taste buds of some people tempt them to eat high-calorie, low-nutrition processed foods, as shown in **Figure 1.** These foods contain large amounts of calories, salt, and fat.

In some parts of the world, people buy and prepare fresh fruits and vegetables every day, as shown in Figure 2. In general, these people have lower rates of obesity and fewer diseases that are common in people who eat more processed foods.

One scientist noted that people with a diet very different from our prehistoric ancestors are more susceptible to heart disease, cancer, diabetes, and other "diseases of civilization." Time to take another bite of your fruits and veggies!

Figure 1 Processing foods increases convenience but removes nutrients and adds calories that could lead to obesity.

Figure 2 People in China shop in markets where farmers sell fresh produce that comes directly from the farms.

Inquiry **MiniLab**
30 minutes

What food would you design?

Suppose you could breed any two fruits or vegetables. What hybrid would you produce?

1 With a partner, discuss qualities of fruits and vegetables that you like and don't like. Then decide on a combination that would have the best qualities of two fruits and/or vegetables.

2 Draw and describe your new food in your Science Journal.

3 Develop a 20-second infomercial advertising the benefits of your new food, and present it to your class.

Analyze and Conclude

1. **Explain** What qualities of the original foods does your hybrid combine?

2. **Predict** Why would people buy your hybrid?

3. **Explain** What are some advantages and disadvantages of your hybrid?

Chapter 20

Matter and Energy in the Environment

THE BIG IDEA How do living things and the nonliving parts of the environment interact?

 **How does the ram survive?**

The ram needs food, air, water, and shelter to survive. The environment provides the ram with all that it needs to survive.

- How does the ram depend on the nonliving things in the photo?

- How might the ram interact with living things in its environment?

Get Ready to Read

What do you think?

Before you read, decide if you agree or disagree with each of these statements. As you read this chapter, see if you change your mind about any of the statements.

1 The air you breathe is mostly oxygen.

2 Living things are made mostly of water.

3 Carbon, nitrogen, and other types of matter are used by living things over and over again.

4 Clouds are made of water vapor.

5 The Sun is the source for all energy used by living things on Earth.

6 All living things get their energy from eating other living things.

ConnectED Your one-stop online resource

connectED.mcgraw-hill.com

🎞 Video   🌐 WebQuest

🔊 Audio   ✓ Assessment

▤ Review   ◉ Concepts in Motion

? Inquiry   g Multilingual eGlossary

Abiotic Factors

Reading Guide

Key Concepts 🔑
ESSENTIAL QUESTIONS

- What are the nonliving parts of an environment?

Vocabulary

ecosystem p. 707

biotic factor p. 707

abiotic factor p. 707

climate p. 708

atmosphere p. 709

 Multilingual eGlossary

 Video BrainPOP®

Inquiry Why So Blue?

Have you ever seen a picture of a bright blue ocean? The water looks so colorful in part because of nonliving factors such as matter in the water and the gases surrounding Earth. These nonliving things change the way you see light from the Sun, another nonliving part of the environment.

Is it living or nonliving?

You are surrounded by living and nonliving things, but it is sometimes difficult to tell what is alive. Some nonliving things may appear to be alive at first glance. Others are alive or were once living, but seem nonliving. In this lab, you will explore which items are alive and which are not.

1 Draw a chart with the headings *Living* and *Nonliving*.

2 Your teacher will provide you with a list of items. Decide if each item is living or nonliving.

Think About This

1. What are some characteristics that the items in the *Living* column share?

2. **Key Concept** How might the nonliving items be a part of your environment?

Living	Nonliving

What is an ecosystem?

Have you ever watched a bee fly from flower to flower? Certain flowers and bees depend on each other. Bees help flowering plants reproduce. In return, flowers provide the nectar that bees use to make honey. Flowers also need nonliving things to survive, such as sunlight and water. For example, if plants don't get enough water, they can die. The bees might die, too, because they feed on the plants. All organisms need both living and nonliving things to survive.

An **ecosystem** *is all the living things and nonliving things in a given area.* Ecosystems vary in size. An entire forest can be an ecosystem, and so can a rotting log on the forest floor. Other examples of ecosystems include a pond, a desert, an ocean, and your neighborhood.

Biotic (bi AH tihk) **factors** *are the living things in an ecosystem.* **Abiotic** (ay bi AH tihk) **factors** *are the nonliving things in an ecosystem, such as sunlight and water.* Biotic factors and abiotic factors depend on each other. If just one factor—either abiotic or biotic—is disturbed, other parts of the ecosystem are affected. For example, severe droughts, or periods of water shortages, occurred in Australia in 2006. Many fish in rivers and lakes died. Animals that fed on the fish had to find food elsewhere. A lack of water, an abiotic factor, affected biotic factors in this ecosystem, such as the fish and the animals that fed on the fish.

WORD ORIGIN · · · · · · · · · · ·

biotic
from Greek *biotikos*, means
"fit for life"

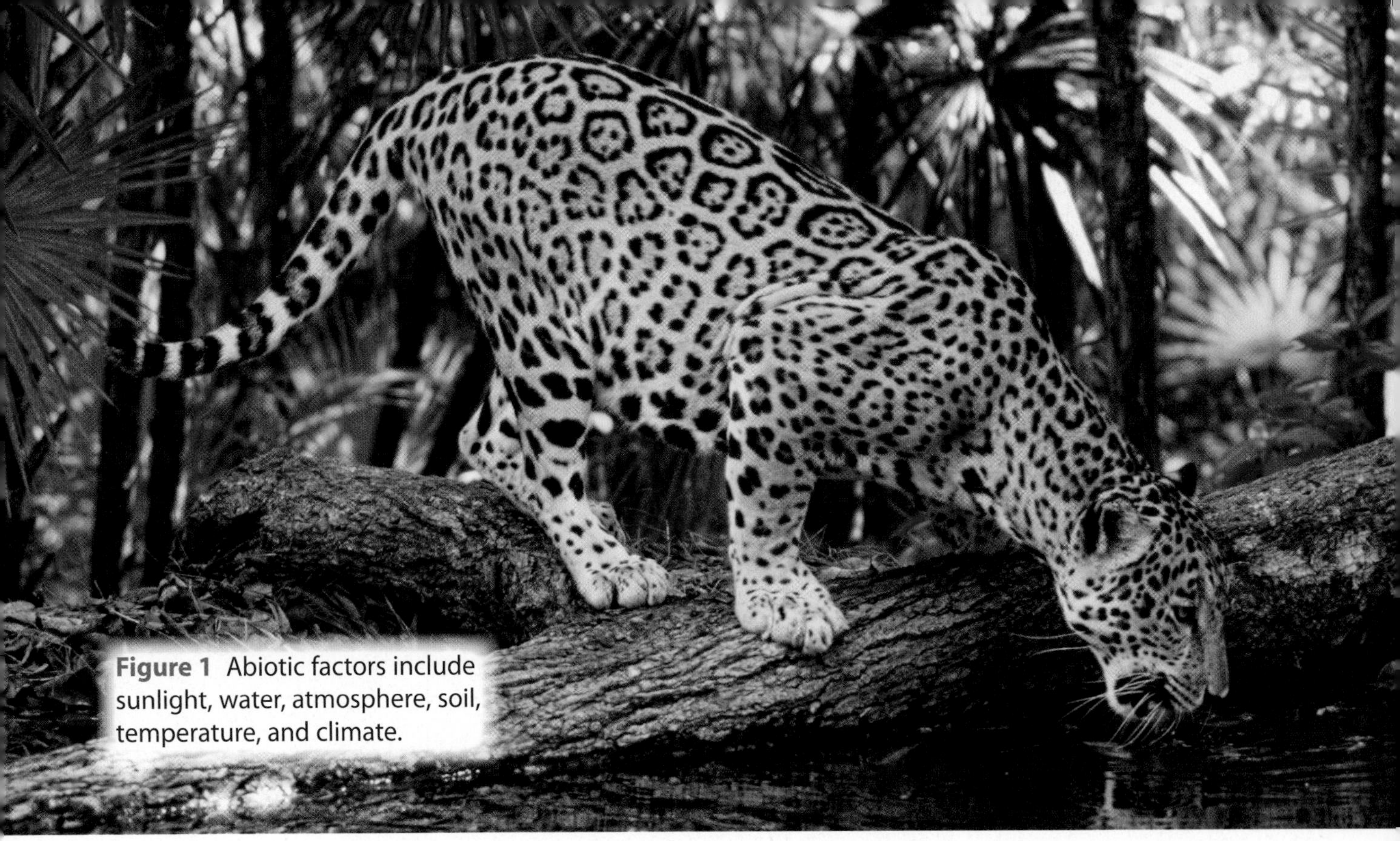

Figure 1 Abiotic factors include sunlight, water, atmosphere, soil, temperature, and climate.

What are the nonliving parts of an ecosystem?

Some abiotic factors in an ecosystem are shown in **Figure 1.** Think about how these factors might affect you. You need sunlight for warmth and air to breathe. You would have no food without water and soil. These nonliving parts of the environment affect all living things.

The Sun

The source of almost all energy on Earth is the Sun. It provides warmth and light. In addition, many plants use sunlight and make food, as you'll read in Lesson 3. The Sun also affects two other abiotic factors—climate and temperature.

Reading Check How do living things use the Sun's energy?

Climate

Polar bears live in the Arctic. The Arctic has a cold, dry climate. **Climate** *describes average weather conditions in an area over time.* These weather conditions include temperature, moisture, and wind.

Climate influences where organisms can live. A desert climate, for example, is dry and often hot. A plant that needs a lot of water could not survive in a desert. In contrast, a cactus is well adapted to a dry climate because it can survive with little water.

Temperature

Is it hot or cold where you live? Temperatures on Earth vary greatly. Temperature is another abiotic factor that influences where organisms can survive. Some organisms, such as tropical birds, thrive in hot conditions. Others, such as polar bears, are well adapted to the cold. Tropical birds don't live in cold ecosystems, and polar bears don't live in warm ecosystems.

Water

All life on Earth requires water. In fact, most organisms are made mostly of water. All organisms need water for important life processes, such as growing and reproducing. Every ecosystem must contain some water to support life.

Fungi

Gases in Atmosphere

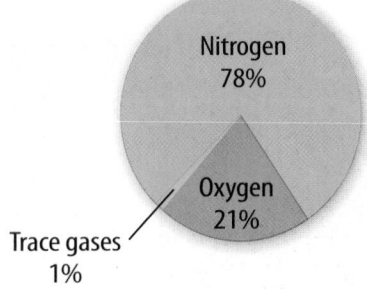

Nitrogen 78%

Oxygen 21%

Trace gases 1%

Climate

Temperature
Precipitation

Precipitation (cm)

Temperature (°C)

Month

Visual Check How does the jaguar interact with the abiotic factors in its ecosystem?

Atmosphere

Every time you take a breath you are interacting with another abiotic factor that is necessary for life—the atmosphere. *The* **atmosphere** (AT muh sfir) *is the layer of gases that surrounds Earth.* The atmosphere is mostly nitrogen and oxygen with trace amounts of other gases, also shown in **Figure 1.** Besides providing living things with oxygen, the atmosphere also protects them from certain harmful rays from the Sun.

Soil

Bits of rocks, water, air, minerals, and the remains of once-living things make up soil. When you think about soil, you might picture a farmer growing crops. Soil provides water and nutrients for the plants we eat. However, it is also a home for many organisms, such as insects, bacteria, and fungi.

Factors such as water, soil texture, and the amount of available nutrients affect the types of organisms that can live in soil. Bacteria break down dead plants and animals, returning nutrients to the soil. Earthworms and insects make small tunnels in the soil, allowing air and water to move through it. Even very dry soil, like that in the desert, is home to living things.

Key Concept Check List the nonliving things in ecosystems.

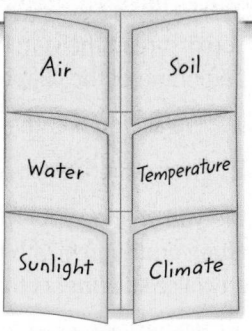

FOLDABLES

Fold and cut a sheet of paper to make a six-door book. Label it as shown. Use it to organize information about the abiotic parts of an ecosystem.

Air	Soil
Water	Temperature
Sunlight	Climate

Lesson 1 Review

Visual Summary

Ecosystems include all the biotic and abiotic factors in an area.

Biotic factors are the living things in ecosystems.

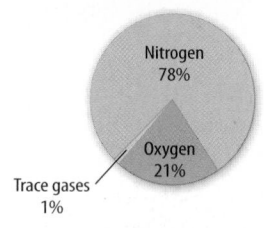

Abiotic factors are the nonliving things in ecosystems, including water, sunlight, temperature, climate, air, and soil.

FOLDABLES

Use your lesson Foldable to review the lesson. Save your Foldable for the project at the end of the chapter.

What do you think NOW?

You first read the statements below at the beginning of the chapter.

1. The air you breathe is mostly oxygen.

2. Living things are made mostly of water.

Did you change your mind about whether you agree or disagree with the statements? Rewrite any false statements to make them true.

Use Vocabulary

1 **Distinguish** between biotic and abiotic factors.

2 **Define** *ecosystem* in your own words.

3 **Use the term** *climate* in a complete sentence.

Understand Key Concepts

4 What role do bacteria play in soil ecosystems?
   A. They add air to soil.
   B. They break down rocks.
   C. They return nutrients to soil.
   D. They tunnel through soil.

5 **Explain** How would a forest ecosystem change if no sunlight were available to it?

Interpret Graphics

6 **Analyze** The graph below shows climate data for an area. How would you describe this climate?

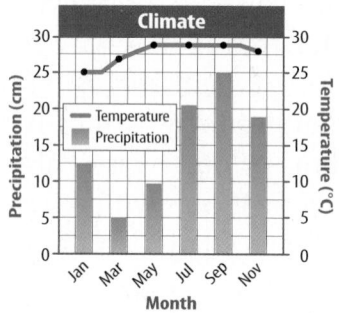

7 **Organize** Copy the graphic organizer below and fill in each oval with an abiotic factor.

Abiotic Factors

Critical Thinking

8 **Predict** Imagine that the soil in an area is carried away by wind and water, leaving only rocks behind. How would this affect the living things in that area?

Terraforming Mars

Life on Another Planet

◄ **Mars is cold and dry, with no sign of life on its dusty, red surface.**

Terraforming is the process of transforming an environment that cannot support life into one that can. Making Mars like Earth would take more than just growing plants and adding water. You would need to consider how every abiotic factor needed to support life would be included in the new environment.

First, consider Mars's temperature. Although Mars gets plenty of sunlight, it is farther from the Sun than Earth is. Air temperatures go no higher than 0°C on a midsummer Martian day. Don't even think about trying to survive a winter night on Mars, as temperatures fall below –89°C.

How could you change the temperature on Mars? Releasing greenhouse gases such as chlorofluorocarbons (CFCs) into the atmosphere can cause the planet to get warmer. Raising the average temperature by only 4°C would melt the polar ice caps, releasing frozen CO_2, another greenhouse gas. This also would cause bodies of water to form. As temperatures rise, liquid water trapped in the soil would turn into a gas, providing the planet with water vapor, an important abiotic factor.

With water and warmer temperatures, plant life could be introduced. While turning light energy into food, plants would introduce another abiotic factor—oxygen. With all the needed abiotic factors accounted for, NASA scientists think that in a few centuries Mars could support life similar to that on Earth.

Life as it is on Earth does not exist on Mars. However, when you compare all the planets in our solar system, Mars is the most like Earth.

It's Your Turn

DEBATE Why would people want to move to Mars? Would this be the right choice? Research these questions and then debate the issues.

Lesson 2

Reading Guide

Key Concepts
ESSENTIAL QUESTIONS

● How does matter move in ecosystems?

Vocabulary

evaporation p. 714

condensation p. 714

precipitation p. 714

nitrogen fixation p. 716

 Multilingual eGlossary

Video BrainPOP®

Cycles of Matter

Inquiry Where does the water go?

All water, including the water in this waterfall, can move throughout an ecosystem in a cycle. It can also change forms. What other forms do you think water takes as it moves through an ecosystem?

 **Launch Lab**

15 minutes

How can you model raindrops?

Like all matter on Earth, water is recycled. It constantly moves between Earth and its atmosphere. You could be drinking the same water that a *Tyrannosaurus rex* drank 65 million years ago!

1. Read and complete a lab safety form.
2. Half-fill a **plastic cup** with warm water.
3. Cover the cup with **plastic wrap.** Secure the plastic with a **rubber band.**
4. Place an **ice cube** on the plastic wrap. Observe the cup for several minutes. Record your observations in your Science Journal.

Think About This

1. What did you observe on the underside of the plastic wrap? Why do you think this happened?

2. How does this activity model the formation of raindrops?

3. 🔑 **Key Concept** Do you think other matter moves through the environment? Explain your answer.

How does matter move in ecosystems?

The water that you used to wash your hands this morning might have once traveled through the roots of a tree in Africa or even have been part of an Antarctic glacier. How can this be? Water moves continuously through ecosystems. It is used over and over again. The same is true of carbon, oxygen, nitrogen, and other types of matter. **Elements** that move through one matter cycle may also play a role in another, such as oxygen's role in the water cycle.

The Water Cycle

Look at a globe or a map. Notice that water surrounds the landmasses. Water covers about 70 percent of Earth's surface.

Most of Earth's water—about 97 percent—is in oceans. Water is also in rivers and streams, lakes, and underground reservoirs. In addition, water is in the atmosphere, icy glaciers, and living things.

Water continually cycles from Earth to its atmosphere and back again. This movement of water is called the water cycle. It involves three processes: evaporation, condensation, and precipitation.

SCIENCE USE V. COMMON USE

element

Science Use one of a class of substances that cannot be separated into simpler substances by chemical means

Common Use a part or piece

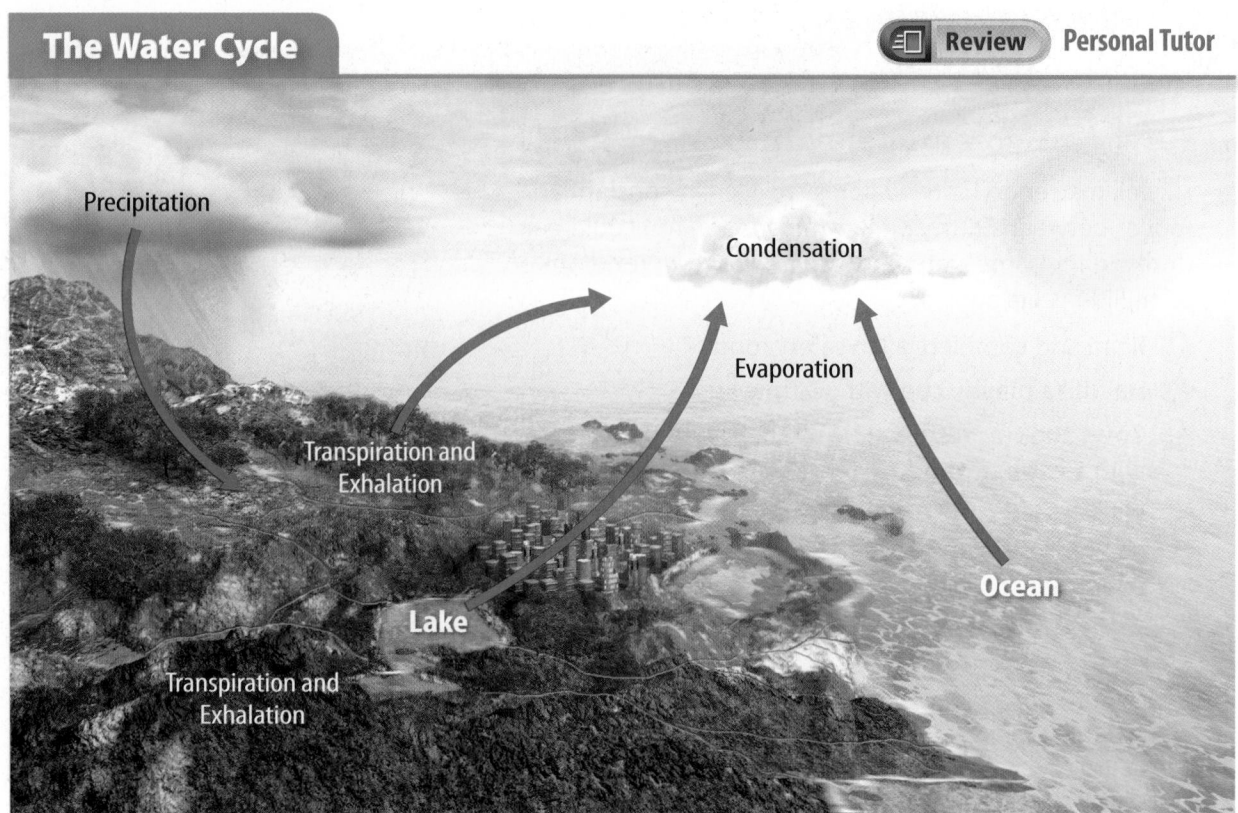

Figure 2 During the water cycle, the processes of evaporation, condensation, and precipitation move water from Earth's surface into the atmosphere and back again.

Evaporation

The Sun supplies the energy for the water cycle, as shown in **Figure 2.** As the Sun heats Earth's surface waters, evaporation occurs. **Evaporation** (ih va puh RAY shun), *is the process during which liquid water changes into a gas called water vapor.* This water vapor rises into the atmosphere. Temperature, humidity, and wind affect how quickly water evaporates.

Water is also released from living things. Transpiration is the release of water vapor from the leaves and stems of plants. Recall that cellular respiration is a process that occurs in many cells. A by-product of cellular respiration is water. This water leaves cells and enters the environment and atmosphere as water vapor.

Condensation

The higher in the atmosphere you are, the cooler the temperature is. As water vapor rises, it cools and condensation occurs.

Condensation (kahn den SAY shun), *is the process during which water vapor changes into liquid water.* Clouds form because of condensation.

Clouds are made of millions of tiny water droplets or crystals of ice. These form when water vapor condenses on particles of dust and other substances in the atmosphere.

Precipitation

Water that falls from clouds to Earth's surface is called **precipitation** (prih sih puh TAY shun). It enters bodies of water or soaks into soil. Precipitation can be rain, snow, sleet, or hail. It forms as water droplets or ice crystals join together in clouds. Eventually, these droplets or crystals become so large and heavy that they fall to Earth. Over time, living things use this precipitation, and the water cycle continues.

Key Concept Check What forms does water take as it moves through ecosystems?

Inquiry MiniLab

20 minutes

Is your soil rich in nitrogen?

Plants get the nitrogen they need to grow from soil. Test the soil near your home to see how much nitrogen it contains. Will the soil support plant growth?

1. Read and complete a lab safety form.
2. Collect a sample of **soil** from around your home.
3. Carefully follow the directions on a **soil nitrogen test kit** and test your soil.
4. Use the color chart to determine the quantity of nitrogen in your soil sample.
5. Compare your results with those of your classmates.

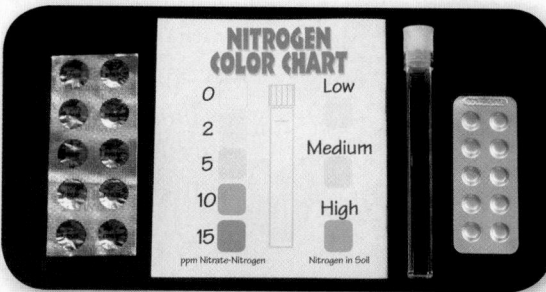

Analyze and Conclude

1. **Determine** if your soil sample has enough nitrogen to support most plant growth.

2. **Hypothesize** why the amount of nitrogen in your soil sample differed from those of your classmates.

3. **Key Concept** Deduce how nitrogen got into your soil sample.

The Nitrogen Cycle

Just as water is necessary for life on Earth, so is the element nitrogen. It is an essential part of proteins, which all organisms need to stay alive. Nitrogen is also an important part of DNA, the molecule that contains genetic information. Nitrogen, like water, cycles between Earth and its atmosphere and back again as shown in **Figure 3**.

Reading Check What do living things use nitrogen for?

Figure 3 Different forms of nitrogen are in the atmosphere, soil, and organisms.

Bacteria in soil convert nitrogen compounds into nitrogen gas, which is released into the air.

Nitrogen gas in atmosphere

Concepts in Motion
Animation

Lightning changes nitrogen gas in the atmosphere to nitrogen compounds. The nitrogen compounds fall to the ground when it rains.

Animals eat plants.

Nitrogen-fixing bacteria on plant roots convert unusable nitrogen in soil to usable nitrogen compounds.

Decaying organic matter and animal waste return nitrogen compounds to the soil.

Plants take in and use nitrogen compounds from the soil.

Nitrogen compounds in soil

From the Environment to Organisms

Recall that the atmosphere is mostly nitrogen. However, this nitrogen is in a form that plants and animals cannot use. How do organisms get nitrogen into their bodies? The nitrogen must first be changed into a different form with the help of certain bacteria that live in soil and water. These bacteria take in nitrogen from the atmosphere and change it into nitrogen compounds that other living things can use. *The process that changes atmospheric nitrogen into nitrogen compounds that are usable by living things is called* **nitrogen fixation** (NI truh jun • fihk SAY shun). Nitrogen fixation is shown in **Figure 4.**

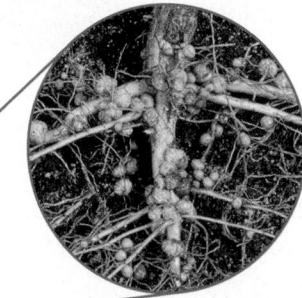

◀ **Figure 4** Certain bacteria convert nitrogen in soil and water into a form usable by plants.

Plants and some other organisms take in this changed nitrogen from the soil and water. Then, animals take in nitrogen when they eat the plants or other organisms.

 Reading Check What is nitrogen fixation?

From Organisms to the Environment

Some types of bacteria can break down the tissues of dead organisms. When organisms die, these bacteria help return the nitrogen in the tissues of dead organisms to the environment. This process is shown in **Figure 5.**

Nitrogen also returns to the environment in the waste products of organisms. Farmers often spread animal wastes, called manure, on their fields during the growing season. The manure provides nitrogen to plants for better growth.

◀ **Figure 5** Bacteria break down the remains of dead plants and animals.

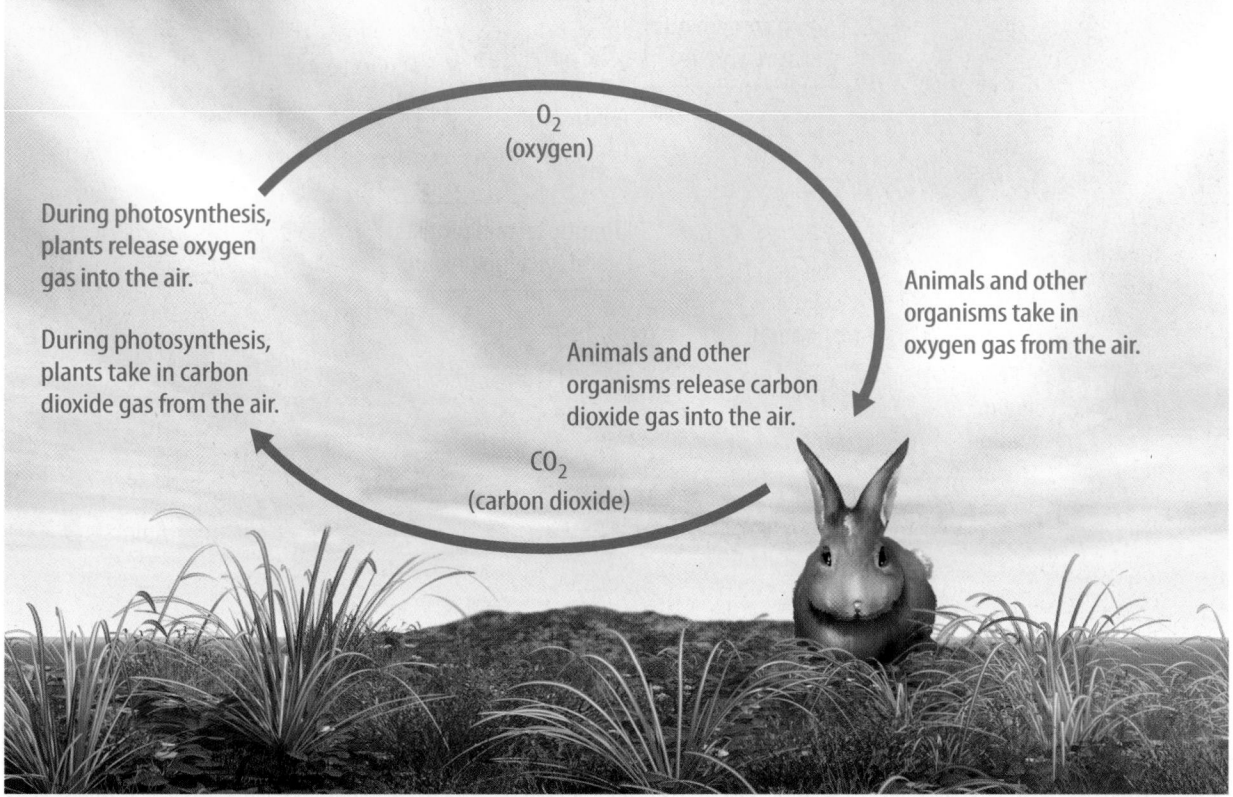

During photosynthesis, plants release oxygen gas into the air.

During photosynthesis, plants take in carbon dioxide gas from the air.

O_2 (oxygen)

Animals and other organisms release carbon dioxide gas into the air.

CO_2 (carbon dioxide)

Animals and other organisms take in oxygen gas from the air.

The Oxygen Cycle

Almost all living things need oxygen for cellular processes that release energy. Oxygen is also part of many substances that are important to life, such as carbon dioxide and water. Oxygen cycles through ecosystems, as shown in **Figure 6.**

Earth's early atmosphere probably did not contain oxygen gas. Oxygen might have entered the atmosphere when certain **bacteria** evolved that could carry out the process of photosynthesis and make their own food. A by-product of photosynthesis is oxygen gas. Over time, other photosynthetic organisms evolved and the amount of oxygen in Earth's atmosphere increased. Today, photosynthesis is the primary source of oxygen in Earth's atmosphere. Some scientists estimate that unicellular organisms in water, called phytoplankton, release more than 50 percent of the oxygen in Earth's atmosphere.

Many living things, including humans, take in the oxygen and release carbon dioxide. The interaction of the carbon and oxygen cycles is one example of a relationship between different types of matter in ecosystems. As the matter cycles through an ecosystem, both the carbon and the oxygen take different forms and play a role in the other element's cycle.

Figure 6 Most oxygen in the air comes from plants and algae.

✓**Visual Check** Describe your part in the oxygen cycle.

REVIEW VOCABULARY

bacteria
a group of microscopic unicellular organisms without a membrane-bound nucleus

The Carbon Cycle diagram:

Carbon compounds in atmosphere

Combustion

Photosynthesis

Photosynthesis

Plants, certain protists, and bacteria on land

Cellular respiration

Cellular respiration

Cellular respiration

Decomposition

Plants, certain protists, and bacteria in water

Decomposition

Animals

Carbon compounds in soil

Decomposition

CO_2 in water

Sediments

Fossil fuels

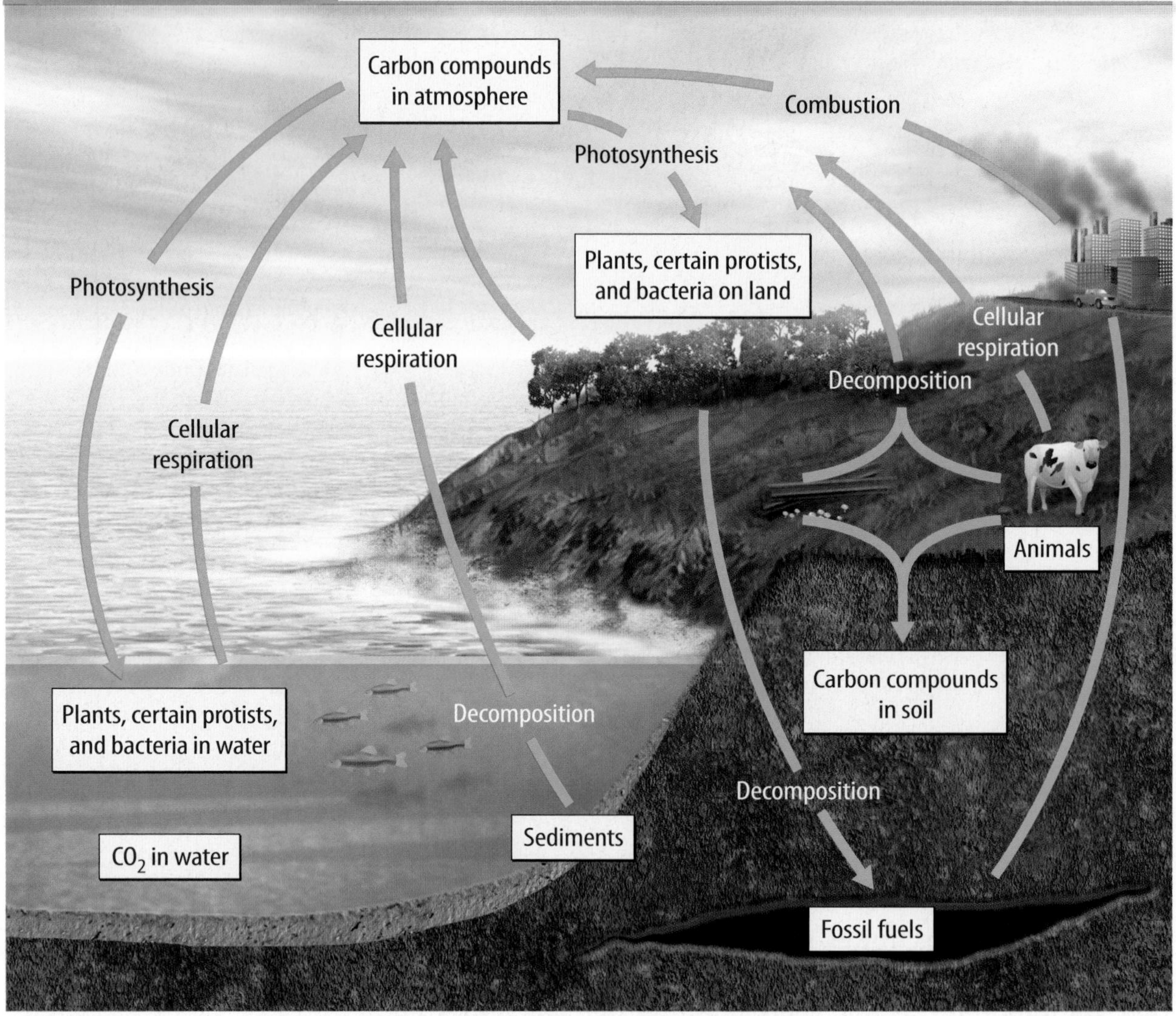

Figure 7 In the carbon cycle, all organisms return carbon to the environment.

The Carbon Cycle

All organisms contain carbon. It is part of proteins, sugars, fats, and DNA. Some organisms, including humans, get carbon from food. Other organisms, such as plants, get carbon from the atmosphere or bodies of water. Like other types of matter, carbon cycles through ecosystems, as shown in **Figure 7.**

Carbon in Soil

Like nitrogen, carbon can enter the environment when organisms die and decompose. This returns carbon compounds to the soil and releases carbon dioxide (CO_2) into the atmosphere for use by other organisms. Carbon is also found in fossil fuels, which formed when decomposing organisms were exposed to pressure, high temperatures, and bacteria over hundreds of millions of years.

FOLDABLES

Make a half book from a sheet of paper. Select a cycle of matter and use your book to organize information about the biotic and abiotic parts of that cycle.

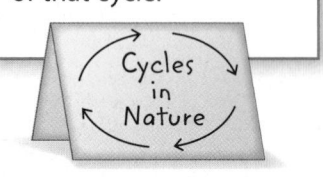

Cycles in Nature

Carbon in Air

Recall that carbon is found in the atmosphere as carbon dioxide. Plants and other photosynthetic organisms take in carbon dioxide and water and produce energy-rich sugars. These sugars are a source of carbon and energy for organisms that eat photosynthetic organisms. When the sugar is broken down by cells and its energy is **released,** carbon dioxide is released as a by-product. This carbon dioxide gas enters the atmosphere, where it can be used again.

The Greenhouse Effect

Carbon dioxide is one of the gases in the atmosphere that absorbs thermal energy from the Sun and keeps Earth warm. This process is called the greenhouse effect. The Sun produces solar radiation, as shown in **Figure 8.** Some of this energy is reflected back into space, and some passes through Earth's atmosphere. Greenhouse gases in Earth's atmosphere absorb thermal energy that reflects off Earth's surface. The more greenhouse gases released, the greater the gas layer becomes and the more thermal energy is absorbed. These gases are one factor that keeps Earth from becoming too hot or too cold.

 Reading Check What is the greenhouse effect?

While the greenhouse effect is essential for life, a steady increase in greenhouse gases can harm ecosystems. For example, carbon is stored in fossil fuels such as coal, oil, and natural gas. When people burn fossil fuels to heat homes, for transportation, or to provide electricity, carbon dioxide gas is released into the atmosphere. The amount of carbon dioxide in the air has increased due to both natural and human activities.

Figure 8 Some thermal energy remains close to the Earth due to greenhouse gases.

Visual Check What might happen if heat were not absorbed by greenhouse gases?

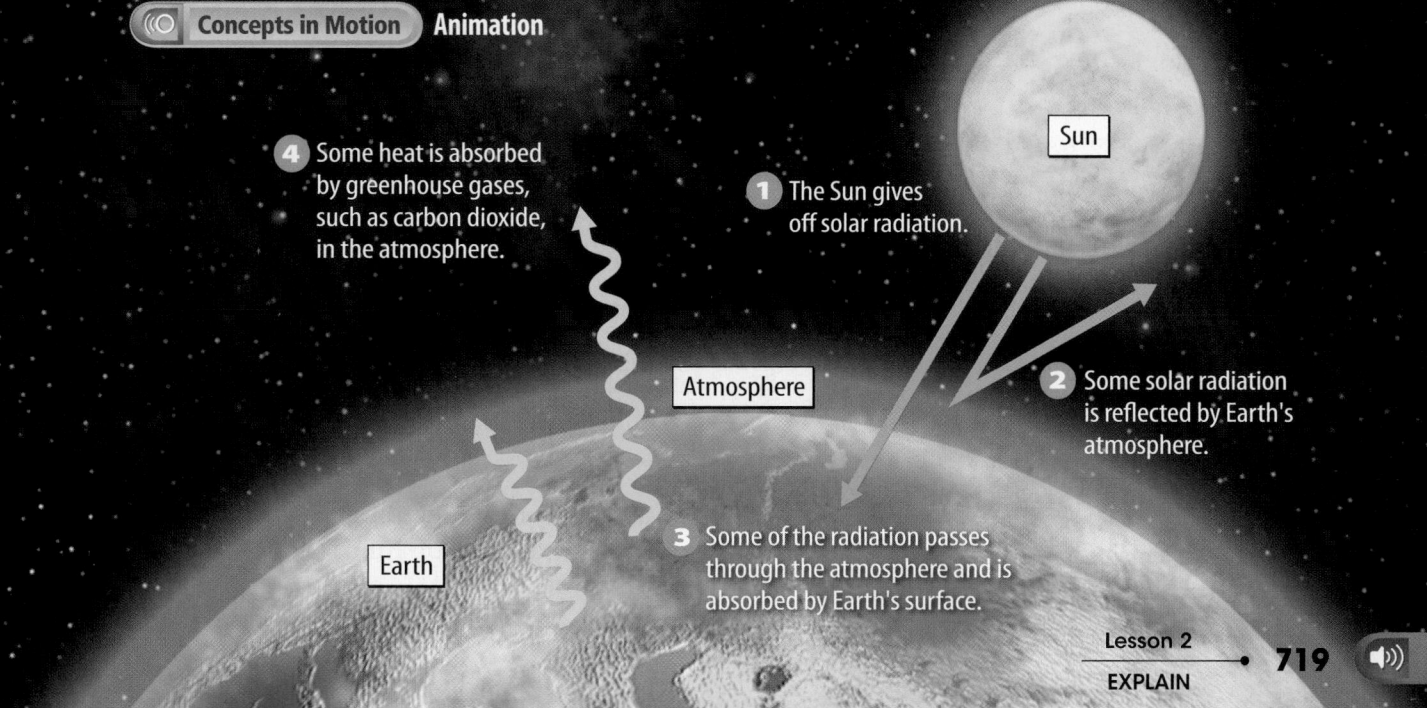

Concepts in Motion Animation

4 Some heat is absorbed by greenhouse gases, such as carbon dioxide, in the atmosphere.

1 The Sun gives off solar radiation.

Sun

Atmosphere

2 Some solar radiation is reflected by Earth's atmosphere.

Earth

3 Some of the radiation passes through the atmosphere and is absorbed by Earth's surface.

Lesson 2 Review

Visual Summary

Matter such as water, oxygen, nitrogen, and carbon cycles through ecosystems.

The three stages of the water cycle are evaporation, condensation, and precipitation.

The greenhouse effect helps keep the Earth from getting too hot or too cold.

FOLDABLES

Use your lesson Foldable to review the lesson. Save your Foldable for the project at the end of the chapter.

What do you think NOW?

You first read the statements below at the beginning of the chapter.

3. Carbon, nitrogen, and other types of matter are used by living things over and over again.

4. Clouds are made of water vapor.

Did you change your mind about whether you agree or disagree with the statements? Rewrite any false statements to make them true.

Use Vocabulary

1 **Distinguish** between evaporation and condensation.

2 **Define** *nitrogen fixation* in your own words.

3 Water that falls from clouds to Earth's surface is called _____.

Understand Key Concepts

4 What is the driving force behind the water cycle?
- A. gravity
- B. plants
- C. sunlight
- D. wind

5 **Infer** Farmers add nitrogen to their fields every year to help their crops grow. Why must farmers continually add nitrogen when this element recycles naturally?

Interpret Graphics

6 **Sequence** Draw a graphic organizer like the one below and sequence the steps in the water cycle.

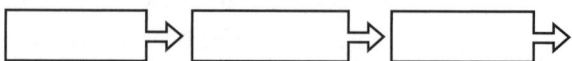

7 **Summarize** how the greenhouse effect moderates temperatures on Earth.

Critical Thinking

8 **Explain** how oxygen cycles through the ecosystem in which you live.

9 **Consider** How might ecosystems be affected if levels of atmospheric CO_2 continue to rise?

How do scientists use variables?

Materials

rubber ball

styrene ball

meterstick

Safety

If you wanted to find out what made one ball bounce higher than another, you might design an experiment that uses variables. You could test whether balls made of one material bounce higher than those made of another. By changing only one variable, the experiment tests only the effect of that factor.

Learn It

When experimenting, scientists often **use variables.** A variable is anything that can be changed. For example, a scientist might want to study the effect that different amounts of water have on a plant's growth. The amount of water is the variable in the experiment. Other factors, such as soil type and amount of sunlight, stay the same.

Try It

1 Read and complete a lab safety form.

2 Examine both the rubber ball and the styrene ball. Predict which ball will bounce higher. Record your prediction in your Science Journal.

3 With your partner, hold the rubber ball 35 cm above the table and drop it. Record how high it bounces. Drop the ball a total of three times, recording the height it bounces each time. Calculate the average height that the rubber ball bounced.

4 Repeat step 3 with the styrene ball.

Apply It

5 Compare the average height of each ball's bounce and determine which bounced higher. Did your data support your prediction?

6 Identify two other variables you could test in this experiment. Would you test them together or separately? Explain.

7 🔑 **Key Concept** What variables might affect a study of the water cycle in your neighborhood?

	Rubber Ball	Styrene Ball
Trial 1		
Trial 2		
Trial 3		
Average bounce		

Lesson 3

Reading Guide

Key Concepts 🔑
ESSENTIAL QUESTIONS

- How does energy move in ecosystems?
- How is the movement of energy in an ecosystem modeled?

Vocabulary

photosynthesis p. 724

chemosynthesis p. 724

food chain p. 726

food web p. 727

energy pyramid p. 728

 Multilingual eGlossary

 Video **BrainPOP®**

Energy in Ecosystems

Inquiry Time for a snack?

All organisms need energy, and many get it from eating other organisms. Can you guess how each of the living things in this picture gets the energy it needs?

Launch Lab

How does energy change form?

Every day, sunlight travels hundreds of millions of kilometers and brings warmth and light to Earth. Energy from the Sun is necessary for nearly all life on Earth. Without it, most life could not exist.

1. Read and complete a lab safety form.

2. Obtain **UV-sensitive beads** from your teacher. Write a description of them in your Science Journal.

3. Place half the beads in a sunny place. Place the other half in a dark place.

4. Wait a few minutes, and then observe both sets of beads. Record your observations in your Science Journal.

Think About This

1. Compare and contrast the two sets of beads after the few minutes. How are they different? How are they the same?

2. Hypothesize why the beads looked different.

3. **Key Concept** How do you think living things use energy?

How does energy move in ecosystems?

When you see a picture of an ecosystem, it often looks quiet and peaceful. However, ecosystems are actually full of movement. Birds squawk and beat their wings, plants sway in the breeze, and insects buzz.

Each movement made by a living thing requires energy. All of life's functions, including growth and reproduction, require energy. The main source of energy for most life on Earth is the Sun. Unlike other resources, such as water and carbon, energy does not cycle through ecosystems. Instead, energy flows in one direction, as shown in **Figure 9.** In most cases, energy flow begins with the Sun, and moves from one organism to another. Many organisms get energy by eating other organisms. Sometimes organisms change energy into different forms as it moves through an ecosystem. Not all the energy an organism gets is used for life processes. Some is released to the environment as thermal energy. You might have read that energy cannot be created or destroyed, but it can change form. This idea is called the law of conservation of energy.

Key Concept Check How do the movements of matter and energy differ?

Cycle and Flow

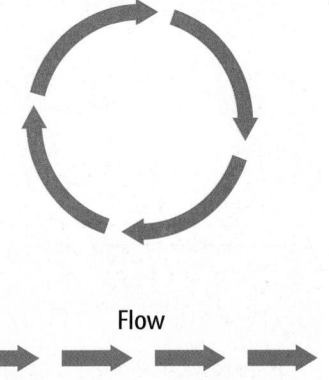

Figure 9 Matter moves in a cycle pattern, and energy moves in a flow pattern.

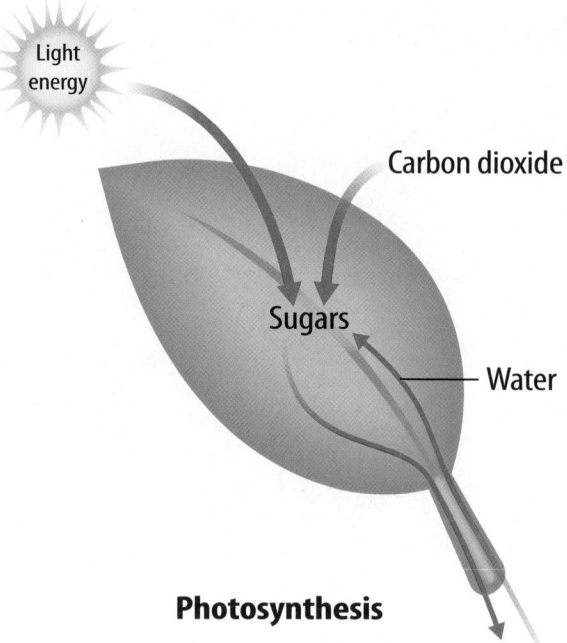

Photosynthesis

▲ **Figure 10** Most producers make their food through the process of photosynthesis.

WORD ORIGIN ·

photosynthesis
from Greek *photo*, meaning "light"; and *synthese*, meaning "synthesis"
· ·

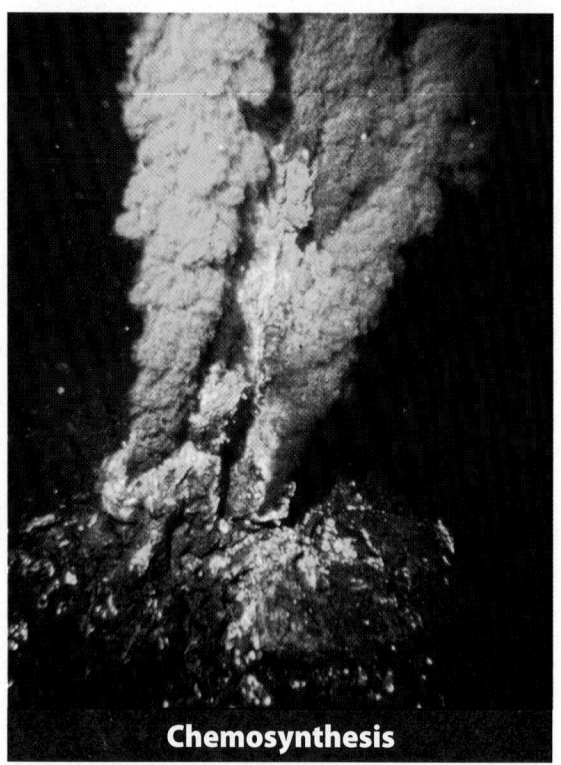

Chemosynthesis

▲ **Figure 11** The producers at a hydrothermal vent make their food using chemosynthesis.

Producers

People who make things or products are often called producers. In a similar way, living things that make their own food are called producers. Producers make their food from materials found in their environments. Most producers are photosynthetic (foh toh sihn THEH tihk). They use the process of photosynthesis (foh toh SIHN thuh sus), which is described below. Grasses, trees, and other plants, algae and some other protists, and certain bacteria are photosynthetic. Other producers, including some bacteria, are chemosynthetic (kee moh sihn THEH tihk). They make their food using chemosynthesis (kee moh SIHN thuh sus).

Photosynthesis Recall that in the carbon cycle, carbon in the atmosphere cycles through producers such as plants, into other organisms, and then back into the atmosphere. This and other matter cycles involve photosynthesis, as shown in **Figure 10. Photosynthesis** *is a series of chemical reactions that convert light energy, water, and carbon dioxide into the food-energy molecule glucose and give off oxygen.*

Chemosynthesis As you read earlier, some producers make food using chemosynthesis. **Chemosynthesis** *is the process during which producers use chemical energy in matter rather than light energy and make food.* One place where chemosynthesis can occur is on the deep ocean floor. There, inorganic compounds that contain hydrogen and sulfur, along with thermal energy from Earth's interior, flow out from cracks in the ocean floor. These cracks are called hydrothermal vents. These vents, such as the one shown in **Figure 11,** are home to chemosynthetic bacteria. These bacteria use the chemical energy contained in inorganic compounds in the hot water and produce food.

Reading Check What materials do producers use to make food during chemosynthesis?

Herbivore

Carnivore

Omnivore

Detritivore

Detritivore—
Decomposer

Figure 12 Organisms can be classified by the type of food that they eat.

Consumers

Some consumers are shown in **Figure 12.** Consumers do not produce their own energy-rich food, as producers do. Instead, they get the energy they need to survive by consuming other organisms.

Consumers can be classified by the type of food that they eat. Herbivores feed on only producers. For example, a deer is an herbivore because it eats only plants. Carnivores eat other animals. They are usually predators, such as lions and wolves. Omnivores eat both producers and other consumers. A bird that eats berries and insects is an omnivore.

Another group of consumers is detritivores (dih TRI tuh vorz). They get their energy by eating the remains of other organisms. Some detritivores, such as insects, eat dead organisms. Other detritivores, such as bacteria and mushrooms, feed on dead organisms and help decompose them. For this reason, these organisms often are called decomposers. During decomposition, decomposers produce carbon dioxide that enters the atmosphere. Some of the decayed matter enters the soil. In this way, detritivores help recycle nutrients through ecosystems. They also help keep ecosystems clean. Without decomposers, dead organisms would pile up in an ecosystem.

Modeling Energy in Ecosystems

Unlike matter, energy does not cycle through ecosystems because it does not return to the Sun. Instead, energy flows through ecosystems. Organisms use some energy for life processes. In addition, organisms store some energy in their bodies as chemical energy. When consumers eat these organisms, this chemical energy moves into the bodies of consumers. However, with each transfer of energy from organism to organism, some energy changes to thermal energy. The bodies of consumers emit excess thermal energy, which then enters the environment. Scientists use models to study this flow of energy through an ecosystem. They use different models depending on how many organisms they are studying.

Food Chains

A **food chain** *is a model that shows how energy flows in an ecosystem through feeding relationships.* In a food chain, arrows show the transfer of energy. A typical food chain is shown in **Figure 13.** Notice that there are not many links in this food chain. That is because the amount of available energy decreases every time it is transferred from one organism to another.

Key Concept Check How does a food chain model energy flow?

Figure 13 Energy moves from the Sun to a plant, a mouse, a snake, and a hawk in this food chain.

Food Chain

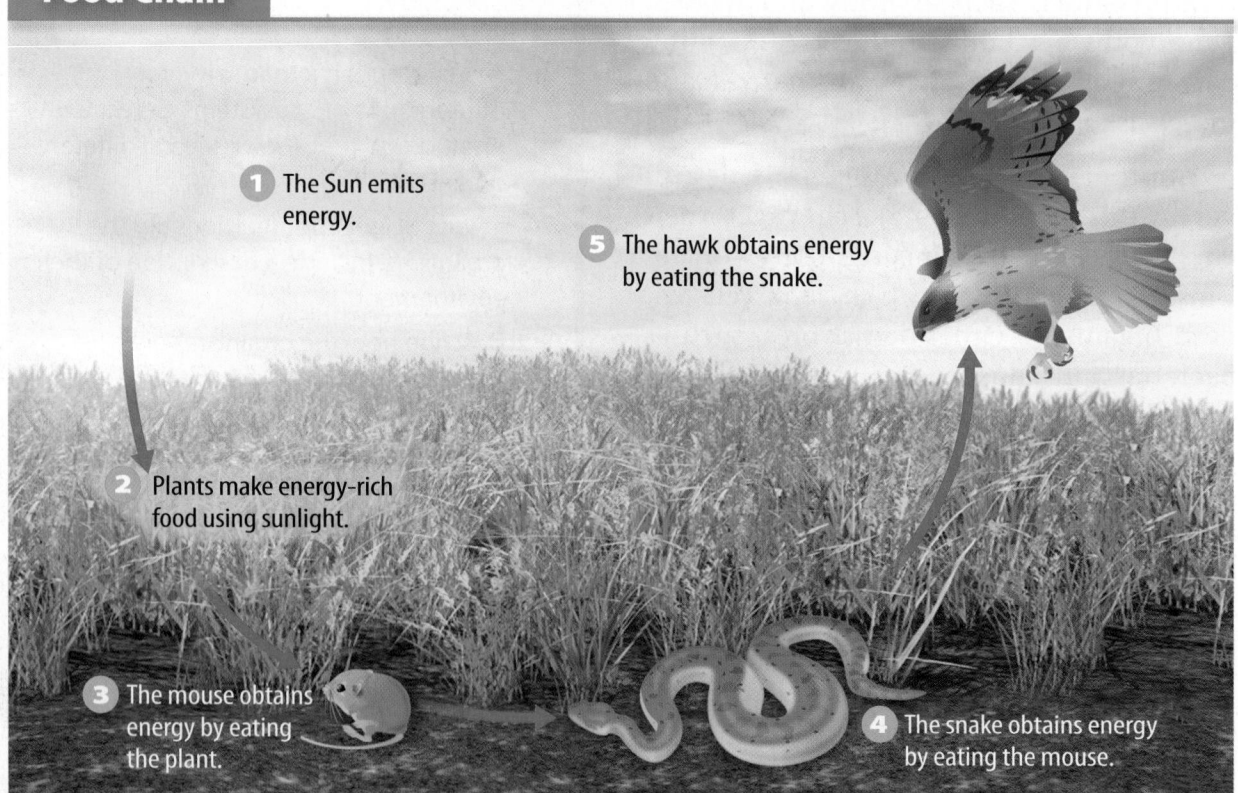

1 The Sun emits energy.

2 Plants make energy-rich food using sunlight.

3 The mouse obtains energy by eating the plant.

4 The snake obtains energy by eating the mouse.

5 The hawk obtains energy by eating the snake.

Food Webs

Imagine you have a jigsaw puzzle of a tropical rain forest. Each piece of the puzzle shows only one small part of the forest. A food chain is like one piece of an ecosystem jigsaw puzzle. It is helpful when studying certain parts of an ecosystem, but it does not show the whole picture.

In the food chain on the previous page, the mouse might also eat the seeds of several producers, such as corn, berries, or grass. The snake might eat other organisms such as frogs, crickets, lizards, or earthworms too. The hawk hunts mice, squirrels, rabbits, and fish, as well as snakes. *Scientists use a model of energy transfer called a* **food web** *to show how food chains in a community are interconnected,* as shown in **Figure 14.** You can think of a food web as many overlapping food chains. Like in a food chain, arrows show how energy flows in a food web. Some organisms in the food web might be part of more than one food chain in that web.

Key Concept Check What models show the transfer of energy in an ecosystem?

Figure 14 A food web shows the complex feeding relationships among organisms in an ecosystem.

Review Personal Tutor

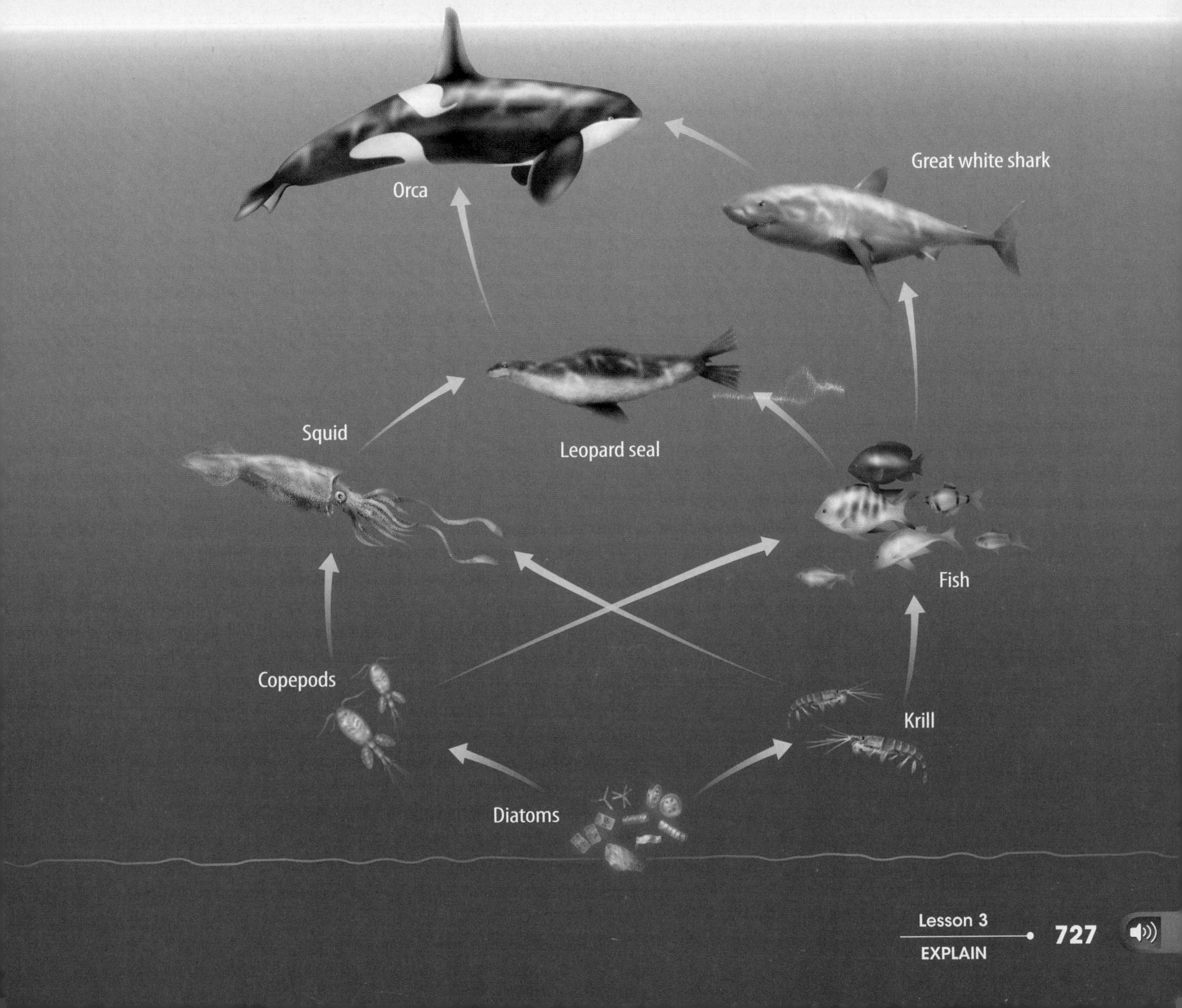
Orca
Great white shark
Squid
Leopard seal
Fish
Copepods
Krill
Diatoms

Math Skills

Use Percentages

The first trophic level—producers—obtains energy from the Sun. They use 90 percent of the energy for their own life processes. Only 10 percent of the energy remains for the second trophic level—herbivores. Assume that each trophic level uses 90 percent of the energy it receives. Use the following steps to calculate how much energy remains for the next trophic level.

First trophic level gets 100 units of energy.

First trophic level uses 90 percent = 90 units

Energy remaining for second trophic level = 10 units

Second trophic level uses 90 percent = 9 units

Energy remaining for third trophic level = 1 unit

Practice

If the first trophic level receives 10,000 units of energy from the Sun, how much energy is available for the second trophic level?

 **Review**

- Math Practice
- Personal Tutor

Energy Pyramids

Food chains and food webs show how energy moves in an ecosystem. However, they do not show how the amount of energy in an ecosystem changes. *Scientists use a model called an* **energy pyramid** *to show the amount of energy available in each step of a food chain,* as shown in **Figure 15.** The steps of an energy pyramid are also called trophic (TROH fihk) levels.

Producers, such as plants, make up the trophic level at the bottom of the pyramid. Consumers that eat producers, such as squirrels, make up the next trophic level. Consumers such as hawks that eat other consumers make up the highest trophic level. Notice that less energy is available for consumers at each higher trophic level. As you read earlier, organisms use some of the energy they get from food for life processes. During life processes, some energy is changed to thermal energy and is transferred to the environment. Only about 10 percent of the energy available at one trophic level transfers on to the next trophic level.

Figure 15 An energy pyramid shows the amount of energy available at each trophic level.

Visual Check How does the amount of available energy change at each trophic level?

 **Concepts in Motion** Animation

Trophic level 3
(1 percent of energy available)

Trophic level 2
(10 percent of energy available)

Trophic level 1
(100 percent of energy available)

Available energy decreases.

✓ **Assessment** Online Quiz

? **Inquiry** Virtual Lab

Visual Summary

Energy flows in ecosystems from producers to consumers.

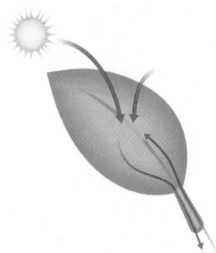

Producers make their own food through the processes of photosynthesis or chemosynthesis.

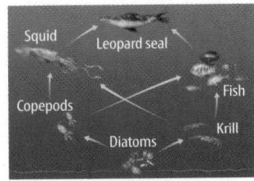

Food chains and food webs model how energy moves in ecosystems.

FOLDABLES

Use your lesson Foldable to review the lesson. Save your Foldable for the project at the end of the chapter.

What do you think NOW?

You first read the statements below at the beginning of the chapter.

5. The Sun is the source for all energy used by living things on Earth.

6. All living things get their energy from eating other living things.

Did you change your mind about whether you agree or disagree with the statements? Rewrite any false statements to make them true.

Use Vocabulary

1 Scientists use a(n) _____ to show how energy moves in an ecosystem.

2 **Distinguish** between photosynthesis and chemosynthesis.

Understand Key Concepts

3 Which organism is a producer?
   A. cow   **C.** grass
   B. dog   **D.** human

4 **Construct** a food chain with four links.

Interpret Graphics

5 **Assess** Which trophic level has the most energy available to living things?

Ecosystem

Trophic level 3

Trophic level 2

Trophic level 1

Critical Thinking

6 **Recommend** A friend wants to show how energy moves in ecosystems. Which model would you recommend? Explain.

Math Skills   📱 Review
——— Math Practice ———

7 The plants in level 1 of a food pyramid obtain 30,000 units of energy from the Sun. How much energy is available for the organisms in level 2? Level 3?

Materials

radish seeds

sand, gravel, potting soil, and humus

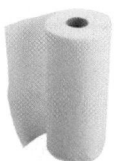

paper towel

planting cups

thermometer

permanent marker

magnifying lens

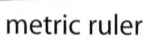

250-mL beaker

metric ruler

Safety

How does soil type affect plant growth?

Plants are producers that make food through the process of photosynthesis. In order for plants to grow, they need the right balance of abiotic factors, such as light, water, air, and soil. Different plants grow well in different conditions. In this lab, you will determine which type of soil is best for growing radishes.

Ask a Question

How does the type of soil affect plant growth?

Make Observations

1. Read and complete a lab safety form.

2. Use the permanent marker to label each cup with the type of soil it will contain: *sand, gravel, potting soil, paper towel,* or *humus.*

3. Add the appropriate soil to each cup to within a thumb's width from the top. Fold the paper towel in half and place it around the inside of the cup.

4. Evenly space four seeds in each cup. Use a pencil tip to push each seed about 1 cm under the surface of the soil.

5. After planting all seeds, use the beaker to add the same amount of water to each cup. Record the amount of water used.

6. Set the cups in the same location, such as a bright windowsill. Place a thermometer next to the cups. The seeds should germinate within several days. Use a magnifying lens to observe your radish seedlings.

7. Record your observations in your Science Journal. Be sure to measure, write, draw, and label what you observe. Also, keep a record of other abiotic factors that affect the plant, such as temperature, amount of water, and hours of light.

Form a Hypothesis

8. Based on your observations, form a hypothesis regarding the effect of soil type on plant growth.

⑦ Type of soil	Observations (Day 1)	Observations (Day 4)	Observations (Day 7)
Sand			
Gravel			
Potting soil			
Humus			
Paper towel			

Test Your Hypothesis

⑨ Repeat your observations of the radish seedlings. Make at least four more sets of observations over the next two weeks.

⑩ About three weeks after the planting date, harvest your crop.

⑪ Gently pull up the radishes to see how they have developed underground.

⑫ Record data about your radish crop. How many radishes did you harvest from each cup? How big were they? What color?

Analyze and Conclude

⑬ **Describe** the abiotic conditions under which your plants grew. Include information about temperature, hours of sunlight, water, and soil type.

⑭ **Compare and Contrast** Share your data with other groups. Compare and contrast rates of growth and size of harvest.

⑮ **The Big Idea** Based on the class data, how does soil affect plant growth? Which type of soil is best for growing radishes?

Communicate Your Results

Combine the class data and create a graph that shows the size of plants in different soil types. Which soil produced the biggest plants? Which produced the fewest plants?

 Extension

Think of another variable besides soil type that might affect the way that radish plants grow. Develop and conduct an experiment to test this variable.

Lab

☑ Do not eat your radish seeds or plants.

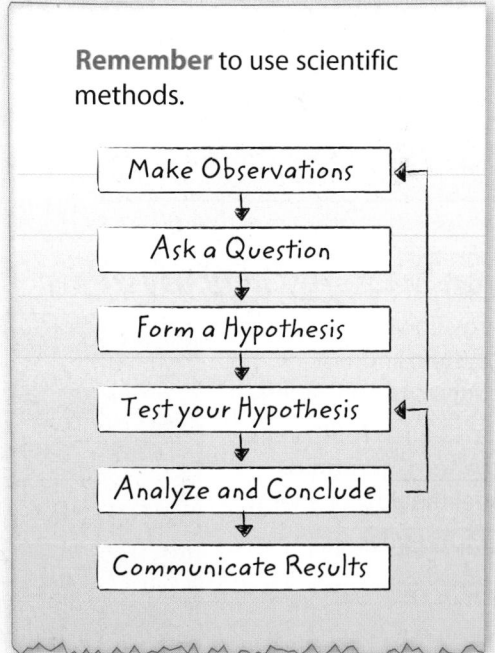

Remember to use scientific methods.

Make Observations → Ask a Question → Form a Hypothesis → Test your Hypothesis → Analyze and Conclude → Communicate Results

Chapter 20 Study Guide

Living things interact with and depend on each other and on the nonliving things in an ecosystem.

Key Concepts Summary	Vocabulary
Lesson 1: Abiotic Factors • The **abiotic factors** in an environment include sunlight, temperature, climate, air, water, and soil. 	**ecosystem** p. 707 **biotic factor** p. 707 **abiotic factor** p. 707 **climate** p. 708 **atmosphere** p. 709
Lesson 2: Cycles of Matter  • Matter such as oxygen, nitrogen, water, carbon, and minerals moves in cycles in the ecosystem.	**evaporation** p. 714 **condensation** p. 714 **precipitation** p. 714 **nitrogen fixation** p. 716
Lesson 3: Energy in Ecosystems • Energy flows through ecosystems from producers to consumers. • **Food chains**, **food webs**, and **energy pyramids** model the flow of energy in ecosystems. 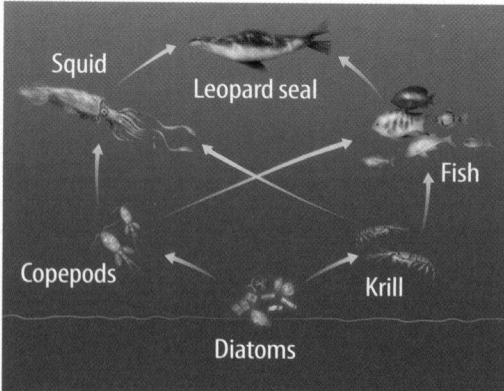	**photosynthesis** p. 724 **chemosynthesis** p. 724 **food chain** p. 726 **food web** p. 727 **energy pyramid** p. 728

FOLDABLES® Chapter Project

Assemble your lesson Foldables as shown to make a Chapter Project. Use the project to review what you have learned in this chapter.

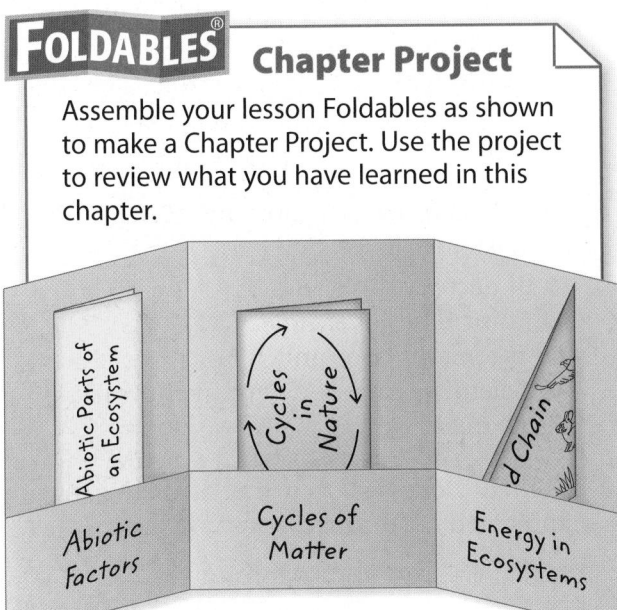

Abiotic Parts of an Ecosystem

Cycles in Nature

Food Chain

Abiotic Factors

Cycles of Matter

Energy in Ecosystems

Use Vocabulary

1 Distinguish between climate and atmosphere.

2 The atmosphere is made mainly of the gases _____ and _____.

3 Living organisms in an ecosystem are called _____, while the nonliving things are called _____.

4 The process of converting nitrogen in the air into a form that can be used by living organisms is called _____ _____.

5 Use the word *precipitation* in a complete sentence.

6 Define *condensation* in your own words.

7 How does a food chain differ from a food web?

8 The process of _____ uses energy from the Sun.

9 Define *chemosynthesis* in your own words.

🔊 **Concepts in Motion** Interactive Concept Map

Link Vocabulary and Key Concepts

Copy this concept map, and then use vocabulary terms from the previous page and other terms from the chapter to complete the concept map.

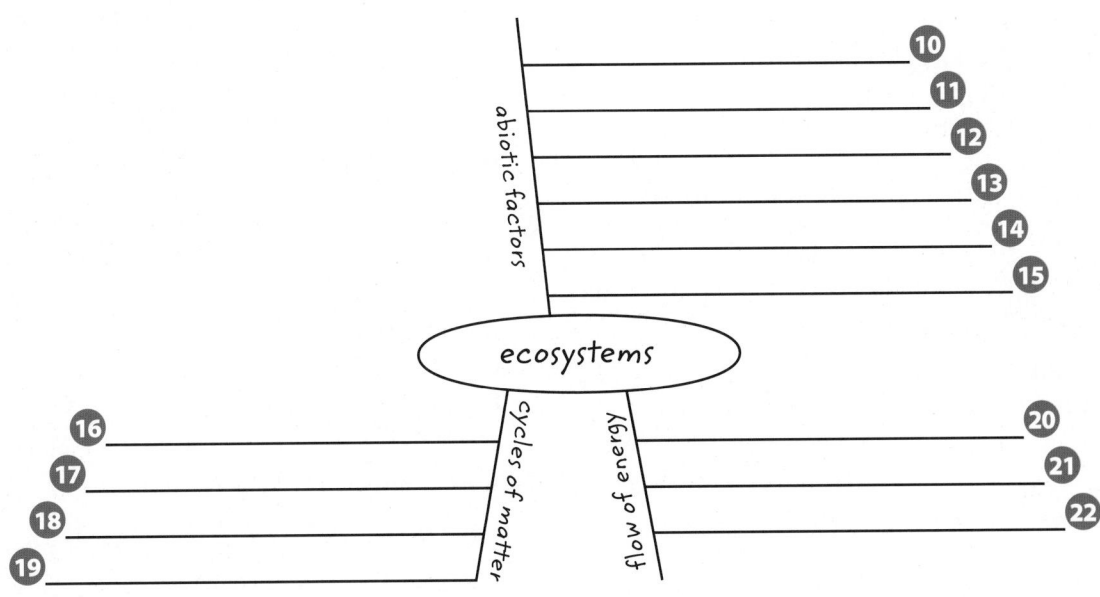

abiotic factors

10

11

12

13

14

15

ecosystems

cycles of matter

flow of energy

16

17

18

19

20

21

22

Chapter 20 Review

Understand Key Concepts 🔑

1 What is the source of most energy on Earth?
A. air
B. soil
C. the Sun
D. water

2 Which is a biotic factor in an ecosystem?
A. a plant living near a stream
B. the amount of rainfall
C. the angle of the Sun
D. the types of minerals present in soil

3 Study the energy pyramid shown here.

Which organism might you expect to find at trophic level I?
A. fox
B. frog
C. grass
D. grasshopper

4 Which includes both an abiotic and a biotic factor?
A. a chicken laying an egg
B. a deer drinking from a stream
C. a rock rolling down a hill
D. a squirrel eating an acorn

5 Which process helps keep temperatures on Earth from becoming too hot or too cold?
A. condensation
B. global warming
C. greenhouse effect
D. nitrogen fixation

6 During the carbon cycle, _____ take in carbon dioxide from the atmosphere.
A. animals
B. consumers
C. decomposers
D. plants

7 Which is true of the amount of matter in ecosystems?
A. It decreases over time.
B. It increases over time.
C. It remains constant.
D. Scientists cannot determine how it changes.

8 Which process is occurring at the location indicated by the arrow?

A. condensation
B. nitrogen fixation
C. precipitation
D. transpiration

9 Which best represents a food chain?
A. Sun ➔ rabbit ➔ fox ➔ grass
B. Sun ➔ grass ➔ rabbit ➔ fox
C. fox ➔ grass ➔ rabbit ➔ Sun
D. grass ➔ rabbit ➔ fox ➔ Sun

10 A person who ate a salad made of lettuce, tomatoes, cheese, and ham is a(n)
A. carnivore.
B. detritivore.
C. herbivore.
D. omnivore.

Critical Thinking

11 **Compare and contrast** the oxygen cycle and the nitrogen cycle.

12 **Create** a plan for making an aquatic ecosystem in a jar. Include both abiotic and biotic factors.

13 **Recommend** a strategy for decreasing the amount of carbon dioxide in the atmosphere.

14 **Role-Play** Working in a group, perform a skit about organisms living near a hydrothermal vent. Be sure to include information about how the organisms obtain energy.

15 **Assess** the usefulness of models as tools for studying ecosystems.

16 Study the food web below. **Classify** each organism according to what it eats.

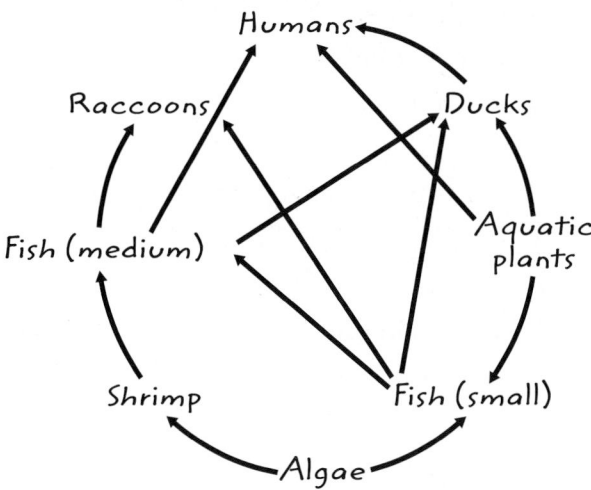

17 **Predict** what would happen if all the nitrogen-fixing bacteria in an ecosystem were removed.

Writing in Science

18 **Write** an argument for or against the following statement. *The energy humans use in cars originally came from the Sun.*

REVIEW **THE BIG IDEA**

19 Describe an interaction between a living thing and a nonliving thing in an ecosystem.

20 How might the ram interact with nonliving things in its environment?

Math Skills ✕ ÷ + –

🔲 **Review**

— **Math Practice** —

Use Percentages

21 A group of plankton, algae, and other ocean plants absorb 150,000 units of energy.

a. How much energy is available for the third trophic level?

b. How much energy would remain for a fourth trophic level?

22 Some organisms, such as humans, are omnivores. They eat both producers and consumers. How much more energy would an omnivore get from eating the same mass of food at the first trophic level than at the second trophic level?

Standardized Test Practice

Record your answers on the answer sheet provided by your teacher or on a sheet of paper.

Multiple Choice

1 In which process do producers use chemical energy and make food?

  A chemosynthesis

  B fermentation

  C glycolysis

  D photosynthesis

Use the image below to answer question 2.

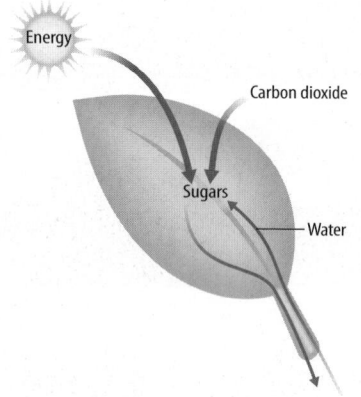

2 What process is shown above?

  A chemosynthesis

  B decomposition

  C nitrogen fixation

  D photosynthesis

3 What organisms help break down dead leaves in an ecosystem?

  A carnivores

  B detritivores

  C herbivores

  D omnivores

4 Which process converts atmospheric nitrogen to a form organisms can use?

  A absorption

  B fixation

  C retention

  D stabilization

Use the diagram below to answer question 5.

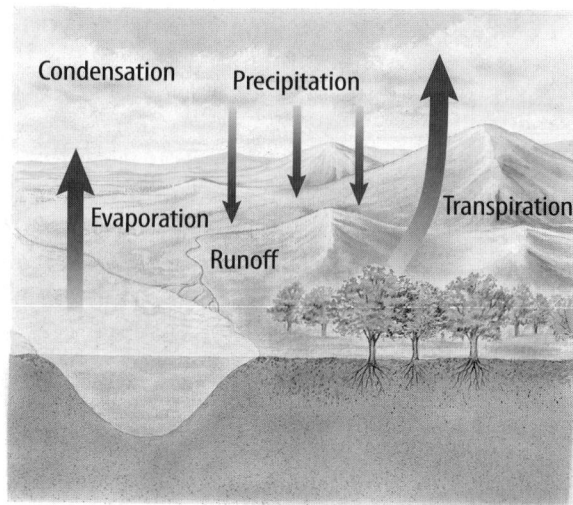

5 Which step of the water cycle shown above occurs in plants?

  A condensation

  B evaporation

  C precipitation

  D transpiration

6 Which is true of energy in ecosystems?

  A It never changes form.

  B It is both created and destroyed.

  C It flows in one direction.

  D It follows a cycle pattern.

7 Which organism would most likely appear at the top of an energy pyramid?

  A grass

  B hawk

  C mouse

  D snake

Use the diagram below to answer questions 8 and 9.

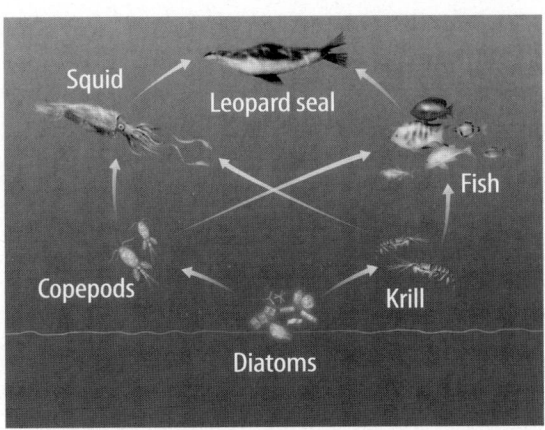

8 How does energy move in the food web pictured above?

  A from leopard seal to squid

  B from diatoms to krill

  C from fish to krill

  D from squid to diatoms

9 Which is an example of a food chain shown above?

  A diatoms → krill → leopard seal

  B fish → krill → squid

  C diatoms → krill → fish

  D squid → fish → leopard seal

10 During which process is oxygen gas released into the atmosphere?

  A chemosynthesis

  B decomposition

  C photosynthesis

  D transpiration

Constructed Response

11 Most ecosystems contain six nonliving factors: atmosphere, climate, soil, temperature, sunlight, and water. Briefly explain how each factor affects the life of a large predator, such as a jaguar, in a jungle ecosystem.

Use the diagram below to answer questions 12 and 13.

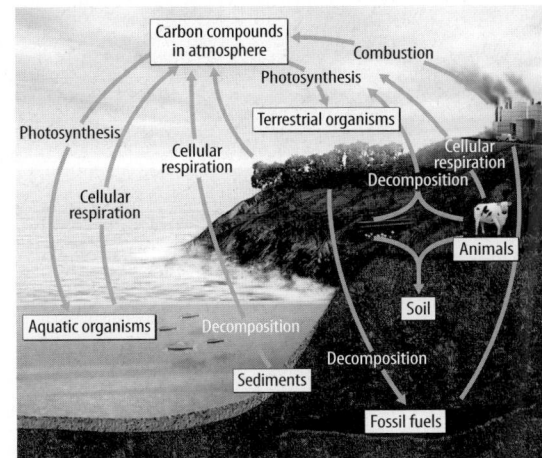

12 Using the image of the carbon cycle shown above, identify three locations of carbon other than the atmosphere. What form does the carbon take in each example?

13 Describe a biological process of the carbon cycle that removes carbon from the atmosphere and a biological process that adds carbon dioxide to the atmosphere.

NEED EXTRA HELP?													
If You Missed Question...	1	2	3	4	5	6	7	8	9	10	11	12	13
Go to Lesson...	3	2	3	2	2	3	3	3	3	2	1	2	2

Chapter 21

Populations and Communities

THE BIG IDEA

How do populations and communities interact and change?

Inquiry: Too Many Pigeons?

This group of pigeons does not depend only on the environment for food. Tourists visiting the area also feed the pigeons. Because so much food is available, more pigeons than normal live in this part of the city.

- Do you think this large number of pigeons affects other organisms in the area?

- How do you think groups of pigeons and other organisms interact and change?

Get Ready to Read

What do you think?

Before you read, decide if you agree or disagree with each of these statements. As you read this chapter, see if you change your mind about any of the statements.

1. Some life exists in the ice caps of the North Pole and the South Pole.

2. A community includes all organisms of one species that live in the same area.

3. Some populations decrease in numbers because of low birthrates.

4. An extinct species has only a few surviving individuals.

5. No more than two species can live in the same habitat.

6. A cow is a producer because it produces food for other organisms.

Populations

Reading Guide

Key Concepts 🔑
ESSENTIAL QUESTIONS

- What defines a population?
- What factors affect the size of a population?

Vocabulary

biosphere p. 741

community p. 742

population p. 742

competition p. 743

limiting factor p. 743

population density p. 744

biotic potential p. 744

carrying capacity p. 745

g Multilingual eGlossary

Inquiry Looking for Something?

Meerkats live in family groups. They help protect each other by watching for danger from eagles, lions, and other hunters of the Kalahari Desert. What other ways might the meerkats interact?

Launch Lab

15 minutes

How many times do you interact?

Every day, you interact with other people in different ways, including talking, writing, or shaking hands. Some interactions involve just one other person, and others happen between many people. Like humans, other organisms interact with each other in their environment.

1. Make a list in your Science Journal of all the ways you have interacted with other people today.

2. Use a **highlighter** to mark the interactions that occurred between you and one other person.

3. Use a **highlighter** of another color to mark interactions that occurred among three or more people.

Think About This

1. Were your interactions mainly with one person or with three or more people?

2. 🔑 **Key Concept** How might your interactions change if the group of people were bigger?

The Biosphere and Ecological Systems

Imagine flying halfway around the world to Africa. When your plane flies over Africa, you might see mountains, rivers, grasslands, and forests. As you get closer to land, you might see a herd of elephants at a watering hole. You also might see a group of meerkats, like the ones on the previous page.

Now imagine hiking through an African forest. You might see monkeys, frogs, insects, spiders, and flowers. Maybe you catch sight of crocodiles sunning themselves by a river or birds perching on trees.

You are exploring Earth's **biosphere** (BI uh sfir)—*the parts of Earth and the surrounding atmosphere where there is life.* The biosphere includes all the land of the continents and islands. It also includes all of Earth's oceans, lakes, and streams, as well as the ice caps at the North Pole and the South Pole.

Parts of the biosphere with large amounts of plants or algae often contain many other organisms as well. The biosphere's distribution of chlorophyll, a green pigment in plants and algae, is shown in **Figure 1**.

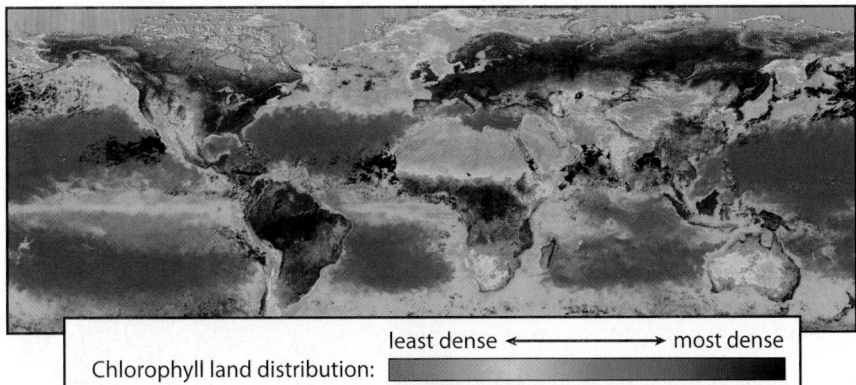

Chlorophyll land distribution: least dense ←——————→ most dense
Chlorophyll water distribution:

Figure 1 The colors in this satellite image represent the densities of chlorophyll, a green pigment found in plants and algae.

✓ **Visual Check** Why might the North Pole have very little green?

What is a population?

The Kalahari Desert in Africa is a part of the Earth's biosphere. A wildlife refuge in the Kalahari Desert is home to several groups of meerkats. Meerkats are small mammals that live in family groups and help each other care for their young.

Meerkats rely on interactions among themselves to survive. They sleep in underground burrows at night and hunt for food during the day. They take turns standing upright to watch for danger and call out warnings to others.

Meerkats are part of an ecosystem, as shown in **Figure 2.** An ecosystem is a group of organisms that lives in an area at one time, as well as the climate, soil, water, and other nonliving parts of the environment. The Kalahari Desert is an ecosystem. The study of all ecosystems on Earth is ecology.

Many species besides meerkats live in the Kalahari Desert. They include scorpions, spiders, insects, snakes, and birds such as eagles and owls. Also, large animals like zebras, giraffes, and lions live there. Plants that grow in the Kalahari Desert include shrubs, grasses, small trees, and melon vines. Together, all these plants, animals, and other organisms form a community. *A* **community** *is all the populations of different species that live together in the same area at the same time.*

All the meerkats in this refuge form a population. *A* **population** *is all the organisms of the same species that live in the same area at the same time.* A species is a group of organisms that have similar traits and are able to produce fertile offspring.

Key Concept Check What defines a population?

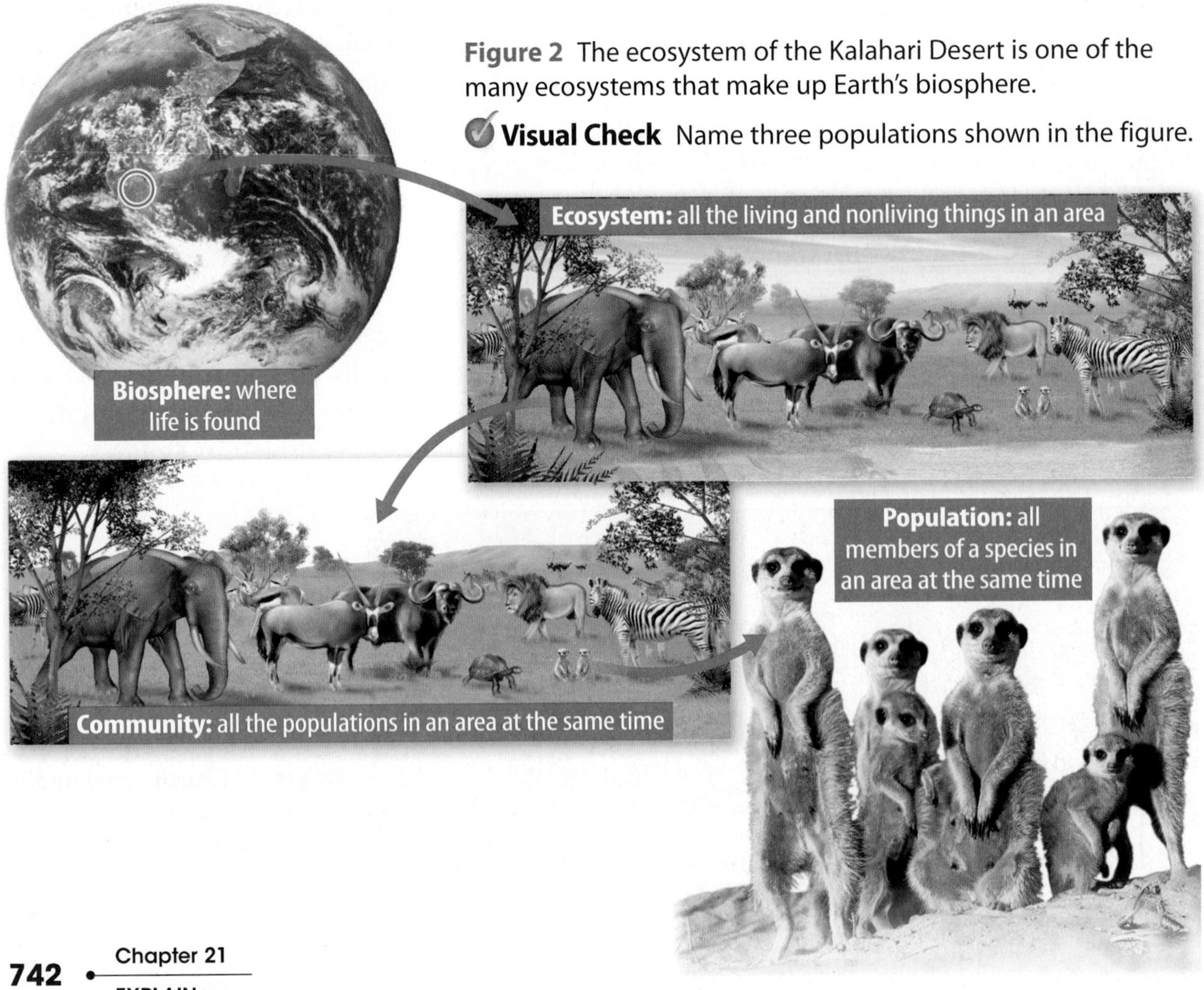
Biosphere: where life is found
Ecosystem: all the living and nonliving things in an area
Community: all the populations in an area at the same time
Population: all members of a species in an area at the same time

Figure 2 The ecosystem of the Kalahari Desert is one of the many ecosystems that make up Earth's biosphere.

Visual Check Name three populations shown in the figure.

Competition

At times, not enough food is available for every organism in a community. Members of a population, including those in the Kalahari Desert, must compete with other populations and each other for enough food to survive. **Competition** *is the demand for resources, such as food, water, and shelter, in short supply in a community.* When there are not enough resources available to survive, there is more competition in a community.

Population Sizes

If the amount of available food decreases, what do you think happens to a population of meerkats? Some meerkats might move away to find food elsewhere. Female meerkats cannot raise as many young. The population becomes smaller. If there is plenty of food, however, the size of the population grows larger as more meerkats survive to adulthood and live longer. Changes in environmental factors can result in population size changes.

Limiting Factors

Environmental factors, such as available water, food, shelter, sunlight, and temperature, are possible limiting factors for a population. *A* **limiting factor** *is anything that restricts the size of a population.* Available sunlight is a limiting factor for most organisms. If there is not enough sunlight, green plants cannot make food by photosynthesis. Organisms that eat plants are affected if little food is available.

Temperature is a limiting factor for some organisms. When the temperature drops below freezing, many organisms die because it is too cold to carry out their life functions. Disease, predators—animals that eat other animals—and natural disasters such as fires or floods are limiting factors as well.

 Key Concept Check What factors affect the size of a population?

Inquiry MiniLab   15 minutes

What are limiting factors?

Certain factors, called limiting factors, can affect the size of a population.

1. Read and complete a lab safety form.
2. Your teacher will divide your class into groups.
3. Using a **meterstick** and **masking tape,** mark a 1-m square on the floor. Place a piece of paper in the middle of the square.
4. All members of your group will stand entirely within the square. While one member keeps time with a **stopwatch,** members of the group will write the alphabet on the sheet of paper one at a time.

5. In your Science Journal, calculate the average time it took each person to write the alphabet.

Analyze and Conclude

1. **Describe** how the space limitations affected each member's ability to complete the task.

2. 🔑 **Key Concept** What functions must an organism perform that can be limited by the amount of available space?

Figure 3 A sedated lynx is fitted with a radio collar and then returned to the wild.

WORD ORIGIN · · · · · · · · · · · ·

population
from Latin *populus*, means "inhabitants"

density
from Latin *densus*, means "thick, crowded"
· · · · · · · · · · · · · · ·

FOLDABLES

Make a horizontal half book and label it as shown. Use it to organize your notes on the relationship between population size and carrying capacity in an ecosystem.

Carrying Capacity

Measuring Population Size

Sometimes it is difficult to determine the size of a population. How would you count scampering meerkats or wild lynx? One method used to count and monitor animal populations is the capture-mark-and-release method. The lynx in **Figure 3** is a member of a population in Poland that is monitored using this method. Biologists using this method sedate animals and fit them with radio collars before releasing them back into the wild. By counting how many observed lynx are wearing collars, scientists can estimate the size of the lynx population. Biologists also use the collars to track the lynx's movements and monitor their activities.

Suppose you want to know how closely together Cumberland azaleas (uh ZAYL yuhz), a type of flower, grow in the Great Smoky Mountains National Park. **Population density** *is the size of a population compared to the amount of space available.* One way of estimating population density is by sample count. Rather than counting every azalea shrub, you count only those in a representative area, such as 1 km². By multiplying the number of square kilometers in the park by the number of azaleas in 1 km², you find the estimated population density of azalea shrubs in the entire park.

Reading Check Describe two ways you can estimate population size.

Biotic Potential

Imagine that a population of raccoons has plenty of food, water, and den space. In addition, there is no disease or danger from other animals. The only limit to the size of this population is the number of offspring the raccoons can produce. **Biotic potential** *is the potential growth of a population if it could grow in perfect conditions with no limiting factors.* No population on Earth ever reaches its biotic potential because no ecosystem has an unlimited supply of natural resources.

Carrying Capacity

What would happen if a population of meerkats reached its biotic potential? It would stop growing when it reached the limit of available resources that the ecosystem could provide, such as food, water, or shelter. *The largest number of individuals of one species that an environment can support is the* **carrying capacity.** A population grows until it reaches the carrying capacity of an environment, as shown in **Figure 4.** Disease, space, predators, and food are some of the factors that limit the carrying capacity of an ecosystem. However, the carrying capacity of an environment is not constant. It increases and decreases as the amount of available resources increases and decreases. At times, a population can temporarily exceed the carrying capacity of an environment.

 Reading Check What is carrying capacity?

Overpopulation

When the size of a population becomes larger than the carrying capacity of its ecosystem, overpopulation occurs. Overpopulation can cause problems for organisms. For example, meerkats eat spiders. An overpopulation of meerkats causes the size of the spider population in that community to decrease. Populations of birds and other animals that eat spiders also decrease when the number of spiders decreases.

Elephants in Africa's wild game parks is another example of overpopulation. Elephants searching for food caused the tree damage shown in **Figure 5.** They push over trees to feed on the uppermost leaves. Other species of animals that use the same trees for food and shelter must compete with the elephants. The loss of trees and plants can also damage soil. Trees and plants might not grow in that area again for a long time.

 Reading Check How can overpopulation affect a community?

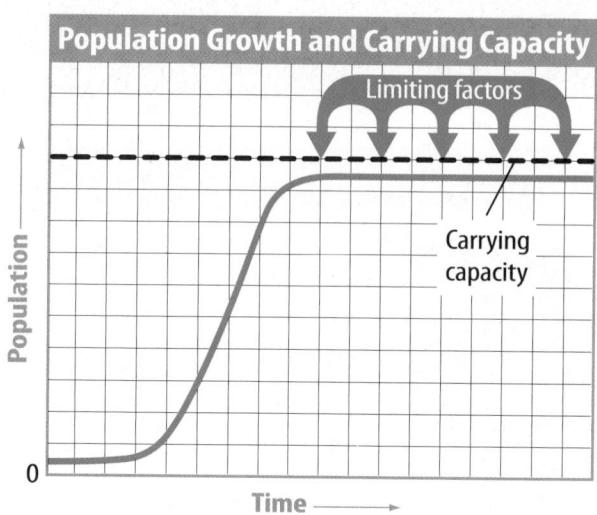

▲ **Figure 4** Carrying capacity is determined in part by limiting factors.

✔ **Visual Check** What factors affect population size in the graph above?

▲ **Figure 5** An overpopulation of elephants can cause damage to trees and other plants as the herd searches for food in the community.

Lesson 1 Review

Visual Summary

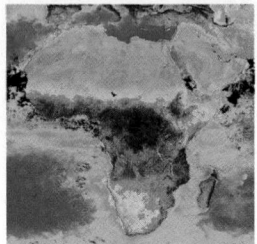

The population density of organisms, including green plants and algae, varies throughout the world.

A community is all the populations of different species that live together in the same area at the same time.

The number of individuals in a population varies as the amount of available resources varies.

FOLDABLES

Use your lesson Foldable to review the lesson. Save your Foldable for the project at the end of the chapter.

What do you think NOW?

You first read the statements below at the beginning of the chapter.

1. Some life exists in the ice caps of the North Pole and the South Pole.

2. A community includes all organisms of one species that live in the same area.

Did you change your mind about whether you agree or disagree with the statements? Rewrite any false statements to make them true.

Use Vocabulary

1 **Define** *population*.

2 **Distinguish** between carrying capacity and biotic potential.

3 Food, water, living space, and disease are examples of _____.

Understand Key Concepts

4 **Explain** how competition could limit the size of a bird population.

5 One example of competition among members of a meerkat population is
   A. fighting over mates.
   B. warning others of danger.
   C. huddling together to stay warm.
   D. teaching young to search for food.

Interpret Graphics

6 **Sequence** Draw a graphic organizer like the one below to show the sequence of steps in one type of population study.

7 **Explain** the changes in population size at each point marked on the graph below.

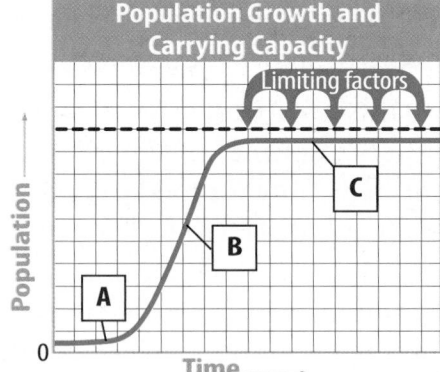

Critical Thinking

8 **Explain** Is the problem of elephants destroying trees in southern Africa overpopulation, competition, or both?

Familiar Birds
in an Unlikely Place

Howling winds blow across the Altiplano—a cold plateau high in the Andes mountain range of South America. There, you might expect to see animals such as llamas, but Felicity Arengo travels to the Altiplano to observe flamingos.

Flamingos usually are associated with tropical regions. However, three species of flamingo—James, Andean, and Chilean—are adapted to the cold, barren Altiplano. Although this region differs from tropical areas where other flamingos live, both have food sources for the birds. The plateau is dotted with salty lakes containing brine shrimp, tiny organisms that flamingos eat.

Scientists have many questions about the flamingos that visit these salty lakes. How large are the flamingo populations? How do they survive when the lakes evaporate? To answer these questions, Arengo and her team visit the lakes and count flamingos there. They also tag flamingos with radio transmitters to track their movements. They have learned that one species, the Andean flamingo, is the rarest flamingo species in the world. Additionally, when the plateau lakes freeze, many flamingos fly to lakes in the lowlands of Argentina, Bolivia, Chile, and Peru.

As human activity changes the Altiplano, flamingos that live there might be in danger. On the plateau, mining operations use and pollute lake water. In the lowlands, ranchers often drain lakes for more land to grow crops or to feed animals.

Arengo and other scientists are working with organizations to protect flamingos' habitats. Scientists have trained park rangers to monitor flamingos' reproductive activities and protect nesting colonies. As scientists collect more data and find new ways to protect flamingos' habitats, a brighter future might be in store for the flamingos of the Altiplano.

▲ **Dr. Arengo tags a flamingo with a radio transmitter. Once she releases the flamingo, satellites will track the flamingo's movement.**

▲ **Flamingos' habitats cover four countries—Argentina, Bolivia, Chile, and Peru. As a well-known species, flamingos help motivate conservation efforts in these countries.**

It's Your Turn

BRAINSTORM With classmates, choose an ecosystem in your area that is in need of conservation. Brainstorm what animal would make a good species to represent the ecosystem, and create a poster designed to raise awareness.

Reading Guide

Key Concepts 🔑
ESSENTIAL QUESTIONS

- How do populations change?

- Why do human populations change?

Vocabulary
birthrate p. 749

death rate p. 749

extinct species p. 751

endangered species p. 751

threatened species p. 751

migration p. 752

g **Multilingual eGlossary**

Video BrainPOP®

Changing Populations

Inquiry Same Mother?

Have you ever seen newly hatched baby spiders? Baby spiders can have hundreds or even thousands of brothers and sisters. What keeps the spider population from growing out of control?

What events can change a population?

Populations can be affected by human-made and environmental changes, such as floods or a good growing season. A population's size can increase or decrease in response to these changes.

1. Read and complete a lab safety form.

2. Record in your Science Journal the number of **counting objects** you have been given. Each object represents an organism, and all the objects together represent a population.

3. Turn over one of the **event cards** you were given and follow the instructions on the card. Determine the event's impact on your population.

4. Repeat step 3 for four more "seasons," or turns.

Think About This

1. Compare the size of your population with other groups. Do you all have the same number of organisms at the end of five seasons?

2. 🔑 **Key Concept** What effect did the different events have on your population?

How Populations Change

Have you ever seen a cluster of spider eggs? Some female spiders lay hundreds or even thousands of eggs in their lifetime. What happens to a population of spiders when a large group of eggs hatches all at once? The population suddenly becomes larger. It doesn't stay that way for long, though. Many spiders die or become food, like the one being eaten in **Figure 6**, before they grow enough to reproduce. The size of the spider population increases when the eggs hatch but decreases as the spiders die.

A population change can be measured by the population's birthrate and death rate. *A population's* **birthrate** *is the number of offspring produced over a given time period. The* **death rate** *is the number of individuals that die over the same time period.* If the birthrate is higher than the death rate, the population increases. If the death rate is higher than the birthrate, the population decreases.

Figure 6 Spiders have a high birthrate, but they usually have a high death rate too. Many spiders die or are eaten before they can reproduce.

Exponential Growth

When a population is in ideal conditions with unlimited resources, it grows in a pattern called **exponential** growth. During exponential growth, the larger a population gets, the faster it grows. *E. coli* bacteria are microscopic organisms that undergo exponential growth. This population doubles in size every half hour, as shown in **Figure 7.** It takes only 10 hours for the *E. coli* population to grow from one organism to more than 1 million. Exponential growth cannot continue for long. Eventually, limiting factors stop population growth.

SCIENCE USE v. COMMON USE

exponential
Science Use a mathematical expression that contains a constant raised to a power, such as 2^3 or x^2

Common Use in great amounts

Exponential Population Growth

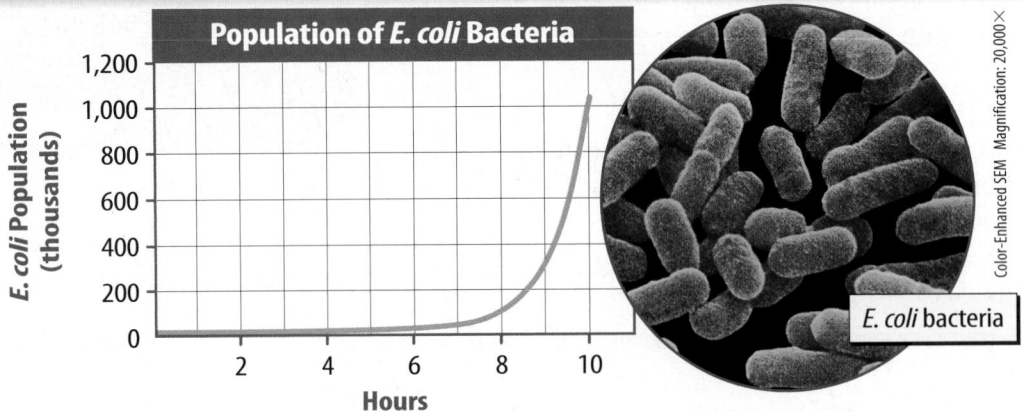

Population of *E. coli* Bacteria

Color-Enhanced SEM Magnification: 20,000×

E. coli bacteria

Figure 7 When grown in the laboratory, this population of *E. coli* bacteria is given everything it needs to briefly achieve exponential growth.

WORD ORIGIN

extinct
from Latin *extinctus*, means "extinguish"

Population Size Decrease

Population size can increase, but it also can decrease. For example, a population of field mice might decrease in size in the winter because there is less food. Some mice might not be able to find enough food and will starve. More mice will die than will be born, so the population size decreases. When food is plentiful, the population size usually increases.

Natural disasters such as floods, fires, or volcanic eruptions also affect population size. For example, if a hurricane rips away part of a coral reef, the populations of coral and other organisms that live on the reef also decrease in size.

Disease is another cause of population decrease. In the mid-1900s, Dutch elm disease spread throughout the United States and destroyed many thousands of elm trees. Because of the disease, the size of population of elm trees decreased.

Predation—the hunting of organisms for food—also reduces population size. For example, a farmer might bring cats into a barn to reduce the size of a mouse population.

Reading Check What are four reasons that a population might decrease in size?

Extinction If populations continue to decrease in numbers, they disappear. *An extinct species is a species that has died out and no individuals are left.* Extinctions can be caused by predation, natural disasters, or damage to the environment.

Some extinctions in Earth's history were large events that involved many species. Most scientists think the extinction of the dinosaurs about 65 million years ago was caused by a meteorite crashing into Earth. The impact would have sent tons of dust into the atmosphere, blocking sunlight. Without sunlight, plants could not grow. Animals, such as dinosaurs, that ate plants probably starved.

Most extinctions involve fewer species. For example, New Zealand was once home to a large, flightless bird called the giant moa, as shown in **Figure 8.** Humans first settled these islands about 700 years ago. They hunted the moa for food. As the size of the human population increased, the size of the moa population decreased. Within 200 years, all the giant moas had been killed and the species became extinct.

Endangered Species The mountain gorillas shown in **Figure 8** are an example of a species that is endangered. *An endangered species is a species whose population is at risk of extinction.*

Threatened Species California sea otters almost became extinct in the early 1900s due to overhunting. In 1977, California sea otters were classified as a **threatened species**—*a species at risk, but not yet endangered.* Laws were passed to protect the otters and by 2007 there were about 3,000 sea otters. Worldwide, there are more than 4,000 species that are classified as endangered or threatened.

Reading Check What is the difference between an endangered species and a threatened species?

Figure 8 Organisms are classified as extinct, endangered, or threatened.

Extinct The giant moa, a large bird that was nearly four meters tall, was hunted to extinction.

Endangered Just over 700 mountain gorillas remain in the wild in Africa.

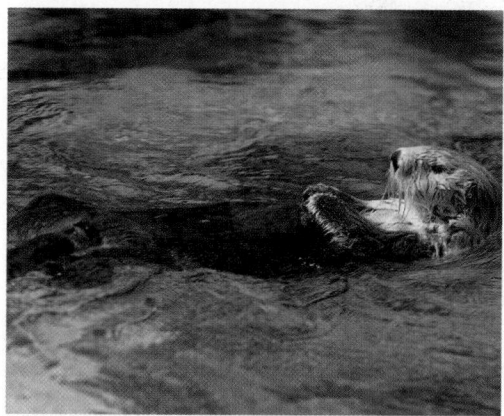

Threatened California sea otters are at risk of becoming endangered because there are so few of them remaining in the wild.

How does migration affect population size?

Your class will model a population of birds that migrates during the fall and the spring.

1. Read and complete a lab safety form.

2. Begin at the summer station. Record in your Science Journal the size of the bird population represented by your class. When your teacher signals, move to the fall station.

3. Pick a piece of **paper** out of the **jar.** If the paper has a minus sign, drop out of the game. If it has a plus sign, bring a classmate into the game.

4. Record the size of the remaining population at the fall station.

5. Migrate to the winter station and repeat steps 3 and 4. Move two more times and repeat for spring and summer.

Analyze and Conclude

1. **Draw Conclusions** What might happen if the birds did not migrate each year?

2. 🔑 **Key Concept** How did the population change throughout the year?

Migration

Figure 9 During the winter, humpback whales mate and give birth in warm ocean waters near the Bahamas. In the summer, they migrate north to food-rich waters along the coast of New England.

Movement

Populations also change when organisms move from place to place. When an animal population becomes overcrowded, some individuals might move to find more food or living space. For example, zebras might overgraze an area and move to areas that are not so heavily grazed.

Plant populations can also move from place to place. Have you ever blown on a dandelion puff full of seeds? Each tiny dandelion seed has a feathery part that enables it to be carried by the wind. Wind often carries seeds far from their parent plants. Animals also help spread plant seeds. For example, some squirrels and woodpeckers collect acorns. They carry the acorns away and store them for a future food source. The animal forgets some acorns, and they sprout and grow into new trees far from their parent trees.

Migration Sometimes an entire population moves from one place to another and later returns to its original location. **Migration** *is the instinctive seasonal movement of a population of organisms from one place to another.* Ducks, geese, and monarch butterflies are examples of organisms that migrate annually. Some fish, frogs, insects, and mammals—including the whales described in **Figure 9**—migrate to find food and shelter.

🔑 **Key Concept Check** List three ways populations change.

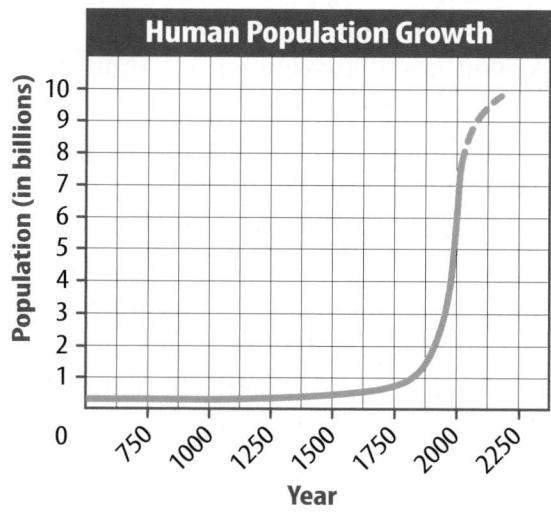

Human Population Growth

◀ **Figure 10** The human population has grown faster in the past 150 years than at any time in Earth's history.

✓ **Visual Check** How does this population curve compare with the graph of the *E. coli* population in **Figure 7**?

Human Population Changes

Human population size is affected by the same three factors that determine the sizes of all populations—birthrate, death rate, and movement. But, unlike other species, humans have developed ways to increase the carrying capacity of their environment. Improved crop yields, domesticated farm animals, and timely methods of transporting foods and other resources enable people to survive in all types of environments.

Scientists **estimate** that there were about 300 million humans on Earth a thousand years ago. Today there are more than 6 billion humans on Earth, as shown in **Figure 10.** By 2050 there could be over 9 billion. No one knows when the human population will reach Earth's carrying capacity. However, some scientists estimate Earth's carrying capacity is about 11 billion.

As the human population grows, people need to build more houses and roads and clear more land for crops. This means less living space, food, and other resources for other species. In addition, people use more energy to heat and cool homes; to fuel cars, airplanes, and other forms of transportation; and to produce electricity. This energy use contributes to pollution that affects other populations.

One example of the consequences of human population growth is the destruction of tropical forests. Each year, humans clear thousands of acres of tropical forest to make room for crops and livestock, as shown in **Figure 11.** Clearing tropical forests is harmful because these forests contain a large variety of species that are not in other ecosystems.

✓ **Reading Check** Explain how human population growth affects other species.

ACADEMIC VOCABULARY

estimate
(verb) to determine roughly the size, nature, or extent of something

Figure 11 Tropical forests are cleared for crops and livestock. The habitats of many organisms are destroyed, resulting in many species becoming endangered or extinct. ▼

Use Graphs

Graphs are used to make large amounts of information easy to interpret. Line graphs show how data changes over a period of time. A circle graph, or pie graph, shows how portions of a set of data compare with the whole set. The circle represents 100 percent and each segment represents one part making up the whole. For example, Figure 14 shows all the moves made by people in the United States during 2004–2005. Fifty-seven percent of all moves were within the same county.

Practice

Based on Figure 14,

1. What percentage of the moves were from one state to another?

2. What percentage of the moves were within the same state?

📖 **Review**

- **Math Practice**
- **Personal Tutor**

Figure 12 Before vaccinations, many children died in infancy. The use of vaccines has significantly reduced death rates.

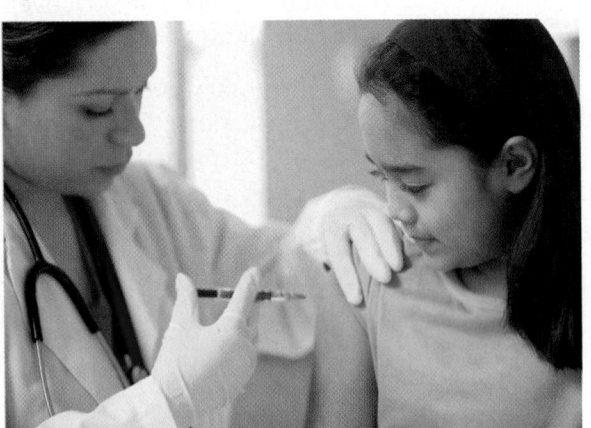

Population Size Increase

Do you know anyone who is more than 100 years old? In 2006, almost 80,000 people living in the United States were at least 100 years old. People are living longer today than in previous generations, and more children reach adulthood. Recall that when the birthrate of a population is higher than its death rate, the population grows. There are several factors that keep the human birthrate higher than its death rate. Some of these factors are discussed below.

Food For some, finding food might be as easy as making a trip to the grocery store, but not everyone can get food as easily. Advances in agriculture have made it possible to produce food for billions of people.

Resources Fossil fuels, cloth, metals, foods, and many other materials are easily transported around the world by planes, trains, trucks, or boats. Today, people have access to more resources because of better transportation methods.

Sanitation As recently as 100 years ago, diseases such as typhoid, cholera, and diphtheria were major causes of death. These diseases spread through unclean water supplies and untreated sewage. Modern water treatment technologies have reduced the occurrence of many diseases. Less expensive and more effective cleaning products are now available to help prevent the spread of disease-causing organisms. As a result, deaths from these illnesses are less common in many countries.

Medical Care Modern medical care is keeping people alive and healthy longer than ever before. As shown in **Figure 12**, scientists have developed vaccines, antibiotics, and other medicines that prevent and treat disease. As a result, fewer people get sick, and human death rates have decreased. Medical technologies and new medicines help people survive heart attacks, cancer, and other major illnesses.

Decreases in Human Population Size

Human populations in some parts of the world are decreasing in size. Diseases such as AIDS and malaria cause high death rates in some countries. Severe drought has resulted in major crop failures and lack of food. Floods, earthquakes, and other natural disasters can cause the deaths of hundreds or even thousands of people at a time. Damage from disasters, such as the damage shown in **Figure 13,** can keep people from living in the area for a long time. All of these factors cause decreases in human population sizes in some areas.

 Reading Check What are three events that can decrease human population size?

Population Movement

Have you ever moved to a different city, state, or country? The size of a human population changes as people move from place to place. The graph in **Figure 14** shows the percentages of each kind of move people make. Like other organisms, populations of humans might move when more resources become available in a different place.

Did your parents, grandparents, or great grandparents come to the United States from another country? Immigration takes place when organisms move into an area. Most of the U.S. population is descended from people who immigrated from Europe, Africa, Asia, and Central and South America.

 Key Concept Check What makes human populations increase or decrease in size?

▲ **Figure 13** Natural disasters such as a tsunami can cause severe damage to people's homes, as well as drastically reduce the population size.

FOLDABLES®

Make a horizontal two-tab book and label it as shown. Use it to summarize why human populations change in size.

Human Population Increase   Human Population Decrease

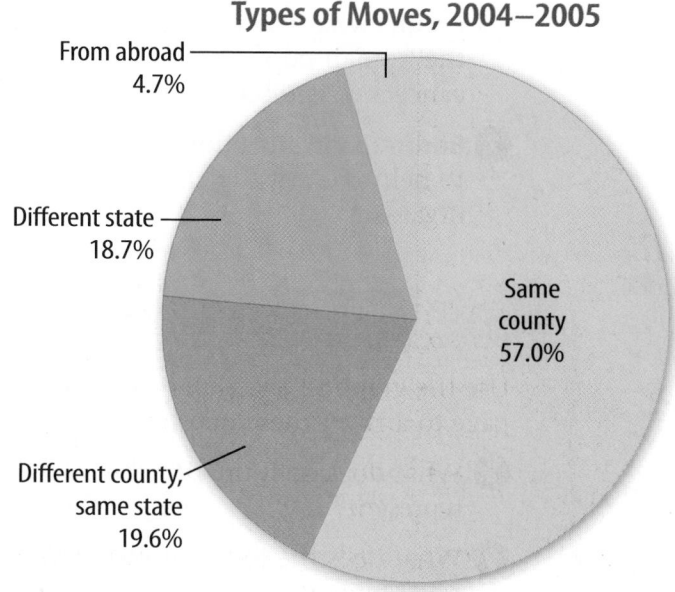

Types of Moves, 2004–2005

From abroad 4.7%

Different state 18.7%

Same county 57.0%

Different county, same state 19.6%

Source: U.S. Census Bureau, Current Population Survey, 2005 Annual Social and Economic Supplement.

◀ **Figure 14** Populations can move between counties and states or even from another country.

Visual Check Which type of move did the largest percentage of the population make?

Lesson 2 Review

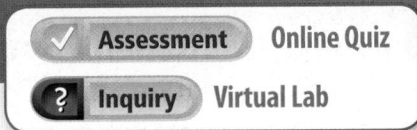

Visual Summary

The birthrate and the death rate of any population affects its population size.

The giant moa is classified as an extinct species because there are no surviving members.

A population that is at risk but not yet endangered is a threatened species.

FOLDABLES

Use your lesson Foldable to review the lesson. Save your Foldable for the project at the end of the chapter.

What do you think NOW?

You first read the statements below at the beginning of the chapter.

3. Some populations decrease in numbers because of low birthrates.

4. An extinct species has only a few surviving individuals.

Did you change your mind about whether you agree or disagree with the statements? Rewrite any false statements to make them true.

Use Vocabulary

1. **Define** *endangered species* in your own words.

2. **Distinguish** between birthrate and death rate.

3. The instinctive movement of a population from one place to another is _____.

Understand Key Concepts

4. Rabbits move into a new field where there is plenty of room to dig new burrows. This is an example of

   A. overpopulation. **C.** carrying capacity.
   B. immigration.   **D.** competition.

Interpret Graphics

5. **Summarize** Copy and fill in the graphic organizer below to identify the three major factors that affect population size.

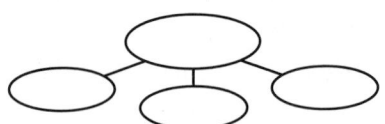

Critical Thinking

6. **Predict** what could happen to the size of the human population if a cure for all cancers were discovered.

7. **Recommend** an action humans could take to help prevent the extinction of tropical organisms.

Math Skills

Review — Math Practice

Use the graph in the Skill Practice on the next page to answer these questions.

8. What does each unit on the *y*-axis represent?

9. What does the lowest point on the blue line represent?

How do populations change in size?

Birthrate and death rate change the size of a population. In the 1700s the death rate of sea otters in central California was extremely high because many people hunted them. By the 1930s only about 50 sea otters remained. Today, the Marine Mammal Protection Act protects sea otters from being hunted. Every spring, scientists survey the central California Coast to determine the numbers of adult and young sea otters (called pups) in the population. The numbers on the graph indicate population sizes at the end of a breeding season.

Learn It

Most scientists collect some type of data when testing a hypothesis. Once data are collected, scientists look for patterns or trends in the data and draw conclusions. This process is called **interpreting data.**

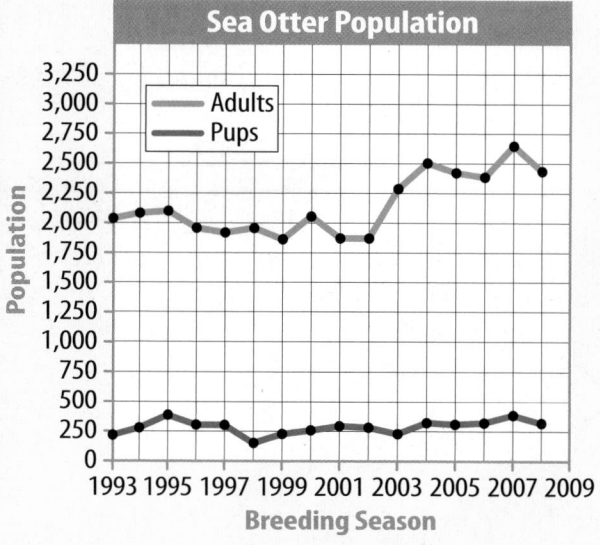

Sea Otter Population

— Adults
— Pups

Population: 0, 250, 500, 750, 1,000, 1,250, 1,500, 1,750, 2,000, 2,250, 2,500, 2,750, 3,000, 3,250

Breeding Season: 1993 1995 1997 1999 2001 2003 2005 2007 2009

Try It

1. The above graph shows changes in adult and pup sea otter populations over many years. Assume that the number of pups seen during the survey represents all the pups that were born and survived in one year—the birthrate. For example, in the 1997 breeding season, the birthrate was 300.

2. In your Science Journal, make a table showing the population size and the birthrate for the 2001 breeding season. Repeat for 2002, 2003, and 2004.

3. In each breeding season, the population increases by the number of pups born and decreases by the number of sea otters that die. Use the following equation to find the death rate for 2002.

   Death rate in 2002 = population size in 2001 + birthrate in 2002 – population size in 2002

Apply It

4. Calculate the death rate in 2004 and compare it to the death rate in 2002.

5. What environmental factors might account for the difference in the death rate between 2002 and 2004?

6. How do you think the population size will change in 2009 and 2010?

7. **Key Concept** Determine how the birthrate compared to the death rate in 2002 and 2004. Explain how these rates affected the population sizes in 2002 and 2004.

Communities

Reading Guide

Key Concepts 🔑
ESSENTIAL QUESTIONS

- What defines a community?
- How do the populations in a community interact?

Vocabulary

habitat p. 759

niche p. 759

producer p. 760

consumer p. 760

symbiosis p. 763

mutualism p. 763

commensalism p. 764

parasitism p. 764

g **Multilingual eGlossary**

Inquiry Time for Lunch?

This Hoopoe (HOO poo) has captured its next meal. Some of the energy needed by this bird for its life processes will come from the energy stored in the body of the lizard. Where did the lizard get its energy?

 **Launch Lab** 15 minutes

What are the roles in your school community?

Within a community, different organisms have different roles. Trees produce their own food from the environment. Then, they become food for other organisms. Mushrooms break down dead organisms and make the nutrients useful to other living things. Think about the members of your school community such as the students, teachers, and custodians. What roles do they have?

1. Draw a table with two columns in your Science Journal. Label one column *Community Member* and the other column *Role in the Community*.

2. Fill in the table with examples from your school.

Community Member	Role in the Community
Principal	Manages school staff including students and teachers

Think About This

1. Are there any community members who have more than one role?

2. What is your role in the school community?

3. 🔑 **Key Concept** Explain how it is beneficial for members of a community to have different roles.

Communities, Habitats, and Niches

High in a rain forest tree, a two-toed sloth munches leaves. Ants crawl on a branch, carrying away a dead beetle. Two birds build a nest. A flowering vine twists around the tree trunk. These organisms are part of a rain forest community. You read in Lesson 1 that a community is made up of all the species that live in the same ecosystem at the same time.

The place within an ecosystem where an organism lives is its **habitat.** A habitat, like the one in **Figure 15,** provides all the resources an organism needs, including food and shelter. A habitat also has the right temperature, water, and other conditions the organism needs to survive.

The rain forest tree described above is a habitat for sloths, insects, birds, vines, and many other species. Each species uses the habitat in a different way. *A* **niche** (NICH) *is what a species does in its habitat to survive.* For example, butterflies feed on flower nectar. Sloths eat leaves. Ants eat insects or plants. These species have different niches in the same environment. Each organism shown in **Figure 15** has its own niche on the tree. The plants anchor themselves to the tree and can capture more sunlight. Termites use the tree for food.

 Key Concept Check What is a community?

WORD ORIGIN ·········

habitat
from Latin *habitus*, means "to live, dwell"

Figure 15 This tree trunk is a habitat for ferns.

How can you model a food web?

Populations interact through feeding relationships. A food web shows overlapping feeding relationships in a community.

1. Read and complete a lab safety form.

2. On a sheet of **paper,** make a list of at least 10 different organisms within a community of your choice. Include a variety of producers and consumers.

3. Use **scissors** to cut out the name of each organism on your list.

4. **Glue** the names onto a piece of **construction paper.**

5. Use **yarn** and glue to connect organisms that have feeding relationships. For example, a piece of yarn would connect a rabbit and grass.

Analyze and Conclude

1. **Use Models** Add the label *Sun* to your model. Which organisms would be connected to the Sun?

2. **Infer** Imagine that you removed three organisms from your food web. How would this affect the community?

3. 🔑 **Key Concept** Which organisms in your model interact through feeding relationships?

Energy in Communities

Sloths are the slowest mammals on Earth. They hardly make a sound, and they sleep 15 to 20 hours a day. Squirrel monkeys, however, chatter as they swing through treetops hunting for fruit, insects, and eggs. Sloths might appear to use no energy at all. However, sloths, squirrel monkeys, and all other organisms need energy to live. All living things use energy and carry out life processes such as growth and reproduction.

Energy Roles

How an organism obtains energy is an important part of its niche. Almost all the energy available to life on Earth originally came from the Sun. However, some organisms, such as those that live near deep-sea vents, are exceptions. They obtain energy from chemicals such as hydrogen sulfide.

Producers *are organisms that get energy from the environment, such as sunlight, and make their own food.* For example, most plants are producers that get their energy from sunlight. They use the process of photosynthesis and make sugar molecules that they use for food. Producers near deep-sea vents use hydrogen sulfide and carbon dioxide and make sugar molecules.

Consumers *are organisms that get energy by eating other organisms.* Consumers are also classified by the type of organisms they eat. Herbivores get their energy by eating plants. Cows and sheep are herbivores. Carnivores get their energy by eating other consumers. Harpy eagles, lions, and wolves are carnivores. Omnivores, such as most humans, get their energy by eating producers and consumers. Detritivores (dee TRI tuh vorz) get their energy by eating dead organisms or parts of dead organisms. Some bacteria and some fungi are detritivores.

✔ **Reading Check** Identify a producer, an herbivore, a carnivore, and an omnivore.

Energy Flow

A food chain is a way of showing how energy moves through a community. In a rain forest community, energy flows from the Sun to a rain forest tree, a producer. The tree uses the energy and grows, producing leaves and other plant structures. Energy moves to consumers, such as the sloth that eats the leaves of the tree, and then to the eagle that eats the sloth. When the eagle dies, detritivores, such as bacteria, feed on its body. That food chain can be written like this:

Sun ⟶ leaves ⟶ sloth ⟶ eagle ⟶ bacteria

A food chain shows only part of the energy flow in a community. A food web, like the one in **Figure 16,** shows many food chains within a community and how they overlap.

Key Concept Check Identify a food chain in a community near your home. List the producers and consumers in your food chain.

Figure 16 Organisms in a rain forest community get their energy in different ways.

Visual Check List the members of two different food chains shown in the figure.

Review Personal Tutor

Food Web

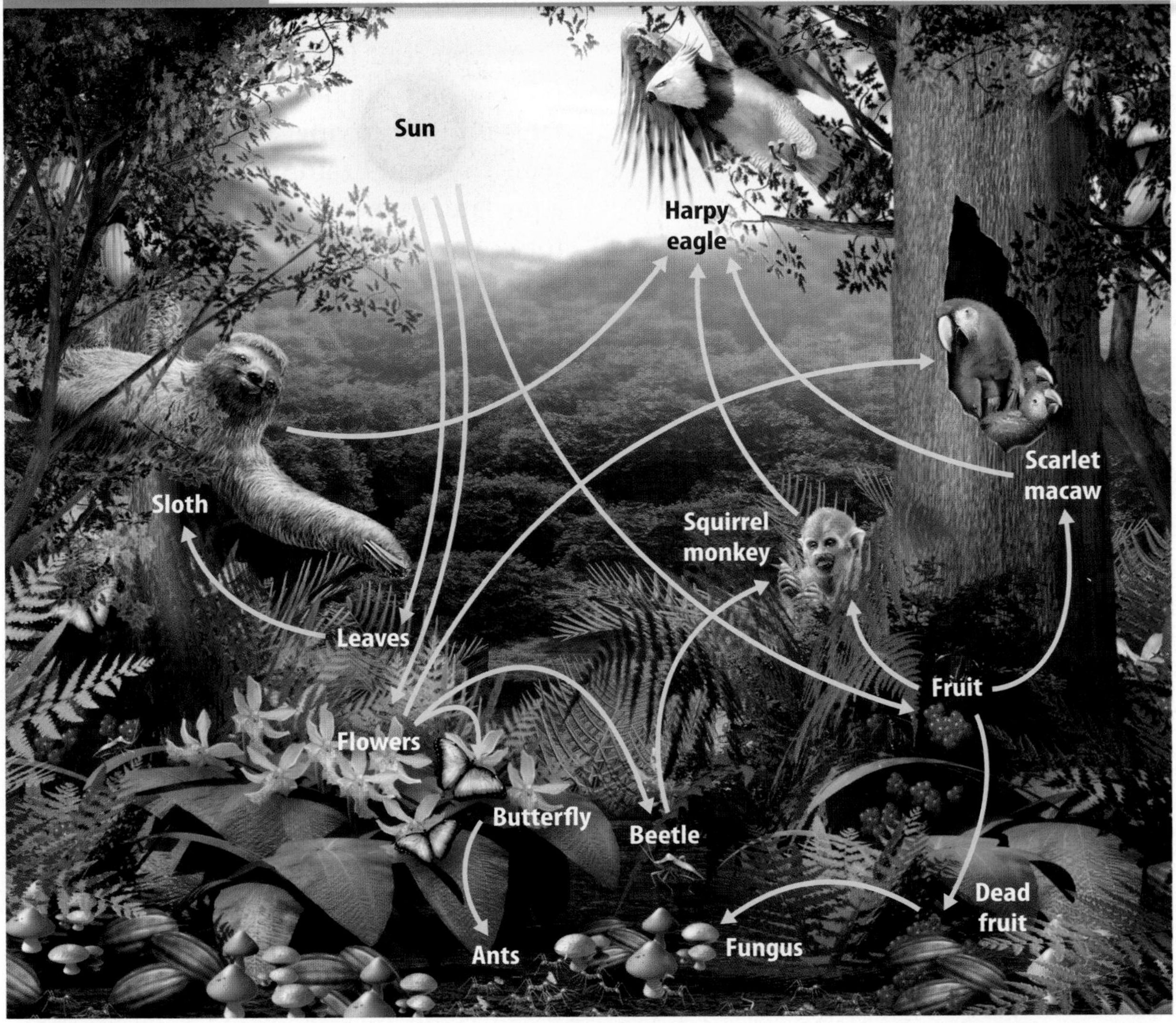
Sun
Harpy eagle
Scarlet macaw
Sloth
Squirrel monkey
Leaves
Fruit
Flowers
Butterfly
Beetle
Dead fruit
Ants
Fungus

Relationships in Communities

The populations that make up a community interact with each other in a variety of ways. Some species have feeding relationships—they either eat or are eaten by another species. Some species interact with another species to get the food or shelter they need.

Predator-Prey Relationships

Hungry squirrel monkeys quarrel over a piece of fruit. They don't notice the harpy eagle above them. Suddenly, the eagle swoops down and grabs one of the monkeys in its talons. Harpy eagles and monkeys have a predator-prey relationship. The eagle, like other **predators,** hunts other animals for food. The hunted animals, such as the squirrel monkey or the lizard shown at the beginning of this lesson, are called prey.

As you read in Lesson 1, predators help prevent prey populations from growing too large for the carrying capacity of the ecosystem. The sand lizard, shown in **Figure 17,** is a predator in most of Europe. Like all predators, they often capture weak or injured individuals of a prey population. When the weak members of a population are removed, there are more resources available for the remaining members. This helps keep the prey population healthy.

 Reading Check Why are predators important to a prey population?

Make a vertical three-tab book and label it as shown. Use it to organize information about the types of relationships that can exist among organisms within a community.

> Predator–Prey Relationships
>
> Cooperative Relationships
>
> Symbiotic Relationships

REVIEW VOCABULARY

predator
an organism that survives by hunting another

Figure 17 Sand lizards eat slugs, spiders, insects, fruits, and flowers.

Visual Check Which type of consumers are sand lizards?

Figure 18 Leaf-cutter ants cooperate while growing food. They work together and cut apart leaves. The ants carry the leaves to an underground nest. The ants' only food is a species of fungus that grows on the leaves.

Cooperative Relationships

The members of some populations work together in cooperative relationships for their survival, like the leaf-cutter ants shown in **Figure 18.** As you read in Lesson 1, meerkats cooperate with each other and raise young and watch for predators. Squirrel monkeys benefit in a similar way by living in groups. They cooperate as they hunt for food and watch for danger.

Symbiotic Relationships

Some species have such close relationships that they are almost always found living together. *A close, long-term relationship between two species that usually involves an exchange of food or energy is called* **symbiosis** (sihm bee OH sus). There are three types of symbiosis—mutualism, commensalism, and parasitism.

Mutualism Boxer crabs and sea anemones share a mutualistic partnership, as shown in **Figure 19.** *A symbiotic relationship in which both partners benefit is called* **mutualism.** Boxer crabs and sea anemones live in tropical coral reef communities. The crabs carry sea anemones in their claws. The sea anemones have stinging cells that help the crabs fight off predators. The sea anemones eat leftovers from the crabs' meals.

◀ Figure 19 Boxer crabs and sea anemones have a mutualistic relationship because both partners benefit from the relationship.

▲ **Figure 20** Epiphytes and trees share a commensal relationship.

Figure 21 Hunting wasps are examples of parasites. The larvae use the paralyzed spider as food while they mature. ▼

Commensalism *A symbiotic relationship that benefits one species but does not harm or benefit the other is* **commensalism.** Plants called epiphytes (EH puh fites), shown in **Figure 20,** grow on the trunks of trees and other objects. The roots of an epiphyte anchor it to the object. The plant's nutrients are absorbed from the air. Epiphytes benefit from attaching to tree trunks by getting more living space and sunlight. The trees are neither helped nor harmed by the plants. Orchids are another example of epiphytes that have commensal relationships with trees.

Parasitism *A symbiotic relationship that benefits one species and harms the other is* **parasitism.** The species that benefits is the parasite. The species that is harmed is the host. Heartworms, tapeworms, fleas, and lice are parasites that feed on a host organism, such as a human or a dog. The parasites benefit by getting food. The host usually is not killed, but it can be weakened. For example, heartworms in a dog can cause the heart to work harder. Eventually, the heart can fail, killing the host. Other common parasites include the fungi that cause ringworm and toenail fungus. The fungi that cause these ailments feed on keratin (KER ah tihn), a protein in skin and nails.

The larvae of the hunting wasp is another example of a parasite. The female wasp, shown in **Figure 21,** stings a spider to paralyze it. Then she lays eggs in its body. When the eggs hatch into larvae, they eat the paralyzed spider's body. Another example of parasitism is the strangler fig. The seeds of the strangler fig sprout on the branches of a host tree. The young strangler fig sends roots into the tree and down into the ground below. The host tree provides the fig with nutrients and a trunk for support. Strangler figs grow fast and they can kill a host tree.

 Key Concept Check List five ways species in a community interact.

Visual Summary

Each organism in a community has its own habitat and niche within the ecosystem.

Within a community, each organism must obtain energy for life processes. Some organisms are producers and some are consumers.

Some organisms have cooperative relationships and some have symbiotic relationships. The hunting wasp and spider have a symbiotic relationship.

FOLDABLES

Use your lesson Foldable to review the lesson. Save your Foldable for the project at the end of the chapter.

What do you think NOW?

You first read the statements below at the beginning of the chapter.

5. No more than two species can live in the same habitat.

6. A cow is a producer because it produces food for other organisms.

Did you change your mind about whether you agree or disagree with the statements? Rewrite any false statements to make them true.

Use Vocabulary

1 **Define** *symbiosis.*

2 **Distinguish** between producers and consumers.

Understand Key Concepts

3 **Explain** how energy from the Sun flows through a rain forest community.

4 **Compare and contrast** predator-prey relationships and cooperative relationships.

5 A shrimp removes and eats the parasites from the gills of a fish. The fish stays healthier because the parasites are removed. This relationship is

   A. commensalism. **C.** mutualism.
   B. competition.   **D.** parasitism.

Interpret Graphics

6 **Organize Information** Copy and fill in the table below with details about the three different types of symbiosis.

7 **Identify** the type of diagram shown below and explain what it means.

Critical Thinking

8 **Predict** what could happen to a population of ants if anteaters, a predator of the ants, disappeared.

9 **Decide** which type of symbiosis this is: Bacteria live in the skin under the eyes of deep-sea fish. The bacteria give off light that helps the fish find food. The bacteria get food from the fish.

Materials

clownfish

symbiosis
cards

How can you model a symbiotic relationship?

As you read earlier, organisms in communities can have many different types of relationships. Symbiotic relationships occur when two organisms live in direct contact and form a relationship. Symbiotic relationships include mutualism, commensalism, and parasitism. Although communities around the world have symbiotic relationships, coral reef communities often include all three types of symbiosis. Many of the organisms in these communities, such as clownfish, sea anemones, and even microscopic copepods, have some type of symbiotic relationship. In this lab, you will research and model one type of symbiosis in a coral reef community.

Question

How do you model a symbiotic relationship and determine its type?

Procedure

1. Read and complete a lab safety form.

2. Get a card from your teacher with the name of an organism that has a symbiotic relationship. Find your partner(s) in the symbiotic relationship.

3. With your partner, brainstorm what type of symbiotic relationship your organism and your partner's organism might have. List and explain your choice(s) in your Science Journal.

4. Using your library and reference books, research your organism with your partner.

5. Develop a visual presentation, such as a skit, a slide presentation, or a series of posters with your partner showing how your symbiotic relationship works and how your organisms interact with other members of the community.

6. Show your presentation to the class.

Analyze and Conclude

7. **Identify** What type of symbiotic relationship did your organism have? What was your organism's role in the relationship?

8. **Compare** How would your organism interact in the community if its partner were not present?

9. **Contrast** What other organisms in a coral reef community have the same type of symbiotic relationship as your organism? If none, explain why.

10. **The Big Idea** How did your organism interact with other members of its population and community?

Communicate Your Results

Make a poster illustrating all the symbiotic relationships you and your classmates studied. Determine what type of relationship each example had. Identify which organisms are hosts, if any.

Inquiry Extension

All of the organisms your class studied are part of the coral reef ecosystem. Create a food web showing how the organisms obtained energy.

Lab Tips

☑ Think about your organism's niche in the ecosystem.

☑ Carefully select resources for accuracy.

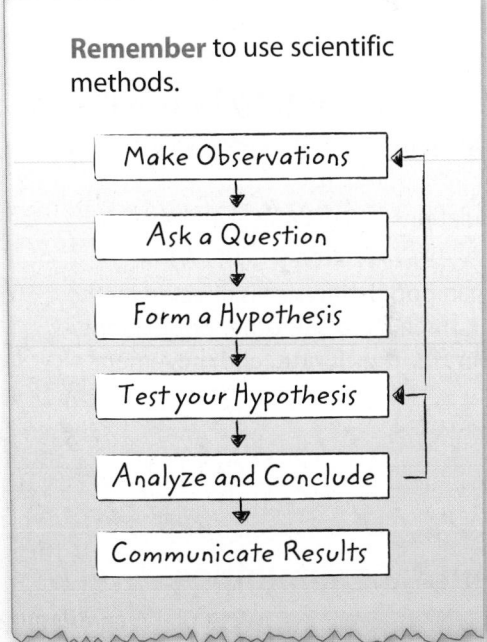

Remember to use scientific methods.

Make Observations

↓

Ask a Question

↓

Form a Hypothesis

↓

Test your Hypothesis

↓

Analyze and Conclude

↓

Communicate Results

THE **BIG IDEA**

A community contains many populations that interact in their energy roles and in their competition for resources. Populations can increase, decrease, and move, affecting the community.

Key Concepts Summary 🔑	Vocabulary

Lesson 1: Populations

- A **population** is all the organisms of the same species that live in the same area at the same time.
- Population sizes vary due to **limiting factors** such as environmental factors and available resources.
- Population size usually does not exceed the **carrying capacity** of the ecosystem.

biosphere p. 741
community p. 742
population p. 742
competition p. 743
limiting factor p. 743
population density p. 744
biotic potential p. 744
carrying capacity p. 745

Lesson 2: Changing Populations

- Populations of living things can increase, decrease, or move.
- Populations can decrease until they are threatened, endangered, or extinct.
- Human population size is affected by the same three factors as other populations—**birthrate**, **death rate**, and movement.

birthrate p. 749
death rate p. 749
extinct species p. 751
endangered species p. 751
threatened species p. 751
migration p. 752

Lesson 3: Communities

- A community is all the populations of different species that live together in the same area at the same time.
- The place within an ecosystem where an organism lives is its **habitat** and what an organism does in its habitat to survive is its **niche.**
- Three types of relationships within a community are predator-prey, cooperative, and symbiotic.

habitat p. 759
niche p. 759
producer p. 760
consumer p. 760
symbiosis p. 763
mutualism p. 763
commensalism p. 764
parasitism p. 764

FOLDABLES®

Assemble your lesson Foldables as shown to make a Chapter Project. Use the project to review what you have learned in this chapter.

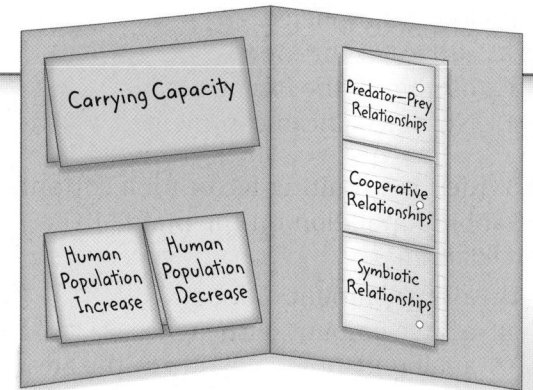

Use Vocabulary

1 The struggle in a community for the same resources is _____.

2 The part of Earth that supports life is the _____.

3 The instinctive movement of a population is _____.

4 A(n) _____ species is one at risk of becoming endangered.

5 A(n) _____ is an organism that gets energy from the environment.

6 The largest number of offspring that can be produced when there are no limiting factors is the _____.

Link Vocabulary and Key Concepts

((◎)) **Concepts in Motion**   Interactive Concept Map

Copy this concept map, and then use vocabulary terms from the previous page to complete the concept map.

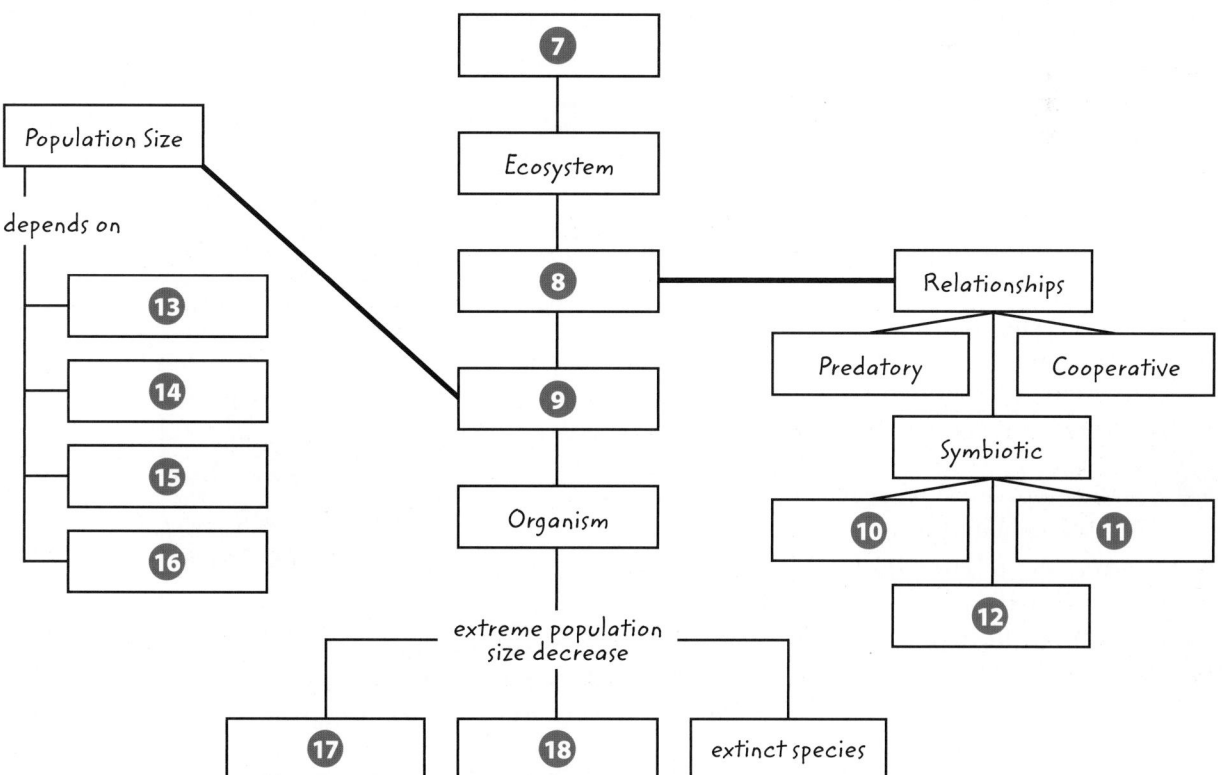

Understand Key Concepts 🔑

1 What does the line indicated by the red arrow in the graph below represent?

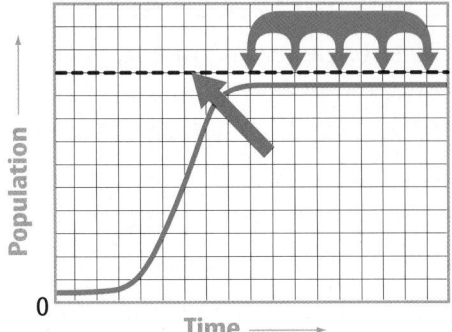

A. competition
B. biotic potential
C. carrying capacity
D. limiting factors

2 The need for organisms to rely on the same resources causes

A. competition.
B. biotic potential.
C. carrying capacity.
D. population growth.

3 The number of organisms in a specific area is

A. a community.
B. the carrying capacity.
C. the population density.
D. the population growth.

4 The number of robins that hatch in a year is the population's

A. biotic potential.
B. birthrate.
C. carrying capacity.
D. exponential growth.

5 A robin population that reaches its biotic potential probably shows

A. exponential growth.
B. low growth.
C. negative growth.
D. no growth.

6 An organism that uses sunlight to make food molecules is a(n)

A. carnivore.
B. consumer.
C. herbivore.
D. producer.

7 Which is NOT part of Earth's biosphere?

A. low atmosphere
B. surface of the Moon
C. bottom of the Pacific ocean
D. North American continent

8 Which is a limiting factor for a cottontail rabbit population on the prairie in Oklahoma?

A. a large amount of food
B. a large amount of shelter space
C. an abundance of coyotes in the area
D. an unpolluted river in the ecosystem

9 Which factor does NOT normally affect human population size?

A. birthrate
B. death rate
C. population movement
D. lack of resources

10 What type of overall population change is shown below?

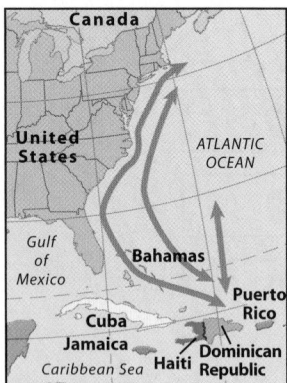

A. immigration
B. migration
C. population decrease
D. population increase

Critical Thinking

11 **Select and draw** three food chains from the food web shown.

12 **Give an Example** What problems might result from overpopulation of pigeons in a city park?

13 **Describe** What are some possible solutions that a city might use to solve a pigeon overpopulation problem?

14 **Decide** Would sample counting or capture-mark-and-release at a specified time and place be the best method for measuring each of these populations: birds, whales, bluebonnet flowers, and oak trees?

15 **Compare and contrast** the feeding habits of carnivores, omnivores, and producers.

16 **Classify** Decide whether each of these relationships is mutualism, commensalism, or parasitism.

- Butterfly pollinates flower while drinking nectar.

- Tapeworm feeds on contents of dog's intestines.

- Fish finds shelter in coral reef.

17 **Draw** a food web that describes energy flow in this community. Insects eat leaves. Spiders eat insects. Birds eat insects and spiders. Frogs eat insects. Birds eat frogs.

Writing in Science

18 **Write** a two-page story that explains how an imaginary population becomes threatened with extinction.

REVIEW THE BIG IDEA

19 Describe three different types of relationships in a community between two different populations of organisms.

20 Do you think this large number of pigeons affects other organisms in the community? Explain your answer.

Math Skills

Review — Math Practice

Use Graphs

Use the graph to answer the questions.

21 During what range of years did the population change the least?

22 The dotted line represents a prediction. What does it predict about population growth beyond the present time?

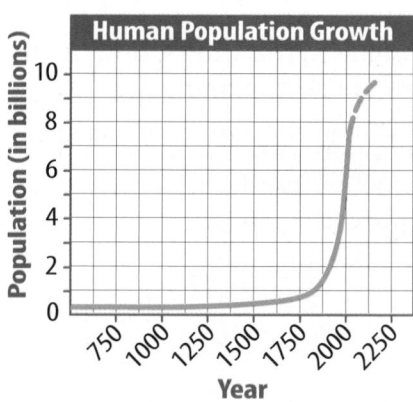

Record your answers on the answer sheet provided by your teacher or on a sheet of paper.

Multiple Choice

1 Which is defined as the demand for resources in short supply in a community?

   A biotic potential

   B competition

   C density

   D limiting factor

Use the diagram below to answer questions 2 and 3.

2 In the diagram above, which number represents an ecosystem?

   A 1

   B 2

   C 3

   D 4

3 According to the arrows, how are the elements of the diagram organized?

   A endangered to overpopulated

   B farthest to nearest

   C largest to smallest

   D nonliving to living

4 Which is NOT a possible result of overpopulation?

   A damage to soil

   B increased carrying capacity

   C loss of trees and plants

   D more competition

Use the diagram below to answer question 5.

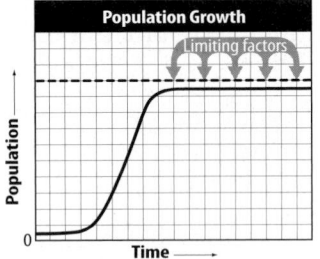

5 What does the dashed line in the diagram represent?

   A biotic potential

   B carrying capacity

   C overpopulation

   D population density

6 What does a population undergo when it has no limiting factors?

   A exponential growth

   B extinction

   C migration

   D population movement

7 What is the term for all species living in the same ecosystem at the same time?

   A biosphere

   B community

   C habitat

   D population

Use the diagram below to answer question 8.

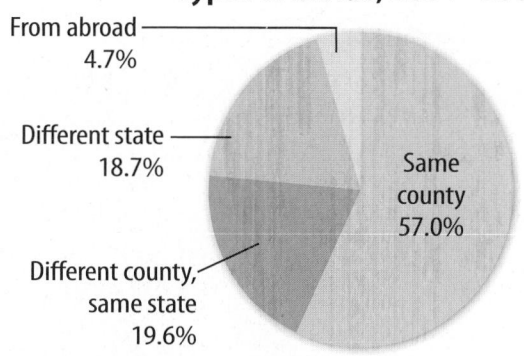

Types of Moves, 2004–2005

From abroad — 4.7%

Different state — 18.7%

Different county, same state 19.6%

Same county 57.0%

Source: U.S. Census Bureau, Current Population Survey, 2005 Annual Social and Economic Supplement.

8 According to the diagram, about how many of those who moved remained within the same state?

  A 20 percent

  B 39 percent

  C 57 percent

  D 77 percent

9 Which type of relationship includes mutualism and parasitism?

  A competition

  B cooperation

  C predation

  D symbiosis

10 Which is a population?

  A all meerkats in a refuge

  B all the types of birds in a forest

  C all the types of cats in a zoo

  D all the types of insects in a swamp

Constructed Response

Use the table below to answer questions 11 and 12.

Growth	Decline

11 In the table, list four factors that contribute to human population growth and four factors that lead to population decline.

12 Select one factor from each column in the table above. Which has the greatest effect on human population today? Explain your reasoning.

13 Describe a negative consequence of human population growth. How can humans minimize the effect of this change?

Use the diagram below to answer question 14.

sunlight → grasses → antelope → lion → bacteria

14 Explain how each organism in the food chain above gets energy. How might the other organisms be affected if the antelope population declines due to disease?

NEED EXTRA HELP?														
If You Missed Question...	1	2	3	4	5	6	7	8	9	10	11	12	13	14
Go to Lesson...	1	1	1	1	1	2	1	2	3	1	2	2	2	3

Biomes and Ecosystems

THE BIG IDEA

How do Earth's biomes and ecosystems differ?

Inquiry **Modern Art?**

Although it might look like a piece of art, this structure was designed to replicate several ecosystems. When Biosphere 2 was built in the 1980s near Tucson, Arizona, it included a rain forest, a desert, a grassland, a coral reef, and a wetland. Today, it is used mostly for research and education.

- How realistic do you think Biosphere 2 is?

- Is it possible to make artificial environments as complex as those in nature?

- How do Earth's biomes and ecosystems differ?

Get Ready to Read

What do you think?

Before you read, decide if you agree or disagree with each of these statements. As you read this chapter, see if you change your mind about any of the statements.

1. Deserts can be cold.

2. There are no rain forests outside the tropics.

3. Estuaries do not protect coastal areas from erosion.

4. Animals form coral reefs.

5. An ecosystem never changes.

6. Nothing grows in the area where a volcano has erupted.

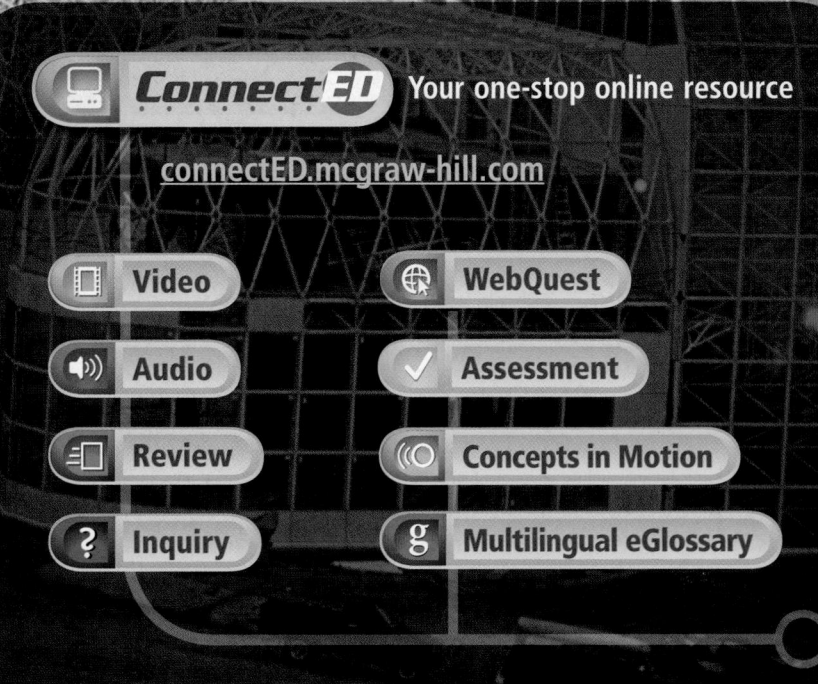

ConnectED Your one-stop online resource

connectED.mcgraw-hill.com

- Video
- WebQuest
- Audio
- Assessment
- Review
- Concepts in Motion
- Inquiry
- Multilingual eGlossary

Reading Guide

Key Concepts 🔑
ESSENTIAL QUESTIONS

- How do Earth's land biomes differ?

- How do humans impact land biomes?

Vocabulary

biome p. 777

desert p. 778

grassland p. 779

temperate p. 781

taiga p. 783

tundra p. 783

g Multilingual eGlossary

Video BrainPOP®

Land Biomes

Inquiry **Plant or Animal?**

Believe it or not, this is a flower. One of the largest flowers in the world, *Rafflesia* (ruh FLEE zhuh), grows naturally in the tropical rain forests of southeast Asia. What do you think would happen if you planted a seed from this plant in a desert? Would it survive?

Inquiry Launch Lab

10 minutes

What is the climate in China?

Beijing, China, and New York, New York, are about the same distance from the equator but on opposite sides of Earth. How do temperature and rainfall compare for these two cities?

1. Locate Beijing and New York on a world map.
2. Copy the table to the right in your Science Journal. From the data and charts provided, find and record the average high and low temperatures in January and in June for each city.
3. Record the average rainfall in January and in June for each city.

High Temperature (°C)	January	June
Beijing		
New York		
Low Temperature (°C)	**January**	**June**
Beijing		
New York		
Rainfall (mm)	**January**	**June**
Beijing		
New York		

Think About This

1. What are the temperature and rainfall ranges for each city?
2. **Key Concept** How do you think the climates of these cities differ year-round?

Land Ecosystems and Biomes

When you go outside, you might notice people, grass, flowers, birds, and insects. You also are probably aware of nonliving things, such as air, sunlight, and water. The living or once-living parts of an environment are the biotic parts. The nonliving parts that the living parts need to survive are the abiotic parts. The biotic and abiotic parts of an environment together make up an ecosystem.

Earth's continents have many different ecosystems, from deserts to rain forests. Scientists classify similar ecosystems in large geographic areas as biomes. *A* **biome** *is a geographic area on Earth that contains ecosystems with similar biotic and abiotic features.* As shown in **Figure 1,** Earth has seven major land biomes. Areas classified as the same biome have similar climates and organisms.

Figure 1 Earth contains seven major biomes.

Concepts in Motion Animation

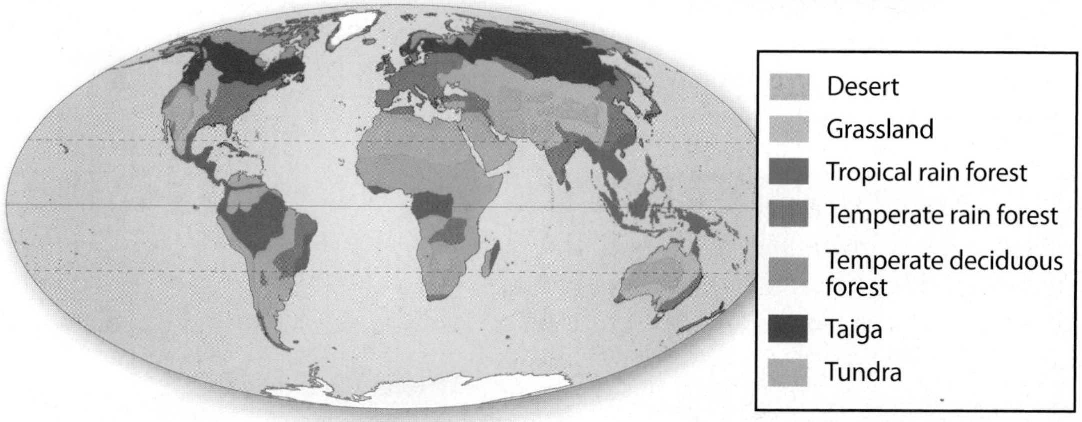

Desert
Grassland
Tropical rain forest
Temperate rain forest
Temperate deciduous forest
Taiga
Tundra

Inquiry MiniLab

20 minutes

How hot is sand?

If you have ever walked barefoot on a sandy beach on a sunny day, you know how hot sand can be. But how hot is the sand below the surface?

1. Read and complete a lab safety form.

2. Position a **desk lamp** over a **container** of **sand** that is at least 7 cm deep.

3. Place one **thermometer** on the surface of the sand and bury the tip of another **thermometer** about 5 cm below the surface. Record the temperature on each thermometer in your Science Journal.

4. Turn on the lamp and record the temperatures again after 10 minutes.

Analyze and Conclude

1. **Describe** the temperatures of the sand at the surface and below the surface.

2. **Predict** what would happen to the temperature of the sand at night.

3. 🔑 **Key Concept** Desert soil contains a high percentage of sand. Based on your results, predict ways in which species are adapted to living in an environment where the soil is mostly sand.

Desert Biome   Woodpeckers

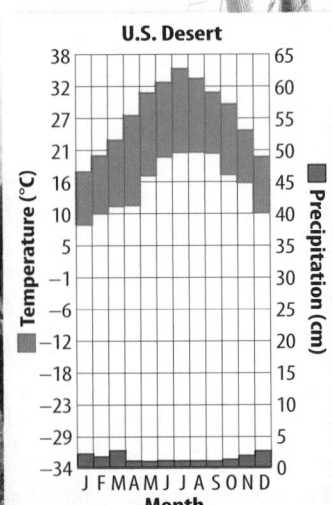

Deserts *are biomes that receive very little rain.* They are on nearly every continent and are Earth's driest ecosystems.

- Most deserts are hot during the day and cold at night. Others, like those in Antarctica, remain cold all of the time.

- Rainwater drains away quickly because of thin, porous soil. Large patches of ground are bare.

Biodiversity

- Animals include lizards, bats, woodpeckers, and snakes. Most animals avoid activity during the hottest parts of the day.

- Plants include spiny cactus and thorny shrubs. Shallow roots absorb water quickly. Some plants have accordion-like stems that expand and store water. Small leaves or spines reduce the loss of water.

Human Impact

- Cities, farms, and recreational areas in deserts use valuable water.

- Desert plants grow slowly. When they are damaged by people or livestock, recovery takes many years.

U.S. Desert

Temperature (°C): 38, 32, 27, 21, 16, 10, 5, −1, −6, −12, −18, −23, −29, −34

Precipitation (cm): 65, 60, 55, 50, 45, 40, 35, 30, 25, 20, 15, 10, 5, 0

Month: J F M A M J J A S O N D

Grassland Biome

Black-footed ferret

Grassland *biomes are areas where grasses are the dominant plants.* Also called prairies, savannas, and meadows, grasslands are the world's "breadbaskets." Wheat, corn, oats, rye, barley, and other important cereal crops are grasses. They grow well in these areas.

- Grasslands have a wet and a dry season.

- Deep, fertile soil supports plant growth.

- Grass roots form a thick mass, called sod, which helps soil absorb and hold water during periods of drought.

Reading Check Why are grasslands called "breadbaskets"?

Biodiversity

- Trees grow along moist banks of streams and rivers. Wildflowers bloom during the wet season.

- In North America, large herbivores, such as bison and elk, graze here. Insects, birds, rabbits, prairie dogs, and snakes find shelter in the grasses.

- Predators in North American grasslands include hawks, ferrets, coyotes, and wolves.

- African savannas are grasslands that contain giraffes, zebras, and lions. Australian grasslands are home to kangaroos, wallabies, and wild dogs.

Human Impact

- People plow large areas of grassland to raise cereal crops. This reduces habitat for wild species.

- Because of hunting and loss of habitat, large herbivores—such as bison—are now uncommon in many grasslands.

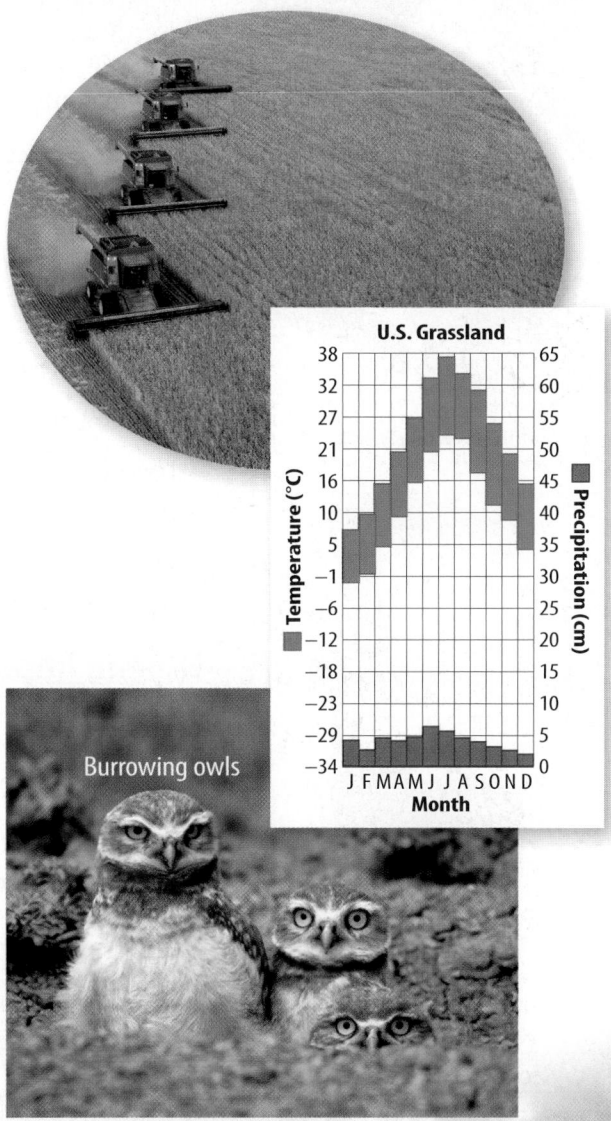

Burrowing owls

U.S. Grassland graph showing Temperature (°C) and Precipitation (cm) by Month (J F M A M J J A S O N D)

Tropical Rain Forest Biome

Ocelot

Toucan

The forests that grow near the equator are called tropical rain forests. These forests receive large amounts of rain and have dense growths of tall, leafy trees.

- Weather is warm and wet year-round.
- The soil is shallow and easily washed away by rain.
- Less than 1 percent of the sunlight that reaches the top of forest trees also reaches the forest floor.
- Half of Earth's species live in tropical rain forests. Most live in the canopy—the uppermost part of the forest.

✓ **Reading Check** Where do most organisms live in a tropical rain forest?

Biodiversity
- Few plants live on the dark forest floor.
- Vines climb the trunks of tall trees.
- Mosses, ferns, and orchids live on branches in the canopy.
- Insects make up the largest group of tropical animals. They include beetles, termites, ants, bees, and butterflies.
- Larger animals include parrots, toucans, snakes, frogs, flying squirrels, fruit bats, monkeys, jaguars, and ocelots.

Human Impact
- People have cleared more than half of Earth's tropical rain forests for lumber, farms, and ranches. Poor soil does not support rapid growth of new trees in cleared areas.
- Some organizations are working to encourage people to use less wood harvested from rain forests.

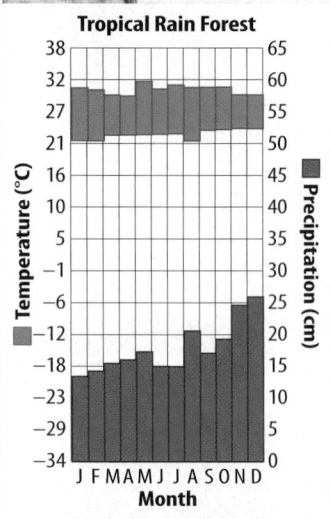

Tropical Rain Forest

Temperature (°C): 38 32 27 21 16 10 5 −1 −6 −12 −18 −23 −29 −34

Precipitation (cm): 65 60 55 50 45 40 35 30 25 20 15 10 5 0

J F M A M J J A S O N D
Month

Temperate Rain Forest Biome

Regions of Earth between the tropics and the polar circles are **temperate** *regions.* Temperate regions have relatively mild climates with distinct seasons. Several biomes are in temperate regions, including rain forests. Temperate rain forests are moist ecosystems mostly in coastal areas. They are not as warm as tropical rain forests.

- Winters are mild and rainy.

- Summers are cool and foggy.

- Soil is rich and moist.

Elk

Biodiversity

- Forests are dominated by spruce, hemlock, cedar, fir, and redwood trees, which can grow very large and tall.

- Fungi, ferns, mosses, vines, and small flowering plants grow on the moist forest floor.

- Animals include mosquitoes, butterflies, frogs, salamanders, woodpeckers, owls, eagles, chipmunks, raccoons, deer, elk, bears, foxes, and cougars.

Human Impact

- Temperate rain forest trees are a source of lumber. Logging can destroy the habitat of forest species.

- Rich soil enables cut forests to grow back. Tree farms help provide lumber without destroying habitat.

 Key Concept Check In what ways do humans affect temperate rain forests?

FOLDABLES

Use a sheet of paper to make a horizontal two-tab book. Record what you learn about desert and temperate rain forest biomes under the tabs, and use the information to compare and contrast these biomes.

Desert Biome | Temperate Rain Forest Biome

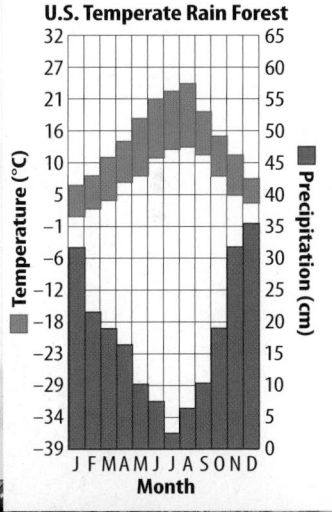

U.S. Temperate Rain Forest

Temperate deciduous forests grow in temperate regions where winter and summer climates have more variation than those in temperate rain forests. These forests are the most common forest ecosystems in the United States. They contain mostly deciduous trees, which lose their leaves in the fall.

- Winter temperatures are often below freezing. Snow is common.

- Summers are hot and humid.

- Soil is rich in nutrients and supports a large amount of diverse plant growth.

Biodiversity

- Most plants, such as maples, oaks, birches, and other deciduous trees, stop growing during the winter and begin growing again in the spring.

- Animals include snakes, ants, butterflies, birds, raccoons, opossums, and foxes.

- Some animals, including chipmunks and bats, spend the winter in hibernation.

- Many birds and some butterflies, such as the monarch, migrate to warmer climates for the winter.

Human Impact

Over the past several hundred years, humans have cleared thousands of acres of Earth's deciduous forests for farms and cities. Today, much of the clearing has stopped and some forests have regrown.

 Key Concept Check How are temperate deciduous rain forests different from temperate rain forests?

U.S. Temperate Deciduous Forest

Temperature (°C) / Precipitation (cm) vs Month (J F M A M J J A S O N D)

Red fox

Taiga Biome

A **taiga** (TI guh) *is a forest biome consisting mostly of cone-bearing evergreen trees.* The taiga biome exists only in the northern hemisphere. It occupies more space on Earth's continents than any other biome.

- Winters are long, cold, and snowy. Summers are short, warm, and moist.

- Soil is thin and acidic.

Biodiversity

- Evergreen trees, such as spruce, pine, and fir, are thin and shed snow easily.

- Animals include owls, mice, moose, bears, and other cold-adapted species.

- Abundant insects in summer attract many birds, which migrate south in winter.

Human Impact

- Tree harvesting reduces taiga habitat.

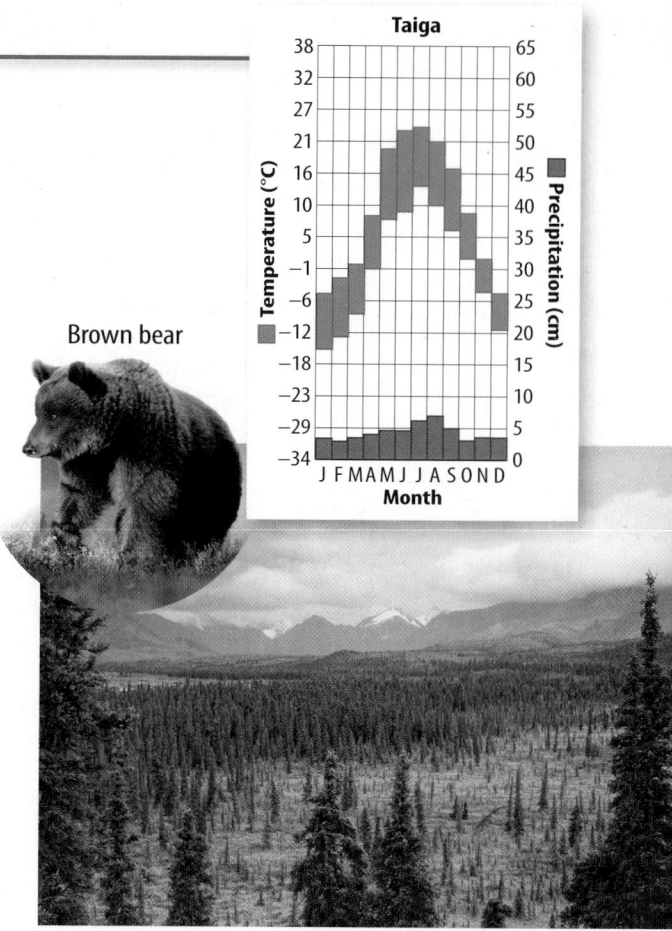

Brown bear

Tundra Biome

A **tundra** (TUN druh) *biome is cold, dry, and treeless.* Most tundra is south of the North Pole, but it also exists in mountainous areas at high altitudes.

- Winters are long, dark, and freezing; summers are short and cool; the growing season is only 50–60 days.

- Permafrost—a layer of permanently frozen soil—prevents deep root growth.

Biodiversity

- Plants include shallow-rooted mosses, lichens, and grasses.

- Many animals hibernate or migrate south during winter. Few animals, including lemmings, live in tundras year-round.

Human Impact

- Drilling for oil and gas can interrupt migration patterns.

Lemming

Visual Summary

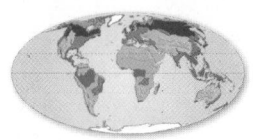

Earth has seven major land biomes, ranging from hot, dry deserts to cold, forested taigas.

Half of Earth's species live in rain forest biomes.

Temperate deciduous forests are the most common forest biome in the United States.

FOLDABLES®

Use your lesson Foldable to review the lesson. Save your Foldable for the project at the end of the chapter.

What do you think NOW?

You first read the statements below at the beginning of the chapter.

1. Deserts can be cold.

2. There are no rain forests outside the tropics.

Did you change your mind about whether you agree or disagree with the statements? Rewrite any false statements to make them true.

Use Vocabulary

1 **Define** *biome* using your own words.

2 **Distinguish** between tropical rain forests and temperate rain forests.

3 A cold, treeless biome is a(n) _____.

Understand Key Concepts 🔑

4 **Explain** why tundra soil cannot support the growth of trees.

5 **Give examples** of how plants and animals adapt to temperate deciduous ecosystems.

Interpret Graphics

6 **Determine** What is the average annual rainfall for the biome represented by the chart to the right?

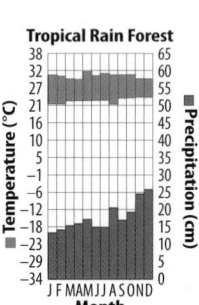

7 **Summarize Information** Copy the graphic organizer below and fill it in with animals and plants of the biome you live in.

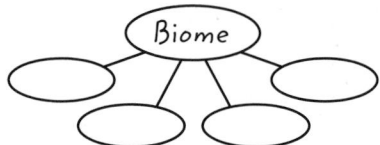

Critical Thinking

8 **Plan** an enclosed zoo exhibit for a desert ecosystem. What abiotic factors should you consider?

9 **Recommend** one or more actions people can take to reduce habitat loss in tropical and taiga forests.

Which biome is it?

Materials
biome data

You have read about the major land biomes found on Earth. Within each biome are ecosystems with similar biotic and abiotic factors. In this lab, you will **interpret data** describing a particular area on Earth to identify which biome it belongs to.

Learn It

Scientists collect and present data in a variety of forms, including graphs and tables. In this activity, you will interpret data in a graph and apply the information to the ideas you learned in the lesson.

Try It

1. Examine the temperature and precipitation data in the graph given you by your teacher.

2. Create a table from these data in your Science Journal. Calculate the average temperature and precipitation during the winter and the summer.

3. Examine the image of the biome and identify some plants and animals in the image.

4. Compare your data to the information on land biomes presented in Lesson 1. Which biome is the most similar?

Apply It

5. Which land biome did your data come from? Why did you choose this biome?

6. Are the data in your graph identical to the data in the graph of the biome in Lesson 1 to which it belongs? Why or why not?

7. Describe this biome. What do you think your biome will be like six months from now?

8. **Key Concept** How might humans affect the organisms in your biome?

Lesson 2

Reading Guide

Key Concept
ESSENTIAL QUESTIONS

- How do Earth's aquatic ecosystems differ?
- How do humans impact aquatic ecosystems?

Vocabulary

salinity p. 787

wetland p. 790

estuary p. 791

intertidal zone p. 793

coral reef p. 793

g **Multilingual eGlossary**

Aquatic Ecosystems

Inquiry Floating Trees?

These plants, called mangroves, are one of the few types of plants that grow in salt water. They usually live along ocean coastlines in tropical ecosystems. What other organisms do you think live near mangroves?

What happens when rivers and oceans mix?

Freshwater and saltwater ecosystems have different characteristics. What happens in areas where freshwater rivers and streams flow into oceans?

1. Read and complete a lab safety form.

2. In a **plastic tub,** add 100 g of **salt** to 2 L of water. Stir with a **long-handled spoon** until the salt dissolves.

3. In another **container,** add 5 drops of **blue food coloring** to 1 L of water. Gently pour the colored water into one corner of the plastic tub. Observe how the color of the water changes in the tub.

4. Observe the tub again in 5 minutes.

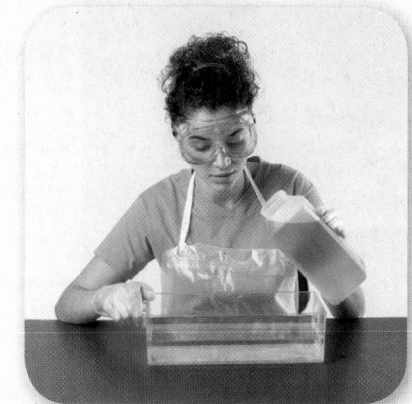

Think About This

1. What bodies of water do the containers represent?

2. What happened to the water in the tub after 5 minutes? What do you think happens to the salt content of the water?

3. 🔑 **Key Concept** How do you think the biodiversity of rivers and oceans differ? What organisms do you think might live at the place where the two meet?

Aquatic Ecosystems

If you've ever spent time near an ocean, a river, or another body of water, you might know that water is full of life. There are four major types of water, or aquatic, ecosystems: freshwater, wetland, estuary, and ocean. Each type of ecosystem contains a unique variety of organisms. Whales, dolphins, and corals live only in ocean ecosystems. Catfish and trout live only in freshwater ecosystems. Many other organisms that do not live under water, such as birds and seals, also depend on aquatic ecosystems for food and shelter.

Important abiotic factors in aquatic ecosystems include temperature, sunlight, and dissolved oxygen gas. Aquatic species have adaptations that enable them to use the oxygen in water. The gills of a fish separate oxygen from water and move it into the fish's bloodstream. Mangrove plants, pictured on the previous page, take in oxygen through small pores in their leaves and roots.

Salinity (say LIH nuh tee) is another important abiotic factor in aquatic ecosystems. **Salinity** *is the amount of salt dissolved in water.* Water in saltwater ecosystems has high salinity compared to water in freshwater ecosystems, which contains little salt.

Salmon

Freshwater ecosystems include streams, rivers, ponds, and lakes. Streams are usually narrow, shallow, and fast-flowing. Rivers are larger, deeper, and flow more slowly.

- Streams form from underground sources of water, such as springs or from runoff from rain and melting snow.

- Stream water is often clear. Soil particles are quickly washed downstream.

- Oxygen levels in streams are high because air mixes into the water as it splashes over rocks.

- Rivers form when streams flow together.

- Soil that washes into a river from streams or nearby land can make river water muddy. Soil also introduces nutrients, such as nitrogen, into rivers.

- Slow-moving river water has higher levels of nutrients and lower levels of dissolved oxygen than fast-moving water.

Biodiversity

- Willows, cottonwoods, and other water-loving plants grow along streams and on riverbanks.

- Species adapted to fast-moving water include trout, salmon, crayfish, and many insects.

- Species adapted to slow-moving water include snails and catfish.

Stonefly larva

Human Impact

- People take water from streams and rivers for drinking, laundry, bathing, crop irrigation, and industrial purposes.

- Hydroelectric plants use the energy in flowing water to generate electricity. Dams stop the water's flow.

- Runoff from cities, industries, and farms is a source of pollution.

Freshwater: Ponds and Lakes

Ponds and lakes contain freshwater that is not flowing downhill. These bodies of water form in low areas on land.

- Ponds are shallow and warm.

- Sunlight reaches the bottom of most ponds.

- Pond water is often high in nutrients.

- Lakes are larger and deeper than ponds.

- Sunlight penetrates into the top few feet of lake water. Deeper water is dark and cold.

Biodiversity

- Plants surround ponds and lake shores.

- Surface water in ponds and lakes contains plants, algae, and microscopic organisms that use sunlight for photosynthesis.

- Organisms living in shallow water near shorelines include cattails, reeds, insects, crayfish, frogs, fish, and turtles.

- Fewer organisms live in the deeper, colder water of lakes where there is little sunlight.

- Lake fish include perch, trout, bass, and walleye.

Smallmouth bass

 **Reading Check** Why do few organisms live in the deep water of lakes?

Human Impact

- Humans fill in ponds and lakes with sediment to create land for houses and other structures.

- Runoff from farms, gardens, and roads washes pollutants into ponds and lakes, disrupting food webs.

Key Concept Check How do ponds and lakes differ?

Common loon

Some types of aquatic ecosystems have mostly shallow water. **Wetlands** *are aquatic ecosystems that have a thin layer of water covering soil that is wet most of the time.* Wetlands contain freshwater, salt water, or both. They are among Earth's most fertile ecosystems.

- Freshwater wetlands form at the edges of lakes and ponds and in low areas on land. Saltwater wetlands form along ocean coasts.

- Nutrient levels and biodiversity are high.

- Wetlands trap sediments and purify water. Plants and micro-scopic organisms filter out pollution and waste materials.

Biodiversity

- Water-tolerant plants include grasses and cattails. Few trees live in saltwater wetlands. Trees in freshwater wetlands include cottonwoods, willows, and swamp oaks.

- Insects are abundant and include flies, mosquitoes, dragon-flies, and butterflies.

- More than one-third of North American bird species, includ-ing ducks, geese, herons, loons, warblers, and egrets, use wet-lands for nesting and feeding.

- Other animals that depend on wetlands for food and breed-ing grounds include alligators, turtles, frogs, snakes, sala-manders, muskrats, and beavers.

Human Impact

- In the past, many people considered wetlands as unimport-ant environments. Water was drained away to build homes and roads and to raise crops.

- Today, many wetlands are being preserved, and drained wet-lands are being restored.

 Key Concept Check How do humans impact wetlands?

Estuaries

Estuaries (ES chuh wer eez) *are regions along coastlines where streams or rivers flow into a body of salt water.* Most estuaries form along coastlines, where freshwater in rivers meets salt water in oceans. Estuary ecosystems have varying degrees of salinity.

- Salinity depends on rainfall, the amount of freshwater flowing from land, and the amount of salt water pushed in by tides.

- Estuaries help protect coastal land from flooding and erosion. Like wetlands, estuaries purify water and filter out pollution.

- Nutrient levels and biodiversity are high.

Biodiversity

- Plants that grow in salt water include mangroves, pickleweeds, and seagrasses.

- Animals include worms, snails, and many species that people use for food, including oysters, shrimp, crabs, and clams.

- Striped bass, salmon, flounder, and many other ocean fish lay their eggs in estuaries.

- Many species of birds depend on estuaries for breeding, nesting, and feeding.

Human Impact

- Large portions of estuaries have been filled with soil to make land for roads and buildings.

- Destruction of estuaries reduces habitat for estuary species and exposes the coastline to flooding and storm damage.

WORD ORIGIN ·

estuary
from Latin *aestuarium*, means "a tidal marsh or opening."

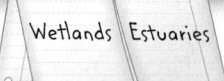

FOLDABLES®

Make a horizontal two-tab book and label it as shown. Use it to compare how biodiversity and human impact differ in wetlands and estuaries.

Wetlands | Estuaries

Harvest mouse

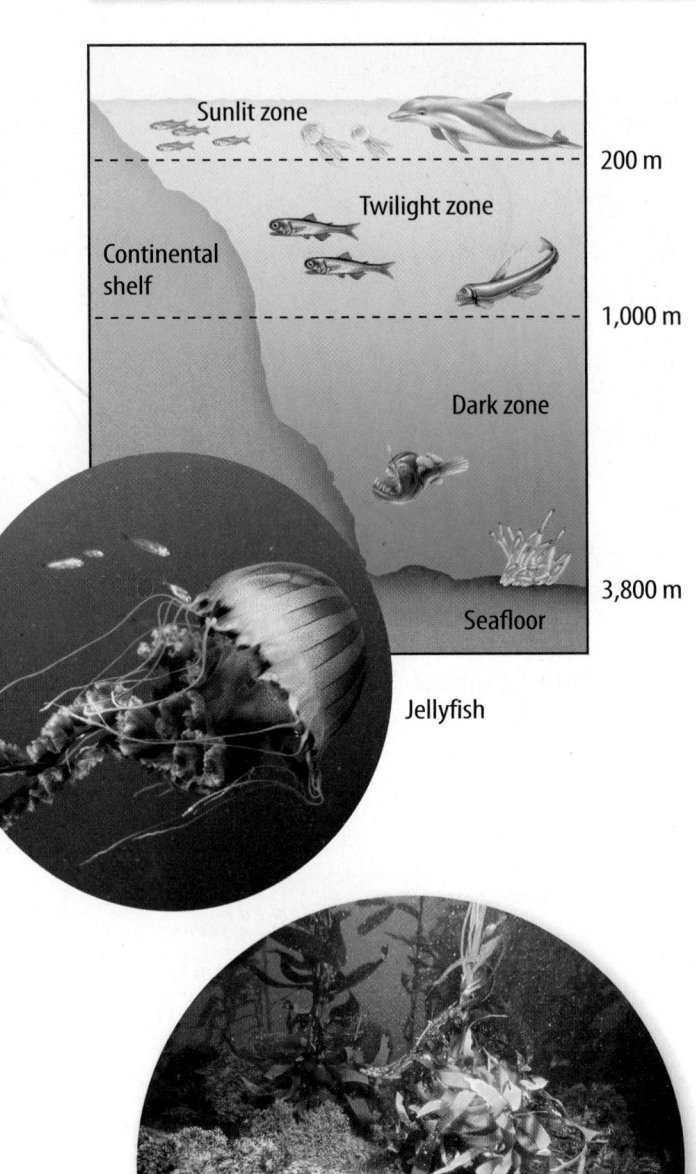

Sunlit zone

200 m

Twilight zone

Continental shelf

1,000 m

Dark zone

3,800 m

Seafloor

Jellyfish

Fur seal

Most of Earth's surface is covered by ocean water with high salinity. The oceans contain different types of ecosystems. If you took a boat trip several kilometers out to sea, you would be in the open ocean—one type of ocean ecosystem. The open ocean extends from the steep edges of continental shelves to the deepest parts of the ocean. The amount of light in the water depends on depth.

- Photosynthesis can take place only in the uppermost, or sunlit, zone. Very little sunlight reaches the twilight zone. None reaches the deepest water, known as the dark zone.

- Decaying matter and nutrients float down from the sunlit zone, through the twilight and dark zones, to the seafloor.

Biodiversity

- Microscopic algae and other producers in the sunlit zone form the base of most ocean food chains. Other organisms living in the sunlit zone are jellyfish, tuna, mackerel, and dolphins.

- Many species of fish stay in the twilight zone during the day and swim to the sunlit zone at night to feed.

- Sea cucumbers, brittle stars, and other bottom-dwelling organisms feed on decaying matter that drifts down from above.

- Many organisms in the dark zone live near cracks in the seafloor where lava erupts and new seafloor forms.

Reading Check Which organisms are at the base of most ocean food chains?

Human Impact

- Overfishing threatens many ocean fish.

- Trash discarded from ocean vessels or washed into oceans from land is a source of pollution. Animals such as seals become tangled in plastic or mistake it for food.

Ocean: Coastal Oceans

Coastal oceans include several types of ecosystems, including continental shelves and intertidal zones. *The **intertidal zone** is the ocean shore between the lowest low tide and the highest high tide.*

- Sunlight reaches the bottom of shallow coastal ecosystems.

- Nutrients washed in from rivers and streams contribute to high biodiversity.

Biodiversity

- The coastal ocean is home to mussels, fish, crabs, sea stars, dolphins, and whales.

- Intertidal species have adaptations for surviving exposure to air during low tides and to heavy waves during high tides.

Human Impact

- Oil spills and other pollution harm coastal organisms.

Ocean: Coral Reefs

Another ocean ecosystem with high biodiversity is the coral reef. *A **coral reef** is an underwater structure made from outside skeletons of tiny, soft-bodied animals called coral.*

- Most coral reefs form in shallow tropical oceans.

- Coral reefs protect coastlines from storm damage and erosion.

Biodiversity

- Coral reefs provide food and shelter for many animals, including parrotfish, groupers, angelfish, eels, shrimp, crabs, scallops, clams, worms, and snails.

Human Impact

- Pollution, overfishing, and harvesting of coral threaten coral reefs.

Sea stars

Inquiry MiniLab
15 minutes

How do ocean ecosystems differ?

Ocean ecosystems include open oceans, coastal oceans, and coral reefs—each one a unique environment with distinctive organisms.

1. Read and complete a lab safety form.

2. In a **large plastic tub,** use **rocks** and **sand** to make a structure representing an open ocean, a coastal ocean, or a coral reef.

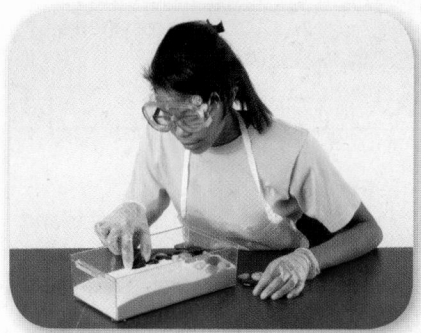

3. Fill the tub with **water.**

4. Make waves by gently moving your hand back and forth in the water.

Analyze and Conclude

1. **Observe** What happened to your structure when you made waves? How might a hurricane affect the organisms that live in the ecosystem you modeled?

2. **Key Concept** Compare your results with results of those who modeled other ecosystems. Suggest what adaptations species might have in each ecosystem.

Grouper

Lesson 2 Review

Visual Summary

Freshwater ecosystems include ponds and lakes.

Wetlands can be saltwater ecosystems or freshwater ecosystems.

Coral reefs and coastal ecosystems have high levels of biodiversity.

FOLDABLES®

Use your lesson Foldable to review the lesson. Save your Foldable for the project at the end of the chapter.

What do you think **NOW?**

You first read the statements below at the beginning of the chapter.

3. Estuaries do not protect coastal areas from erosion.

4. Animals form coral reefs.

Did you change your mind about whether you agree or disagree with the statements? Rewrite any false statements to make them true.

Use Vocabulary

1. **Define** the term *salinity*.

2. **Distinguish** between a wetland and an estuary.

3. An ocean ecosystem formed from the skeletons of animals is a(n) _____.

Understand Key Concepts

4. Which ecosystem contains both salt water and freshwater?
   - **A.** estuary
   - **B.** lake
   - **C.** pond
   - **D.** stream

5. **Describe** what might happen to a coastal area if its estuary were filled in to build houses.

Interpret Graphics

6. **Describe** Copy the drawing to the right and label the light zones. Describe characteristics of each zone.

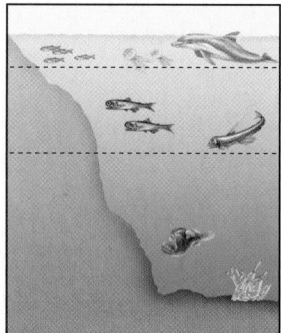

Critical Thinking

7. **Recommend** actions people might take to prevent pollutants from entering coastal ecosystems.

Math Skills

— Math Practice —

8. The salinity of the Baltic Sea is about 10 PPT. What weight of salt is present in 2,000 g of its seawater?

Saving an Underwater Wilderness

A researcher takes a water sample from a marine reserve. ▼

How do scientists help protect coral reefs?

Pollution and human activities, such as mining and tourism, have damaged many ecosystems, including coral reefs. Scientists and conservation groups are working together to help protect and restore coral reefs and areas that surround them. One way is to create marine reserves where no fishing or collection of organisms is allowed.

A team of scientists, including marine ecologists Dr. Dan Brumbaugh and Kate Holmes from the American Museum of Natural History, are investigating how well reserves are working. These scientists compare how many fish of one species live both inside and outside reserves. Their results indicate that more species of fish and greater numbers of each species live inside reserves than outside—one sign that reefs in the area are improving.

Reef ecosystems do not have to be part of a reserve in order to improve, however. Scientists can work with local governments to find ways to limit damage to reef ecosystems. One way is to prevent overfishing by limiting the number of fish caught. Other ways include eliminating the use of destructive fishing practices that can harm reefs and reducing runoff from farms and factories.

By creating marine reserves, regulating fishing practices, and reducing runoff, humans can help reefs that were once in danger become healthy again.

Kate Holmes examines a coral reef. ▶

It's Your Turn

WRITE Write a persuasive essay to a town near a marine reserve describing why coral reefs are important habitats.

AMERICAN MUSEUM OF NATURAL HISTORY

How Ecosystems Change

Reading Guide

Key Concepts 🔑
ESSENTIAL QUESTIONS

- How do land ecosystems change over time?
- How do aquatic ecosystems change over time?

Vocabulary

ecological succession p. 797

climax community p. 797

pioneer species p. 798

eutrophication p. 800

 Multilingual eGlossary

 Video

- Science Video
- What's Science Got to do With It?

Inquiry How did this happen?

This object was once part of a mining system used to move copper and iron ore. Today, so many forest plants have grown around it that it is barely recognizable. How do you think this happened? What do you think this object will look like after 500 more years?

How do communities change?

An ecosystem can change over time. Change usually happens so gradually that you might not notice differences from day to day.

❶ Your teacher has given you **two pictures of ecosystem communities.** One is labeled *A* and the other is labeled *B*.

❷ Imagine community A changed and became like community B. On a blank piece of **paper**, draw what you think community A might look like midway in its change to becoming like community B.

Think About This

1. What changes did you imagine? How long do you think it would take for community A to become like community B?

2. 🔑 **Key Concept** Summarize the changes you think would happen as the community changed from A to B.

How Land Ecosystems Change

Have you ever seen weeds growing up through cracks in a concrete sidewalk? If they were not removed, the weeds would keep growing. The crack would widen, making room for more weeds. Over time, the sidewalk would break apart. Shrubs and vines would move in. Their leaves and branches would grow large enough to cover the concrete. Eventually, trees could start growing there.

This process is an example of **ecological succession**—*the process of one ecological community gradually changing into another.* Ecological succession occurs in a series of steps. These steps can usually be predicted. For example, small plants usually grow first. Larger plants, such as trees, usually grow last.

The final stage of ecological succession in a land ecosystem is a **climax community**—*a stable community that no longer goes through major ecological changes.* Climax communities differ depending on the type of biome they are in. In a tropical forest biome, a climax community would be a mature tropical forest. In a grassland biome, a climax community would be a mature grassland. Climax communities are usually stable over hundreds of years. As plants in a climax community die, new plants of the same species grow and take their places. The community will continue to contain the same kinds of plants as long as the climate remains the same.

🔑 **Key Concept Check** What is a climax community?

FOLDABLES

Fold a sheet of paper into fourths. Use two sections on one side of the paper to describe and illustrate what land might look like before secondary succession and the other side to describe and illustrate the land after secondary succession is complete.

REVIEW VOCABULARY ·······

community
all the organisms that live in one area at the same time

Primary Succession

What do you think happens to a lava-filled landscape when a volcanic eruption is over? As shown in **Figure 2,** volcanic lava eventually becomes new soil that supports plant growth. Ecological succession in new areas of land with little or no soil, such as on a lava flow, a sand dune, or exposed rock, is primary succession. *The first species that colonize new or undisturbed land are* **pioneer species.** The lichens and mosses in **Figure 2** are pioneer species.

Figure 2 Following a volcanic eruption, a landscape undergoes primary succession.

During a volcanic eruption, molten lava flows over the ground and into the water. After the eruption is over, the lava cools and hardens into bare rock.

Lichen spores carried on the wind settle on the rock. Lichens release acid that helps break down the rock and create soil. Lichens add nutrients to the soil as they die and decay.

Airborne spores from mosses and ferns settle onto the thin soil and add to the soil when they die. The soil gradually becomes thick enough to hold water. Insects and other small organisms move into the area.

After many years the soil is deep and has enough nutrients for grasses, wildflowers, shrubs, and trees. The new ecosystem provides habitats for many animals. Eventually, a climax community develops.

Secondary Succession

In areas where existing ecosystems have been disturbed or destroyed, secondary succession can occur. One example is forestland in New England that early colonists cleared hundreds of years ago. Some of the cleared land was not planted with crops. This land gradually grew back to a climax forest community of beech and maple trees, as illustrated in **Figure 3**.

 Reading Check Where does secondary succession occur?

Figure 3 When disturbed land grows back, secondary succession occurs.

Concepts in Motion

Animation

Settlers in New England cleared many acres of forests to create cropland. In places where people stopped planting crops, the forest began to grow back.

Seeds of grasses, wildflowers, and other plants quickly began to sprout and grow. Young shrubs and trees also started growing. These plants provided habitats for insects and other small animals, such as mice.

White pines and poplars were the first trees in the area to grow to their full height. They provided shade and protection to slower growing trees, such as beech and maple.

Eventually, a climax community of beech and maple trees developed. As older trees die, new beech and maple seedlings grow and replace them.

Aquatic succession begins with a body of water such as a pond.

Over time, sediments and decaying organisms build up and create soil. This soil fills the bottom of the pond or lake.

Eventually the pond or lake fills completely with soil and a land ecosystem develops.

Figure 4 The water in a pond is slowly replaced by soil. Eventually, land plants take over and the pond disappears.

How Freshwater Ecosystems Change

Like land ecosystems, freshwater ecosystems change over time in a natural, predictable process. This process is called aquatic succession.

Aquatic Succession

Aquatic succession is illustrated in **Figure 4.** Sediments carried by rainwater and streams accumulate on the bottoms of ponds, lakes, and wetlands. The decomposed remains of dead organisms add to the buildup of soil. As time passes, more and more soil accumulates. Eventually, so much soil has collected that the water disappears and the area becomes land.

 Key Concept Check What happens to a pond, a lake, or a wetland over time?

Eutrophication

As decaying organisms fall to the bottom of a pond, a lake, or a wetland, they add nutrients to the water. **Eutrophication** (yoo troh fuh KAY shun) *is the process of a body of water becoming nutrient-rich.*

Eutrophication is a natural part of aquatic succession. However, humans also contribute to eutrophication. The fertilizers that farmers use on crops and the waste from farm animals can be very high in nutrients. So can other forms of pollution. When fertilizers and pollution run off into a pond or lake, nutrient concentrations increase. High nutrient levels support large populations of algae and other microscopic organisms. These organisms use most of the dissolved oxygen in the water and less oxygen is available for fish and other pond or lake organisms. As a result, many of these organisms die. Their bodies decay and add to the buildup of soil, speeding up succession.

WORD ORIGIN

eutrophication
from Greek *eutrophos,* means "nourishing"

Lesson 3 Review

Visual Summary

Ecosystems change in predictable ways through ecological succession.

The final stage of ecological succession in a land ecosystem is a climax community.

The final stage of aquatic succession is a land ecosystem.

FOLDABLES

Use your lesson Foldable to review the lesson. Save your Foldable for the project at the end of the chapter.

What do you think NOW?

You first read the statements below at the beginning of the chapter.

5. An ecosystem never changes.

6. Nothing grows in the area where a volcano has erupted.

Did you change your mind about whether you agree or disagree with the statements? Rewrite any false statements to make them true.

Use Vocabulary

1 **Define** *pioneer species* in your own words.

2 The process of one ecological community changing into another is _____.

3 **Compare and contrast** succession and eutrophication in freshwater ecosystems.

Understand Key Concepts

4 **Draw** a picture of what your school might look like in 500 years if it were abandoned.

5 Which process occurs after a forest fire?
  A. eutrophication
  B. photosynthesis
  C. primary succession
  D. secondary succession

Interpret Graphics

6 **Determine** What kind of succession—primary or secondary—might occur in the environment pictured to the right? Explain.

7 **Summarize Information** Copy the graphic organizer below and fill it with the types of succession an ecosystem can go through.

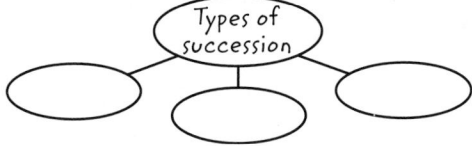

Critical Thinking

8 **Reflect** What kinds of abiotic factors might cause a grassland climax community to slowly become a forest?

9 **Recommend** actions people can take to help prevent the loss of wetland and estuary habitats.

A Biome for Radishes

Materials

paper towels

small jar

plastic wrap

jar lid

radish seeds

desk lamp

magnifying lens

Safety

Biomes contain plant and animal species adapted to particular climate conditions. Many organisms can live only in one type of biome. Others can survive in more than one biome. A radish is a plant grown around the world. How do you think radish seeds grow in different biomes? In this lab, you will model four different biomes and ecosystems—a temperate deciduous forest, a temperate rain forest, a desert, and a pond—and determine which biome the radishes grow best in.

Ask a Question

Which biome do radishes grow best in?

Make Observations

1. Read and complete a lab safety form.

2. Fold two pieces of paper towel lengthwise. Place the paper towels on opposite sides of the top of a small jar, as shown, with one end of each towel inside the jar and one end outside. Add water until about 10 cm of the paper towels are in the water. The area inside the jar models a pond ecosystem.

3. Place a piece of plastic wrap loosely over the end of one of the paper towels hanging over the jar's edge. Do not completely cover the paper towel. This paper towel models a temperate rain forest ecosystem. The paper towel without plastic wrap models a temperate deciduous forest.

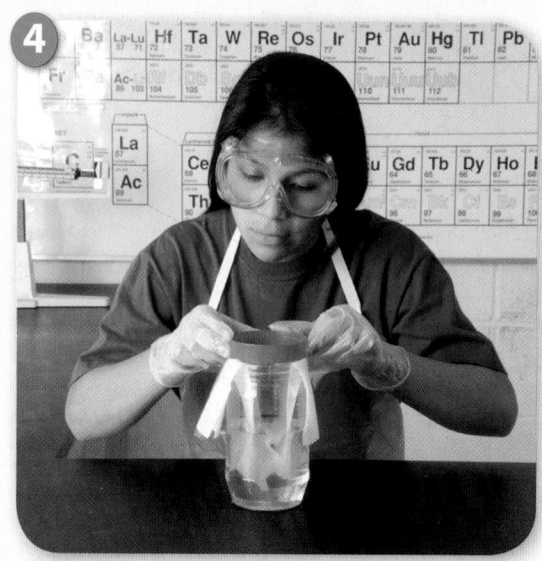

4. Place the jar lid upside-down on the top of the jar. The area in the lid models a desert.

Form a Hypothesis

5. Observe the four biomes and ecosystems you have modeled. Based on your observations and your knowledge of the abiotic factors a plant requires, hypothesize which biome or ecosystem you think radish seeds will grow best in.

By permission of TOPS Learning Systems, www.topscience.org.

Test Your Hypothesis

6 Place three radish seeds in each biome: pond, temperate forest, temperate rain forest, and desert. Gently press the seeds to the paper towel until they stick.

7 Place your jar near a window or under a desk lamp that can be turned on during the day.

8 In your Science Journal, record your observations of the seeds and the paper towel.

9 After five days, use a magnifying lens to observe the seeds and the paper towels again. Record your observations.

Analyze and Conclude

10 **Compare and Contrast** How did the appearance of the seeds change after five days in each model biome?

11 **Critique** Evaluate your hypothesis. Did the seeds grow the way you expected? In which biome did the seeds grow the most?

12 **The Big Idea** In the biome with the most growth, what characteristics do you think made the seeds grow best?

Lab Tips

☑ Do not eat the radish seeds.

☑ If your seeds fall off the paper towel strips, do not replace them.

Communicate Your Results

Working in a group of three or four, create a table showing results for each biome. Present the table to the class.

Inquiry Extension

In this lab, you determined which biome produced the most growth of radish seeds. Seeds of different species might sprout in several different biomes. However, not all sprouted seeds grow to adulthood. Design a lab to test what conditions are necessary for radishes to grow to adulthood.

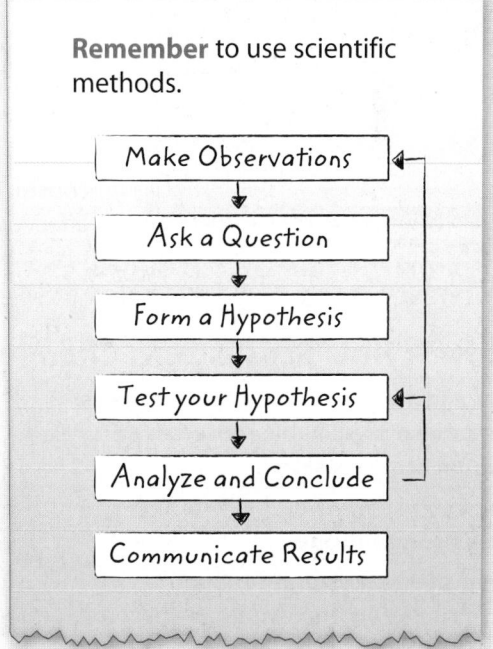

Remember to use scientific methods.

Make Observations
↓
Ask a Question
↓
Form a Hypothesis
↓
Test your Hypothesis
↓
Analyze and Conclude
↓
Communicate Results

Chapter 22 Study Guide

 **THE BIG IDEA** Each of Earth's land biomes and aquatic ecosystems is characterized by distinct environments and organisms. Biomes and ecosystems change by natural processes of ecological succession and by human activities.

Key Concepts Summary

Lesson 1: Land Biomes

- Each land **biome** has a distinct climate and contains animals and plants well adapted to the environment. Biomes include **deserts**, **grasslands**, tropical rain forests, **temperate** rain forests, deciduous forests, **taigas**, and **tundras.**

- Humans affect land biomes through agriculture, construction, and other activities.

Lesson 2: Aquatic Ecosystems

- Earth's aquatic ecosystems include freshwater and saltwater ecosystems. **Wetlands** can contain either salt water or freshwater. The **salinity** of **estuaries** varies.

- Human activities such as construction and fishing can affect aquatic ecosystems.

Lesson 3: How Ecosystems Change

- Land and aquatic ecosystems change over time in predictable processes of **ecological succession.**

- Land ecosystems eventually form **climax communities.**

- Freshwater ecosystems undergo **eutrophication** and eventually become land ecosystems.

Vocabulary

biome p. 777
desert p. 778
grassland p. 779
temperate p. 781
taiga p. 783
tundra p. 783

salinity p. 787
wetland p. 790
estuary p. 791
intertidal zone p. 793
coral reef p. 793

ecological succession p. 797
climax community p. 797
pioneer species p. 798
eutrophication p. 800

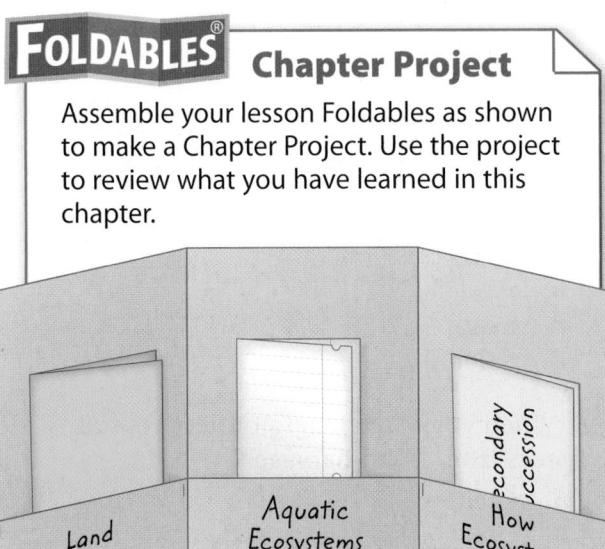
FOLDABLES® Chapter Project

Assemble your lesson Foldables as shown to make a Chapter Project. Use the project to review what you have learned in this chapter.

Land Biomes

Aquatic Ecosystems

How Ecosystems Change

Secondary Succession

Use Vocabulary

Choose the vocabulary word that fits each description.

1 group of ecosystems with similar climate

2 area between the tropics and the polar circles

3 land biome with a layer of permafrost

4 the amount of salt dissolved in water

5 area where a river empties into an ocean

6 coastal zone between the highest high tide and the lowest low tide

7 process of one ecological community gradually changing into another

8 a stable community that no longer goes through major changes

9 the first species to grow on new or disturbed land

Link Vocabulary and Key Concepts

Concepts in Motion Interactive Concept Map

Copy this concept map, and then use vocabulary terms from the previous page and other terms from this chapter to complete the concept map.

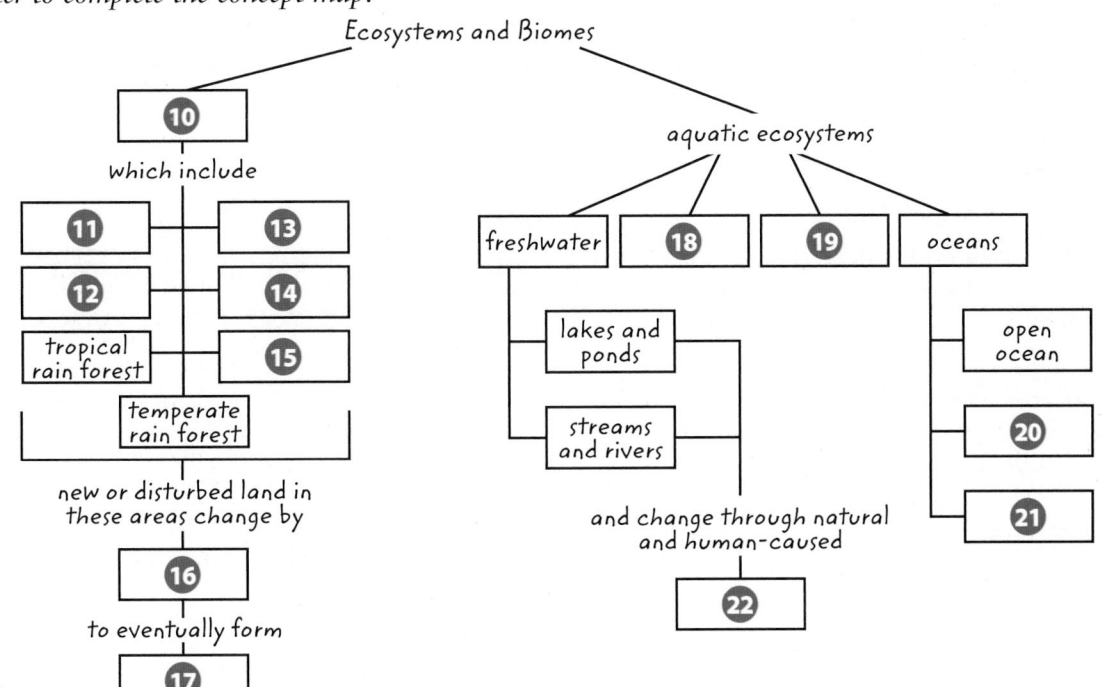

Ecosystems and Biomes

10

which include

11 **13**

12 **14**

tropical rain forest **15**

temperate rain forest

new or disturbed land in these areas change by

16

to eventually form

17

aquatic ecosystems

freshwater **18** **19** oceans

lakes and ponds

streams and rivers

and change through natural and human-caused

22

open ocean

20

21

Understand Key Concepts 🔑

1. Where would you find plants with stems that can store large amounts of water?
   A. desert
   B. grassland
   C. taiga
   D. tundra

2. What does the pink area on the map below represent?

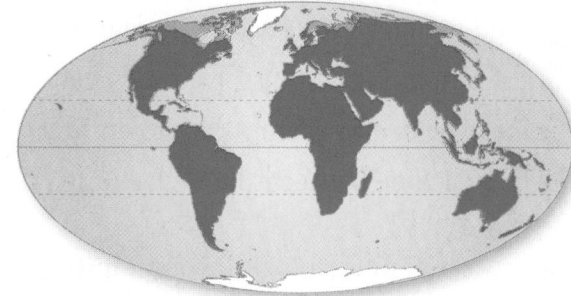

   A. taiga
   B. tundra
   C. temperate deciduous forest
   D. temperate rain forest

3. Where would you find trees that have no leaves during the winter?
   A. estuary
   B. tundra
   C. temperate deciduous forest
   D. temperate rain forest

4. Which biomes have rich, fertile soil?
   A. grassland and taiga
   B. grassland and tundra
   C. grassland and tropical rain forest
   D. grassland and temperate deciduous forest

5. Which is NOT a freshwater ecosystem?
   A. oceans
   B. ponds
   C. rivers
   D. streams

6. Where would you find species adapted to withstand strong wave action?
   A. estuaries
   B. wetlands
   C. intertidal zone
   D. twilight zone

7. Which ecosystem has flowing water?
   A. estuary
   B. lake
   C. stream
   D. wetland

8. Which ecosystems help protect coastal areas from flood damage?
   A. estuaries
   B. ponds
   C. rivers
   D. streams

9. Which organism below would be the first to grow in an area that has been buried in lava?

   A. A
   B. B
   C. C
   D. D

10. What is a forest called that has had the same species of trees for 200 years?
    A. climax community
    B. pioneer species
    C. primary succession
    D. secondary succession

11. What is eutrophication?
    A. decreasing nutrients
    B. decreasing salinity
    C. increasing nutrients
    D. increasing salinity

Critical Thinking

12 **Compare** mammals that live in tundra biomes with those that live in desert biomes. What adaptations does each group have that help them survive?

13 **Analyze** You are invited to go on a trip to South America. Before you leave, you read a travel guide that says the country you will be visiting has hot summers, cold winters, and many wheat farms. What biome will you be visiting? Explain your reasoning.

14 **Contrast** How are ecosystems in the deep water of lakes and oceans different?

15 **Analyze** Which type of ocean ecosystem is likely to have the highest levels of dissolved oxygen? Why?

16 **Hypothesize** Why are the first plants that appear in primary succession small?

17 **Interpret Graphics** The following climate data were recorded for a forest ecosystem. To which biome does this ecosystem likely belong?

Climate Data	June	July	August
Average temperature (°C)	16.0	16.5	17.0
Average rainfall (cm)	3.0	2.0	2.0

Writing in Science

18 **Write** a paragraph explaining the succession process that might occur in a small pond on a cow pasture. Include a main idea, supporting details, and concluding sentence.

REVIEW THE BIG IDEA

19 Earth contains a wide variety of organisms that live in different conditions. How do Earth's biomes and ecosystems differ?

20 The photo below shows Biosphere 2, built in Arizona as an artificial Earth. Imagine that you have been asked to build a biome of your choice for Biosphere 3. What biotic and abiotic features should you consider?

Math Skills

Review

— Math Practice —

Use Proportions

21 At its highest salinity, the water in Utah's Great Salt Lake contained about 14.5 g of salt in 50 g of lake water. What was the salinity of the lake?

22 The seawater in Puget Sound off the coast of Oregon has a salinity of about 24 PPT. What weight of salt is there in 1,000 g of seawater?

Record your answers on the answer sheet provided by your teacher or on a sheet of paper.

Multiple Choice

1 Which aquatic ecosystem contains a mixture of freshwater and salt water?

   A coral reef

   B estuary

   C pond

   D river

Use the diagram below to answer question 2.

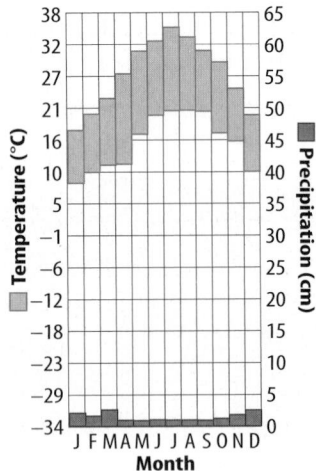

2 The diagram above most likely illustrates the climate of which biome?

   A desert

   B grassland

   C tropical rain forest

   D tundra

3 Which occurs during the first stage of ecological succession?

   A eutrophication

   B settlement

   C development of climax community

   D growth of pioneer species

4 Which biome has lost more than half its trees to logging activity?

   A grassland

   B taiga

   C temperate deciduous forest

   D tropical rain forest

Use the diagram below to answer question 5.

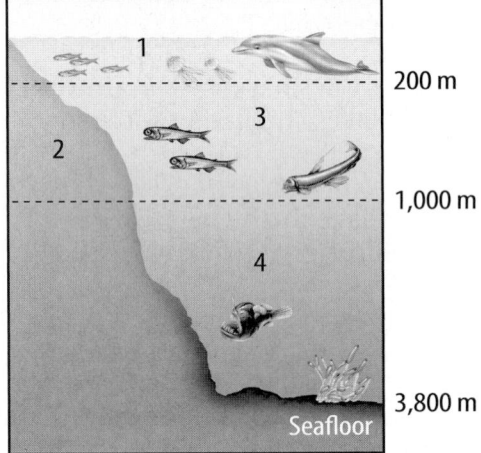

5 In the diagram above, where might you find microscopic photosynthetic organisms?

   A 1

   B 2

   C 3

   D 4

6 During aquatic succession, freshwater ponds

   A become saltwater ponds.

   B fill with soil.

   C gain organisms.

   D increase in depth.

Use the diagram below to answer question 7.

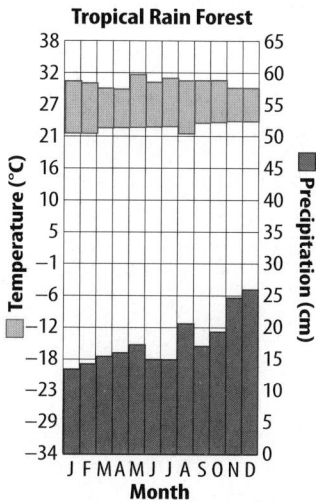

7 Based on the diagram above, which is true of the tropical rain forest biome?

   A Precipitation increases as temperatures rise.

   B Rainfall is greatest mid-year.

   C Temperatures rise at year-end.

   D Temperatures vary less than rainfall amounts.

8 Which aquatic biome typically has many varieties of nesting ducks, geese, herons, and egrets?

   A coral reefs

   B intertidal zones

   C lakes

   D wetlands

Constructed Response

Use the table below to answer questions 9 and 10.

Land Biome	Climate and Plant Life	Location
Desert		
Grassland		
Taiga		
Temperate deciduous forest		
Temperate rain forest		
Tropical rain forest		
Tundra		

9 Briefly describe the characteristics of Earth's seven land biomes. List one example of each biome, including its location.

10 How does human activity affect each land biome?

Use the table below to answer question 11.

Aquatic Ecosystem	Aquatic Animal
Coastal ocean	
Coral reefs	
Estuaries	
Lakes and ponds	
Open ocean	

11 Complete the table above with the name of an aquatic animal that lives in each of Earth's aquatic ecosystems.

NEED EXTRA HELP?											
If You Missed Question...	1	2	3	4	5	6	7	8	9	10	11
Go to Lesson...	2	1	2	3	2	2	2	2	1	1	

Using Natural Resources

THE BIG IDEA How can people protect Earth's resources?

Inquiry A Typical Day at Work?

These technicians are working on a wind farm off the coast of Denmark. Wind energy meets about 20 percent of Denmark's energy needs.

- How do you think wind energy works?
- What might be some advantages of using wind as an energy source?
- What might be some disadvantages?
- How can people protect Earth's resources?

Get Ready to Read

What do you think?

Before you read, decide if you agree or disagree with each of these statements. As you read this chapter, see if you change your mind about any of the statements.

1. The world's supply of coal will never run out.

2. You should include minerals in your diet.

3. Global warming causes acid rain.

4. Smog can affect human health.

5. Oil left over from frying potatoes can be used as automobile fuel.

6. Hybrid electric vehicles cannot travel far or go fast.

ConnectED Your one-stop online resource

connectED.mcgraw-hill.com

- Video
- WebQuest
- Audio
- Assessment
- Review
- Concepts in Motion
- ? Inquiry
- g Multilingual eGlossary

Lesson 1

Reading Guide

Key Concepts 🔑

ESSENTIAL QUESTIONS

- What are natural resources?
- How do the three types of natural resources differ?

Vocabulary

natural resource p. 813
nonrenewable resource p. 814
renewable resource p. 816
inexhaustible resource p. 818
geothermal energy p. 819

 Multilingual eGlossary

 Video BrainPOP®

Earth's Resources

Inquiry A River in the Desert?

People in dry areas sometimes build structures such as this aqueduct to carry water to their cities. Why do you think water is such an important resource? Do you think Earth's supply of water will ever run out?

Where does it come from?

Almost everything you use comes from natural resources, or materials that come from the environment. Can you identify the natural resources used to make a common object?

1. Read and complete a lab safety form.

2. Choose a common **object** from around your classroom or in your backpack.

3. Create a data table like the one below in your Science Journal. In the first column of your data table, list the object you will investigate.

4. In the second column, determine all the natural resources required to make the object. The example table shown here lists some natural resources used to make a pencil.

Natural Resources in a Pencil	
Object	Natural Resources Required
Pencil	1. wood
	2. graphite
	3.
	4.

Think About This

1. Which natural resource was hardest to identify? How did you figure it out?

2. Compare your data table to a classmate's. Which natural resources were on both lists?

3. **Key Concept** What type of natural resource was most common? Why might this be?

Natural Resources

You walk into a room and switch on a light. Where does the electricity to power the light come from? It might come from a power plant that burns coal or natural gas. Or, it might come from rooftop solar panels made with silicon, a mineral found in sand.

The smallest microbe and the largest whale both rely on materials and energy from the environment. The same is true for humans. People depend on the environment for food, clothing, and fuels to heat and light their homes. *Parts of the environment that supply materials useful or necessary for the survival of living things are called* **natural resources.** Natural resources include land, air, minerals, and fuels. The trees and water in **Figure 1** also are natural resources.

 Key Concept Check What are natural resources?

Figure 1 All parts of the environment that are important to living things are natural resources.

Nonrenewable Resources

How often do you travel in a vehicle that runs on gasoline? Do you drink soda from aluminum cans or sip water from plastic bottles? Gasoline, aluminum, and plastic are made from nonrenewable resources.

Nonrenewable resources *are natural resources that are being used up faster than they can be replaced by natural processes.* Nonrenewable resources form slowly, usually over thousands or millions of years. If they are used faster than they form, they will run out. Nonrenewable resources include fossil fuels and minerals.

 Reading Check What characteristic makes a resource nonrenewable?

Fossil Fuels

Fossil fuels include coal, oil, and natural gas. The fossil fuels we use today formed from the decayed remains of organisms that died millions of years ago. Although fossil fuels are forming all the time, we use them much more quickly than nature replaces them. Fossil fuels form underground. As shown in **Figure 2,** coal is mined from the ground. Oil and natural gas are drilled from the ground.

Fossil fuels are used primarily as sources of energy. Many electric power plants burn coal or natural gas to heat water and make steam that powers generators. Natural gas also is used to heat homes and businesses. Gasoline, jet fuel, diesel fuel, kerosene, and other fuels are made from oil. Most plastics also are made from oil.

FOLDABLES®

Make a small horizontal tri-fold book. Label it as shown. Use it to identify similarities and differences among the types of resources.

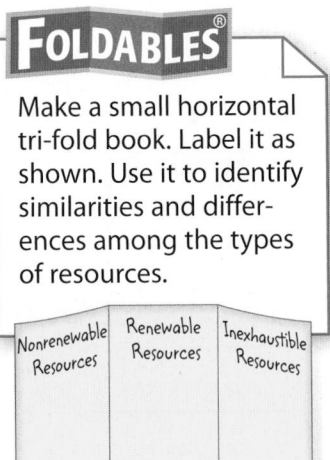

Nonrenewable Resources | Renewable Resources | Inexhaustible Resources

Figure 2 The black rock layer is a seam of coal. It formed from the decayed remains of trees, ferns, and other swamp plants that died 300–400 million years ago.

Uranium

((O)) **Concepts in Motion** Animation

Figure 3 Uranium is the fuel used to generate electricity in nuclear power plants.

✅ **Visual Check** What do you think is being emitted by the tower?

Minerals

Have you ever added fertilizer to a plant's soil? Fertilizers contain phosphorus and potassium, two minerals that promote plant growth. The human body also needs minerals for good health, including calcium and magnesium.

Minerals are nonliving substances found in Earth's crust. People use minerals for many purposes. Gypsum is used in wall board and cement. Silicon is important for the manufacture of computers and other electronic devices. Copper is used in electrical wiring.

Uranium is a mineral that can be used as a source of energy. In a nuclear power plant, such as the one shown in **Figure 3,** the nuclei of uranium atoms are split apart in a reaction known as nuclear fission. Some of the energy that held the nuclei together is released as heat, which is then used to boil water and produce steam to generate electricity.

Like fossil fuels, minerals are formed underground by geologic processes that take millions of years. For that reason, most minerals are considered nonrenewable. Some minerals, such as calcium, are plentiful. Others, such as large rubies, are rare.

✅ **Reading Check** Why are minerals nonrenewable?

Renewable Resources

Supplies of many natural resources are constantly renewed by natural cycles. The water cycle is an example. When liquid water evaporates, it rises into the **atmosphere** as water vapor. Water vapor condenses and falls back to the ground as rain or snow. Water is a renewable resource.

Renewable resources *are natural resources that can be replenished by natural processes at least as quickly as they are used.* These resources do not run out because they are replaced in a relatively short period of time. They include water, air, land, and living things.

Renewable resources are replenished by natural processes. Still, they must be used wisely. If people use any resource faster than it is replaced, it becomes nonrenewable. As shown in **Figure 4,** forests are sometimes nonrenewable resources.

 Reading Check In what way are renewable and nonrenewable resources similar?

Figure 4 Forests can be nonrenewable if trees are cut down faster than they can grow back.

Air

Did you know that plants produce almost all of the oxygen in the air we breathe? Oxygen is a product of photosynthesis. You might recall that photosynthesis is a series of chemical reactions in plants that use energy from light and produce sugars. Without plants, Earth's atmosphere would not contain enough oxygen to support most forms of life.

Air also contains carbon dioxide (CO_2), which plants need for photosynthesis. CO_2 is released into the air when dead plants and animals decay, when fossil fuels or wood are burned, and as a product of cellular respiration in plants and animals. Recall that cellular respiration is a series of chemical reactions that convert energy from food into a form usable by cells. Without CO_2, photosynthesis would not be possible.

Land

Fertile soil is an important resource. Topsoil is the upper layer of soil that contains most of the nutrients plants need. Gardeners know that topsoil can be replenished by the decay of plant material. The carbon, nitrogen, and other elements in the decomposing plants become available for the growth of new plants.

Topsoil can be classified as a renewable resource. However, if it is carried away by water or wind, it can take hundreds of years to rebuild.

Land resources also include wildlife and ecosystems, such as forests, grasslands, deserts, and coral reefs.

 Reading Check How is topsoil replenished by natural processes?

Water

Can you imagine a world without water? All organisms require water to live. People need a reliable supply of freshwater for drinking, washing, and irrigating crops. People also use water to run power plants and factories. Oceans, lakes, and rivers serve as major transportation routes and recreational areas. They are important habitats for many species, including some that people depend on for food.

Most of Earth's surface is covered by water. But only a small amount is freshwater that people can use, and this water must be cleaned before you can drink it. Freshwater is renewed through the water cycle, but the total amount of water on Earth always remains the same.

Has your community ever been asked to conserve water because of a drought? A drought can cause supplies of freshwater to run short. In many large cities, water is transported from hundreds of miles away to meet the needs of residents. In some parts of the world, people travel long distances every day to get the water they need.

 **MiniLab** **20 minutes**

How clean is the water?

Did you drink water or use water to wash today? Clean water is an important natural resource. It must be cleaned before it is used by people. Many water treatment plants clean water by passing it through a series of filtration steps.

1. Read and complete a lab safety form.
2. Obtain a cup of **dirty water.** Write a description of the water's appearance in a data table in your Science Journal.
3. Place a **funnel** in a **beaker.** Place a **paper towel** in the funnel. Pour the water through the paper towel. Record your observations in the table.
4. Repeat step 3, but use two layers of paper towels. Record your observations.
5. Repeat step 3, but use four layers of paper towels. Record your observations.

Step	Observations
Initial water	
1st filtration	
2nd filtration	
3rd filtration	

Analyze and Conclude

1. **Observe** How did the appearance of the water change with each filtration?

2. **Recommend** Do you think the water you produced in step 4 is clean enough to use in your home? Why or why not?

3. 🔑 **Key Concept** Summarize how people and other living things use water.

Inexhaustible Resources

An **inexhaustible resource** *is a natural resource that will not run out, no matter how much of it people use.* Energy from the Sun, solar energy, is inexhaustible. So is wind, which is generated by the Sun's uneven heating of Earth's lower atmosphere. Another inexhaustible resource is thermal energy from within Earth.

 Key Concept Check How do inexhaustible resources differ from renewable and nonrenewable resources?

Use Percentages

Converting a ratio to a percentage often makes it easier to visualize a set of numbers. For example, in 2007, 101.5 quadrillion units (quads) of energy were used in the United States. Of that, 6.813 quads were produced from renewable energy sources. What percentage of U.S. energy was produced from renewable energy sources?

Set up a ratio of the part over the whole.

$$\frac{6.813 \text{ quads}}{101.5 \text{ quads}}$$

Rewrite the fraction as a decimal.

$$\frac{6.813 \text{ quads}}{101.5 \text{ quads}} = 0.0671$$

Multiply by 100 and add %.

$$0.0671 \times 100 = 6.71\%$$

Practice

Of the 101.5 quads of energy used in 2007, 0.341 quads were from wind energy. What percentage of U.S. energy came from wind?

 **Review**

- **Math Practice**
- **Personal Tutor**

Solar Energy

Without heat and light from the Sun, life as it is on Earth would not be possible. If you've studied food chains, you know that energy from the Sun is used by plants and other producers during photosynthesis to make food. Consumers are organisms that get energy by eating producers or other consumers. The energy in food chains always is traced back to the Sun.

Solar energy can be harnessed for many uses. Greenhouses trap heat. They make it possible to grow warm-weather plants in cool climates. Solar cookers concentrate the Sun's heat to cook food. Large solar-power plants provide electricity to many homes. Solar energy also can be used to heat water for individual homes, as shown in **Figure 5.**

Energy from an Inexhaustible Resource 🔑

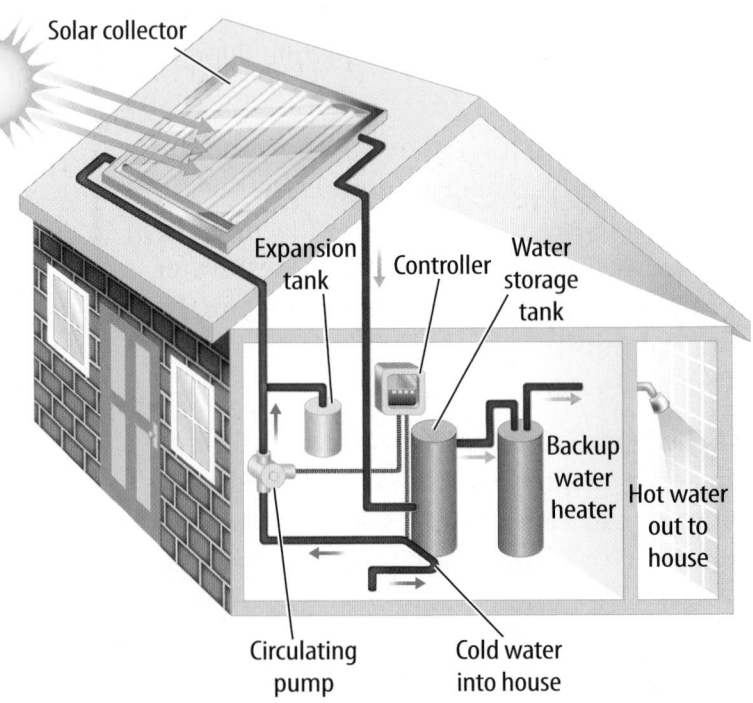

Figure 5 A solar water heater uses energy from the Sun to heat water. The hot water can be stored in a tank until it is needed.

🔵 **Visual Check** In which part of the system is water heated by the Sun?

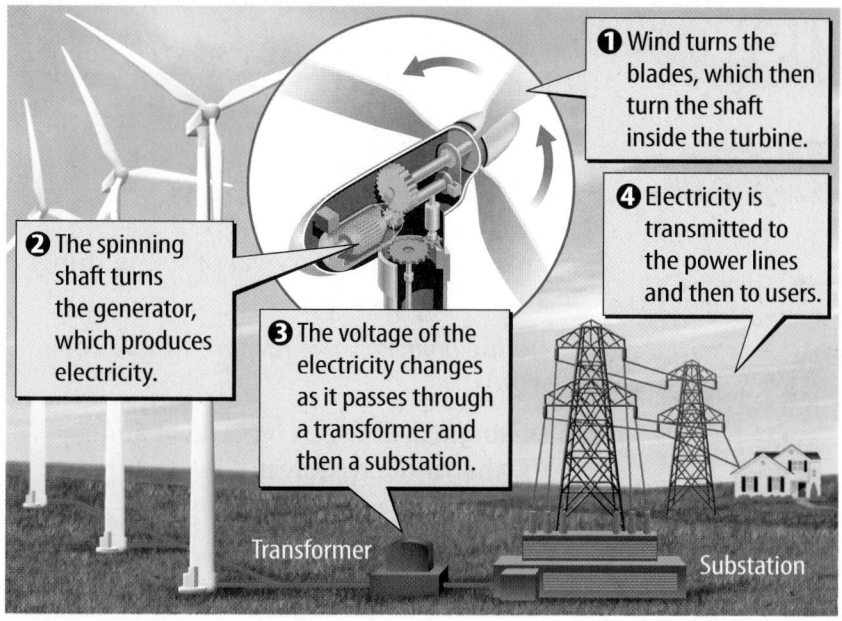

❶ Wind turns the blades, which then turn the shaft inside the turbine.

❷ The spinning shaft turns the generator, which produces electricity.

❸ The voltage of the electricity changes as it passes through a transformer and then a substation.

❹ Electricity is transmitted to the power lines and then to users.

Transformer   Substation

◀ **Figure 6** The wind spins the blades of a wind turbine, which in turn powers a generator that produces electricity.

☑ **Visual Check** What happens to the electricity as it passes through a transformer and a substation?

Wind Power

What do sailboats, kites, and windmills have in common? All are powered by wind—the movement of air over Earth's surface. Wind is an inexhaustible resource produced by the uneven heating of the atmosphere by the Sun.

If you live in an area with frequent, strong winds, you might have seen giant wind turbines. These turbines, such as the ones shown in **Figure 6,** can be used to produce electricity.

Geothermal Energy

Another inexhaustible resource is geothermal energy. **Geothermal energy** *is thermal energy from within Earth.* Pockets of molten rock, or magma, rise close to the surface of some parts of Earth's crust. The magma heats underground water and rocks. The heated water produces steam used to generate electricity. In California and other regions, geothermal energy produces electricity on a large scale, as shown in **Figure 7.**

WORD ORIGIN

geothermal
from Greek *geo-*, means "earth"; and Greek *therme*, means "heat"

Figure 7 Geothermal power plants use heat from within Earth to generate electricity. ▼

((◎)) **Concepts in Motion** **Animation**

Lesson 1 Review

Visual Summary

Living things depend on natural resources such as water, air, and land to meet their needs.

Water is considered a renewable resource.

Wind energy can be transformed into electricity.

FOLDABLES

Use your lesson Foldable to review the lesson. Save your Foldable for the project at the end of the chapter.

What do you think NOW?

You first read the statements below at the beginning of the chapter.

1. The world's supply of coal will never run out.

2. You should include minerals in your diet.

Did you change your mind about whether you agree or disagree with the statements? Rewrite any false statements to make them true.

Use Vocabulary

1 Parts of the environment that are important to the survival of living things are _____.

2 **Define** *nonrenewable resource* in your own words.

3 **Distinguish** between renewable and inexhaustible resources.

Understand Key Concepts

4 Which is a nonrenewable resource?
   A. freshwater   C. sunlight
   B. natural gas   D. wood

5 **Explain** why inexhaustible resources also could be considered renewable.

Interpret Graphics

6 **Identify** the natural resource the device below uses, and explain how it works.

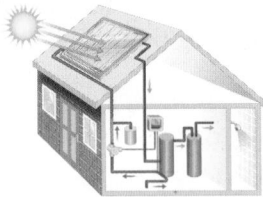

7 **Organize Information** Copy the graphic organizer below, and use it to list ways people use sunlight as a natural resource.

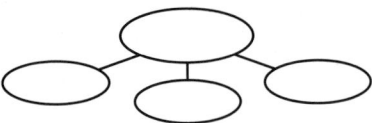

Critical Thinking

8 **Hypothesize** What measures could be taken on a farm to ensure that topsoil remains renewable?

Math Skills

Review
— Math Practice —

9 Of the 101.5 quads of energy used in 2007, only 0.081 quads were from solar energy. What percentage of U.S. energy came from solar energy?

Clean Energy from Underground

AMERICAN MUSEUM OF NATURAL HISTORY

Using Geothermal Energy to Heat—and Cool

Most of the energy we use comes from burning fossil fuels such as coal and oil. This releases carbon dioxide (CO_2) into the atmosphere, which causes global surface temperatures to rise. To lower CO_2 emissions, some people are switching to clean, renewable energy sources. One source is geothermal energy, thermal energy from inside Earth.

Geothermal Heat Pumps Even as the air cools in winter and warms in summer, temperatures a few meters below Earth's surface stay pretty much the same—around 13°C. Geothermal heat pumps use the temperature difference between air and ground to heat or cool buildings, depending on the season. A geothermal heat pump moves fluid through pipes from a building into the ground and then back again. In winter, the fluid carries thermal energy from the ground to warm the building. In summer, it moves thermal energy from the building to the ground and returns with cooler fluid. Each year, approximately 50,000 geothermal heat pumps are installed in the United States.

Outside air temperature less than 13°C

Warmed air circulates through the house.

Cooler air returns to furnace.

Warmed air circulates through the house.

Cooler air returns to furnace.

Fluid releases thermal energy to the circulating air.

Cold fluid enters ground pipes.

Ground temperature around 13°C

Fluid absorbs thermal energy from the warm ground and flows back into the house.

Geothermal Power Plants Geothermal energy also can produce electricity. At one time, geothermal power plants were located only near geysers and hot springs where geothermal energy is released near Earth's surface. Today, they can be almost anywhere. These plants pump water far underground where temperatures reach up to 200°C. The water boils, and the steam is captured and brought to the surface. The steam turns turbines, which run generators that produce electricity. And it's clean energy, too: geothermal plants release only 1 percent of the carbon dioxide that coal-burning power plants produce.

It's Your Turn

RESEARCH Geothermal heat pumps have been available since the 1940s. Why do you think more homes are not using them? Research this question, and write a short report about your findings.

Pollution

Reading Guide

Key Concepts 🔑
ESSENTIAL QUESTIONS

- How does pollution affect air resources?
- How does pollution affect water resources?
- How does pollution affect land resources?

Vocabulary

pollution p. 823

ozone layer p. 824

photochemical smog p. 824

global warming p. 825

acid precipitation p. 825

 Multilingual eGlossary

 Video

- BrainPOP®
- What's Science Got to do With It?

Inquiry Orange Drink?

Runoff from a mine turned the water in this stream orange. How do you think the runoff affects the organisms that live in the stream? How do you think it affects the organisms that rely on the stream as a source of freshwater?

How do air pollutants move?

Small particles of pollutants can be transported by air movement. Once a pollutant is in the air, how far can it travel?

1. Read and complete a lab safety form.
2. Use a **tape measure** to determine the distance from your desk to the **lab candle.** Record your measurement in your Science Journal.
3. As soon as your teacher blows out the candle, start a **timer.**
4. Stop the timer when you smell the blown-out candle. Record the time in your Science Journal.

Think About This

1. Divide your distance from the lab candle by the time it took you to smell the blown-out candle. How fast did the smell move?

2. Compare your results with students in different parts of the room. Why do you think the speeds varied?

3. 🔑 **Key Concept** How do you think the movement of the smell from the blown-out candle is similar to the movement of a pollutant in the air?

What is pollution?

What happens when smoke gets in the air or toxic chemicals leak into soil? Smoke is a mixture of gases and tiny particles that make breathing difficult, especially for people who have health problems. Toxic chemicals that leak into soil can kill plants and soil organisms. These substances cause pollution. **Pollution** *is the contamination of the environment with substances that are harmful to life.* An example of pollution is shown in **Figure 8.** The oil-covered animals might not survive. Other wildlife also are affected negatively, including fish that people rely on for food.

Most pollution occurs because of human actions, such as burning fossil fuels or spilling toxic materials. However, pollution also can come from natural disasters. Wildfires create smoke. Volcanic eruptions send ash and toxic gases into the atmosphere. Regardless of its source, pollution affects air, water, and land resources.

Figure 8 Oil spills pollute water and harm wildlife.

Air Pollution

Many large cities issue alerts about air quality when air pollution levels are high. On such days, people are asked to avoid activities that contribute to air pollution, such as driving cars, using gasoline-powered lawn mowers, or cooking on charcoal grills. To avoid breathing problems, people also are advised to exercise in the early morning when the air is cleaner. Air pollution that can affect human health and recreational activities can be caused by ozone loss, photochemical smog, global warming, and acid precipitation.

Ozone Loss

Ozone is a molecule composed of three oxygen atoms. In the upper atmosphere, it forms a protective layer around Earth. *The **ozone layer** prevents most harmful ultraviolet (UV) radiation from reaching Earth.* UV radiation from the Sun can cause cancer and cataracts and can damage crops.

In the 1980s, scientists warned that Earth's protective ozone layer was getting thinner. The problem was caused primarily by chlorofluorocarbons (CFCs). CFCs are compounds used in refrigerators, air conditioners, and aerosol sprays. Governments around the world have phased out the use of CFCs and other ozone-depleting gases. As a result, the ozone layer is expected to recover within several decades.

Photochemical Smog

Sunlight reacts with waste gases from the burning of fossil fuels and forms a type of air pollution called **photochemical smog.** As shown in **Figure 9,** smog darkens the air and also can smell bad. It is formed of particles and gases that irritate the respiratory system. One of the gases in smog is ozone. In the upper atmosphere, ozone is helpful. But in the lower atmosphere, it is a pollutant that can harm organisms and cause lung damage.

FOLDABLES®

Make a horizontal three-tab book with a tab top. Label it as shown. Use it to explain the effects of pollution.

Effects of Pollution on...

| Air Resources | Water Resources | Land Resources |

WORD ORIGIN · · · · · · · · · ·

photochemical smog
from Greek *photo-*, means "light"; Latin *chemic*, means "alchemy"; and modern English *smog*, blend of "smoke" and "fog"

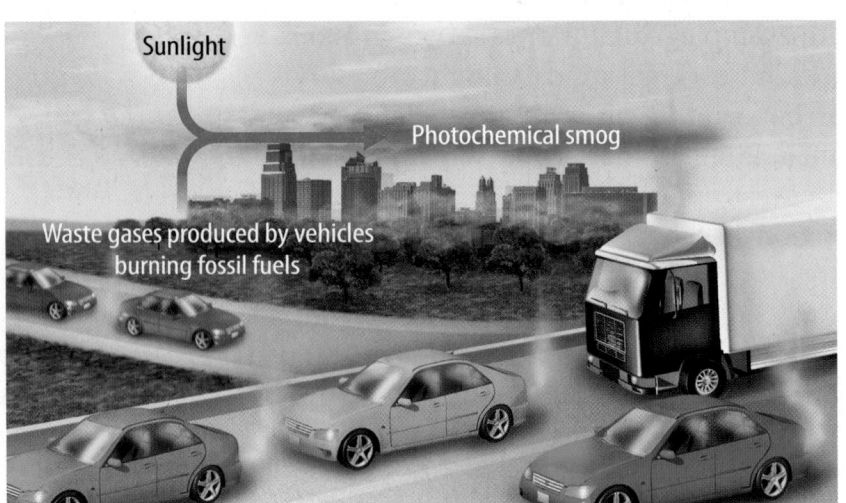

Figure 9 🔑
Photochemical smog can worsen throughout the day as chemicals continue to react with sunlight.

✓ **Visual Check** What activities contribute to the formation of smog?

Global Warming

You might have heard news reports about the melting of glaciers and sea ice. Earth is getting warmer. **Global warming** *is the scientific observation that Earth's average surface temperature is increasing.* Global warming can lead to climate change—changing weather conditions, changes to ecosystems and food webs, increases in the number and severity of floods and droughts, and increased coastal flooding as sea ice melts and sea level rises.

Data indicate that Earth's average surface temperature and increases in atmospheric carbon dioxide (CO_2) follow the same general trend. CO_2 is a greenhouse gas. This means it traps heat, helping to keep Earth warm. Greenhouse gases occur naturally. Without them, Earth would be too cold to support life. But human activities add greenhouse gases to the atmosphere, especially CO_2 from the burning of fossil fuels. Most scientists, including those on the United Nations Intergovernmental Panel on Climate Change, agree that increases in atmospheric CO_2 are contributing to global warming.

ACADEMIC VOCABULARY

occur
(verb) to appear or happen

Acid Precipitation

Gases produced by the burning of fossil fuels also create other forms of air pollution, including acid precipitation. **Acid precipitation** *is acidic rain or snow that forms when waste gases from automobiles and power plants combine with moisture in the air.* Coal-burning power plants produce sulfur dioxide gas that combines with moisture to form sulfuric acid. Cars and trucks produce nitrous oxide gases that form nitric acid. Acid precipitation pollutes soil and can kill plants, including trees, as shown in **Figure 10.** It also contributes to water pollution and can damage buildings.

Figure 10 Acid rain can harm soil organisms and plant roots.

Visual Check How did acid rain affect this ecosystem?

 Key Concept Check How does pollution affect air resources?

Review   Personal Tutor

How fast can you turn a sand castle into sediment?

Runoff can move sediment into streams. Sediment blocks stream flow, clogs the feeding structures of animals, and decreases the amount of light for aquatic plants. How does the flow of water affect rates of sedimentation?

1. Read and complete a lab safety form.

2. Use a **foam cup** to build a **sand** castle in a **plastic container.** Measure its height with a **metric ruler.** Record the data in your Science Journal.

3. Fill a **spray bottle** with water. Adjust the tip of the bottle so it sprays a mist.

4. Using a **timer,** spray your sand castle for 30 s. Measure and record the height of your sand castle.

5. Readjust the tip of the spray bottle so it sprays a stream of water. Then, rebuild your castle with fresh sand and repeat step 4.

6. Rebuild your sand castle with fresh sand. Poke three holes in the bottom of the foam cup with a **pencil.** Put your finger over the holes and fill the cup with water. Repeat step 4, letting water run out of the holes onto your castle.

Analyze and Conclude

1. **Evaluate** Which trial caused the largest change in the height of the sand castle?

2. **Model** What natural events could each of your trials represent?

3. **Key Concept** How might these natural events affect the quality of water resources?

Water Pollution

Have you ever seen a stream covered with thick green algae? The stream might have been polluted with fertilizers from nearby lawns or farms. It might contain chemicals from nearby factories. Water pollution can come from chemical runoff and other agricultural, residential, and industrial sources.

Wastewater

You might have been warned not to pour paint or used motor oil into storm drains. In most cities, rainwater that flows into storm drains goes directly into nearby waterways. Materials that go in the drain, including grease and oil washed from the street, can contribute to water pollution.

The wastewater that drains from showers, sinks, and toilets contains harmful viruses and bacteria. To safeguard health, this wastewater usually is purified in a sewage treatment plant before it is released into streams or used to irrigate crops. In some parts of the world, there is little or no sewage treatment. People might have to use polluted water.

Wastewater that comes from industries and mining operations also contains pollutants. It requires treatment before it can be returned to the environment. Even after treatment, some harmful substances might remain and impact water quality.

Runoff and Sediments

When it rains, water can flow over the land. This water, called runoff, flows across lawns and farmland. Along the way, it picks up pesticides, herbicides, and fertilizers. Runoff carries these pollutants into streams, where they can harm insects, fish, and other organisms. Runoff also carries sediment particles into streams. Too much sediment can damage stream habitats, clog waterways, and cause flooding.

Key Concept Check How does pollution affect water resources?

Figure 11   Fertilizers and irrigation water contain salts that can build up in soil, as shown in the photo on the left. The photo on the right shows a mining technique that disturbs ecosystems.

Land Pollution

Have you ever helped clean up litter? Foam containers, plastic bags, bottles, cans, and even furniture and appliances get dumped along roadsides. Litter is more than an eyesore. It can pollute soil and water and disturb wildlife. Sources of land pollution include homes, farms, industry, and mines.

Agriculture

Farmers use pesticides and other agricultural chemicals to help plants grow. But these chemicals become pollutants if they are used in excess or disposed of improperly. Herbicides kill weeds. But if they flow into streams, they can kill algae and plants, and harm fish and amphibians. Some farming practices contaminate soil, as shown in **Figure 11.**

Industry and Mining

Many industrial facilities, including oil refineries and ore processors, produce toxic wastes. For example, coal ash sludge is produced when coal is burned in power plants. The sludge contains mercury, lead, arsenic, and other potentially harmful metals. If toxic wastes such as these are incorrectly stored or disposed of, they contaminate soil and water. The health of people, plants, and wildlife can be affected.

Mining of fossil fuels and minerals can disturb or destroy entire ecosystems, as shown in **Figure 11.** Some coal-mining techniques can release toxic substances that were buried in rock. After the coal has been removed, the area can be restored. But it is difficult or impossible to replace the original ecosystem.

Key Concept Check How does pollution affect land resources?

Lesson 2 Review

Visual Summary

Pollution, the introduction of harmful substances into the environment, can harm humans and other living things.

Smog, ozone loss, global warming, and acid precipitation are caused by air pollutants.

Land and water can be polluted by littering and chemical runoff from homes, factories, mines, and farms.

FOLDABLES

Use your lesson Foldable to review the lesson. Save your Foldable for the project at the end of the chapter.

What do you think NOW?

You first read the statements below at the beginning of the chapter.

3. Global warming causes acid rain.

4. Smog can affect human health.

Did you change your mind about whether you agree or disagree with the statements? Rewrite any false statements to make them true.

Use Vocabulary

1. **Define** *photochemical smog* in your own words.

2. **Distinguish** between global warming and acid precipitation.

3. The layer of atmosphere that prevents UV radiation from reaching Earth is the _____.

Understand Key Concepts

4. Which is NOT a source of pollution?
   A. burning coal   C. photosynthesis
   B. mining minerals D. volcanic eruptions

5. **Explain** the difference between ozone in the lower atmosphere and ozone in the upper atmosphere.

6. **Describe** how pollution affects water resources.

Interpret Graphics

7. **Compare and Contrast** Copy and fill in the table below to compare and contrast air, water, and land pollution.

Type of Pollution	Similarities	Differences
Air		
Water		
Land		

Critical Thinking

8. **Hypothesize** The water in a stream that flows through farmland has always been clear. After a hard rain, the water in the stream became muddy. What caused the change?

9. **Apply** How do trees and other plants help lessen global warming? How might deforestation, or cutting down trees, contribute to global warming?

How can you communicate about pollution?

You have read about different types of pollutants in this chapter. Now it's your turn to communicate what you have learned. A public service announcement (PSA) is like a commercial that explains an important issue.

Materials

stopwatch

computer

Learn It

Communication of ideas is an important part of the work of scientists. A scientific idea that is not reported will not advance scientific knowledge or the public's understanding of science. Scientists often **communicate** their ideas in presentations.

Try It

1 Read and complete a lab safety form.

2 Choose a pollutant you read about in this chapter or a different pollutant in which you have an interest.

3 Research your pollutant. Find out as much as you can about how it is produced, how it enters the environment, what problems it causes, and how its effects can be reduced.

4 Write a 1-min script for a PSA that communicates the information you gathered in step 3.

5 Practice your script until you feel comfortable speaking it before a group. If recording equipment is available, record your PSA.

Apply It

6 Present your PSA to your class.

7 Take questions from the class. Ask your classmates what they learned. Record their comments in your Science Journal.

8 **Critique** your PSA. Did the class understand the message you were trying to communicate? How could you improve your presentation?

9 **Key Concept** How does the pollutant you researched affect natural resources?

Protecting Earth

Reading Guide

Key Concepts
ESSENTIAL QUESTIONS

- How can people monitor resource use?

- How can people conserve resources?

Vocabulary
sustainability p. 835

recycling p. 836

g **Multilingual eGlossary**

Inquiry **A Better View?**

This image taken from a satellite shows an eruption on a volcanic island. What parts of the environment do you see in the image? How can images taken from satellites help scientists study Earth?

How can you turn trash into art?

Reusing materials helps reduce the natural resources needed to make something new. It also reduces the amount of trash discarded in landfills. Some environmentally friendly artists reuse materials to create new art. In this lab, you will create something new from objects you usually might throw away.

1 Read and complete a lab safety form.

2 Carefully consider the materials in the **trash collection.**

3 Using **craft materials,** create a piece of art out of the trash. Try to convey a message with your art. For example, your message might be "Protect Earth."

4 Display your artwork to the class.

Think About This

1. Describe your artwork. What kind of trash did you use? What kind of art did you create?

2. What message did you try to convey?

3. 🔑 **Key Concept** How do you think reusing materials helps conserve resources?

Monitoring Human Impact on Earth

Earth's human population is expected to grow to 7 billion by 2012. As the population increases, so does humans' impact on the planet. Scientists, governments, and concerned citizens around the world are working to identify environmental problems, educate the public about them, and help find solutions.

Scientists collect data on a variety of environmental conditions by placing detectors on satellites, aircraft, high-altitude balloons, and ground-based monitoring stations. For example, the United States and the European Union have launched satellites into orbit around Earth to gather data on greenhouse gases, ozone, ecosystem changes, melting glaciers and sea ice, climate patterns, and ocean health.

The U.S. Environmental Protection Agency (EPA) is a government organization that monitors the health of the environment and looks for ways to reduce human impacts. The EPA enforces environmental laws and supports research at universities and national laboratories. It also works with citizens and organizations to identify superfund sites—abandoned areas that have been contaminated by toxic wastes—and develops plans for cleaning them up.

🔑 **Key Concept Check** How can people monitor resource use?

FOLDABLES

Make a small shutter-fold book. Label it as shown. Use it to identify technology and methods that protect natural resources.

Monitoring Natural Resources

Conserving Natural Resources

Developing Technologies

Many technologies have been developed to protect Earth's resources, and more are on the way. These advances often focus on saving energy and reducing pollution.

Water-Saving Technologies

It takes energy to clean water and to transport it to homes and businesses. So technologies that conserve water also save energy. Low-flow showerheads and toilets help reduce water use. Drip irrigation systems, such as the one shown in **Figure 12**, decrease water waste.

Energy-Saving Technologies

Saving energy can make Earth's supply of fossil fuels last longer. Relying more on renewable energy sources can reduce fossil fuel use. Some of these sources can be expensive, but designs are constantly improving and costs are going down. Researchers estimate that solar electricity soon will cost no more than electricity produced by burning fossil fuels. Burning fewer fossil fuels also creates less pollution.

Other energy-saving advances include compact fluorescent lightbulbs (CFLs). They use about one-fourth the energy of incandescent bulbs and can last ten times longer. In 2007, Americans reduced greenhouse gas emissions by an amount equal to removing 2 million cars from the road just by switching to CFLs.

Figure 12 Drip irrigation slowly delivers water to the roots of plants. Less water is lost to runoff and evaporation.

Inquiry MiniLab

20 minutes each day

What's in the air?

Air pollution made of particles that float in the air is called particulate matter, or PM. The Clean Air Act requires the EPA to monitor PM.

1. Read and complete a lab safety form.
2. To make a PM collector, coat two **plastic container lids** with a layer of **petroleum jelly.**

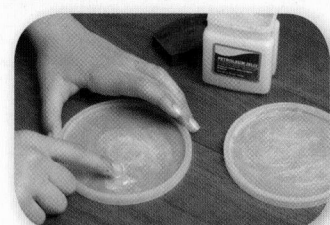

3. Leave each PM collector in a different location around your school. Record the location, the date, and the time in your Science Journal.

4. On the following day, retrieve the collectors. Record the date and time.
5. Use a **magnifying lens** to observe the PM. Record your observations.

Analyze and Conclude

1. **Describe** What types of PM did you find on your collectors?

2. **Compare** the amount and type of PM found in the different locations. Formulate a reason for any differences you observe.

3. **Key Concept** What conclusions about air quality in your school can you draw from your data?

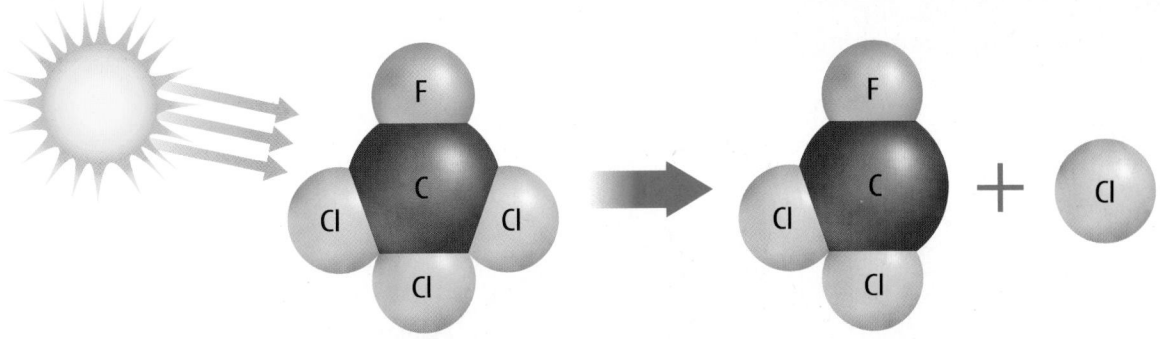

Sunlight reacts with a CFC molecule, causing a chlorine atom to break away.

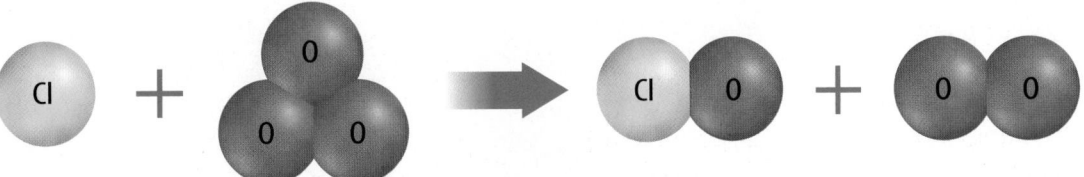

The chlorine atom reacts with and breaks apart an ozone molecule.

CFC Replacements

You have read that CFCs cause thinning of the ozone layer. How does this happen? The chlorine atoms in CFC molecules react with sunlight to destroy ozone, as shown in **Figure 13.** All CFCs soon will be phased out and replaced with chemicals that do not contain chlorine. Replacements include hydrofluorocarbons (HFCs) and perfluorocarbons (PFCs). Even after CFCs are no longer in use, it will take decades for the ozone layer to recover.

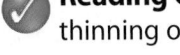 **Reading Check** What steps have been taken to reverse the thinning of the ozone layer?

Alternative Fuels

Gasohol and biodiesel are alternative fuels that help reduce humans' use of fossil fuels. They also help reduce air pollution.

Gasohol is a mixture of 90 percent gasoline and 10 percent ethanol. Ethanol is alcohol made from corn, sugar cane, or other plants. Using gasohol helps reduce emissions of carbon monoxide, an air pollutant that contributes to smog. The carbon in ethanol comes from plants rather than fossil fuels. So, using gasohol can help reduce emissions that contribute to global warming.

Biodiesel is made from renewable resources, primarily vegetable oils and animal fats—including oil left over from frying foods in restaurants. Biodiesel can be burned in diesel engines in farm and industrial machinery, trucks, and cars. It produces fewer pollutants than regular diesel fuel, and it reduces CO_2 emissions by 78 percent.

Figure 13 When CFC molecules reach the upper atmosphere, sunlight breaks off chlorine atoms. Each free chlorine atom can destroy an ozone molecule and prevent another from forming.

Visual Check How do CFCs affect ozone molecules?

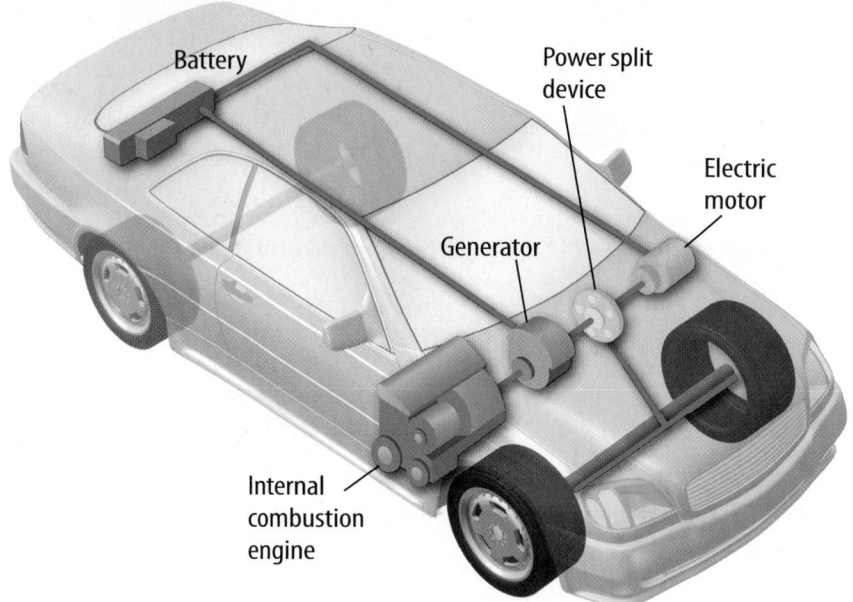

Figure 14 A hybrid vehicle uses a battery to power an electric motor. A small gasoline engine provides additional power.

✓ **Visual Check** What are the power sources in a hybrid vehicle?

Automobile Technologies

If you were buying a car, you would want to know how many miles it travels per gallon of fuel—miles per gallon, or mpg. The higher a car's mpg, the less pollution it will add to the environment. A car with a high mpg also will use up fewer fossil-fuel resources.

One of your choices might be a **hybrid** electric vehicle (HEV). HEVs combine a small gasoline engine with an electric motor powered by batteries, as shown in **Figure 14.** HEVs run on battery power as much as possible, with a boost from the engine for longer trips, higher speeds, and steep hills. The engine also charges the batteries. HEVs can get up to twice the mileage of a conventional car—close to 50 mpg in some recent car models.

In the future, another automobile alternative might be a fuel-cell vehicle (FCV). Inside a fuel cell, oxygen from the air chemically combines with hydrogen to produce electricity. The primary waste product is water. Tailpipe emissions from FCVs are nearly pollution-free. However, obtaining hydrogen fuel requires using methane or other fossil fuels. Researchers are looking for alternatives.

✓ **Reading Check** Compare HEVs and FCVs.

Making a Difference

Do you turn off the lights when you leave a room or recycle bottles and cans? If so, you are helping reduce your impact on the environment. You can help protect Earth's resources in other ways as well, such as cleaning up a stream, educating others about environmental issues, analyzing the choices you make as a consumer, and following some of the suggestions you will read about next.

Sustainability

When people talk about environmental issues, they often use the word *sustainability*. **Sustainability** *means meeting human needs in ways that ensure future generations also will be able to meet their needs*. When you turn off the lights as you leave a room, you are saving energy—and you are also helping to ensure a sustainable future. **Figure 15** shows other actions that lead toward a sustainable future.

 Reading Check What is sustainability?

Sustainable Actions 🔑

Figure 15 Planting trees, composting, and picking up litter help sustain the environment.

Restore and Rethink

Restoring damaged habitats and ecosystems to their original state is one way to make a difference. For example, picking up trash can restore water habitats.

You also can rethink the way you perform everyday activities. Instead of riding in a vehicle to nearby places, you could ride your bike or walk.

Reduce and Reuse

You can reduce the amount of waste you create simply by reducing the amount of material you use. For example, avoid products with too much packaging. Or, bring your own bags for carrying purchases, as shown in **Figure 16.**

Reusing items also helps reduce waste. Instead of buying new, reuse something that will work just as well. You also can donate used items to charities or resell them.

Figure 16 Reusable bags help save energy and reduce waste.

WORD ORIGIN · · · · · · · · · · ·

recycle
from Latin *re-*, means "again"; and Greek *kyklos*, means "circle"

Recycle

If an item cannot be reused, you might be able to recycle it. **Recycling** *is manufacturing new products out of used products.* This process reduces wastes and extends our supply of natural resources. Computers and other electronics contain valuable metals that can be recycled, as well as toxic materials that can contribute to pollution. So recycling also helps makes sure that toxins are properly disposed of.

Compost Leaves, grass clippings, and vegetable scraps can be recycled by composting. In a compost pile, these materials decay into nutrient-rich soil that goes back into the garden.

Buy Recycled Separating recyclables from the rest of the trash is just one step. To keep the cycle going, buy and use recycled products. You can find shoes, clothing, paper, and carpets made from recycled materials.

Key Concept Check How can you conserve resources?

Lesson 3 Review

Visual Summary

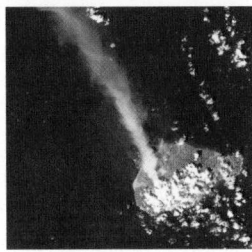

Scientists use a variety of techniques to monitor the use of natural resources, including satellites, aircraft, high-altitude balloons, and ground-based monitoring stations.

New technologies such as HEVs and alternative fuels conserve resources and produce less pollution.

People can help protect resources by reducing their use of resources, reusing products, and recycling products.

FOLDABLES®

Use your lesson Foldable to review the lesson. Save your Foldable for the project at the end of the chapter.

What do you think NOW?

You first read the statements below at the beginning of the chapter.

5. Oil left over from frying potatoes can be used as automobile fuel.

6. Hybrid electric vehicles cannot travel far or go fast.

Did you change your mind about whether you agree or disagree with the statements? Rewrite any false statements to make them true.

Use Vocabulary

1 **Define** *sustainability* in your own words.

Understand Key Concepts

2 Which produces water as its primary waste product?
   A. biodiesel   C. gasohol
   B. FCV   D. HEV

3 **Analyze** Compare the tailpipe emissions of an HEV with a car that has only a gasoline engine.

4 **Apply** What water-saving and energy-saving techniques could you use in your kitchen?

Interpret Graphics

5 **Explain** how the process below affects the environment.

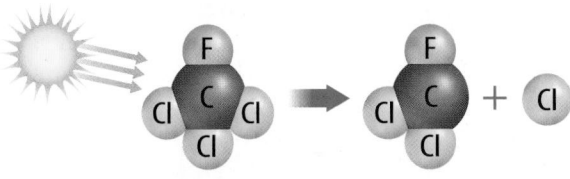

6 **Identify** Copy and fill in the graphic organizer below to identify three ways people can limit waste production.

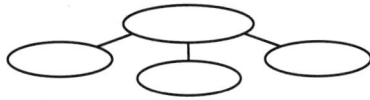

Critical Thinking

7 **Hypothesize** The same delivery truck passes you almost every morning as you walk to school. Each time it goes by, you smell fried potatoes. What could be the reason?

8 **Recommend** The school cafeteria throws out mounds of vegetable peelings and leftover food every day. The school gardener would like to plant vegetables, but the soil is too thin. What sustainable actions could you recommend?

How can you conserve a natural resource?

You have read about natural resources and about how they can be affected by human activities. Even though you are just one person, your actions can help conserve natural resources. Your task is to develop a realistic plan to conserve a natural resource.

Ask Questions

How do your daily activities affect natural resources? What actions could you take to conserve a natural resource?

Make Observations

1. Read and complete a lab safety form.

2. Select the natural resource you want to help conserve. In your Science Journal, describe how the resource is used. Also discuss the problems that threaten the natural resource.

3. Review the list of conservation activities below. Choose activities from the list or come up with your own ideas. Explain how the activities would conserve the resource you have chosen.

4. Write a plan that details how you will enact these activities in your everyday life. Describe the materials you will need and the steps you will follow. Make a time line showing how you will implement the plan.

5. Remember, your plan must be realistic. Conduct research as you do this investigation to help you learn more about natural resources and conservation plans.

Conservation Activities
Change showerheads and faucets to low-flow.
Install rain barrels to use for watering gardens.
Start a compost pile for food scraps or yard waste.
Provide recycling bins at sporting events.
Replace incandescent lights with CFLs or LEDs.
Clean up a local road or pond.
Replace car trips with bicycling or walking whenever possible.
Lower the heating thermostat in winter and raise the air-conditioner thermostat in summer.

Form a Hypothesis

6 State the major goal or goals of your plan in the form of a hypothesis.

Test your Hypothesis

7 Discuss your plan with a classmate. Does he or she think it will work? Is the plan realistic, or will it require large amounts of money, time, and resources? Modify your plan based on your classmate's input.

8 Implement your plan over a scheduled period of time. Follow your time line. Record your observations and any quantifiable data.

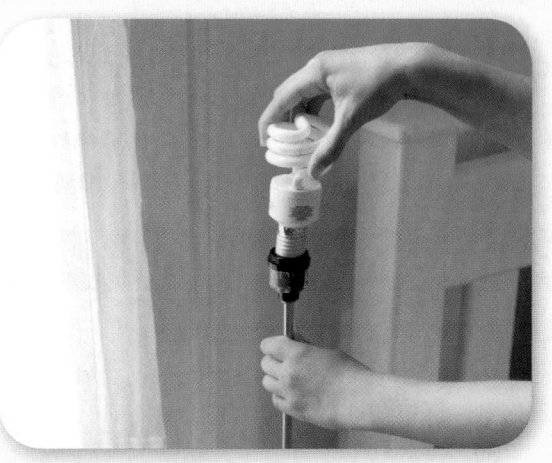

Analyze and Conclude

9 **Assess** How did your plan affect the natural resource? Which impacts were you able to quantify? Which impacts were difficult to quantify?

10 **Evaluate** Did you see any limitations to your plan? For example, can it be implemented on a larger scale?

11 **The Big Idea** Why is it important to actively work to conserve Earth's resources?

Lab Tips

☑ If you are having trouble deciding on a topic, think about your activities as you go about your day. What things do you do that use a lot of natural resources?

☑ Be flexible. Propose more than one way to solve a problem.

☑ Be creative, but keep your plan realistic.

Communicate Your Results

Create an assessment report of your plan. Make your report engaging and informative. Provide a comprehensive description of your results. Include a proposal for extending the time period of the plan.

Inquiry Extension

Create a 1-min PSA describing your plan. The PSA should encourage others to follow the plan. Include a graph or other visual that shows the positive impact of your plan on the natural resource. Project how this impact would increase if everyone in the class followed your plan. Project the impact of your plan on county, state, and national levels.

Remember to use scientific methods.

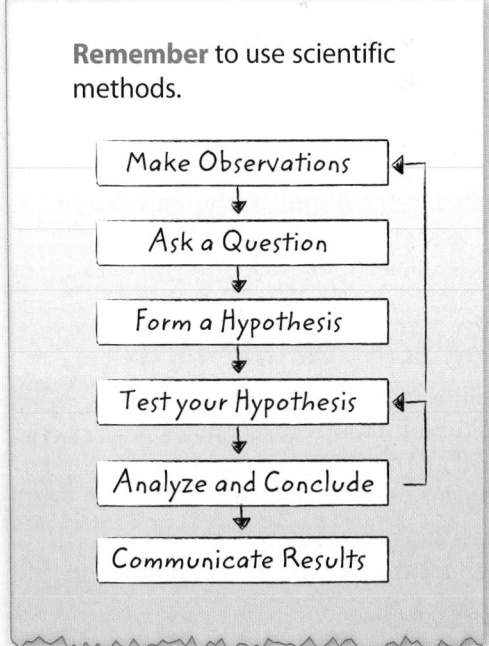

Make Observations → Ask a Question → Form a Hypothesis → Test your Hypothesis → Analyze and Conclude → Communicate Results

Chapter 23 Study Guide

THE BIG IDEA

People can protect Earth's resources by understanding how their use of natural resources affects the environment, knowing which natural resources are in limited supply, and making decisions toward a more sustainable future.

Key Concepts Summary 🔑	Vocabulary
Lesson 1: Earth's Resources • **Natural resources** are raw materials and forms of energy that are important to living things. • Resources can be **renewable** or **nonrenewable.** Some renewable resources are **inexhaustible.** 	**natural resource** p. 813 **nonrenewable resource** p. 814 **renewable resource** p. 816 **inexhaustible resource** p. 818 **geothermal energy** p. 819
Lesson 2: Pollution • Air pollutants cause **photochemical smog,** ozone loss, **global warming,** and **acid precipitation.** • Chemical runoff can damage lakes, streams, and water supplies. Sediment runoff from land can disturb aquatic habitats. • Litter and pollutants can contaminate soil, harm organisms, and reduce land's ability to support life. Mining can disturb ecosystems and create toxic wastes. 	**pollution** p. 823 **ozone layer** p. 824 **photochemical smog** p. 824 **global warming** p. 825 **acid precipitation** p. 825
Lesson 3: Protecting Earth • Satellites, aircraft, and ground-based monitoring stations collect data on pollution. The EPA monitors pollution and helps develop clean-up plans. • People can protect Earth's resources by reducing, reusing, and **recycling.** 	**sustainability** p. 835 **recycling** p. 836

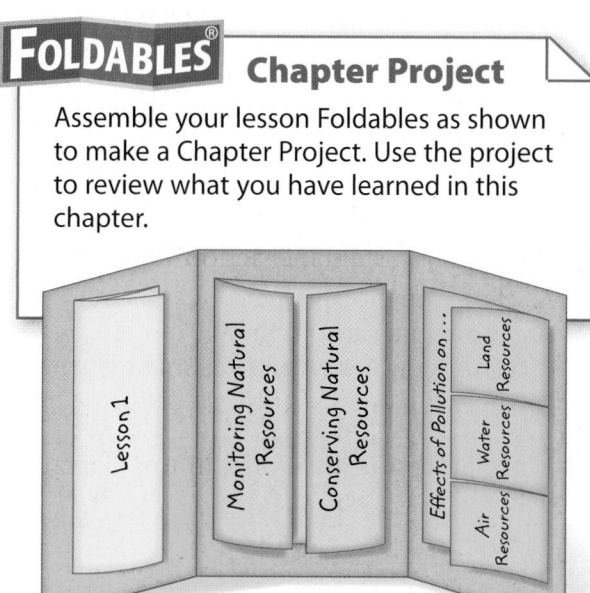

FOLDABLES® **Chapter Project**

Assemble your lesson Foldables as shown to make a Chapter Project. Use the project to review what you have learned in this chapter.

Use Vocabulary

1 Sunshine, oil, coal, uranium, trees, oxygen, and streams are examples of _____.

2 Distinguish between recycling, reusing, and reducing.

3 A tropical forest that takes 1,000 years to recover from being burned down is a(n) _____ resource.

4 Use the term *sustainability* in a sentence.

5 Rainfall that keeps a pond full is a(n) _____ resource.

6 Define *global warming* in your own words.

Link Vocabulary and Key Concepts

Concepts in Motion Interactive Concept Map

Copy this concept map, and then use vocabulary terms from the previous page and other terms from the chapter to complete the concept map.

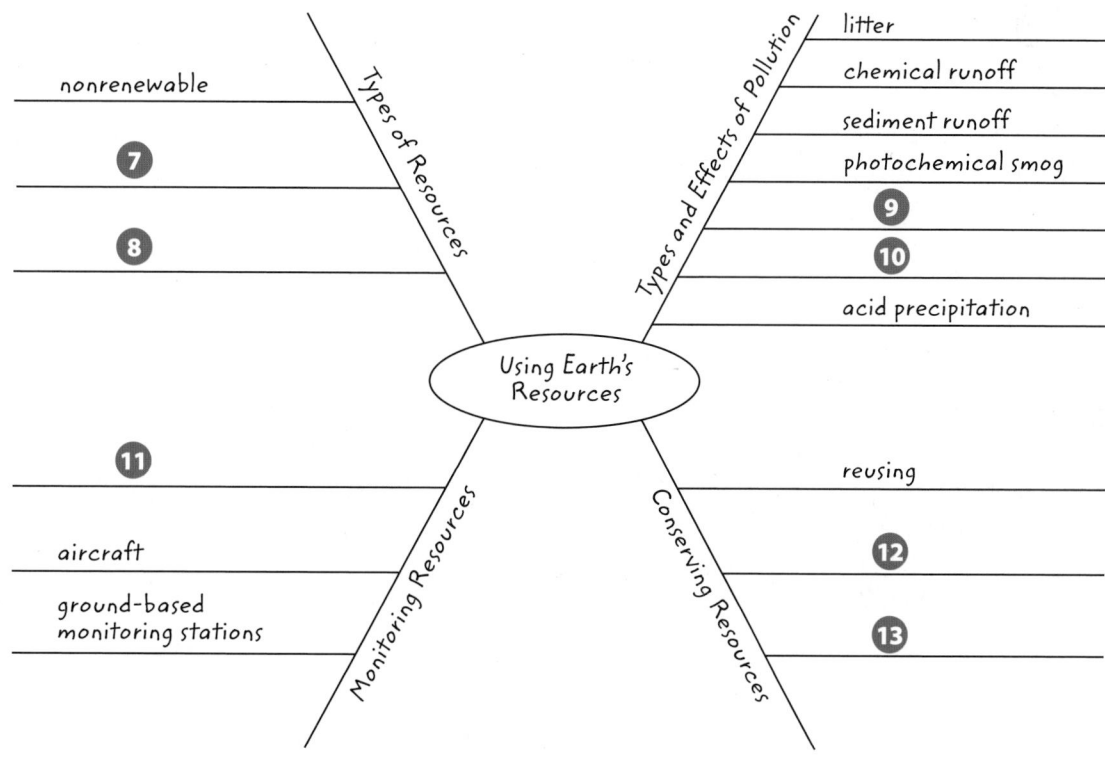

Understand Key Concepts

1 Which is an inexhaustible resource?

A. air
B. land
C. water
D. wind

2 What are the items below made of?

A. inexhaustible resources
B. nonrecyclable resources
C. nonrenewable resources
D. renewable resources

3 Greenhouse gases contribute to which environmental problem?

A. acid rain
B. global warming
C. ozone depletion
D. photochemical smog

4 Biodiesel can be made from which resource?

A. ethanol
B. gasoline
C. hydrogen gas
D. vegetable oil

5 Which technology produces electricity using sunlight?

A. fuel cells
B. solar cookers
C. solar power plants
D. solar water heaters

6 What kind of pollution results when sunlight reacts with sulfur dioxide produced by the burning of fossil fuels?

A. acid rain
B. global warming
C. ozone depletion
D. photochemical smog

7 Which is a sustainable action?

A. carpooling to a game
B. riding in a car to school
C. running water when brushing teeth
D. throwing out a slightly used shirt

8 What process is illustrated in the diagram below?

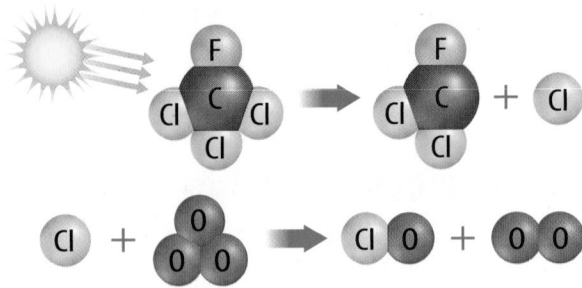

A. acid rain
B. global warming
C. ozone depletion
D. smog formation

9 Uranium is classified as what?

A. a fossil fuel
B. a greenhouse gas
C. a mineral resource
D. a renewable resource

10 Which is a renewable resource?

A. coal
B. sunlight
C. water
D. wind

Critical Thinking

11 **Classify** each of the following as renewable, nonrenewable, or inexhaustible: notebook paper, flashlight batteries, and heat from a volcano.

12 **Explain** why geothermal energy is considered an inexhaustible resource.

13 **Design** an experiment to determine how acid rain affects plants.

14 **Interpret Scientific Illustrations** Describe how the process below affects human health.

15 **Create** a poster explaining why items such as used motor oil or leftover paint should be recycled rather than poured down a storm drain or dumped on soil.

16 **Summarize** how people can help prevent land pollution.

17 **Compare** the emissions of a gasoline-powered automobile, a hybrid electric vehicle, and a fuel-cell vehicle. Which vehicle contributes the least amount of air pollution?

18 **Give** an example of how people can reduce the amount of trash they produce.

Writing in Science

19 **Write** a letter to a younger student about sustainability. Explain what it means, why it is important to his or her generation, and how it involves considering future needs, not just current ones.

REVIEW THE BIG IDEA

20 Give examples of what a government and an individual could do to protect Earth's resources.

21 How can using wind energy help conserve Earth's resources?

Math Skills

 **Review**

Math Practice

Use Percentages

22 Between 2003 and 2006, the amount of U.S. energy produced from renewable sources increased from 6.15 quads to 6.91 quads. What was the percentage increase?

23 Wind energy usage increased from 0.115 quads to 0.341 quads between 2003 and 2007. What was the percentage increase?

24 In 2006, only 6.92 percent of U.S. energy was produced from renewable sources. If the total energy consumption was 99.8 quads, how much energy was produced from renewable sources?

Record your answers on the answer sheet provided by your teacher or on a sheet of paper.

Multiple Choice

1 Why is coal a nonrenewable resource?

  A Coal is used faster than it forms.

  B Coal cannot be recycled like glass or plastic.

  C Humans do not know how to make coal.

  D Coal formed in the past and no longer forms today.

2 Which is an effect of photochemical smog?

  A global warming

  B lung damage

  C skin cancer

  D acid precipitation

Use the diagram to answer questions 3 and 4.

3 The diagram shows a chlorofluorocarbon (CFCs) reaction. Where does this reaction occur?

  A in water

  B on land

  C in an automobile

  D in the atmosphere

4 How does this reaction affect the environment?

  A It depletes the ozone layer.

  B It pollutes water.

  C It produces acid rain.

  D It produces photochemical smog.

5 Which government agency monitors the health of the environment and works to reduce human impacts?

  A CFC

  B CFL

  C EPA

  D HEV

6 Which material is NOT a fossil fuel?

  A coal

  B copper

  C natural gas

  D oil

Use the diagram to answer question 7.

7 Nika is reading a pamphlet about the proper disposal of different materials. The pamphlet includes the image shown above. What would happen if someone performed the action shown in the image?

  A The oil would cause photochemical smog.

  B The oil would be washed into nearby streams or lakes.

  C The oil would evaporate and cause ozone depletion.

  D The oil would remain in the storm drain and not cause harm.

8 Which action recycles yard waste and kitchen waste?

   A composting

   B planting trees

   C using drip irrigation

   D using compact fluorescent lightbulbs

Use the diagram to answer question 9.

9 What type of energy resource is shown in the diagram?

   A geothermal

   B solar

   C water

   D wind

10 Which is a renewable resource that can become nonrenewable if it is used up too quickly?

   A oil

   B forests

   C coal

   D natural gas

Constructed Response

11 What action could you take to help conserve resources and reduce the amount of waste that enters landfills?

Use the diagram to answer question 12.

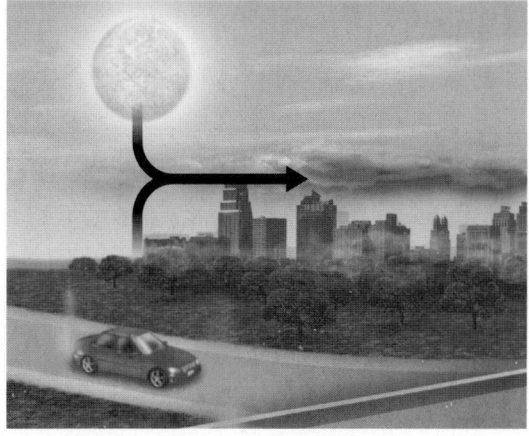

12 Which part of the environment is most affected by the activity shown here? Explain your answer.

13 Describe how rethinking your everyday activities contributes to a sustainable future.

14 Identify one renewable resource and one inexhaustible resource. Then, describe similarities and differences between the two resources.

NEED EXTRA HELP?														
If You Missed Question...	1	2	3	4	5	6	7	8	9	10	11	12	13	14
Go to Lesson...	1	2	3	3	3	1	3	3	1, 3	1	3	2,3	3	1

Student Resources

For Students and Parents/Guardians

These resources are designed to help you achieve success in science. You will find useful information on laboratory safety, math skills, and science skills. In addition, science reference materials are found in the Reference Handbook. You'll find the information you need to learn and sharpen your skills in these resources.

Table of Contents

Scientific Methods

Scientists use an orderly approach called the scientific method to solve problems. This includes organizing and recording data so others can understand them. Scientists use many variations in this method when they solve problems.

Identify a Question

The first step in a scientific investigation or experiment is to identify a question to be answered or a problem to be solved. For example, you might ask which gasoline is the most efficient.

Gather and Organize Information

After you have identified your question, begin gathering and organizing information. There are many ways to gather information, such as researching in a library, interviewing those knowledgeable about the subject, and testing and working in the laboratory and field. Fieldwork is investigations and observations done outside of a laboratory.

Researching Information Before moving in a new direction, it is important to gather the information that already is known about the subject. Start by asking yourself questions to determine exactly what you need to know. Then you will look for the information in various reference sources, like the student is doing in **Figure 1.** Some sources may include textbooks, encyclopedias, government documents, professional journals, science magazines, and the Internet. Always list the sources of your information.

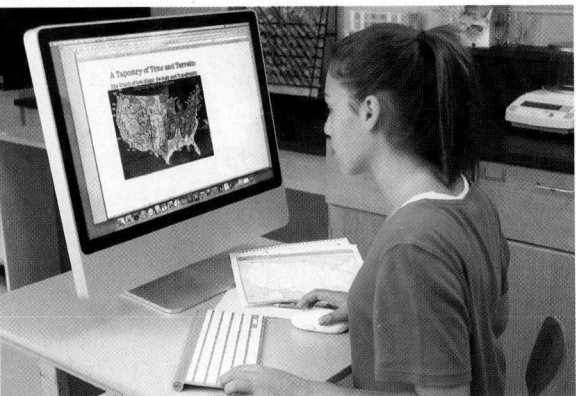

Figure 1 The Internet can be a valuable research tool.

Evaluate Sources of Information Not all sources of information are reliable. You should evaluate all of your sources of information, and use only those you know to be dependable. For example, if you are researching ways to make homes more energy efficient, a site written by the U.S. Department of Energy would be more reliable than a site written by a company that is trying to sell a new type of weatherproofing material. Also, remember that research always is changing. Consult the most current resources available to you. For example, a 1985 resource about saving energy would not reflect the most recent findings.

Sometimes scientists use data that they did not collect themselves, or conclusions drawn by other researchers. This data must be evaluated carefully. Ask questions about how the data were obtained, if the investigation was carried out properly, and if it has been duplicated exactly with the same results. Would you reach the same conclusion from the data? Only when you have confidence in the data can you believe it is true and feel comfortable using it.

SCIENCE SKILL HANDBOOK

MATH SKILL HANDBOOK

FOLDABLES HANDBOOK

REFERENCE HANDBOOK

GLOSSARY/ GLOSARIO

INDEX

Interpret Scientific Illustrations As you research a topic in science, you will see drawings, diagrams, and photographs to help you understand what you read. Some illustrations are included to help you understand an idea that you can't see easily by yourself, like the tiny particles in an atom in **Figure 2.** A drawing helps many people to remember details more easily and provides examples that clarify difficult concepts or give additional information about the topic you are studying. Most illustrations have labels or a caption to identify or to provide more information.

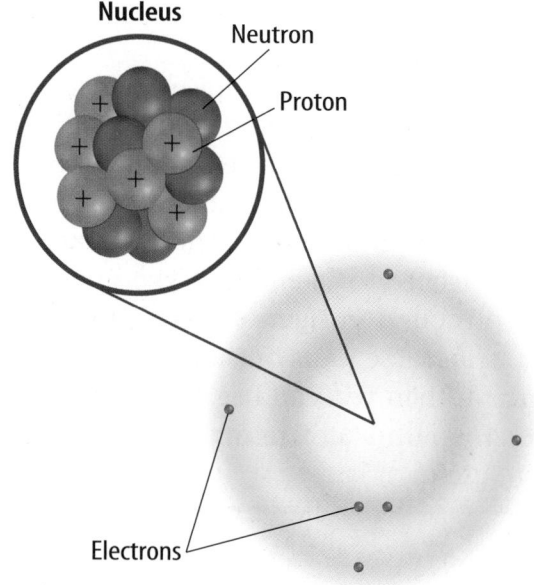

Figure 2 This drawing shows an atom of carbon with its six protons, six neutrons, and six electrons.

Concept Maps One way to organize data is to draw a diagram that shows relationships among ideas (or concepts). A concept map can help make the meanings of ideas and terms more clear, and help you understand and remember what you are studying. Concept maps are useful for breaking large concepts down into smaller parts, making learning easier.

Network Tree A type of concept map that not only shows a relationship, but how the concepts are related is a network tree, shown in **Figure 3.** In a network tree, the words are written in the ovals, while the description of the type of relationship is written across the connecting lines.

When constructing a network tree, write down the topic and all major topics on separate pieces of paper or notecards. Then arrange them in order from general to specific. Branch the related concepts from the major concept and describe the relationship on the connecting line. Continue to more specific concepts until finished.

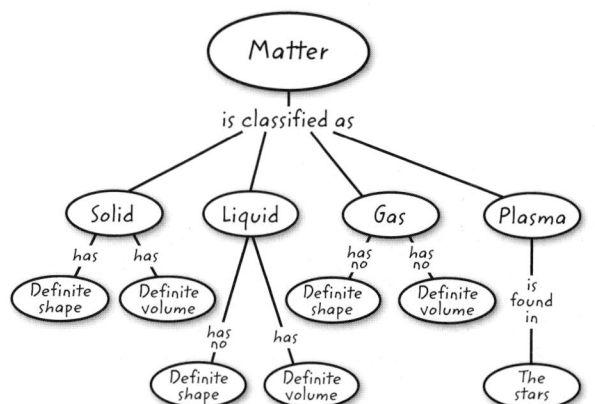

Figure 3 A network tree shows how concepts or objects are related.

Events Chain Another type of concept map is an events chain. Sometimes called a flow chart, it models the order or sequence of items. An events chain can be used to describe a sequence of events, the steps in a procedure, or the stages of a process.

When making an events chain, first find the one event that starts the chain. This event is called the initiating event. Then, find the next event and continue until the outcome is reached, as shown in **Figure 4** on the next page.

SCIENCE SKILL HANDBOOK

MATH SKILL HANDBOOK

FOLDABLES HANDBOOK

REFERENCE HANDBOOK

GLOSSARY/ GLOSARIO

INDEX

SCIENCE SKILL HANDBOOK

MATH SKILL HANDBOOK

FOLDABLES HANDBOOK

REFERENCE HANDBOOK

GLOSSARY/ GLOSARIO

INDEX

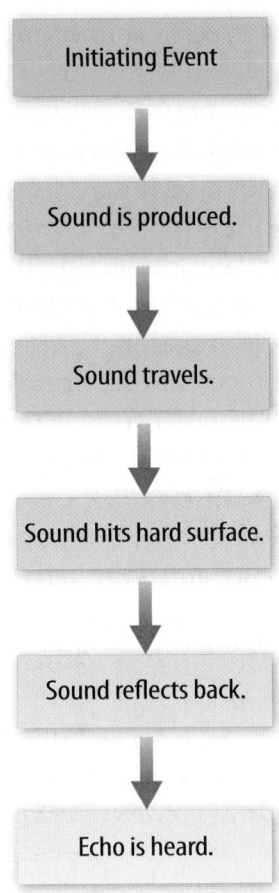

Figure 4 Events-chain concept maps show the order of steps in a process or event. This concept map shows how a sound makes an echo.

Cycle Map A specific type of events chain is a cycle map. It is used when the series of events do not produce a final outcome, but instead relate back to the beginning event, such as in **Figure 5.** Therefore, the cycle repeats itself.

To make a cycle map, first decide what event is the beginning event. This is also called the initiating event. Then list the next events in the order that they occur, with the last event relating back to the initiating event. Words can be written between the events that describe what happens from one event to the next. The number of events in a cycle map can vary, but usually contain three or more events.

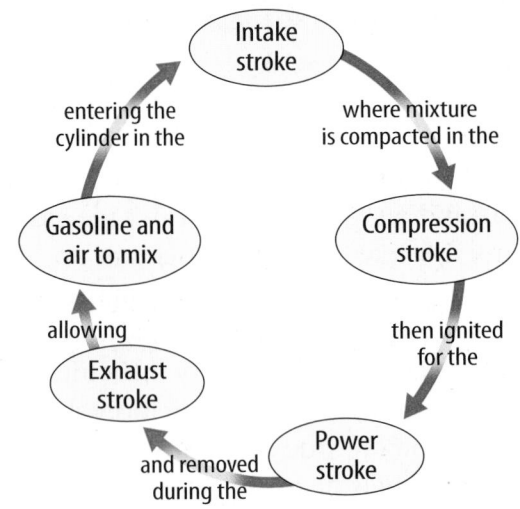

Figure 5 A cycle map shows events that occur in a cycle.

Spider Map A type of concept map that you can use for brainstorming is the spider map. When you have a central idea, you might find that you have a jumble of ideas that relate to it but are not necessarily clearly related to each other. The spider map on sound in **Figure 6** shows that if you write these ideas outside the main concept, then you can begin to separate and group unrelated terms so they become more useful.

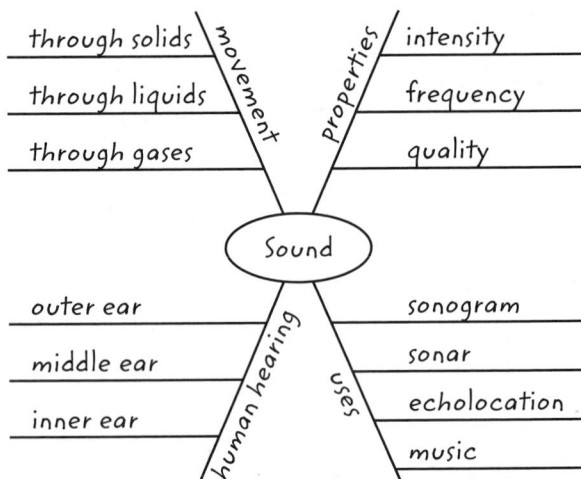

Figure 6 A spider map allows you to list ideas that relate to a central topic but not necessarily to one another.

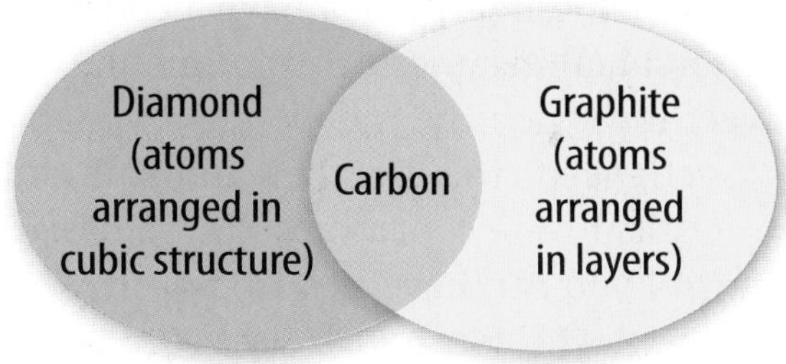

Figure 7 This Venn diagram compares and contrasts two substances made from carbon.

Venn Diagram To illustrate how two subjects compare and contrast you can use a Venn diagram. You can see the characteristics that the subjects have in common and those that they do not, shown in **Figure 7.**

To create a Venn diagram, draw two overlapping ovals that are big enough to write in. List the characteristics unique to one subject in one oval, and the characteristics of the other subject in the other oval. The characteristics in common are listed in the overlapping section.

Make and Use Tables One way to organize information so it is easier to understand is to use a table. Tables can contain numbers, words, or both.

To make a table, list the items to be compared in the first column and the characteristics to be compared in the first row. The title should clearly indicate the content of the table, and the column or row heads should be clear. Notice that in **Table 1** the units are included.

Table 1 Recyclables Collected During Week			
Day of Week	**Paper (kg)**	**Aluminum (kg)**	**Glass (kg)**
Monday	5.0	4.0	12.0
Wednesday	4.0	1.0	10.0
Friday	2.5	2.0	10.0

Make a Model One way to help you better understand the parts of a structure, the way a process works, or to show things too large or small for viewing is to make a model. For example, an atomic model made of a plastic-ball nucleus and chenille stem electron shells can help you visualize how the parts of an atom relate to each other. Other types of models can be devised on a computer or represented by equations.

Form a Hypothesis

A possible explanation based on previous knowledge and observations is called a hypothesis. After researching gasoline types and recalling previous experiences in your family's car you form a hypothesis—our car runs more efficiently because we use premium gasoline. To be valid, a hypothesis has to be something you can test by using an investigation.

Predict When you apply a hypothesis to a specific situation, you predict something about that situation. A prediction makes a statement in advance, based on prior observation, experience, or scientific reasoning. People use predictions to make everyday decisions. Scientists test predictions by performing investigations. Based on previous observations and experiences, you might form a prediction that cars are more efficient with premium gasoline. The prediction can be tested in an investigation.

Design an Experiment A scientist needs to make many decisions before beginning an investigation. Some of these include: how to carry out the investigation, what steps to follow, how to record the data, and how the investigation will answer the question. It also is important to address any safety concerns.

SCIENCE SKILL HANDBOOK

MATH SKILL HANDBOOK

FOLDABLES HANDBOOK

REFERENCE HANDBOOK

GLOSSARY/ GLOSARIO

INDEX

Test the Hypothesis

Now that you have formed your hypothesis, you need to test it. Using an investigation, you will make observations and collect data, or information. This data might either support or not support your hypothesis. Scientists collect and organize data as numbers and descriptions.

Follow a Procedure In order to know what materials to use, as well as how and in what order to use them, you must follow a procedure. **Figure 8** shows a procedure you might follow to test your hypothesis.

Procedure

Step 1	Use regular gasoline for two weeks.
Step 2	Record the number of kilometers between fill-ups and the amount of gasoline used.
Step 3	Switch to premium gasoline for two weeks.
Step 4	Record the number of kilometers between fill-ups and the amount of gasoline used.

Figure 8 A procedure tells you what to do step-by-step.

Identify and Manipulate Variables and Controls In any experiment, it is important to keep everything the same except for the item you are testing. The one factor you change is called the independent variable. The change that results is the dependent variable. Make sure you have only one independent variable, to assure yourself of the cause of the changes you observe in the dependent variable. For example, in your gasoline experiment the type of fuel is the independent variable. The dependent variable is the efficiency.

Many experiments also have a control—an individual instance or experimental subject for which the independent variable is not changed. You can then compare the test results to the control results. To design a control you can have two cars of the same type. The control car uses regular gasoline for four weeks. After you are done with the test, you can compare the experimental results to the control results.

Collect Data

Whether you are carrying out an investigation or a short observational experiment, you will collect data, as shown in **Figure 9.** Scientists collect data as numbers and descriptions and organize them in specific ways.

Observe Scientists observe items and events, then record what they see. When they use only words to describe an observation, it is called qualitative data. Scientists' observations also can describe how much there is of something. These observations use numbers, as well as words, in the description and are called quantitative data. For example, if a sample of the element gold is described as being "shiny and very dense" the data are qualitative. Quantitative data on this sample of gold might include "a mass of 30 g and a density of 19.3 g/cm^3."

Figure 9 Collecting data is one way to gather information directly.

Figure 10 Record data neatly and clearly so it is easy to understand.

When you make observations you should examine the entire object or situation first, and then look carefully for details. It is important to record observations accurately and completely. Always record your notes immediately as you make them, so you do not miss details or make a mistake when recording results from memory. Never put unidentified observations on scraps of paper. Instead they should be recorded in a notebook, like the one in **Figure 10.** Write your data neatly so you can easily read it later. At each point in the experiment, record your observations and label them. That way, you will not have to determine what the figures mean when you look at your notes later. Set up any tables that you will need to use ahead of time, so you can record any observations right away. Remember to avoid bias when collecting data by not including personal thoughts when you record observations. Record only what you observe.

Estimate Scientific work also involves estimating. To estimate is to make a judgment about the size or the number of something without measuring or counting. This is important when the number or size of an object or population is too large or too difficult to accurately count or measure.

Sample Scientists may use a sample or a portion of the total number as a type of estimation. To sample is to take a small, representative portion of the objects or organisms of a population for research. By making careful observations or manipulating variables within that portion of the group, information is discovered and conclusions are drawn that might apply to the whole population. A poorly chosen sample can be unrepresentative of the whole. If you were trying to determine the rainfall in an area, it would not be best to take a rainfall sample from under a tree.

Measure You use measurements every day. Scientists also take measurements when collecting data. When taking measurements, it is important to know how to use measuring tools properly. Accuracy also is important.

Length To measure length, the distance between two points, scientists use meters. Smaller measurements might be measured in centimeters or millimeters.

Length is measured using a metric ruler or meterstick. When using a metric ruler, line up the 0-cm mark with the end of the object being measured and read the number of the unit where the object ends. Look at the metric ruler shown in **Figure 11.** The centimeter lines are the long, numbered lines, and the shorter lines are millimeter lines. In this instance, the length would be 4.50 cm.

Figure 11 This metric ruler has centimeter and millimeter divisions.

SCIENCE SKILL HANDBOOK

MATH SKILL HANDBOOK

FOLDABLES HANDBOOK

REFERENCE HANDBOOK

GLOSSARY/ GLOSARIO

INDEX

SCIENCE SKILL HANDBOOK

MATH SKILL HANDBOOK

FOLDABLES HANDBOOK

REFERENCE HANDBOOK

GLOSSARY/ GLOSARIO

INDEX

Mass The SI unit for mass is the kilogram (kg). Scientists can measure mass using units formed by adding metric prefixes to the unit gram (g), such as milligram (mg). To measure mass, you might use a triple-beam balance similar to the one shown in **Figure 12.** The balance has a pan on one side and a set of beams on the other side. Each beam has a rider that slides on the beam.

When using a triple-beam balance, place an object on the pan. Slide the largest rider along its beam until the pointer drops below zero. Then move it back one notch. Repeat the process for each rider proceeding from the larger to smaller until the pointer swings an equal distance above and below the zero point. Sum the masses on each beam to find the mass of the object. Move all riders back to zero when finished.

Instead of putting materials directly on the balance, scientists often take a tare of a container. A tare is the mass of a container into which objects or substances are placed for measuring their masses. To find the mass of objects or substances, find the mass of a clean container. Remove the container from the pan, and place the object or substances in the container. Find the mass of the container with the materials in it. Subtract the mass of the empty container from the mass of the filled container to find the mass of the materials you are using.

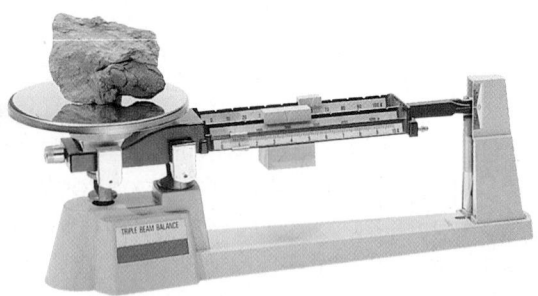

Figure 12 A triple-beam balance is used to determine the mass of an object.

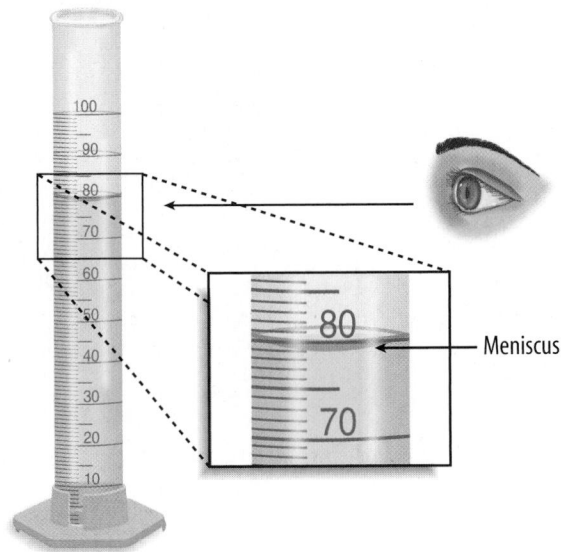

Figure 13 Graduated cylinders measure liquid volume.

Liquid Volume To measure liquids, the unit used is the liter. When a smaller unit is needed, scientists might use a milliliter. Because a milliliter takes up the volume of a cube measuring 1 cm on each side it also can be called a cubic centimeter ($cm^3 = cm \times cm \times cm$).

You can use beakers and graduated cylinders to measure liquid volume. A graduated cylinder, shown in **Figure 13,** is marked from bottom to top in milliliters. In lab, you might use a 10-mL graduated cylinder or a 100-mL graduated cylinder. When measuring liquids, notice that the liquid has a curved surface. Look at the surface at eye level, and measure the bottom of the curve. This is called the meniscus. The graduated cylinder in **Figure 13** contains 79.0 mL, or 79.0 cm^3, of a liquid.

Temperature Scientists often measure temperature using the Celsius scale. Pure water has a freezing point of 0°C and boiling point of 100°C. The unit of measurement is degrees Celsius. Two other scales often used are the Fahrenheit and Kelvin scales.

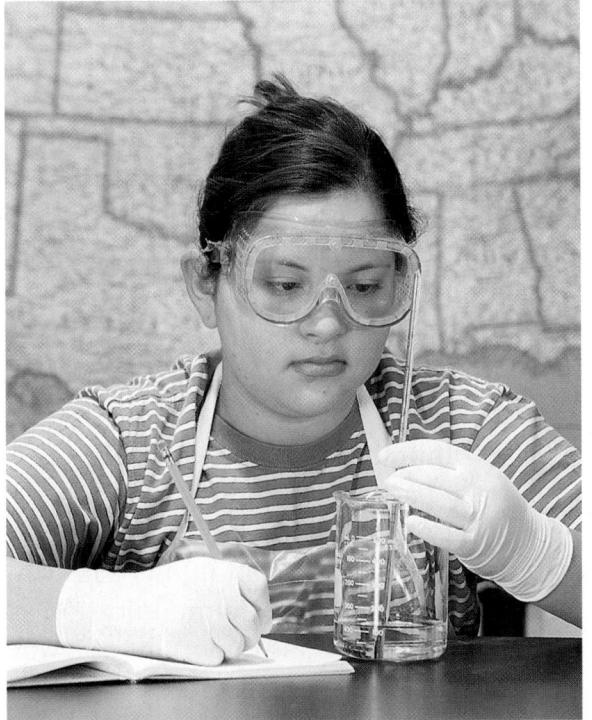

Figure 14 A thermometer measures the temperature of an object.

Scientists use a thermometer to measure temperature. Most thermometers in a laboratory are glass tubes with a bulb at the bottom end containing a liquid such as colored alcohol. The liquid rises or falls with a change in temperature. To read a glass thermometer like the thermometer in **Figure 14,** rotate it slowly until a red line appears. Read the temperature where the red line ends.

Form Operational Definitions An operational definition defines an object by how it functions, works, or behaves. For example, when you are playing hide and seek and a tree is home base, you have created an operational definition for a tree.

Objects can have more than one operational definition. For example, a ruler can be defined as a tool that measures the length of an object (how it is used). It can also be a tool with a series of marks used as a standard when measuring (how it works).

Analyze the Data

To determine the meaning of your observations and investigation results, you will need to look for patterns in the data. Then you must think critically to determine what the data mean. Scientists use several approaches when they analyze the data they have collected and recorded. Each approach is useful for identifying specific patterns.

Interpret Data The word *interpret* means "to explain the meaning of something." When analyzing data from an experiment, try to find out what the data show. Identify the control group and the test group to see whether changes in the independent variable have had an effect. Look for differences in the dependent variable between the control and test groups.

Classify Sorting objects or events into groups based on common features is called classifying. When classifying, first observe the objects or events to be classified. Then select one feature that is shared by some members in the group, but not by all. Place those members that share that feature in a subgroup. You can classify members into smaller and smaller subgroups based on characteristics. Remember that when you classify, you are grouping objects or events for a purpose. Keep your purpose in mind as you select the features to form groups and subgroups.

Compare and Contrast Observations can be analyzed by noting the similarities and differences between two or more objects or events that you observe. When you look at objects or events to see how they are similar, you are comparing them. Contrasting is looking for differences in objects or events.

SCIENCE SKILL HANDBOOK

MATH SKILL HANDBOOK

FOLDABLES HANDBOOK

REFERENCE HANDBOOK

GLOSSARY/ GLOSARIO

INDEX

SCIENCE SKILL HANDBOOK

MATH SKILL HANDBOOK

FOLDABLES HANDBOOK

REFERENCE HANDBOOK

GLOSSARY/ GLOSARIO

INDEX

Recognize Cause and Effect A cause is a reason for an action or condition. The effect is that action or condition. When two events happen together, it is not necessarily true that one event caused the other. Scientists must design a controlled investigation to recognize the exact cause and effect.

Draw Conclusions

When scientists have analyzed the data they collected, they proceed to draw conclusions about the data. These conclusions are sometimes stated in words similar to the hypothesis that you formed earlier. They may confirm a hypothesis, or lead you to a new hypothesis.

Infer Scientists often make inferences based on their observations. An inference is an attempt to explain observations or to indicate a cause. An inference is not a fact, but a logical conclusion that needs further investigation. For example, you may infer that a fire has caused smoke. Until you investigate, however, you do not know for sure.

Apply When you draw a conclusion, you must apply those conclusions to determine whether the data supports the hypothesis. If your data do not support your hypothesis, it does not mean that the hypothesis is wrong. It means only that the result of the investigation did not support the hypothesis. Maybe the experiment needs to be redesigned, or some of the initial observations on which the hypothesis was based were incomplete or biased. Perhaps more observation or research is needed to refine your hypothesis. A successful investigation does not always come out the way you originally predicted.

Avoid Bias Sometimes a scientific investigation involves making judgments. When you make a judgment, you form an opinion. It is important to be honest and not to allow any expectations of results to bias your judgments. This is important throughout the entire investigation, from researching to collecting data to drawing conclusions.

Communicate

The communication of ideas is an important part of the work of scientists. A discovery that is not reported will not advance the scientific community's understanding or knowledge. Communication among scientists also is important as a way of improving their investigations.

Scientists communicate in many ways, from writing articles in journals and magazines that explain their investigations and experiments, to announcing important discoveries on television and radio. Scientists also share ideas with colleagues on the Internet or present them as lectures, like the student is doing in **Figure 15.**

Figure 15 A student communicates to his peers about his investigation.

These safety symbols are used in laboratory and field investigations in this book to indicate possible hazards. Learn the meaning of each symbol and refer to this page often. *Remember to wash your hands thoroughly after completing lab procedures.*

PROTECTIVE EQUIPMENT Do not begin any lab without the proper protection equipment.

|  GOGGLES | Proper eye protection must be worn when performing or observing science activities that involve items or conditions as listed below. |  APRON | Wear an approved apron when using substances that could stain, wet, or destroy cloth. |  SOAP | Wash hands with soap and water before removing goggles and after all lab activities. |  GLOVES | Wear gloves when working with biological materials, chemicals, animals, or materials that can stain or irritate hands. |

LABORATORY HAZARDS

Symbols	Potential Hazards	Precaution	Response
DISPOSAL	contamination of classroom or environment due to improper disposal of materials such as chemicals and live specimens	• DO NOT dispose of hazardous materials in the sink or trash can. • Dispose of wastes as directed by your teacher.	• If hazardous materials are disposed of improperly, notify your teacher immediately.
EXTREME TEMPERATURE	skin burns due to extremely hot or cold materials such as hot glass, liquids, or metals; liquid nitrogen; dry ice	• Use proper protective equipment, such as hot mitts and/or tongs, when handling objects with extreme temperatures.	• If injury occurs, notify your teacher immediately.
SHARP OBJECTS	punctures or cuts from sharp objects such as razor blades, pins, scalpels, and broken glass	• Handle glassware carefully to avoid breakage. • Walk with sharp objects pointed downward, away from you and others.	• If broken glass or injury occurs, notify your teacher immediately.
ELECTRICAL	electric shock or skin burn due to improper grounding, short circuits, liquid spills, or exposed wires	• Check condition of wires and apparatus for fraying or uninsulated wires, and broken or cracked equipment. • Use only GFCI-protected outlets	• DO NOT attempt to fix electrical problems. Notify your teacher immediately.
CHEMICAL	skin irritation or burns, breathing difficulty, and/or poisoning due to touching, swallowing, or inhalation of chemicals such as acids, bases, bleach, metal compounds, iodine, poinsettias, pollen, ammonia, acetone, nail polish remover, heated chemicals, mothballs, and any other chemicals labeled or known to be dangerous	• Wear proper protective equipment such as goggles, apron, and gloves when using chemicals. • Ensure proper room ventilation or use a fume hood when using materials that produce fumes. • NEVER smell fumes directly. • NEVER taste or eat any material in the laboratory.	• If contact occurs, immediately flush affected area with water and notify your teacher. • If a spill occurs, leave the area immediately and notify your teacher.
FLAMMABLE	unexpected fire due to liquids or gases that ignite easily such as rubbing alcohol	• Avoid open flames, sparks, or heat when flammable liquids are present.	• If a fire occurs, leave the area immediately and notify your teacher.
OPEN FLAME	burns or fire due to open flame from matches, Bunsen burners, or burning materials	• Tie back loose hair and clothing. • Keep flame away from all materials. • Follow teacher instructions when lighting and extinguishing flames. • Use proper protection, such as hot mitts or tongs, when handling hot objects.	• If a fire occurs, leave the area immediately and notify your teacher.
ANIMAL SAFETY	injury to or from laboratory animals	• Wear proper protective equipment such as gloves, apron, and goggles when working with animals. • Wash hands after handling animals.	• If injury occurs, notify your teacher immediately.
BIOLOGICAL	infection or adverse reaction due to contact with organisms such as bacteria, fungi, and biological materials such as blood, animal or plant materials	• Wear proper protective equipment such as gloves, goggles, and apron when working with biological materials. • Avoid skin contact with an organism or any part of the organism. • Wash hands after handling organisms.	• If contact occurs, wash the affected area and notify your teacher immediately.
FUME	breathing difficulties from inhalation of fumes from substances such as ammonia, acetone, nail polish remover, heated chemicals, and mothballs	• Wear goggles, apron, and gloves. • Ensure proper room ventilation or use a fume hood when using substances that produce fumes. • NEVER smell fumes directly.	• If a spill occurs, leave area and notify your teacher immediately.
IRRITANT	irritation of skin, mucous membranes, or respiratory tract due to materials such as acids, bases, bleach, pollen, mothballs, steel wool, and potassium permanganate	• Wear goggles, apron, and gloves. • Wear a dust mask to protect against fine particles.	• If skin contact occurs, immediately flush the affected area with water and notify your teacher.
RADIOACTIVE	excessive exposure from alpha, beta, and gamma particles	• Remove gloves and wash hands with soap and water before removing remainder of protective equipment.	• If cracks or holes are found in the container, notify your teacher immediately.

SCIENCE SKILL HANDBOOK

MATH SKILL HANDBOOK

FOLDABLES HANDBOOK

REFERENCE HANDBOOK

GLOSSARY/ GLOSARIO

INDEX

Safety in the Science Laboratory

Introduction to Science Safety

The science laboratory is a safe place to work if you follow standard safety procedures. Being responsible for your own safety helps to make the entire laboratory a safer place for everyone. When performing any lab, read and apply the caution statements and safety symbol listed at the beginning of the lab.

General Safety Rules

1. Complete the *Lab Safety Form* or other safety contract BEFORE starting any science lab.

2. Study the procedure. Ask your teacher any questions. Be sure you understand safety symbols shown on the page.

3. Notify your teacher about allergies or other health conditions that can affect your participation in a lab.

4. Learn and follow use and safety procedures for your equipment. If unsure, ask your teacher.

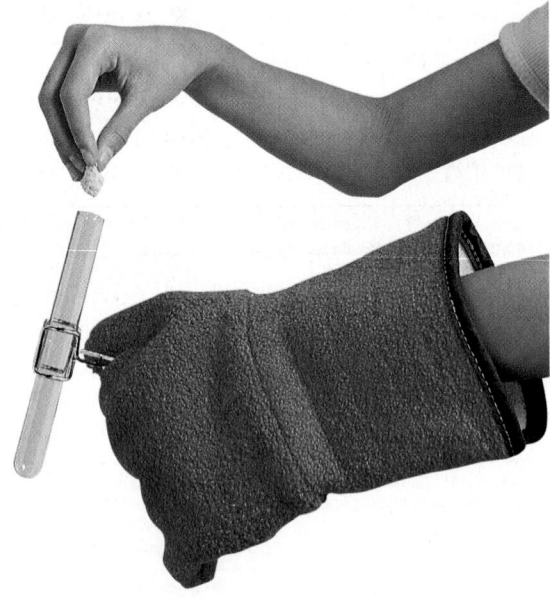

5. Never eat, drink, chew gum, apply cosmetics, or do any personal grooming in the lab. Never use lab glassware as food or drink containers. Keep your hands away from your face and mouth.

6. Know the location and proper use of the safety shower, eye wash, fire blanket, and fire alarm.

Prevent Accidents

1. Use the safety equipment provided to you. Goggles and a safety apron should be worn during investigations.

2. Do NOT use hair spray, mousse, or other flammable hair products. Tie back long hair and tie down loose clothing.

3. Do NOT wear sandals or other open-toed shoes in the lab.

4. Remove jewelry on hands and wrists. Loose jewelry, such as chains and long necklaces, should be removed to prevent them from getting caught in equipment.

5. Do not taste any substances or draw any material into a tube with your mouth.

6. Proper behavior is expected in the lab. Practical jokes and fooling around can lead to accidents and injury.

7. Keep your work area uncluttered.

Laboratory Work

1. Collect and carry all equipment and materials to your work area before beginning a lab.

2. Remain in your own work area unless given permission by your teacher to leave it.

3. Always slant test tubes away from yourself and others when heating them, adding substances to them, or rinsing them.

4. If instructed to smell a substance in a container, hold the container a short distance away and fan vapors toward your nose.

5. Do NOT substitute other chemicals/substances for those in the materials list unless instructed to do so by your teacher.

6. Do NOT take any materials or chemicals outside of the laboratory.

7. Stay out of storage areas unless instructed to be there and supervised by your teacher.

Laboratory Cleanup

1. Turn off all burners, water, and gas, and disconnect all electrical devices.

2. Clean all pieces of equipment and return all materials to their proper places.

3. Dispose of chemicals and other materials as directed by your teacher. Place broken glass and solid substances in the proper containers. Never discard materials in the sink.

4. Clean your work area.

5. Wash your hands with soap and water thoroughly BEFORE removing your goggles.

Emergencies

1. Report any fire, electrical shock, glassware breakage, spill, or injury, no matter how small, to your teacher immediately. Follow his or her instructions.

2. If your clothing should catch fire, STOP, DROP, and ROLL. If possible, smother it with the fire blanket or get under a safety shower. NEVER RUN.

3. If a fire should occur, turn off all gas and leave the room according to established procedures.

4. In most instances, your teacher will clean up spills. Do NOT attempt to clean up spills unless you are given permission and instructions to do so.

5. If chemicals come into contact with your eyes or skin, notify your teacher immediately. Use the eyewash, or flush your skin or eyes with large quantities of water.

6. The fire extinguisher and first-aid kit should only be used by your teacher unless it is an extreme emergency and you have been given permission.

7. If someone is injured or becomes ill, only a professional medical provider or someone certified in first aid should perform first-aid procedures.

SCIENCE SKILL HANDBOOK

MATH SKILL HANDBOOK

FOLDABLES HANDBOOK

REFERENCE HANDBOOK

GLOSSARY/ GLOSARIO

INDEX

Use Fractions

A fraction compares a part to a whole. In the fraction $\frac{2}{3}$, the 2 represents the part and is the numerator. The 3 represents the whole and is the denominator.

Reduce Fractions To reduce a fraction, you must find the largest factor that is common to both the numerator and the denominator, the greatest common factor (GCF). Divide both numbers by the GCF. The fraction has then been reduced, or it is in its simplest form.

Example

Twelve of the 20 chemicals in the science lab are in powder form. What fraction of the chemicals used in the lab are in powder form?

Step 1   Write the fraction.

$$\frac{\text{part}}{\text{whole}} = \frac{12}{20}$$

Step 2   To find the GCF of the numerator and denominator, list all of the factors of each number.

Factors of 12: 1, 2, 3, 4, 6, 12 (the numbers that divide evenly into 12)

Factors of 20: 1, 2, 4, 5, 10, 20 (the numbers that divide evenly into 20)

Step 3   List the common factors.

1, 2, 4

Step 4   Choose the greatest factor in the list. The GCF of 12 and 20 is 4.

Step 5   Divide the numerator and denominator by the GCF.

$$\frac{12 \div 4}{20 \div 4} = \frac{3}{5}$$

In the lab, $\frac{3}{5}$ of the chemicals are in powder form.

Practice Problem At an amusement park, 66 of 90 rides have a height restriction. What fraction of the rides, in its simplest form, has a height restriction?

Add and Subtract Fractions with Like Denominators To add or subtract fractions with the same denominator, add or subtract the numerators and write the sum or difference over the denominator. After finding the sum or difference, find the simplest form for your fraction.

Example 1

In the forest outside your house, $\frac{1}{8}$ of the animals are rabbits, $\frac{3}{8}$ are squirrels, and the remainder are birds and insects. How many are mammals?

Step 1   Add the numerators.

$$\frac{1}{8} + \frac{3}{8} = \frac{(1 + 3)}{8} = \frac{4}{8}$$

Step 2   Find the GCF.

$$\frac{4}{8} \text{ (GCF, 4)}$$

Step 3   Divide the numerator and denominator by the GCF.

$$\frac{4 \div 4}{8 \div 4} = \frac{1}{2}$$

$\frac{1}{2}$ of the animals are mammals.

Example 2

If $\frac{7}{16}$ of the Earth is covered by freshwater, and $\frac{1}{16}$ of that is in glaciers, how much freshwater is not frozen?

Step 1   Subtract the numerators.

$$\frac{7}{16} - \frac{1}{16} = \frac{(7 - 1)}{16} = \frac{6}{16}$$

Step 2   Find the GCF.

$$\frac{6}{16} \text{ (GCF, 2)}$$

Step 3   Divide the numerator and denominator by the GCF.

$$\frac{6 \div 2}{16 \div 2} = \frac{3}{8}$$

$\frac{3}{8}$ of the freshwater is not frozen.

Practice Problem A bicycle rider is riding at a rate of 15 km/h for $\frac{4}{9}$ of his ride, 10 km/h for $\frac{2}{9}$ of his ride, and 8 km/h for the remainder of the ride. How much of his ride is he riding at a rate greater than 8 km/h?

SCIENCE SKILL HANDBOOK

MATH SKILL HANDBOOK

FOLDABLES HANDBOOK

REFERENCE HANDBOOK

GLOSSARY/ GLOSARIO

INDEX

Add and Subtract Fractions with Unlike Denominators To add or subtract fractions with unlike denominators, first find the least common denominator (LCD). This is the smallest number that is a common multiple of both denominators. Rename each fraction with the LCD, and then add or subtract. Find the simplest form if necessary.

Example 1

A chemist makes a paste that is $\frac{1}{2}$ table salt (NaCl), $\frac{1}{3}$ sugar ($C_6H_{12}O_6$), and the remainder is water (H_2O). How much of the paste is a solid?

Step 1 Find the LCD of the fractions.

$$\frac{1}{2} + \frac{1}{3} \text{ (LCD, 6)}$$

Step 2 Rename each numerator and each denominator with the LCD.

Step 3 Add the numerators.

$$\frac{3}{6} + \frac{2}{6} = \frac{(3+2)}{6} = \frac{5}{6}$$

$\frac{5}{6}$ of the paste is a solid.

Example 2

The average precipitation in Grand Junction, CO, is $\frac{7}{10}$ inch in November, and $\frac{3}{5}$ inch in December. What is the total average precipitation?

Step 1 Find the LCD of the fractions.

$$\frac{7}{10} + \frac{3}{5} \text{ (LCD, 10)}$$

Step 2 Rename each numerator and each denominator with the LCD.

Step 3 Add the numerators.

$$\frac{7}{10} + \frac{6}{10} = \frac{(7+6)}{10} = \frac{13}{10}$$

$\frac{13}{10}$ inches total precipitation, or $1\frac{3}{10}$ inches.

Practice Problem On an electric bill, about $\frac{1}{8}$ of the energy is from solar energy and about $\frac{1}{10}$ is from wind power. How much of the total bill is from solar energy and wind power combined?

Example 3

In your body, $\frac{7}{10}$ of your muscle contractions are involuntary (cardiac and smooth muscle tissue). Smooth muscle makes $\frac{3}{15}$ of your muscle contractions. How many of your muscle contractions are made by cardiac muscle?

Step 1 Find the LCD of the fractions.

$$\frac{7}{10} - \frac{3}{15} \text{ (LCD, 30)}$$

Step 2 Rename each numerator and each denominator with the LCD.

$$\frac{7 \times 3}{10 \times 3} = \frac{21}{30}$$

$$\frac{3 \times 2}{15 \times 2} = \frac{6}{30}$$

Step 3 Subtract the numerators.

$$\frac{21}{30} - \frac{6}{30} = \frac{(21-6)}{30} = \frac{15}{30}$$

Step 4 Find the GCF.

$$\frac{15}{30} \text{ (GCF, 15)}$$

$$\frac{1}{2}$$

$\frac{1}{2}$ of all muscle contractions are cardiac muscle.

Example 4

Tony wants to make cookies that call for $\frac{3}{4}$ of a cup of flour, but he only has $\frac{1}{3}$ of a cup. How much more flour does he need?

Step 1 Find the LCD of the fractions.

$$\frac{3}{4} - \frac{1}{3} \text{ (LCD, 12)}$$

Step 2 Rename each numerator and each denominator with the LCD.

$$\frac{3 \times 3}{4 \times 3} = \frac{9}{12}$$

$$\frac{1 \times 4}{3 \times 4} = \frac{4}{12}$$

Step 3 Subtract the numerators.

$$\frac{9}{12} - \frac{4}{12} = \frac{(9-4)}{12} = \frac{5}{12}$$

$\frac{5}{12}$ of a cup of flour

Practice Problem Using the information provided to you in Example 3 above, determine how many muscle contractions are voluntary (skeletal muscle).

SCIENCE SKILL HANDBOOK

MATH SKILL HANDBOOK

FOLDABLES HANDBOOK

REFERENCE HANDBOOK

GLOSSARY/ GLOSARIO

INDEX

SCIENCE SKILL HANDBOOK

MATH SKILL HANDBOOK

FOLDABLES HANDBOOK

REFERENCE HANDBOOK

GLOSSARY/ GLOSARIO

INDEX

Multiply Fractions To multiply with fractions, multiply the numerators and multiply the denominators. Find the simplest form if necessary.

Example

Multiply $\frac{3}{5}$ by $\frac{1}{3}$.

Step 1 Multiply the numerators and denominators.

$$\frac{3}{5} \times \frac{1}{3} = \frac{(3 \times 1)}{(5 \times 3)} \, \frac{3}{15}$$

Step 2 Find the GCF.

$$\frac{3}{15} \text{ (GCF, 3)}$$

Step 3 Divide the numerator and denominator by the GCF.

$$\frac{3 \div 3}{15 \div 3} = \frac{1}{5}$$

$\frac{3}{5}$ multiplied by $\frac{1}{3}$ is $\frac{1}{5}$.

Practice Problem Multiply $\frac{3}{14}$ by $\frac{5}{16}$.

Find a Reciprocal Two numbers whose product is 1 are called multiplicative inverses, or reciprocals.

Example

Find the reciprocal of $\frac{3}{8}$.

Step 1 Inverse the fraction by putting the denominator on top and the numerator on the bottom.

$$\frac{8}{3}$$

The reciprocal of $\frac{3}{8}$ is $\frac{8}{3}$.

Practice Problem Find the reciprocal of $\frac{4}{9}$.

Divide Fractions To divide one fraction by another fraction, multiply the dividend by the reciprocal of the divisor. Find the simplest form if necessary.

Example 1

Divide $\frac{1}{9}$ by $\frac{1}{3}$.

Step 1 Find the reciprocal of the divisor.

The reciprocal of $\frac{1}{3}$ is $\frac{3}{1}$.

Step 2 Multiply the dividend by the reciprocal of the divisor.

$$\frac{\frac{1}{9}}{\frac{1}{3}} = \frac{1}{9} \times \frac{3}{1} = \frac{(1 \times 3)}{(9 \times 1)} = \frac{3}{9}$$

Step 3 Find the GCF.

$$\frac{3}{9} \text{ (GCF, 3)}$$

Step 4 Divide the numerator and denominator by the GCF.

$$\frac{3 \div 3}{9 \div 3} = \frac{1}{3}$$

$\frac{1}{9}$ divided by $\frac{1}{3}$ is $\frac{1}{3}$.

Example 2

Divide $\frac{3}{5}$ by $\frac{1}{4}$.

Step 1 Find the reciprocal of the divisor.

The reciprocal of $\frac{1}{4}$ is $\frac{4}{1}$.

Step 2 Multiply the dividend by the reciprocal of the divisor.

$$\frac{\frac{3}{5}}{\frac{1}{4}} = \frac{3}{5} \times \frac{4}{1} = \frac{(3 \times 4)}{(5 \times 1)} = \frac{12}{5}$$

$\frac{3}{5}$ divided by $\frac{1}{4}$ is $\frac{12}{5}$ or $2\frac{2}{5}$.

Practice Problem Divide $\frac{3}{11}$ by $\frac{7}{10}$.

Use Ratios

When you compare two numbers by division, you are using a ratio. Ratios can be written 3 to 5, 3:5, or $\frac{3}{5}$. Ratios, like fractions, also can be written in simplest form.

Ratios can represent one type of probability, called odds. This is a ratio that compares the number of ways a certain outcome occurs to the number of possible outcomes. For example, if you flip a coin 100 times, what are the odds that it will come up heads? There are two possible outcomes, heads or tails, so the odds of coming up heads are 50:100. Another way to say this is that 50 out of 100 times the coin will come up heads. In its simplest form, the ratio is 1:2.

Example 1

A chemical solution contains 40 g of salt and 64 g of baking soda. What is the ratio of salt to baking soda as a fraction in simplest form?

Step 1 Write the ratio as a fraction.

$$\frac{salt}{baking\ soda} = \frac{40}{64}$$

Step 2 Express the fraction in simplest form. The GCF of 40 and 64 is 8.

$$\frac{40}{64} = \frac{40 \div 8}{64 \div 8} = \frac{5}{8}$$

The ratio of salt to baking soda in the sample is 5:8.

Example 2

Sean rolls a 6-sided die 6 times. What are the odds that the side with a 3 will show?

Step 1 Write the ratio as a fraction.

$$\frac{number\ of\ sides\ with\ a\ 3}{number\ of\ possible\ sides} = \frac{1}{6}$$

Step 2 Multiply by the number of attempts.

$$\frac{1}{6} \times 6\ attempts = \frac{6}{6}\ attempts = 1\ attempt$$

1 attempt out of 6 will show a 3.

Practice Problem Two metal rods measure 100 cm and 144 cm in length. What is the ratio of their lengths in simplest form?

Use Decimals

A fraction with a denominator that is a power of ten can be written as a decimal. For example, 0.27 means $\frac{27}{100}$. The decimal point separates the ones place from the tenths place.

Any fraction can be written as a decimal using division. For example, the fraction $\frac{5}{8}$ can be written as a decimal by dividing 5 by 8. Written as a decimal, it is 0.625.

Add or Subtract Decimals When adding and subtracting decimals, line up the decimal points before carrying out the operation.

Example 1

Find the sum of 47.68 and 7.80.

Step 1 Line up the decimal places when you write the numbers.

$$\begin{array}{r} 47.68 \\ + 7.80 \\ \hline \end{array}$$

Step 2 Add the decimals.

$$\begin{array}{r} \overset{1\ 1}{47.68} \\ + 7.80 \\ \hline 55.48 \end{array}$$

The sum of 47.68 and 7.80 is 55.48.

Example 2

Find the difference of 42.17 and 15.85.

Step 1 Line up the decimal places when you write the number.

$$\begin{array}{r} 42.17 \\ -15.85 \\ \hline \end{array}$$

Step 2 Subtract the decimals.

$$\begin{array}{r} \overset{3\ 11}{4\cancel{2}.1\cancel{7}} \\ -15.85 \\ \hline 26.32 \end{array}$$

The difference of 42.17 and 15.85 is 26.32.

Practice Problem Find the sum of 1.245 and 3.842.

SCIENCE SKILL HANDBOOK

MATH SKILL HANDBOOK

FOLDABLES HANDBOOK

REFERENCE HANDBOOK

GLOSSARY/ GLOSARIO

INDEX

SCIENCE SKILL HANDBOOK

MATH SKILL HANDBOOK

FOLDABLES HANDBOOK

REFERENCE HANDBOOK

GLOSSARY/ GLOSARIO

INDEX

Multiply Decimals To multiply decimals, multiply the numbers like numbers without decimal points. Count the decimal places in each factor. The product will have the same number of decimal places as the sum of the decimal places in the factors.

Example

Multiply 2.4 by 5.9.

Step 1 Multiply the factors like two whole numbers.

$24 \times 59 = 1416$

Step 2 Find the sum of the number of decimal places in the factors. Each factor has one decimal place, for a sum of two decimal places.

Step 3 The product will have two decimal places.

14.16

The product of 2.4 and 5.9 is 14.16.

Practice Problem Multiply 4.6 by 2.2.

Divide Decimals When dividing decimals, change the divisor to a whole number. To do this, multiply both the divisor and the dividend by the same power of ten. Then place the decimal point in the quotient directly above the decimal point in the dividend. Then divide as you do with whole numbers.

Example

Divide 8.84 by 3.4.

Step 1 Multiply both factors by 10.

$3.4 \times 10 = 34, 8.84 \times 10 = 88.4$

Step 2 Divide 88.4 by 34.

$$
\begin{array}{r}
2.6 \\
34{\overline{\smash{\big)}\,88.4}} \\
\underline{-68} \\
204 \\
\underline{-204} \\
0
\end{array}
$$

8.84 divided by 3.4 is 2.6.

Practice Problem Divide 75.6 by 3.6.

Use Proportions

An equation that shows that two ratios are equivalent is a proportion. The ratios $\frac{2}{4}$ and $\frac{5}{10}$ are equivalent, so they can be written as $\frac{2}{4} = \frac{5}{10}$. This equation is a proportion.

When two ratios form a proportion, the cross products are equal. To find the cross products in the proportion $\frac{2}{4} = \frac{5}{10}$, multiply the 2 and the 10, and the 4 and the 5. Therefore $2 \times 10 = 4 \times 5$, or $20 = 20$.

Because you know that both ratios are equal, you can use cross products to find a missing term in a proportion. This is known as solving the proportion.

Example

The heights of a tree and a pole are proportional to the lengths of their shadows. The tree casts a shadow of 24 m when a 6-m pole casts a shadow of 4 m. What is the height of the tree?

Step 1 Write a proportion.

$$\frac{\text{height of tree}}{\text{height of pole}} = \frac{\text{length of tree's shadow}}{\text{length of pole's shadow}}$$

Step 2 Substitute the known values into the proportion. Let h represent the unknown value, the height of the tree.

$$\frac{h}{6} \times \frac{24}{4}$$

Step 3 Find the cross products.

$$h \times 4 = 6 \times 24$$

Step 4 Simplify the equation.

$$4h \times 144$$

Step 5 Divide each side by 4.

$$\frac{4h}{4} \times \frac{144}{4}$$

$$h = 36$$

The height of the tree is 36 m.

Practice Problem The ratios of the weights of two objects on the Moon and on Earth are in proportion. A rock weighing 3 N on the Moon weighs 18 N on Earth. How much would a rock that weighs 5 N on the Moon weigh on Earth?

Use Percentages

The word *percent* means "out of one hundred." It is a ratio that compares a number to 100. Suppose you read that 77 percent of Earth's surface is covered by water. That is the same as reading that the fraction of Earth's surface covered by water is $\frac{77}{100}$. To express a fraction as a percent, first find the equivalent decimal for the fraction. Then, multiply the decimal by 100 and add the percent symbol.

Example 1

Express $\frac{13}{20}$ as a percent.

Step 1 Find the equivalent decimal for the fraction.

$$
\begin{array}{r}
0.65 \\
20\overline{)13.00} \\
\underline{12\,0} \\
1\,00 \\
\underline{1\,00} \\
0
\end{array}
$$

Step 2 Rewrite the fraction $\frac{13}{20}$ as 0.65.

Step 3 Multiply 0.65 by 100 and add the % symbol.

$$0.65 \times 100 = 65 = 65\%$$

So, $\frac{13}{20} = 65\%$.

This also can be solved as a proportion.

Example 2

Express $\frac{13}{20}$ as a percent.

Step 1 Write a proportion.

$$\frac{13}{20} = \frac{x}{100}$$

Step 2 Find the cross products.

$$1300 = 20x$$

Step 3 Divide each side by 20.

$$\frac{1300}{20} = \frac{20x}{20}$$

$$65\% = x$$

Practice Problem In one year, 73 of 365 days were rainy in one city. What percent of the days in that city were rainy?

Solve One-Step Equations

A statement that two expressions are equal is an equation. For example, $A = B$ is an equation that states that A is equal to B.

An equation is solved when a variable is replaced with a value that makes both sides of the equation equal. To make both sides equal the inverse operation is used. Addition and subtraction are inverses, and multiplication and division are inverses.

Example 1

Solve the equation $x - 10 = 35$.

Step 1 Find the solution by adding 10 to each side of the equation.

$$x - 10 = 35$$
$$x - 10 + 10 = 35 - 10$$
$$x = 45$$

Step 2 Check the solution.

$$x - 10 = 35$$
$$45 - 10 = 35$$
$$35 = 35$$

Both sides of the equation are equal, so $x = 45$.

Example 2

In the formula $a = bc$, find the value of c if $a = 20$ and $b = 2$.

Step 1 Rearrange the formula so the unknown value is by itself on one side of the equation by dividing both sides by b.

$$a = bc$$
$$\frac{a}{b} = \frac{bc}{b}$$
$$\frac{a}{b} = c$$

Step 2 Replace the variables a and b with the values that are given.

$$\frac{a}{b} = c$$
$$\frac{20}{2} = c$$
$$10 = c$$

Step 3 Check the solution.

$$a = bc$$
$$20 = 2 \times 10$$
$$20 = 20$$

Both sides of the equation are equal, so $c = 10$ is the solution when $a = 20$ and $b = 2$.

Practice Problem In the formula $h = gd$, find the value of d if $g = 12.3$ and $h = 17.4$.

SCIENCE SKILL HANDBOOK

MATH SKILL HANDBOOK

FOLDABLES HANDBOOK

REFERENCE HANDBOOK

GLOSSARY/ GLOSARIO

INDEX

Use Statistics

The branch of mathematics that deals with collecting, analyzing, and presenting data is statistics. In statistics, there are three common ways to summarize data with a single number—the mean, the median, and the mode.

The **mean** of a set of data is the arithmetic average. It is found by adding the numbers in the data set and dividing by the number of items in the set.

The **median** is the middle number in a set of data when the data are arranged in numerical order. If there were an even number of data points, the median would be the mean of the two middle numbers.

The **mode** of a set of data is the number or item that appears most often.

Another number that often is used to describe a set of data is the range. The **range** is the difference between the largest number and the smallest number in a set of data.

Example

The speeds (in m/s) for a race car during five different time trials are 39, 37, 44, 36, and 44.

To find the mean:

Step 1 Find the sum of the numbers.

$39 + 37 + 44 + 36 + 44 = 200$

Step 2 Divide the sum by the number of items, which is 5.

$200 \div 5 = 40$

The mean is 40 m/s.

To find the median:

Step 1 Arrange the measures from least to greatest.

36, 37, 39, 44, 44

Step 2 Determine the middle measure.

36, 37, 39, 44, 44

The median is 39 m/s.

To find the mode:

Step 1 Group the numbers that are the same together.

44, 44, 36, 37, 39

Step 2 Determine the number that occurs most in the set.

44, 44, 36, 37, 39

The mode is 44 m/s.

To find the range:

Step 1 Arrange the measures from greatest to least.

44, 44, 39, 37, 36

Step 2 Determine the greatest and least measures in the set.

44, 44, 39, 37, 36

Step 3 Find the difference between the greatest and least measures.

$44 - 36 = 8$

The range is 8 m/s.

Practice Problem Find the mean, median, mode, and range for the data set 8, 4, 12, 8, 11, 14, 16.

A **frequency table** shows how many times each piece of data occurs, usually in a survey. **Table 1** below shows the results of a student survey on favorite color.

Table 1 Student Color Choice		
Color	Tally	Frequency
red	IIII	4
blue	IIII	5
black	II	2
green	III	3
purple	IIII II	7
yellow	IIII I	6

Based on the frequency table data, which color is the favorite?

Use Geometry

The branch of mathematics that deals with the measurement, properties, and relationships of points, lines, angles, surfaces, and solids is called geometry.

Perimeter The **perimeter** (P) is the distance around a geometric figure. To find the perimeter of a rectangle, add the length and width and multiply that sum by two, or $2(l + w)$. To find perimeters of irregular figures, add the length of the sides.

Example 1

Find the perimeter of a rectangle that is 3 m long and 5 m wide.

Step 1 You know that the perimeter is 2 times the sum of the width and length.

$P = 2(3 \text{ m} + 5 \text{ m})$

Step 2 Find the sum of the width and length.

$P = 2(8 \text{ m})$

Step 3 Multiply by 2.

$P = 16 \text{ m}$

The perimeter is 16 m.

Example 2

Find the perimeter of a shape with sides measuring 2 cm, 5 cm, 6 cm, 3 cm.

Step 1 You know that the perimeter is the sum of all the sides.

$P = 2 + 5 + 6 + 3$

Step 2 Find the sum of the sides.

$P = 2 + 5 + 6 + 3$

$P = 16$

The perimeter is 16 cm.

Practice Problem Find the perimeter of a rectangle with a length of 18 m and a width of 7 m.

Practice Problem Find the perimeter of a triangle measuring 1.6 cm by 2.4 cm by 2.4 cm.

Area of a Rectangle The **area** (A) is the number of square units needed to cover a surface. To find the area of a rectangle, multiply the length times the width, or $l \times w$. When finding area, the units also are multiplied. Area is given in square units.

Example

Find the area of a rectangle with a length of 1 cm and a width of 10 cm.

Step 1 You know that the area is the length multiplied by the width.

$A = (1 \text{ cm} \times 10 \text{ cm})$

Step 2 Multiply the length by the width. Also multiply the units.

$A = 10 \text{ cm}^2$

The area is 10 cm².

Practice Problem Find the area of a square whose sides measure 4 m.

Area of a Triangle To find the area of a triangle, use the formula:

$A = \frac{1}{2}(\text{base} \times \text{height})$

The base of a triangle can be any of its sides. The height is the perpendicular distance from a base to the opposite endpoint, or vertex.

Example

Find the area of a triangle with a base of 18 m and a height of 7 m.

Step 1 You know that the area is $\frac{1}{2}$ the base times the height.

$A = \frac{1}{2}(18 \text{ m} \times 7 \text{ m})$

Step 2 Multiply $\frac{1}{2}$ by the product of 18×7. Multiply the units.

$A = \frac{1}{2}(126 \text{ m}^2)$

$A = 63 \text{ m}^2$

The area is 63 m².

Practice Problem Find the area of a triangle with a base of 27 cm and a height of 17 cm.

SCIENCE SKILL HANDBOOK

MATH SKILL HANDBOOK

FOLDABLES HANDBOOK

REFERENCE HANDBOOK

GLOSSARY/ GLOSARIO

INDEX

Circumference of a Circle The **diameter** (*d*) of a circle is the distance across the circle through its center, and the **radius** (r) is the distance from the center to any point on the circle. The radius is half of the diameter. The distance around the circle is called the **circumference** (C). The formula for finding the circumference is:

$$C = 2\pi r \ \text{ or } \ C = \pi d$$

The circumference divided by the diameter is always equal to 3.1415926… This nonterminating and nonrepeating number is represented by the Greek letter π (pi). An approximation often used for π is 3.14.

Example 1

Find the circumference of a circle with a radius of 3 m.

Step 1 You know the formula for the circumference is 2 times the radius times π.

$$C = 2\pi(3)$$

Step 2 Multiply 2 times the radius.

$$C = 6\pi$$

Step 3 Multiply by π.

$$C \approx 19 \ \text{m}$$

The circumference is about 19 m.

Example 2

Find the circumference of a circle with a diameter of 24.0 cm.

Step 1 You know the formula for the circumference is the diameter times π.

$$C = \pi(24.0)$$

Step 2 Multiply the diameter by π.

$$C \approx 75.4 \ \text{cm}$$

The circumference is about 75.4 cm.

Practice Problem Find the circumference of a circle with a radius of 19 cm.

Area of a Circle The formula for the area of a circle is: $A = \pi r^2$

Example 1

Find the area of a circle with a radius of 4.0 cm.

Step 1 $A = \pi(4.0)^2$

Step 2 Find the square of the radius.

$$A = 16\pi$$

Step 3 Multiply the square of the radius by π.

$$A \approx 50 \ \text{cm}^2$$

The area of the circle is about 50 cm².

Example 2

Find the area of a circle with a radius of 225 m.

Step 1 $A = \pi(225)^2$

Step 2 Find the square of the radius.

$$A = 50625\pi$$

Step 3 Multiply the square of the radius by π.

$$A \approx 159043.1$$

The area of the circle is about 159043.1 m².

Example 3

Find the area of a circle whose diameter is 20.0 mm.

Step 1 Remember that the radius is half of the diameter.

$$A = \pi\left(\frac{20.0}{2}\right)^2$$

Step 2 Find the radius.

$$A = \pi(10.0)^2$$

Step 3 Find the square of the radius.

$$A = 100\pi$$

Step 4 Multiply the square of the radius by π.

$$A \approx 314 \ \text{mm}^2$$

The area of the circle is about 314 mm².

Practice Problem Find the area of a circle with a radius of 16 m.

SCIENCE SKILL HANDBOOK

MATH SKILL HANDBOOK

FOLDABLES HANDBOOK

REFERENCE HANDBOOK

GLOSSARY/ GLOSARIO

INDEX

Volume The measure of space occupied by a solid is the **volume** (V). To find the volume of a rectangular solid multiply the length times width times height, or $V = l \times w \times h$. It is measured in cubic units, such as cubic centimeters (cm^3).

Example

Find the volume of a rectangular solid with a length of 2.0 m, a width of 4.0 m, and a height of 3.0 m.

Step 1 You know the formula for volume is the length times the width times the height.

$$V = 2.0 \text{ m} \times 4.0 \text{ m} \times 3.0 \text{ m}$$

Step 2 Multiply the length times the width times the height.

$$V = 24 \text{ m}^3$$

The volume is 24 m^3.

Practice Problem Find the volume of a rectangular solid that is 8 m long, 4 m wide, and 4 m high.

To find the volume of other solids, multiply the area of the base times the height.

Example 1

Find the volume of a solid that has a triangular base with a length of 8.0 m and a height of 7.0 m. The height of the entire solid is 15.0 m.

Step 1 You know that the base is a triangle, and the area of a triangle is $\frac{1}{2}$ the base times the height, and the volume is the area of the base times the height.

$$V = \left[\frac{1}{2}(b \times h)\right] \times 15$$

Step 2 Find the area of the base.

$$V = \left[\frac{1}{2}(8 \times 7)\right] \times 15$$

$$V = \left(\frac{1}{2} \times 56\right) \times 15$$

Step 3 Multiply the area of the base by the height of the solid.

$$V = 28 \times 15$$

$$V = 420 \text{ m}^3$$

The volume is 420 m^3.

Example 2

Find the volume of a cylinder that has a base with a radius of 12.0 cm, and a height of 21.0 cm.

Step 1 You know that the base is a circle, and the area of a circle is the square of the radius times π, and the volume is the area of the base times the height.

$$V = (\pi r^2) \times 21$$

$$V = (\pi 12^2) \times 21$$

Step 2 Find the area of the base.

$$V = 144\pi \times 21$$

$$V = 452 \times 21$$

Step 3 Multiply the area of the base by the height of the solid.

$$V \approx 9{,}500 \text{ cm}^3$$

The volume is about 9,500 cm^3.

Example 3

Find the volume of a cylinder that has a diameter of 15 mm and a height of 4.8 mm.

Step 1 You know that the base is a circle with an area equal to the square of the radius times π. The radius is one-half the diameter. The volume is the area of the base times the height.

$$V = (\pi r^2) \times 4.8$$

$$V = \left[\pi\left(\frac{1}{2} \times 15\right)^2\right] \times 4.8$$

$$V = (\pi 7.5^2) \times 4.8$$

Step 2 Find the area of the base.

$$V = 56.25\pi \times 4.8$$

$$V \approx 176.71 \times 4.8$$

Step 3 Multiply the area of the base by the height of the solid.

$$V \approx 848.2$$

The volume is about 848.2 mm^3.

Practice Problem Find the volume of a cylinder with a diameter of 7 cm in the base and a height of 16 cm.

SCIENCE SKILL HANDBOOK

MATH SKILL HANDBOOK

FOLDABLES HANDBOOK

REFERENCE HANDBOOK

GLOSSARY/ GLOSARIO

INDEX

Science Applications

Measure in SI

The metric system of measurement was developed in 1795. A modern form of the metric system, called the International System (SI), was adopted in 1960 and provides the standard measurements that all scientists around the world can understand.

The SI system is convenient because unit sizes vary by powers of 10. Prefixes are used to name units. Look at **Table 2** for some common SI prefixes and their meanings.

Table 2 Common SI Prefixes

Prefix	Symbol	Meaning	
kilo–	k	1,000	thousandth
hecto–	h	100	hundred
deka–	da	10	ten
deci–	d	0.1	tenth
centi–	c	0.01	hundreth
milli–	m	0.001	thousandth

Example

How many grams equal one kilogram?

Step 1   Find the prefix *kilo–* in **Table 2.**

Step 2   Using **Table 2,** determine the meaning of *kilo–*. According to the table, it means 1,000. When the prefix *kilo–* is added to a unit, it means that there are 1,000 of the units in a "kilounit."

Step 3   Apply the prefix to the units in the question. The units in the question are grams. There are 1,000 grams in a kilogram.

Practice Problem Is a milligram larger or smaller than a gram? How many of the smaller units equal one larger unit? What fraction of the larger unit does one smaller unit represent?

Dimensional Analysis

Convert SI Units In science, quantities such as length, mass, and time sometimes are measured using different units. A process called dimensional analysis can be used to change one unit of measure to another. This process involves multiplying your starting quantity and units by one or more conversion factors. A conversion factor is a ratio equal to one and can be made from any two equal quantities with different units. If 1,000 mL equal 1 L then two ratios can be made.

$$\frac{1,000 \text{ mL}}{1 \text{ L}} = \frac{1 \text{ L}}{1,000 \text{ mL}} = 1$$

One can convert between units in the SI system by using the equivalents in **Table 2** to make conversion factors.

Example

How many cm are in 4 m?

Step 1   Write conversion factors for the units given. From **Table 2,** you know that 100 cm = 1 m. The conversion factors are

$$\frac{100 \text{ cm}}{1 \text{ m}} \text{ and } \frac{1 \text{ m}}{100 \text{ cm}}$$

Step 2   Decide which conversion factor to use. Select the factor that has the units you are converting from (m) in the denominator and the units you are converting to (cm) in the numerator.

$$\frac{100 \text{ cm}}{1 \text{ m}}$$

Step 3   Multiply the starting quantity and units by the conversion factor. Cancel the starting units with the units in the denominator. There are 400 cm in 4 m.

$$4 \text{ m} = \frac{100 \text{ cm}}{1 \text{ m}} = 400 \text{ cm}$$

Practice Problem How many milligrams are in one kilogram? (Hint: You will need to use two conversion factors from **Table 2.**)

Table 3 Unit System Equivalents

Type of Measurement	Equivalent
Length	1 in = 2.54 cm 1 yd = 0.91 m 1 mi = 1.61 km
Mass and weight*	1 oz = 28.35 g 1 lb = 0.45 kg 1 ton (short) = 0.91 tonnes (metric tons) 1 lb = 4.45 N
Volume	$1 \text{ in}^3 = 16.39 \text{ cm}^3$ 1 qt = 0.95 L 1 gal = 3.78 L
Area	$1 \text{ in}^2 = 6.45 \text{ cm}^2$ $1 \text{ yd}^2 = 0.83 \text{ m}^2$ $1 \text{ mi}^2 = 2.59 \text{ km}^2$ 1 acre = 0.40 hectares
Temperature	$°C = \frac{(°F - 32)}{1.8}$ K = °C + 273

*Weight is measured in standard Earth gravity.

Convert Between Unit Systems **Table 3** gives a list of equivalents that can be used to convert between English and SI units.

Example

If a meterstick has a length of 100 cm, how long is the meterstick in inches?

Step 1 Write the conversion factors for the units given. From **Table 3,** 1 in = 2.54 cm.

$$\frac{1 \text{ in}}{2.54 \text{ cm}} \quad and \quad \frac{2.54 \text{ cm}}{1 \text{ in}}$$

Step 2 Determine which conversion factor to use. You are converting from cm to in. Use the conversion factor with cm on the bottom.

$$\frac{1 \text{ in}}{2.54 \text{ cm}}$$

Step 3 Multiply the starting quantity and units by the conversion factor. Cancel the starting units with the units in the denominator. Round your answer to the nearest tenth.

$$100 \text{ cm} \times \frac{1 \text{ in}}{2.54 \text{ cm}} = 39.37 \text{ in}$$

The meterstick is about 39.4 in long.

Practice Problem 1 A book has a mass of 5 lb. What is the mass of the book in kg?

Practice Problem 2 Use the equivalent for in and cm (1 in = 2.54 cm) to show how $1 \text{ in}^3 \approx 16.39 \text{ cm}^3$.

SCIENCE SKILL HANDBOOK

MATH SKILL HANDBOOK

FOLDABLES HANDBOOK

REFERENCE HANDBOOK

GLOSSARY/ GLOSARIO

INDEX

SCIENCE SKILL HANDBOOK

MATH SKILL HANDBOOK

FOLDABLES HANDBOOK

REFERENCE HANDBOOK

GLOSSARY/ GLOSARIO

INDEX

Precision and Significant Digits

When you make a measurement, the value you record depends on the precision of the measuring instrument. This precision is represented by the number of significant digits recorded in the measurement. When counting the number of significant digits, all digits are counted except zeros at the end of a number with no decimal point such as 2,050, and zeros at the beginning of a decimal such as 0.03020. When adding or subtracting numbers with different precision, round the answer to the smallest number of decimal places of any number in the sum or difference. When multiplying or dividing, the answer is rounded to the smallest number of significant digits of any number being multiplied or divided.

Example

The lengths 5.28 and 5.2 are measured in meters. Find the sum of these lengths and record your answer using the correct number of significant digits.

Step 1 Find the sum.

5.28 m	2 digits after the decimal
+ 5.2 m	1 digit after the decimal
10.48 m	

Step 2 Round to one digit after the decimal because the least number of digits after the decimal of the numbers being added is 1.

The sum is 10.5 m.

Practice Problem 1 How many significant digits are in the measurement 7,071,301 m? How many significant digits are in the measurement 0.003010 g?

Practice Problem 2 Multiply 5.28 and 5.2 using the rule for multiplying and dividing. Record the answer using the correct number of significant digits.

Scientific Notation

Many times numbers used in science are very small or very large. Because these numbers are difficult to work with scientists use scientific notation. To write numbers in scientific notation, move the decimal point until only one non-zero digit remains on the left. Then count the number of places you moved the decimal point and use that number as a power of ten. For example, the average distance from the Sun to Mars is 227,800,000,000 m. In scientific notation, this distance is 2.278×10^{11} m. Because you moved the decimal point to the left, the number is a positive power of ten.

The mass of an electron is about 0.000 000 000 000 000 000 000 000 000 000 911 kg. Expressed in scientific notation, this mass is 9.11×10^{-31} kg. Because the decimal point was moved to the right, the number is a negative power of ten.

Example

Earth is 149,600,000 km from the Sun. Express this in scientific notation.

Step 1 Move the decimal point until one non-zero digit remains on the left.

1.496 000 00

Step 2 Count the number of decimal places you have moved. In this case, eight.

Step 2 Show that number as a power of ten, 10^8.

Earth is 1.496×10^8 km from the Sun.

Practice Problem 1 How many significant digits are in 149,600,000 km? How many significant digits are in 1.496×10^8 km?

Practice Problem 2 Parts used in a high performance car must be measured to 7×10^{-6} m. Express this number as a decimal.

Practice Problem 3 A CD is spinning at 539 revolutions per minute. Express this number in scientific notation.

Make and Use Graphs

Data in tables can be displayed in a graph—a visual representation of data. Common graph types include line graphs, bar graphs, and circle graphs.

Line Graph A line graph shows a relationship between two variables that change continuously. The independent variable is changed and is plotted on the x-axis. The dependent variable is observed, and is plotted on the y-axis.

Example

Draw a line graph of the data below from a cyclist in a long-distance race.

Table 4	**Bicycle Race Data**
Time (h)	**Distance (km)**
0	0
1	8
2	16
3	24
4	32
5	40

Step 1 Determine the x-axis and y-axis variables. Time varies independently of distance and is plotted on the x-axis. Distance is dependent on time and is plotted on the y-axis.

Step 2 Determine the scale of each axis. The x-axis data ranges from 0 to 5. The y-axis data ranges from 0 to 50.

Step 3 Using graph paper, draw and label the axes. Include units in the labels.

Step 4 Draw a point at the intersection of the time value on the x-axis and corresponding distance value on the y-axis. Connect the points and label the graph with a title, as shown in **Figure 8.**

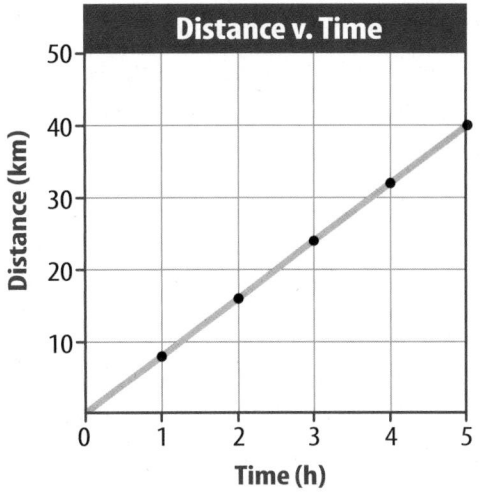

Figure 8 This line graph shows the relationship between distance and time during a bicycle ride.

Practice Problem A puppy's shoulder height is measured during the first year of her life. The following measurements were collected: (3 mo, 52 cm), (6 mo, 72 cm), (9 mo, 83 cm), (12 mo, 86 cm). Graph this data.

Find a Slope The slope of a straight line is the ratio of the vertical change, rise, to the horizontal change, run.

$$\text{Slope} = \frac{\text{vertical change (rise)}}{\text{horizontal change (run)}} = \frac{\text{change in } y}{\text{change in } x}$$

Example

Find the slope of the graph in **Figure 8**.

Step 1 You know that the slope is the change in y divided by the change in x.

$$\text{Slope} = \frac{\text{change in } y}{\text{change in } x}$$

Step 2 Determine the data points you will be using. For a straight line, choose the two sets of points that are the farthest apart.

$$\text{Slope} = \frac{(40 - 0) \text{ km}}{(5 - 0) \text{ h}}$$

Step 3 Find the change in y and x.

$$\text{Slope} = \frac{40 \text{ km}}{5 \text{ h}}$$

Step 4 Divide the change in y by the change in x.

$$\text{Slope} = \frac{8 \text{ km}}{\text{h}}$$

The slope of the graph is 8 km/h.

SCIENCE SKILL HANDBOOK

MATH SKILL HANDBOOK

FOLDABLES HANDBOOK

REFERENCE HANDBOOK

GLOSSARY/ GLOSARIO

INDEX

Bar Graph To compare data that does not change continuously you might choose a bar graph. A bar graph uses bars to show the relationships between variables. The *x*-axis variable is divided into parts. The parts can be numbers such as years, or a category such as a type of animal. The *y*-axis is a number and increases continuously along the axis.

Example

A recycling center collects 4.0 kg of aluminum on Monday, 1.0 kg on Wednesday, and 2.0 kg on Friday. Create a bar graph of this data.

Step 1 Select the *x*-axis and *y*-axis variables. The measured numbers (the masses of aluminum) should be placed on the *y*-axis. The variable divided into parts (collection days) is placed on the *x*-axis.

Step 2 Create a graph grid like you would for a line graph. Include labels and units.

Step 3 For each measured number, draw a vertical bar above the *x*-axis value up to the *y*-axis value. For the first data point, draw a vertical bar above Monday up to 4.0 kg.

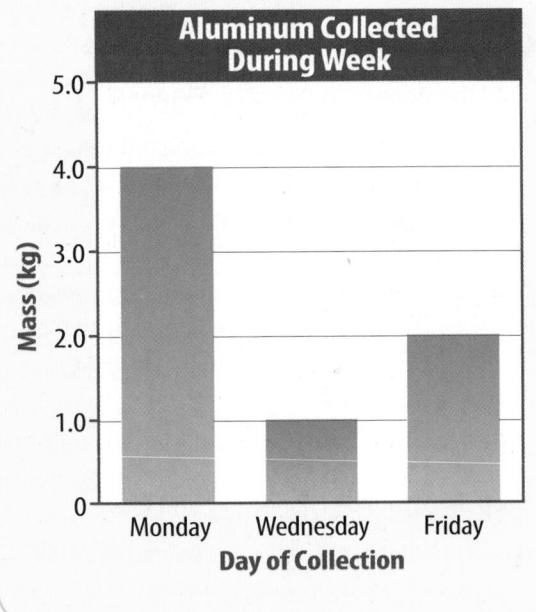

Practice Problem Draw a bar graph of the gases in air: 78% nitrogen, 21% oxygen, 1% other gases.

Circle Graph To display data as parts of a whole, you might use a circle graph. A circle graph is a circle divided into sections that represent the relative size of each piece of data. The entire circle represents 100%, half represents 50%, and so on.

Example

Air is made up of 78% nitrogen, 21% oxygen, and 1% other gases. Display the composition of air in a circle graph.

Step 1 Multiply each percent by 360° and divide by 100 to find the angle of each section in the circle.

$$78\% \times \frac{360°}{100} = 280.8°$$

$$21\% \times \frac{360°}{100} = 75.6°$$

$$1\% \times \frac{360°}{100} = 3.6°$$

Step 2 Use a compass to draw a circle and to mark the center of the circle. Draw a straight line from the center to the edge of the circle.

Step 3 Use a protractor and the angles you calculated to divide the circle into parts. Place the center of the protractor over the center of the circle and line the base of the protractor over the straight line.

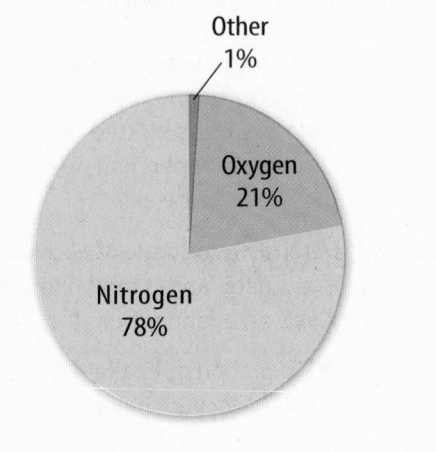

Practice Problem Draw a circle graph to represent the amount of aluminum collected during the week shown in the bar graph to the left.

Student Study Guides & Instructions
By Dinah Zike

1. You will find suggestions for Study Guides, also known as Foldables or books, in each chapter lesson and as a final project. Look at the end of the chapter to determine the project format and glue the Foldables in place as you progress through the chapter lessons.

2. Creating the Foldables or books is simple and easy to do by using copy paper, art paper, and internet printouts. Photocopies of maps, diagrams, or your own illustrations may also be used for some of the Foldables. Notebook paper is the most common source of material for study guides and 83% of all Foldables are created from it. When folded to make books, notebook paper Foldables easily fit into 11″ × 17″ or 12″ × 18″ chapter projects with space left over. Foldables made using photocopy paper are slightly larger and they fit into Projects, but snugly. Use the least amount of glue, tape, and staples needed to assemble the Foldables.

3. Seven of the Foldables can be made using either small or large paper. When 11″ × 17″ or 12″ × 18″ paper is used, these become projects for housing smaller Foldables. Project format boxes are located within the instructions to remind you of this option.

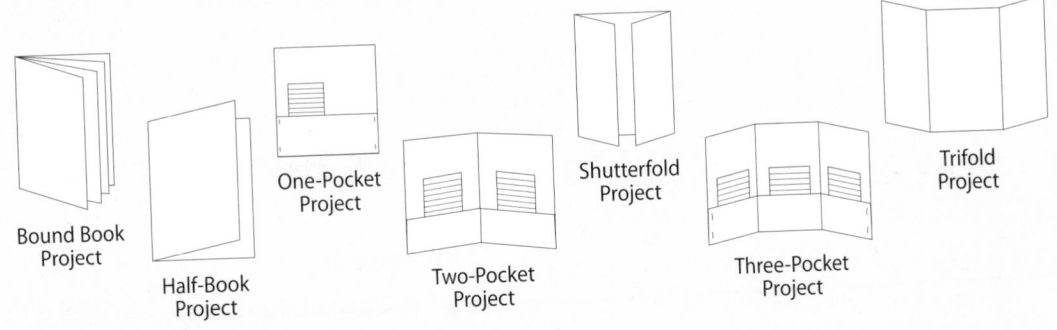

Bound Book Project

Half-Book Project

One-Pocket Project

Two-Pocket Project

Shutterfold Project

Three-Pocket Project

Trifold Project

4. Use one-gallon self-locking plastic bags to store your projects. Place strips of two-inch clear tape along the left, long side of the bag and punch holes through the taped edge. Cut the bottom corners off the bag so it will not hold air. Store this Project Portfolio inside a three-hole binder. To store a large collection of project bags, use a giant laundry-soap box. Holes can be punched in some of the Foldable Projects so they can be stored in a three-hole binder without using a plastic bag. Punch holes in the pocket books before gluing or stapling the pocket.

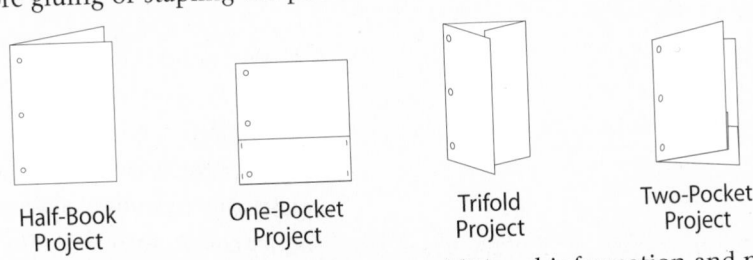

Half-Book Project

One-Pocket Project

Trifold Project

Two-Pocket Project

5. Maximize the use of the projects by collecting additional information and placing it on the back of the project and other unused spaces of the large Foldables.

SCIENCE SKILL HANDBOOK

MATH SKILL HANDBOOK

FOLDABLES HANDBOOK

REFERENCE HANDBOOK

GLOSSARY/ GLOSARIO

INDEX

Half-Book Foldable® By Dinah Zike

Step 1 Fold a sheet of notebook or copy paper in half.

Label the exterior tab and use the inside space to write information.

PROJECT FORMAT
Use 11" × 17" or 12" × 18" paper on the horizontal axis to make a large project book.

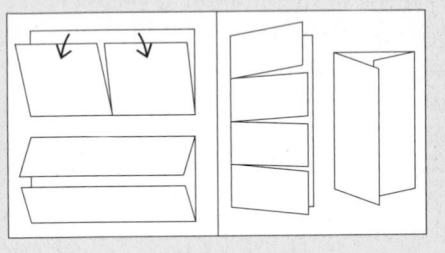

Variations

Paper can be folded horizontally, like a *hamburger* or vertically, like a *hot dog*.

A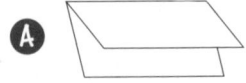

B

C Half-books can be folded so that one side is ½ inch longer than the other side. A title or question can be written on the extended tab.

Worksheet Foldable or Folded Book® By Dinah Zike

Step 1 Make a half-book (see above) using work sheets, internet print-outs, diagrams, or maps.

Step 2 Fold it in half again.

Variations

A This folded sheet as a small book with two pages can be used for comparing and contrasting, cause and effect, or other skills.

B When the sheet of paper is open, the four sections can be used separately or used collectively to show sequences or steps.

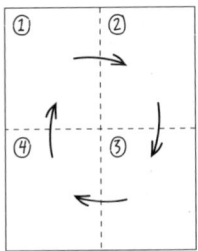

SCIENCE SKILL HANDBOOK

MATH SKILL HANDBOOK

FOLDABLES HANDBOOK

REFERENCE HANDBOOK

GLOSSARY/ GLOSARIO

INDEX

Two-Tab and Concept-Map Foldable® By Dinah Zike

Step 1 Fold a sheet of notebook or copy paper in half vertically or horizontally.

Step 2 Fold it in half again, as shown.

Step 3 Unfold once and cut along the fold line or valley of the top flap to make two flaps.

Variations

A Concept maps can be made by leaving a ½ inch tab at the top when folding the paper in half. Use arrows and labels to relate topics to the primary concept.

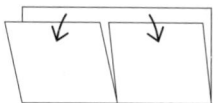

B Use two sheets of paper to make multiple page tab books. Glue or staple books together at the top fold.

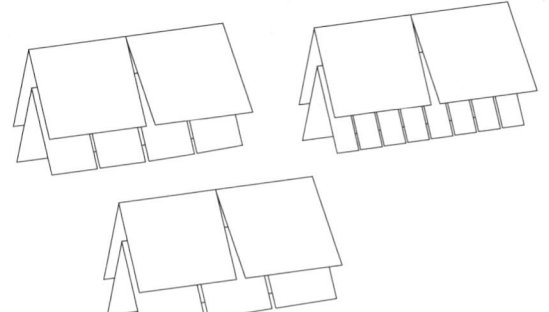

Three-Quarter Foldable® By Dinah Zike

Step 1 Make a two-tab book (see above) and cut the left tab off at the top of the fold line.

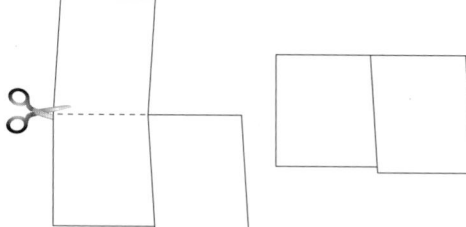

Variations

A Use this book to draw a diagram or a map on the exposed left tab. Write questions about the illustration on the top right tab and provide complete answers on the space under the tab.

B Compose a self-test using multiple choice answers for your questions. Include the correct answer with three wrong responses. The correct answers can be written on the back of the book or upside down on the bottom of the inside page.

SCIENCE SKILL HANDBOOK

MATH SKILL HANDBOOK

FOLDABLES HANDBOOK

REFERENCE HANDBOOK

GLOSSARY/ GLOSARIO

INDEX

Science Skill Handbook

Math Skill Handbook

Foldables Handbook

Reference Handbook

Glossary/Glosario

Index

Three-Tab Foldable® By Dinah Zike

Step 1 Fold a sheet of paper in half horizontally.

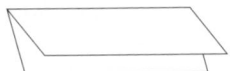

Step 2 Fold into thirds.

Step 3 Unfold and cut along the folds of the top flap to make three sections.

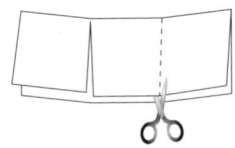

Variations

A Before cutting the three tabs draw a Venn diagram across the front of the book.

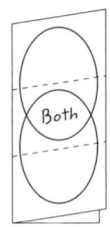

B Make a space to use for titles or concept maps by leaving a ½ inch tab at the top when folding the paper in half.

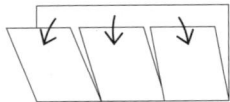

Four-Tab Foldable® By Dinah Zike

Step 1 Fold a sheet of paper in half horizontally.

Step 2 Fold in half and then fold each half as shown below.

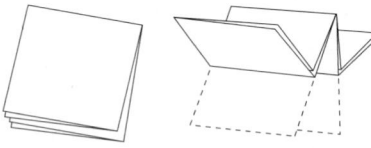

Step 3 Unfold and cut along the fold lines of the top flap to make four tabs.

Variations

A Make a space to use for titles or concept maps by leaving a ½ inch tab at the top when folding the paper in half.

B Use the book on the vertical axis, with or without an extended tab.

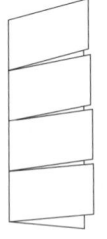

Folding Fifths for a Foldable® By Dinah Zike

Step 1 Fold a sheet of paper in half horizontally.

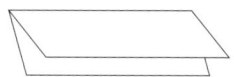

Step 2 Fold again so one-third of the paper is exposed and two-thirds are covered.

Step 3 Fold the two-thirds section in half.

Step 4 Fold the one-third section, a single thickness, backward to make a fold line.

Variations

A Unfold and cut along the fold lines to make five tabs.

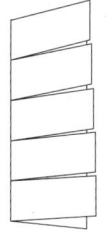

B Make a five-tab book with a ½ inch tab at the top (see two-tab instructions).

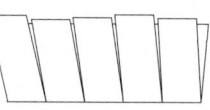

C Use 11″ × 17″ or 12″ × 18″ paper and fold into fifths for a five-column and/or row table or chart.

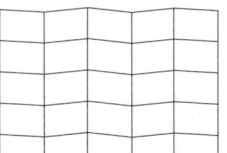

SCIENCE SKILL HANDBOOK

MATH SKILL HANDBOOK

FOLDABLES HANDBOOK

REFERENCE HANDBOOK

GLOSSARY/ GLOSARIO

INDEX

Folded Table or Chart, and Trifold Foldable® By Dinah Zike

Step 1 Fold a sheet of paper in the required number of vertical columns for the table or chart.

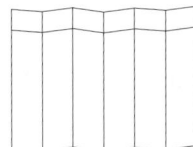

Step 2 Fold the horizontal rows needed for the table or chart.

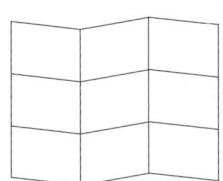

PROJECT FORMAT
Use 11″ × 17″ or 12″ × 18″ paper and fold it to make a large trifold project book or larger tables and charts.

Variations

A Make a trifold by folding the paper into thirds vertically or horizontally.

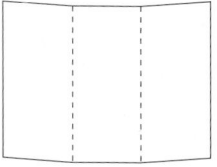

B Make a trifold book. Unfold it and draw a Venn diagram on the inside.

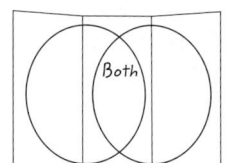

Two or Three-Pockets Foldable® By Dinah Zike

Step 1 Fold up the long side of a horizontal sheet of paper about 5 cm.

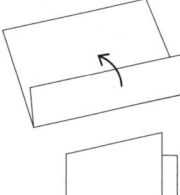

Step 2 Fold the paper in half.

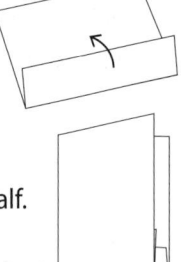

Step 3 Open the paper and glue or staple the outer edges to make two compartments.

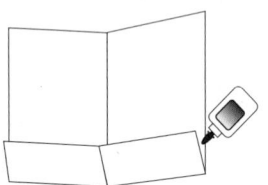

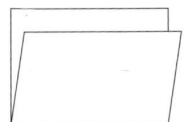

Variations

A Make a multi-page booklet by gluing several pocket books together.

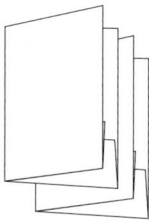

B Make a three-pocket book by using a trifold (see previous instructions).

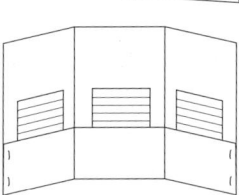

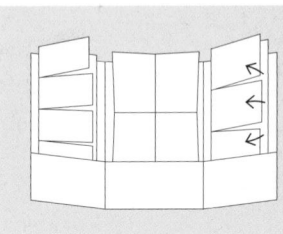

PROJECT FORMAT
Use 11″ × 17″ or 12″ × 18″ paper and fold it horizontally to make a large multi-pocket project.

- -

Matchbook Foldable® By Dinah Zike

Step 1 Fold a sheet of paper almost in half and make the back edge about 1–2 cm longer than the front edge.

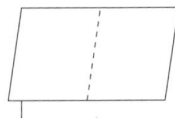

Step 2 Find the midpoint of the shorter flap.

Step 3 Open the paper and cut the short side along the midpoint making two tabs.

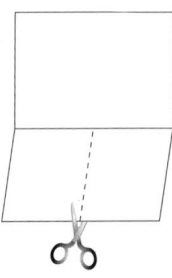

Step 4 Close the book and fold the tab over the short side.

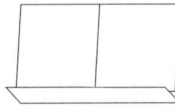

Variations

A Make a single-tab matchbook by skipping Steps 2 and 3.

B Make two smaller matchbooks by cutting the single-tab matchbook in half.

SCIENCE SKILL HANDBOOK

MATH SKILL HANDBOOK

FOLDABLES HANDBOOK

REFERENCE HANDBOOK

GLOSSARY/ GLOSARIO

INDEX

Shutterfold Foldable® By Dinah Zike

Step 1 Begin as if you were folding a vertical sheet of paper in half, but instead of creasing the paper, pinch it to show the midpoint.

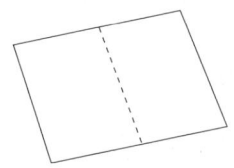

PROJECT FORMAT
Use 11" × 17" or 12" × 18" paper and fold it to make a large shutterfold project.

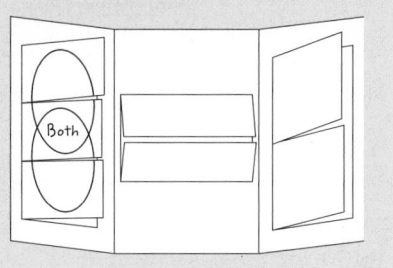

Step 2 Fold the top and bottom to the middle and crease the folds.

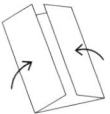

Variations

A Use the shutterfold on the horizontal axis.

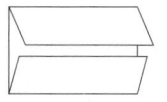

B Create a center tab by leaving .5–2 cm between the flaps in Step 2.

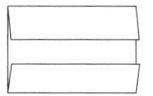

Four-Door Foldable® By Dinah Zike

Step 1 Make a shutterfold (see above).

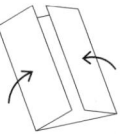

Step 2 Fold the sheet of paper in half.

Step 3 Open the last fold and cut along the inside fold lines to make four tabs.

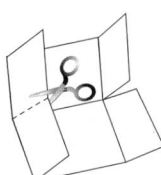

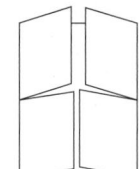

Variations

A Use the four-door book on the opposite axis.

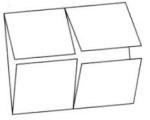

B Create a center tab by leaving .5–2 cm between the flaps in Step 1.

SCIENCE SKILL HANDBOOK

MATH SKILL HANDBOOK

FOLDABLES HANDBOOK

REFERENCE HANDBOOK

GLOSSARY/ GLOSARIO

INDEX

Bound Book Foldable® By Dinah Zike

Step 1 Fold three sheets of paper in half. Place the papers in a stack, leaving about .5 cm between each top fold. Mark all three sheets about 3 cm from the outer edges.

Step 2 Using two of the sheets, cut from the outer edges to the marked spots on each side. On the other sheet, cut between the marked spots.

Step 3 Take the two sheets from Step 1 and slide them through the cut in the third sheet to make a 12-page book.

Step 4 Fold the bound pages in half to form a book.

Variation

A Use two sheets of paper to make an eight-page book, or increase the number of pages by using more than three sheets.

PROJECT FORMAT
Use two or more sheets of 11″ × 17″ or 12″ × 18″ paper and fold it to make a large bound book project.

- -

Accordian Foldable® By Dinah Zike

Step 1 Fold the selected paper in half vertically, like a *hamburger*.

Step 2 Cut each sheet of folded paper in half along the fold lines.

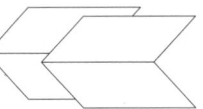

Step 3 Fold each half-sheet almost in half, leaving a 2 cm tab at the top.

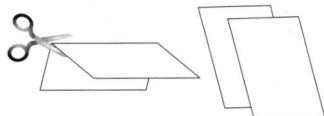

Step 4 Fold the top tab over the short side, then fold it in the opposite direction.

Variations

A Glue the straight edge of one paper inside the tab of another sheet. Leave a tab at the end of the book to add more pages.

B Tape the straight edge of one paper to the tab of another sheet, or just tape the straight edges of nonfolded paper end to end to make an accordian.

C Use whole sheets of paper to make a large accordian.

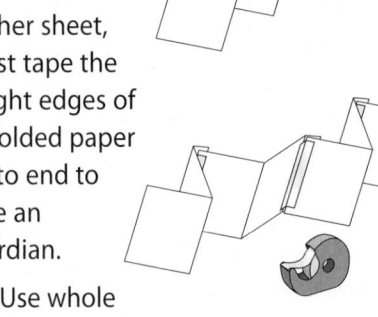

SCIENCE SKILL HANDBOOK

MATH SKILL HANDBOOK

FOLDABLES HANDBOOK

REFERENCE HANDBOOK

GLOSSARY/ GLOSARIO

INDEX

Layered Foldable® By Dinah Zike

Step 1 Stack two sheets of paper about 1–2 cm apart. Keep the right and left edges even.

Step 2 Fold up the bottom edges to form four tabs. Crease the fold to hold the tabs in place.

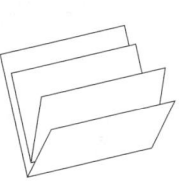

Step 3 Staple along the folded edge, or open and glue the papers together at the fold line.

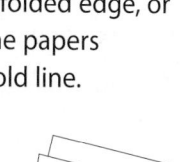

Variations

A Rotate the book so the fold is at the top or to the side.

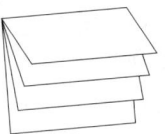

B Extend the book by using more than two sheets of paper.

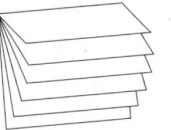

Envelope Foldable® By Dinah Zike

Step 1 Fold a sheet of paper into a *taco*. Cut off the tab at the top.

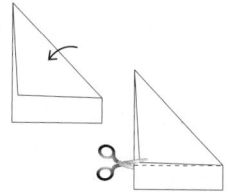

Step 2 Open the *taco* and fold it the opposite way making another *taco* and an X-fold pattern on the sheet of paper.

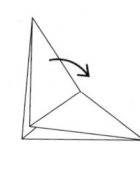

Step 3 Cut a map, illustration, or diagram to fit the inside of the envelope.

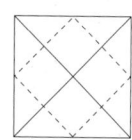

Step 4 Use the outside tabs for labels and inside tabs for writing information.

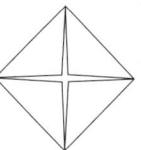

Variations

A Use 11″ × 17″ or 12″ × 18″ paper to make a large envelope.

B Cut off the points of the four tabs to make a window in the middle of the book.

SCIENCE SKILL HANDBOOK

MATH SKILL HANDBOOK

FOLDABLES HANDBOOK

REFERENCE HANDBOOK

GLOSSARY/ GLOSARIO

INDEX

Sentence Strip Foldable® By Dinah Zike

Step 1 Fold two sheets of paper in half vertically, like a *hamburger*.

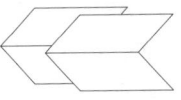

Step 2 Unfold and cut along fold lines making four half sheets.

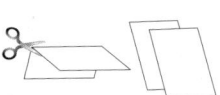

Step 3 Fold each half sheet in half horizontally, like a *hot dog*.

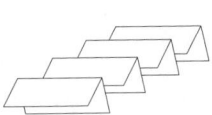

Step 4 Stack folded horizontal sheets evenly and staple together on the left side.

Step 5 Open the top flap of the first sentence strip and make a cut about 2 cm from the stapled edge to the fold line. This forms a flap that can be raisied and lowered. Repeat this step for each sentence strip.

Variations

A Expand this book by using more than two sheets of paper.

B Use whole sheets of paper to make large books.

Pyramid Foldable® By Dinah Zike

Step 1 Fold a sheet of paper into a *taco*. Crease the fold line, but do not cut it off.

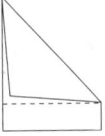

Step 2 Open the folded sheet and refold it like a *taco* in the opposite direction to create an X-fold pattern.

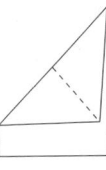

Step 3 Cut one fold line as shown, stopping at the center of the X-fold to make a flap.

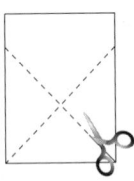

Step 4 Outline the fold lines of the X-fold. Label the three front sections and use the inside spaces for notes. Use the tab for the title.

Step 5 Glue the tab into a project book or notebook. Use the space under the pyramid for other information.

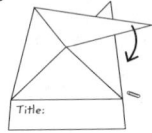

Step 6 To display the pyramid, fold the flap under and secure with a paper clip, if needed.

SCIENCE SKILL HANDBOOK

MATH SKILL HANDBOOK

FOLDABLES HANDBOOK

REFERENCE HANDBOOK

GLOSSARY/ GLOSARIO

INDEX

Single-Pocket or One-Pocket Foldable® By Dinah Zike

Step 1 Using a large piece of paper on a vertical axis, fold the bottom edge of the paper upwards, about 5 cm.

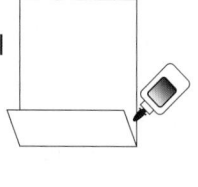

Step 2 Glue or staple the outer edges to make a large pocket.

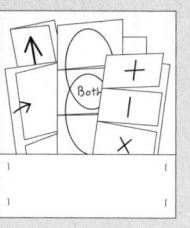

Variations

A Make the one-pocket project using the paper on the horizontal axis.

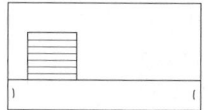

B To store materials securely inside, fold the top of the paper almost to the center, leaving about 2–4 cm between the paper edges. Slip the Foldables through the opening and under the top and bottom pockets.

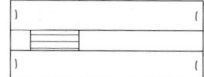

Multi-Tab Foldable® By Dinah Zike

Step 1 Fold a sheet of notebook paper in half like a *hot dog*.

Step 2 Open the paper and on one side cut every third line. This makes ten tabs on wide ruled notebook paper and twelve tabs on college ruled.

Step 3 Label the tabs on the front side and use the inside space for definitions or other information.

Variation

A Make a tab for a title by folding the paper so the holes remain uncovered. This allows the notebook Foldable to be stored in a three-hole binder.

SCIENCE SKILL HANDBOOK

MATH SKILL HANDBOOK

FOLDABLES HANDBOOK

REFERENCE HANDBOOK

GLOSSARY/ GLOSARIO

INDEX

Reference Handbook

PERIODIC TABLE OF THE ELEMENTS

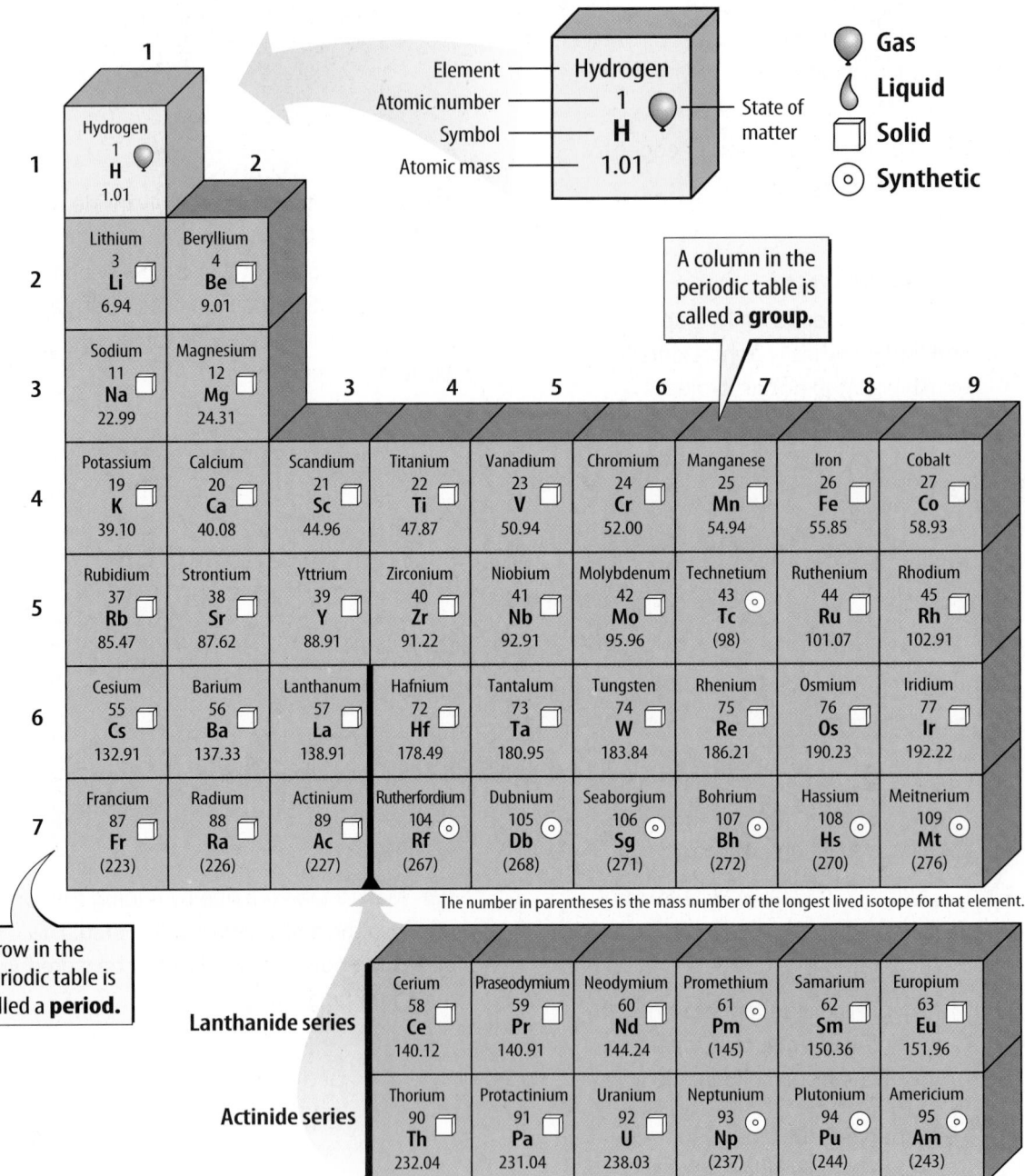

SCIENCE SKILL HANDBOOK

MATH SKILL HANDBOOK

FOLDABLES HANDBOOK

REFERENCE HANDBOOK

GLOSSARY/GLOSARIO

INDEX

Periodic Table (portion)

Legend:
- Metal
- Metalloid
- Nonmetal
- Recently discovered

18
Helium 2 **He** 4.00

13	14	15	16	17
Boron 5 **B** 10.81	Carbon 6 **C** 12.01	Nitrogen 7 **N** 14.01	Oxygen 8 **O** 16.00	Fluorine 9 **F** 19.00	Neon 10 **Ne** 20.18

10	11	12	13	14	15	16	17	18
			Aluminum 13 **Al** 26.98	Silicon 14 **Si** 28.09	Phosphorus 15 **P** 30.97	Sulfur 16 **S** 32.07	Chlorine 17 **Cl** 35.45	Argon 18 **Ar** 39.95
Nickel 28 **Ni** 58.69	Copper 29 **Cu** 63.55	Zinc 30 **Zn** 65.38	Gallium 31 **Ga** 69.72	Germanium 32 **Ge** 72.64	Arsenic 33 **As** 74.92	Selenium 34 **Se** 78.96	Bromine 35 **Br** 79.90	Krypton 36 **Kr** 83.80
Palladium 46 **Pd** 106.42	Silver 47 **Ag** 107.87	Cadmium 48 **Cd** 112.41	Indium 49 **In** 114.82	Tin 50 **Sn** 118.71	Antimony 51 **Sb** 121.76	Tellurium 52 **Te** 127.60	Iodine 53 **I** 126.90	Xenon 54 **Xe** 131.29
Platinum 78 **Pt** 195.08	Gold 79 **Au** 196.97	Mercury 80 **Hg** 200.59	Thallium 81 **Tl** 204.38	Lead 82 **Pb** 207.20	Bismuth 83 **Bi** 208.98	Polonium 84 **Po** (209)	Astatine 85 **At** (210)	Radon 86 **Rn** (222)
Darmstadtium 110 **Ds** (281)	Roentgenium 111 **Rg** (280)	Copernicium 112 **Cn** (285)	* Ununtrium 113 **Uut** (284)	* Ununquadium 114 **Uuq** (289)	* Ununpentium 115 **Uup** (288)	* Ununhexium 116 **Uuh** (293)		* Ununoctium 118 **Uuo** (294)

*The names and symbols for elements 113–116 and 118 are temporary. Final names will be selected when the elements' discoveries are verified.

Gadolinium 64 **Gd** 157.25	Terbium 65 **Tb** 158.93	Dysprosium 66 **Dy** 162.50	Holmium 67 **Ho** 164.93	Erbium 68 **Er** 167.26	Thulium 69 **Tm** 168.93	Ytterbium 70 **Yb** 173.05	Lutetium 71 **Lu** 174.97
Curium 96 **Cm** (247)	Berkelium 97 **Bk** (247)	Californium 98 **Cf** (251)	Einsteinium 99 **Es** (252)	Fermium 100 **Fm** (257)	Mendelevium 101 **Md** (258)	Nobelium 102 **No** (259)	Lawrencium 103 **Lr** (262)

SCIENCE SKILL HANDBOOK

MATH SKILL HANDBOOK

FOLDABLES HANDBOOK

REFERENCE HANDBOOK

GLOSSARY/ GLOSARIO

INDEX

SCIENCE SKILL HANDBOOK

MATH SKILL HANDBOOK

FOLDABLES HANDBOOK

REFERENCE HANDBOOK

GLOSSARY/ GLOSARIO

INDEX

Diversity of Life: Classification of Living Organisms

A six-kingdom system of classification of organisms is used today. Two kingdoms—Kingdom Archaebacteria and Kingdom Eubacteria—contain organisms that do not have a nucleus and that lack membrane-bound structures in the cytoplasm of their cells. The members of the other four kingdoms have a cell or cells that contain a nucleus and structures in the cytoplasm, some of which are surrounded by membranes. These kingdoms are Kingdom Protista, Kingdom Fungi, Kingdom Plantae, and Kingdom Animalia.

Kingdom Archaebacteria

one-celled; some absorb food from their surroundings; some are photosynthetic; some are chemosynthetic; many are found in extremely harsh environments including salt ponds, hot springs, swamps, and deep-sea hydrothermal vents

Kingdom Eubacteria

one-celled; most absorb food from their surroundings; some are photosynthetic; some are chemosynthetic; many are parasites; many are round, spiral, or rod-shaped; some form colonies

Kingdom Protista

Phylum Euglenophyta one-celled; photosynthetic or take in food; most have one flagellum; euglenoids

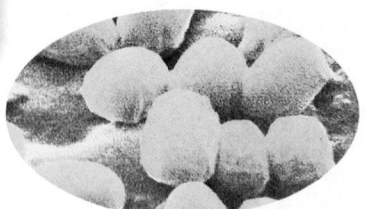

Kingdom Eubacteria
Bacillus anthracis

Phylum Chlorophyta
Desmids

Phylum Bacillariophyta one-celled; photosynthetic; have unique double shells made of silica; diatoms

Phylum Dinoflagellata one-celled; photosynthetic; contain red pigments; have two flagella; dinoflagellates

Phylum Chlorophyta one-celled, many-celled, or colonies; photosynthetic; contain chlorophyll; live on land, in freshwater, or salt water; green algae

Phylum Rhodophyta most are many-celled; photosynthetic; contain red pigments; most live in deep, saltwater environments; red algae

Phylum Phaeophyta most are many-celled; photosynthetic; contain brown pigments; most live in saltwater environments; brown algae

Phylum Rhizopoda one-celled; take in food; are free-living or parasitic; move by means of pseudopods; amoebas

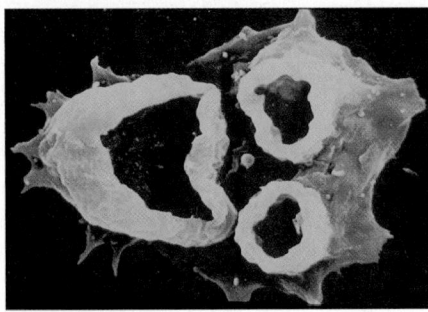

Amoeba

Phylum Zoomastigina one-celled; take in food; free-living or parasitic; have one or more flagella; zoomastigotes

Phylum Ciliophora one-celled; take in food; have large numbers of cilia; ciliates

Phylum Sporozoa one-celled; take in food; have no means of movement; are parasites in animals; sporozoans

Phylum Myxomycota
Slime mold

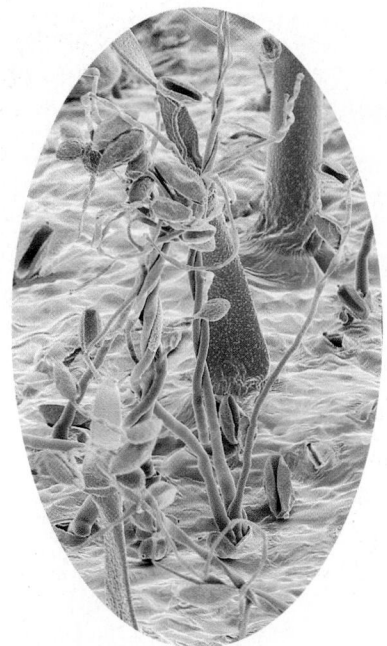

Phylum Oomycota
Phytophthora infestans

Phyla Myxomycota and Acrasiomycota one- or many-celled; absorb food; change form during life cycle; cellular and plasmodial slime molds

Phylum Oomycota many-celled; are either parasites or decomposers; live in freshwater or salt water; water molds, rusts and downy mildews

Kingdom Fungi

Phylum Zygomycota many-celled; absorb food; spores are produced in sporangia; zygote fungi; bread mold

Phylum Ascomycota one- and many-celled; absorb food; spores produced in asci; sac fungi; yeast

Phylum Basidiomycota many-celled; absorb food; spores produced in basidia; club fungi; mushrooms

Phylum Deuteromycota members with unknown reproductive structures; imperfect fungi; *Penicillium*

Phylum Mycophycota organisms formed by symbiotic relationship between an ascomycote or a basidiomycote and green alga or cyanobacterium; lichens

Lichens

SCIENCE SKILL HANDBOOK

MATH SKILL HANDBOOK

FOLDABLES HANDBOOK

REFERENCE HANDBOOK

GLOSSARY/ GLOSARIO

INDEX

Kingdom Plantae

Divisions Bryophyta (mosses), **Anthocerophyta** (hornworts), **Hepaticophyta** (liverworts), **Psilophyta** (whisk ferns) many-celled non-vascular plants; reproduce by spores produced in capsules; green; grow in moist, land environments

Division Lycophyta many-celled vascular plants; spores are produced in conelike structures; live on land; are photosynthetic; club mosses

Division Arthrophyta vascular plants; ribbed and jointed stems; scalelike leaves; spores produced in conelike structures; horsetails

Division Pterophyta vascular plants; leaves called fronds; spores produced in clusters of sporangia called sori; live on land or in water; ferns

Division Ginkgophyta deciduous trees; only one living species; have fan-shaped leaves with branching veins and fleshy cones with seeds; ginkgoes

Division Cycadophyta palmlike plants; have large, featherlike leaves; produces seeds in cones; cycads

Division Coniferophyta deciduous or evergreen; trees or shrubs; have needlelike or scalelike leaves; seeds produced in cones; conifers

Division Anthophyta
Tomato plant

**Phylum
Platyhelminthes**
Flatworm

Division Gnetophyta shrubs or woody vines; seeds are produced in cones; division contains only three genera; gnetum

Division Anthophyta dominant group of plants; flowering plants; have fruits with seeds

Kingdom Animalia

Phylum Porifera aquatic organisms that lack true tissues and organs; are asymmetrical and sessile; sponges

Phylum Cnidaria radially symmetrical organisms; have a digestive cavity with one opening; most have tentacles armed with stinging cells; live in aquatic environments singly or in colonies; includes jellyfish, corals, hydra, and sea anemones

Phylum Platyhelminthes bilaterally symmetrical worms; have flattened bodies; digestive system has one opening; parasitic and free-living species; flatworms

Division Bryophyta
Liverwort

Phylum Chordata

Phylum Nematoda round, bilaterally symmetrical body; have digestive system with two openings; free-living forms and parasitic forms; roundworms

Phylum Mollusca soft-bodied animals, many with a hard shell and soft foot or footlike appendage; a mantle covers the soft body; aquatic and terrestrial species; includes clams, snails, squid, and octopuses

Phylum Annelida bilaterally symmetrical worms; have round, segmented bodies; terrestrial and aquatic species; includes earthworms, leeches, and marine polychaetes

Phylum Arthropoda largest animal group; have hard exoskeletons, segmented bodies, and pairs of jointed appendages; land and aquatic species; includes insects, crustaceans, and spiders

Phylum Echinodermata marine organisms; have spiny or leathery skin and a water-vascular system with tube feet; are radially symmetrical; includes sea stars, sand dollars, and sea urchins

Phylum Chordata organisms with internal skeletons and specialized body systems; most have paired appendages; all at some time have a notochord, nerve cord, gill slits, and a post-anal tail; include fish, amphibians, reptiles, birds, and mammals

SCIENCE SKILL HANDBOOK

MATH SKILL HANDBOOK

FOLDABLES HANDBOOK

REFERENCE HANDBOOK

GLOSSARY/ GLOSARIO

INDEX

Use and Care of a Microscope

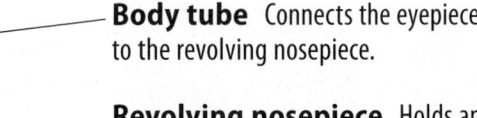

Eyepiece Contains magnifying lenses you look through.

Arm Supports the body tube.

Low-power objective Contains the lens with the lowest power magnification.

Stage clips Hold the microscope slide in place.

Coarse adjustment Focuses the image under low power.

Fine adjustment Sharpens the image under high magnification.

ocular lens

objective lens(s)

Body tube Connects the eyepiece to the revolving nosepiece.

Revolving nosepiece Holds and turns the objectives into viewing position.

High-power objective Contains the lens with the highest magnification.

Stage Supports the microscope slide.

Light source Provides light that passes upward through the diaphragm, the specimen, and the lenses.

Base Provides support for the microscope.

Caring for a Microscope

1. Always carry the microscope holding the arm with one hand and supporting the base with the other hand.

2. Don't touch the lenses with your fingers.

3. The coarse adjustment knob is used only when looking through the lowest-power objective lens. The fine adjustment knob is used when the high-power objective is in place.

4. Cover the microscope when you store it.

Using a Microscope

1. Place the microscope on a flat surface that is clear of objects. The arm should be toward you.

2. Look through the eyepiece. Adjust the diaphragm so light comes through the opening in the stage.

3. Place a slide on the stage so the specimen is in the field of view. Hold it firmly in place by using the stage clips.

4. Always focus with the coarse adjustment and the low-power objective lens first. After the object is in focus on low power, turn the nosepiece until the high-power objective is in place. Use ONLY the fine adjustment to focus with the high-power objective lens.

Making a Wet-Mount Slide

1. Carefully place the item you want to look at in the center of a clean, glass slide. Make sure the sample is thin enough for light to pass through.

2. Use a dropper to place one or two drops of water on the sample.

3. Hold a clean coverslip by the edges and place it at one edge of the water. Slowly lower the coverslip onto the water until it lies flat.

4. If you have too much water or a lot of air bubbles, touch the edge of a paper towel to the edge of the coverslip to draw off extra water and draw out unwanted air.

SCIENCE SKILL HANDBOOK

MATH SKILL HANDBOOK

FOLDABLES HANDBOOK

REFERENCE HANDBOOK

GLOSSARY/ GLOSARIO

INDEX

Glossary/Glosario

Cómo usar el glosario en español:
1. Busca el término en inglés que desees encontrar.
2. El término en español, junto con la definición, se encuentran en la columna de la derecha.

Pronunciation Key

Use the following key to help you sound out words in the glossary:

a	b**a**ck (BAK)		ew	f**oo**d (FEWD)
ay	d**ay** (DAY)		yoo	p**u**re (PYOOR)
ah	f**a**ther (FAH thur)		yew	f**ew** (FYEW)
ow	fl**ow**er (FLOW ur)		uh	comm**a** (CAH muh)
ar	c**ar** (CAR)		u (+ con)	r**u**b (RUB)
e	l**e**ss (LES)		sh	**sh**elf (SHELF)
ee	l**ea**f (LEEF)		ch	na**t**ure (NAY chur)
ih	tr**i**p (TRIHP)		g	**g**ift (GIHFT)
i (i + con + e) .	**i**dea (i DEE uh)		j	**g**em (JEM)
oh	g**o** (GOH)		ing	s**ing** (SING)
aw	s**o**ft (SAWFT)		zh	vi**si**on (VIH zhun)
or	**or**bit (OR buht)		k	ca**k**e (KAYK)
oy	c**oi**n (COYN)		s	**s**eed, **c**ent (SEED, SENT)
oo	f**oo**t (FOOT)		z	**z**one, rai**s**e (ZOHN, RAYZ)

English — **A** — **Español**

abiotic factor/active immunity

abiotic factor (ay bi AH tihk • FAK tuhr): a nonliving thing in an ecosystem. (p. 707)

absorption: the process in which nutrients from digested food are taken into the body. (p. 433)

accuracy: a description of how close a measurement is to an accepted or true value. (p. NOS 14)

acid precipitation: acidic rain or snow that forms when waste gases from automobiles and power plants combine with moisture in the air. (p. 825)

active immunity: the process by which the human body produces antibodies in response to an antigen. (p. 617)

factor abiótico/inmunidad activa

factor abiótico: componente no vivo de un ecosistema. (pág. 707)

absorción: proceso en el cual los nutrientes del alimento digerido son alojados dentro del cuerpo. (pág. 433)

exactitud: descripción de qué tan cerca está una medida a un valor aceptable. (pág. NOS 14)

precipitación ácida: lluvia o nieve ácidas que se forman cuando los gases residuales de automóviles o de plantas de energía se mezclan con la humedad en el aire. (pág. 825)

inmunidad activa: proceso por el cual el cuerpo humano produce anticuerpos en respuesta a un antígeno. (pág. 617)

active transport: the movement of substances through a cell membrane using the cell's energy. (p. 64)

adaptation (a dap TAY shun): an inherited trait that increases an organism's chance of surviving and reproducing in a particular environment. (p. 203)

aggression: a forceful behavior used to dominate or control another animal. (p. 461)

alga (plural, algae): a plantlike protist that produces food through photosynthesis using light energy and carbon dioxide. (p. 266)

allele (uh LEEL): a different form of a gene. (p. 160)

allergy: an overly sensitive immune response to common antigens. (p. 616)

alternation of generations: process that occurs when the life cycle of an organism alternates between diploid and haploid generations. (p. 352)

alveolus (al VEE uh lus; plural, alveoli): microscopic sacs or pouches at the end of the bronchioles where gas exchange occurs. (p. 561)

amoeba (uh MEE buh): one common sarcodine with an unusual adaptation for movement and getting nutrients. (p. 271)

analogous (uh NAH luh gus) structures: body parts that perform a similar function but differ in structure. (p. 211)

antibiotic (an ti bi AH tihk): a medicine that stops the growth and reproduction of bacteria. (pp. 242, 624)

antibody: a protein that can attach to a pathogen and make it useless. (pp. 251, 616)

antigen: a substance that causes an immune response. (p. 616)

appendage: a structure, such as a leg or an arm, that extends from the central part of the body. (p. 387)

artery: a vessel that carries blood away from the heart. (p. 570)

transporte activo: movimiento de sustancias a través de la membrana celular usando la energía de la célula. (pág. 64)

adaptación: rasgo heredado que aumenta la oportunidad de un organismo de sobrevivir y reproducirse en su medioambiente. (pág. 203)

agresión: comportamiento contundente usado para dominar o controlar otro animal. (pág. 461)

alga (plural, algas): protista parecida a una planta que produce el alimento por medio de la fotosíntesis, usando la energía lumínica y el dióxido de carbono. (pág. 266)

alelo: forma diferente de un gen. (pág. 160)

alergia: respuesta inmune demasiado sensible a los antígenos comunes. (pág. 616)

alternancia de generaciones: proceso que ocurre cuando el ciclo de vida de un organismo se alterna entre generaciones diploides y haploides. (pág. 352)

alveolo (plural, alveolos): bolsas o sacos microscópicos en los extremos de los bronquiolos donde ocurre el intercambio de gas. (pág. 561)

ameba: sarcodina común con una adaptación inusual para moverse y obtener nutrientes. (pág. 271)

estructuras análogas: partes del cuerpo que ejecutan una función similar pero tienen una estructura distinta. (pág. 211)

antibiótico: medicina que detiene el crecimiento y reproducción de las bacterias. (pág. 242, 624)

anticuerpo: proteína que se adhiere a un patógeno y lo hace inútil. (pág. 251, 616)

antígeno: sustancia que causa una respuesta inmune. (pág. 616)

apéndice: estructura, como una pierna o un brazo, que se prolonga de la parte central del cuerpo. (pág. 387)

arteria: vaso que lleva sangre fuera del corazón. (pág. 570)

SCIENCE SKILL HANDBOOK

MATH SKILL HANDBOOK

FOLDABLES HANDBOOK

REFERENCE HANDBOOK

GLOSSARY/ GLOSARIO

INDEX

SCIENCE SKILL HANDBOOK

MATH SKILL HANDBOOK

FOLDABLES HANDBOOK

REFERENCE HANDBOOK

GLOSSARY/ GLOSARIO

INDEX

arthritis (ar THRI tus): a disease in which joints become irritated or inflamed, such as when cartilage in joints is damaged or wears away. (p. 492)

ascus (AS kuhs): the reproductive structure where spores develop on sac fungi. (p. 279)

asexual reproduction: a type of reproduction in which one parent organism produces offspring without meiosis and fertilization. (p. 129)

asymmetry: a body plan in which an organism cannot be divided into any two parts that are nearly mirror images of each other. (p. 377)

atherosclerosis (a thuh roh skluh ROH sus): the buildup of fatty material within the walls of arteries. (p. 572)

atmosphere (AT muh sfir): a thin layer of gases surrounding Earth. (p. 709)

atria (AY tree uh; singular, atrium): the upper two chambers of the heart. (p. 568)

artritis: enfermedad en la que las articulaciones se irritan o inflaman, como cuando el cartílago en las articulaciones se lastima o desgasta. (pág. 492)

ascus: estructura reproductiva donde se desarrollan las esporas en un hongo con saco. (pág. 279)

reproducción asexual: tipo de reproducción en la cual un organismo parental produce crías sin mitosis ni fertilización. (pág. 129)

asimetría: plano de un cuerpo en el cual un organismo no se puede dividir en dos partes que sean casi imágenes al espejo una de otra. (pág. 377)

arteriosclerosis: acumulación de material graso en el interior de las paredes de las arterias. (pág. 572)

atmósfera: capa delgada de gases que rodean la Tierra. (pág. 709)

atrios (singular, atrio): las dos cámaras superiores del corazón. (pág. 568)

B

B cell: a type of white blood cell that forms and matures in the bone marrow and secretes antibodies into the blood. (p. 616)

bacterium: a microscopic prokaryote. (p. 231)

basidium (buh SIH dee uhm): reproductive structure that produces sexual spores inside the basidiocarp. (p. 278)

behavior: the way an organism reacts to other organisms or to its environment. (p. 447)

bilateral symmetry: a body plan in which an organism can be divided into two parts that are nearly mirror images of each other. (p. 377)

binomial nomenclature: a naming system that gives each organism a two-word scientific name. (p. 21)

biological evolution: the change over time in populations of related organisms. (p. 195)

célula B: tipo de glóbulo blanco que se forma y madura en la médula ósea y secreta anticuerpos a la sangre. (pág. 616)

bacteria: procariota microscópica. (pág. 231)

basidio: estructura reproductiva que produce esporas sexuales en el interior de un basidiocarpo. (pág. 278)

comportamiento: forma en la que un organismo reacciona hacia otros organismos o hacia su medioambiente. (pág. 447)

simetría bilateral: plano corporal en el cual un organismo se puede dividir en dos partes que sean casi imágenes al espejo una de otra. (pág. 377)

nomenclatura binomial: sistema de nombrar que le da a cada organismo un nombre científico de dos palabras. (pág. 21)

evolución biológica: cambio a través del tiempo en las poblaciones de organismos relacionados. (pág. 195)

bioluminescence (BI oh lew muh NE sunts): the ability of certain living things to give off light. (p. 458)

biome: a geographic area on Earth that contains ecosystems with similar biotic and abiotic features. (p. 777)

bioremediation (bi oh rih mee dee AY shun): the use of organisms, such as bacteria, to clean up environmental pollution. (p. 241)

biosphere (BI uh sfihr): the parts of Earth and the surrounding atmosphere where there is life. (p. 741)

biotic factor (bi AH tihk • FAK tuhr): a living or once-living thing in an ecosystem. (p. 707)

biotic potential: the potential growth of a population if it could grow in perfect conditions with no limiting factors. (p. 744)

birthrate: the number of offspring produced by a population over a given time period. (p. 749)

bladder: a muscular sac that holds urine until the urine is excreted. (p. 545)

brain stem: the area of the brain that controls involuntary functions. (p. 641)

breathing: the movement of air into and out of the lungs. (p. 559)

bronchus (BRAHN kus; plural, bronchi): one of two narrow tubes that carry air into the lungs from the trachea. (p. 561)

bruise: an injury where blood vessels in the skin are broken, but the skin is not cut or opened. (p. 508)

budding: the process during which a new organism grows by mitosis and cell division on the body of its parent. (p. 131)

bioluminiscencia: capacidad de ciertos seres vivos de producir luz. (pág. 458)

bioma: área geográfica en la Tierra que contiene ecosistemas con características bióticas y abióticas similares. (pág. 777)

biorremediación: uso de microorganismos, como bacterias, para limpiar la contaminación del medioambiente. (pág. 241)

biosfera: partes de la Tierra y de la atmósfera que la rodea donde hay vida. (pág. 741)

factor biótico: vida cosa o anteriormente vida cosa en un ecosistema. (pág. 707)

potencial biótico: crecimiento potencial de una población si esta puede crecer en condiciones perfectas sin factores limitantes. (pág. 744)

tasa de nacimientos: número de crías que tiene una población durante un período de tiempo dado. (pág. 749)

vejiga: bolsa muscular que contiene la orina hasta que se excreta. (pág. 545)

tallo cerebral: área del cerebro que controla funciones involuntarias. (pág. 641)

respiración: movimiento de aire hacia adentro y hacia afuera de los pulmones. (pág. 559)

bronquio (plural, bronquios): uno de los dos tubos delgados que llevan aire de la tráquea a los pulmones. (pág. 561)

moretón: herida en la cual los vasos sanguíneos de la piel se rompen, pero la piel no se corta ni abre. (pág. 508)

germinación: proceso durante el cual un organismo nuevo crece por medio de mitosis y división celular en el cuerpo de su progenitor. (pág. 131)

C

Calorie: the amount of energy it takes to raise the temperature of 1 kg of water by 1°C. (p. 523)

cambium: a layer of tissue that produces new vascular tissue and grows between xylem and phloem. (p. 314)

caloría: cantidad de energía necesaria para aumentar la temperatura de 1 kg de agua a 1°C. (pág. 523)

cámbium: capa de tejido que produce tejido vascular nuevo y crece en medio del xilema y el floema. (pág. 314)

SCIENCE SKILL HANDBOOK

MATH SKILL HANDBOOK

FOLDABLES HANDBOOK

REFERENCE HANDBOOK

GLOSSARY/ GLOSARIO

INDEX

SCIENCE SKILL HANDBOOK

MATH SKILL HANDBOOK

FOLDABLES HANDBOOK

REFERENCE HANDBOOK

GLOSSARY/ GLOSARIO

INDEX

camouflage (KAM uh flahj): an adaptation that enables a species to blend in with its environment. (p. 204)

cancer: a disease in which cells reproduce uncontrollably without the usual signals to stop. (p. 607)

capillary: a tiny blood vessel that delivers supplies to an individual cell and takes away waste materials. (p. 570)

carbohydrate (kar boh HI drayt): a macromolecule made up of one or more sugar molecules, which are composed of carbon, hydrogen, and oxygen; usually the body's major source of energy. (pp. 47, 524)

cardiac (KAR dee ak) muscle: muscle found only in the heart. (p. 500)

carrying capacity: the largest number of individuals of one species that an ecosystem can support over time. (p. 745)

cartilage (KAR tuh lihj): a strong, flexible tissue that covers the ends of bones. (p. 490)

cast: a fossil copy of an organism made when a mold of the organism is filled with sediment or mineral deposits. (p. 191)

cell: the smallest unit of life. (p. 10)

cell cycle: a cycle of growth, development, and division that most cells in an organism go through. (p. 85)

cell differentiation (dihf uh ren shee AY shun): the process by which cells become different types of cells. (p. 99)

cell membrane: a flexible covering that protects the inside of a cell from the environment outside the cell. (p. 52)

cell theory: the theory that states that all living things are made of one or more cells, the cell is the smallest unit of life, and all new cells come from preexisting cells. (p. 44)

cell wall: a stiff structure outside the cell membrane that protects a cell from attack by viruses and other harmful organisms. (p. 52)

camuflaje: adaptación que permite a las especies mezclarse con su medioambiente. (pág. 204)

cáncer: enfermedad en la cual las células se reproducen sin control sin las señales usuales para detenerse. (pág. 607)

capilar: vaso sanguíneo diminuto que entrega suministros a una célula individual y extrae los materiales de desecho. (pág. 570)

carbohidrato: macromolécula constituida de una o más moléculas de azúcar, las cuales están compuestas de carbono, hidrógeno y oxígeno; usualmente es la mayor fuente de energía del cuerpo. (pág. 47, 524)

músculo cardíaco: músculo que sólo se encuentra en el corazón. (pág. 500)

capacidad de carga: número mayor de individuos de una especie que un medioambiente puede mantener. (pág. 745)

cartílago: tejido fuerte y flexible que reviste los extremos de los huesos. (pág. 490)

contramolde: copia fósil de un organismo compuesto en un molde de el organismo está lleno de sedimentos o los depósitos de minerales. (pág. 191)

célula: unidad más pequeña de vida. (pág. 10)

ciclo celular: ciclo de crecimiento, desarrollo y división por el que pasan la mayoría de células de un organismo. (pág. 85)

diferenciación celular: proceso por el cual las células se convierten en diferentes tipos de células. (pág. 99)

membrana celular: cubierta flexible que protege el interior de una célula del ambiente externo de la célula. (pág. 52)

teoría celular: teoría que establece que todos los seres vivos están constituidos de una o más células (la célula es la unidad más pequeña de vida) y que las células nuevas provienen de células preexistentes. (pág.44)

pared celular: estructura rígida en el exterior de la membrana celular que protege la célula del ataque de virus y otros organismos dañinos. (pág. 52)

cellular respiration: a series of chemical reactions that convert the energy in food molecules into a usable form of energy called ATP. (pp. 69, 336)

cellulose: an organic compound made of chains of glucose molecules. (p. 299)

central nervous system (CNS): system made up of the brain and the spinal cord. (p. 640)

centromere: a structure that holds sister chromatids together. (p. 88)

cerebellum (ser uh BEH lum): the part of the brain that coordinates voluntary muscle movement and regulates balance and posture. (p. 640)

cerebrum (suh REE brum): the part of the brain that controls memory, language, and thought. (p. 640)

cervix (SUR vihks): a small structure between the uterus and the vagina. (p. 688)

chemical digestion: a process in which chemical reactions break down pieces of food into small molecules. (p. 532)

chemosynthesis (kee moh sihn THUH sus): the process during which producers use chemical energy in matter rather than light energy to make food. (p. 724)

chemotherapy: a type of cancer treatment in which chemicals are used to kill the cells that are reproducing uncontrollably. (p. 624)

chloroplast (KLOR uh plast): a membrane-bound organelle that uses light energy and makes food—a sugar called glucose— from water and carbon dioxide in a process known as photosynthesis. (p. 57)

chordate (KOR dayt): an animal that has a notochord, a nerve cord, a tail, and structures called pharyngeal pouches at some point in its life. (p. 393)

chyme (KIME): a thin, watery liquid made of broken down food molecules and gastric juice. (p. 535)

cilia (SIH lee uh): short, hairlike structures that grow on the surface of some protists. (p. 270)

respiración celular: serie de reacciones químicas que convierten la energía de las moléculas de alimento en una forma de energía utilizable llamada ATP. (pág. 69, 336)

celulosa: compuesto orgánico constituido de cadenas de moléculas de glucosa. (pág. 299)

sistema nervioso central (SNC): sistema constituido por el cerebro y la médula espinal. (pág. 640)

centrómero: estructura que mantiene unidas las cromátidas hermanas. (pág. 88)

cerebelo: parte del cerebro que coordina el movimiento muscular voluntario y regula el equilibrio y la postura. (pág. 640)

cerebrum: parte del cerebro que controla la memoria, el lenguaje y el pensamiento. (pág. 640)

cérvix: estructura pequeña entre el útero y la vagina. (pág. 688)

digestión química: proceso por el cual las reacciones químicas descomponen partes del alimento en moléculas pequeñas. (pág. 532)

quimiosíntesis: proceso durante el cual los productores usan la energía química en la materia en vez de la energía lumínica, para elaborar alimento. (pág. 724)

quimioterapia: tipo de tratamiento para el cáncer, en el cual se usan químicos para matar las células que se están reproduciendo sin control. (pág. 624)

cloroplasto: organelo limitado por una membrana que usa la energía lumínica para producir alimento –un azúcar llamado glucosa– del agua y del dióxido de carbono en un proceso llamado fotosíntesis. (pág. 57)

cordado: animal que en algún momento de su vida tiene notocordio, cordón nervioso, cola y estructuras llamadas bolsas faríngeas. (pág. 393)

quimo: líquido diluido y acuoso constituido de moléculas de alimento descompuestas y jugos gástricos. (pág. 535)

cilios: estructuras cortas parecidas a un cabello que crecen en la superficie de algunos protistas. (pág. 270)

SCIENCE SKILL HANDBOOK

MATH SKILL HANDBOOK

FOLDABLES HANDBOOK

REFERENCE HANDBOOK

GLOSSARY/ GLOSARIO

INDEX

cladogram: a branched diagram that shows the relationships among organisms, including common ancestors. (p. 23)

climate: the long-term average weather conditions that occur in a particular region. (p. 708)

climax community: a stable community that no longer goes through major ecological changes. (p. 797)

cloning: a type of asexual reproduction performed in a laboratory that produces identical individuals from a cell or a cluster of cells taken from a multicellular organism. (p. 134)

closed circulatory system: a system that transports materials through blood using vessels. (p. 425)

codominance: an inheritance pattern in which both alleles can be observed in a phenotype. (p. 164)

coelom (SEE lum): a fluid-filled cavity in the body of an animal. (p. 412)

commensalism: a symbiotic relationship that benefits one species but does not harm or benefit the other. (p. 764)

community: all the populations living in an ecosystem at the same time. (p. 742)

comparative anatomy: the study of similarities and differences among structures of living species. (p. 210)

competition: the demand for resources, such as food, water, and shelter, in short supply in a community. (p. 743)

compound microscope: a light microscope that uses more than one lens to magnify an object. (p. 28)

condensation (kahn den SAY shun): the process during which water vapor changes into liquid water. (p. 714)

conditioning: a way of learning new behaviors where a behavior is modified so that a response to one stimulus becomes associated with a different stimulus. (p. 453)

cladograma: diagrama de brazos que muestra las relaciones entre los organismos, incluidos los ancestros comunes. (pág. 23)

clima: promedio a largo plazo de las condiciones del tiempo atmosférico de una región en particular. (pág. 708)

comunidad clímax: comunidad estable que ya no sufrirá mayores cambios ecológicos. (pág. 797)

clonación: tipo de reproducción asexual realizada en un laboratorio que produce individuos idénticos a partir de una célula o grupo de células tomadas de un organismo pluricelular. (pág. 134)

sistema circulatorio cerrado: sistema que transporta materiales a través de la sangre usando vasos. (pág. 425)

condominante: patrón heredado en el cual los dos alelos se observan en un fenotipo. (pág. 164)

celoma: cavidad llena de fluido en el cuerpo de un animal. (pág. 412)

comensalismo: relación simbiótica que beneficia a una especie pero no causa daño ni beneficia a la otra. (pág. 764)

comunidad: todas las poblaciones que viven en un ecosistema, al mismo tiempo. (pág. 742)

anatomía comparativa: estudio de las similitudes y diferencias entre las estructuras de las especies vivas. (pág. 210)

competición: demanda de recursos, tales como alimento, agua y refugio, cuyo suministro es escaso en una comunidad. (pág. 743)

microscopio compuesto: microscopio de luz que usa más de un lente para aumentar la imagen de un objeto. (pág. 28)

condensación: proceso durante el cual el vapor de agua cambia en agua líquida. (pág. 714)

condicionamiento: forma de aprender comportamientos en la cual se modifica una conducta, de tal manera que la respuesta a un estímulo se asocia con un estímulo diferente. (pág. 453)

conjugation (kahn juh GAY shun): a process during which two bacteria of the same species attach to each other and combine their genetic material. (p. 234)

constants: the factors in an experiment that remain the same. (p. NOS 20)

consumer: an organism that cannot make its own food and gets energy by eating other organisms. (p. 760)

coral reef: an underwater structure made from outside skeletons of tiny, soft-bodied animals called coral. (p. 793)

coronary circulation: the network of arteries and veins that supplies blood to all the cells of the heart. (p. 571)

critical thinking: comparing what you already know with information you are given in order to decide whether you agree with it. (p. NOS 10)

crop: a specialized structure in the digestive system where ingested material is stored. (p. 432)

cuticle: a waxy, protective layer on the leaves, stems, and flowers of plants. (p. 299)

cytokinesis (si toh kuh NEE sus): a process during which the cytoplasm and its contents divide. (p. 89)

cytoplasm: the liquid part of a cell inside the cell membrane; contains salts and other molecules. (p. 53)

cytoskeleton: a network of threadlike proteins joined together that gives a cell its shape and helps it move. (p. 53)

conjugación: proceso durante el cual dos bacterias de la misma especie se adhieren una a la otra y combinan sus material genético. (pág. 234)

constantes: factores en un experimento que permanecen iguales. (pág. NOS 20)

consumidor: organismo que no puede hacer sus propios alimentos y obtiene energía comiendo otros organismos. (pág. 760)

arrecife de coral: estructura bajo el agua formada por exoesqueletos de animales diminutos y de cuerpo blando. (pág. 793)

circulación coronaria: red de arterias y venas que suministran sangre a todas las células del corazón. (pág. 571)

pensamiento crítico: comparación que se hace cuando se sabe algo acerca de información nueva, y se decide si se está o no de acuerdo con ella. (pág. NOS 10)

buche: estructura especializada en el sistema digestivo donde el material ingerido se almacena. (pág. 432)

cutícula: capa cerosa de protección que tienen las hojas, los tallos y las flores de las plantas. (pág. 299)

citocinesis: proceso durante el cual el citoplasma y sus contenidos se dividen. (pág. 89)

citoplasma: fluido en el interior de una célula que contiene sales y otras moléculas. (pág. 53)

citoesqueleto: red de proteínas en forma de filamentos unidos que le da forma a la célula y le ayuda a moverse. (pág. 53)

D

daughter cells: the two new cells that result from mitosis and cytokinesis. (p. 89)

death rate: the number of individuals in a population that die over a given time period. (p. 749)

decomposition: the breaking down of dead organisms and organic waste. (p. 240)

dependent variable: the factor a scientist observes or measures during an experiment. (p. NOS 20)

células hija: las dos células nuevas que resultan de la mitosis y la citocinesis. (pág. 89)

tasa de mortalidad: número de individuos que mueren en una población en un período de tiempo dado. (pág. 749)

descomposición: degradación de organismos muertos y desecho orgánico. (pág. 240)

variable dependiente: factor que el científico observa o mide durante un experimento. (pág. NOS 20)

SCIENCE SKILL HANDBOOK

MATH SKILL HANDBOOK

FOLDABLES HANDBOOK

REFERENCE HANDBOOK

GLOSSARY/ GLOSARIO

INDEX

dermis: a thick layer of skin that gives skin strength, nourishment, and flexibility. (p. 507)

description: a spoken or written summary of an observation. (p. NOS 12)

desert: a biome that receives very little rain. (p. 778)

diaphragm (DI uh fram): a large muscle below the lungs that contracts and relaxes as air moves into and out of the lungs. (p. 562)

diatom (DI uh tahm): a type of microscopic plantlike protist with a hard outer wall. (p. 267)

dichotomous key: a series of descriptions arranged in pairs that leads the user to the identification of an unknown organism. (p. 22)

diffusion: the movement of substances from an area of higher concentration to an area of lower concentration. (pp. 62, 422)

digestion: the mechanical and chemical breakdown of food into small particles and molecules that your body can absorb and use. (p. 531)

diploid: a cell that has pairs of chromosomes. (p. 118)

DNA: the abbreviation for deoxyribonucleic (dee AHK sih ri boh noo klee ihk) acid, an organism's genetic material. (p. 170)

dominant (DAH muh nunt) trait: a genetic factor that blocks another genetic factor. (p. 155)

dermis: capa gruesa de piel que le proporciona a la piel fuerza, nutrimento y flexibilidad. (pág. 507)

descripción: resumen oral o escrito de una observación de. (pág. NOS 12)

desierto: bioma que recibe muy poca lluvia. (pág. 778)

diafragma: músculo grande debajo de los pulmones que se contrae y relaja a medida que el aire entra y sale a los pulmones. (pág. 562)

diatomea: tipo de protista microscópico parecido a una planta que tiene una pared externa dura. (pág. 267)

clave dicotómica: serie de descripciones organizadas en pares que dan al usuario la identificación de un organismo desconocido. (pág. 22)

difusión: movimiento de sustancias de un área de mayor concentración a un área de menor concentración. (pág. 62, 422)

digestión: descomposición mecánica y química del alimento en partículas y moléculas pequeñas que el cuerpo absorbe y usa. (pág. 531)

diploide: célula que tiene pares de cromosomas. (pág. 118)

ADN: abreviatura para ácido desoxirribonucleico, material genético de un organismo. (pág. 170)

rasgo dominante: factor genético que bloquea otro factor genético. (pág. 155)

E

eardrum: a thin membrane between the outer ear and the inner ear. (p. 650)

ecological succession: the process of one ecological community gradually changing into another. (p. 797)

ecosystem: all the living things and nonliving things in a given area. (p. 707)

egg: the female reproductive, or sex, cell; forms in an ovary (pp. 117, 673)

tímpano: membrana delgada en medio del oído externo y del oído interno. (pág. 650)

sucesión ecológica: proceso en el que una comunidad ecológica cambia gradualmente en otra. (pág. 797)

ecosistema: todos los seres vivos y los componentes no vivos de un área dada. (pág. 707)

óvulo: célula reproductiva femenina o sexual; forma en un ovario. (pág. 117, 673)

SCIENCE SKILL HANDBOOK

MATH SKILL HANDBOOK

FOLDABLES HANDBOOK

REFERENCE HANDBOOK

GLOSSARY/ GLOSARIO

INDEX

electron microscope: a microscope that uses a magnetic field to focus a beam of electrons through an object or onto an object's surface. (p. 29)

embryo: an immature diploid plant that develops from the zygote. (p. 354); a developing human from the time it attaches to the uterus until the eighth week of pregnancy. (p. 686)

embryology (em bree AH luh jee): the science of the development of embryos from fertilization to birth. (p. 212)

endangered species: a species whose population is at risk of extinction. (p. 751)

endocrine (EN duh krun) system: system consisting of groups of organs and tissues that release chemical messages into the bloodstream. (p. 657)

endocytosis (en duh si TOH sus): the process during which a cell takes in a substance by surrounding it with the cell membrane. (p. 64)

endospore (EN doh spor): a thick internal wall that a bacterium builds around its chromosome and part of its cytoplasm. (p. 235)

energy pyramid: a model that shows the amount of energy available in each link of a food chain (p. 728)

enzyme (EN zime): a protein that helps break down larger molecules into smaller molecules and speeds up, or catalyzes, the rate of chemical reactions. (p. 532)

epidermis (eh puh DUR mus): the outermost layer of skin and the only layer in direct contact with the outside environment. (p. 507)

esophagus (ih SAH fuh gus): a muscular tube that connects the mouth to the stomach. (p. 534)

estuary (ES chuh wer ee): a coastal area where freshwater from rivers and streams mixes with salt water from seas or oceans. (p. 791)

eutrophication (yoo troh fuh KAY shun): the process of a body of water becoming nutrient-rich. (p. 800)

evaporation (ih va puh RAY shun): the process of a liquid changing to a gas at the surface of the liquid. (p. 714)

microscopio electrónico: microscopio que usa un campo magnético para enfocar un haz de electrones a través de un objeto o sobre la superficie de un objeto. (pág. 29)

embrión: planta diploide inmadura que se desarrolla de un zigoto. (pág. 354) ser humano en desarrollo desde el momento en que se adhiere al útero hasta la octava semana de embarazo. (pág. 686)

embriología: ciencia que trata el desarrollo de embriones desde la fertilización hasta el nacimiento. (pág. 212)

especie en peligro: especie cuya población se encuentra en riesgo de extinción. (pág. 751)

sistema endocrino: sistema que consta de grupos de órganos y tejidos que liberan mensajes químicos en la corriente sanguínea. (pág. 657)

endocitosis: proceso durante el cual una célula absorbe una sustancia rodeándola con la membrana celular. (pág. 64)

endospora: pared interna gruesa que una bacteria produce alrededor del cromosoma y parte del citoplasma. (pág. 235)

pirámide energética: modelo que explica la cantidad de energía disponible en cada vínculo de una cadena alimentaria. (pág. 728)

enzima: proteína que descompone moléculas más grandes en moléculas más pequeñas y acelera, o cataliza, la velocidad de las reacciones químicas. (pág. 532)

epidermis: capa más externa de la piel y la única capa que está en contacto directo con el medioambiente externo. (pág. 507)

esófago: tubo muscular que conecta la boca al estómago. (pág. 534)

estuario: zona costera donde el agua dulce de los ríos y arroyos se mezcla con el agua salada de los mares y los océanos. (pág. 791)

eutrofización: proceso por el cual un cuerpo de agua se vuelve rico en nutrientes. (pág. 800)

evaporación: proceso de cambio de un líquido a un gas en la superficie del líquido. (pág. 714)

SCIENCE SKILL HANDBOOK

MATH SKILL HANDBOOK

FOLDABLES HANDBOOK

REFERENCE HANDBOOK

GLOSSARY/ GLOSARIO

INDEX

excretory system: the system that collects and eliminates wastes from the body and regulates the level of fluid in the body. (p. 541)

exocytosis (ek soh si TOH sus): the process during which a cell's vesicles release their contents outside the cell. (p. 64)

exoskeleton: a thick, hard outer covering; protects and supports an animal's body. (p. 387)

explanation: an interpretation of observations. (p. NOS 12)

extinct species: a species that has died out and no individuals are left. (p. 751)

extinction (ihk STINGK shun): event that occurs when the last individual organism of a species dies. (p. 194)

sistema excretor: sistema que recolecta y elimina los desperdicios del cuerpo y regula el nivel de fluidos en el cuerpo. (pág. 541)

exocitosis: proceso durante el cual las vesículas de una célula liberan sus contenidos fuera de la célula. (pág. 64)

exoesqueleto: cubierta externa, gruesa y dura; protege y soporta el cuerpo de un animal. (pág. 387)

explicación: interpretación que se hace de las observaciones. (pág. NOS 12)

especie extinta: especie que ha dejado de existir y no quedan individuos de ella. (pág. 751)

extinción: evento que ocurre cuando el último organismo individual de una especie muere. (pág. 194)

F

facilitated diffusion: the process by which molecules pass through a cell membrane using special proteins called transport proteins. (p. 63)

fat: also called a lipid, a substance in the body that provides energy and helps your body absorb vitamins. (p. 525)

fermentation: a reaction that eukaryotic and prokaryotic cells can use to obtain energy from food when oxygen levels are low. (p. 70)

fertilization (fur tuh luh ZAY shun): a reproductive process in which a sperm joins with an egg. (pp. 117, 466, 679)

fetus: term used to describe a developing human from the ninth week of the pregnancy until birth. (p. 686)

fission: cell division that forms two genetically identical cells. (pp. 130, 234)

flagellum (fluh JEH lum): a long whiplike structure on many bacteria. (p. 234)

food chain: a model that shows how energy flows in an ecosystem through feeding relationships. (p. 726)

difusión facilitada: proceso por el cual las moléculas pasan a través de la membrana celular usando proteínas especiales, llamadas proteínas de transporte. (pág. 63)

grasa: también llamada lípido, sustancia en el cuerpo que proporciona energía y ayuda al cuerpo a absorber vitaminas. (pág. 525)

fermentación: reacción que las células eucarióticas y procarióticas usan para obtener energía del alimento cuando los niveles de oxígeno son bajos. (pág. 70)

fertilización: proceso reproductivo en el cual un espermatozoide se une con un óvulo. (pág. 117, 466, 679)

feto: término usado para describir al ser humano en desarrollo desde la novena semana de embarazo hasta el nacimiento. (pág. 686)

fisión: división celular que forma dos células genéticamente idénticas. (pág. 130, 234)

flagelo: estructura larga similar a un látigo que tienen muchas bacterias. (pág. 234)

cadena alimentaria: modelo que explica cómo la energía fluye en un ecosistema a través de relaciones alimentarias. (pág. 726)

food web: a model of energy transfer that can show how the food chains in a community are interconnected (p. 727)

fossil record: record of all the fossils ever discovered on Earth. (p. 189)

frond: a leaf of a fern. (p. 309)

fruit: plant structure that contains one or more seeds; develops from the ovary and sometimes other parts of the flower. (p. 357)

red alimentaria: modelo de transferencia de energía que explica cómo las cadenas alimentarias están interconectadas en una comunidad. (pág. 727)

registro fósil: registro de todos los fósiles descubiertos en la Tierra. (pág. 189)

fronda: hoja de un helecho. (pág. 309)

fruta: estructura de la planta que contiene una o más semillas; se desarrolla del ovario y algunas veces de otras partes de la flor. (pág. 357)

gene (JEEN): a section of DNA on a chromosome that has genetic information for one trait. (p. 160)

genetics: the study of how traits are passed from parents to offspring. (p. 149)

genotype (JEE nuh tipe): the alleles of all the genes on an organism's chromosomes; controls an organism's phenotype. (p. 160)

genus (JEE nus): a group of similar species. (p. 21)

geologic time scale: a chart that divides Earth's history into different time units based on changes in the rocks and fossils. (p. 193)

geothermal energy: thermal energy from Earth's interior. (p. 819)

gill: an organ that exchanges carbon dioxide for oxygen in water. (p. 423)

gizzard: a muscular pouch similar to a stomach that is used to grind food. (p. 432)

global warming: an increase in the average temperature of Earth's surface. (p. 825)

glycolysis: a process by which glucose, a sugar, is broken down into smaller molecules. (p. 69)

grassland: a biome where grasses are the dominant plants. (p. 779)

gen: parte del ADN en un cromosoma que contiene información genética para un rasgo. (pág. 160)

genética: estudio de cómo los rasgos pasan de los padres a los hijos. (pág. 149)

genotipo: de los alelos de todos los genes en los cromosomas de un organismo, los controles de fenotipo de un organismo. (pág. 160)

género: grupo de especies similares. (pág. 21)

escala de tiempo geológico: tabla que divide la historia de la Tierra en diferentes unidades de tiempo, basado en los cambios en las rocas y fósiles de. (pág. 193)

energía geotérmica: energía térmica del interior de la Tierra. (pág. 819)

Branquia: órgano que intercambia dióxido de carbono por oxígeno en el agua. (pág. 423)

molleja: bolsa muscular similar al estómago que sirve para triturar el alimento. (pág. 432)

calentamiento global: aumento en la temperatura media de la superficie de la Tierra. (pág. 825)

glucólisis: proceso por el cual la glucosa, un azúcar, se divide en moléculas más pequeñas. (pág. 69)

pradera: bioma donde los pastos son las plantas dominantes. (pág. 779)

SCIENCE SKILL HANDBOOK

MATH SKILL HANDBOOK

FOLDABLES HANDBOOK

REFERENCE HANDBOOK

GLOSSARY/ GLOSARIO

INDEX

H

habitat: the place within an ecosystem where an organism lives; provides the biotic and abiotic factors an organism needs to survive and reproduce. (p. 759)

haploid: a cell that has only one chromosome from each pair. (p. 119)

heredity (huh REH duh tee): the passing of traits from parents to offspring. (p. 149)

heterozygous (he tuh roh ZI gus): a genotype in which the two alleles of a gene are different. (p. 161)

hibernation: a response in which an animal's body temperature, activity, heart rate, and breathing rate decrease during periods of cold weather. (p. 451)

homeostasis (hoh mee oh STAY sus): an organism's ability to maintain steady internal conditions when outside conditions change. (p. 13)

homologous (huh MAH luh gus) chromosomes: pairs of chromosomes that have genes for the same traits arranged in the same order. (p. 118)

homologous (huh MAH luh gus) structures: body parts of organisms that are similar in structure and position but different in function. (p. 210)

homozygous (hoh muh ZI gus): a genotype in which the two alleles of a gene are the same. (p. 161)

hormone: a chemical signal that is produced by an endocrine gland in one part of an organism and carried in the bloodstream to another part of the organism (p. 657)

hydrostatic skeleton: a fluid-filled internal cavity surrounded by muscle tissue. (p. 412)

hyphae (HI fee): long, threadlike structures that make up the body of fungi and also form an underground structure that absorbs minerals and water. (p. 277)

hypothesis: a possible explanation for an observation that can be tested by scientific investigations. (p. NOS 6)

hábitat: lugar en un ecosistema donde vive un organismo; proporciona los factores bióticos y abióticos de un organismo necesita para sobrevivir y reproducirse. (pág. 759)

haploide: célula que tiene solamente un cromosoma de cada par. (pág. 119)

herencia: paso de rasgos de los padres a los hijos. (pág. 149)

heterocigoto: genotipo en el cual los dos alelos de un gen son diferentes. (pág. 161)

hibernación: respuesta en la cual la temperatura corporal, el ritmo cardíaco y la tasa de respiración de un animal disminuyen durante los periodos fríos. (pág. 451)

homeostasis: capacidad de un organismo de mantener las condiciones internas estables cuando las condiciones externas cambian. (pág. 13)

cromosomas homólogos: pares de cromosomas que tienen genes de iguales rasgos dispuestos en el mismo orden. (pág. 118)

estructuras homólogas: partes del cuerpo de los organismos que son similares en estructura y posición pero diferentes en función. (pág. 210)

homocigoto: genotipo en el cual los dos alelos de un gen son iguales. (pág. 161)

hormona: señal química producido por una glándula endocrina en una parte de un organismo y llevado en la corriente sanguínea a otra parte del organismo. (pág. 657)

hidroesqueleto: cavidad interna llena de fluido rodeada por tejido muscular. (pág. 412)

hifas: estructuras largas en forma de filamentos que constituyen el cuerpo de los hongos y que también forman una estructura subterránea que absorbe minerales y agua. (pág. 277)

hipótesis: explicación posible de una observación que se puede probar por medio de investigaciones científicas. (pág. NOS 6)

I

immunity: the resistance to specific pathogens. (p. 617)

imprinting: behavior that occurs when an animal forms an attachment to an organism or place within a specific time period after birth or hatching. (p. 452)

incomplete dominance: an inheritance pattern in which an offspring's phenotype is a combination of the parents' phenotypes. (p. 164)

independent variable: the factor that is changed by the investigator to observe how it affects a dependent variable. (p. NOS 20)

inexhaustible resource: a natural resource that will not run out, no matter how much of it people use. (p. 818)

infectious disease: a disease caused by a pathogen that can be transmitted from one person to another. (p. 605)

inference: a logical explanation of an observation that is drawn from prior knowledge or experience. (p. NOS 6)

inflammation: a process that causes a bodily area to become red and swollen. (p. 615)

innate behavior: a behavior that is inherited rather than learned. (p. 449)

instinct (IHN stingt): a complex pattern of innate behaviors. (p. 450)

integumentary (ihn teg gyuh MEN tuh ree) system: the body system that includes all the external coverings of the body, including the skin, nails, and hair. (p. 505)

International System of Units (SI): the internationally accepted system of measurement. (p. NOS 12)

interphase: the period during the cell cycle of a cell's growth and development. (p. 86)

intertidal zone: the ocean shore between the lowest low tide and the highest high tide. (p. 793)

invertebrate (ihn VUR tuh brayt): an animal that does not have a backbone. (p. 376)

inmunidad: resistencia a patógeno específicos. (pág. 617)

impronta: comportamiento que ocurre cuando un animal forma un apego a otro organismo o lugar dentro de un período específico de tiempo, después de nacer o eclosionar. (pág. 452)

dominancia incompleta: patrón heredado en el cual el fenotipo de un hijo es una combinación de los fenotipos de los padres. (pág. 164)

variable independiente: factor que el investigador cambia para observar cómo afecta la variable dependiente. (pág. NOS 20)

recurso inagotable: recurso natural que no se acabará, sin importar cuánto lo usen las personas. (pág. 818)

enfermedad infecciosa: enfermedad causada por un patógeno que se puede transmitir de una persona a otra. (pág. 605)

inferencia: explicación lógica de una observación que se extrae de un conocimiento previo o experiencia. (pág. NOS 6)

inflamación: proceso que causa que un área del cuerpo se vuelva roja e hinchada. (pág. 615)

comportamiento innato: comportamiento heredado más que aprendido. (pág. 449)

instinto: patrón complejo de comportamientos innatos. (pág. 450)

sistema tegumentario: sistema corporal que comprende todas las coberturas externas del cuerpo, incluidos la piel, las uñas y el cabello. (pág. 505)

Sistema Internacional de Unidades (SI): sistema de medidas aceptado internacionalmente. (pág. NOS 12)

interfase: período durante el ciclo celular del crecimiento y desarrollo de una célula. (pág. 86)

zona intermareal: playa en medio de la marea baja más baja y la marea alta más alta. (pág. 793)

invertebrado: animal que no tiene columna vertebral. (pág. 376)

SCIENCE SKILL HANDBOOK

MATH SKILL HANDBOOK

FOLDABLES HANDBOOK

REFERENCE HANDBOOK

GLOSSARY/GLOSARIO

INDEX

involuntary muscle: muscle you cannot consciously control. (p. 500)

músculos involuntarios: músculo que se controla conscientemente. (pág. 500)

J

joint: where two or more bones meet. (p. 491)

articulación: donde dos o más huesos se unen. (pág. 491)

K

kidney: a bean-shaped organ that filters, or removes, wastes from blood. (p. 543)

riñón: órgano con forma de frijol que filtra, o extrae, los desechos de la sangre. (pág. 543)

L

larynx (LER ingks): a triangle shaped area into which air passes from the pharynx; also called the voice box. (p. 560)

laringe: área en forma de triángulo dentro de la cual pasa el aire proveniente de la faringe; también se le llama caja sonora de voz. (pág. 560)

lichen (LI kun): a structure formed when fungi and certain other photosynthetic organisms grow together. (p. 284)

líquen: estructura formada cuando crecen juntos los hongos y algunos organismos que realizan la fotosíntesis. (pág. 284)

ligament (LIH guh munt): the tissue that connects bones to other bones. (p. 491)

ligamento: tejido que conecta los huesos con otros huesos. (pág. 491)

light microscope: a microscope that uses light and lenses to enlarge an image of an object. (p. 28)

microscopio de luz: microscopio que usa luz y lentes para aumentar la imagen de un objeto. (pág. 28)

limiting factor: a factor that can limit the growth of a population. (p. 743)

factor limitante: factor que puede limitar el crecimiento de una población. (pág. 743)

lipid: a large macromolecule that does not dissolve in water. (p. 47)

lípido: macromolécula extensa que no se disuelve en agua. (pág. 47)

lungs: the main organs of the respiratory system. (p. 561)

pulmones: órganos principales del sistema respiratorio. (pág. 561)

lymph: tissue fluid that has diffused into lymph vessels. (p. 586)

linfa: fluido de los tejidos que se esparce en los vasos linfáticos. (pág. 586)

lymph node: a small spongy structure that filters particles from lymph. (p. 586)

nódulo linfático: estructura pequeña y esponjosa que filtra partículas de la linfa. (pág. 586)

lymphatic system: part of the immune system that helps destroy microorganisms that enter the body. (p. 585)

sistema linfático: parte del sistema inmune que destruye los microorganismos que entran al cuerpo. (pág. 585)

M

macromolecule: substance in cells that forms when many small molecules join together. (p. 45)

macromolécula: sustancia en las células que se forma cuando mucha moléculas pequeñas se unen. (pág. 45)

mechanical digestion: a process in which food is physically broken into smaller pieces. (p. 532)

digestión mecánica: proceso por el cual el alimento se descompone físicamente en pedazos más pequeños. (pág. 532)

meiosis: a process in which one diploid cell divides to make four haploid sex cells. (p. 119)

melanin (MEH luh nun): a pigment that protects the body by absorbing some of the Sun's damaging ultraviolet rays. (p. 507)

menstrual (MEN stroo ul) cycle: a process of reproductive-related changes involving the ovaries and uterus. (p. 678)

metamorphosis (me tuh MOR fuh sihs): a developmental process in which the body form of an animal changes as it grows from an egg to an adult. (p. 470)

migration: the instinctive, seasonal movement of a population of organisms from one place to another. (pp. 451, 752)

mimicry (MIH mih kree): an adaptation in which one species looks like another species. (p. 204)

mineral: any of several inorganic nutrients that help the body regulate many chemical reactions. (p. 525)

mitosis (mi TOH sus): a process during which the nucleus and its contents divide. (p. 89)

mold: the impression of an organism in a rock. (p. 191)

multicellular: a living thing that is made up of two or more cells. (p. 10)

muscle: strong body tissue that can contract in an orderly way. (p. 497)

mutation: a permanent change in the sequence of DNA, or the nucleotides, in a gene or a chromosome. (p. 175)

mutualism: a symbiotic relationship in which both organisms benefit. (p. 763)

mycelium (mi SEE lee um): an underground network of hyphae. (p. 277)

mycorrhiza (mi kuh RI zuh): a structure formed when the roots of a plant and the hyphae of a fungus weave together. (p. 282)

meiosis: proceso en el cual una célula diploide se divide para constituir cuatro células sexuales haploides. (pág. 119)

melanina: pigmento que protege el cuerpo absorbiendo parte de los rayos ultravioleta dañinos del sol. (pág. 507)

ciclo menstrual: proceso de cambios relacionados con la reproducción que involucra los ovarios y el útero. (pág. 678)

metamorfosis: proceso de desarrollo en el cual la forma del cuerpo de un animal cambia a medida que crece del huevo al adulto. (pág. 470)

migración: movimiento instintivo de temporada de una población de organismos de un lugar a otro. (pág. 451, 752)

mimetismo: una adaptación en el cual una especie se parece a otra especie. (pág. 204)

mineral: cualquiera de los varios nutrientes inorgánicos que ayudan al cuerpo a regular muchas reacciones químicas. (pág. 525)

mitosis: proceso durante el cual el núcleo y sus contenidos se divide. (pág. 89)

molde: impresión de un organismo en una roca. (pág. 191)

pluricelular: ser vivo formado por dos o más células. (pág. 10)

músculo: tejido corporal fuerte que se contrae de manera sistemática. (pág. 497)

mutación: cambio permanente en la secuencia de ADN, de los nucleótidos, en un gen o en un cromosoma. (pág. 175)

mutualismo: relación simbiótica en la cual los dos organismos se benefician. (pág. 763)

micelio: red subterránea de hifas. (pág. 277)

micorriza: estructura formada cuando las raíces de una planta y las hifas de de un hongo se entrelazan. (pág. 282)

natural resource: part of the environment that supplies material useful or necessary for the survival of living things. (p. 813)

recurso natural: parte del medioambiente que suministra material útil o necesario para que los seres vivos sobrevivan. (pág. 813)

SCIENCE SKILL HANDBOOK

MATH SKILL HANDBOOK

FOLDABLES HANDBOOK

REFERENCE HANDBOOK

GLOSSARY/ GLOSARIO

INDEX

natural selection: the process by which organisms with variations that help them survive in their environment live longer, compete better, and reproduce more than those that do not have the variations. (p. 202)

naturalist: a person who studies plants and animals by observing them. (p. 199)

negative feedback: a control system in which the effect of a hormone inhibits further release of the hormone; sends a signal to stop a response. (p. 660)

nephron (NEH frahn): a network of capillaries and small tubes, or tubules, where filtration of blood occurs. (p. 543)

nerve net: a netlike control system that sends signals to and from all parts of the body. (p. 414)

nervous system: the part of an organism that gathers, processes, and responds to information. (p. 637)

neuron (NOO rahn): the basic functioning unit of the nervous system; a nerve cell (p. 639)

niche (NICH): the way a species interacts with abiotic and biotic factors to obtain food, find shelter, and fulfill other needs. (p. 759)

nitrogen fixation (NI truh jun • fihk SAY shun): the process that changes atmospheric nitrogen into nitrogen compounds that are usable by living things. (pp. 240, 716)

noninfectious disease: a disease that cannot pass from person to person. (p. 606)

nonrenewable resource: a natural resource that is being used up faster than it can be replaced by natural processes. (p. 814)

notochord: a flexible, rod-shaped structure that supports the body of a developing chordate. (p. 393)

nucleic acid: a macromolecule that forms when long chains of molecules called nucleotides join together. (p. 46)

nucleotide: a molecule made of a nitrogen base, a sugar, and a phosphate group. (p. 171)

selección natural: proceso por el cual los organismos con variaciones que las ayudan a sobrevivir en sus medioambientes viven más, compiten mejor y se reproducen más que aquellas que no tienen esas variaciones. (pág. 202)

naturalista: persona que estudia las plantas y los animales por medio de la observación. (pág. 199)

retroalimentación negativa: sistema de control en el cual el efecto de una hormona inhibe más liberación de la hormona; envía una señal para detener una respuesta. (pág. 660)

nefrona: red de capilares y tubos pequeños, o túbulos, donde ocurre la filtración de la sangre. (pág. 543)

red nerviosa: sistema de control parecido a una red que envía señales hacia y desde todas las partes del cuerpo. (pág. 414)

sistema nervioso: parte de un organismo que recoge, procesa y responde a la información. (pág. 637)

neurona: unidad básica de funcionamiento del sistema nervioso; célula nerviosa. (pág. 639)

nicho: forma de una especie interacciona con los factores abióticos y bióticos para obtener comida, encontrar refugio, y satisfacer otras necesidades. (pág. 759)

fijación del nitrógeno: proceso que cambia el nitrógeno atmosférico en componentes de nitrógeno útiles para los seres vivos. (pág. 240, 716)

enfermedad no infecciosa: enfermedad que no se puede pasar de una persona a otra. (pág. 606)

recurso no renovable: recurso natural que se está agotando más rápidamente de lo que se puede reemplazar mediante procesos naturales. (pág. 814)

notocordio: estructura flexible con forma de varilla que soporta el cuerpo de un cordado en desarrollo. (pág. 393)

ácido nucléico: macromolécula que se forma cuando cadenas largas de moléculas llamadas nucleótidos se unen. (pág. 46)

nucelótido: molécula constituida de una base de nitrógeno, azúcar y un grupo de fosfato. (pág. 171)

nucleus: part of a eukaryotic cell that directs cell activity and contains genetic information stored in DNA. (p. 55)

núcleo: parte de la célula eucariótica que gobierna la actividad celular y contiene la información genética almacenada en el ADN. (pág. 55)

O

observation: the act of using one or more of your senses to gather information and take note of what occurs. (p. NOS 6)

open circulatory system: a system that transports blood and other fluids into open spaces that surround organs in the body. (p. 424)

organ: a group of different tissues working together to perform a particular job. (p. 102)

organ system: a group of organs that work together and perform a specific task. (p. 103)

organelle: membrane-surrounded component of a eukaryotic cell with a specialized function. (p. 54)

organism: something that has all the characteristics of life. (p. 9)

osmosis: the diffusion of water molecules only through a membrane. (p. 62)

osteoporosis (ahs tee oh puh ROH sus): a bone disease that causes bones to weaken and become brittle. (p. 492)

ovary (OH va ree): a flower structure located at the base of the style of a flower that contains one or more ovules (p. 356); the female reproductive organ that produces egg cells; stores oocytes which mature into ova (pp. 466, 676)

ovulation: a process occurring near the end of phase 2 of the menstrual cycle in which hormones cause an egg to be released from the ovary. (p. 678)

ovule: female reproductive structure of a seed plant where the haploid egg develops. (p. 354)

ozone layer: the layer of atmosphere that prevents most harmful ultraviolet (UV) radiation from reaching Earth. (p. 824)

observación: acción de usar uno o más sentidos para reunir información y tomar notar de lo que ocurre. (pág. NOS 6)

sistema circulatorio abierto: sistema que transporta sangre y otros fluidos hacia espacios abiertos que rodean a los órganos en el cuerpo. (pág. 424)

órgano: grupo de diferentes tejidos que trabajan juntos para realizar una función específica. (pág. 102)

sistema de órganos: grupo de órganos que trabajan juntos y realizar una función específica. (pág. 103)

organelo: componente de una célula eucariótica rodeado de una membrana con una función especializada. (pág. 54)

organismo: algo que tiene todas las características de la vida. (pág. 9)

ósmosis: difusión de las moléculas de agua únicamente a través de una membrana. (pág. 62)

osteoporosis: enfermedad de los huesos que los debilita y los vuelve quebradizos. (pág. 492)

ovario: estructura de flores situado en la base del estilo de una flor que contiene uno o más óvulos. (pág.356); el órgano reproductivo femenino que produce óvulos; tiendas de ovocitos que maduran en los óvulos. (pág. 466, 676)

ovulación: proceso que ocurre cerca de la finalización de la segunda fase del ciclo menstrual en el cual las hormonas causan la liberación de un óvulo del ovario. (pág. 678)

óvulo: estructura reproductiva femenina de la semilla de una planta donde el huevo haploide se desarrolla. (pág. 354)

capa de ozono: capa de la atmósfera que evita que la mayor parte de la radiación ultravioleta dañina llegue a la Tierra. (pág. 824)

SCIENCE SKILL HANDBOOK

MATH SKILL HANDBOOK

FOLDABLES HANDBOOK

REFERENCE HANDBOOK

GLOSSARY/GLOSARIO

INDEX

P

paramecium (pa ruh MEE see um): a protist with cilia and types of two nuclei. (p. 270)

parasitism: a symbiotic relationship in which one organism benefits and the other is harmed. (p. 764)

passive immunity: the introduction of antibodies that were produced outside the body. (p. 617)

passive transport: the movement of substances through a cell membrane without using the cell's energy. (p. 61)

pasteurization (pas chuh ruh ZAY shun): a process of heating food or liquid to a temperature that kills most harmful bacteria. (pp. 243, 603)

pathogen (PA thuh jun): an agent that causes disease. (pp. 242, 601)

penis: a tubelike structure that delivers sperm to the female reproductive system. (p. 674)

periosteum (per ee AHS tee um): a membrane that surrounds bone. (p. 490)

peripheral nervous system (PNS): system made of sensory and motor neurons that transmit information between the central nervous system (CNS) and the rest of the body. (p. 641)

peristalsis (per uh STAHL sus): waves of muscle contractions that move food through the digestive tract. (p. 534)

pharynx (FER ingks): a tubelike passageway at the top of the throat that receives air, food, and liquids from the mouth or nose. (p. 560)

phenotype (FEE nuh tipe): how a trait appears or is expressed. (p. 160)

pheromone (FER uh mohn): a chemical that is produced by one animal and influences the behavior of another animal of the same species. (p. 459)

phloem (FLOH em): a type of vascular tissue that carries dissolved sugars throughout a plant. (p. 315)

Paramecio: protista con cilios y dos tipos de núcleos. (pág. 270)

parasitismo: relación simbiótica en la cual se perjudica organismo se beneficia y el otro. (pág. 764)

inmunidad pasiva: introducción de anticuerpos producidos fuera del cuerpo. (pág. 617)

transporte pasivo: movimiento de sustancias a través de una membrana celular sin usar la energía de la célula. (pág. 61)

pasteurización: proceso en el cual se calientan los alimentos o líquidos para matar la mayoría de bacterias dañinas. (pág. 243, 603)

patógeno: agente que causa enfermedad. (pág. 242, 601)

pene: estructura en forma de tubo que deposita esperma en el sistema reproductor femenino. (pág. 674)

periostio: membrana que recubre los huesos. (pág. 490)

sistema nervioso periférico (SNP): sistema formado por neuronas sensoriales y motoras que transmiten información entre el sistema nervioso central (SNC) y el resto del cuerpo. (pág. 641)

peristalsis: ondas de contracciones musculares que mueven el alimento por el tracto digestivo. (pág. 534)

faringe: pasadizo parecido a un tubo en la parte superior de la garganta que recibe el aire, el alimento y los líquidos provenientes de la boca o de la nariz. (pág. 560)

fenotipo: forma como aparece o se expresa un rasgo. (pág. 160)

feronoma: químico que es producido por un animal y que influye en el comportamiento de otro animal de la misma especie. (pág. 459)

floema: tipo de tejido vascular que transporta azúcares disueltos por toda la planta. (pág. 315)

SCIENCE SKILL HANDBOOK

MATH SKILL HANDBOOK

FOLDABLES HANDBOOK

REFERENCE HANDBOOK

GLOSSARY/ GLOSARIO

INDEX

photochemical smog: air pollution that forms from the interaction between chemicals in the air and sunlight (p. 824)

photoperiodism: a plant's response to the number of hours of darkness in its environment. (p. 344)

photosynthesis (foh toh SIHN thuh sus): a series of chemical reactions that convert light energy, water, and carbon dioxide into the food-energy molecule glucose and give off oxygen. (pp. 71, 334, 724)

pioneer species: the first species that colonizes new or undisturbed land. (p. 798)

pistil: female reproductive organ of a flower. (p. 356)

placenta (pluh SEN tuh): an organ formed by the outer cells of the zygote and cells from the uterus. (p. 685)

plant hormone: a substance that acts as a chemical messenger within a plant. (p. 345)

plasma: the yellowish, liquid part of blood that transports blood cells. (p. 579)

platelet: a small, irregularly shaped piece of a cell that plugs wounds to stop bleeding. (p. 579)

pollen (PAH lun) grain: spore that forms from tissue in a male reproductive structure of a seed plant. (p. 354)

pollination (pah luh NAY shun): the process that occurs when pollen grains land on a female reproductive structure of a plant that is the same species as the pollen grains. (p. 354)

pollution: the contamination of the environment with substances that are harmful to life. (p. 823)

polygenic inheritance: an inheritance pattern in which multiple genes determine the phenotype of a trait. (p. 165)

population: all the organisms of the same species that live in the same area at the same time. (p. 742)

population density: the size of a population compared to the amount of space available. (p. 744)

smog fotoquímico: contaminación del aire que se forma por la interacción entre los productos químicos en el aire y la luz del sol. (pág. 824)

fotoperiodismo: respuesta de una planta al número de horas de oscuridad en su medioambiente. (pág. 344)

fotosíntesis: serie de reacciones químicas que convierte la energía lumínica, el agua y el dióxido de carbono en glucosa, una molécula de energía alimentaria, y libera oxígeno. (pág. 71, 334, 724)

especie pionera: primera especie que coloniza tierra nueva o tierra virgen. (pág. 798)

pistilo: órgano reproductor femenino de una flor. (pág. 356)

placenta: órgano formado por las células externas del cigoto y células del útero. (pág. 685)

fitohormona: sustancia que actúa como mensajero químico dentro de una planta. (pág. 345)

plasma: parte líquida y amarillenta de la sangre que transporta las células sanguíneas. (pág. 579)

plaqueta: fragmento de una célula, pequeño y de forma irregular, que tapona las heridas para detener el sangrado. (pág. 579)

grano de polen: espora que se forma de tejido en una estructura reproductiva masculina de una planta de semilla. (pág. 354)

polinización: proceso que ocurre cuando los granos de polen posan sobre una estructura reproductiva femenina de una planta que es de la misma especie que los granos de polen. (pág. 354)

polución: contaminación del medioambiente con sustancias dañinas para la vida. (pág. 823)

herencia poligénica: patrón de herencia en el cual genes múltiples determinan el fenotipo de un rasgo. (pág. 165)

población: todos los organismos de la misma especie que viven en la misma área al mismo tiempo. (pág. 742)

densidad poblacional: tamaño de una población comparado con la cantidad de espacio disponible. (pág. 744)

SCIENCE SKILL HANDBOOK

MATH SKILL HANDBOOK

FOLDABLES HANDBOOK

REFERENCE HANDBOOK

GLOSSARY/GLOSARIO

INDEX

positive feedback: a control system in which the effect of a hormone causes more of the hormone to be released; sends a signal to increase a response (p. 660)

precipitation (prih sih puh TAY shun): water, in liquid or solid form, that falls from the atmosphere (p. 714)

precision: a description of how similar or close measurements are to each other. (p. NOS 14)

prediction: a statement of what will happen next in a sequence of events. (p. NOS 7)

pregnancy: the period of human development from fertilized egg to birth. (p. 685)

producer: an organism that uses an outside energy source, such as the Sun, and produces its own food (pp. 298, 760)

protein: a long chain of amino acid molecules; contains carbon, hydrogen, oxygen, nitrogen, and sometimes sulfur (pp. 47, 524)

protist: a member of a group of eukaryotic organisms, which have a membrane-bound nucleus. (p. 265)

protozoan (proh tuh ZOH un): a protist that resembles a tiny animal. (p. 270)

pseudopod: a temporary "foot" that forms as the organism pushes part of its body outward. (p. 271)

puberty (PYEW bur tee): the process by which the reproductive system matures during adolescence. (p. 690)

pulmonary circulation: the network of vessels that carries blood to and from the lungs. (p. 571)

Punnett square: a model that is used to show the probability of all possible genotypes and phenotypes of offspring. (p. 162)

retroalimentación positiva: sistema de control en el cual el efecto de una hormona causa más liberación de la hormona; envía una señal para aumentar la respuesta. (pág. 660)

precipitación: agua, en forma líquida o sólida, que cae de la atmósfera. (pág. 714)

precisión: sescripción de qué tan similar o cercana están las mediciones una de otra. (pág. NOS 14)

predicción: afirmación de lo que ocurrirá a continuación en una secuencia de eventos. (pág. NOS 7)

embarazo: período del desarrollo del ser humano desde que se fertiliza el óvulo hasta el nacimiento. (pág. 685)

productor: organismo que usa una fuente de energía externa, como el Sol, y fabricar su propio alimento. (pág. 298, 760)

proteína: larga cadena de aminoácidos; contiene carbono, hidrógeno, oxígeno, nitrógeno y, algunas veces, sulfuro. (pág. 47, 524)

protista: miembro de un grupo de organismos eucarióticos que tienen un núcleo limitado por una membrana. (pág. 265)

protozoario: protista que parece un animal pequeño. (pág. 270)

Seudópodo: "pata" temporal que se forma a medida que el organismo empuja parte del cuerpo hacia afuera. (pág. 271)

pubertad: proceso por el cual el sistema reproductor madura durante la adolescencia. (pág. 690)

circulación pulmonar: red de vasos que lleva sangre hacia y desde los pulmones. (pág. 571)

cuadro de Punnett: modelo que se utiliza para demostrar la probabilidad de que todos los genotipos y fenotipos posibles de cría. (pág. 162)

R

radial symmetry: a body plan in which an organism can be divided into two parts that are nearly mirror images of each other anywhere through its central axis. (p. 377)

simetría radial: plano corporal en el cual un organismo se puede dividir en dos partes para que sean casi imágenes al espejo una de la otra, en cualquier parte del eje axial. (pág. 377)

receptor: special structures in all parts of the sensory system that detect stimuli. (p. 647)

recessive (rih SE sihv) trait: a genetic factor that is blocked by the presence of a dominant factor. (p. 155)

recycling: manufacturing new products out of used products. (p. 836)

reflex: an automatic movement in response to a stimulus. (p. 642)

regeneration: a type of asexual reproduction that occurs when an offspring grows from a piece of its parent. (p. 132)

renewable resource: a natural resource that can be replenished by natural processes at least as quickly as it is used. (p. 816)

replication: the process of copying a DNA molecule to make another DNA molecule. (p. 172)

retina (RET nuh): an area at the back of the eye that includes two types of cells—rod cells and cone cells—that contain photoreceptors. (p. 648)

Rh factor: a protein found on red blood cells; a chemical marker. (p. 581)

rhizoid: a structure that anchors a nonvascular seedless plant to a surface. (p. 307)

RNA: ribonucleic acid, a type of nucleic acid that carries the code for making proteins from the nucleus to the cytoplasm. (p. 173)

receptor: estructuras especiales en todas partes del sistema sensorial que detectan los estímulos. (pág. 647)

rasgo recesivo: factor genético boqueado por la presencia de un factor dominante. (pág. 155)

reciclaje: fabricación de productos nuevos hechos de productos usados. (pág. 836)

reflejo: movimiento automático en respuesta a un estímulo. (pág. 642)

regeneración: tipo de reproducción asexual que ocurre cuando un organismo se origina de una parte de su progenitor. (pág. 132)

recurso renovable: recurso natural que se reabastece mediante procesos naturales tan rápidamente como se usa. (pág. 816)

replicación: proceso por el cual se copia una molécula de ADN para hacer otra molécula de ADN. (pág. 172)

retina: área en la parte posterior del ojo que incluye dos tipos de células –bastones y conos– que contienen fotorreceptores. (pág. 648)

factor Rh: proteína que se encuentra en los glóbulos rojos; es un marcador químico. (pág. 581)

rizoide: estructura que sujeta una planta sin sistema vascular ni semillas a la superficie. (pág. 307)

ARN: ácido ribonucleico, un tipo de ácido nucléico que contiene el código para hacer proteínas del núcleo para el citoplasma. (pág. 173)

S

salinity (say LIH nuh tee): a measure of the mass of dissolved salts in a mass of water. (p. 787)

science: the investigation and exploration of natural events and of the new information that results from those investigations. (p. NOS 4)

scientific law: a rule that describes a pattern in nature. (p. NOS 9)

scientific theory: an explanation of observations or events that is based on knowledge gained from many observations and investigations. (p. NOS 9)

salinidad: medida de la masa de sales disueltas en una masa de agua. (pág. 787)

ciencia: la investigación y exploración de los eventos naturales y de la información nueva que es el resultado de estas investigaciones. (pág. NOS 4)

ley científica: regla que describe un patrón dado en la naturaleza. (pág. NOS 9)

teoría científica: explicación de observaciones o eventos con base en conocimiento obtenido de muchas observaciones e investigaciones. (pág. NOS 9)

seed: a plant embryo, its food supply, and a protective covering (p. 354)

selective breeding: the selection and breeding of organisms for desired traits. (p. 205)

semen: (SEE mun): a mixture of sperm and fluids produced by several glands. (p. 674)

sensory system: the part of your nervous system that detects or senses the environment. (p. 647)

sexual reproduction: type of reproduction in which the genetic material from two different cells—a sperm and an egg—combine, producing an offspring. (pp. 117, 465)

significant digits: the number of digits in a measurement that are known with a certain degree of reliability. (p. NOS 15)

sister chromatids: two identical chromosomes that make up a duplicated chromosome. (p. 88)

skeletal muscle: a type of muscle that attaches to bones. (p. 499)

skeletal system: body system that contains bones as well as other structures that connect and protect the bones and that support other functions in the body. (p. 487)

smooth muscle: involuntary muscle named for its smooth appearance. (p. 500)

society: a group of animals of the same species living and working together in an organized way. (p. 460)

species (SPEE sheez): a group of organisms that have similar traits and are able to produce fertile offspring. (p. 21)

sperm: a male reproductive, or sex, cell; forms in a testis (pp. 117, 673)

spinal cord: a tubelike structure of neurons that sends signals to and from the brain. (p. 641)

spiracle: a tiny hole on the surface of an organism where oxygen enters the body and carbon dioxide leaves the body. (p. 422)

spleen: an organ of the lymphatic system that recycles worn-out red blood cells and produces and stores lymphocytes. (p. 587)

semilla: embrión de una planta, su suministro de alimento y cubierta protectora. (pág. 354)

cría selectiva: selección y la cría de organismos para las características deseadas. (pág. 205)

semen: mezcla de esperma y fluidos producidos por varias glándulas. (pág. 674)

sistema sensorial: parte del sistema nervioso que detecta o siente el medioambiente. (pág. 647)

reproducción sexual: tipo de reproducción en la cual el material genético de dos células diferentes de un espermatozoide y un óvulo se combinan, produciendo una cría. (pág. 117, 465)

cifras significativas: número de dígitos que se conoce con cierto grado de fiabilidad en una medida. (pág. NOS 15)

cromátidas hermanas: dos cromosomas idénticos que constituyen un cromosoma duplicado. (pág. 88)

músculo esquelético: Tipo de músculo que se adhiere a los huesos. (pág. 499)

sistema esquelético: Sistema corporal que comprende los huesos al igual que otras estructuras que conectan y protegen los huesos y que apoyan otras funciones en el cuerpo. (pág. 487)

músculo liso: Músculo involuntario llamado así por su apariencia lisa. (pág. 500)

sociedad: grupo de animales de la misma especie que viven y trabajan juntos de una forma organizada. (pág. 460)

especie: grupo de organismos que tienen rasgos similares y que están en capacidad de producir crías fértiles. (pág. 21)

esperma: célula reproductora masculina o sexual; forma en un testículo. (pág. 117, 673)

médula espinal: estructura de neuronas en forma de tubo que envía señales hacia y del cerebro. (pág. 641)

espiráculo: hueco diminuto en la superficie de un organismo por donde entra oxígeno al cuerpo y sale dióxido de carbono. (pág. 422)

bazo: órgano del sistema linfático que recicla los glóbulos rojos muertos y produce y almacena linfocitos. (pág. 587)

spore: a daughter cell produced from a haploid structure (p. 352)

stamen: the male reproductive organ of a flower (p. 356)

stem cell: an unspecialized cell that is able to develop into many different cell types. (p. 100)

stimulus (STIHM yuh lus): a change in an organism's environment that causes a response. (pp. 341, 638)

stoma (STOH muh): a small opening in the epidermis, or surface layer, of a leaf. (p. 317)

sustainability: meeting human needs in ways that ensure future generations also will be able to meet their needs. (p. 835)

symbiosis (sihm bee OH sus): a close, long-term relationship between two species that usually involves an exchange of food or energy. (p. 763)

synapse (SIH naps): the gap between two neurons. (p. 639)

systemic circulation: the network of vessels that carry blood from the heart to the body and from the body back to the heart. (p. 571)

espora: célula hija producida de una estructura haploide. (pág. 352)

estambre: órgano reproductor masculino de una flor. (pág. 356)

célula madre: célula no especializada que tiene la capacidad de desarrollarse en diferentes tipos de células. (pág. 100)

estímulo: cualquier cambio en el medioambiente de un organismo que causa una respuesta. (pág. 341, 638)

estoma: abertura pequeña en la epidermis, o capa superficial, de una hoja. (pág. 317)

sostenibilidad: satisfacción de las necesidades humanas de forma que se asegure que las generaciones futuras también podrán satisfacer sus necesidades. (pág. 835)

simbiosis: relación intrínseca a largo plazo entre dos especies que generalmente involucra intercambio de alimento o energía. (pág. 763)

sinapsis: espacio en medio de dos neuronas. (pág. 639)

circulación sistémica: red de vasos que llevan sangre del corazón al cuerpo y de regreso del cuerpo al corazón. (pág. 571)

T

T cell: a type of white blood cell that forms in the bone marrow and matures in the thymus gland; produces a protein antibody that becomes part of the cell membrane. (p. 616)

taiga (TI guh): a forest biome consisting mostly of cone-bearing evergreen trees. (p. 783)

technology: the practical use of scientific knowledge, especially for industrial or commercial use. (p. NOS 8)

temperate: the term describing any region of Earth between the tropics and the polar circles. (p. 781)

territory: an area that is set up and defended by animals for feeding, mating, and raising young. (p. 461)

testis (TES tihs): the male reproductive organ that produces sperm. (pp. 466, 674)

célula T: tipo de glóbulo blanco que se forma en la médula ósea y madura en la glándula del timo; produce un anticuerpo de proteína que se vuelve parte de la membrana celular. (pág. 616)

taiga: bioma de bosque constituido en su mayoría por coníferas perennes. (pág. 783)

tecnología: uso práctico del conocimiento científico, especialmente para uso industrial o comercial. (pág. NOS 8)

temperatura: término que describe cualquier región de la Tierra entre los trópicos y los círculos polares. (pág. 781)

territorio: área que un grupo de animales establece y defiende para alimentarse, aparearse y criar su descendencia. (pág. 461)

testículos: Órgano reproductivo masculino que produce espermatozoides. (pág. 466, 674)

SCIENCE SKILL HANDBOOK

MATH SKILL HANDBOOK

FOLDABLES HANDBOOK

REFERENCE HANDBOOK

GLOSSARY/ GLOSARIO

INDEX

threatened species: a species at risk, but not yet endangered. (p. 751)

thymus: the organ of the lymphatic system in which T cells complete their development. (p. 587)

tissue: a group of similar types of cells that work together to carry out specific tasks. (p. 101)

trace fossil: the preserved evidence of the activity of an organism. (p. 191)

trachea (TRAY kee uh): a tube that is held open by C-shaped rings of cartilage; connects the larynx and the bronchi. (p. 560)

transcription: the process of making mRNA from DNA. (p. 173)

translation: the process of making a protein from RNA. (p. 174)

tropism (TROH pih zum): plant growth toward or away from an external stimulus (p. 342)

tundra (TUN druh): a biome that is cold, dry, and treeless. (p. 783)

especie amenazada: especie en riesgo, pero que todavía no está en peligro. (pág. 751)

timo: órgano del sistema linfático en el cual las células T completan su desarrollo. (pág. 587)

tejido: grupo de tipos similares de células que trabajan juntas para llevar a cabo diferentes funciones. (pág. 101)

traza fósil: evidencia conservada de la actividad de un organismo.(pág. 191)

tráquea: tubo que los anillos en forma de C del cartílago mantienen abierto; este conecta la laringe y los bronquios. (pág. 560)

transcripción: proceso por el cual se hace mARN de ADN. (pág. 173)

traslación: proceso por el cual se hacen proteínas a partir de ARN. (pág. 174)

tropismo: crecimiento de las plantas hacia o lejos de un estímulo externo. (pág. 342)

tundra: bioma frío, seco y sin árboles. (pág. 783)

U

umbilical (um BIH lih kul) cord: a rope-like structure formed by the outer zygote cells that attaches the developing offspring to the placenta. (p. 685)

undulation (un juh LAY shun): the wavelike motion of some animals. (p. 416)

unicellular: a living thing that is made up of only one cell. (p. 10)

ureter (YOO ruh tur): a tube through which urine leaves each kidney. (p. 545)

urethra (yoo REE thruh): a tube through which urine leaves the bladder. (p. 545)

urine: the fluid produced when blood is filtered by the kidneys. (p. 543)

cordón umbilical: Estructura parecida a una cuerda formada por las células externas del cigoto que unen el hijo a la placenta. (pág. 685)

ondulación: movimiento de algunos animales parecido a una ola. (pág. 416)

unicelular: ser vivo formado por una sola célula. (pág. 10)

uréter: tubo por el cual la orina sale de cada riñón. (pág. 545)

uretra: tubo por el cual la orina sale de la vejiga. (pág. 545)

orina: fluido que se produce cuando los riñones filtran la sangre. (pág. 543)

V

vaccination: weakened or dead pathogens placed in the body, usually by injection or by mouth. (p. 617)

vaccine: a mixture containing material from one or more deactivated pathogens, such as viruses. (p. 252)

vacunación: patógenos debilitados o muertos introducidos en el cuerpo, generalmente por medio de una inyección o por la boca. (pág. 617)

vacuna: mezcla que contiene material de uno o más patógenos desactivados, como los virus. (pág. 252)

SCIENCE SKILL HANDBOOK

MATH SKILL HANDBOOK

FOLDABLES HANDBOOK

REFERENCE HANDBOOK

GLOSSARY/ GLOSARIO

INDEX

vagina: the part of the female reproductive system that connects the uterus to the outside of the body. (p. 676)

variable: any factor that can have more than one value. (p. NOS 20)

variation: a slight difference in an inherited trait among individual members of a species. (p. 201)

vascular tissue: specialized plant tissue composed of tubelike cells that transport water and nutrients in some plants. (p. 300)

vector: a disease-carrying organism that does not develop the disease. (p. 605)

vegetative reproduction: a form of asexual reproduction in which offspring grow from a part of a parent plant. (p. 133)

vein: a vessel that carries blood toward the heart. (p. 570)

ventricles (VEN trih kul): the lower two chambers of the heart. (p. 568)

vertebrate (VUR tuh brayt): an animal with a backbone. (p. 376)

vestigial (veh STIH jee ul) structure: body part that has lost its original function through evolution. (p. 211)

villus (VIH luhs): a fingerlike projection, many of which cover the folds of the small intestine. (p. 536)

virus: a strand of DNA or RNA surrounded by a layer of protein that can infect and replicate in a host cell. (p. 247)

vitamin: any of several nutrients that are needed in small amounts for growth, regulation of body functions, and prevention of some diseases. (p. 525)

voluntary muscle: muscle that you can consciously control. (p. 499)

vagina: Parte del sistema reproductor femenino que une el útero con el exterior del cuerpo. (p. 676)

variable: cualquier factor que tenga más de un valor. (pág. NOS 20)

variación: ligera diferencia en un rasgo hereditario entre los miembros individuales de una especie. (pág. 201)

tejido vascular: tejido especializado de la planta compuesto de células tubulares que transportan agua y nutrientes en algunas plantas. (pág. 300)

vector: organismo portador de una enfermedad pero que no la desarrolla. (pág. 605)

reproducción vegetativa: forma de reproducción asexual en la cual el organismo se origina a partir de una planta parental. (pág. 133)

vena: vaso que lleva sangre hacia el corazón. (pág. 570)

ventrículos: las dos cámaras inferiores del corazón. (pág. 568)

vertebrado: animal con columna vertebral. (pág. 376)

estructura vestigial: Parte del cuerpo que a través de la evolución perdió la función original. (pág. 211)

vellosidad: proyección parecida a un dedo, muchas de las cuales cubren los pliegues del intestino delgado. (pág. 536)

virus: filamento de ADN o de ARN rodeado por una capa de proteína que puede infectar una célula huésped y replicarse en ella. (pág. 247)

vitamina: cualquiera de los varios nutrientes que se necesitan en cantidades pequeñas para el crecimiento, para regulación de las funciones del cuerpo y para prevención de algunas enfermedades. (pág. 525)

musculares voluntarios: Músculo que controlas conscientemente. (pág. 499)

W

wetland: an aquatic ecosystem that has a thin layer of water covering soil that is wet most of the time. (p. 790)

Humedal: ecosistema acuático que tiene una capa delgada de suelo cubierto de agua que permanece húmedo la mayor parte del tiempo. (pág. 790)

SCIENCE SKILL HANDBOOK

MATH SKILL HANDBOOK

FOLDABLES HANDBOOK

REFERENCE HANDBOOK

GLOSSARY/ GLOSARIO

INDEX

SCIENCE SKILL HANDBOOK

MATH SKILL HANDBOOK

FOLDABLES HANDBOOK

REFERENCE HANDBOOK

GLOSSARY/ GLOSARIO

INDEX

X

xylem (ZI lum): a type of vascular tissue that carries water and dissolved nutrients from the roots to the stem and the leaves. (p. 314)

xilema: tipo de tejido vascular que transporta agua y nutrientes disueltos desde las raíces hacia el tallo y las hojas. (pág. 314)

Z

zygosporangia (zi guh spor AN jee uh): tiny stalks formed when a zygote fungus under goes sexual reproduction. (p. 279)

zygote (ZI goht): the new cell that forms when a sperm cell fertilizes an egg cell (pp. 117, 466, 684)

zigosporangia: tallos diminutos que se forman cuando un hongo zigoto se somete a reproducción sexual.(pág. 279)

zigoto: Célula nueva que se forma cuando un espermatozoide fertiliza un óvulo. (pág. 117, 466, 684)

Index

Italic numbers = illustration/photo   **Bold numbers** = vocabulary term
lab = indicates entry is used in a lab on this page

SCIENCE SKILL HANDBOOK

MATH SKILL HANDBOOK

FOLDABLES HANDBOOK

REFERENCE HANDBOOK

GLOSSARY/ GLOSARIO

INDEX

A

Abiotic factors
in aquatic ecosystems, 787
effects of, 711
explanation of, **707,** *708*
interaction between animals and, *709*
plant growth and, 730–731 *lab*
types of, 708–709, 732
ABO blood types, 165, *165*
ABO system, 580, *580*
Absolute-age dating, 192, *192*
Absorption, 433, 531
Academic Vocabulary, NOS 11, 17, 30, 52, 102, 132, 165, 201, 270, 300, 336, 383, 424, 465, 501, 546, 573, 614, 642, 687, **719,** 753, 825
Accuracy, NOS **14,** NOS 15
Achilles tendon, 498
Acid, 535
Acid precipitation, 825
Acquired immunodeficiency syndrome (AIDS), 605
Active immunity, 617
Active transport, *64,* **64**
Active viruses, 248
Adaptations
environmental, 204, 216–217 *lab*
explanation of, **203**
types of, 203, *203*
Adenine, 171
Adenosine triphosphate (ATP)
explanation of, 56, 69
glucose converted into, 71
use of, 70
Adolescence, 690
Adrenal glands, *659*
Aerobic bacteria, 233
Affect, 687
Aggression, *461,* **461**
Aging, 690
Agriculture, 827, *827*
Air-breathing catfish, 17
Air pollution. *See also* **Pollution**
explanation of, 816, 824, 832 *lab*
sources of, *824,* 824–825, *825*
Air pressure, 562, *562*
Alcohol consumption
fetal development and, 687, *687*
health issues and, 622
Alcohol fermentation, 71
Algae
explanation of, *266,* **266**
importance of, 269, *269,* 275
types of, 268, *268*

Alleles
dominant and recessive, 161, *161,* 162, 163
explanation of, **160,** *160,* 606
multiple, 165
Allergy, 616
Alternation of generations, *352,* **352,** 353
Alternative fuels, 833
Alveoli, *561,* **561**
Amino acids
explanation of, 524
proteins made from, 174, *174*
Amoeba, 98, *98*
explanation of, 271, **271**
movement of, 271 *lab*
reproduction in, 131, *131*
Amphibia, 395
Amphibians
explanation of, **395,** *395*
hearts in, 425
Amylase, 47
Analogous structures, 211
Analysis, NOS 7, NOS 25
Anaphase, 91, *91,* 120, *120,* 121, *121*
Anaerobic bacteria, 233
Anatomy, comparative, 210–211
Ancestry, 210
Anemia, 581
Angiosperms
explanation of, *319,* 319–320, *320,* 356
leaves of, 317
life cycle of, 357, *357*
types of, 319, *319*
Animal behaviors
based on seasons, 451
conditions that change, 472–473 *lab*
courtship as, 461
explanation of, **447**
innate, 449–451, *450, 451*
learned, 452–453, *453*
societies and, *460,* 460–461, *461*
stimuli and responses and, *448,* 448–449, *449*
territorial, 461
Animal cells, *53,* 59 *lab,* 297, *297*
Animal cloning, 135, *135*
Animalcules, 603
Animalia, 20, *20*
Animal-like protists
explanation of, 266, *266*
protozoans as, 270, 272, *272*
types of, *270,* 270–271, *271*
Animal regeneration, 132, *132*
Animals
adapted for unique environments, 436–437 *lab*
bacteria living in, 239, *239*

characteristics of, 375, 375 *lab,* 411, 427
circulation in, 421, *424,* 424–425, *425*
classification of, *376,* 376–378, 376 *lab, 377, 378, 379*
control structures in, *414,* 414–415, *415*
gas exchange in, 421–423, *423*
reproduction in, 375
symmetry in, 377, *377*
types of movement in, *416,* 416–417, *417, 419*
Annelida, 386
Annelid worms, 386, *386*
Annual plants, 320
Antibiotics
explanation of, **242,** 251, **599,** 624
from fungi, 281, 283, *283*
horseshoe crab blood extract as, 583
resistance to, 242–243, *243,* 283
Antibodies
explanation of, **251, 616**
function of, 252 *lab*
vaccinations producing, 617
Antigens, 580, *580,* **616**
Aorta, 570
Appendages
cell, 53, *53*
explanation of, **387**
jointed, 387, 388 *lab*
Aquatic ecosystems
estuary, 791, *791*
explanation of, 787
freshwater, 787 *lab,* 788, 788–789, *789*
ocean, 787 *lab,* 792, 792–793, *793*
wetland, 790, *790*
Aquatic Species Program (ASP) (Department of Energy), NOS 21, NOS 23, NOS 24
Aquatic succession, 800, *800*
Aquino, Adriana, 17
Arachnids, 388
Arachnologists, 127
Araschnia levana, 166
Archaea, 20, **20,** 231, 235
Area, 546
Arengo, Felicity, 747
Aristotle, 19
Armored catfish, 17
Arms
bionic, 495, *495*
Arteries, 570, *570,* 572
Arterioles, 570, *570*
Arthritis, 492
Arthropods, *387,* 387–388, *388*
Artificial selection, 205
Ascus, 279
Aseptic techniques, 609 *lab*

SCIENCE SKILL HANDBOOK

MATH SKILL HANDBOOK

FOLDABLES HANDBOOK

REFERENCE HANDBOOK

GLOSSARY/ GLOSARIO

INDEX

Science Skill Handbook
Math Skill Handbook
Foldables Handbook
Reference Handbook
Glossary/Glosario
Index

C

D

Darwin, Charles

SCIENCE SKILL HANDBOOK

MATH SKILL HANDBOOK

FOLDABLES HANDBOOK

REFERENCE HANDBOOK

GLOSSARY/ GLOSARIO

INDEX

SCIENCE SKILL HANDBOOK

MATH SKILL HANDBOOK

FOLDABLES HANDBOOK

REFERENCE HANDBOOK

GLOSSARY/ GLOSARIO

INDEX

SCIENCE SKILL HANDBOOK
MATH SKILL HANDBOOK
FOLDABLES HANDBOOK
REFERENCE HANDBOOK
GLOSSARY/GLOSARIO
INDEX

SCIENCE SKILL HANDBOOK
MATH SKILL HANDBOOK
FOLDABLES HANDBOOK
REFERENCE HANDBOOK
GLOSSARY/ GLOSARIO
INDEX

SCIENCE SKILL HANDBOOK
MATH SKILL HANDBOOK
FOLDABLES HANDBOOK
REFERENCE HANDBOOK
GLOSSARY/GLOSARIO
INDEX

Science Skill Handbook

Math Skill Handbook

Foldables Handbook

Reference Handbook

Glossary/ Glosario

Index

Credits

Art Acknowledgements:

The McGraw-Hill Companies, Zoo Botanica, Pronk & Associates, Articulate Graphics, Emily Damstra, Argosy.

Photo Credits

Front Cover, Spine Photodisc/Getty Images; **Back Cover** Thinkstock/Getty Images; **Inside front,back cover** Thinkstock/Getty Images; **Connect Ed** (t)Richard Hutchings, (c)Getty Images, (b)Jupiter Images/Thinkstock/Alamy; **i** Thinkstock/Getty Images; **iv** Ransom Studios viii–ix The McGraw-Hill Companies; **ix** (b)Fancy Photography/Veer; **NOS 2–NOS 3** Images & Stories/Alamy; **NOS 4** (l)Natural Visions/Alamy, (r)Kelly Jett/Alamy; **NOS 5** (c)Frans Lanting/CORBIS, (b)Hank Morgan - Rainbow/Science Faction/CORBIS; **NOS 6** Lynn Keddie/Photolibrary; **NOS 7** Jose Luis Pelaez, Inc./CORBIS; **NOS 8** (t)David S. Holloway/Getty Images, (c)Klaus Guldbrandsen/Photo Researchers, (b)Giovanni Chaves-Portilla/Fundación Ecodiversidad Colombia; **NOS 9** Dennis Kunkel Microscopy, Inc./PHOTOTAKE/Alamy; **NOS 11** Plush Studios/Getty Images; **NOS 12** Richard Peters/Alamy; **NOS 13** PETE OXFORD/MINDEN PICTURES/National Geographic Stock; **NOS 16** (tl)Charles D. Winters/Photo Researchers, (tr)Matt Meadows, (c)Louis Rosenstock/The McGraw-Hill Companies, (bl)David Chasey/Getty Images, (br)Biosphoto/NouN/Peter Arnold, Inc.; **NOS 17** (t)Lauren Burke/Getty Images, (b)Richard T. Nowitz/CORBIS; **NOS 18** (tl)Stockbyte/Getty Images, (tr)Don Farrall/Getty Images, (bl)Medicimage/Visulas Unlimited, Inc., (br)Hutchings Photography/Digital Light Source; **NOS 19** (l to r, t to b,2,4)Hutchings Photography/Digital Light Source, (1,3)The Mcgraw-Hill Companies; **NOS 20** NREL/US Department of Energy/Photo Researchers; **NOS 21** (l)akg-images, (r)Stefan Puchner/UPPA/Photoshot; **NOS 22** (l)Pat Watson/The McGraw-Hill Companies, Inc., (r)Jan Hinsch/Photo Researchers; **NOS 23** (t)Hank Morgan/Photo Researchers/Getty Images, (c)Andrew Kaufman, (b)Ashley Cooper/Alamy; **NOS 24** Colin Braley/AP Images; **NOS 25** (t)MARK MOFFETT/MINDEN PICTURES/National Geographic Stock; **NOS 26** (t)Hank Morgan/Photo Researchers/Getty Images; **NOS 27** Courtesy Seambiotic Ltd; **NOS 28** (l to r, t to b)Hutchings Photography/Digital Light Source, (1)The Mcgraw-Hill Companies; **6–7** Vaughn Fleming/Garden Picture Library/Photolibrary; **8** Angela Wyant/Getty Images; **9** (t)Hutchings Photography/Digital Light Source, (b)Mark Gibson; **10** (l)BRUCE COLEMAN, INC./Alamy, (c)Mark Smith/Photo Researchers, (r)Gary Meszaros/Photo Researchers; **11** (l)Joe McDonald/CORBIS, (r)BRUCE COLEMAN INC./Alamy; **12** (l)John Kaprielian/Photo Researchers, (c)Gary Gaugler/The Medical File/The Medical File/Peter Arnold, Inc.; **13** (r)Hutchings Photography/Digital Light Source; **14** Michael Abbey/Visuals Unlimited; **15** (t)Digital Vision/PunchStock, (tc)Robert Clay/Alamy, (c)John Kaprielian/Photo Researchers, (c)Splinter Images/Alamy, (b)Lee Rentz, (bc)liquidlibrary/PictureQuest; **16** (t)Mark Smith/Photo Researchers, (c)Michael Abbey/Visuals Unlimited, (b)liquidlibrary/PictureQuest, (inset)D. Finn/American Museum of Natural History, (bkgd)Reinaldo Minillo/Getty Images; **17** Spencer Grant/Photolibrary; **18** (t)Hutchings Photography/Digital Light Source, (b)PhotoLink/Getty Images; **21** Shin Yoshino/Minden Pictures/Getty Images; **22** Mark Steinmetz; **24** Shin Yoshino/Minden Pictures/Getty Images; **25** (t)Frank Greenaway/Getty Images, (tc)Adam Jones/Danita Delimont Agency, (b)Jill Van Doren/Alamy, (bc)Mark Steinmetz; **26** Eye of Science/Photo Researchers; **27** (t)Hutchings Photography/Digital Light Source, (c) Dr Jeremy Burgess/Photo Researchers, (b)Imagestate/Photolibrary; **28** (l)Steve Gschmeissner/Photo Researchers, (r)JGI/Getty Images; **29** (l)Stephen Schauer/Getty Images, (cl)ISM/Phototake, (cr)A. Syred/Photo Researchers, (r)age fotostock/SuperStock; **30** (t) Dr Jeremy Burgess/Photo Researchers; Hutchings Photography/Digital Light Source; **31** (l)Steve Gschmeissner/Photo Researchers, (tc)JGI/Blend Images/Getty Images, (r)A. Syred/Photo Researchers, (b)ISM/Phototake, (bc)Stephen Schauer/Getty Images; **32** (l,r)Hutchings Photography/Digital Light Source; **33** Hutchings Photography/Digital Light Source; **34** (t)Joe McDonald/CORBIS, (b)age fotostock/SuperStock; **36** Creatas/PunchStock; **37** (l)The McGraw-Hill Companies, (r)Vaughn Fleming/Garden Picture Library/Photolibrary; **40** (c)Dr. Donald Fawcett/Visuals Unlimited/Getty Images; **40–41** Dr. Dennis Kunkel/Visuals Unlimited/Getty Images; **42** Tui De Roy/Minden Pictures; **43** (t)Hutchings Photography/Digital Light Source, (c)Bon Appetit/Alamy, (b)Omikron/Photo Researchers; **44** (tl)Tim Fitzharris/Minden Pictures/Getty Images, (tc)Biophoto Associates/Photo Researchers, (tr)James M. Bell/Photo Researchers, (bl,bc,br)Dr. Richard Kessel & Dr. Gene Shih/Visuals Unlimited/Getty Images; **45** FoodCollection/SuperStock; **46** Dr. Gopal Murti/Photo Researchers; **47** Ed Reschke/Peter Arnold, Inc.; **48** (t)James M. Bell/Photo Researchers, (b)Dr. Gopal Murti/Photo Researchers; **49** (l)VICTOR SHAHIN, PROF. DR. H.OBERLEITHNER, UNIVERSITY HOSPITAL OF MUENSTER/Photo Researchers, (r)NASA-JPL; **50** Eye of Science/Photo Researchers; **51** Hutchings Photography/Digital Light Source; **53** SPL/Photo Researchers; **54** Hutchings Photography/Digital Light Source; **55** Dr. Donald Fawcett/Visuals Unlimited/Getty Images; **56** (l)Dr. Donald Fawcett/Visuals Unlimited/Getty Images, (r)Dennis Kunkel / Phototake; **57** (l)Dr. R. Howard Berg/Visuals Unlimited/Getty Images, (r)Dennis Kunkel / Phototake; **58** Dr. R. Howard Berg/Visuals Unlimited/Getty Images; **59** (c)Macmillan/McGraw-Hill; (others)Hutchings Photography/Digital Light Source; **60** LIU JIN/AFP/Getty Images; **61** Macmillan/McGraw-Hill; **63** Hutchings Photography/Digital Light Source; **67** (c)Macmillan/McGraw-Hill; Colin Milkins/Photolibrary, (others)Hutchings Photography/Digital Light Source; **69** Hutchings Photography/Digital Light Source; **71** (t)Biology Media/Photo Researchers, (b)Andrew Syred/Photo Researchers; **72** Michael & Patricia Fogden/Minden Pictures; **73** Biology Media/Photo Researchers; **74** (tc,bc)Macmillan/McGraw-Hill, (others)Hutchings Photography/Digital Light Source; **76** Dr. Richard Kessel & Dr. Gene Shih/Visuals Unlimited/Getty Images; **79** Dr. Dennis Kunkel/Visuals Unlimited/Getty Images; **82–83** Robert Pickett/CORBIS; **84** Michael Abbey/Photo Researchers; **85** (t)Hutchings Photography/Digital Light Source, (b)Bill Brooks/Alamy; **87** (bl)Ed Reschke/Peter Arnold, Inc., (br)Biophoto Associates/Photo Researchers, (others)Dr. Richard Kessel & Dr. Gene Shih/Visuals Unlimited; **88** Don W. Fawcett/Photo Researchers; **89,90,91** (l)Ed Reschke/Peter Arnold, Inc.; **92** (l)P.M. Motta & D. Palermo/Photo Researchers, (r)Manfred Kage/Peter Arnold, Inc.; **93** Hutchings Photography/Digital Light Source; **94** (t)Biophoto Associates/Photo Researchers, (b)P.M. Motta & D. Palermo/Photo Researchers; **95** (l)Alex Wilson/Marshall University/AP Images, (r)Bananastock/Alamy; **96** (inset)Biosphoto/Lopez Georges/Peter Arnold, Inc., (bkgd)Biosphoto/Bringard Denis/Peter Arnold, Inc.; **97** (t)Hutchings Photography/Digital Light Source, (c)Steve Gschmeissner/Photo Researchers, (b)Cyril Ruoso/ JH Editorial/Minden Pictures; **98** (t)Wim van Egmond/Visuals Unlimited/Getty Images, (c)Jeff Vanuga/CORBIS, (b)Alfred Pasieka/Photo Researchers; **99** (l)Biophoto Associates/Photo Researchers; **101** (r)Andrew Syred/Photo Researchers; **102** (inset)Ed Reschke/Peter Arnold, Inc., (bkgd)Michael Drane/Alamy; **103** Hutchings Photography/Digital Light Source; **105** Wim van Egmond/Visuals Unlimited/Getty Images; **106,107** Hutchings Photography/Digital Light Source; **111** Robert Pickett/CORBIS; **114–115** Bill Coster/Getty Images; **116** Science Pictures Ltd./Photo Researchers; **117** Hutchings Photography/Digital Light Source; **120,121** (t)Ed Reschke/Peter Arnold, Inc.; **122** (t,c)Nature's Images/Photo Researchers, (b)Jeremy West/Getty Images; **124** (l)Rob Walls/Alamy, (r)Nigel Cattlin/Alamy; **125** (tl)Stockbyte/Getty Images, (tr)Craig Lovell/CORBIS, (c)Piotr & Irena Kolasa/Alamy, (bl)image100/SuperStock, (br)Wally Eberhart/Visuals Unlimited/Getty Images; **126** Bill Coster/Getty Images; **127** (bl)Greg Broussard, (bkgd)David Thompson/Photolibrary; **128** Dr. Brad Mogen/Visuals Unlimited; **129** Horizons Companies; **130** CNRI/Photo Researchers; **131** (l,c,r)Biophoto Associates/Photo Researchers; **133** (l)sciencephotos/Alamy, (t)Wally Eberhart/Visuals Unlimited, (r)DEA/G.CIGOLINI/Getty Images, (b)Jerome Wexler/Photo Researchers; **135** Roslin Institute; **136** Mark Steinmetz; **137** (t)Dr. Brad Mogen/Visuals Unlimited, (c)Roslin Institute, (b)Mark Steinmetz; **138** (t,c,b)Hutchings Photography/Digital Light Source; **139** Hutchings Photography/Digital Light Source; **140** (t)Science Pictures Ltd./Photo Researchers, (b)CNRI/Photo Researchers; **143** Bill Coster/Getty Images; **146–147** Tom and Pat Leesson; **148** Nigel Cattlin/Visuals Unlimited; **149** (tl)Geoff du Feu/Alamy, (tr)Ken Karp/McGraw-Hill Companies, (cl)Glow Images/Getty Images, (cr)Getty Images, (bl,br)The Mcgraw-Hill Companies; **150** (l,r)Wally Eberhart/Visuals Unlimited; **151** (t)Tom and Pat Leesson, (bl)DEA PICTURE LIBRARY/Photolibrary, (br)WILDLIFE/Peter Arnold, Inc.; **152,153** (purple flower)DEA PICTURE LIBRARY/Photolibrary, (white flower)WILDLIFE/Peter Arnold, Inc.; **157** (t)Pixtal/age Fotostock, (c)World History Archive/age Fotostock, (b)Tek Image/Photo Researchers, (bkgd)Jason Reed/Getty Images; **158** (l to r, t to b,2,5–10)Getty Images, (3)Punchstock, (4,11,12)CORBIS; **159** (t)Hutchings Photography/Digital Light Source, (b)Biophoto Associates/Photo Researchers; **161** (t,b)Martin Shields/Photo Researchers; **163** (l)Maya Barnes/The Image Works, (r)Bill Aron/PhotoEdit; **164** (l)Peter Smithers/CORBIS, (tr)Geoff Bryant/Photo Researchers, (c)Bill Ross/CORBIS, (bl)J. Schwanke/Alamy, (bc,br)Yann Arthus-Bertrand/CORBIS; **165** Chris Clinton/Getty Images; **166** (tl)Picture Net/Corbis, (tr)June Green/Alamy Images, (c)Carolyn A. McKeone/Photo Researchers, (bl,br)Hania Arensten-Berdys/www.gardensafari.net; **167** Chris Clinton/Getty Images; **168** (l,r)Kristina Yu/Exploratorium Store; **169** PHOTOTAKE Inc./Alamy; **170** Hutchings Photography/Digital Light Source; **178** (all)Hutchings Photography/Digital Light Source; **179** (tr)The McGraw-Hill Companies; (others)Hutchings Photography/Digital Light Source; **180** (cl)WILDLIFE/Peter Arnold, Inc., (purple flower)DEA PICTURE LIBRARY/Photolibrary; **183** Tom and Pat Leesson; **184** (bc)Gary W. Carter/CORBIS, (br)Alamy Images, (others)Ted Kinsman/Photo Researchers; **185** (t)Alamy Images, (c)Frank Krahmer/zefa/CORBIS, (b)Geoff du Feu/Alamy; **186–187** William Osborn/Minden Pictures; **188** Florida Museum of Natural History photo by Eric Zamora ©2008; Hutchings Photography/Digital Light Source; **190** (l)B.A.E. Inc./Alamy, (r)The Natural History Museum/Alamy; **191** (l)Mark Steinmetz, (c)Tom Bean/CORBIS, (r)Dorling Kindersely/Getty Images; **195** Hutchings Photography/Digital Light Source; **196** Dorling Kindersely/Getty Images; **197** (t)Ryan McVay/Getty Images, (c)C Squared Studios/Getty Images, (b)Richard Broadwell/Alamy; C Squared Studios/Getty Images; Getty Images; Tim O'Hara/Corbis; **198** DLILLC/CORBIS; **199** Hutchings Photography/Digital Light Source; **200** (l)Jeffrey Greenberg/Photo Researchers, (c)David Hosking/Alamy, (r)Mark Jones/Photolibrary; **201** Chip Clark; **203** (l)Carey Alan & Sandy/Photolibrary, (c)Robert Shantz/Alamy, (r)Stan Osolinski/Photolibrary; **204** (l)Paul Sutherland/National Geographic/Getty Images, (t)NHPA/Photoshot, (r)Kay Nietfeld/dpa/CORBIS, (b)Mitsuhiko Imamori/Minden Pictures; **205** (l)ARCO/D. Usher/age Fotostock, (t)Photodisc/Getty Images, (r)Joe Blossom/NHPA/Photoshot, (b)Hutchings Photography/Digital Light Source; **206** (t)Mark Jones/Photolibrary, (tc)Chip Clark, (b)Don Mammoser/Bruce Coleman, Inc./Photoshot, (bc)Paul Sutherland/National Geographic/Getty Images; **207** (t)D. Parer & E. Parer-Cook, (b)B. Rosemary Grant/AP Images, (bkgd)Skan9/Getty Images; **208** Joseph Van Os/Getty Images; **209** Hutchings Photography/Digital Light Source; **214** T. Daeschler/The Academy of Natural Sciences/VIREO; **215** Joseph Van Os/Getty Images; **216** (t to b,5Hutchings Photography/Digital Light Source, (2–4)Macmillan/McGraw-Hill, (br)Mary Plage/Photolibrary, (cr)USGS; **218** Mark Steinmetz; **221** William Osborn/Minden Pictures; **226** (t)Eric Audras/Getty Images, (cl)David Fischer/Getty Images, (c)CORBIS/age fotostock, (cr)NASA Spinoff; **227** (tl)NOAA, (cl)Patrick Landmann / Photo Researchers, Inc., (r)NASA, (bl)courtesy of Polar Products, Inc.; **228–229** Eye of Science/Photo Researchers; **230** Dr. Tony Brain/Photo Researchers; **231** Hutchings Photography/Digital Light Source; **232** (l)Dr. David M.

Phillips/Visuals Unlimited/Getty Images, (c)Medical-on-Line/Alamy, (r)Visuals Unlimited/CORBIS; **233** (t)Hutchings Photography/Digital Light Source, (b)Stefan Sollfors/Getty Images; **234** Science VU/Visuals Unlimited/Getty Images; **235** (l)Richard Du Toit/Minden Pictures, (r)Beverly Joubert/National Geographic/Getty Images; **236** Stefan Sollfors/Getty Images; **237** (tl)Photodisc/Getty Images; (tr)Michael Rosenfeld/Getty Images, (c)Rich Legg/iStockphoto, (bl)Science Source/Photo Researchers, (br)Hercules Robinson/Alamy, (bkgd)Lawrence Lawry/Getty Images; **238** Dante Fenolio/Photo Researchers; **239** (t)Hutchings Photography/Digital Light Source, (b)CORBIS; **240** (t)Wally Eberhart/Visuals Unlimited/Getty Images, (b)Hutchings Photography/Digital Light Source; **241** (inset)Eye of Science/Photo Researchers, (bkgd)Debra Reid/AP Images; **242** Zephyr/Photo Researchers; **244** (tl)Eye of Science/Photo Researchers, (r)CORBIS, (bl)Zephyr/Photo Researchers; **245** (t to b,2)Macmillan/McGraw-Hill, (r,3–5)Hutchings Photography/Digital Light Source; **246** Juliette Wade/Gap Photo/Visuals Unlimited; **252** (br)Hutchings Photography/Digital Light Source; **254** (t to b)Hutchings Photography/Digital Light Source, (4)Macmillan/McGraw-Hill; **255** Hutchings Photography/Digital Light Source; **256** Wally Eberhart/Visuals Unlimited/Getty Images; **259** Eye of Science/Photo Researchers; **262–263** Ed Reschke/Peter Arnold, Inc.; **264** Visuals Unlimited/CORBIS; **265** (t)Hutchings Photography/Digital Light Source, (b)Flip Nicklin/Minden Pictures/Getty Images; **266** (l)Flip Nicklin/Minden Pictures/Getty Images, (c)Michael Abbey/Photo Researchers, (r)Matt Meadows/Peter Arnold, Inc., (b)NASA Spinoff; **266–267** StockTrek/Getty Images; **267** (t)Manfred Kage/Peter Arnold, Inc., (c,b)Wim van Egmond/Visuals Unlimited/Getty Images; **268** (tl)Melba Photo Agency/PunchStock, (tr)WILDLIFE/Peter Arnold, Inc., (bl)M. I. Walker/Photo Researchers, (br)blickwinkel/Alamy; **269** (t)Images&Stories/Alamy, (b)Bill Bachman/Photo Researchers; **271** (l,r,b)Michael Abbey/Photo Researchers, (t)Hutchings Photography/Digital Light Source; **273** Mark Steinmetz; **274** (t)Visuals Unlimited/CORBIS, (b)Manfred Kage/Peter Arnold, Inc.; **275** (l)Ashley Cooper/Alamy, (r)JUPITERIMAGES/Brand X /Alamy, (bkgd)Kaz Chiba/Getty Images; **276** Felix Labhardt/Getty Images; **277** Hutchings Photography/Digital Light Source; **278** Mark Steinmetz; **279** (t,tc,bc)Hutchings Photography/Digital Light Source, (b)Gregory G. Dimijian/Photo Researchers; **280** Hutchings Photography/Digital Light Source; **281** (l,r)www.offwell.info, (c)Hutchings Photography/Digital Light Source; **283** C. James Webb / Phototake; **284** David Robertson/stockscotland; **285** (l)David Robertson/stockscotland, (r)Mark Steinmetz; **286** (tr,bc)Macmillan/McGraw-Hill, (t)Hutchings Photography/Digital Light Source; **288** (l)Flip Nicklin/Minden Pictures/Getty Images, (t)Michael Abbey/Photo Researchers, (r)Matt Meadows/Peter Arnold, Inc., (b)David Robertson/stockscotland; **291** Ed Reschke/Peter Arnold, Inc.; **294–295** Edmunds Dana/Photolibrary; **296** Dr. Martha Powell/Visuals Unlimited/Getty Images; **297** (l to r)Art Wolfe/Getty Images, (1)Mark Steinmetz, (2)Photos Horticultural/Photoshot, (3)Beverly Joubert/National Geographic/Getty Images, (4)SuperStock/SuperStock, (5)Renaud Visage/Getty Images; **298** (l)Biophoto Associates/Photo Researchers, (r)James Randklev/Photolibrary; **299** Siede Preis/Getty Images; **300** (l)H. Stanley Johnson/SuperStock, (c)Darryl Torckler/Getty Images, (r)Mark Steinmetz; **301** (tl)Biophoto Associates/Photo Researchers, (tr)Darrell Gulin/CORBIS, (bl)David Maitland/Getty Images, (br)Chromorange RM/Photolibrary; **302** (tl)Steven P. Lynch/The McGraw-Hill Companies, Inc., (tr)Mark Bowler/Photoshot, (c)David Maitland/Getty Images, (bl)Biophoto Associates/Photo Researchers, (br)Mark Steinmetz; **303** (tl)Janis Burger/Bruce Coleman, Inc./Photoshot, (tr)Darrell Gulin/CORBIS, (cl)Dr. Carleton Ray/Photo Researchers, (cr)WILDLIFE/Peter Arnold, Inc., (bl)Mark Steinmetz, (br)Russell Illig/Photodisc/Getty Images; **304** (t)Chromorange RM/Photolibrary, (c)Mark Steinmetz, (b)Biophoto Associates/Photo Researchers; **305** (t)TIM LAMAN/National Geographic Stock, (c)Gilbert S. Grant/Photo Researchers, (b)Reinhard Dirscherl/Water Frame/Getty Images; **306** Ern Mainka/Alamy;

Credits

307 Hutchings Photography/Digital Light Source; **308** (l)WILDLIFE/Peter Arnold, Inc., (cl)David Whitaker/Alamy, (cr)Ed Reschke/Peter Arnold, Inc., (r)Steven P. Lynch/The McGraw-Hill Companies, Inc.; **309** (t)Mark Bowler/Photoshot, (c)Mark Steinmetz, (b)Janis Burger/Bruce Coleman, Inc./Photoshot; **310** (tl)Mark Bowler/Photoshot, (tr)David Whitaker/Alamy, (bl)Mark Steinmetz, (br)Mark Steinmetz; **311** (tl)Macmillan/McGraw-Hill, (tr)Burke/Triolo Productions / Getty Images, (bl)CORBIS, (br)Kristy-Anne Glubish/Design Pics/CORBIS; **312** Donald M. Jones/Minden Pictures; **313** (t)studiomode/Alamy, (tl)Comstock Images/Alamy, (tr)Burke Triolo Productions/Getty Images, (b)Michael Rosenfeld/Getty Images, (bl)Bon Appetit/Alamy, (br)Walter Cimbal/Getty Images; **315** JIM RICHARDSON/National Geographic Stock; **316** (l)Mark Steinmetz, (r)Burke/Triolo Productions/Getty Images; **317** (l)Siede Preis/Getty Images, (r)Dr. Gerald Van Dyke/Visuals Unlimited/Getty Images; **318** (t)Brian Gadsby/Photo Researchers, (tl)Robert Harding Picture Library/SuperStock, (tr)Steve Solum/Bruce Coleman, Inc./Photoshot, (b)JTB/Photoshot, (bl)WILDLIFE / Peter Arnold, Inc., (br)Dr. Carleton Ray/Photo Researchers; **319** (t)Mark Steinmetz, (c)Russell Illig/Photodisc/Getty Images, (b)Wally Eberhart/Visuals Unlimited/Getty Images; **320** (tl)Ed Reschke/Peter Arnold, Inc., (tr)CORBIS, (cl)Clive Nichols/Getty Images, (cr)Travelscapes/Alamy, (bl,br)The McGraw-Hill Companies; **321** (t)Russell Illig/Photodisc/Getty Images, (c)JIM RICHARDSON/National Geographic Stock, (b)Bon Appetit/Alamy; **322** (tl)The Mcgraw-Hill Companies, (tr)Daisy Gilardini/Getty Images, (c)Digital Vision/Getty Images, (b)Natalie Fobes/Getty Images; **324** (t)H. Stanley Johnson/SuperStock, (c)WILDLIFE/Peter Arnold, Inc., (b)Michael Rosenfeld/Getty Images; **326** Steven P. Lynch/The McGraw-Hill Companies, Inc.; **327** Edmunds Dana/Photolibrary; **330–331** Mark Moffett/Minden Pictures; **332** Dr. Dennis Kunkel/Visuals Unlimited/Getty Images; **333** (t)Hutchings Photography/Digital Light Source, (b)The McGraw-Hill Companies; **334** Siede Preis/Getty Images; **335** The Mcgraw-Hill Companies; **336** Hutchings Photography/Digital Light Source; **338** (t,b)The McGraw-Hill Companies; **339** (t)Jacques Jangoux/Photolibrary, (b)MARK EDWARDS/Peter Arnold, Inc., (bkgd)Digital Vision/Getty Images; **340** NHPA/Photoshot; **341** (t)Hutchings Photography/Digital Light Source, (b)Cathlyn Melloan/Getty Images; **343** (l)Martin Shields/Photo Researchers, (c)Stephen Dalton/Minden Pictures, (r)Martin Shields/Photo Researchers; **346** Sylvan Wittwer/Visuals Unlimited; **347** (tl)Monty Rakusen/Getty Images, (tr)Nigel Cattlin/Photo Researchers, (c)Nigel Cattlin/Alamy, (bl)B. ANTHONY STEWART/National Geographic Stock, (br)GardenPhotos.com/Alamy; **348** (t,b)Martin Shields/Photo Researchers; **349** (1,2,3,6)The Mcgraw-Hill Companies; (others)Hutchings Photography/Digital Light Source; **350** Bjorn Rorslett/Photo Researchers; **351** (t)Ingram Publishing/SuperStock, (b)Wally Eberhart/Visuals Unlimited/Getty Images; **353** (l)CARR CLIFTON/ MINDEN PICTURES/National Geographic Stock, (r)Ed Reschke/Peter Arnold Inc.; **354** Eye of Science/Photo Researchers; **355** (t)Andrew Brown; Ecoscene/CORBIS, (b)Dr. Daniel Nickrent/Southern Illinois University; **356** Hutchings Photography/Digital Light Source; **358** (t)Don Klumpp/Getty Images, (1)Alan & Linda Detrick/Photo Researchers, (2)Comstock/PunchStock, (3)Brad Mogen/Visuals Unlimited, (4)Walter H. Hodge/Peter Arnold, Inc., (5)Siede Preis/Getty Images, (6)Renee Morris/Alamy, (7)Elizabeth Whiting & Associates/Alamy, (8)USDA/Photo Researchers, (9)Adam Jones/Photo Researchers, (10)CORBIS, (11)Ingram Publishing/SuperStock, (12)Gary Meszaros/Visuals Unlimited/Getty Images; **359** (t)CARR CLIFTON/ MINDEN PICTURES/National Geographic Stock, (b)Eye of Science/Photo Researchers; **360** (r)Hutchings Photography/Digital Light Source; Stockdisc/PunchStock; **362** The Mcgraw-Hill Companies; **364** (l)Scott Camazine/Photo Researchers, (r)Mark Steinmetz; **365** (l)Cathlyn Melloan/Getty Images, (r)Mark Moffett/Minden Pictures; **370** Wayne R Bilenduke/Getty Images; **372–373** Gary Bell/Getty Images; **373** Darrell Gulin/Getty Images; **375** (t)Hutchings Photography/Digital Light Source, (b)John Cancalosi/Alamy; **376** Geoff Brightling/Getty Images; **377** (l)Brand X Pictures/PunchStock, (c)Paul Nicklen/National Geographic/Getty Images, (r)Design Pics/Carson Ganci; **378** (t)Ingram Publishing/Alamy, (c)Francesco Rovero, (b)Frank Greenaway/Getty Images; **380** (t)John Cancalosi/Alamy, (b)Paul Nicklen/National Geographic/Getty Images; **381** (c)age fotostock/SuperStock, (inset)N. Simmons/American Museum of Natural History, (bkgd)Heath Korvola/Getty Images; **382** Matthew Oldfield, Scubazoo/Photo Researchers; **383** Hutchings Photography/Digital Light Source; **385** (t)James H. Robinson/Photo Researchers, (b)Sinclair Stammers/Photo Researchers; **386** (t)Ingram Publishing/Alamy, (b)Doug Perrine/SeaPics.com; **388** (t)Ingram Publishing/Alamy, (c)Hutchings Photography/Digital Light Source, (b)Jeremy Woodhouse/Getty Images; **390** (t)Ingram Publishing/Alamy, (b)Jeremy Woodhouse/Getty Images; **391** (l to r, t to b)C Squared Studios/Getty Images, (1)Siede Preis/Getty Images, (2)Brand X Pictures/PunchStock, (3)John Foxx / Alamy, (4)Photodisc / Getty Images, (5)Creatas/PunchStock, (6)Hutchings Photography/Digital Light Source, (7)Siede Preis/Getty Images, (8)Brand X Pictures/PunchStock, (9)Siede Preis/Getty Images; **392** FRANS LANTING/National Geographic Stock; **393** Hutchings Photography/Digital Light Source; **394** Pacific Stock/SuperStock; **396** (inset)Daniel Heuclin/NHPA/Photoshot, (bkgd)JH Pete Carmichael/Getty Images; **398** Steve Kaufman/CORBIS; **399** (t)Daniel Heuclin/NHPA/Photoshot, (c)Steve Kaufman/CORBIS, (b)www.flickr.com/photos/twobigpaws/Flickr/Getty Images; **400** (t,c)Macmillan/McGraw-Hill, (b)Hutchings Photography/Digital Light Source; **401** Hutchings Photography/Digital Light Source; **402** (t)John Cancalosi/Alamy, (b)Doug Perrine/SeaPics.com; **404** (l)Frederic Pacorel/Getty Images, (r)IT Stock Free/Alamy; **405** (l)Ingram Publishing/Alamy, (c)David Fleetham/Visuals Unlimited/Getty Images, (r)Gary Bell/Getty Images; **408–409** J. Keith Rankin/Alamy; **410** Neil Lucas/Minden Pictures; **411** (t)Mark Steinmetz, (b)Vincent Leblic/Photolibrary; **413** (t)Jeff Foott/Getty Images, (b)Dorling Kindersley/Getty Images; **414** Hutchings Photography/Digital Light Source; **416** (l)Mark Strickland/SeaPics.com, (r)Ken Usami/Getty Images; **417** (t)Art Wolfe/Getty Images, (c)Nicholas Bergkessel, Jr./Photo Researchers, (b)Brand X Pictures/PunchStock; **418** (t)Vincent Leblic/Photolibrary, (b)Brand X Pictures/PunchStock; **419** Prisma/SuperStock; 420 Microfield Scientific Ltd/Photo Researchers; **421** Hutchings Photography/Digital Light Source; **422** Hutchings Photography/Digital Light Source; **427** Macmillan/McGraw-Hill; **428** Martin Shields/Alamy; **429** (t)Ken Lucas/Visuals Unlimited, (b)Lester Lefkowitz/Getty Images; **430** (t)Heinrich van den Berg/Getty Images, (c)E. & P. Bauer/CORBIS, (b)Merlin Tuttle/BCI/Photo Researchers; **431** (l)Bartomeu Borrell/age fotostock, (r)H. Robinson James/Getty Images; **432** The Mcgraw-Hill Companies; **434** Creatas/PunchStock; **435** (t)Merlin Tuttle/BCI/Photo Researchers, (b)Creatas/PunchStock; **436** The McGraw-Hill Companies; **437** Hutchings Photography/Digital Light Source; **438** Dorling Kindersley/Getty Images; **440** (l)John Foxx/Alamy, (r)Creatas/PunchStock; **441** Scott Linstead/Tom Stack & Associates; **444–445** Anup Shah/Minden Pictures; **446** Worldwide Picture Library/Alamy; **447** (t)Hutchings Photography/Digital Light Source, (b)Eric Gay/AP Images; **448** (l)Mark Steinmetz, (r)Joseph Devenney/Getty Images; **449** Steve Bloom/Getty Images; **450** Bianca Lavies/National Geographic/Getty Images; **451** age fotostock/SuperStock; **453** (l,r)Mark Steinmetz, (c)Thomas & Pat Leeson/Photo Researchers; **454** (t)Joseph Devenney/Getty Images, (c)Bianca Lavies/National Geographic/Getty Images, (b)Mark Steinmetz; **455** (t,tc)Macmillan/McGraw-Hill, (b,bc)Hutchings Photography/Digital Light Source; **456** Anna Henly/Getty Images; **457** (t)Hutchings Photography/Digital Light Source, (b)Photography EPC/Photolibrary; **458** (t)Hutchings Photography/Digital Light Source, (b)Satoshi Kuribayashi/Photolibrary; **460** SUZI ESZTERHAS/MINDEN PICTURES/National Geographic Stock; **461** (t)Arco Images GmbH/Alamy, (b)Dave Watts/Tom Stack & Associates; **462** (t)SUZI ESZTERHAS/MINDEN PICTURES/National Geographic Stock, (c)Dave Watts/Tom Stack & Associates, (b)Arco Images GmbH/Alamy; **463** (inset)TIM LAMAN/National Geographic Stock, (bkgd)Getty Images; **464** Thomas Marent/Minden Pictures; **465** (l to r, t to b)David J Green/Getty Images, (1)Purestock/PunchStock, (2)NPS Photo, (3)IT Stock/age fotostock, (4)Richard Wear/Design Pics/CORBIS, (5)CORBIS, (6)Leonard Lee Rue III/

Photo Researchers; **466** (l)Tim Hawley/Getty Images, (r)Michael Winokur/Getty Images; **467** John Cancalosi/Photolibrary; **468** (inset)Daniel Heuclin/NHPA/Photoshot, (bkgd)PHONE PHONE - Auteurs Cordier Sylvain/Peter Arnold, Inc.; **469** David Higgs/NHPA/Photoshot; **471** (t)Leonard Lee Rue III/Photo Researchers, (tc)John Cancalosi/Photolibrary, (b)John Cancalosi/Photolibrary, (bc)PHONE PHONE - Auteurs Cordier Sylvain/Peter Arnold, Inc.; **472** (l to r, t to b,2,5,6)Macmillan/McGraw-Hill, (others)Hutchings Photography/Digital Light Source; **473** Hutchings Photography/Digital Light Source; **474** (t)Thomas & Pat Leeson/Photo Researchers, (c)Anna Henly/Getty Images, (b)Daniel Heuclin/NHPA/Photoshot; **476** Bianca Lavies/National Geographic/Getty Images; **477** (l)Dave Watts/Tom Stack & Associates, (r)Anup Shah/Minden Pictures; **482** (l)Nick Laham/Getty Images, (r)Nick Laham/Getty Images; AFP/Getty Images; **484–485** Charlie Schuck/Getty Images; **486** Gustoimages/Photo Researchers; **487** (t)Hutchings Photography/Digital Light Source, (b)CMCD/Getty Images; **488** Hutchings Photography/Digital Light Source; **492** Mark Steinmetz; **493** (l)Dennis MacDonald/PhotoEdit, (c)Daniel Dempster Photography/Alamy, (r)Bob Daemmrich/PhotoEdit; **494** (b)CMCD/Getty Images; **495** (bkgd)Tomi/PhotoLink/Getty Images; **496** Phil Loftus/Capital Pictures; **497** Hutchings Photography/Digital Light Source; **498** CMCD/Getty Images; **499** Innerspace Imaging/Photo Researchers; **500** (t)Dr, Gladden Willis/Visuals Unlimited/Getty Images, (b)Dr, Gladden Willis/Visuals Unlimited/Getty Images; **503** (t,b)Hutchings Photography/Digital Light Source; **504** Steve Gschmeissner/Photo Researchers; **505** (t)Hutchings Photography/Digital Light Source, (b)Comstock/Jupiterimages; **506** (t)Thomas Barwick/Getty Images, (b)Hutchings Photography/Digital Light Source; **508** (l)Stephen J. Krasemann/Photo Researchers, (c)Scientifica/Visuals Unlimited, (r)Ian Leonard/Alamy; **510** Stockbyte/Getty Images; **511** (tl)Comstock/Jupiterimages, (r)Scientifica/Visuals Unlimited, (bl)Steve Gschmeissner/Photo Researchers; **512** (all)Hutchings Photography/Digital Light Source; **513** Hutchings Photography/Digital Light Source; **517** Charlie Schuck/Getty Images; **520–521** MedicalRF.com/Getty Images; **522** Peter Menzel; **523** Hutchings Photography/Digital Light Source; **524** (t)Dorling Kindersley/Getty Images, (b)Hutchings Photography/Digital Light Source; **525** (t)The McGraw-Hill Companies, (b)Michael Rosenfeld/Getty Images; **526** Hutchings Photography/Digital Light Source; **527** (l)David Young-Wolff/PhotoEdit, (r)Mark Steinmetz; **528** (t)Peter Menzel, (tc)Dorling Kindersley/Getty Images, (b)Mark Steinmetz, (bc)David Young-Wolff / PhotoEdit; **529** (tl.tr)Macmillan/McGraw-Hill, (others)Hutchings Photography/Digital Light Source; **530** Steve Gschmeissner/Photo Researchers; **531,532,534** Hutchings Photography/Digital Light Source; **537** (l)Scimat/Photo Researchers, (r)CNRI/Photo Researchers; **538** Hutchings Photography/Digital Light Source; **539** (inset)Dr. Dennis Kunkel/Visuals Unlimited, (bkgd)Dr. Dennis Kunkel/Visuals Unlimited/Getty Images; **540** Wolf Fahrenbach/Visuals Unlimited/Getty Images; **541** Hutchings Photography/Digital Light Source; **543** Photodisc/Getty Images; **545** Hutchings Photography/Digital Light Source; **547** Wolf Fahrenbach/Visuals Unlimited/Getty Images; **548** (tl,cr,br)Hutchings Photography/Digital Light Source, (others)Macmillan/McGraw-Hill; **550** (t,b)Hutchings Photography/Digital Light Source, (c)Photodisc/Getty Images; **552** Hutchings Photography/Digital Light Source; **553** MedicalRF.com/Getty Images; **556–557** Bo Tornvig/Getty Images; **558** Juergen Berger/Photo Researchers; **559** Hutchings Photography/Digital Light Source; **560** Holger Winkler/zefa/CORBIS; **563** James Cavallini/Photo Researchers; **564** Holger Winkler/zefa/CORBIS; **565** (t to b,2,3,5)Macmillan/McGraw-Hill, (c,r,4)Hutchings Photography/Digital Light Source; **566** Ron Chapple/Getty Images; **567** Hutchings Photography/Digital Light Source; **568** Image Source/Jupiterimages; **571** Image Source/Jupiterimages; **572** Hutchings Photography/Digital Light Source; **575** (all)Hutchings Photography/Digital Light Source; **576** Nati Harnik/AP Images; **577,579** Hutchings Photography/Digital Light Source; **583** (t)Andrew J. Martinez/Photo Researchers, (b)Steve Hamblin/Alamy, (bkgd)Jeffrey L. Rotman/CORBIS; **584** Dr P. Marazzi/Photo Researchers, Inc.; **585** Hutchings Photography/Digital Light Source; **586** C Squared Studios/Getty Images; **589** (l,r)C Squared Studios/Getty Images; **590** (tl,r)Hutchings Photography/Digital Light Source, (cl)Macmillan/McGraw-Hill, (bl)Science Source/Photo Researchers; **591** (all)Science Source/Photo Researchers; **592** (t)Holger Winkler/zefa/CORBIS, (c)Image Source/Jupiterimages, (b)C Squared Studios/Getty Images; **595** Bo Tornvig/Getty Images; **598–599** Steve Gschmeissner/Photo Researchers; **600** (inset)Scott Camazine/Photo Researchers, (bkgd)Science Source/Photo Researchers; **601** (t)Hutchings Photography/Digital Light Source, (b)Eurelios/Photo Researchers; **602** (l)Wellcome Library, London, (r)Michael Abbey/Photo Researchers; **603** The McGraw-Hill Companies; **604** Dr. Dennis Kunkel/Visuals Unlimited/Getty Images; **605** Hutchings Photography/Digital Light Source; **607** (tl)Tomi/PhotoLink/Getty Images, (tr)Zephyr/Photo Researchers, (bl,br)St Bartholomew's Hospital/Photo Researchers; **608** (t)Michael Abbey/Photo Researchers, (b)St Bartholomew's Hospital/Photo Researchers; **609** (tcl)Macmillan/McGraw-Hill, (others)Hutchings Photography/Digital Light Source; **610** Science Pictures Ltd/Photo Researchers; **611** (tr)Hutchings Photography/Digital Light Source; **612** Hutchings Photography/Digital Light Source; **613** (tl)SPL Photo Researchers, (tr)Dr. Kessel & Dr. Kardon/Tissues & Organs/Visuals Unlimited/Getty Image, (c)RubberBall Productions, (cr)Eye of Science/Photo Researchers, (bl)Eye of Science/Photo Researchers, (br)Purestock/Getty Images; **614,618** PHOTOTAKE Inc./Alamy; **619** (t)Image Source/Getty Images, (b)George Musil/Visuals Unlimited/Getty Images, (bkgd)Stockbyte/SuperStock; **620** OJO Images/SuperStock; **621** (tr)Hutchings Photography/Digital Light Source; **622** (t)C Squared Studios/Getty Images, (bl)C Squared Studios/Getty Images, (br)D. Hurst/Alamy; **623** (t)George Diebold/Getty Images, (b)Hutchings Photography/Digital Light Source; **624** JUPITERIMAGES/Thinkstock/Alamy; **625** (tl)George Diebold/Getty Images, (cl)Creatas/PunchStock, (r)D. Hurst/Alamy, (bl)C Squared Studios/Getty Images; **626** (tr,br)Hutchings Photography/Digital Light Source, (t to b)Oleg Shpak/Alamy, (2–5,9)Hutchings Photography/Digital Light Source, (6)Macmillan/McGraw-Hill; **628** (t)Science Source/Photo Researchers, (b)OJO Images/SuperStock; **631** Steve Gschmeissner / Photo Researchers, Inc.; **634–635** Aflo Foto Agency/Photolibrary; **636** Dr. John Mazziotta et al./Photo Researchers; **637** Hutchings Photography/Digital Light Source; **638** David Stoecklein/CORBIS; **640** Doug Pensinger/Getty Images; **643** Hutchings Photography/Digital Light Source; **644** Doug Pensinger/Getty Images; **645** Hutchings Photography/Digital Light Source; **646** Steven Puetzer/Getty Images; **647** Hutchings Photography/Digital Light Source; **651** (l,r)CORBIS/Alamy; **653** Hutchings Photography/Digital Light Source; **654** Steven Puetzer/Getty Images; **655** (l)David J. Green - technology/Alamy, (r)Digital Vision/PunchStock; **656** ISM/Phototake; **657** Hutchings Photography/Digital Light Source; **659** Mark Andersen/Getty Images; **662** Hutchings Photography/Digital Light Source; **663** Hutchings Photography/Digital Light Source; **664** (t)Doug Pensinger/Getty Images, (c)Corbis Premium RF/Alamy, (b)ISM/Phototake; **667** Aflo Foto Agency/Photolibrary; **670–671** Yorgos Nikas/Getty Images; **672** P.M. Motta & J. Van Blerkom/Photo Researchers; **673** (tr)Hutchings Photography/Digital Light Source; **676** Eye of Science/Photo Researchers; **677** Yorgos Nikas/Getty Images; **679** (r)Hutchings Photography/Digital Light Source; **680** Eye of Science/Photo Researchers; **681** (t)Y. Nikas/Biol Reprod/Getty Images, (c)Keystone/Getty Images, (b)Mauro Fermariello/Photo Researchers; **682** Steve Allen/Getty Images; **683** (t)Vincenzo Lombardo/Getty Images, (b)Yellow Dog Productions/Getty Images; **685** (t)Visual&Written SL/Alamy, (b)Tony Freeman/PhotoEdit; **686** (tl)Dr G. Moscoso/Photo Researchers, (tc,tr)Anatomical Travelogue/Photo Researchers, (bl)Biophoto Associates/Photo Researchers, (br)Neil Bromhall/Photolibrary; **690** (t)Digital Vision, (b)Hutchings Photography/Digital Light Source; **691** (t,b)Biophoto Associates/Photo Researchers, (c)Anatomical Travelogue/Photo Researchers;

Credits

692 (t,b,bc)The McGraw-Hill Companies, (tc)Hutchings Photography/Digital Light Source; 693 (all)Marjorie L. Foreman; 694 (t)Eye of Science/Photo Researchers, (b)Yorgos Nikas/Getty Images; 697 Yorgos Nikas/Getty Images; 702 (t to b)Georg Gerster / Photo Researchers, Inc., (2)Keren Su/Getty Images, (3)Smneedham/Getty Images, (4)Courtesy of the University of Central Florida; 703 (t)SuperStock / SuperStock, (b)Stuart Fox/Getty Images; 704–705 MICHAEL S. QUINTON/National Geographic Image Collection; 706 (c)George H.H. Huey; 708–709 Gerry Ellis/Minden Pictures/Getty Images; 709 Nigel Cattlin/Alamy; 710 (t)MICHAEL S. QUINTON/National Geographic Image Collection, (b)Gerry Ellis/Minden Pictures/Getty Images; 711 NASA-JPL; 712 IIC/ Axiom/Gatty Images; 713 Hutchings Photography/Digital Light Source; 715 Horizons Companies; 716 (t)Visuals Unlimited/CORBIS, (b) Melbourne Etc/Alamy; 720 Melbourne Etc/Alamy; 721 (all)Hutchings Photography/Digital Light Source; 722 (c)Art Wolfe/Getty Images; 723 Hutchings Photography/Digital Light Source; 724 NOAA; 725 (l)Digital Vision/PunchStock, (cl) SA Team/ Foto Natura/Minden Pictures, (c)BananaStock/Punchstock, (cr)Colin Young-Wolff/PhotoEdit, (r)Mark Steinmetz; 730 (6)Macmillan/McGraw-Hill, (others)Hutchings Photography/Digital Light Source; 732 George H.H. Huey; 735 MICHAEL S. QUINTON/National Geographic Image Collection; 738–739 Heidi & Hans-Jurgen Koch/Minden Pictures; 740 Martin Harvey/CORBIS; 741 (t)Hutchings Photography/Digital Light Source, (b)NASA Goddard Space Flight Center (NASA-GSFC); 742 (l)NASA, (r)Nigel J. Dennis/Gallo Images/CORBIS; 743 Hutchings Photography/Digital Light Source; 744 (t,b)Raymond Gehman/CORBIS; 745 (t)Riaan Janse van Rensburg/Alamy, (b)Gerry Ellis/Minden Pictures/Getty Images; 746 (t)NASA Goddard Space Flight Center (NASA-GSFC), (b)Nigel J. Dennis/Gallo Images/CORBIS; 747 (t)Andoni Canela/Photolibrary, (c)O. Rocha/American Museum of Natural History, (b)Pete Oxford/Minden Pictures; 748 Dr Jeremy Burgess/Photo Researchers; 749 (t)Hutchings Photography/Digital Light Source, (b)TomVezo.com; 750 Dr. David Phillips/Visuals Unlimited/Getty Images; 751 (t)Mary Evans Picture Library/Alamy, (c)Paul Souders/CORBIS, (b)Tom Brakefield/Getty Images; 752 Hutchings Photography/Digital Light Source; 753 Ricardo Beliel/BrazilPhotos; 754 Blend Images/Jupiterimages; 755 BEAWIHARTA/Reuters/CORBIS; 756 (t)TomVezo.com, (c)Mary Evans Picture Library/Alamy, (b)Tom Brakefield/Getty Images; 757 Tom & Pat Leeson; 758 Duncan Usher/Minden Pictures; 759 Jacques Jangoux/Photo Researchers; 760 (t)Hutchings Photography/Digital Light Source; 762 Bach/zefa/CORBIS; 763 (t)CORBIS, (b)Mark Strickland/SeaPics.com; 764 (t)Carol & Don Spencer/Visual Unlimited/Getty Images, (b)Michael & Patricia Fogden/Minden Pictures/Getty Images; 765 (t)Jacques Jangoux/Photo Researchers, (c)Bach/zefa/CORBIS, (b)Michael & Patricia Fogden/Minden Pictures/Getty Images; 766 (l,br)Hutchings Photography/Digital Light Source, (tr)Digital Vision / Getty Images; 768 (t)Nigel J. Dennis/Gallo Images/CORBIS, (c)Dr Jeremy Burgess/Photo Researchers, (b)CORBIS; 771 Heidi & Hans-Jurgen Koch/Minden Pictures; 774–775 Roger Ressmeyer/CORBIS; 776 Frans Lanting/CORBIS; 778 (t)Tom Vezo/Minden Pictures/Getty Images, (c)Hutchings Photography/Digital Light Source, (b)David Muench; 779 (t)Laura Romin & Larry Dalton/Alamy, (tc)Jim Brandenburg/Minden Pictures, (b)Chuck Haney / DanitaDelimont.com, (bc)Comstock/PunchStock; 780 (tl)age fotostock/Photolibrary, (tr)Gavriel Jecan/Getty Images, (bl)Jacques Jangoux/Mira.com, (br)Frans Lanting/CORBIS; 781 (t)M DeFreitas/Getty Images, (bl)Doug Sherman/Geofile, (br)Comstock Images/Alamy; 782 (t)Tom Till, (bl)Bruce Lichtenberger/Peter Arnold, Inc., (br)Russ Munn/CORBIS; 783 (t)age fotostock/SuperStock, (tc)Marvin Dembinsky Photo Associates/Alamy, (b)Andre Gallant/Getty Images, (bc)age fotostock/SuperStock; 784 (t)Frans Lanting/CORBIS, (b)Tom Till; 785 (b)Andre Gallant/Getty Images, (bcr)Andre Gallant/Getty Images; 786 Woodfall/Photoshot; 787 (tr)Hutchings Photography/Digital Light Source; 788 (tl)Comstock/PunchStock, (tr)Arthur Morris/Visuals Unlimited/Getty Images, (cl)Paul Nicklen/NGS/Getty Images, (cr)Stephen Dalton/Minden Pictures, (b)Medioimages/PunchStock, (bcl)Dr. Marli Mill/Visuals Unlimited/Getty Images; 789 (t)Jean-Paul Ferrero/Minden Picture, (tc)Lynn & Donna Rogers/Peter Arnold, Inc., (b)Image Ideas/PictureQuest, (bc)Photograph by Tim McCabe, courtesy USDA Natural Resources Conservation Service; 790 (t)Michael S. Quinton/National Geographic/Getty Images, (c)James L. Amos/Peter Arnold, Inc., (b)Steve Bly/Getty Images; 791 (t)Tom & Therisa Stack/Tom Stack & Associates, (bl)B. Moose Peterson, (br)David Noton Photography/Alamy; 792 (t)Camille Lusardi/Photolibrary, (c)Gregory Ochocki/Photo Researchers, (b)Doug Allan/Getty Images; 793 (t)Gavriel Jecan/Photolibrary, (b)Comstock Images/PictureQuest, (br)Hutchings Photography/Digital Light Source; 794 (t)Jean-Paul Ferrero/Minden Picture, (c)Steve Bly/Getty Images, (b)Comstock Images/PictureQuest; 795 (t)K. Holmes/American Museum of Natural History, (c)K. Frey/American Museum of Natural History, (b)Stephen Frink/Getty Images, (bkgd)Wayne Levin/Getty Images; 796 Paul Bradforth/Alamy; 802 (others)Hutchings Photography/Digital Light Source, (2,3,4)Macmillan/McGraw-Hill; 803 (tr)Hutchings Photography/Digital Light Source; 804 (t)David Muench, (c)Tom & Therisa Stack/Tom Stack & Associates; 807 Roger Ressmeyer/CORBIS; 808 (6)Macmillan/McGraw-Hill; 810–811 Sarah Leen/National Geographic/Getty Images; 812 Ron Chapple Stock/Alamy; 813 Creatas/PunchStock; 814 CHRIS JAMES/Peter Arnold, Inc.; 815 (l)Mark Steinmetz, (r)ImageState/age fotostock; 816 Gary Braasch/Getty Images; 819 inga spence/Alamy; 820 (t)Creatas/PunchStock, (b)Ron Chapple Stock/Alamy; 821 PhotoLink/Getty Images; 822 Thomas R. Fletcher/Alamy; 823 (t)Hutchings Photography/Digital Light Source, (b)NATALIE B. FOBES/National Geographic Stock; 825 Robert Jureit/Getty Images; 826 Hutchings Photography/Digital Light Source; 827 (l)Scott Bauer/USDA; 827 (r)Harrison Shull/Getty Images; 828 (t)NATALIE B. FOBES/National Geographic Stock, (c)Robert Jureit/Getty Images, (b)Harrison Shull/Getty Images; 829 (t)The Mcgraw-Hill Companies, (c)Rob Melnychuk/Brand X/CORBIS, (b)Hutchings Photography/Digital Light Source; 830 NASA Jet Propulsion Laboratory (NASA-JPL); 831 Butch Martin/Getty Images; 832 (t)JAMES L. STANFIELD/National Geographic Stock, (b)Mark Steinmetz; 835 (l)Jonathan Nourok/PhotoEdit, (c)Steve Skjold/Alamy Images, (r)David Young-Wolff/PhotoEdit; 836 (l)Peter Starman/Getty Images, (r)Tony Craddock/Photo Researchers; 837 (t)NASA Jet Propulsion Laboratory (NASA-JPL), (b)Tony Craddock/Photo Researchers; 839 Mark Steinmetz; 840 (t)Mark Steinmetz, (c)Thomas R. Fletcher/Alamy, (b)JAMES L. STANFIELD/National Geographic Stock; 843 Sarah Leen/National Geographic/Getty Images; SR-00–SR-01 (bkgd)Gallo Images - Neil Overy/Getty Images; SR-02 Hutchings Photography/Digital Light Source; SR-06 Michell D. Bridwell/PhotoEdit; SR-07 (t)The McGraw-Hill Companies, (b)Dominic Oldershaw; SR-08 StudiOhio; SR-09 Timothy Fuller; SR-10 Aaron Haupt; SR-42 (c)NIBSC / Photo Researchers, Inc., (r)Science VU/Drs. D.T. John & T.B. Cole/Visuals Unlimited, Inc.; Stephen Durr; SR-43 (t)Mark Steinmetz, (r)Andrew Syred/Science Photo Library/Photo Researchers, (br)Rich Brommer; SR-44 (l)Lynn Keddie/Photolibrary, (tr)G.R. Roberts; David Fleetham/Visuals Unlimited/Getty Images; SR-45 Gallo Images/CORBIS; SR-46 Matt Meadows

PERIODIC TABLE OF THE ELEMENTS

Element —— Hydrogen
Atomic number —— 1
Symbol —— H —— State of matter
Atomic mass —— 1.01

- 🎈 Gas
- 💧 Liquid
- ⬜ Solid
- ⊙ Synthetic

A column in the periodic table is called a **group.**

A row in the periodic table is called a **period.**

	1	2	3	4	5	6	7	8	9
1	Hydrogen 1 H 1.01								
2	Lithium 3 Li 6.94	Beryllium 4 Be 9.01							
3	Sodium 11 Na 22.99	Magnesium 12 Mg 24.31							
4	Potassium 19 K 39.10	Calcium 20 Ca 40.08	Scandium 21 Sc 44.96	Titanium 22 Ti 47.87	Vanadium 23 V 50.94	Chromium 24 Cr 52.00	Manganese 25 Mn 54.94	Iron 26 Fe 55.85	Cobalt 27 Co 58.93
5	Rubidium 37 Rb 85.47	Strontium 38 Sr 87.62	Yttrium 39 Y 88.91	Zirconium 40 Zr 91.22	Niobium 41 Nb 92.91	Molybdenum 42 Mo 95.96	Technetium 43 Tc (98)	Ruthenium 44 Ru 101.07	Rhodium 45 Rh 102.91
6	Cesium 55 Cs 132.91	Barium 56 Ba 137.33	Lanthanum 57 La 138.91	Hafnium 72 Hf 178.49	Tantalum 73 Ta 180.95	Tungsten 74 W 183.84	Rhenium 75 Re 186.21	Osmium 76 Os 190.23	Iridium 77 Ir 192.22
7	Francium 87 Fr (223)	Radium 88 Ra (226)	Actinium 89 Ac (227)	Rutherfordium 104 Rf (267)	Dubnium 105 Db (268)	Seaborgium 106 Sg (271)	Bohrium 107 Bh (272)	Hassium 108 Hs (270)	Meitnerium 109 Mt (276)

The number in parentheses is the mass number of the longest lived isotope for that element.

Lanthanide series Cerium 58 Ce 140.12	Praseodymium 59 Pr 140.91	Neodymium 60 Nd 144.24	Promethium 61 Pm (145)	Samarium 62 Sm 150.36	Europium 63 Eu 151.96
Actinide series Thorium 90 Th 232.04	Protactinium 91 Pa 231.04	Uranium 92 U 238.03	Neptunium 93 Np (237)	Plutonium 94 Pu (244)	Americium 95 Am (243)